John Levens

Kuwait
May 1999

DAYS OF FEAR

DEDICATION

For those who did not return,
And their families;

And for those who are yet to return,
And their families.

JOHN LEVINS **DAYS OF**

FEAR

**THE INSIDE STORY OF THE IRAQI INVASION
AND OCCUPATION OF KUWAIT**

To Ted and Gloria Wang,
With my very best wishes,
and deepest appreciation
for your service here.
I hope that this helps to
give you a deeper understanding
of Kuwait,

John Levins

Kuwait
May 1999

MOTIVATE
PUBLISHING

Motivate Publishing
Dubai: PO Box 2331, Dubai, UAE
Abu Dhabi: PO Box 43072, Abu Dhabi, UAE
London: Macmillan House, 96 Kensington High Street
London W8 4SG

First published by Motivate Publishing 1997

ISBN 1 873544 98 7

British Library Cataloguing-in-Publication Data.
A catalogue record for this book is available from the
British Library.

Printed by Emirates Printing Press, Dubai

Note on maps: All international boundaries between
Iraq and Kuwait shown on the maps in this book
are as per the decisions of the UN Iraq-Kuwait
Boundary Demarcation Commission.

CONTENTS

Appendices

August, 1997

P. O. Box 1558,
13016, Safat, Kuwait
Telephone and fax:
(965) ~~246-1058~~
371-7827

LETTER TO PARTICIPANTS

This letter is addressed to all those people whose lives were directly affected by the Iraqi invasion of Kuwait, and the subsequent occupation. It is especially intended for those who were in Kuwait at the time, and spent a substantial part of the occupation there, or in Iraqi custody. This includes the Kuwaitis themselves, the Westerners, particularly those used as Human Shields, the Arab and Asian expatriates, and their families at home.

Seven years ago, our peaceful worlds were turned dramatically upside down by the invading Iraqi Army. It would be seven long months before Kuwait was liberated. The images of the 42-day air war and the 100-hour ground war which achieved that, and the raging oilfield fires, will remain seared into the world's consciousness as hopefully the last 'big war' of the millennium.

Yet, as all of us who were there know, the war was only part of the story; the inconclusive endgame, if you like. The military and political campaign to defeat Iraq and free Kuwait has been exhaustively documented, and rightly so, but the equally momentous story of the occupation – of what happened inside occupied Kuwait and in Iraq itself, including military operations inside Kuwait itself during both the invasion and the liberation – has gone largely untold until now. Those days will forever remain with us as the most memorable of our lives, but few of us at the time could see the whole picture. This book aims to rectify that. It is your story.

My original objective in writing this book was to distill the essence of our various disparate experiences, and to link these into a coherent tapestry. Most of us have bounced back into normal life; others are still, even now, suffering. A few have tragically succumbed to suicide. My prayer is that this book will be a healing for those of us who need it. If you can read this book with a sense of, 'Yes, that's the way it was. That's how I felt. Now I know the whole story!' and then say, 'It's all behind me now....', it will have served its purpose. I want to give you a sense of release, a finality. For those of you who have no need of such healing, I hope that the book will be a valuable record of an important part of your life. The need for this is even more obvious than it was before: the first printing of 5,000 copies was sold out within three months; this reprint represents a similar number. I am gratified by the support received.

In Australia: P. O. Box 276, Applecross WA 6153, AUSTRALIA. Fax: 61-89-367-2878

We must also remember that the crisis is not yet over, especially for the estimated 604 missing Kuwaitis and other nationals still unaccounted for by Iraq, and their families. We must also remember the surviving victims of torture and rape. Some of them are leading a life of living death. In a way, the dead and their families are the lucky ones. They have a sense of closure; the families can complete the grieving process. The loved ones of those still missing can only hope against all hope, and pray that if their people are no more, that the end came quickly. Their grief has no end.

On a broader level, Iraq has yet to comply fully with the terms of the March 1991 ceasefire. Although Baghdad has in recent years improved its cooperation with UN weapons inspections, particularly after being forced to do so by high-level defections in 1995, and recognised Kuwait's sovereignty and borders in November 1994, it is still hiding information on its weapons of mass destruction, and only admitting to it when presented with the evidence. Allied warplanes still patrol expanded no-fly zones over northern and southern Iraq, Saddam is still imposing an internal embargo on his northern Kurdish provinces, and has devastated the historic southern marshes in an attempt to contain opposition in the south. The West has its own hostages and POWs back, but Saddam Hussein still holds the entire Iraqi nation hostage.

You may notice a bias in this book towards the Kuwaitis. I make no apologies for that. I have lived in Kuwait for over a decade and seen the best and worst that is in any nationality. During the occupation, the Kuwaitis in Kuwait demonstrated the very best of the human spirit, in courage, selflessness, honour, hospitality, loyalty, even a willingness to lay down their lives for their friends and country. Some of them, male and female, Sunni and Shia, Muslim and Christian, took incredible risks to support people they didn't even know simply because it was the right thing to do. Over the years, oil wealth has robbed many of them of some of the finer traditional qualities. Their performance during the occupation proved conclusively that those qualities were not far beneath the surface. They bought back in blood what had been stolen from them by oil. I have nothing but admiration for them as a people.

You will also notice a bias in the content of the book towards the experiences of the Westerners. This I do apologise for, but it is unavoidable. It is the source of my own experience, and what English-speaking readers want to know. There are numerous books in Arabic about the occupation, especially covering the brave Kuwaiti Resistance. In time, I hope that these are translated into English to compensate for the current dearth in this area. Other stories cannot yet be told because the people involved may still be in Iraqi custody.

I have sought to make the book as accurate and as comprehensive as possible, but no research is perfect, and any book is a sum of many compromises. I am acutely aware that even minor errors in an account of such a major part of your life can steal the experience from you. Although it has been impossible to speak with everyone who was involved (and different people invariably see the same events through different eyes), I am confident that the research is solid; from the entire first edition which went worldwide – often to major figures. I received only a handful of substantive comments. All of these have been incorporated into this printing. Nevertheless, if you are seeing this book for the first time and notice any material omissions or mistakes, please accept my apologies and write to me with the corrections. I will try to include them in any future editions.

Similarly, I have tried to include my own personal experiences only where they illustrate key aspects of the story. If you have a better illustration, let me know and I will replace my own with it. Additionally, some readers may feel that I have been unduly critical or bitter about certain players in the crisis, particularly members of the electronic media, those people known as 'grovellers', and certain politicians and others. I bear these people no personal grudge. My objective was to convey the feelings of those involved towards such individuals at the time; sometimes those feelings ran very high.

One particularly unfortunate group of people were – and are – the Palestinians. A small minority let their compatriots down by engaging in looting and collaboration. This is a fact of history, and had been recorded as such. I do not for one moment imply that the Palestinian people as a whole were at fault, although I cannot accept their leadership's stance during the crisis.

Above all, this book is about ordinary people caught up in an extraordinary situation, and how they dealt with the challenges and dangers they faced. We all know that since the invasion, we will never be quite the same as anyone else. I hope that those who were not there can glimpse through this book a little of how that difference came about. I pray that they never have to go through a similar experience.

On behalf of everyone who was in Kuwait at the time, I would like to express our deepest appreciation to the world leaders and their public and troops who made the country's liberation possible. Foremost amongst these are George Bush and Margaret Thatcher. For the Westerners among us, our unending gratitude must also go to those brave diplomats serving in Kuwait and Iraq who allowed us to remain in touch with our families, however tenuously. In particular, we cannot forget those who gave their lives on active service.

There are so many people to thank for their contribution to this book that I have had to do so elsewhere, but this letter would not be complete without a word of gratitude to the Kuwaiti people who endured the occupation in their own country. They made Kuwait worth living in, and worth liberating.

John Levins

ACKNOWLEDGEMENTS

This book would not have been possible without the generosity, support, and assistance of many people, some of whom would prefer that they not be recognised.

It is impossible to specifically mention the hundreds of people who were responsible, in ways great and small, for helping this book see the light of day. Some of them have rendered great service merely by answering several key questions. Others have spent many, many hours with me. Each has been critically important in their own way. For those I forget, my apologies, and gratitude.

A work of this nature necessarily involves talking to a wide cross-section of people on very sensitive issues. A number of these lost dear friends and relatives during the crisis, and trusted me to treat their story with the sensitivity it demands. I sincerely hope that trust has been vindicated in these pages.

For services which those involved are best aware of, my thanks go to Mohammed J. Abdul Salam, Dr Yousef Abdul-Moati, Maha Al-Abdulrazzak, John and Dianne Abi-Hanna, Roy Abraham, Ibrahim Abu Lail, Samya Al-Adwani, Sheikh Athbi Fahad Al-Ahmad, Ernest Alexander, Hala Alghanim, Akhtar Ali, Sheikh Ali Jaber Al-Ali, Dr Sheikh Ali Salem Al-Ali, Shawkat Hussein Ali, Ray Alamango, Ken Allen, Miriam Amie, Talal Al-Arab, Norma Armstrong, Alla Assad, Brian, Gloria and Glen Ashwell, Walid Al-Awadi, Lieutenant-General Mohammed Al-Bader, Amy Bahman, Seraj Al-Baker, Nasser and Rukhsana Bakir, Tony and Pauline Barlow, Neil Beevor, Dr Hashem and Dr Ebraheem Behbehani, John Bentley, Nicola Benwell, Ken and Jo Best, Bernhard Bischoff, Jerry and Jackie Blears, Sandy Blindell, Barbara K. Bodine, Colonel Mahmoud Boushahri, Aisa Bou-Yabes, Richard Brook, Steven and Josie Brookes, Tim Brosnan, Colin Brown, Danny Brown, Paul and Gale Brown, Warrant Officer Adel Bu Arki, Abdulatief Bukannan, Dr Garry Burns, Steve and Wendy Bushby, Peter and Terry Byrnes, Blair Cameron, John Carlough, Nick Cate, Alan and Suzanne Cattermole, Chris and Mary Chambers, Andy Charles, George and Anna, and Paul and Susanne Cienciala, Phil Coggin, Bill and Luz Marina Colwell, Barry and Diane Cooper, Captain Pat Cooper USN, Colin Crispin, Ryan Crocker, Leo Cruise, Sawson Dajani, Chris Dawkins, General Sir Peter de la Billière, Mike and Lesley Devey, Saud Al-Deham, Janet Dolman, David and Sue Dorrington, Brigadier Mahmoud Al-Dossari, Andrew Dowdy, the late Ian Dron, Colonel Bruce Duncan, Sylvain and Anna Duporge, Major Nasser Al-Duwailah, Dr Hassan Al-Ebraheem, Janet and Steve Edwards, Jeffrey Eggen, Samir Elbaba, Senator Gareth Evans, Peter Eyles, Kevin and Laverne Fallon, Colonel Mohammed Al-Farsi, Kholoud Al-Feeley, Nick Fitzsimon, David Forsdike, Tim Frank, Jerry and Rosemary Fronabarger, William and Arlene Fullerton, Lieutenant-Colonel Tom Funk, Mel and Carol Gage, Christian and Betty Geargeoura, Lee Getchell, Dalal Al-Ghanem, Diraar Y. Alghanim, Lulwa Al-Ghanim, Tannous Ghosn, Dr Abdullah Al-Ghunaim, Faris Glubb, Edward Gnehm, Peter and Dorothy Goodwin, Maurice and Laurie Graham, Dene Green, Geoff Green, Mick Grosvenor, Faisal Al-Habishi, Saleh and

Barbara Al-Hadoud, Mae Al-Hajjaj, Mrs Amal Al-Hamad, Hamad Al-Hamad, Brigadier Mohammed Al-Harmi, John D. Harris, Oriole Hart, Dr Samir Hawana, Julie Henderson, Liselotte Hertz, Patrick Herbert, Sue Hewer, Odessa Higgins, Butch Hoffman, Anthony Hordern, General Charles Horner, Craig Hosking, David Hough, W. Nat and Margie Howell, Ken and Magda Hoyle, Colonel Nasser Husainan, Aziza Ibrahim, Hiyam Al-Ibrahim, Tareq Al-Iesa, Bob Jaggard, Yousef Al-Jalahma, Nirmala Janssen, Emad Al-Jaouni, Mohammed Al-Jazzaf, David Joachim, Niju John, Colonel Jesse L. Johnson, Robert F. Johnson, Lieutenant-Colonel Mahdi Al-Jumah, Dr Fouad Al-Khadra, Ahmad and Cathy Khajah, Nazeeh Khajah, Ibrahim Al-Khaldi, Paul Kennedy, Kholoud Al-Khamis, Bader Al-Khashti, Nick and Linda Koblyk, Joe Kunicki, Mathew Kuruvilla, Rose Lambert, Tom Laming, Toufic and Michelle Lawand, Mario Lazo, John and Delilah Lewinton, Peter and Libby Lloyd, Robert and Rosemary Lloyd, Alick Longhurst, Henk and Ann Looy, Luan Low, Rick MacDermott, Fiona MacDonald, Brigadier Hamish McGregor, Keith and DeeDee McKenzie, Sandy and Barbara Macmillan, Greg Maine, Victor Mallet, Ivan Manning, Soheila Marafie, Connie Mataki, Brock and Christopher Matthews, Sunny Mathews, Zahra Matran, Bennie Mitchell, Colonel John and Mrs Ellen Mooneyham, Major Mohammed Jassim Mousalem, Dr Haya Al-Mughni, Colonel Ahmad Al-Mulla, Lief and Lis Munksgaard, Caryle Murphy, Susi Al-Mutawa, Dr Fatma Nader, Sheikh Saud Nasir, Sheikh Sabah Nasir, Dave Neal, Andrew Nobbay, Kirsty Norman, Rajeh Saad Al-Omair, Dr Warren Osmond, Abdulrazzak Al-Othman, Bart Ouvry, Trevor Owen, John Ernest and Shanti Paramanandam, Connie Parrish, Bruce, Edna and Giles Parry, Beth Payne, Mike Penniman, Bill Petersen, Elvis Pinto, Daniel Pipes, J. Christopher Poole, Dr Rodica Pospoi, the Al-Qabandi family, particularly Adnan, Ghassan and Iqbal, and especially Anwar, Ali and Ibrahim, Narjis Qabazard, Mahmoud Qabazard, Ahmad Al-Qaoud, Colonel Ahmad Al-Rahmani, John Raine, Jehan Rajab, Menal Al-Rashid, Sergeant Exkchart Rattanachai, Ahmad Al-Rayyis, Dennis Reid, George and Susan Reid, Tony Rodrigues, Gale Rogers, Salem R. Al-Roomi, Fawzya Al-Roumi, Captain Sami Al-Rushoud, David Rutter, Ali Hmoud Al-Sabah, Ali Jaber Ali-Ali Al-Sabah, Mishal Al-Sabah, Dr Rasha Al-Sabah, Talal K. A. Al-Sabah, Abdulatief Al-Sabeeh, Nouriya Al-Sadani, Harcharan and Paramjit Singh Saini, Adnan Al-Saleh, Mohammed Al-Saleh, Brigadier Qais Al-Saleh, B. George and Debra Saloom, Major-General Salem Al-Sarour, Dave Saunders, General H. Norman Schwarzkopf, Guy Seago, Christopher Segar, Abdulaziz F.O. Al-Serri, Dr Habib and Mrs Christine Al-Shaban, Ahmad Al-Shaddad, Gunvant Shah, Dr Ali Al-Shamlan, Faisal Al-Shammeri, Sergeant Eid Al-Shammery, Ghanim Al-Shammery, Captain Ali Al-Shanfa, Dr Abdullah Al-Shayeji, C. Miles Sheldon, Janet M. Shields, Dave and Aiden Short, Talal Showaish, Yvonne Sidani, Sohaila Al-Sijari, Alan and Joan Sinclair, Stewart Skelhorn, Emil and Dorothea Skodon, Ric Smith, Colonel Cliff Squires, Major-General Saber Al-Suwaidan, David C. Tait, James Tansley, Caroline Tshering, Paul Tyson, Tonya Ugoretz Buzby, Fiona Underwood, Laurens and Mona Van Egelen, Thomas Varghese, H. S.Vedi, C. R. Vinod, Bruce Watkins, Dick Wearn, Ron Webster, Sir Michael Weston, Mark Williams, Ralph and Colleen Williams, Fred Winter, Ken Woodside, Uwe Wruck, Sabah Al-Yacoub, Musab Al-Yaseen, and Nariman Zaarour.

An essential source of information and verification was diaries kept at the time. For the use of these, and other valuable assistance, I am particularly indebted to Chris and Lesley Bell, George Cienciala, Janet Edwards, Gordon Johnson, the late Don Latham, Glenda Lockwood, Bishop Francis Micallef, Paul Scogna, Hermann Simon, Joan Sinclair, Ray and Vonzy Washer, and Phillip Wearne.

For photographs, I gratefully acknowledge the Kuwait Ministry of Information, particularly Abdullatif Bukannan; the Kuwait News Agency, particularly Anwar Al-Hasawi, Ali Al-Roumi and Tareq Al-Shatti; the Saudi Information Office, Kuwait; the Kuwait Air Force; the Kuwait Navy; Colonel Mahmoud Boushahri, Dr Hassan Al-Ebraheem, Sharon Fronabarger, Colonel Jesse and Mrs Judith Johnson, Jeff Jugar and Connie Parrish, Bader Al-Khashti, Mathew Kuruvilla, Muna Al-Mousa, Anwar Al-Qabandi, Sheikh Sabah Nasir Al-Sabah, Mohammed J. Abdul Salam, Christopher Segar, Emil Skodon and Jack Wozniak.

No author works in a vacuum. Every book on a crisis such as this is part of a wider family of literature. I would like to make special mention of Lawrence Freedman's and Efraim Karsh's unparalleled *The Gulf Crisis 1990-1991*, John Simpson for his excellent *From The House Of War*, with his accounts of life in Baghdad, and two *Washington Post* reporters, Molly Moore with her *A Woman At War* and Rick Atkinson with his *Crusade*. Finally, Brian Keenan, with his insightful *An Evil Cradling*, put into words what so many of us felt but found difficulty describing, although none of us can claim to have suffered as he did.

A special note of thanks is due to John Gregory, Bob Jaggard, and B. Paul and Lesley Scogna in Dubai, Andrew Barbour in London, Larry and Liz Banks in Hamburg, Shauna Roberts, Alba Sequeira, and Paul and Gale Brown in the US, for their hospitality, generosity and forbearance in the international research part of the book. Without them, it simply could not have been done.

There are several individuals without whom this work would have been impossible to finish. I would like to pay particular tribute to Hajji Bader Al-Bazie Al-Yaseen, John Carlough, Keith McKenzie, the late Don Latham, and his wife, Maria, and Abu Abdullah.

As importantly, I must pay particular recognition to those eagle-eyed individuals who proof-read and edited the earlier, drafts of this book, and turned it into something which I hope is readable. A special thanks to Wendy Beddison, Suzanne Cattermole, Tanya Shirazi, Maggie Yerolatsitis, Lucia Mihaela Gheorghe and Paul Cienciala. Any remaining errors are my responsibility alone.

I would also like to thank Mel Gage and Armando D. Lipana of Fahad Al-Mazouk Printing Press, Kuwait, and David Forsdike for work on the cover. And no acknowledgement would be complete without recognising the professional contribution of those involved at Motivate Publishing in Dubai, in particular Ian Fairservice, Catherine Demangeot, Zelda Pinto, Dejan Vrbanovic and Nadeem Ansari.

Above all, my eternal gratitude goes out to my family who put up with my obsession over the years it took to research and write the book, and gave me the encouragement and moral support to complete the project. I cannot thank them enough for suffering through the crisis itself with great strength, patience, and love.

1. INVASION

It was 5.40 a.m., Thursday, 2 August 1990. The telephone was ringing. I was half-asleep ... 'Who could it be, at this time of the morning?', I wondered, my mind struggling to emerge from slumber. Outside, the sun was up: the start of another hot summer's day in Kuwait.

My apartment was on the eighth floor of the massive 400-unit Al-Muthanna Residential Complex, looming like a fortress over central Kuwait City. The 13-storey building formed three sides of a square surrounding a central courtyard, with the 17-storey Plaza Hotel filling the fourth side. I could see north-west across the city's main thoroughfare, past hotels and office buildings, to Jorn Utzon's beautiful National Assembly Building and the glistening waters of Kuwait Bay.

The call was from Lawrence Miall, a British friend living in ten kilometres to the east, on Kuwait Bay. 'John?' Lawrence's voice was uncertain. He had just been called by friends. 'They say Iraq has invaded. They're in the city!'

I was suddenly wide awake. The tension between Kuwait and Iraq during the past fortnight had been common knowledge, but few had anticipated a fully-fledged invasion. At most, we expected Iraq might grab a border oilfield, or two islands 80km to the north, but not come all the way to Kuwait City. Besides, Kuwait had helped Iraq extensively during the recent Iran-Iraq war. It just couldn't be... but Lawrence wasn't one for practical jokes.

I looked out of the living-room window. Eight floors below, beyond the Plaza Hotel, a lone Iraqi soldier, Kalashnikov in hand, sauntered past the British Airways office. There could be no mistake. In my five years in the Emirate, I had never seen a Kuwaiti soldier carrying the distinctive Kalashnikov with its long, curved magazine, but I had seen plenty of Iraqi soldiers during business and holiday trips to Iraq. The man could only be Iraqi.

'Lawrence!' I felt my heart beating faster. 'One just walked down the street. Definitely Iraqi.' Lawrence had heard jet aircraft pass low overhead minutes earlier, but had been unable to identify them. He had seen no troops.

Then I heard it, a sound that would become all too familiar: the rattle of light automatic fire. It was impossible to tell where it was coming from. 'Lawrence,' I said, 'I must ring Arlene' She was a mutual friend, living nearby. I felt secure in this massive building, but Arlene's flat overlooked the Kuwaiti National Assembly building. It would be a prime target in any invasion.

I called Arlene. Her father had just been ordered back home from his way to work at the airport by Iraqi soldiers on the street. Moments later, a colleague had called to say that the Iraqis were at the airport. The family was safe, barricaded inside, staying away from the windows.

If the Iraqis were at the airport and in the city centre, they must have the country virtually wrapped up. I had been awake less than five minutes. This was shaping up to be a very full morning.

My mind was racing. Who do I know in the Kuwaiti Army? I hope they know what's going on. Nabil! That's it, Nabil and Nadine. Nabil was a reservist, like many young Kuwaiti men. He lived near Lawrence. His English wife, Nadine, had the misfortune to be a holder of an Iraqi passport, a legacy of her father. I dialled again. 'Nadine?' Her voice was sleepy. No one had roused her yet this morning. There was a pause as she looked at her watch. 'What are you doing calling at this time?'

'Nadine, the Iraqi Army is in the city. We've been invaded! Tell Nabil'

'You're kidding. There's nothing going on here.'

'Nadine, I'm not kidding. Tell Nabil to call his unit.'

My doorbell rang. 'Nadine, someone's at the door. I have to go.' The caller was my neighbour from across the hall, an American dentist, with a young mustachioed stranger whom he introduced as Phil Balmforth, his wife's visiting nephew. Phil was Canadian, in his early twenties. His father was with the UN in Jordan.

'John, the Iraqis are here,' the American said. 'We think they're near the lights. We're going down to have a look.' He indicated a narrow window at the end of the corridor which would afford a better view of the main intersection in central Kuwait City.

At that moment we heard the dull, hollow thud of an explosion. Directly across from us, on the other side of the graveyard in central Kuwait City, a small missile streaked 500 metres eastwards towards the Ministry of Information building, next to the radio and TV station, holing it three-quarters of the way up. Bits of debris flew out, almost in slow motion, with a puff of smoke but no flames. The sprinklers must have been working.

The rocket had come from behind the Salhiya Complex, a long, seven-storey commercial complex backing onto the Meridien Hotel, which faced our building. We could see soldiers running a few hundred metres away on the other side of the adjacent graveyard, but could not identify them. There was the sound of plenty of small-arms fire. We couldn't see from where, but it was obvious that the Iraqis were attacking the TV station.

Our attention was drawn suddenly to the street eight floors below, near the offices of Saudi Arabian Airlines. Two policemen were usually on duty there, guarding the offices. We could see them now, sitting on their chairs in the shade of the verandah, smoking, pistols in holsters, wondering about all the firing and explosions. They looked at each other in bewilderment.

'Wake up' we wanted to scream at them. 'Get under cover! Go for your guns! Get on your radios! Find out what's going on!' Incredibly, isolated cars were still driving past them down the street towards the main intersection. It was too early for a regular traffic jam, but one was forming directly in front of the Meridien Hotel. The reason was obvious to us, but the curve of the road hid the view from the two stunned policemen. About a dozen Iraqi troops were advancing up the street from the intersection, stopping cars and ordering people out, onto the footpath.

Our minds were racing. The Kuwait Governorate and Ministries Complex were nearby. Four kilometres beyond lay Dasman Palace, the Amir's home, and the British and US embassies. If the troops we could see now were advancing in that direction, and if the airport to the south was taken, then we must be witnessing the northern arm of a pincer movement. It was a classic take-over strategy. Neutralize the TV and radio stations, and capture the airport. We had no idea whether they had also attacked the Dasman Palace. We could see no smoke from that direction. Perhaps the Kuwaitis were making a stand there, perhaps they had already been overrun ... The broader questions had to wait: another drama was about to unfold at our feet.

The two cops saw the first Iraqi, but remained seated, frozen in shock. The Iraqi initially didn't see them, and was going about his work of stopping cars and ejecting the occupants, when suddenly his commander ran down the central reservation, waving a pistol. He saw the policemen and screamed at the lead trooper, who saw them simultaneously. The muzzle of his Kalashnikov swung towards them as he pulled the weapon into his shoulder, ready to fire.

Still sitting down, the two policemen put their hands straight up, over their heads, staring wildly at the Iraqi. They could see death seconds away. The Iraqi yelled at them to place their hands on their heads, and then stand up. They obeyed, trembling. One at a time, the Iraqi ordered them to remove their pistol belts and caps, and then to lie face down on the footpath, hands on the backs of their necks. We breathed a collective sigh of relief for the cops. Our hearts went out to them. Their relief at being spared was palpable eight floors above.

The policemen were soon joined by the occupants of the growing stream of cars being stopped by the troops. Obviously the civilians driving into work early knew nothing of the invasion. For them to have got this far, there must have been no troops in the suburbs or on the major intersections leading into the city centre. The invasion must still be in its early stages.

The men were made to get out of their cars, and join the policemen, but allowed to sit up. Some of the men were Indians. The contrast was not lost on us. In Kuwait, Asians are often looked down upon as manual labour. Now, the two cops were lying on their faces, and the Indians sitting comfortably beside them. They were soon joined by a few captured Kuwaiti National Guardsmen.

One of the few women, an elegantly dressed Lebanese or Palestinian, protested. We had to laugh at the spectacle. Even in an invasion, it wasn't the done thing to make a woman sit down on the street with a crowd of male strangers. The Iraqi relented. War or no war, Arab manners had to be respected. The woman was allowed to go back and sit in her car.

The spell was broken. The noise of firing was all around us now, fairly sporadic, but we could not see any further action. The men sat on the footpath below us, their cars abandoned nearby, doors open.

I thought of my family at home in Australia. I had to let them know. The Iraqis had hit the TV station and would soon take the Ministry of Communications. My neighbour's telephone had an international line. He said I could use it. Gratefully I dialled Australia, five hours ahead.

The phone seemed to ring for an eternity. Finally, my father's secretary, answered. 'Tracey, John here. Can I please speak to Dad?' I tried to keep my voice steady. My father came on the line.

'Dad, hi, John here. Er, Dad, you know that fax I sent you a week ago, saying that the Iraqis hadn't got here yet ...?' There had been some concern when I had recently left to return to Kuwait, but I had assured my family that it was probably just a storm in a teacup, merely Arab politicking.

'Well, Dad, they're here. It looks as though they've taken over.'

'Are you OK?' My father's voice was calm. He always handles crises well.

'Yeah, fine. Civilians are being treated OK. They're taking Kuwaiti soldiers and police prisoner, not shooting them. Actually, it's all very polite.'

'How do you feel?' I could tell he was concerned. What else could I expect? I was not sure how I felt. It occurred to me that I'd just been watching the opening stages of a real invasion, and felt more elation than fear. That probably comes later, I thought.

'Remember that TV interview during the Falklands War, with a British Harrier pilot who had just returned from a bombing mission?' I said. We both remembered the interview. The reporter had asked the pilot how he felt, and the pilot had looked him straight in the eye and said, 'Scared shitless'.

We laughed. It got the message across. We had both thought the pilot very sensible, without any pretence. That was just what I wanted to convey, rather than the fear. In other words, it's a bit scary, but I'll act sensibly.

We chatted for a while. I told him not to worry, to explain the situation to my mother and siblings, and tell them that I'd get out as soon as I could. He was happy that the troops seemed to be disciplined. We rang off, not knowing when we would speak again, but promising to call regularly.

The next call was to the Australian Broadcasting Corporation. I thought the world needed to know what was going on, especially that the Iraqis did not seem to be hurting people. A reporter called Wendy Everrett came on the line, excited at breaking the story. I could feel her trying to reach out over the airwaves with the biggest story of her life. A real-life invasion story being broken in time for the midday news. Local man on the scene. And she had it.

I explained as best I could what we had witnessed, stressing that the troops seemed disciplined. We did not want people overseas to get the impression that those in Kuwait were being murdered indiscriminately. I told Wendy that the Pizza Hut at the bottom of the apartment tower had been looted in the few minutes since the capture of the policemen. This seemed to bring the crisis to a local level. Everyone could identify with the local Pizza Hut.

My neighbour wanted to call his family and his home radio station, so I returned to my own flat. The indicator light on the answering machine was flashing. I pushed the button. Nadine's voice clicked on: 'John, Nadine here. Someone's pulling your leg. Go back to bed.' Click. Barely 20 minutes had passed since we had spoken'

I called her back. 'Nadine, it's no joke.' Her voice was subdued. 'I know,' she said, 'Nabil's put his uniform on and gone out. He couldn't get his unit on the phone. It's chaos.'

I was speechless. What do you say to a woman whose husband has just gone off to war without a rifle when his country has been overrun by her father's countrymen? It was not yet 7.00 a.m. in Kuwait. It was approaching midnight of the previous day in New York; 4.00 a.m. in London, and early afternoon in Japan and Australia. A major new crisis had just dawned.

2. COMBAT, CAPTURE, CROSSFIRE

Kuwait is squeezed between north-east Saudi Arabia and south-east Iraq, shaped somewhat like a huge head, facing east across the Arabian Gulf towards Iran. It is only 160km north to south, from the northern farming settlement of Abdaly to Wafra on the Saudi border. West to east it extends 150km from Salmi, near the triple border with Saudi Arabia and Iraq, to the Arabian Gulf. Its 18,000km^2 area is similar that of the American state of New Jersey. The landscape is generally flat, sandy desert, rising to a low plateau in the west where the Wadi Al-Batin forms the western border with Iraq.

Kuwait's largest offshore island, Bubiyan, is an 863km^2 mudflat, wedged between the forehead of the Kuwaiti mainland and Iraq's Fao Peninsula. On Bubiyan's north flank is tiny Warba Island – only 37km^2 – guarding the entrance of the Khor Abdullah, Iraq's second outlet to the Gulf after the Shatt Al-Arab waterway to the east. Another larger island, Failaka, which was populated, lies south of Bubiyan.

Kuwait's major geographic feature is Kuwait Bay, extending 40km into the interior as far as the town of Jahra, beneath a low desert escarpment known as Mutla'a Ridge – more correctly the Zoor Escarpment. This ridge, one of the country's few natural barriers, extends 60km along the northern shore of the bay to Subiya, where a road bridge connects Bubiyan to the mainland.

The settled area of Kuwait is confined almost exclusively to the southern shore of Kuwait Bay, and half-way down the coast from there to the Saudi border. The road pattern of Greater Kuwait City is best described as a chessboard, with six east–west major ring roads, numbered consecutively from First Ring to Sixth, and six north–south arteries, mostly modern six-lane freeways. The squares of the chessboard are the suburbs, with Kuwait City itself occupying the northern squares.

The main road to the west, out of the city, is Jahra Road. It runs to Jahra itself, along the town's northern boundary, then turns north at Mutla'a, and continues for 80km to the Iraqi border.

The outer three ring roads run inland from the coast, west beyond the edge of the chessboard. Fourth Ring terminates 20km inland, at Jahra Road. Fifth Ring runs to 10km beyond this. Sixth Ring continues inland then loops west around Jahra, crosses Jahra Road, and joins the road along the northern edge of Kuwait Bay. West of Jahra, another road branches south-west off Sixth Ring at Atraf, and runs 100km west to the Saudi border to Salmi. Another major internal road, Seventh Ring, branches off Sixth Ring 30km inland, dog-legs south, and then runs east to the Arabian Gulf. The International Airport is sandwiched between Sixth and Seventh Rings, on the southern edge of the chessboard. These road systems were to prove vital to the defence of Kuwait.

Two north–south freeways, the Fahaheel Expressway and Maghreb-Assafar Motorway, connect the urban area to Kuwait's principal oil refinery complex at

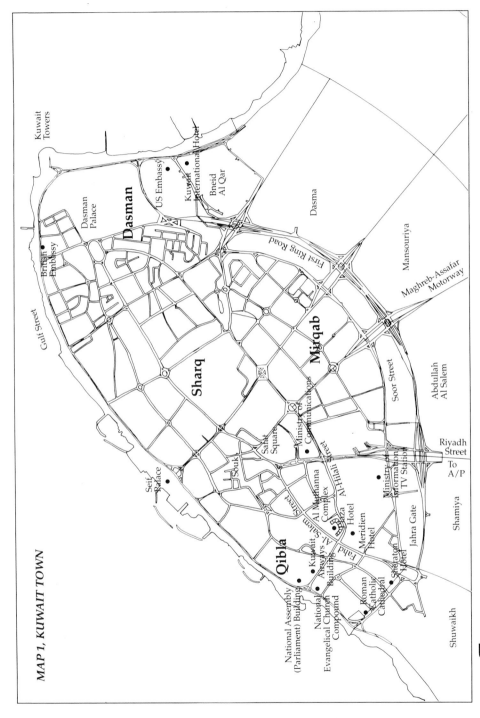

MAP 1, KUWAIT TOWN

Kuwait Towers

US Embassy

Kuwait International Hotel

Bneid Al Qar

Dasman Palace

Dasman

British Embassy

First Ring Road

Dasma

Mansouriya

Gulf Street

Maghreb-Assafar Motorway

Mirqab

Soor Street

Sharq

Abdullah Al Salem

Ministry of Communications

Sahat Square

Riyadh Street

To A/P

Souk

Al-Hilali Street

Ministry of Information TV Station

Seif Palace

Al Muthanna Complex

Al Salem Street

Plaza Hotel

Meridien Hotel

Fahd

Jahra Gate

Shamiya

Qibla

Kuwait Airways Building

Roman Catholic Cathedral

Sheraton Hotel

National Assembly (Parliament) Building

National Evangelical Church Compound

Shuwaikh

BASE MAPS ©

SALEM AL-MARZOUK AND SABAH ABI-HANNA WLL

Ahmadi and Fahaheel. They then merge into a single road to Saudi Arabia. In a good car, it takes a little over an hour to reach the Saudi border from central Kuwait City.

The regular population of Kuwait at the time of the invasion was about 2 million, but perhaps only about 1.5 million were actually in the country on 2 August, with many Kuwaitis and more affluent expatriates escaping the searing summer heat on holidays abroad.

The Kuwaiti armed forces - under the command of Chief of Staff Major-General Misyad Al-Sane and his deputy Major-General Jaber Al-Khalid, were concentrated in the southern, populated half of the country, with only one minor base in the north. Because of the short distances and excellent road systems, most Kuwaiti servicemen commuted daily. With the Iraqi invasion launched in the early morning hours, many of those men who were in the country at the time were not at their bases, or were unable to get to them.

Kuwait's Navy was based at Ras Al-Jalayh, 35km north of the Saudi border, under Colonel Qais Al-Saleh. Its main punch lay in eight German-built Lurssen fast patrol boats – two of 57-metres and six of 45-metres. All eight vessels were armed with a forward 76mm Melara automatic gun, aft twin-barrelled Breda 40mm guns, and Exocet anti-ship missiles. The only other armed vessels were 15 small Coastguard anti-smuggling patrol craft, with light machine guns, and a few barges anchored off the coast as offshore Coastguard posts. The Coastguard operated as part of the police, not the Navy.

The Kuwait Air Force (KAF), commanded by Brigadier Daoud Alghanim, had three major bases with 64 fixed-wing combat aircraft. Ahmad Al-Jaber base, 40km inland from Ahmadi, hosted 30 A-4 Skyhawks and 12 BAe Hawks; Ali Al-Salem base, 10km west of Jahra, had 23 Mirage F-1s, and KAF Headquarters was situated at International Base, just south of the International Airport, and shared its runway. The Air Operations Centre, from which all flight operations were co-ordinated, was underground in a bunker at the Air Defence Base, east of the International Airport, separate from the headquarters.

The KAF also had 16 Puma and Super Puma heavy helicopters, and 20 Gazelle light anti-tank helicopters armed with TOW missiles, all at Ali Al-Salem. The four Hercules C-130 transports and two DC-9 executive jets were at the International Airport. Ground-based air defences comprised four batteries of US Improved-HAWK missiles, and shoulder-fired anti-aircraft missiles. At the time of the invasion, the HAWKs had one battery on Failaka Island, a second near Ahmadi, a third south of Ras Al-Jalayh and one near Mutla'a.

The Army Land Forces, commanded by Brigadier Abdul Aziz Al-Bargash, comprised three independent regular armoured brigades. The heaviest were 35 Brigade and 15 Brigade, equipped with upgraded British Chieftain tanks, US M-113 APCs with TOW anti-tank missiles, and Soviet BMP-2s. Artillery consisted of US M-109 155mm and French 155mm self-propelled howitzers. The third armoured brigade, 6 Brigade, was little more than a reinforced battalion, with older British Vickers tanks and various APCs. It was based 40km south of the Iraqi border, on the eastern side of the Jahra-Abdaly Road.

The army's 35 Brigade, under Colonel Salem Al-Sarour, comprised the 7th and 8th Armoured Battalions, 57th Mechanized Infantry Battalion, and 51st Artillery Battalion, plus support companies. Its camp was 23km south-west of Ali Al-Salem KAF base, on the southern side of the Salmi Road. 15 Brigade, commanded by Colonel Mohammed Al-Harmi, based a few kilometres north of Ras Al-Jalayh naval base, had the 151st and 152nd Armoured Battalions, the 2nd Mechanized Infantry Battalion, plus its artillery.

A British-trained Amiri Guard brigade, equipped with British Saracen armoured cars, was the élite of the army. Its principal role was the defence of the Amir himself, and the Crown Prince and Prime Minister. The final major army unit, designated 80 Brigade and based in Jahra, was little more than a reserve mechanized infantry unit. A Special Forces battalion, in reality a reinforced company, was based in Jahra at the Military Academy and Armour School, equipped with British Scorpion light tanks.

Kuwait also had a National Guard brigade, reporting directly to the Amiri Diwan, not to the Ministry of Defence. Its main role, equipped as light armoured infantry with US Commando armoured cars, was the security of vital installations and the Amiri residences and work-places.

In metropolitan Kuwait, Jiwan/Mubarak Camp between Jahra Road and Fourth Ring, housed the National Guard, Defence Ministry Headquarters, and GHQ, with a fall-back command bunker at the Air Defence Base at Sabhan, south of Sixth Ring, near the International Airport.

The Kuwaiti military also had their own eye-in-the-sky – a huge TCOM observation blimp on lease from the US Navy, fitted with a sophisticated TPS-63 ground surveillance radar. Tethered at Jahra, this device could see almost all the way to Basra when flown at its maximum altitude of 4600m. It downloaded directly to the GHQ, and by reading the width of the strobe from the radar, the Kuwaitis could almost identify the type of vehicle on the screen: wide for armour, thin for soft-skinned vehicles.

The Kuwaitis were aware that the Iraqi forces had massed and were deployed to attack if they so chose. The question was whether they would move into Kuwait, and if so, what they would take, and when. In the weeks before the invasion, Kuwait's armed forces were stood down to avoid aggravating the tense political situation. The Government did not want to give Saddam any pretext to attack. In any event, they would have had no chance of holding out against his vastly superior forces without assistance. All their hopes were pinned, until the very last moment, on negotiations.

The first indications of serious trouble came shortly after sunset on the night of 1 August. The Kuwaitis had been watching the massive Iraqi forces poised on their northern frontier through their own border posts and the airborne ground surveillance radar on the TCOM balloon. The Iraqis seemed to be moving all the way along the border, about ten kilometres inside Iraq. Some troops were moving to the west; others were closing up to the border.

At about 8.00 p.m., Kuwait Air Force Operations Officer and Deputy Commander, Colonel Fahd Al-Ameer called Deputy Chief of Staff Major-General Jaber Al-Khalid to report the Iraqi movements. Al-Khalid rushed to the

GHQ Operations Room, advised the Minister of Defence and Chief of Staff of the situation, and called in the Land Forces, Air Force and Navy commanders. National Guard commanders were also alerted. Orders from the Government continued to be to do nothing to aggravate the Iraqis. Saddam was definitely sabre-rattling, but if his troops crossed over, they were expected to take only a small border strip. Talks between the Iraqis and the Kuwaiti Crown Prince and Prime Minister were scheduled for Saturday, 4 August, in Baghdad, so a full invasion was unthinkable.

At about 9.15 p.m., Iraqi forces on the border asked Kuwaiti troops to stop conducting border patrols. By 10.00 p.m., the Kuwaiti General Staff had told the Land Forces and Air Force commanders to call in their unit commanders and staffs, and to load ammunition up to the limit of their existing authority. Government orders were still to do nothing. An hour later, light Iraqi units crossed the border and started surrounding five Kuwaiti border posts on Kuwaiti territory. A Kuwaiti patrol was fired on, but suffered no casualties. The incidents were reported to the Minister of Defence, but his order was for the patrols hold their fire and to remain in their posts. The Cabinet was in session, considering its response.

Shortly after midnight, the Iraqis moved in on the first border post, capturing it. Other posts fell in rapid succession. At about 12.30 a.m., the Kuwaiti generals finally received a verbal order to go on alert. With their airborne ground surveillance radar, they could see the movement of massive formations of Iraqi armour just across the border, but they had yet to cross over.

Iraq had been planning the invasion for at least a month, if not more. It was not a spur of the moment action. It takes time to assemble and task the massive forces used.

The initial Iraqi objectives were to neutralize the armed forces, and kill or capture the Amir and the Crown Prince – who also served as Prime Minister – to eliminate the Kuwaiti leadership. They would surround the metropolitan area, cutting it off from the south, and also any reinforcements which might come from the GCC's (Gulf Cooperation Council) Peninsula Shield force in Saudi Arabia. The Iraqis need not have worried. The Peninsula Shield existed more on paper than in reality.

The Iraqi assault plan was a classic combined arms envelopment operation, well-planned but hastily executed. Prior to the invasion, Iraq had infiltrated hundreds of agents into the country, and brought their weapons in through their embassy's diplomatic baggage. The hotels were full of Iraqis who had checked in during the past week. They had also slipped men into the Ras Al-Jalayh area, near the navy base. This was not difficult as the area is dotted with beach chalets, and heavily trafficked with private fishing boats.

The first attacks in Kuwait City were made at about 4.00 a.m. by these infiltrators, dressed in civilian clothes and using private cars as cover for what the Iraqis would later claim was a domestic coup attempt. They could not overwhelm the Amiri Guard at the Amir's Dasman Palace residence, so contented themselves with shooting up the area to create a diversion, and preparing to guide in heliborne reinforcements to take the palace.

One of the first casualties of the invasion was an Egyptian car park attendant at the Kuwait International Hotel, opposite the US Embassy. His life was saved as he was dozing in his booth with his head down. One bullet went over his head. Another went lower, and hit him in the leg.

On Wednesday evening, 1 August, before the Iraqi infiltrators started terrorizing Kuwait City, a large Iraqi naval force left Iraq's Umm Qasr naval base, near the Kuwaiti border, heading for three main points on the Kuwaiti mainland: the Salmiya residential area on the southern lip of Kuwait Bay, the Shuaiba port, south of the oil complex, and the Ras Al-Jalayh naval base.

At the time, the Iraqi Navy was thought to have eight Soviet-built Osa fast attack craft, armed with Styx anti-ship missiles or 56mm forward guns, and 38mm aft guns. The Osas were an excellent craft, very fast. They also had numerous smaller vessels, including hovercraft, amphibious vehicles, locally-built small landing craft, and three large *Polnochy* class landing craft.

To complete the flotilla, numerous small civilian craft had apparently been pressed into service. Quite literally scores of Iraqi vessels were swarming towards Kuwait's shores, each of the three waves led by several Osas. With the sea state glassy calm, and a light haze, they had no problem navigating the 160 kilometres to bring them offshore from their targets by dawn.

At about 1.00 a.m. on 2 August, shortly after Iraqi forces captured the first Kuwaiti border posts, the main Iraqi force of 300 tanks and armoured vehicles, with artillery, swept across the northern border.

The main axis of the Iraqi ground advance was straight south. Its core consisted of two of the four Republican Guard divisions tasked to the invasion, the *Hammurabi*, followed by the *Nebuchadnezzar* as the second wave. The *Hammurabi's* two armoured brigades headed down the Abdaly Road towards Jahra. Its third brigade, of mechanized infantry, crossed over at Umm Qasr, drove straight down the road on the Kuwaiti mainland opposite Bubiyan Island, secured the Bubiyan bridge, and then turned west along the northern shore of Kuwait Bay below the Zoor Escarpment, before linking up again with the main column at Mutla'a. Once there, the *Hammurabi* would split into two columns again, one heading into the heart of Kuwait City along Jahra Road, and the other heading along Sixth Ring Road to the International Airport and beyond. Elements of the *Hammurabi* were to surround the Ali Al-Salem KAF base, after it had been bombed by the Iraqi Air Force.

To the west, about half-way along the Wadi Al-Batin, the other two Republican Guard divisions, the *Medina* and the *Tawakalna*, entered Kuwait across the desert. Their orders were to intersect the Salmi Road and drive east up it past Ali Al-Salem to the Sixth Ring intersection at Atraf, and then on into southern Kuwait. They were slower than expected in crossing as they had to contend with poor roads on the Iraqi side of the border. The lead division, the *Medina*, would not reach the Salmi Road until late morning.

Seeing the initial Iraqi movements on their radar in the early hours of 2 August, the panicked Kuwaiti generals could be in no doubt that the Iraqis were going to advance more than a few kilometres. They quickly abandoned any hope of holding the Iraqis in the north. The priority was now to defend the metropolitan area.

At 2.00 a.m., the Land Forces commander was ordered to hold a line at Mutla'a Ridge to Subiya, the only natural barrier available to the Kuwaitis, while 6 Brigade, with barely a battalion in its base, was ordered to withdraw to Mutla'a before it was cut off. Once there, it was to link up with Colonel Suleiman Al-Bargash's 80 Brigade and a Kuwaiti Special Forces company under Lieutenant-Colonel Abdulwahab Al-Anzi and try to hold the pass where the road from Abdaly cuts through Mutla'a Ridge. Meanwhile, 35 Brigade received orders to deploy into the open desert north of Ali Al-Salem, to defend the base and flank the Iraqis, while 15 Brigade was to rush from its base far in the south to help 6 Brigade. However, neither 15 Brigade nor 35 Brigade were yet in a position to leave their camps. Both heavy units were frantically trying to load their vehicles and find crews for them.

By 2.30 a.m., the Crown Prince and Prime Minister and most of the Cabinet were at the GHQ Operations Room, monitoring the situation with the generals. Chaos reigned in both the GHQ and the bases as rumours abounded and orders were given and countermanded. Officers and men were still being called in from their homes, if they could be found.

By about 3.30 a.m., the first wave of the Iraqi *Hammurabi* Division had reached Jahra, 18km from the GHQ. Its vanguard was briefly engaged as it came down Mutla'a Ridge by several hastily-deployed Kuwaiti Saladin armoured cars, but they were hopelessly outgunned. The Kuwaitis withdrew after incurring casualties and running out of ammunition. The Iraqis had not expected a fight. They were surprised at the resistance, but quickly crushed it.

Incredibly, events were moving so swiftly that Colonel Fahd Al-Issa, the Commander of 6 Brigade, found himself driving south parallel to an Iraqi column from the *Hammurabi* as he was withdrawing to Jahra. The Iraqis were on the main road, and the Kuwaitis on a nearby track. The Iraqis, presumably believing their own story that they were entering Kuwait to help with a revolution, did not fire at the Kuwaiti vehicles, apparently thinking that they were joining them in their drive into the city. In the confusion, Al-Issa was unable to link up with 80 Brigade or the Special Forces. His forces were scattered in the dark. There would be nothing but a few platoons of National Guard to stop the Iraqis until they reached the Mubarak Camp GHQ.

In Washington DC, the Pentagon and CIA were reportedly aware at midnight Kuwait time that the invasion was imminent. However, like the Kuwaitis, they had no way of telling how far the Iraqis would go. The considered assessment of both the US Central Command and the CIA was that it would only be a border land-grab. Reports from Western embassies in Baghdad told them little more than what was available in the press. In fact, at the time, White House staff were still preparing a message to Saddam urging restraint.

The US and British embassies in Kuwait were both on half-alert that evening. On the afternoon of 1 August, before the staff of the US Embassy had gone home for the weekend, the senior diplomats had been told not to go anywhere they could not be reached by phone. Ambassador Nat Howell had told the duty officer for the night, Kevin Briscoe, to call him, but not to be too concerned if he received any unusual messages.

The British were similarly placed. As late as the afternoon of 1 August, the embassy's Political and Information Officer, John Raine, had briefed visiting journalists that the Iraqis were most unlikely to cross the border, but that if they did, they would remain in the largely uninhabited northern half. Little fighting was expected. After all, the Kuwaiti Crown Prince and Prime Minister was still meeting with the Iraqis in Jeddah, and further talks were planned for Baghdad the following week. Several senior British journalists, including Patrick Bishop from *The Telegraph* newspaper, Michael Macmillan from BBC TV, and Tim Llewelyn from the BBC in Cyprus, had visited Kuwait in the light of the Iraqi threats. They apparently concluded that there was not going to be a big story, and departed. A number of lesser journalists, including a *Times* stringer, Giancarlo Gumuccio, Caryle Murphy of the *Washington Post's* Cairo bureau, and Hettie Lubberding from Dutch Radio were still in town, but preparing to leave.

Nevertheless, the British Embassy was manned overnight at a higher level than usual. Ambassador Michael Weston was joined overnight in his Residence on the compound by his Deputy, Tony Millson, the local MI-6 man, Tony Paice, and one other official. The diplomats were not to be disappointed. At about 3.00 a.m., Kevin Briscoe in the US Embassy received a message from the Kuwaiti military reporting that the Iraqis had crossed the border and had captured several border posts. The British received similar advice. American Ambassador Nat Howell was roused and briefed. He reported to Washington, but it was still unclear that the incursion – which had been anticipated – was the precursor of a fully-fledged invasion. The Kuwaiti generals were too preoccupied in trying to find out what was going on and mobilize their forces to brief the embassies fully.

By about 4.00 a.m., Howell had his own direct confirmation that the invasion would go all the way to Kuwait City. The Iraqis infiltrated into the city during the previous week were firing into the air outside his compound walls in front of the Kuwait International Hotel. The British were even closer to the action. Only a small strip of vacant land separated them from the Amir's Dasman Palace, a major Iraqi target.

The embassies went on a crisis footing and called in their staff. At 4.10 a.m., British DHM Tony Millson called John Raine at home, and asked him to get the word out. Reuters was briefed by 4.30 a.m. The BBC would carry the news on its World Service bulletin at 6.00 a.m. Other diplomats were being roused, and told to report to their embassies if it was safe to do so. Everyone was scrambling for information. Was the crisis an external invasion, or an internal insurrection? Who was fighting whom?

Western forces in the region were helpless. The US Navy had several warships in the Gulf, but only one, the USS *Robert G. Bradley*, was near Kuwait. The Royal Navy Armilla Patrol had four warships on duty in the Gulf at the time, but none close to the scene. In any event, the Kuwaitis had not asked formally for assistance, and it was impossible to contact anyone in authority from the Kuwaiti Government. At about 5.00 a.m., the US Ambassador received a desperate call from a functionary at the Kuwaiti Ministry of Foreign Affairs saying, 'Now is the time for America to come to the aid of Kuwait!', but it was too late to do anything.

As the Iraqi ground forces crossed the border, the Kuwait Navy base at Ras Al-Jalayh was staffed with only an overnight skeleton crew of perhaps 50 men. One of the eight Lurssen fast patrol boats, *Sanbouk*, had been on patrol at sea for two days, and was about 40km south of Failaka island.

At 2.00 a.m., Major Jassim Al-Ansari, the Acting Commander of the Navy's 1st Squadron and skipper of *Istiqlal*, the Navy's flagship, was ordered to his base from home. Sensing that something was not right, Al-Ansari was still awake when the call came. He kissed his wife and children good-bye, something he had seldom done on his way out to work, even when the Navy had been deployed during the Iran-Iraq war. It would be seven long months before he would speak to or see them again.

Arriving at Ras Al-Jalayh at 3.00 a.m., Al-Ansari went straight to his vessel, ordered the duty officer to call in all the crew from home, and to prepare for sea. He then reported to the base headquarters, but the only news the navy had then was that Iraqi artillery had fired on the northern borders.

The roads had been quiet on the 60km drive from suburban Kuwait, and the skipper of the patrolling *Sanbouk*, Captain Yacoub Al-Muhanna, reported no movement on his radar. There was no guidance from GHQ, so the officers decided to call in all available navy personnel to ready those vessels they could for sea. One of the eight fast patrol boats was in dry-dock and a second had been stripped of her weapons and ammunition in preparation for dry-docking. The Kuwaitis had only six vessels at their disposal, and the only one of these with a full crew was the patrolling *Sanbouk*.

In the meantime, the KAF had been in action. At 3.45 a.m., the Air Operations Centre advised Ali Al-Salem of incoming aircraft – about 70 helicopters, heading for the base and Kuwait City. The base commander, Colonel Saber Al-Suwaidan, scrambled four of his Mirage interceptors at 3.55 a.m., each armed with two MAGIC-1 missiles and 30mm cannon. The pilots, Captain Mohammed Al-Dossari, and Lieutenants Habis Al-Mutairi, Abdullah Suwailim, and Ali Al-Anzi, each shot down two helicopters with their MAGICs. Another two Mirages were launched an hour later. Major Taher Al-Taher in one shot down two helicopters with his missiles - one of which was trying to jam the HAWK missile radars on Failaka Island - and then a third with his 30mm cannon. His colleague, Lieutenant Bassam Al-Jouaid, got one.

The Iraqis were not long in retaliating. As the sky lightened, they attacked all three KAF bases simultaneously at 5.25 a.m. with about six aircraft each, using Sukhoi bombers, escorted by their own Mirages, hitting the runways, taxiways, and the lubrication shop at Ali Al-Salem. It was a well-coordinated attack. Another aircraft hit the Umm Al-Haiman telephone exchange to disrupt communications with the Ras Al-Jalayh Naval Base further south, putting a bomb in the precise room needed to knock it out.

At the time, Ali Al-Salem had several aircraft aloft. They were ordered to divert to Al-Jaber base, or the Al-Adamy Border Station with Saudi Arabia.

When the Mirages arrived over Al-Jaber, they found that it too had been bombed. Air-dropped mines were scattered all over the runway. Clearance crews were unavailable to deal with them, and the Mirages had insufficient fuel to reach Saudi Arabia safely.

The pilots were faced with attempting a suicidal landing on bombed runways, or ejecting and abandoning their aircraft, when someone suggested that they try a security road which ran just inside the perimeter fence of the base. The road was 2,700 metres long and 4.5 metres wide, hardly enough for two cars to pass side by side, but just wide enough for a Mirage undercarriage. The pilots brought their aircraft in safely, and ground crews rushed out to retrieve the pilots and refuel the aircraft.

This incident proved to be particularly significant in the defence of Kuwait. At the time, the commanders of Al-Jaber base thought that they would be unable to operate their A-4s from their damaged and mined runways, but now, using the road, they would be able to fight.

At 6.00 a.m., all operational Gazelles, Pumas and Super Puma helicopters at Ali Al-Salem, and the BAe Hawks at Al-Jaber were ordered to the border. A number of the helicopters from Ali Al-Salem went first to International Base. It was then under attack by Iraqi ground forces, so they diverted to Al-Jaber, and landed to refuel. From there, they later went to Saudi Arabia. Some of the helicopters remained at Ali Al-Salem and Al-Jaber until they could be readied for escape later. Six of the 12 Hawks flew out to Bahrain, and six under maintenance at the time were later captured. Three of the four C-130s and one of the two DC-9s at the International Base also managed to fly out.

The Mirages – most of which were still at Ali Al-Salem – were not out of the fight yet. Two more took off at 6.30 a.m. from the undamaged parts of the runways, shooting down two Iraqi helicopters before flying to Al-Jaber and landing on the perimeter road to refuel. Over the next three hours, all but eight of the 23 Mirages managed to take off for Saudi Arabia. One of these shot down an Iraqi helicopter to bring the total for the Mirages for the morning to 15.

Meanwhile, three of the four HAWK air defence missile batteries were also in action. Only the Mutla'a battery was unable to operate. The others were straining at the leash. They had Iraqi aircraft on their radars, but with the confusion in the Air Operations Centre were unable to get the order to fire. Several of them took matters into their own hands.

The first battery in action was the one on Failaka Island, at 4.50 a.m., taking down an Iraqi fighter. Over the next three hours, it shot down a further confirmed three fighters, and one unconfirmed. At 9.15 a.m., it engaged three helicopters with a missile each, but was unable to confirm the kills. It destroyed one at 2.30 p.m. with its last missile.

During the day, the Kuwaitis fired 24 HAWK missiles for a confirmed toll of ten Iraqi helicopters and four fixed-wing fighters, with three unconfirmed helicopters and one unconfirmed fighter. Tragically, one of the Pumas fell victim to a Kuwaiti HAWK near Ahmadi, killing two officers and two enlisted men. The battery sites on the mainland had little or no perimeter defence, and were overrun in the afternoon.

As the KAF bases were dealing with incoming Iraqi aircraft from the north, Iraqi Special Forces were flying east across the Gulf by helicopter from Iraq to reinforce the infiltrators preparing to attack the Amir's residence.

At this time, the Crown Prince and Prime Minister, Sheikh Sa'ad Al-Abdullah, had been at the Ministry of Defence Mubarak Camp GHQ with most of the Cabinet since about 2.30 a.m. The Amir was still at the Dasman Palace. At about 4.00 a.m., with the sound of tanks and gunfire ever closer, the senior Kuwaiti officers at GHQ advised Sheikh Sa'ad and the Ministers to leave. The intention was for the Cabinet and generals to relocate to a fall-back underground command bunker at the Air Defence Base, leaving Director of Operations Brigadier Jassim Shehab and his staff in command at the GHQ.

The Cabinet and senior officers left the GHQ in a convoy of cars. Navy Commander Colonel Qais Al-Saleh headed for his own base at Ras Al-Jalayh, 70km away. It was obvious now that the Iraqis intended to take the city, if not the entire country. Sheikh Sa'ad realized that the Amir would be a priority target, and that the Amiri Guard could not possibly hold out for long against the massive armoured force now driving headlong into the city. It was vital for the integrity of the Government and the country that the Iraqis did not capture or kill the Amir. Instead of following the generals, Sheikh Sa'ad called the Amir on his car phone, saying he was coming to the Dasman Palace to get him, to relocate him out of harm's way. Arriving at the palace at 4.35 a.m., Sheikh Sa'ad persuaded the reluctant Amir to leave. They left the palace shortly before 5.00 a.m. and sped south towards Saudi Arabia.

Shortly after 5.00 a.m., the Iraqi infiltrators, reinforced by helicopter-borne Special Forces, launched their attack on the Amiri Guard at the palace. The Amir's youngest brother, Sheikh Fahd Al-Ahmad, unaware of the developments of the past few hours, arrived at the palace gate with two companions less than 30 minutes after the Amir's departure, and was killed by a stray shot in the head in his car just outside the gates.

By this time, the Amir and key elements of his Government were safe in the far south of the country. They had had an extremely narrow escape. Over the next few hours, the Kuwaiti Amiri Guard in and around the Dasman Palace put up a fierce fight, but they were hopelessly outnumbered. Skirmishes continued around the palace until about 2.00 p.m., but scattered shots could be heard from inside its walls and in the surrounding suburbs until that evening. Two Amiri Guards and two civilian employees of the Amir were killed, as was a National Guardsman at the Amiri Diwan.

The most notable casualty that morning, Sheikh Fahd Al-Ahmad, was one of the most popular and accessible members of the ruling family. As Chief of the Kuwait Football Association and Chairman of the Asian Olympic Committee, he was a leading international and national figure in the sports world. The Iraqis realized only later who they had killed, but by the time they went to look for his body it had been spirited away to a mortuary by the Kuwaitis and was later buried under a false name.

The death of a prominent member of the ruling family in the invasion was of great significance to the Kuwaiti people. The Al-Sabah family had shared directly in the nation's loss of life and suffering. The escape of the Amir and

Crown Prince and Prime Minister was even more important as it allowed the Kuwaiti Government to remain intact throughout the crisis.

At 4.13 a.m., as Iraqi forces closed in on the city, British Airways Flight BA149 from Heathrow to Kuala Lumpur via Kuwait and Madras, under Captain Richard Brunyate, landed at Kuwait International Airport, minutes before British diplomats in Kuwait advised Reuters of the invasion. The 747 aircraft carried 367 passengers. Eleven were children; 63 were British nationals. Most of the others were Indians or Malaysians, with a sprinkling of Americans, four Australians, a Canadian, four French, two Italians, a New Zealander, a Spaniard, and four West Germans.

BA149's timing was most unfortunate. If it had landed half an hour earlier, it may have been able to take off again before the airport was closed. Had it been half an hour later, it would have been warned off just before landing, and could have diverted safely. Instead, the 747 was cleared to land by Kuwait Air Traffic Control at a time when the invasion had been under way for at least three hours, and the KAF was already in action against incoming Iraqi aircraft. The airport was finally closed shortly after 5.00 a.m.

Before leaving London, Captain Brunyate and the BA operations management had been sufficiently concerned about news reports of the tension between Kuwait and Iraq to make enquiries of the FCO (Foreign and Commonwealth Office). They were given the same answer as the local BA manager: the situation was normal. Furthermore, during the flight, Brunyate had spoken by radio with London-bound flight BA148 which had left Kuwait at 1.30 a.m. The other pilot reported nothing out of the ordinary. BA had serviced Kuwait without disruption throughout the entire Iran-Iraq War from 1980 to 1988, and despite the current tension, Iraq and Kuwait were still Arab neighbours. An invasion was the last thing anyone expected.

There was only a handful of disembarking passengers, an American family and an Arab man in First Class, and about a dozen people in Economy. Most of the passengers were going on to Madras and Kuala Lumpur.

The American family in First Class comprised Mr B. George Saloom, his wife Debra, and his son G. Preston, from San Diego. Saloom was arriving in Kuwait for the first time to take up a post with a local bank. Two of the Economy Class passengers were Mel Gage, a long-time British resident of Kuwait who would later become a key part of the British community in hiding, and a London *Financial Times* journalist, Victor Mallet.

The Salooms disembarked without incident, and collected their baggage. There was an air of tension which they could not quite put their finger on, but they were new to Kuwait, and thought little of it. The airport was quiet, and virtually empty, and the regular guards were still on duty. They passed through immigration and customs unusually quickly, and were met by a driver.

The Economy passengers disembarked next. Before deplaning, one of them saw a member of the BA ground staff who was a personal friend. He was told, 'If you're going to get off, get off quickly.' The ground crew were unsure what the problem was, but something was obviously wrong. This passenger came from the rear of Economy, where 32 British SAS men were later alleged to have boarded the aircraft through the rear door several minutes before take-off, and later disembarked in Kuwait. He saw no evidence of this.

As the Saloom family left the airport they heard what sounded like thunder, and asked their driver what it was. His English was poor, but he said, 'Not to worry'. They saw no evidence of military activity on the drive north into the city, but as they turned the last street corner before the hotel there were two loud, hollow explosions, like a car backfiring. Then, as they were checking into the hotel there was a burst of automatic fire outside the front door. They turned around to see troops outside. The family could not identify their nationality, but they were Iraqis – the very same men my neighbour and I watched capturing the two Kuwaiti policemen minutes later.

The Economy passengers followed the First Class passengers and aircrew through immigration quickly, also noticing that it was unusually quiet. Several of the passengers, including Mel Gage and the journalist, waited at the luggage carousel for their bags to appear. After about 20 minutes, the BA ground staff told them that nothing else was coming off. Annoyed, Mel turned to go home, and Mallet decided to check into his hotel, intending to retrieve their bags the following day. As they left the terminal it seemed that all the airport staff were leaving.

Victor Mallet took a taxi for the Sheraton Hotel, in central Kuwait City. He would never arrive there. Mel Gage hailed a taxi home. His route took him north up the freeway from the terminal, and as he neared Sixth Ring, about 20 tanks passed him, heading south towards the airport on the other side of the road. He was unable to identify the tanks, but assumed they were Kuwaiti. They were not. Within half an hour the first bombs exploded on the runway as several Iraqi bombers streaked by after attacking the nearby KAF Headquarters. The remaining crew and the luckless BA transit passengers were hurried off the plane and into the relative safety of the terminal building as puffs of black smoke and muffled booms came from scattered tanks now visible around the airport perimeter. The southern arm of the Iraqi armoured pincer was encircling the airport from its thrust along Seventh Ring.

By 4.30 a.m., at the Kuwait Navy's Ras Al-Jalayh base, a few more officers and men had reported, but those officers on the base trying to call their colleagues at home were having great problems getting through to the city. The telephone lines seemed to have been either jammed or cut. *Istiqlal* had established a data link with *Sanbouk*, but there still did not appear to be a threat from the sea. Major Al-Ansari on *Istiqlal* was seething with frustration. Only three of his officers and seven crew were available to run a vessel with a normal complement of 45.

Suddenly, reports came in of Iraqi paratroopers landing on Al-Jaber KAF base, and of Iraqi ground forces penetrating northern Kuwait and closing in on Kuwait City. The leading Iraqi tanks had indeed passed Jahra, but the reports of paratroopers were false. There was little the Navy could do to support the city, but they assumed that if the Iraqis were landing on Al-Jaber base, then Ras Al-Jalayh would be next.

Shortly afterwards, *Sanbouk* sent a flash message from sea saying she had Iraqi vessels and helicopters on her radar screens, moving towards Kuwait from the east. There was no indication of the type of vessels, or their number, but a seaward threat seemed to be developing. Earlier plans were revised: it was decided that *Istiqlal* - the only vessel with barely enough crew - would put to sea and engage the enemy.

As soon as Al-Ansari cleared the base around 5.00 a.m. and was able to bring *Istiqlal's* radar up, he saw scores of small Kuwaiti fishing boats running for land in front of literally scores of what could only be presumed to be small Iraqi vessels. There were small contacts in a 180° arc on his radar screens. At the same time, Captain Al-Muhanna on *Sanbouk* clarified his earlier flash message, reporting that the Iraqis were heading towards the coast in three waves. They had cleverly skirted the edge of the Kuwaitis' radar radius by swinging far out into the Gulf, and then racing in from the east. Without their Exocets on board, *Istiqlal* and *Sanbouk* could only prepare for action when the Osas came within the 16km range of their 76mm forward guns.

As *Istiqlal* was putting to sea, Colonel Qais Al-Saleh was nearing the base after the 70km drive from the GHQ. On the way, he had hardly seen another car on the road until the Amir's convoy with its red escort cars hurtled past him at high speed, several kilometres north of the base, near 15 Brigade's camp, heading south towards Saudi Arabia. At the time, Al-Saleh was aware that northern Kuwait was in Iraqi hands, and that they would now be closing on the GHQ. To him, the country seemed lost, but he was determined that his vessels would still fight if they could.

Arriving at the base, he immediately called the Deputy Chief of Staff, Major General Jaber Al-Khalid, now at the fall-back command bunker at the Air Defence Base, and asked for Air Force or Army support. 'Sorry,' said Al-Khalid. 'I cannot support you. You're on your own.'

Al-Saleh took stock of his situation. It was next to hopeless. Barely 100 men were on the base. Apart from weapons on the boats, they only had a couple of light machine guns, a few rifles used by the gate sentries - each with a handful of bullets - and a few pistols. Only four of the six remaining Lurssens at the base were not under repair or in dry-dock. His men were still trying to call in the crews for the missile boats, but most of them lived in the Jahra and Sulaibikhat areas, which the Iraqis had already passed, and sealed off. The base telephone exchange was jammed with incoming and outgoing calls. He issued his orders. 'We will support our vessels at sea to whatever extent we can, and try to get the others out. But if the Iraqis land at the base, we will consider it no longer under our control.' Al-Saleh was not about to throw his men's lives away in futile heroics. He ordered to *Istiqlal* and *Sanbouk* to stop any Iraqi vessels from reaching the base, if at all possible.

The Iraqi propaganda attack was co-ordinated with the military in a futile effort to provide some cover for the naked aggression, but was a little too early to be credible. At 5.45 a.m., ten minutes after Iraqi jets had screamed over Kuwait's suburbs and as Iraqi troops were still taking the city centre, Baghdad Radio announced that Kuwaiti revolutionary students and republicans were launching a coup against the ruling Al-Sabah, and warned against foreign intervention. Fifteen minutes later it declared that the Al-Sabah Government had been overthrown, and that Iraqi troops were entering Kuwait at the invitation of the new rulers to assist with the revolution.

The deceit was transparent. Not only was Kuwait far too stable for a motley group of dissidents to overthrow the Government, but the announcements were made up to six hours after the launch of an invasion which had taken weeks, if not months, to plan. Not every Kuwaiti agreed with the Government, but they were unanimous that it was *their* Government.

The Iraqis were not the only people driving into Kuwait City that morning. Hundreds of civilians were on their way to work, oblivious of the invasion. Inevitably, many of them would run into the Iraqis.

At 4.50 a.m., Tom Laming, a British manager who lived within sight of the Dasman Palace noticed helicopters over the palace. This was unusual, but he dismissed it as a Kuwaiti forces exercise. Tom got into his car as usual at 5.00 a.m., and drove west on First Ring towards his office on the other side of the city. The roads were usually empty at that time, so he noticed nothing unusual. However, as he stopped at a set of lights, he heard distant explosions and the crack of gunfire. As a retired army man, this did not sound to him like an exercise. Nevertheless, he could see no troops, and so pressed on, towards the Sheraton Hotel. It was 5.10 a.m. He was the only car on the road.

Suddenly, as he passed under a flyover opposite the Ministry of Information, several soldiers ran out onto the road firing their weapons into the air. Tom braked hard, stopped, and was pulled out of the car. The Iraqis were not violent. They were obviously scared – but they were disciplined. Tom was taken to a park on the roadside, and made to sit down with a small group of Asian workers captured earlier. The Saloom family, which had just disembarked from BA149, had passed unhindered along the same road only minutes earlier on their way to the Meridien Hotel.

Meanwhile, Victor Mallet, also from BA149, was in a taxi heading towards the Sheraton, wondering when he could retrieve his lost baggage. The taxi turned off the road from the airport onto First Ring, and almost immediately ran into a traffic jam of stationary cars which included Tom's. Victor and the taxi-driver were ordered from the car at gunpoint and taken to another nearby park. A few minutes made all the difference between safety and captivity.

On the other side of the city, near the Dasman Palace, the British Consul, Larry Banks, was having his own problems. He had been called at home at 5.16 a.m., and told to get into the embassy. As he left home, the Iraqi jets that had just bombed the airport screamed overhead.

Reaching the edge of the city centre at 5.45 a.m., he tried to turn onto the road running past the Dasman Palace to the embassy, but it was blocked by a Kuwaiti police car. The officers refused to let him through. This probably saved his life. He would have driven straight into the crossfire between the Iraqis attacking the palace, and the Amiri guards.

Larry carried on, planning to intersect the Gulf Road further on, and then drive back along it towards the embassy. He reached the coast without further incident and was within sight of the embassy when he was stopped by a soldier, taken out of his car, and manhandled onto the beach outside the embassy with several hundred other civilians, mainly Indians and Arabs who had been caught on their way to work, one of the embassy's Indian security guards, P.V.C. Joseph, and another Englishman, Mike Meade. Unknown to Larry, two of the people who joined the group were Sheikh Rashid and another man who had been with Sheikh Fahd Al-Ahmad when he was killed barely half an hour earlier. The Iraqis had herded all their prisoners from the Dasman Palace onto the beach, not knowing who they were.

By this time the Iraqis were shooting at anything that moved or refused to stop, even at dhows on Kuwait Bay. Larry could hear rounds cracking over his head, and looked up from the beach to see his car, still on the road, riddled by bullets. First things first. Larry searched around for rocks on the beach to build a little wall to shelter behind, and dug in. The situation was chaotic. It was a full hour before he realized that the attackers were actually Iraqis.

Larry's colleague, John Raine, who had advised Reuters of the invasion earlier, was more fortunate. He had made his way towards the embassy, but was merely turned back, and not captured. Some of the American diplomats were even luckier. Most of the senior American officials lived on or next to their compound, and could walk in across the road. They were further from the Dasman Palace, and out of the immediate line of fire: nevertheless, they could hear the intense gunfire from the battle less than a kilometre away.

Far to the west, near Jahra, Stewart Griffiths, a British Wood Group engineer in his late forties, ran straight into the Iraqi Army on his way to work.

He had left his apartment at 5.30 a.m. for the hour's drive along Sixth Ring to work in northern Kuwait.The drive was perfectly normal until he sighted several smoke plumes in the distance. He was diverted by Kuwaiti police off the main road, through Jahra, and eventually back onto the main road. The police had said nothing to him about an invasion. The plumes of smoke, which were burning vehicles or helicopters, could have been from oilfield flares to a civilian on his way to work. Several kilometres beyond Jahra, as the road rises up the Mutla'a Ridge, Stewart was stopped by soldiers he presumed were Kuwaiti. They asked him where he was going. He told them where he worked, and showed them his pass. They waved him on without comment.

At the top of the ridge, a kilometre or two further on, he encountered more troops. They were not as friendly. They ordered him out of his car at gunpoint, and over to the side of the road to join three Indian colleagues already there. When pressed, an officer explained that Stewart was now a prisoner of the Iraqi Army which had entered Kuwait to support the Revolution. Stewart was astounded. It was the start of a four-month ordeal.

Thirty kilometres beyond Mutla'a, Colonel Al-Sarour at Kuwait's 35 Brigade had finally left his camp at 4.30 a.m., with a reinforced TOW platoon, his command vehicle and a jeep, leaving orders with his battalion commanders to catch up with him as soon as they could. The situation was developing so rapidly that the GHQ could not keep up with it. To aggravate matters, there were rumours that Iraqi paratroops had landed on Ali Al-Salem. Al-Sarour's impossible three-way mission was to defend Ali Al-Salem 23km to his north-east, secure the junction at Atraf where Sixth Ring meets the road from Salmi, and block the north–south road to the Iraqi border at Mutla'a Ridge.

Back at 35 Brigade's camp, confusion reigned. False reports were coming in that Ali Al-Salem, the Jiwan/Mubarak Camp GHQ in the city, and the Special

Forces camp in Jahra had all been captured, together with the (correct) news that 6 Brigade had fallen, and that 80 Brigade was surrounded in Jahra. The Commander of the 7th Armoured Battalion, Lieutenant-Colonel Ahmad Al-Wazzan, started to lay plans for a withdrawal from the camp to Saudi Arabia. However, within minutes the incorrect reports were clarified, and Al-Wazzan received orders to follow Al-Sarour to defend Mutla'a.

Al-Sarour headed slowly towards Jahra up the Salmi Road with Al-Wazzan's 25 Chieftains, now fully armed and fuelled, catching up with him. Nearing the intersection of Sixth Ring just before 6.00 a.m., he encountered a lone Kuwaiti soldier who had just escaped from Jahra. Apparently the Iraqis were already there, and had surrounded a force of Kuwaitis in a local school. The Iraqis had told them to surrender, or be annihilated.

Colonel Al-Sarour's men could hear the engines of the Iraqi vehicles, and the squeak and clank of their tracks, along Sixth Ring, just below a slight ridge ahead of them, but the Kuwaitis could not yet see them. Al-Sarour turned north off the road onto high ground overlooking Jahra, and sighted the Iraqis pouring southwards on Sixth Ring. Al-Wazzan soon caught up and quickly deployed his tanks, apparently unseen by the Iraqis.

At 6.45 a.m., 35 Brigade's Chieftains opened fire on the right flank of the Iraqi column at a range of about two kilometres. This second wave of the *Hammurabi* Republican Guard did not expect such stiff opposition after the successful passage of the first wave. They were on the road in column, and had not reconnoitered or secured their flanks in their haste to reach their objectives. 35 Brigade could hear the panic on the Iraqi radios.

Curiously, the Iraqis were using old T-55s, against the Kuwaiti Chieftains. With their modern laser sights, the Kuwaitis could initially pick off the Iraqi vehicles before the Iraqis could range on them. Fortunately, the more capable Iraqi T-72s were being brought down to Kuwait on low-loader transporters, and were not used in the initial fighting.

By the time 35 Brigade was in action, the Iraqis had taken the city centre north of First Ring, the airport, and Sixth and Seventh Rings. It was almost three hours since the first Iraqi tanks had passed through the intersection on their way to the airport, and moments after the unfortunate Stewart Griffiths was captured at Mutla'a on his way to work. Metropolitan Kuwait was surrounded, except for the suburbs down the coastal strip and the oil suburbs of Ahmadi and Fahaheel. The Iraqis then proceeded to fill the pocket, bringing in waves of troops in helicopters, trucks, and buses. Their next targets were the Amir's workplace in the Bayan Palace on the southern edge of Fifth Ring, and the Residence of the Crown Prince and Prime Minister at Sha'ab on the coast.

As 35 Brigade was setting up its positions, 15 Brigade far to the south under Colonel Mohammed Al-Harmi was trying to get to the city. Al-Harmi had gathered 14 tanks and their crews, and a dozen BMPs, loaded them onto transporters, and left camp at 4.15 a.m., with urgent orders to assist 6 Brigade beyond Mutla'a. At the time, 6 Brigade had already been passed by the Iraqis but in the chaos, the GHQ had not updated him. Al-Harmi told his deputy, Colonel Tawfiq Al-Abdulrazzak, to follow him as soon as he could with more vehicles and the brigade artillery. His plan was to head north, turn west onto Seventh Ring Road, skirt Jahra, and drive up the Abdaly Road to 6 Brigade.

By the time Al-Harmi's convoy had reached Shuaiba, about 25 km north of their camp, they received word from the Land Forces that an Iraqi armoured brigade which had bypassed the GHQ was headed towards them. They dismounted their tanks and BMPs from the transporters so that they would be ready to fight, and continued warily north, watching out for the Iraqi armour.

At 5.00 a.m., Al-Harmi received a message from Colonel Abdulhamid Al-Taher in the Land Forces Headquarters, asking where he was going. 'To help 6 Brigade, as ordered earlier!' he replied.

'Forget it,' said Al-Taher. '6 Brigade is already finished. The Iraqis are well past Mutla'a. We need help at the GHQ.'

Sensing the confusion at the GHQ, Al-Harmi requested a clear order. Soon after, the Commander Land Forces, Colonel Abdul Aziz Al-Bargash and the Director of Operations called him with orders to make all haste to the GHQ, and to deploy an armoured section to defend the Air Defence Base, where the Minister of Defence and the senior officers had relocated. Al-Harmi bypassed Seventh Ring, and continued directly into the metropolitan area, turning onto Fourth Ring, and speeding along it towards the GHQ.

By 7.00 a.m., Al-Harmi and his two dozen armoured vehicles, with trucks and jeeps, reached the Shuwaikh industrial area, separated from the GHQ only by a flyover. They stopped on the side of the road to reassemble, within earshot of scattered shooting around the camps, invisible to them on the other other side of the bridge. They did not want to approach too hastily, and be misidentified as Iraqis. Suddenly, several light Iraqi vehicles drove down the road, oblivious to the Kuwaiti tanks. They were engaged and destroyed.

Meanwhile, three more tanks from the 151st Armoured Battalion had left 15 Brigade's base, heading north under Lieutenant-Colonel Faisal Al-Adwani. Within the metropolitan area, near the intersection of Fifth Ring and the Maghreb-Assafar Motorway, they encountered three or four light Iraqi vehicles bringing Iraqi troops to attack the nearby Bayan Palace. The Kuwaitis opened fire, destroying the vehicles, and continued on.

At sea, at around 6.00 a.m., the Kuwait Navy's *Istiqlal* and its skeleton crew were closing in on Kubbar Island. Its skipper, Major Al-Ansari, was trying to put himself in a position to support *Sanbouk*. Suddenly, three large high-speed contacts appeared on *Istiqlal's* radar, 12km east of Kubbar. They were turning west towards Ras Al-Jalayh. Al-Ansari was unsure what they were. By the time he had identified the lead vessel, it was 12km south of him. In fact, it was an Iraqi Osa, heading for Ras Al-Jalayh at an incredible 38 knots. This was in excess of *Istiqlal's* own top speed, but the Osa would have to slow down as he neared the coast. *Istiqlal* turned around, and sped off in pursuit.

Al-Ansari radioed Major Khalid Al-Faraj at the base that the Iraqi vessel was heading towards them, and received a direct order to fire warning shots. *Istiqlal* opened fire with her forward 76mm gun at a range of about 11km. The shells landed just in front of the speeding Iraqi, but he kept going. Al-Ansari requested and received permission to destroy him.

Just then, things started to go badly wrong. Al-Ansari's targeting screen lost its vertical hold. Without his technicians on board, he had to make do. He fired several shells almost blind at the speeding Osa, without effect.

In the meantime, *Sanbouk* was in action against another Osa north of Kubbar. However, Al-Muhanna was also suffering systems failures, and had to withdraw towards Ras Al-Jalayh to give his crew time to rectify the problems. Electronic gremlins had launched their own attacks on both Kuwaiti vessels at the most critical moment.

At about 6.15 a.m., the Osa being pursued by *Istiqlal* closed on the base. The Iraqis had packed the boat with Republican Guards, and knew their target well. In fact, they had visited the base on a friendly visit six weeks earlier. The chief of that delegation was now commanding the Iraqi naval task force.

The Kuwaiti craft still in the base were moored in an artificial basin formed by two concrete sea walls with a single narrow entrance, facing north. The Iraqi Osa headed straight for this entrance from the northeast, but the opening was partially obstructed by a Kuwaiti landing craft trying to get out to sea, with one of the Kuwait missile boats trying to get out from behind it. The Iraqi commander veered away from the entrance, and headed for a construction contractor's jetty outside the basin, on the northern edge of the base. From the jetty, it was only a short distance to the northern gate, through which most of the Kuwait Navy men reporting to the base would normally come. By landing there, not only would the Iraqis be protected from the Kuwaiti boats' guns by the Kuwaitis' own sea walls, but they would be able to seal off the base from landward reinforcements much quicker.

Watching from the sea, *Istiqlal* could see the Osa heading for the contractor's jetty, expecting with mounting anticipation to see him run aground any moment on two rocks known to obstruct the jetty's approaches. But the Iraqi was incredibly lucky. His dog-leg away from the entrance inadvertently put him in a narrow strip of safe water between the rocks and the shore. He reached the jetty safely. Al-Ansari could not now fire on him for fear of hitting his own colleagues in the base. The Osa turned its forward 56mm gun towards the exit of the basin, trapping all the Kuwaiti vessels inside. From now on, to bring their own guns to bear, the Kuwaitis would have to first clear the exit, by which time the Iraqis could fire. Apart from *Istiqlal* and *Sanbouk*, the Kuwait Navy was in checkmate.

About 50 Republican Guard commandos leapt off the Osa, and deployed ashore cautiously. They were outside the main base area where most of the Kuwaitis were, beyond a brick wall which bisected the base internally. The wall would not stop them for long. Seeing this, Colonel Qais Al-Saleh sent an officer to the access road to the main gate to stop any other Kuwaitis approaching the base from there, then jumped into his car and drove across the base and through a gate in the wall, towards the landing point. The leading Republican Guards stopped him by pointing an RPG at his car as he neared them, ordered him from the vehicle, and escorted him towards the docked Osa. Al-Saleh remembers that they seemed to be completely brainwashed that the Kuwaitis had been stealing their money. They had obviously been hyped up for the mission by their officers.

At the Osa, Al-Saleh recognised the Iraqi Navy colonel in charge of the operation from his recent visit. In fact, he had known him from earlier co-operation during the Iran-Iraq War. He was even shocked to recognise the Osa as a recently purchased vessel which had been delivered to a Kuwaiti port for the Iraqis, and which the Kuwait Navy had towed to Umm Qasr for them.

'What the hell are you doing here?' Al-Saleh shouted at the Iraqi. The Iraqi, seemingly totally relaxed, smiled, saluted, and said: 'Good morning, Sir. We are here on a training mission.'

'Then why didn't you tell us?' replied Al-Saleh, sarcastically. The Iraqi, still incredibly relaxed said: 'The objective was to surprise you.'

In the meantime, more Republican Guards were moving inland, towards the main base. One Iraqi was lying on the jetty, writhing in pain from having crushed his foot between the boat and the jetty as he jumped off. Other than that, the Iraqis seemed to have everything their own way. Knowing that his sailors were no match for these troops, Al-Saleh told the colonel to tell his men not to shoot. 'They have orders not to shoot unless they are fired upon,' said the colonel reassuringly.

'I want to go back to my people,' said Al-Saleh. 'I'm sorry,' said the Iraqi. 'You will stay with me,' and took him aboard the Osa.

The Iraqi infantry soon took the northern gate and sealed it off, preventing further Kuwaitis from entering the base. A Kuwaiti officer on the main gate turned a machine gun from the guard post onto the Iraqis advancing on him from inside his own base, and fired a few shots. The Iraqis replied with an RPG which, fortunately for the Kuwaiti, glanced off the concrete and exploded harmlessly beyond. He gave up.

By now, two more Kuwaiti 45-metre vessels, *Al-Ahmadi* and *Al-Abdaly*, had slipped their moorings, and had been trying to get to sea with skeleton crews. They were now trapped by the Osa, and had no choice but to return to their berths and await capture.

Majors Al-Ansari on *Istiqlal* and Khalid Al-Faraj at the base headquarters were still in radio contact. Al-Faraj was reporting that the Iraqis were moving towards the base headquarters. 'This could be the last time we speak,' he said to Al-Ansari. He went off the air shortly thereafter as he was captured.

By 7.00 a.m., the Iraqis controlled most of the Ras Al-Jalayh, with *Istiqlal* looking on helplessly five kilometres out to sea. Al-Ansari could only stand offshore and prevent further Iraqi seaborne reinforcements from reaching the base, and hope that his colleagues on land could cope with the commandos. With communications cut, he was not to know that they had already been overpowered, but feared the worst.

On land, the Iraqis gathered the Kuwaitis as prisoners, and brought the other senior officers - four lieutenant-colonels - to the Osa. Al-Saleh was then taken to the communications centre with Lieutenant-Colonel Khalid Al-Shatti. The Iraqis wanted him to tell the two boats to return to base, and the Kuwaitis were trying to figure out how to surreptitiously tell *Istiqlal* and *Sanbouk* to go south. However, incredibly, before they could make any contact with the boats, the escorting Republican Guard officer started smashing the communications equipment with his pistol. One of his men joined in, using the butt of his Kalashnikov. The two Kuwaitis looked at each other, bemused. No one would be able to issue any orders now to *Istiqlal* and *Sanbouk*. They could only hope that the skippers would act of their own accord.

Miraculously, the Kuwaitis lost only one man dead, Lieutenant Jamal Al-Salem, a marine commando and diver. He had driven up to the northern gate in his pick-up. The Iraqis told him to go home - the fighting was over - but he insisted, apparently reaching for his pistol in the glove box, and was shot in the thigh. The Iraqis left him bleeding profusely on the road in the morning heat, and initially prevented his colleagues from giving him First Aid. They then dumped him in the back of his own truck, and took him to their commander and Al-Saleh on the Osa. By then, his clothes were covered in blood from having rolled around the back of the truck in own blood. Al-Saleh told the Iraqis that he would have to go direct to the hospital, as the base did not have the facilities or sufficient plasma to treat him, but the Iraqis brought him to the sick bay instead, By the time he got there, he had lost even more blood. He died around noon. The only Iraqi casualties in the initial assault force were the man who caught his foot between the Osa and jetty as he jumped off, and one with a slight bullet wound to his forearm.

The Iraqis, however, did not escape significant casualties. At around 7.25 a.m., they tried to reinforce their men at Ras Al-Jalayh with helicopter-borne forces. They had reckoned without the Kuwaiti HAWK air defence missile battery ten kilometres to the south, under Captain Abdullah Al-Asfoor. He fired three missiles and took down a large Iraqi helicopter, before the Iraqis changed their flight approach paths and avoided the area.

Perhaps the most relieved man at Ras Al-Jalayh that morning was the Iraqi commander. He later told Kuwaiti officers taken prisoner that when he was handed the mission of taking Ras Al-Jalayh, he had initially considered it as suicidal. He knew the potential of the Kuwaiti Navy from the days he had worked with them during the Iran-Iraq War, and later exchange visits. 'The only thing which saved us was that your Government stood you down before we attacked,' he told the Kuwaitis. 'If you had been on alert, you would have blown me out of the water.'

Other people, on land, were having their own problems. On the ridge above Jahra, the little group of prisoners including Stewart Griffiths were kept waiting until after 7.00 a.m., watching tanks and trucks full of Iraqi soldiers roll by. They were not tied up, but could go nowhere. Then suddenly the captives were ordered into their cars, and told to drive a few kilometres north, where they were ordered out again and made to kneel in the desert. The Iraqi troops were tense, impatient and nervous, presumably because of the unexpected resistance from 35 Brigade, and the helicopter losses at the hands of the KAF. It seemed to Stewart that they could be shot here and buried in the desert without anyone being any the wiser. Iraqi casualties from below the ridge began to trickle up to their position, to be evacuated to Iraq in cars commandeered from the Arab civilians. The Kuwaitis were having an effect.

Shortly after 9.00 a.m., one of the Iraqi officers ordered Stewart to drive him back down south to a command post at the ridge. When he arrived, several large Iraqi helicopters were being engaged by a Kuwaiti Mirage – presumably that of Lieutenant Faisal Al-Hamoud – flying the last combat sortie from Ali Al-Salem. Stewart saw one helicopter brought down with a missile as the Iraqis fired back with small arms, without effect. Stewart took advantage of the diversion to try to escape by running into the desert, but an officer stopped him by firing two shots over his head.

When the firing ceased, the Englishman was ordered to drive back to where his Indian colleagues were waiting. They then drove up to the border post at Abdaly, past burnt-out Iraqi tanks, APCs and the charred carcass of an Iraqi helicopter 20km north of the ridge, and straight through the abandoned Kuwaiti post, and the Iraqi post on the other side of what had been no-man's land, to a military camp near the Iraqi town of Safwan. Here, seven long months later, General Schwarzkopf would meet the defeated Iraqi generals.

At the camp, they were asked for their passports. No one had them, so they had to enact the farce of going back to the border post to register. Incredibly, the Iraqis were sticking to bureaucratic details in the midst of an invasion. Stewart was forced to leave his car behind with promises that they would come back tomorrow. He would never see it again. The three Indians were allowed to go, but Stewart and two Turks who had joined him were held. At about 4.30 p.m., they were put into a covered wagon and taken to another military installation where the Turks were freed. In response to his repeated protests, Stewart was told that he was being 'held for his own safety', with promises that 'maybe he could to return to Kuwait the following day'. It was a pattern that many of us would become familiar with.

Thirteen other Westerners – eleven Americans and a Canadian working on Santa Fe International Corporation oil rigs in northern Kuwait, and a German surveyor working on Bubiyan – were also captured that morning. They were the first members of what would become Saddam Hussein's Human Shield.

As 35 Brigade was stalling the second wave of Iraqis at Mutla'a, civilians elsewhere in Kuwait continued to try to get to work, ignorant of the invasion.

At the western edge of Kuwait City centre, near the Sheraton Roundabout, Geoff Green, a British marine superintendent at Kuwait Oil Tanker Company (KOTC), was sitting on a patch of desert at 7.00 a.m., wondering how the day had gone so wrong. The Iraqi Republican Guard infantrymen guarding him and several dozen other men - mainly Arabs and Asians - left no doubt as to who was in charge of the country, or at least the city centre. Tom Laming and Victor Mallet were huddled in other groups nearby, nursing the same thoughts.

Geoff had left his home in Fintas, 25km to the south, at 6.10 a.m., for an early start at the office. His girlfriend, Julie, a pharmacist at the Amiri Hospital, followed him in her own car. Both turned west off the Maghreb-Assafar Motorway onto First Ring Road, winding through 300 metres of roadworks, towards the Sheraton. A kilometre east of the roundabout, Geoff noticed a long line of stationary cars blocking the road ahead. He assumed that an accident had occurred on the roundabout, and pulled up behind the rearmost vehicle. Julie was a little quicker. Sensing something was seriously wrong, she made a quick U-turn on the motorway, and headed back the way she had come, on the wrong side of the road.

Before Julie's action could register, there was a tap on Geoff's car window and he found himself looking into the eyes of a lean, fit Arab soldier, in camouflage and a red beret, parachute wings on his chest. The soldier was armed with the unmistakable Kalashnikov AK-47. It did not yet occur to Geoff that the soldier was Iraqi.

Geoff lowered the window. The soldier spoke in Arabic, gesturing for Geoff to leave the car. *'Mafi Arabi'* ('No Arabic'), said Geoff, trying to avoid the inconvenience. The muzzle of the Kalashnikov was raised to his face. The message was unmistakable. Geoff turned off his engine, and started to extract the key. The soldier told him to leave it in the ignition.

The trooper was joined by others, herding people from other stopped cars. The prisoners were directed along the road towards the Sheraton, in the direction they had been driving moments before. The troops were businesslike, not deliberately threatening, but clearly expecting to be obeyed. Unsure of who the soldiers were, the captives discussed among themselves whether they were Kuwaiti or Iraqi, whether this was a coup or an invasion.

Close to the roundabout, they were directed to a patch of open desert where a steadily growing group of men were being collected from the stalled cars and surrounding area. This is where Geoff found himself at 7.00 a.m. when he should have been safely in his office.

The prisoners should have considered themselves lucky. Less than 100 metres away an Indian man lay dead, riddled with Kalashnikov bullets. This unfortunate individual was a cook in an Indian restaurant nearby. Upon hearing the firing outside, he had come outside to investigate, still holding the kitchen knife he had been using . An Iraqi soldier had mistaken him for a defender in the half-light, and cut him down with a burst of fire. A Filipino security guard from the Sheraton Hotel also lay dead.

At 7.30 a.m., New Zealander Michelle Lawand, a bank systems analyst, crossed First Ring on her way to work. She noticed nothing unusual, except that the roads were a little quiet for a Thursday morning. She apparently drove straight through a gap in the Iraqi lines. It was not until she arrived at work that other early risers broke the news of the invasion. In fact, the first her husband, Toufic, heard of it was when he was awoken by a phone call from his sister-in-law in New Zealand. Michelle now had a problem. She had to get home, 15 kilometres away, through the Iraqi Army, and it was too risky for Toufic to come in. She was alone, and had no idea how the Iraqis were treating women. This was not working out to be a good morning.

In the western city centre, the small groups of captive civilians held by the roadside were becoming increasingly worried. As the sun rose in the summer sky, it became obvious that they were caught in the first stages of a fully-fledged invasion.

In one of these groups, Geoff Green did not see another Westerner until about 8.30 a.m. when a colleague, Dave Smith, joined him. Heavy trucks and armour from the northern arm of the main Iraqi force passed by towards the city centre. Bursts of fire continued to ring out, but it was difficult to tell whether these were directed into the air, or were part of a firefight. At least no one was shooting directly at them. Their guards seemed relaxed. They were undoubtedly professionals, and seemed to be trying to ensure that the prisoners were not harmed. Although exposed, the captives felt strangely safe.

Nearby, in another group, Tom Laming tried to make a run for it. He had edged his way over to a running irrigation hose to get a drink of water, then rose to his feet and tried to dash around some buildings when the Iraqis were not looking. Unfortunately for Tom, he ran straight into an Iraqi soldier coming the other way. The man was more terrified than Tom, and instinctively fired a burst from his Kalashnikov over Tom's head, so close that the burnt cordite fell in his hair. Tom was promptly returned to captivity, and thought better of any further escape attempts.

Around 9.00 a.m., with the temperature already above 30°C, the prisoners were suddenly ordered to return to their cars and go home. This sounded too good to be true, but they weren't out of harm's way yet. As they rose, fresh bursts of fire, much closer than the earlier ones, rang out from the direction of a Ministry of Interior complex on the other side of First Ring. Some Kuwaitis were using the cover of the houses adjoining the road to snipe at the Iraqis, oblivious to the safety of the civilians. Geoff could hear the rounds striking the ground, then the Iraqis behind him returning the fire, with the rounds whistling over his head. He was in the middle of a real firefight. The men dropped flat, but the Iraqis told them to get up again, firing bursts alternately towards the unseen assailants, and then into the air to herd the men onto the relative safety of the road, which was slightly below ground level.

Geoff and Dave ran, crouching, all the way back to their cars. Their keys were still in their ignitions, miraculously untouched after two and a half hours. Geoff turned around on the motorway, heading back down it the wrong way as Julie had done earlier, and then south, towards home.

Tom went to his own car. It had been looted, but the key was also still in the ignition. Vic Mallet was not as fortunate. The Sheraton was obviously not a good place to stay, with the nearby roundabout rapidly turning into an Iraqi camp. His taxi-driver had disappeared. He finally flagged down a pick-up driver, asking him about any other hotels. The man was trying to get to his own home, near the airport. The Holiday Inn was nearby. He would take Vic.

Tom managed to get home without any problems, but as Geoff reached the intersection of the motorway with Third Ring, he found it blocked by Kuwaiti policemen, directing what sparse southbound traffic there was to the west onto Third Ring. The police were in uniform, armed only with their revolvers. No Kuwaiti or Iraqi soldiers were in sight. Geoff could hardly believe it. The Iraqi Republican Guard had had the city centre for the past three hours, but the police were still controlling the central suburbs.

He headed west as directed, then turned onto the next road towards home. This led him past the airport, where he was confronted by three Iraqi tanks abreast on the road facing him, with more behind. There were about 36 in all, the best part of an armoured battalion. The road itself was impassable, but the soldiers were not aggressive. In fact, most were leaning against the tanks or walking around, chatting and smoking. Geoff did not want to spend another few hours in the sun. He mounted the side reservation without stopping, and simply drove past them, arriving home at 10.30 a.m. It was not until 5.00 p.m. that Julie returned. She had spent the day at work in the hospital as the wounded from the battle at Dasman Palace were being brought in.

In the meantime, the British Consul, Larry Banks, and the hundreds of others on the beach outside the British Embassy were trying to keep their heads down. No one else had been able to get into the embassy. The only staff inside were those who had been there overnight, and the Indian gatekeeper. To make matters worse, none of those inside knew how to take incoming calls through the switchboard. Hundreds of frantic British nationals calling up for advice received a busy signal, the answering machine, or the Indian gatekeeper who could tell them nothing at all. The Americans, being further removed from the action, had been more successful in getting their staff in and were frantically working their phones, telling their people to stay inside.

Suddenly, at 8.45 a.m. the firing over Larry's head intensified sharply. Kuwaiti Amiri Guard and National Guard reinforcements called to the Dasman Palace were counter-attacking. The Iraqis guarding the civilians on the beach turned and ran. The prisoners seized their opportunity, and ran as soon as there was a lull in the firing. Larry left his shot-up car on the road, and dashed into the embassy compound with his Indian colleague, Mike Meade, and a pregnant Englishwoman who had joined them. For the first time in over three hours, he felt safe behind the concrete walls and gates. That feeling soon disappeared. He checked the so-called armoured gate later that day, and found that a round had gone right through it.

Michelle Lawand also made her move. She withdrew as much money as she could from a nearby ATM, and started driving tentatively south. Amazingly, she made it across First Ring without incident, and then tried to stick to back roads as much as possible. Eventually, she was forced to take a major intersection. As she turned onto the main road, she glanced to her right, back towards Kuwait City. The Iraqis were at the previous intersection, right behind her. She turned sharply south, and sped home as fast as she could.

At sea, the Kuwait Navy was not quite out of the fight, but there was little they could do. They were only two vessels – without missiles and low on ammunition – one with only eleven crew out of a complement of 45, and a jammed forward gun.

The only option seemed to try to take the pressure off Kuwaiti forces ashore by preventing further naval landings in the main urban area. The two vessels turned north towards Ahmadi, still with scores of Iraqi small craft on their radars, but these scattered as soon as they saw them coming. It was impossible to find a decent target. All the Iraqi Osas were staying well out of range.

The two Kuwaiti vessels could see numerous large Iraqi helicopters over the land and water in the distance, but neither the aircraft nor the Osas made any overt moves. However, one helicopter came within two kilometres, on the seaward side of the Kuwaitis, at around 9.15 a.m., apparently checking out the boats. The Iraqis may have thought they were safe from the Kuwaitis' guns at that range, but they had not counted on Captain Al-Asfoor's HAWK battery south of Ras Al-Jalayh. He locked on to the helicopter at a range of about 20 km, launched his fourth missile of the day, and shot it out of the sky.

Al-Ansari and Al-Muhanna later learned from their captured colleagues after their release in 1991 that the helicopter was apparently carrying senior Iraqi Navy officers who were supervising the naval attack. The Iraqi orders were apparently to capture the Kuwaiti boats, not to destroy them, which may explain the reluctance of the Iraqis to engage them.

At around 8.30 a.m., *Istiqlal* managed to speak on a VHF radio channel with Captain Fadel Al-Wathiqi in Ras Al-Jalayh. Although the Iraqis controlled most of the base, Al-Wathiqi was still on one of the four Loadmaster landing craft in the harbour. The Iraqis had not yet reached him. 'They captured our Daddy,' said Al-Wathiqi, referring in code to Chief of Naval Forces Colonel Qais Al-Saleh, and were holding him on the Osa. Kuwaiti crews were still on several of the boats in the harbour, but the Iraqis had control of the base on land.

The two vessels, unaware that the Kuwaiti Army had been almost overrun, tried to raise any Kuwaiti authority on land to request resupply and orders. Their usual chain of communication was through Ras Al-Jalayh, but that was out of action. The only way they could reach anyone was through Captain Al-Muhanna's personal mobile telephone. He finally managed to get through to the GHQ at 9.30 a.m. and requested a resupply of ammunition and missiles at Khiran Resort harbour, in the south of the country. He was told to withdraw to Saudi Arabia. Al-Muhanna relayed this to Al-Ansari, who was reluctant to withdraw that far south. It would be tantamount to leaving the fight.

With the foray up the coast looking ever more futile, *Istiqlal* and *Sanbouk* rendezvoused at a point 20km east of the base, where they divided *Sanbouk's* crew more evenly between the two vessels, and fixed *Istiqlal's* forward main gun. By now, it was after 10.30 a.m. Their radar picture of Ras Al-Jalayh showed the Osa that *Istiqlal* had chased at the contractor's jetty, a second Osa which had come in when they had gone north, and a few other small Iraqi craft. Actually, the Iraqis had brought in reinforcements on at least two fast hovercraft. Colonel Qais Al-Saleh and his four lieutenant-colonels had been put on one of these at about 10.30 a.m., and it had left for the Iraqi Navy base at Umm Qasr. With the exception of the doctor at the sick bay and several other civilians, the remaining Kuwait Navy men - including the boat crews - were now all held in a hangar near the jetty where the first Osa had docked.

Al-Ansari and Al-Muhanna came up with a desperate plan to try at least to save some of the Kuwaiti vessels still there, assuming their crews were aboard. They set a plan for both vessels to attack the Osas, and for *Sanbouk*, being the smaller, more manoeuverable vessel, to enter the harbour, and attack the Iraqis there with her guns and machine guns. *Istiqlal* would stand outside, and prevent Iraqi reinforcements from arriving.

The first phase of attack with the Kuwaiti vessels closing in on the Osas went according to plan. *Istiqlal* was in the lead, with *Sanbouk* a kilometre behind on the port quarter. They were helped by an unexpected diversion as the nearby HAWK missile battery shot down its third Iraqi helicopter of the day. *Istiqlal* opened fire on the Osas with its 76mm forward Melara gun, but it soon jammed again. *Sanbouk* had to take over. One Osa was reportedly hit, but not sunk.

However, after the earlier engagement, *Sanbouk* herself soon ran out of ammunition. With *Istiqlal's* gun jammed, there was no point in pursuing the plan. With other Iraqi vessels now closing in, the two Kuwaiti vessels withdrew at about 11.30 a.m. to a coastguard station further south.

During the battle for Ras Al-Jalayh, another ship's captain was coping with his own drama. Captain Robert McNeill was the master of the *Chesapeake City*, a 80,000-ton American-flagged, Kuwaiti oil product carrier. His vessel had loaded some cargo from a pier off Ahmadi the previous evening, and then moved at about 1.00 a.m. on 2 August to another terminal off the Mina Abdullah refinery, about 20 kilometres north of Ras Al-Jalayh.

All other ships in Kuwaiti ports at the time - about half a dozen in all - were Kuwaiti, except for an Indian rice ship, the *Al-Safir*. This was unusual. The world's shippers seemed to have smelled trouble, and stayed away.

At 4.00 a.m., as Captain McNeill was taking on cargo, an alert was sounded through the port authorities, but cancelled an hour later as a false alarm. McNeill was not convinced. There was no sound of firing or military activity, but things did not seem right. He called the US Embassy at 6.00 a.m. on his ship's satellite telephone, and miraculously reached a US Naval officer immediately, who confirmed that Kuwait had indeed been invaded, and that he should sail if he could.

Using his VHF, McNeill asked the port authorities to disconnect him from the terminal, but the harbourmaster refused. 'An invasion isn't possible,' he said. 'Men who live in the city have just come to work, and have seen no trouble at all.' McNeill insisted that the US Embassy had confirmed that the country had been invaded. The argument went back and forth for some time before it was settled, with every other vessel within radio range listening to it. This was enough for one container ship entering Kuwait. She turned tail and sailed back down the Gulf, escaping possible capture.

Chesapeake City was finally released, and set sail at 8.00 a.m., by which time Ras Al-Jalayh had fallen, and Iraqi troops were in Kuwaiti City. McNeill did not consider his vessel out of danger yet. He had served on tankers in the Gulf during the Iran-Iraq War when Iranian speedboats armed with machine guns and RPGs had been the main danger to shipping, after mines. He radioed the US Navy in Bahrain, requesting protection.

Fortunately, the USS *Robert G. Bradley*, a frigate under Commander Kevin Cosgriff, was nearby. *Bradley* had been deployed to the northern Gulf for the previous fortnight to monitor Iraqi movements, following Saddam's threats against Kuwait. She turned towards the coast as the tanker came out to sea. The two vessels linked up, and *Chesapeake City* was escorted to safety.

The sole American-flagged ship in port had escaped, removing a factor which could have greatly complicated matters in the days ahead. Over the next 12 hours, all Kuwaiti oil tankers in port slipped their moorings, and set sail. The Iraqis had not reacted quickly enough to stop them. Only the Indian cargo ship in Shuwaikh Port, which was well inside Kuwait Bay, and a number of smaller vessels in port and drydock were captured.

In the meantime, the Kuwait Air Force was back in action, this time with the A-4 Skyhawks from Al-Jaber base. At about 8.30 a.m., Majors Ala'a Al-Sayegh and Hussein Al-Qattan each shot down an Iraqi helicopter, and two more fell to the Skyhawks at 10.00 a.m.

By 8.30 a.m., Ali Al-Salem had been surrounded by Iraqi tanks and armoured vehicles. They were probably no more than a company strong, but 35 Brigade's

7th Armoured Battalion, barely eight kilometres away to the east at Atraf intersection, was fully involved with the second wave of the *Hammurabi* Republican Guard, and so was unable to offer any assistance. In any event, there was no direct communication between Ali Al-Salem and 35 Brigade, and communication through the GHQ was impossible.

Colonel Al-Sarour was eventually reinforced on his right flank by 16 Chieftains from the 8th Armoured Battalion, under Lieutenant-Colonel Ali Al-Mulla at 9.00 a.m., and later by elements of the 57th Mechanized Infantry Battalion in their M-113s and BMPs, who brought their machine guns and 30mm cannon to bear. The Iraqis at Ali Al-Salem were not yet strong enough to attack 35 Brigade in the rear, and seemed to have orders to simply lay siege to the trapped airmen.

The 8th Armoured Battalion's 3rd Company, with 10 Chieftains under Captain Ali Abdulkarim was initially directed to move across Sixth Ring Road into Jahra to free 80 Brigade, which was surrounded in their camp. This was a particularly difficult task. Sixth Ring is a six-lane divided road with concrete barriers separating the north and sound lanes, too high for even a tank to climb. The Iraqis were at both nearby interchanges, and the next interchange was beyond Jahra. The mission proved impossible. Abdulkarim was ordered to take up positions on the south side of the Salmi Road, with the 7th Battalion on their north, and to engage Iraqi targets on Sixth Ring.

This move almost led to tragedy. Communications were patchy at best. As Abdulkarim's tanks closed up, the 7th Battalion's Lieutenant-Colonel Al-Wazzan did not recognise them in the morning haze as Kuwaiti. He feared that they were Iraqis trying to turn his flank from the south, and deployed a TOW platoon against them.

Abdulkarim saw the TOWs trained on him, but could not raise Al-Wazzan on the radio. He ordered his gunners to sight on the TOW launchers, and to fire if they fired. A TOW missile is guided onto its target by the gunner using wires and a joystick device. Abdulkarim was betting that a tank round would be faster than the missile in the hope it would strike the TOW gunners before they could guide the missiles onto his tanks. His gunners protested that they would be firing on their colleagues. 'Its either us or them!'said Abdulkarim.

After a few very tense minutes, Al-Wazzan recognised the tanks as Kuwaiti Chieftains, and called off the TOWs.

The Kuwaitis held a position on high ground back from the intersection of Sixth Ring and the Salmi Road, anchored at a huge car storage lot. They were never able to build up beyond a battalion-sized force, but part of the Iraqi second wave was temporarily stalled. With tanks on both sides of the Salmi Road oriented onto Sixth Ring, they could limit movement along the road, but little else. It was a hopeless battle. More troops were pouring into Kuwait from Iraq, and the Iraqis were organizing a counter-attack. To complicate matters, the Iraqi officers were using civilian cars. The Kuwaitis could not differentiate between them and *bona fide* civilians caught in the cross-fire.

Despite 35 Brigade's efforts, the Iraqi infantry was reaching its objectives by helicopter, and further Iraqi armour was pouring into Kuwait along Jahra Road five kilometres away, out of range of Al-Sarour's tanks. His artillery had the range to reach them, but he had no spotters in place to direct their fire. His requests for reinforcements from GHQ - itself then under attack - had been met with the reply that there was nothing available.

Even if Kuwaiti artillery could not hit the Iraqis coming down Mutla'a, the invaders still had to contend with the Kuwait Air Force. By mid-morning, with Iraqi armour in Kuwait City, the infantry followed on buses. Several Kuwaiti A-4s from Al-Jaber base caught a convoy of these at Mutla'a, and strafed them, killing many of the Iraqis, and setting the buses alight.

A lull settled on 35 Brigade's battle by mid-morning. The Kuwaiti artillery, set some six kilometres back from the Atraf intersection, engaged Iraqis from the *Hammurabi* sheltering among the wrecks of their vehicles and behind the Sixth Ring embankment. Some attempted to surrender, but the Kuwaitis could not handle prisoners, and waved them away. The brigade took advantage of the respite to send four trucks back to their camp to replenish ammunition.

Around 11.00 a.m., the brigade received news of an armoured column approaching their positions from the rear. The first encounter was almost comical. The commander of the 51st Artillery Battalion's 2nd battery, Captain Ghassan Daoud, was standing beside the Salmi Road with some of 35 Brigade's reserve tanks, near the brigade's artillery positions, when he saw the column approaching. Several of the tanks were flying green flags, which were initially mistaken for Saudi flags. He assumed that the tanks were from the GCC Peninsula Shield force at Hafr Al-Batin, sent into Kuwait to reinforce the Kuwaitis. It would have taken them this long to reach Atraf.

Daoud walked forward to greet them, when he suddenly realized that they were T-72s and BMPs, nothing at all like Saudi armour. He was too committed to turn back, so asked the crew of the lead vehicle their identity and the location of their commander. They were the 14th Brigade of the *Medina* Republican Guard, which had entered Kuwait from the west. Trying desperately to retain his cool, Daoud thanked them, walked back to his own vehicle, and informed Colonel Al-Sarour of the new development by radio.

The Iraqis, obviously thinking that the Kuwaitis were part of the revolution story they had been fed, did not move against the nearby Kuwaiti reserve tanks and artillery, but continued up the road to the intersection. The Kuwaiti tankers overlooking Sixth Ring held their breath as the column – about a battalion strong – passed by.

At the intersection, Kuwait's 7th and 8th Armoured Battalions had little time to react. The Iraqis, presumably thinking that the Kuwaiti tanks on both sides of the road were no threat, passed between them, and started to turn right onto Sixth Ring. Fortunately for the Kuwaitis, there was no direct communication between the now-bruised *Hammurabi* and the newly-arrived *Medina*, and the *Medina* arrived in the midst of a lull in the battle, otherwise they would have been forewarned by the sound of firing.

The Kuwaitis held their fire until a full company of the *Medina* were on Sixth Ring. The 8th Armoured Battalion then opened fire their right flank, as the 7th Armoured Battalion turned its guns onto the Iraqi tanks still on the Salmi Road.

Those Iraqis who could withdrew hastily back down the Salmi Road to regroup at a truck-weighing station 3,000 metres from the intersection. The Kuwaiti artillery that they had bypassed earlier was still in position – farther west, and on the south side of the Salmi Road – and shelled the Iraqi vehicles, causing them to withdraw farther west, towards Ali Al-Salem.

As the Kuwaiti artillery were engaging the *Medina*, a single Kuwaiti A-4 Skyhawk appeared, flown by Major Majed Al-Ahmad. It circled the Kuwaiti artillery position twice. The Kuwaiti gunners held their breath. There was no air-to-ground communication between them and the little bomber. They feared they might be targeted as they were so close to the Iraqis. They had good reason for concern. The Kuwaiti pilots could not identify the Kuwaiti Chieftains from the air. Information from the GHQ was non-existent, so they had little or no pre-mission briefing. For all they knew, every vehicle on the ground was Iraqi. Fortunately for the Kuwaiti artillery, Al-Ahmad chose the Iraqi column closer to Ali Al-Salem as the better target, and bombed it.

Although surrounded, Ali Al-Salem was not yet out of the fight. From 1.30 p.m., the tower vectored a further seven sorties of A-4s from Al-Jaber base onto the new column. The Iraqis had no air cover. After their mauling at the hands of the Kuwaiti HAWK batteries earlier in the morning, the Iraqi Air Force was staying out of harm's way. The A-4s rolled in on the Iraqi ground troops, dropping 500-lb bombs, and firing Zuni air-to-ground rockets. By an incredible stroke of good fortune, one of the A-4s hit an ammunition truck in a group of bunched-up vehicles, which blew up, destroying many other vehicles.

Despite this success, flights of up to 30 Iraqi Mi-8 *Hip* helicopters were ferrying Iraqi troops over the heads of 35 Brigade into Kuwait City to the east. The KAF could not handle the volume of Iraqi aircraft. The HAWK battery at Mutla'a, one of the most critical in the country, had not been in action, and was now captured. All the serviceable Mirages had evacuated to Saudi Arabia, but Lieutenant Adnan Abdul Rasool in an A-4 shot down a single helicopter at 1.00 p.m., the last of the five destroyed by the Skyhawks.

The *Medina* was not long in hitting back. With one of its brigades badly mauled, the other two – and the survivors of the first – were out for revenge. They set up their own artillery and 81mm mortar positions north of the Salmi Road, and started shelling the Kuwaiti artillery, seriously wounding battalion commander Lieutenant-Colonel Fahd Asush. They then threatened the Kuwaitis with an attack by BMPs, but did not press it. The Kuwaiti artillery withdrew to less exposed positions further south and east.

The Kuwaiti tanks were having their own problems. Most were down to two or three rounds of main gun ammunition, and neither supplies nor reinforcements were available. Fatigue and thirst were taking their toll on 35 Brigade which had the *Hammurabi* Republican Guard to their front, and the *Medina* in their rear, between them and their base. The *Medina* were advancing on the Kuwaitis, who were now starting to take casualties.

It was obvious that 35 Brigade would be completely surrounded if it maintained its present position. Colonel Al-Sarour decided on a withdrawal south, to a broadcasting station on the north–south road between Jahra and Al-

Jaber KAF base. During the move, the brigade received orders from the GHQ to cross the desert to 15 Brigade's camp, and replenish. However, communications were tenuous at best. It was thought at the time that the Iraqis were already at 15 Brigade, so GHQ told Al-Sarour to take whatever action he considered necessary. He decided to withdraw past Al-Jaber, and position himself against the Saudi border to protect his flanks and rear.

By nightfall, most of the 7th and 8th Armoured Battalions and some of the artillery were near the border. The mechanized infantry was near Al-Jaber. Colonel Al-Sarour made contact with Saudi Lieutenant-Colonel Saleh Al-Belouwi. At 8.00 p.m., the Saudis requested them to cross over in case the Iraqis followed them to the border. The Saudis did not want a clash with the numerically superior Iraqis at that stage. They provided the Kuwaitis with food, water, fuel and tents, but no ammunition.

At 2.00 a.m. on 3 August, 35 Brigade crossed into Saudi Arabia. Further south, a mechanized infantry company from 15 Brigade made good their escape through Kuwait's southern oilfields.

Kuwait's main armoured forces were now out of the battle, but some were alive to fight another day. A few more fierce final stands would be made in Kuwait City, and the KAF bases were still holding out, but the Iraqis had broken the back of the outnumbered Kuwaiti defences. The late Kuwaiti mobilization probably saved a great many lives on both sides as the battles were not as hard fought as they might otherwise have been.

As 35 Brigade were commencing their mid-afternoon withdrawal, the two surviving Kuwait Navy vessels were nearing the island of Umm Al-Maradem, where the Kuwait coastguard had a large barge, *Sawahil 35.*

The Iraqis had trailed them, but did not fire on them, for whatever reason. However, Captain Al-Asfoor at the Kuwaiti HAWK missile battery south of Ras Al-Jalayh had no such reservations about holding his fire. The Iraqis sent another helicopter into the area, perhaps to scout for the Iraqi boats, and he shot it down. His battery had by then fired six missiles and downed four helicopters. He later fired two HAWKs at an Iraqi fighter, but these missed.

As the Kuwaiti boats reached Umm Al-Maradem at around 2.00 p.m., the pursuing Iraqis slowed down and kept their distance, presumably unaware of the Kuwaitis' weapons problems. During the trip, Captain Al-Muhanna was again in contact with the GHQ on his mobile phone, and relayed orders to Major Al-Ansari that they were to withdraw to Khafji. Al-Ansari did not want to give up the fight yet, and wanted to speak directly to the GHQ. When they reached *Sawahil 35*, he tried to call them from a mobile phone on the barge, but could not get through. He then tried the Coastguard Headquarters in Shuwaikh, and spoke to a Major Abdullah Al-Khail.

The Coastguard were surrounded by Iraqi tanks and could do nothing. The Iraqis seemed happy to sit outside the building, and wait for them to surrender. Al-Ansari asked Al-Khail to get on his hotline to the GHQ, and request an ammunition resupply at the port for the nearby Khiran Resort. The GHQ, apparently trying to get Al-Ansari out of their hair, told him OK, but he would have to go to Khafji in Saudi Arabia, not Khiran.

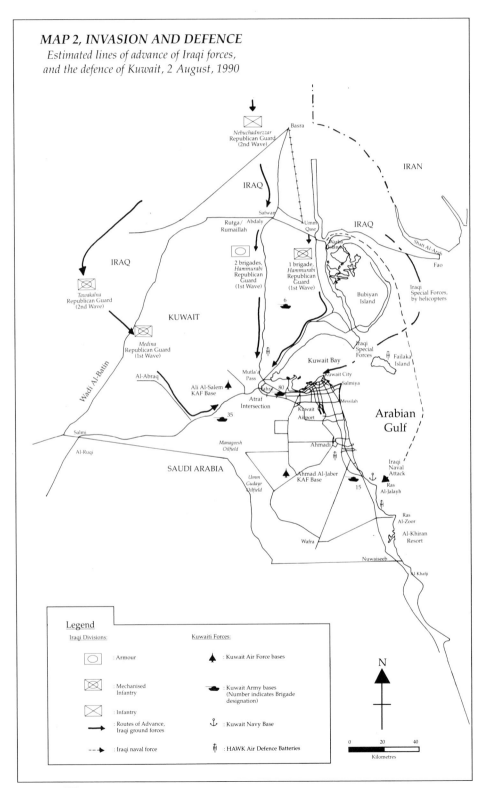

MAP 2, INVASION AND DEFENCE
Estimated lines of advance of Iraqi forces,
and the defence of Kuwait, 2 August, 1990

IRAN

Basra

Nebuchadnezzar
Republican Guard
(2nd Wave)

IRAQ

Satwan

Rutga /
Rumaillah   Abdaly

Umm
Qasr   IRAQ

Shatt Al-Arab

Fao

Tawakalna
Republican Guard
(2nd Wave)

IRAQ

2 brigades,
Hammurabi
Republican
Guard
(1st Wave)

1 brigade,
Hammurabi
Republican
Guard
(1st Wave)

Warba
Island

Iraqi
Special Forces,
by helicopters

KUWAIT

Bubiyan
Island

6

Medina
Republican Guard
(1st Wave)

Al-Abraq

Ali Al-Salem
KAF Base

Mutla'a
Pass

Fahti

Atraf
Intersection

80

Iraqi
Special
Forces

Kuwait Bay

Kuwait City
Salmiya

Messilah

Failaka
Island

**Arabian
Gulf**

Wadi Al-Batin

Salmi

Al-Ruqi

35

*Manageesh
Oilfield*

Kuwait
Airport

Ahmadi

Iraqi
Naval
Attack

SAUDI ARABIA

*Umm
Gudayr
Oilfield*

Ahmad Al-Jaber
KAF Base

15

Ras
Al-Jalayh

Ras
Al-Zoor

Al-Khiran
Resort

Wafra

Nuwaiseeb

Al-Khafji

Legend

Iraqi Divisions: Kuwaiti Forces:

◯   : Armour   ▲ : Kuwait Air Force bases

⊠   : Mechanised
          Infantry   : Kuwait Army bases
                                              (Number indicates Brigade
                                              designation)

⊠   : Infantry

→   : Routes of Advance,
          Iraqi ground forces   ⚓ : Kuwait Navy Base

- - ▸ : Iraqi naval force   : HAWK Air Defence Batteries

N

0   20   40

Kilometres

Explanatory notes to Map 2, Invasion and Defence

1. 1 August, 9.00 p.m.: Iraqi troops on border order Kuwaiti forces to cease patrols. Initial assessment is that Iraqis are only trying to occupy northern strip of land.

2. 11.00 p.m.: Iraqis surround five Kuwaiti border posts. Kuwaiti armed forces alerted. Iraqi incursion feared imminent after failure of Jeddah talks, but full-scale invasion still not yet apparent .

3. 2 August, 1.00 a.m.: Iraq's *Hammurabi* Republican Guard Division crosses the northern border at Abdaly and Umm Qasr. *Nebuchadnezzar* Republican Guard follows *Hammurabi*. *Medina* Republican Guard cross over in the west, followed by *Tawakalna*.

4. 2.00 a.m.: Kuwait's 6 Brigade withdraws towards Jahra.

5. 3.00 a.m.: Lead Iraqis engaged by Kuwaiti armoured cars outside Jahra. Kuwaitis, outgunned and outnumbered, withdraw after taking casualties. 35 Brigade and 15 Brigade continue mobilizing.

6. 3.55 a.m.: KAF Mirages from Ali Al-Salem scramble against incoming Iraqi helicopters.

7. 4.00 a.m.: Iraqi infiltrators in Kuwait City attack Amir's Dasman Palace. Iraqi vanguard reaches Kuwait's outer suburbs.

8. 4.13 a.m.: British Airways flight BA149 lands at Kuwait International Airport.

9. 4.15 a.m.: Elements of 15 Brigade leave camp, heading for 6 Brigade. Later diverted to GHQ.

10. 4.30 a.m.: Command element of 35 Brigade leaves camp. Crown Prince and Prime Minister leaves Ministry of Defence GHQ. Collects Amir from Dasman Palace at 4.45 a.m., and drives south towards Saudi Arabia. Senior Kuwaiti generals evacuate GHQ to fall-back command bunker .

11. 4.45 a.m.: Iraqi Special Force helicopters arrive over Dasman Palace.

12. Shortly after 5.00 a.m.: Iraqi troops, apparently unaware of the escape of the Amir, attack Dasman Palace, killing the Amir's brother, an Amiri Guard, and two other men.

13. 5.30 a.m.: Both major KAF bases and KAF HQ near International Airport bombed. KAF Mirages in the air at the time ordered to divert to Al-Jaber base, or Saudi Arabia. Other Iraqi forces shell runway of Kuwait International Airport, and adjacent KAF base.

14. Dawn: Kuwait Navy Base overwhelmed, one man killed, by commandos landed by Osa fast patrol boat. Kuwaiti fast attack craft *Istiqlal* and *Sanbouk*, the only Kuwaiti vessels at sea, attempt to take on Iraqi vessels with guns. *Istiqlal* and *Sanbouk* later escape to Saudi Arabia.

15. 6.00 a.m.: KAF Gazelle, Puma and Super Puma helicopters and six of the twelve BAe Hawks leave Ali Al-Salem base for Saudi Arabia.

16. 6.45 a.m.: 35 Brigade engages second wave of Iraqi forces as they travel down Sixth Ring Road from Mutla'a. Other Iraqi forces are already well into the city, moving virtually unopposed along Jahra Road. Heliborne Iraqi troops reinforce their colleagues in the city.

17. 8.30 a.m. on: Skyhawks from Al-Jaber, based farther away from direct line of advance of Iraqis, engage Iraqi helicopters and ground forces.

18. 35 Brigade's engagement lasts throughout the morning and into the afternoon. Eventually outnumbered and outflanked, with four dead, the brigade retreats towards Saudi Arabia, reaching the border around 6.00 p.m.

19. 3 August, 2.00 a.m.: 35 Brigade crosses over into Saudi Arabia.

The two Kuwaiti vessels left *Sawahil 35* , arriving at Khafji at dusk, only to find that no one there knew anything about an ammunition resupply. In fact, the Saudis were desperate to know what was going on inside Kuwait. The Coastguard men from the barge followed in small boats. The Saudis told the Kuwaitis that their Amir and Crown Prince and Prime Minister were in the residence of the Governor of Khafji. Several Kuwaiti Gazelle and Puma helicopters and their pilots were also in town. Al-Ansari and Al-Muhanna were received by Sheikh Jaber and Sheikh Sa'ad. They were shocked by the state they found the two men in, having narrowly escaped death earlier that day. The Amir was aware that his younger brother was dead, and it seemed that the country was lost, and hundreds of his people killed.

Despondent, the two skippers returned to their vessels, and were ordered by the Saudi authorities to move to Jubail, further down the coast.

By midday the Iraqis had effectively captured Kuwait City. The military camps and the GHQ between Fourth Ring and Jahra Road would hold out until late that night, together with the last valiant defenders at the Ministry of Interior Headquarters and the Bayan Palace. Both major KAF bases would not be captured until the following day, but were all but out of the fight.

The State of Kuwait north of Seventh Ring was virtually under Iraqi control. The invaders then proceeded to tighten their grip, and to extend it to the Saudi border. It would be nearly seven long months before they left.

3. THE FIRST DAY

Radio Kuwait's Arabic Service announced the invasion at 6.00 a.m., half an hour after Iraqi jets screamed low over the city's suburbs. The first scant reports appeared on the BBC World Service at the same time. By 7.00 a.m., the BBC was reporting tanks and fighting in the city on the basis of FCO briefings and hurriedly telephoned reports from inside Kuwait.

In Washington, the National Security Council was alerted as 35 Brigade was setting up its defence below Mutla'a Ridge. At 7.20 a.m., Kuwait time, President Bush strongly condemned the invasion, calling for an immediate and unconditional Iraqi withdrawal. Treasuries world-wide started freezing Iraqi assets, and also Kuwait's multi-billion dollar investment portfolio to prevent Saddam accessing it. The world was waking up to a new, great crisis.

In the Al-Muthanna Complex, at around 6.00 a.m., a group gathered in my American neighbour's apartment as the Iraqi troops moved away from us, down the street. Within an hour there were six of us, all Westerners. We were soon joined by an Iraqi friend living in the building, and a Sudanese doctor.

At about 7.00 a.m., the civilians taken from their cars on their way to work seem to have been allowed to leave the footpath where they had been held. The captured Kuwaiti policemen and National Guard were formed up into two ranks, and marched off with their hands clasped behind their necks.

The city centre went very quiet after 7.30 a.m. The cars below our windows remained abandoned. Occasionally, a commandeered pick-up drove past with captive Kuwaiti policemen squeezed in the back, their heads down between their knees, guarded by one or two Iraqi soldiers. Other than that, the only life on the streets was an occasional Iraqi jeep flying a small, square, red flag from a stubby flagstaff on its front wing, or a lone pedestrian soldier.

People throughout the city were on the phone to each other, or gathering in similar groups. Many had been woken up by the jets, but dismissed it as low flying by the Kuwait Air Force. Few had seen any action. Only those living near Dasman Palace and the western city centre, or along the main Iraqi route of advance, had seen any troops. The suburbs were still controlled by the Kuwaiti police, but the Iraqis held the main routes into and out of the city.

In the Al-Muthanna Complex, we considered our next move. Strangely, in the midst of a crisis, it was prosaic to say the least: breakfast. The American's apartment soon became the source of endless cups of coffee and sandwiches. We realized that the Iraqis were here to stay for at least a few days, if not more. The country would be severely disrupted; there would be no work, no income, for some time. We did not know if or when we would be able to leave, but presumed it would not be long. Some of us thought we would be back at work in a week or so. Looking back, our naivety was astounding.

My American neighbour got through to the US Embassy, and Phil to the Canadian. Advice from both was to stay indoors and keep our heads down.

We had no Britons in our group at the time so had no contact with the British Embassy. It would have made little difference. Her Majesty's Ambassador Michael Weston and the handful of diplomats with him had enough on their hands without answering the phone. Their lines were busy trying to contact other staff, including the missing Consul, Larry Banks, who was still held on the beach outside. On top of that, they had to destroy sensitive documents in case the Iraqis moved in. They could do virtually nothing for their community. By mid-morning, most of the British community were under the mistaken impression that the embassy was unmanned.

The US Embassy, on the other hand, had been frantically calling its registered nationals, telling them to stay at home. It was largely because of this quick action that the only Americans captured on the first morning were those on desert oil rigs in the path of the advancing troops, or on BA149.

Besides US Ambassador Nat Howell and his domestic staff, a six-man Marine guard under Staff Sergeant Jimmy Smith lived on the embassy compound. The Deputy Chief of Mission (DCM), Barbara Bodine, the local CIA man, J. Hunter Downes, and several other officers lived directly opposite the compound. The new Consul, Mrs Gale Rogers, who had only recently arrived in town, was also nearby. Those who could not get into the compound were the military personnel, most of whom were part of the US Liaison Office Kuwait (USLOK), and other diplomats living out in the suburbs.

The scene in the US compound was a mixture of pandemonium, panic and procedure. There was a mad scramble to destroy every classified piece of material, including computers with information on the hard disks. With insufficient time to shred everything, the diplomats built a fire in the embassy yard, and fed it frantically. In their haste, they reportedly destroyed even money from the safe, and the evacuation plan. Later, when people had to go out to buy food, they had to take up a collection.

Later in the morning, phone lines from some areas to the embassy failed. One group of coastal suburbs between Sixth Ring and Ahmadi was out of telephone communication with the rest of the country from the early hours of the invasion and throughout the occupation when an Iraqi tank backed into a local exchange. With their switchboards swamped for most of the first day, it was almost impossible to contact the two major Western embassies in Kuwait.

Most of the US diplomats and military living in the suburbs were in the Jabriya area, a block away from the Japanese Embassy. They were initially instructed to go to their own embassy in the city, but as they were leaving their homes they received another call saying it was too dangerous with fighting around the compound. They were to stay where they were.

Unfortunately, the Jabriya Americans were also near the home of the Amir's sister, and an Al-Sabah *diwaniah* (traditional gathering place of Kuwaitis and their guests). Throughout the morning, Al-Sabah women and children gathered at the *diwaniah* in Chevy and GMC wagons, apparently in preparation for a dash to Saudi Arabia. The area looked increasingly risky. The Americans feared that the Iraqis would come looking for the Al-Sabah families, and stumble across them. A smart Iraqi officer would soon figure out that the strapping 'diplomats' with short haircuts were US military.

The senior American diplomat in the area, 36-year-old Economic Counsellor Emil Skodon, advised the Embassy of their predicament, and was told to seek sanctuary at the Japanese Embassy. Besides Skodon, his wife Dorothea, and their two small daughters, the 16-strong Jabriya contingent included the Commander of USLOK, Colonel John Mooneyham and his family, three other USLOK men and their families, a civilian attached to USLOK, and his wife, a US Navy enlisted man, and a civilian teacher.

Skodon approached Japanese *chargé d'affaires*, Akio Shirota for refuge. He agreed with little hesitation. His one condition was that the Americans stayed completely incognito. They were put into the Embassy basement.

It took time to adjust to the reality of the invasion. Incredibly, some people felt they had pressing matters at work, so went in regardless. Many employees turned up late for work, armed with the excuse that the buses were not running. For much of the first day, many people simply carried on as normal.

The Iraqi columns that had skirted the city on Sixth and Seventh Ring were so intent on reaching their objectives that they seldom dropped off any forces along the way to secure their flanks. People who pulled up at traffic lights minutes after the Iraqis had rumbled through had no way of knowing they had ever been there. By the time most people were on their way to work after 6.00 a.m., the main roads on the outer edge of the urban area were almost devoid of Iraqi troops. Those troops whose mission was to take the International Airport were inside the perimeter, not outside, and their colleagues had disappeared south towards the Saudi border. People driving towards the airport at that time saw nothing unusual. In the first hours of the invasion, the Iraqis were more interested in preventing the escape of the Kuwaiti Government by air, and neutralizing the nearby KAF International Base, than they were in capturing offices. Kuwait Airways Corporation (KAC) office staff continued to turn up for work, unhindered, for some time.

One of these was Paul Eliopoulos, a Greek-American Arthur Andersen computer consultant seconded to KAC. He arrived at work to discover that the invasion had occurred. Instead of going home, he proceeded to shut down the mainframes. At the time, Iraqi Airways' passenger reservations system was hosted off KAC computers. As the machines came down, Iraqi Airways in Baghdad, apparently ignorant of the invasion, sent an electronic message querying the move and asking that the system be kept going. Paul replied that: 'For their information, Kuwait had just been invaded by Iraq, and he was going to shut the system down.' The Iraqis protested, saying they had a contract..... KAC could not shut the system down unilaterally!

Paul shot back a short, defiant '*F_ _ k you !*' and completed the job. Days later, he was captured by the Iraqis, and held hostage; he worried for months whether the consequences of his brave, futile protest would be visited on him.

In the hours immediately after the Iraqis took the city centre, there was more danger on the roads from panicked motorists than from the Iraqi Army. The

Kuwait Police tried in vain to stop people from travelling into the city, but were eventually forced to abandon their own checkpoints by the advancing Iraqis. Those people who had arrived at work before the Iraqis had taken the city rushed back towards their homes in the suburbs, sometimes battling their way through the second wave of Iraqi trucks and armoured vehicles which suddenly appeared on the arterial roads. They were joined by hundreds of others, all heading for the relative safety of the suburbs. Drivers were running red lights, bumping over central reservations, and driving on the wrong side of the road in panic. The roads were soon strewn with smashed cars and broken glass. Some of the cars had caught fire, and looked as if they had been shot up. A number of Iraqis added to the destruction by smashing the windscreens of Kuwaiti cars they stopped, and ordering the drivers to abandon their vehicles. Incredibly, other people were still queuing for the non-existent buses.

Initial reactions to the invasion differed sharply. While some people, especially those who had seen little action, treated it as a great adventure and took advantage of the day off work to go swimming or play tennis, others turned their homes into bunkers, taped up their windows to prevent them shattering from blast, and filled every container they could find with water.

Those of us who had witnessed the early action were under no illusion that things were normal. Whatever happened, it would be wise to stock up on food. That required money, which meant the bank. The banks were not open, but Kuwait is a modern cash society, and ATM cash dispensers are used widely.

The time was approaching 8.30 a.m. The firing had died away and the streets were deserted. The bank was no more than 50 metres from my building. It seemed safe and if I did not go soon, the ATM would be empty. I left the building by a back entrance nearest to the Gulf Bank, peering around the edge of the buildings for any troops. The only vehicles apart from those left overnight at parking meters were an ambulance which had crashed into the sidewalk, and a yellow school bus. The doors of the ambulance were open, the crew and patient, if there had been one, gone. The bus also seemed empty.

I turned the corner to the ATM, past the smashed window of a Rolex watch shop. A heavy safe lay outside, showing marks of unsuccessful attempts to open it. All the displays were gone, leaving only the plastic stands and open boxes, but the thieves were nowhere to be seen. In fact, there was no one on the street, even at the ATM. I inserted the plastic card, feeling very vulnerable. I had perhaps a week's food in my flat, and no more than KD40 (US$133) in my pocket. I had to survive. My heart sank as the screen flashed unhelpfully that the service was not available. There was nothing more I could do.

The streets were still eerily quiet, so I crossed the road to Arlene's flat to see how the family was. They also wanted to get cash, but their bank was 500 metres away. Four of us, including Arlene as the only woman, decided to try it. We used back lanes where possible, and arrived at the bank after ten minutes.

The family was more fortunate. Their ATM worked. They each withdrew the maximum, KD250, concealing it within their clothes as they did so. Hurrying homewards, we encountered our first Iraqi soldier face-to-face. He was in a nondescript khaki uniform with a Kalashnikov hanging from his shoulder, his arm resting on the forestock. He was guarding the street corner, obviously not enjoying his new job in the heat. The man called Arlene over, asking her if she was Kuwaiti. She put on her haughtiest look, pulled out her identification card, and looked down her nose at him, saying: *'La, Hindia!'* (No, Indian!) He looked at the card quizzically, as if he could not read it, even though it was in Arabic. He was a country lad, scruffy, but with an open, friendly face, trying to be tough. We pointed out the nationality on the card to him. He nodded. *'Ameriki?'* (American?) he asked me. *'La, Australi.'* (No, Australian) I replied. He seemed satisfied, and sent us on our way.

By mid-morning the Iraqis held the city centre and Sixth Ring, and were completing their envelopment of the city.

In the suburbs, people who could get into shops stripped the shelves bare, with fist fights sometimes breaking out in the panic. Curiously, whenever Westerners appeared, the Kuwaitis often pushed them to the front of the queue. They seemed embarrassed that the expatriates were caught in such an inconvenient situation in their country. The more cynical commented that the Kuwaitis were already aware of where their salvation would come from, and it would not be entirely from brother Arabs.

In the city centre, the situation was far too tense for many shopkeepers to venture forth. Most of the shops had already been looted by 9.00 a.m. Windows of electronics and camera shops were smashed. Anything within arm's reach disappeared. Many gold *souq* jewellers ran the gauntlet of Iraqi troops only to arrive at their shops to find them picked clean. The Iraqi Army or local opportunists had got there first. A few quick dealers had got into the *souq* early, and rather than risk carrying their gold out, hid it under the floorboards or elsewhere with the intention of retrieving it later.

Other shop owners who had managed to make it into the city without being detained, or who lived above the premises, stood by nervously, afraid to open the grills and retrieve their stock in case it was taken from them at gunpoint. Within days, most of the bars themselves were hacked off, or even ripped open with forklift trucks. Whatever remained disappeared in minutes.

I arrived back from my trip to the banks to be greeted by the news of a full battalion of about 50 Iraqi tanks, all T-72s, coming down Fahd Al-Salem Street from the direction of the Sheraton. The heavy troops of the first wave had arrived. The armour clanked down both sides of the road, most of it turning left at the main intersection towards Kuwait Bay. It was quite a sight, their long guns protruding from their turrets like the lances of great armoured knights. I breathed a sigh of relief. I had just walked across that same road.

The advance of these ponderous beasts proved comical as well as awesome. The drivers were obviously unused to manoeuvring in city streets. Several mounted the kerbs, crushing the concrete before crashing back down onto the road. One knocked over a traffic light as it turned, and continued towards the bay on the wrong side of the road as his colleagues dutifully chugged up the other side. Unknown to the wrong-way Iraqi tank driver, his destruction of this one very visible traffic light in central Kuwait City gave rise to a false rumour which came to be believed as the Gospel truth worldwide, that the Iraqis were even stealing the traffic lights.

The tanks chugged between the Evangelical Church compound on their left, and the National Assembly on their right, belching blue diesel fumes. Some were flying red flags, similar to those on the officers' jeeps darting around the city. At the Gulf Road T-junction, a few went to the left, the rest to the right. They then peeled off in the same manner as the other tanks deploying further down the coast, mounting the central reservation, crushing the greenery under their tracks and parking there with their guns aimed out over Kuwait Bay.

Unknown to us, another tank battalion was doing the same from the south, moving up the coast road from Sixth Ring in a column. Individual tanks peeled off and deployed every 200 metres on the coastal parking lots, their guns pointing out across the Gulf. They were obviously preparing to repulse any amphibious attack. The only force capable of mounting such an operation was the US Marines. Even at that stage, the Iraqis knew their real enemy.

This procedure was repeated all the way along the 36km from the Shuwaikh Port, until the two tank battalions joined up. By noon, a hundred tanks, one every 200 or 300 metres, formed a line of steel along the north and eastern coasts of the urban area. Other troops held Sixth Ring and the International Airport along the southern edge. Thousands more continued to pour in from Iraq in trucks and buses. Kuwait was in checkmate.

During the morning, brief skirmishes were fought at the Messila Palace, the residence of the Minister of Commerce and Industry, on the coast a kilometre south of Sixth Ring, and at the nearby Army Officers' Club. Most Kuwaiti troops in these locations had mustered straight from their homes, with few weapons, so they were quickly surrounded and had to surrender.

Further up the coast at Sha'ab, the Iraqi Air Force attacked the residence of Crown Prince and Prime Minister Sheikh Sa'ad Al-Abdullah twice, causing heavy damage and setting it alight, while at Bayan Palace, on Fifth Ring, flights of Mi-8 helicopter gunships circled the complex at mid-morning, strafing the guard posts. Iraqi jets had rocketed it earlier in the morning. Scattered fighting continued around Bayan Palace until mid-afternoon.

At the Jiwan and Mubarak camps and GHQ, a force of several hundred Kuwaitis were holding out. These men, hastily called in from their homes earlier that morning, had been ordered at around 8.30 a.m. by the Director of Operations, Brigadier Jassim Al-Shehab, not to resist, and to surrender their weapons. They had no armour, only small-arms, and were outflanked with Iraqi troops to their north on Jahra Road and in the hospitals complex, and behind them in the city. Iraqi tanks and infantry were to the west as well, near the intersection of Fourth Ring and Jahra Road. The National Guard, whose camp was closest to the intersection, were exchanging limited fire with the Iraqis and had no immediate plans to surrender, but they had no armour or anti-tank weapons, only light mortars. The Iraqis had not yet made a concerted effort to capture the camps, but it was only a matter of time.

By then, following his dash from his camp far to the south, 15 Brigade's Colonel Mohammed Al-Harmi had regrouped his little force of a couple of dozen Chieftains and BMPs on Fourth Ring east of the camps. He sent an officer forward to to assess the situation, but the man was mistaken for an Iraqi, and was wounded in the arm by nervous Kuwaitis firing from inside the camps. It took some time to arrange safe passage for Al-Harmi's vehicles into the camps, through the south gate of Jiwan on Fourth Ring. Once inside, he discovered that the Kuwaitis were preparing to surrender. He contacted Al-Shehab. 'We are here,' Al-Harmi said. 'You now have armour.'

'OK,'replied Al-Shehab. 'We will fight until we die.'

Al-Harmi then deployed his tanks on each gate of the Jiwan and Mubarak camps, both on the north and south sides, and waited for the Iraqis.

Everything remained relatively peaceful until about 10.00 a.m., when a convoy of Iraqi Army trucks drove east down Fourth Ring in the middle of the civilian traffic, towards Jiwan. Suddenly, everything seemed to happen at once. Iraqi light artillery opened up on the camps, and the Kuwaitis inside fired on the Iraqi trucks. The Iraqis jumped out to find cover as the civilian cars scattered. 15 Brigade's tanks then started engaging Iraqi tanks which appeared to the west, on Fourth Ring. The Iraqi infantry pulled back, and the battle settled down to a stalemate tank duel for the next two hours.

Fortunately for the Kuwaitis, the Iraqi artillery and mortar batteries were initially firing blind. They were positioned north of the camps in the grounds of the Al-Sabah Hospital, and in a cinema car park several kilometres west of the Fourth Ring/ Jahra Road intersection, but had few spotters close to the camps. Nevertheless, before the bombardment, Iraqi officers had gone around to residential buildings likely to fall within their field of fire, warning people to take shelter. They made a genuine effort to avoid harming civilians.

On the southern edge of the camps, Englishman Brock Matthews was in his apartment on Fourth Ring, overlooking the south entrance of the camps. He and his Australian son, Chris, answered a knock at the door shortly after 10.00 a.m. to five Kuwaiti National Guardsmen armed with G3 automatic rifles. They politely asked him if they could use his balcony as an observation post. It was hardly a request that could be refused.

The Kuwaitis' mission was to direct the fire of two of 15 Brigade's tanks inside the camps onto the Iraqis outside, but they were totally unprepared. They had brought no binoculars or radios. They had the determination and even some of the arms to fight, but not the leadership to do so effectively.

Throughout the late morning, the Iraqi bombardment concentrated on the Jahra Road headquarters entrance on the northern edge of the Mubarak Camp, the Ministry of Defence building, the military college, and the medical centre. Eventually, the Iraqis placed spotters atop the dome of the nearby Medical Centre Mosque to the north, and their fire became more effective. Some reports put other spotters on top of the nearby ten-storey Ministry of Electricity and Water (MEW) building, on Fourth Ring, west of the camps.

The Kuwaitis concentrated on blinding these eyes of the Iraqi gunners. A platoon of National Guard reportedly killed the spotters on the MEW building, occupied the roof, and fired on the Iraqis below, just within rifle range. Despite this, the besieged Kuwaitis did not have the time or the leadership to plan a proper defence, and little defence against the artillery. With the exception of 15

Brigade and some National Guard companies, they were a gathering of random soldiers and policemen, not formed units. They fought with whatever weapons they could lay their hands on, which was precious little. Most small-arms ammunition was locked away elsewhere.

In the city centre, a lull set in after the passage of the tanks down Fahd Al-Salem Street, and their deployment along the coast. In the street below our windows, some people started drifting back to reclaim their abandoned cars.

Our constant phone calls around the city turned up only snippets of information. The BBC could only tell us that the invasion had occurred, that the Amir and Government were safe in Saudi Arabia. The UN Security Council was meeting to discuss the crisis, and the Arab League Foreign Ministers were convening in Cairo. The spot price of oil was rocketing. A crisis of global proportions was in the making.

Suddenly, at 10.40 a.m., a flight of about 15 large Iraqi helicopters thundered by with a shattering roar, level with our windows, heading east. We could even see the crewmen's moustaches. They were gone in a moment, the eerie silence outside soon restored. We discovered later that the helicopters' mission was to land troops at the Shuwaikh Port. Most people in Kuwait that day observed fleets of helicopters flying low across the city. One flew too low, and hit power lines in the Palestinian enclave of Hawally. The others continued on. The severely burned pilot was later treated at Kuwait's Mubarak Al-Kabeer Hospital. The blackened corpses of other men in the charred machine provided a major attraction for sightseers for several days.

As the morning wore on, we became more curious to see what was going on at street level. Apart from my brief trip to the banks, no one in our group had been outside that morning. Most, quite sensibly, wanted to stay put. Mary, an American woman who had joined us, and I decided to venture out onto the broadwalk of the shopping centre below for a peek. In retrospect it was a stupid thing to do, but natural curiosity and excitement got the better of us.

As we exited the elevator on the ground floor we noticed a bullet hole in the nearby glass door, and a chip out of the wall. A chill went up our spines. Someone had been shooting at our building. Whether it was by accident or not was irrelevant. The result would be the same if you got in the way of a bullet.

Nevertheless, the sense of adventure drove us on. We could see the smashed door of the Pizza Hut ahead of us, and a wrecked city bus and cars on the road beyond, but our view of the interior of the restaurant was obscured. So much had happened in the past five hours that I forgot we had seen troops looting it earlier. We tiptoed out tentatively onto the boardwalk, when suddenly a cheerful Arabic voice called: '*Fadl, Ahlan wa Sahlan!*' (Welcome. Join us !)

We spun around. Inside the Pizza Hut were half a dozen young Iraqi troops tucking into a breakfast of bread, pizza toppings, and Pepsi. The restaurant cash box lay smashed and empty on the floor alongside their Kalashnikovs.

'We have plenty,' one said, in Arabic, grinning, indicating the food.

In the Arab world, with its great tradition of hospitality, it is difficult to pass a group of people whom one knows, even fleetingly, when they are eating, and not be invited to join them. A failure to extend an invitation would dishonour them, but it is perfectly acceptable, even expected, to decline with elaborate excuses.

Mary and I looked at each other. This was not a rampaging army. These were kids on a new adventure. We did not feel threatened, although Mary would have felt differently had she been alone. We declined gracefully, and resumed our reconnaissance, joining up with Tony Ghosn, a Lebanese neighbour who had also ventured outside, and several other Lebanese.

The scene from the broadwalk was disturbing. Besides the Pizza Hut, many shop windows were smashed, especially those with watches, jewellery, and electronics. Computer diskettes, useless to the Iraqis, were scattered in the dirt with discarded timepiece cases and instructions for cassette players.

About half the cars had been retrieved by their owners or driven away by the soldiers, but dozens remained, their owners either taken away for some reason by the Iraqis, or too scared to return. Some still had their engines running. The occupants had not been allowed to turn them off before being taken prisoner. The bus had run up onto the central reservation. We were to find out why later. It was an eerie sight. An entire street of empty cars.

A lone Iraqi soldier on the street beckoned us over, smiling. He had been reversing an abandoned Toyota the wrong way up the street, towards a Mercedes. He was a fit, solid man in his thirties, in camouflage and a red beret, with parachute wings on his left breast. He was sweating, but looked fresh. His webbing, crude but functional, held several magazines in pouches around his midriff, with grenades in two small pockets on each side. The number '2' in Arabic script, in a white circle, was stencilled onto the middle pouch. I could see no badges of rank, but he looked like an enlisted man. He held his weapon with professional familiarity, but not threateningly. This was apparently a member of the much-vaunted Republican Guard.

We walked over to the low balcony, intrigued, looking down at him, not daring to venture onto the sidewalk. He began to speak in Arabic and sign language, addressing himself to me and ignoring Mary, as manners dictated. It appeared he wanted a tube, or a hose to siphon petrol.

I had some plastic tubing in my apartment upstairs. So far, the troops seemed friendly. Their manners were impeccable, at least towards Westerners. This one would get the petrol either way, with or without my help. It seemed best to be civil. I asked him to come with me so that he would not think I was trying to avoid him, and left Mary in the care of Tony. We rode the elevator upstairs, with the soldier glancing quizzically at the lights designating the floors. He stood respectfully in the foyer of my flat as I searched for the tubing. The day was hot. He had obviously been in the sun for a while. I offered him a cold Pepsi from the fridge, but he refused it. I opened it, took a sip myself, then offered it to him. He took one sip for politeness.

We returned downstairs, with him still looking strangely at the elevator. Then it struck me. He may have been a seasoned paratrooper, but this looked like his first ride in an elevator. He smiled nervously as it jolted to a stop on the ground floor. We exited, and he went about his task of siphoning fuel out of the Toyota into the Mercedes. After finishing, he walked back to the Toyota, coiled the hose neatly, held it aloft in the air for me to see, and placed it on top of the car with a gesture of thanks. He then drove off in the Mercedes, crashing the automatic transmission as if it had a manual gearbox.

The whole incident was surreal. It had been perfectly acceptable for the soldier to loot an abandoned Mercedes from some absent Kuwaiti in preference to the Toyota , but he would not drink my Pepsi, and returned the hose I lent him when he may have needed it himself later. It would have been so easy for him to take it. I have often wondered if he was just a particularly well-mannered fellow with an aversion to Pepsi. I felt a twinge of the guilt of collaboration, and remorse for the unknown Mercedes owner.

Emboldened, Mary and I ventured down onto the sidewalk, collecting several spent cartridge casings, and an empty ammunition box with 'GHQ, Ministry of Defence, Jordan' stencilled on it. This was our first evidence of Jordanian collaboration in the invasion, but for all we knew, the ammunition may have been stockpiled from the Iran-Iraq War, and paid for by Kuwait. There had obviously been shooting around here, but there was no evidence of casualties about, no bodies, no bloodstains on the street. Perhaps they had just been firing into the air for effect.

Our next discovery soon dispelled that assumption. We boarded the crashed city bus, noticing that several windows were smashed. A thick trail of heavy, congealed blood led from the driver's seat to the rear door. Flies were already feasting on it. The driver had obviously been badly wounded, and had lost a lot of blood, perhaps been killed, but was nowhere to be seen. The unfortunate man must have been fired upon in panic or reaction when he surprised the Iraqi squad we had first seen advancing eastwards. This explained why the bus had crashed. The adventure had turned sour. We headed back to our apartments. This was no game. Innocent people were paying the price in blood.

Meanwhile, to the west, the siege of the Jiwan and Mubarak camps continued unabated.

In late morning, with the Kuwaiti National Guard holding Fourth Ring on the south side of the camps, the Iraqis tried to outflank the Kuwaiti tanks with an infantry assault from the north, across Jahra Road. They killed several Kuwaiti soldiers at the main entrance of the Ministry of Defence Headquarters, and captured the signals building in the Mubarak Camp itself, killing a number of Kuwaiti signallers, and temporarily installing artillery spotters on the roof of the building. They were targeting the GHQ nerve centre of the Kuwaiti Armed Forces, and knew exactly where to go. They also occupied the nearby Police College. Kuwaitis in the camps fought back, preventing further Iraqi advances, and eventually pushing them back across Jahra Road. However, the Iraqis maintained a toehold in the Police College.

The Kuwaitis then counterattacked across Jahra Road, supported by four of 15 Brigade's tanks. The Iraqi infantry in the hospitals complex were taken by surprise. They had not expected a counterattack, certainly not with Kuwaiti tanks. Their own supporting armour was too far away to be of much use, and they themselves were exhausted, not having slept since the Tuesday night.

About 600 of them, including a colonel, gave up almost without a fight and were shepherded back into the Mubarak Camp, to be locked up.

However, as the Kuwaitis were withdrawing back across Jahra Road with their prisoners, one of their tanks, commanded by Captain Hamid Al-Kandari, was too slow. It presented a profile target to Iraqi gunners farther down the road. They scored a direct hit, killing or fatally wounding three crewmen. Al-Kandari only survived because he was high up in the turret.

After this engagement, the Iraqis stopped trying to send tanks down Jahra Road. There was no need for them to risk their forces unnecessarily after such losses. They could send more armour into the city on Jamal Abdul Nasser Street, on the other side of the hospitals complex, without risk.

Nevertheless, the stubborn Kuwaiti resistance at the camps was proving annoying to the Iraqis, who needed to get further forces into the Kuwaiti suburbs to secure them, to reinforce their colleagues already holding the coast, and push more forces south. They could do this along Fifth and Sixth Ring, but they were also keen to take the now barely-functioning Kuwaiti GHQ in the Mubarak Camp, if only as a symbolic victory.

At about 2.00 p.m., the Iraqis started trying to push down Fourth Ring, past the National Guard.The weight of numbers and the Iraqi shelling began to tell. The 700 National Guardsmen were exhausted after holding out in the summer heat since early morning. Answering a plea for help, Colonel Al-Harmi pulled four tanks and four BMPs off his northern perimeter to reinforce them. Although the Jiwan and Mubarak camps complex is adjacent to the National Guard camp, there were no connecting gates. The Kuwaiti tanks therefore had to break through the internal walls to reach the National Guard camp. Once inside, they deployed at the gates overlooking Fourth Ring, and opened fire, driving the Iraqis back towards the Jahra Road intersection.

For the remainder of the afternoon, the Kuwaitis prevented the Iraqis from moving down either Fourth Ring or Jahra Road. The Iraqis, for their part, concentrated on bringing up reinforcements and shelling the camp intermittently. For some reason, they did not turn around their troops and tanks already in the city and try to take the camps from the east.

The large Iraqi helicopters and gunships were not the only aircraft in action over the city at the time. The Kuwait Air Force was still fighting back, with the A-4s from Al-Jaber base.

In late morning, two A-4s loaded with 500lb bombs were on their way to bomb an Iraqi column at Mutla'a when their base received reports of the Iraqi concentration near the Sheraton. The two aircraft split up, with Lieutenant Ali Saud diverting to the Sheraton, and his colleague continuing on to Mutla'a. Saud rolled in on the Iraqis gathered on an open area in front of the Roman Catholic Cathedral and dropped his bombs, shaking windows and rattling nerves throughout the city centre, before returning safely to base.

Shortly afterwards, in the Al-Muthanna, we were jolted by the roar of fighter planes nearby. Then someone spotted them circling perhaps 500 metres away, at the level of the thirteenth floor. We rushed to a bedroom window to get a better view. They were close enough for us to see the pilots' white helmets under the canopies, but moving too quickly to identify any markings. I thought they looked like Kuwaiti Skyhawks, but we could not be sure.

The two jets swooped and banked in figures-of-eight 500 feet above the city centre, as if they were dancing. They seemed to be trying to see something on the ground below. Scattered black puffs of anti-aircraft fire clawed towards them. We could not be certain where the fire was coming from.

Suddenly both jets dived one after the other, at an angle of 45°. Halfway into the dive they each fired two rockets from under their wings, the propellant leaving a line of white hot fire behind each speeding missile. As the weapons cleared the aircraft, each jet turned sharply out of the dive as if they had hit an invisible trampoline. It was an instant change of direction. Both aircraft immediately turned northwest and sped away.

We could not tell at the time whose jets they were. Some maintained they were Iraqi, but by then the Iraqis had control of that area. They would hardly call in an air strike on their own troops. We never even discovered for sure what they were firing at. The only real damage we saw in that area later was a burned-out police station, but there were no holes in its roof. Whatever the target was, someone was going to a lot of trouble to hit it. If the planes were Kuwaiti, we were greatly heartened that they were putting up a fight.

Several other A-4 sorties were flown against Iraqi ground troops, but it was a hopeless battle. There were just too many Iraqis, and they were already deep into Kuwait. Furthermore, with the Kuwaitis being dependent on expatriate ground crew, they were unable to use all their aircraft or to turn them around as quickly as they should have been able to.

During the afternoon, responding to reports of Iraqi vessels approaching the coast, two A-4s intercepted a large landing craft escorted by a fast attack craft near Failaka. One dropped cluster bombs on the larger vessel, but was unable to confirm any damage. The last sorties of the day were flown by Lieutenants Salem Ajmi and Adnan Hammadi on the Salmi Road at about 4.30 p.m.

In the Al-Muthanna, our next contact with the troops several hours later was not as pleasant as the first. I was in my apartment, alone, when the doorbell rang. Thinking it was a neighbour, I opened it, to be faced by a Republican Guard with a scruffy, uncertain-looking trooper behind him in the cotton khaki uniform of what we later learned was the Regular Army. The Guardsman's air of professionalism was unmistakable. He asked if he could enter. It was obvious he did not expect to be refused.

The other man stayed outside, fidgeting nervously, while the Guardsman quickly scanned the interior of the apartment. He checked only the view of the courtyard separating the residential complex from the Plaza Hotel. I never found out what he was looking for, but he left within 30 seconds, nodding curtly. The two men then proceeded across the corridor to my neighbour's place, without allowing me a chance to warn him of the impending visit.

My neighbour opened the door unsuspectingly, as I had. We had yet to realize this was unwise. As the two soldiers entered, with me following, the second man noticed the big group sitting in the living room. He cocked his weapon with a loud *click-click*, bringing it up to cover the group. They froze.

'Schwea, schwea, Hajji. Mafi mushkilla. Mafi jundi moujoud!' (Easy, Sir. No problem. No soldier here!), I said. He lowered the gun, but kept it pointed in the general direction of the group. The Guardsman went about his business, looking out of windows in the bedrooms, returning after seconds.

He asked people's nationalities. We were a mixed bunch. Several British by now, two Australians, a few Americans, a Sudanese doctor, and Hadi Al-Omari, the Iraqi Personnel Manager of Kuwait Drilling Company. The Guardsman glowered at Hadi, and asked him why he as an Iraqi was here in the company of foreigners. Hadi shot back: 'I live here in Kuwait, in this building, and these people are my friends. What's the problem? You are the ones coming into our house, this country, uninvited.'

The Guardsman seemed dissatisfied, but did not pursue the matter. We were left with the impression that he did not approve of Iraqis who lived in Kuwait. They left as quickly as they had come.

Meanwhile, in the Airport Hotel, the passengers and crew of BA149 were increasingly concerned about their fate. Soldiers were in the hotel, but they were not threatening. In fact, they seemed genuinely concerned for their prisoners' safety. Some bored troops even began to play with the children.

Settling in was an exercise in chaos. The hotel, a transit facility, has only 200 rooms. There were over 400 individuals on the premises. Some had to share rooms with total strangers, or bed down in the foyer. A simple breakfast was prepared by the BA crew as most of the hotel staff, except the cook, had fled. They lunched on what was to become a staple diet of chicken and rice, with a few vegetables. Some BA staff joked that they had been caught in what was probably just another Third World coup which would soon blow over. Most people expected they would soon be allowed to fly out in the refuelled 747 parked barely 500 metres away. It was not until 7.00 p.m. that Captain Clark announced that there was no possibility of leaving that day.

The incoming crew, now at the Regency Palace Hotel, and those with the passengers at the Airport Hotel, were not the only aircrew in Kuwait. British Airways had two other crews, both from Tristars, in the Regency. Air France, Japanese Airlines and Egypt Air all had crews on layover in town, but no aircraft at the airport. The Egyptians would eventually be allowed to leave. The Japanese would later join the British as Saddam's hostages. The French – and a few of the British crew – would remain successfully in hiding.

In addition to the passengers and aircrew, over 100 Western and Japanese guests were in Kuwait's hotels. Many of these people would become hostages, or be forced into hiding for four long months.

Ken and Jo Best, a British couple, were living on the Gulf coast south of Sixth Ring. They had a view of the beaches at the front, and the Fahaheel fish market, behind which was the IBI Residential Camp, named after the contractor that built it. IBI housed most of the British NCOs from the British Liaison Team (BLT) attached to the Kuwaiti forces, and their families.

The BLT comprised 6 Army and 2 RAF officers, plus 69 Army and RAF Warrant Officers and Senior NCOs, a total of 77 men, most of whom were accompanied by their families. Their role was to advise the Kuwaitis on maintaining and operating their Chieftain tanks and BAe Hawk Mk64 jet trainers. Although seconded to the Kuwaiti forces, they had no war role. At the time of the invasion, 66 BLT men and over 150 dependants were in Kuwait. They lived at eleven different locations in the country, the heaviest concentration being at IBI, with 33 of the 66.

The team's secondment had been automatically rescinded the moment the Iraqis crossed the border, but that was now of academic interest. Fortunately for them, the invasion happened at a time of the week, and at a time of day, when they were not at their regular workplaces on the Kuwaiti bases. Unfortunately, unlike their American counterparts in USLOK, they and their families did not have diplomatic passports.

Ken and Jo had seen Iraqi trucks deposit infantry on the beaches at 9.00 a.m. The troops were just left there, in small groups, with their small-arms. At about 11.00 a.m., Ken was on the phone to the senior Warrant Officer at IBI, RSM Mike Haynes. Jo was looking out of the window at what she thought were four small boats motoring towards the coast. She remarked to Ken that they were going awfully fast towards the beach, when all of a sudden they drove up out of the water onto the land. They were Iraqi amphibious craft.

Similar-sized amphibious units had been landing on beaches all the way down the Gulf coast. It seemed strangely comical. The troops who had arrived by truck already held the beaches. It looked as if some Iraqi Marine commander wanted to give his men a bit of practice.

Ken warned Mike Haynes at IBI. From his apartment, Ken could see the Iraqis who had just landed walking south towards IBI. Haynes had already told the few Kuwaiti troops guarding the camp to hide their weapons. There was no point resisting. It would only get people killed.

A squad of ten Iraqi Republican Guards entered the camp, and were shocked at finding British soldiers and their families there, all in civilian clothes. They had a quick look around, and then left, without leaving anyone behind.

The commander of the BLT, Colonel Bruce Duncan, who lived near central Kuwait City, had called Haynes at 5.00 a.m. with the news of the invasion, and told all the men to gather in the mess. The women and children were to implement Phase I of the evacuation plan, which was to pack all the cars with rations for 24 hours, spare fuel, valuables and documents. The men were to stand by to help with any mass evacuation of British civilians. The women and children had the option of leaving Kuwait by driving south to Saudi Arabia. Not unexpectedly, they decided to a woman to stay with their husbands. No one knew what the situation was like on the road south, although it was perhaps only a 40 minute fast drive from IBI to the border.

Later in the day, around 5.00 p.m., the Iraqis returned, locked the camp gates, and posted guards there, and at every house. The 33 men inside, their families, and two colleagues who had come from elsewhere to collect packing cases were trapped. The window of opportunity for escape was closed.

In the Al-Muthanna, as noon approached, we noticed battered Iraqi buses in groups of five or six, carrying men in scruffy civilian clothes towards the

Sheraton Hotel. We did not know what or who they were, but they were actually the Popular Army – those who had survived the strafing by the KAF on Mutla'a Ridge – being shipped in to occupy the city while the professional troops were deployed where real fighting might occur.

Within half an hour, a line of buses stretched from the Sheraton hundreds of metres east down Fahd Al-Salem Street. There must have been thousands of men. Strangely, they came from the opposite direction to the troops who had first taken the city, and the tanks. We later surmised that they must have had to skirt the city because of continuing Kuwaiti resistance at the Jiwan and Mubarak camps. There was a scare that they were going to occupy our building and evict us. Scores of them suddenly disembarked from the buses in front of the building, but only to collect buckets of water from the ornamental fountains, and then re-board the buses. With the noon-time temperature pushing 50°C, it must have been hell in those unair-conditioned buses.

Throughout the first day of the invasion, and into the second, people who had access to international lines were calling home to their families, friends and employers abroad, usually in an upbeat mood. To those at home, the greatest burden was ignorance. Media reports were sketchy, and often alarmist. The story was breaking too quickly to verify properly. The few foreign journalists in Kuwait, including the *Washington Post's* Caryle Murphy at the Kuwait International Hotel, and the *Financial Times'* Victor Mallet and Dutch Radio's Hettie Lubberding at the Holiday Inn were frantically trying to find out what was going on, and file before international communications were cut.

TV stations worldwide were showing file footage of Iraqi armour racing across the desert. Accounts of those in Kuwait who had witnessed action were naturally given prominence over the many more who had seen nothing at all. It was as if all of Kuwait were devastated. Some people outside Kuwait had no idea whether their relatives and friends were alive or dead, whether their daughters or wives had been raped. Imagination played havoc with them. Some went into shock. Others fully expected the crisis to pass within days, and for their loved ones to come home with a few exciting stories.

The surprisingly positive tone of many phone calls out of Kuwait that day was a function of individuals' experiences, and a desire to reassure their loved ones. Most had indeed seen no action at all, and only heard gunfire in the distance. The invasion was not affecting them directly, other than preventing them from going to work. For the most part, electricity, water and phones stayed on. The almost light-hearted nature of many calls was quite genuine. Incredibly, I recall one of my earlier irrational concerns being that a dance scheduled for that evening at the SAS Hotel would be cancelled.

The reaction of Kuwaitis still in the country was quite different from that of the expatriates. For one thing, it was their country that had been invaded. Some of them, such as my friend Nabil, tried to join their units - some successfully - just as their colleagues were being overwhelmed. About 700 Kuwaiti officers and several thousand enlisted men were eventually captured. Hundreds of others escaped, shedding their uniforms and melting into the suburbs. Some kept their sidearms, or obtained sporting weapons from home, and sniped at the Iraqis throughout the ensuing days. The Kuwait Police hastily emptied out the armouries in their suburban stations to arm the nascent Resistance. The Kuwaiti suburbs were initially no-go areas for the Iraqis. They were relatively safe in strength on the main roads and in expatriate suburbs, but initially dared not venture into the maze of unfamiliar streets in pursuit of the Kuwaitis.

The Kuwaitis had no doubts that the coup story was a concoction, but could do little about it. It was obvious to them from the huge scope of the invading force that the Iraqis were here to stay. Like the expatriates, the Kuwaitis stocked up on food and water, and retrieved what money they could from the ATMs. A number offered refuge to Westerners, particularly Americans, well aware that these people would eventually be in great danger from the Iraqis.

Late in the day, a radio station claiming to be Radio Kuwait broadcast that the Provisional Free Kuwait Government (PFKG) had overthrown the Amir and invited in the Iraqis. No one believed it, particularly Arabs, not least because of the announcers' Iraqi accents. The real Kuwait TV stayed on the air throughout the day on its regular channel. The Iraqis had captured the main transmitter, but could not find the back-up. There were even rumours that the Kuwaitis were broadcasting from Khafji in Saudi Arabia. Most of the transmission was of patriotic songs, and file tape of KAF Mirages and Skyhawks flying over Kuwait City, or Kuwaiti armour on manoeuvres. This was interspersed with footage of the Amir and Crown Prince in happier times.

The station broadcast that the Amir and other members of the Government had escaped to Saudi Arabia, and that the Amir's brother, Sheikh Fahd Al-Ahmad had been killed at Dasman Palace. It was initially reported that Crown Prince and Prime Minister Sheikh Sa'ad Al-Abdullah was co-ordinating the defence of Kuwait from an underground crisis centre, but later bulletins reported that he too was safely in Saudi Arabia. Sheikh Sa'ad eventually went on TV live to prove that the legitimate government was still intact, and to appeal for resistance. 'They have come to kill the sons of Kuwait and its women,' he said. 'Our patriotic Army is repelling the aggression. Patriotic Kuwaitis should stand behind them.'

In fact, the Army had been all but routed but Sheikh Sa'ad need not have worried about his citizenry. They were firmly behind him, and already putting together what would later prove to be a unique and extremely effective underground Resistance.

The wheel of history had turned full circle. The Al-Sabah had given refuge to the Al-Saud in the late 1800s, enabling them to retake their fallen capital at Riyadh in 1902, and eventually to build Saudi Arabia. The Saudis were now giving refuge to the Al-Sabah, and would eventually enable them to regain their country with their Allies' help.

Throughout the world, Kuwaitis on holiday or business abroad flocked to their embassies for news. Several hundred Kuwaiti men in Saudi Arabia crossed back into Kuwait across the desert before the Iraqis consolidated their positions. They would continue to do so over the next few weeks.

As the day progressed, residents of the city centre discovered over the phones that friends in the suburbs were moving around freely. Kuwaitis were being hassled, even beaten and robbed, but non-Kuwaitis were largely being left alone. In the end, so many people in the city centre ventured outside during the early afternoon that in order to send people back to their homes, the Iraqis spread a rumour that Government buildings in the city would be bombed at 4.00 p.m. The streets emptied as the news spread, growing in the telling, with someone even mentioning chemical warfare. This really worried people. Everyone knew that Saddam had used it before.

Spirited debates ensued in groups as to whether it was best to shelter in basements with more protection from blast, or on top floors of high buildings where they would be marginally safer from chemical weapons. Our naivety was astounding. The state of mind of people at the time was such that they actually believed the Iraqis might bomb or gas their new conquest on the first afternoon, for no military advantage. Nevertheless, the ploy worked. The city centre was soon deserted. The Iraqis could get on with consolidating their hold on the city, or looting, or whatever their task was, without civilians getting in the way. From the first day of the invasion, a dusk to dawn curfew was imposed, under threat of being arrested or shot.

The situation in the suburbs was remarkably different. The shops were open, with people still panic shopping. Incredibly, although fighting was continuing elsewhere, especially at the Jiwan and Mubarak camps, some of the Iraqi soldiers in the units that had sealed off the coast seemed to have been given time off, and were in the supermarkets actually helping the shoppers to load their trolleys, and paying for their own purchases in Kuwaiti dinars.

By mid-afternoon, the leading Iraqi troops, perhaps less than a battalion strong, were about ten kilometres north of Kuwait's south-eastern border with Saudi Arabia, on the road leading down the Gulf coast to the oil cities of Dhahran, Dammam and Al-Khobar. The *Medina* Republican Guard, which had entered Kuwait from the west, controlled the east–west Salmi Road which ran parallel to Kuwait's south-western border with Saudi Arabia, but the *Medina* did not pose a real threat to the Saudis. The real lines of communication into the Saudi heartland ran down the coast.

The Iraqi vanguard bypassed the Kuwaiti oil centre of Ahmadi, and 15 Brigade's camp farther south. They dropped off sub-units to hold the intersections around 15 Brigade, but would not move into the camp for another two days. The Kuwaiti troops still inside were all but trapped. Further Iraqi units reinforced those already holding the Ras Al-Jalayh naval base, and overran the HAWK air defence battery beyond that. They had travelled over 200km in the heat of high summer, moving and fighting since early morning. By the time they neared the Saudi border, they were exhausted and low on fuel, food and ammunition. They could have been pushed back by a relatively modest fresh force, and air power, if any had been available.

The Kuwaiti Minister of Defence, Chief of Staff, his deputy, the Air Force Commander and several other senior officers had been at the fall-back command bunker at the Air Defence Base, 500 metres east of the International Airport, since early morning, after withdrawing from the GHQ. The generals were all but powerless. Communications with the GHQ were patchy at best.

They didn't even have a radio net set up. Confusion reigned. They could still talk to the air bases, but could give them little guidance. In effect, the Kuwaiti high command had lost control of their forces by breakfast time. Those units and bases still holding out were doing so entirely independently.

Although hardly able to contact his own forces, Deputy Chief of Staff Major-General Jaber Al-Khalid was in hotline contact with the Saudis. Under the terms of the GCC mutual defence arrangements, the Saudis were within their rights, even obliged, to come to Kuwait's assistance, but they were just as surprised as Kuwait by the invasion, and in the same poor state of readiness. They had a powerful air force, but it was not prepared for stopping the Iraqi armoured behemoth, and had no forward air controllers. Even if the Saudis could have sent troops into Kuwait, they were reluctant to do so for fear of finding themselves engaged with Iraqi forces in Kuwait, but outflanked by an Iraqi thrust into Saudi Arabia from another direction. For the time being, Saudi Arabia preferred to husband her forces and defend her own territory.

By 2.00 p.m., the Kuwaiti generals considered Kuwait already lost. They recommended to the Defence Minister that he leave the bunker, and follow the Government out to Saudi Arabia. If Kuwait were to survive, it would have to be with the help of its foreign friends, but those friends had little to offer for now. No American or British forces were within striking distance. Both major Western governments were still working on a political solution, and had no treaty obligations to come to Kuwait's defence. The Kuwaiti Ambassador in Washington, Sheikh Saud Nasir, who for most of that first morning was the only ranking member of the Kuwaiti Government capable of doing anything at all, had asked for Western forces, but there was no suggestion that the Saudis would agree to a counter-attack on Iraq, or into Kuwait, from their soil.

That afternoon, another Kuwaiti officer was having his own personal confrontation with the Iraqis. Chief of Naval Forces Colonel Qais Al-Saleh had been captured that morning, and brought with his four lieutenant-colonels to the Iraqi naval base at Umm Qasr, on the Kuwaiti border, arriving at about 1.30 p.m. At the time, with the GHQ, Air Defence Base, and the KAF bases still holding out, they were the seniormost Kuwaiti officers in Iraqi hands.

At Umm Qasr, Al-Saleh was separated from his colleagues, and taken to an office in the Iraqi Navy Headquarters. He was not restrained or interrogated, and was treated politely. An Iraqi Navy colonel whom he knew came to speak to him. It was obvious that the Iraqi was unhappy at what had transpired, but was obliged to follow orders. As they were talking, the Iraqi Chief of Naval Staff, a brigadier, also known to Al-Saleh, entered the building, walked past the open door of the room, and went straight to his own office. The Iraqi colonel with Al-Saleh went and told the brigadier that Al-Saleh was there, whereupon the brigadier left the building immediately - without stopping to talk to the Kuwaiti - and drove away in a yellow Mercedes.

An hour later, a senior Iraqi intelligence officer came for Al-Saleh, and took him to a depot outside the base. It looked like a construction camp, except for the many small helicopters and expensive cars parked nearby. Al-Saleh was brought to a massive underground bunker, at least 30 metres in length, where about two dozen senior officers were gathered. The most junior among them was a full colonel. Most were brigadiers and generals, from all the Iraqi military services and corps: Republican Guard, Regular Army, Artillery, Air Force, Air Defence, Navy, and the *Mukhabarat*. On the wall were large military maps depicting the invasion routes into Kuwait. It was obvious to Al-Saleh that he was in the command bunker for the entire invasion operation, and these men were running it. He instantly recognised the man in charge: Lieutenant-General Hussein Kamil Al-Majeed Al-Takriti, Saddam's first cousin and son-in-law, who would later become known to the world as the architect of Saddam's nuclear, biological and chemical weapons programme.

Al-Saleh was brought before Al-Takriti, and took an instant dislike to the man. He radiated evil. His manners were coarse. He behaved with all the class of a street thug in a general's uniform, with the power of life-and-death to match it. Every other man in the room seemed to be in mortal fear of him.

'Tell us what you know!' snapped Al-Takriti, to the Kuwaiti.

'I know nothing,' shot back Al-Saleh, fixing the Iraqi with a cold stare.

'Ah, come on now. You, the head of the Kuwaiti Navy, and you know nothing?' replied Al-Takriti, sarcastically.

Al-Saleh wanted to get away from this man. He had little patience for him, and was seething inside. 'Listen,' he said, trying to keep his voice level, 'When I was called from my house to the GHQ, it was dark. I left the GHQ for my base, and it was dark. When I got to the base, it was still dark. Then your people captured me and put me in their boat. It was dark inside. Then they put me and my men inside a hovercraft, and brought me here, and it was dark in the hovercraft. Also,' added Al-Saleh, his anger rising, 'if I close my eyes and try to imagine that this.... invasion .... would have ever happened from a brother Arab, it will also be dark, and I could not imagine it.'

The Iraqi looked at him for a moment, then said, almost softly, 'You will suffer two or three days. We have suffered from you for years.'

Al-Saleh was taken aback, remembering the substantial assistance given by Kuwait to Iraq during the course of the Iran-Iraq War, and especially the close co-operation between their respective navies. 'What do you mean?'

The Iraqi general turned and pointed to one of the wall maps, almost shouting, 'Look at the map! Your border is at Mutla'a, not at Safwan! Who brought you to Safwan? The British did. Iraq has been denied its rights of full access to the Gulf for all these years. We are righting the wrong.'

Al-Saleh was tiring of the discussion. It would go nowhere. 'I'm a military man,' he said. 'If you want to discuss borders, that is a matter for the politicians.' The Iraqi was also tiring of his game, and had an invasion to run. He turned to the other officers. 'Does anyone have any questions?' he asked them, indicating Al-Saleh. No one spoke.

'You may go,' he said, and Al-Saleh was driven to Basra, where he was kept in a house used by Iraqi intelligence until the following afternoon.

Reflecting on his episode with Al-Takriti, Al-Saleh was convinced that the original Iraqi intention was to take Kuwait just as far south as Mutla'a - giving Saddam all of northern Kuwait with Bubiyan, Warba, and the northern shore of Kuwait Bay, with Kuwait City in range of his artillery and beholden to Baghdad

- but to do so, he would first take the entire country, destroy its armed forces and its Government, install a puppet regime, and then withdraw to Mutla'a as a 'compromise' in the face of the expected international condemnation. Saddam seemed to have known that he could not get away with extinguishing Kuwait entirely, but if he left a rump Kuwait and spun a sufficiently good story about being a victim of British imperial map-making, then he could possibly keep the crisis within the Arab fold, and get away with it. With Saddam's military power, Kuwait's neighbours would be relieved at having 'negotiated' the continued existence of even half of Kuwait. If successful, Saddam would also be able to make Saudi Arabia dance to his tune and pay his bills through extortion without having to put one Iraqi soldier on Saudi soil, and even gain access to Kuwait's substantial overseas assets. Later events would reinforce this conclusion.

In New York, the UN Security Council convened at 9.00 a.m., Kuwait time, 2 August. Within hours, it passed Resolution 660 condemning the Iraqi invasion, demanding an immediate and unconditional withdrawal, and calling for immediate intensive negotiations between Iraq and Kuwait to resolve their differences, with the support of the Arab League. It would be the first of thirteen Security Council resolutions on the crisis over the next seven months. There were no dissenting votes. The only abstention was Yemen, which had not received instructions from its capital as it was the Islamic weekend.

The Americans then considered their next move. The option of quick retaliatory air strikes using US Navy carrier aircraft was dismissed as being potentially more provocative than effective. At the time, it was thought that if Iraq could not be persuaded to leave Kuwait by diplomatic means and economic sanctions, a much larger military force would be needed. Few seemed to have realised at the time that Saddam's bluff - thinly stretched as he was - could have been called with a quick and relatively limited counter attack.

At 3.30 p.m. Kuwait time, the full National Security Council (NSC) convened at the White House, chaired by President Bush. The US Administration was still catching its breath. Bush told reporters covering the meeting that the NSC was not discussing intervention, nor contemplating sending troops. In a thinly veiled reference to Saudi Arabia, he said - correctly - there was no evidence that any other countries were threatened, but he wanted Iraq out of Kuwait. US hopes at this stage were pinned on diplomacy. The NSC meeting ended inconclusively, with Bush leaving for Colorado to meet with visiting British Prime Minister, Margaret Thatcher.

With the capture of Kuwait, Saddam now controlled 20% of the world's oil reserves. If he took Saudi Arabia, he would have 40%. The price of oil rose with the prospect of an oil embargo on Iraq and Kuwait, and disruption to supplies. The West was caught very much off-balance. The invasion was obviously a threat to US interests, but there was insufficient political co-operation and too few military forces in place to counter it in a timely manner.

Washington's real interests in the Gulf lay in Saudi Arabia, not Kuwait. As far as the market was concerned, buying Kuwaiti oil from Iraq was the same as buying it from Kuwait. In fact, at the time, the US was importing about 200,000 barrels per day (bpd) from Kuwait – only 10% of its production – but

550,000 bpd, or 20%, of Iraqi production. Market pressures would force prices down again unless Saddam was able to dictate Saudi oil policy at the point of a gun. This was the main danger to the oil market. The invasion was virtually a *fait accompli*. The immediate American task was to stop Saddam going any farther, if that was what he intended. The CIA estimated that he could be in Riyadh within three days, but the real issue was the eastern Saudi oilfields.

The opportunity presented by the invasion to do something about Saddam's nuclear, biological and chemical weapons programmes was only just being recognized. More importantly, if handled correctly, the crisis could be an opportunity to remove decisively the Iraqi threat to the entire region. There was certainly no crusade to liberate Kuwait at this stage. As General Colin Powell, the Chairman of the US Joint Chiefs of Staff, confided to General Schwarzkopf that day, 'I think we'd go to war over Saudi Arabia, but I doubt we'd go to war over Kuwait.'

In Kuwait, the situation at the Jiwan and Mubarak camps settled into a standoff throughout the late afternoon. Although the Iraqis had not closed on the camps again, and the shelling had become intermittent, the Kuwaitis realized they would soon be overrun. The Iraqis held the initiative and were bringing up reinforcements.

The battle was telling on the Kuwaitis. 15 Brigade's tanks were running desperately low on ammunition, and suffering mechanical breakdowns. There was no chance of resupply, and there were no mechanics. The men were tired, hungry, scared, and concerned about their families at home. At around 5.00 p.m., Colonel Al-Harmi had phoned Director of Operations, Brigadier Jassim Al-Shehab, to confer on the situation. 'We will fight on,' said Al-Shehab.

Dusk fell without incident. Then, around 7.30 p.m., the Iraqis started moving armour into the hospitals complex north of the camps. It was obvious they would try another assault before long. Al-Harmi went to the Operations Room to see Al-Shehab, but found only one soldier there. Sometime in the past two hours, Al-Shehab and his staff had left through the unthreatened eastern gates of the camp, not telling the men who were doing the fighting.

Incensed, Al-Harmi ordered the men on the pressured northern flank to withdraw through the south gate. An officer was sent to tell the men at the south-west end of the camps overlooking Fourth Ring to pull back to the south gate, but many of them had already done so.

Over the next two hours, after disabling and abandoning most of their vehicles, the Kuwaiti troops melted out of the camps, mainly through the south gate, into the surrounding suburbs. Lieutenant-Colonel Mohammed Al-Salahi of the 152nd Armoured Battalion managed to salvage one Chieftain and four BMPs, and rendezvoused at 10.00 p.m. with Al-Harmi and Land Forces Commander Brigadier Abdul Aziz Al-Bargash at the police station in the nearby suburb of Keifan, two kilometres to the east. Lieutenant-Colonel Alghanim of the 2nd Infantry Battalion brought more men out with him, arriving at about midnight. In the dark and confusion, orders went astray and unheard. Most of the men from inside the camps went home, but several hundred made it to the Keifan rendezvous. They regrouped, moved the tank and BMPs away from the houses to safeguard the civilians, and, exhausted, settled down for the night in the police station and surrounding houses.

As the Kuwaitis were withdrawing from the camps, there ensued one of the tragedies of war where brave men die after ceasing to fight. The National Guards in Brock Matthews' apartment overlooking Jiwan received word that the Iraqis were withdrawing, and that so should they. They were left with the impression that the Iraqis, whose fire had slackened, had pulled back.

Some of the soldiers from the camps lived west of the Jahra Road/ Fourth Ring intersection where the Iraqis had concentrated, so drove out of the complex in their private cars, turning right down Fourth Ring towards the intersection. The Iraqis had not withdrawn. Some Kuwaitis were captured. Others were slaughtered. In the darkness, Brock, Chris, and the five National Guardsmen could see the muzzle flashes of rifles being fired into the cars as the Kuwaitis were shot mercilessly. The Iraqis were exacting a terrible revenge for their casualties.

The Kuwait Coastguard was not yet out of the fight either. Several of their small vessels were at sea on patrol at the time of the invasion. Their mission was anti-smuggling and illegal immigrant patrols, so they were lightly armed. However, one skipper, Sergeant Salem Al-Mulla, sailed directly into Kuwait Bay at 6.00 p.m., surprising the tanks and troops which had been deployed peacefully on the beach since morning. Residents of the beachside suburb of Salmiya found themselves caught in a short, sharp, crossfire as the Kuwaitis opened fire with everything they had, and then beat a hasty retreat. Those outside dived frantically behind walls for cover. Fortunately for the Kuwaitis, the Iraqis were poor shots, and they escaped unscathed.

At the Air Defence Base, where the Kuwaiti generals were still in the fall-back command bunker, Iraqi tanks approached the complex at about 5.00 p.m. They stopped a few hundred metres away, apparently reluctant to venture closer with the approaching dark, and unaware that the generals were inside. In any event, the base did not present a military threat. The Iraqis seemed content to pull back and surround the general area, and wait until morning.

At dusk, the base commander, Colonel Yacoub Al-Suwaiti, ordered all personnel to assemble in the barracks building for safety, and they ate for the first time. Their number included Tom Kreuzeman, the only American advisor to make it to his post that day. Lights were blacked out as they sat in darkness, sharing their few remaining cigarettes. There was a major scare at about 8.00 p.m., when trucks and armour were heard on the road barely 100 metres from the perimeter, but the Iraqis still did not move into the base.

The Kuwaiti generals decided to slip out under cover of darkness before the Iraqis completely sealed off the area. Chief of Staff Major-General Misyad Al-Sane, his deputy, Major-General Jaber Al-Khalid, and Air Force Commander Brigadier Daoud Alghanim moved to the nearby Logistics Camp to tell the men there to leave. KAF Operations Commander Colonel Fahd Al-Ameer stayed behind for a while to maintain contact with Ali Al-Salem and Al-Jaber bases, and to supervise the evacuation of the Air Defence Base itself.

The two generals and the brigadier finally slipped out of the camps successfully, and made their way to the house of one of their colleagues. They were exhausted, having been awake under incredible strain since Wednesday morning. Al-Khalid called his home. An Indian employee answered. 'Don't come home, Sir,' the man said. 'The Iraqis are here waiting for you.'

At this time, the two outlying KAF bases were still holding out, with Ali Al-Salem surrounded. A few helicopters were still there, and eight Mirages which were unable to fly out. Most of the A-4 Skyhawks and six BAe Hawks were still at Al-Jaber, which Iraqi ground troops had not yet reached. Most of the retreating 35 Brigade was past the base, and nearing the Saudi border, but elements of the 57th Mechanized Infantry Battalion, under Lieutenant-Colonel Nasser Al-Zaibi went to the base. Al-Zaibi's intention was to contact 15 Brigade from Al-Jaber, and to rearm from their stocks. Just as he found the operations bunker at 5.45 p.m., several Iraqi aircraft bombed the base, inflicting no casualties. Al-Zaibi was saved by having just closed the bunker door behind him seconds before an Iraqi bomb landed nearby. His contacts with 15 Brigade's base came to naught. They were surrounded themselves.

An hour later, the Iraqis bombed Ali Al-Salem, hitting the Commander's office, killing Warrant Officer Walid Al-Thufeiri, and wounding another man. The Kuwaiti airmen tried to move the wounded man to the hospital in Jahra, but the Iraqis would not let them pass through their lines.

Over the next few hours, senior officers from the International Base, including Brigadier Ghazi Al-Abdulrazzak, made their way to Al-Jaber. At 8.30 p.m., the KAF base commanders heard from the Air Operations Centre that all organised resistance had collapsed. They were now completely on their own, not knowing what to expect. Shortly afterwards, they received orders from Colonel Fahd Al-Ameer to send all remaining serviceable aircraft to Saudi Arabia in the morning, as soon as it became light enough to fly.

At the Air Defence Base, the Kuwaiti soldiers stripped to their underwear, put on whatever civilian clothes they could find, took their weapons, and gradually slipped out of the base with their car lights blacked out. Tom Kreuzeman, went with them, escorted by a Kuwaiti sergeant, finally reaching his home by 2.00 a.m. on 3 August.

In the city centre, as darkness fell, and along with it a sort of calm, we gazed from our windows on the city below and the suburbs beyond. Everything was still, the silence punctuated periodically by a distant burst of gunfire and flash of tracer. Roads throughout the city were deserted except for the occasional Iraqi jeep, and cars abandoned from the early morning.

To the west, we could hear muffled booms from the siege of the Jiwan and Mubarak camps, although we did know what it was at the time. All the city lights were ablaze, having switched on automatically. They would come on every night throughout the occupation until January 1991, when the Iraqis switched them off after the first night of the air war.

On CNN that night, transmitted into Kuwait from other Gulf States, the Kuwaiti Ambassador to the US, a visibly shocked Sheikh Saud Nasir, was seen asking for immediate American military assistance. This drove the situation home to many of us. In order to maintain their independence, the Kuwaitis had studiously avoided giving Western powers bases in Kuwait, even when the US Navy had been escorting Kuwaiti vessels during the Iran-Iraq War. They had always tried to depend principally on their Arab allies, even during earlier Iraqi threats in 1961 and 1973. Now, the only hope for Kuwait's salvation lay with the West. We expected a quick military response. We were not to know that it would take seven long months to arrive.

Late that evening, Kuwait time, George Bush met with Margaret Thatcher in Aspen, Colorado. Bush had left Washington earlier in the day without any firm decision on a course of action other than the freezing of Iraqi and Kuwaiti assets, UN condemnation of the invasion, and moves to build broad support for economic sanctions. Mrs Thatcher was far more forceful. Although Bush had been to Kuwait many years earlier as an oilman – and joked (inaccurately) of drilling the nation's only dry hole – Thatcher had visited the country as Prime Minister, and knew the Kuwaitis well. As far as she was concerned, the invasion would not stand. Saddam would be punished, period.

The meeting was the start of a campaign to liberate Kuwait where the Americans would be seen by those in Kuwait as supplying the muscle, and on-again, off-again resolution, and the British the determination and further military muscle to ensure that they followed through.

That evening, Bush spoke to King Fahd of Saudi Arabia. They discussed what Saddam's ultimate intentions might be, and possible US assistance to Saudi Arabia. No course of action was settled on. King Fahd had reportedly spoken to Saddam earlier about the movement of his troops towards Saudi Arabia. The Iraqi President had dismissed the move as a military exercise, and was not contactable after that.

Later, Bush spoke with Egyptian President Hosni Mubarak, and King Hussein of Jordan. It was apparent now that Jordan would not take advantage of the situation to threaten Saudi Arabia, and that the Arab Cooperation Council with Saddam was now dead. Their advice to Bush was to give the Arabs time to handle the crisis themselves. Bush made it clear that the invasion was more than a simple regional dispute but at the time, an Arab solution was one of the few immediate options available. The Arabs would have their chance to get Saddam out of Kuwait peacefully.

Total Kuwaiti military and police casualties during the invasion were about 65 dead and 500 wounded. Most of the casualties came from the hard-fought siege of the Jiwan and Mubarak camps. The numbers in absolute terms seemed remarkably low, but the dead represented about one-half of one percent of Kuwait's entire armed forces.

The Kuwait Air Force's fixed-wing losses in the invasion were eight Mirages captured, leaving 15; ten A-4s, leaving 20; and six of the 12 BAe Hawks. Helicopter losses were four of the 20 Gazelles, one of which crashed near the Saudi border the following morning in still unclear circumstances, killing all four crewmen; four of the ten Pumas, one of which fell to a Kuwaiti HAWK missile, killing four; and three of the six Super Pumas, one of which was destroyed on the ground at Ali Al-Salem. The A-4s and Mirages that escaped later took part in Operation Desert Storm. The Gazelles worked with the UAE ground forces, and the Pumas and Super Pumas with the British.

The entire Kuwait Navy fleet except for *Istiqlal* and *Sanbouk* was captured, and subsequently became a priority target of the Coalition forces because of its potential mine-laying and anti-ship capacity. Kuwait Navy officers serving on British vessels in the Gulf in February 1991 had to watch on radar screens as a Royal Navy Lynx helicopter disabled *Istiqlal's* sister ship, *Sabhan*, with Sea Skua missiles, and US Navy aircraft finished her off.

The Kuwait Army lost a large part of 35 Brigade's armour which could not be taken out to Saudi Arabia, most of 15 Brigade's equipment, and all of 6 and 80 Brigades', totalling several hundred armoured vehicles. Elements of two Kuwaiti brigades, especially 35 Brigade, escaped into Saudi Arabia, and were eventually reconstituted with the addition of soldiers who had been on leave or serving abroad at the time, volunteers and Yugoslav M84 tanks.

Several senior Iraqi officers apparently became unexpected casualties of the invasion as a result of the stiff Kuwaiti resistance. According to unconfirmed reports, Saddam was so unimpressed by the performance of his forces in what had been expected to be a walk-over, and especially by their failure to kill or capture the Amir, that he ordered the execution in September 1990 of a number of senior officers who had planned the invasion.

The invasion had not been as bloodless for civilians as we thought. Apart from the Indian restaurant cook, and the Filipino at the Sheraton, several other individuals lost their lives. One of these was an Egyptian security guard at the Kuwait University Shuwaikh residential complex. He was unfortunate enough to surprise Iraqi scouts as they advanced into the city centre in the pre-dawn darkness. Another two were Thai garbage collectors in Ahmadi.

A week later, I discovered the legacy of the yellow school bus opposite my bank. We had noticed a curious stench when walking down the street in the early days, but thought it nothing more than rotting garbage. The Iraqis had also noticed the odour. I was at a window of a high floor of the Plaza Hotel, looking out across Kuwait Bay with several other men when we saw three Iraqis in boiler suits opening the back door of the bus. They shut it rapidly again as the smell overpowered them. The driver had been lying dead in there for six days, in daytime temperatures exceeding 50 °C.

Throughout the next week, we were to hear tales of unfortunate Arab and Asian individuals who had simply been in the wrong place at the wrong time, usually on their way to an early start at work, or returning from an overnight shift. In the main, the Iraqis seemed to go out of their way to avoid civilian casualties, but there were inevitable tragedies in an operation of that scale.

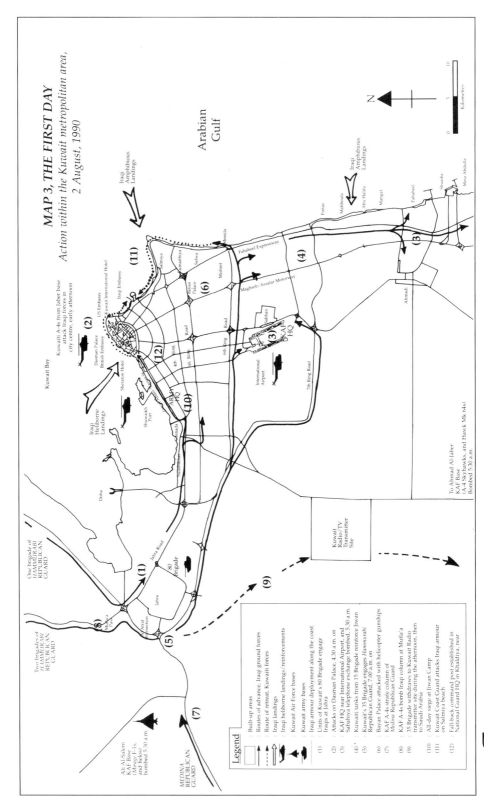

MAP 3, THE FIRST DAY
*Action within the Kuwait metropolitan area,
2 August, 1990*

Arabian
Gulf

Kuwait Bay

One brigade of
HAMMURABI
REPUBLICAN
GUARD

Two brigades of
HAMMURABI
REPUBLICAN
GUARD

MEDINA
REPUBLICAN
GUARD

Ali Al-Salem
KAF Base
(Mirage F-1s,
and heles)
bombed 5.30 a.m.

Iraqi Heliborne
Landings

Iraqi
Amphibious
Landings

Iraqi
Amphibious
Landings

Kuwaiti A-4s from Jaber base
attack Iraqi forces in
city centre, early afternoon

Dasman Palace
British Embassy

US Embassy

Iraqi Embassy

Sheraton Hotel

Kuwait International Hotel

Messila

Salmiya

Jumathra

Salwa

Mishref

Bayan Palace

Fahaheel Expressway

Maghreb / Assafar Motorway

6th Ring Road

5th Ring Road

4th Ring Road

7th Ring Road

International
Airport

KAF
HQ

ARMY
HQ

Shuwaikh Port

Doha

Jahra Road

Mutla'a
Pass

Atraf
Section

Jahra

80
Brigade

Ardiya

Sulaibiya

Sabhan

Ahmadi

Fintas

Mahboula

Abu Halifa

Mangaf

Fahaheel

Shuaiba

Mina Abdulla

To Ahmad Al-Jaber
KAF Base
(A-4 Skyhawks, and Hawk Mk 64s)
Bombed 5.30 a.m.

Kuwait Radio/TV
Transmitter
Site

N

0   5   10
Kilometres

Legend

	: Built-up areas
	: Routes of advance, Iraqi ground forces
	: Route of retreat, Kuwaiti forces
	: Iraqi landings
	: Iraqi heliborne landings / reinforcements
	: Kuwait Air Force bases
	: Kuwait army bases
	: Iraqi armour deployment along the coast
(1)	: Units of Kuwait's 80 Brigade engage Iraqis at Jahra
(2)	: Attacks on Dasman Palace, 4.30 a.m. on
(3)	: KAF HQ near International Airport, and Sabahiya telephone exchange bombed, 5.30 a.m.
(4)*	: Kuwaiti tanks from 15 Brigade reinforce Jiwan
(5)	: Kuwait's 35 Brigade engages *Hammurabi* Republican Guard, 7.00 a.m. on
(6)	: Bayan Palace attacked with helicopter gunships
(7)	: KAF A-4s strafe column of *Medina* Republican Guard
(8)	: KAF A-4s bomb Iraqi column at Mutla'a
(9)	: 35 Brigade withdraws to Kuwait Radio transmitter site during the afternoon, then to Saudi Arabia
(10)	: All-day siege at Jiwan Camp
(11)	: Kuwait Coast Guard attacks Iraqi armour on Salmiya beach
(12)	: Fall-back command post established in National Guard HQ in Khaldiya, near

Explanatory notes to Map 3, Metropolitan Action, 2 August, 1990

1. 7.00 a.m. onwards: Iraqi troops secure the city centre.
2. Approx. 8.00 a.m. onwards: Iraqi heliborne troops reinforce ground columns. Kuwait Air Force and HAWK air defence missiles shoot down a number of these helicopters.
3. Approx. 8.30 a.m. onwards: Iraqi helicopter gunships strafe Bayan Palace and Dasman Palace.
4. Approx. 9.30 a.m. onwards: Iraqi armour deploys in two columns along the coast of Kuwait Bay and the Arabian Gulf. The northern column travels through the city centre, and deposits a vehicle every 200 metres along the coast of Kuwait Bay. The southern column travels along Sixth Ring, turns north at the Arabian Gulf, and deploys similarly until the two columns meet.
5. Kuwaiti troops holding out at Army Officers' Club at Messila meet these forces, and are eventually overwhelmed.
6. Approx. 10.00 a.m.: Iraqi troops shell Kuwait International Airport, accompanied by American, British and Canadian oilmen taken from oil rigs during their advance. Iraqis commence artillery and infantry attack on Jiwan and Mubarak Camps complex. Kuwaiti troops and police hold them off until after dark.
7. Approx. 10.40 a.m.: About 15 Iraqi Mi-8 helicopters fly in airborne troops through the streets of Kuwait City, to take Shuwaikh Port, trapping an Indian merchant ship and a KOTC workboat.
8. Approx. 11.00 a.m.: Iraqi amphibious troops land at several locations on the Kuwaiti coast.
9. Late morning through late afternoon: Iraqi forces consolidate their positions in the city, and start moving into the suburbs. Iraqi Popular Army troops brought in to occupy Kuwait City as regulars prepare to deploy further south. The siege of Jiwan and Mubarak Camps continues. Kuwaitis in the Ministry of Interior HQ in the suburb of Salhiya south of First Ring, near city centre, continue to snipe at Iraqis. The southern column of Iraqi forces forges south, as far as ten kilometres north of the Saudi Arabian border, by-passing Ahmadi and Fahaheel and 15 Brigade's camp.
10. Early afternoon: Kuwaiti A-4 jets attack Iraqi forces on the ground in central Kuwait City.
11. 5.00 p.m.: British servicemen working with the British Liaison Team, and their families resident in IBI Camp near Fahaheel, are sealed in by Iraqi troops.
12. 5.45 p.m.: Ahmad Al-Jaber base bombed for the second time.
13. Approx. 6.00 p.m.: Kuwait Coastguard boat sails into Kuwait Bay, exchanges fire with Iraqi armour deployed on the beach, and then withdraws.
14. 6.45 p.m.: Ali Al-Salem base bombed, killing one man and wounding another.
15. Approx. 8.00 p.m.: Iraqi troops enter Ahmadi.
16. Approx. 9.00 p.m. onwards: Kuwait defenders at Jiwan and Mubarak camps complex withdraw into nearby suburbs. A number of men are stopped by Iraqi troops to the west of the camps, and executed in their cars.
17. Kuwaiti troops evacuate Air Defence Maintenance Base, without casualties.

4. WHO ARE THE KUWAITIS?

Around the world, news of the invasion raised questions on just who were the Kuwaitis. The popular stereotype was of oil-rich high rollers. This image had a grain of truth, but its perpetrators were a tiny minority. The reality is that Kuwait in July 1990 was generally a sophisticated, educated and undeniably wealthy place. Not every Kuwaiti was rich, but a beneficent government ensured that no citizen went without food, shelter, education or medical care, and that most adult males had jobs.

Kuwait had her problems, as any country does, but the famous oil wealth was barely a generation old. The first exports were made shortly after World War II, but the real money only came with the 1973 oil crisis. Before oil, Kuwait and her Gulf neighbours eked out a precarious existence with trade, pearling, and limited agriculture. Illiteracy was widespread, disease rife, sanitation poor. The only regular medical service in Kuwait up to the 1950s was an American missionary hospital, established as a clinic in 1910.

Many Kuwaitis attribute foreign resentment of their wealth to sour grapes at being beaten at the West's own capitalist game. When OPEC sold oil at market rates in the 1970s and 1980s, they simply met demand at a market price. The oil exporters were under no obligation to subsidize their customers' thirst for cheap energy any more than the oil importers were obliged to offer discounts on their exports to the Gulf. Kuwait does not expect any special favours when the oil runs out.

Kuwait's earliest recorded history dates back three centuries before Christ when Alexander the Great, and his Seleucid successors, ruled from Syria through Mesopotamia, Kuwait, and Persia.

Alexander's admirals were attracted to Kuwait by the same features that interested the Turkish, Russian, German, and British Empires 2,000 years later: her strategic position at the head of the Arabian Gulf on the trade route between Europe and the Far East, and into the Arabian interior; a reliable fresh water supply; and the largest sheltered natural harbour on the Gulf.

Before Alexander, Kuwait was probably part of the federation of the ancient kingdom of Dilmun, whose capital was in present-day Bahrain. Dilmun linked the coastal settlements of the Arabian Gulf as important *entrepôts* for the trade between India and Bronze Age Mesopotamia. The Dilmunites were culturally and religiously distinct from, and largely independent of, the more powerful Mesopotamians, the predecessors of most modern Iraqis. After the decline of the Greeks and Seleucids in the 2nd Century AD, Kuwait was controlled by the second great Persian Empire, the Sasanids. She retained her trading role, and emerged as an important pearling centre, a role which continued into the early 20th Century.

When Islam swept the region in the 7th Century AD, Kuwait fell under the influence of the Abbasids, descendants of the Prophet Mohammed's uncle, who ruled from Baghdad, until replaced by the Mongols in 1258. A thousand years before Columbus, trade passing through Kuwait came from as far away as

China. Her inhabitants at the time were probably a cosmopolitan mix of Arabs from the Arabian Peninsula and Mesopotamia, and Persians.

In the 16th Century, the first powers from outside the immediate region since Alexander turned towards the Gulf. The Portuguese conquered from Hormuz to as far north as Bahrain; by 1536, the Ottomans took Mesopotamia - including Baghdad - south to the head of the Gulf, but the European powers and Ottomans were generally happy to leave the administration of the tiny impoverished coastal settlements and interior to the local sheikhs.

With the formation in the early 18th Century of the English East India Company, and the Dutch East India Company, and expulsion of the Portuguese from the Gulf by a Persian-British alliance, the English and Dutch became the regional maritime powers, but continued to leave the local sheikhs to their own devices, and tried to maintain good relations with the Ottomans. Their main concern was their trade routes, and it was in the sheikhs' interests to profit from the trade that the Europeans brought. The Ottomans paid scant attention to this desolate part of their far-flung empire, so the sheikhs began to assert their own authority under nominal Ottoman suzerainty.

By the first half of the 18th Century, the prevailing powers in the Arabian interior, and on the Arabian Gulf, were federations of nomadic tribal families. One of these was the *Bani Khalid*. They had consolidated their power from south of present-day Basra to Qatar, and into parts of the interior.

A sub-federation of the *Bani Khalid*, a group of families known as the *Utub*, or the *Anayzah*, settled Kuwait permanently around 1714. The Utbis were driven from their lands in the Nejd, in central Arabia, during the 17th Century by a prolonged drought. They initially re-settled in modern day Qatar, where they acquired maritime skills, before finally moving to Kuwait.

In the 1750s, the inhabitants of Kuwait elected as their ruling sheikh, or Amir, one Sabah bin Jaber, who became the first in the line of Kuwait's present-day ruling family. By 1758, when the east coast of America was still a string of British colonies, Sabah's authority was firmly established in Kuwait and the nearby area. The resultant security and the unique geographical position encouraged Kuwait's rapid development. By 1764, Kuwait had a population of around 10,000, with 800 small pearling boats sailing south each year to harvest the rich pearl beds off Bahrain and Qatar.

With Kuwait's success, the dominant but poorer *Bani Khalid* tried unsuccessfully to subjugate the *Utbi* Al-Sabah. Whenever the nomadic bedouin *Bani Khalid* forces arrived, the maritime Kuwaitis abandoned their mainland settlement for nearby Failaka Island. The *Bani Khalid* would eventually tire of the expedition. As nomads, they had little use for an abandoned town. Lacking the naval forces to take Failaka, they went back to the desert. The Al-Sabah offset the power of the *Bani Khalid* by gaining recognition by the Ottomans in Baghdad. It was the start of Kuwait's policy of balancing regional powers against each other which would become a hallmark of her ability to survive as a distinct entity in the centuries to come.

Kuwait's security and independence in the following years was greatly helped by disputes between the rival regional powers. The *Bani Khalid* to the south were attacked by an alliance of the Islamist Wahabis and the Al-Saud family from the interior of Arabia. To the north, the Persians captured Ottoman Basra in 1776 and held it for five years. Insecurity elsewhere drove more trade through Kuwait, so that by the late 1770s, all Indian trade with Baghdad, Aleppo and Constantinople passed through it.

This period saw the beginnings of the long and ultimately fruitful Kuwaiti association with the British, although the relationship was always ruled by self-interest. In 1775, the English East India Company started dispatching its desert mail from the Gulf to Aleppo through Kuwait. Britain's war with France also meant that it was safer to use Arab vessels for cargoes and mail.

By the late 1700s, the Wahabi–Saudi alliance had conquered the *Bani Khalid* strongholds on the Gulf coast, and turned its attention to Kuwait. Various reports suggest that the initial Wahabi–Saudi raids were little more than skirmishes, but on one occasion, a British warship anchored in Kuwait Bay, and the Indian Sepoy guard, are reported to have helped the Kuwaitis repel an attacking force of about 4,000 men, mounted on 2,000 camels.

Kuwait was again saved by outside events in 1813, when Saudi and Wahabi designs on the town were diverted by the Ottoman–Egyptian campaign to recapture Mecca and Medina, which the Saudis and Wahabis had taken in 1802. The desert tribesmen were completely outclassed by the Turks, and routed with great bloodshed by 1819. With this Ottoman victory, the threat to Kuwait from other regional Arab tribes dissipated temporarily.

After breaking the Saudis, the Turks withdrew to western Arabia. They were still very much in control of Mesopotamia, but although they considered Kuwait as part of their empire, they exercised little practical control over it. Kuwait maintained her autonomy through a combination of co-operation and diplomacy with the Turks, and by maintaining friendly but informal relations with the increasingly powerful British.

Kuwaiti relations with the Ottomans at the time were generally cordial, and conducted on equal terms. On occasions, the Al-Sabah helped the Turks in local military expeditions, and defended the area south of Basra from raiders. Her vessels flew the Ottoman flag as a convenience for protection against piracy, and in recognition of the Ottomans as the pre-eminent Muslim religious authority at the time, rather than as an Ottoman subject. Over 160 years later, the Kuwaitis would make use of the flag of a new superpower, the US, to protect her vessels from other attacks.

In the meantime, the relationship between the Kuwaitis and Saudis improved into an uneasy alliance, and later into friendship. The Ottoman–Egyptians had again marched from central Arabia to the Gulf in 1838, routing the Saudis, before withdrawing. On several occasions in the 1840s, Kuwait gave refuge to various Saudi leaders in time of need.

In 1871, the Ottomans returned to central Arabia in force, and occupied the western Gulf coast. Kuwait actually contributed 300 vessels and some cavalry to the campaign as a Turkish ally, but the Turks did not annex Kuwait. Instead, the Kuwaiti Amir was nominally appointed '*Qaim-Maqam*', or Provincial Governor, by the Turks, whose intention at the time was to ward off British influence rather than incorporate Kuwait into their empire.

The adjoining Ottoman province of Basra had earlier been divided into three sub-divisions, Amara, Muntafiq and Basra itself. Under the Governorship arrangement, Kuwait was autonomous, but supposed to report to Basra. However, the Amir had a free hand in handling his internal affairs, and the town was exempt from Ottoman taxes. The sheikh's laws rather than Ottoman law applied. Any Ottoman suzerainty over Kuwait at the time was purely nominal, and for all practical purposes was limited to religious affiliation with the Caliphate in Constantinople.

In the meantime, the Saudis were facing more problems. A second great Arabian family, the Rasheedis, chased them from their capital, Riyadh, in the spring of 1891. The displaced Al-Saud eventually reached Kuwait in 1894, among them the teenage Abdul Aziz bin Abdul Rahman Al-Saud, or Ibn Saud, who would become the founder of modern Saudi Arabia.

In May 1896, two years after the Al-Saud's arrival, Mubarak Al-Sabah became Amir in the only Kuwaiti transition of power in history in which blood has been spilled. A cool and ruthless leader, later described as having the political skills of a Machiavelli and the ambition of a Richelieu, he would rule until 1915, and guide Kuwait through some of her most difficult years as the Great Powers coveted her strategic position. He is still revered in Kuwait today as Mubarak Al-Kabeer (the Great), and the Kuwaiti Constitution specifies in effect that the line of succession shall come from his sons.

In Mubarak's time, Kuwait was a thriving centre of Arab seafaring. Every autumn, hundreds of huge wooden *boum* merchantmen, some over 60 metres long, would set off along the ancient trade routes, riding the trade winds to the west coast of India and Ceylon, and then back the following spring, or to Aden and then Zanzibar on the East African coast, trading dates, pearls and Arab horses for salt, spices, timber, ivory and ghee. Another 400 vessels harvested the pearl banks, employing up to 10,000 divers at the height of the season.

The population was a mix of nomadic and settled Arab bedouins, Persians, Jews with their own synagogue, and several thousand Africans. There were even bordellos, confined to the southern corners of town, but the prosperity and diversity lived alongside grinding poverty for many of the townspeople.

Mubarak continued to give refuge to the Saudis, but his motives were not entirely altruistic. He knew that Kuwait was most secure when those with designs on her were busy elsewhere. This was part of the same logic that led Kuwait to play the Ottomans off against the *Bani Khalid* in the 1700s, and support Iraq during its futile 1980-1988 war with Iran. As long as Iraq was fighting Iran, Saddam could not threaten Kuwait. This was Kuwait's defence. Sheltering the Al-Saud allowed Mubarak to balance the powerful Rasheedis.

By February 1897, the Ottomans were making serious threats against Kuwaiti independence. Mubarak tried to enlist British support against the Turks by offering Britain his assistance in maintaining regional law and order in return for an agreement similar to the treaty signed in 1820 with the sheikhs in what later became the UAE. The British declined. At the time, they had no wish to come into direct conflict with the Ottomans.

Developments the following year led the British to reassess their position. The Russians, Britain's arch-rival at the time, were negotiating with the Ottomans for the construction of a railway from the Mediterranean to the Gulf. Mubarak let it be known that he was considering granting a concession to the Russians for a coal-loading station in Kuwait. The British feared this would give rise to Russian territorial rights in Kuwait and hurried back to him. The Kuwaitis had again successfully played off the big powers against each other. This led to a secret agreement between Mubarak and the British on 23 January 1899, which effectively placed Kuwait's foreign affairs in British hands. Mubarak undertook not to receive agents or representatives of any foreign power, nor to allow any part of his land to be used or sold to any other power or their nationals without the consent of the British, in return for the 'good offices' of the British, a term left conveniently undefined.

The Treaty came just in time for Kuwait. When the Turks continued to press their claim to Kuwait, the Royal Navy stationed HMS *Lapwing* nearby. Mubarak reasserted his independence in May 1899 by raising customs duties on all imports, including those from Basra and other Turkish ports, and refused to receive a Turkish harbour-master who arrived to take over Kuwait's port.

The Turks further pressed the matter the following year by trying to re-establish a customs house at Kuwait, and connect a telegraph line from their territory on the nearby Fao Peninsula to their possessions in the Arabian interior, through Kuwait. The line would have required troops to guard it, with attendant loss of Kuwaiti sovereignty. The British Minister in Constantinople warned off the Turks.

In the meantime, an Imperial German commission had visited Kuwait, also with a view to establishing a railway terminus for the proposed Berlin-Baghdad railway. The Germans had been dealing with the Ottomans over the acquisition of 20 square miles of land at the head of Kuwait Bay. Mubarak sent them packing, making it clear that he was in charge of Kuwait, not the Turks, and he did not want any railway terminus in his jurisdiction. The British told both the Germans and Turks that Mubarak could not grant any territory to the Baghdad Railway Commission without British consent. With the 1899 Treaty no longer a secret, the Turks were reluctant to come into direct conflict with the British. They and the Germans backed down.

The Turks, however, continued to pursue their ambitions in Kuwait through their Rasheedi surrogates, promising them they could replace the Al-Sabah in Kuwait if they captured it. Later that year, in December 1900, Mubarak and the Saudis marched against the Rasheedis, attacking them in their heartland around Hail, 600km to the west. The Kuwaitis and Saudis were trounced, and retreated to Kuwait in the spring of 1901 to lick their wounds, as the Rasheedis prepared to retaliate.

Upon Mubarak's chastened return to Kuwait, senior Ottoman officials from Basra visited him to convince him of the need for a Turkish garrison for protection against the Rasheedis. It was sheer blackmail. Mubarak declined the offer as it would have led to *de facto* Turkish occupation of Kuwait. He turned to the British for support. This time, however, Her Majesty's Government were reluctant to further upset the Turks: however, they did send a gunboat, HMS *Perseus*, to keep an eye on Turkish and German moves.

Mubarak evaded the Turkish demands throughout the summer, but could not stop the Rasheedis. By September, they were three days' march from Kuwait, so *Perseus* landed machine guns at Jahra, and two additional gunboats were ordered to Kuwait from Bombay. The Rasheedis could not take on the combined forces of Mubarak, the Saudis and the Royal Navy, and withdrew north into present-day Iraq to confer with their Ottoman paymasters.

In Kuwait, young Ibn Saud jumped at the chance. His family's capital of Rasheedi-occupied Riyadh was lightly defended, with the bulk of his foe's army headed in the opposite direction. He left Kuwait in late 1901 with a small band of followers and recaptured Riyadh on 16 January 1902. It was the first of a series of conquests with Kuwaiti help which eventually led to the formation of modern Saudi Arabia.

The Turks, however, did not give up entirely. During 1902, they occupied Umm Qasr and Safwan in northern Kuwait, and Bubiyan Island, and continued sponsoring Rasheedi raids. The British were prepared to defend territory adjoining Kuwait Bay, but only as long as Mubarak did not go chasing the Rasheedis in the interior. Then, other peoples' wars took the pressure off the Kuwaitis again when young Ibn Saud's remarkable military successes in central Arabia distracted both the Ottomans and the Rasheedis from Kuwait.

In 1903 the British decided to establish closer relations with Mubarak, so Captain S.G. Knox arrived in Kuwait in August 1904 as Political Agent. He was in effect the first British Ambassador to Kuwait. The Treaty of 1899 had outlived its usefulness, so the British began work on the basis of a new agreement with the Ottomans to define the position of Kuwait. In the meantime, Mubarak concluded more agreements with the British, eventually undertaking in 1913 not to grant an oil concession without British approval.

The wily Mubarak knew he would be of use to the British only while he served their interests, so while the British considered how they would deal with the issue of Kuwait and the Ottoman Empire, Mubarak sought to balance the British by improving his own relations with the Turks. At one stage he acted as intermediary between them and the Saudis, and in 1906 even attempted a reconciliation between the Rasheedis and Saudis.

In July of 1908, the Young Turks deposed Constantinople's Sultan-Caliph, leading in time to renewed Ottoman attempts to subjugate Kuwait. However, wars in Libya and the Balkans drove the Turks to settle their problems with the British over Kuwait and the Gulf in the hope of gaining British support elsewhere. This led to discussions opening in February 1911 which resulted in the signing, pending ratification, of the Anglo-Ottoman Convention on the Gulf on 29 July 1913. This treaty broke Kuwait's territory into two zones. The inner one was a semi-circle of 65km radius, centred on Kuwait City, including the offshore islands. Within this, the Amir exercised complete independence, free of Ottoman laws. The second, outer zone extended Kuwaiti territory west to the Wadi Al-Batin - Kuwait's present-day western border with Iraq - and south into what is now Saudi Arabia. Kuwait's southern border then was 125km south of where it is today, and her area three times as large. The tribes within this second zone were the Amir's subjects, to be administered in accordance with his role of Ottoman *Qaim - Maqam*.

However, with war clouds looming in Europe, and the prospect of Turkey's entry into the war on Germany's side, this agreement was never ratified. It would, nevertheless, in the absence of a better guide, later form the basis of the delineation of Kuwait's northern and western borders with Iraq.

As war broke out in Europe in 1914, Britain was desperate for all the help she could get. She therefore agreed to recognize Kuwait as independent of the Ottoman Empire in exchange for Mubarak's support against Turkey. Knox, now a Colonel and Acting British Resident for the Gulf, promised Mubarak that Kuwait would become an independent Sheikhdom under British protection if he took the British side. He agreed. Kuwait was now effectively a minor ally of Britain against the Axis Powers, well removed from Ottoman dominance.

As Muslims, it was very difficult for many Kuwaitis to align themselves with the British against the Ottomans. Nevertheless, Mubarak convinced his old *protegé*, Ibn Saud, to join the Allies. Unlike the Hashemites in western Arabia with T.E. Lawrence, neither man actually attacked the Turks. The Kuwaitis continued to look to their own interests as the Great Powers looked to theirs. They traded and smuggled with all-comers, including the Turks. In their poverty, other people's wars provided opportunity to prosper.

However, Kuwait's fortunes declined as the war progressed when Mubarak passed away in 1915. He was succeeded by his eldest son, Jaber, the grandfather of the present-day Amir of Kuwait. Jaber leaned towards the Turks, but he only ruled for 14 months. His younger brother, Salem, the grandfather of the current Crown Prince and Prime Minister, took over in 1917. Salem shifted more overtly to the Turkish side. He had masterminded the smuggling to the Ottomans under his father, but was now more open about it.

To make matters worse, Salem did not get on with Ibn Saud. Kuwaiti forces under Salem had been sent by Mubarak in 1915 to help Ibn Saud in one of his wars. However, once the enemy was routed, Salem, following his father's brief, declined to give Ibn Saud the help he needed to crush them decisively. Ibn Saud did not forget this. The British were also unhappy. It had taken them two and a half years and 98,000 casualties to capture Baghdad from the Turks in March 1917, and they were bitter about the lack of real assistance from Mubarak's sons, and Salem's duplicitous wartime policy. They imposed a naval blockade in early 1918 which was not lifted until after the war.

Salem's friction with Ibn Saud eventually led to a Saudi land blockade and incursions. On 10 October 1920, the Ikhwan Wahabis attacked Jahra from Saudi territory. The British, seeking to balance rising Saudi power, and preferring to see Kuwait autonomous, landed guns and Royal Marines from HMS *Emerald*. The Ikhwan withdrew, and the British High Commissioner to the new nation of Iraq, Sir Percy Cox, promised to resolve the Saudi-Kuwait border dispute the following year.

Salem died on 22 February 1921, and with him most of the feud with Ibn Saud. He was succeeded by his nephew, Ahmad, who became the father of the current Amir.

Following Turkey's defeat in World War I, the British mandate granted over captured Ottoman territory by the League of Nations' April 1920 San Remo

Agreement formed the two ex-Ottoman provinces of Baghdad and Basra into Iraq. Mosul joined in 1923 to form present-day Iraq. The Hashemite King Faisal I, who had led the Arab revolt against the Turks in western Arabia and modern-day Jordan and Syria, was installed in Iraq by the British as a constitutional monarch in June 1921. Fatefully, this brought Iraq and Kuwait under the control of a single international power.

One of the British problems was the late Mubarak's old *protegé*, Ibn Saud, and the propensity for his tribesmen to raid Iraq and Jordan. International borders as we know them today were an anachronism to tribal Arabs. A sheikh's lands extended only as far as his wisdom and strength allowed. His successor was not necessarily entitled to keep those lands by virtue of inheritance. But this was the 1920s, and fixed borders were important. In particular, with the emergence of oil as the fuel of the 20th Century, and discoveries in nearby Persia, the British needed to clarify sovereignty over concession areas to be leased to oil companies.

In 1922, true to his word, Sir Percy Cox summoned Ibn Saud to the tiny Gulf port of Uqair near Bahrain. The primary purpose of the meeting was to define the borders between Saudi Arabia and Iraq. Kuwait was unavoidably part of this, and was represented by her British Political Agent, Major J.C. More. The Kuwait-Iraq borders were delineated largely in accordance with the unratified Anglo-Ottoman Convention of 1913. However, Sir Percy allocated to Iraq a large area of land which had been claimed by the Saudis. To compensate the Saudis for this, and punish Kuwait for her collaboration with the Turks during the war, Cox gave two-thirds of Kuwait to the Saudis, and a northern strip of Kuwaiti land to Iraq. Kuwait was the double loser. In no position to argue, she had to accept her dismemberment.

The border between Kuwait and Iraq was confirmed in an exchange of correspondence in April 1923 between Sheikh Ahmad, Cox, and More. When the British mandate in Iraq ended nine years later in 1932, and Britain sponsored Iraq's application to join the League of Nations, its first Prime Minister, Nuri Al-Said, was unhappy with the border position as it was, and openly advocated the annexation of Kuwait. He felt that he was being railroaded by the British into recognizing the borders, but eventually confirmed them in a letter to the then British High Commissioner in Iraq, Sir Francis Humphrie, on 21 July 1932. These borders are those in existence today, as recently demarcated by the UN following the Gulf War.

Whilst her modern borders were being defined, Kuwait – not under threat from outside powers for the first time in her history – was gradually recovering from the war years. By 1926, her estimated population was about 50,000, comprising mainly Arabs, Persians and Africans, a few Jews, and some Chaldean Christians from Iraq, in addition to the handful of American missionaries running the only hospital.

The allocation of two-thirds of her territory to Saudi Arabia in 1922 was not Kuwait's only great loss of that decade. The Gulf pearl industry, one of her principal sources of income, collapsed with the development of cultured pearls by a Japanese noodle-vendor, Kokichi Mikimoto. The continuing friction with Saudi Arabia and later the Great Depression brought great hardship. The emerging hope that oil might be found in Kuwait, as it had been in Persia, did little to relieve this. It would be two decades until the money flowed.

Because of his loss of territory at Sir Percy Cox's Uqair conference in 1922, Sheikh Ahmad was reluctant to award an oil concession to a British company, despite Britain's importance. As a compromise, Kuwait Oil Company (KOC), a joint venture between the predecessor of modern-day BP, which was exploiting the new Persian fields, and Gulf Oil of America, which later merged into Chevron, was formed was formed in London on 2 February 1934. Sheikh Ahmad had found another power to balance British influence. KOC was granted an exclusive concession by Sheikh Ahmad to search for and produce oil, and on 22 February 1938 the first successful well, still in production today and known as Burgan 1, was capped.

Despite this good fortune, trouble was brewing. Iraq conveniently forgot its earlier recognition of its borders with Kuwait shortly after gaining its League of Nations membership. The first renewed calls for annexation came in 1933, but grew more serious in 1938 when King Faisal I's successor, Ghazi, launched a propaganda campaign ostensibly to liberate Kuwait from British rule.

The attacks, although couched in pan-Arab rhetoric, were motivated by Iraq's realization of Kuwait's oil potential, and by the territorial concessions Iraq itself had made to Iran in 1937, thus limiting further its already narrow access to the Gulf. Iraq was also genuinely concerned about the vulnerability of its main port, Basra, to Persia, and wanted to develop another secure outlet to the sea. Iraq became more belligerent and the British warned Baghdad that they would intervene militarily against any move on Kuwait, but Ghazi persisted. However, fate smiled yet again on Kuwait. Young King Ghazi brought his reign to a premature end by slamming his sports car into a lamp-post on the night of 4 April 1939, and the threat receded for the time being.

Development of Kuwait's oil was delayed by World War II, but by 1946 the first exports were flowing. Even with oil selling at less than US$2 a barrel, the industry developed rapidly. By 1950, Kuwait had an estimated population of 150,000, three times that of a generation earlier. The new KOC town servicing the oilfields was named 'Ahmadi' after the Amir who had overseen the birth of the oil industry. Sheikh Ahmad died in 1950, and was succeeded by Sheikh Abdullah, the father of the present-day Crown Prince and Prime Minister.

Oil changed Kuwait almost overnight. Schools, power stations, and hospitals to eventually replace the American medical mission were built. Perhaps most importantly, the oil financed water desalination plants. During the mid-1950s, Kuwait and Iraq were on the verge of agreeing to a demarcation which would have given Iraq a 99-year lease on parts of northern Kuwait and Warba Island in exchange for guaranteed supplies of fresh water. Sheikh Abdullah decided not to proceed as this would have given Iraq a stranglehold over Kuwait. His country had survived for 200 years without oil, but she could not survive without control of her own water. The desalination plants enabled Kuwait to seal her independence by replacing the need to ship water from Iraq, much to Baghdad's ire.

Iraqi ambitions over Kuwait resurfaced in the late 1950s when Nuri Al-Said, still Prime Minister in Baghdad and conveniently forgetting his own 1932 acceptance of Kuwait's independence, attempted to have Kuwait join the newly-formed Arab Hashemite Union linking Jordan and Iraq. Fate intervened on Kuwait's behalf yet again. On 14 July 1958, Al-Said and the Iraqi royal family were overthrown in a coup. The king's body and that of his uncle were hung from lamp-posts by their feet; Al-Said's mutilated corpse was dragged through the streets of Baghdad. One witness to this barbarism was a young British traveller, Michael Charles Swift Weston who, as British Ambassador to Kuwait 32 years later, would again witness Iraq's darker side.

The new revolutionary government in Baghdad headed by Brigadier Abdul Karim Qassim at first seemed a definite improvement on Hashemite royalty, even backing Kuwait's bids to join Arab and international organizations before she was fully independent of Britain, but the honeymoon would not last long.

On 19 June 1961, Kuwait signed the Treaty of Independence with Britain which abrogated the 1899 treaty and disentangled various agreements linking the two countries. Kuwait thus became a fully independent sovereign state.

Kuwait wisely remained neutral between the conservative and radical wings of the Arab League, and declared her Cold War non-alignment by establishing relations with both the US and the USSR. From a practical point of view, nothing enhanced Kuwait's position more than sharing her new oil wealth. In 1961, the Kuwait Fund for Arab Economic Development was established to provide long-term, low-interest loans for development projects in poorer Arab states. This fund, the pioneer in its field, continues to this day.

Despite earlier positive signs, Kuwait's independence did not please Qassim in Baghdad. Less than a week after the abrogation of the 1899 treaty, he renewed the old Ottoman claim to Kuwait which Saddam Hussein would use again 29 years later, claiming that Kuwait was part of Basra, and promising to appoint the Amir an area executive administrator, reporting to Basra.

At the time, although not a military giant, Iraq still posed a credible threat. The Kuwaiti Army had only 1,500 men, 16 tanks and one battery of field artillery. But Kuwait's defences lay in foresight, not firepower. Her pre-independence diplomacy and contractual defence arrangements with the UK paid off handsomely. Other Arab states rallied to her side. Egypt's President Nasser publicly opposed Qassim's claims. Britain dispatched a paratroop battalion from Cyprus, and Royal Marines from Bahrain. An infantry brigade followed. Within 48 hours, 8,000 British troops had been deployed. With the arrival of the aircraft carrier HMS *Victorious* on 9 July, Qassim backed down, denying that he had ever intended to invade, but the tension remained.

Interestingly, Egyptian intelligence apparently passed evidence to Riyadh that Qassim was coveting not only Kuwait, but also the Saudi territory carved off Kuwait at Uqair in 1922. This may have been to distract the Saudis from their war with the Egyptian-backed Yemeni republicans, but it was taken seriously. The Saudis also sent troops. Saddam learned from this in 1990, and went to great lengths to reassure the Saudis that he was not after their land.

Both sides complained to the UN Security Council, which was impotent to act because of Cold War stalemates. The matter was therefore left to the Arab League and Britain. A month after the abrogation of the 1899 treaty, on 20 July 1961, Kuwait became a member of the League, which subsequently sent troops to replace the British, and supported Kuwait's application to join the UN.

Iraq responded to this wave of support for Kuwait by withdrawing from the Arab League in December 1961, and redrawing its map to include Kuwait. Baghdad shot itself in the foot by announcing that it would sever diplomatic relations with any State recognizing Kuwait. As the list of countries accepting Kuwaiti envoys grew, so too did the number of Iraqi ambassadors making their way home. Iraq became more isolated. The crisis subsided, but did not end completely until Qassim met his own violent end. On 8 February 1963 he was overthrown and assassinated by the first Ba'ath Party coup.

Iraq's only real success during the crisis was to delay Kuwait's admission to the UN, but on 7 May 1963 Kuwait became the UN's 111th member. However, the 1963 coup had another more far-reaching effect. It paved the way for a 25 year-old Saddam Hussein to return from exile in Egypt where he had taken refuge after a botched attempt on Qassim's life. He subsequently took over the Ba'ath's intelligence function, from which he was to build his power base.

During the 1961-1963 crisis with Iraq, Kuwait continued to build the democratic institutions of a modern independent state. A constituent assembly of 20 elected and 11 appointed members prepared a written Constitution, which was approved by Sheikh Abdullah on 11 November 1962. It came into effect on 29 January 1963 when Kuwait's first National Assembly convened following a general election based on a limited adult male electorate.

Following Qassim's fall, the new Iraqi regime reassured Kuwait. Talks between the Iraqi and Kuwaiti Prime Ministers and transfers of funds later in the year led to Ba'athi Iraq recognising the independence of Kuwait, and its sovereignty over its boundaries as defined in the exchange of letters between the two governments upon Iraq gaining its own independence in 1932.

The years following this crisis passed relatively peacefully for Kuwait, helped by the internal political turmoil in Iraq as governments fell, and the Ba'ath Party built itself into the terror machine it is today.

During the 1960s, Kuwait developed a cradle-to-grave welfare state for her citizens, established her University, and became a leading member of OPEC, of which she had been a founding member. The much-loved Sheikh Abdullah passed away in 1965, and was succeeded by his brother, Sabah.

The main tensions in the ensuing years arose from the Arab-Israeli wars of 1967 and 1973, and the damage this caused to Kuwait as an Arab state in her relations with the West. In 1964, the year after Baghdad had reaffirmed Iraq's recognition of Kuwait's sovereignty, talks commenced on actually demarcating the border. However, the Ba'ath had been overthrown in November 1963 by a coup within a coup, and the new regime had little enthusiasm for border demarcation. They not only hindered it, but encroached into undisputed areas. In 1966, Iraq temporarily overran Kuwait's Bubiyan Island in protest against talks between Kuwait and Iran over the division of their continental shelf regions, conducted without Iraq's participation.

In April 1967, Iraq again crossed into Kuwait's northern region as part of an application for loans to assist with dam construction. Once the loans were extended, the troops were withdrawn, and the Iraqis became more amenable, but never quite got around to border demarcation surveys.

In 1969, Baghdad asked Kuwait to allow Iraqi troops to be stationed on the Kuwaiti side of their common border to protect the Iraqi coast against Iran. This time, the same Ba'ath party that had confirmed the borders ten years earlier was back in power. Saddam Hussein, although Vice-President, held the real power in Baghdad, after having been restored on 17 July, 1968. The Kuwaitis were evasive, but Saddam went ahead and deployed soldiers in a narrow border strip, then sent his officials to Kuwait City to present the *fait accompli* to the Amir, and gain his formal approval. It was not forthcoming.

On 20 March 1973, the Iraqi troops at Samta inside Kuwait were reinforced. However, the agenda now had superpower implications. In April 1972, Saddam had signed a 15-year friendship treaty with the USSR which included a defence co-operation clause. Iraq wanted to build a naval port at Umm Qasr which would give the Soviets a naval base in the Gulf. Iraq moved armour into Kuwait, killing two Kuwaiti border guards, Lieutenant Saud Al-Sahali and Corporal Rael Al-Thufeiri. Kuwait mobilized, Saudi forces moved into Kuwait in a show of force, and US-backed Iran warned off Iraq.

A combination of Arab League mediation and a large Kuwaiti loan finally persuaded the Iraqis to withdraw most of the troops, but elements of the Iraqi Army remained on Kuwaiti territory for some years until well into the Iran-Iraq War. Whenever Kuwait protested, the Iraqis argued that the troops could not be pulled out as long as the border was not precisely demarcated.

In August 1973, Saddam proposed building oil pipelines from southern Iraqi oilfields across Bubiyan to the Gulf. This was rejected by Kuwait as it would have led to *de facto* Iraqi occupation of Bubiyan, and Warba Island. Saddam's next ploy was to offer to demarcate the borders in return for the two islands. Again, the Kuwaitis refused. They saw no need to give away land for a demarcation that Iraq had already long agreed to, but was not implementing.

Saddam did not try again in earnest until 1975, following his Algiers Agreement with Iran whereby he ceded disputed areas of the Shatt Al-Arab to the Shah, thus removing Iranian and US support for the rebellious Iraqi Kurds. This time Iraq demanded that Kuwait cede Warba to it, and lease Bubiyan for 99 years. Again, Kuwait refused and the matter was left unresolved, only to be renewed again in 1978. The following year, the Shah of Iran fell, and both Iraq and Kuwait had more than border issues on their minds.

The greatest challenge confronting Kuwait and her neighbours in the early 1980s was the new fundamentalist regime of the Ayatollah Khomeini in Iran, and the fear that the Islamic Revolution would be forcibly exported across the Gulf. In retrospect, this fear was largely unfounded. Like all revolutions, the Iranian version would have run out of steam in its early years had Saddam not tried to take advantage of the situation and retrieve what he had signed away at Algiers in 1975. Iran never had territorial ambitions on Kuwait; she had enough land of her own, and plenty of maritime outlets. By attacking Iran, Saddam unwittingly helped to consolidate Khomeini's Islamic Revolution, and gave it an enemy other than the US to focus on.

The Iran-Iraq war was a mixed blessing for Kuwait. As long as Iraq was fighting Iran, it could not menace Kuwait. However, Kuwait and her Gulf neighbours were justifiably concerned at the hornets' nest Iraq had stirred up. The fear was that if the Iranians broke through the Iraqis, they would attack the Gulf States in retaliation for their support of Iraq. The fighting was so close to Kuwait at times that the artillery could be heard on still mornings.

Kuwait's dilemma was complex. She was obliged to support the Iraqis morally and financially as fellow Arabs, despite Iraq's previous designs on her, but doing so caused offence to Iran. However, Kuwait's best protection from Saddam was to ensure that he had enough resources to keep on fighting, but insufficient to win. It was an unpleasantly pragmatic path to take.

Kuwait bolstered her own defences when, on 25 May 1981 she formed the Gulf Co-operation Council (GCC), with Bahrain, Oman, Qatar, Saudi Arabia and the UAE. This was a loose alliance whose unspoken objective was the common defence of its members. The GCC was supposed to lead to an integrated military structure but the result was merely a division-sized joint force, known as the Peninsula Shield, based south of the Kuwaiti border in Saudi Arabia.

As the Iran-Iraq war settled into bloody stalemate, Kuwait was increasingly drawn into the crisis with Iranian-sponsored terrorist attacks on Kuwaiti coffee-houses, and the French and American embassies, in December 1983. This led to the arrest, conviction and imprisonment of seventeen individuals, several of whom were related to the pro-Iranian Hezbollah in Lebanon. None of these men were executed despite the loss of life they caused, and capital punishment being on the Kuwaiti statute books for such crimes.

In Lebanon, the relatives of the jailed terrorists tried to pressurize Western governments into forcing Kuwait to release these terrorists by kidnapping Westerners in Beirut, including the local CIA Chief, William Buckley. Buckley was tortured to death. Others were held for years, but the Kuwaitis refused to be bullied, even when a Kuwaiti Airbus was hijacked in December 1984, and an assassination attempt was made on the Amir in May 1985.

More bombings and hijackings followed, but the terrorists had received due process, and would have to serve their time. Back-door attempts by glory-seeking Western politicians such as Jesse Jackson who visited Kuwait in November 1987 in an attempt to gain the release of the Western hostages by doing a deal on the prisoners were politely rebuffed. Some of these terrorists were released upon completion of their sentences in the late 1980s, and the remainder by Iraqi troops in August 1990. The surviving Western hostages in Lebanon were gradually freed after that.

In the meantime, Iraq was on the defensive. The Iranian capture of the Fao Peninsula in 1986 forced Iraq to export oil using pipelines through Turkey and Saudi Arabia. If Saddam couldn't export oil through the Gulf, then he was not going to allow the Iranians to do so. He therefore started the tanker war by attacking vessels carrying Iranian oil. Naturally enough, Iran retaliated by hitting ships carrying oil from those States financing Iraq, including Kuwait, and by firing surface-to-surface missiles at Kuwaiti refineries and oil ports.

This led in 1987 to an increased US Navy presence in the Gulf on the Iraqi side. The Americans reportedly began giving covert aid to Iraqi forces by passing satellite intelligence to their land forces, and guiding their aircraft onto Iranian maritime targets. This led to the incident on 17 May 1987 when an Iraqi Mirage fighter-bomber supposedly accidentally attacked the USS *Stark*, one of two radar-picket frigates, with Exocet missiles. Thirty-seven American sailors died. There is some speculation that the attack was an Iraqi ploy to draw more US vessels into the Gulf. Iraq co-operated with the US investigation to a certain extent, even agreeing to pay compensation, but refused to allow the Mirage pilot to be interviewed.

Kuwait was feeling the effect of the attacks on her shipping, but could do little about it on her own. She therefore asked the Americans for protection by placing a number of her oil tankers under the US flag. Like the British earlier in the century, the Americans were reluctant to get further involved, but the Kuwaitis were old hands at this game. Kuwait Oil Tanker Company leased three Soviet tankers. The Americans promptly put eleven Kuwaiti tankers under the Stars and Stripes. Within months, Kuwaiti tankers were operating under US, British and Soviet flags - and Kuwait's - with escorts by the three big powers. Kuwait had brought the world's navies to the Gulf in strength.

The *Stark* incident led to a change in the rules of engagement for the US Navy in the Gulf. Local commanders were given greater latitude to fire on potential threats. This inevitably led to clashes with the Iranians. The major beneficiary was embattled Iraq. By September 1987, the US naval force in the Gulf had risen to about 80 vessels. In effect, America protected Iraqi and allied GCC shipping, whilst allowing Iraq to attack Iranian vessels. The US had effectively entered the Iran-Iraq War on the side of Saddam, and would eventually sink or disable most of the Iranian Navy over the coming months.

American-Iraqi co-operation reached a high point on 17 April 1988 when US vessels apparently conducted diversions against Iran by jamming its radar and attacking Iranian targets as the Iraqis launched an all-out effort to recapture the Fao Peninsula. Further Iraqi attacks with covert US help over the next six weeks put Iran firmly on the defensive. A final blow came on 3 July 1988 when the USS *Vincennes* mistakenly shot down an Iranian Airbus on a scheduled flight to Dubai, killing all 290 passengers and crew. Iran seemed convinced it had been a deliberate act, and realized it could not fight a superpower and Iraq. On 18 July 1988, Khomeini agreed to UN Security Council Resolution 598 calling for a ceasefire. It was the effective end of the Iran-Iraq War. The fighting eventually ceased on 8 August, 1988, although a final settlement was not reached and prisoners continued to be held by both sides.

Having successfully helped extract Iraq from a debilitating war by bringing America in on Iraq's side, and financing a large part of Saddam's war effort, few people in Kuwait imagined that Iraq would again turn its attention to Kuwait. Those with an eye on history knew otherwise. Iraq would be back. The question was when, and for how much.

On the eve of the 1990 Iraqi invasion, Kuwait was a glistening cosmopolitan metropolis of 2 million people, of which about 650,000 were Kuwaitis. An estimated further 200,000 people had the ethnic characteristics of Kuwaitis – many were related by blood and marriage to Kuwaitis – but were not Kuwaiti citizens. They were known as the *bidoon*, or 'without nationalities'. They were essentially those unable or unwilling to prove that they did not have another nationality, and had not come from elsewhere more recently in search of the benefits of Kuwaiti citizenship. Some were descendants of desert bedouin who had been unaware of the need to register as citizens in the 1960s. Others were Saudis, Iranians and Iraqis.

These Kuwaitis and *bidoons* were a diverse mix. They had originally come from all the surrounding countries, and even from as far away as Lebanon and Syria. The *Utbi* migrants from central Arabia in the 1700s had intermarried with other arrivals over the past 250 years, and even with Indian and African women in the ports where Kuwaiti merchants traded. Over 99% of Kuwaitis were Muslims, of the Sunni and Shia persuasions. The non-Muslim Kuwaitis are a few Christians of Iraqi and Lebanese origin. Most of the younger generation, particularly women, are University-educated and speak English.

The remainder of the population were expatriates, who had to have jobs or be sponsored to live in Kuwait. About 400,000 were Palestinians or Jordanians. The rest came from all corners of the earth. Perhaps only 15,000 were Westerners and Japanese. The remaining 735,000 were primarily Indians, Egyptians, Pakistanis, Bangladeshis, Filipinos, Lebanese, Sri Lankans, Syrians, Thais, Iranians and Iraqis. Economically, Kuwait was a very effective mechanism for the transfer of oil wealth - and stability - to the Third World through the export of skills and labour for hard currency.

The Palestinians had the best deal of all expatriates, and guarded it jealously. They filled most middle-level positions, were highly educated, and many spoke English. No other country except Jordan hosted them in such numbers. As such, they had a powerful network which looked after its own. They could even keep some Kuwaitis out of jobs they were qualified for.

Kuwait had played host to about 10% of the worldwide population of Palestinians for over a generation. The first Palestinians were welcomed with open arms as refugees in 1948. A problem was brewing in that Kuwaitis were on the verge of being outnumbered by Palestinians in their own country, but this had not reached a head. Besides educating them, giving them free medical care, and a head start to migrate to Western countries, Kuwait regularly paid substantial amounts of direct financial aid to the PLO and to Palestinian hospitals and charities in the Israeli-occupied Jordanian West Bank, and provided significant political support for the Palestinian cause.

Yasser Arafat had learned his English at the American Mission Hospital in Kuwait, and made his fortune as a contractor in the boom years of the early 1960s. He regularly visited Kuwait to collect funds, and was warmly received. As with old Sheikh Mubarak's policy of giving refuge to the Al-Saud in their time of need, this modern example of brotherhood had its own agenda. The Palestinians are a powerful, emotive force in Arab politics, and Kuwait had invested heavily in them. The Kuwaiti sense of outrage and betrayal at Arafat's support for Saddam after the invasion is more understandable in this light. Simply, the Palestinians did not pay the bill when it was presented.

Kuwait's greatest social problem other than the *bidoon* dilemma was maintaining the work ethic in Kuwaitis when a ready supply of labour was prepared to do all that was required for less than the nationals expected to be paid. The oil wealth had weakened the link between effort and reward, and was turning modern Kuwaitis into a sedentary race.

Politically, the Al-Sabah held power, but Kuwait had been the only Gulf State with an elected parliament of any sort and demands for the elected National Assembly to be re-established had resulted in the appointment of a National Council as a precursor to this. The broader National Assembly had been suspended in 1986 on security grounds during the Iran-Iraq war. With the August 1988 ceasefire holding between Iraq and Iran, the Kuwaiti public saw a need for further progress in their political rights.

Culturally, Kuwait is a conservative Muslim country, but not as strict as some of her neighbours. The synagogues have long since gone, a casualty of Zionism, but there is no objection to the entry of Jews into Kuwait, although not on an Israeli passport. Kuwait boasts about 22 churches of most denominations. The Roman Catholics even have a cathedral, and a local Bishop. Christians are generally free to worship as they wish. Hindu and Buddhist temples are proscribed as these religions are inconsistent to monotheistic Islam, but there is no objection to private worship. It is a policy of live and let live.

Kuwait in 1990 was a safer place than many others worldwide. The prevailing Muslim culture, a strict jail regime, and deportation of expatriate offenders saw to that. Capital punishment was reserved for murder, rape, and terrorism, but was infrequently applied, and normally commuted to a custodial sentence. In any event, these crimes are rare. Bank hold-ups simply did not happen. Thieves receive jail as punishment, not amputation. Islamic Sharia law applies only to the law of personal status such as marriage, divorce and inheritance. People take sensible precautions such as locking their doors, but they are far safer than in most Western or Asian cities.

In her finances, Kuwait had invested wisely, to such an extent that she was later able to pay in cash for much of the cost of her liberation from Iraq. Oil income at the time of the invasion accounted for less than 50% of state revenues. The remainder came not from taxes, but from foreign investments.

In essence, Kuwait in mid-1990 was an independent, safe, stable, respected, and profitable country. It simply got on with what it did best, and tried to stay out of harm's way. It was so quiet that most people in the West could not even place it on a world map. The events of 2 August 1990 would change all that. Kuwait, her people and her region would never be the same again.

5. THE ROAD TO WAR

With the August 1988 ceasefire in the Iran–Iraq War holding, but the Iraqi economy wrecked and Saddam's ego undented, the stage was set for the invasion of Kuwait. The greatest surprise of the crisis in retrospect is just how obvious this was. There were at least five major signals from Saddam that he was up to no good, from February through to July 1990, but few observers predicted the full extent of the invasion in sufficient time to prevent it.

Saddam's challenge in the summer of 1988 was to win the peace. Eight years of bloody combat had left Iraq bankrupt. Saddam had fought the war on credit. Iran had done so on current account, beholden to no one.

But all that credit had financed a formidable military machine. At the cessation of hostilities, Saddam had a million men under arms, half of them reservists, an estimated 5,500 main battle tanks, and 689 combat aircraft. About one in four Iraqi men were in uniform. Quality aside, the sheer volume of Iraq's forces, and Saddam's propensity to use them, posed a great threat.

More alarmingly, Saddam was developing long-range missiles, chemical weapons, biological weapons, ultra-long range artillery and, most frightening of all, nuclear weapons. He had used the missiles and chemicals to effect in his war with Iran, but was still developing the other three.

Peace with Iran did not bring about an Iraqi demobilization, or a termination of the strategic weapons programmes. There was some justification for Saddam keeping his army mobilized as treaty negotiations with Iran soon stalemated, but the only conceivable reason for continuing the development of strategic weapons was further expansionism.

The Iran–Iraq ceasefire brought a great sense of relief to Kuwait. In the short term, there was a tremendous opportunity for business in helping Iraq to recover from the war, and for rebuilding relations with Iran. No one could know at that stage just how soon disaster would strike.

Saddam's concentration on transforming Iraq into a regional superpower, and his likely ambitions, were not lost on Kuwait. He made the requisite threatening noises against Israel, but wise heads in Kuwait knew better. In the five major Arab–Israeli conflicts from 1948 to 1985, Iraqi forces had been conspicuous by their absence. In that time, Iraq had launched two serious attempts on Kuwait, in 1961 and 1973, and numerous minor incursions.

Within days of the ceasefire with Iran, Iraq accused Kuwait of effectively shifting her borders north by moving her customs post from Mutla'a Ridge to Abdaly, 75km to the north. To underline the point, Iraqi troops made a minor incursion, but withdrew. It was a ridiculous ploy. Kuwait had indeed built a post at Mutla'a many years before, more for convenience than anything else. Administratively, in the days before Kuwait's superhighways, with little more than desert between Mutla'a and Abdaly, it was easier to support a post closer to the city. The real Kuwaiti border post at Abdaly was still within Kuwait. As a matter of fact, the Iraqi post opposite Abdaly at Safwan was also in Kuwaiti territory, as later demarcated by the UN in 1991 and 1992.

The incident confirmed Kuwaiti fears that Saddam had little gratitude for their wartime help. It also fed later assessments that Saddam only wanted northern Kuwait, perhaps only as far south as Mutla'a.

Kuwait strengthened her defences on four fronts: diplomatic, financial, military and demographic. The diplomatic moves were the steady, quiet building of relationships with her regional Arab allies and the superpowers, and now also Iran, having incurred Iranian displeasure during the Iran-Iraq War. Financially, she boosted her economy by turning on the oil taps. At the 1989 OPEC summit, Kuwait negotiated approval of an increased two million barrels per day (bpd) quota to regularize the *de facto* position. Other OPEC states, including Iraq, were unhappy but accepted it as a *fait accompli.*

Militarily, Kuwait sought to replace her ageing A-4 Skyhawks and Mirage F-1s with 48 top-of-the-line US F/A-18s. It was not as easy for her to buy the F/A-18s as one might expect. American lawmakers were not as perceptive to the Iraqi danger. In particular, the Israel lobby was fixated with the perceived Arab threat to Israel. Incredibly, they seemed to fear that Kuwaiti F/A-18s might be used against Israel! They initially blocked the sale, but the Kuwaitis knew how to handle this. In the same week as the Kuwaiti Crown Prince and Prime Minister visited Washington to negotiate the F/A-18 purchase, British Defence Secretary George Younger was in Kuwait after the successful conclusion of a major Saudi-British defence deal, and a senior Soviet general in full uniform, with a delegation, was conspicuous in Kuwait's Meridien Hotel. The message to Washington was clear. Kuwait was prepared to go elsewhere, and quickly. The Americans heard, and approved the sale.

At the same time, Kuwait upgraded her air defence missile systems, and plans were made to buy more tanks from Britain and Yugoslavia, and APCs from the Soviet Union and Egypt. Kuwait was truly ecumenical in her choice of suppliers. The arms purchases from major powers included an element not written into any contract: the implicit agreement to come to Kuwait's aid if required. Kuwait was buying goodwill along with the hardware.

Demographically, Kuwait announced plans to build a new city, a power station and a university on the largely uninhabited north shore of Kuwait Bay. At the time, I was puzzled at this; there was plenty of land available around Kuwait City itself. But the real agenda had little to do with town planning. Kuwait was asserting her own sovereignty over her northern half.

At the time, the US seemed more concerned with Saddam's human rights record than his military threat. Throughout the Iran–Iraq War, Washington had supported Saddam as the perceived lesser of two evils: the Reagan Administration had no wish to see revolutionary Iran emerge as the dominant power in the Gulf without an Iraqi counterbalance. It was a distasteful choice, given the nature of Saddam's regime, but necessary.

With the August 1988 ceasefire holding, America found itself less obliged to hold its tongue on Iraqi human rights excesses. On 8 September 1988, when Iraqi Foreign Minister Tareq Aziz visited Washington for a meeting with Secretary of

State George Schultz, he was greeted with condemnation of Iraq's latest use of chemical weapons against its Kurds, two weeks earlier, and a unanimous US Senate vote for some of the strongest sanctions ever applied under the 1988 *Prevention of Genocide Act*.

True to form, Saddam took the message personally. Three days after the American condemnation, a reported 100,000 Iraqis demonstrated outside the US Embassy in Baghdad, the first such anti-American protest since the 1967 Arab-Israeli War. Two months later, the embassy's chief political officer, Haywood Rankin, was expelled. Washington retaliated by expelling an Iraqi diplomat. Saddam now had what he wanted – a foreign enemy to focus his countrymen's minds on to distract them from his robbery of their lives. In the months to follow, he would add Britain, Israel, Kuwait and the UAE to the mix to feed the myth of a major international conspiracy against Iraq.

Despite these problems, late 1988 and early 1989 passed peacefully enough. There were unprecedented moves towards political openness in Iraq, including hints at an end to the Ba'ath monopoly on power, a democratic multi-party system, and direct free elections for the Presidency. Price controls were lifted, certain State enterprises privatized, and attempts made to attract capital from the Gulf and elsewhere. Iraq seemed to be genuinely moving from Stalinism to socialism. The economic changes were real enough, and necessary to get the moribund economy moving. The political reforms were pure charade.

Internationally, despite his human rights spat with the West, Saddam acted positively. In late 1988 he was instrumental, with Egyptian President Hosni Mubarak, in having the PLO recognise Israel's right to exist. He continued to build his links with Egypt, but Mubarak was acutely aware of his duplicity. In March 1979, Saddam had hosted the Arab League summit which had expelled Egypt for making peace with Israel, only to come rushing back to Egypt the following year for military assistance against Iran.

However, co-operation with Saddam served Egyptian interests. Iraq owed Cairo US$3.5 billion for arms purchases, and another US$850 million to Egyptian expatriates in Iraq. However much Mubarak personally disliked Saddam, it would be easier to influence him positively with closer links. This led on 19 February, 1989 to the formation of the Arab Co-operation Council (ACC) linking Egypt, Iraq, Jordan and Yemen in a loose economic alliance. For Jordan and impoverished Yemen, it was a good deal, and a counterbalance to the GCC. Three months later, Egypt was back in the Arab League.

The West was pleased that Saddam was now grouped with such respected and pragmatic moderates as Mubarak and King Hussein. Kuwait was relatively pleased as the ACC was expected to divert Saddam's attention away from them to the broader Arab role he cherished. The future looked bright for Arab politics, and regional peace.

But all was not as it seemed. Saudi Arabia was unhappy with what was effectively now an Iraqi threat on its south - through Yemen - as well as the north, through both Iraq and Jordan. The Saudis had not been on good terms with Yemen since annexing its two oil rich provinces in 1934, and a proxy war in the 1960s. Jordan's Hashemites still nursed a grudge at the loss of the western Hijaz part of Saudi Arabia to Ibn Saud in the 1920s.

Around this time, the Saudis apparently concluded they were unlikely to recover the money they had loaned to Saddam, so converted these huge amounts into outright grants. In return, Saddam entered into a non-aggression pact with Saudi Arabia. This caused some surprise in Western capitals, as, by definition, the need for such a pact arises only with the prospect of aggression. Saddam was obviously up to something, but his agenda was still unclear.

About a week before the ACC was formed, Iraq had reportedly offered a similar pact to Kuwait, but the price was too high: cession of some of the northern lands, including the Rumaillah/ Ratga oilfield, and leasing Warba and Bubiyan Islands to Iraq, plus forgiveness of the estimated US$14 billion of loans, and more cash. Not only would this have meant caving in to extortion, but it would have compromised Kuwait's improving relations with Iran, and her neutrality in the stalled Iran-Iraq treaty negotiations.

Then, in March 1989, an agreement was suddenly announced for a deal whereby 350 million gallons per day of potable water, and 500 million gallons of irrigation water would be piped to Kuwait from Iraqi rivers, in return for electricity from Kuwaiti power stations. This caused a great deal of surprise as Kuwait already generated her drinking water from her desalination plants. The piped water would be cheaper, and allow development of the arid lands of Kuwait. The agreement was never implemented, but at the time it suggested that progress could be made on other issues.

In May 1989 I visited Iraq with several American friends over a holiday weekend. At the time, Iraq was a good, cheap holiday. It had the historical sites of Babylon, Nimrod and Ur. You could see the green valleys and streams of Kurdistan for the price of a five-star dinner for two in Kuwait. Basra was fascinating with its canals and palm trees, and reconstruction, while the great Shi'ite shrines of Najaf and Kerbala exuded history. The southern marshes were fascinating, like a step into another world. For expatriates whose short trips out of Kuwait had been limited to an expensive few days in Bahrain or Dubai, Iraq was a Godsend. You could even drive there from Kuwait.

For the ordinary people of Iraq the realities of life were very different. The first thing that struck us was the poverty. It hit you the moment you crossed the border. On the Kuwaiti side, uniformed immigration officials sat behind computers, and Asian janitors in orange boiler-suits kept their offices clean. In Iraq, you were immediately surrounded by flies and smells of something rotting. The officials, although not unfriendly, conducted their business with manual ledgers, and dressed in street clothes. The sole cleaner was an old Shi'ite crone in a black *abaya*, using a bunch of twigs as a brush.

We soon learned that in Iraq, Saddam poured millions into his pet projects, at the expense of his people. Baghdad was a stark contrast to the impoverished hinterland. Whilst it could not be described as wealthy, it had more than its fair share of five-star hotels, huge ministry buildings, and most impressive of all, a magnificent unfinished museum and memorial to the Iran–Iraq War, referred to euphemistically as Saddam's *Qadassiyah* after an ancient historical Arab victory over the Persians.

The people themselves were exceedingly friendly, and polite, a diverse mix of Christian, Sunni and Shi'ite Arabs, and Kurds, all of them simply trying to get on with life. They were very proud of their country, and delighted to see visitors after the years of war and isolation. There was no animosity at all towards Americans or other Westerners. We could feel the tremendous sense of relief after the war, and a great hope for the future.

The aspect of greatest note, however, was the pervasiveness of Saddam. It was eerie. Pictures of him were everywhere, some six metres high and floodlit. People discussed him only with the party line on their lips. In any event, we had been warned not to discuss politics in Iraq, and especially not to say anything that might be construed as against Saddam. That weekend, Saddam himself was on a trip to Kurdistan. TVs in the lobbies of every hotel ran continuous coverage of him walking benignly among his Kurdish subjects, at a safe distance, as they adulated him in a transparent choreography. It struck us that these were the same people whose kin he had bombed with chemical weapons, but such inconsistencies were not mentioned in Iraq.

Mid-1989 passed quietly as Saddam got on with his reconstruction efforts. His main domestic task was the demobilization of army reservists. This was not easy. Iraq's shattered economy simply could not absorb tens of thousands of young men whose only life experience had been the military. To make matters worse, the soldiers came home to find an estimated 1.2 million expatriate Egyptian and Sudanese workers in jobs which they felt they were entitled to, and Iraqi women married to many of the Egyptians. It was a recipe for disaster. Internationally, he concentrated on championing the Palestinian cause, and developing the view among the poorer Arabs of their entitlement to a greater share of the Gulf States' oil wealth.

At the time, Kuwait was re-establishing relations with Iran. On 29 September 1989 the new Iranian Ambassador took up his post in Kuwait. Saddam was put out by Kuwaiti *rapprochement* with his arch-enemy, especially given the stalemate in the peace treaty negotiations with Iran. To make the point, Iraqi troops moved briefly into northern Kuwaiti in October 1989, then withdrew. It was apparent that Saddam wanted to be treated with the respect due to the local neighbourhood heavy.

Further evidence of Saddam's attitudes came almost unnoticed, in November 1989, with the Iraqi TV appearance of a bruised and beaten 31-year-old Farzad Bazoft, an Iranian-born journalist with British travel papers, working for London's *Observer* newspaper. Bazoft had been arrested in September for allegedly spying at the site of a recent huge explosion at the Al-Qa'qa weapons plant outside Hilla, 100km south of Baghdad. Reports had said that about 700 people had been killed in the incident.

A confession that he had been working for Israeli and British intelligence had been tortured out of Bazoft, but he had done less than many other Western journalists in Iraq at the time, merely driving around the perimeter of the site, and taking some samples of ash residue on the roadside near the entrance, in full view of the sentries. He had even gone there with the knowledge of the Iraqi Ministry of Information, and Foreign Ministry Undersecretary Nizar Hamdoun. Bazoft would make another - far more tragic - appearance four months later.

Despite setbacks such as those at Hilla, on 5 December Iraq successfully tested a three-stage liquid-fuelled rocket, supposedly designed to carry a satellite. Known as *'Tammuz-1'*, it was basically a number of SCUD-B boosters fastened together, with obvious applications as a long-range ballistic missile.

Iraq had ended the Iran–Iraq war with hundreds of intermediate range missiles, designated *'Al-Hussein'*, and *'Al-Abbas'*, based on the SCUD-B, a Soviet-designed weapon using World War II rocket technology. They had been used with limited success to bombard Iranian cities. The *Al-Hussein* had a range of 650km with a 136kg payload. *Al-Abbas* could reach 900km with 300kg. Both were relatively inaccurate, but could threaten cities and large troop concentrations, particularly with the right type of warhead.

Later that month, Iraq tested an intermediate-range ballistic missile known as *'Al-Abed'* with a 2,000km range and a 750kg payload. This was a generation beyond *Al-Hussein* and *Al-Abbas*. The West sat up and took notice. *Al-Abed* could not be justified on the grounds of self-defence. Concern further increased in February 1990 when US satellites detected the construction in western Iraq of five fixed missile launch sites within range of Israel.

In 1990, Iraq apparently planned to spend US$9 billion on war reconstruction, and clear up to US$5 billion of its estimated US$80 billion foreign debt. The total cost of reconstruction was estimated by Western economists at US$230 billion. With the low oil prices of the late 1980s, Iraq had earned only US$13 billion from oil in 1989, down from US$26 billion in 1980, and had spent a total of about US$24 billion. Not only was Saddam's income now half what it had been ten years previously, but his expenses were higher. He needed money, lots of it, and quickly. For a man like him, the obvious source of further funds was extortion. But first, he had to prepare the ground.

Saddam's first opportunity for this came at an ACC Foreign Ministers' meeting in Baghdad on 19 February, the first anniversary of the ACC's founding. He demanded that the few remaining elements of the US Navy be completely withdrawn from the Gulf, and was clearly bent on resurrecting the bogeyman of neo-colonialism. America's assistance in helping to force the ceasefire with Iran only 18 months earlier was conveniently forgotten.

He repeated this call at the first ACC summit in Amman the following week, this time adding a demand that oil-rich Arab states withdraw their funds from the US, and invest in Arab countries, the USSR and Eastern Europe. He even began to talk of liberating Jerusalem. President Mubarak and King Hussein were taken aback. As Saddam's ACC colleagues, they had no wish to be drawn into dictating how the US should deploy her forces, telling the GCC states how to invest their cash, and talk of attacking Israel.

The following day Saddam made his play. He reportedly told Mubarak and Hussein, 'I need US$30 billion in fresh cash. Go and tell the Gulf States that if they do not give Iraq this money, we will know how to get it.' Few Western analysts took note of this first explicit extortion threat, just five months before the invasion, used as they were to windy Arab rhetoric. Nevertheless, a sense of unease began to crystallize. What was Saddam up to?

The heat was turned up on 15 March with the execution in Baghdad of the unfortunate Farzad Bazoft. Iraq had ignored calls, since his arrest, to either release him, or give him a fair trial, but the suddenness of the trial on 10 March, and the verdict, shocked the world.

Bazoft was tried by little more than a kangaroo court. His real crime was to be a means for Saddam to send a message far and wide that he was not to be trifled with. As an Iranian with Western connections, Bazoft was fair game.

In response to the execution, Britain temporarily recalled its recently-appointed Ambassador, Harold Walker, cancelled trade and Ministerial visits, and sent home six Iraqis on Ministry of Defence courses. That was all: no economic sanctions or severing of diplomatic relations. Walker would return in May with orders to resume a dialogue with Saddam. Britain needed Iraqi business, as did many other countries. One dead Iranian working for a British newspaper did not warrant cutting off valuable channels of trade and communication. The prevailing view at the time was that such action would only harm Western interests, and reduce the opportunity to moderate Saddam.

Nevertheless, Bazoft's death as a British journalist focused the attention of the Western and Israeli press, which may have been exactly what Saddam wanted. There were notable inconsistencies in the way Bazoft's execution was handled, which suggested that its real purpose was to publicize Iraq's military potential, and to obtain assurances that Israel would not attack Iraq. For one thing, death sentences in Iraq are normally carried within a day of the verdict, if not immediately. The five-day delay gave the media plenty of time to build their outrage. A further week's delay between the body being handed over to the British Embassy helped this. It was inevitable that the media would turn to the subject of Bazoft's investigations: Iraq's strategic weapons. This in turn led to renewed speculation that Israel would be well-advised to destroy these systems before they became a real threat.

I travelled to Iraq on business in March, 1990, the week after Bazoft's execution, flying from Basra to Baghdad on Iraqi Airways. Surprisingly, for a country supposedly at peace, half of the passengers were Army officers of every rank up to brigadier. But there was no pride in these men. In the departure hall, the various ranks sat separately. The juniors never saluted their superiors. I queried this with a captain beside me. He laughed, saying: 'In Iraq, we are all good socialists! Every officer is the same as the other.'

The truth came out later in the flight. They were all sick of the Army, and just wanted to get back to normal family life. But even if they were demobilised, there were no jobs. No one, including the Gulf States, was prepared to invest in an economy subject to Saddam's whims.

In Baghdad, the mood had changed noticeably from my earlier visit ten months earlier. Thousands of jobless demobilised soldiers wandered aimlessly around the streets. The hope for a better future was gone. In fact, there was great resentment of Kuwait and anything Kuwaiti. There was a feeling that the Kuwaitis were taking advantage of Iraq when it was down, driving up to Baghdad and Basra in their fancy cars, and buying up the country.

There was an element of truth in this. In the war-shattered Iraqi economy, everything was sold at bargain basement prices. Everyone was desperate for hard currency. It was their only form of security. Thousands of young men had been killed and wounded needlessly in the war with Iran. The peace was being lost as surely as the war had been a disaster. Almost everything Iraq could provide - food, carpets, scrap, fertilizer, antiques, entertainment - was being sold for a fraction of its value, and the Iraqis didn't like this.

The mood was captured for me by a senior diplomat. 'My driver,' he said 'says that you can't even get a decent woman in Baghdad these days. They're all down in Basra with the Gulfies!' It was true. On the Baghdad's streets, there were plenty of Gulf tourists with girls who obviously were not their sisters. At an Arab League conference two months later, Iraqi Foreign Minister Tareq Aziz would pledge that his country would not kneel, their children would not starve, and their women would not be driven to prostitution. The truth was the reverse. Saddam had driven his people so far into the ground that some Iraqi women were being forced to sell themselves to survive.

On 28 March, less than two weeks after Farzad Bazoft's execution, American and British customs inspectors intercepted a consignment of 40 US-manufactured krytrons, or high-voltage capacitors which could be used in the detonation mechanism of a nuclear bomb. The arrested Iraqis were apparently trying to smuggle them from the US to Iraq through London.

The implications of this were far-reaching. It was becoming apparent that Iraq was closer than previously thought to developing an operational nuclear weapon, and that Israel's 1981 attack on Iraq's Osirak nuclear reactor had slowed down but not stopped Saddam's nuclear programme. With his long-range missiles operational, he could target anywhere from Greece to Pakistan. This included all of the Arabian Peninsula, Israel, Egypt, and Iran. The only type of warhead justified by such a weapon was nuclear. No one expected that Saddam would nuke Athens or Karachi, but he could hold a nuclear pistol at the head of the entire region, and demand ransom on a gigantic scale.

But as with Bazoft's execution, there were inconsistencies. The krytrons bust seemed all too easy. There was suspicion in some quarters that Iraqi intelligence had let themselves be caught to focus more attention on Iraq's strategic weapons potential, with resultant calls in Israel for a pre-emptive strike. Whether intended or not, this was the effect. The Arabs reacted to the prospect of an Israeli raid as they have always done with any external threat to an Arab state: they fell in behind Saddam, at least publicly.

The row over Farzad Bazoft's execution and the capture of the krytrons were portrayed by Saddam as a US–British–Israeli conspiracy to prevent him from completing his weapons programme.

On 2 April, five days after the krytrons incident, Saddam addressed the General Command of the Iraqi Armed Forces, saying he would attack Israel with binary chemical weapons if Israel attacked Iraq. This was his second explicit signal that trouble was brewing. These comments did not go down well in the West or Israel, even though on a careful reading they were a threat of retaliation if attacked, not a unilateral threat. The US described them as 'inflammatory, outrageous, and irresponsible'. What the speech did do, however, was divert attentions from Saddam's real objective: Kuwait.

This alarm was just what Saddam wanted. It prompted a flurry of shuttle diplomacy. The Saudi Ambassador to the US, Prince Bandar Sultan, flew to Baghdad to obtain Saddam's assurances to President Bush and King Fahd that he would not attack Israel, unless Israel attacked first. Bush obtained Israeli assurances that she would not move against Iraq, and passed this back to Saddam. Iraq had some of what it wanted: a secure western flank with Israel, the 1989 non-aggression pact with Saudi Arabia, and an exhausted Iran to its east. On 4 April Saddam sent a private letter to the Iranian President offering to restart the stalled treaty negotiations and exchange POWs. He was freeing himself for action against Kuwait, four months thence.

Ten days after Saddam's 2 April speech, a delegation of five US Senators met Saddam in Mosul. They mentioned their concern about nuclear, chemical and biological weapons, but were more interested in trade and money. They did not even mention the late Farzad Bazoft. In fact, they blamed most of the problems between Iraq and the US on the Western press, not Saddam's human rights record and his weapons programmes. Their grovelling, led by later Presidential-hopeful Senator Robert Dole, only reassured Saddam that as long as he provided business for the West, he could virtually do as he liked.

A few days after the US Senators left Iraq, British Customs impounded a shipment of precision-machined steel pipes ostensibly manufactured for the Iraqi oil industry. They were in fact part of what became known as the 'supergun', a massive artillery piece designed to fire shells hundreds, if not thousands, of miles. In the following days and weeks, other parts for this weapon were found across Europe, destined for Iraq. Many were sceptical that such a gun was even feasible, but news of the mysterious murder in March of its designer, Canadian Dr Gerald Bull, and revelations about his previous involvement in such a project for the US military, raised fears that there was more to Saddam's ambitions than met the eye. The supergun was indeed technically feasible. Saddam's missile programmes and chemical weapons capacity were well known, but the supergun was a whole new dimension. More seriously, it was conceivable that it could deliver nuclear warheads.

By May 1990, the tension in Iraq between the returning soldiers and the Egyptian expatriate workers had passed breaking point. Hundreds of Egyptian bodies began arriving at Cairo airport from Baghdad each week with evidence of violent death: bullet wounds, bludgeoning, stab marks. It was far more than could be explained by normal mishaps. There was obviously a campaign of violence in Iraq to force out the Egyptians.

Cairo's press kept fairly quiet about this, but Egyptian public opinion began to move against Iraq, with Egypt becoming increasingly uncomfortable at being in the ACC alliance with an unreformed Saddam. By shooting Egyptian workers, the Iraqis were alienating the leading Arab power.

In May, Saddam sent out his third explicit signal of impending mischief. This time the target was his wealthy Gulf neighbours. At the end of the month, Saddam hosted an Arab League summit in Baghdad. Its ostensible purpose was to condemn the growing emigration of Soviet Jews to Israel. Many of the leaders realized that Saddam would try to use the summit for his own ends, so Saudi Arabia, Morocco and Oman sent deputies. Syria boycotted it.

Their fears were justified. Saddam initially rehashed his anti-Americanism and threats against Israel, and identified the perceived conspiracy. He then proceeded to pressure Kuwait and the UAE to cut their oil production and force the oil price up to the level he wanted. Iraqi Foreign Minister Tareq Aziz made Saddam's attitude to the Gulf States clear, arguing that Iraq had protected them from the dangers of Iranian fundamentalism. Aziz claimed that this service had cost far more than Kuwait and other GCC States had paid; the loans were only part-payment for services rendered.

Saddam concluded the summit by suggesting that Kuwait's and the UAE's high-volume oil production policies which were supposedly depressing the value of Iraq's oil exports amounted to a kind of economic war against Iraq. He demanded US$27 billion from Kuwait in return for oil he claimed had been pumped by Kuwait from Iraq's section of the Rumaillah/Ratga oilfield, but left the door open for a response by hinting that he did not really believe that the economic war was intentional. It was a crude, thinly-veiled threat.

Saddam waited through the first two weeks of June 1990 for a response to his demands, but the Kuwaitis essentially ignored him. They saw no need to give in to Iraqi blackmail. If they did, he would only come back later for more.

Saddam's Deputy Prime Minister and Chief Economic Advisor, Sa'doun Hammadi, visited Kuwait in late June, after meeting with King Fahd in Riyadh to request US$10 billion each of the Saudis and the UAE. He reportedly renewed the Iraqi request for forgiveness of Kuwaiti wartime loans, a cut in oil production to force the price up, and US$10 billion in cash.

The Kuwaiti Amir reportedly replied that the demand was absurd. Even Kuwait did not have such a large amount readily available. He was prepared to give Iraq US$500 million over three years as an act of charity from one Arab brother to another, but that was all. As for the oil production, he would discuss that if Iraq settled the border demarcation issue.

But time was short. Saddam could not afford to wait. He demanded from Kuwait an amount of money equivalent to the production of the Kuwaiti end of the shared Rumaillah/Ratga field and accused Kuwait – unjustifiably – of stealing its oil by directional drilling under the frontier. In any event, claimed Iraq, the entire area was its property, so it was entitled to all the oil. In fact, Kuwait had been producing an average of 10,000 bpd, over 5% of her production, from her part of this field for more than ten years, and this was the first time Iraq had raised the issue publicly.

With tension running high, Kuwait agreed in a meeting of Gulf Oil Ministers in Jeddah, on 10 July, 1990, to abide by her OPEC quota, and started liquidating funds in case a payout was required. The production cut was expected to increase the price. The tension seemed to subside.

Another little-noticed incident on 11 July caused Saddam concern. Iranian Foreign Minister Ali Akbar Velayati called in to Kuwait on his way home from unsuccessful peace treaty talks with Tareq Aziz in Geneva. Kuwait had provided significant aid to Iran after a recent terrible earthquake. Saddam apparently became worried that Kuwait might seek Iranian protection. If so much as an Iranian battalion arrived in Kuwait, he would be unable to invade for fear of restarting the Iran-Iraq war. He harboured similar fears about the West. He did not want to face *any* foreign troops in Kuwait, and had to move before they arrived. Time, at least then, was not on his side.

In mid-July, the Iraqis gave their fourth and clearest signal yet that Saddam was intent on causing trouble.

On 15 July at an Arab League Foreign Ministers' meeting in Tunis, Iraqi Foreign Minister Tareq Aziz presented a 37-page memo to Secretary-General Chadli Klibi, accusing Kuwait of deliberately driving the oil price down to damage the Iraqi economy, and encroaching on Iraqi territory when Iraq had been preoccupied with Iran. There was none of Saddam's hedging from the Arab League summit in May about the economic warfare being unintentional. Aziz was adamant that this supposed anti-Iraqi policy was quite deliberate.

With remarkable precision, he estimated that the low oil-price policy, starting in 1981, had cost the Arab world US$500 billion in revenue, of which Iraq's share was US$89 billion. Furthermore, the oil supposedly stolen by Kuwait from Rumaillah/Ratga was valued at US$2.4 billion.

At the same meeting, the PLO and Iraq criticised their ACC colleague, Egypt, for siding with the Gulf States, its closer ties to the US, and for its *rapprochement* with Syria. Cairo, seeing itself as the leader of the Arab world, was most displeased, particularly with the continuing stream of dead Egyptians arriving home from Baghdad. The Arabs were forming into separate camps two weeks before Saddam's tanks moved into Kuwait.

Kuwait and the UAE hardly had time to catch their breath before Saddam built on Aziz's statements in his Revolution Day speech on 17 July, saying: 'If Kuwait had deliberately robbed Iraq, it was because Kuwait was in an anti-Iraq conspiracy with America, Britain, Israel and the UAE.' According to Saddam, Iraq would not tolerate this much longer; if negotiations did not give Iraq the protection it demanded, then it had no option but to take action. 'Cutting necks', he said, 'is better than cutting the means of living'. In effect, if Kuwait and the UAE did not pay up, Saddam would come after them.

Saddam had taken a proverbial pistol from its holster, and was waving it in the direction of Kuwait and the UAE. He may not have been contemplating a fully-fledged invasion at that stage. His need was for funds, not another war. The conventional wisdom was that if Kuwait did not comply then, at most Iraq would take the oilfield and islands, nothing further.

On 17 July, the day of Saddam's speech, the Iraqi leader gave his fifth and final signal of intent by dispatching lead elements of the *Hammurabi* Republican

Guard armoured division from its base in central Iraq to just north of the Kuwaiti border, followed two days later by the *Medina* and *Tawakalna*. The three divisions totalled about 35,000 men, with perhaps 1,000 armoured vehicles. The pistol pointed at Kuwait was being loaded.

Kuwaiti diplomats in Iraq started picking up intelligence on the Iraqi troop movements. The Kuwaiti Deputy Chief of Staff, Major-General Jaber Al-Khalid, put his forces on alert within the limit of his authority, which meant that he could not hold the alert for more than 24 hours without Cabinet approval. Even this was difficult as many Kuwaiti servicemen - including the Chief of Staff - were already abroad on summer holiday. The military had been on alert all the way during the Iran-Iraq War. This was the first year in which a normal summer leave programme had been reimplemented.

Only a few international observers picked up the full seriousness of the latest moves. Most hedged their bets. Hardly anyone, with the exception of *The Economist*, was prepared to make predictions. In its 21 July edition, printed several days earlier, the newspaper said presciently that Saddam's comments 'sounded alarmingly like a pretext for invasion'.

On 18 July the Iraqi Parliament voted Saddam President for life, also proposing an amendment to a new draft constitution which said that presidential elections should be held for the first time since the Ba'ath coup of 1968, with the head of state serving an eight-year term. Not surprisingly, there was no mention of any challengers to Saddam.

On the day of Saddam's Presidential life-appointment charade, the Kuwaiti Cabinet met to discuss his threats, and rejected them as extortion in an indignant letter to Klibi. The prevailing view was that they were more of a bargaining position than an ultimatum. Some concessions might be necessary, but Kuwait would do everything in her power to reduce them to the barest minimum. In any deal, the Iraqi *quid pro quo* would have to be the border demarcation. Military action could not be ruled out, but was believed to involve at most a border crossing up to ten kilometres into Kuwait, followed by a withdrawal after a payoff. Major-General Jaber Al-Khalid was asked to take his forces off alert so as not to aggravate the situation.

In Baghdad that day, US Ambassador April Glaspie visited the Iraqi Ministry of Foreign Affairs (MFA) to seek clarification on the threats against Kuwait. It was the first of seven daily visits over the next week during which she conveyed messages from the State Department that the US insisted that disputes be settled peaceably, and that America was strongly committed to the defence of her friends in the Gulf.

Washington then issued a public statement to the same effect. This was reinforced on 19 July by Secretary of Defence Dick Cheney. At this stage, the Iraqi troop movements were not public knowledge. Iraq's Ambassador to Washington was summoned to the State Department and told that the US would continue to support the sovereignty and integrity of the Gulf States, and insisted that disputes be settled peacefully. In the meantime, the US Congress was finally doing something about Iraq's weapons programme. The Senate Banking Committee unanimously approved legislation to deny Iraq agricultural credits, and bar the sale of technological items with military applications. These were, in effect, sanctions against Iraq, but far too late to stop Saddam from building the military machine he would soon use.

The sudden eruption of the crisis caused a flurry of diplomacy in the Gulf and Egypt. The Iraqi propaganda campaign against Kuwait and the UAE was particularly virulent. Arab diplomacy is generally conducted with grace and good manners. Not so in this case. Older Kuwaitis commented that they had never heard anything like it, even when Iraq had threatened Kuwait in 1961-63, and 1973, or at the height of Iraqi–Syrian tensions.

The Arab League's Klibi flew to Kuwait on 20 July, as Saudi Arabia's King Fahd and Egypt's Hosni Mubarak called for moderation. Kuwait sent envoys to every Arab capital, except Baghdad, to garner support. On 21 July, news of the Iraqi deployments reached the Western press, and through that the public in Kuwait. The tension rose further. That same day, Klibi left Kuwait for his headquarters in Tunis instead of going to Baghdad as planned. He had put his mediation efforts on hold until the Iraqis were willing to co-operate.

Kuwait, alarmed that an Arab solution may come to naught, hedged her bets by informing the UN Secretary-General of the crisis on 22 July. This drew immediate Iraqi claims that Kuwait was trying to internationalize the row. Saddam needed to keep the rest of the world sidelined; his muscle would have far more leverage if he kept the affair within the Arab family.

In the meantime, the Arab League appointed Hosni Mubarak as its mediator. On 24 July, following a meeting with King Hussein of Jordan and Tareq Aziz in Alexandria, he arrived in Baghdad to see Saddam, with plans to travel on to Kuwait. According to the Iraqi version of the meeting, Saddam told Mubarak that he would not use force as long as talks were ongoing between Iraq and Kuwait, and would not intervene militarily before he had exhausted all possibilities for negotiation. The Egyptian version carries no record of conditionality. Saddam explained his troop build-up on the Kuwaiti border as 'normal routine exercises', but asked Mubarak not to tell the Kuwaitis this so as to maintain the pressure on them. He also agreed to stop the vitriolic propaganda attacks.

In the meantime, Kuwait stepped up her campaign for Arab support by sending parliamentary delegations to Arab capitals in the wake of the earlier special envoys, and the Arab League's Klibi flew to Baghdad after receiving the necessary assurances of Iraqi co-operation. A resolution seemed in sight. The tension subsided again, but little came of his meetings with the Iraqis.

Mubarak left Baghdad on the 25th for Kuwait with no intention of collaborating with Saddam's game of bluff. He was also annoyed by a false Iraqi statement released while he was still on his way to Kuwait, saying that there had been no discussion of the Kuwaiti question. Mubarak relayed to the Kuwaitis that Saddam had said he did not intend to invade, and advised them to be flexible in their negotiations. In Mubarak's assessment, Saddam's real objective was money, for which he was desperate.

Those following matters closely thought they knew what Saddam was up to. An OPEC summit was scheduled for 26 July. Iraq wanted to increase the crude oil benchmark price from US$18 to US$25. Saddam's actions were seen as pressure on Kuwait and the UAE for funds, and a price-boosting production cut. The troop movements were described as 'sabre-rattling'.

Most Arab states were taken aback by the strength of the US diplomatic response to Saddam's July 17th speech, to the extent that some feared it might inflame the situation. Not so the UAE. They were unconvinced that Saddam would not use force and had secretly requested the US to deploy two KC-135 aerial refuelling tankers so they could maintain around-the-clock air patrols with their Mirage interceptors. The US provided the planes, and the four US Navy warships in the Gulf was reinforced with another two vessels. On 24 July, the Americans announced the deployment of both the ships and the KC-135s, saying that her forces had commenced a limited exercise with the UAE. In an unpublicized move, one of the newly-arrived vessels, the USS *Robert G. Bradley*, was sent to the northern Gulf to keep an eye on Iraqi movements.

For the US, the exercises were a means of sending a message to Saddam that the US would support Kuwait and the UAE. Doubts were growing in Washington as to whether he was really bluffing. Kuwait for her part, to avoid aggravating the tension, was sticking to her long-established policy of not inviting foreign forces onto her soil.

In Baghdad, at midnight on 24 July, US Ambassador Glaspie received a protest over the 'exercises'. The following morning, the Iraqi press was full of complaints about 'foreign threats'. Glaspie then delivered to the Iraqi MFA a copy of a State Department announcement which stated that 'there is no place for coercion and intimidation in a civilized world', and reaffirmed the US commitment to its friends in the area. At noon, she was summoned on one hour's notice to meet Saddam for the first time, and explain the manoeuvres.

Ambassador Glaspie's meeting with Saddam became one of the most misunderstood parts of the crisis. The impression given by the Iraqis and elements of the Western media was that she gave Saddam *carte blanche* to enter Kuwait, or at the very least did nothing to discourage the invasion, by saying that the US had no opinion on Iraq's border dispute with Kuwait. In fact, this aspect was only a small part of a long and complex meeting between the President of sovereign Iraq, and the Ambassador of a major power which was not then at war, and did not see itself going to war, against Iraq. Glaspie's famous statement that the US had no opinion on the border matter was perfectly true, but was reported out of context. The US position was and is that it is up to sovereign countries to solve their own differences peacefully, preferably with the help of regional organizations such as the Arab League. Unlike Britain, the US had nothing to do with setting the borders in the first place. For America to have voiced an opinion would have compromised her neutrality. Ambassador Glaspie actually expressed the hope, quite appropriately, that the problem would be solved quickly by mediation by Arab League Secretary-General Chadli Klibi, or mediator Hosni Mubarak.

At the close of the meeting, Saddam asked Glaspie to convey a personal message to George Bush, promising that there would be no invasion. This was the same undertaking he had given to Hosni Mubarak, and King Hussein.

Ambassador Glaspie later described this series of promises as 'a deception on a massive scale.' With the OPEC meeting scheduled for the next day in Geneva, and expectations of the price rise which Saddam was after, many could be forgiven for concluding that Saddam had almost got what he wanted, so an invasion was simply unnecessary.

Meanwhile, as US satellites kept watch, the three Iraqi Republican Guard divisions that had deployed between 17 and 19 July were joined by a further four infantry divisions and one special forces brigade, bringing the Iraqi force on the Kuwaiti border to about 100,000, or 20% of the regular Iraqi military.

Iraq did not even try to hide this massive force. It was meant to intimidate. If the US had missed it, UNIIMOG (UN Iran-Iraq Military Observer Group) would have seen it: it was their job to monitor troop movements near the Iranian border. There was no failure of Western intelligence in actually knowing about the troops. The failure lay in not predicting far enough ahead to pre-empt the invasion in which Saddam would use them.

To be fair to the spooks, several factors indicated that Saddam would not invade. First, Iraq followed the Soviet military doctrine, which called for large-scale rehearsals of major operations. The Americans had seen none. Secondly, in the Americans' opinion, insufficient communications networks were in place to allow a large operation. Finally, stocks of matériel necessary to support a major offensive operation had not been deployed with the troops.

By 26 July, after Saddam's meeting with Ambassador Glaspie, the prevailing opinion was that the intimidation would continue until the Kuwaitis paid up, but that Iraq would not invade. Nevertheless, on 25 July, Kuwait's Military Attaché in Basra, Colonel Sa'id Matar, had reportedly advised Kuwait that Iraq would move in. This may have been discounted with Saddam's reassurances conveyed via Hosni Mubarak on the same day, and his separate assurances to King Fahd and King Hussein.

General Schwarzkopf, the Commander of the US Central Command, which covered the Gulf, reportedly told the Chairman of the Joint Chiefs, General Powell, that it looked at most as if Iraq was poised to launch a punitive but limited strike into Kuwait. The British apparently came to the same conclusion. The pistol in Saddam's hand had been loaded, but not yet cocked.

The OPEC meeting at the Sheraton in Geneva opened on 26 July with the existing benchmark price of US$18. However, oil was actually trading at US$14. Iraq demanded an increase to US$25, After much haggling, a price of US$21, the highest the Saudis would accept, was struck on 27 July with a corresponding production cut. Iraq seemed to have got some of what it wanted. It simply remained for Kuwait and the UAE to provide some ready cash. The crisis seemed on its way to a resolution, however unsatisfactorily.

On 26 July, Kuwaiti newspapers picked up Hosni Mubarak's announcement that Iraq and Kuwait would hold direct talks in Jeddah, scheduled for the 28th or 29th. Banner headlines proclaimed: 'IT'S OVER.' Saudi Arabia hailed the announcement as a breakthrough. The level of talks were expected to be at Prime Minister level. Arab League Secretary-General Chadli Klibi had arrived in

Kuwait from Baghdad the previous evening after conferring with Saddam. The Kuwaiti press might have been forgiven its optimism.

As the Arab week opened on Saturday, 28 July, it seemed only a matter of time and money before the crisis was defused completely. On that day and the next, barely 72 hours before the invasion, two separate Iraqi Ministers told US Ambassador Glaspie that Iraq would not invade. She was apparently satisfied that the Arabs were handling the crisis satisfactorily themselves, although the previous day she had visited the Kuwaiti Ambassador to Baghdad, Ibrahim Al-Bah'oo, and warned him that in her opinion there could be a military operation. Nevertheless, Glaspie had been scheduled to leave Iraq for medical treatment and annual leave, but this had been deferred since the flare-up of the crisis with Saddam's April 'burn half of Israel' speech. She could wait no longer, so left Baghdad on Monday, 30 July, only two days before the invasion, leaving the Embassy in the hands of *chargé d'affaires*, Joe Wilson. At the time, Iraqi infiltrators were already in Kuwait, some of them checked into city hotels, awaiting the word to move.

The moderate Arab leaders continued to reassure the Americans. The Arabs would handle the problem themselves; it would be best if the US could maintain a low profile. The Americans complied.

However, sometime during that week, Saddam apparently concluded that the US would not in fact fight, at least not for Kuwait. He may have assumed that Saudi Arabia would never agree to the stationing on her soil of sufficient US forces to eject him from Kuwait once he had taken and reinforced it. It seems he concluded that if he played a big enough hand, then no one could beat him. The gamble came very close to working. Documents left behind by retreating Iraqi troops seven months later confirmed that Iraqi brigade commanders had been briefed on the invasion by 31 July at the latest.

Developments on the ground did not support the relaxed assessments in Western capitals as diplomats arrived at work that Monday morning, 30 July. Around that time, Saddam seems to have moved two squadrons of MiG fighters to his Yemeni ACC ally. This was hardly noticed at the time, and reported only briefly in the immediate aftermath of the invasion. The Iraqi planes in themselves could hardly threaten Saudi Arabia's modern air force and air defence system, even with North Yemen's and South Yemen's ageing MiGs, Sukhois, and F-5s, but it was a brilliant diversionary move which prevented Saudi Arabia from being in a position to come to Kuwait's aid militarily by forcing her to think of defending her own southern borders first.

Similarly, Egyptian intelligence reportedly advised Mubarak on 28 and 29 July that an invasion was likely within a week. UNIIMOG had come to a similar conclusion, but its warnings were discounted. Truck drivers and tourists entering Kuwait from Iraq reported long delays on Iraqi roads near Basra with huge military convoys, and acres of roadside military encampments. In Paris, French intelligence, with their close links to the Iraqi forces in several areas, warned Kuwaiti Ambassador Tareq Al-Razouki that: 'it is not possible for the troops to stay where they are..... they will either move in or pull back.' Al-Razouki was so alarmed at this that he took the first plane back to Kuwait on 30 July to warn his superiors personally.

The direct Kuwait-Iraq talks scheduled for that Saturday and Sunday were deferred until Tuesday, 31 July after Iraq issued a statement outlining the demands it expected to be met. These comprised Kuwait undertaking not to exceed the OPEC quota agreed at the weekend, to hand over to Iraq the Rumaillah/ Ratga oilfield, to pay Iraq US$2.4 billion, write off Iraq's massive debts to Kuwait, and provide an additional US$10 billion compensation. They were totally unsatisfactory to Kuwait. She was not prepared to pay such a heavy price, and had been reportedly assured by British Prime Minister Margaret Thatcher that Britain and the US would support her fully if she did not accede to Saddam's demands.

In Washington, satellite photos still showed eight Iraqi divisions on the Kuwaiti border, with others further north. They had been partially reinforced with artillery, logistics and aircraft. The size of the force was out of all proportion to that required to merely intimidate Kuwait. With logistics in place, it could conceivably take all of Kuwait, and eastern Saudi Arabia.

However, by the afternoon of 30 July, the conclusion of both the CIA and US military intelligence officers whose job it was to predict the almost unpredictable was that Saddam would move into Kuwait, but take only the northern border strip with the Rumaillah/ Ratga oilfield, and Bubiyan and Warba Islands. The word from key Arab leaders was still that Saddam would not invade. He was simply maintaining the pressure to get his cash. Saddam's loaded pistol was cocked, but the safety catch was still on.

In Kuwait, the week before the invasion, the military were worried. Chief of Staff Major-General Misyad Al-Sane had returned from leave on 26 July, and reassumed command from his deputy, Major-General Jaber Al-Khalid.

Repeated requests from the Kuwaiti generals to be allowed to deploy their forces outside their camps for safety and to release ammunition stocks, so that they could respond quickly to any move, were turned down. Instructions from the Cabinet were to do nothing that might give the Iraqis a pretext for acting.

Not only the generals wanted to upgrade their readiness. A number of line officers in Kuwait's main armoured force, 35 Brigade, were convinced that the Iraqis would cross over, but were unsure just how far they would come. They and others in the armed forces had their own intelligence from sources in Iraq: friends, relatives, even some of their own colleagues returning from holiday. At the time, the officers felt that the Iraqis might come only ten kilometres into Kuwait, or as far as Mutla'a at the most. Their major tactical concern was that the Iraqis would cause trouble at the border to draw the Army north, and then sweep in from the west, behind them. Any Kuwaiti forces in the north would then be split off from Kuwait City, and effectively surrounded.

These concerns were conveyed to Land Forces Headquarters, with a request from brigade commander Colonel Salem Al-Sarour that the unit be put on alert. The request was turned down. Hopes in the Government were still pinned on a satisfactory outcome of the ongoing OPEC meetings, and diplomacy.

However, by Saturday, 28 July, despite the official optimism expressed in the press, the Kuwaiti Government was far from convinced that the crisis was over. Prime Minister Sheikh Sa'ad Al-Abdullah reportedly met with the Chief of Staff and key military commanders, and asked them how much time they would need to go on alert. He was apparently told that the Army would require 30 minutes for 6 Brigade, 90 minutes for 35 Brigade, and that 15 Brigade would take a little longer because of a lack of tank transporters.

35 Brigade's officers were incensed when they heard of this meeting. At the time, the tanks had not been armed, and 25% of the Army was still out of Kuwait on summer leave. They advised the GHQ that they would require at least half a day to deploy, and then only if all the men were on the base. More seriously, their contingency plans had envisaged defending against Iranian infantry from the north-east, or Iraqi forces trying to cross Kuwaiti territory to flank the Iranians, not Iraqi armour coming from the north and west.

On his own initiative, Lieutenant-Colonel Ahmad Al-Wazzan, the Commander of 35 Brigade's main armoured unit, 7th Armoured Battalion, put his own unit on alert unofficially, and pre-loaded everything he could onto his vehicles, short of ammunition, which could only be released from the stores on the authority of the GHQ and Ministry of Defence.

The following day, word of 7th Battalion's move reached the GHQ. They told Colonel Al-Sarour that there were no orders to stand to. Al-Wazzan was to stand down. However, this had not been completed by the time the Iraqis crossed the border – 36 hours later – so his unit was the only full Kuwaiti ground force in a position to move against them.

The Kuwaiti Navy was similarly placed. Although the Chief of Naval Forces, Colonel Qais Al-Saleh, was on duty, his deputy was in London on his honeymoon, and one of his two squadron commanders was also away. A week earlier, the Navy had proposed putting two vessels on full alert, in addition to the usual vessel on patrol at sea. Acting on Ministry of Defence orders, the GHQ refused the request. In fact, they ordered all the Exocet MM-40 missiles taken off the Navy's combat vessels for 'maintenance', and for preparations for the dry-docking of *Sabhan*, one of the two larger vessels, to proceed. The Navy had also been ordered not to patrol the northern Kuwaiti territorial waters near Iraq. They were to go no farther north than Failaka Island.

The Air Force also wanted to go on alert. Director of Technical Affairs Brigadier Ghazi Al-Abdulrazzak was reportedly near tears with frustration as he told his men that permission to release ammunition had been refused.

By the morning of Tuesday 31 July, news of the 100,000 troops was in the *Washington Post*, and the *Telegraph* in London, but not in the Kuwaiti newspapers. People abroad with friends and relatives in Kuwait telephoned with concern, but most of those in Kuwait were either unaware of the news, or dismissed it as just another local spat. Their mindset, mine included, was two years behind the game, still in the Iran-Iraq War. After all, we argued dismissively, Kuwait had poured billions into the Iraqi war effort against Iran. Why should Iraq invade Kuwait? It was inconceivable. The local papers were saying that it was all over. The Western papers must be uninformed.

Both the American and British Embassies called meetings of their wardens, volunteers whose task it was to maintain contact with their local communities in a crisis. The Americans had taken the lead earlier in the week, and the British held their own meeting at short notice on the evening of 31 July to address the newspaper reports. The British meeting was addressed by Consul Larry Banks, and Colonel Bruce Duncan, Commander of the British Liaison Team. The wardens were advised that in London's opinion, if the Iraqis did cross the border, they would probably only take the disputed Rumaillah/ Ratga oilfield, and Bubiyan and Warba, and come no further south than Mutla'a. There was no cause for alarm among those living in Kuwait City. The wardens were told that it was advisable to stock up on water and supplies as a standard precaution, whether or not there was an Iraqi threat, but that the situation did not warrant putting out general advice to this effect.

The embassies were taking their lead from their capitals, who had access to satellite imagery, reports from their missions in Baghdad, and contact with major Arab leaders. The embassies would later come in for a great deal of criticism for not warning their people to get out before the Iraqis invaded. They were not the only ones who were fooled. Virtually the entire Western intelligence community worldwide was caught by surprise at the extent of the invasion.

One serious problem became apparent during the meetings. As with the Kuwaiti military, many wardens were away on annual leave. The embassies scrambled to fill the gaps. They would still be doing so when the Iraqis invaded a day and a half later. Neither embassy issued travel advisories. In fact, several people returning from abroad checked with their embassies in Kuwait before flying back, and were told that there was no problem.

When direct talks between the Kuwaitis and Iraqis opened in Jeddah on Tuesday, 31 July, the three leading Iraqis in their delegation, Izzat Ibrahim, Saddam's Deputy, Sa'doun Hammadi, the Deputy Prime Minister, and Ali Hassan Al-Majeed, the supposed Local Government Minister, architect of many of Saddam's atrocities, and future Iraqi Governor of Occupied Kuwait, were surprised at the firmness of Kuwaiti Crown Prince and Prime Minister, Sheikh Sa'ad Al-Abdullah and Foreign Minister Sheikh Sabah Al-Ahmad. In fact, the Kuwaitis had come with a delegation of about 70, including oil, border and legal experts. They were serious. The Iraqi officials were apparently outnumbered by their own aircraft's crew.

The Iraqis had expected the Kuwaitis to be intimidated. Instead, they were not prepared to concede one inch of territory. They were prepared to agree to the already settled oil quota, to write off the irrecoverable debt, and lend Iraq US$9 billion, but that was as far as it went. Sheikh Sa'ad also wanted the border issue settled once and for all.

The talks did not go well, even when the Saudis reportedly offered to make up the US$1 billion difference between the Iraqi demands for cash and the Kuwaiti offer. Sheikh Sa'ad and his team left for Kuwait in the afternoon of 1 August, and the Iraqis for Baghdad earlier, apparently without even taking their leave of host, King Fahd. On Kuwait TV that night, a worried-looking Sheikh Sa'ad was seen arriving at the airport, amid reports that the talks would resume in Baghdad the following week.

In Washington, on 1 August, seven hours behind Kuwait, the US issued a statement expressing hope that the next meeting would be more successful, and that coercion and intimidation would have no future. The Americans were reportedly ready to offer forces to Kuwait, but the Kuwaitis were still reluctant to call in non-Arab troops. The State Department also spoke to the Iraqi Ambassador in Washington who assured them that there was no need to worry; Iraq was not going to move against anybody.

However, at about 2.00 p.m. Kuwait time on that day, less than 12 hours before the invasion, the latest satellite photos sent US intelligence analysts scurrying. The *Hammurabi* had moved to within five kilometres of Kuwait's northern border, and other divisions had moved in behind them. Eighty troop-carrying helicopters and gunships had been moved forward with the infantry.

By then, the border had been closed. Shortly afterwards, both the CIA and Egyptian intelligence came to the conclusion that Saddam would probably cross the border, but neither service indicated how far he would go. The assessment was clouded by continuing reports that the logistics to support an invasion were not in place, and news of the talks in Jeddah. The safety catch had been taken off the pistol; the finger was firmly on the trigger.

When the Iraqi delegation from Jeddah reached Baghdad, Saddam convened his Cabinet, the Revolutionary Command Council. It was probably then that the decision to invade, which had been made at least the day before, was confirmed. The timing of the original decision, before the Jeddah talks started, was later confirmed not only by captured Iraqi documents, but by the movement by Iraq of millions of dollars from European and various Middle East banks into the Jordanian Central Bank during the past few days.

Just three hours before Iraqi troops crossed into Kuwait, General Schwarzkopf started briefing the US Secretary of Defense and the Joint Chiefs of Staff in the Pentagon. His assessment was that the Iraqis would stage a limited move to seize Rumaillah/Ratga, Bubiyan and Warba. There was little that the US could do militarily in the short term. Furthermore, no arrangements were in place with Kuwait to come to her aid if attacked. Schwarzkopf wrapped up his briefing a mere 90 minutes before the Iraqis took the first Kuwaiti border posts.

In Kuwait, most of the soldiers who had been at the bases went home. They were not on alert, and it looked as if the talks would resume on Saturday. It was also the solemn Shia occasion of *Ashura*. Saddam would use Egypt's and Syria's tactic of the 1973 Yom Kippur war with Israel. He would attack when his targets – fellow Muslims – were at prayer.

Late that evening, the Kuwaiti newspapers for Thursday, 2 August were printed, reporting the failure of the Jeddah talks, and saying 'MORE TALKS NEEDED'. These were to get under way in Baghdad on Saturday. The reports were redundant even before those newspapers came off the presses. Saddam had pulled the trigger. His infiltrators were already poised to strike. The first bullet was on its way to the target. With Kuwaiti troops frantically trying to mobilize, Saddam's tanks were on their way to Kuwait City.

6. THE FIRST WEEK

In Kuwait City, the pre-dawn hours of Friday, 3 August were broken by sporadic gunfire. Bursts of red tracer would suddenly split the night sky, arcing beautifully, lazily, unbelievably slowly through the dark. Now and then we were shaken by a heavier explosion. It was impossible to see from where the fire originated. More often than not, the gunfire was nervous Iraqis firing at shadows. Sometimes it was far more serious. The embryonic Kuwaiti Resistance was fighting back with a mixture of amateurism and courage.

Those with family and friends who had disappeared on the first day were sick with worry. Fear and ignorance gnawed at them, sending their imaginations wild, alternating between hope and despair. The Iraqis eventually took captured Kuwaiti military men - especially officers - to Iraq. It would be several weeks before the relatives knew their men's fate. The Iraqis argued that the invasion was an internal affair within Iraq, and thus they were under no obligation to follow International Committee of the Red Cross (ICRC) reporting procedures on POWs. Thankfully, these Kuwaitis were in the custody of the regular Iraqi military, and were reasonably well treated until their release in March 1991. Not so other Kuwaiti prisoners later on.

The families of the captured Westerners were advised by their embassies within 48 hours that their men were held in hotels in Baghdad. They were alive and well, and had been visited by their Baghdad-based diplomats.

Strangely, at this stage, with the exception of women whose husbands were out of the country – particularly if they had small children – few of us were greatly concerned for our own safety, or at least we pretended not to be. Our main concern was to let people at home know that we were safe.

The media were particularly persistent as long as communications lasted, even calling at 2.00 a.m. Most of us were emotionally exhausted from the first day, and gave them short shrift. We just wanted to sleep, war or no war.

Other calls were more matter-of-fact. I recall looking out of the window late in the morning, speaking to my father on what would be one of the last international calls before the lines were cut, telling him that things had quietened down. 'There's a tank at the petrol station across the road.' I said. My father asked what he was doing. 'Looks like he's filling up,' I said.

'Is he paying for it?' asked my father, in jest.

'Can't see either way, Dad, but no one's going to argue with him.'

Most people woke early on the second day, almost wondering if the dream were over. From our vantage point over the suburbs we could see little movement other than smoke from half a dozen fires. The city streets were deserted except for the occasional military jeep, a few pedestrian soldiers, and more of the battered Iraqi coaches bringing the Popular Army in.

Kuwaitis in the Interior Ministry offices in Shamiya near the city centre held out for most of that day, but eventually surrendered. There were further skirmishes at Dasman Palace, and the Iraqis pounded the nearby Kuwait Intelligence building. We never learned for certain what happened to the defenders, but a story circulated that the Iraqis simply told them to go home.

Suburbs elsewhere were teeming with people stocking up with food, cigarettes, petrol and cooking gas, or preparing to flee the country. Shops had opened once the fighting passed, their owners deciding it was better to sell out or to give their stock away rather than have it looted. A number of car dealers reportedly started giving cars away, first to their own staff and anyone who worked with affiliated companies, and then to all-comers. The suburbs fell quiet only after dark, when a dusk to dawn curfew was enforced.

The rumour machine soon started. Before long, the Lebanese grapevine sang with the word that a deal had been struck whereby Saddam would withdraw for US$30 billion, a strip of northern land, and the non-return of the Al-Sabah. BBC World Service reports of Kuwaiti casualties suggested 800 dead and wounded. The actual number of Kuwaiti dead was less than a tenth of this, although the wounded numbered hundreds. Iraqi casualties were never confirmed, but were certainly higher than Kuwaiti.

With the loss of the international lines, and disruption to the local service, the gravity of the situation sank in. The only means of communication with the outside world was through the secure embassy satellite systems, private satellite telephones or ham radios, of which there were few. These systems simply could not serve the thousands stranded in Kuwait.

The two major KAF bases were still in Kuwaiti hands on the morning of 3 August, but only just. Most of the A-4 Skyhawks and some helicopters were still at Al-Jaber base 24 hours after the invasion. A few helicopters were at Ali Al-Salem. The last Gazelle took off for Saudi Arabia at 3.30 a.m. but later crashed in undetermined circumstances near the Saudi border, killing four Kuwaiti officers. Following orders issued the previous evening, all serviceable Skyhawks took off before dawn, and flew safely to Dhahran.

The Iraqi Air Force attacked Al-Jaber base again at 9.30 a.m. with four Sukhois, escorted by two Mirages. The Kuwaitis did not take it lying down, shooting down one Mirage with a SAM-7 'Strella' shoulder-launched missile. This was the last of eight Strellas fired by the Kuwaitis. The others had brought down three confirmed helicopters over the Air Defence Base the previous day. Two other hits were unconfirmed.

In the meantime, the Iraqi Army was moving to take over the surrounded Ali Al-Salem base. At 9.00 a.m., the front gate called the Commander's office. An Iraqi colonel wanted to talk. Base Commander Colonel Saber Al-Suwaidan met the officer, who requested that he surrender to avoid further bloodshed. Hardly in a position to argue, Al-Suwaidan agreed provided that the safety of his men was guaranteed. The Iraqi gave his word of honour, and the wounded Kuwaitis were moved through the Iraqi lines to Jahra Hospital.

Al-Suwaidan gathered his 92 officers in the Officers' Club, and the several hundred enlisted men in the base gym, although a few officers managed to bluff their way out through the Iraqis as civilian technicians. At 1.00 p.m., they were taken in trucks to the Sulaibikhat Fire Station, where the senior officers were brought before three Iraqi generals. One was a lieutenant-general, probably by the name of Baraq, who seemed to be in command of the invasion force. Another was a major-general, and the third was a Brigadier Qais. Baraq seemed particularly concerned about FROG surface-to-surface missiles which he thought were at Ali Al-Salem. Colonel Al-Suwaidan knew nothing of these, and was taken aback when Baraq virtually accused him of lying. The Iraqi's intelligence was good, but out of date. The missiles had been there, but only up to 1985, before Al-Suwaidan took over command.

At about 1.00 p.m., the Iraqis moved into Al-Jaber base, and took the surrender from the senior officer there, Brigadier Ghazi Al-Abdulrazzak.

The captive airmen from both bases had their hands tied with electrical wire, and were taken north in buses towards Umm Qasr, where they met up shortly after dark with other POWs from the Army, Navy, National Guard and Police. The hundreds of prisoners were driven around the southern part of Basra for several hours, with the Iraqis not seeming to know where to take them. Finally, at around 2.00 a.m., they arrived at a small army camp in Zubair just north of the Kuwaiti border, and were kept on the buses until dawn.

The Kuwaiti A-4s which had evacuated to Saudi Arabia were not entirely idle once they arrived.

To complicate matters for the Saudis, Yemen seemed to be siding with Saddam, at least politically, and several Iraqi Air Force squadrons which had been moved there shortly before the invasion were causing concern. With the Saudis distracted by Iraq, Yemen could conceivably move into the coveted mountainous Saudi provinces of Asir, Jizan and Najran, up to the border of Mecca Province. Early fears - however unrealistic in retrospect - that the Iraqi invasion of Kuwait might be part of a three-way conspiracy whereby Jordan would move south into the western Saudi coastal provinces of Qurayyat, Tabuk, Medina and Mecca, linking up with Yemeni forces from the south, with Iraq taking the eastern Saudi seaboard, were very real. King Hussein had a definite interest. The four north-western Saudi provinces comprised much of the *Hijaz* region of Saudi Arabia which had been lost by his family to Ibn Saud in the 1920s. At the time, anything seemed possible.

The Saudis moved a Pakistani-manned brigade to the Yemeni border, and beefed up their Khamis Mushayt air base in the south-west. Some KAF A-4s were moved there from Dhahran until the Yemeni threat dissipated.

Iraq's recent non-aggression pact with Saudi Arabia was now seen for what it was: an attempt to lull the Saudis into a false sense of security. The Saudis did not want to commit forces against Iraq in Kuwait, only to find themselves fighting what could be a three-front war against Iraq, Yemen, and Jordan.

The Kuwaiti Army was not yet quite out of the fight, although it would inflict little further damage on the Iraqis. The remnants of 15 Brigade, which had withdrawn from the Jiwan and Mubarak camps the previous evening, were still in the suburb of Keifan, with a single tank and four BMPs. Early in the morning, the Iraqis were moving armoured vehicles further into the city along Jahra Road, which borders Keifan, when Lieutenant Mohammed Al-Jassar hit one with a

Sagger anti-tank missile from a BMP. The Iraqis moved swiftly into the suburb, firing indiscriminately, even at houses. The Kuwaitis knew they could not hold out, and their presence was endangering the local civilians, so they quickly disabled their vehicles and slipped out of the area. Some of the men went home. The senior officers, now in civilian clothes, rendezvoused at the home of Lieutenant-Colonel Talal Musallem, where they were joined by the KAF Director of Operations, Colonel Fahd Al-Ameer.

Elsewhere, Chief of Staff Major-General Misyad Al-Sane and his deputy Major-General Jaber Al-Khalid were trying to put together the pieces. At one stage, Al-Khalid managed to reach the Commander of 80 Brigade in Jahra, on a mobile phone. He was still in his camp with several hundred men, surrounded by the Iraqis, and said he was going to try to break out. This proved to be little more than a dream. 80 Brigade soon surrendered.

The only major army camp still in Kuwaiti hands on the second day was 15 Brigade's, near Ras Al-Jalayh, but the Iraqis seemed happy to simply cut them off and let them wither on the vine. They posed no military threat. The Iraqis finally entered the camp on Saturday morning, over 48 hours after the invasion. They told the Kuwaiti troops, some of whom were still manning their tanks, to change into any civilian clothes they had in the barracks. They would be released to go home. Most complied, but one officer suspected a ploy, and slipped out through a back gate with some of his men. He was right. The others were taken away, to Basra, and then by train to Baghdad where they eventually joined their colleagues in the POW camps.

Throughout Kuwait, many people gathered in one central apartment or house overnight for safety and reassurance. Everyone was debating what the next step should be. Arguments ranged between sitting tight and hoping the crisis would blow over, and making a run for the Saudi border, a mere 90km away.

Saudi Arabia has always been a difficult place to enter, even with a visa. Many of us doubted the Saudis would let us in, but others figured that if they arrived at the border with the Iraqi Army at their heels, the Saudis would hardly turn them away. Official advice at the time, both from the embassies when we could contact them, and that relayed over the BBC World Service and VOA, was to stay indoors and keep a low profile. Most of us complied. Others plotted escape attempts.

Rumours of an impending evacuation of Westerners abounded. These grew from statements from embassies that they would organize evacuations at the earliest opportunity. People came to believe what they wanted to hear, assuming that evacuations were imminent. Others decided to stay, regardless, in the belief that the crisis would blow over in a matter of weeks.

The Iraqi propaganda machine was still claiming that the Iraqis had come to the aid of a group of revolutionary students to overthrow the Al-Sabah. No one believed this. When a foreign radio interviewer told me about it during one of the earlier telephone calls, my only answer was: 'That's bullshit!'

At 7.15 p.m. on 3 August, the Iraqis broadcast a communique on Kuwait TV's regular channel saying that the 'national power' had decided to leave the country, and promised a 'new era of democracy' for Kuwait. The announcer spoke with an Iraqi accent, and had been dressed up in Kuwaiti costume, but did not know how to wear it properly! He praised Kuwait's 'temporary, free government', the 'Provisional Free Kuwait Government' (PFKG). The operative word was 'temporary'. In fact, the Iraqis were unable to cobble together a press-ganged puppet PFKG until the following day. They would not appear for almost a week, and then only to offer amalgamation with Iraq.

From the second day, the Iraqis installed portraits of Saddam throughout the city. One of the first was outside the wrecked Jiwan and Mubarak camps, where the Kuwaitis had held out bravely during 2 August. Even as Iraq was telling the world that Kuwait had a new, revolutionary, indigenous government, those in Kuwait were left in no doubt where the real power lay.

A few brave Kuwaiti Ministry of Information employees managed to maintain radio and TV transmissions for several days using a mobile transmitter until the Iraqis either found the station or jammed it. It seemed pitiful resistance with the Iraqis firmly in control, but it had to be admired.

Other Kuwaitis sniped at Iraqi soldiers with small arms, or engaged in drive-by shootings, but their actions were largely ineffectual and unco-ordinated. With over 100,000 Iraqi troops in the country, the deaths of a few were insignificant, and only served to antagonize the rest. Nevertheless, the Iraqis were taken aback at the ferocity of the resistance. According to their own captured documents, they had simply not anticipated it.

Some Kuwaitis acted with an eye to the future, to a time when they could organize a more effective resistance. At great personal risk, a number of Kuwaiti military officers entered local military depots and ammunition stores, before the Iraqis had established full control, and carried off whatever weapons and ammunition they could in their private cars, including explosives and hand-held ground-to-air SAM-7 'Strella' missiles. The basis of a meaningful military resistance was already being put in place.

On the evening of 3 August, the Iraqis reached western Ahmadi, where Kuwait Oil Company's 290-bed hospital is located. They wanted to take it over entirely as a military hospital. The doctors had to explain to them that it was the only one in the immediate area, and served 60,000 oil sector employees and their dependents. The Iraqis eventually relented, and allowed the Kuwaitis to keep a small section of the hospital for civilians, but they would run the hospital themselves. For the next two months, it was full of Iraqi wounded, suffering from bullet wounds and the results of car bombings.

There was one particularly distressing incident shortly after the Iraqis moved into the hospital. Two premature babies were on respirators in the area taken over by the Iraqis. Two hours later, they were dead. The Iraqis gave no explanation, and simply handed the bodies over to the Kuwaitis. It was never clear whether they simply did not know how to care for babies in intensive care or had let them die, as such babies are allowed to in Iraq.

During the first two days, the mystery of the missing Iraqi logistics tail, which had helped convince US intelligence that the Iraqis would go no further than the border strip, was solved. Simply, there was no tail.

The Iraqis had come in with whatever they carried in their vehicles. There was little reserve supply of ammunition, or even food. They could use captured Kuwaiti fuel, but most Kuwaiti ammunition did not fit their weapons, and they had to forage for rations. For several weeks, until their logistics caught up with them, many were starving. They could not have invaded Saudi Arabia even if they had wanted to.

In fact, the Iraqis seemed to have orders to treat Saudis with particular respect. Cars with Saudi plates passed virtually unhindered on Kuwaiti roads, and when Iraqi troops on the border wandered into Saudi territory, they withdrew immediately with apologies as soon as they were challenged.

In Kuwait, we listened religiously to the BBC World Service and VOA news every hour, and tuned in to every Gulf TV station we could. To our surprise, the Gulf countries hardly mentioned the invasion for several days, and then only as the 'current crisis facing the Arab nation.' We soon gave up on VOA and settled on the BBC. The American service was difficult to pick up, and invariably at least an hour behind the BBC.

Coverage by Gulf TV initially focused on the safe arrival of the Amir and the Kuwait Government in Saudi Arabia. It then shifted to the UN debate. I distinctly remember Sheikh Saud Nasir, the Kuwaiti Ambassador to the US, being asked if Kuwait was requesting US troops. The harried diplomat, usually a picture of control, gave the simple answer: 'Yes.'

In the first hours of the invasion, centres of authority formed throughout the country. The initial focus was naturally on the embassies. People looked to them to provide national leadership in a crisis. Unfortunately, most of the embassies were just as much in shock as their nationals, perhaps more so. Most of the British diplomats could not even get into their embassy for the first two days because of the Iraqi troop presence nearby. The only men inside the compound were those who had spent the night of 1 August there, and Consul Larry Banks, his Indian security colleague, and a few civilians who had passed most of the first morning avoiding bullets on the beach outside. For the first two days, these people were busy destroying documents, and trying to find out what was going on themselves.

The Americans were more fortunate. Not counting USLOK and other seconded military personnel, and the six Marine guards, there were 26 accredited American diplomats in the country, and most of them were able to make it into their compound. The US Embassy instructed its nationals not to engage in any activities against the occupying forces. The last thing anyone needed was some Rambo drawing unwelcome attention to the Westerners.

The most effective leadership at this point came from a number of Westerners who had been resident in Kuwait for many years, some of whom had been appointed wardens of their embassies. Their function was generally to maintain contact with fellow nationals in their area, usually a suburb, and to liaise between these people and the embassy. The system had become all but dormant without the focus of the Iran–Iraq War, but now the embassies and wardens scrambled to recover.

Several individuals came rapidly to the fore. One of the key groups was established by Mike Devey, an ex-British Army NCO, Mel Gage, the printing executive who had returned to Kuwait on the ill-fated BA149, and Geoff French, a computer consultant. They formed what later became known in some circles as 'Command Central', a co-ordinating body in the suburbs, using phone lines from several adjoining houses. The concentration of three key wardens in one place was a grave security risk, but facilitated the quick consultation vital in the early days. They were later joined by businessman Brian Ashwell.

This organization became so effective that when we later heard of General Schwarzkopf's 'Central Command', we jokingly suggested suing the General for breach of copyright if he didn't hurry up and come to our rescue. Command Central was not the senior wardens' body, nor was there ever a single chief warden, but with several key men involved, it was one of the most important.

Other individuals operating on their own were just as crucial. The British Consul's wife, Liz Banks, and her children ran an information clearing house from their home on a 24-hour telephone roster, allocating people to wardens by suburb. Two other British diplomats did the same, as did the French diplomats, basing their warden network on the diplomats' residences. When all but one of the phone lines to the American Embassy failed, the retiring US Consul's wife, Luz Marina Colwell, set up a phone network from her suburban home and relayed information to the embassy by radio.

The biggest and most crucial task of the wardens was to compile lists of Westerners in Kuwait, and to determine their contact details, location, and any immediate problems. The other side of the job was to determine whether people actually on the embassy lists were in the country. The lists were hopelessly out of date as most people had failed to register at their embassies when they first arrived in or finally left Kuwait. Others were away on leave. Figures were published from Western capitals suggesting there were 3,500 British and 2,500 Americans in Kuwait. In fact, with the usual summer exodus, there were probably only about 2,000 British and 800 Americans, but it would take several weeks to confirm this. The next function was to address any immediate medical problems, food, and escape plans.

One British warden, Richard Hattersley, compiled his list by standing outside the local supermarket as people were doing their panic shopping, and approaching anyone who looked like a Westerner. Another leading warden, Scotsman Sandy Macmillan, inveigled people into coming to him. He put the word out that anyone who wanted to be evacuated should contact him. He was flooded with calls, and ended up with a list in the hundreds.

The area most in need of effective wardens comprised the coastal suburbs of Fintas, Abu Halifa, Mahboula and Mangaf between Sixth Ring and Ahmadi, all of which were out of phone contact with the rest of the country. They felt completely cut off, even abandoned. A formidable woman by the name of Dorothy Goodwin came to the fore here, helped by Kevin Fallon, a BLT man who lived outside IBI, Ray Washer, and several other Australian and British men and women. Mrs Goodwin, who was locally employed at the British Embassy, made a lot of enemies with her forceful ways, but she had the drive and courage to step into a leadership vacuum. Another British man, George Reid, and his neighbours, set up their own network in conjunction with Mrs Goodwin. Several American engineers working for Kay and Associates, technical advisors to the KAF, maintained contact with the US Embassy initially through a mobile phone.

The British in these areas had no back-up radio or accredited diplomats living nearby, so Goodwin enlisted the local US warden, Mrs Odessa Higgins, to pass messages for her to the British Embassy via the US Embassy on her walkie-talkie. This arrangement fell apart when Mrs Higgins and her husband took refuge in the US Embassy after several days, taking her radio with them. Another American, Tal Ledford, braved the 30km of roadblocks to the US Embassy to get another radio and take over from Higgins.

It was impossible to keep everyone happy in the circumstances. Many took to consuming large amounts of their home-brew alcohol. Experienced men who should have taken the lead simply fell apart, leaving the task of organizing those around them to less qualified men, and women. Strong personalities with set ideas on how to handle the crisis clashed almost violently with others. Some people complained like schoolchildren about others hiding food. Most groups worked well together, but there were significant problems. The wardens, especially in these cut-off areas, were in a no-win situation.

The British warden function was initially limited to Britons in view of the enormity of the task, and the fact that the other Western embassies, all with fewer nationals in Kuwait, were setting up their own systems. Curiously, the American warden system, which had been the best prepared prior to the invasion, virtually collapsed within days. There were several notable exceptions, but the general impression of most Americans at the time was that they simply did not have a warden system. Later, the Americans had to rely to a large extent on the Canadians, Australians and New Zealanders.

In the city centre, we began to build our own network. I made contact in the adjacent Plaza Hotel with a very capable and brave gentleman, David Cunningham, the Food and Beverage Manager. Although only a new arrival himself, he was forced into the role of General Manager when his Arab manager fell to pieces, and locked himself in his office. The Plaza's phones had failed, and David was facing an impossible job with a major hotel full of scared people. His female staff were terrified of rape. He needed all the help he could get. We were able to compile lists of his guests and staff, and passed them through our working phone lines to the respective embassies.

Several other hotels in the city centre had Westerners as guests, including the Meridien, Sheraton and Salam Palace. The American manager of the Meridien, Keaton Woods, was in contact with his embassy and had one of their walkie-talkies. The Sheraton and Salam Palace were occupied by the Iraqis, so we had to write them off. I concentrated on building links with the Plaza, and compiling a list of all the people in our apartment complex.

The Meridien was particularly unfortunate. Its newly-arrived pastrychef, a young Frenchman by the name of Rene, had poked his head out of the door to see what was going on after hearing noises in the first moments of the invasion. The Iraqis had promptly arrested him, leaving behind a distressed wife and young children with no idea what had happened to him. Apart from this, three

Egyptair stewardesses were apparently raped there on 3 August. Woods never let this be widely known, but we could well believe it. After that he kept all his female staff out of sight of the Iraqis, hidden in back rooms, and made them use back elevators and stairs.

Outside my immediate area, the largest hotel was the huge Kuwait International, with over 400 guests, 64 of whom were Westerners. General Manager Hermann Simon's greatest fear was that the Iraqis would bomb the hotel, mistaking it for the nearby US Embassy. He had spread a Red Cross flag on the roof, and set up a First Aid post in a ground floor conference room. Like other hoteliers around town, he quietly removed the lobby portraits of the Amir and Crown Prince and Prime Minister, and lowered the Kuwaiti flag. He then gathered his guests and staff in the ballroom for a briefing, asking them not to sleep in their rooms, recommending instead the basement, now stocked with bread and water, in case of fire or bombardment. He had even emptied the fuel tanks of vehicles in the car park above the basement to minimize the risk of fire. If people were uncomfortable with the basement, they were welcome to use the ballroom or even the lobby. Guests were asked not to waste food at meals in case they had to 'spend a few more days there'. Everyone was to take a shower that night, and fill up the bathtub. No one knew whether the water mains would still be connected the following day.

As the Iraqis consolidated their positions in Ahmadi and Fahaheel late on the second day, they revisited the BLT's IBI camp. It had been sealed off, with 35 British NCOs and their 73 dependants, and one young man who had the misfortune to be visiting them, plus teenage Glen Ashwell, who had been baby-sitting over the weekend, and Danny Tonks, a young boy who had come to spend the weekend with a friend.

The Iraqis had been cordial when they first entered the camp the previous day. There was some concern when they returned later that evening and posted guards, but they did not seem threatening. This changed when an Iraqi captain and a lieutenant arrived after dark on Friday with a detail of troops.

The British men were ordered to line up on the road outside their houses. Several men did not come out initially as they were reluctant to leave their families. To move things along, the senior British NCO, WO1 Mike Haynes, sounded the fire alarm siren. This sent the Iraqis into a frenzy, suspecting it was some kind of secret signal or diversion. They entered the houses, and dragged the remaining men out bodily. They were then marched off to the mess, without an opportunity to say goodbye to their families or retrieve their passports. The Iraqis also wanted to take three of the older boys, but one of the men, WO2 Jerry Blears, convinced them otherwise.

After a great deal of protest, 28 of the 35 men were loaded into an 18-seater minibus, and the others into two cars stolen from the camp, and taken away. The oldest male left behind in the camp was a 16-year-old boy.

There were only three Iraqi guards on the bus. The British soldiers could have overpowered them easily, but were concerned for their families. The vehicles drove to a command post in the adjacent Mina Al-Ahmadi refinery, and then back to Fahaheel where they almost returned to the camp. The Iraqis were actually lost. They eventually arrived at the Ahmadi Governorate around midnight, where the men were reassured that if they just gave their names and addresses, they could return home within half an hour. Unknown to them, this was a classic Iraqi ploy to get their co-operation.

They saw an Iraqi major-general who told them they were going to Baghdad for their own protection. They said that if they were going anywhere, they wanted their families with them. The general initially refused even to consider this, assuring them that their families would be safe, but after heated argument, it was agreed that they would return to IBI for the families. They got as far as the access road to the camp before meeting an officer who refused to have anything to do with the new arrangement. The men, greatly concerned for their families, were then driven off into the night to the Basra Sheraton, where they arrived the following day.

The women back at IBI were stunned when their men were first taken away. They rang around the camp on the internal phones to check that everyone was OK. No one had been harmed, but the Iraqis were still in the camp, and soon started coming into houses, saying they wanted the military uniforms, which the men had destroyed on the first day. The women were near to panic, not knowing what had happened to the men. Whenever they asked the Iraqis when they were coming back, they were told: 'a few hours', then 'tomorrow', then 'in a couple of days'. On one occasion, several of the women heard bursts of automatic fire nearby, and feared that their men had been executed.

The women and children gathered in six houses for security. They tried unsuccessfully to call the BLT Commanding Officer, Colonel Bruce Duncan, or his deputy, Wing-Commander Wes Jones, but the areas where the officers lived were affected by the disruption to the local phone system. They then tried to reach the British Embassy, unsuccessfully. One woman was able to reach the home of the British Consul, Larry Banks, where his wife Liz was. Liz could communicate with the embassy, but the BLT women could not initially speak directly to anyone in authority.

There was little anyone could do for those at IBI at the time. With the curfew in effect, even British diplomats could not get to the camp, and other British men living nearby could not go there in case they too were arrested.

The BLT husbands' fears were justified. The families endured a night of terror huddled in the six houses, behind barricaded doors and barred windows. As soon as the Iraqi officers left the camp, the soldiers started banging on the doors of the houses and rattling the windows. Drunken troops hot-wired some of the British servicemen's cars, and played dodgems within the camp until they ran out of petrol. When an officer made a brief appearance, the women complained, and he stopped the men. However, later on, after he left, the soldiers entered some of the empty houses, looting whatever they could find of value, and vandalizing the homes.

During the first two days, a large number of people of all nationalities simply drove down the three main roads to Saudi Arabia. The Iraqis, through their as-yet-unseen puppet PFKG, declared the Saudi border closed, but were initially unable to deploy enough troops to enforce this. The same announcement said that people were free to leave Kuwait for Iraq, but did not say whether they could go any farther. Saudi Arabia had opened its borders to Westerners, although many other nationalities slipped through as well. Kuwaitis and other GCC nationals did not need visas. Nevertheless, the Saudis were aware of the risk of Iraqi infiltrators slipping into the Kingdom with Kuwaitis and other Arabs, and subjected them to close scrutiny.

News filtered back on the Gulf States' TV, BBC and VOA that people were getting out. However, many escapees did not inform their embassies in Riyadh, and information on those who did was not always relayed back to Kuwait. This created a great deal of uncertainty as to whether people had actually got out, died in the desert heat or had been detained by the Iraqis. In fact, no Westerners died on escape attempts until the following week.

The first few days were the window of opportunity for escape. The official advice against going was to cause great bitterness in the months to come.

At the Airport Hotel, concern amongst the BA149 passengers and crew mounted as the crisis entered its second day. A senior Iraqi officer ordered everyone to assemble in the lobby at 8.00 a.m. He assured BA Captain Clark that they were not prisoners, but this was greeted with scepticism.

Life was eased a little when the hand luggage was brought off the aircraft an hour later, but the passengers' and crew's main luggage remained on the aircraft and was never recovered. Staff from the Malaysian Embassy visited their nationals at about 10.00 a.m., and the French four hours later, buoying up the passengers' spirits. People in authority now knew where they were. The Indian Embassy visited the following day; the Italians, Canadians and Greeks later. The passengers did not see any British diplomats until they had left the Airport Hotel. The embassy did phone, but it was overwhelmed trying to service the large British community and deal with the BLT crisis. The local BA managers, Laurie O'Toole and Trevor Owen, were looking after the passengers better than any diplomats could.

At 4.00 p.m., 208 passengers, mainly Indian nationals, and some crew, were moved to the Regency Palace and SAS Hotels, on the Gulf coast, leaving 161 in the Airport Hotel. This eased the overcrowding, but the doors were still locked and the guests were advised not to leave the premises for their personal safety. When some intrepid French and Italians found an open door and ventured forth to sightsee and chat with the soldiers outside, they were returned at gunpoint before they had gone a hundred metres.

Those who were not initially moved to other hotels passed their time mainly in boredom, interspersed with flurries of excitement as columns of armoured vehicles passed nearby, or Iraqi helicopters landed at the airport. They were periodically asked to muster in the lobby for transfer to other hotels, only to return to their rooms after several futile hours. On 4 August, some passengers observed the Iraqis stealing the first Kuwait Airways (KAC) jets, and flying them out. The looting was in full swing, and official.

Throughout the first two days, the Arab states conducted frantic diplomacy in an attempt to resolve the crisis. King Hussein and President Mubarak met in

Alexandria on 3 August. The King had spoken to Saddam at 1.00 p.m. on the day of the invasion, and was reportedly told that Iraqi troops would leave Kuwait soon, provided there was no condemnation from the Arabs, and no outside interference. It was in Saddam's interests to keep the crisis in the Arab arena, but the wide-ranging ramifications of the invasion made this impossible. There was little expectation that Saddam would withdraw from all of the country, but some believed he would at least evacuate the urban area, and establish a new line at Mutla'a.

The Arabs had most to lose from outside intervention, and so tried desperately for several days to broker a peaceful solution. This explained the lack of immediate condemnation of the invasion from their camp.

King Hussein and President Mubarak tried to convene a limited Arab summit in Jeddah for 5 August with the participation of Saudi Arabia, Egypt, Jordan, Iraq and the Kuwaiti Amir. The King arrived in Baghdad at 9.30 a.m. on 3 August, reportedly obtaining Saddam's agreement to attend the mini-summit, and withdraw. Iraq announced that it would start withdrawing from 5 August, but there was to be no question of restoring the Al-Sabah.

With King Hussein visiting Saddam in Baghdad, Iraqi Vice-President Izzat Ibrahim was in Riyadh, telling King Fahd that Kuwait was history. Iraqi Prime Minister Sa'doun Hammadi delivered the same message in Cairo to the Arab League Foreign Ministers. It was becoming increasingly obvious that Saddam had no intention of restoring the *status quo ante*, and was trying to use the Arab League to forestall broader international action.

The Egyptian version of 3 August says that King Hussein failed to insist on two preconditions for the Jeddah mini-summit with Saddam: the withdrawal of Iraqi forces, and restoration of the Al-Sabah. Mubarak would not support the summit before these two conditions were met, and Saddam was not prepared to meet them before the summit. In fact, Saddam was not even prepared to have the Kuwaiti Amir at Jeddah. When the Arab League, under pressure from Saudi Arabia and Syria, condemned the invasion and called for an unconditional withdrawal on the evening of 3 August, any residual hopes for the mini-summit quickly evaporated. The condemnation was not, however, unanimous. Of the 21 members, six besides Iraq did not vote for it: Djibouti, Jordan, Libya, Palestine, Sudan and Yemen.

This was not quite the end of Arab efforts to resolve the crisis. Yasser Arafat flew to Baghdad on 5 August, and was asked by Saddam to tell the Saudis that Iraq was ready to talk. Arafat then went to Cairo to consult with Mubarak, who was becoming more openly hostile to Iraq. The Egyptian President was incensed at Saddam not only because of the invasion, and the treatment of Egyptians in Iraq. He had been lied to when Saddam told him he would not invade, and had unwittingly passed those lies on to the Kuwaitis and Saudis, thus lulling them into a false sense of security. Embarrassed and humiliated, Mubarak was in no mood to concede anything to Saddam.

There was a growing realization in Arab capitals that force would be required, and that a solution where Saddam kept half of Kuwait was no solution. Morocco promised a battalion to Saudi Arabia, and Egypt considered its own contribution. By the evening of 3 August, King Fahd had given up on an

Arab solution. The crisis was far too big for that, and the perceived threat to his country too great. He realized that if force had to be used to defend Saudi Arabia – and perhaps later to liberate Kuwait – there was only one source this could come from. He started sounding out the Americans through his Ambassador in Washington to determine whether the Americans would come in, with sufficient force to do the job, and then leave when the job was done.

In Kuwait early on the morning of Saturday, 4 August, the British NCOs' wives at IBI ventured tentatively out of the houses they had sheltered in after a night of fear and desperation. They still had no idea what had happened to their men. A few Iraqi soldiers were wandering around the camp, but they did not initially bother the women, some of whom went back to their own homes. They were horrified at the wanton looting and vandalism, and returned quickly to the shelter of their colleagues.

At about 9.00 a.m., just over 12 hours after their husbands had been taken away, the women heard from the British Embassy that the men had been taken to Baghdad. The news was both a great relief and a source of concern. They wondered how they would be able to rejoin the men, but they first had to survive in their current situation. The embassy had been unable to send anyone down to protect them, so they stayed behind barricaded doors, watching the Iraqis outside through gaps in their drawn curtains, tuning in to the BBC news, and checking around town on the phones with anyone they could contact.

Throughout this first day the Yemeni caretaker of the compound, Mr Mahmoud, did his best to care for the women. He could have fled to safety with his wife and six small children, but chose to stay behind. He spoke with an Iraqi officer, and obtained permission to go into town to buy supplies for the women. They collected the money, and Mahmoud went off shopping.

At the time, the seven British officers in the country were having their own problems. Colonel Duncan's house was surrounded by soldiers camped inconveniently around it, seemingly ignorant of who he was. On the same day, the Iraqis entered the Pearl Marzook building in Salmiya where three of the remaining British officers lived. The Iraqis knew they were there. One Major Ben Tyler escaped after a telephone tip-off from another officer as the Iraqis entered his apartment. A second major, Alex Boyd, and Army Air Corps Captain Colin Dunscombe were captured and taken to the KAC Club for initial questioning, and then overland to Baghdad via the Basra Sheraton.

That same afternoon, after lunch in the Basra Sheraton, a group of 60 captured Westerners, including the 35 BLT NCOs from IBI and the civilian men captured during the previous two days, had been flown from Basra to Baghdad in a four-engined Antonov *Candid*. The BLT men had arrived just as the civilians were going to lunch, dressed only in the shorts, T-shirts and sandals they were wearing when taken away from IBI the previous night.

Upon arrival at Baghdad's Al-Muthanna inner city airport, they were welcomed like honoured guests in the VIP suite, and told they only needed to ask to receive anything they wanted. 'What about being sent home?' said one man, but this was not on the wish list. They were then separated into four groups: the Americans and the lone Canadian, all oilmen; the 35 British military and six civilians, including two oilmen; Rene the Frenchman; and Herbert Hunsdorf, a West German surveyor captured from Bubiyan Island.

Each group went to a different hotel; the British to the Mansour Melia, the Americans and Canadian to the Al-Rasheed, Rene to the Palestine Meridien, and Herbert to the Oberoi. They were taken in by a side entrance, given coffee and cake, and then a buffet supper. The large groups received a pep-talk from an Iraqi major, who expressed the hope that they would be comfortable. Their requests to contact their embassies were denied. The major was unable to tell them what would happen, only that he was following orders.

Eventually, the larger groups were split up, and brought through the kitchens and service lifts to rooms on the upper floors, with two men to each room, and guards at the end of each corridor. The room phones had been removed, so they were unable to contact anyone else in Baghdad.

Back in Kuwait, at IBI, the BLT NCOs' families spent a second terrifying night alone with only the teenage boys and Mahmoud for protection. By then, news of their husbands' arrival in Baghdad was on the BBC. They were in the Mansour Melia Hotel, where they were soon visited by the British Military Attaché in Baghdad, Colonel John Cochrane.

Besides the foreign civilians, the Iraqis were holding the Kuwaiti military POWs at Zubair. The Iraqis also had a problem. After announcing that revolutionaries had taken over Kuwait, and called in Iraqi forces to help, they could not find a single Kuwaiti political figure – opposition or otherwise – to go along with their charade. Even the head of the Kuwaiti branch of their own Ba'ath Party had refused. They did, however, have the POWs.

At about 6.00 a.m., 4 August, the Kuwaiti POWs were let off the buses that had brought them to the camp four hours earlier, and put into huts. A number of Iraqi official cars, all white Mercedes, then arrived at the camp, and the officials started trying to talk several of the senior officers into acting as members of a Provisional Government of Kuwait. They would have nothing to do with it. The Iraqis then moved on to some of the younger officers, seemingly at random. Several of these men were taken away to Baghdad in the cars, to form the Provisional Free Kuwait Government (PFKG) under duress.

This puppet PFKG was headed by an unknown Colonel Ala'a Hussein Ali, with a cast of seven equally unknown Ministers. Colonel Ala'a had a particularly heavy workload, being Prime Minister, Commander-in-Chief of the armed forces, Defence Minister, and Minister of the Interior.

At first, the legitimate Kuwaiti Government, now in exile, denied that Ali was even a Kuwaiti, citing his accent. He was in fact a 31-year-old Baghdad-educated Kuwaiti accountant, of Iraqi origin, who worked for a local cardboard manufacturer. As a Navy reservist subaltern, he had been captured on the morning of the invasion, and forced into his new role under duress.

Another, more senior Kuwaiti Naval officer, Chief of Naval Forces Colonel Qais Al-Saleh was also having an unusual day, and clocking up an inordinate amount of travel between Baghdad and southern Iraq. After his encounter with Iraq's Lieutenant-General Hussein Kamil Majeed on the afternoon of the invasion, Al-Saleh had been kept by Iraqi Intelligence in Basra until the following afternoon. That evening, he had been driven overnight to Baghdad's Al-Rasheed Army Camp, the capital's biggest. He arrived early Saturday morning, just as most of the other Kuwaiti POWs were being let off the buses at Zubair. Al-Saleh was initially questioned by an intelligence brigadier about the organisation of the Kuwaiti military. He laughed at the Iraqi. 'You've captured my entire country. You already know everything!'

At 9.30 a.m., a Colonel Mumtaz, the Al-Rasheed camp commander, came to visit Al-Saleh. 'Come,' he said, 'You will be sent back to Kuwait with all your officers.' Al-Saleh had been in Baghdad barely three hours, and now the Iraqis were sending him back! Sure enough, he was soon reunited on a minibus with his four lieutenant-colonels. The Iraqis suddenly seemed very friendly. They were taken to the VIP lounge of Baghdad's inner city Al-Muthanna airport, through which the captive Westerners would pass later that afternoon, and the Iraqis began to make apologetic comments about unfortunate misunderstandings, and disputes between brothers being things which can be solved. The Kuwaitis grew increasingly puzzled.

They were flown to Iraq's Shuaiba Air Force Base, near Zubair, where, unknown to them, the other Kuwaiti POWs were being held. In less than 24 hours, Al-Saleh and his men had been taken 600km from Basra to Baghdad, and then back again almost to where they had started from. The solicitous Iraqi treatment continued, with a good meal being served. In retrospect, it was apparent that they were being softened up as candidates for the PFKG, and the Iraqis who were looking after them were unaware at the time that their colleagues at Zubair already had Ala'a Hussein Ali as their puppet.

That evening, at 6.00 p.m., the other Kuwaiti POWs at Zubair were bussed first to Shuaiba Railway Station. Al-Saleh and his officers were also taken from Shuaiba Air Force Base to the station in stolen Kuwait Public Transport Company buses, where they met their colleagues. The combined group then went on the overnight train from Basra to Baghdad. On the train, they put together the story of how the puppet government had been formed.

In Baghdad the following morning, the officers were taken to the Al-Rasheed Army Camp, where Al-Saleh had been barely 24 hours earlier, and the enlisted men to Takrit, Saddam's birthplace. Upon his arrival at Al-Rasheed, Al-Saleh met a puzzled Colonel Mumtaz again. 'What are you doing here?' asked the Iraqi, thinking that Al-Saleh had been sent back to Kuwait, and that Kuwait had been restored under a new government. 'Ask your own government!' replied an equally puzzled Al-Saleh.

This time, however, the conditions - at both Al-Rasheed and Takrit - were not as pleasant as on Al-Saleh's earlier visit. There was one toilet for up to 100 men, open sewers, no air conditioning or even electric fans in the heat of summer, and only bread, lentil soup, and dirty water for rations. They had no blankets or mattresses, and only the clothes they were captured in. The Kuwaitis would remain in Al-Rasheed and Takrit for another three weeks, until they were moved by train to Mosul.

In retrospect, it was probably sometime during Saturday, 4 August, that Saddam decided, in the face of strong international condemnation that he was unlikely to get away with what seems to have been his original plan of taking all of Kuwait, installing a puppet government in what would become a disarmed vassal state comprising southern Kuwait, returning the Kuwaiti POWs, and keeping the entire northern half. The momentum of his military's moves and his public relations campaign was such that a staged partial withdrawal would take place the following day, and be broadcast as planned, but from then on, he seemed resolved to keep all of the country. The message from Arab and Western capitals was that he had to get out of all of the country, period. In response, he would keep all of it. In this were sown the seeds of his defeat. Had he left southern Kuwait at that point, the perceived threat to Saudi Arabia would have been greatly reduced, and the Coalition which eventually defeated him may never have been put together in the way it was. By keeping everything, he lost everything.

During the first few days of the occupation, the 60 embassies and diplomatic missions in Kuwait scrambled to recover from the initial shock. A major problem for the ambassadors was in finding an Iraqi in authority to talk to. The senior Iraqi Army officers in Kuwait had apparently been told to stay away from the major Western embassies. The Iraqi diplomats themselves maintained the charade of a takeover by revolutionary Kuwaitis, with Iraq merely lending a hand, so they simply changed the accreditation to the new puppet Government. The regular Iraqi Ambassador was nowhere to be found.

The roles of the embassies changed drastically as soon as the crisis broke. Almost immediately, they lost most of their autonomy. Crisis Centres were set up in their respective home capitals to manage the crisis from a higher level. The embassies themselves became primarily consular arms of the Foreign Ministries, and a means of 'flying the flag'. This had some advantages in that it allowed the embassies' actions to be more effectively co-ordinated with the other arms of foreign and military policy, and the embassies in Baghdad, but it also meant that more decisions had to be referred to superiors at home who often had less of a grasp on the situation than people on the ground.

The British Embassy held their first wardens' meeting on Saturday 4 August, and a second later in the week. The main topic was sending messages back to families at home through the embassy's communications system. This was impossible with over 1,000 British family units. The Americans also held meetings every three to four days with phone updates in between.

The embassies could tell their wardens very little at the early meetings. This was extremely frustrating for communities with an insatiable thirst for information and advice. Many people came to believe erroneously that the embassies were holding back information, or were paralysed. The diplomats' main advice was to lie low, stay indoors or close to home, stock up on essential supplies, and not risk escape attempts across the desert. 'Keep a low profile!' became a local catchphrase.

This last piece of advice was hotly disputed as people had made it out to Saudi Arabia in the first couple of days, and were continuing to do so. However, the embassies were obliged to give such advice for the overall safety of their communities. In the long experience of their capitals, aggressors in modern conflicts generally allow foreign nationals and possible witnesses to leave as soon as possible after the initial fighting. Few expected that the Iraqis would do otherwise. Furthermore, the Iraqi troops in the city did not seem to be harming Westerners; but no one could guarantee the behaviour of nervous troops in the desert. Several terrible rapes - including one of the British wife of a Kuwaiti who was gang-raped by six Iraqi soldiers in her home in Ahmadi - would come to light later, but at the time the troops seemed relatively well behaved. More importantly, a cross-desert trip in a Kuwaiti summer is a dangerous undertaking at the best of times. It was a venture only for hardy souls with desert-driving experience and four-wheel drive vehicles. To have recommended such escapes to thousands of urbanites in family cars, many with small children, would have been irresponsible.

From the very beginning of the crisis, the approaches of the American and British embassies differed significantly. The Americans initially adopted a siege mentality, and tried to bring all their diplomats and dependents into the compound. Within days, over 100 individuals were living on the premises. Other Americans seeking refuge were housed in the Consul's house in the suburbs. The British, however, would not accept any civilians into their compound, and most of their diplomats remained in their homes. They argued, not quite accurately, that they did not have the same space as the Americans, and could not feed a large number of refugees. They did have space, but also a much larger community. If they had let some people in, they would have had to let in everyone, plus people they were responsible for such as the Australians, Irish and New Zealanders who did not have local embassies.

Few of the American diplomats ventured beyond their fortified walls during the first week. The British Ambassador, however, told his men to 'put on the old school tie, and get out there and find out what's going on'. Two of them, Consul Larry Banks and John Raine visited American Ambassador Nat Howell on 4 August. He was apparently shocked that they were out and about. They were equally shocked at the condition they found him in.

The US Ambassador's office in Kuwait at the time was essentially an underground bunker, built after a 1983 terrorist attack on the compound. It was literally a windowless steel box in a basement, suitably decorated inside, accessible only through a staircase and a series of security doors. At their first meeting, Larry and John found Ambassador Howell sitting at his desk with a Marine guard and his M-16 rifle on the settee beside him.

Howell was fortunate to have as his Deputy Chief of Mission (DCM) a very capable young woman, Barbara Bodine. He needed this. His number three man, Economic Counselor Emil Skodon, and the senior US military advisor, Colonel John Mooneyham, would be holed up in the Japanese Embassy for most of the first two weeks. To protect both the Japanese sheltering them and the Americans themselves, communication was limited to one quick daily phone call. The US Consul, Gale Rogers, had just arrived in town. Her predecessor, Bill Colwell, had his household packed up, ready to go. In effect, most of Howell's senior people were either incommunicado, or new.

A perception quickly developed among the US community and some people in their embassy that a serious leadership vacuum existed, partially attributable to the fog of war and the siege mentality. Those who were in the compound at the time saw it as Miss Bodine stepping bravely into a leadership gap for which she was unqualified. According to several senior military people there - who had the luxury of not being in the hot seat - there seemed to be little effective delegation, and poor staff work. All decisions seemed to go directly from Miss Bodine to everyone else, without proper consultation. Any information fed into the system seemed to disappear into a black hole, with little or no feedback.

For most of the first week, the Americans lived in fear of the Iraqis coming over the wall. The Marine guards were still armed and in uniform, and would have resisted if the Ambassador had felt this was necessary. With the embassy looking increasingly dangerous, and becoming uncomfortably crowded, the diplomats reversed their earlier policy and advised people to stay in their own homes. Refuge was limited to US diplomats, locally-hired staff, the military, their families, and desperate cases.

Other countries were also giving refuge. The Swiss had 27 people in their tiny mission, most of whom had brought nothing useful with them. Others were in the diplomats' residences. The Japanese, with their famed community discipline, were perhaps the most notable case of this. Almost the entire community of 295 Japanese, including the 14 diplomats and the 26-strong stranded JAL aircrew under Captain Hiroshi Shibata and Chief Stewardess Masako Ando came into the embassy during the first week. They lived in the basement with the 16 Americans who had arrived on the first day. Paradoxically, this discipline would eventually prove to be their undoing.

At IBI, where the families of the BLT NCOs' wives had just spent their second night alone, conditions continued to deteriorate. On the morning of Sunday, 5 August, the soldiers started looting empty houses wholesale, and a few began to harass the women. On one occasion, five of them broke into a house. One held a knife to the throat of the RSM's wife, Elaine Haynes, and molested her in front of four terrified children. Another woman in the house was also attacked. Fortunately, an Iraqi NCO came by. He was infuriated at the younger men, and marched them away. The women never saw them again.

At the time of the incident, Mrs Haynes was on the phone to the British Embassy – the lines now working – and left the receiver off the hook. The diplomats on the other end could hear everything, but were helpless. Panic spread throughout the rest of the women.

By late afternoon, the embassy had obtained Iraqi permission for Commercial Attaché Don Macauley to go to the camp. He arrived with Ambassador Michael Weston, and they went straight to the Haynes' house, where they were greeted by a barrage of righteous criticism for not getting there sooner. Weston and Macauley spoke to the Iraqi officers who had appeared at the camp, and things quietened down. There was no further harassment or joyriding in stolen vehicles.

The women berated Weston for the advice to sit tight when they could have escaped on the first day. He tried to explain to them that the embassy had thought the Iraqis would just come over the border, not all the way into Kuwait. It was very difficult to get the women, in their fear and their concern for their men, to focus on the situation as it was. In the end, all Mr Weston could do was reassure them that their men were safe in Baghdad, and that the embassy was doing its best to move them to a safer location. Macauley was ordered by the Ambassador to stay with the families and to accompany them wherever they went or were taken, whether it was Saudi Arabia, Iraq, or even Bahrain. The following day, the embassy started making attempts to move the families to the Messila Beach Hotel, or the Kuwait International, which was closer to the embassy.

Harassment of women was not confined to IBI. On the Sunday evening we learned another lesson in the dangers of occupation. We had heard stories of Filipinas being raped, and suspected that many of them were true. The Iraqi soldiers we encountered occasionally in the corridors of our complex were friendly to us, but often asked about Filipinas.

I had just returned to my apartment from an improvised church service in the adjoining Plaza Hotel when there was a frantic visit from Paul Kennedy, the Irishman one floor above. Paul's Thai wife was out of the country at the time, but his sister-in-law, two other Thai girls, and the husband of one of the girls, Pon, were sharing his large apartment.

At 4.45 p.m., Paul and Pon had noticed a line of tanks going down the street. They went to the other side of the apartment complex to see which way they were going. As luck would have it they encountered two soldiers prowling the corridors. They asked for Paul's ID, read the apartment number from it, and insisted on accompanying the men back to the flat. They noticed the girls, showing obvious interest, but left.

Ninety minutes later, the two soldiers returned with three colleagues, one of whom was in a red beret, and knocked on the door. Paul initially refused to open it. The girls ran to prepared hiding places as the soldiers started trying to kick in the door. Paul opened it, and was rewarded with a backhanded slap across the face for the delay. One soldier clamped Paul's chest with his arm, and put a large knife under his chin as the other soldiers started searching the apartment. Paul and Pon were then moved into the dining room, as one of the soldiers covered them with his gun.

Within minutes, they heard screams as two of the girls were found in the bedroom. The red beret, who had been involved in the search for the girls, nodded to the soldier who had been covering the two men, unfolded the stock of his Kalashnikov, released the safety catch, and pointed it at them from five metres away. The other man went to the bedroom.

Suddenly, there were sounds of a scuffle from the other end of the apartment as the third girl was found. She came running down the corridor, screaming at the soldiers in Arabic they were not good Muslims. Paul told her to stand by him, and say they were married. She did so, maintaining her tirade against the soldiers, as the man who had found her came into the room.

The red beret, who had looked uncomfortable about the whole affair, became upset, and started shouting towards the bedrooms. The other men shouted back angrily, in Arabic. Paul, Pon and the third girl heard the sounds of doors slamming. Both girls at the other end of the apartment had been released by the soldiers, and had run into the bathroom.

After some discussion between themselves, the soldiers ordered the men and the third girl to sit on a sofa, then sat down with them, and asked for tea.

Incredibly, one started pulling watches, which had obviously been looted from the shopping complex downstairs, from his pockets and ammunition pouches, and pressing them onto the men. It may have been in apology, or a bribe so that they would not be reported. Eventually, they left.

After this, we heard stories of soldiers breaking into an Indian family's home to rape a maid, and tremendous courage as the head of the house told them they would have to kill him first before they touched her. The troops said they didn't want his own daughters, who were also there, but what was the maid to him? The man persisted, and the soldiers backed down.

In another incident, Iraqi soldiers apparently entered the Residence of Filipino Ambassador Mohammed Tamano to rape Filipinas taking refuge there. Mr Tamano initially tried to stop them, until they threatened to beat him up. Two older Filipinas then stepped forward and told the soldiers to take them rather than the younger women. They went with the men, and all news of them was lost. Such courage was unfathomable.

Rape was not confined to Asian women, and the presence of husbands did not necessarily deter the troops. A German woman in Salwa was raped in front of her husband on the same day. The man was tied up and had to watch the ordeal. After that, the soldiers forced the couple to make them tea, just like the visitors to Paul's apartment. Several British women, and probably other Western, Asian and Arab women were raped, but most women chose to keep their ordeal within their families. Many of the spouses of these women also suffered terribly, and continue to do so today, with a profound sense of failure and impotence at their inability to defend their women.

The Iraqi Army, however, seemed to officially condemn rape. During the move of some BA149 people from the Airport Hotel to the SAS Hotel on 3 August, a stewardess of Indian extraction was indecently assaulted. Captain Clark complained to the Iraqi officer in charge, who had the woman identify the soldier. According to several unconfirmed reports, he was made to kneel throughout a full day on the beach, in the boiling sun – with August temperatures reaching over 40 °C – and then shot by firing squad at dusk.

This news, when it circulated, was of no consolation to those women who were raped. Besides, to which Iraqi authority could they complain? Nevertheless, it may explain the Iraqi rapists' consistent habit of offering their victims expensive looted watches, perhaps in a feeble plea for silence.

The broader Western problem at the time was not so much the loss of Kuwait, but the Iraqi threat to Saudi Arabia. Saddam did not have to invade Saudi Arabia to influence its oil policy. He could sit in Kuwait, dictate the OPEC price and production levels, and extract non-repayable loans. The threat of force was more useful than the exercise of it. The risk – however unjustified – was that the Saudis would adjust to the new set of realities. Saddam would then keep Kuwait, eventually riding out world condemnation. No one could oblige Saddam to leave Kuwait without strong Saudi support. This meant access to land bases, something which the Kingdom had consistently declined to grant. More importantly, Saddam would have the time and money to complete his weapons of mass destruction, and become an even greater threat.

The Saudi dilemma was more stark. They could either appease Saddam, or rely on the US to defend them. Neither option was palatable. Appeasement could compromise Saudi independence, whereas bringing in the Americans would open the country to charges that it was incapable of carrying out its principal role of defending the Holy Cities of Islam.

Along with the perceived military threat to Saudi Arabia, Saddam's invasion of Kuwait provided the Americans with a perfect reason to act against his strategic weapons programme, which had been causing great concern to them, Israel, and most of the Arab States. The three-fold objective thus became the defence of Saudi Arabia and the economic stability arising from its low oil price policy, the curtailment of Saddam's weapons programmes, and the liberation of Kuwait. The latter objective was to be the means of achieving the other two.

On 3 August, NSC Advisor Brent Scowcroft met with Saudi Ambassador Prince Bandar Sultan. The Saudis' main concern was that if they allowed the Americans in, they must do the job properly, and then leave. That evening, 48 hours after the invasion, Bandar was briefed on US military options and shown intelligence on the Iraqi forces. The Americans were adamant that the Iraqis in Kuwait posed a threat to the Kingdom. Bandar briefed King Fahd directly. The Americans were serious. Saudi and American interests converged sufficiently in this new crisis that most of the old rules no longer applied.

President Bush spoke to King Fahd the following afternoon. The King had already decided after consultation with his advisors to ask the Americans in, but did not yet formally approve the move. He asked Bush to send a briefing team. Bush also reportedly spoke to the Kuwaiti Amir that evening, promising that the US would help win back his country. On 5 August, Defense Secretary Dick Cheney left Washington for Jeddah with a delegation including US Ambassador to Saudi Arabia Charles W. Freeman, General Schwarzkopf, his Air Chief, Lieutenant-General Horner, and a CIA man.

In parallel with the military moves, an economic blockade was established to backstop the diplomatic condemnation. Turkey agreed to close the twin Iraqi 1,200km pipelines which run across its territory to the Mediterranean, pending a UN sanctions resolution. These pipelines, with a capacity of 1.7 million bpd, carried two-thirds of Iraq's exports. The Saudis also considered closing an 800,000 bpd Iraqi pipeline across Saudi Arabia to the Red Sea port of Yanbu, but held off until they had decided to accept US forces. In any event, the unofficial embargo on Iraqi oil was preventing uplifts from the terminals. On 4 August, Canada and the EC approved a broad range of sanctions including an oil embargo, and an assets freeze. The following day, Japan embargoed Iraqi and Kuwaiti oil. Support was building for formal sanctions.

That same evening, with the UN Security Council moving towards the sanctions resolution in response to Iraq's indifference to Resolution 660 demanding its immediate withdrawal, Saddam used his puppet PFKG, in a sinister change from its earlier statement allowing all foreigners to leave Kuwait for Iraq, to broadcast that:

'Countries which resort to punitive measures against the PFKG and brotherly Iraq should remember that they have interests and nationals in Kuwait. If these countries insist on aggression against Kuwait and Iraq, the Kuwait Government will reconsider

the methods of dealing with those countries. They should not expect us to act honourably at a time when they are aggressively conspiring against us and our Iraqi brothers.'

It was a thinly veiled threat to trade off the foreigners in Kuwait against sanctions, frozen assets, and the likely military build-up. In Baghdad, Saddam reportedly advised that shutting off Iraq's oil exports would provoke an attack on Saudi Arabia. He could hardly have given the Saudis more reason for asking in US troops, and the US for being willing to send them.

People in Kuwait were on an emotional roller coaster. Most of those who had been undecided about leaving now firmly resolved to get out if they could.

A glimmer of hope appeared in Kuwait on 5 August when Iraq announced it was withdrawing on schedule, as promised two days earlier. TV footage showed tanks being loaded onto transporters, and driving along Kuwaiti motorways with smiling, waving Iraqi soldiers perched on top.

The staged withdrawal fooled no one. Some Iraqi troops were indeed leaving Kuwait, but they were merely re-deploying. The Republican Guard units that had led the invasion were pulling back to the Iraqi side of the border but other forces were replacing them in Kuwait. Meanwhile, Special Forces and other units remained firmly in control in Kuwait City.

Suspicion - and wishful thinking - grew within Kuwait that Iraq had now realized it had bitten off more than it could chew, and might withdraw to Mutla'a after stripping bare the Kuwaiti infrastructure. This was soon dispelled as the Iraqi civil administration started moving in. The Iraqis had well and truly come to stay.

There was delight late that evening when we heard on the BBC World Service that George Bush finally seemed to be talking tough. Up to that point, his main message had been that he was not considering military intervention. Now, in an interview on the White House lawn, under pressure from reporters, a new line came out. 'This aggression against Kuwait will not stand,' said Bush. No longer was he just drawing a line in the sand at the Saudi border. He was now talking of reversing the invasion, implying that if sanctions did not work – as no one in Kuwait expected them to – then he would go further.

At 7.00 a.m. on Monday 6 August, with Dick Cheney still on his way to Saudi Arabia, the BBC World Service carried the first news of US military moves. The US Third Fleet had been diverted to the region, B-52 bombers were said to be on alert, and there was talk of bombing Baghdad. For those in Kuwait, the prospect of being caught up in the middle of a battlefield, and being expendable in the overall scheme of things, suddenly became very real.

Even as the Iraqis announced they were withdrawing from Kuwait, they were moving more Western hostages from Kuwait to Baghdad. The Salam Palace Hotel was cleared out in the morning of 5 August. The Kuwait Sheraton followed that evening.

In Baghdad, most hostages had already had some contact with their diplomats. The US Embassy had found out about the Americans in the Al-Rasheed, and were visiting them. They had passed on news of the British in the Mansour Melia to their colleagues at the British Embassy.

The local British Consul, Pauline Waugh, had been to the Mansour Melia three times during the night of 4 August. Each time, the receptionists had denied any knowledge of the hostages. However, another British couple staying at the hotel confirmed that they had seen a bus-load of Europeans coming in. The diplomats had badgered the hotel people until they admitted to the hostages, and took them up to see the BLT men during the night.

When the diplomats returned the next morning, this was the first opportunity for the hostages to find out what was going on, and to send messages back to their wives and children. Their consular officials would be allowed access to them for the next ten days. They learned that the Iraqi borders were closed, all internal and international flights into and out of Iraq had been stopped, and the fighting in Kuwait was over. Most importantly, according to Iraqi TV, the Iraqi Army would start withdrawing soon. This was a great relief to the men, as it implied that their families would be safe.

These prisoners were not allowed to leave the hotels, or to communicate with other regular guests. It was an eerie existence. US Consul Melvin Ang was only able to tell them that he thought they would be there for a long time, but he could not say for how long. The British felt similarly.

The regular guests at the hotel were largely unaware of the hostages' plight. It was not until several days later, when someone commented about an American woman swimming in the pool in her clothes, that they realized they were hostages from Kuwait: the woman had nothing else to wear. The following day, the Baghdad residents brought in swimming costumes, and left them in the changing rooms for the hostages. The diplomats brought in other clothes, and toiletries and other requirements donated by the local Western communities, the diplomats themselves, and the US Embassy Marine guards.

The following morning, before Dick Cheney and his party had even landed in Saudi Arabia, the American, British, French and German BA149 passengers in the Kuwait Airport Hotel were separated from the others and informed that they would be taken to the Messila Beach Hotel, and well looked after. A number of these people with spouses of a different nationality were left behind at the Airport Hotel for the time being. The larger group of 58 had their passports taken from them. They were indeed bussed to the Messila Beach Hotel. However, once there, they stayed on the buses, and linked up with another coach carrying staff and guests of the same nationalities from that hotel. Both groups were then taken to Basra and later Baghdad to become part of the Human Shield.

This was a ploy repeated time and again by the Iraqis with groups of prisoners. They would gather them together and ensure co-operation by promising good news, only to reveal their true intentions once the group was firmly under control.

The remaining 100 or so persons at the Airport Hotel, comprising the BA crew, Australians, Indians, Italians, Malaysians, New Zealanders and Swiss, spent the rest of the day observing the Iraqis stealing more KAC planes, until they had taken all 15 at the airport, flying them north, and also shipping out stolen airport equipment.

As soon as news of the removal of people from hotels reached the embassies, West German diplomats visited all other hotels still containing their nationals, and took them to the homes of German residents of Kuwait, or diplomats. The Americans, British and French left their people in the hotels for the time being. The British were even still planning to move the BLT families into one.

Later that day, Saddam used the PFKG puppet government to announce again that: 'All foreigners and Kuwaiti nationals are free to leave for Iraq, for any reason whatsoever, using the land route. The airport has been closed.' This meant that we could not leave by land to Saudi Arabia, or by air, not that any planes other than Iraqi ones and stolen KAC aircraft were leaving Kuwait at the time. The announcement did not say that people could leave Iraq once they got there. In the charade being played out by Saddam, that would be for the Iraqi Government itself, not the PFKG, to decide.

This announcement sent a flurry of concern throughout the Western communities in Kuwait. Until then, they had thought they might eventually be able to leave through Saudi Arabia, but it now seemed that any evacuation would have to be through Jordan, via Baghdad. This was an entirely different proposition. Saudi Arabia was a mere 100km drive; Jordan was 1,600km away, across an unfamiliar and potentially hostile country, in midsummer.

Saddam then further complicated the issue. He ordered the borders of Iraq closed. Kuwait's borders with Saudi Arabia were already shut, but not entirely sealed. Now refugees, including hundreds of thousands of Asian and Egyptian guest workers, could not even leave Iraq. The prospects of any sort of evacuation organized with Iraqi co-operation faded rapidly.

In the early hours of Monday, 6 August, the Amir of Kuwait made his first televised appearance since the invasion. It was transmitted into Kuwait by GCC TV stations. The Amir looked a shell of his former self, as he read from notes. He had lost not only his country, but also his youngest brother, Fahd, and had narrowly escaped capture and possible death himself.

There were mixed feelings in Kuwait about this address. Most Kuwaitis appreciated the wisdom of the legitimate Government getting out, but there was an underlying bitterness that the Government had not negotiated its way out of the invasion happening in the first place. The Al-Sabah's image had taken a beating, but its legitimacy was unquestioned.

That same morning, with news of the previous day's round-ups from the Sheraton and Salam Palace hotels on the grapevine, and in the light of the ominous PFKG threat, Western guests in some of the other hotels were ordered to their rooms by the management, and asked to keep a low profile. Later, news of the Airport Hotel and Messila Beach Hotel pick-ups increased the concern. Senior Iraqi officials, both civilian and military, started moving into the major hotels. As they did, those Westerners who could moved out.

On the afternoon of Monday, 6 August, the US *Chargé d'Affaires* in Baghdad, Joe Wilson, met with Saddam. His brief was to determine Saddam's intentions as to Saudi Arabia, and secure the safety of US nationals in Kuwait.

Saddam was obviously preoccupied with Dick Cheney's imminent visit to

Saudi Arabia. He sought to reassure Wilson that he had no designs on Saudi Arabia, reminding him of his non-aggression treaty with the Kingdom, and accusing the US of using the crisis as a pretext to put troops into the Gulf. He considered the invasion of Kuwait a *fait accompli*, and the Al-Sabah as history. Saddam argued that the invasion of itself posed no direct threat to American interests, and said he was prepared to safeguard such interests once the Americans spelled them out.

He then went on to explain to Wilson that his promises in July to King Hussein and President Mubarak not to invade Kuwait had been conditional on the 31 July and 1 August Jeddah talks with the Kuwaitis, and that the invasion had been launched only when these failed, and Iraq had 'received a call for help from Kuwaiti revolutionaries'.

When Wilson later pursued the matter of his citizens with Iraqi officials, he was told that Saddam had yet to make a decision. All foreigners from Kuwait had freedom to travel anywhere in Iraq, but no one - including Iraqis - was allowed to leave Iraq. This restriction applied not only to Americans, and Wilson was told to rest assured about the fate of his citizens in Kuwait. Saddam was presumably waiting for the outcome of Cheney's meeting with King Fahd in Jeddah, and seemed suspicious that the Americans only wanted their people out of the way in the event of a bombing attack on Baghdad.

On 6 August, the Iraqis ordered everyone in Kuwait to return to work, or face loss of pay and termination of their jobs. This announcement was treated as a joke. It was a poor attempt to establish the fiction that Kuwait was functioning normally under benevolent Iraqi rule.

Virtually the entire economy had been at a standstill since the invasion, except for essential services, barbers, a few scattered mechanics, and grocery supermarkets. A few factories kept going, but only long enough to shut down their furnaces safely, while essential services workers had been ordered to remain at their posts by the Amir from exile in Saudi Arabia. With these exceptions, the Kuwaitis stayed away from work in droves.

Some Kuwaitis did attend work, but only to secure computer files and other records under the very noses of the Iraqis who had no idea what a byte was. One story circulated about an Iraqi walking into an office of the National Bank of Kuwait, and seeing computer terminals on the desks. 'Why,' he asked, 'does everyone have a television? Do they sit here all day watching TV?'

In Jeddah, on the evening of 6 August, American Defense Secretary Dick Cheney and his delegation met King Fahd and his advisors.

The Saudi king was shown American satellite photos of the Iraqi forces on his border, although only a trained analyst could tell what the vehicles in the sand were, or how capable they were of moving south. By this time, an estimated 200,000 Iraqi troops and 2,000 tanks were in Kuwait, together with seven SCUD missile launchers. It was insufficient to invade and occupy such a large, alerted country. Saddam could reinforce these troops in a few weeks, although in doing so he would dangerously expose his Iranian flank, and a move into Saudi Arabia would leave his supply lines hopelessly vulnerable.

The Iraqis were deployed in a thin line about 10km north of the Saudi-Kuwaiti border, with few reserves behind them. It was essentially a 160km-long screen to seal the border, with a tank or APC every 500 metres or so. The main units were the 12th Division near Salmi in the west, and then the 5th, 10th, 11th, 17th and 6th Divisions across to the Gulf, all either armour or mechanized infantry. They were regular Army, not Republican Guard, but still a formidable force, even if they were not organized to move south with vigour.

The Iraqis were under no illusions that the Americans would fight if Saudi Arabia were attacked. It was an entirely different scenario to the invasion of Kuwait. Even the CIA man with Cheney felt that the threat to Saudi Arabia was real, but not imminent. In fact, a story later emerged that the CIA man had a briefing that there was at most a 30% chance of the Iraqis moving into Saudi Arabia, and that Schwarzkopf had ordered him to hand this over to him so that he could deliver it to King Fahd himself - which he didn't. It was further later alleged that the Iraqi bulldozers which were digging defensive, static positions for the tanks had been airbrushed out of the satellite photos.

King Fahd had already decided to invite the Americans in, but he needed to let them understand they would be coming to his country with the eventual objective of crushing Saddam, and then leaving. At the end of the meeting, King Fahd told Cheney that his forces were welcome. Cheney called Bush to advise him of this at 10.00 p.m. Kuwait time, Monday, 6 August.

In the early hours of Tuesday, shortly after King Fahd and Cheney concluded their meeting, and as more Western hostages from Kuwait arrived in Baghdad, the UN Security Council passed Resolution 661 imposing the toughest sanctions in its history on Iraq, and freezing all Iraqi and Kuwaiti assets abroad. Three hours later, the Turkish pipelines were officially closed, followed by the Saudi line. On that day, for the first time in its history, neutral Switzerland imposed sanctions. With the occupation only five days old, the foundations of the triple pillars of diplomatic condemnation, economic embargo and military deployment against Iraq had been laid.

The deployment of Western troops, primarily naval forces, started even before Cheney met King Fahd, but navies alone would be insufficient to counter Saddam. This needed heavy tank and ground forces, and land-based aircraft.

The aircraft carrier USS *Eisenhower* and its battle group were sent to the Eastern Mediterranean. Its sister carrier, *Independence*, which had been on its way to the Gulf at the time of the invasion, was moved from the Indian Ocean to the Straits of Hormuz. The French sent a frigate to the area. On 6 August, Britain announced that it was sending frigates and deploying RAF jets to Bahrain. The American Military Airlift Command and ground forces, including the US 82nd Airborne Division's readiness brigade, were alerted. Australia soon followed suit with a frigate, a destroyer, and a supply vessel.

Cheney called on President Mubarak of Egypt on his way back from Saudi Arabia on 7 August for consultations, and to clear *Eisenhower's* passage through the Suez Canal into the Red Sea. He then visited King Hassan of Morocco, the first Arab leader outside the Gulf to have offered troops.

Within hours of King Fahd's invitation, 48 US Air Force F-15s were on their way to Saudi Arabia. By 1.00 a.m. Kuwait time, the US 82nd Airborne Division were taking off for the same destination. The aircraft carrier USS *Saratoga* and the battleship USS *Wisconsin* and their escorts left for the Gulf shortly afterwards. The 7th Marine Expeditionary Brigade, the men who would actually liberate Kuwait itself, were despatched to the Gulf. This was the nucleus of I Marine Expeditionary Force, which would grow to an 84,500-strong force of two ground divisions, an aircraft wing, and supporting units.

The US had to square the perceived threat to Saudi Arabia, which provided the basis for the dispatch of the forces, with Saddam's assurance to Joe Wilson in Baghdad that he would not invade the Kingdom. This was simple. No one believed Saddam any more.

In Kuwait, we followed these developments with increasing dread, and a sense of being trapped in the middle as the two sides dug in. Any sense of adventure which some may have felt in the first few days quickly disappeared as the prospect of military action became more likely.

We also had to cope with rumours. I was telephoned by someone with news that US Marines had just landed in Salmiya, a coastal suburb. Another friend staying with German and Swiss diplomats was asked to confirm a rumour that the Americans intended to bomb Kuwait in two hours. Another story was of two Kuwaiti aircraft either returning from Saudi Arabia or flying from Al-Jaber KAF Base, and bombing the occupied Ali Al-Salem KAF Base, or Jahra police station. Someone else reported Allied ships being sighted off the coast.

With the removal of people from four of the Kuwait hotels, the fear of detention rose markedly. People had visions of Japanese World War II internment camps, of families being split up, as had already happened to the BLT. After five days of lying low, and half-hearted escape attempts, the mood among most of the Westerners changed to one of desperation, and determination to get out of Kuwait, to Saudi Arabia.

This fear was exacerbated by news of opinion polls in the US suggesting that the public wanted quick military action against Iraq. This was impossible at the time, other than a quick bombing campaign, but few people in Kuwait appreciated this. In fact, we expected it. On 8 August, the BBC announced that the US was launching its biggest overseas deployment since Vietnam. Bush obviously meant business. Many people in Kuwait feared being caught in the middle of a shooting war within days, or even hours.

People had started to pack in the first days in the expectation of an evacuation. As the crisis worsened, they refined this. Most had individual 'run-for-your-life' bags, with essential papers, a change of clothes, and absolutely necessary items. It was usually something which could be carried as hand luggage. Then there was a suitcase which people expected to have to leave behind in the event of anything other than an orderly evacuation. Most groups also had a bag with food, water, medical supplies and room for a short-wave radio. Somehow, the preparedness allayed some of the fear.

At the time, British Ambassador Michael Weston was still trying unsuccessfully to secure the safety of the BLT NCOs' wives and children at IBI, now under the protection of Commercial Attaché Don Macauley. He had more success with Colonel Bruce Duncan, the Commanding Officer of the BLT, who was with his wife and family at his home near Shuwaikh Port and the administrative offices for the Kuwait Coastguard. The Iraqis were encamped around his house. They were not deliberately surrounding the house, or overtly threatening the family. It was just where they had chosen to set up camp.

Duncan was particularly concerned for his wife and teenage daughters, and that the Iraqis would discover his identity. Several unsuccessful attempts were made to move him before Weston and Consul Larry Banks drove up to the house on 7 August in an official car, Union Flag fluttering from the flagstaff. They told the Iraqis around the house that they had come to take one their subjects and his family to a safer location. The Iraqis wanted to know who he was. 'Just an engineer,' said Weston. The Iraqis did not press the matter, and allowed the family to leave with the diplomats.

However, they had gone no more than 200 metres before they were arrested at a roadblock, and taken to a nearby Iraqi headquarters. After a very tense two-and-a-half-hours, a sharp young Iraqi lieutenant-colonel arrived, and delivered a lengthy explanation as to why Iraq had come to assist the oppressed people of Kuwait. He then apologized for the inconvenience, and seemed on the verge of releasing them when he suddenly asked the Ambassador 'Is this man your military attaché?' Mr Weston looked the Iraqi straight in the eye, saying, 'We don't have a military attaché in the British Embassy here', without elaborating. The distinction was barely close enough to the truth not to be a lie. They were allowed to go.

The British were not the only people moving their military that day. The six members of USLOK and their families who had not taken refuge in the Japanese Embassy, 12 people in all, headed by Lieutenant-Colonel Tom Funk and Major Fred Hart, moved into the US embassy. They were joined by the Naval Liaison Officer and his three Navy communicators.

A number of the US military people went into their embassy against their better judgement. They had been monitoring the tense situation there on their radios, and were unconvinced that it was the best place to be. The diplomats were unable to tell them whether it was safe to drive to the compound without being picked up by the Iraqis, and they were haunted by the memory of the Iranian hostage crisis. They felt safe in their homes, where they had at least a fighting chance of staying hidden. But the order came directly from the Ambassador. In their words, they 'saluted smartly, and moved out'.

The military personnel were shocked at the sight that greeted them. About 175 people were now living in the compound, housed mainly in the small six-man Marine barracks, the Ambassador's Residence, and a few storerooms. There seemed to be little organization. Hart's wife volunteered with a State Department wife to do the cooking, whilst her husband, Funk and CWO4 Dave Forties, another USLOK man, sat down to plan where to get the food from. At the time, those on the compound were living off whatever food they had brought in with them, supplies in the Ambassador's Residence and Marine barracks, and the snack bar.

As soon as the military men discovered that they could move around, especially on their diplomatic passports, Forties and Hart went on shopping trips with Commercial Attaché Paul Scogna. They first returned to their own homes and emptied out the freezers and cupboards, and then stocked up with literally tonnes of food from The Sultan Center and Americana Safeway warehouses. Some merchants allowed them credit, but where cash was required, they had to take up a collection from the people in the compound.

Living conditions in the compound were crowded, and relations became strained living in such close proximity to others, under the constant fear that the Iraqis would come over the wall. Everyone who had moved in had been asked to bring whatever food, bottled water, and cooking gas bottles that they could. Those who did had it taken from them and placed in a communal supply. Resentments festered. Those who had been organized were annoyed when they had to scrounge for items they had originally supplied.

Another group of American men who could have been of critical importance to the Iraqis were also called in to the embassy. These were six engineers who worked for Raytheon Corporation or the Kuwait Ministry of Defence on the Improved-HAWK anti-aircraft missiles, some of which had been captured intact by the Iraqis. They became known later as the 'HAWK men of Kuwait'.

Five of these men, Felipe Alayon, Lloyd Culbertson, Tal Ledford, Bennie Mitchell, and his wife and infant son, and Guy Seago reported to the embassy. A sixth, Tom Kreuzeman, who had been the only American advisor to muster with his Kuwait colleagues on 2 August, refused. He later became legendary for his feats in hiding from the Iraqis.

In the embassy, the five men were told to destroy any documents, including their passports with visas, which could link them to Raytheon or the Kuwaiti forces. They were given replacement embassy IDs, but not diplomatic passports as these are generally only issued from Washington. They were then debriefed on the operational status of the HAWK missiles. The diplomats told them, 'You are with us. You will go out with us whenever we do.' They were put to work answering the phones to American citizens. Their instructions were to tell American callers that there was an evacuation plan, that they were on it, and that everyone would go out together.

With the increasing desperation to get out of Kuwait to Saudi Arabia, those people who had not already done so rushed to retrieve their passports from their employers' offices where they are usually held for safe-keeping, sometimes breaking into their own work-places if they did not have the keys. Rumours circulated of bedouins who knew the desert offering to lead convoys out for KD500. They may have had some Kuwaiti takers, but no known Westerners had to pay a guide. A number - probably no more than a score - were in fact guided out free by bedouins. Many more would have paid if they had the money, and could connect with a guide.

Not everyone heeded the official advice to stay put. The number of people making escape attempts across the desert into Saudi Arabia soared. The Iraqis seemed to be allowing out non-Kuwaiti Arabs and Asians, but not Kuwaitis and Westerners. Most people were turned back before they got anywhere near the border, but over 100 Westerners made it out into Saudi Arabia that week.

Throughout the first six days, the Iraqis tried to bluff their way through the crisis. It became obvious that Saddam had expected to get away with his seizure of Kuwait if the US did not object too forcefully. For most of the first week, Saddam maintained the transparent charade of an internal Kuwaiti revolution, with Iraqi troops coming to the assistance of Kuwaiti republicans.

Saddam certainly expected the sanctions. He had prepared by buying in huge quantities of basic food supplies – on credit – and by transferring most of Iraq's funds from Western and Japanese banks to Jordan. Sanctions would make life uncomfortable for the Iraqis, but not impossible, and would eventually break up under the combined pressure of an Iraqi international PR campaign and the world's thirst for cheap oil. The Saudis would simply have to accept the new menace on their borders, and follow Saddam's bidding. The Kuwaitis, for their part, could either become Iraqis, or another exiled people.

When his threats of retaliation against foreign nationals failed to forestall the embargo, or prevent the despatch of Western forces, Saddam began implementing his Human Shield policy in earnest.

In the meantime, the Kuwaiti Resistance was emerging as a popular, broad-based movement, incorporating almost every Kuwaiti in the country to one extent or another.

The most obvious were the active military groups who staged nightly hit-and-run attacks on the Iraqis with sporting pistols, rifles and weapons salvaged from army, navy and police armouries. The Iraqis could not travel safely at night in small groups. Lone vehicles in the suburbs would be destroyed with weapons as primitive as Molotov cocktails.

The Kuwaitis were ingenious. A Kuwaiti friend came to my apartment with a colleague asking for guns from the Western embassies, or if I knew where they could get cyanide to inject into oranges to offer the hungry Iraqi troops. I could not help them with weapons, nor would the embassies have risked their positions by doing so, but some of their colleagues must have found the poison. Within days, the Iraqis were refusing any food offered to them by Kuwaitis.

The resistance was also passive. Men started growing their beards in a classic Arab show of disapproval. This was not a hollow gesture. Apart from certain religious groups, Kuwaiti men usually sport only a moustache. The Iraqis knew this, and ordered them to shave the beards, pulling them out with pliers if they didn't. Children painted anti-Iraqi graffiti on walls.

At midnight on 7 August the Kuwaitis assembled on their rooftops in the first mass-organized demonstration to shout defiance at the Iraqis and 'Allah u-Akhbar!' (God is Great!). They were apparently encouraged to do so at this time by a rumour that spy satellites were passing overhead then. The satellites probably saw little, but the Iraqis certainly heard it. After five days of occupation, the Kuwaiti message was that they were most unwelcome.

The Kuwaiti women played perhaps a more effective role than the men in the early days in showing the world that they were a people worthy of salvation. Throughout the first week, the women, playing on the proper Arabic courtesies to women, held several peaceful demonstrations against the Iraqis, with pictures of the Amir and Crown Prince and Prime Minister, and the national crest. These demonstrations were filmed and photographed, and the record smuggled out of Kuwait, but the demonstrations were not without risk. On several occasions, the Iraqis first fired over the heads of the demonstrators to disperse them, and then directly into the crowd. At least one young college student, Miss Sana'a Al-Foderi was killed. An engineering student, Abdulrahman Hassan, was killed in a separate demonstration.

Other women carried weapons and ammunition for the men, both under their *abayas* and hidden in their cars. Some even engaged in the attacks. In the early days, women could get away without being searched at roadblocks. It was actually a more dangerous mission than the attacks themselves, as if discovered they would have had no chance of escape.

Less dangerous forms of Resistance included Kuwaiti youths removing street signs at night to confuse the Iraqis, and distributing newsletters by fax, or slipping them under doors. The circulars urged people not to report for work in areas other than essential services. They also addressed the need for hard information. Some bilingual Kuwaitis translated BBC World Service bulletins into Arabic, and included them in the newsletters. Other people raised the Kuwaiti flag over their houses, and hung pictures of the Amir and the Crown Prince and Prime Minister from road signs and bridges.

Most importantly, the structure for a meaningful resistance, loosely co-ordinated with the Kuwaiti Government-in-exile in Saudi Arabia, was being established. Several members of the Al-Sabah family had remained in Kuwait, notably Sheikh Sabah Nasir, the brother of the Kuwaiti Ambassador to the US, Sheikh Athbi Fahd Al-Ahmad, the son of the Amir's brother who had been killed on the first morning, and the Crown Prince and Prime Minister's daughter Hussa. Others who had been out of the country at the time, including Sheikh Ali Salem Al-Ali, the son of the Commander of the National Guard, returned across the desert from Saudi Arabia through the Iraqi front line. Two key senior officers, Major-General Abdul Wahab Al-Muzain and Brigadier Yousif Mishari also infiltrated back into Kuwait in the first week, with full authority from the Kuwaiti Government-in-exile.

Together with Major-General Mohammed Al-Bader, who was working for the Cabinet, and a number of other military officers who had escaped capture, such as KAF Colonel Fahd Al-Ameer, 15 Brigade Commander Colonel Mohammed Al-Harmi, and retired National Guard Major-General Khalid Boodai, these men started building a Resistance network to harass the Iraqis and maintain the welfare of the Kuwaitis and expatriates under occupation.

The civilian and military wings of the Resistance eventually established a form of higher committee with representatives of all major groups in Kuwait, particularly the military, merchants, Shi'ites, and various Islamist groups. They tried to divide up the work, and to allocate responsibility for various suburbs. With people not working, they would eventually need money for food. Sources of funds such as the takings from the Kuwait National Petroleum Company petrol stations were tapped, and policy guidelines for distribution of food from local co-operative societies and funds were laid down. This committee was never in a position to give orders, but by the end of the first week, they had a network covering all of Kuwait.

For their part, the military wing tried to impose some order on the *ad hoc* military campaign by establishing contact with military officers in every area, and co-ordinating operations. Colonel Fahd Al-Ameer emerged as the key military leader. They ended up with about 34 groups throughout Kuwait, with varying degrees of activity and varying levels of co-ordination.

Despite this organization and the involvement of senior individuals, the Resistance was made up of ordinary Kuwaitis. One of the most active was a US-educated Ministry of Foreign Affairs computer expert, Miss Asrar Al-Qabandi. She was a stoutly-built pint-sized powerhouse of energy who had almost single-handedly established the Khalifa School, Kuwait's first private institution for autistic children. During the first days of the occupation, Asrar and her friend, epidemiologist Miss Hind Al-Bahar, had moved into the school, an old villa overlooking the coast at Salmiya. There, they plotted Iraqi positions to send out to Allied forces in Saudi Arabia, but when it became apparent that the Marines would be a long time coming, they turned their attentions to helping people survive the occupation.

Sheikh Ali Salem Al-Ali had obtained a satellite phone with which he planned to re-establish communication with the Government-in-exile. The two young women went looking for a safe place to operate it from. On the fourth day of the occupation, they came to the home of an oil executive, Ahmad Khajah, in the suburb of Mishref. He arranged for them to use the nearby house of Mrs Abbasa Behbehani as a base. The first communications with the Kuwaiti Government-in-exile, and with the Kuwaiti Embassy in Washington, commenced at the end of the first week.

The Resistance could never hope to defeat the huge Iraqi war machine on its own, but it would soon demonstrate a courage, ingenuity and resilience in ordinary Kuwaitis that surprised even many of their own people.

On the morning of 8 August, the British Embassy's efforts to relocate the BLT families from IBI to somewhere safer finally bore fruit. At 10.20 a.m., the women were given 20 minutes to be ready to leave for Kuwait City, and told to take only one bag per family. The Ambassador was coming down to the camp with a detail of Iraqi troops to escort them. There was a mad panic to pack and repack, and to find transport from the vehicles the Iraqis had been playing with. Only one in four of the vehicles on the compound was usable.

At the time, in an attempt to lighten the atmosphere and maintain morale, Macauley had dressed up in cut-off shorts, a BLT T-shirt, his Royal Navy tie, odd socks and shoes, and a woman's large straw hat. When Ambassador Weston arrived and saw him he exclaimed, 'My God, you've flipped too!'

On Macauley's order, 73 women and children piled out of their homes, crowded into a dozen vehicles, and locked all the doors and windows. They were ordered to follow the diplomats to the Kuwait International Hotel, 40 km north, in convoy.

The drive was an eye-opener for the women. They had been confined to the camp since the invasion. The sight of the tanks and troops dug in all the way along the coast, and the signs of damage, particularly stripped cars, took them aback. The city itself was even more distressing. To get to the hotel, they had to pass a number of burned buildings, some of which were still smouldering.

The contradictions of the invasion became even more stark when they checked in. The women were astounded at the contrast between the polite, courteous Iraqi officers at the hotel, and the rabble they had had to deal with. They felt safe in the hotel. It was close to the embassy, and General Manager Hermann Simon was successfully retaining an air of near-normalcy.

On Wednesday, 8 August, at 4.00 p.m. Kuwait time, President Bush announced the deployment of US forces to the Gulf, emphasising that the action was being taken to assist the Saudi Government in the defence of its homeland. Their mission was defensive, not offensive. Much to the disgust of those in Kuwait, he specifically said that the troops were not being sent to force Iraq out of Kuwait. That task seemed to be left to sanctions and the economic embargo. We were delighted that these had been imposed in principle, but did not believe they would work, at least within a reasonable timeframe.

Bush's four objectives were Iraq's immediate and unconditional withdrawal from Kuwait, the restoration of the legitimate Government, the security of the Gulf region, and finally, the protection of American lives. A number of Americans in Kuwait, including my neighbour, were incensed that they were the last item on the list, but that was the way it had to be.

King Fahd's speech of the following day explaining his decision to call in foreign forces also gave us little hope. While demanding the restoration of Kuwait and its Government, he too stressed that his military moves were defensive only, and threatened no one. At the time, with only a brigade of Saudi National Guard between Saddam and the Saudi heartland, it was a wise stance, but not what we wanted to hear. Without action, we were stuck.

8 August was also Victory Day in Baghdad, to celebrate the 1988 ceasefire in the Iran-Iraq war.

Several of the hostages in the Baghdad hotels had a rude awakening at 5.00 a.m., with the sound of heavy-calibre gunfire nearby. With the news of the deployment of US forces, some of the them initially thought that the war had begun. They were under direct Iraqi guard in Baghdad, and held little hope for their own survival if this happened. However, there was a simpler reason for the gunplay. As part of a curious Iraqi means of celebration, the Iraqis were firing off various weapons around the city. It took the Mansour Melia hostages a while to pinpoint the source of the noise, but they eventually located it as an anti-aircraft gun about a kilometre away, on the banks of the Tigris. They could see the muzzle flashes, but the absence of tracer lines indicated that the gun was firing blanks. All the street lights were still on. The war had not yet started.

That day, Iraq's ruling Revolutionary Command Council finally gave up the charade of an internal revolution in Kuwait by issuing a resolution annexing Kuwait as Iraq's 19th Province, renaming Kuwait City as 'Kazimah'. In line with the apparently original plan to take just the northern part of the country, Kuwait north of Mutla'a Ridge was added to Basra Province, with the remainder designated a separate Province of Kuwait. The annexation was to be formally ratified on 28 August. According to Iraq, the PFKG, which only 30 hours earlier had declared the 'Kuwait Republic', had requested that Iraq absorb Kuwait, thus re-establishing what Iraq claimed was the correct historical position, or 'the return of the branch to the root.'

Since their embassies had first made contact with them, the hostages in the Baghdad hotels had been allowed visits by their diplomats three times a day. The officials had done a great job of bringing in games and books to replace the *Baghdad Observer*, the propaganda sheet provided by the Iraqis as the only reading material, and were trying to find the hostages changes of clothes. One game brought in by the diplomats was particularly appropriate in the circumstances. It was called RISK, and involved armies from various countries conquering certain regions of the world.

Most of their first day had been spent in their rooms, watching Iraqi TV and recounting their various experiences. They were initially served meals in their rooms, but then allowed to eat in the banqueting hall as the Iraqis relaxed a little. By the 6th, they were allowed to use the swimming pools. Although they were no longer confined to service lifts, they were always under escort when they were away from their floors, and kept in small groups.

The following day, they were joined by the two BLT officers who had been captured from their homes in Kuwait , and the first people moved up from the hotels in Kuwait, including some BA149 passengers. Both of the British officers were in uniform. The Mansour Melia now held over 150 British, with a lesser number of Americans at the Al-Rasheed, and a sprinkling of French and West Germans at the Meridien and Oberoi respectively.

On the evening of 8 August, the hostages in the Baghdad hotels had a ringside view of the Victory Day celebrations on the Tigris River, with fireworks over the water, and a dozen illuminated river craft cruising by. The most bizarre thing about the spectacle was the absence of spectators. From their hotel balconies, the hostages could see normal traffic on the bridges over the river. There were no crowds on the river bank, despite the glorious summer evening. The Iraqi people cared little for Saddam's mini-Nuremburg.

7. THE SECOND WEEK

The UN was swift to condemn Saddam's annexation of Kuwait, declaring it null and void in Security Council Resolution 662 on 9 August.

The coincidence of Iraq's Victory over Iran Day, and Kuwait Annexation Day did not go unnoticed. Saddam seemed to be digging himself a bigger hole. At the time, despite a ceasefire, he was still officially at war with Iran. An estimated 150,000 Iraqi troops were still deployed along the Iranian border. Saddam's actions were unfathomable. He was not on speaking terms with Syria, the Turks were staunch members of the infant Coalition, and he was opening another front in Kuwait. His only friendly neighbour was Jordan. All others either had guns pointed at him, or were blockading him.

We had actually expected Iran to take advantage of the situation and at any moment drive Iraq from Iranian border territory it still held. We even expected the US Marines to come marching up the road from Saudi Arabia within hours. Iraq would not have had the reserves to hold Kuwait, and repel the Iran. After eight years of aiding Iraq against Iran, Kuwaitis now prayed that the Iranians would attack. We did not see how Saddam could survive.

However, he was at his best with his back against the wall. By the end of the second week, he would have removed the Iranian threat, at a price, and generated substantial political support in the Arab world by playing the Palestinian card. At that stage, the only Western countries that had actually committed forces were the US, Britain, France and Australia. Others would soon follow suit, but it was by no means clear that the world would eventually have the resolve to expel Saddam from Kuwait.

Saddam's first victory of the second week was not entirely of his own making. It occurred when the Arabs shot themselves in the foot at a hastily convened and acrimonious Arab League summit in Cairo on 10 August.

The summit split almost down the middle. Egypt, Lebanon, Syria, Morocco and the GCC States sided with Kuwait, while Jordan, Palestine, Yemen, Algeria, Libya, Mauritania and Sudan abstained. Tunisia, which had served as the League's headquarters since Egypt's expulsion after the Camp David accords - and perhaps annoyed that the League had met in Cairo for the first time since then - did not attend. The Gulf Arabs were furious, especially after the substantial support they had given the Palestinians and poorer Arab states over the years. The abstentions were not necessarily votes for Iraq, but from then on, the Arab League's irrelevance was sealed.

Significantly, the chief of the Iraqi delegation, Taha Yassin Ramadan, went to great lengths to reassure the Saudis that Iraq had no hostile intent against them. The Iraqis were trying hard to limit Saudi enthusiasm for inviting in foreign forces.

Saddam capitalized on this Arab League division by issuing his so-called initiative of 12 August. Iraqi TV and radio gave this a big build-up, hinting that it involved withdrawal from Kuwait. This proved to be partially true, but Saddam linked it to Israeli withdrawal from the West Bank, Gaza, Golan Heights and south

Lebanon. It was an impossible bargain, but it demonstrated his astuteness. With some justification, he insisted that if UN resolutions against him were to be enforced, then so too should those against Israel.

This seemed quite reasonable to many in the West, now increasingly concerned at Israel's brutal suppression of the *intifada*. To many non-GCC Arabs who felt strongly about the Palestinian issue, the image of a strong Arab leader standing up to the West was heady stuff. Thousands of Jordanians and Palestinians rallied behind Saddam, even volunteering to fight in Kuwait, while Kuwait itself became irrelevant. Popular support for governments in those non-GCC Arab states that officially supported Kuwait was eroded.

The major exception was Egypt, where President Mubarak's press increased its reporting of the Egyptian workers murdered in Iraq over recent months. Egyptian opposition to Saddam actually became quite strident. Mubarak said that he saw no possibility of a peaceful solution. Few of us believed he was serious. At that stage, he had earmarked only 5,000 troops to go to Saudi Arabia. Nevertheless, hopes for a peaceful solution were fading rapidly.

In Kuwait, after a week of the Western ambassadors trying to find someone to talk to, the Iraqis finally provided them with Mr Abdel Jaber Ghani, a former Ambassador to Kuwait, and Dean of the Diplomatic Corps. Ghani was now in uniform, with a reputation for closeness to Saddam, and toughness.

His first meeting with the ambassadors was not particularly pleasant. He told them that their embassies could continue functioning only up to 24 August. They could work until then as consular arms of their missions in Baghdad, which, said Ghani, was the appropriate place for embassies in what was now one country. No political work would be allowed. That was the sole province of the embassies in Baghdad. If his troops believed that the diplomats were sheltering anyone other than their own nationals, they would feel free to enter the missions. More seriously, the citizens of Australia, Canada, New Zealand, the US and Western Europe could not leave Kuwait, except to go to Baghdad. Everyone else was free to go to Jordan, through Iraq, but not through Saudi Arabia. After 24 August, the diplomats would have to relocate to Baghdad, whence they would be allowed to leave Iraq.

The US Embassy had their own internal drama on this day. During the previous night, with heavy firing nearby, the diplomats had reported to Washington their fears that the Iraqis would storm the compound. The State Department then sent a message to their embassies in Baghdad and Kuwait, ordering them to disable any excess weapons. The reason was to prevent anyone with access to a firearm, other than the disciplined Marine guards, shooting at the Iraqis and causing death or injury among civilians in the compound. The intention was simply to disable the weapons by removing the firing pins or bolts, and securing them in a safe place.

The Regional Security Officer in Kuwait, Michael Bender, took the message literally. The Marines were ordered, against their better judgement, to physically wreck their weapons. They were then taken out of uniform. When Ambassador Howell gave Bender a treasured pistol which had been passed down from his father, he expected to get it back minus the firing pin. It came back in pieces. The embassy in Kuwait then had absolutely nothing to defend themselves with, even against a mob. Their colleagues in Baghdad received the same message, but only pulled the firing pins and bolts.

The destruction of embassy resources in Kuwait went further than firearms. The USLOK and the CIA station chiefs each had a radio set with which they could communicate with Washington. The diplomats had already destroyed their own secondary communications systems so they only had one system to disable if the Iraqis came in quickly. Ambassador Howell did not want any freelancing outside channels, so ordered both sets destroyed. The CIA man reportedly stood over his, saying that only the Director of Central Intelligence could order him to destroy the equipment. Howell let it be known that he was in charge in Kuwait. The CIA set ended up in pieces.

It was during this second week that I made contact with Command Central. At the time, I could not pass information to the British Embassy on their nationals in the Plaza Hotel because the telephones there had failed completely. The British Embassy phones seemed constantly engaged.

I explained to Mike Devey where we were, who was in our group, the situation in our area, and the problem with contacting the British Embassy on behalf of the Plaza. Command Central had no warden for the central city area. Mike needed a contact, and asked me if I'd do it. That is how I became the British Embassy warden for the central city area. There was no training, no official appointment, no guidance. Just do what you can, and keep in contact.

Although the city centre was primarily a commercial area, it also had several major residential complexes, five-star hotels, and a few smaller hotels. By then, the number of Westerners in it was little more than two dozen, most of them in the Al-Muthanna and the Plaza. Those in the Sheraton had been taken to Baghdad. The remaining several hundred Westerners who usually lived in the area had fled to friends in the suburbs or to Saudi Arabia.

On 9 August Saddam delivered another blow to those in Kuwait when he declared that the Iraqi and Kuwaiti dinars were at parity, one-for-one, effectively cutting the value of our funds in the bank by 90%. The change was largely academic at the time as the banks would not open for another ten days, but it was sickening to think that the savings of years of hard work had been wiped out overnight.

After a week under occupation, people slowly adjusted to the situation. Although they were greatly concerned with food and security, most were in good health, and safe. Most days that week dawned bright, clear and hot. One could be forgiven for thinking that the invasion was just a bad dream.

Very few people knew anyone killed in the fighting, and without the pressures of work, some actually began to treat every day as a weekend. Alcohol was now freely available in Kuwait, especially Iraqi *arak*, beer, and genuine Heineken. Incredibly, some people were still enjoying the excitement, but few fooled themselves that the situation could carry on indefinitely. Those with children were desperate to get them out.

A small core of perhaps less than a hundred Westerners had decided to stay, at least until everyone else who wanted to go had done so. A number of these were the

British wardens such as Sandy Macmillan who had been in Kuwait for many years, and whose local knowledge would be invaluable in evacuating others safely. They felt a responsibility to see through the bad times, having enjoyed Kuwait in the good ones. A number of Western women, especially those with Kuwaiti husbands or boyfriends, were also firmly resolved to stay. Personally, I was ambivalent. If the opportunity arose, I would leave for the sake of my family at home, but I was not going to risk a desert escape or take up a seat which more rightfully belonged to a child or woman.

For news of what was going on outside we had to rely primarily on the BBC, and TV news from Saudi Arabia. There were no regular newspapers in Kuwait any more, although the Iraqis had taken over the premises of a leading local daily, *Al-Qabas*, and were trying to produce their own propaganda sheet. Its title was to be *Al-Nida'a*, or *The Call*, in reference to the now discredited ploy that Kuwaiti revolutionaries had invited in the Iraqi Army.

As time went on, we were pleasantly surprised at the international military response. We heard on 10 August that West Germany was sending ships, and that US Secretary of State James Baker was discussing the question of NATO sending forces. The evening of 11 August brought news of Egyptian and Syrian troops leaving for Saudi Arabia, and Morocco and Turkey giving airfield space to the US. On 13 August, The Netherlands committed two vessels. Even Iran offered to send troops to the UAE, Oman and Bahrain, but was politely rebuffed. Everyone seemed to be joining in. Pakistan sent ground forces to defend Mecca and Medina, and Belgium and Italy sent warships to bring the total Allied naval deployment in the Gulf to 70 ships.

The Western diplomats and US military in Kuwait were also moving around that week. US Commercial Counsellor Paul Scogna was constantly out picking up Americans who felt they were in exposed locations, arranging food for them, and visiting hotels to liaise with the managers and his nationals there. He seemed to be thoroughly enjoying himself, doing a good job, and relishing the prospect of escaping from the tense and overcrowded embassy compound.

When Norwegian Ambassador Hans Longva, whose wife is Vietnamese, advised the Americans of the dire state of affairs at the Philippines Embassy, US Ambassador Howell arranged a US$15,000 line of credit through Washington and Manila, paid outside Kuwait, to pay for rice and other staples for the 3,000 desperate Filipinos sheltering in and around the embassy. Scogna and his colleagues tapped their contacts with Kuwaiti storehouses and the Kuwait Danish Dairy to obtain supplies. A number of American civilians were vocal about their diplomats spending time helping Third World nationals, but no American was in danger of starving.

Another individual highly regarded by the people sheltering in the US compound was USLOK Lieutenant-Colonel Tom Funk, a short, solid man, whose size belied a big heart. He went out of his way to try to make these people comfortable in whatever basic accommodation they had. He and his colleagues spent their days acquiring food and supplies from throughout Kuwait, and were later credited with getting in sufficient food to enable the embassy to withstand a three-and-a-half-month siege.

The role of the wardens also expanded rapidly in the second week as new needs arose, and as they became more organized. After collating lists of people in the country, their attention turned towards providing for those who had lost everything, building up food supplies, and helping others escape.

Command Central's Mel Gage knew a Kuwaiti food merchant who simply opened up his warehouse. 'Take anything,' he said. They stocked up on tinned and dried goods, rice, pasta – anything that would last - and farmed out frozen food to freezers all over the city. By the end of the week, they had access to enough food for several hundred individuals for six months. The problem now was to keep it out of Iraqi hands, distribute it fairly, and avoid hoarding.

As for escapes, some wardens passed on the embassies' advice to lie low. Others, in their personal capacities, gave every assistance they could to those wishing to mount escape attempts. This involved distributing cross-desert route maps, and establishing rendezvous points for departing convoys. Unfortunately, the wardens' personal and official roles were easily confused, so some members of the community thought that the warden system itself was sending conflicting messages about going. The foreign media got half of the story from the escapees, and ran articles saying that the British Embassy was officially telling people to stay put, but handing out maps on the quiet. This was not so. Much to the anger of the diplomats, the reports risked compromising their delicate relations with the Iraqis.

Information was always imperfect, and the embassies and wardens could only advise, never order. This distinction, and the concept that people had to take responsibility for their own choices, albeit with the counsel of more experienced heads, was lost on many. Some expected to be led all the way by the wardens who, at the same time, were trying to sustain their own families.

At the Al-Muthanna we watched as endless streams of Iraqi buses brought in more Popular Army men. Some of us became concerned that the Iraqis would take over the building as accommodation for their troops. Then the phones failed for several days, and we were unable to contact the embassies at all.

However, before the phones failed, we had discovered that other Westerners were moving about freely. It seemed safe to venture out again. We rationalized that the BLT men had been picked up because they were military. We did not know about the other isolated pick-ups of men on the first and second days, or the people moved to Baghdad from the hotels simply because our information links were still in their infancy.

To call in to the US Embassy and Command Central, we would drive to a nearby suburb, and use the phone in the house of the departing US Consul, Bill Colwell. The contrast between the city and the Bill's area in the upmarket Kuwaiti suburb of Abdullah Al-Salem could not have been greater. In the city, looters rubbed shoulders with hordes of scruffy Iraqi troops. In the suburbs, life was almost normal. Shops were selling their stock in an orderly fashion, and there was little evidence of the Iraqi Army, except at the local police station.

After tasting security in the suburbs for several days, my American neighbour and several other people from the Al-Muthanna decided to relocate there. Paul Kennedy and I decided to stay. We felt less threatened by the Iraqis, and preferred to remain in our own homes. More importantly, we had several female friends living nearby, and we were concerned for their safety. We could do little if the Iraqis came looking for the girls in earnest, but at least we were two other men nearby. It was naive, but we were still learning.

Throughout the first fortnight and beyond, the embassies endured a great deal of criticism, mostly out of frustration. Many people blamed the diplomats for not warning them to leave before the invasion in the mistaken belief that they had advance knowledge of Saddam's plans. Others railed against them when friends on desert escape attempts - despite advice against such attempts - went missing for days, before turning up in Riyadh or elsewhere.

A split between civilians and diplomats became stark when news of the embassy closure order of 9 August was made public on 12 August. Up to then, the US Embassy had been telling its people that everyone would go out together, but that evening the State Department broadcast on VOA that non-essential embassy personnel would leave for Baghdad as soon as possible. The private citizens were told to prepare themselves in case an evacuation became possible, and were again advised against crossing the border into Saudi Arabia. The British and others were making similar plans.

The communities were incensed that the diplomats might run out on the civilians. After a week of being told that everyone would leave together, the State Department now seemed to be looking after its own and leaving everyone else. This was unfair as skeleton staffs would stay behind, but the tension was so high that people lashed out at anything they could. To soothe the concerns of the civilians, the US Embassy offered to send brief messages for its citizens to their families at home. It reversed its line the following day, citing communication difficulties, and advised people to keep on listening to the BBC, VOA and CNN for evacuation notices.

The embassies had actually been able to provide little practical support to most members of their communities, but they were an important psychological factor, and provided a focus for authority. Most importantly, they were a tenuous communication link to the outside world. Suddenly, the foreign communities were faced with the prospect of not having any diplomatic representation or communications at all.

Nevertheless, at their Wardens' Meetings on 11 August, the major embassies made it clear to their people that they were going to stay, and that the Iraqis would have to move them by force, although the British were awaiting further instructions from London. A new respect for the diplomats gradually took hold. People were not going to be abandoned if their Governments could possibly avoid it.

A number of hotels in Kuwait City still housed guests. The largest group was in the International, comprising mainly the BLT families. For these, the five-star luxury and comfort was in stark contrast to the week of terror at IBI. They could sit in the air-conditioned coffee shop with a curious air of detachment, overlooking the sparkling waters of Kuwait Bay, and watch sweating Iraqi troops prepare their fortifications outside. They rubbed shoulders with senior Iraqi officers and administrators who arrived to consummate the annexation.

The Iraqis in the hotel were polite, even sympathetic. They followed Arab manners of not speaking directly to the women unless they had to, but it was perfectly appropriate to chat with the children. One soldier, unaware of what had happened to the BLT men, asked a boy where his dad was. When told that other soldiers had taken him away, the Iraqi apologised sincerely and turned away. He knew that being taken away in Iraq was not a good sign.

The women were initially advised by their embassy not to communicate with their friends outside in case the lines were tapped, and the Iraqis tracked down other British through this. They were still military wives, and about 30 BLT families, with their men, were still at large. This fear dissipated as they settled in, and some of the women's civilian friends actually managed to visit them, with clothes and little comforts. Despite their trials, the BLT women were more fortunate than their compatriots in one way. They were a high priority of the embassy. Unlike other Britons in Kuwait, they could send brief messages home through the embassy's communications.

The BLT families were not the only people at the hotel. One unfortunate American couple had been due to leave Kuwait on the day of the invasion. They had sent their household goods out, and were spending the last days of their contract in the hotel. Others were caught on one-day business trips. The BLT families would have to stay until the British Embassy could reunite them with their men in Baghdad, but General Manager Hermann Simon smuggled many of the other people out of the hotel, sometimes in laundry baskets with the help of Don Macauley and one of his sons. One was young Glen Ashwell, who had been baby-sitting at IBI. His father, Brian, of Command Central, was gravely concerned for his teenage son. Glen was finally reunited with his parents on 11 August. Another younger child, Danny Tonks, who had been staying overnight with a friend at IBI was also slipped back to his family.

In Baghdad, the BLT women's husbands and other hostages were also relatively comfortable in their hotels, but equally concerned for their families' safety. The numbers increased during the week as about 20 people picked up trying to leave Kuwait across the desert came in. On 11 August, the Baghdad hostages were consolidated into two hotels, with the French, now numbering about 30, and the eight Germans joining the British in the Mansour Melia. The Americans stayed in the Al-Rasheed, although the two Canadians were released to their embassy. The Iraqi Human Shield policy of incarcerating only certain key nationalities was set as early as the second week, but it took several weeks for the news to filter back to those in Kuwait.

Four days later, an unusual British group came into the hotel. The women were dressed in *abayas*, and looked like Indians or Pakistanis, but spoke with London accents. They were English pilgrims who had been visiting the holy Shi'ite shrines in Iraq, and had been prevented from leaving because of the suspended flights. They would later be let out before the other hostages.

The British hostages were not visited by their Ambassador to Baghdad, Mr Harold Walker until 12 August. Like the US and several other ambassadors, he was out of the country at the time of the invasion, but returned immediately. It was not until this date that the men, military and civilian alike, who had been separated from their families, were able to send messages back to them in Kuwait.

By 12 August, most of the Iraqi armour in Kuwait City had deployed either south towards Saudi Arabia, or back into Iraq. A large armoured reserve, the Iraqi IV

Corps' 6th Armoured Division and 1st Mechanized Infantry Division, based itself near Jahra, from where it could move easily in any direction. The rest of Kuwait was held by Iraq's III Corps, with nine divisions strung out along the Saudi border and the coast, and the 3rd Armoured Division and 5th Mechanized Infantry Division behind them in the Burgan oilfield as reserves.

Most of the Iraqis in the city and suburbs were surprisingly well behaved. Apart from the looting, which seemed to be carried out as much by local Palestinians, Indians and a few Kuwaitis, the Iraqis generally paid for their purchases. Kuwait was a bargain for them. With the new currency parity, they were buying goods for 10% of their real price. Other soldiers were seen handing out bottles of cooking gas, melons, and bread to poorer Asians and Arabs. They still knocked on doors or stopped cars, asking politely for food, water and cigarettes, but seldom entered houses forcefully, and the initial spate of rapes subsided as the officers brought their men under control.

Many of the soldiers went out of their way to apologise to the Kuwaitis, and explain that they had not wanted to come to Kuwait, but had been ordered to do so. They seemed genuinely embarrassed. Most of them realized that if it had not been for Saddam and his war with Iran, they could have been as well off as the Kuwaitis. The morale of the ordinary troops was rock-bottom. The tragedy of this became apparent when medical staff in Kuwaiti hospitals found themselves treating gunshot wounds to the left hand, or foot, especially among teenage soldiers. It dawned on them after several cases that these boys were shooting themselves to avoid being sent to the front line.

In Kuwait City, we continued to stock up where we could, although we had little money. I recall trying to pay for groceries at a co-operative supermarket checkout with my ATM card. The cashier was sympathetic, but refused. A Kuwaiti behind me, even though he was buying for his own big family, insisted on paying, and would not even give me his name and address so that I could reimburse him after liberation. All I could say was thank you, and that we would get his country back for him, of that I was sure. He looked me straight in the eye and said, 'Yes, I know you will. *Insha Allah* (God Willing).' Even in those early days, the Kuwaitis kept the faith.

Other Westerners caught with a lack of funds told how some supermarkets refused to take money from them. The cashiers would ring up the purchase for the sake of nearby Iraqis, and then cancel it. I heard of one occasion where a customer gave the cashier a ten dinar note for a small purchase. The cashier took the note, put it in the till, and counted out ten one dinar notes for the man, with a wink. Many shops ignored the order to accept Kuwaiti currency at parity to the Iraqi, and exchanged it at the going rate of ten to one.

Elsewhere, panic shopping had subsided slightly, partially because people had stocked up, and the shops were rationing supplies carefully. The local co-operatives instituted a system whereby only people resident in their particular area could buy from that store. It had to be flexible to allow for people who had fled from their own areas, but it worked very effectively.

As part of our own organization in the city centre, I had visited my office on 9 August, and photocopied a notice for all 400 apartments in our residential complex.

It asked people to leave their names, nationalities, passport numbers, contact details of next-of-kin abroad, apartment numbers, phone numbers, and any particular problems they were experiencing, in an envelope in the garbage room in a block some distance from our apartments. I would collect the details. We were becoming more careful. I did not want the Iraqis to trace the notice back to my apartment. The idea was to appoint wardens for floors or blocks, and meet together if the situation deteriorated. I promised to try to pass on the details to the respective embassies.

The response was overwhelming. Most replies were from Filipinos low on food, or whose women feared being raped. Others were from Egyptians or Lebanese. However, most of these people were able to leave within weeks.

As a result of this circular and other contacts, we formed a group of eleven Westerners, comprising an elderly British couple in their 60s, Ken and Magda Hoyle, a British–Irish couple, Chris and Mary Chambers, a single British woman, Jane Anderson, and five men who were either single, or with wives and families outside the country at the time. All other Westerners in the building had moved out to the suburbs in the first week. A final – and eminently welcome – addition was Imad Ghawji, a US-educated Syrian engineer whom I knew fleetingly. Imad would be our life-saver on many occasions during the occupation, and refused to leave Kuwait until we could.

One of the greatest fears at the time was the continuation of our water supplies. Most homes in Kuwait are connected to the mains, but many are still supplied by tankers which call fortnightly to fill rooftop tanks. People on the mains supply had the doubtful security of continued supply, at no cost, if the tanker drivers left, but had no alternate supply if the mains failed.

Fortunately, the mains supply continued until the air war in January 1991. To their eternal credit, many tanker drivers, mainly Egyptians, Iranians and Palestinians, remained on duty and did not take undue advantage of their customers. Nevertheless, people filled every container they had, and those with tanks husbanded water very carefully. Some took things to the extreme and even washed their clothes in the bath water, and then rinsed the dishes in it before washing them with clean water in the kitchen sink. Finally, the overworked water was used to flush the toilets.

Electrical supplies continued uninterrupted for the most part. This was critical for running refrigeration, air-conditioning and water pumps in the scorching summer heat. Most blackouts were due to mechanical failures in the buildings themselves rather than in the mains supply. We had several scares in the Al-Muthanna when either the air-conditioning or power, or both, failed, but our guardian angel, Imad, always managed to get it going again.

We started to eat food more from the freezer than from the refrigerator or drygood stores so that our supplies would last longer if the power failed. Some people turned freezers up full, then sealed them with tape so that the food would take longer to thaw in the event of a power failure.

The supply of cooking gas was also a major concern, particularly for lower-income groups. This is usually very cheap in Kuwait, and distributed in gas bottles. Somehow, small quantities of gas bottles found their way onto the market. Nevertheless, those who could used electric hotplates or microwaves whilst the power lasted, and pooled these to save the precious gas. In our complex, we regularly cooked for 12 people on a two-plate electric cooker.

Throughout most of the second week, the 16 military, diplomatic and civilian Americans who had sought shelter in the Japanese Embassy were still sharing a crowded basement with over 300 Japanese. They had been joined by three Western women: a Canadian, an American, and an Englishwoman.

The accommodation was one floor of what had originally been designed as a large house for a Kuwaiti family. There was one kitchen, two showers, and two toilets, only one of which worked. The 19 non-Japanese were crowded into a few small rooms in the basement. For security reasons, the Japanese *chargé d'affaires*, Akio Shirota, had told his people to simply ignore their presence.

Colonel Mooneyham and the military men had a particularly difficult time. Sitting impotently in the basement ran counter to everything in their natures and professions. They felt they should be out in the action, taking care of their people, but it was more important to Washington that they stay hidden and evade capture. To aggravate matters, the ranking American diplomat, Mr Emil Skodon, was younger than most of the military, and had the unenviable task of conveying the Ambassador's instructions to stay put. It took a special type of discipline for the military men to accept these orders.

The Americans were finally ordered to their own compound on Tuesday, 14 August, when it became apparent that the Iraqis were not targeting American officers, as they had the British. The British had been a higher profile unit, even wearing Kuwaiti uniforms, but they did not have diplomatic passports.

Mr Shirota was a hero in the eyes of the Americans. He continued to keep their embassy advised on the whereabouts of Americans with whom he was in contact, and at one stage during the first week, may have been instrumental in preventing an Iraqi forced entry into the American compound. At the time, several Japanese were still in their own homes, some near the US Embassy. One day, they were told to move amidst a sudden increase in military activity in the area. Shirota suspected that the Iraqis were moving civilians out of the way in preparation for the assault. He reported this to Mr Skodon, who relayed it to Ambassador Howell. The fears were conveyed to Washington, who then contacted Joe Wilson in Baghdad, who in turn contacted his Iraqi contacts, and ensured that any assault, if one was planned at all, was quashed.

On the day the Americans from the Japanese Embassy relocated to their own compound, the local CIA man, J. Hunter Downs, got his daughter, Courtney, across the border into Saudi Arabia, using his local contacts. This later caused a great deal of bitterness amongst the civilians, who saw the diplomats as telling them to stay put, and then getting their own people out.

The move into the embassy brought another, unexpected benefit. Colonel Mooneyham had kept his Beretta service pistol with him. With all the other weapons in the compound having been disabled, this was the sole functioning firearm they had against the entire Iraqi Army. The person most in need of it was the senior communicator, Jeff Jugar, who might have to hold off the Iraqis for the vital few minutes he and his colleague would need to destroy their equipment if the Iraqis forced their way in. Jeff got the gun.

The fear of chemical attack, present from the first days, also spread, especially after the media scrambled for background stories on Saddam to fill the gaps in the news. They recalled in vivid detail the Iraqi gassing of the Iranians and Kurds. We would have preferred it if they had avoided this. Not only did it worry us, but it terrified our families at home.

On 13 August, we saw the first footage of the invasion taken out by people who had escaped into Saudi Arabia. It had been shot from a building overlooking the Dasman Palace and British Embassy, and showed tanks in the streets, with smoke rising from the Palace. We were fascinated: this had happened in our own town, and few of us had seen it. We then realized that our families at home would be seeing it too, and would think it was still going on. CNN had failed to explain that the city was now relatively quiet. We developed a love-hate relationship with the media. We craved their news, but greatly resented their sensationalism and incomplete reporting.

Reports started to circulate in Kuwait of large missiles heading south on trucks, probably SCUDs. The Iraqis did not try to hide the movement, which would have been easy to do by skirting the city, or using desert tracks. It seems they wanted the missiles to be seen. Other eyewitnesses saw gas masks and mobile equipment which seemed to be for decontamination facilities.

The British Embassy took the threat of chemical attack so seriously as to allow Ray Washer, one of the Mahboula wardens who had served in the British Army, to brief a wardens' meeting on the principles of chemical protection. The embassy also obtained extracts of a manual on nuclear warfare precautions, and distributed copies at the next meeting. I received one, full of black marks where words had been scored out, as if censoring a naughty novel. We finally figured out what the deletions were. The manual was an old civil defence publication on how to protect oneself from radioactive fallout. Presumably, whoever had provided it did not want to panic people into thinking that they might be facing a nuclear attack. This was particularly thoughtful, but the censoring was so obvious that it only served to highlight the deletions. The manual was all but irrelevant to chemical warfare.

All around town, people prepared airtight rooms in inner rooms or bathrooms, and sealed doors and windows with duct tape. It did not occur to many of us that Saddam had no conceivable reason to bomb Kuwait with gas when so many of his own troops were there, most without chemical protection gear. Still, a few suggested that if Allied troops came in, the Iraqis might pull back, and then shell the city from the north with chemicals.

As the crisis deepened, more people planned escapes across the desert to Saudi Arabia. The main roads were now closed, and the Iraqis were turning people back opposite Ras Al-Jalayh, near the Kuwait Navy Base, 40km north of the border. They had also blocked the western Salmi Road. The only way out was across the desert, which the Iraqis could not seal completely, but this was difficult for people more used to driving on six-lane highways.

Some people who were turned back at Ras Al-Jalayh drove only as far back as the Mina Abdullah refinery, 20km north, and then onto the south-west road to Wafra, a farming town 10km north of the border. They would then turn off that road before occupied Wafra, and cut across the desert westwards, then south into Saudi Arabia. The Iraqis soon blocked the Mina Abdullah turnoff.

There were two other major routes. First, people drove west along the Sixth or Seventh Ring towards Jahra, and then cut off on desert tracks to the south-west near a huge car graveyard, heading for the point 50km away where the Kuwaiti border with Saudi Arabia turns sharply south, at Managish, in an area known as the 'elbow'. The main landmark was a line of power pylons heading directly for the border. People in two-wheel drive vehicles could drive on the compacted sand below the wires.

This route was known as 'Oscar', or 'The Pipeline'. It had been trailblazed by a German amateur rally driver, Ottmar Lange who had taken three groups to the border in the early days, and returned to Kuwait. On the return leg of his third trip, he had been shot at by Iraqis, so decided against any more desert jaunts. However, he had then drawn a map of the route. Mike Devey from Command Central came around, and copied it for distribution. One of the men passing the map around apparently mistook Ottmar's name for 'Oscar', so the route was misnamed in perpetuity. 'Pylons' was read as 'pipelines', on the mistaken assumption that there was a pipeline to Saudi Arabia which could be followed. There was, but on the Iraqi side of the border, 70 km to the west.

The second route led through the same car graveyard, then westwards either through the desert or along the axis of the Salmi Road towards the Wadi Al-Batin, Kuwait's western border with Iraq. The cars then turned south into Saudi Arabia, hoping to slip through a gap in the line of Iraqi vehicles facing the border. It was impossible to go along the Salmi Road itself as it was blocked. The secret was to stay off the roads. This route was much longer, but there were fewer troops in this remote, desolate part of Kuwait.

Desert escapes were not simple at all. The desert is not of uniform composition. There was a great risk of becoming bogged down in soft sand, and getting stuck in the 50°C heat. Most people trying to escape had never driven in the desert before, and were using two-wheel drive vehicles. Those cars that did get into the desert had to travel as light and as fast as possible across the sand, dodging rocks and dips, in order to avoid getting stuck. Luggage was limited to important papers, survival supplies and a change of clothes.

Once the convoys reached the Saudi border, they were confronted by an insurmountable sand berm which discourages smugglers. Unless they happened upon a Saudi border post, they had to drive parallel to the berm, still in Kuwait, until they reached the crossing point. There, unsure whether the post was in Saudi or Iraqi hands, they had to approach cautiously.

The Saudis were only accepting GCC nationals, Americans, Australians, Canadians, New Zealanders and West Europeans. Unless other people were with a convoy whose permissible nationals would argue for them, or be responsible for them leaving the Kingdom, they had to return to Kuwait.

From our own group, two cars with my American neighbour and Phil Balmforth in one, a BMW, and an American couple in the other, tried the southern routes first, early one morning. They were turned back, so decided to try the route off Sixth Ring. The BMW lost the second car somewhere on Sixth Ring. They assumed it had turned back, so they continued on alone.

By this time, the sun was high in the sky. Thousands of vehicles with occupants of almost every nationality were trying the same thing, all making for the Saudi border. The track into the desert through a hole in the motorway fence off Sixth Ring was a huge traffic jam.

They attempted several times to find a way through before finding clear ground. They had gone no more than 100 metres before the BMW bogged in soft sand. They dug it out with the help of some people in similar straits nearby, only to become hopelessly stuck after another 100 metres.

They abandoned the BMW, intending to come back for it with a Kuwaiti friend's four-wheel drive, and hitched a ride back to the city with a carload of Pakistanis who had also abandoned their attempt. Once home, they discovered that the people in the second car were not there. They later learned that they had turned off earlier onto a track with hard sand which took them all the way to Saudi Arabia. It was very much a matter of luck. The two cars had set out on the same day, at the same time, only one had turned off earlier and made it out. The other had failed. They were never able to recover the car, and soon moved back into the Al-Muthanna.

Several British men lost their car in even more dangerous circumstances on 15 August. They had gone into the desert on a scouting expedition with a Pajero four-wheel drive prior to bringing their families out on a fully-fledged escape attempt. They were returning home when they were stopped by a group of soldiers. The Iraqis threw them out of the vehicle, and drove off in it, leaving the men to walk home in the summer heat. After several hours, they were picked up by a Kuwaiti who had given up his attempt. They eventually arrived home dehydrated and exhausted.

Escape attempts across the desert continued into the latter half of the second week. Literally thousands of cars were trying to get out, only some of them four-wheel drives. Success was often a matter of prayer, planning and providence. An American friend, Jerry Fronabarger was typical. He set off in the early morning of 12 August with his wife and two teenage daughters in a five vehicle convoy comprising ten Americans, six Filipinos, four Italians, two Russians and a dog. Their Mitsubishi Galant was packed with extra fuel, water, tools and food in case they were stuck in the desert. Extra food and water was packed to bribe the Iraqis into letting them pass.

They turned off Sixth Ring near Jahra into the desert, trying to maintain a heading of 210 degrees, roughly south-west, purposely avoiding power lines and oil pipelines. The desert track soon disappeared and they were in open desert. They stopped whenever they could on hard sand to top up their fuel tanks, check their bearings, and have a drink. After two and a half hours, they reached the berm, and negotiated their way along it for 20km until they reached the border post. Hundreds of cars and thousands of people were milling around on the Kuwaiti side. They approached with great trepidation, fearing that the Iraqis held the post, but finally spied the familiar green Saudi flag on a jeep darting around the massed cars.

After identifying themselves and haggling with the Saudis to get the

Russians and Filipinos through, the five cars were allowed to enter. As soon as they reached the paved road on the Saudi side, they jumped out of the cars, hugging each other, crying, some even kissing the ground.

The day before Jerry's convoy got through, a 49-year-old Briton, Douglas Croskery, the only Westerner to die during a desert escape attempt, was shot and killed almost within sight of the border. The incident was nothing but a ghastly accident, although many other cars were fired upon, and several hit.

Croskery was part of a mixed convoy of 20 Kuwaitis and 3 Britons in six cars, led by a Kuwaiti. His wife, Thelma, was back home in the UK. The group was about eight kilometres from the border, near the Managish 'elbow', with Croskery bringing up the rear of the convoy in a Daihatsu Rocky. The 17 year-old brother of the convoy leader was in the passenger seat, with a Kuwaiti woman and two children in the back. Their heavier car had become stuck in soft sand earlier, and abandoned. The passengers had been distributed throughout the other cars in the convoy, including Croskery's Daihatsu.

As they neared the border, they encountered a fork in the desert track. The left fork was actually the route to the border post, but the right fork looked like the main route. It actually led to an oil installation, and a dead-end, but this was not apparent for several hundred metres. At that stage, the only way to regain the correct route was to turn around, and return to the fork.

The convoy had apparently taken the right fork before the leader realised his mistake. What happened next is unclear, but it is thought that a group of Iraqi troops had placed themselves between the two routes, several hundred metres from the fork, and were holding up and looting cars nearing the border on the left fork. The convoy had come up on the Iraqis from behind, but was still about 50 metres from them when they turned around. The Iraqis seem to have realised that this convoy was about to escape, and ran onto the right fork, just as the convoy completed its U-turn.

Croskery's Daihatsu was the last vehicle in the convoy. The Iraqis may have shouted at him to stop, but he either did not hear them, or kept going regardless. Either way, at least one of the Iraqis fired a burst from his Kalashnikov in the direction of the car to get it to stop.

Most of the rounds went wide, but one passed through the rear window of the Rocky - miraculously missing the woman and children in the back - pierced the headrest of Croskery's seat, and smashed into the back of his head, killing him instantly. The four other people in the car screamed as the contents of Croskery's skull were sprayed across the inside of the windshield. The driverless jeep ground to a halt.

The troops ran to the car, thinking the driver had merely stopped in response to the warning shots. They were horrified to find a dead Briton slumped over the wheel, and a hysterical woman, two children, and the youth in the car. They pulled Croskery's body from the vehicle, and told the youth to drive the others back into Kuwait. He headed back up the track, then circled around onto the left fork, towards Saudi Arabia, and caught up with the other cars. No one saw what the troops did with the body, although several unconfirmed reports say that later escapees saw it by the roadside.

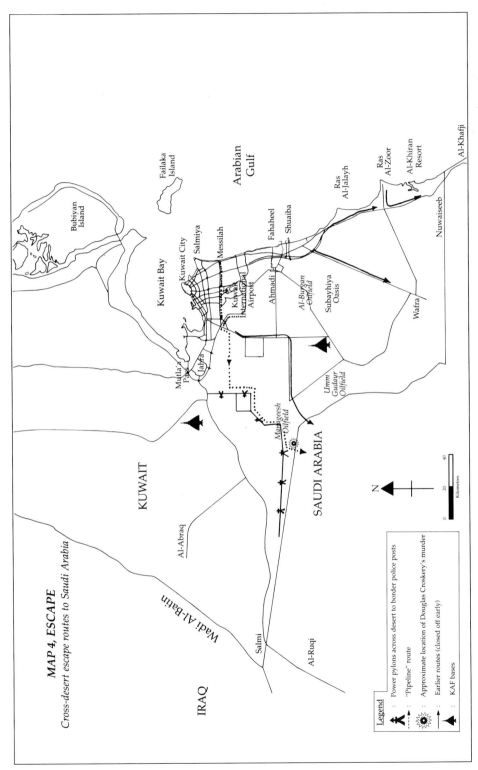

MAP 4, ESCAPE
Cross-desert escape routes to Saudi Arabia

Legend

- ✦ : Power pylons across desert to border police posts
- ···· : "Pipeline" route
- ✺ : Approximate location of Douglas Croskery's murder
- ◄ : Earlier routes (closed off early)
- ◄ : KAF bases

BASE MAPS © SALEM AL-MARZOUK AND SABAH ABI-HANNA WLL

The convoy left the Daihatsu at the border post. The surviving passengers were then taken 40km west to the nearest major Saudi post near Salmi, where the story was apparently narrated to a British sergeant from the Defence Attaché's office at the British Embassy in Riyadh. Somehow, in the confusion, a message was passed back to the embassy in Kuwait that the incident had happened two km east of Salmi, instead of closer to the elbow.

The British Consul in Kuwait, Larry Banks, contacted the Iraqi Ambassador in Kuwait - with whom the embassies now had a dialogue of sorts - as soon as he received the message on 12 August. He requested to be allowed to travel to the border area to recover the body. The Iraqi told him that he had no information on the incident, but that if the embassy insisted, the Iraqi Army would help. The British had one further problem. They had no body bag, and did not expect to be able to recover the body until the following day. By then, it would be in no fit state to carry back in a car. Fortunately, the US Embassy came to the rescue and provided one.

The following morning, the Iraqis provided an escort of a lieutenant and two small busloads of troops. They headed due south on the Fahaheel Expressway, directly towards Saudi Arabia. This was not the most direct route to Salmi, and Banks soon realised that the Iraqi officer had no idea where he was supposed to be going. Despite Banks' protests, the lieutenant insisted on going south, until they encountered a road block south of Ahmadi, and were told they could go no further. They returned to Kuwait City after a wasted trip. That afternoon, the British Ambassador and Banks met with the Iraqi Ambassador, and complained to him. He told them to come back the next morning, and he would provide a better escort.

The Iraqi was as good as his word. On 14 August, three days after Mr Croskery was shot, a Colonel Hashem was provided to Mr Banks, with an escort. Two soldiers travelled in the pick-up with Colonel Hashem, Banks, and a British civilian, Ken Robinson, who came along to help.

This time, they headed towards Salmi. Colonel Hashem was sympathetic, even helpful and apologetic. They reached the reported site of the incident, but the Iraqi soldiers there knew nothing of it. They themselves were barely surviving, with little food or fuel. Nevertheless, they shared whatever rations they had with the two Englishmen and Colonel Hashem over lunch.

The search team quartered the area, but were unable to find anything. On one occasion, they met a Saudi border patrol, but there were no hostilities. The crisis was far too tense and fresh to risk a shooting war this early. The Saudis could not help them either.

Mr Banks was obliged to return to Kuwait City after a fruitless search. There was nothing more he could do. There were thousands of living Britons in Kuwait to be looked after. It simply had to be assumed that Croskery had been buried somewhere by the men who had killed him.

Seven months later, after the war was over, Mr Banks went looking for Croskery again. This time, the car had been traced to the border post where it still stood, abandoned and caked with the unfortunate man's blood. The British FCO had now debriefed the witnesses properly, so they knew the approximate area of the incident. British Military Police conducted a thorough search of the area, but the body has never been found. The car, however, was eventually driven back to Kuwait, cleaned up, and sold.

This unfortunate incident contained two lessons, at a tragically high price. The first was that desert escape attempts were very risky undertakings. The embassies felt that it vindicated their advice to lie low but refrained admirably from saying 'We told you so.' The second lesson, which seems to have been lost, was being able to see firsthand just how thin the Iraqi defenses on the Saudi border were at the time.

Back in Kuwait City, people were periodically shaken violently from the false sense of security that had settled over some after the first week of relative calm.

On 9 August, the Iraqis learned their own lesson about how bitter the Kuwaitis were. They had brought a TV crew down from Baghdad to film street scenes of people apparently going about their business, and the usual Mercedes sedans driving around Kuwait, unhindered. According to the story, one Kuwaiti Mercedes was more than it seemed. It pulled up next to the camera crew and their escort, and the Kuwaitis inside opened up with automatic weapons, Chicago-style, killing or wounding several Iraqis. The incident became known as the 'Video Street Massacre'.

That afternoon, the Kuwaiti Resistance attacked a broken-down Iraqi ammunition truck on the Fahaheel Expressway, near Fifth Ring. A 20-minute fireworks display ensued. Shrapnel was flung up to a kilometre away. Harry Delaney, an Australian in the nearby suburb of Bayan, watched the spectacular explosions from his roof at what he thought was a safe distance. 'Great video footage!', he thought, and turned to go downstairs for his camera. As he entered the stairwell, a projectile from the exploding truck shattered the wall he had been standing by seconds earlier, ricocheted downwards, sliced through the steel front gate, and came to rest out in the street.

Other civilians had equally narrow escapes. On the night of 15 August, in the 19-storey Fintas Towers residential complex in Mahboula, a Kuwaiti sniper fired from the upper floors at Iraqis in the Defence Minister's residence across the road. The Iraqis replied with .50 calibre anti-aircraft machine guns. The rounds not only smashed windows, but penetrated the reinforced concrete walls. The families retreated into the depths of the apartments as far as they could, and huddled on the floor until well after the firing ceased.

The following morning, at 5.30 a.m., an Iraqi colonel led a door-to-door search of the building. His troops found footsteps in the dust on the emergency staircase, but no sign of the sniper. Instead, they came across the frightened families who they had nearly killed the previous night. The colonel went ashen-faced when he realized that there had been children in the building. He took one of the Irishmen who lived on the upper floors to a window, and pointed down at a tank, several hundred metres away on the south side the building. 'You see that tank?' he said to the man. 'After the firing last night, I gave orders for it to blow the top off this building if there was one more shot fired from it. You and your family and friends are very lucky to be alive.'

In the city centre, we witnessed our own version of Iraqi brutality. The looting had apparently got out of hand and led to fighting among the troops.

The Iraqis had decided to crack down. One afternoon, while sitting in an apartment overlooking the street, we had noticed a crowd of people gathering outside the Capital Governorate building, several hundred metres up the road. It was too far to see what was going on, but we presumed that it was merely an unusually large crowd of Palestinians and Egyptians getting papers from the authorities so that they could move their own household goods.

Tragically, we were wrong. The crowd was there for a more macabre purpose. The Iraqis had shot a blindfolded man, tied his hands behind his back, and suspended the body above the road from a mobile crane. The hook of the crane had been slipped through the ropes tying his hands, and the boom placed so that he hung directly over the road, facing down. His stockinged feet almost brushed the tops of cars which were forced to pass underneath on their way out of the city centre. We saw this unfortunate man later that afternoon on a trip to the embassies. There was an Arabic sign nearby saying he was a major, and had been executed for stealing a pair of shoes.

This shock drove home the seriousness of the situation. The man had certainly not deserved such a fate for looting when most Iraqis and many Palestinians in Kuwait were engaging in exactly the same activity, and the Iraqi official looting of parts of Kuwait's infrastructure ranging from airliners to university libraries was in full swing. Reports on the shortwave services told of US$3 to US$4 billion in gold bullion, foreign currencies and securities being looted from Kuwait's Central Bank and taken to Baghdad. The Iraqis justified this by saying it was part of their national assets being relocated to the national capital. If they were to apply their own rules consistently, half their Army and hundreds of Iraqi and Palestinian civilians would be swinging from cranes. The story of the hanging major, was, however, to provide unexpected service to the Westerners when they later went into hiding.

On Wednesday, 15 August, Saddam secured his eastern flank with Iran by agreeing to Teheran's conditions for a permanent ceasefire.

This initiative was astounding. Saddam simply gave away overnight everything his country had fought for over eight years, at the price of – by conservative estimates – over 100,000 dead, and several hundred thousand wounded, all in a country of only 18 million people. The man who had signed the 1975 Algiers Agreement with the Shah of Iran over the Shatt Al-Arab waterway dividing the southernmost border of Iraq and Iran, and who had shredded it on television in 1980 to begin the Iran–Iraq War, now agreed to its terms with Ayatollah Khomeini's successors. His troops soon withdrew from Iranian territory to the pre-war borders, and the long-delayed exchanges of tens of thousands of Iraqi and Iranian POWs began, providing more men, albeit men devastated by years of brutal captivity, for Saddam's forces in Kuwait.

Expectations grew that Saddam would be overthrown by his own people for this insult to the war dead. Rumours had been rife about coup attempts in Baghdad. We could not see how the Iraqi masses could accept this latest news. They were indeed grateful for peace with their largest neighbour and the start of the return of what was left of their menfolk, but Saddam with one fell swoop had rendered their sufferings of the past decade meaningless.

Yet Saddam's security was so good, and his people so cowed, that any overthrow attempt that may have been made was rapidly crushed. The people were even forced to rally behind him in this new crisis against a bigger, more *infidel* enemy. The Iranians, wisely, did not actively pursue this opportunity further. They knew that the West was far more capable than they of punishing their old enemy, and that it would be in their own long-term interests if they stayed on the sidelines.

The offer did more than secure Iraq's eastern flank, and free POWs. It also reportedly freed 30 Army divisions which had been deployed along the Iranian border. The number of men may not have been quite as large as this, but it was nevertheless substantial, and most were available for duty in Kuwait. The Saudis were not at all convinced that Saddam would not now move on them. Getting the Iranians off his back only heightened the risk. At that stage, there were only about 8,000 combat-ready Saudi and GCC troops on the border. American ground forces were still to arrive in significant numbers, although US air power was rapidly falling into place.

An announcement of more concern to the Westerners in Kuwait was broadcast at 9.00 a.m. that morning, 15 August. Baghdad was now calling us 'restrictees' who would have to remain in Iraq for 'the duration of the crisis'. It was unclear exactly what this meant, but it was certainly a turn for the worse.

Later that day, the British Embassy held what was to be its last wardens' meeting of the crisis. Mike Devey had asked me to attend as the warden for the city centre area. The meeting was held in the elegant drawing room of the Ambassador's Residence. About 50 people were crowded in, including some of the BA149 flight crew. Consul Larry Banks was in charge. It was a measure of the fast-developing situation that when I raised a question, he asked me who I was, and what I was doing there. 'As far as I know,' I said, 'I'm your warden for the central city area. If there's anyone else covering that area, let me know, and I'll hand over to him.' There was no one. I was allowed to speak.

The meeting was instructive. At the previous one, on 12 August, Ambassador Michael Weston had apologized for the earlier advice to lie low and not try to escape, when many people had done so successfully. At this meeting, Mr Banks advised us that Mr Weston and the US Ambassador had visited the Iraqi Ambassador to protest at the situation, and secure the safety of their nationals. The Iraqi had been most unwelcoming, and advised them that no one was allowed to leave via Saudi Arabia. The main product of the meeting was a warning that the troops had orders to shoot anyone trying to escape. Douglas Croskery's death on 11 August was sufficient warning that this was possible, despite the Iraqis' initial assistance in trying to recover the body.

Nevertheless, no one stopped the wardens who advised the meeting who to see for escape maps. Everyone sympathized with Mr Croskery's fate, but they wanted to be able to take their own chances. The embassy did not hand out maps themselves, but did not prevent anyone from doing so.

The main topic of the wardens' meeting was how various organizations were being established throughout the city, such as a medical centre, and various wardens briefed others on how their networks were operating.

At the time, the ambassadors were still trying to clarify the Iraqi advice that Westerners in Kuwait would have to stay until the crisis was resolved, so it was not widely discussed. The major concern of those in Kuwait was still getting messages out to family at home. The embassy pleaded that they did not have the secretarial staff available to do this. One man volunteered that his wife would be delighted to type up the messages, which could then presumably be transmitted on the embassy secure systems. Banks undertook to consider the offer, and set a date for the next meeting, two days hence.

The Americans held their own wardens' meeting that afternoon, with about 75 of the 800 Americans in Kuwait. It was more of a community meeting as most people there had come to find out at first hand what was going on. There was great speculation about the embassy closing down and the diplomats relocating to Baghdad. Few of the civilians, if any, wanted to go there.

At the previous day's meeting between the Iraqi Ambassador and the US and British ambassadors, the Iraqi had pressured the diplomats to leave. The American told him that he still had people in Kuwait, so could not leave. The Iraqi offered to provide the diplomats with an escort to Baghdad, and then out through Jordan, but it was clear that the civilians would not be allowed to leave Iraq. Ambassador Howell said he was not prepared to countenance an overland evacuation through hostile territory, and suggested Kuwait Airport instead. The Iraqi argued it wasn't safe, to which Howell countered 'Why not? No one is going to attack a planeload of Americans.' He got nowhere.

Another officer addressed the meeting, urging Americans to avoid moving into the embassy as it was already overcrowded. He did not give numbers, but indicated it was in excess of 100. In fact, it was double that, plus dogs and cats. However, no American seeking refuge would be turned away, although they might have to sleep on the floor and bring their own food and bedding.

The question session at the end of the meeting would have been comical if it were not so tragic. Questions included: 'What do I do if I'm raped?'; 'Is it better to stay on the upper floors or go into the basement if shelling starts?'; and 'What is the exchange rate between the Kuwaiti dinar, Iraqi dinar, and US dollar.' After two weeks, people still had not answered these questions for themselves. It was suggested later, somewhat chauvinistically, that the answer to all three questions should have been, 'Try not to worry about it!'

Nevertheless, the Americans' morale was buoyed with news that the 82nd Airborne Division was now in Saudi Arabia and 7th Marine Expeditionary Brigade were landing in Jubail. Expectations grew in some quarters that paratroopers would capture Kuwait International Airport to evacuate the Westerners. Some of the military people in the embassy compound even prepared a landing zone for Delta Force commandos. It was wishful thinking.

At that last wardens' meeting, the British Embassy announced that an escorted convoy to Baghdad of non-essential diplomatic staff, their dependents, and any dependents of the diplomats who would be remaining in Kuwait for the time being would leave on Thursday, 16 August. The embassy staff was being reduced to a skeleton of ten men, headed by the Ambassador. Any British civilians who wanted to join the convoy were welcome, but would have to provide their own transport and supplies for the trip.

The convoy would be led by the local MI-6 man, Tony Paice. The Anglican priest in Ahmadi, Reverend Michael Jones, his wife Jean, and friend Dick Wearn came along for moral support. Several people in Ahmadi were not impressed at what they saw as the Padre running out on them, but it was his choice. The families of the BLT men who had been captured two weeks earlier were included, so they could rejoin the men in Baghdad.

Many of the women wanted to go together in a bus, but both the Iraqis and the embassy said this was impossible. The diplomats were unable to give them a firm indication of how long the trip would take; perhaps 12 to 15 hours was the best estimate. It would take double that.

The women arranged themselves so that most cars had two drivers so that they could relieve each other. It also meant that some families would be spread across several cars, but it was unavoidable, and they expected that the entire convoy would stick together. They left the hotel to meet outside the British Embassy for departure at 8.00 a.m. on the 16th, taking letters to post for the Asian and Egyptian hotel staff who had looked after them so well.

At the time, Baghdad had issued an order the previous evening for the Westerners in Kuwait to report to specified hotels, but the news had not yet filtered down to the Iraqis in Kuwait. I went to meet the convoy with Anna Cienciala, whose husband, George, was being held in Baghdad, to deliver a parcel of his clothes and his passport to the Reverend. It was obvious from the start that the BLT women's fears were justified. There was little organization, and even less co-ordination with the Iraqis.

We waited for some time for the Iraqi escort, but they never showed. More civilian women and children trickled in to join the convoy. Eventually, 29 vehicles lined up outside the embassy, with 80 civilians, mainly women and children, and twelve British diplomats. The diplomats went into the building to phone the Iraqi Embassy, but still no escort arrived. The August sun turned the waiting cars into ovens, but the women could not use their air-conditioning as they had to preserve the precious petrol. All this in a country with 10% of the world's oil reserves. They were growing increasingly angry.

At about 9.00 a.m., Paice decided to lead the convoy to the Iraqi Embassy, several kilometres down the Gulf Road. Anna and I returned to our homes. The convoy then proceeded into the suburbs to rendezvous with a Russian convoy of diplomats and civilians, losing six British cars within minutes. A couple of embassy cars went off to try to find them, as the others went ahead to meet the Russians. This came as a surprise to many of the women. They had no idea they were joining up with anyone.

The convoy finally left the city for the border at Abdaly, driving through a summer sandstorm, past the sites of 35 Brigade's battle west of Jahra, and more Iraqi troops pouring into Kuwait from the north. One of the British women was particularly distraught. Her 17 year-old son was with the six missing cars. No one seemed to know what had happened to them, other than the vague idea that they may rendezvous with them at the border.

They could only go as fast as the slowest car. Several vehicles soon broke down and stopped for repairs while the others continued. The convoy had now split into three, still in Kuwait. The better-organised Russians sped ahead on their own towards Abdaly. The remaining cars reached Abdaly at about 2.00 p.m. After six hours, they were still less than 150km from Kuwait City.

The Iraqis at the border held them up for several hours, haggling about passports which many of the people did not have. Many of the BLT women were incensed. They had handed their passports in to the Iraqis at the Kuwait International against their better judgement, on the advice of the British diplomats, with assurances that if anything went wrong, the embassy could reissue documents for them 'in 15 minutes.' They never got them back.

The Iraqis eventually cleared them to proceed, and provided an escort of six *Mukhabarat* Toyota Land Cruisers. Then, as they walked out of the immigration building to their vehicles, the missing cars turned up. They had been found by some Iraqi soldiers in Kuwait City, and driven around, looking for rest of the convoy. When they failed to find it, they had decided to head for the border, and try to meet them there. The mother of the missing boy was beside herself with relief, and flung herself into her son's arms.

The convoy eventually proceeded up the older, northern road to Baghdad, past Basra, along the Tigris, instead of along the faster southern highway. It was a long, slow, hot trip in the heat of the day, without air-conditioning. Refuelling could take up to an hour as the 29 vehicles descended on a petrol station. Then they had to stop every half an hour or so for the escorts to check they had lost no one along the way. Several cars broke down and were abandoned, with the occupants squeezing in with others.

Despite their demands for more haste, the escorting Iraqis were generally friendly and concerned, and organized. They had escort vehicles at either end of the convoy, and another which drove up and down alongside like a collie shepherding its flock. When several of the women became too fatigued to drive, an Iraqi took over to give them a break at the wheel.

Finally, a rest stop was called in the early hours of 17 August, at Kut, over 400km from Safwan. The drivers were exhausted. They slept fitfully in their vehicles or on the ground for a couple of hours before setting off again towards Baghdad, 300km away. On this last leg, one of the teenagers became badly dehydrated. There was a further delay as the escorting Iraqis took him to a nearby hospital for treatment. The boy was still very sick at the next refuelling stop, so the Iraqis put him, his mother and sister in one of their Land Cruisers, and sped off ahead to Baghdad. Another car joined them with two other women, both of whose small children had also become dehydrated.

The main convoy arrived at the first major checkpoint in metropolitan Baghdad at 11.00 a.m. The more sinister Iraqi officialdom now became apparent. The genial escorts from Abdaly put on stern faces to match their Baghdadi colleagues. All passports were collected from those who had them, and the Iraqis argued again with the diplomats, this time about not being able to book them into hotels without passports, as is the law in Iraq.

They waited another 90 minutes in the morning heat, sticky, sweaty and hungry, having been on the road for 27 hours. Suddenly, they were split into two groups. Those with diplomatic passports were to go direct to the British

Embassy. They drove off with local British Embassy officials, without telling the others what was going on. The Iraqi escorts from Safwan then came around the BLT women and three civilians to say goodbye, wish them well, and apologise for the ordeal they were being put through. The women were told that their men were waiting for them at the Mansour Melia, and set off hopefully under a fresh Iraqi escort of local *Mukhabarat*.

The BLT wives were to be bitterly disappointed. In a cruel move which no one accepted as coincidence, all but four of the men had been moved out to a strategic site at Baiji Army Camp while the women had been on the road the previous night. The only remaining men were Major Boyd, RSM Haynes, and two other men. This was the final straw for the women. They turned on Haynes in uproar, but he could only tell them that as far as he knew, the men had been taken to other hotels around Baghdad, and it seemed to have been just a big Iraqi mistake which would soon be rectified. A further 80 individuals were now in direct Iraqi custody as part of the Human Shield, having driven themselves to Baghdad for the Iraqis.

The news of the separation of the elements of the convoy soon reached Kuwait on the BBC. At that time, the Iraqis started to enforce their order for certain nationalities to gather at specified hotels by picking up whoever they could find. This first British convoy was perhaps the unfortunate victim of bad timing in the rapidly-developing crisis, but those still in Kuwait breathed a sigh of relief that they had not been in it.

The Iraqis in Baghdad corrected themselves the following day. After spending the night of 17 August in the Mansour Melia, half of the BLT families were taken to Baiji to join their men. The husbands of the remaining women came back into the Mansour Melia, where they spent several nights before returning to the sites. Major Boyd was less fortunate. He had been marked as a leader, so was shipped off with a group of German captives, where it was felt he would have less scope for causing trouble for the Iraqis.

It was a moving and intensely emotional time as husbands, wives, children and fathers who had thought they might never see each other again were reunited. The men told of the atrocious conditions they had been held under at the sites, the women of their terror on the night the men had been taken away from IBI Camp, and the harrowing journey from Kuwait.

8. ROUND-UP: THE SECOND FORTNIGHT

Iraqi TV, evening, Wednesday, 15 August, 1990:

'All Americans, West Europeans, and Australians will report to hotels in Kuwait City, or face unspecified difficulties!'

The order was chilling, the menace apparent. Obey... or else. The vagueness of the consequences of not complying made them all the more sinister. It was also specific, mentioning nationalities by name. The Iraqis meant business.

In Kuwait, we saw the original announcement on Iraqi TV the following afternoon. It was in Arabic, by Saddam's usual presenter, delivered in his deep, bass, measured tones, but sub-titled in English. The only inconsistency I recall was the omission of the Japanese who in practice became the fifth nationality - in addition to Americans, British, French and West Germans - incarcerated at strategic sites. We had previously heard rumours that these four major Western nationalities might be held. They represented the three Western Permanent Members of the UN Security Council, plus the economic giant of Germany. The Iraqis could have no surer way of holding the world's attention. The Japanese would complete the set.

This was the first time that all Europeans and Australians were specifically included in an incarceration order. Curiously, Canadians and New Zealanders were not mentioned. We presumed that this was an Iraqi oversight. We were wrong. When these people were caught, they were freed either in Baghdad or Kuwait. Others, such as Australians and Irish, were arrested, but released later. Curiously, some West Europeans besides the British, French and West Germans were also released, despite also having been told to report to hotels.

The tone of the announcement was later softened to imply that the move was for our own protection, and that it was really to help the Iraqis to help us. Few believed the soft sell.

On 16 August, the Iraqi Ambassador in Kuwait made sure that those in Kuwait got the message. He called the US and British ambassadors and several other envoys to the Iraqi Embassy, and told them that their people must report to the major hotels 'for their own protection'. Those who did not comply would face unspecified disciplinary action. The Iraqis wanted the Western ambassadors to arrange for the round-up of their own people.

The Iraqi insisted that he wanted everyone. When he asked US Ambassador Nat Howell to tell him where all the Americans were, 'so that we may protect them', Howell replied 'America is not a police state: it does not keep track of its citizens in that manner. I would not be at liberty to tell you where the Americans in Kuwait are, even if I wanted to. This order is not only a practical impossibility: I have no power to order my people to move.'

The Iraqi replied to the effect of 'Come off it ! Even we know where 90% of your citizens are!' Howell shot back, 'Then could you please give me your list so that I can contact them.' The Iraqi's bluff had been called, but his men would soon start hunting down recalcitrant Americans and other Westerners.

Howell apparently talked the Iraqi into specifying the Kuwait International Hotel for his people. It was next to his compound, and would allow him to service them more conveniently. The British Embassy was farther from any major hotel, but the Regency Palace was particularly convenient as most Britons in Kuwait lived within three kilometres of it. Presumably the French were to go to the Meridien. Apparently the rest of us were free to choose any hotel of our preference.

One critical victory arose from the meeting. The ambassadors told the Iraqi it was impossible for them to gather their nationals without their phones working. He agreed to have the lines restored, and they continued working on and off for the rest of the time the embassies were staffed.

The ambassadors were not the only ones horrified at the order. The Kuwait International and Regency Palace between them had about 650 rooms. At the time, it was thought that there were about 6,000 Americans and British in Kuwait. The hotels could not possibly accommodate them all. The real numbers were barely a third of that, but still far beyond the hotels' capacity, particularly with difficulties in getting food, and fleeing staff.

It would hardly have mattered if we had missed the announcements on Iraqi TV. At 6.00 p.m. on 16 August, the BBC World Service, acting on an FCO communique drafted in consultation with the British Embassy in Kuwait, virtually repeated it verbatim, with elaboration, as if it were endorsed by the British Government. They effectively relayed the message for the Iraqis.

The communique read as follows:

'In a very grave and sinister development, the Iraqi authorities have advised that the British community should assemble at a single point in Kuwait. The United States community has received a similar instruction.

'The Iraqi authorities have advised that, in order to better protect the British community, they want all British citizens located in one place in Kuwait. They have said that British citizens must move to the Regency Palace Hotel on 16 August. The Iraqis have stated that if the British community does not move voluntarily, it will face unspecified difficulties. The embassy takes this to mean that the Iraqis will take measures to ensure that British citizens are moved to one location. If you choose to move, please take all food from your residence with you to give to the hotel management to help with their food stocks. We suggest that you take no more than one suitcase per person with you to the hotel.

'The border with Saudi Arabia is officially closed. The Iraqis have said that foreigners may travel to Baghdad but are not permitted to leave Iraq.

'As for those British citizens in hotels in Baghdad, the British Embassy in Baghdad is doing all that it can to assist them. Items such as toiletries, books and games are being provided by the embassy and the British community in Baghdad. A doctor is on duty and the embassy is helping to provide any medicines as required.'

The BBC said that people had two hours to report to the hotels.

Technically, it was the British wardens' function to pass on this advice to the community. Almost to a man, they refused, or made it clear that it was embassy advice, not theirs, and that they would not be complying. Most of the Western community ignored the order, and were flabbergasted at the British Embassy's stand. In our group, there was never any suggestion of complying. If the Iraqis wanted us, they would have to come and find us.

The BBC advice was misleading, although on careful reading it did give individuals the option of complying or not. First, it suggested that the Americans were issuing the same advice, or were going to comply. This apparently incensed the US Embassy as some Americans may have followed the instructions issued on the highly respected BBC. Second, it implied that it was safe to travel to Baghdad and that people could stay in hotels with embassy assistance. In fact, most Westerners who ventured out on the streets of Kuwait in the following days were incarcerated first in hotels, and later at strategic sites, with little or no access to their diplomats in Baghdad.

As a result of the BBC announcement, a few Americans and several British families did report to the hotels, only to be told by the staff, and diplomats who had been posted there to receive them, that they were not expected. The Palestinian Manager of the Regency Palace Hotel, Ghassan Rwanjhi, warned those British who turned up at his door of the Iraqis' real intentions, and advised them to go home while they still could.

The timing of the BBC announcement was such that those who complied on the evening of 16 August had to travel there just before curfew. Their trip home was nerve-wracking as some expected to be shot from afar as curfew violators. Strangely, despite the announcement, those travelling around Kuwaiti that day had no more than the usual trouble at Iraqi checkpoints. The troops certainly had not received the orders.

By the morning of 17 August, the BBC was still telling people to go to the hotels, but the British wardens and VOA were saying to stay inside until clarification had been obtained. That afternoon the FCO and BBC did a U-turn and fell in line with the prevailing wisdom when the embassy realized the real reasons for the Iraqi demand. The advice from all sources was now to stay inside, but to go peacefully if the Iraqis came for you.

On the afternoon of 16 August, the Americans and Britons already held in the Kuwait International and Regency Palace Hotels had their passports taken from them in preparation for being moved out. That evening, those BA aircrew who had not already slipped out into the suburbs were taken from the SAS Hotel to the Kuwait International. Several dozen Britons and a sprinkling of Australians, New Zealanders and French BA 149 passengers remained at the SAS, along with a number of Indians, but only for the time being.

Amazingly, while other embassies were frantically trying to keep their people out of Iraqi hands, the British continued to promote the Iraqi order. Two British diplomats visited the Plaza Hotel with a minibus, and offered to take the acting Manager, David Cunningham and the 12 other Britons there to the Regency Palace Hotel. The diplomats were shocked when their nationals declined ungraciously, explaining that the last place they wanted to be was where the Iraqis were rounding up Westerners. By this time, the Americans and Canadians had been collected from the hotel by their diplomats. The British were the only Westerners left at the Plaza.

Two young men in the Plaza, David Hough and Neal Beevor, got the key of a vacant staff apartment in the Al-Muthanna from David Cunningham, and moved in with only hand luggage and food for a few days. Our group was now up to 13. The Iraqis sealed off the Plaza before Cunningham could send them more promised supplies. Two families, the Liddles and Bignells, were trapped with him. We could have hidden them all in the Al-Muthanna, but were too slow. I still regret this failure. They all went to strategic sites in Iraq.

On the evening of 17 August, the first reports filtered in of Westerners picked up from their homes. Rumours circulated in Kuwait that Westerners would be used as Human Shields at strategic sites to prevent an Allied attack, and that many captive Westerners had already been placed at such sites. They were soon confirmed as true. The Iraqis were serious. There was no distinction at the time between men, women and children. All were fair game, but the four major Western nationalities and later the Japanese were particularly vulnerable. After two weeks of relative freedom of movement, this marked the start of the deep hiding stage.

The UN was quick to react to this. On 18 August, the Security Council passed Resolution 664 demanding the immediate release of foreigners in Iraq and Kuwait. The Iraqis replied by threatening to use their 'guests' as Human Shields to prevent what they claimed was an imminent Allied attack. The West abandoned its previously euphemistic language, and began unequivocally to use the word 'hostage'. The two words were later combined by those in Baghdad to coin the hybrid 'guestage'. Saddam would soon rise to new heights of cynicism and term them 'Heroes of Peace'. Whatever their label, it was clear they would be released only in return for the withdrawal of US and British forces from Saudi Arabia, and an end to the sanctions. This deal was firmly rejected by both governments.

In Kuwait, the dialogue between ambassadors continued. US Ambassador Nat Howell told his Iraqi counterpart on 18 August that the Americans were more comfortable in their own homes, and that any attempt to round them up would 'not be taken as a friendly action.' The Iraqi said he would have to report to Baghdad, but assured Howell that they did not intend to round anyone up, implying with injured innocence that they were not the Gestapo, and that the step was for the safety and protection of the Westerners.

It seemed that a standoff would now ensue. The tension rose daily. President Bush authorized the call-up of certain military reserves on 18 August and there was speculation that Soviet troops would join the Americans in Saudi Arabia. We listened intently to hourly shortwave news broadcasts. Our fate was in the hands of powerful men and women in Baghdad, Washington, London and New York.

Saddam responded to UN Security Council Resolution 664 by personally laying out his plans for the hostages. In an open letter to the families of those being held, he expressed his 'pain' at being forced to confine their loved ones in

Iraq, and tried to blame the US and Britain for their predicament. His twisted logic argued that this move was designed to help open a deeper dialogue for a peaceful resolution of the crisis. He promised that if the Western forces withdrew from the Gulf and undertook not to attack Iraq, then the hostages would be released immediately. It was direct blackmail.

This letter was reinforced by a repetition of its main points by Iraqi diplomats at the UN. More ominously, for those in Kuwait, Saddam later declared that anyone who harboured foreigners, regardless of nationality, was guilty of espionage, which was punishable by hanging. He confirmed this on 26 August with Revolutionary Command Council Resolution 341.

Around this time, the Iraqis managed to get enough Palestinians and others to return to work, and reopen a few of the banks. They initially tried to reprogram the ATMs to allow people to use their cards, but eventually had to revert to manual records, where they simply marked withdrawals off the 1 August balances printout. No one was depositing money. Queues 100 metres long formed outside banks to withdraw the maximum of 200 dinars each week. It was of little use to the hidden Westerners. One had to make a personal appearance to get the money, and that meant capture.

The rush for what money there was available was so great that the Iraqi troops were called in to maintain order. On one occasion, a soldier fired into the air. One round hit an Indian man in the head as it returned to earth, critically wounding him. He went into a coma, and died later in hospital.

In Kuwait, BA149 passengers of Indian origin with Western passports scrambled to obtain Indian papers. Most succeeded, thanks to the 20 and 21 August visit to Kuwait of Indian Foreign Minister Mr Gujral, the only senior foreign Government Minister allowed into Kuwait throughout the occupation.

Gujral was filmed embracing Saddam in Baghdad, much to the disgust of almost everyone in Kuwait, before flying to Kuwait in an Indian Air Force transport. However, with 172,000 nationals in Kuwait, India was in a difficult position. Most were low-income people who could not possibly survive for long in the environment of Occupied Kuwait. Gujral had to deal with the Devil first to feed them, and then get them out. Typically, though, those who would benefit most in the immediate future were the rich Indians.

Another major meeting was held between the Iraqis and the leading diplomats on 19 August, at which almost all the ambassadors stationed in Kuwait except the American one were present. Its purpose was to discuss the status of the embassies after 24 August. Although the Iraqis were courteous, the atmosphere was tense.

Several of the envoys tried to sound out the Iraqis on the still-unclear consequences if the embassies refused to shut down by 24 August. A number put forward hypothetical situations to try to circumvent the order, with the Danish Ambassador asking, 'What if I want to stay in my personal capacity, say if I have a Kuwaiti girlfriend. Would I be allowed to stay?' The Iraqi Ambassador laughed and told the Dane that his personal problems could be discussed later.

He would not budge on the closure deadline, and continued to be vague on the consequences of not complying.

During the third week of August, certain diplomats continued to move around relatively freely, although most of their nationals had gone into hiding. The Iraqis were scrupulous in sticking to their own deadlines once set. The diplomats would have freedom of movement up to the closure deadline of noon, 24 August, but not a minute beyond, even if their nationals didn't. On 20 August, the Norwegian and US envoys, and British representatives, visited various hotels, and were allowed to speak to the guests. The diplomats said that they were going to defy the closure order, and remain in Kuwait.

The British diplomats had reversed their earlier co-operation with the Iraqis, and told their nationals in the SAS Hotel that they were in the best possible place. This was hardly so. They would have been far better off hidden among the large British community. The following day, news leaked out that the all British diplomats would go on the 24th, leaving behind two local staff. This was soon countermanded. Whitehall apparently told the diplomats to reduce the staff to an absolute minimum, but at least the Ambassador and Consul would be staying.

In the week leading up to the embassy closure deadline, the various Heads of Missions who were going to stay held a series of meetings. There were obviously varying levels of commitment. Some, such as the Canadians, were going to stay no matter what as a matter of principle. Others were there only because their governments had directly ordered them to. These men were looking for the first chance to get out. A few of the points raised were mundane, but relevant. The Korean Ambassador wondered whether the country was now on Iraqi summer time, which was one hour ahead of Kuwait time. It did not seem a big deal at the time, but the Americans would later regret not paying more attention to the clock-watching Korean.

During the third week of August, the Iraqis allowed Baghdad-based representatives of countries not directly represented in Kuwait to visit briefly in a consular capacity. In Iraqi eyes, it abetted the claim that Kuwait was part of Iraq, but the embassies in Baghdad carefully avoided explicit admission of this when requesting permission to visit.

The first to arrive were Australian Consul Brian Rowe, and Michelle and Jeff Wood from the New Zealand Embassy. Rowe was accompanied by a particularly courageous individual, Toufic Lawand, who was acting as his guide and translator. Lawand, an Australian of Lebanese extraction, had driven to Baghdad from Kuwait on 14 August with his wife, Michelle. They had encountered little trouble on the way. However, no one in the Australian Embassy in Baghdad knew Kuwait. Having escaped from Kuwait, Lawand actually went back into it, leaving his wife safe in Baghdad.

The role of these visiting diplomats was to assess the situation on the ground, and contact as many of their nationals in Kuwait as possible. This was not without its risks, not necessarily from the Iraqis. On the evening of 20 August, Toufic and Brian were visiting several Australian families in the Mishref area. Their driver was waiting outside, with the car. The vehicle had Iraqi diplomatic plates, but the local Kuwait Resistance only recognised it as Iraqi. They opened fire in a drive-by attack, hitting the car, and narrowly missing the driver. It was another reminder after Douglas Croskery's death that the situation was deadly serious.

The visits of these Baghdad-based diplomats was the first opportunity many people had to get any sort of message to family in the outside world since the international lines had failed. Unfortunately, these brave officials had insufficient time to visit everybody, but they at least made phone contact with as many of their nationals as they could. In fact, several people did not want a personal visit in case it drew attention to their location.

It was at this stage that the duties of Australian warden for Kuwait were added to those I already held as British warden for the city centre. I had compiled a list of about two dozen Australians with whom I was in contact. There had been no Australian warden for Kuwait before the invasion, but the embassy needed one now. Brian Rowe was only allowed to stay in Kuwait for a couple of days, and was unsure if he would be permitted to return.

The main requirement was to compile a list of the hundred or so Australians still in Kuwait, and maintain contact with them and the embassy in Baghdad. Brian gave me the list he had over the phone. With the help of several other Australians, I proceeded to try to locate all the people on it, and, as importantly, those not on it.

I was not given any communication equipment with which to contact Baghdad, nor were any formal arrangements made by the diplomats with other local missions. The Canadians were supposed to handle our communications, but they had their own communication problems, and an even bigger community to care for. Fortunately, I had a good friend in the Swiss Embassy, DCM Bernhard Bischoff, who agreed to help. There were few Swiss nationals in Kuwait, and several Swiss diplomats were going to stay after the closure deadline. He could handle it.

The New Zealanders had also formed a well-organized warden system, headed by two rugby-playing chemists, Alistair Lane and Ron Houston, from the Kuwait Danish Dairy. They were in contact with their nationals from BA149 in the SAS Hotel, and with most of their two-dozen strong community. Their communications were handled by the Danish Embassy, and later by the Belgian Embassy's Bart Ouvry. Together, the Australians, New Zealanders and Danes formed a loose and effective partnership, gradually expanding our network, and swapping information with the Americans and the British.

The Canadians had also set up their warden system, co-ordinated by their local Consul, Ron Waugh, a Swedtel telecoms engineer, Fred Skovberg, and later architect Eoin MacDougald and newly-arrived lawyer Britt Mockridge. The French and West Germans did the same. The Irish, also without a local embassy, were led by a visiting Aer Lingus computer engineer, Cathal O'Connell, who had been in Kuwait for only five days before the invasion.

Several other wardens later found themselves in their position purely by accident. One, Chris Bell, took over a small group in co-ordination with Command Central when his own warden, Alan Jardine, went out to buy cigarettes and was captured. Gulf Bank computer analyst Dave Dorrington, found himself in the role when his colleague, who had been a warden, escaped across the desert without first telling those he was responsible for, leaving Dave's telephone number on his answering machine. Dave ended up sheltering a number of the BA149 crew, BLT men who had evaded capture, and the overflow of people seeking refuge with Command Central.

Amazingly, the Americans continued to hold wardens' meetings in their embassy and elsewhere for a week after the round-up order, when US civilians were liable to be picked up from the streets. The wardens had to run the gauntlet of Iraqi roadblocks to attend these. Miraculously, no one was captured. Within a week of the round-up order, most Western nationals were covered by their indigenous warden systems, or consuls in local embassies.

With the prospect of serving as Iraqi hostages if caught, the Western communities in Kuwait went underground.

Stricter security precautions were implemented as each successful day in hiding passed. People in apartments did not use lights at night, or placed drapes or blankets over windows so that no light would show. Those in houses scattered rubbish outside or moved the furniture from rooms that might be visible from the road to make the house appear vacant. Cars were brought in off the street if possible, or hidden in friends' garages or yards. People who might be seen from other apartments, houses or the street, dressed in traditional Arab clothing when moving around inside, or when venturing outdoors to bury rubbish or collect food delivered by Kuwaiti, Arab or Asian friends who were free to move around.

Some people feared that the Iraqis would find their addresses from employers' records, especially at Ministries, and moved out to wherever they could find. My American neighbour had no such option, so took an Arabic-language nameplate from the door of Arab friends who had left, and placed it on his door to fool any casual callers that they were outside the home of Amer Al-Arabi. He then removed his apartment number from the outside wall, and swopped it with one from a nearby Indian's abandoned apartment. To complete the deception, he removed from the Indian's apartment any items that would identify the previous occupant, and replaced them with enough of his own family photos, books and papers to mislead the Iraqis that it was his vacated apartment. Hopefully, if the Iraqis found his address, they would conclude that he was no longer in the complex.

Several curious gaps in Kuwaiti peacetime organization greatly helped those in hiding. First, the Kuwaiti street naming and numbering system away from the main roads is almost random. A system does exist, but few people understand it. To frustrate the invaders, the Kuwaiti Resistance and others began to swap around what street signs there were, turn them around to point the wrong direction, or remove them altogether.

Second, Kuwait has no printed telephone directory in the Western style showing subscribers' names, addresses and numbers. Mail, including telephone invoices, is delivered to postboxes, not to street addresses, so the physical address is not contained in the accounting system.

At the time, the Kuwaiti Ministry of Communications was developing a computer system to match phone numbers to physical addresses with the assistance of Swedtel, headed locally by Canadian Fred Skovberg. It was not yet operational, but Fred had accessed the test system through his home PC, using local phone lines, and had changed the access codes remotely so that no one, not even his staff, could operate it. However, despite Fred's assurances, many people preferred to play safe and kept their calls to an absolute minimum, or even refused to use the phone at all.

Nevertheless, there was no doubt that phones were being monitored. Numerous people reported unusual clicks and voices on the phone. Two Indian men speaking in their native tongue were told by a sharp voice on the line to speak in either Arabic or English. People never gave their locations or any clues as to their hiding places over the phone. The Irish frustrated attempts to eavesdrop by speaking in Gaelic. It may have made no difference, but they had the satisfaction of being one up on the Iraqis.

Despite these precautions, it was impossible for everyone to evade capture. Within a week of the round-up order, the Iraqis were holding about 142 Britons, and less than a hundred each of Americans, French and West Germans. They had also found a number of senior Kuwaiti military personnel and bureaucrats. A few Japanese were held directly by the Iraqis, in Baghdad, but almost 300 of them were holed up in their own embassy in Kuwait.

In some cases, people were forced out by the need to seek medical attention. Trevor Pedley and his eight-months pregnant wife, Christine, were captured in this way on their way back from a clinic. The Iraqis took them even despite her condition, but gave her the best of treatment. She delivered safely.

Mrs Pedley's treatment was in stark contrast to that accorded some Kuwaiti and Asian women who were evicted from maternity wards within hours of delivering their babies. The Iraqis wanted to show that they were caring for their Western guests humanely in the true spirit of Arab hospitality. The same courtesy was not extended to others who lacked a powerful news media.

For those in hiding, our only links with the world outside were by local phone, if it was still working, shortwave radio news services, and TV from Iraq and several nearby GCC countries.

We watched an inordinate amount of this TV. Some of it was heart-wrenching Iraqi footage showing hundreds of shattered POWs returning from years of captivity in Iran. Many of these men carried posters of Saddam which had obviously been thrust into their hands for the benefit of the cameras. Nevertheless, the joy at being finally home was unmistakable as man after man fell to the ground and kissed it, often in tears. Others sat listlessly in wheelchairs. No voices were broadcast, just a continuous stream of returning men, against a background of 'Somewhere Over The Rainbow'. It was as surreal as it was tragic. The colleagues of these shattered men had just turned our lives upside down, but we were moved to tears at their plight.

Other Iraqi TV was more outrageous. Between programmes, they showed a new map of Iraq, with Kuwait tacked on to the southern end. They said that 40% of Americans had AIDS, and were coming to Saudi Arabia to spread it there. Then they put the Kuwait Ambassador to Baghdad, Mr Ibrahim Al-Bah'oo, and a young captive member of the Al-Sabah on TV, and forced them to speak against the Kuwaiti Government and praise the Iraqi intervention.

The Iraqis repeated the order for Westerners to report to hotels on several occasions over a week until it became clear that no one was going to comply voluntarily. Western governments now consistently advised their people to stay inside if at all possible, and complained to Baghdad that they didn't order their people around, and didn't want the Iraqi Government to do so either. Nevertheless, the Iraqis were already taking action. Most Westerners held in the Regency Palace Hotel were sent to four hostage sites within Kuwait in the early hours of 19 August.

For most of the week after the issue of Iraq's Revolutionary Command Council Resolution 341, Iraqi TV repeated the death threat for anyone helping foreigners. No one doubted that the Iraqis meant it. Some elements of the Kuwaiti Resistance quickly countered this by promising to kill or burn down the house of anyone who turned in a Westerner. A few Kuwaiti landlords asked their Western tenants to move, but the vast majority of Kuwaitis erected a wall of silence around them. They continued to harbour and in some cases feed the tenants, despite the threat to their own lives.

Our fear increased further as the barbaric nature of the Iraqi regime became more widely known. Many people had seen or heard of the hanging of the Iraqi Army major outside the Kuwait Governorate, and other Iraqis executed similarly around town. If the Iraqis could hang one of their own as an example for stealing a pair of shoes, then surely they could do at least that to anyone else. We were constantly reminded of Saddam's brutality to his own people, especially the gassing of the Kurds, and the treatment of Iranian POWs. It would not be long before that same brutality would be visited on Kuwait.

To their eternal credit, most Asians and Arabs, including many resident Iraqis, did not inform on Westerners, even under this threat of death. Nevertheless there was always the fear that if it were discovered that they knew where Westerners were hiding and had not volunteered the information, they would meet their end at the end of a rope, or with a bullet in the head.

The death threat was taken seriously. We heard stories of sons of Kuwaitis married to British women being threatened for harbouring their own mothers. Up until the time of the round-up announcement, Andrew Nobbay, a close Indian friend, had regularly visited my apartment. After the announcement, he continued to bring us fresh food which we could not go out and get ourselves. When his mother heard of this, she ordered him to stop, and called me, asking me to understand that she only had one son. I understood. Andrew's life was worth more than a few fresh vegetables.

We do not know of a single confirmed incident where a Westerner was captured because of information given to the Iraqis by a Kuwaiti, although one report told of a French family being turned in on 19 August after a disagreement with their landlord.

The Palestinians were quite a different story. Saddam had tried to align their cause with his, and Yasser Arafat had foolishly sided with him. His entrance into the Arab League meeting of 10 August, hand in hand with Iraqi Foreign Minister Tareq Aziz had incensed the Kuwaitis, especially after their substantial financial and political support to Palestinians over the years.

This lead from the PLO led to a small but significant minority actively collaborating with the Iraqis. Besides informing on Westerners and Kuwaitis, these Judases, including a few Egyptians and Kuwaitis, collaborated by joining the Iraqi Popular Army, manning roadblocks, helping to publish Iraqi newspapers in Kuwait, and assisting the Iraqis to strip Kuwait of its infrastructure. Incredibly, few of those Iraqis ordinarily resident in Kuwait cooperated with the invaders. Most were firmly on the side of the Kuwaitis and Westerners, even hiding them in several cases.

This minority was most definitely just that. Most Palestinians were honourable people. Many Westerners in Kuwait knew at least several Palestinians. Our concern was not necessarily about those we knew, but that our Palestinian friends would unwittingly let it slip within earshot of an informer that they knew a Westerner, and maybe even unwittingly cause their own death for concealing it. As such, the rule was to avoid all Palestinians. This was vindicated on several occasions when men who had been captured phoned us from hotels they were initially taken to in Kuwait, and told us that a Palestinian acquaintance had been with the Iraqis who arrested them.

Life for those in hiding became more and more difficult, particularly for those with children. People who had been been moving around Kuwait relatively freely in the first two weeks, but who had not tried to escape, found themselves scared, frustrated and bored, losing control of their own destiny.

Our main fear in the Al-Muthanna Complex was that the troops who had conducted the earlier house-to-house searches would be back. Thankfully we never saw them. Others had given Iraqi soldiers outside their homes water and bread, even shelter from the searing summer heat, and lived in fear that they would return, this time to take them away.

Some parents began to make arrangements to leave their babies or small children with Arab or Asian friends in case they were captured. The adults fully expected to be sent to strategic sites where they might lose their lives in the impending war. Few people had faith in sanctions.

People listened to the radio avidly. We would eat our evening meal, and then watch the evening TV news successively from Bahrain, Qatar, and finally Dubai, reception permitting. Qatar usually had the best coverage, but was hardest to pick up. We saw endless news clips of US forces arriving in Saudi Arabia: muscular, fit US Marines spoiling for a fight. It seemed inconceivable that the ill-disciplined conscript Iraqis we could see around us were holding off the cream of the West's fighting men. They weren't: the Western politicians were. Of course, we were unaware of the quality of the hundreds of thousands of Iraqi forces deployed between ourselves and the Marines, but on the surface it seemed such an uneven match.

George Bush was the target for a great deal of criticism in Kuwait for continuing his scheduled holiday while Americans were held hostage and US troops prepared for war in a faraway land. Among his sharpest critics were his own citizens in hiding in Kuwait, and several local US diplomats. He may have been sending a message to Saddam, but the hostages and those in hiding felt that he had all but abandoned them. Up to 20 August, Bush refused to use the term 'hostage', and talked mainly of defending Saudi Arabia, not of liberating Kuwait. The Baghdad newspapers picked up on his penchant for the links, lambasting him with cartoons headed 'Golf Crisis'.

British Prime Minister Margaret Thatcher was far more strident. She became the darling of many Americans hiding in Kuwait, and the Kuwaitis. She had the backbone and sense of purpose that Bush seemed to lack. Her more bellicose statements caused considerable concern that the Iraqis would react by making things worse for the British they held, but her firm stand was nevertheless widely applauded by many in hiding.

To be fair to Mr Bush, we did not appreciate the complexities of the Coalition he was building at the time. An immediate attack would have meant a far bloodier and less conclusive outcome, especially for the hostages, but at the time the matter seemed to deserve more attention than his golf.

Tension increased daily as the US sent F-117 'Stealth' bombers to Saudi Arabia, Egypt started shipping armour across the Red Sea, and Iraq let it be known that it had indeed moved SCUD missiles into Kuwait. The Americans rejected Iraqi calls for talks while Iraq occupied Kuwait and held hostages. Selected US military reserves were called up, and Iraq informed UN representatives in Baghdad that the fate of thousands of foreigners in its control would be decided by US military action. Margaret Thatcher continued to berate Saddam as a despot and tyrant hiding behind the skirts of women and children. War looked imminent within weeks.

As the deadline for the closure of the embassies in Kuwait drew near, several European missions, excluding the unfortunate British, French and West Germans, decided that the safety of their women and children lay in getting them to Baghdad where at least the Iraqis were recognizing their accreditation and there was regular communication with the outside world.

Baghdad was now a media circus. These women and children would be safer if they could be seen, and have access to food and medical attention. It was becoming clear that such people would not be placed on sites, but could not leave Iraq. There was even the hope they could drive out to Turkey. This had to be weighed against the risk of being caught in Baghdad if the war started.

The relocation argument won. A convoy of Austrians, Norwegians and Swiss, with their diplomats, drove to Baghdad on 21 August. The Swedes and Danes followed. I had put George Cienciala's Austrian-born wife, Anna, in touch with the Austrian Embassy through a German diplomat friend. She joined the convoy. Such was the nature of the network we were building.

The Austrians left the others in Baghdad, and drove to Zakho, on Iraq's northern border with Turkey, without any firm guarantees of being allowed to leave. At the border, the Iraqis would allow the diplomats out, but not the civilians. The story goes that the Austrians had succeeded in bribing the officer on duty to allow them all to cross into Turkey, when his superior drove up and withdrew the permission. The entire convoy was forced to return to the regional capital of Mosul, where they stayed in the local Oberoi Hotel for three days. The Swedes followed the Austrians to Zakho, and back to Mosul.

The Dutch and Belgians planned an evacuation of all their people from Kuwait, including men, for 22 August, but cancelled it after hearing of the problems the others had experienced. The non-essential Italian diplomats and some civilians left Kuwait for Baghdad in a minibus on 23 August, the day before the embassy closure order went into effect. They took with them most of the New Zealand and many of the Irish women and children, leaving an embassy skeleton staff. The Soviets also evacuated all their nationals who had not left on 16 August, declaring in a delightful piece of diplomatic double-speak that their embassy was not closed, merely temporarily unstaffed.

In the meantime, Austrian President and past UN Secretary-General Kurt Waldheim had arrived in Baghdad to plead his compatriots' case. Austria was playing a clever double game by capitalizing on its ostensible neutrality, and publicly denying the US military overflight rights until all Austrians who wanted to leave Iraq and Kuwait had done so. They used to the full their longstanding pro-Arab record, and the barely suppressed admiration which many Arabs had for Waldheim's wartime service in the anti-Jewish Nazi SS.

Saddam sent his personal aircraft to Mosul to collect the 95 Austrians. They met Waldheim amidst the smiles and TV cameras of the Iraqi propaganda machine. Then it was to the VIP lounge at Saddam International Airport, where they were delayed sufficiently to allow time for the TV footage to be transmitted to Vienna for the evening news, in time for their arrival home. The cynical Iraqi public relations machine was in full swing. However, the Swedes and Danes, without a figure to plead for them, had to stay.

The Iraqis were also moving people. On 22 August, the last 28 Westerners in the Kuwait International Hotel, including some BA crew, went to Baghdad.

The Japanese community was also moving out, taking their civilian nationals with them. Unknowingly, they would be playing into the Iraqis' hands.

It had been unclear whether or not the Iraqis intended to add the Japanese to the Human Shield, but the inclusion of Japanese *chargé d'affaires* Akio Shirota with the Western diplomats at the meeting with the Iraqi Ambassador on 19 August suggested that they were being viewed differently from other Asians. It was also obvious that the Japanese Embassy could not possibly remain as home to almost 300 individuals, especially if the Iraqis cut the water and power supplies after 24 August.

The Japanese Government in consultation with Mr Shirota decided to give their people the option of moving to Baghdad. About 100 Japanese decided to take their chances: others preferred to stay in the embassy for the time being. This first group left in the early hours of 22 August and made their way to the airport, where they paid their own way to Baghdad on the new Iraqi Airways 'domestic' service, which few people know about. The payment was a fine point of honour to establish that they were moving themselves, not being moved. Nevertheless, they were not happy, expecting at least another few days in Baghdad, with no guarantees that they could leave Iraq.

The 200 Japanese remaining behind - including about 20 infants and children -

prepared themselves for the the next escalation. They did not have long to wait. The Iraqis contacted Mr Shirota, requesting that he accept 'Iraqi protection' for the Japanese community. He refused. The Iraqis then demanded that he hand over everyone in the embassy. Again, he refused. It was now apparent that the Japanese were indeed in the same boat as the Westerners. By mid-afternoon, the Iraqis had surrounded the embassy, with their guns trained on it. The Japanese had become the first mission to be sealed off.

In the meantime, Canadian *chargé d'affaires* Bill Bowden, whose Ambassador's Residence was nearby, talked his way past the encircling Iraqis to see Shirota, and advised him of the nature of the Iraqis' deployment, and their equipment. It was obvious that the Iraqis were serious.

Long and agonizing discussions followed between Shirota and Tokyo on the embassy's secure communications systems. They were in a no-win situation. Shirota finally decided to recommend to his people that they all move to Baghdad, where it was thought they would have more of a chance to survive than in an embassy on the verge of being stormed. He gathered them and said 'I am not speaking to you as the *chargé d'affaires*, but in my own capacity. I am requesting that you move to Baghdad. You may be held there as hostages, but you will not be killed on the spot as we might be here. At any moment, the Iraqis might come in. Until now, we have lived through this situation as far as possible on our own terms. The decision to move should be made in our way.'

Early the following morning, everyone except Shirota prepared to leave the embassy for Baghdad. Tokyo had instructed that one officer remain in the embassy. The number was limited to one to minimize the expected casualties. It was apparently expected that whoever stayed behind might not survive. This was to be Shirota. It sounded melodramatic, but such was the prevailing atmosphere. Suddenly, as the group was leaving the premises, orders came that another man was to stay. It was not clear why two men should survive better than one, but orders were orders. A young, single male Arabist diplomat stayed with Shirota until both of them relocated to Baghdad a week later.

By the afternoon of 23 August, the Iraqis had almost 300 additional hostages in Baghdad. The Japanese civilians were kept at hotels, and the diplomats allowed to go to their embassy. The Japanese civilian men would eventually be sent to sites with the Americans, British, French and West Germans, and the women and children were released.

On 23 August, the Americans decided to evacuate 112 diplomatic and military personnel and dependents from their embassy compound, by road to Baghdad. The Iraqis had promised that they would be allowed to leave Iraq through Turkey. This would later be known in American circles as the 'Convoy to Hell'.

The Americans had agonized for days over whether to send the convoy at all. The Iraqis had promised an escort, but were becoming more difficult as the closure deadline drew near. Most people on the convoy did not want to go. They were nervous at leaving the relative safety of the embassy for an 800-kilometre drive to Baghdad. To make matters worse, news had filtered back on the BBC about the difficulties encountered by the British Embassy convoy of 16 August, and those of the other Europeans.

Nevertheless, the State Department had broader considerations. It needed the diplomats to stay as long as there were still Americans in hiding, and to maintain a political presence, if at all possible. Moving out people who could not contribute to that objective and who could go would save food and enable the embassy to hold out longer. It might even get those people out of Iraq.

The convoy was led by Emil Skodon, the Embassy's number three man, and had been organized by USLOK Lieutenant-Colonel Tom Funk. The plan was classic military organization. Each car was marked with a rooftop 'X' in contrasting tape so that it could be monitored from reconnaissance satellites. The 30 vehicles were grouped in 'march-units' of six cars each. Each unit would travel at five-minute intervals from the next to avoid a potentially dangerous accordion effect; each was stocked with food, water, and tools, and had spare places to accommodate people if one car broke down and had to be abandoned. Families were kept together, and each unit had a radio. A 'drag car' at the rear of the convoy was assigned to round up any stragglers.

The convoy hit trouble even before the Americans left their compound. The Iraqi escort failed to show at the appointed time of 3.00 a.m. The Americans were then told that there would be no escort unless every last diplomat on the embassy staff left in the convoy, and the embassy shut down. The Americans told the Iraqis 'no deal'. The convoy would go anyway, escort or no escort.

The escort and an Iraqi Ministry of Foreign Affairs (MFA) man eventually turned up at 5.00 a.m., together with an American diplomat from Baghdad, Charlie Sidel. The MFA man said that either all went, or only 50. A great deal of argument ensued within the American ranks between 'at least let's save the 50', and 'the entire convoy of 112, or nothing'. The Americans eventually decided that the 50 would go, and once they were on their way, the rest of the cars would simply drive out of the gate, follow the convoy, and try to bluff their way through. The last-minute change of plans wrecked Tom Funk's careful organization. Ten cars were pulled out of their march-units, and cobbled together into an *ad hoc* convoy for the official 50. The Iraqis refused to let any radios out of the compound, so the cars could not maintain voice contact with each other.

It was a traumatic parting. Eight diplomats and several dozen civilian men, women and children were staying behind. No one knew whether they would see them alive again. No one without a diplomatic passport could go. One of these was the baby son of one of the HAWK men, Bennie Mitchell, and his Filipina wife. In desperation and compassion, USLOK Master Sergeant Al Allen and his Korean wife took the boy with them in the hope of passing him off as their own. However, this put 51 individuals on the official convoy.

The first group sped off at 6.00 a.m., led by Ambassador Howell in his armoured limousine. Howell would accompany them to Abdaly, the farthest point to which he could travel without actually leaving Kuwait. Two locally-employed Palestinian drivers accompanied the convoy to provide whatever help they could. The second group of 61 left shortly afterwards in about 20 cars, trying desperately to catch up with the speeding Ambassador.

It was a recipe for disaster. Few people had slept much in the past days. They were scared and tired, driving at high speed, trying to keep up with the cars ahead. The first accident happened before they had even left the urban area. Apparently the driver of one of the last cars mistook a hitch-hiking Iraqi soldier for a checkpoint and slowed, but the following vehicle, driven by Mr Bobby Higgins, didn't. The ensuing collision dislocated his wife Odessa's right leg at the hip. Amazingly, only Mrs Higgins was seriously injured.

Lieutenant-Colonel Funk and several of the Marines in the drag car soon came across the scene, with people milling around in confusion. The rest of the convoy had carried on ahead, unaware of the accident. Mrs Higgins had to be taken to a hospital quickly, but whoever took her back might be interned by the Iraqis, now that their diplomatic immunity was uncertain. There was no choice. Funk and one of the Marines, Corporal Dan Hudson, took Higgins and her husband back to the embassy, nearly an hour away. She was in agony and barely conscious. Corporal Hudson sat in the back with her, and nursed her all the way. He is credited with saving her life by keeping her out of shock.

At the embassy, Mrs Higgins was examined by Dr James Carroll, a paediatrician taking refuge there. He gave her a shot of morphine. The three men then took Mr and Mrs Higgins to the nearby Amiri Hospital. Mrs Higgins was admitted and treated, and her husband hidden by Filipino medical staff.

Funk, Hudson, and Dr Carroll returned to the embassy. The two servicemen discussed whether they should stay, or risk trying to catch up with the convoy. They chose to take their chances, and took to the road again.

Meanwhile, the 51 members of the first part of the convoy had arrived at the border. Ambassador Howell had stopped at Abdaly, while the rest of the convoy proceeded across the one kilometre border strip to Safwan. The Iraqis there said they had no permission to allow the convoy through. Emil Skodon and Charlie Sidel told them to check with Baghdad. The Americans waited for what seemed like an eternity in the stifling heat as the Iraqis tried to find someone in authority in Baghdad to talk to.

The British, at the same time, had decided to reduce their skeleton embassy staff from the remaining ten men to four, having already sent their families to Baghdad a week earlier in the ill-fated convoy of 16 August. The six departing British diplomats, led by DHM Tony Millson, passed through the border largely unhindered, overtaking the stalled Americans, but could do little for them other than carry news of their fate to Baghdad.

The Iraqis finally told Skodon and Sidel that they had one more than the agreed number, and that they could only let 50 go through. There was an additional problem with the Mitchell infant in Master Sergeant Allen's care not having his own passport. Skodon said it was either all or nothing. Some of the Americans backed Skodon. Others suggested that one person go back so that at least the 50 could get through.

Then the second group turned up, with an additional 57 people, followed some time later by Lieutenant-Colonel Funk and Corporal Hudson. This more than doubled the problem for the Iraqis, but Skodon continued haranguing them. Finally, the Iraqis said they had to verify that every individual was either a diplomat, or a member of a diplomatic family. In fact, almost half of the men on the convoy were military, but on diplomatic passports.

The Iraqis eventually allowed the convoy to pass through intact after three hours, as Ambassador Howell, his driver, and the two Palestinian staffers returned to Kuwait City. The convoy finally arrived at the US Embassy in Baghdad at 1.45 a.m. on 24 August, after a 19-hour ordeal, expecting to rest for a few hours before carrying on to Turkey. They were greeted with the news that the Iraqis had reneged on their promise. They could go no further unless the embassy in Kuwait closed down completely.

Five people who should have been on the convoy were the HAWK missile men who had reported to the embassy on State Department instructions. They had been told that they would go out with the evacuated diplomats, and to tell other American citizens the same thing. However, their names got lost somewhere in the system, and they were not allowed to leave. Strangely, men seconded from Federal Highways to Kuwait were on the convoy. Someone in Washington apparently assigned more priority to road engineers than missile experts who could show the Iraqis how to shoot down US warplanes.

Two of the men, Tal Ledford and Guy Seago - incensed at being denied the chance to escape earlier - decided to take their chances and try to get to Saudi Arabia after the convoy left. The Iraqis soon captured them. The other three elected to stay in the compound. A sixth, Tom Kreuzeman, who had refused to come in, remained successfully in hiding, feeling greatly vindicated.

Thursday, 23 August also saw one of the worst Iraqi public relations blunders of the whole crisis. The Iraqis had been particularly stung by criticism of their treatment of the hostages, so they televized a visit by Saddam himself to a group of British families in a camp.

In Kuwait, we could hardly believe our eyes when we saw Saddam walk into the room, dressed in a smart grey suit and silk tie, complete with matching handkerchief in the breast pocket of the jacket. He was accompanied by his personal translator, Dr Saadoun Joubaydi, and an Air Force colonel and Army lieutenant-colonel, both armed with pistols. Dr Joubaydi would later become known as 'Mr Smoothie' for his extremely polished English accent and instantaneous translation.

The 25 hostages themselves seemed just as surprised, and slightly intimidated. They were a mixture of British BLT families, with children, and BA149 passengers. One was an unaccompanied 15-year-old British boy, Alan Barnett, who had been on his way to Malaysia to join his family.

Saddam smiled and shook the hands of the nervous men, then sat on an upright chair, facing the group, looking very relaxed and in charge. The officers stood respectfully behind him, with Dr Joubaydi to his side. There were insufficient seats to go around. Many of the women sat; most of the men stood. Outside the building, unseen by the cameras, a company of crack Special Forces surrounded the complex, providing security.

The Iraqi President launched into a speech, expressing concern for the hostages' welfare and explaining that he had come to see their conditions for himself. There was no hint of apology for their detention. More hostages, hurriedly gathered from elsewhere, continued to enter the room.

The most memorable scene was when Saddam called over five-year-old

Stuart Lockwood, whose father, Derek, was a BLT Warrant Officer, and a slightly older boy, Ian Martin. Those who knew Stuart from Kuwait thought him an obnoxious brat, but now he was a picture of terrified innocence, with his fine, fair hair, summer shorts, and *Le Coq Sportif* T-shirt. Ian kept on glancing at his parents. Stuart did the same, constantly folding and unfolding his arms as Saddam put his own arm around him and stroked his hair.

In Kuwait, we could barely believe the evidence of our eyes. This was so cynical. The Iraqis had misjudged the Western mind terribly if they thought this would portray Saddam as the kindly uncle. One of our group broke the silence by shouting out: *'Go on, Stuart! Piss on his knee. Piss on it!'*

Unknown to us, and edited out by Iraqi TV, another child called Dale actually kicked Saddam's ankle, and is probably the only person to have done so since Saddam was in school, and escape with his life.

Stuart held his bladder and Saddam's knee stayed dry, but the colonel behind, entering into the spirit of the kindly tyrant, tousled the boy's hair, and patted his cheek, smiling paternally as if Stuart were his own nephew.

Stuart looked increasingly uncomfortable as the session continued, never once meeting Saddam's eye or uttering a word as questions went back and forth between Saddam and the boy's father on Stuart's nutrition, especially milk and cornflakes. The significance of the subject was not lost on us. The Iraqis' main line of attack against the UN sanctions was that they prevented the importation of baby formula, thus causing the deaths of Iraqi babies through malnutrition. This was ludicrous. Iraq is an incredibly fertile land, and its women are not renowned for their lactation deficiencies. More relevantly, humanitarian supplies were specifically excluded from the embargo.

Mr Lockwood was polite and terse, although visibly nervous, and desperate to get his son back. He gave Saddam no opening. The dictator knew better than to pursue the matter. He changed tack, launching into a political lecture.

The hostages themselves soon bounced back, especially the women. A lady doctor by the name of Marla, a BA149 passenger, bombarded Saddam with cleverly-crafted questions as to why, if they really were guests, they could not leave as guests are normally free to do. Saddam took this in his stride, avoiding a direct answer, but reiterating that they were serving a great purpose in preventing a war, even appealing to their sense of duty in doing so.

The questions moved onto the children, and the practical question of getting them back to school in time for the September term. 'They have exams coming up,' explained one of the women. It was suggested that the children should be let go, so that their education would not be disturbed. The women were clever. They appealed to the natural Arab concern for children and family. Saddam was not taken in. He promised to have the Iraqi Women's Federation and government teachers attend to the ladies' concerns. There was no hint that they would be released in the near future, let alone in time to start school.

One of the group's main concerns was that their families at home were made aware that they were safe and well. Saddam told them they could write letters and take photographs, and that they would be forwarded.

Saddam spent a full two hours with the group. During that time, one of the women complained about being thrown out of her home in Kuwait, and being forced to leave all her possessions behind. Amazingly, Saddam apologized, and promised that everyone would be fully compensated. The greatest triumph for the hostages came at the end of the meeting, just before a group photo was taken, when young Alan Barnett's situation was explained. Saddam agreed that he could go, even giving him a US$500 parting gift.

A full third of the session was televised, suitably edited by the Iraqis. The entire Western world was outraged. Every parent could identify with it. The media had a field day. Margaret Thatcher launched into further tirades against Saddam, with her most vehement accusations that he was something less than a complete man. 'Way to go, Maggie!' we cried, but many people in the camps wished she had held her tongue while they were in Iraqi custody.

Gone was the image of stoical expatriates keeping a stiff upper lip in temporary difficulties, and a squabble between Third World Arab neighbours. The crisis now became personal to the West. Innocent children were being manipulated by evil despots and swarthy men in dark uniforms with guns.

The Iraqis then tried to drive a wedge through the UN Security Council by offering to release an unspecified number of the 560 French nationals in Iraq and Kuwait as a sign of trust, and in the hope that France would withdraw its forces being sent to Saudi Arabia. The French denounced this, insisting on the immediate and unconditional release of all hostages, without exception.

True to Saddam's word, the Iraqi Women's Federation arrived that very afternoon, and young Alan Barnett left for home, as did 10-year-old American Penelope Nabakov, who had also been travelling unaccompanied on BA149.

The following day, Friday 24 August, the Iraqi order to close the embassies went into effect. Tension mounted noticeably in the hours leading up to this. Everyone waited to see what would happen in this first real face-to-face showdown between Iraq and the Western governments – ignorant as we were of what had happened with the Japanese. We were fearful for the individual diplomats in the compounds. As direct instruments of their governments' defiance of Saddam, we presumed that they would be singled out for harsh treatment. The air of countdown rivalled that of any Apollo moon mission.

The courage and *sang froid* of many of these young diplomats was commendable. Most were volunteers who had had option of moving to their missions in Baghdad. Several of the ambassadors simply fell apart, leaving the task of maintaining their country's presence to their deputies and staff.

Curiously, even the time of the deadline was confused. Different embassies were dreading different hours. The British and several others seemed to think the deadline was midnight on 23 August when it was apparently noon on the 24th. The four remaining British diplomats packed their bags, expecting the Iraqis to turn up at midnight, demanding that they leave. They were going to refuse, and expected to be marched out at gunpoint. That afternoon, the electricity was cut, reinforcing their assumption that the closure time was that night. The four men dined later by candlelight, than opened up their secure communications with London, and waited for midnight. When nothing happened an hour or so after midnight, Don Macauley was locked into the communications centre so that he would have time to get the word out in case the Iraqis came in. The Ambassador and the other two men went to bed.

The following morning, the Americans – who had been counting down to a noon deadline – discovered to their detriment how meticulous the Iraqis could be. The Korean Ambassador's earlier concern over whether they should be following Kuwaiti or Iraqi summer time was justified. At 10.45 a.m. Kuwait time, a friendly Palestinian was driving a tanker truck of diesel fuel towards the embassy. The fuel was required to power the generators required for communications if the Iraqis cut the power to the embassies, as they subsequently did. The truck was stopped, and the driver told that the embassy was sealed off. The diplomats protested that there were still 75 minutes to go. The Iraqis replied that it was now 11.45 a.m. Iraq time, and that as Kuwait was part of Iraq, it was now 11.45 a.m. Kuwait time. The truck would not be able to get in and out of the embassy within 15 minutes. It was not allowed in.

Everyone except the Iraqis had been ignoring the hour's summertime difference between Iraq and Kuwait. The lack of this vital diesel would later have potentially serious consequences for the Americans. Ambassador Howell was later reported as saying, with the sense for an historical quip which diplomats reserve for such occasions: 'Well, I guess midnight came early.'

At the time, the media conjured up images of embassies ringed with battalions of tanks. This was far removed from the truth. The heaviest guard on any of them was a squad of soldiers. The Iraqis needed nothing else. The diplomats were hardly going to put up a fight, and had said they were going to stay.

When nothing happened to the embassies immediately after the closure deadline, there was a great sense of relief and anti-climax. In fact, it suited the Iraqis to have the diplomats remain in their missions. Their presence provided yet another layer of Human Shields in Kuwait City itself, and these hostages would feed themselves. Any diplomats who did leave were usually escorted politely to Baghdad, but not sent to strategic sites.

Nevertheless, the Iraqis did not make it easy for the defiant diplomats. On 25 August, they cut off their electricity, mains water, and some of the phones. Curiously, they did not cut all the lines. The West Germans reconnected their phones to their lesser known fax line, and operated quite successfully. The British and Americans had some lines cut, but were always contactable.

The same day, the UN Security Council passed Resolution 665 authorizing the use of force by naval blockade to enforce the earlier sanctions. However, George Bush continued to stress the defence of Saudi Arabia, still avoiding any specific mention of liberating Kuwait. He seemed to be relying on sanctions to force Saddam out. However, Margaret Thatcher's focus was always on Kuwait. The distinction was not lost on the Kuwaitis. They needed American firepower and forces, but Mrs Thatcher was their real hero.

On 25 August, the day after the US Embassy's 'Convoy to Hell' arrived in Baghdad, the diplomats' dependants were allowed to leave Iraq via Turkey. The men and the three female diplomats had to stay, although these women were also allowed to leave later. Their greatest fears – of the families being broken up

– were realized, but the women had to go for the sake of the children. Only one American male diplomat, Charlie Sidel, was allowed to accompany them to the border at Zakho. The normal six-hour drive took three times as long. Once there, they were again held up in the heat while the Iraqis argued whether three 18-year-old boys and a 15-year-old girl without diplomatic passports could go. The border was a mass of heaving humanity, with tens of thousands of Asian refugees trying to get into Turkey. There was no water, no food, and only overflowing concrete trenches for toilets.

The American women were now as angry as they were scared. One made her own little protest. She changed her baby's diaper, and then threw the soiled one out of the car. Her eldest daughter protested, saying 'Mommy, you're not supposed to do that!' She replied 'Only in this country, dear. Only here...'

The Iraqis finally settled on who could go, but only allowed cars with diplomatic plates to cross. Those with regular Kuwaiti plates had to be left on the Iraqi side. The three young men had to return to Baghdad with Mr Sidel, but the girl was allowed to go. The 20 American women and 27 children were finally told to proceed. As they drove north through the soft sand, a bridge came into view, with an arched sign saying 'Welcome To Turkey'.

On 28 August Saddam finally turned on his Saudi neighbours, thus hardening their stance against him. He seemed to be wanting to make enemies.

Earlier in the month, the Iraqis had gone to great lengths to reassure the Saudis that they were safe, and that Iraq had no designs on their lands. Up to that time, the Saudis' aims were to have Saddam withdraw inside his own borders. They did not want to fight brother Arabs. Saddam had been flaying the Saudis for inviting in foreign forces, but had not specifically threatened them. They could absorb this rhetoric as long as it did not get more serious.

Then Saddam suddenly declared a *jihad* against the Saudis – a step not taken lightly in Islam. He called for the overthrow of the Saudi monarchy, and threatened to destroy the Kuwaiti and Saudi oilfields if sanctions against him were not lifted. It was the same day that his annexation of Kuwait as Iraq's 19th Province came into effect.

This was not something that the Saudis could ignore, especially with their pre-eminent role as the guardians of Islam's holiest places. It was at this point that the West's and the Saudis' war aims began converging rapidly. No longer would the Saudis be happy for Saddam to withdraw with his forces intact. Like the Americans and British, they now wanted his war machine put out of action to prevent it becoming an even greater threat in the future. They would now support an attack on Iraq itself, in the context of liberating Kuwait.

In Saudi Arabia, Allied forces were flooding into the country faster than the Saudis could accommodate them. Many of these were Kuwaiti servicemen who had been on leave outside Kuwait at the time of the invasion, or who had escaped from Kuwait through the desert, or Iran.

One of these new arrivals was Major-General Jaber Al-Khalid, the Kuwaiti Deputy Chief of Staff. He had spent the first three weeks of the occupation in Kuwait, feeling increasingly redundant. Other officers were leading the

Resistance, and as a general he felt of little use without troops. He, Chief of Staff Misyad Al-Sane and KAF Commander Brigadier Daoud Alghanim decided that their place lay with their forces outside Kuwait.

On 22 August, the three generals had slipped out across the desert in a Chevrolet Suburban through the Minagish oilfield. They carried cartons of cigarettes to bribe any Iraqis they encountered, joking nervously that it would be a good catch for the Iraqis to find all three of them together in one car.

The escape was easier than they expected. The Iraqis hardly bothered them once a few cigarettes changed hands. They reached Hafr Al-Batin safely, called the Kuwaiti Government in Taif, and were ordered to fly there immediately. They were desperately needed to help reconstitute their forces.

In late August, Al-Khalid, now Acting Chief of Staff, addressed his mustered troops at Hafr Al-Batin, saying:

'We owe a great deal of thanks to our Arab brothers and our Western friends who will assist us in reclaiming our country.

'But the first blood to be spilled must be the blood of a Kuwaiti, and the first Kuwaiti blood must be that of your officers as you lead your troops.'

He then contacted General Schwarzkopf. 'I have a special request. The forces that lead the attack to liberate Kuwait must be Kuwaiti.' Schwarzkopf replied: 'Your request is granted.'

The American was as good as his word. When the war started, Kuwait Air Force planes were among the first into Kuwait, and suffered one of the first casualties. Fortunately, the pilot survived, becoming a POW. The Kuwait Navy, with US Navy assistance, would be the first to engage the Iraqis at sea, and would be the first to liberate Kuwaiti soil, an offshore island. On land, Kuwaiti scouts led US Marines across the border, and provided liaison and intelligence to every other major Allied formation. Six small Kuwaiti brigades took part in the ground fighting. The main mission of routing the Iraqi forces had to be given to the more powerful Western forces, but their limit of advance was Sixth Ring. The potentially bloody mission of fighting the Iraqis out of the urban area fell to the Kuwaitis and their Arab allies.

But that was far in the future. At the time, in late August, the only people actually fighting for Kuwait were the Kuwaiti Resistance, inside Kuwait. We could hear their sudden, sharp battles almost every night, and even sometimes daytime sniping attacks and car bombs. They would inflict casualties, and incur many themselves, but the message to the Iraqis was clear: 'This is our country. Get out!'

Brothers in history, cycles in time....
Mubarak Al-Kabeer (top left, ruled 1896-1915) who, with his predecessor, gave refuge to the Al-Saud when they were chased from their lands in the early 1890s by the rival Rasheedis. From Kuwait, the young Abdulaziz Ibn Saud (top right, in later life) reclaimed Riyadh in 1902, with the help of Kuwaiti cavalry and other allies, and built what is today the Kingdom of Saudi Arabia. Eighty-eight years later, Ibn Saud's son, King Fahd (bottom right) returned the favour by granting refuge to Mubarak's grandsons, Amir Sheikh Jaber Al-Ahmad, (bottom left) and Crown Prince and Prime Minister Sheikh Saad Al-Abdullah (bottom centre) and their people, thus enabling them and their allies to reclaim Kuwait.

As Kuwait newspapers were rolling off the presses in the pre-dawn hours of 2 August, 1990, expressing hopes for further talks, Iraqi tanks were rolling towards Kuwait City. Saddam never had any intention of talking. It was complete strategic surprise.

The week before the invasion, Kuwaiti newspapers hailed the imminent settlement of the crisis which had blown up during the previous fortnight. In Baghdad on 25 July, 1990, Saddam told US Ambassador April Glaspie 'We aren't going to do it'. Egyptian President Hosni Mubarak, who had just left Baghdad for Kuwait, was similarly misled. King Hussein of Jordan's role is less clear.

Eye-in-the-sky... With the TPS-63 ground surveillance radar on the T-COM observation balloon tethered near Jahra, the Kuwait High Command could virtually count the Iraqi tanks arrayed against them, but the political assessment until it was too late was that Saddam was bluffing.

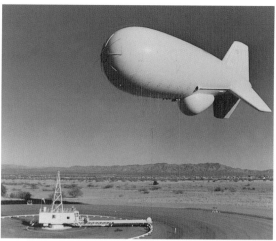

Kuwaiti Mirage F-1 interceptors scramble at dawn from Ali Al-Salem KAF base. Commanded by Colonel Saber Al-Suwaidan (shown left), Mirages such as those shown downed sixteen confirmed Iraqi aircraft; the A-4 Skyhawks from Ahmad Al-Jaber base downed five, and flew ground attack missions against Republican Guard columns.

A Kuwaiti Improved-Hawk air defence missile takes to the air. Kuwaiti Hawks, in four batteries, three of which were in action, accounted for ten confirmed Iraqi helicopters, four fixed-wing fighters, three unconfirmed helicopters, one unconfirmed fighter, and - tragically - one Kuwait Puma helicopter.

Kuwait Navy 57-metre fast patrol boat, KNS Istiqlal *, which, with* KNS Sanbouk, *took on Iraqi naval forces on the morning of 2 August, 1990.*

Iraq armoured personnel carriers approach central Kuwait City from the south on the Maghreb-Assafar Motorway. Notice how local citizens have painted over the bottom half of the street sign on the right in a desperate but futile attempt to deny the Iraqis directions.

Iraqi armour outside the Armed Forces Club in Salwa. The aircraft in the background is an old Kuwait fighter on display.

Alone against the world. From the first hours of the invasion, the Iraqis deployed armour along the coast in defense against an amphibious attack, which never came.

As Iraqi armour poured into Kuwait City in a well-planned pincer, elements of Kuwait's 35 Armoured Brigade under Colonel Salem Al-Sarour (shown later as a Major-General) fought a fierce but one-sided battle against elements of two Iraqi Republican Guard divisions west of the city.

Within days of the invasion, Kuwaiti civilians, mainly women and students, went onto the streets in organised, unarmed demonstrations in protest. Iraqi troops fired on a number of these demonstrations, killing students Sana Al-Foderi, 20, and Waheed Safri, 19, in separate incidents. Several other individuals were wounded.

Ego trip... Name change to Saddam's preference

Door-to-door searches became a regular feature of life as the Iraqis hunted down members of the Kuwait ruling family, military and police, and Westerners. The man in the white safari suit is Mukhabarat, who generally commanded the search teams. The troops are most likely Special Forces, known universally at the time in Kuwait as the 'red berets', and sometimes confused with the Republican Guard.

Cars were stripped of wheels and engine parts, even licence plates, and the showrooms burned. One story circulated that one major car dealer - Alghanims - gave whatever cars they could away to their staff, then burned their showroom with the remaining stock inside to prevent the Iraqis from getting it.

A panorama of the US Embassy compound, Kuwait, seen from an Iraqi's eye-view, from the roof of the nearby Kuwait International Hotel. The besieged diplomats and civilians held out for almost four months, without mains power and water. British and American Human Shields were held in atrocious conditions in the villas in the left background. Any rescue attempt would have meant killing at least some civilians in the hotel. Said US Ambassador Howell, 'the longest embassy siege since 55 days at Peking'.

British Ambassador Michael Weston (on right) and Consul Larry Banks, the last Western diplomats to leave Kuwait in December 1990, and the first to return in February 1991, seen after liberation.

Camp Kuwait - the group of US diplomats and civilians who held out in their besieged embassy until their release in December 1990.

Japanese Chargé d'Affaires Akio Shirota, hailed as a hero by James Baker. Shirota gave refuge to US military personnel, US diplomats, and their families during the first weeks of the occupation. The Japanese were the first embassy sealed off by the Iraqis.

The blockaded diplomats in both the American and British embassies dug wells. The American well, dubbed 'Brownie's Hole', was the brainchild of Ohio engineer Paul Brown who persisted despite the doubts and jibes of his countrymen.

US Ambassador Nat Howell, and Deputy Chief of Mission Barbara Bodine, who actually ran the compound.

9. THE ANATOMY OF A PICK–UP

A 'pick-up' was the process whereby the Iraqis captured Westerners and Japanese, and usually placed them on strategic sites as 'Human Shields'. Most were conducted in an extraordinarily civil fashion. There were numerous notable exceptions, but the general pattern was one of respect and reassurance – quite the opposite of when the Iraqis arrested Kuwaitis, a large number of whom were either held for ransom, or transported to jails in Iraq.

Once picked–up in Kuwait, captive Westerners were generally taken to the Regency Palace Hotel, where they were housed in five-star luxury for several days. They were then bussed or flown to Baghdad for another few days in the Mansour Melia Hotel, while the Iraqis decided which site to send them to.

There were several variations on this theme, depending on the stage of the crisis. Apart from the BA149 people, the Japanese community, and the BLT men taken from their homes, the four main types of pick-ups were from the street in Kuwait, especially in the first and third weeks of the crisis; hotels in Kuwait; the desert, during escape attempts, and homes. A number of men, particularly Americans, British and French, who were resident in or visiting Iraq were also taken in Baghdad in late August when the Iraqis were apparently unable to find enough Human Shields from Kuwait.

Pick-ups from the streets in Kuwait were generally confined to the first week of the crisis, when people were unaware that Westerners were being taken, and late in the third week, immediately after the round-up order, when some people thought it was still safe to drive around.

During the first week, there was little consistency. Most pick-ups then were of people who were simply in the wrong place at the wrong time. Those who found themselves in Baghdad in these early days were accommodated at the Mansour Melia or Al-Rasheed Hotels. They were initially allowed limited consular access, until mid-August, just before they were despatched to sites.

Whereas the early captives of 2/3 August were first taken to Army camps near Basra, and then to Baghdad, other people captured from Kuwait's streets later in the first week were taken to the nearest hotel that had been sealed off by the Iraqis, and detained. At the same time, incredibly, other Westerners were moving around Kuwait completely unmolested.

Most early street pick-ups were done by the Army, usually Special Forces or the Republican Guard (it was hard to distinguish them, as they both wore red berets) and not by the *Mukhabarat*. It could be a particularly unpleasant experience as the soldiers lacked the interpersonal skills of the secret police. One American captured on the street, Paul Eliopoulos, had his glasses broken by the troops and recalls his main fear at the time was of being raped by them. Such incidents of direct physical violence were, however, rare.

More importantly, when women were involved, there were no publicized incidents of serious assault by the troops, although their behaviour towards some women could be classified as sexual harassment. However, the soldiers seldom allowed people captured on the streets to go home to inform their families, collect their passports, or even pack a change of clothes. They were taken as they were. In some early cases, men were forcibly separated from their wives at gunpoint. The women were allowed to go free, but their protests fell on deaf ears. However, after the first few days, families were always taken away as a group, and when the women were later allowed to leave Iraq, they were given the option of staying with their men.

The Army usually turned over captured people to the *Mukhabarat* as soon as they could, usually within 24 hours. The army seemed to dislike the job handling civilian prisoners, appearing to consider it beneath them.

This first phase of capturing Westerners from the street lasted about four days. Then, inexplicably, it stopped. The Iraqis may have found themselves unprepared to handle the several hundred people they suddenly found themselves burdened with. They were swamped. The invasion took the Iraqi bureaucracy as much by surprise as anyone else.

At that stage, many Westerners had been moving around, largely unhindered, since 2 August, getting supplies of food and petrol, sightseeing and plotting escape routes. Perhaps a score out of thousands of Westerners had been captured from the streets. The rest of those under direct Iraqi control in the early days were from three major hotels, oil installations and survey sites in the desert, the BLT and BA149.

Most people were unaware of the civilian captures that had occurred: others were aware of them but had encountered no direct problems with the Iraqis, and so continued moving around. When they met friendly Iraqis, this only convinced them that the people who had been captured were just plain unlucky. The captives were incommunicado, so we could not discover the truth.

Street pick-ups in Kuwait resumed on about 19 August, four days after the round-up order. It took the Iraqis that long to get organized. Most Westerners at that time were staying inside, but a few ventured out to get food, or to return to their own apartments after moving in with others, and were captured. This usually involved a visit to a local police station or school where the local battalion was headquartered, registration with the army, and finally a drive to be turned over to the *Mukhabarat* at the Regency Palace or SAS Hotels.

This second phase of pick-ups from the streets was much more organized. The Iraqis had their own procedures clear in their minds. The Army was merely acting for the *Mukhabarat*, who were actually running the Human Shield programme. People were handed over to the *Mukhabarat* in Kuwait almost immediately instead of being first taken to Basra Army camps.

Pick-ups from hotels occurred from the second day of the occupation until the end of August.

Removal of people from hotels must be distinguished from the use of these facilities as holding points for people captured in other circumstances. At the time of the invasion, there were about 200 Westerners and Japanese in the ten major Kuwait hotels. The treatment of these people depended greatly on the officer in charge. There were no set rules. When staff and guests were taken from the Sheraton they could not even go back to their rooms for their passports or clothes, but at the Salam Palace, on the same day, the guests could pack and the phones were turned on so that they could call their embassies or friends and tell them what was happening.

The most unfortunate hotel guests were those in the Sheraton, where a nearby park was taken over by the Iraqis early on the first morning as a staging area. The guests were forced outside into the park opposite the hotel, where they had to sit for several hours with bullets flying over their heads, Iraqi armour driving past into the city, and helicopters landing nearby, before being eventually allowed back into the hotel and sealed in.

On 5 August, after the Iraqis had released most of the non-Westerners, the others were taken to Basra in three buses late the following day. Apparently one of the buses went to the Basra Prison instead of the Basra Sheraton, and the unfortunate 26 male passengers spent the night in atrocious conditions. The people on the other two Kuwait Sheraton buses were more fortunate, and went to their hotel's namesake in Basra.

The Salam Palace Hotel was sealed off early on the morning of 3 August. The troops entered the hotel, very politely, at 7.30 a.m. The 200 guests and staff of various nationalities were called to the lobby, and told by the officers that they were checking the hotel for members of the Al-Sabah. The management were ordered to take down pictures of the Amir and Crown Prince and Prime Minister. Kuwaitis and Arab guests were allowed to leave, but the others were warned to refrain from going outside for their own safety. Access to phone lines and all TV stations except Baghdad were cut.

Three days later, at 9.20 a.m., 58 of the Americans, British, French and Germans among the 161 BA149 passengers then at the Airport Hotel and the 17 Western staff and guests from the Messila Beach Hotel were taken to Basra in three minibuses. Captain Peter Clark and the BA crew stayed behind at the Airport Hotel with remaining passengers, primarily Malaysians, Australians and Italians, and a few Britons with non-British spouses.

The sole American, two Germans, and seven British at the Salam Palace - including Mary Hall, a Baghdad-based diplomat who had been visiting Kuwait on a shopping trip with her children at the time of the invasion - were then taken to the Sheraton in Basra. The normal two-hour drive took 15 hours, with the escorting Iraqis constantly apologizing for the inconvenience, and assuring them that the move to Baghdad was for their own safety.

The people from these four hotels in Kuwait, the two BLT officers captured on 4 August, and a few other captives, now totalling over 100, were consolidated at the Basra Sheraton on the afternoon of 6 August. The Salam Palace and Kuwait Sheraton people and a few others were eventually bussed to Baghdad just after 3.00 p.m.; the Messila Beach people and the BA passengers from the Airport Hotel went by overnight train, in sleeper cars. For the trip, the Iraqis kept the groups together according to their original source.

One of the captured men in Baghdad was a Canadian oilman, Graham Pierce. He was initially kept with his American and British colleagues in the Al-Rasheed, but released to his embassy on 7 August. Even at this early stage - five days into the crisis - the Iraqis had selected the key nationalities for the Human Shield programme, but it would be some time before we became generally aware of that.

The people in the remaining six major Kuwaiti hotels were more fortunate, at least for the next 12 days. The West Germans cleared all their nationals from these hotels as soon as they heard of the Messila Beach pick-up, but other embassies left their people where they were. All Westerners in the Holiday Inn escaped across the desert, or went into hiding. The Iraqis initially seem to have forgotten about it, and did not seal it off until 18 August.

Four hostage sites were established in Kuwait early the following morning. The first moves from the Regency Palace and SAS Hotels to the sites were not made until then, by which time some of the staff and guests, including Richard Brunyate, the British Airways Captain who had landed BA149 in Kuwait, and several of his crew, had escaped into the suburbs and into hiding. Brunyate was later nicknamed 'Captain Fantastic' for his escapades in always staying one step ahead of the Iraqis. In the early hours of 19 August, the Regency was almost completely emptied of Westerners in preparation for receiving people from the next major phase of pick-ups, from homes.

The Kuwait International was cleared out on 22 August. General Manager Hermann Simon started the crisis with 64 Western guests. Others had since come and gone. By the time the Iraqis came for the remaining Westerners, Simon had smuggled out all but 28. Those remaining were BA crew, moved in by the Iraqis on 16 August, and others who were not prepared to risk an escape.

Simon was summoned to explain the missing people. Fearing for his life, he could only explain as diplomatically as possible that he had no idea the Iraqis were coming for the people; perhaps they had simply found alternative accommodation. The Iraqi was upset, but gave his word that Simon would come to no harm because of the missing guests. Simon was left behind as Austrians were not wanted, and the Iraqis left his German wife with him.

The other Westerners in the hotel at that stage had their passports collected without warning in the afternoon. Soon afterwards, a British diplomat came to the hotel, and was told to leave. Two American diplomats who visited later were ordered away at gunpoint.

In the two weeks since the Iraqis had last cleared out a Kuwaiti hotel, they had still not quite organized themselves as much as they might have. The 28 hostages were bussed in an old, dilapidated coach to a military camp in Jahra where they were put in a barracks room with camp beds for the night. The following day, they were split into three groups, and spent that night in separate locations near Jahra, and were then reunited at an army camp near Abdaly, where they spent another night in Nissen huts. They finally returned to five-star accommodation at the Mansour Melia in Baghdad on 25 August. It had taken them three days from Kuwait to Baghdad.

The last people to be taken from Kuwaiti hotels were moved out to Baghdad on 30/31 August. When the few remaining Westerners in the Plaza, which had been sealed off on 16 August, were first moved out of the Plaza, they thought they were going direct to Baghdad, but were simply moved across the road to the Meridien and consolidated with others there.

People who had been captured and held in the Regency Palace since the

Kuwait hostage camps were set up on 19 August were moved out on the morning of 30 August. Several dozen Britons and French, together with other Europeans, Australians and New Zealanders in the SAS Hotel at the time left by bus for Baghdad at 8.15 a.m. on the 31st, and were joined by those from the Meridien and Plaza.

The Iraqis had used the past week to catch up on their organization. Instead of staging people through Basra, they were taken directly to Baghdad. From there, the American, British, French, German and Japanese men were eventually sent to sites. The others were eventually released to their embassies, and the women and children allowed to leave Iraq.

Like street pick-ups, pick-ups from the Kuwaiti desert during attempts to escape to Saudi Arabia were very few in the first week, stopped almost entirely during the second week, and recommenced with renewed vigour shortly after the round-up order as people made last-ditch efforts to escape.

Pick-ups of this type were potentially very dangerous as shots were fired on several occasions, particularly from the second week of August. The Iraqis generally aimed over and in front of fleeing vehicles, but in the circumstances it was impossible to tell whether they were firing in earnest and were merely poor shots, or whether they were genuine warning shots. Anyway, the safest thing to do was usually stop and surrender. In retrospect, it is amazing that only one Westerner and two known Kuwaitis were killed in this way.

Even then, until mid-August perhaps only 20 people were actually detained, out of the hundreds attempting desert escapes. Many Kuwaitis simply bribed their way past the troops. Few escape attempts were made by Westerners after 19 August as people still in Kuwait decided they had little chance of success and went into hiding, although the last successful escape occurred in the first week of September, on the 'Oscar' route. At the time, the Iraqis were simply not expecting a carload of Westerners to be on the roads or in the desert two weeks after most of them had gone into hiding; they sailed through without any problems.

The first people despatched to camps in Iraq itself were those held in the Baghdad hotels. The French and Germans were first to leave, from the Mansour Melia, early on the evening of 16 August. The Americans from the Al-Rasheed followed an hour later, then the British, including most of the BLT men. The other hostages had come mainly from Kuwait's Messila Beach, Sheraton and Salam Palace Hotels, and BA149. All the Americans were taken to the Al-Qaim nuclear site in western Iraq. The British, French and Germans went to several different camps. Even as they left the hotels, some of their Iraqi escorts were wishing them well, and seemed genuinely concerned.

Over the next six days, all the hostages in the Baghdad hotels left for the sites. Transport was by bus, usually leaving after dark. Most of the trips to sites in Iraq were just hot, boring night-time rides of up to eight hours through the Iraqi countryside. Some sites were near Baghdad, but most were in the far west, near Jordan, in the north, in Kurdistan, and in the south, near Basra. Invariably, the Iraqis never told the hostages where they were going. Some hostages never learned the real names or the natures of their sites.

The worst burden for the hostages during these trips was the uncertainty over their fate. The greatest fear in the minds of many of the women was rape, although the Iraqis had generally behaved civilly in the hotels. The men were equally concerned that they were helpless to protect the women.

Once people were moved out of hotels they felt they had lost any last control they might have had over their lives. They were totally at the mercy of the Iraqis. Their governments were even less able to help them now. In Baghdad, they had enjoyed limited consular access until 16 August. Now they were completely cut off. They knew that they were part of the Human Shield programme, but did not quite know what that meant.

Some of the trips were particularly unsettling, more out of Iraqi ineptitude than deliberate intimidation. The Iraqis sometimes got lost taking people to camps. Roads in rural Iraq are poorly sign-posted, and many strategic sites, being military installations, are not marked at all. This was frustrating for the Iraqis, but terrifying to the hostages, who felt that the Iraqis knew exactly what they were doing, and were playing a game with them.

The Iraqis did indeed make a deliberate effort to disorient at least some of the hostages. A number of them reported being taken on three-hour trips to places they later learned were less than an hour from Baghdad. Most transfers from the hotels to the sites may have been conducted at night to minimize the risk of satellite surveillance identifying where the hostages were being taken, or of the buses being followed. They certainly fooled the hostages. Few of them had any idea where they were, although those taken to dams and to sites in the south were generally aware of their location.

Like many other people who had tried to escape previously, Ken Best and his wife Jo were driven into another, final attempt by the round-up order, and the BBC news that people from the Baghdad hotels had been sent to sites. At this stage, people were desperate to get out.

They left home early on the morning of 18 August, in a small convoy of four-wheel drive vehicles with a few British couples and a Canadian architect, Eoin MacDougald. They made good progress across the desert until they encountered a line of Iraqi tanks close to the Saudi border, spaced at several hundred metres, all the way across the horizon. They tried to drive west to the end of the line, but it went on kilometre after kilometre. They eventually encountered some Iraqi soldiers who told them to come back in the afternoon.

By then, each vehicle was low on fuel, so they decided to return home, fill up, and try again later. The Iraqis had not let them through, but had not otherwise troubled them, despite the round-up order being over 48 hours old. However, on the way home, they were stopped at a roadblock by an Iraqi major who tried to arrest them. Ken asked a passing colonel to sort out the problem, but the major said that his orders were from Baghdad. The colonel promised to check, and said he or his driver would be back in half an hour.

True to his word, the colonel's man returned, and took the group off the major's hands. The major's orders were correct. They were taken to a nearby brigade headquarters, then to the Iraqi Embassy, and finally to the Regency Palace where the Iraqis checked them in as if they were regular guests.

That same afternoon, other groups of Westerners were also trying to leave across the desert, encouraged by news that 50 people had made it out the previous day. One of these groups, in two cars, consisted of four British men, an Austrian woman, Hanna Schluet, and a young British woman, Kirsty Norman, all disguised in Arab dress – hoping vainly that from a distance they might be mistaken for bedouins. However, they were stopped by the Iraqis only a couple of kilometres into the desert. The troops knew about the route. Unknown to the group, Ken Best and his ill-fated convoy had passed through the same point unhindered that same morning.

The soldiers were singularly unamused by the Westerners' Arab dress, and were obviously unhappy at having to stand out in the hot sun stopping people driving into the desert, but they simply ordered the cars back to Kuwait City.

Suddenly, the lead vehicle, driven by one of the men, with a second man and Hanna Schluet on board, hurtled forward and off into the desert in a wide arc, crashing and thumping over the uneven ground at high speed, before heading back towards the soldiers and the second car. The driver had apparently suffered a sudden nervous breakdown. The male passenger jumped from the vehicle, and Hanna was preparing to do so when the driver slid to a halt in a cloud of dust and sand within a foot of the terrified Iraqis.

Hanna threw herself out into the arms of a surprised Iraqi. The soldier's colleagues dragged the driver from the car, and started pushing, berating and beating him, eventually forcing him to sit cross-legged on the hot sand. In the meantime, a line of other cars which had followed them into the desert saw that the scene was turning ugly, turned around, and fled back towards the city.

The women pleaded with the Iraqis that it was all a terrible mistake, but one of the soldiers started beating Kirsty on the arm with the flat side of a small spade, shouting at her. The mood was so aggressive that for ten minutes they believed they would have been summarily shot there and then if the driver had killed or injured one of the soldiers.

Tempers gradually subsided, helped by the need to fetch an officer, and by the assistance of a nearby English-speaking Kuwaiti who translated the Westerners' apologies and explanations to the soldiers. The group was then ordered to a headquarters in a commandeered Kuwaiti Ministry of Electricity and Water complex closer to the city.

The spectacle of the five Westerners was the highlight of the day for the officers in the headquarters, who gathered to listen to the proceedings. They were not threatening. The group was fed in the headquarters canteen and drove their own cars under escort to the Iraqi Embassy at the opposite end of the metropolis. It was bizarre, driving through a beautiful Gulf summer sunset, under friendly armed guard, on deserted streets where Kuwaiti families would normally be out, enjoying the evening breeze. It was the first time they had been through the city, or along the coast of Kuwait Bay, since the invasion. They were shocked at the large number of abandoned and cannibalized cars by the roadside, and the transformation of the beautiful, landscaped waterfront area into a warren of sandbagged trenches and bunkers.

The Iraqi Embassy was heavily guarded, with a tank at its entrance. It was an eerie feeling to be so close to the centre of the invading force, but still to remain totally unscathed, as if they were invisible. They waited outside for some time, before being told that they were going to a hotel. They assumed it would be the Regency Palace, but headed in the opposite direction.

This time their destination was another headquarters at the main campus of the Kuwait Institute for Scientific Research. There they had to wait for an hour for various papers to be signed by a general before they were driven briefly back to the Iraqi Embassy, and then finally, at around 11.00 p.m. to the Regency Palace, where Ken and Jo Best and their group had been since that afternoon. The hotel was filling up.

Another group of Westerners with several uncaptured BLT NCOs and their families, an ex-BLT man, Ray Washer and his wife and daughter, Dorothy Goodwin, the British Embassy warden for Fintas and nearby areas, and her husband Peter, made an escape attempt on the same day, 18 August. Six vehicles with 29 people left at 3.00 a.m., turned off Seventh Ring, and headed south-west across a desert track towards the Saudi border, 40 km away.

The little convoy drove through an Iraqi Army encampment about ten km into the desert, just as the troops were waking up. The soldiers were wandering around scratching themselves in their long underwear. The British waved at the troops, who waved back, seemingly unconcerned. However, the track beyond was blocked by Iraqi military vehicles, so they turned south-east. After a few more kilometres, they saw tanks and guns ahead in the distance, so turned back onto a south-west heading, having bypassed the blocked track.

Within 15 km of the border, they breasted a ridge, to find themselves looking down on troops in trenches a hundred metres away. Three of the cars turned back, but the others kept going, trying to bluff their way past the Iraqis. They were less than quarter of an hour from the border.

Suddenly, some of the Iraqis opened fire with their Kalashnikovs, the bullets kicking up spurts of sand a metre in front of the lead vehicle of BLT WO Kevin Fallon. They stopped, shaken. The Iraqis approached the vehicles but did not arrest them, only telling them firmly to go home.

The convoy turned around towards Kuwait City, but once out of sight of the Iraqis, circled around back towards the south-west. They passed a lone tank in the distance, which fired warning shots towards them. The six cars retreated again, regrouped, and decided to go further west, before turning south again.

However, they soon encountered an APC, which told them to go back. They back-tracked for about 300 metres and stopped, but the APC suddenly came after them at speed, almost hitting several of the stationary vehicles. They were taken back to the point where they had been first fired upon, where they briefly met a brigadier. He had given the order to capture the convoy after the first firing incident. They had been unfortunate to run into the APC just before its commander received the order over his radio.

After some time, the six cars were told to follow an Iraqi jeep towards Ali Al-Salem base on the Salmi Road. Five kilometres from the base, they had a terrifying scare. The jeep stopped to allow a convoy of senior officers' cars to pass. Two Arabs, dressed in civilian *dishdashas*, hopped out of the jeep, with shovels, and went off into the desert. Several of the Westerners initially thought

Illustration 1. Welcome To Baghdad

GENERAL DIRECTORATE OF TOURISM   مـديـريـة الـسـيـا حـة الـعـامـة

Ref.   الاشارة :

Date   التاريخ :

Dear Guest ,   ضيفنـــا المـــــزيـــــز ٠

We welcome you to Iraq and hope   نرحـب بـكـم فـي الــــــراق ٠
that you have a pleasant stay   ونتمنى لكـم اقـــامـــة طيبـــة ٠
here. The Ministry of Informa-   وطبقا للاتفـاق مـن وزارة الثقافـة والاعلم ٠
tion and Culture extends its
hospitality and offers you the   فـان الضيـــافـة تشـمـل مـايـلـــي :
following facilities :

1.   Accommodation   ١ــ اجـــور الـسـكـن ٠

2.   Meals and Soft Drinks   ٢ــ اجـــور الطمام والمرطبات لشخص واحـد
3.   Lunadary   ٣ــ اللـــورنـدكت
Payments for other services must   يرجى ملاحظـة أن كافـة الخدمـات الاخـرى
be paid for in foreign currency.   يجـب أن تدفـع بالعملـة الاجنبيـــة ٠

Please do not hesitate to contact   مرة اخرى نتمنى لكـم اقـامـة طيبـــة
us in case you need anything   فـي ربـــــوع الـــــراق ٠
further. Warm regards ,

THE MANAGEMENT   .   الادارة ٠

Haifa St. P, O, Box 6153 Baghdad Tel. 5370041   ٥٣٧٠٠٤١ هاتف   ٦١٥٣ شارع حيفا ص. ب
Telex   212768- 212970- 212976 Melia IK   ٢١٢٩٧٦ ـ ٢١٢٩٧٠ ـ ٢١٢٧٦٨ تلكس   ميليا آك

  Melia International Hotels

that the men had gone to dig graves, and they would be then shot and buried in the desert. To their great relief, the jeep resumed its journey, with their six cars following it. They never saw the men with the shovels again.

From Ali Al-Salem, they were taken to the Jahra Police Station for three hours. All this time, they were in Army custody. From Jahra, they left for Jiwan Camp, again driving their own vehicles. Most of the cars then had Iraqi troops in them, but not the Goodwins'. Seizing his chance, Mr Goodwin did a quick U-turn at a traffic light, and headed back towards the police station, the last place he thought the Iraqis would come looking for him. After lying low for a while, he and his wife eventually made their way home.

Meanwhile, the people in the other five cars arrived at Jiwan with the Iraqis greatly annoyed at losing one car. They were questioned until 10.00 p.m. as to who they were, their jobs, and what they were doing in the desert. They had been on the road since 3.00 a.m. that morning, and were exhausted with fatigue and fear. Finally, they were taken to the residential premises of the Kuwait University Medical Faculty, adjacent to Shuwaikh Port.

The group - now down to 27 - were initially kept and fed in a huge oval room. Eight of them, comprising the Fallon and Hall families and a single man were then taken at 2.00 a.m. to a barely-completed villa near the Dasman Palace. Another small group was taken to the Messila Palace, on the coast, several kilometres south of Sixth Ring. The remaining people were split into groups of between four and eight, and accommodated overnight in the looted villas of the university residences.

These were the first people to be put in what would eventually be four hostage camps in Kuwait itself. At the same time, the smaller group with Kirsty Norman, Hanna Schluet, and the unbalanced driver were waiting for their papers to be signed by the general, only a kilometre away, before being taken back to the Regency Palace. The Kuwait camps were being set up.

At 1.30 a.m. on 19 August, shortly after the first Kuwait hostage site was set up at the university residential complex in Shuwaikh, the Americans, British and French in the Regency Palace Hotel were roused from their beds with a phone call from reception.

They were called down to the lobby, allowed one bag each, and divided into families and singles. There were no Germans or Japanese in the hotel at that stage. Other nationalities were to stay behind. It was a traumatic experience. An officer told them they were being taken to the Meridien or Sheraton in Baghdad. At this stage, it was 60 hours since the first hostages in Baghdad had gone out to their sites. The Iraqis seemed to have come under pressure from above to get the hostages dispersed as soon as possible.

The BA crew in the nearby SAS Hotel were mustered at about the same time. The BA passengers in the hotel simply awoke the next morning to find the crew gone. Most of the BA crew in the two hotels, although not married to each other, had paired off into couples in case they were separated by sex. The different family names in their passports did not alert the Iraqis to the ploy as Arab women keep their own family name after marriage.

The scene in the Regency Palace's lobby was remarkably normal. The BA crew were all in uniform, looking as cheerful and efficient as their advertisements. The atmosphere was almost relaxed. It was more like a crowd of aircrew and tourists checking out on their way to a flight, only their journey and destinations would be unlike anything they had ever experienced.

The groups, about 100 individuals in all, were put on separate buses for the four sites in Kuwait: the three places where people were being held or sent to from the Shuwaikh university complex at that very moment, and the IBI Camp at Fahaheel, home of the captive BLT NCOs.

Forty-nine people went to IBI, a dozen each to the Messila Palace and the Dasman villa, and ten to the university residences. Over the next few days, a few more individuals joined those at Messila Palace to bring the total to 44. Each site had some BA people. Most of the people on these sites were British, with a sprinkling of Americans and French. After that, there were no additions to the Kuwait sites. They stayed that way until the women were evacuated at the end of August, the French in October, and the remaining men were all relocated to Baghdad in late November.

Thereafter, all other captives, including those held at the time in the other Kuwait hotels, were sent to Baghdad. The Iraqis needed time to actually figure out where to put people. Baghdad's bureaucrats suddenly had to find places for hundreds of Western men, women and children, and co-ordinate with Saddam's office, their Ministry of Defence and other organizations, to decide which sites they should go to. Within days, they would have almost 300 Japanese from Kuwait to cope with too. It was an administrative nightmare. The solution was to ship those in Baghdad to the few readily available sites, and send those captured in Kuwait to local sites, at least until the Iraqi bureaucracy could catch up.

In the midst of this distribution of people to sites, one little thing went almost unnoticed. The nationals who had been left behind in the Regency Palace Hotel, and who lived in Kuwait, including the Canadian architect Eoin MacDougald captured with Ken Best, and the Austrian woman, Hanna Schluet, taken with the five Britons after the driving incident in the desert, were released and allowed to return to their homes in Kuwait that day.

The Iraqis had settled on who they wanted, and who could have freedom of movement. Some other individuals who were not of the five targeted nationalities continued to be held in the SAS Hotel, but they were predominantly BA passengers with nowhere else to go. They were unaware that they were free to go as their British companions could not leave, and the Iraqis did not enlighten them.

This was the beginning of the realisation in Kuwait that some Westerners might have freedom of movement, although Canadian Graham Pierce had been released to his embassy in Baghdad 12 days earlier.

Pick-ups from homes started in earnest a week after the 15 August round-up order. The general procedure was for one or two *Mukhabarat*, reinforced by a section of Special Forces troops, to go directly to the homes of the Westerners, knock on the door, and give them no more than half an hour to pack.

Ironically, the main feature of these home pick-ups was the extraordinarily civil way in which most of them were conducted. The Iraqis obviously had orders to be gentle with the Westerners. They were especially sympathetic to women, and went out of their way to reassure them they would not be harmed. They seemed embarrassed at involving women and children against Arab tradition in what was essentially men's work.

The pick-up teams were usually led by an officer with excellent English who informed the Westerners they were now guests of the Iraqi Government, and would they please pack a few things. If the Westerners did not answer the door, and the Iraqis were certain that they were inside, the soldiers simply broke it down. There were numerous incidents of Westerners lying low when they saw the troops coming, and the Iraqis going away if they were not quite sure of their ground. If the Iraqis did force their way in, the troops poured through the door with their guns at the ready, and secured the premises before the *Mukhabarat* came in. It was a very slick, professional military operation. Initially, the soldiers were understandably nervous, but seldom touched the Westerners. Instead, they simply covered them with their Kalashnikovs, asking whether they were Americans, and where their weapons were. It was less violent than many American TV show arrests.

Once the troops realized they were in no immediate danger, they calmed down, and their officer or the *Mukhabarat* took over. If the officer spoke English, the *Mukhabarat* man usually stayed in the background, but was obviously in charge. The soldiers would then search the home, going through it room by room, rummaging through drawers and cupboards, presumably for weapons or other incriminating material, but usually casing it for loot.

The captives were rarely taken directly to the Regency Palace. They seemed to drive around to a series of places, often headquarters, other times just to houses with no apparent function. In some cases, it seemed as though the Iraqi snatch team had been given the cars for a day, and were trying to do all their errands, including capturing hostages and shopping, at the same time.

The Iraqis were more interested in Americans and British than others: in fact, captured documents dated early September 1990 ordered the Special Forces to conduct house-to-house searches, and to concentrate specifically on Americans as they still held an insufficient number of them in custody. It had apparently become an embarrassment to the administrators of the Human Shield programme in Baghdad to have so many British, but so few Americans. Saddam needed more ammunition against the largest power in the Coalition.

Despite the generally civil nature of the pick-ups, there were several particularly aggressive incidents involving violence against Westerners. The occasion involving the greatest number of people occurred on the morning of 4 September in the southern coastal suburb of Abu Halifa. At the time, the women and children had just left the apartments on their way to the rendezvous point for an evacuation to Baghdad, and out of Iraq.

The Iraqis had arranged to sweep a number of apartment blocks in the area, starting at about 6.30 a.m. It was a well-planned operation. A platoon of soldiers was assigned to each building. The troops were in teams. One squad surrounded and sealed off the buildings, while another scaled the walls and stood guard on the roofs of the carports to prevent anybody sneaking out. Then an assault team entered the block, and began breaking down every door.

Some of the destruction was wanton. One soldier threw a TV set against a wall; another came after one British man with a garden chain, as if to hang him. Another was struck hard in the face with a rifle butt atop a staircase when he did not move fast enough for the troops. One man barricaded himself on the roof of his building, and only came down when the Iraqis threatened to blow it up with RPGs.

The prisoners were taken downstairs to wait for the officer running the operation. By then, the soldiers had calmed down. The officer was almost apologetic. About 50 men, mainly British and American, and a few women who had stayed behind, were captured. At least two men evaded capture by hiding in a cupboard in a disused apartment.

On the same day as the people from Abu Halifa were captured, an American money manager, Miles Hoffman, was shot in the arm trying to evade capture. Hoffman was in a first-floor apartment in the suburb of Jabriya with another American. At about 2.00 p.m., when his companion was sunning himself on the roof, the Iraqis came and banged on the door. Hoffman climbed out of the window onto a low wall, and ran along it towards a nearby free apartment.

The Iraqis burst into the apartment. One of them rushed across to the open window, raised his rifle, and fired on Hoffman with about nine rounds. One hit Hoffman just below the left elbow, shattering the bone. He collapsed, screaming in pain. His companion was more fortunate. On hearing the commotion, he came down the stairs, and walked straight into the soldiers, surrendered and was detained peacefully.

The news of this shooting terrified those of us still in hiding. It demonstrated that the Iraqis were prepared to fire on unarmed civilians. However, the Iraqis were acutely embarrassed at this. They took Hoffman to the nearby Mubarak Al-Kabeer hospital, and ensured that he was given the best available treatment. They then contacted the US Embassy, and allowed locally-employed staff to visit him. Hoffman's injuries did not save him from becoming a hostage. Four days later, he found himself on a site near Baghdad.

The coastal area of Fintas and the nearby suburbs south of Sixth Ring, which were cut off from phone contact with the rest of the country, were garrisoned from September by mainly Iraqi Kurdish units, thought to be from the Iraqi 19th Infantry Division, with Arab or Kurdish officers. The Kurds, however, tended to be more sympathetic to the Westerners.

In one incident, three British men had successfully hidden for over three months in an apartment where a unit of Kurdish troops was camped in the courtyard. The building had 62 apartments. By then, the Iraqis had looted the other 61. The men had barricaded their door. The Iraqis had tried several times to break it down, but always left for easier pickings elsewhere.

Finally, late one evening, the Iraqis made a serious effort to get in, then went away after some time. The men knew they would be back, and did not want to antagonize them further, so dismantled the barricade. When the Iraqis resumed their efforts in the early hours of the morning, the door gave way with ease. The officer walked into the darkened apartment, asking his men why it had taken them so long before. Then he saw the three men, sitting at the dining table, drinks in hand, packed and ready to go. He was horrified that they had hidden there for three months, ever since he and his unit had been bivouacked in the complex. He seemed extremely concerned that he would be disciplined for harbouring them for so long.

The officer reportedly initially suggested sealing the apartment back up again, or driving the men into the desert and letting them go, but the Britons were concerned for their safety now that the Iraqis knew where they were, even if they were Kurds. The men and the soldiers are said to have convinced the officer that he had to hand them in, so he asked them to spend the rest of the night there, and he would bring the appropriate people after daylight.

In the morning, the *Mukhabarat* came, and the men went through the usual procedure, ending up in Baghdad. They never found out what happened to the Iraqi Kurdish officer, but he had been genuinely concerned for his safety.

This was not the only incident of Iraqi Kurdish troops being reluctant to hand over Westerners. On another occasion, a group of British men in an apartment block in this area had carelessly left the stairwell door on the ground floor unlocked. Some Kurdish troops came upstairs, encountered the men in the corridor, and simply told them to be more careful in future, and lock their door. The Kurds reportedly explained that they would have been taken away if Iraqi Arab troops had found them. They asked the British to say nothing about the incident if they were caught later, and left.

Some home pick-ups produced the strangest stories. On one occasion, a man was on the phone to a friend when the knock came on the door. He checked who it was through the peephole, and said matter-of-factly 'Have to go, old chap. The Iraqis are here. I'll call you from the Regency Palace shortly. Cheers!' It was as simple as that. People had resigned themselves to their fate.

Other men with a more defiant attitude could actually see the Iraqis coming up the stairs or corridor towards their flats, banging on or breaking down doors on their way. I recall one man in a building being searched calling in progress reports. 'They're just on the landing...' Next call: 'They're into the Indian's apartment three doors away...' Five minutes later: 'They're in Ali the Palestinian's apartment two doors away.' After another few minutes: 'They're trashing next door...' Then: 'They're banging on my door. The bastards can bloody well break it in. I'm f - - - - d if I'm going to open it for them.'

There were no calls for another 15 minutes. Finally, we called him. An Iraqi answered. We hurriedly disconnected. Within hours, the man called us from the Regency Palace. The Iraqis had been annoyed at having to break down the door, but had accepted his not opening it as fair play, and not mistreated him.

Sometimes, when the phone rang during a pick-up, the Iraqis either answered it, or told a captive to do so, and listened in. The new prisoners hinted to the callers that they were compromised, or pretended it was a wrong number. In any event, by late September, telephone security procedures were in place, so the caller usually took the hint, disconnected quickly, and informed the relevant warden or embassy.

In our building, we woke one morning to find the doors of all the apartments in the adjoining corridor, except one, broken open, and the contents looted. We had not heard a thing. The looters, whoever it had been, had not even knocked on our doors. It was simply the luck of the draw.

Captive Westerners were usually questioned, but the interviews could hardly be called interrogations. A few simple questions might be asked at the pick-up by the officer in charge, who was seldom more senior than a captain. A longer interview might be conducted elsewhere by a lieutenant-colonel or colonel, or a *Mukhabarat* man, before the hostages were taken to the Regency Palace.

The Iraqis usually simply asked the captive's name and where he worked. Most people were asked, particularly during late August and September, why they had not reported to the hotels as ordered. The prisoners replied that they had been following their embassies' instructions. This sometimes annoyed the Iraqis. As far as they seemed to be concerned, they - and not the embassies - were the authority in Kuwait, but they did not press the matter.

On occasions, when captured people had a particularly good food supply, the Iraqis asked where the stocks had come from. They seemed to be looking for Kuwaitis who were helping Westerners, but were generally satisfied when told by the people that they had been well-stocked before the invasion, or had been supplied by Arab or Indian friends who had since left Kuwait. In other instances, when asked about their jobs, those in sensitive positions lied that they served in a more innocuous capacity. The Iraqis were particularly interested in people working as advisors for the Kuwaiti Ministry of Defence. Sometimes the men were caught out as the Iraqis had found their personnel files in the companies or bases they had taken over, but the *Mukhabarat* were not unpleasant about the deception. They seemed to expect it.

The Iraqis were seldom forceful or threatening to captured Westerners, although several British women captured on their way to evacuation buses in September were intimidated into saying where their husbands or fathers were hiding. It was different for any Arabs they caught helping Westerners. Some were beaten up, or threatened with torture, to force them to disclose where the Western men were. There are no confirmed cases of Arabs or other people being executed for harbouring Westerners: nevertheless, the threat was taken very seriously, and captured Iraqi documents later proved that the soldiers had full authority from their own chain of command to do this.

The Iraqis initially used several hotels in Kuwait and Baghdad during August for hostages, but then reverted exclusively to the Regency Palace Hotel in Kuwait, and the Mansour Melia in Baghdad. The Iraqis responsible for the 'Special Guests' established their people in these two hotels.

The food was generally good, although it deteriorated over time as sanctions began to bite. Treatment in the hotels was generally civil, although one man in the Mansour Melia was apparently hit in the knee with a rifle butt when he was watching TV in the presence of English-speaking Iraqis, and Mrs Thatcher made a particularly inflammatory comment. Another man who tried to escape from the hotel was badly beaten. The Iraqis were very serious about ensuring people did not escape. It seemed they would be severely disciplined if they lost a hostage. They gave the hostages relative freedom of movement on the floors they were held on, but not beyond that. They behaved reasonably if you played by their rules, but could be nasty if you didn't.

Some hostages with a sense of humour dubbed the Mansour Melia 'Hotel California', after The Eagles' song of that name...... '*We are programmed to receive; you can check out any time you like, but you can never leave...*' The metaphor was imperfect, although close. They left, but to strategic sites.

It was never quite clear which organization was in charge of the hostages in the Mansour Melia: the *Mukhabarat*, or the Iraqi Ministry of Interior. The Iraqis may have been deliberately vague, but the main figure in the Mansour Melia, at least during August, seemed to be a Mr Saif, who said he was from the Protocol Department of the Ministry of Interior. He had a difficult and distasteful job, but tried to do it with as much grace as he could muster.

Several other regular visitors to the Mansour Melia were more welcome than Mr Saif. A young American diplomat, Steve Theibault, made a point of visiting the hostages daily, even though few of them were Americans. He dressed casually, and brought in six-packs of beer, distributing them regardless of nationality. He had an utter contempt for the Iraqis, which he did his best to display, and was a tremendous morale booster for the prisoners.

Another individual was Father Kevin, a Catholic priest apparently associated with Mother Theresa's Daughters of Charity order. He visited the hotel regularly, with his Bible, and was very supportive. In several cases, where elderly or sick hostages were being held, he went personally to the Iraqi authorities to try to get them released, or at least not sent to sites.

The greatest burden during the course of a pick-up was ignorance of what lay ahead. This was particularly prevalent during the early days, before the Human Shield programme was implemented. Later, once people knew they were going to sites, there was still an element of fear, but they also knew that others had gone through the process unharmed, and that the Iraqis were not deliberately harming Westerners.

Perhaps the most curious widespread emotion in the early stages of a pick-up was relief, although this was by no means universal. It was often apparent in the voices of people when we spoke to them on the phone in the Regency Palace. Many were actually on a high. The ordeal of hiding or trying to escape across the desert was over. No more agonizing; no more desperate plans; no more anxious attention to the sound of every vehicle outside closed curtains, or footfalls on the landing; no more terror at having the door broken down by looters or soldiers; no more hoarding or rationing of food, or fear of phones being tapped. One described it as like a delayed visit to the dentist; you knew it had to happen eventually, but it wasn't as bad as expected when it did.

For many of the women, and their husbands, the fear of rape by roaming soldiers or Palestinians disappeared when they were in *Mukhabarat* custody. It was apparent that all the other Iraqis feared these men, and that the Westerners were quite safe with them. Best of all for some people who had been isolated alone in hiding was the human company of other captives, even the Iraqis, and the friendly hotel staff.

Another strange reaction was an air of detachment. People would go through the experience as if it were happening to someone else. They were unharmed, the Iraqis seemed to be concerned for their safety, if not their freedom. They were in the bizarre situation of being hostages in a five-star hotel, prisoners in a gilded cage. No one was tied up, there was plenty of food, and the *Mukhabarat* treated them with respect. It was nothing at all like the popular image of hostages buried away in a dark cell in a Beirut slum, with a gang of scruffy desperadoes. To some, the experience seemed like a dream they hoped to wake up from soon.

Some pick-ups had their funny side, brought about more through sheer good fortune in timing and Iraqi incompetence than anything else. The most memorable case was British warden and Gulf Bank computer analyst, Dave Dorrington and his guests, 3 BLT men, and a BA149 flight engineer and purser, during their pick-up in November.

When the Iraqis entered the house, one of the British servicemen, David Dutson, dived under a bed, but the Iraqis found the others. However, David's foot was protruding from under the bed, visible to anyone entering the room. As an Iraqi escorted one of the other men into the room to collect his baggage, the second man noticed David's foot, and began to sing, in English, *'Yer foot's stickin' out; Yer foot's stickin' out. Pull it in, pull it in; Yer foot's stickin' out.'*

David promptly did so, remained hidden, and the Iraqis took the others away without him! The other five men were eventually taken to the Regency Palace, where they met three British youths who had just had their freedom negotiated, and five West Germans who had reported there after the general release of their countrymen. The Iraqis were going to release them, but the five British men were destined for sites.

By this stage, the security of those in hiding was generally so good, and the remaining Americans and Britons so well-hidden, that the Iraqis were catching only the odd group of hostages every few days. There were not enough men in captivity for a busload, and Iraqi Airways was operating daily flights to Baghdad from Ali Al-Salem KAF Base, so the 13 men were put on a plane for Baghdad, along with an escort.

However, the Iraqis in Kuwait had put all the passports, including those of the British youths and Germans into one envelope, and given it to the escort. This Iraqi had not been involved in their capture, and did not know which men were which nationality. On the aircraft, the Germans commiserated with the British about their fate, after hiding successfully for over three months. One of the Germans, Uwe Wruck, who was a warden for his community in Kuwait, noticed that the Iraqi had all the passports in the unopened envelope, and began to plot how they might help the British.

Curiously, both the Iraqi security and the British Embassy representatives to meet the three youths failed to turn up at Saddam International Airport in

Baghdad, but West German Consul Andrew Schrieder did. Uwe spoke quickly to him in German, half-jokingly, asking if there was anything he could do for the five British. Schrieder turned around and asked the escorting Iraqi for the envelope. He opened it, saw the British passports with the German passports, and then quickly closed it with a nod of approval, keeping it firmly in his hand as if all the documents were for his people. The Iraqi was obviously confused as he knew that most of the men were to be released, but he did not object. Besides, this German official seemed to have some authority.

The British played along, but had to wait around as if nothing was amiss until their baggage came off the carousel. They were still within the airport confines, and would not be free until they were in the German diplomatic car and past the checkpoint at the airport perimeter. The bags arrived after what seemed like an eternity, and the group walked as fast as was inconspicuously possible to Schrieder's vehicle, where they were whisked away to safety at the West German Embassy.

The German Ambassador was delighted at his little coup, and offered them full Teutonic hospitality. He had a sense of humour too, reportedly telling the men, 'Ve haf vays to make you talk to your wives!' and directing them to the embassy's phone. This was precisely what the men wanted to do most at the time. They were then taken away again in the safety of a German diplomatic vehicle to the old East German Embassy, where they spent the rest of their time in Iraq before being released in early December.

The experiences of the Westerners during pick-ups paled into insignificance beside those of the Kuwaitis and a number of other Arabs. Kuwaiti pick-ups started in the second week of the occupation, and continued through to liberation in February 1991, with a sudden and massive increase in the week before the Iraqi withdrawal.

The Iraqis picked up Kuwaitis for a variety of reasons. A number were for valid Iraqi security concerns and to capture suspected members of the Kuwait Resistance, but most were to steal property, or extort ransoms from their friends and family. The same reasons applied to other Arabs. In the later days, especially February 1991, it was to take hostages as bargaining chips. Up to six hundred of these individuals are still missing, some presumed dead.

Whereas the Westerners were accommodated initially in luxury hotels in Kuwait and Baghdad, and fully accounted for, the Kuwaitis were usually thrown into bare police cells. On some occasions they were taken to special holding or torture centres. Some were never seen alive again. They had no embassy to call. The International Red Cross and other such humanitarian agencies were banned from Kuwait, in blatant contravention of the Geneva Conventions to which Iraq was a High Contracting Party.

The two main sources of Kuwaiti pick-ups were at Iraqi checkpoints, and from homes. Men, and women on occasions, were taken from their cars on the pretext of their papers not being in order, or even no pretext at all. Kuwaiti homes were usually entered during sweeps for Resistance members and weapons, usually after a nearby Resistance attack. The Iraqi troops on these occasions were usually rough, as they were concerned for their own safety, and vengeful of their colleagues' deaths. The usual procedure was for regular Iraqi Army or Popular Army to throw a cordon around a suburb or a section of it, and for the Special Forces or Republican Guard to conduct the house-to-house search with the *Mukhabarat*. This was invariably done in the daytime as the Resistance was particularly active at night, and found it easier to evade the troops in the back streets. On some occasions, the Iraqis would turn off the phone service to the area to frustrate Kuwaiti efforts to warn each other.

There were no known incidents of Kuwaitis being killed during the searches, but beatings of Kuwaiti men, and rapes of the women and female domestic staff did occur. Children were asked whether their daddy ever went to work in a uniform, or had a gun, to try to catch them out about their father's occupation. The danger of troops coming back in small groups after the search was over, usually to take women or property they had noticed during the official search, was as great as the danger during the search itself. The Kuwaitis therefore usually moved to relatives' homes in other suburbs immediately after the search had passed through the area.

After being picked up, the Kuwaiti men were usually beaten, some lightly, others more severely. Suspected Resistance people were singled out for particularly vicious treatment. The Iraqis were constantly trying to break the Resistance and build up intelligence on the Kuwaitis, so seldom executed anyone summarily. Bodies of Kuwaiti murder victims turned up days, weeks or even months after their pick-up, frequently with signs of torture.

Families and friends of captured Kuwaitis were seldom told where their people had been taken. They had to go looking for them, starting at the local police station or school being used as a headquarters. There, they met the first layer of the Iraqi ransom system. An officer would agree to help them in return for a bribe of cash, electronics or a car, although a few officers did help out of genuine concern for the families' plight. There was no guarantee that the first officer would be able to deliver, so this process had to be repeated at several likely starting points. It generally took a few days to find out where the person was held. It was then a matter of trying to bribe them out of custody. Sometimes there would be charges pending against them. The Iraqi judicial system, insofar as it existed, participated in the self-enrichment programme.

The bribes did not always work. Sometimes the prisoners were taken to camps in Iraq. Others were later executed. On a number of occasions, the Iraqis played a particularly cruel trick on the families in a deliberate programme of terror and intimidation. The prisoner was taken to his home after the bribe had been paid, and the family asked to identify him. He was then allowed to walk from the Iraqis towards his family's welcoming arms. As he neared them, an Iraqi officer raised a pistol, and shot him in the back of the head.

Although the Westerners picked up by the Iraqis were generally unaware of these incidents, they could count themselves fortunate that the worst most of them would suffer was three to four months in Iraqi camps.

10. THE HUMAN SHIELDS

During the crisis, Iraq held over 1,000 Western and Japanese men, women and children as 'Human Shields' at about 70 sites throughout Iraq, and four in Kuwait. The total held at any one time peaked in mid-October at about 800, mostly men, before selective releases commenced. Of the 800, about 350 were British, 120 American, 100 French, 80 German and 150 Japanese.

The British were particularly well represented for several reasons. First, there were more British expatriates in Kuwait, so more were available for capture. Secondly, large groups such as BA passengers and crew and the BLT were easy targets for the Iraqis. Thirdly, some British civilians drove themselves to Baghdad with their embassy convoy of 16 August. Finally, unlike other major embassies, the British Embassy in Kuwait did not clear their nationals out of the hotels before the Iraqis sealed them off. Those Britons who got out of the hotels in time did so on their own initiative.

Several other factors worked in favour of the Americans. Many members of the 110-member US Embassy convoy to Baghdad on 23 August, although military, had diplomatic passports. US civilian airliners do not fly into Kuwait, so they had no aircrew or passengers in town.

The Japanese were also disproportionately represented as most of them, with the exception of one family, the Moriwakis, had taken refuge in the Japanese Embassy, and had flown themselves to Baghdad on 22/23 August.

Saddam's hostage policy had several interconnected objectives. Militarily, he wanted to put public pressure on Western governments to forego military action, or at least keep a war limited to Kuwait. He was playing for time until the Coalition fell apart under its own internal political and financial pressures. If an attack did occur, the hostages' ultimate role was to be seen dead on Western TV screens, thus forcing Western leaders to cease the attack.

Economically, he tried to undermine the blockade against Iraq by reinforcing his warning that foreigners would share the deprivations suffered by Iraqis as a result of the sanctions. He was particularly cynical in his threats to ensure that foreign children suffered equally with Iraqi children due to any shortages of baby milk and medicines.

Politically, Saddam sought to divide the Coalition by rewarding those countries who hinted at a more flexible attitude with selective releases. This was reflected in the relatively harsher treatment and fewer releases of the Americans and British, whose governments took a particularly hard line. He also used the hostage issue, with a limited degree of success, to portray himself as the reasonable leader of a historically wronged country.

Legally, the holding of the hostages breached the 1949 Geneva Convention Relative to the Protection of Civilian Persons in Time of War, to which Iraq was a signatory. When Iraq invaded Kuwait, Kuwaitis in both Iraq and Kuwait became 'protected persons' under this Convention. When

Iraq refused to allow non-Kuwaitis to leave Kuwait and Iraq, they too became 'protected persons'. The Iraqis denied that the Convention applied as it refused to admit that they were an occupying power in Kuwait. To them, the crisis was a domestic matter within their own country.

There seemed to be a genuine cultural gap between the world and Iraq on the Human Shields. To Iraq, it was a perfectly acceptable tactic, whereas almost everyone else was outraged. Iraq had also used civilian hostages extensively in the Iran–Iraq War. It was nothing new. Iraq, dehumanized by years of oppression and war, may have seen nothing wrong with holding other countries' nationals to prevent an attack. The logic that it was to the greater benefit of all concerned made sense to them: the theft of large chunks of thousands of individuals' lives did not compare to the perceived pay-off in protection. Iraqi officialdom could not seem to understand why taking hostages actually increased the West's resolve instead of forcing it to be more conciliatory. This view was not shared by many ordinary Iraqis who frequently apologized to the hostages for their ordeal. Perhaps forgotten in all the heat of the crisis was the fact that holding people in such a manner was a breach of due process under the Iraqi Constitution and law.

The overall hostage policy was controlled by a 'Central Committee for Guest Relations'. The day-to-day administration seemed to be carried out by the Ministry of Interior's Protocol Department, or the *Mukhabarat*. Behind all this lurked Saddam Hussein and his inner circle.

The basic rule was to incarcerate American, British, French, German and Japanese nationals, excluding diplomats, who lived in or were visiting or transiting Kuwait from somewhere other than Iraq, at the time of the invasion. With a couple of dozen exceptions, persons of those nationalities resident in Iraq were not sent to sites, but could not leave the country. Kuwait-based diplomats from the 'big five' nations were allowed to move around Baghdad, but not beyond the city limits, although the Iraqis classified them as ordinary citizens, and not diplomats.

With the exception of those held at sites in Kuwait, the hostages were generally allocated to various Iraqi ministries for the duration of their captivity. Men who were initially sent to dams were generally always held at dams, even when they were moved between sites. They were the responsibility of the State Commission for Dams, part of the Iraqi Ministry for Irrigation and Water Projects. Other people held in fertilizer plants, often a cover for uranium enrichment or ammunition factories, came under the State Enterprise for Phosphates. Those with the Civil Aviation authorities usually went to one of the two Baghdad airports, or Basra International Airport. There was minor shifting between ministries, but not much.

Some of the Iraqis in charge of the hostages seemed to sincerely believe in making an unpleasant experience as bearable as possible. Others possessed a particularly nasty streak which they exercised by telling hostages that they would be released soon, or were being moved to Baghdad in preparation for being flown home, only to dash their hopes cruelly. Nevertheless, there was a deliberate policy to play off America and Britain against the other countries with nationals held hostage by not allowing through comfort packages or mail. At other times, it was seldom clear whether the Iraqis were trying in their own clumsy way to be kind, or were simply downright nasty. In one case, they withheld news of the murder at home of an American hostage's wife as they felt he had enough to worry about being at a site. The only consistent kindness, if it may be so termed, was that no hostage was to be allowed to die, even from natural causes, if at all possible.

The Iraqis did make some mistakes, even with their own rules. Two British Schlumberger men working for the Iraqi Oil Company were picked up on 21 August, and Morton Brown, an American with Bechtel Corporation, working on an Iraqi Government dam project near Turkey, was picked up with his family on 26 August, apparently after visiting the residence office to get an exit visa for his wife. He was taken to a camp, after being told earlier by the authorities that there would be no problem. His family were let go.

After Brown had been in a camp for seven weeks, a senior *Mukhabarat* officer arrived to tell him 'Your being taken as a 'Special Guest' was a mistake. If you write a report on the problems with the dams, you may be sent back to work, or can go home if you choose.' The Iraqi promised a decision in the next two days. Mr Brown wrote the report, but remained at the site.

At least four other Americans working in or visiting Iraq were also interned. Several Britons and Frenchmen were confined to the sites on which they were working in Iraq. Other American and British men, and Westerners and Japanese working in Iraq, were generally left alone to carry on with their jobs, although they were not allowed to leave Iraq.

The selective nature of the Human Shield programme had bizarre results. In one incident, a Cypriot and a Yugoslav living in Kuwait travelled to Basra to try to register their vehicles with the Iraqi authorities. They were aware that Britons and Germans were being picked up in Kuwait, so were astounded to meet one of each national in the Sheraton Hotel, Basra. 'You guys should be in hiding!' said the Cypriot. 'The Iraqis will get you!'

'Oh, no,' said the Briton. 'I'm Iraqi British. My friend is Iraqi German. We're not Kuwaiti British or Kuwaiti German. We can't leave Iraq, but we don't have to go to a site. In fact, near my office is a camp with Kuwaiti Brits, Kuwaiti Americans, and Kuwaiti Germans.' These two men could actually see their own countrymen held as hostages, but could do nothing to help them.

However, at several other camps, the hostages were in regular contact with American or European managers who were still working on their contracts, and who would take their names and mail into the embassies in Baghdad whenever they visited the capital. The Iraqis must have known this, but still allowed the men working for them to have contact with the hostages.

With the exception of the four hostage locations in Kuwait, the strategic sites were exactly that: installations vital to Iraq's war-fighting capability, including power generation, oil refining and the development of its strategic weapons. Most sites were in fact attacked during the Gulf War. The Human Shields were in the direct firing line. The risk to their lives was very real.

Lieutenant-General Sir Peter de la Billière, Commander of British Forces in the Gulf, later wrote that the British SAS, the world's finest Special Forces unit, had been tasked with planning to rescue these hostages during the early part of the military build up in Saudi Arabia and Turkey, but that they did not expect to be able to get more than half out alive. Casualties among the hostages, not to mention the rescue teams, would have been in the hundreds.

There were nine distinct categories of site in Iraq itself:

- about twelve Air Force bases, and civilian airports in Baghdad and Basra;
- six to ten Army camps, especially close to Baghdad: some of these were adjacent to weapons manufacturing or development sites, and it was seldom clear what the function of a particular army site was;
- major communications facilities, such as the Baghdad General Post Office, and the central telecommunications exchange;
- about twelve conventional weapons manufacturing facilities: these included tank factories, foundries, and ordnance manufacturing plants;
- about six dams and hydroelectric generation plants, in Kurdistan;
- about four ports and naval bases, all near Basra, and Umm Qasr;
- at least eight nuclear, chemical and biological weapons plants, including uranium enrichment facilities: these sites often went under the name of fertilizer plants, and were in fact dual use facilities;
- about a dozen oil and gas installations, mainly refineries;
- about a dozen oil-fired power stations.

The four locations in Kuwait, used between 19 August and 25 November, were not strategic sites as they did not protect any Iraqi military capacity. However, two of these were on the Gulf coast, so may have been seen by the Iraqis as providing protection against an amphibious attack, together with the Regency Palace Hotel which generally had up to several dozen captured Westerners in transit. A third site was between the US and British embassies, nearer the former, so may have been thought to provide protection against an attempt to rescue those under siege in the two embassies.

However, the coastal locations were unsuitable for amphibious landings. The US Marines had selected a site at Shuaiba, six kilometres south of the nearest Kuwait camp, for any amphibious operation they might have had to conduct, but it was never a serious proposition in General Schwarzkopf's plans. In any event, any embassy rescue mission could have either avoided the nearby hostages, or included them. The real reason for the Kuwait sites is probably that the Iraqis simply needed somewhere convenient to hold the hostages at the time. They were only moved to Baghdad when releases of the French, Germans, and some others created vacancies at the Iraq sites.

Each of the sites in Iraq had between four and thirty hostages, with the average at each site about a dozen. One camp, at Al-Qaim in western Iraq, initially had 37 Americans – all the Americans the Iraqis had in custody at the time. However, once the Iraqis got organized, ten men were moved out to other locations on 19 August, and mixed with the British and others. The women and children left ten days later, reducing the number to 20. The numbers on most other sites were cut by up to a half on 29 August with the release of the women and children.

Most sites had a mix of nationalities, but few sites held citizens of all five targeted countries. In fact, it was difficult for the Iraqis to spread the Americans, French and Germans across the sites as they had only about one or two of each for every site.

Initial living conditions in the camps varied from disgraceful to reasonably comfortable. In August, most of the accommodation was actually either immediately outside, or some distance from, the sites the hostages were protecting, mainly in functional prefabricated buildings in vacated or disused construction contractors' camps. In fact, despite being cut off from their diplomats, many hostages who had been held in the Baghdad hotels preferred the more relaxed atmosphere of the sites, where there was a less overt official Iraqi presence, and they were later allowed outside for exercise.

Families and couples were always kept together if captured together. However, spouses captured separately were held at different sites, with no knowledge of each other's whereabouts. Stewart Griffiths, the British man who drove into the Iraqi Army on Mutla'a Ridge on the morning of 2 August, was held at a dam for four months, while his wife Barbara was held in IBI Camp in Kuwait after she was captured in mid-August.

It was obvious to the first people who arrived at the sites in August that the Iraqis had just prepared them. In fact, the initial accommodation was often quite makeshift. The rooms that some of the BLT men were put in after being moved out of the Mansour Melia Hotel had been uninhabited for years, and were infested with insects. Others were more fortunate, being housed in well-appointed holiday villages. Still others were put into houses hastily vacated by the site's factory manager.

Some people were put in huts with windows freshly painted over, boarded up, or covered with corrugated iron so they could not see what was going on at the site. They were only allowed outside a few days later after the Iraqis had built a fence around their huts. Occasionally, the Iraqis were still installing Western-style toilets when the hostages arrived, or did so at their request. The Iraqis could just as easily have left the people in the Baghdad hotels for another couple of days until they were ready, but they were under great pressure from their hierarchy to get them out of the hotels and into camps.

At Al-Qaim, the accommodation was an industrial camp, previously used by construction contractors. This site was the main Iraqi uranium enrichment facility, close to Israel and reasonably well-known. It may have been the first site protected by the Human Shield because Iraq feared an Israeli attack on it. The Al-Qaim hostages were held in small two-bedroom prefabricated chalet-style huts, with a small living room, kitchen, bathroom and small shower stall. Two men, or a couple or family, were allocated to each hut.

Hostages at another site were held in 40 villas in a compound 280 metres long by 200 metres wide, surrounded by a 3-metre chain-link and barbed-wire fence. They had total freedom of movement within the compound which even had two bomb shelters left over from the Iran–Iraq War. Each villa had a refrigerator which was kept stocked with bottled water, soft drinks, eggs, a few fruits and vegetables, and the fixings for tea, coffee and breakfast. It was basic, but not quite hardship.

Hostages at military installations lived in officers' barracks, recreation rooms, or in the firemen's quarters at airfields. At the Baghdad Post Office they were held on the mezzanine floor which had been converted into two bedrooms, and could use the business floor at night for exercise and recreation. The Iraqis even set up a table tennis table for them.

In the early days, before conditions deteriorated, most people lived in single rooms, or shared with one other individual. Some men even had their own villa or bungalow in a compound. With a few exceptions, families were seldom obliged to share a room with other people, but some had to do so during the first couple of weeks while the Iraqis got themselves organized.

The idea of unmarried men and women sharing the same accommodation caused the Iraqis some consternation. It is unacceptable in Arab society to have mixed dormitories. Initially, at one site in Kuwait, only two rooms were available. The Iraqis tried to put the men in one, and the women in the other, but the hostages refused. They did not want the women to be alone, without whatever little protection the men might be able to provide. From later experience, the Iraqi guards would have been seriously disciplined if they had even touched any of the women, but the hostages were not to know this.

Many of the hostages had only the summer clothes they were captured in, or tracksuits and other sundry clothes donated by their embassies, or scrounged from other hostages. This was a major issue, and never adequately addressed by the Iraqis until late October or November when, incredibly, the Iraqis provided some of the men with winter clothes or new shoes and even new well-tailored suits, presumably to smarten them up for their release soon afterwards. Several men survived four months of incarceration with one shirt, a pair of trousers, and one set of underwear. The Iraqis supplied bedding, which was usually clean and passable, if basic.

Strangely, despite being in what were essentially civilian prisoner-of-war camps, the hostages in Iraq itself, but not those at the four Kuwait camps, had to do very little of their own housework unless they wanted to. The Iraqis generally brought in local people as cleaners.

Once the camps were organized, the hostages were usually provided with a washing machine, a TV, a video player and a shortwave radio. Some men had brought their portable stereos with them, so they had a little entertainment. The only TV stations most hostages could pick up was the Iraqi State channel. Nevertheless, there were some highlights. Iraqi TV apparently ran 'ET' before the BBC. Ironically, most of the English-language programmes were re-runs of American serials such as 'I Love Lucy' and 'Petrocelli'. Several British hostages maintained in jest that this in itself was a form of torture.

Initially, some of the senior guards prevented the hostages from listening to the BBC on their own radios as, according to the Iraqis, 'it might confuse them as to the true story'. The Iraqis confiscated the radios, and replaced them with Iraqi TV, and the *Baghdad Observer*. This, however, seemed to be on the initiative of the local managers. The Iraqis themselves were still finding their way around the hostage programme. Within several weeks, most of the hostages' personal shortwave sets had been returned, and the Iraqis even provided sets to some groups who did not have them, but not foreign papers.

Where possible, the hostages tried to engage in sports and other activities to keep themselves fit and occupied. The favourite Iraqi group sports seemed to be volleyball, soccer and badminton, and if facilities were not readily accessible, the guards set up a net between two street lamp posts, and the men played in the street. At one camp, the Americans and Britons taught the guards and the Japanese how to play tennis. Later, the Japanese teamed up with the Americans to teach the British softball. In return, the British introduced the Americans to the mysteries of cricket. This had a particular appeal, as the games took longer, and helped to pass the time.

For evenings, or when it was too warm for sports, a number of hostages made up bingo cards, and held their own bingo nights. One Hispanic American gave Spanish lessons to three Japanese who were scheduled to go to Spain for their companies; and he and other English-speaking hostages learned French from one of the Frenchmen. Most men who maintained a positive attitude came out of their camps more knowledgeable about something than when they went in.

The food varied greatly from site to site, ranging from subsistence rations of rice and tomato paste to quite a respectable menu. Mostly, it was similar every day, but the quality and quantity deteriorated over time. In one typical camp, the hostages had freshly-baked unleavened Arabic bread and tea for breakfast. Later on, they were supplied with dry cereal, whole milk and sugar. Lunch and dinner usually consisted of rice, cucumbers, eggplant and tomatoes. The fortunate camps had fruit or tapioca pudding for dessert. Some had chicken or fish, usually carp, served regularly, but the chicken was often so tough that they could only feed it to the wild dogs around the camps.

Mutton, cheese, yoghurt, eggs and fresh fruit were freely available in some camps; in others they were a rarity. Fruit was seasonal, progressing from watermelons and cantaloupes to pomegranates, grapes, apples, oranges and dates. When mutton was available, it usually comprised more fat and gristle than meat. Few, if any, hostages saw beef during their incarceration.

Many hostages, especially after September, were genuinely concerned that they were not getting a balanced diet. Even the quantities of the staples they were allowed were fairly small. Some, but not all, of the Iraqis creamed off supplies for themselves and their families. As a result, most hostages who were in camps for more than several weeks lost a great deal of weight.

In one camp, the manager was married to a British woman. The hostages never met her, but they did meet his sons, one of whom had returned to Iraq from school in the UK. This man replaced an earlier manager who had been cool towards the hostages. As soon as he arrived, their conditions improved. Beer and eggs, which had been discontinued, returned, and the new manager visited them daily to see if there was anything he could do. When one hostage asked if they could have a chocolate cake, the man's wife baked one for them.

The food was usually cooked by the Iraqis, although more often than not, the cook was simply a worker from the factory floor. Where the kitchen was in the vicinity of the hostages' accommodation, they often had to show the cook what to do, and teach him basic food hygiene. Where cooking facilities were in the hostages' accommodation, many men preferred to cook their own meals. In the early days, meals were prepared at nearby hotels or canteens, and brought to the hostages in their rooms or a dining hall in tinfoil containers, like TV meals, but was often cold by the time it got to the hostages.

The food supply was helped later in the crisis by 'comfort packages' from the embassies in Baghdad, especially the Germans, French and Japanese who sent excellent military ration packs. The most welcome aspect of these packages was the variety in diet they provided. They usually also contained notepaper and envelopes, socks and underwear, cassette tape players, tapes and books, playing cards, shaving gear, toiletries, basic medicines, and running shoes and track suits. They were a Godsend. The French packages were the favourite. Their military rations included wine.

In some camps, the Iraqis provided a case of beer every second day between four or five men. The women were given Pepsi. This ration sometimes had to be discontinued when some men became aggressive after a few drinks. The beer ration was reduced later in the crisis to one case a week, or one every fortnight, and then reinstituted in the weeks before their release in December.

Smokers usually received a packet or two of cigarettes each day, starting with Western brands in the early days, and then Iraqi Sumer cigarettes as the sanctions began to bite. Men and women who did not smoke took their ration to pass on to others. On occasions, especially after the women left, cigarettes would be withdrawn from the men as punishment for aggressive behaviour, or when the Allies announced troop reinforcements in Saudi Arabia.

Many men, while not seriously contemplating an escape attempt, hoarded enough supplies to last them for several days in case they had to make a run for it in the event of war. They used wrappings from cigarettes packets and any plastic bags available to store small quantities of food, mainly bread and sugar. It may have had no practical value, but it gave them an important sense of preparedness at a time when every little mental boost was critical.

The Iraqis were concerned about the hostages' health, if not their diet. They had their own reasons, besides the genuine concern of some individual Iraqis. It was not good publicity for them to have hostages die in custody. A dead Human Shield was not a Human Shield. They took hostages to hospitals whenever they were aware of any serious or life-threatening conditions, and those who suffered from stress-induced migraines were examined by opticians and neurologists.

Each camp either had a physician at the site, or one nearby, but some hostage physicians were unimpressed at the professional abilities of their Iraqi colleagues. The title 'Doctor' in the Arab world is used loosely, even to describe pharmacists and opticians. The so-called Iraqi 'doctors' may have been little more than interns or Army medics. They did not hesitate to refer cases to better qualified people. Nevertheless, some of them, particularly the female doctors, were highly thought of by the hostages. Incredibly, a few British men found themselves being treated by medicos who had lived in their own home towns, and even knew the countryside around their areas.

Those hostages who visited hospitals were shocked at the level of health care available. There were some very skilled specialists, but most Iraqis had sub-standard medical care. The conditions were unbelievably unhygienic. Iraq's considerable resources had been squandered on war, and palaces and monuments for Saddam, instead of on basic public services. Premature or retarded babies were left to die. Saddam's society had no place for weaklings.

Most hostages developed severe diarrhoea as a result of stress and poor food hygiene, and a number of people caught hepatitis. Several would be treated for up to three years after their release for parasites acquired in the camp. Some men suffered severe headaches and depression from constant apprehension. Others became dehydrated and had to be put on drips.

The greatest scars were often the invisible psychological ones which the Iraqis could not, or would not treat. Several men attempted suicide during their incarceration. At least one Englishman and a Frenchman in the Kuwait camps had nervous breakdowns, as did several others in Iraq. Many of them are still suffering from the symptoms of post-traumatic stress disorder, including insomnia, irrational fears, rage, guilt, impotence and impaired ability to function and concentrate.

Three elderly men, an American and two British, died in camps from heart attacks. The Iraqis could not have foreseen this, but with better care and diet, and less stress, the men might have survived. Several others did not recover psychologically after their release, and have since taken their own lives.

After the camps were established, the Iraqis moved people around between sites to keep the Western military and diplomats guessing as to their exact whereabouts. The first moves were merely reallocations from larger camps established to get people out of the Baghdad hotels. The real 'shell game', described after the game where a small object is hidden under one of several identical upturned cups, or 'shells', and one party moves the shells around quickly by sleight of hand while the other tries to guess which shell the object is under, started in late September, once more camps had been organized.

Some hostages were moved to five or six locations: others spent their entire incarceration at one site. The Iraqis often seemed to leave a core of perhaps three out of the original dozen arrivals at the camp, and move the rest. In other cases, they swapped entire camps. Some men arrived at a new camp to find hostages there packed to move to where they had just come from.

Moves between sites, as with the initial transportation to sites, were usually carried out at nighttime, perhaps to confound the Baghdad embassies' efforts to track their people. If so, it worked. The embassies knew approximately how many people were at which locations, especially when the departing women were debriefed, and others were released later, but they could never pin everyone down to an exact location at any given time.

The execution of the shell game was as inconsistent as most other aspects of the Human Shield programme. In some cases, hostages were given only a few minutes to pack their few possessions, with the Iraqis waiting impatiently. At other times, the Iraqis would give them reasonable notice, and turn up on time. On yet other occasions, they were told they would be moving within an hour or so, but nothing happened until the next day. The orders regarding who was to move, and to where, apparently came from a central point in Baghdad.

Sometimes names were specified. At other times, just numbers.

The moves could be extremely demoralizing for hostages, especially when they involved being separated from companions. Ignorance of where they were going, or what was going to happen, emphasized their total lack of control over their own lives. Small groups which provided mutual support were broken up, destroying what little vital social fabric they had.

Each site had a camp manager and three to five guards, otherwise known as 'minders', who were on duty during the day, with one man on duty at night, depending on the number of hostages.

Some of the camp managers were middle-class professionals with a surprising amount in common with the hostages. Many of them spoke English. Some had even received part of their training in the West. At Basra Airport, for example, the mainly British and Japanese hostages were visited daily by the Airport General Manager, his deputy, two lady engineers, and the Senior Air Traffic Controller. The GM had lived in the UK for 15 months, and the Air Traffic Controller had learned his trade at Heathrow. The airport personnel did their best, and were apologetic without actually saying so. It was difficult for the hostages to have anything against them personally.

The camps in Kuwait were initially guarded by young conscripts. One female hostage described them as decent, pathetic boys, ruled by fear. They most definitely did not want to be there. Later, they were replaced by older men, in their 50s or 60s, as the younger men were sent to the front.

The guards in Iraq itself were usually young, or elderly, poorly-educated Arab or Kurdish Muslims, although a number were Christian Iraqis or Armenians. They certainly were not hardened troops, although many spoke schoolboy English. The hostages were generally middle-aged, professionally or technically qualified Westerners or Japanese from a Christian or Shinto tradition respectively. There was little common ground.

The guards generally left the hostages alone during the day. They were present at a daily roll-call and mealtimes, but otherwise unseen. In some camps, in the early days, where the accommodation was in a fenced-in compound, the guards asked the hostages not to go outside at night, but did not lock them in. In family camps in particular, the guards were under strict orders not to enter the hostages' living spaces, or even venture near the huts, especially where women were concerned. At least one group of guards went out of their way to be solicitous, planting a bed of roses for some British families.

Most were armed, if at all, with only a Soviet-made Marakov automatic pistol in a waistband holster. The majority of the guards in Iraq itself dressed in civilian clothes, and were either low-level *Mukhabarat*, or civilians drafted into the job. They were seldom hard-core *Mukhabarat* or Ba'athi, although a number of the camp commanders were. The four camps in Kuwait and the military in Iraq had soldiers as guards, armed with Kalashnikovs. The Iraqis often told the hostages that the weapons were merely to protect them from the ubiquitous wild dogs, and any members of the local populace who might take a dislike to the hostages because of the sanctions.

In fact, the Iraqi soldiers serving as camp guards were usually very poorly trained. In one camp in Kuwait, an ex-soldier hostage had to show them how to clean their weapons. One man's rifle was so dirty that the barrel could have burst if the weapon had been fired. On other occasions, when arguments between the guards and hostages led to a soldier pointing his weapon at one of the men, the hostage simply took the weapon from the soldier's hands, removed the magazine, and threw the weapon in a corner.

Some hostages deliberately tried to build a rapport with the guards, on the assumption that this would make it far more difficult for the Iraqis to follow any orders to shoot them. It soon became apparent that most guards were not generally the type of people who could murder in cold blood.

The guards often sat and listened to the radio with the hostages, especially from September when the international shortwave services broadcast messages from families. They were elated for the hostages whenever they received a message. There was certainly no obvious attempt by the guards to eavesdrop on or record the messages. On one occasion, when a message came over the BBC for a man who had recently been moved to another site, the camp manager contacted the new site to make sure the man got it.

Many guards and hostages never became personally close, but there were funny incidents. In one camp, a new guard entered the hostages' quarters with a pistol tucked into the waistband at the back of his trousers. This was uncalled for as the hostages were certainly not going to attempt to overpower the armed guards. Bringing a weapon into the accommodation area was downright arrogant. One man asked this guard whether he was any good with the pistol. 'Why?' asked the Iraqi at this seemingly genuine enquiry as to his marksmanship. 'Because,' said the hostage, looking him straight in the eye, 'if your first shot misses, that thing goes up your arse!' The guard never brought a pistol into the hostages' quarters again.

In another incident, a fellow hostage came running to the same man in a panic saying that he had seen dynamite in the guard's hut, so they were going to be blown up. The man went to see the guard to ask him what it was all about. 'Oh, it's nothing really,' replied the guard with a smile. 'I just stole the dynamite so that I can go fishing with it in the river next week-end. Do you want to come along?' The guard had a sense of humour. 'Fine,' said the hostage, 'I'll just see if I have any prior arrangements.'

Although the guards publicly praised Saddam, a number of them began to sympathize more with the hostages than with their national leadership. For their own safety, they never openly criticized Saddam or the regime, but their loathing was evident. The guards' main concern was to get back to a normal family life after the years of war, and for the hostages to be allowed to go home. The sympathy was sometimes mutual. The hostages knew how the lives of these men had been hijacked, and how their enforced Army service had prevented them from gaining an education, a career, or a wife and family.

While most camp managers, commanders, and guards were reasonable men with a distasteful job, some could be extremely unpleasant. Perhaps the most serious reported incident occurred at a power station at Duara, on the Tigris River. One night, the camp manager, a Ba'athi officer with an intense dislike for the hostages, took several of them into the desert in a truck, and lined them up alongside a trench being dug by an excavator. The officer had reportedly placed soldiers with rifles opposite the men, when a more senior officer drove out of the dark, and ordered the men back into the truck. The senior Iraqi was apparently furious at his colleague for subjecting the men to such a scare.

While many hostages attempted to get along amicably with their guards, others made a point of baiting them to see how far they could push them, especially when the Iraqis were hostile. One American said little else to his guards during his entire confinement but two words: 'F - - - - Off!' Every time they spoke to him, it was the same. 'Good morning, Mister.' Reply: 'F - - - - Off!'; 'Come for dinner, Mister.' Reply: 'F - - - - Off!'; 'You must come with us, now. You go to another place. Please pack.' Reply: 'F - - - - Off!'

This same man had a record of creative insubordination. On his first site, he had volunteered to clean up the swimming pool area in the old construction camp they were held in. The Iraqis were initially quite happy for him to do this, but soon moved him when they discovered his true intentions. He had made a sign with rocks, presumably visible from reconnaissance satellites saying '19 HOSTAGES HERE'.

Some hostages would tell the guards that the Americans were watching them from their satellites, and could see everything, even at night. They disobeyed them, swore at them, and responded slowly to instructions to see how far they would go. In a few cases, they even staged riots, throwing flower pots at the walls, and chanting 'Down, down, Saddam! Down, Saddam!' in parody of the anti-American demonstrations in Baghdad on Iraqi TV.

Other camps were more subtle. The baiting was designed to put one over on the Iraqis rather than to annoy them. One group made a point of using the *Baghdad Observer*, which invariably had Saddam's face on the front page, as the chief weapon in a daily fly-swatting competition. Every time they killed an insect, they yelled out 'D-I-F!' for 'Dirty Iraqi Fly!' Eventually, the Iraqis asked what 'D-I-F' meant and were told 'Dear Iraqi Friend.' They did not appreciate the joke. The hostages wondered whether they ever realized that Saddam's face was being treated in this manner.

Several other hostages were a little more crafty, but less successful, in their attempts to outwit the guards. At one camp, before the women and children left, the men were missing their beer, which they usually brewed themselves in Kuwait and which the Iraqis had not yet supplied. A golden opportunity presented itself when one of the boys turned fourteen. The men tried to convince the guards that it was an important rite of passage for the young man to have his first beer on his fourteenth birthday, and that the other men were supposed to drink his health. The Iraqis did not buy it. They did, however, provide a cake and birthday cards for the lad, and held a beerless party for him with the other hostages, complete with balloons.

At one camp in southern Iraq, a group of hostages who objected to being moved at the end of September appointed a committee of three men to represent all 21 hostages at the site, and told the Iraqis that they would have to deal exclusively with the committee. They also demanded hot showers and Western-style toilets instead of the hole-in-the-ground facilities. The guards tried to break the committee by talking directly to the other 18 hostages, but the others maintained their solidarity. Eventually, the Iraqis moved the site's office personnel into the warehouse, and the hostages into the vacated offices. Proper toilets were installed, and also three hot showers. The victory was not quite complete. The toilets were kindergarten sized, for children, which presented further problems, but it was a distinct improvement.

On another occasion, two American hostages at a camp near Safwan, both of whom were committed Christians, asked to be taken to church. The Iraqis initially refused, so the men made a point of being obvious about praying at the table before eating. This went on for seven weeks until the Iraqis eventually took all 21 men to the Evangelical Church in Basra, for two weeks in a row. It was another small victory, but was discontinued when the guards saw the warm reception that the men got from the Iraqi congregation, and feared that the Iraqi churchgoers might help the hostages in some way.

Despite a few lighter moments, a hostage's life was usually a daily grind, with little to do other than write diaries, or letters home, or read books. A chore such as the laundry became the highlight of the day for some people. The boredom was compounded by the indeterminate sentence. In a way, it was worse than being in jail. There was no light at the end of the tunnel.

For the first two months in the camps, from mid-August through to October, the international emphasis was on sanctions. The hostages found this absolutely ridiculous. They were aware of how long Cuba, Rhodesia and South Africa had held out. Few had any faith that sanctions would work in a reasonable timeframe. Many of them prayed for military action. With very few exceptions, their consular officials did not see them after they had left the Baghdad hotels until their release in December. This caused the hostages great concern as they realized that only the Iraqis knew where they were, and they could quite conceivably disappear without a trace.

The immediate stress on the male hostages was lessened somewhat when the women and children left. They were grateful that their families were out of Iraq, but the resulting isolation was a two-edged sword. Even with other men around, many hostages experienced a crushing sense of loneliness and sheer helplessness at being parted from their families. Some who had been separated from their wives in Kuwait were not even sure that their wives were out until late October, when they heard their first message from them on the shortwave message services.

The lack of freedom preyed constantly on the minds of men who had previously been normal, active family men. Some of them held in southern Iraq recall being overcome with emotion, gazing wistfully at storks rising on the thermals above nearby power station cooling towers, and wishing they could simply float up and join the birds in their freedom.

The frustration was caused to a certain extent by a sense of abandonment on the part of their governments. Whilst many hostages agreed in principle with their countries' stance against Saddam, they felt that not enough was being done at home to get them out. The news seemed to concentrate on sanctions and the military. The hostages were seldom a leading news item after the women and children until late October, when the first missions by various politicians and other individuals to Baghdad to try to secure their release occurred.

Several hostages later expressed the feeling that when you are held against your will, incommunicado, you feel alone, worthless, and abandoned. One later said that, while neither he nor any of his fellow-hostages would ever claim to have suffered as greatly as people such as Brian Keenan, held for four years by terrorists in Beirut, the Irishman had later described the feelings of being a hostage perfectly as a crucifying loneliness. Others with a magnanimity not justified by their own dire situation, even maintained that the term hostage as applied to them devalued the terrible ordeal of the Beirut hostages. They felt that it overstated their position.

The frustration of incarceration was exacerbated in some cases by tensions between some of the hostages, and later by the claustrophobia of being held in confined areas with little to do. Most were unused to being forced to spend time together with other men who had been perfect strangers. The only thing most of them had in common was their time in Kuwait. The BA passengers and crew, and the Japanese Airlines crew did not even have that.

Some men became short-tempered, resentful, even petty with each other and their guards. They felt that the situation was going nowhere. This was not helped by the lack of incoming mail from families, and a suspicion that letters they had sent were not getting out of Iraq. The guards generally tried to absorb this, but it became harder to do as the military build-up continued and they realized that their country might very well go to war. A few men stole communal food, and other little things. As most people had very few possessions, it soon became apparent who the thieves were, and they were promptly ostracized.

Tension rose and fell with the news, the condition of the men, and their particular situation. When they heard on the BBC on 30 September that letters mailed by hostages had arrived in the UK, those who had sent them were delighted, but Americans and others who were unsure whether theirs had arrived, and hostages in some of the Kuwait camps who had been unable to send any letters at all became more depressed and irritable.

In public, the hostages usually put on a cheerful, even aggressive face in a pretense that the situation was not getting to them. But behind closed doors, there was a great deal of fear, prayer and tears. Many were haunted by nightmares, often of Iraqis coming to take them away in the middle of the night, a dream that came true all too often. Others, held next to an oil refinery, had visions of swimming in burning oil when the refinery exploded.

Most companions were sensitive and supportive. Couples who stayed together depended greatly on each other. In fact, the starkness of their situation, and sharper focus of values, led several married couples to start families in captivity. This was abetted by the lack of contraceptives, but also by the sharper realization of their mortality. Other hostages continually told and retold their own story, and harped on about their own experiences. The other hostages generally let them talk, and get it off their chests, but sometimes people had to be told to shut-up, and cease their self-pity.

People coped with the psychological burdens of life as a hostage in their own ways. One man, Ken Hoyle, had been a World War II POW of the Germans. An Iraqi prison camp hardly bothered him, even in his sixties, especially as his wife Magda was with him. She herself had lived through the Nazi occupation of Czechoslovakia, so took the ordeal pretty much in her stride, apart from severe food-induced illness.

Most men turned to prayer, even if they were not particularly religious previously. Others had their existing faith to sustain them. To some, the times in the camp were almost like a holiday from the intense pressures of work. Several of them eventually returned home tanned, fitter and more relaxed than they had been in years: others became nervous wrecks.

Men such as marine engineers from KOTC who had spent time at sea were perhaps better prepared to handle the situation. They were used to living in confined spaces in an all-male environment, and in some cases having to live quietly by themselves to avoid conflict. The BLT men, being soldiers, were particularly aware of the importance of maintaining morale. They took some of the civilians under their wing, and even out jogging along the perimeter fences of the sites when this was possible. When some men were down, others would almost literally drag them out of their rooms for some exercise.

In one isolated camp near Basra, the hostages persuaded the Iraqis to allow them to set up a golf course outside the perimeter fence. They used golf clubs left behind by the Japanese contractors who had built the nearby installation, and little pieces of rubber hose for golf balls. They eventually built a rough nine-hole golf course, complete with fairways and greens, distinguished by different types of sand. The links served several purposes. Not only did it provide exercise, maintain morale, and keep the hostages occupied, but they felt that the safest place for them to be in the event of a sudden Allied attack on the nearby site was outside, away from buildings which would be targets.

Other men found resilience through humour and laughing at the situation, the guards, even the antics of their fellow captives. They made a point of cracking jokes, playing silly games, even imitating popular TV characters. One man described it as retreating back to childhood, to a time when they had no responsibilities, simply to retain their sanity.

The camp humour was very black at times, and poked fun at everything from Saddam to the Iraqi and Kuwaiti armies. A favourite joke was 'What is yellow, and looks good on President Saddam?' Answer: 'A bulldozer!' The British dreamed up a whole series of 'knock-knock' jokes with 'Knock-knock.', 'Who's there?', 'Saddam.', 'Saddam Who?', 'S'damn shame we can't go home.' Another was a variation on the old Jewish joke of how to get 50 of them into a phone box: for the Iraqis, instead of putting ten cents in, you merely tell them it belongs to someone else.

Some coped by simply burying themselves in projects. A Frenchman, Gabriel, read Tom Clancy's 800-page *Clear and Present Danger*, all 300,000 words of it, with an English-French dictionary. One man at IBI took apart and reassembled a car engine. An intrepid few concentrated on escape plans, or on collecting every bit of relevant information about their sites to pass along to military intelligence in the event that they or fellow-captives were released. In essence, those who found a means of coping with the forced inactivity, even if it was just maintaining a stiff upper lip and studied nonchalance, survived in a far better state than those who had no such structure.

The time in the camps could either make or break men. Many found a previously unknown inner strength; the values in their lives became more sharply focused. These centred on family and loved ones, rather than career and possessions. When everything else was taken away from them, the only thing that mattered was other people, and to those with faith, God.

The mail situation did improve as the crisis progressed. Some hostages in Iraq were allowed to send letters out from as early as 24 August, although they had previously been able to get some out with their diplomats during their time in the Baghdad hotels. Even in the first weeks in the camps, they were to use the Hotel Mansour Melia, Baghdad, Iraq, as the return address, but it was soon changed to P.O. Box 3990, Haifa Street, Baghdad. By November, most camps had mail privileges. However, not every camp, particularly the four in Kuwait, was able to send out mail.

Most letters sent out through the Iraqis did arrive at their destinations, although it was early October before most hostages were aware of this through messages over the BBC or VOA. Incoming mail was not delivered as diligently. It often took at least five weeks to arrive. Men sometimes received more than a dozen letters at a time after a drought of several weeks. Mail into Iraq was affected by the sanctions as well as by Iraqi capriciousness. One hostage got 17 of the 20 letters he received from his wife throughout his detention on a single day in mid-November. Another later calculated that he received only 18 out of over 300 letters posted to him during his confinement.

Mail was always a tangible, intensely emotional attachment to home. It was not unusual for men to weep when they received it. However, it could be a mixed blessing. For those who did not receive mail, the sight of others with a simple envelope could push them over the emotional brink. At times, incoming mail also confirmed how difficult a time families were having coping with the separation, and living in the real world without a breadwinner.

There were just four major occasions when men could get letters out and be reasonably certain of having them delivered uncensored: in late August with the women and children; two months later when the French were released in October; early in November when over 100 Germans and some Americans left; and a fortnight later with the last of the Germans. Even then, the Iraqis took some of the letters from the released hostages on their way out.

The Iraqis were as inconsistent with the mail as they were with almost everything else. In some camps, they actually collected the mail from the hostages, and made sure that it got out. In other cases, hostages gave mail to men who were being released early, in front of the guards, and the letters were subsequently taken from the departees before they left Iraq by other Iraqis. Other camps had no such problems at all. In fact, the Iraqis even forwarded mail received for some hostages after they had left in December. On some occasions where hostages could send letters out, especially from camps in Iraq itself, the Iraqis photographed the men, and told them to put the photographs in the envelopes, but leave them unsealed. The letters were censored. More importantly, the *Mukhabarat* could get the addresses of the men's families from the envelopes, and in some cases used these to contact their wives, and invite them to Iraq to visit the men for propaganda purposes.

To most people, the social fabric of their little groups was vital. Many who spent time together, even if it were only a couple of weeks, have remained close. They can only relate to the experience with other people who shared it.

One consistent feature which developed was the desire to be released only with their companions. There was nothing heroic about this. Those who had the opportunity to leave before others almost exclusively took it. There was no reason to prolong the suffering of families at home by standing on a principle, but some men who could have been released earlier by asking their wives to come to Iraq and plead their cases told their spouses they wanted to be released with all the others. The shared ordeal brought some people incredibly close. The circumstances bred intense loyalties. Others reacted differently, and have since been unable to talk to their camp companions.

The hostages were continually used for propaganda by the Iraqis, even after the Stuart Lockwood debacle, and the cynicism of an infamous later session in which husbands were cobbled together with wives and children from other families, to appear as if they were real families.

As early as 4 September the Iraqis tried to get some hostages to go on TV and criticize their governments. The Iraqi purpose was three-fold: to promote their propaganda in the West, to underline the risk faced by Western and Japanese citizens in the event of an attack, and to portray their so-called humane side by showing how well the hostages were being looked after. The head of the Iraqi TV team was usually a Mr Hilal, who became a familiar sight to many of the hostages. Unlike captive Allied airmen paraded on TV later during Desert Storm, the hostages were not physically forced to participate. Some were even able to ask the Iraqis where the interviews would take place, and whether foreign journalists would be present. The answer to the first was 'probably at the site'; the second was a definite 'No'.

Nevertheless, the hostages were in the same dilemma as the downed flyers. The psychological pressure to participate was tremendous. At that stage, they had no other way of telling their families that they were safe, but also had no wish to collaborate. Some went on camera; others declined. This half-hour nightly programme was called 'Guests' News,' or 'The Peace Broadcast.' Some hostages who did not participate called it 'Traitors' Half Hour,' but this was patently unfair in the circumstances, especially as the Iraqis edited the programme judiciously.

Those hostages who went on TV tried to be as innocuous as possible. They may have looked fine to the general public, but those of us who knew them could see they had lost weight, and looked decidedly uncomfortable. It was another incentive to stay in hiding. We had anticipated shortly after the round-up order that the Iraqis would pull such a stunt, and discussed it among ourselves while still in hiding. Several men who appeared on Iraqi TV unwittingly caused us a great deal of concern when they failed to drop prearranged code words to indicate that they were safe and well.

Feedback on the Western public's reaction to the initial sessions did cause a shift in emphasis. The Iraqis gradually learned how to play to their audience. Whereas to the Iraqi mind, Saddam's famous first session of 23 August with the British families was perfectly acceptable, and portrayed him as a kindly uncle, Western viewers saw it as the ultimate in cynicism, verging on the perverted. Later photo sessions of Saddam with foreign children and other hostages were handled far more skillfully.

The four sites in Kuwait were in a class of their own. Initially, when established on the night of 18/19 August, they held a total of about 135 men, women and children, mainly British, with a few Americans and French, but no Germans or Japanese. About 75 individuals remained after most of the women and children left at the end of August. All of these sites contained a mixture of Kuwait residents, hotel staff or guests, and BA passengers and crew. All four initially had children.

Upon arrival at IBI in the early morning of 19 August, the Iraqis took the families with the seven children to their accommodation, and left the others to their own devices. This was as far as the allocation went. The single or unaccompanied women shared houses with the men for protection, rather than having segregated houses. All the hostages were British, except for one American couple and three young Frenchmen from BA149.

The camp comprised a series of small semi-detatched houses, two to a building. The hostages were appalled at the state of the homes. As with the other Kuwait sites, they had been looted, and in some cases vandalized, during the previous two weeks. The Iraqis had opened the freezers and refrigerators, taken whatever food they wanted, and left the doors open so that the remaining frozen food rotted. Drygoods had been thrown around and ground underfoot. Cans of food had been punctured and left to fester. The destruction was wanton. A favourite Iraqi means of vandalism, practised with a vengeance at IBI, was to defaecate on the floors, and leave the toilets unflushed. The accumulated stink was putrid, overpowering.

The hostages' first task was to clear up the mess, and instill some semblance of order. Fortunately, the power was still on, so they could use whatever appliances had not been looted or smashed, and they had hot water. The smell lingered for some time, but they gradually got used to it. In a way, the destruction and the need to build a comfortable living space was a blessing. It gave them a sense of purpose and a job in the first few difficult days.

Under the mess, the hostages found homes in a state of suspended animation. The camp had the air of a wrecked *Marie Celeste*. Some family photos were still there. The hostages could match some names to faces from the personal papers in the houses. It was apparent that the women had left their homes suddenly, some even leaving behind important documents.

The sole American woman on the camp, Charlene Williams-Coutre, later went around the houses and gardens, picking up the photographs strewn on the ground, and tried to sort out whose they were. She later carried them out of Kuwait with her, and miraculously managed to get some to men held at other sites. Others were posted to whatever home addresses she had found. The BLT women were extremely grateful for this kindness. Several of their men were overcome when a couple of family snapshots arrived at their camps.

In an extraordinary coincidence, IBI was particularly fortunate as two of the British hostages there, Ken and Jo Best, had lived there several years earlier. They knew exactly where everything was, and where it should be. Ken became one of the natural leaders of the camp, along with George Parris, a BA senior steward. Ken spoke reasonable Arabic, so was able to converse more readily with the guards. He was typecast for the role as a British prison camp captain with his drive and organizational skill, and Army background. At times, he was also accused of being overbearing, but he had no choice but to establish his authority over a large group of disparate and scared people.

Ken and Jo called a meeting at their house on the first afternoon so that people could introduce themselves to those they did not already know, and to give them the good news that the camp came fully equipped with home-made ethanol, wine and beer cellars. The BLT women had poured much of the alcohol down the drains in the first couple of days of the occupation for fear of the Iraqi troops getting too drunk and coming after them, but there was still plenty around. The camp also had a mess, gym, swimming pool and disco. It was all in a dreadful state, but with little else to do, they could easily sort it out. Every evening after that, the hostages gathered at Ken and Jo's house, which they dubbed St. George's Square, for roll-call. Afterwards, most of them retired to the Mess for the social event of the evening.

One of the first priorities after cleaning space to live in was contingency plans in the event of an attack, or an explosion in the adjacent refinery. Most of the weatherboard houses would offer scant protection even from rifle fire, so they agreed to gather in the sole concrete building in the event of an emergency. It would at least keep out small-arms bullets and shrapnel. Later, they dug shelters, even making them airtight, and installed SCUBA tanks salvaged from the diving club to provide oxygen in case of gas attack.

The first communal area cleared was the Sergeants' Mess, to provide a meeting place. This was considered critical to prevent people from becoming isolated in their own quarters, and thus succumbing to depression. It was also important to establish a sense of community for the children. The Mess had a bar which became the focal point of the camp. Kirsty Norman, the young woman who had been captured in the desert on 18 August, became the first barmaid as a reward for mucking out the bar.

The Iraqis distributed rations on the first afternoon, mainly rice and assorted canned goods, and resupplied them every other day, in meagre quantities. However, the hostages salvaged some dry goods and cans from the wreckage of the kitchens to supplement their diet. George Parris took over the distribution of the rations, and the custody of the salvaged canned goods, to make it centralized and equitable. The main shortage was fresh fruit and vegetables. A BA stewardess, Nicky Love, a physiotherapist, was the only one with medical training, so she became the camp nurse. The Iraqis had a doctor at the camp, but the hostages preferred to go to Nicky first.

Within days, the camp had a fully functioning social life, with fancy dress birthday parties, barbeques, brewing committees, and formal dinner parties where they drank a toast to the Queen. The cheerfulness was brittle at times, but it was a very British reaction to stress, even with the American couple and three Frenchmen. The main concern, however, was for the children. They had no idea how long they would be there. It could be months or even years, so it became even more important to establish a sense of normality.

Most of the BA people had only their hand luggage with them as the Iraqis had not allowed them to retrieve their hold baggage. Those who had been caught trying to escape across the desert had taken few clothes with them, and only survival rations. To acquire clothes, food and equipment, the hostages had to raid the previous occupants' homes. There was an initial reluctance to loot other people's' possessions, but they doubted that the families would return or mind in the circumstances, and soon they were going through wardrobes, trying on items for size, and selecting their favourite ones.

After some time, the lack of protein in their diet became a concern, so Ken and George asked the Iraqis if they could have a sheep, expecting a carcass. They received some chicken and a piece of mutton, but then the Iraqis brought a live sheep. The hostages looked at it, and then at each other. If they wanted meat, they would have to kill it. Eventually, David Mayers, the British Food and Beverage Manager of the Regency Palace, who was at the site, slaughtered and butchered it. This was repeated later with two goats.

The group at IBI had an extraordinary range of talents. One man, David Eddy, started a prayer group. Another, John Chappell, was an electronics advisor to the Indian Army, and found a radio telephone which the BLT had to communicate with the British Embassy in an emergency. The Iraqis had fired a bullet into it, and stabbed it with a screwdriver, but miraculously failed to do any serious damage. Chappell repaired the set. The hostages tried to use it once to contact the British Embassy but otherwise kept it hidden ready for a real emergency. They did not want to use it in case the Iraqis intercepted the transmissions, and traced them.

Initially, with the new school term approaching and no prospect of an early release, one of the mothers, an English and drama teacher from the Island School in Hong Kong, became concerned for the children's education. They therefore laid plans to start a tiny school, with an *ad hoc* curriculum. The youngest of the seven children was two, the eldest 17. David Eddy was a recently graduated engineer, so he could handle the maths and science; another man was a qualified swimming instructor and ran the physical education classes; Kirsty Norman was an archaeological conservator, so could do history. The three Frenchmen could tutor conversational French. They even had a composer and conductor. He could teach music, and even composed a 'Camp Song'. One of the BA stewardesses started aerobics lessons with salvaged music tapes and a sound system wired up in the Sergeants' Mess.

The second major Kuwait site, the Messila Palace, home of Sheikh Salem Al-Duaij, the Kuwaiti Minister for Commerce and Industry, was not as grand as it sounded, but nevertheless quite luxurious. It was little more than a very large coastal villa, attached to a splendid reception and entertaining area, 20km north of IBI. It had been looted, but not severely. There was little of the wanton vandalism that greeted the IBI people.

For the first couple of weeks, the Iraqis maintained an operations room in the *diwaniah* outside the palace gate. It seemed to be the headquarters for the local beach defences. The hostages passed by it once, and noticed tactical maps on the walls and tables, and senior officers. The headquarters was later moved, perhaps because it was within range of Kuwait Resistance attacks from the nearby expressway.

The locks on every door in the palace had been smashed during the looting, but many of the bedrooms still had sumptuous double beds, with silk sheets and thick pile carpets and rugs. The Iraqis brought in camp cots to make up the shortage of beds. The 41 British and three American hostages were initially accommodated two or three to a room. Nevertheless, the women felt vulnerable without locks on the bedroom doors, so the Iraqis installed some.

Although the food was poor, the soldiers shared most of what they had with the hostages. In fact, many of the hostages felt that they ate better than their guards. They were fortunate to have in their numbers a BA steward with a culinary passion who could do wonders with the meagre rations and a few salvaged spices. Like IBI, the Iraqis brought them a live sheep one day.

The hostages had relative freedom of movement in their own quarters, but were kept segregated from the main part of the palace, which was used by Iraqi officers. Some of the outbuildings served as a barracks, but the troops did not come near the hostages. The main complaint apart from the food was that they were allowed outside for only few minutes each day, and had no communal area. Unlike IBI, there was no lounging around the pool, or central meeting point other than the dining room. This became a particular problem when the air-conditioning insisted on breaking down in the heat of summer.

Some of the experiences of the Messila Palace were surreal. One hostage recalls lying on Sheikh Salem's bed, dressed in a *dishdasha* salvaged from his wardrobe, watching him on TV in Saudi Arabia. Sheikh Salem was an art collector, so they were surrounded by exotic silk wall hangings, million-dollar paintings, and ornate vases. They ate their ration of rice, vegetables and watermelon from the very best china, with expensive gold and silver cutlery, and crystal, in an impeccably furnished formal dining room. Incredibly, the palace also had satellite TV, which gave them access to CNN and GCC TV.

The medical care was similar to the other camps. In fact, a 26-year-old American of Indian extraction with high blood pressure was taken to Baghdad where the Iraqis could better care for him. On one occasion, when a BA person fainted from influenza, complicated by weakness from the poor food, the group wrote a letter of complaint to the Iraqi Governor of Kuwait, Ali Hassan Majeed, with a copy to the UN. The Governor apparently visited the palace the next day. Conditions then improved somewhat.

The third site in Kuwait – but the first to be set up – used two villas at the university residential complex at Shuwaikh. The villas were about 500 metres apart. Each had tree-shaded gardens, and was well secluded, so the hostages could venture outside, and were later allowed to wander around much of the complex. The first villa initially held eight hostages: two families and some singles who had been picked up during a desert escape attempt on 18 August. The second held BA passengers and cabin crew, and the French chef from the Regency Palace. Numbers dropped to three and eleven respectively after the women and children left. Except for the chef, all were British.

As with the other sites, the villas had been looted. There was no bedding left at all, so the hostages had to use towels for sheets and blankets. Fortunately they had little need of warmth during the hot summer nights. Those who had been captured during escape attempts still had their cars with them, so salvaged some home comforts from these. The Iraqis even allowed one of the Britons, Ray Washer, to run the engine of his Pajero periodically to keep the battery charged. With smaller numbers than at IBI and Messila Palace, the guards were more relaxed, and chatted freely with the hostages.

Despite living so close, the two small groups were unaware of each other until the guards told the first group about the second after four weeks in custody. Ray Washer talked his guards into taking him to visit the others. From then on, they were in contact almost every evening. The three Britons from the first villa were delighted to meet the Frenchman, who was adept at making the rations more palatable. Previously, they had subsisted on what they described as 'rice and red goop'.

In contrast to the luxuries of Messila Palace, and the relative comfort and freedom of IBI and the university villas, the final and most unfortunate Kuwait site was a villa near the Dasman Palace.

The Dasman villa, as it became known, had initially been set up at 2.00 a.m. on 19 August with eight British people – two families and a single man – all of whom had been captured earlier during a desert escape attempt.

When they awoke later that morning, they found that a further twelve people had been brought from the Regency Palace. These were mainly BA passengers and crew, including three stewardesses, and the man who had snapped and almost run down the Iraqi soldiers in the desert the previous afternoon. There were now ten men, and ten women and children at the site.

Conditions were extremely basic. The villa had no previous occupants' property and food that could be salvaged. The builders had barely completed it. The first eight arrivals found bare rooms, and few beds. One of the couples, BLT Warrant Officer Kevin Fallon and his wife Laverne, who had been living outside IBI, insisted on a bed for their daughter, Sarah. The other family, the Halls, had two single beds for two adults and two children. The single man had no bed at all. He and the Fallons initially slept on the floor. Eventually, the arrangements settled down to three bedrooms for the 20 people, with mattresses on the floor, and one small communal room, with a TV.

It did not initially seem that food would be a problem. The villa had large stocks of food, fruit, and cigarettes, presumably brought in specially by the Iraqis. However, this disappeared before the hostages could enjoy it, leaving only subsistence rations. On one occasion, they had eight small pieces of chicken to feed 20. The food met barely half of their nutritional requirements. Fortunately, one of the women had multivitamins which they used to supplement their diet. The Iraqis guarding them aggravated matters by taking things very casually, sometimes only feeding them at 10.00 p.m.

When the remaining nine British and one American, all that remained after the women and children left on 30 August, were moved to another nearby villa, the supplies of food, furniture, and what few personal possessions they had were loaded onto a truck. The hostages followed on foot, under guard. By the time they arrived, the truck had been thoroughly pilfered.

The new accommodation was also a two-storey villa, also in the final stages of construction. There was not a single item of furniture, no hot water, and the air-conditioning had not been connected. Thankfully, with the scorching heat of summer, one of the men was an air-conditioning mechanic, and got it going. They each had a foam mattress to sleep on, and a blanket. The hostages lived on the first floor. The guards, under a Lieutenant Adnan, stayed on the ground floor.

Conditions were even worse in this new villa. The rest of September and all of October passed without them setting foot outdoors once. They could see the sun-drenched streets outside, and the trees at the Kuwait Engineers' Society across the road, and hear the lapping waters of Kuwait Bay, a hundred metres away, but could do nothing about it. The mental condition of the man who had snapped in the desert worsened, but the Iraqis seemed unconcerned.

Their situation only improved after they were visited by an Iraqi major-general, with an entourage of colonels, on 1 November. The general was shocked at the conditions the men had endured, and apologized. The rations were increased and varied immediately, and they were allowed outside for exercise. More furniture was brought in. However, they only spent a further three weeks in Kuwait before they were moved to Baghdad with the remaining people from the other three Kuwait sites.

Incredibly, the hostages in three of the Kuwait camps found working phones which enabled them to contact people intermittently, without the Iraqis' knowledge. The exception was the unfortunate Dasman group. The Iraqis had gone through the camps, removing any phones they found, but the mess their own men had made concealed one set each at IBI and Messila Palace, and in each of the two villas in the Shuwaikh university complex.

At IBI, one of the men called an Irish nurse, Mary Dredges, still in hiding in nearby Ahmadi, as soon as they arrived, and told her where they were, and how many. Mary passed the news on to the British Embassy, expecting it to be treated properly. The next day, it was on the BBC that the UK Government knew the whereabouts of some 48 of the people taken away. Someone in the British FCO had no idea of the danger they could place people in.

The Iraqis obviously monitored the BBC. The next day, an officer visited the camp, demanding to know if they had a phone, and asking some of the people where they had lived. The hostages denied having the phone, but the incident scared them into not using it again. They suspected that the Iraqis could tap all lines out of IBI, and they were in enough trouble as it was.

The Messila Palace hostages found their phone attached to a fax machine. They assumed that the Iraqis had left it because they did not know what a fax was. They were unsure if it was bugged, so only used it once a week or so to contact friends still hiding in Kuwait. The men at the university residential complex had no such reservations about using their phones. They contacted Command Central and their embassies almost daily, after finding the phone on 22 August, and passed on news of their conditions, and whatever little information they could put together on movements at the nearby port.

In fact, Ray Washer, one of the men at Shuwaikh, had been a Royal Engineer explosives specialist. He advised the Kuwait Resistance over the phone, through Command Central, on how to make better car bombs with ammonium nitrate fertiliser and diesel, and packing it around a small core of conventional explosives. The situation was bizarre. The hostages were being incarcerated by Iraqis, while they were telling the Kuwaitis how to go about killing more Iraqis, and teaching the Iraqis how to clean their Kalashnikovs.

The phones were a mixed blessing. The initial problem with the Shuwaikh phones was that the hostages did not know their own numbers, so could make but not receive calls. More seriously, one of the British women at the camp, a Kuwait Airways stewardess, was married to a Palestinian, and had no idea where he was. They finally tracked him down through Command Central. On 31 August, he turned up at the camp with Kalashnikov in hand. The men were horrified. He was a collaborator, and he had been in contact with Command Central. Its security might have been compromised; it had no choice but to move. As soon as they had advised Command Central of the danger it was in, the hostages did not use the phone for several days.

The Palestinian was eventually allowed to take his English wife with him, but the Iraqi officer was suspicious of how he had known where to come, and questioned the hostages. They lied that the news of their location had been on the BBC World Service, and that a senior officer who had not given them his name had previously asked for the husband's phone number. Apparently the Palestinian either did not know that the men had a phone, or kept quiet about it once he got his wife back.

The Shuwaikh phones had a more humanitarian use than helping the Kuwaiti Resistance kill Iraqis. By virtue of its position, the camp was always the last point of call for any major movement of people out of the camps, such as the evacuation of the women and children, or a transfer of all the remaining people to Baghdad in November. The Iraqis would first call to IBI, then Messila Palace and the Dasman villa before Shuwaikh. As such, Ray Washer could usually get a list of names of all the people being moved out, and call it through to the British Embassy or Command Central. The Western Governments could then be alerted to watch out for them at the Mansour Melia in Baghdad in the next eight to twelve hours.

Getting the information was never simple, as the Iraqis tried to keep those being moved from other camps separate from those staying behind at camps visited along the way. Nevertheless, lists were passed across hidden in cigarette packets, and the information got out.

There were very few successful escapes from camps, although on 25 August, the BBC news reported that hostage rescue squads were in Saudi Arabia, preparing for action. That night was spent nervously by those who had heard the news. At that early stage in the crisis, some hostages genuinely expected that the SAS or Green Berets would swoop down on the camps. In any event, this false alarm proved to be media hype. With hundreds of hostages held throughout Iraq and Kuwait, and thousands of other Western civilians and diplomats, including women and children, still in Baghdad, such a rescue mission was impossible.

Notwithstanding their generally civil nature, when it came to escape attempts by the hostages, the guards were deadly serious about preventing them. It seemed that the only circumstances in which the guards were allowed to fire on hostages was if they were escaping, and there was no other way of stopping them. Fortunately, the only incident of a hostage being hit by Iraqi fire was Miles Hoffman's arm injury during his capture in Kuwait.

It was extremely difficult for men in the camps in Iraq to make a successful escape. Most of them stood out as Westerners or Japanese, and very few spoke Arabic. A determined man could get outside the perimeter, but once outside he had no transport, and hardly knew where he was. Without maps, compasses, disguises, fluency in Arabic, and a helpful local population, he had no chance.

In theory, those near Jordan, Iran, Turkey or Syria could try to reach those countries, but there was always the risk of landmines. There was also the risk of being shot by border patrols from those countries, even though they countries said on 26 August that they would assist anyone crossing their borders in their escape from Iraq. Men closer to Baghdad could try for refuge at a Western mission, but it meant walking conspicuously into Baghdad, and asking directions. No Iraqi would willingly give an escapee hostage a lift into Baghdad for fear of being shot by the *Mukhabarat*.

A further problem for hostages in the Iraqi hinterland was the packs of wild dogs roaming the countryside. It was unsafe to travel on foot off the main roads, especially at night. A BLT officer reportedly escaped from the camp in Kurdistan one night, and was making his way towards Syria when he encountered a pack. He thought better of the venture, and broke back into the camp. The guards never knew he had gone.

One group of three British and two French engineers did manage to escape from a camp near Basra by stealing a boat and sailing into the Gulf, where they were picked up off Khafji. Another group of hostages had an idea which never got off the ground, literally. They were held at Basra International Airport, where the Iraqis were storing the looted Kuwait Airways Boeing 767s and Airbuses. As luck would have it, one of the hostages at the site was Captain Hiroshi Shibata, the Japanese Airlines pilot caught in Kuwait. He could actually see the Kuwaiti aircraft on the apron from his accommodation, only 200 metres from the main fuel dump. 'All I need is a power pack!' he would say, but there was no chance. The planes were too well guarded.

The situation was a little different in the Kuwait camps. A number of the people who ordinarily lived in Kuwait could have escaped any time they wanted, especially from IBI or the Shuwaikh villas. They knew exactly where they were, where to go and how to hide once they were away from the camps. What stopped them was the prospect of retribution against their companions and their own guards. In fact, the guards told them on several occasions that they themselves would be executed if the hostages escaped.

Strangely, at IBI, the speedboats and dinghies used by the BLT's diving club, complete with outboard motors, had not been touched by the Iraqis. The group hatched contingency plans to get everyone into the boats and out to sea if hostilities erupted, or if the adjacent Mina Al-Ahmadi refinery were blown up. It was a last resort, as each of the two perimeter fences running down to the water had tank emplacements just outside them. Fortunately, they never had to put the plan into action. It was just as well. When the women got to Baghdad during the first evacuation, they met with BLT women who told them that they had sabotaged the boats so that they would have sunk before getting very far offshore, in the expectation that the Iraqis would use them.

In one instance at IBI, the lone American couple and one of the BA people tried to escape. The American man had cut through the fence, and returned to his hut to bide his time, but kept the piece of cut wire with him. The chief guard had found the cut fence on his rounds, suspected the American, and went to the hostage leaders, Ken Best and George Parris. They went together to talk to the American, who denied all knowledge of it, despite the piece of wire being in his possession. During the argument, the American said that 'this situation is crazy'. The Iraqi was upset enough already at the prospect of severe disciplinary action against himself if the attempt had been successful. This pushed him too far. He grabbed the American, drew his pistol, and held it against the man's temple, assuring him that he was not crazy. Ken Best had to calm the Iraqi, take the weapon from him, and replace it in his holster.

The American was left in no doubt by the other hostages that they had no wish to pay for his escape by having their conditions worsen. The Iraqi in charge later pleaded with the hostages not to escape as then he would be shot. 'What more can I do for you?' he asked plaintively. 'I've done everything in my power to make life comfortable for you.' Despite the situation, the Iraqi was sincere. He was just a functionary forced into a situation he did not want to be in.

Attitudes of the Human Shields to an Allied attack, even one in which they might die or be killed by their captors, were predominantly in favour of prompt military action. This was not false heroics. After several weeks in the camps, most men just wanted to get the situation over and done with either way. It was simply a fact of life to which they resigned themselves.

When the UN Security Council on 29 November authorized the use of force against Iraq if it were not out of Kuwait by 15 January, the men still in the camps at that time had their date with destiny. Strangely, it lifted morale rather than dashing it. The ordeal now had a time-limit. Fortunately, their reprieve came a week later when they were released.

The guards in one camp were stunned when they found that the hostages were running a sweepstake on the date of the attack. One of the more aggressive men replied to the guard's query with: 'Because that's the day you're going to die, Sunshine! If they attack here with you guarding us, you're dead.' After the guard recovered his composure, he said: 'But you will also be dead!' to which the hostage replied: 'So what?'

Curiously, many guards told the hostages that in the event of an attack, they had strict orders to get them to shelters as quickly as possible, even if it meant pushing other Iraqis aside. This actually happened at one stage at a camp near Basra when a nearby practice firing of heavy weapons by the Iraqi Army panicked the guards into thinking that the war had started.

The Western and Japanese hostages were actually a minority of the people held by the Iraqis during the crisis. During the first week of the occupation, several thousand Kuwaiti military POWs were taken, including about 700 commissioned officers up to the rank of brigadier. These men were from all five military and security services: the Army, Air Force, Navy, National Guard, and Police. Most were captured on the first few days of the occupation.

There were five main camps, all of them near sites where Western and Japanese hostages were held: at Mosul, 400km north of Baghdad; Takrit, near Saddam's birthplace north of Baghdad; and at Ba'qouba, Al-Rashed and Ramadi, all near Baghdad. Several other camps and detention centres in Iraq and Kuwait held Kuwaiti civilians arrested on suspicion of involvement in the Kuwaiti Resistance. Another civilian detention camp was near Basra.

Most of these camps had been used recently for Iranian POWs. When the Kuwaiti servicemen arrived in August, they met Iranian soldiers, some of whom had been held for ten years. They were shadows of their former selves. This was unnerving. At the time, the Kuwaitis had no idea how long the crisis would go on for, and were ignorant of world reaction to the invasion. Some of them recall looking at the pathetic Iranians and seeing themselves ten years hence.

The Kuwaitis at home were greatly concerned for the welfare of their captive men. They knew of the privations suffered by Iranian POWs at the hands of the Iraqis, and feared for the lives and sanity of their men. In contravention of the Geneva Conventions, the Iraqis did not advise their families of their capture or condition through the ICRC. The prisoners themselves were in a dilemma as they did not wish to expose their families to Iraqi harassment by asking the Iraqis to inform them of their whereabouts.

The first major camp for Kuwaiti officers in Mosul had nine large halls, each holding about 70 men, cooled with overhead electric fans. The POWs were given thin mattresses and blankets, and just enough room to lie down. There was a roll-call three times a day during which they had to sit in ranks on the floor, and be counted. They were fed usually once a day, in groups of ten, with rice or rough bread. Most of them lost a great deal of weight. Some required medical treatment after their return, although none died in custody.

After they got over the initial shock and depression of defeat and captivity, the Kuwaiti POWs' morale was generally high, particularly once they heard that US and British forces were deploying in Saudi Arabia. A few could listen to foreign news broadcasts on smuggled shortwave radio sets. Some made the rudiments of board games from whatever they could, and rosaries from date stones, or soap carvings in the best tradition of World War II POW camps. They passed their time cooking, cleaning, and playing chequers with home-made sets.

Some organized classes in recitation of the Holy Koran. One of the captive officers, KAF Colonel Saber Al-Suwaidan, the Commander of Ali Al-Salem base, spent his time planning the re-establishment of the Air Force from captivity, with his colleagues.

During the first weeks of the occupation, the Iraqis took some of the POWs, particularly KAF technical people, back to Kuwait to help them move captured military equipment to Iraq. The Iraqis, who had some excellent test pilots and their own Mirages, were able to fly the eight captured Mirages and six BAe Hawks to Iraq, but needed help elsewhere. The POWs were promised they could see their families if they helped. Almost to a man, they refused, even though most were then only half an hour's drive from their homes.

It took six weeks for the Kuwaiti families to discover where their men were held through constant enquiries of Iraqi friends and relatives. Thereafter, to the Iraqis' credit, the families were allowed to visit the men weekly until the start of the air war. By November 1990, the Baghdad hotels were filled with Kuwaiti families on their way to POW camps. The visits were a tremendous morale boost, and allowed the families to bring the men food and clothing.

While the Westerners and Japanese were often the focus of the world media and their own governments, very little attention was given to the more numerous Kuwaiti hostages. Most spent almost eight months in detention, until March 1991. Their Government was in no position to help them. Their ordeal was far worse than those experienced by the Westerners and Japanese.

In other cases, especially where men were captured as part of the Resistance, they were held 40 to a small cell, with no room to all to lie down at once, and no toilet facilities. They had to defaecate in a corner, and literally lived in their own waste. They were hardly fed. Most had been arrested with only the clothes on their backs, and had to cuddle up to each other at night for warmth. Torture was gratuitously frequent and hideously primitive.

A number of these people were Kuwaiti politicians and ex-Parliamentarians – especially members of the Ba'ath movement in Kuwait – who Saddam had hoped to use to form his puppet PFKG. To a man, they refused, and one has not been seen again.

The conditions suffered by Kuwaiti civilians rounded up in Kuwait during the occupation, especially in February 1991 when Allied forces were closing in on Kuwait City, were far worse than those of the military POWs. Several died upon return from captivity as a result of the ordeal. The tragedy of the Kuwaiti detainees continues to this day. Every Western and Japanese hostage has been released or accounted for. The body of only one dead Westerner has never been found, but 600 Kuwaitis and other Arab and Asian individuals are still missing, and unaccounted for.

11. EVACUATION

Late on the evening of 28 August, another Iraqi TV announcement stunned those in hiding, those at sites, and the world:

' President Saddam Hussein has ordered that all foreign women and children in Iraq have the option of either remaining in Iraq, or leaving whenever they wished, including those hosted by Iraq, effective the following day, Wednesday, August 29th.'

It sounded too good to be true. Saddam may have shown himself capable of great duplicity, but one thing was certain: when he made a major announcement such as this on Iraqi TV, you believed him.

Everyone in Kuwait knew that Saddam considered Kuwait part of Iraq, so the announcement included their women and children. It was unclear whether youths between 16 and 21 would qualify as children, but one thing was crystal clear: the women could go, but the men would stay.

The actual release announcement followed another of Saddam's hostage charades. This time, the set-up was far more sophisticated. Instead of using complete families, the Iraqis assembled about 20 American, British, French and Japanese mothers and children from some families, and husbands from others, so that all adults present would have their spouse still in a camp, separated from them, and would therefore behave themselves. The venue was the Conference Centre opposite the Al-Rasheed Hotel.

These chosen few hostages were taken from camps to the Mansour Melia. Some of them had been told that they were going to meet Saddam, and decided among themselves that they would at least ask for the release of the women and children. Once in Baghdad, they were given a huge breakfast, and then taken to the Conference Centre in buses with the windows blacked out. The state of mind of a few of them at the time was such that they feared they were being taken away to be shot. Several spouses left behind in the camps feared that they would not see their husbands or wives again.

One of the British women was Mrs Jackie Blears, the wife of a BLT Warrant Officer. She and her two small children had been brought in from the Daura Army Camp. When they arrived at the Conference Centre and saw the Iraqi TV crews, Mrs Blears realised what was likely to happen and asked one of the Iraqis whether the transmission would be going to the UK. It would, so she asked them if they could focus on her six-year-old daughter, Rachel. It was her birthday, and she wanted the child's grandparents at home to know that she was safe, and when. At that stage, no one knew what their eventual fate would be, or whether the Iraqis would identify the date of the meeting.

The TV men mentioned the request to Saddam's tranlator, Dr Joubaydi, who came across to Mrs Blears to confirm that it was indeed Rachel's birthday. The Iraqis were obviously looking for a chance to charm. Dr Joubaydi asked Rachel if she would like a cake, and then arranged presents for all the children there.

Shortly afterwards, Saddam appeared, and was introduced individually to all the hostages. When he came to the Blears family, Dr Joubaydi mentioned that it was Rachel's birthday. Saddam nodded, and carried on. He was trying very hard to be pleasant and friendly, but his eyes said it all. People there described them universally as being as cold as a shark's.

Saddam was apparently also suffering from a shortage of clothes, or butlers. He was dressed in the same smart, double-breasted silk suit he had worn to visit the other British hostages five days earlier, but the trousers were creased at the crotch as if he had been sitting in them for a long time. This was later airbrushed out in publicly released photographs, and cleverly hidden by Iraqi photographers placing hostages in front of him in other photos.

After the introductions, the group was subjected to a 38-minute diatribe during which Saddam sought to justify his actions. He turned on the charm by telling the hostages that he was pained by their plight, saying that if he or his family were in the same position, he would feel similarly. According to him, the hostages were there to save the lives of many more women and children in Iraq. His country had no option but to place them at key installations to prevent the US and other forces from bombing them.

'I hope the hospitality forced on you will not last long,' Saddam said, repeating his line to the earlier group. Several of the kids, unimpressed, fell asleep as he droned on, a point he did not fail to notice. The adults thought silently to themselves that this was hospitality they could well do without.

The lecture was followed by a question-and-answer session, but the ploy of separating the spouses flopped. A British woman, Jackie Joyce, taking a leaf from Margaret Thatcher's book, asked Saddam why, if he was a man, was he hiding behind the skirts of women and children. An American BA149 passenger, Kevin Bazner, asked Saddam to release the women and children as a symbol of Iraq's good faith. Another woman asked how he could use children as pawns in something they didn't understand.

Saddam either simply acknowledged or evaded the questions, but announced a willingness to engage Margaret Thatcher and George Bush in a TV debate. The State Department later called the offer 'sick', and 'undeserving of even a response'. This was a world crisis, not an election campaign.

Interestingly, Saddam was aware of the criticism of his earlier hostage session. 'I don't see why they should be annoyed,' he said disingenuously, referring to the critics. 'It seems to me those officials were annoyed by my meeting the British group because they do not want the facts to be told except by them and through their channels.' It had apparently not occurred to him that expressing concern for the welfare of children was inconsistent with holding them and their parents as Human Shields.

At the end of the session, a group photograph was taken, with the two Blears children standing in front of Saddam, his hands on their shoulders. Suddenly, Saddam turned to Mrs Blears and said, 'It is my wish that your family go free for Rachel's birthday.' Mrs Blears was quick off the mark. 'Including my husband ?' she asked. 'Yes,' said Saddam.

At that stage, despite Saddam's 23 August offer to release some of the French, there was still no indication that the release would apply to anyone other than the Blears family, but something seemed about to happen. Jackie Blears and her children returned to Daura at 7.00 p.m. to collect her husband, and the other hostages went back to their own camps. That evening, at 10.00 p.m., it was announced on Iraqi TV that all women and children could go.

Iraqi TV later said that the decision to release the women and children was in response to the unnamed woman's question on why children were being used as pawns. However, Saddam seems to have decided on this between his earlier session with the hostages on 23 August, and the second. He merely needed a stage to squeeze maximum propaganda out of it. This was later reinforced by the speed with which the Iraqis moved once the announcement was made. Some guards had even told the hostages on the sites several hours before the announcement that women and children who wanted to go would probably be freed in a day or so. Whatever the reason, it was a victory for us, with the real possibility that the women and children would get out.

August 28th was, however, soured by the death of James Worthington, a 56-year-old American hostage, of a heart attack at a site near Basra.

The announcement that the women and children could leave Iraq produced a stream of conflicting reactions in Kuwait, and in the camps and hotels.

On the one hand, there was a tremendous sense of relief. Others were understandably sceptical that it was a ploy to capture more Westerners. Even after some women and children had left Iraq successfully in the following days, a number of the more suspicious among us feared that those let out were bait to lure the far greater numbers still in hiding to come out, and get caught.

There was no immediate rush to leave. Any departure would have to be through Baghdad, then probably to Jordan or Turkey. This was impossible without official assistance. Those in the camps would have to be taken to Baghdad by the Iraqis. Most of us in Kuwait were unaware that Iraqi Airways had been flying a so-called 'domestic' Kuwait-Baghdad service between since mid-August. The only way to Baghdad seemed to be overland. With the risk to their personal security, women could not simply drive the 700 kilometres there through what was essentially enemy territory.

Westerners in hiding in Kuwait turned to their embassies, expecting that national evacuations would be organized, but the diplomats were waiting for the situation to clarify itself. The picture was further confused as the Iraqis continued picking up Westerners, including women and children. We were now familiar with the time-lag of the trickle-down of official Iraqi announcements to the troops on the streets. No one wanted to risk venturing out only to find that the troops were unaware that women and children could go.

The only Western women and children who had left Iraq at that stage were the Austrians with Kurt Waldheim on 25 August, 15-year-old Alan Barnett, and a 10-year-old American girl, Penelope Nabakov, both of whom had been travelling alone on BA149 and were seen as special cases.

Many of the hostages in Iraq heard of the announcement on the 11.00 p.m. Iraqi TV news, but their guards had to wait for orders from Baghdad, although they did suggest that the announcement was serious. The hostages in Kuwait heard about the release on their shortwave radios in the early hours of 29 August, but expected nothing to happen for a few days.

Even after the announcement, it was still unclear exactly who could go. At several camps, senior Iraqis visited to do a head count, and check who was married and who was single. This prompted some hostages to think that the families would be released as a gesture, but that the singles would stay.

On 29 August, within 12 hours of the announcement, the Iraqis in Kuwait suddenly told women and children at IBI that they had 20 minutes to pack if they wanted to go. Some men with children, especially those without an accompanying wife, were initially told that they would be allowed to accompany their families to Baghdad, but this was later countermanded. All men at the sites would be staying behind, even if they were the only parent.

For the women, the decision to go or stay was extremely painful, especially at such short notice. Mothers found themselves in an invidious dilemma. They either had to abandon their husbands to an uncertain fate, when they desperately wanted to be with them, or they had to risk the lives of their children to remain together as a family. Some initially decided to stay together, arguing with varying degrees of conviction that the children would suffer more from being separated from their fathers. Other women wanted to send the children out to be cared for by relatives, and stay behind themselves. A few childless married women, or those whose children were grown, were adamant that they would stay, as were some teenagers. Few men agreed. Every person out was a bonus, and they stood a better chance of surviving in the event of war with fewer people. Most women who initially chose to stay were persuaded to leave by their men, and to take the teenagers with them.

The final decision for families was usually that the wife and children had to go for the sake of the youngsters. The children had priority, and their mothers had to go with them. Similarly, parents with children abroad felt that if the mother got out, then the children would have at least one parent. It was that simple. If you were an female or a child, even a male teenager, you would live; if you were an adult male, you were likely to die.

A number of single women in Kuwait stayed either because their boyfriends or fiancés were there, or simply because it was their home. It was an act of personal defiance and solidarity. We were concerned for their safety, but admired their courage. Several of them, notably a stunning Dane, Liselotte Hertz, would later become a vital link to the survival of many of those in hiding. Two of the BA149 air stewardesses at IBI decided to stay with their boyfriends, as did several wives, and one woman who had struck up an affair with a BA steward. A few women without children also stayed in the Iraqi camps. Most went. Only one or two children stayed.

Many families spent this brief time on last-minute instructions for personal and financial affairs, or just holding each other. It was impossible to squeeze the hopes and plans of a lifetime, the love, the friendship, into a sudden few minutes of farewell. Grown men had to turn away in tears, their children and wives clinging to them for the last few minutes. As the coaches disappeared towards Baghdad, many of the women and children, and the men waving good-bye, feared that this would be the last time they would see each other.

The first Iraqi convoy to take women and children out of Kuwait left late on the morning of Wednesday, 29 August. It comprised several coaches holding over a hundred women and children from the four strategic sites in Kuwait.

The 50 remaining Westerners in the Regency Palace Hotel, and eight in the Meridien, followed the next day. In contrast to the rule for the camps, the men in the Kuwait hotels were allowed to accompany their families to Baghdad, but from there they would be going to camps in Iraq itself. The following day about 40 people left from the last remaining hotel, the SAS, on two coaches.

The first convoy from the Kuwait strategic sites to Baghdad took 18 hours on a scorching summer day, in unair-conditioned buses. The buses left IBI in late morning, then called at the other three sites in Kuwait during the afternoon. None of the people at the latter three sites were given any notice that they were leaving. The hostages already on the buses had to wait while the others packed and said good-bye. It was a long and tedious process.

The first stop was after leaving the Kuwait urban area was after sunset, at the Iraqi border post of Safwan. The passports were checked while the women remained on board the stifling buses. For the rest of the trip, they only had what little food and water they had been able to bring with them, and a bunch of crunchy dates which the Iraqis cut down for them to munch on.

The convoy and its exhausted passengers finally arrived at the Mansour Melia in Baghdad at 6.00 a.m. the next day. There, they met some of the women and children from the BLT who had driven themselves to Baghdad in the British Embassy convoy two weeks earlier, and others who had been brought in from sites closer to Baghdad the previous day.

The smaller Iraqi convoys from the Kuwait hotels in the last two days of August followed the same route, but the trips took only 12 hours against the earlier 18, not having to stop at a series of camps along the way. The men were not immediately separated from their families. Keeping them together for the time being made it easier for the Iraqis to handle them, and the Human Shield puppeteers were still trying to figure out where to put them.

The women and children, numbering about 500, were held at the Mansour Melia, with 180 men, until 1 September while the Iraqis and the embassies tried to arrange transport out of Iraq. In fact, the delay was partially because no one was prepared to evacuate such numbers at short notice. Aircraft had to be chartered, and landing clearance obtained, a task greatly complicated by the sanctions then in force.

The situation in the hotels was incongruous. The women and children generally spent the time in their rooms, took their meals together in the ballroom, and could use the swimming pool in the morning. In the afternoon, other Westerners resident in Baghdad, and of the same nationalities as the hostages, used the same pool, and came and went as they pleased.

The women were livid when they found that they would have to wait at least 24 hours before actually leaving, and protested strongly to the Iraqis. They would have preferred to spend the time with their husbands and friends at the sites. Some of them initially told the Iraqis that they wanted to return to the sites, but reconsidered when they realised that their men would simply send them back, and they would have to relive the agony of the separation.

The hotel was more relaxed than two weeks previously, when some of the women from the Iraqi sites had been there. The security was less overt, and the hostages could move relatively freely between floors. The Iraqi guards were generally friendlier than they had been before, even solicitous.

Rumours abounded as to who would leave, when, and by what route. It was uncertain whether they would go overland, or by air to Jordan or Turkey, or even directly to Europe by air. No one seemed to know whether national aircraft would be allowed to fly in, or whether Iraqi planes would have to be used. There was no definite information. Some of them became quite upset at the prospect of having to spend even more time in Baghdad.

The Iraqi propaganda machine took full advantage of the situation. On the morning of 30 August they brought in their TV crews to interview some of the women in the hotel foyer. A few women complied, but in one instance the Iraqis bit off more than they could chew. A British woman told them angrily that they had better smarten up their ideas, as the Americans would shortly flatten the country. That footage never found its way anywhere.

The following day, the Iraqis brought in packs of Western media, who at that stage were just arriving in Baghdad, and told the women that they were free to say anything they liked. This would have been all very well if their men had not still been Human Shields. Their comments were understandably muted, although they used the opportunity to make the point that after 48 hours in the hotel, they still had no firm word on their departure. Surprisingly, the women found the Iraqi media more courteous than most of the Western go-getters. Several reporters received a lesson in manners at the sharp end of a British woman's tongue.

The Baghdad embassies were allowed to visit the women and children from the afternoon of 30 August, but were denied access to the men. It was apparent that preparations were being made, however slowly, for the departure of the families, but that the men would soon go to strategic sites.

Many of the women and children had lost their passports in the invasion, so there was a rush to issue temporary documents so that everyone could leave when the flights were available. The British Embassy, even a month after the invasion, was apparently suffering from a lack of stationery, film, and passports. Jerry Blears, who was to be the sole man released, had to be taken around Baghdad by the Iraqis looking for an instant photographic booth. His embassy then issued him with a 100-page passport, valid for 30 days.

Despite the delays, most of the women were impressed at the Baghdad diplomats' efforts on their behalf, which contrasted sharply with their perceptions of their embassies in Kuwait. The comparison was unfair, as the Baghdad embassies had had time to catch their breath, were fully staffed, and were not operating under war conditions. There was nevertheless a feeling that they would have been in less trouble if their Kuwait embassies had been as competent. The diplomats also debriefed most of the women about the sites they had been held on in order to build up a picture of who was being held where, and presumably to help in building a target list for the Allied forces.

Meanwhile, most European embassies in Kuwait, excluding those of the three targeted West European nationalities, had accepted the Iraqis' assurances at face value, and decided to evacuate their women and children, along with non-essential staff from their missions. Of the EC countries, only Ireland, Luxembourg and Portugal were not represented by their own embassies in Kuwait, so their nationals generally teamed up with others.

The Dutch left in one coach on 31 August, taking all three dozen Dutch women and children, several Arab women on Dutch passports, a few Belgians, a Swede married to a Kuwaiti, two British women – one of whom was married to a Dutchman and had been given Dutch travel papers – and an Irish woman in a similar situation. Two Dutch male diplomats, and all the Dutch civilian men, were left behind. An Arab embassy staffer accompanied the women on the bus. The Spanish followed, and the Greeks and Portuguese, by car.

The next day, the Italians left on a minibus, accompanied by Arabist Kuwait-based diplomats, taking with them most of the New Zealand women and children, an Australian, and some Irish.

The morning of 1 September saw a flurry of activity in Baghdad. The women and children who had been brought in from the camps were told they would definitely be leaving that day. They assembled early in the morning, and finally left for Saddam International Airport in mid-afternoon for one of two flights which were due to leave at 6.00 p.m. The first was an Iraqi Airways 747 to Paris, London and Washington. The second was an Iraqi charter flight from Baghdad to Amman arranged by the Japanese for their women and children. Lufthansa was also sending in an Airbus for the Germans.

The families who had been bussed up intact from Kuwait now had to face their own trauma of separation. As the women were leaving, one BA149 passenger, who had been on his way to Kuala Lumpur on his honeymoon, was told to pack for an unknown destination, while his bride left for the airport.

Saddam International was crowded with a myriad of nationalities, all anxious to get out of Iraq but despondent at leaving the men behind. A few of the women would never see their husbands alive again. Their embassy staff were there to ease the passage, but there was little they could do. The Iraqis were running the show. The crowd was tense. The Iraqis could change their mind at any moment, and send them straight back to the hotels or the sites. A further cause for the delay was the manual check-in. In a piece of poetic justice, the Iraqis could not use their computerised check-in facilities as Iraqi Airways was hosted off Kuwait Airways' now defunct computer in Kuwait.

By this time, the Western media had found their way to the airport, and were interviewing the hostages on their way home. One of them noticed Jerry Blears, trying to look as inconspicuous as possible among all the women and children. 'You're a man!' said Brent Sadler of ITN. 'No kidding!' said Blears. 'Now please don't draw that patently obvious fact to the attention of too many Iraqis, or I'm not getting out of here, regardless of what Saddam said.'

By 6.00 p.m., the scheduled departure time, there was no sign that departure was imminent. The 17 American passengers from the camps were boarded at 6.30 p.m., but were then de-planed when it was apparent that there would be further delays. People were extremely restless, but it took them some time to find out what the delay was.

Apparently, the Iraqi Airways 747 on which the Americans, British and

French were to leave was waiting for the radical American politician Jesse Jackson to arrive from Kuwait. He had flown there as a journalist, complete with camera crew, to contribute to Saddam's propaganda in return for the release of a token batch of Americans on health and compassionate grounds. He had inexplicably extended his time by several hours to argue for the release of an American woman, Mrs Furiel Allen, who had been hiding in the Kuwait International Hotel despite the fact that Saddam's release announcement was now three and a half days old and Mrs Allen was free to go.

However, Jackson had brought very few of the American women and children from Kuwait with him. His party was mainly from the US Embassy compound, Odessa Higgins with her dislocated hip from the American 'Convoy to Hell', Mr Higgins, and Mrs Allen. The reasons are still unclear. Either the US State Department was still unsure about the release announcement, or Jackson already had enough token releases. The most charitable interpretation is that he knew that the women, but not the men, were allowed to go, and so concentrated on getting out what sick men he could.

The British Embassy in Kuwait had tried to get two seriously ill British men onto Jackson's flight, but this had not been cleared with Baghdad. One, Mike Brown, apparently had serious liver trouble. The other, Tony Wilbraham, had lung cancer. Saddam's personal interpreter, Dr Saadoun Joubaydi, was escorting Jackson's group. Joubaydi, a quintessential gentleman in front of the cameras but quite another person otherwise, refused to take the men despite the medical evidence. The Iraqis had given away enough for one day, and Jackson had enough glory for the time being.

Finally, in mid-evening, the Japanese were the first to leave for Amman with 68 of their own people and over 30 other nationalities, to be met by a Japanese Airlines flight in Amman. This was a great relief to the waiting Westerners. The Iraqis were honouring their word to let them out.

The passengers for the Lufthansa flight, including the Dutch and the two English women from Kuwait, arrived at the airport as the last of the passengers for the Paris, London and Washington flight were entering the departure lounge, only to be told at 8.00 p.m. that their flight was cancelled. The West German Ambassador protested vociferously, and successfully. Lufthansa left Baghdad at midnight, for Frankfurt, carrying over 300 people, mainly Germans, and people from eight other nationalities. They were the first substantial numbers of Western women and children to escape from Iraq.

Jackson's group eventually arrived in Baghdad from Kuwait shortly after midnight with 29 American women and children, and 15 men, several of whom were from the US Embassy compound in Kuwait. The now thoroughly disgusted American, British and French passengers boarded the aircraft by nationality, after waiting eight hours. Jackson boarded after they were seated, walking up and down the aisles with his minders and TV crew, waving at the evacuees, and saying how he had rescued them. Several irate women told him to 'sit down and shut up'; they had been waiting long enough because of him. He retreated to the first-class cabin with his entourage.

The Iraqi 747 with 265 passengers, comprising 199 Britons, 22 French and 44 Americans, and Jackson's group, finally took off at about 2.00 a.m. on 2

September, with a great cheer and round of applause as the wheels cleared the ground. The joy soon subsided as the passengers succumbed to exhaustion, and their concerns for the men left behind. The flight landed first at Orly to allow the French to disembark and Jackson to bask in the limelight. The Iraqis did not allow French, American or British officials onto the aircraft, which left an hour later for Heathrow, before proceeding on to Washington.

By that morning, nearly 700 Western and Japanese women and children, mainly from the camps, or resident in Iraq, had left Baghdad on four aircraft. Hundreds more would follow. Some of them recall travelling in a daze, hardly believing that they were finally leaving, a month to the day after the invasion which had turned their lives upside down. For most of them, their hearts were still in Kuwait or Iraq with their menfolk and friends.

The war of words between Saddam and Western leaders, especially Margaret Thatcher, continued unabated throughout this early stage of the evacuation. Mrs Thatcher had been given much of the credit by those in Kuwait for shaming Saddam into releasing the women and children, but once this had been achieved it was felt that she should have held her tongue until they were all safely home. Hundreds of women and children were still hiding in Kuwait, and arrangements had yet to be made for their repatriation.

Thatcher was adamant that the hostages would not stand in the way of military action to free Kuwait. Her way of protecting the hostages was by threatening the Iraqis with dire consequences if any harm befell them. She implied that Saddam and those acting under his orders could be tried as war criminals, and accused him, amongst other things, of 'lacking in regard for basic human rights and dignity'. Despite the wider considerations facing Mrs Thatcher, it was a patently inappropriate approach for the moment.

George Bush's remarks were far more temperate. His resolve was amply demonstrated by the massive US deployment in Saudi Arabia although, unlike Mrs Thatcher, he was not yet talking about liberating Kuwait.

Perhaps as a result of this tension, the Iraqis threatened to drop what they described as their moral commitment to safeguard the lives of foreigners in Iraq and Kuwait. The empty justification of only days earlier that the detainees were held for humanitarian reasons, was dropped. Iraq was quite explicit that the Western and Japanese men were to be held at strategic sites as a deterrent against an Allied attack. If the Iraqis expected gratitude for releasing the women and children, they certainly did not receive any, and acted accordingly. Saddam then banned all foreign aircraft from flying into Baghdad: only Iraqi aircraft would take out passengers, greatly complicating the evacuation, and helping to finance the Iraqi economy.

In Kuwait, attention turned to the embassies for assistance in actually getting the women and children out. About 80 German women and children left on 2 September, the same day as the first flights reached the West. The British and French embassies said only that they were not organizing convoys. The Americans were working on an air evacuation, but nothing was definite yet.

Actually, State Department spokeswoman Margaret Tutweiler had said as early as 29 August that the preferred course of action was chartering flights from Kuwait to Baghdad, but her colleagues in Baghdad were having trouble arranging this with the Iraqis. The US diplomats in Kuwait asked their citizens to stay inside for the time being. The dangers of trying to get out without official assistance were illustrated when several women took the initiative to go to the Iraqi Embassy in Kuwait to apply for exit visas. They were traced back to their homes, and they and ten men were picked up.

The smaller countries which had not already sent their women and children north were galvanized into action once the first planes of women and children arrived home on the morning of 2 September. The approximately one thousand women and children still in hiding in Kuwait were now fairly certain that they really would be let go, and by the evening of 2 September every country except the US, UK, Canada and France, whose nationals comprised the vast majority of Westerners in Kuwait, had either evacuated their women and children to Baghdad, or had firm plans to do so within the next 36 hours. Unknown to us, things would move so quickly the following day that the evacuation effort for those in hiding would fall over its own feet.

The Australian Embassy in Baghdad sent two coaches from Baghdad to Kuwait, followed by the Australian Consul, Phil Coggan, in a car. The buses rendezvoused at the Swiss Embassy, which we were using for our communications to Baghdad in the absence of a local mission.

Once Coggan arrived, late on 2 September, the buses were parked at the Messila Beach Hotel. Suddenly, in the crazy logic prevailing in Kuwait at the time, not having a local embassy turned from a drawback into a distinct advantage as the Iraqis allowed Baghdad-based diplomats of countries which were not represented locally to visit and assist with the evacuations.

Coggan then collected all the women and children who could not make their own way to the hotel safely, using his car with Iraqi diplomatic plates, and the Messila Beach minibus. He wanted everyone at the hotel the night before the planned departure on 4 September, and was prepared to pay for their food and accommodation. Coggan ran an exhausting one-man shuttle service between half of the suburbs in Kuwait, and the hotel.

An Australian schoolteacher, Julie Henderson, organized things at the hotel, checking off people as they arrived, and seeing that they were accommodated and had seats on the coaches. She reported back to Phil, and to me as the Australian warden, to ensure that no one was missed. The Egyptian manager who had taken over the hotel after the British General Manager, Tony Barlow, was incarcerated in early August, provided exemplary care with breakfast, lunch, sandwiches and games for the children.

Phil Coggan's shuttle service was not without its problems, especially when ferrying people in from the outlying suburbs of Ahmadi and Fintas. That entire coastal area was by now heavily defended against an amphibious attack, and the soldiers were no respecters of Phil's diplomatic pass and permit to visit Kuwait, even though he was accredited to Baghdad. He and his passengers were arrested on several occasions, once within 200 metres of being released from the previous arrest. The drive which normally takes less than half an hour took over two and a half with stops at commandeered schools, with Coggan trying to explain to uninterested Iraqi officers – if he could find any – that Saddam was allowing the women and children to go, and that he was a Baghdad-based diplomat helping them to do so.

At the time, I was co-ordinating things with the Irish warden, Cathal O'Connell. A number of Irish women and children had already gone to Baghdad with the Italians, but Cathal had no word from his own embassy there about evacuating the rest. I asked the Australian Ambassador in Baghdad, through our communications link with the Swiss Embassy in Kuwait, if we could also take the Irish. He said we could take anyone we wanted to and could fit in. Cathal jumped at the chance, and soon any Irish women we could contact were allocated seats on the Australian coaches.

By a twin stroke of good fortune, several of these were nurses. Another passenger already booked on the bus was Dr Josephine Dryden, an elderly British anaesthetist who had been evicted from the local Hadi Clinic by the Palestinian manager. We now had virtually a full medical team on board.

I then turned to the far more numerous British, suggesting to their embassy that the Australians take out British women and children, starting with the pregnant, sick or elderly, and those with infants. I explained that we had medical personnel on our buses, which would be escorted by a Baghdad-based Australian diplomat. At that time, the morning of 3 September, there was no indication that the British and French were organizing evacuations. The British Commercial Attaché, Don Macauley, who had been one of the most fearless and hardest-working diplomats during the first weeks of the crisis, told me, 'if the British Government did organize a convoy – and this was not being presently contemplated – the evacuees would have to pay for it in accordance with standard practice. As such, he would advise any British women who wanted to leave to go with the Australians.'

The entire British community was astounded that their embassy was not organizing a convoy when almost every other nation had done so, or was doing so, and people were particularly incensed that in a time of war their Government was requiring people to pay for their evacuation.

The real story was that London had apparently given little thought to an evacuation of those in hiding in Kuwait, or had kept the diplomats in Kuwait ignorant of plans for an air evacuation, so the local diplomats were merely following standard procedures. The British diplomats in Kuwait, all but helpless in their besieged embassy, had been contacting their colleagues in Baghdad about arranging an air evacuation since the release announcement was first made late on 28 August. They had not received a reply in five days, and were desperately fielding mounting criticism from their own community.

Nevertheless, after speaking with the British Embassy in Kuwait I passed the Australian offer to take out medical cases and pregnant women, and the embassy's comments, around the British warden network. Within hours, we registered 18 British, one Canadian and 20 Irish women and children on our buses, in addition to a dozen Australians. It was no longer simply an Australian evacuation. It was turning into an international affair. I was concerned that we would not have enough buses, but Phil Coggan said he would hire more if necessary. He would not leave behind anyone who wanted to go, including the British, if it was in his power to take them.

The two seriously ill Britons who had earlier been turned away from Jesse Jackson's flight, together with Mrs Wilbraham, decided to try to join us.

At the same time, another evacuation initiative was bearing fruit. Two British investment bankers with Gulf Investment Corporation (GIC), Colin Crispin and Patrick Herbert, were hiding with their families in the Zahra Residential Complex in Salmiya, overlooking the Italian Embassy. They had seen the Italian buses leaving with the Irish on 1 September, and knew of the Dutch, Belgian and Spanish departures, and the preparations for the Australian convoy. In fact, Crispin's family was booked on the Australian buses. They had spoken to the British Embassy about getting their people out, but had been told to wait for them to organize an air evacuation.

Crispin decided that the sooner the women and children were out, the better. Many British, however unfairly, were still bitter at their embassy's lack of warning about the invasion and the advice to lie low in the first few days when they could have made it across the Saudi border, and had no confidence in its ability to organize anything. Crispin obtained details of a bus company from the Continental diplomats, and hired three coaches for US$2,500 each, payable by GIC outside Kuwait. We arranged to amalgamate these buses into the Australian convoy. There was now no need for the Australians to hire more buses for the British. Mr Crispin's buses would rendezvous at the Zahra Complex the following morning for anyone who wanted to go. The Australian buses escorted by Phil Coggan would pass by on their way north from the Messila Beach and collect them.

Once his buses were confirmed, Mr Crispin contacted the British Embassy and told them he had three buses with a total of 150 seats. He needed a few of these for his family, and Mr Herbert's, but the rest of the British community was welcome to the remaining seats, courtesy of GIC.

The British Embassy's reaction was unexpected. They told him that they couldn't have a private initiative. Apparently this was confirmed by advice from London. The FCO did not want groups of unescorted British women and children travelling across Iraq. They wanted him to call off the buses.

Crispin explained that the buses were leaving the following morning, regardless of London's feelings, unless the embassy had confirmed alternative arrangements in place, and that they would be escorted to Baghdad by an Australian diplomat. It had been five-and-a-half days since the release announcement and it seemed that everyone except the Americans, British and Canadians were getting their people out. Time was of the essence, and none of these embassies had been able to provide a firm date for an air evacuation.

The early afternoon passed frantically with phone call after phone call to book people on the three buses, and arrange safe transport for them to the Zahra Complex. Suddenly, at 2.00 p.m., Don Macauley, the British diplomat who had earlier that day told me that the British were not organizing an evacuation, rang Mr Crispin and asked him if he could hire a further seven buses. There had apparently been a change of heart in London. Crispin, now feeling somewhat vindicated, referred them to the bus companies.

Unfortunately, the diplomats did not phone either Phil Coggan or myself to advise us so that we could liaise with them, and ensure that the two convoys met up, and had an escort.

The British Embassy got two of their senior locally-employed staff, Vice-Consul Raj Gopolan, an Indian, and Mr Musallim, a Palestinian, to speak to the bus companies during the afternoon, and arranged a further seven buses. That evening, at around 6.00 p.m., the British Embassy told its wardens to advise their nationals to meet the buses in the carpark of The Sultan Center Supermarket in Salmiya, early the following morning, 4 September. The announcement was repeated several times that evening on the BBC World Service to ensure that even those who were out of phone contact heard it.

At the same time, the French Embassy had also been talking to bus companies, and advised its nationals to report to its embassy in Jabriya at 6.00 a.m. for a convoy that would leave at 8.00 a.m.

The British Sultan Center rendezvous, only a few hundred metres from the Zahra Complex, was relatively sensible. Most of the British in Kuwait knew it well, lived within five kilometres of it, and could make their way there largely unhindered by Iraqi checkpoints. However, it was almost impossible to reach safely from the outlying suburbs south of Sixth Ring without passing through numerous checkpoints and travelling during curfew. Fortunately for the French, most of them lived within easy reach of their embassy.

There was no indication that the British convoy had been cleared with the Iraqis. It was apparently assumed by the embassy that Saddam's announcement a week earlier was sufficient authorization for the local Iraqi forces to allow the convoy to pass unhindered. It would not be escorted by British diplomats, although Raj and Musallim would be at The Sultan Center.

Everyone was allowed one suitcase and hand baggage. Saying good-bye was as difficult as it had been for the Human Shields in the camps, if not more so. Those in hiding had more time, but as they were not in Iraqi custody, there was more temptation to stay, especially if they were well stocked with food. For those low on food, the decision to go or stay was a little easier. It was a matter of physical survival. Again, many men had to order their wives to go.

A major problem at the time was deciding who was eligible to leave. There was no definitive guidance from the Iraqis, the British embassies in Baghdad or Kuwait, or the BBC. The main concern was for young men 16 to 20, and students 21 and over. The British argument was that males under 21 and students should be classified as children. The Iraqis seemed to consider that the cut-off point was 18, or even as low as 16, as they had boys of that age in their Army. The decision as to whether the young men should risk it was left to the individual families. Many turned to their wardens for advice. The only guidance they could give was that if a young man of 18 was particularly swarthy and well-built, then he might be wise to take his chances in Kuwait with his father instead of risking becoming a Human Shield; if he could pass for 16, and had 'lost' his passport, then he should consider going.

The sudden news of the British convoy threw the plans for what had been the joint Crispin-Australian convoy, into near chaos. The three rendezvous points and the respective arrangements became hopelessly confused. Some people were told the Zahra Complex; others correctly that it was The Sultan Center, to which the British rendezvous had been changed, and still others the Messila Beach Hotel, from which only the Australian buses were leaving.

At one stage, I was called by an individual who told me adamantly that the Australian convoy was leaving from the Zahra Complex, when I knew very well that it was going from the Messila Beach. Someone else told me that there was no Australian convoy, only a British one. I was livid at the interference to our carefully co-ordinated plans. I eventually became so frustrated that I simply told people that if they wanted to be sure of getting out, escorted by a diplomat, then get to the Messila Beach, end of story. If the British wanted to reorganize things without telling those who were going to be responsible for escorting them to Baghdad, then there was little we could do. It had to be on their heads. I washed my hands of the British convoy.

To aggravate matters, some of the British and Irish who were booked for the Australian buses, but who were not already at the Messila Beach, started to drop out. There was a natural tendency to want to go with one's own friends, so they switched to the British convoy, thinking that it too would be escorted. It would also allow them to have a last night at home with the men. I spent the rest of that evening on the phone trying to establish exactly who was going on which convoy. Most people who initially dropped out switched back when they learned that the British one would not have a diplomatic escort.

Arranging safe transport to The Sultan Center dawn rendezvous at 12 hours' notice, overnight, was particularly difficult. This was precisely why the Australians had Phil Coggan collect anyone who could not be absolutely certain of getting safely to the Messila Beach on the morning of the departure.

There were then several hundred British families in Kuwait, with over 600 women and children. Some wardens and Westerners had Arab or Asian friends who were prepared to transport them to the rendezvous, but there was simply insufficient time to collect everyone, or enough safe people to do so. The threat of an Iraqi death sentence for aiding Westerners was taken very seriously. The men could not take their own families for fear of being caught and sent to sites. Some taxi companies were still operating, but these were operated largely by Palestinians, so were an unacceptable security risk.

The fears of the British community were realized when they tried to get to the buses on the morning of 4 September. Many women who still had cars had to drive them to the Sultan Center and abandon them there. Where possible, they formed small convoys for protection. Those living in the nearby suburbs had little trouble at the few checkpoints operating in the early hours of the morning. Several were delayed and intimidated, but there were no confirmed reports of physical abuse, although at least one Kuwaiti who brought his British wife to the buses was reportedly beaten by the Iraqi troops before their officer intervened. Fortunately, those who turned up at the Zahra Complex were easily redirected to the nearby Sultan Center.

Several men, including three BLT NCOs who had escaped the initial round-up of their colleagues, were so desperate to get their families out that they drove them to the buses themselves, and were arrested by the Iraqis. Another 100 or so other British women and children, mainly from the Ahmadi and the southern suburbs south of Sixth Ring where the Australian Consul had experienced such trouble were stopped and arrested. As feared, the troops on the street knew nothing of the permission for them to leave.

About 300 British and 80 French women and children arrived at the respective rendezvous points largely unhindered. Two women and two children on the British buses were Americans, as there was still no word on an American evacuation, and a German woman, Mrs Monika Simon, the wife of the General Manager of the International Hotel, was on the French buses.

At the Sultan Center, the women had to wait for several fearful hours under the increasing scrutiny of Iraqi troops for the buses to turn up. The only British Embassy representatives there were Raj and Musallim, but they could do little about the Iraqis. The only British man was the elderly Jim Wright, who, with his wife Mary, had been visiting his son in Kuwait at the time of the invasion. He had decided to take his chances that he would be allowed on the buses, and then out of Iraq in deference to his age. It was a vain hope. He got to Baghdad, but no further. The Iraqis even kept old men.

In the meantime, those who had been arrested on their way in from the southern suburbs were being questioned by bemused Iraqi officers, who seemed quite taken aback by the numbers of Western women and children suddenly appearing on the streets in the early morning. After several worrisome hours - in some cases the entire day - being driven around town from one headquarters to another, the Iraqis finally took them mainly to the Regency Palace and Meridien Hotels. They would not be going to Baghdad that day.

Two French buses left the French Embassy at 8.00 a.m., along with a Palestinian man who seemed to be organizing the convoy. They stopped at a house in the suburbs, where he got off, and reboarded with an attaché case full of Iraqi currency. The French buses then proceeded to another rendezvous point, where they waited for the British buses to join them.

The British buses pulled away from The Sultan Center at about the same time. Only seven of the ten buses were needed because the women who had been arrested on their way to The Sultan Center had not turned up.

Each bus had an Iraqi, Jordanian or Palestinian driver and assistant, some of whom were openly hostile. The vehicles were old, little more than city buses, without on-board toilet facilities. The women had to rely on whatever supplies they had brought with them. There were no official escorts, either from the British Embassy, or Baghdad, or from Iraqi security.

The drivers did not seem to know where they were going, and drove around Kuwait's suburbs for about an hour. Unknown to the women, they were looking for the rendezvous with the French buses, but the uncertainty caused the women a great deal of concern. Many of them had been waiting in the car-park, without ablution facilities, for several hours. When they finally found the two French buses, the drivers were reluctantly obliged to wait for the passengers to go to the toilet in what appeared to be a commandeered Kuwaiti house. It was after 10.00 a.m. before they finally got onto the road out of town.

A number of the drivers and assistants started to intimidate the British women before they even left Kuwait City, and refused to turn on the air-conditioning in the stifling summer heat. In contrast, when the women on a French bus complained that the air-conditioning did not seem to be working, the driver's assistant cleaned out the vents, and made sure that it did. Several drivers made the trip as uncomfortable as possible, frequently swerving, braking hard, and hitting potholes either through incompetence, or sheer nastiness. The aged suspension of the buses did not help.

The route of the seven British and two French coaches, and two accompanying private vehicles, took them alongside Jahra, and up the Mutla'a Ridge, past the wrecked Iraqi armoured vehicles, trucks and helicopters destroyed by the Kuwaiti forces on the morning of the invasion. It was the first evidence the women had seen of the intensity of the fighting.

They were accompanied on the road north by columns of looted Kuwaiti cars being taken to Iraq, and Iraqi and Jordanian trucks loaded with goods, some of it the property of homeward-bound Egyptians, Jordanians, Lebanese and Palestinians, but much of it presumably looted. The other side of the dual carriageway had streams of cars and trucks going into Kuwait to continue the looting, or retrieve what was left of the occupants' homes.

The main delay was at the border at Safwan where they were held up for several hours. The scene was pandemonium, with thousands of Arabs and Asians in cars, trucks and buses trying to get out of Kuwait with whatever possessions they could carry. The Iraqis were systematically looting the Asians of whatever pitiful possessions they had. One unfortunate Asian bus had just broken its axle. Iraqi bedouin shepherd women in black *abayas* stood on the back of pick-ups, Kalashnikovs in hand, surrounded by their herds, watching the exodus. The Iraqis did not seem to know what to do with the British and French women, and eventually let them proceed.

After Safwan, the convoy took the longer, rougher and slower northern road past Basra, around the eastern edge of the Iraqi marshes, parallel to the Iranian frontier. Some of the drivers became increasingly intoxicated, and their driving more erratic, as they consumed the beer they had bought at roadside shops. They stopped only when they wanted to, despite pleas from the women that the children were sick or needed to relieve themselves.

As the cool of the desert night fell after a scorching eleven hours on the road, some of the drivers turned the air-conditioning on full so that the women froze, and switched on the lights and music to deny them sleep. They finally arrived in Baghdad at about 10.00 pm, but their ordeal was not yet over.

The Iraqi public relations machine, now looking for fresh meat after the departure of most women and children from the camps four days earlier, swung into action as soon as the British and French convoys hit Baghdad.

The British Embassy in Baghdad had arranged accommodation at four top hotels, the Sheraton, Mansour Melia, Novotel and Al-Rasheed, and had planned to meet the buses near Babylon on the southern road into Baghdad. Instead, the buses came into Baghdad on the south-east road, and went straight to the Al-Rasheed. The exhausted passengers were met by the glare of Iraqi TV cameras, while the harried embassy staff at the hotel were prevented from speaking to them. Once the Iraqi media had their footage of how well the women were being accommodated, they were forced back onto the coaches, under protest, and taken to the Mansour Melia where the performance was repeated. The diplomats were again prevented from assisting their nationals, and the group was again reloaded onto the buses once the Iraqis had their footage, and headed towards the Sheraton.

On this last leg, the Iraqi propaganda effort backfired. A British ITN crew flagged down one of the British buses which was lagging behing the others, and filmed the exhausted, dishevelled women and children on board. Most women refused to give their names for fear of the fate of their husbands in Kuwait, but the footage was a great relief to the men in hiding when it was seen on GCC TV channels the following day. They knew their wives and children had arrived safely in Baghdad.

They finally arrived at the Sheraton only to be told that it was full, but the hotel was persuaded to take some of the Britons, and the remainder were accommodated in the Novotel and back in the Mansour Melia. The French were taken to their own embassy, and then to the three-star ATAP Hotel.

The Australian buses had been scheduled to leave Kuwait at the same time as the British, but did not depart until 1.00 p.m. Phil Coggan waited until he was satisfied that everyone who wanted to be on the convoy had arrived, and that pleas to the Iraqis to allow the two sick British men to accompany them had been exhausted. He did a final shuttle run to collect a few more Irish from the southern suburbs which were out of phone contact with the rest of Kuwait.

The original plan had been for Coggan, as a diplomat accredited to Baghdad, to escort Mr Crispin's British buses to Baghdad, and thus provide them with some measure of official protection. However, this fell by the wayside when the British Embassy took over the organization of their own convoy. The men listening to the BBC back in Kuwait had to laugh when the BBC broadcast an FCO bulletin saying that the British buses were on their way to Baghdad, followed by the Australian buses. It sounded as if the FCO was trying to race the Australians to Baghdad.

At the time, we were still calling around the hotels, trying to sort out who had been arrested on their way to the British buses. I could see some of them in the Meridien across the road from my apartment. The women were being allowed out to their vehicles to bring their possessions into the hotel. It was an eerie feeling, looking at these prisoners less than 50 metres below our hiding place. Eventually, we got a fix on who was involved, and where they were. It seemed that the Iraqis had plans to take them north themselves.

At the Messila Beach, Tony Wilbraham, the man stricken with cancer, had been a perfect gentleman, hardly complaining despite his terminal condition. His wife Maureen was a model of stoicism. Mike Brown, on the other hand, was described by one of the women at the hotel as '...a real liability'. The women were surprised at the good grace with which the Iraqis tolerated him. The result was that everyone was deeply disappointed when Mr Wilbraham was not allowed to board the bus, but felt that they were better off without Mike Brown. The Iraqis promised to evacuate them in two or three days, and in fact did eventually take them to Baghdad. Despite their life-threatening conditions, they did not leave Baghdad for several months.

The Australian buses had a reasonably comfortable trip in the circumstances. The women were in the more comfortable air-conditioned bus, with the baggage in the second. The driver and his assistant, a Jordanian, were sensitive gentlemen who sympathized with the women. They even kept a primus stove going to ensure that hot water was available for the babies' bottles. Phil Coggan drove behind the buses in his car with Iraqi diplomatic plates, and a permit which eased their way through the checkpoints.

They followed the same route as the British and French buses to the Kuwait–Iraq border, past the detritus of battle at Mutla'a and beyond, in the midst of the refugee and looter traffic. They experienced a delay at the border while the Iraqis liaised with a checkpoint further up the road to let them pass. It was a busy day at the Safwan border for the Iraqi immigration people.

The women's passports were collected, and they had to complete visa application forms. The Irish nurses and Dr Dryden were apparently concerned that they might not be allowed to leave, as Iraq was supposedly retaining medical personnel in case of war. Most of the women simply listed their professions as housewives, although a story later emerged that if questioned about the inconsistency on their papers, the Irish nursing sisters would say that they were nuns, or sisters, in a Kuwait-based Irish Catholic religious order, and that Dr Dryden, their Mother Superior, was a Doctor of Theology.

After clearing the border, the buses, two cars, and their escorting diplomatic car proceeded on the six-lane southern highway towards Nassiriyah, a town on the western edge of the marshes, arriving at 7.30 p.m. The Iraqi bus company had thoughtfully arranged a relief stop at a hotel. Later, the convoy was flagged down by a British diplomat near Babylon. He was still waiting for the British buses which had left five hours earlier, but were on the older road, far to the east. The Australians finally arrived in Baghdad at 3.30 a.m. on 5 September, after a 14-hour trip.

The buses stopped at the suburban Australian Embassy, where Ambassador Peter Lloyd, his wife, Libby, and staff were waiting. They were directed to a three-star dive pretentiously called the 'Baghdad Towers'. It was a most uncomfortable place, more like a student hostel, with a number of Iraqi men hanging around the lobby in the small hours of the morning. It had been chosen by the embassy in preference to the five-star hotels as it would be easier to get the women out of it, and into the embassy itself, in case of an emergency. Ambassador Lloyd provided all the women with spending money, and contacted the respective embassies for the non-Australian women.

Two of the women with small children felt particularly uncomfortable with the Iraqi men around, especially without locks on the bedroom doors. Ambassador Lloyd and his wife took them to their own home for the night. The rest of the women teamed up at least two to a room. Some barricaded their doors with whatever furniture was available. Very few of them slept.

By the morning of 4 September, most of the women and children from the strategic sites, and the earlier smaller European convoys from Kuwait, together with the New Zealanders and some of the Irish, had left Baghdad. During that morning and the next, most remaining American, British, French and German men in the Mansour Melia were moved to sites with the Iraqis saying it was to make room for the women and children expected from Kuwait.

The only Westerners left in the hotels when the Australian, British and French convoys arrived were three British couples, a British male diabetic, an ill American, and assorted men in what was known as 'the grey group', comprising those other than the five major wanted nationalities. These 'grey group' men expected it would simply be a matter of time before they too would be sent to sites, but that afternoon they were released into the custody of their embassies in Baghdad. It was a tremendous relief, but they still could not leave Iraq. The Iraqis had drawn a definite line between the five key nationalities and the rest of the Western world. Previously, only Canadian and some Irish men had been released. Now others were included.

It was some time before news of this filtered down to Kuwait. Even then, we were unsure whether it meant that we would be free from incarceration only in Baghdad under the care of our embassies there, or whether we would enjoy similar freedom in Kuwait. In any event, the news of this development came far too late for non-American and non-British men in Kuwait to be of further use in organizing the evacuation of the women and children.

Early on the afternoon of 5 September, the Australians and French were escorted to Baghdad's Saddam International Airport by their embassy staff, and left Baghdad for Amman at 3.30 p.m. on a French-chartered Iraqi jet, within 12 hours of their arrival in the city. In Amman, the French were transferred to an Air France flight home, while the Australians were met by their local Ambassador, Bob Bowker. They were taken to an Amman hotel to freshen up, and speak to the media on their own terms, before boarding the Australian Prime Minister's RAAF Falcon *Mystere* executive jet for home.

Meanwhile, the British women were still in Baghdad. The only American women and children who had got out of Kuwait at that stage were the few who had left on the British buses, and the handful with Jesse Jackson.

That evening, 5 September, the Iraqis cleared out the Kuwait Meridien and Regency Palace Hotels where they were holding those arrested on their way to the previous day's British convoy, and men captured in the first week of September. Approximately 180 people went to Baghdad in seven coaches.

The journey to Baghdad took 12 hours but was mercifully through the cooler hours of darkness. The drivers were exhausted even before they started. They had just driven down from Baghdad, and had to stop for a break every three hours just to keep awake. When they got back on the darkened roads, they seemed to try to make up for the stops by racing each other and narrowly missed scores of trucks coming down to Kuwait. In the midst of the truckloads of loot heading north, they were astounded to see 4-metre long missiles, presumably captured Kuwaiti HAWKs, being hauled towards Baghdad.

A second British Embassy bus convoy of women and children left Kuwait on 6 September in three coaches, with one American. Most of the passengers were women who either could not get to the earlier convoy because of the short notice, or who had finally been persuaded to get out while they could.

The situation in our building was typical. When the first convoy left, the only two married women in our group decided to stay with their husbands. The third woman, Jane Anderson, left. The two wives simply could not tear themselves away at such short notice. One, Magda Hoyle, an elderly lady, was resolved that she would stay with her husband Ken, even if they had to starve together. The other, Mary Chambers, a vivacious Irish blond, went on this second convoy against her better judgement. We were very sorry to see her go, but our main concern was for her safety. We knew we would be helpless to protect her if Iraqi troops or marauding Palestinians came after her.

The treatment on this second official British convoy was not so bad as that on the first. The convoy also had a higher proportion of children, which may explain the better treatment by the drivers and assistants. Nevertheless, the drivers still drove violently, drank throughout the journey, and had to be forced to stop to allow the women and children to relieve themselves.

One of the passengers on this convoy did not fit the description of a woman or a child. He was Peter Goodwin, an ex-RAF fighter pilot, now a middle-aged KAC airline pilot. Goodwin certainly had plenty of gumption. His wife, Dorothy, had dressed him up in a wig and lady's blouse, and they had made their way to the Regency Palace Hotel rendezvous with forged drivers' licences which identified them in Arabic as Czechoslovakian.

Goodwin was using the passport of a Mrs Elizabeth Price, the British mother-in-law of a Kuwaiti colleague. The passport had been sent into Kuwait ahead of Mrs Price so that she could get rebated KAC tickets.

Many of the women on the coaches were irate when they noticed Goodwin, who had managed to board unseen by the Iraqis. They felt that he was putting them and their children in danger, but they could not deny him the chance to escape. They had to grudgingly admire his courage and initiative.

However, when their husbands learned of this attempt later, many would have cheerfully lynched both Goodwins. Some vowed to take legal action, or worse, against them in the UK if ever they got out. The men's nerves were on a hair trigger from the moment their families left their hiding places until they had confirmation that they were safely out of Iraq. The atmosphere was so tense, and the concern for them so great, that anything that might conceivably compromise their safety was seen as high treason. The British Embassy in Kuwait was similarly scathing that Mrs Goodwin, one of its own employees, albeit not a diplomat, had been party to the scheme.

Goodwin's disguise did not fool the Iraqis for long. He got as far as Safwan. There, the passports were collected, and the Palestinian and Sudanese couriers on the bus went into the immigration building. The Iraqis came out, and ordered everyone off the vehicles. The women, children, and Mr Goodwin, had to file into a room to be checked physically against the documents. An Iraqi officer called out the names, and each individual had to approach a desk in the center of the room. When Mrs Price's name was called, Mr Goodwin had no option but to comply. The officer took one look at Mr Goodwin in his wig and blouse, glanced at Mrs Price's photograph, and then blew his top. Goodwin was immediately taken away into a back room.

The Iraqis were not amused. 'What the hell is going on?' demanded the senior officer. 'Take this thing off!' he said, touching the wig. Goodwin replied that he couldn't as his wife had done such a good job of attaching the wig that only she could remove it. The officer sent back into the main room for Mrs Goodwin, who had her husband's real passport with her. In the back room, the senior Iraqi officer was still seething. As Mrs Goodwin walked in, her husband, still dressed up as a woman in the midst of the Iraqi officers, indicated the wig lamely, saying: 'You'll have to take this off.' She produced his passport to prove who he really was, and then started extracting hairclips and pins, as the Iraqi gradually calmed down.

The Iraqis sent back to Kuwait for the British Embassy's Raj Gopolan, who had liaised with them on the convoy. It took him several hours to arrive, during which time the buses were held up at Safwan, with Mr Goodwin feeling increasingly guilty about the delay he had caused.

When Raj finally arrived, he denied all knowledge of Mr Goodwin, although he knew the couple well. The Iraqi accepted his explanation, sent Raj on his way, told Mr Goodwin to sit down, and orderedthe buses to proceed.

At this point, Mrs Goodwin stated that she would stay with her husband. The Iraqi told her that he was staying, but she was going on to Baghdad. Mrs Goodwin stood her ground firmly, and the argument became heated. Finally, the officer had enough. He drew his pistol, cocked it, pointed it at Mrs Goodwin's face, and told her, 'Get the hell out of my office!' Mrs Goodwin was escorted onto the bus, while Mr Goodwin remained behind, still in his padding and lady's blouse, but now minus his wig.

He was eventually taken to Basra by a very courteous *Mukhabarat* man, then put on an overnight sleeper to Baghdad. Ten hours later, he was sent back to Basra and on to the Khor Zubair Power Station - barely 30 minutes from Safwan - in a pick-up. It was not the last he would hear of his escape attempt.

As the second British road convoy was wending its way across Iraq on 6 September, the Canadians were undertaking the first air evacuation from Kuwait, using a chartered Iraqi aircraft. The Japanese had actually been the first to leave Kuwait by air, almost two weeks earlier, but that was almost the entire community together, and prior to the release of the women and children. The Canadian Government pulled out all stops to evacuate their people, including asking for *agrément* for their new Ambassador to Baghdad, J. Christopher Poole, after the invasion. They even had their own chartered aircraft sitting on the tarmac in Cyprus, ready to go in.

Poole did not get into Baghdad until after the evacuation, but the Kuwait end was organized – in conjunction with the local Canadian diplomats besieged in their mission – by Jean-Paul Gautier, a Baghdad-based Arabist diplomat who had once served in Kuwait. Gautier had driven to Kuwait with Iraqi permission. The rendezvous was the Hadi Clinic, in Jabriya, near the Canadian Ambassador's Residence. With the Ambassador on leave at the time of the invasion, the embassy was under *chargé d'affaires* Bill Bowden.

The Canadians had similar problems to the British in getting to the dawn rendezvous, but managed. They were given the same amount of short notice, but there were many Canadians in town of Arab and Indian extraction who had reverted back to their original documents, and could help.

Unknown to most of us at the time, a number of what became known as the 'real' Canadian men were moving around relatively freely. One of them was architect Eoin MacDougald, who had been arrested on a desert escape attempt on 18 August, and released the following morning. A few other Canadians had heard of this, taken the plunge, and found that the Iraqis arrested them now and then, but let them go as soon as they got to an officer. A few of these men were helping on the ground with the evacuation. Others had elected to go to Baghdad with the women, even though they would not be allowed out of Iraq.

The main Canadian problem was actually Mr Gautier, who was seen as a bit of a maverick. He apparently got aggressive with the Iraqis, who felt they should be treated with a little more respect, so they held up the convoy from the Hadi Clinic to Kuwait International Airport.

In the meantime, the Iraqi plane had arrived, with the Ambassador's secretary, Janice Atree-Smith, on board. When she discovered that the civilians had not yet arrived at the airport, she, a lone woman in occupied territory, set off to the rendezvous and sorted out the unpleasantness between Gautier and the Iraqis. The aircraft left some time later, on an hour long flight to Baghdad. It was in stark contrast to the torturous day-long road convoys. By 2.00 p.m. that day, the Canadians were on a flight to Ankara.

Meanwhile, the women and children from the first British convoy had handed their passports to their diplomats in Baghdad to have their exit visas processed. They spent the night of 5 September, the day of their arrival, in various hotels before their planned departure the following day. A few stayed longer to have replacement passports issued. Those in the Mansour Melia were joined early on the morning of 6 September by the people who had been captured on their way to the buses on the morning of the 4th, and others who had been picked up during the previous week. The British Embassy staff were granted access to the women, but were not allowed to speak with the men held separately on the top floors of the Mansour Melia.

The women learned that the embassy was chartering two Iraqi aircraft to take them to Amman, where they would be met by a British Airways flight. This was different from the experience of the women from the camps, who had left four days earlier. They had flown directly to Europe and the US, some on Iraqi charters, others on national aircraft which had flown into Baghdad. Saddam's reaction to the increasingly bitter attacks on him by Margaret Thatcher, and the UN embargo on Iraq, was to ban foreign aircraft from operating into Baghdad. There was even speculation that Iraqi planes would be denied landing rights at foreign airports, and that the women and children might have to endure another long, overland journey to Amman or Turkey.

The situation in the hotels was incongruous in the extreme. Regular Western residents of Baghdad, and the visiting media now pouring into Iraq, were allowed to move around the city relatively freely and even use hotel facilities, while the British and French women, and the men destined for the Human Shield, were confined to these same five-star hotels.

Baghdad was strangely peaceful for the capital of a country on the brink of war, but the women found it a sinister place, with portraits of Saddam on every wall and street corner, and a constant *Mukhabarat* presence. No one felt secure. It was assumed that the hotel rooms and public areas were bugged, so the women could not speak freely, least of all about their men back in hiding. A number of women found that their suitcases had been rifled in their rooms.

More seriously, reports later emerged of several women being assaulted by Iraqis in their rooms, some in front of their children. Given the security around the hotels at the time, this could only have been done by or with the collusion of the *Mukhabarat*. As far as is known, all the victims of these attacks kept it largely to themselves for fear it might delay their departure from Iraq, or affect the fate of their husbands still in hiding.

On 6 September the Iraqis tried to take away some of the British youths over 16 years of age, having previously assured them that they could leave, and also the elderly Mr Jim Wright, who had accompanied the first convoy to Baghdad. At 11.30 a.m., they loaded the women and children who had arrived that morning onto buses to take them from the Mansour Melia to the Al-Rasheed. The men were left behind. Once they were on the bus, they tried to take away a 19-year-old British boy, who was accompanied by his mother. His father was still in hiding in Kuwait. The women pleaded with the Iraqis to let him go, but they said that they had boys of 16 in their army, so at 19 he was a man. They refused to relent, so his mother got off the bus with him.

The Iraqis were less successful with Mr Wright and his wife. They were spirited away by UK Ambassador Harold Walker to his Official Residence, where they stayed until the release of all Western hostages in December.

Throughout 6 September, the British women who had arrived in Baghdad on the first convoy were repeatedly told that their departure was imminent, only for this to be contradicted. Finally, at 5.00 p.m., all those who had exit visas boarded coaches for the journey to the airport, only to wait for a further three hours while further documents were processed. When they finally arrived at the airport, they had to pick up their passports from the floor where the Iraqis had thrown them, and undergo luggage and body searches.

Once in the departure lounge, they were told that there was no aircraft available. The Western ambassadors who had accompanied the women intervened. Aircraft were found, but there were further delays as they were prepared. Two aircraft holding mainly British women and children finally left on the hour-long flight for Amman late that evening, followed by a planeload of Americans and others. Upon arrival, the passengers were transferred directly, past the waiting media, onto their national airlines. The British went to the promised BA flight, where there were medical personnel, a chaplain, FCO and Ministry of Defence officials, and a social worker.

The relief to be on one's own airline, smothered with attention, after the trials of the past weeks was delightful, but tinged with concern for the men left behind. The British women had nothing but praise for the BA crew. The same could not be said for the press. After five weeks of only radio and TV news, the front-page stories on the Western newspapers on board were not of their evacuation or of the men left behind, but the rising price of oil. Their true value fell sharply into perspective.

The only Americans who left at that stage were those from Iraq, the camps, or the first British convoy. Most US women and children from Kuwait, besides those few who had come out with Jesse Jackson, were still there, in hiding. The Americans in Kuwait were told that there would probably be an air evacuation, but that it was likely to take a week to organize.

Further groups of women and children flew out of Iraq over the ensuing days as they arrived in Baghdad and had their exit visas processed. Those from the second British convoy of 6 September, and those detained on their way to the first convoy had to wait in Baghdad until 9 September. Nevertheless, the process was well established by then. The British diplomats had learned from the earlier flights. They were at the airport in force, and even enlisted the help of the Western TV crews to keep their cameras on the women to deter the Iraqis from stealing their gold on the way out.

In contrast to the European and Australian road evacuations, the Americans and Canadians travelled in style, by air, without having to stay in Baghdad.

The American evacuation took several days longer to organize than the road evacuations as the US Embassy in Baghdad had to consult the Canadians to find out how to do it, and then negotiate the charter with the Iraqis, and arrange a blanket visa to allow their citizens to transfer directly to a flight out of Baghdad. For two days after the Australian and British women had left, the Americans in Kuwait thought that their embassy was doing nothing, but when TV images of the exhausted British women arriving in Baghdad were seen in Kuwait, some of them felt they were better off in Kuwait.

The Americans chartered an Iraqi flight into Kuwait on the morning of 7 September, the day after the Canadian air evacuation and second British Embassy convoy. This was a great surprise to the people in hiding. They had been told that it would take at least a week, but now they had one plane, with a second flight scheduled for the following day.

It was now their turn to tear themselves away from their husbands and friends at short notice. They were advised not to take any documents showing their husbands' addresses in case the Iraqis used them to trace the men, and to try to arrange a neutral national to drive them to the early-morning rendezvous. Like the British, many of the women had to drive their own cars and then abandon them. They were allowed only whatever luggage they could carry themselves, usually one suitcase and hand baggage.

The 170 Americans for the first flight met at 7.30 a.m. at the carpark of a popular supermarket near the airport, the appropriately named Americana Safeway. Several Canadian men, notably Eoin MacDougald and Britt Mockridge, who had helped with the Canadian flight, were on hand to provide invaluable co-ordination and organization at the rendezvous. Their presence seemed to keep any Iraqi harassment at bay.

The women were shocked during their trip to Safeway at the trash piled up on the roadsides, and the burned-out Iraqi vehicles, the victims of Resistance attacks, littering the main highways. A greater surprise greeted them at Safeway. It was completely burned out. What had previously been a glittering hypermarket, pure middle-America, was now a mass of blackened concrete pillars, twisted metal and ashes. It was the first real evidence many of the women had seen of the destruction in the city.

Despite the tension, the scene at the Safeway carpark had its amusing moments. A number of the American women had dressed up in *abayas* and *hejab* (conservative Muslim female dress) to disguise their nationalities at roadblocks, and reduce the risk of harassment. However, they were unused to wearing the flowing robes, and constantly tripped over the skirts when taking long American strides. They had to adjust to walking with little steps.

The evacuees on this first American flight were crowded into old buses for the ten-minute ride to the airport, with their luggage on another bus. Once loaded, the buses did not move for two hours. They were left parked in the blazing sun, with little ventilation and no air-conditioning. The babies and children became fractious. There was another hour's delay at the airport before they were allowed to board the blessed relief of the Iraqi Airways plane. Eoin MacDougald and Britt Mockridge's main problem then, after helping the women to board, was in being actually allowed off the plane.

The Americans disembarked in Baghdad before lunchtime, into the arms of their embassy staff and American and French media. Most elected not to talk to the press until they were well out of Iraq. Others felt that a TV interview was the best way to let their men in Kuwait, and their families back in the US, know that they were safe and well.

There was a further delay in Baghdad while exit visas were arranged, and new travel documents issued for those who had lost their passports, but they eventually boarded a second Iraqi flight to Amman. They had no real problems in Baghdad. A number of the women attributed this to the ruckus being kicked up by the State Department about the shooting and wounding of Miles Hoffman in Kuwait several days earlier.

Arrivals from the first flight were received in Amman by US Ambassador Roger Harrison, and taken to an airport hotel in Amman to wait for the onward flight. It would be 36 hours before it arrived, but at least they were out of Iraq, and could call their families at home. Jordan was like a breath of fresh air after the fear of Kuwait and the tension of the evacuation.

The second flight from Kuwait on 8 September initially went as smoothly as the first, but there were long delays in Baghdad. The main cause was Kuwaiti children with American mothers trying to leave on their Kuwaiti passports. The Iraqis considered these children to be Iraqi. They were also apparently getting desperate to find more American men for the Human Shield, and wanted the women's civil ID cards, which had their home addresses on them. The aircraft finally left for Amman in the early hours of 9 September, arriving only 15 minutes before the scheduled departure of the Northwest Airlines flight which was to take the first people to Frankfurt.

The evacuees from the second flight were quickly consolidated onto the Northwest aircraft, but their problems were not quite over. There was a security scare, so they had to deplane and identify their baggage individually. Once this was done, they were in Germany within hours.

Poignantly, the Northwest airliner had just deposited US troops in Saudi Arabia. A number of the women found notes from the American soldiers in ashtrays, and slipped into the bulkhead trimmings, wishing them all the best, and asking the women to write and pray for them.

The week after the British bus convoys, a young Baghdad-based Arabist British diplomat, James Tansley, and the Baghdad Consuls from Australia, Canada, Ireland, The Netherlands and the US were allowed to fly to Kuwait on one of the US flights, to help arrange the departure of any remaining women and children, and to encourage any who were still in Kuwait to leave.

Tansley's presence would have been a Godsend on the British bus convoys, but was now virtually a waste of time. He was not even allowed into the British Embassy. However, Dr Niall Holohan, the Irish Consul, on the first post-invasion visit by an Irish diplomat, was able to visit a number of his countrymen in hiding, and issue Irish travel documents to some of them who were carrying British or US passports.

The Americans took out any other Westerners who wanted to go. With the exception of one special flight for the French when they were released in October, all other evacuations of the Western women and children, regardless of nationality, were run by the Americans. There were 12 such flights prior to the release of their men in December: 10 in September, and one each in October and November. They became known as 'Air Rogers' flights after the US Consul in Kuwait, Mrs Gale Rogers, who co-ordinated the Kuwait end of them.

The American flight of 22 September from Kuwait had to be touted as the 'very last one', as people had begun to hang on for a later flight, and the aircraft were going to Baghdad half-empty. The major beneficiaries of the flights in the third week of September turned out to be Arab nationals with US connections and the Iraqi Treasury, rather than real American civilians. They took out mainly Arab-Americans, or Egyptian and Palestinian families with a child holding an American passport by virtue of birth in the US.

One particular individual who left on that flight was Dame Violet Dickson, the widow of Colonel Harold Dickson, one of the most distinguished British figures in Kuwait's history. Dame Violet was in her 90s, senile, bedridden, and had been terminally ill in hospital since before Easter that year. The British Embassy had even prepared a grave for her in their grounds.

The British Embassy had arranged for only two seats, one for Dame Violet, and one for a companion, despite the old woman being bedridden. They had also made no provision for getting her to the aircraft. When the Americans discovered this, they blocked a whole row of seats for her to lie down on, and to seat two nurses and the attending physician, and arranged with the Iraqis to get her ambulance to the door of the plane.

The Americans evacuated over 2,000 US women, children, and their non-American families, and nationals from some 30 other countries.

After the contrast between the two modes of evacuation - overland and by air - became known, there was intense criticism of the European Embassies, in both Baghdad and Kuwait, for not organising an air evacuation. The diplomats' response was the quite honest explanation that speed was of the essence in getting the women and children out, and that the air evacuations took longer to organise. Jesse Jackson may have been able to fly to Kuwait on 1 September in an Iraqi aircraft for his contribution to Saddam's propaganda, but at the time the British buses were organised, the embassies were apparently having great difficulty arranging charter flights. The delay in organising the Canadian and American flights was evidence of this, although the fact that the Japanese had been able to fly up to Baghdad almost two weeks earlier on a scheduled Iraqi Airways service suggested that it was possible.

To be fair to the British Government, they were trying to organise an air evacuation at the time, but were taking so long about it that Mr Crispin's private initiative and the Australian convoy simply overtook them. If they had told their people that an air evacuation was being prepared, but would take a day or two to organise, people might have waited. As it was, the men in hiding in Kuwait wanted to get their families out as soon as possible, and an air evacuation did not even occur to most of them. Few of us knew at the time that the airport was operating, or that Jesse Jackson had been in town.

Later, the British apparently declined to co-host the 'Air Rogers' flights, saying that there were only 30 to 40 people who were eligible to leave. The British position seemed to be that if such individuals had not gone out earlier, they were not entitled to official assistance. The British played virtually no role in the US flights, including the evacuation of their own nationals, Commonwealth citizens, or other EC nationals nominally under their care. In fact, a great deal of animosity occurred between the two embassies in Kuwait when the British started booking people on the US flights without liaising with the Americans. At one stage, the US and British officials, the closest of allies in Saudi Arabia, were not even talking to each other in Kuwait.

There were several other categories of women and children in Iraq. Some were ordinarily resident in Iraq with their own jobs, or as wives of men working there. Others were visitors such as pilgrims, tourists, or businesswomen. Most had no real problems in leaving. The travel ban on foreigners who had been in Iraq prior to the invasion was effectively lifted as far as they were concerned.

Even after most of the women and children had left, some women, notably British and Irish nurses working for the Aer Lingus company, PARC, at Baghdad's Ibn Al-Bitar hospital, had difficulty leaving. At first, they were allowed to go on the condition that PARC sent replacements for them, but this was virtually impossible. It was several months before the Iraqis relented.

12. SEPTEMBER 1990: SETTLING IN

The early days of September 1990 were not the finest hours for the Coalition. The world seemed prepared to defend Saudi Arabia, but with the notable exception of Mrs Thatcher, preferred for the time-being to rely on sanctions to edge Iraq out of Kuwait. There seemed to be little stomach for military action. George Bush had drawn his line in the sand at the Kuwaiti–Saudi border from his Kennebunkport golf course, but we were on the wrong side of it.

Almost without exception, those in Kuwait, and the hostages, were convinced that the sanctions, even the embargo of Iraqi oil sales and military imports, were merely symbolic. Iraq had massive armament stockpiles, and its own indigenous arms and oil industries. The idea of Saddam mending his ways in response to sanctions was simply naive. We had no doubt that the only way he would leave Kuwait was at the point of a gun.

However, matters did improve. By late September, elements of most military forces that eventually liberated Kuwait were in Saudi Arabia, although the political will to use force still seemed weak.

The continuing departures of women and children were a great relief to us. It not only got them out of the way of a shooting war, but for those of us still in Kuwait, the limited food supplies would go further as we awaited liberation.

Our first great disappointment in September was the statement by the Saudi Defence Minister, Prince Sultan bin Abdul Aziz, that his country could not be used as a staging ground by the American military for rescuing hostages under Iraqi control, or for launching offensive operations against Iraq. American forces were in his country only to defend it. 'The Kingdom of Saudi Arabia is not a theatre for any action that is not in defence of Saudi Arabia', he said.

Prince Sultan was no doubt seeking to calm the situation by countering earlier US media speculation that hostage rescue squads were preparing for action in Saudi Arabia, and to give the military the time they needed to build a credible defence. He was delivering the official line at the time.

General Schwarzkopf was similarly unhelpful, saying there would be fighting only if Iraq attacked. Indeed, it was only at this time that the Saudis, reacting to Iraqi threats, began to align their war aims with the West's, that is, to put paid to Saddam's potential for future greater mischief.

A collective groan arose from those in Kuwait and on the sites at these comments. Military action was patently impossible without Saudi support, and the US going on the offensive. It appeared at the time that both Saudi Arabia and the US were willing to write off Kuwait. In the meantime, we would be stuck indefinitely. Those of us in hiding knew that we could hold out for no more than a few months, and might be faced with the choice of giving ourselves up to the Iraqis, or starving. The Human Shields' main hope for salvation lay in war, which at the time seemed a more realistic proposition than a unilateral release by Saddam.

The Kuwaitis themselves knew that the longer it took for liberation, the less of their country would be left. Each day, they could see hundreds of Iraqi trucks shipping it north piecemeal. Each day meant more Kuwaiti dead.

Initial hopes for a diplomatic solution were dashed when talks in Amman between Iraqi Foreign Minister Tareq Aziz and UN Secretary General Javier Perez de Cuellar on 30/31 August ended inconclusively. At the same time, King Hussein of Jordan met with Mrs Thatcher in London, but they were unable to agree on a common approach. King Hussein was caught between his two great friends: Iraq, his major trading partner, and the West. To complicate the King's situation, Saddam's championing of the Palestinian cause was creating domestic pressure from the 60% of Jordanians of Palestinian origin.

Aziz arrived back in Baghdad from Amman on 1 September. He was immediately despatched to Moscow to ease the Soviet Union's condemnation of the invasion, but Soviet President Mikhail Gorbachev maintained his unequivocal demand that all Iraqi troops withdraw immediately from Kuwait, and that its independence and sovereignty be restored. Aziz emerged from the talks looking somewhat anguished, his previously sunny disposition gone. He left Moscow rebuffed, with the Soviets accusing Iraq of aggression.

Pope John Paul II joined the Soviets by rebuking Iraq, but said that military action by US-led forces could bring 'more evil' to the Gulf. As far as we in Kuwait were concerned, there was already enough evil in the Gulf in the form of the Iraqi Army. It was about time to replace it with the US Marines.

We were similarly unimpressed when US Secretary of State James Baker said that the US Administration expected a long stand-off. US officials were then saying that sanctions could take more than a year to cripple Iraq. This really worried us. We, and Kuwait, simply did not have that long. Escape from Kuwait was now virtually impossible. The only solution to our ordeal seemed to be war. Those Westerners hiding in Kuwait favouring sanctions over war were an ever-shrinking minority. The Human Shields, some now in their fifth week of incarceration, were similarly disposed. Only a handful of Kuwaitis of Iraqi or Palestinian origin were against war.

The first week of September was not without its bright spots. Saddam continued to allow Western and Japanese women and children to leave Kuwait and Iraq, and the Arab League met in Cairo where 13 of the 21 members demanded that Saddam not only leave Kuwait, but also pay reparations.

The Arabs had shifted, by a slim margin, from searching for a face-saving formula for Saddam to outright opposition. The myth of Arab brotherhood was abandoned. The way was now clear for the rest of the world to get on with solving the problem without riding roughshod over the Arab League. The only sour note was the resignation of the League's respected Secretary-General, Chadli Klibi, in reaction to Saudi and Syrian claims that he did not do enough to get more Arab States to send troops to Saudi Arabia. At that time, the only non-GCC Arab troops in Saudi Arabia were 2,000 Egyptians, 3,000 Syrians and 2,000 Moroccans. They were militarily inconsequential alongside the 100,000 US troops then in the region, but were of immense political value.

President Bush also announced on 2 September that he would meet with Gorbachev in Helsinki on the 9th. It was now apparent that the Soviets would not back their previous Iraqi client, and news of the summit raised hopes that they might even take an active part against Iraq.

In an effort to cut the ground from under Saddam on the Palestinian issue, which had great appeal to the Arab public, Israel and the US agreed to work together on a credible Arab–Israeli peace process. Concurrently, Israel said that it would view any Iraqi move into Jordan as an intolerable threat to which it would respond. This did little for Coalition cohesion. The Saudis and Syrians were horrified at the prospect of being on Israel's side in a war with Arab Iraq, but it reminded Saddam that he also risked taking on Israel.

On 4 September, James Baker outlined a new regional security structure to counter the strategic threat from Iraq, based partially on a US commitment to maintain a long-term military presence in the Gulf, even if Iraq withdrew from Kuwait, within the framework of a NATO-style alliance. In one month, Saddam had given the Americans what they had tried unsuccessfully to get for decades: invitations to set up military bases in the GCC countries.

Saddam did not take the criticism lying down. In a fit of born-again Islam, he renewed his call for *jihad* against US troops in Saudi Arabia, and called for the toppling of King Fahd and Hosni Mubarak. His new-found enthusiasm for Islam was all the more incongruous when his chief diplomat, Tareq Aziz, professed to be a Christian. He then rounded on the Israelis by vowing to drive them out of Jerusalem, and defeat all foreign forces arrayed against him.

Aware that his greatest allies were time, and the innate differences between the disparate members of the Coalition, Saddam continued to try to play off the Arabs against the West, the US against the Europeans, and the poorer Arabs of North Africa against their wealthier GCC brothers.

In response to the embargo, the Iraqis made a show of asking city dwellers to join relatives in the countryside. Rationing was introduced. Saddam was telling his people to dig in for the long haul. To gain Arab public sympathy, he said that Iraqi children were dying because of shortages of milk formula and medicines caused by sanctions. He did not get far with this. Western diplomats pointed out that milk was still widely available, although at a higher price, and that there were no sanctions on humanitarian supplies.

In Kuwait, the embargo was a joke. There was no real food shortage. The problem was distribution, and money to buy it. Fresh produce flooded into Kuwait from Iraq to take advantage of the higher prices. Even truckloads of beer, whisky and *araq*, much of it imported from Jordan, and cigarettes, found their way into the previously dry Emirate. Street markets selling cucumbers, tomatoes, watermelons, eggs, and alcohol flourished as Palestinians and Indians set up shop. We did not see why the Iraqis were complaining about baby formula when they could smoke and drink to their heart's content.

Saddam then issued new maps of Iraq, showing Kuwait split into two, with the northern half attached to Basra Province, and the southern half as Iraq's new Nineteenth Province. It was hardly the setting of the stage for a face-saving solution. He also sought to link the embargo to the plight of the trapped

Westerners and Japanese, saying that their countries should immediately send food for them. It was an attempt to reduce Western public support for the sanctions. They could tolerate Iraqis suffering hardship, but their own people starving was another matter.

The debate over whether to eventually use force to evict Saddam from Kuwait, or rely on sanctions, overshadowed the far greater long-term danger posed by his nuclear, chemical and biological weapons programme. Up to that point, only a few sharp Western journalists had even raised this aspect publicly, but it was foremost in the minds of the politicians and generals. The Coalition knew that these weapons would have to be dealt with sooner or later. Some chemical weapons plants were vulnerable to Allied bombing, but US intelligence could not find the hundreds of secret chemical stockpiles, and knew even less about Saddam's nuclear and biological weapons programmes.

The real Allied agenda was to remove the long-term threat of the Iraqi military. The Allies had not created the crisis, but it provided them with a golden opportunity to do what would eventually have to be done. The liberation of Kuwait was certainly a key consideration, but the longer–term interests of the US and the Middle East rested on removing Saddam's potential for regional hegemony. An Iraqi withdrawal from Kuwait, with its military intact, would be more of a long-term defeat than a victory.

In the midst of all this, the Israelis were uncommonly smug about having bombed Iraq's Osirak nuclear reactor in 1981. Several sources suggested – with some justification as post-war evidence indicated – that had they not done so, the Coalition would now be facing an Iraqi nuclear bomb.

The pick-ups in Kuwait intensified following the evacuation of the women and children. Some of the men in hiding in Kuwait feared the Iraqis must have taken the women's Kuwaiti civil IDs from them on the way out of Iraq, and were using the addresses on the cards to find the men. The day we realized this, husbands scurried to check their wives' bedside lockers to search for the cards. Those who did not find them lived in a heightened state of fear until the pick-ups gradually abated in late September after the Iraqis had taken most of those who were most vulnerable, or most at risk from informers.

Security precautions were tightened. One of the most widespread was with phone calls, whereby the caller would let the other phone ring three times, then hang up, and redial. The other party would then know that it was a friend, and answer on the first ring. Even so, we usually answered the phone in Arabic, or waited for the other party to speak first. Some individuals even imposed a two or three minute time limit on phone calls.

One major rule was that there were to be no Palestinian visitors as a small minority of them were collaborating, and there had been several reports of people being captured because of Palestinian acquaintances. This rule against Palestinians caused some trouble. The Irishman with us disagreed with it, and received his Palestinian colleagues once when they insisted on visiting him. The group reaction was brutal. We ostracized him for several days.

Other rules were as basic as not using the corridors unless absolutely necessary, such as at mealtimes, or about going on the roof to sunbathe.

There was a constant fine balance between security and mental and physical health. We could not survive without social contact, and mealtimes were always the best opportunities for this. Similarly, several men insisted that they needed to spend time on the roof each day for fresh air. This was quite reasonable, but they had to stay out of the line of sight of the upper floors of the Plaza Hotel.

There were other important rules. It was forbidden to speak English in the corridors in case we were overheard as we passed a flat with potential informers in it. Hard shoes were banned in order to minimize footfall noise.

Out in the suburbs, men in houses made their residences look as uninhabited as possible. Furniture was moved out of rooms visible from the street, gardens were allowed to die back, and paths were left unswept to give the place an unoccupied look. Whenever they had to venture outside to collect food dropped off for them, or take some sun, they walked only on the grass or the raised borders of the footpaths to avoid leaving footprints. When in the garden or front rooms, the men dressed in *dishdashas* so that a casual observer would mistake them for Arabs. Many men grew beards in hiding, to make it difficult to identify them as Westerners from a distance. They lived with minimal lighting in almost complete silence behind closed curtains.

Many people constructed bolt-holes in case the search got too close. One American, George Daher, had the good fortune to live in a large villa with the twin benefits of a swimming pool and Danuta, a formidable Polish lady doctor. Whenever the Iraqis came calling, George headed straight for the pool pump-room and Danuta answered the door, sometimes in her white coat, and told the Iraqis that she was the only one there. Other men had hiding places in air-conditioning ducts inside or outside their flats, or in their attics.

Several men with handyman skills went to incredible lengths. One group took out a door jamb from the entrance to a small room at the rear of a flat, inserted a cupboard into the space, and finished the area around it with trim salvaged from a skirting board. The entrance to the hideaway was through the rear of the cupboard, which they could lock from the inside. They put food, water and even a microwave oven in their bolt-hole. The room was invisible to anyone unfamiliar with the layout of the flat. It merely seemed as if there was a built-in cupboard at the end of the corridor. It proved critical at one stage when the Iraqis came in and looted the rest of the house, oblivious to the men hiding a few feet away, behind the cupboard.

Those in apartment blocks had less scope for security, more risk of being found, and fewer escape routes. Men in houses could usually see the Iraqis coming down the street, and hightail it over the back wall if things got desperate. People in high-rises could hardly jump out of the window. Nevertheless, we did what we could. Those without peepholes in our front doors took them from looted or abandoned flats. We then noticed that whenever someone inside looked through the peephole, the person outside could see the disturbance to the interior light through the lens. The solution was to stick a piece of paper with a pinprick in it over the peephole on the inside, so the light would not show, but the man inside could still see out.

The two young British men, Neil Beevor and David Hough, who had joined us from the Plaza Hotel, were occupying a flat with its entrance in an elevator lobby. Some of these lobbies had utility rooms, so they prised *'Electricity'*, *'No Smoking'* and *'Keep Out'* signs, in Arabic and English, off the utility rooms on other floors, and glued them onto the wall outside their flat and onto their door. To complete the deception, they taped up the doorbell switch.

Whenever we moved between flats, we phoned ahead. The occupant of the destination flat first checked to see if the corridor was clear. We timed the trip to the second, and the door was opened quietly as soon as the visitor arrived, and shut quickly behind him. Exposed time in stairwells and corridors was reduced to an absolute minimum. We never, absolutely never, used elevators as no one knew where they would stop and who might get in.

In houses, but especially in flats, the prevailing rule was silence. This could never be total as people still had to talk, listen to the radio and TV, and do the chores. However, we minimized noise as much as possible. My American neighbour took his showers at 3.00 a.m. when he felt that there was less chance of Iraqis wandering past his flat and hearing the plumbing.

The noisiest activities were cooking and washing up. This was especially critical for our group as all our kitchens were near the front doors, and the clatter was audible to anyone in the corridor outside. We cleaned one item of crockery at a time, and placed each item of cutlery on a teatowel as we dried it to eliminate any sound. The TV and radio were kept in a back room, and turned low. The ringer on the phone was always turned down.

We later went to the extent of nailing blankets over the insides of our front doors, and placing cushions along the base of the door to block any accidental noise. Similarly, if curtains were too thin to block all light, we hung blankets against the windows, and placed pillows along the bottom edge of floor-to-ceiling windows. The precautions were not just paranoia. We continually heard of people being captured because of the most elementary security slips.

The main consideration after security was food. We were extremely careful with everything. Teabags were reused several times. If we did not finish a cup of tea or coffee, it was reheated in the microwave later on. Chicken bones and skin were saved for stock or soup. Oil from canned sardines was used to flavour rice. Nothing was wasted. Most men had very little meat. The main component of their evening meals was pasta and rice, with a few vegetables for flavouring. Cooking actually became quite therapeutic.

Reactions to the enforced incarceration differed greatly. One Briton in our group was so upset by the departure of his wife that he drank heavily, while the American became fastidious to the point of fanaticism about cleanliness, and washed his kitchen floor daily. He developed such an extremely sensitive sense of smell that he would not even sit next to someone who had not showered in the past six hours. He then worked up a deep-seated bitterness towards the US Embassy and his Government. He could not understand why paratroopers had not jumped in during the early days and established a *cordon sanitaire* along the coast road from Kuwait City to Saudi Arabia, with helicopters and fighter planes flying cover. He then read William Manchester's *'American Caesar'* about the life of General Douglas MacArthur several times, and wrote letters to George Bush telling him how MacArthur would have run the crisis. All we could do was humour him.

Other men in the group shone. Cliff Pickard, a middle-aged Englishman and a real loner, took exemplary care of the man who was drinking. The two young Englishmen served with distinction. They had a wonderful, dry sense of humour, and took it upon themselves to maintain the American's spirits by telling him jokes, inviting him for dinner, and just listening to his ramblings.

Others in our group who gave us a sense of stability were the elderly couple, Ken and Magda Hoyle. Magda became our mother figure, and was held in great respect for her decision to stay against our entreaties to go. She explained that her children were grown up, most of them with families of their own, so her place was with her husband. The other women, she said, did not have that luxury. Ken was also great for putting things in perspective. He had a great sense of humour, and a perpetual twinkle in his eye. As importantly, we all knew that he had been a POW of the Germans in World War II. He never spoke about it, but the knowledge that we had a real ex-POW in our midst helped us to see our own ordeal in a more balanced light.

Things really started moving on the diplomatic front on 9 September, when George Bush and Mikhail Gorbachev met in Helsinki, hoping to co-ordinate their approaches to the crisis. Bush wanted a stronger Soviet commitment, possibly including the Soviet military, but Gorbachev, fresh from his meeting with Tareq Aziz, emphasized his new diplomatic initiative, including a Middle East peace conference which the US had until then strongly opposed.

Neither man got everything he had wanted, but each got far more than he might have expected. After seven hours of talks they issued a joint pledge to act 'individually and in concert' to reverse Iraq's conquest of Kuwait, even if peaceful means failed. The US did not get Soviet troops but did get stronger Soviet diplomatic support; the Soviets did not get a peace conference just yet, but the Americans dropped their long-standing opposition to it, provided Iraq's occupation of Kuwait was not on the agenda. They were united in their view that Iraq had to leave Kuwait. Gorbachev made the telling point that during past Middle East crises, the US and USSR had been on opposite sides, and even on the brink of war. Now they were of one mind in principle, but merely differed on the means to achieve the ends. In Kuwait, we were delighted. The results exceeded our wildest expectations.

Saddam had sought to pre-empt this superpower union by sending an open message to Bush and Gorbachev on the eve of their meeting, reaffirming his intention to keep Kuwait, and saying that the crisis was one for the Arab nations to solve, not the superpowers. However, at this stage, an Arab solution was long dead, if not quite buried. The letters had no effect.

With Bush and Gorbachev meeting in Helsinki, Tareq Aziz's route back from Moscow had taken him to Teheran to see Iranian Foreign Minister Ali Akbar Velayati in an unsuccessfully attempt to coax the Iranians into circumventing the UN embargo. The Iranians reiterated their condemnation of the invasion, but also criticized the regional build-up of foreign forces. Aziz's one victory was to resume diplomatic relations with Iran. This was granted more significance than it deserved: Iran and Iraq had gone through most of their own bitter conflict with diplomatic relations intact. That they could now talk to each other a little more conveniently was of little consequence.

At the same time, Arab governments aligned against Iraq were speaking in private of what they saw as the need for military action to eliminate Saddam and his military might. Tacit consensus on the inevitability of war emerged, despite repeated public statements to the contrary by Arab leaders.

Saddam began to look increasingly desperate when, on 10 September, he offered free oil to developing countries willing to break the UN trade sanctions, if only they would come and get it. The *quid pro quo* was obviously political support. It was a tempting offer for poorer Asian countries which had been dealt a triple blow with the loss of remittances from their nationals working in Kuwait, the cost of resettling those people, and higher oil prices: but there were no takers. The naval blockade would have stopped them.

Iraq could not even win a trick on the sporting front. The Olympic Council of Asia, which had held the murdered Sheikh Fahd Al-Ahmad in high regard, banned Iraq from the 11th Asian Games in Peking, and expelled it from its membership. This was a painful defeat for Iraq as most of the voting countries were Third World nations, rather than the Western powers which Iraq blamed for trying to isolate it. Iraq, a mover in the Non-Aligned Movement, had been firmly rejected by its own club. Kuwait, to prove the point that, although occupied, it was not beaten, said a reduced Kuwaiti team of 65 would compete. This was down from the regular 300, with eleven members thought to have been killed in the invasion, others still in Kuwait, and more joining the military in the US, the UK, and Saudi Arabia.

One of the big winners of the crisis was Egypt. Her key role consummated her rehabilitation into the Arab world after years of ostracism in the wake of the Camp David accords. The seal was set on this when the Arab League relocated its headquarters from Tunis to its original site in Cairo. Another beneficiary was Syria, who came in from the international cold when James Baker visited Hafez Al-Assad in Damascus. Even deep-seated US differences with Syria on state-sponsored terrorism did not obstruct the *rapprochement.*

Within a week, there was another astounding diplomatic development. Saudi Arabia and the Soviet Union restored diplomatic relations, which had been broken 52 years earlier. Saudi Foreign Minister Prince Saud Al-Faisal even left Moscow saying that he would welcome Soviet troops as part of the Coalition against Saddam.

Upon his return from Helsinki, President Bush addressed a joint session of Congress saying that the US would not be blackmailed by Saddam over hostages, and making it clear that force would be used if necessary to prevent Iraq from retaining Kuwait. This was exactly what most of us in Kuwait and Iraq wanted to hear. Disparaging remarks about Bush being a wimp subsided as we recognized the fine manner in which he was handling the crisis. His performance in a joint press conference with Gorbachev in Helsinki had been masterly. He was now deftly preparing America for the prospect of war.

Things were also happening in London. Foreign Secretary Douglas Hurd had just returned from a whirlwind tour of the Gulf and Yemen. Hurd's meeting in

Jeddah with the Saudi Foreign Minister had been particularly productive. Parliament had been recalled, and on 6 September, with the Western women and children still arriving home, engaged in an emergency debate on the crisis. An overwhelming majority supported the steps taken to date, but there was dispute on the preconditions for military intervention.

One area in which the British Government came in for a great deal of criticism was in the handling of the plight of the British community in Kuwait. It was apparent that they had dropped the ball in a big way. One of the earliest evacuees, Kirsty Norman, had written a scathing letter to the *Times* on the British Embassy's perceived incompetence. Her husband, a Reuters man who knew which strings to pull, had been told by the FCO that she was safe with a Swiss diplomat, when in fact she was on a strategic site.

The FCO Minister of State, William Waldegrave, had replied in a letter full of errors of fact. In truth, the embassy had simply been overwhelmed, but Waldegrave would not admit this. The letters coincided with the Parliamentary debate, and were read into the record. It was a great boost for us still in Kuwait and Iraq to know that the evacuated women were batting for us, but with all the other aspects of the crisis demanding attention, the hostages and those in hiding were soon put on the back burner.

The second week of September was also a distinct improvement for the Coalition on the military front. In contrast to General Schwarzkopf's recent emphasis on the defensive nature of the US deployment, the Pentagon now said that US forces in or near Saudi Arabia would be strong enough by 15 October to mount offensive action against Iraq, or Iraqi-occupied Kuwait, or both. By mid-September, the air deployment would be virtually complete.

Belgium and The Netherlands sent warships to help enforce the embargo. Britain and France indicated that they would consider sending further forces. We began to anticipate a two-week bombing campaign starting on 1 October, with the troops coming in a fortnight later. At that time, we could last until the end of October, just, and started to pin our hopes on such a timetable.

September 14 was a red letter day for all those in hiding, and in the camps, as country after country committed specific forces. With a bipartisan Parliamentary majority behind her, Mrs Thatcher ordered the first substantial European ground forces to the Gulf in the form of the British Army of the Rhine's 7th Armoured Brigade. This unit comprised two regiments with 120 Challenger tanks, an armoured infantry battalion, an armoured reconnaissance squadron, and an artillery regiment. It was expected to arrive within three weeks, preceded by additional Tornado aircraft. To our unschooled military minds, this fitted perfectly into our imagined timetable.

Egyptian President Mubarak had committed 30,000 more troops to Saudi Arabia a week earlier. Now Syria's President Hafez Al-Assad hinted that he would despatch 10,000 more men, and 300 tanks – a full armoured division. Turkish President Turgut Ozal prepared his country for a possible military role. NATO agreed to consider a US proposal to commit ground forces to Saudi Arabia, and to provide transport for Arab troops. Italy committed eight Tornados, and a fourth warship, but no ground forces. Canada eventually became the fourth largest non-Arab military contributor after the US, UK and France, overhauling Australia, which had been among the first to send ships, with a squadron of CF-18 Hornets, two frigates and a supply ship.

These commitments above and beyond the requirements for a purely defensive role were seen as another indication that the Coalition was not going to wait forever for Iraq to withdraw from Kuwait.

Finance for this deployment started to fall into place. Saudi Arabia promised to pay the multi-million dollar operating costs of US forces in the region, and to contribute billions in aid to Arab countries in the anti-Iraq Coalition. On 8 September, James Baker met with the Kuwaiti Amir in Taif, and received promises of financial assistance. In fact, Washington expected to defray almost all expenses incurred in the operation with US$2.5 billion from Kuwait, and contributions from Bahrain, Qatar, Saudi Arabia, the UAE, Japan and Western Europe. Kuwait also contributed a further US$2.5 billion to countries such as Jordan, Egypt and Turkey which were hurting economically because of the UN embargo. The EC announced it would help similarly. Even neutral Sweden and Finland joined in the condemnation of Iraq, and sent funds to Jordan and Turkey to help them cope with their refugee crisis.

This was a great deal for the US military, and for most of the Gulf States except beleaguered Kuwait. The GCC contributions were financed in part by a combination of higher oil prices caused by the crisis, and increased production to replace the 4 million bpd of sanctioned Kuwaiti and Iraqi exports that had disappeared from the market. The Japanese, Western and Asian public who were the ultimate consumers of Gulf oil and gas were paying higher prices to their suppliers, which in turn financed the non-Kuwaiti GCC contributions to the US deployment and sanctions-affected countries. Iran was an even bigger winner. It benefitted from the higher prices, higher production, and Iraqi overtures, without having to pay any financial contributions.

The major non-combatant Coalition countries also dug deep. West Germany offered transport planes and ships, military equipment and economic assistance of US$1.87 billion, and US$250 million in aid for nations hardest hit by the embargo. Japan approved US$3 billion in aid, in addition to a previous US$1 billion, and sought to pass a law allowing its troops to serve as non-combatants in the Gulf. There was much US media criticism of Japan over its constitutional ban on sending men, with the critics conveniently forgetting that America itself had imposed the now inconvenient Constitution on Japan. At the time, the early Japanese role in hiding US military and diplomats in Kuwait could not be revealed, so the Japanese had to take it on the chin.

James Baker returned home on 15 September from a nine-nation tour with US$16 billion in pledges. Eventually, the total aid committed by the Gulf States, Europe, and Japan amounted to about US$20 billion.

In the midst of the hordes of troops flooding into Saudi Arabia from all corners of the world, one tiny force at the heart of the crisis was trying its best to make an impact.

The remnants of the Kuwait Armed Forces were gradually reorganizing themselves under Acting Chief of Staff Major-General Jaber Al-Khalid.

Hundreds of servicemen who had been on leave outside Kuwait were reporting for duty. Hundreds more volunteers were clamouring for training, and camps were established for them in Saudi Arabia and the UAE, often on the initiative of individual officers. US Special Forces were eventually assigned to train them. Except for the men from 35 Brigade and a few from 15 Brigade, the Kuwaitis had no uniforms, no weapons, no vehicles, and precious little of anything else. Fortunately, Al-Khalid had trained in the US with the Commander of the US Special Operations Forces, Colonel Jesse Johnson, so a profitable working relationship was in place once they were reunited.

Eventually, the Yugoslav M84 tanks which Kuwait had had on order before the invasion were delivered, and re-equipped 35 Brigade. *Fahd* wheeled APCs arrived from Egypt for the infantry. Slowly, the Kuwaitis put together six small brigades, each barely more than a battalion, all of which would serve under Saudi command. Hundreds of bilingual Kuwaitis were assigned to Western units as liaison officers, and to advise on conditions inside Kuwait.

The KAF fixed-wing aircraft that had escaped the Iraqis were integrated into the Allied air plan, although the Mirages were kept largely grounded as it was feared that they might be mistaken for similar Iraqi aircraft.

The Kuwait Navy was also keen to do its bit, but had only two surviving combat vessels and the coastguard barge retrieved from Kuwaiti waters by the Saudis. The Navy Chief, Colonel Qais Al-Saleh was a POW, so his deputy, Lieutenant-Colonel Ahmad Al-Mulla, took over. All the light arms and ammunition were taken off the vessels and sent into Kuwait with people infiltrated across the border. The three vessels had remained at Mishab in Saudi Arabia for August, then moved to Bahrain. This was the logical place for them as Bahrain also had Lurssens. The Bahraini Navy provided excellent support, even putting the Kuwaitis on their payroll, and allowing them access to their spares and ammunition, even Exocet missiles.

Perhaps as important as the re-equipping and training were the command arrangements. Al-Mulla was concerned firstly that the Arab forces would not be directly involved in operations against the Iraqis when the liberation commenced. Then, even if they were, he feared that the Saudis would sideline the Kuwaitis. At a major conference in September between the Allies and the GCC states, Al-Mulla got Major-General Al-Khalid to put the Kuwait Navy under US command to ensure that it would be integrated into the operations.

From then on, the Kuwait Navy was directly involved in the US Navy's plans. The Coastguard barge was dry docked and upgraded to act as a support ship for the two Lurssens, and for US Navy SEAL commandos who would later conduct frogman and mini-submarine operations against the Kuwaiti coast. Someone nicknamed it 'Happy Duck', and that's the way it stayed. *Happy Duck* could eventually take any US helicopter other than the largest Chinooks, would provide a floating forward sick bay, and accommodated the volunteer force which would reclaim the first liberated Kuwaiti territory.

The Kuwaitis were able to download invaluable data from *Istiqlal's* and *Sanbouk's* computers on virtually all Iraqi and Iranian naval vessels in the northern Gulf, information built up over the years, for the Americans, enabling them to more readily identify Iraqi ships - and even various types of missiles -

through their radar signatures and electromagnetic emissions. The two boats even staged mock attacks on US vessels to help ready them in case the Iraqis used the six captured Kuwaiti Lurssens with their Exocets against the Allies.

A great morale boost to the men in hiding and the hostages occurred on Friday, 7 September. The BBC World Service started its *Gulf Link* programme.

The first broadcast included an interview with the leaders of one of the volunteer support groups being set up in the UK to help the families and friends of those affected by the crisis. Thereafter, *Gulf Link* sent short, individually-recorded messages to those in Kuwait and Iraq. It instantly became compulsory listening and a major part of the daily routine.

Initially, it lasted 15 minutes, with a daily average of 35 messages. It was transmitted at 7.45 p.m. Kuwait time, with a repeat early the following morning, every Western weekday. To cope with demand, it was later extended to 30 minutes, allowing 90 messages, and then to 45 minutes, seven days a week, until it went off the air in December after the release of the hostages.

The programme was financed by the FCO, and started after lobbying from relatives and the support groups which had sprung up in August. By the time the women and children arrived home in early September, the programme was almost ready to roll, and served a vital need in allowing them to communicate with the men stranded back in the Gulf.

Gulf Link catered mainly to the British as the largest community of Westerners in Kuwait and Iraq. Other countries had their own services, some of which started weeks before *Gulf Link*. The VOA's was *Messages from Home*. The Australians, Canadians, Dutch, French and Germans all had their own services. Message senders were counselled to use only first names or codenames, never surnames, and to avoid giving any clue as to where people might be hiding. Nevertheless, there were some terrible security gaffes, but in the end no harm seems to have been done.

Over its three-month life, *Gulf Link* sent an estimated 8,000 messages, or 100 a day at its peak. During November 1990, when most of the men in camps were allowed to phone home, priority was given to those in Kuwait, who had no direct contact with their families. The average gap between messages was about ten days for *Gulf Link* and *Messages from Home*, although exceptions were made for birthday and anniversary messages, and particularly urgent transmissions. The smaller countries had a same-day service.

The VOA service could be particularly painful to listen to. While most British and other relatives remained upbeat, many of the Americans became emotional on air. The other women felt that there was little point in telling their men how much they loved them. This was patently obvious. Football scores and news of the children's progress at school were far more useful.

The programmes also broadcast a few basic recipes for the men, and provided expert speakers on nutrition and the psychology of surviving in the situation. Radio Australia even featured a famous football hero and professional motivator who advised us to use the time in hiding productively by getting fit, and learning Arabic! You had to appreciate the initiative.

Throughout September, the media were the battlefield for far more serious matters. The propaganda war continued unabated, with exaggerated claims by both the Kuwaitis and Iraqis.

On the one hand, the Kuwaitis were trying to hurry along Western military action by reporting an increasingly desperate situation in their occupied country, with lack of fresh food, and frequent failures in the electricity and sewage systems. The Iraqis, for their part, showed staged videos, later with CNN collaboration, of a Kuwaiti hospital operating normally, and apparently peaceful street scenes. Both views had an element of truth, but were blown out of proportion. The Iraqis had evicted most Kuwaiti patients from hospitals – CNN was set up and fell for it – and the set-up street scenes were hardly representative. None showed the checkpoints, or the nervous looks on the faces of the troops at the threat of Resistance attacks.

A far more effective and convincing form of propaganda came from the Kuwait Resistance itself, inside Kuwait, with the help of Westerners in hiding. One of these Resistance groups, headed by Sheikh Sabah Nasir and Sheikh Ali Salem Al-Ali, had a young woman, Asrar Al-Qabandi and a satellite telephone system. Asrar organized satellite phone interviews with US, British and French TV networks to keep Kuwait in the public focus. The first calls had gone to ITN in the UK in the third week of August, but had been overshadowed by the Stuart Lockwood episode, and other concerns for the hostages, including – still – many women and children. In September, Asrar's group started working the American networks, particularly CNN, CBS, the ABC and Ted Koppell's *Nightline*. The initially tried VOA, but gave up after being put on hold, and told to 'Call back on Monday'.

One group of four Americans hiding in Mishref, Don Latham, his stepfather Gene Hughes, Joe Lammerding, and Fritz Cameron, and a Briton, John Bridger, were particularly fortunate to be in the care of Asrar and her colleagues. She first contacted them on 12 September, asking if they would like to talk to ABC anchor, Barbara Walters. They had to provide their social security numbers to verify to ABC that it was not a hoax. Asrar then connected them to the US. Each of the men spoke to Walters for about 15 minutes, telling her of the plight of Westerners in Kuwait, and the brutality of the occupation. They then used the same channel to speak privately with their families.

It was a remarkable piece of public relations, and drove home to the American public the suffering of the Kuwaitis and their own nationals under the occupation. It brought the Kuwaitis into Western living rooms as resourceful individuals sustaining Americans and Britons being hunted by Saddam, and countering the media stereotype of a moneyed bourgeois. Young Kuwaiti men and women were fighting for their land as the massive Allied military force sat on its backside in the Saudi desert. Don, a Vietnam War Special Forces veteran, returned the favour by showing other Resistance people how to make better bombs.

Some of the other propaganda could be quite ridiculous. At one stage, Iraq announced its intention of trying George Bush for planning war and genocide against Iraq, and for aggression against Grenada and Panama, shortly after US officials had suggested trying Saddam for his chemical attacks on the Kurds. More seriously, Iraq warned the US that its Middle East presence left it open to terrorist attacks in retaliation for 'crimes and insults' against Islamic countries. The US responded by advising that it would hold Saddam personally responsible for any such attacks. Behind the scenes, Syria and the PLO were pressured to keep guerilla groups affiliated with them in check.

The pick-ups of civilians in hiding continued unabated into mid-September. However, a series of raids on the official residences of Western Ambassadors in Kuwait caused far more trouble for Saddam than for the diplomats.

By then, three weeks after the embassy closure order, only 17 diplomatic missions remained manned, mainly the US, Canada, the major European countries, and a few Arab and Asian posts. On 13 September the Iraqis entered the Dutch Ambassador's Residence in a move which seemed designed to pressure the European missions to close down. When there was little response, they hit the French, Canadian and Belgian Residences the following day.

The first was the French. The Ambassador was out of Kuwait at the time of the invasion and five of the six French diplomats remaining in Kuwait were in the embassy itself, but the Military Attaché, Colonel Edouard Crespin, and three French civilians were in the Residence. All four were taken away.

When the Iraqis entered the Canadian Residence - next door to the French - later that day, they found themselves with far more people than expected. Several Baghdad-based Consuls, including Melvin Ang from the US, Australia's Phil Coggan, Canada's Jean-Paul Gautier, and Ireland's Dr Niall Holohan were there on what would be their last Iraqi-permitted trip to Kuwait to assist with the evacuation of the women and children. Also there were Irish warden Cathal O'Connell and his team of Aer Lingus computer consultants, who had been convinced to relocate to Baghdad.

The diplomats and the six Irish civilians were first held in the Residence for an hour, before being taken away to a local headquarters, where they were told they would have to go to Jahra. This was 30km away, on the way to Iraq. The diplomats became increasingly concerned, particularly Mr Ang, who had arranged the evacuation flight that was due to leave for Baghdad within hours. Despite their protests of diplomatic immunity and the production of passes from Baghdad, they were loaded onto a minibus for Jahra.

Upon arrival at Jahra - at what was probably the HQ for Iraq's III Corps - the group met up with Colonel Crespin and the three French civilians. They were held for a further hour, with Mr Ang becoming increasingly concerned about his people at the airport. The Iraqis eventually told the diplomats and Irish that they could go, but the three French civilians were taken away to join the Human Shield. The diplomats and the Irish civilians were eventually driven back to the Canadian Residence, but detained in the bus until the *Mukhabarat* arrived and cleared their release. They then hurried to the airport where, much to Mr Ang's relief, the American civilians had organized themselves with the help of several Canadian men.

The Belgian diplomats were also raided on the same day, but had less trouble. The soldiers simply told them to leave, but departed when the two diplomats retreated from the embassy into the adjoining residence.

At the time, it was uncertain whether the raids were part of a normal search for Westerners or a deliberate breach of diplomatic immunity. They seemed to be co-ordinated, at least on the local level, as the Iraqis also entered Bangladeshi and Tunisian premises. The raids also came days after Bangladesh, Belgium, Canada and The Netherlands had committed forces, so it hardly looked co-incidental, but it is unlikely the events were related, given the time-lag required to organize anything on Baghdad's instructions. France and Tunisia were the exceptions, but President Mitterrand had been making belligerent noises. We were never able to figure out why Tunisia was hit, but then again, we never could fathom Iraqi logic.

However, the senior Iraqi officials in Baghdad who received vehement diplomatic protests seemed genuinely surprised, and immediately denied that the raids had taken place at all. Some officer serving in Kuwait would obviously have to do a great deal of explaining.

Regardless of whether the embassy raids were the initiative of some Iraqi officer in Kuwait or a deliberate move by Baghdad, they suited French President François Mitterrand perfectly. At the time, he was looking for a good excuse to send ground forces. France was lagging behind the British, Canadians, and even the Italians. However, Mitterrand had faced Cabinet opposition, including that of Defence Minister Jean-Pierre Chevenement, a founding member of the Franco–Iraqi Friendship Society. Characteristically, the French were trying to avoid appearing as running dogs of the Americans. Mitterrand had specifically said on 9 August that France would not be associated with the multinational force proposed by Washington. France could just about accept her civilians being taken hostage, but a raid on a French Ambassador's Residence was an entirely different matter.

Up to then, the French commitment had been limited to a naval deployment totalling about 3,500 personnel. On 15 September, Mitterrand announced that the raids seemed to be a test of Coalition solidarity, and despatched 4,200 extra men, 48 AMX-10 tanks, 30 Mirage and Jaguar warplanes, and 48 helicopters. He then started to press for a UN air embargo on Iraq and expelled some 40 Iraqi diplomats and other personnel. The French in Kuwait were delighted. Their military commitment now exceeded the British, which only made the British in Kuwait more hawkish.

In an apparent Iraqi attempt to mollify Mitterrand, all the sick and elderly French were allowed out of Iraq with former Algerian President, Ahmad Ben-Bella. Iraq finally apologized for the raids on 23 September, admitting them, but it was too late. The French Foreign Legion was on its way to Saudi Arabia, and the UN Security Council had issued yet another Resolution, 667, condemning acts of violence against the embassies in Kuwait.

Not only France reacted to the raids. The EC expelled all Iraqi Military Attachés and restricted Iraqi diplomats' movements to the same radius around their capitals as Western diplomats in Baghdad were limited to. This set off a round of tit-for-tat expulsions from Baghdad.

The Coalition forces in Saudi Arabia were now less concerned about their ability to stop a determined Iraqi attack into Saudi Arabia. However, despite talk that the military deployment was shifting from the defence of Saudi Arabia to building an offensive capacity, Iraq still remained a formidable foe.

On 15 September, without warning, the Iraqis opened the Kuwaiti border with Saudi Arabia at Nuwaisib to let Kuwaitis depart. This followed several weeks of increased repression in Kuwait, particularly after a number of successful Kuwait Resistance attacks.

At this stage, about 60 Kuwaitis had been killed, most by execution, in addition to those who lost their lives in the fighting on 2 August. Rape was on the increase as the Iraqis settled into the city. Both men and women were being picked up from the roads, and held for ransom or torture. The Iraqis had built up a pressure-cooker of fear in Kuwait. Now, when they opened the valve, thousands of Kuwaitis flowed out.

At the time of the invasion, perhaps 400,000 out of 650,000 Kuwaitis were in the country. The rest were abroad on business, studies or holiday. In the first six weeks, perhaps 130,000 had escaped into Iran or Jordan, through Iraq, using forged papers, or across the desert into Saudi Arabia. Within days of the border being opened, some 10,000 Kuwaitis had crossed over. Another 150,000 would follow over the next four months.

The first major roadblock before the border was only about two kilometres north of it. The regular border crossing was sealed off, so the Kuwaitis had to drive into the desert for some distance, and then turn south across the border. The Iraqis took all identity documents and passports from the Kuwaitis, as well as any money and valuables that were not secreted away. More seriously, after the border had been open for a couple of days, the Iraqis started seizing men aged 17 to 45. There were many different reports of what happened to them. Some suggested that they were pressed into the Iraqi Army, others that they were jailed. It seems that most were simply sent back to Kuwait City while the women, children and older men were allowed to leave. In some cases, it was possible to bribe the Iraqis to allow the men out.

The Iraqis seemed to have several objectives with this policy of terrorizing Kuwaitis out of their own country. The most obvious was to deprive the Resistance of its support, and make them easier to find. The repression did not cause Kuwaitis to turn against the Resistance, but it did make it harder for them to hide. Secondly, the Iraqis started colonizing certain lower income areas of Kuwait with their own people. The idea seemed to be to stack the country with Iraqis and Palestinians who would support a domestic plebiscite on the future of the country which Iraq hoped to bluff through the UN, and to undermine the credibility of the legitimate Government of Kuwait by demonstrating that the Kuwaitis were abandoning their own country.

There was also speculation that Iraq was trying to create a refugee problem for the Saudis, but the Kuwaiti Government was able to resettle its people with the help of its GCC allies. More seriously, Iraq tried to sneak some agents into Saudi Arabia with the departees, but Kuwaiti and Saudi security at the border foiled this. In a close-knit nation of 650,000 based on an extended family structure, it took only a few questions to establish a person's *bona fides*.

The evening of 16 September saw one of the strangest phenomena of the crisis. President Bush spoke directly to the Iraqi people on Iraqi TV in an eight-minute address prepared at Iraq's suggestion, with a VOA Arabic translation. There had been scepticism that the tape would be shown in its entirety, but it was. However, Iraqi TV gave no advance notice of the broadcast so that thousands of Iraqis had not even tuned in.

Bush told the Iraqis that their leaders had brought them to the brink of war with the West and the Arab world, that Saddam had lied about the invasion, and that Iraq now stood isolated and alone. He assured them that Americans hoped for a peaceful solution, but were prepared to fight if forced to, and that Saddam alone was to blame for any suffering from the sanctions.

Bush was followed immediately on Iraqi TV by a 35-minute monologue from Saddam's spokesman calling Bush a liar. Apparently, many Iraqis had watched Bush out of curiosity, but turned off when Saddam's man came on.

The return match was played on 25 September. Saddam addressed the American people through an interpreter, saying, in an incredible denial of the truth, that Iraq was not the invader of Kuwait, but the 'victim of previous annexations and conspiracies'. Bush was accused of sending his soldiers to war unnecessarily, and was warned of 'violence in a bottomless abyss'.

The spectacle of the two principal figures in the crisis addressing each other's public was weird to say the least. Bush seemed unaware that public opinion was of little consequence in Iraq, and that there was a tremendous gap between Saddam's rhetoric and the feelings of ordinary Iraqis. Neither man succeeded in convincing the other's public of the virtue of his position, but that was hardly the point. They could both now say they had at least tried.

Another senior American in the news on 17 September was General Michael J. Dugan, the US Air Force Chief of Staff. He was fired for unguarded comments made to journalists on a trip to Saudi Arabia. He had effectively said that the Allies would bomb Baghdad, go after Saddam, his mistress, and his generals. How Dugan knew how to find Saddam's fancy lady and what her war role was remains a mystery, but it sounded great to us.

At the time, most talk of military action was in the context of the blockade, or of liberating Kuwait, not of hitting Iraq itself. The real objective of neutralizing Saddam's nuclear, chemical and biological weapons had been kept off the public agenda. Dugan had almost let the cat out of the bag.

Although a villain in Washington, Dugan was a great hero in Kuwait. He had said exactly what we wanted to hear. We wanted him to take over from Generals Powell or Schwarzkopf. Some even suggested that he replace Bush. There was no point bringing all that military might to Saudi Arabia to sit there for years while the sanctions puttered along and Saddam kept Kuwait. Dugan's crime was more of timing than indiscretion. If he had said the same thing four months later, it would have gone down splendidly.

In Kuwait on the day of General Dugan's dismissal, the Board of the Kuwait Red Crescent Society (KRCS) were facing an even more uncertain future. They had been picked up *en masse* by the *Mukhabarat*. This incident seems to have a case of Iraqi bureaucracy tripping over itself, but the eminent doctors sitting blindfolded in an Iraqi cell were not to know this.

The KRCS had been trying to keep the hospitals running after many of the staff had fled or gone into hiding. This had not been easy. The Iraqis had banned volunteers from working in the hospitals as Kuwaitis were boycotting their regular work, and resupply of medicines was almost impossible.

One of the KRCS's jobs had been to get food to the various hospitals in Kuwait, including the one in Jahra, which held most of the Iraqi wounded from the battles on 2 August. However, the road to Jahra was not secure. The volunteers were scared to drive along it with a truckload of food.

In fact, the KRCS was walking a very fine line. On the one hand, individual members were active in the Resistance, even running clinics treating wounded fighters. Yet, the organization as a whole had to work with the Iraqis where it could in order to discharge its humanitarian functions.

On the morning of 17 September, several members of the Board were invited to what seemed to be a regular meeting at the Jabriya Polyclinic with a Captain Ibrahim, chief of the local Iraqi-occupied police station. Unknown to them, he was *Mukhabarat*. After tea, the doctors were invited to reconvene at the nearby premises of the Kuwait Association of Medical Professionals, where the Board had set up its temporary headquarters. Things then began to look serious. Their cars were escorted from the polyclinic by several carloads of armed men to the Kuwait Governorate at the Naif Palace, which was a security headquarters.

Once there, they were introduced to a *Mukhabarat* brigadier. Captain Ibrahim and a colleague disappeared into the brigadier's office for half an hour, leaving the worried doctors outside. After another unsettling ten minutes, they were blindfolded and led downstairs into a locked room. They were now in fear of their lives, with the prospect of torture playing on their minds. After some time the blindfolds were removed, and they were allowed to visit the toilet, but the guards checked on them every five minutes.

In the meantime, their colleagues were frantically trying to track them down. They eventually pieced together what had happened. One of the Resistance people, Miss Asrar Al-Qabandi, using her group's satellite telephone, informed her brother Adnan, who was working with the Government-in-exile in Taif, of the arrests. He in turn spread the word, and the ICRC in Geneva was able to put pressure on the Iraqis even before the Iraqi Government in Baghdad was aware of the arrests. The Resistance might not be able to spring the doctors from Iraqi custody, but they could make it more difficult for the Iraqis to get rid of them, and get away with it.

Back in the locked room at the Naif Palace, the afternoon dragged on fearfully for the captive doctors. No one told them what the problem was until one of them was taken away just before the evening prayer. His colleagues had no idea where he had gone, and performed their prayers fervently, fearing the worst. Then, to their great relief, he returned, unharmed. The other men were then questioned individually. They realized that the problem was the supplies for the Jahra Hospital and the Iraqi wounded. In fact, the interrogators actually congratulated them on their work, and seemed to understand the problem when it was explained to them.

Although the Iraqi officers seemed satisfied, the doctors were held for another 26 days. Apparently, Ali Hassan Majeed, the Iraqi Governor of Kuwait, had asked for them, so they could not be released until cleared by him. Then the brigadier went to Baghdad on leave. At the time, most officers in Kuwait did two weeks duty, with a week off at home. The officer acting for the brigadier would not release them until the other man returned.

During this time, they were fed sparingly, with very poor food. On some days they were forgotten entirely. Before being released on 11 October, they had to give the *Mukhabarat* details of their relatives, including parents, siblings, uncles and aunts both from their own side of family, and from their wives'. The Iraqis wanted to know about jobs, political affiliations, virtually everything. To top it all, they had to sign a pledge that the information was 100% correct, under penalty of hanging. They were told to report back regularly. The Iraqis were trying to use them to spy on other Kuwaitis.

To their colleagues outside, it was as if they had come back from the dead. They were debriefed by one of the Resistance leaders, Sheikh Sabah Nasir, who told them to humour the Iraqis for the time being, for their own safety.

Within a couple of days, one of the men, Dr Ebraheem Behbehani, received a phone call from the Iraqis saying that orders had come down from the Deputy Iraqi Prime Minister, Taha Yassin Ramadan, that the KRCS would become the Kuwait Division of the Iraqi Red Crescent. This was a breach of the Geneva Conventions, but Behbehani was hardly in a position to object. He reported back to Sheikh Sabah, and his colleague, Sheikh Ali Salem Al-Ali, who advised him to get out of the country, as he was in danger. Once the Iraqis had their hooks into him, they would not let go. If they wanted to take over the KRCS, then they would have to do it on their own. A week later, Dr Behbehani left Kuwait, on a false passport made up by Sheikh Ali. Four days later, he was in Geneva, testifying to the International Federation of Red Cross and Red Crescent Societies on the situation in Kuwait. He later travelled to New York to testify before the UN, and brief President Bush.

Both sides continued to build up their forces throughout September. On the 19th, we heard that the Iraqis now had an estimated 360,000 men, 2,800 tanks, 650 artillery pieces, and 2,000 APCs in or near Kuwait - roughly half in Kuwait itself, and half in southern Iraq - an increase of 30% over the previous two weeks. Less than a week later, US Secretary of Defense Dick Cheney said that a further 70,000 Iraqi troops and 700 tanks had been moved in.

On 20 September, Argentina announced that it was sending two warships. It was the only Latin American country to send forces. Some of the British were quite amused at Argentine and British forces being on the same side only eight years after the Falklands War. Spain then announced it was sending three ships. One wag noted that there were now so many frigates in the Gulf and Red Sea that traffic lights, in Spanish and English, would have to installed. The ships were in more danger from bumping into each other than from Iraq.

There was a serious side to this. Warships were a relatively risk-free means of providing forces. As General Schwarzkopf later remarked to the British Commander, Lieutenant-General de la Billière when the Englishman pressed for the aircraft carrier HMS *Ark Royal* to be deployed, 'I'm running out of water to put ships on.' What the Coalition really needed was tanks.

Saddam did not let up with his rhetoric. His Information Minister, Latif Jassim, issued a threat which became all too real only five months later by saying that Iraq would blow up the oil fields in the Gulf if it were attacked.

On 21 September, Saddam issued his most bellicose statement of the crisis to date by urging his citizens to prepare for the 'Mother Of All Battles', backed up by expulsions of several US, European and Egyptian diplomats in response to the expulsions by Europe after the embassy raids in Kuwait. The British Military Attaché in Baghdad, Colonel Cochrane, was sent packing on the 20th. The US then expelled three Iraqi diplomats in addition to the 36 sent home earlier.

Two days later, Saddam threatened to attack Saudi oilfields, and Israel if Iraq was strangled by the UN sanctions, which he blamed on the US. He also implied that he might harm the hostages, and dug his heels in by saying there were no conditions under which Iraq would leave Kuwait. Whenever the US offered any type of olive branch, he snubbed it. When a senior American official suggested that if Iraq left Kuwait, its claims against Kuwait could be considered, possibly by the International Court of Justice in The Hague, Iraq dismissed this out of hand. He seemed implacably opposed to any compromise, which only brought the likelihood of war closer.

At the same time, according to news reports, Iraqi units along the Kuwaiti border were preparing conspicuous chemical decontamination sites in what may have been a warning that Iraq was prepared to use chemical weapons.

Despite the rhetoric, serious discussions were going on. After Saddam had agreed in mid-August to the settlement of his war with Iran on Iranian terms, there had been great concern in Coalition quarters that not only had a further threat to Saddam been removed, and his troops manning the Iranian border freed for operations in Kuwait, but that Iran might conceivably join with Iraq against the Coalition. Iran was hardly a friend of America, or indeed Saudi Arabia. Neither country had much pull with Iran, but Syria's Hafez Al-Assad did, especially after his support for Teheran against Baghdad during the Iran–Iraq War. On a visit to Teheran from 22-25 September, Al-Assad secured guarantees from Iran that she would not take advantage of the situation. The Coalition had one less thing to worry about.

After the initial shock of the invasion, the religious institutions in Kuwait bounced back, despite disruption to their staff, and looting and harassment.

The two main churches in Kuwait are the National Evangelical Church, and the Roman Catholic Cathedral. The Evangelicals were particularly badly affected, with one of its American Pastors on leave outside of Kuwait at the time of the invasion, another holed up in the US Embassy, and the Arab pastor too scared to come to the compound. It was kept going only by a few dedicated lay members. The main Anglican Church, St. Paul's, in Ahmadi, virtually ceased to function for the duration of the occupation. Most of its members were British and either hostages, abroad, or in hiding. Its priest, the Reverend Michael Jones, was a Human Shield in Iraq.

The Roman Catholics were more fortunate. The Bishop, Monsignor Francis Micallef, was Maltese. His priests, mainly Indians, Filipinos, or Arabs, were generally free to move around and minister to their flock. They even continued to perform marriages, and hold Mass.

The Iraqis largely respected the churches themselves, if not the residences of the clergy. Some of the churches were protected by Christian Iraqi soldiers, a number of whom attended the services, with their Kalashnikovs on the pews beside them. The Evangelical Church and the Cathedral became centres for food collection from people leaving Kuwait. They were very effective in spreading the limited supplies, and keeping people in touch with one another.

The Muslim organizations in the country were just as effective. Neighbourhood mosques became meeting as well as religious centres. The Iraqis did not always accord them their due respect as they were often suspected of harbouring Resistance people, which in some cases was true. It was a small victory each day to hear the *muzzein's* call to prayer, as in peacetime, and to see the Kuwaiti men flocking to the mosque on Fridays. The Iraqis might be able to hijack the country, but they did not shake its faith.

However, one young imam, or prayer leader, paid the ultimate price for his defiance of the Iraqis. Salah Al-Rafie was arrested from his home in late September when he refused to honour Saddam in his Friday sermons, and was found with anti-Iraqi leaflets and firearms in his house. He was killed in front of his own mosque on 3 October with a gunshot to the back of the head.

Perhaps the greatest example of generosity of the human spirit, Kuwaiti or otherwise, occurred one afternoon when I received a call from Stephen Tubb, another Australian who was also acting as a warden. The Iraqis were clearing out the orphanage; the staff had two hours to find places for the children. He asked if I knew anyone who could help. I made a few calls, unsuccessfully, and got back to him within an hour. He told me not to worry. Each of the hundred or so kids had already been placed with a Kuwaiti family.

During the second half of September, the UN Security Council considered a French-initiated draft Resolution for an air cargo embargo against Iraq.

Security Council Resolution 670, imposing an air embargo, excluding humanitarian and UNIIMOG flights, and authorizing the detention of Iraqi ships, was passed on 25 September. Only Cuba voted against it. The Resolution also condemned Iraq's treatment of Kuwaitis, the measures to force them out of Kuwait, and the holding of hostages. The embargo was largely symbolic as the only meaningful air traffic into and out of Iraq and occupied Kuwait were the evacuation flights for foreign women and children, and the Amman-Baghdad shuttle. Nevertheless, the message was clear.

To our great delight, Soviet Foreign Minister Eduard Shevardnadze took the opportunity of the passing of the resolution to issue a blunt warning to Saddam that war was close unless Iraq withdrew from Kuwait.

The Human Shields became the direct victims of the increasing belligerence. Until then, most of them had been held in reasonably comfortable quarters. Now, those in Iraq were moved further into the sites, into offices, laboratories and other rooms specially converted to house them. They were placed in the direct line of any Allied air strikes, instead of in accommodation on the periphery of the sites. Several Iraqi camp managers objected to Baghdad that the new accommodation was inadequate, but were told to follow orders.

The accommodation deteriorated virtually across the board, except for the camps in Kuwait which were not moved at all. In one Iraqi location, two dozen men who were moved from cabins into an office block had to share four small rooms, with two wash basins, four urinals, two Asian 'hole-in-the-floor' toilets, one of which had a shower head above it, and a single Western-style toilet. More importantly, they were prevented from going outside for exercise.

The Iraqis also made sure that their so-called 'Special Guests' felt the effects of the sanctions. A ration of one and a half kilos of rice, one kilo of sugar, 100 grams of tea, 500 grams of cooking oil, one bar of soap, one small packet of washing powder, per person per month, and one loaf of bread per meal per person, was introduced in the camps in the middle of the month.

Despite the deterioration in conditions, the September moves were the source of some amusement when it brought the hostages into closer contact with ordinary Iraqis. At one camp, the hostages were now held on the first floor of an office block, with a typing pool of pretty young Iraqi women on the ground floor. Instead of guards, the Iraqis posted two old crones, swathed in black *abayas*, outside the hostages' accommodation, to ensure that there was no fraternization. The hostages nicknamed one 'Charles Bronson' because she was so ugly, and the other one 'Happy', because she always looked so miserable. At first the old women were terrified of the all-male hostages, but gradually warmed to them. The men, however, never got anywhere near the young ladies, but they found that they were providing a source of amusement for the girls. They used to dress casually during the hot summer days, and the young ladies had apparently never seen Western men wearing shorts before.

In Kuwait, the pick-ups continued. During mid-September, Dubai TV confirmed what had until then only been a good rumour: the Iraqis were offering substantial rewards for information about the location of foreigners. We had mixed feelings about this. There was a perverse satisfaction that we were so well hidden that Saddam had to place a price on our heads, but also the fear that it would increase the risk of our being caught.

However, the pick-ups would settle at about ten per week for the next two months, although this was still a great loss. We felt that it was only a matter of time before the Iraqis did a house-to-house search of all of Kuwait. For the 1,000 men in hiding, it was a race against time between being captured, starving, or being released by Allied forces.

The Western men who were perhaps in the worst position in Kuwait were those several dozen in areas where phone services had been lost. They were almost totally isolated. The only link some of them had with the outside world was the BBC World Service, if they had a shortwave radio. Some did not even have that. They were fortunate to be in small groups of relatively resilient men. It is incredible that some of them survived for over three months in such isolation. Later in the crisis, when some nationalities could move around, we were able to visit these groups, and get them radios, but at least one group of three British men hid in an apartment building, part of which the Iraqis were using as a barracks. We did not even know they were there. Even if we had, we could not have got anywhere near them.

In Kuwait, the rumour machine continued to give false hopes and new twists to the crisis. One of the better tales, which first arose on 20 September, was that several senior Iraqi officers had been executed in Baghdad for treason, presumably for plotting against Saddam. This raised hopes that Saddam's regime was crumbling, and that a coup might topple him.

Another, first heard three days later, was that people were to stay off the streets for the next few days to clear them for Army traffic, as the Iraqis were pulling back to Mutla'a Ridge, and their new border between Basra and Kuwait 'Provinces'. At about this time, we noticed Asian street cleaners picking up litter along the main thoroughfares. This was unusual, as there had been no municipal services since the invasion. Someone suggested that it was not a withdrawal, but that Saddam might be coming to visit, and the streets were being spruced up for his benefit. Sure enough, a week or so later, Iraqi TV showed footage of Saddam visiting Kuwait. The broadcast did not specify when the visit had occurred, but it was probably in the past few days.

Withdrawal rumours, often based on heartfelt wishful thinking, cropped up with incredible regularity. They were invariably accompanied by a definite date for the withdrawal, and frequently based on an alleged conversation with 'an Iraqi officer related by marriage to Saddam'. One of the worst culprits was the Arabic language Radio Monte Carlo. They were invariably wrong, but this did not stop people believing them. A far more reliable source, sometimes hours ahead of the BBC, was Radio Israel.

Then, on 24 September, people were given 12 days to exchange their Kuwaiti dinars for Iraqi currency. The Iraqis had already decreed that the two currencies were at parity, but there was still a healthy black market for Kuwaiti dinars, worth ten times their Iraqi equivalent before 2 August, but now trading at between 3 and 6 Iraqi dinars. Iraq now wanted to cancel them entirely. After the deadline, it would be a crime to hold Kuwaiti currency.

Three days later, the Iraqis gave the Kuwaitis until 31 October to change their citizenship to Iraqi. This set off a new flood of Kuwaiti departees to Saudi Arabia through the open southern border, but many stayed, with no intention at all of changing nationalities.

For the first eight weeks of the crisis, the Kuwaiti Government had been preoccupied with re-establishing itself in exile in Taif, caring for its *diaspora*, organizing support for those still inside Kuwait, and re-equipping its armed forces to join the Coalition military in Saudi Arabia.

The most visible Kuwaiti had been the Ambassador to the US, Canada and Venezuela, Sheikh Saud Nasir. News of the situation in Kuwait had filtered out through Western, Asian, Kuwaiti and other Arab departees, and through a series of satellite phone link-ups between Americans and British in hiding in Kuwait and Western TV networks by Asrar Al-Qabandi and others.

Sheikh Saud's polished performance, and these Resistance-organized interviews, had been very effective in conveying the sense of fear, and the repression, destruction and looting going on in Kuwait. The Kuwaitis then brought their big guns to bear. On 27 September, the Amir, Sheikh Jaber Al-Ahmad, addressed the UN General Assembly, pleading for his country's liberation. He urged the UN to stand by the sanctions, and offered developing Third-World countries relief on their debts to Kuwait, most of which were already soft loans. The Amir, usually a reticent man, made a forceful case for a quick liberation. He was given a standing ovation as the Iraqi delegation walked out in a huff in silent protest.

Sheikh Jaber's speech was strenuously endorsed by most Arab Foreign Ministers, and followed by a moving address by Bangladeshi President Mohammed Ershad, describing the hardship his country was suffering as a result of the crisis. It was a poignant reminder that Saddam had not only declared war on a little rich state, but also on the poor nations of southern Asia who depended greatly on Kuwait for much of their economic stability.

The Amir then met with President Bush and National Security Advisor General Brent Scowcroft in Washington, and warned them that Iraq was systematically destroying Kuwait by plunder. There was consensus that waiting for the embargo to work would mean the end for Kuwait. Sheikh Jaber later met with the US Cabinet, and then with Secretary of Defense Dick Cheney, and Chairman of the Joint Chiefs of Staff, General Colin Powell.

The Iraqis were not the Amir's only enemies. Elements within the US Administration who did not fully appreciate the political and historical link of Kuwaitis to their ruling family tried to make Iraqi withdrawal from Kuwait and restoration of the Al-Sabah into separate issues. The Amir successfully quashed this, and left a powerful impression on those he met. A visibly moved Scowcroft said that the destruction of Kuwait shortened the time the US could wait for economic sanctions to work. Bush himself said that the UN would be asked to look at a military option if sanctions did not work, but did not specify a timetable for this. In fact, at that time, the five permanent members of the Security Council were still saying that sanctions must be given time to work, but this was sounding less convincing by the day.

In Kuwait, the break-down in law and order led to encounters with looters as well as with troops searching for Westerners.

Security preparations we had made earlier proved to be absolutely necessary. Several British men in Ahmadi had close escapes. A group of three of them, comprising John Plater, Dennis Reid and Alan Sinclair had established bolt-holes in ceiling cavities, and on one occasion had made it into them just before Iraqi looters broke down the door. They had to stay hidden for several hours while they watched the Iraqis beneath them through the air vents, systematically looting their house. They feared that the Iraqis would be back, so hurriedly moved to another house, only to have the same thing happen again the following night, and again the night after.

Another group set up their own 'electric fence' – a fly screen wired to a 13-amp socket – in the corridor of their house to deter looters, and hid in the loft when they came in. The screen was conspicuously visible, and they hoped that it would deter any looters, or at least that anyone making their way through the house would stumble into it, and get a nasty shock. However, the looters were determined individuals. They knocked it out of their way with a broom.

Our own experiences were not so bad, but there were some real scares. One day, two individuals who looked like Iraqis or Palestinians in civilian clothes came to my door and rang the bell, but then moved on to my American neighbour's flat. They rang his bell, and looked at his decoy nameplate, identifying the occupant as an Arab. He watched them for what seemed like an eternity through the peephole, hardly daring to breathe until they eventually left. We later discovered that they may have been Kuwait Resistance people in disguise coming around to see if we needed any help.

It was not only the Westerners who were at risk. One afternoon, my American neighbour heard some men in the corridor. I was out, so he called our Indian neighbours, Arnu and Shirin Monteiro to see if they could check what was going on. Shirin was alone in the flat, but walked down the corridors towards our end of the building. As she passed one of the looted flats with its door open, she heard a noise inside, and poked her head in. An Iraqi soldier was in the bathroom, pulling his trousers up. She was so taken aback that she indignantly asked the soldier what he was doing there. The soldier asked her the same. They stood there interrogating each other until Shirin realized that she was all alone and fair game. She turned around, and dashed back to her own flat, bolting the door behind her. The soldier went away, now suitably relieved, and never bothered us.

The rest of the group were incensed when we heard the story that evening. We would rather have had the American captured than Shirin raped. She should not have gone down the corridor alone, but she was a brave woman, and concerned about us. She had done so in response to the American's appeal. We had a new security rule from then on: do not involve other people in our security, especially women, if there is any risk of placing them in danger.

Some of the looting experiences were quite bizarre, as well as terrifying. The local General Manager of DHL, Steve Bushby, and his friend, Bill Petersen, were preparing to retire late one night when four men armed with pistols came in the door. They were looters, not soldiers: one Iraqi and three Palestinians. They bound Steve and Bill with the flex from bedside lamps, and then proceeded to loot the villa. They walked Bill around the house, asking if there were any women, or any other people there. It was unclear whether they would have raped any women they found, but Steve and Bill were profoundly grateful that their families had left four weeks previously.

Steve and Bill were eventually untied, and seated on a mattress in the lounge. At first, they were told to go to sleep, but this was hardly the time for that. They feared they might be shot the moment they nodded off. The looting continued for about an hour or so, with the men stacking the loot in the entrance hall, but showing no sign of leaving. Steve and Bill were wondering if the looters were trying to work up the courage to shoot them, when they suddenly realized that they were waiting for curfew to be lifted at dawn.

At about 3.00 a.m., Bill was sent into the kitchen to make tea, and they all sat around making polite conversation, after which two of the looters dozed off. The leader, the Iraqi, seemed overcome with remorse, but not to the extent of returning their property. He explained that he was very poor, his children in Iraq were starving, and he had been driven to this. He even showed the two

Westerners where he had been wounded during the Iran–Iraq War.

Steve and Bill had some home-brew beer that was not quite ready. The visitors started drinking it, with the half-fermented brew exploding out of the necks of the bottles as they opened them. The two men offered them some more palatable home-made wine, but the looters preferred the beer. Then one of them found a bottle of ethanol, which Steve used as hard liquor, and asked what it was for. Steve and Bill did not want them getting drunk on this, and working up the courage to shoot them, so said it was a medicine for skin conditions. The Iraqi's eye lit up. He pulled off his shoes and socks, and started rubbing it on his feet, which were afflicted with sores.

Just before first light, the remorseful Iraqi said that he would like to do something for the men. Bill and Steve were going to suggest that they left the loot behind – especially the radio. The Iraqi suddenly had a flash of inspiration, noting their concern about missing messages from their wives on *Gulf Link*, and asked them if they would like to be home with their families. The two men did not see how he could manage that.

'Easy,' said the Iraqi. 'I can't do much today because I'm tired after driving down from Baghdad, and staying up all night like this. Today I have a big job taking care of all this', he said indicating their property. 'But I will return in a few days and call you. I will then take you to Baghdad. You can stay with my family there, and then we can go to Kurdistan. Near the border with Turkey, I will put you on donkeys, and in 15 miles you will be in Turkey.'

'That sounds all very well,' said the men with a great deal of scepticism, 'but how are you going to call us? You've taken all the phones. Besides, what about the checkpoints between here and Baghdad, and Turkey?'

'No problem.' replied the Iraqi, and told one of his colleagues to bring a phone back in from the pile of loot, the cheapest one. 'As for the checkpoints, I can get you through. You can bribe these people with a few dollars.'

Steve and Bill had no intention of being around to receive any phone calls or follow-up visits. They were on the phone to me and the other wardens as soon as the looters left - also taking Bill's car - trying to organize a place to move to. Norma Armstrong, a British woman who had decided to stay in Kuwait and was looking after a number of other displaced fellows, took them in.

Several other men had similar terrifying experiences. An elderly Briton, Ron Barker, and his wife, were looted of almost everything, as was a Mr Derek Wright. All of them counted themselves lucky to escape with his lives. It would have been incredibly easy for the looters simply to shoot their victims. There was no way they could have been brought to justice.

Inexplicably, after the build-up of the political and military pressure on Iraq throughout September, George Bush seemed to soften his tone. In a speech to the UN General Assembly on 1 October, he said that he still hoped for a diplomatic solution. He then turned Saddam's attempted linkage of his occupation of Kuwait with the Israeli occupation of the West Bank back onto the Iraqis by saying that Iraq's unconditional withdrawal from Kuwait could lead to opportunities for settling Iraqi–Kuwaiti differences as well as the Arab–Israeli conflict, but the two could not be addressed together.

In retrospect, this was a wise move to garner further support from a world wary of war, but at the time it appeared to be a gesture to Saddam. It was not what we wanted to hear. The past two months had been an emotional roller coaster of tough talk and military build-up, followed by back-downs and hints of peaceful solutions. With the alternating periods of relative quiet when the Iraqis were leaving us alone, and the almost sheer panic when they were nearby, the occupation was an exhausting experience. We knew that the sanctions were useless, and could see Kuwait being systematically trucked to Iraq before our eyes. We wanted war, now, even if we were in the way.

Saddam seemed to go quiet during the last week of September, possibly because he was busy visiting Kuwait. In fact, the crisis almost seemed to slip from the headlines for a day or so. In Kuwait on 25 September, we were shocked when the BBC hardly mentioned the crisis at all, for the first time in two months. We felt a curious sense of abandonment, almost as if we deserved to be on every bulletin, but were being forgotten.

Some of us in Kuwait tried to do our own little bit for the PR effort, even if we lacked Resistance friends with one of the few satellite phones. Although unable to call home, we had neighbours leaving who could take out videos.

The catalyst for one of these videos was a TV transmission in late September which showed a British computer salesman in Kuwait, his face shaded out, and his identity concealed. The man was generally despised around town, especially as he was said to have moved his Filipina mistress in shortly after his wife – a delightfully sweet woman – had been evacuated. There were other rumours that he was looting the vacant flats of nearby fellow Britons, and selling the goods to Iraqis, Syrians and Palestinians. It was not so much his alleged infidelity and collaboration which incensed us, but the way he begged world leaders to keep talking peace. He spoke for an ever-decreasing minority of men in Kuwait.

My American neighbour and I decided to make a counter-video to send out with Arnu and Shirin when they left in early October. I salvaged a video camera from a nearby looted flat, and we set up a light behind each other's heads to keep our faces in shadow, and then interviewed each other.

The message was crystal clear. There were terrible atrocities going on in Kuwait, and no reason why Allied forces should not be here. In case King Fahd and President Bush had any qualms about the risk to the Westerners in hiding in the case of war, we assured them we would prefer to take our chances rather than continue our limbo existence of constant fear. We were unaware of the extent of Iraqi forces in the desert, but from what we could see of them in the street below us, they were no match for professional Western or Arab troops.

The video was eventually shown worldwide in late October. The message was unmistakable. Come in now, before there is no Kuwait left to liberate.

13. FREEDOM OF MOVEMENT

The next major development for the Westerners in hiding in Kuwait, after the women's and children's evacuations, was the freedom of certain nationalities to move around Kuwait – and even Iraq – without becoming Human Shields.

This freedom was relative. Until mid-October, it was uncertain whether we could return to Kuwait if we went to Baghdad, so most of us with freedom of movement stayed in Kuwait. No one wanted to be in Baghdad when the shooting started, and there was no question of being allowed to leave Iraq. In Kuwait, we were not allowed south of Ahmadi, or west of Ali Al-Salem. Those in Iraq itself had to stay at least ten kilometres away from the borders, and well away from military installations, and Saddam's residences.

Even this restricted movement was a great relief after weeks of hiding. More importantly, it allowed a number of us to help the Americans, British, French and Germans still in hiding with mail, food, and other supplies.

The realization that some of us in Kuwait might have freedom of movement occurred over a period of almost five weeks. Even then, we could not be certain of it until someone from each nationality was arrested, and released.

In retrospect, indications that only certain nationalities qualified for the Human Shield existed as early as the first week of the occupation, but they were sufficiently ambiguous, and our information network still so patchy, that it was hard to draw firm conclusions. The earliest clue was when a Canadian Santa Fe oilman captured in Kuwait, Graham Pierce, was released to his Baghdad embassy on 7 August. However, few people in Kuwait knew of this.

The next indication came on 19 August, when Eoin MacDougald, a Canadian captured in Kuwait the previous day with some British friends was released. His friends became Human Shields. However, Australians, Irish and New Zealanders were still being picked up, and BA149 people of those nationalities were being held. Several other Canadians then began to move around tentatively. They were at a particular advantage as Canada had a local embassy. The diplomats could tie up Eoin's experience with that of Canadians in Iraq. Many others, without local missions, were not so fortunate.

There seemed to be no consistency. We thought that nationals of countries that had committed fewer military forces to the Coalition would be safer, yet Canada was sending more forces than many other countries, and while her nationals seemed to be free, those of Ireland and New Zealand, which had sent no forces at all, were being arrested and might qualify as Human Shields. This assumption was reinforced for the Australians and New Zealanders in late August when an Australian woman, Wendy Reid, New Zealander Ian Mills, and a Briton, Colin MacGregor, were captured and sent to Baghdad. Then, on 31 August, Australians, Italians, Norwegians, New Zealanders and others from BA149 who had been held at Kuwait hotels followed them.

However, unknown to most of us, on the same day, the Iraqis revisited the Fintas Towers residential complex in the southern suburbs, which were cut off from phone contact with the rest of Kuwait. Most Americans and British living there had been taken away a week earlier. This time, the Iraqis went door-to-door, and took everyone down to the lobby. The major in charge asked Americans, British, French, Germans or Japanese to go to one side. The only remaining Britons were a woman whose husband was out of the country, and her 14-year-old son. They were taken away. The only American was an elderly man, Bill Mills. He stayed hidden in his flat while his Iranian wife tried to bluff her way through. However, some of the Jordanian and Indian residents were scared, and wanted to give him away. He eventually came down, looking sick, and explaining that he had a bad heart. The Iraqis told him to stay. The last thing they needed was a hostage dying in their custody.

Unknown to those in the lobby, the Iraqis had already taken away a 58-year-old Australian Kuwait Airways pilot, Jim Strong, in what would turn out to be a combination of terror and farce. He had been taken from his flat without even a chance to turn off a leg of lamb he had roasting in the oven, and put in the back seat of a car with several Iraqis. However, the Iraqis were somewhat unprepared. One of them had to go back into the lobby to get bandages from the the building's First Aid kit to blindfold Jim. They then forced him into the footwell of the back seat, and drove off.

In the meantime, other Iraqis who had been searching the flats brought down the second Australian, another KAC pilot, Greg Wood, but found the car gone. They now presumably faced the prospect of walking back to their own headquarters. Much to Greg's relief, they let him go.

Meanwhile, Jim was being driven around blindfolded on the floor of the car in what seemed like an endless trip, with several men who looked as if they were quite capable of shooting him on a whim. Eventually, they came to a hotel which the Iraqis said was the Basra Sheraton. Jim recognized it as the Kuwait Regency Palace. He was taken inside, much relieved to be out of the car and on his way to some sort of authority. There was another pleasant surprise. The Iraqis at the hotel told him that he 'was the wrong man', and that he could go. Jim was finally returned to Fintas, five hours after his arrest, greatly shaken, with his leg of lamb now thoroughly overdone.

It was now clear to the Fintas people that at least Australians, Danes and Irish could move around with relative freedom, but they could not tell us because of their failed phones, even if they had known about us. The warden system elsewhere in Kuwait was now quite strong, but had no links to cut-off areas such as Fintas. At that time, the women and children had not yet left. No one wanted to leave their families unattended to go out visiting friends.

Things developed further in early September. People other than Americans, British, French and Germans who had been taken to Baghdad by the Iraqis in late August were released to their embassies on 5 September. Within days, this news had reached us in Kuwait. However, we were still unsure if the freedom of movement applied only to those in Baghdad, and feared that if we poked our heads outside, we would be taken north, and released to the embassies. We felt it would be like jumping out of the frying pan into a fire which was not yet lit, but soon would be when the Americans attacked.

In Kuwait, a few of those who were certain that they could move around started taking their first tentative steps, although most stayed in hiding in case they attracted Iraqi attention to American or British neighbours. The Fintas Towers people - three Irish families, the two Australians, and some Danes - had no such fears. All of their 'wanted' neighbours except Bill Mills had been taken away, and the Iraqis knew about him.

In the meantime, another Irishman had started moving around, under special circumstances. He was Patrick Dower, a senior manager for a hospital caterer. The Iraqis needed him, so he was issued with a pass to allow him to do his job. The Irishman in our group was in contact with Patrick, and told us of his difficulties at checkpoints. We assumed that he was being allowed to move around solely because of his job, and his arrests suggested that any other Irish people who ventured out would not be safe.

In fact, the local Iraqis seemed to be particularly efficient, and intent on implementing a working civilian administration. On September 2, a group of civilian Iraqis, escorted by soldiers, called on one of the Fintas Towers Irishmen, KOTC marine engineer Dave Short, to conduct a census. It was all very civilized as they sat down over a cup of tea, and filled in the forms.

In this surreal environment, the greatest danger sometimes came not from the soldiers. One of the Iraqis had left his Kalashnikov lying on the dining room table where the Westerners were going over the census paperwork. The children were playing on the floor when one of the young lads noticed the gun, reached up, and grasped the trigger. The adults froze, praying that the weapon was not loaded. It wasn't. The embarrassed Iraqi gently retrieved the weapon from the child's grasp, and they went on with their business.

On 5 September, the day after the women and children left, Dave Short and Jim Strong ventured forth into their local area by car. They encountered mainly friendly troops, and returned home without incident. Two days later they tried a longer trip to try to contact friends in the main urban area. They went through nine checkpoints with few problems, and returned home safely.

With the disrupted phones, both men were largely ignorant of the warden systems functioning elsewhere in the city, so we did not find out about each other until much later. While they were moving around relatively freely, most of the rest of us, except the Canadians, were still in hiding. A few other nationalities with local embassies, such as the Dutch, were also taking their own first steps, but news of this was slow to filter through the networks.

On September 9, Dave and Jim tried another expedition, to try to contact Dave's Kuwaiti boss. This time they were not so fortunate. They were arrested at a checkpoint, and locked up for five hours in a commandeered school. They were never questioned beyond their names and nationalities, and were finally released. Shaken, they stayed at home for the next few days.

Elsewhere in Kuwait, on 10 September, an apartment building in Salwa with several New Zealanders and Danes was raided by the Iraqis. The *Mukhabarat* came in, looked at their passports, made a phone call, and told them that they should go to Baghdad for their own safety. There was no arrest, no coercion to go, only a strong suggestion. The New Zealanders and Danes did not press the point as they wanted to be rid of the Iraqis as soon as possible. Nevertheless, it was the first raid we were aware of in which people were not taken away to the Regency Palace Hotel.

The New Zealanders gave the matter some thought, and decided they would venture out. Two of them, Alistair Lane and Ron Houston, worked at the Kuwait Danish Dairy (KDD), which was still functioning. It was an essential service, so they decided to return to work. Even after the New Zealanders' experience, the Australians were still uncertain that they would be allowed to stay in Kuwait, especially as Australia had committed warships. If captured, they expected to be released only to their embassy in Baghdad. The Irish were in similar straits. Although they had sent no forces, they were very much part of the EC diplomatic front.

On 13 September, Dr Niall Holohan, an Irish diplomat from Baghdad who had been allowed into Kuwait to help with the evacuation of any remaining Irish women and children made the first tentative link between the Fintas Towers Irishmen and those elsewhere in Kuwait. He told the Fintas men about the Irish warden system, but it would be another two weeks before they made contact. More importantly, Dr Holohan brought the first firm news that the women and children who had left a week earlier were now safely home.

Two days later, the Irish Aer Lingus visitors under Irish warden Cathal O'Connell were caught up in the Iraqi raids of the embassy residences, but were eventually allowed to go on their way. Cathal, in his usual efficient manner, let us know about this before he left. However, as they were headed for Baghdad, and Dr Holohan had not briefed us on Dave Short's experiences, it was still uncertain whether all Irish in Kuwait could move around.

With Cathal's departure, Paul Kennedy, the Irishman in my building, took over as Irish warden, but it took him time to pick up the pieces. September 13 was the first time he heard of Dave and his two compatriots, but we assumed that they were in the same situation as ourselves.

Another few days passed. The Canadians, New Zealanders, Pat Dower, and a few other Europeans were moving around with little trouble, but the other nationalities were not so sure. No one wanted to be the first to test the water in case the Iraqis had special rules for us. It was extremely difficult to find out what, if any, rules applied, so most people decided to stay hidden.

A couple of days later, a Lebanese Australian, Samir Elbaba, came on the scene. Like Pat Dower, he too was in the hospital catering business, but was using Lebanese papers. He was an extremely brave and resourceful individual, and had been using his cover to help as many people as he could with food and false identification, including members of the Al-Sabah.

One of Samir's French colleagues, Jean-Michel Chinou, had been captured and was in the Regency Palace. Samir brazenly visited the hotel, and tried unsuccessfully to get him out. He asked the Iraqis in passing whether Australians and others could move around and stay in Kuwait. He did not get a straight answer, but it seemed they would not be forced to go to Baghdad.

Samir passed this on to the other Australians, but we were still a little nervous. However, after another day or so, I decided we had to do something to determine our status. To aggravate matters, one of our number, Graham Lightfoot, a shipping executive who had been visiting Kuwait on business, had developed a severe ear infection. Another Lebanese Australian, John Abi-Hanna, had smuggled him to a doctor, but Graham needed hospitalization. I therefore rang the Iraqi Embassy, explained to them that I was an Australian, and asked them if they wanted me as a hostage, and if not, would I have to go to Baghdad, or could I stay in Kuwait?

The Iraqi on the other end of the line, a Mr Mohammed Ali, was appalled at the word 'hostage'. He insisted that we were guests of the Iraqi Government, so I had to go along with the charade. Nevertheless, after checking with a colleague, he told me I was free to move around Iraq, but would not give me a straight answer as to whether I could stay in Kuwait. 'Iraq and Kuwait,' he said, 'are one'. He encouraged me to go to Baghdad for my own safety, saying that I could call by the embassy, and he would give me the papers to allow us to travel there. There was no insistence, merely a suggestion that it was better to go. I relayed this to other Australians I was in contact with, and via the Swiss Embassy to our embassy in Baghdad, who replied the next day saying, in effect, 'don't trust the Iraqis in Kuwait.

It seemed that someone would have to go out and test the waters. The trouble was that my car was not operational and I had no transport. Samir Elbaba came to the rescue again. He had decided to leave Kuwait because he feared that the Iraqis were gradually closing in on his activities to support the Resistance. He had been helping the Kuwait Red Crescent Society extensively with hospital catering. Most of the KRCS Board had been arrested on 17 September, and was thought to have been implicated with the Resistance. Samir was worried that he might hang if he was associated with any Resistance activities. Fortunately, Samir's absent wife had a car, and he offered me the use of it. He arranged for one of his Filipino staffers to pick me up and take me to his house. It was 28 September.

The first steps towards freedom were very tentative. The American in our group was against my going out, although Dr Holohan had already arranged a valid Irish travel document for him. Nevertheless, we were running low on food. Our guardian angel, Imad Ghawji, could only do so much.

I climbed down the fire escape stairs, and left through a little-known exit where there was less chance of encountering any Iraqis guarding the building. The choice was right. No one was around. We could see the footpath from our windows eight floors above, but the sight of the shopping centre at ground level was a shock. Absolutely everything had been looted. Windows had been smashed, and the soldiers had defaecated on the shop floors. It was a most unsettling scene. There were no pedestrians, but this was hardly surprising. There was nothing left to steal. I prayed that Samir's man would be on time. Sure enough, he was, in a white pick-up. His name was Mario Lazo. I was delighted to see a friendly face in the midst of such devastation.

Mario was remarkably cool. 'As a matter of fact, he said, 'the Iraqis give me less trouble at the checkpoints than the Kuwaiti police in normal times.' I could not help thinking that the Iraqis had threatened execution for anyone helping Westerners, and here he was driving one around.

It dawned on me that I had just come out of 44 days of hiding, and he had been moving around since 2 August. As we drove, all the tension, the fear, of the previous weeks just ebbed away. I was outside. Until then, I had not realized how much stress we were under, and began to feel more for our broken American. I lowered the window and let the hot summer air rush against my face. No more hiding, cocking an ear for every sound. Freedom tasted so sweet.

Samir's house was in Salmiya, about 20 minutes away. Mario knew how to avoid the checkpoints, so by the time we got there I had still not encountered an Iraqi since before going into hiding. It was quite a surprise to meet Samir for the first time. We had been talking on the phone for weeks. I expected a middle-aged executive, in his forties. Instead, he was in his mid-thirties; a short, smiling man who obviously ate well. He exuded energy, and was constantly on the phone arranging things for people. He was due to leave for Baghdad within hours, but was still running around helping others. He was a professional guardian angel with an endless range of resources and contacts.

We chatted, and had a bite to eat. He wrote a letter in Arabic, ostensibly selling his wife's car to me. We got it started, and took our leave. I was very grateful to him. Here he was, giving his wife's car to a near total stranger. An incredible fellow. Before he left, he gave me directions to his office and warehouse, and told me to take as much food from there as I wanted.

I drove out onto the main road, alone. The car was absolutely perfect. An old, battered Nissan Cherry which only the most desperate looter would covet. The mere act of driving was ecstasy; the freedom was indescribable. I was the only Westerner on the road, so seemed to attract a lot of glances, but no hostility. The wheels made an unusual hum from passing over the indentations made in the road surface by the Iraqi tracked vehicles.

I drove down the motorway for about 15km without any problems. There were troops around, usually walking by the side of the road, in scruffy uniforms, every one of them with a Kalashnikov slung over his shoulder, but there were no checkpoints. Then, a few hundred metres before I had to turn off, one of them waved me down. He was not hostile, but he had a gun.

I stopped. He walked in front of the car, and pointed at what I thought was the licence plate. 'Oh no!' I thought. 'He's saying that it should be an Iraqi plate, not a Kuwaiti one.' I got out to show him the registration book and Samir's letter, and started to try to explain in pidgin Arabic that I didn't know where I had to go to change the plate. The soldier just stood there, smiling, and pointing. As I came around to the front of the car, I realized what he was pointing at. A big piece of scrubby bush was lodged in the front bumper. He was simply telling me this. We both laughed, and I removed the bush.

The next approach was not quite so friendly. He pointed to his left wrist. There was no watch on it. I thought he was asking the time, so I told him, in Arabic. He indicated his wrist again. I thought that he couldn't understand me, so showed him the watchface. He tapped it with one gnarled finger. Then it dawned on me. He wanted the watch! By this time, I was developing a measure of confidence, and was still on a high with my new-found freedom. I turned, got straight back into the car, and drove off. He did not try to stop me.

Back home, I was careful to park in the underground carpark several blocks away from the elevator shafts leading to the apartments of the American and British, and check that there was no one around before getting out. With the exception of the American, the group was delighted that one of us could now move around, and that we had another food supply.

I rang the other Australians I was in contact with to tell them of the experience. Paul Kennedy informed his countrymen, most of whom were also still in hiding. They were all a bit sceptical as I had not had my papers checked, but agreed that it looked promising. The only way to check it was to go through a checkpoint, so told them I'd go out again and see what happened.

Again, there was no trouble on the road, at least at first. I headed towards the eastern end of town, and was a hundred metres from the US Embassy and the International Hotel when I ran into a checkpoint. These soldiers were firm. I was ordered over to the side of the road, and left there, becoming increasingly worried, while the soldiers checked the other cars through.

After a few minutes, the NCO came over to me. I showed him my passport, but he could not read English. He was not hostile, but not friendly, and kept the passport. A Palestinian stopped to translate, and told me that the soldier would send me to his officer. My stomach knotted. Australians might be on the list after all. I started to feel angry at myself, and then foolish, and wished I was back in the safe claustrophobia of my flat. I did not want to think about it, but the idea of being sent to Baghdad sent chills down my spine.

I was expecting the Iraqis to put me in a jeep for the trip to their officer. No such luck. I had to drive myself into custody. The NCO told an old soldier who must have been at least 50 but looked 70 to get into the passenger seat, gave him my passport, and off we went. It must have been his first ride in a car for a long time. He seemed very nervous and just smiled at me.

I parked outside the neighbourhood school where the officer was stationed, and was told to wait outside while the old soldier went in. There was no one else around. I could have made a run for it, but that would have meant abandoning the car, and my passport. I decided it was not a good idea.

After some time, I was asked inside, and had to wait again. He arrived after a while, a young lieutenant, looking sleepy. Despite his interrupted nap, he was not unfriendly, but not warm. His English was excellent. We shook hands out of politeness, and he asked me a few general questions, and for my Kuwaiti civil ID card, which I showed him. He asked me where I lived, so I sketched a little map which would have been impossible to follow. He seemed convinced that he knew where it was, then looked me in the eye and asked if there were any Americans or British there.

'Just Egyptians, Filipinos, Syrians and an Irishman,' I lied, immediately regretting mentioning the Irishman. He seemed satisfied, slapped my passport into my hand and said, smiling: '*Tafaddal* (Welcome). Welcome to Iraq.'

I breathed a sigh of relief. It was as official as we could expect. An officer had gone through my papers, and they didn't want me. It felt great. I asked him if I could give the old soldier a lift back to his checkpoint. He declined. I did not push my luck. All I wanted to do now was get home.

Once home, I found that everything was happening that day. Dave Short and the other two Irishmen and Greg Wood from Fintas Towers had visited Paul

Kennedy in my building. They had related their story, and the news that the two Australians in Fintas had been moving around for over three weeks. I called the other Australians and told them. They were convinced. Within hours, Australians and Irishmen were moving all around Kuwait, getting arrested themselves, and released. It was freedom, of sorts, and we loved it.

By 1 October, most non-US, British, French and German Westerners in Kuwait, and the sole remaining Japanese family, the Moriwakis, were moving around.

The strangest thing about freedom was being able to see for the first time people we had come to know almost intimately over the phone. For almost two months, we had known their voices, their jobs, the names of their wives and children, even how long they had been in Kuwait, their moods, likes and dislikes. The crisis had formed an uncommon sense of intimacy and community. When we came face to face, the appearance seldom matched our expectations. Some were taller, shorter, older, younger, fatter, or just plain different from our mental image. It was an object lesson in preconceived notions!

The first task of those with freedom of movement after getting people who were ill - such as Graham Lightfoot - to Baghdad, was to stock up our own groups with food, and then start supplying friends in other groups. At the time, many people were down to only a few weeks' rations. The free Westerners thus became a primary source of resupply for those in hiding.

This was not as easy as it sounds. With the exception of the New Zealanders who had gone back to work at KDD and a few other people, we had no income, and very little money. A few of us had managed to change dollars and Kuwaiti dinars into Iraqi dinars, but it wasn't much. The Irish were probably the best catered for. Their visiting Consul had given them US$300 each. Unknown to us at the time, money would soon start coming in from the Kuwaiti Government via the Kuwaiti Resistance, ID200 per man, but until it reached us, we had to make do.

Samir Elbaba came to the rescue again. We could take anything we needed from his company's warehouse, free. He had left, but his Asian staff were staying behind for the time being. They were tremendous, particularly the Sri Lankan manager, Mr John Ratnam. These men could have sold off thousands of dollars worth of canned, frozen and dry goods, but they opened their hearts to us. We soon had enough food to last until beyond Christmas.

Samir's men were of service to us in another extremely valuable way. One of his Filipino employees took tremendous risks to bring down from Baghdad an Australian passport for the local DHL General Manager, Steve Bushby, and a Polaroid camera. Steve was entitled to Australian citizenship but had never formally acquired it, and was still using his British passport. Paul Kennedy and I had arranged an Irish temporary travel document for him, but that document had not yet been tested in a confrontation with the Iraqis. Steve felt much safer with a full passport. The Polaroid camera was a Godsend. It meant we could now take photographs for false driving licences for those men who had no photos of their own. The courage of this Filipino man in helping others he did not even know was incredible. The *Mukhabarat* would not have thought twice about shooting him for smuggling a Polaroid camera.

The Lebanese-Australians proved very helpful again when John Abi-Hanna and his family left in late October. They gave us enough to feed our group of 12 for several months. The Irish catering manager, Pat Dower, who had been moving around on his special pass, also got bulk supplies, but people had to pay for it. Within the space of one week, we had gone from the prospect of running out of food within a month, to having enough to last until Easter. There was so much that we started to distribute it to other groups.

The New Zealanders working at KDD provided their own dairy delivery service to many of the men in hiding. Each day, they returned from work with their cars laden with cartons of milk and fruit juices. Each evening they and the two Danish ladies staying with them, Liselotte Hertz and Vicky Hill, went out to deliver these to men in hiding. Alistair Lane's living room resembled a supermarket milk-and-fruit-juice cabinet, with shrink-wrapped boxes of litre cartons of anything the dairy produced arranged in neat rows.

An Australian who managed the local Pizza Hut and Hungry Bunny hamburger chains, Paul Tonkin, had supplies of almost anything that went into a pizza or hamburger, other than fresh produce. As importantly, he had sold some of this, and with the takings from a number of the restaurants had several thousand Iraqi dinars which he distributed among his people. It was a great comfort to have something in our pockets with which to pay for petrol.

With these sources and the help of Kuwaitis and departing Indian and Arab friends, and Command Central's secret stockpile, the Westerners in hiding eventually had enough food to last well into the New Year. A few people were hoarding, but there was no longer any real risk of people starving as long as they had a phone.

An *ad hoc* system slowly developed whereby free Westerners started looking after their own American and British friends for resupply, food and mail. The French seemed to have their own network of Lebanese, and the Germans had many of their countrywomen married to Kuwaitis. These systems expanded in conjunction with the wardens to encompass people who did not have any free Westerner friends. The people doing the resupply became known as 'minders'.

This was not simple. We had to be very careful not to compromise the security of people we were resupplying by drawing the attention of Iraqi troops or collaborators to them. You could not just walk up to the front door with a bag of groceries, and ring the bell. Often, you simply walked or drove past the building, and dropped the bag near a gate, never seeing the men inside. Other times, you drove directly into the carport, and the men in hiding came out disguised as Kuwaitis to open the gate. Often, we had to do the drops at night, between dusk and the curfew at 10.00 p.m.

A number of people besides the New Zealanders and Danes were particularly active. One of the most important, and certainly among the bravest, was Peter Byrnes, an unassuming Australian engineer living in Ahmadi. There were 14 British men hiding in that isolated suburb, with only one road in and out. Another four men were hiding in nearby Fahaheel, which was more accessible, but still tense. Pete, as he was known, was the only free Westerner in the area, and could have moved closer to the city and lived in relative comfort.

Pete's first taste of freedom was not quite so sweet as for the rest of us, which made it all the more surprising that he stayed in his own area. When he first ventured out in early October, he was arrested, held in the local police station, and told he was going to Baghdad. Pete explained to the Iraqi in charge that as far as he knew, Australians were free to move around. The Iraqi did not think this was so, but went off to the Regency Palace Hotel to check. Meanwhile, Pete was left overnight in a bare room, without even a mattress or blanket. The Iraqi returned, slightly apologetic, saying to Pete, 'You apparently know more about the situation than I do. You are free to go.'

Upon returning home, he found that his TV and other electronics had been looted. Relishing his new-found freedom, he returned to the police station to complain. The Iraqis eventually admitted sheepishly that they had 'taken them for safe-keeping'. Some, but not all, were returned to him.

To make matters worse, the Iraqi Army and Police were having a turf war over loot in Ahmadi, and Pete was caught up in this on several occasions. He was arrested by one of the parties and spent another night in the cells, only to be taken out by the other party and have his passport and car – but not his money – restored to him. On several other occasions, he was roughed up, and slapped by armed Palestinians. Nevertheless, Pete stayed in Ahmadi, without any other free Westerners nearby, and kept the 14 men supplied until they were allowed to leave in December. He was helped in this by a Syrian KNPC engineer, Haitham Shaheen, Ahmadi's version of our Imad Ghawji.

Another important individual was Canadian Eoin MacDougald, who had been moving around since 19 August. At one stage, before other people became mobile, he was minding in excess of one hundred people. The most noticeable thing about men such as Pete and Eoin was that they never, ever, made a fuss about what they were doing. They simply went ahead and did it, day by day, because it was a job that needed to be done, and they were in a position to do it.

For those of us who were moving around, the euphoria soon wore off. Kuwait was no longer the bustling city we had known. It was a ghost town. Trash was strewn over the normally pristine motorways. You could hardly drive a kilometre without seeing cars up on blocks by the roadside, their wheels gone and bonnets open, batteries, distributors, even headlights missing. The only shops functioning were grocery co-operatives, a few private supermarkets, bakeries, and barbers. Every electronics outlet, video shop and clothes boutique had been looted. It was a depressing experience just to be on the street.

The depression was nothing compared to the stress of continually going through checkpoints, and wondering if the Iraqis would give you a hard time. We just never knew when the rules might change, and we might be snatched off the street to join the Human Shield. The soldiers' behaviour depended on their moods, and the discipline in their units. It was nearly impossible to build up a long-term friendly relationship with troops in a particular area as they were invariably moved or went on leave every couple of weeks. Those of us who were moving around would come home each evening, absolutely drained from the nervous energy of dealing with the Iraqis. After the first week of freedom, I had to stay inside for a day or so just to rest. If there had not been other people outside who needed our services, I would have gladly remained inside, and waited for the US Marines to arrive.

The Iraqi officers who planned the key checkpoints obviously knew what they were doing. There were few, if any, on the main motorways except where the north-south roads converged into the city centre, near the airport, or at Ahmadi in the south. However, it was almost impossible to get off the motorways into a suburb without encountering a checkpoint. My good fortune in passing through no checkpoints on my first trip out was seldom repeated.

Within suburbs, checkpoints were usually set up around corners, so that you could not turn into a driveway, or another area, or even make a U-turn, after you had seen them and they had seen you. You even had to go through them between parts of suburbs. Kuwait's extensive system of dual carriageways and fenced-off suburbs worked like the corridors and cells of a huge open prison.

A checkpoint was usually manned by four to six men, seldom more, and they seemed to work six-hour shifts. It was unusual to see officers or Iraqi civilian police on checkpoints, although on occasions the *Mukhabarat* would set up their own checkpoints, with young, hard, Saddam lookalikes in smart slacks and leather jackets, a pistol stuck in a waistband holster.

The checkpoints themselves were initially improvized affairs which became more sophisticated with time. Their main feature was an obstruction extending half-way across the road from the right-hand kerb, and then another a few metres further on, this time from the central reservation. The idea was to force cars to slow down and weave between the two blockages, presenting themselves at an angle to the troops. The obstructions started out as a couple of concrete breeze-blocks, or police crowd barriers. More permanent checkpoints featured a few weighted 44-gallon drums painted yellow with a black strip around the middle, with wooden planks on top.

Other checkpoints, especially those set up by surprise, or on narrow roads, did not even have obstructions. The troops just stood on the kerb, or in the road. The message was clear. Stop. No one argued. They had guns. Nevertheless, it was unusual for a machine gun to be set up to cover the checkpoint approaches. For all their effectiveness they were remarkably casual affairs.

The soldiers were invariably armed with Kalashnikov assault rifles. On larger checkpoints, especially on main roads, one or two men had RPGs. The troops tended to sling their rifles horizontally from their shoulders, resting their arms on the forestock. The effect of this when they leaned over to peer in the driver's window was to have the barrel pointing straight at us, at a distance of 30 centimetres. At that angle, it was impossible to see whether the safety catch was on. I lost count of the number of Kalashnikov barrels I looked down. An image of the curious appearance of the muzzle, which looks as if someone has whittled off a piece of the metal, is still emblazoned in my mind.

Despite this casual appearance, the troops did not hesitate to use their weapons. Two Westerners hiding in Salmiya heard a massive explosion one day, and peered out from behind closed curtains to see a car in flames about 50 metres beyond a nearby checkpoint. The car had tried to run the checkpoint. The Iraqis had fired an RPG into it. No one could have got out of that alive.

Mostly, the troops were friendly, even deferential, particularly in areas with a regular traffic of free Westerners. Their favourite sentence was *'Ullah uh-sadiq'*, which meant nothing to us. It did not even occur to me that it was a greeting, as they usually said it in response to the more common *'Salaam alikoom'* (Peace be with you), to which the correct reply is *'Alikoom salaam'*. I eventually asked a Palestinian friend what this meant, as the Iraqi accent is quite distinct from other Arab accents. My friend laughed, saying: 'It means 'God be with you'.' I had to laugh too. Here was the Iraqi Army occupying us while wishing us the blessings of the Almighty.

However, other troops could be downright difficult, especially with Kuwaitis. On one occasion, an elderly Kuwaiti's car was stopped ahead of me at a checkpoint. The senior Iraqi NCO at the post, a warrant officer with stars of his collar, was obviously harassing the Kuwaiti. He took every piece of identification the man had, including his car registration and insurance papers. I waited, caught in the queue, unable to back out, growing increasingly concerned for the Kuwaiti, and selfishly fearing I might be next. The Kuwaiti was eventually told to get out of the car. As he did so, the Iraqi slapped him hard across the head, and then came over to me. I cringed as far back in the seat as I could, greeted him warily, and handed over every piece of paperwork I could lay my hands on. He just looked at my civil ID card which identified my nationality. *'Ullah uh-sadiq'* he said, and waved me through.

There was no one best way to deal with the Iraqis at the checkpoints. Some people treated them with icy coolness, even contempt, on the basis that you had to be firm. Others felt that it was best to be civil. I chose the more pleasant option, which seemed to work. There were times when a nasty individual might take this as a sign of weakness, but then you could always become curt. The trick was never to appear intimidated.

The Western women with freedom of movement could be particularly vulnerable. One of the most active of these was Liselotte Hertz. She would drive around Kuwait to deliver food and visit people in a sporty white Honda CRX, with a Danish flag decal on the back. She refused to dress in an *abaya*, but for her own safety was usually accompanied by Robin Van Kempen, a huge New Zealand chef from the Kuwait International Hotel.

One day, Lise and Robin ran into a troublesome checkpoint, and were taken to a headquarters where they were shown upstairs to the captain's private quarters. Robin was told he was free to go. The captain wanted to question Lise alone. It was apparent that his intentions were less than honourable. Robin folded his arms, looked down at the armed Iraqi, and said he was going nowhere without Lise. Eventually, the captain could see that he would have to shoot Robin if he was to have his way with Lise, and dismissed them both.

Few of us had such harrowing experiences, but whenever we became a little too confident with our freedom, something invariably happened to shake us out of our complacency. At first, we were always home by dark, even though the curfew now went into effect at 10.00 p.m. As time went on, we pushed it to the limit, often slipping in with minutes to spare. Once, however, I nearly gave up night driving completely. The reason was not the Iraqis, but the Kuwaitis. By this time, the Resistance had become much better organized. They no longer took daylight potshots at random Iraqis, but launched selective, well-coordinated night-time attacks on Iraqi billets.

The night attacks gave the Kuwaitis a distinct advantage. They knew the areas better than the Iraqis, and there were fewer checkpoints. Furthermore, at night, there was less chance of civilians getting caught in a crossfire. The Kuwaiti tactic was to fire a few rounds, then move, so that the Iraqis could not draw a bead on them. The Iraqis would open up in almost every direction with everything they had. Thus, with a dozen rounds, the Kuwaitis prompted the Iraqis to fire off hundreds of rounds, and kept them worried.

One of these Iraqi billets was in a school near the main New Zealanders' apartment, now known affectionately as 'Kiwi House'. Late one evening, Steve Bushby and I visited Kiwi House, parking my battered car in the street outside. No sooner were we in the door than all hell seemed to break loose outside. We could hear the crump of several RPGs over the chatter of automatic weapons. The din was unbelievable. I could imagine the rounds whipping down the street, chopping my car to pieces.

The Danes and New Zealanders seemed unconcerned. No one hit the floor, although Steve and I certainly felt like doing so. The others were obviously used to this, and knew they were not in the line of fire. 'No problem,' said Alistair Lane. 'This happens every couple of nights. Nothing's ever hit the building. It's a bit early tonight, though.'

The action went on for what seemed like half an hour, and then silence. We sipped coffees, waiting for a decent interval to go out and check the car. Miraculously, it was untouched. None of the buildings seemed to have been hit. There were no broken windows or smashed street lights. We could not even find any spent rounds on the road. It was almost as if the attack had never happened. We beat a quick retreat back to our own place. Incredibly, the nearby checkpoint was still manned. We approached, expecting a stiff search. '*Ullah uh-sadiq,* ' said the Republican Guard, and waved us through.

A number of encounters with the Iraqis were decidedly surreal. In order to get through more troublesome checkpoints, we developed the ploy of picking up hitch-hiking Iraqi soldiers a few hundred metres before the checkpoint, and driving through it with them in the car. The men at the checkpoint would usually wave us through when they saw their colleagues in the car. We did not consider this to be collaboration as it was using the Iraqis to our advantage, and they were seldom in the car for more than ten minutes. Therefore we did not feel at risk from the Kuwaiti Resistance. However, there were times when I bit off more than I could chew.

One such incident occurred in October. I had given a soldier a lift to Hawally, a Palestinian area, and during the course of the drive had tried to strike up a conversation. His English was poor, but he was uncommonly friendly. Arabs are invariably fiercely proud of their rich language, and delighted when anyone shows interest in it. He was no different. I made the mistake of asking him what the Army officers' ranks were in Arabic. He told me, all ten ranks from second lieutenant through full general, plus Saddam's.

This was all very well, until he started testing me, and I couldn't recite them word-perfect. The man must have been a drafted schoolteacher. We reached where I had to drop him off, but he would not leave me until I knew all the ranks, straight up and down. He even drew the badges of rank with stars and eagles on a piece of cardboard to make sure I had them right. There I was, sitting on a main road, next to a Palestinian enclave, talking to an Iraqi soldier who was drawing pictures for me, and wondering whether the Resistance had just placed me on a hit list. I have never learned any other ten Arabic words so quickly, and can still recite them perfectly to this day.

From then on, every time I had to deal with an Iraqi officer, I addressed him by his rank. They were delighted, but it did not go down well with some other Westerners. Pete Byrnes, despite his own immense personal courage, was horrified. 'John,' he said, 'if you do that, they'll think you're a spy.'

Throughout the early weeks of our new-found freedom, our embassies in Baghdad had encouraged us to go to Baghdad. Most of us had declined, but this looked more and more attractive as it became apparent that an Allied attack was not imminent. Few of us wanted to stay in Baghdad, but we would be able to phone our families from there, and have access to loans from the embassies to help us survive in Kuwait. Our main concern was that we would not be able to return to Kuwait, where most of us felt much safer.

Arab and Asian friends had been shuttling between Kuwait and Baghdad from the second week of the occupation on all sorts of errands, such as making international calls, and organizing air tickets to evacuate people to Jordan.

Perhaps the exploit with the greatest cheek was that of Lucia Topalian, a Lebanese-Armenian artist with friends in the Al-Sabah family. She stayed in Baghdad's Al-Rasheed Hotel directly above what was thought to be Saddam's bunker, and called her friends in Saudi Arabia. They slammed the phone down when she said she was calling from Baghdad, but she called them again, and reassured them that their people still in Kuwait were safe.

Few of the Westerners who wanted to remain in Kuwait were prepared to risk being stuck in Baghdad if the Americans did decide to hit it, so only those who intended to stay there went north at first. Then, as usual, it was the New Zealanders who broke the ice. One of their number, Ian Mills, who had been captured and taken to Baghdad in August, arrived in Kuwait by taxi to retrieve the remains of his personal effects. This proved that you could return from Baghdad, almost like coming back from the dead. You merely had to show your Kuwaiti civil ID card at the checkpoints to prove that you were resident in Kuwait. So much for annexation. The only documents the Iraqis could depend on were those issued by the Government they had displaced.

The first known Westerners to travel voluntarily to Baghdad, and return, since Toufic Lawand had accompanied a Baghdad-based diplomat on a brief visit in August, were the New Zealand warden, Alistair Lane, and one of the Danes, Vicky Hill. It was a relatively simple matter. The New Zealand Consul, Michelle Wood, had given them a map drawn by her husband, Jeff, when they had visited Kuwait. It was a work of art, even including distances between major towns, major checkpoints, tips on where to get fuel, and how to avoid the centres of country towns. For the more adventurous, the map showed the distances from Baghdad to Turkey (496km), and Jordan (560km).

MAP 5, THE ROAD TO BAGHDAD

*Map provided by New Zealand Embassy, Baghdad of overland routes
form Kuwait to Baghdad*

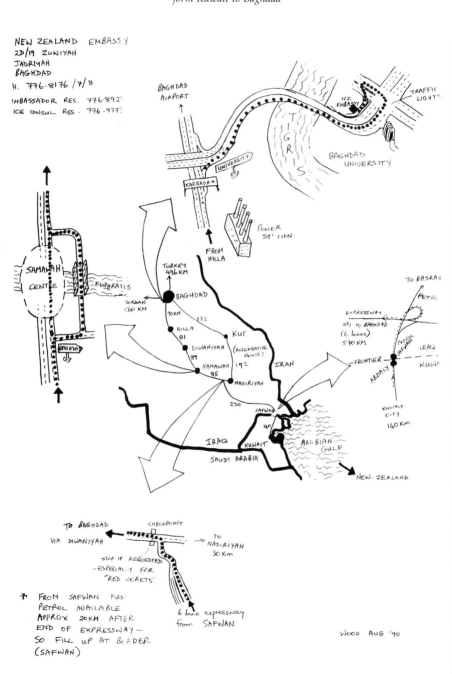

The 713-km trip to Baghdad took nine hours in a good car, instead of the 12-24 hour horror trips of the bus evacuations. The difference was that the Iraqis had taken the buses on the rougher, longer northern road. The road on Jeff's map – the famed 'Highway 8' later taken by the US XVIII Corps in February 1991 – was a six-lane expressway for most of the 230km between Safwan and Nassiriyah, and a good highway for the remaining 343km to Baghdad.

It was possible to take taxis as Ian Mills had done, and quite inexpensive, but Alistair decided to drive himself. They almost did not make it. He wanted an early start, so set off shortly before curfew was lifted. The Iraqis were nervous about any car on the road at that time. Alistair took a wrong turn when still in the urban area, realized it, and turned around to get back onto the main road. Unknown to him, there was a barely visible checkpoint on the road he had turned into. A soldier had seen a car turn into the road, stop, then turn away, in the dim light. It looked suspicious, so he raised his rifle. Fortunately, Vicky glimpsed this in the gathering light, and stopped Alistair. It took some time to sort things out, but they were finally allowed to proceed, and arrived in Baghdad without further mishap.

When they returned several days later, laden with food, spirits and beer, we had our first real idea of life in Baghdad. There was no doubt now that we could go there and return, but Alistair had some chilling news for us. He had spoken to the embassies, who described the atrocious conditions endured by the Human Shields at some strategic sites. At that stage, a number of men in hiding had considered giving themselves up as they felt that being in an Iraqi camp could be no worse than the constant stress and fear of hiding from the Iraqis in Kuwait. Alistair's news changed their minds.

Road transport was not the only means of getting to and from Baghdad. Iraqi Airways operated daily 'domestic' flights between Kuwait and Baghdad from mid-August. The procedure was a little more involved than a normal flight, but did the job. You had to be dropped off at a freeway overpass a kilometre from Kuwait International Airport. It was then a five dinar (US$1) bus ride to the terminal where you bought a ticket, which cost ID100 (US$22) return economy class, or ID120 (US$27) first class. The only difference between first and economy was that you got your tea in a proper cup and saucer instead of a styrofoam cup, were assured of a seat, and had a red boarding card.

You then had to wait around for a bus to Ali Al-Salem KAF Base, 60km away. Flights had been leaving from there ever since the Kuwaiti Resistance attacked an Iraqi aircraft leaving the International Airport with an anti-aircraft missile. Once at Ali Al-Salem, there was another wait, a security search, and then a flight of a little over an hour in a rickety Iraqi Airways 727 to Saddam International Airport, Baghdad.

The bus to Ali Al-Salem cost ID3 (67 cents), and the taxi from Saddam International into Baghdad ID15 (US$3), so the round trip cost the equivalent of US$38, first class. Someone returning from Baghdad could report to the airport at 8.30 a.m. for a 9.30 a.m. flight, and be home in Kuwait by lunchtime. There was also an afternoon flight. One could not quite go to Baghdad in the morning, phone home, and be back in Kuwait that night, but you could do the round trip in 35 hours by staying overnight in Baghdad.

Over the next few weeks, most free Westerners in Kuwait made at least one trip to Baghdad to see their embassies there, ensure that they were on the list being submitted to the Iraqis for exit visas, and call their families. Most returned. Their home was Kuwait. Even though Baghdad was relatively safe and much more normal than Kuwait at that time, no one wanted to be caught 700km behind enemy lines when General Schwarzkopf finally made his move.

The good General's intelligence people actually owe a great deal more to the free Westerners than most people imagine. The dozens of men who shuttled to Baghdad from Kuwait provided a wealth of intelligence on the Iraqi Army in Kuwait. We could not count all the tanks, but we could tell the Baghdad diplomats about the Iraqis' morale, the urban defenses, obvious changes, and the quality of the troops. Mostly, our reports served to confirm or complement those of the Kuwaiti Resistance, but we had no way of knowing that.

Some of this intelligence was actually quite specific. One man solved a nagging query for the defence people. With their satellites, they had a good overhead view of the beach defences. However, they could not always differentiate between decoys and the real thing. The Iraqis had dug in tanks and artillery along the beach against an amphibious assault. In front of these weapons was a wire fence, somewhat like chicken wire. Apparently, skilled tacticians deploy a special type of fence in front of equipment which might be subject to guided missile attack. This confuses the missile's radar. The military needed to know what type of wire it was so that they could plan how to attack these defences. This man told them that it was regular fencing wire as he had seen where the Iraqis had cut it down from a nearby tennis court.

Other information was not readily ascertainable from the satellites. For example, people in the 18-storey Fintas Towers, which overlooked the beach, could plot the tanks, as the satellites could. However, the men could see that some heavy tanks were hopelessly bogged in the sand. The Iraqis were apparently used to operating on desert sand, not wet beach sand. The bogged tanks had become little more than fixed pieces of artillery, and sitting ducks.

Later, Peter Byrnes, the Australian taking care of the British in Ahmadi, noticed armoured vehicles among trees on the southern edges of Ahmadi. We were unsure whether the satellites could see these as they were under cover, and were able to get close enough simply by driving down the suburb's perimeter road alongside the trees to count them, and identify the vehicle type. They turned out to be part of the reserve armour of Iraq's III Corps.

The main concern of the US defence people in Baghdad was SCUD and SCALEBACK missiles. They gave a few of us quick briefings on how to identify the different missile types and their launchers, but we never saw any. We learned to identify a T-72 from a T-55 or T-62 by counting drive wheels, the shape of the turret, and the style of the gun. They were also particularly concerned about anti-aircraft missiles, especially captured Kuwaiti HAWKs. We were unable to help them with that, but one set of anti-aircraft missiles at Atraf on the way to Ali Al-Salem KAF Base for the flight to Baghdad must have been the most widely-reported battery in Kuwait.

In November, it became apparent that the US Embassy was having trouble with its generators, or was running low on fuel for them, or both. The staff had reduced their nationals' ration of messages, and the non-US wardens working through them could only send and receive messages every second day. The US DCM, Barbara Bodine, was never explicit about the problem over the phone in case the line was tapped, but she was concerned. If they lost the generators, they lost their communications with Washington. They would have been of no use to anyone, and would have had to either stay in the embassy without secure communications, or relocate to Baghdad. With the second option, the 19 civilians taking refuge with them would have ended up as Human Shields.

Miss Bodine need not have bothered being so secretive. Her own State Department had released news of the low fuel supplies to the Press. Apparently, someone in Washington either had no idea of the situation in Kuwait, or was playing a clever game with the Iraqis to convince them that those inside the embassy would soon have to come out of their own accord. The trouble was, they seemed not to have let Miss Bodine in on the game.

For Westerners in Kuwait, this was serious. The US Embassy was the only reliable means of secure communication out of Kuwait. The French had left a couple of weeks earlier, and the British Embassy had a voice link to Abu Dhabi which could be eavesdropped on by the Iraqis, and serviced only the British. If we lost the American channel, we were in big trouble.

We started considering how to get power into the embassy. This would obviously have to be by extension cord from a nearby power source, but we could not simply walk up to the embassy wall, throw a cord across, and plug it in. Even if we could do this unseen, the soldiers guarding the compound were sure to see the cable hanging over the wall, or running across the street.

The embassy compound was sandwiched between the Gulf Road and a small access road to its main pedestrian entrance. This entrance was next to a bullet-proof glass reception booth where the Americans could sit and observe the Iraqis on the access road. The most promising power source was a line of seven abandoned houses which backed onto the access road. Most of these had been tenanted by US diplomats, and were now looted. They faced onto another road, parallel to the access road. We estimated the access road was 12 metres wide, from the walls of the houses' back yards to the embassy compound wall.

Our problem was therefore to get the power from one of the houses, across the access road and into the embassy. The most critical part was the road, which formed a type of quarantine zone around the embassy. The garden walls of the first three houses, and the last, which happened to be Barbara's, were high enough to prevent any troops outside them from seeing an electric cable running through the garden. The fact that the houses had been thoroughly looted was a blessing. No one was living in them, not even Iraqi soldiers.

We suggested this idea to Barbara over the phone, cryptically. She seemed to think that it was a long shot, and warned us not to put ourselves in danger, but delegated one of the civilians with her, Mike Penniman, to liaise with us.

Our first reconnaissance trip was to the home of the Westerner in hiding closest to the embassy. This was Tom Laming, a Briton who lived in a block of flats on the third road back from the embassy, parallel to the access road. Tom was bored stiff, and itching for a bit of action. He had served in Malaya with the British Army in the 1950s, and the idea of being able to get back at the Iraqis and give the Americans a helping hand appealed to him greatly.

We called Mike from Tom's flat, and arranged for him to climb out onto the flat roof of the tallest building in the compound, so that we could see him. He was in full view of the Iraqis around the embassy, but they did not bother him. We then went onto the flat roof of Tom's building, being very careful to ensure that no patrolling Iraqis could see us, peered over the parapet, and sighted Mike. He was 200 metres distant, across two rows of houses, but it was a delicious small victory to be able to see one of the blockaded Americans.

However, that did not solve the power problem. It was too far to sling a cable between Tom's building and the embassy. Furthermore, if the Iraqis found it, they could follow it back to Tom's hiding place. It seemed that the only way we could get the cable in unseen was to put it underground. This could only be done from was the back yard of one of the houses into the embassy, or vice versa. Apart from the safety aspect, this would take so much effort and time that it would surely alert the Iraqis. A tunnel under 12 metres of road would have to be at least 16 metres long to allow an entrance at each end, and big enough to accommodate a man. It would have entailed excavating over 12 cubic metres of sand. This was obviously impractical.

Then one of the Australians, Tony Hordern, a BA149 passenger who had worked as an outback surveyor, suggested that we 'water-bore' a tunnel just big enough for the cable. He explained that when road workers needed to run a small pipe or cable under a country road without digging it up, they excavate a working pit about a metre deep, perpendicular to the road, and then a smaller intercept trench of the same depth on the opposite side of the road. A long, 40 to 50mm diameter steel pipe with a hose through it is then placed horizontally in the working pit, stuck into the wall nearest the road, and aimed at the intercept pit on the other side of the road using levelling blocks. The water is turned on, and the pipe gradually jacked, twisted and pushed forward under the road as the flow of water washes away the sand in front of it. The idea is for the pipe to reach the intercept pit on the other side. The hose could then be withdrawn, and a cable inserted. Tony explained that in this case, the hole would probably have to be bored at a depth of at least two metres to avoid hitting sewerage and drainage systems under the road.

This seemed like a brilliant idea. The water-boring would have to be done by the Americans inside. They had more cover, and the water. Our job would be to dig the intercept pit in the back yard of one of the houses, and then wire the cable up to a power source in the house.

I knew the layout of the western edge of the embassy compound. Trees and a small toilet block inside the wall could provide cover to the American water-borers from the Iraqis who could see into much of the compound from the nearby Kuwait International Hotel. There was even better cover at the compound's north-west corner opposite Barbara's house, but from Tom Laming's roof we had noticed troops billeted in the nearby Kuwait Girl Guides Association. They were so close that they would probably hear the Americans and ourselves digging if we chose Barbara's house. We therefore opted for one of the first three houses, which were further from the billets.

Another reconnaissance was in order. The most promising house was the third one, which had been occupied by Mr J. Hunter Downes, the local CIA man. It was directly opposite the reception booth. As importantly, we knew who had lived there, so we had a cover story if the Iraqis caught us snooping around.

Tony and I went with Harry Delaney, another Australian, to see what potential Downes' house offered. There were no troops guarding the road, so we walked straight through the open front gate. Harry went inside to check the house, and Tony and I went around the back to see how it lined up with the embassy. It was perfect. We could see the US flag flapping languidly in the compound on the other side of the wall. Then we noticed a *mulhuq* (a small one-bedroom apartment, usually for domestic staff) at the rear of the garden, about 30 metres from the house, against the concrete wall of the back yard.

The *mulhuq* could not have been better. In fact, its back windows were in the wall itself. We would not have to run a cable from the house. It could be done from the *mulhuq*, without the risk of of casual looters or Iraqi troops visiting the house and finding a cable running across the garden. There was far less chance of the Iraqis visiting the *mulhuq* as it was unlikely to hold anything of value. Even better for our purposes, the toilet had backed up and stank. With the smell detectable from outside the *mulhuq* door, no one would want to go in.

To our delight we could see directly from the *mulhuq* bathroom window into the reception booth of the embassy. The Americans there would be able to signal to us when the coast was clear to start digging. As an added bonus, there was a sewer manhole cover just outside the *mulhuq*, a couple of feet from the wall. It was perfect for hiding the dirt from the intercept pit. There was even a water pipe in the wall which the American water-borers could aim at.

Just then, when everything seemed to be going our way, our luck ran out. Tony and I were still in the *mulhuq* when we glanced back at the house and saw Harry with several Iraqi soldiers around him. They were not physically restraining him, but we could see they were unhappy about him being there. Tony and I debated what to do. The Iraqis may have seen us walk into the house from their billets at the Girl Guides Association, but they might not know that there were three of us. It was apparent that Harry had not told them about us yet, otherwise they would have come for us. We could either hide in the *mulhuq*, and hope they didn't find us, and that Harry was able to talk his way out, or we could give ourselves up. There was really no choice.

Tony and I walked out of the *mulhuq*, our hearts in our mouths. The Iraqis were as surprised to see us as Harry was delighted. We shook hands with them out of politeness, but they were curt. The senior one asked us in patchy English what we were doing there. We told him that we had come to check on Mr Joe's house. He told us that whoever was here before was gone, and that we should not be in this area, an obvious reference to the embassy.

The best defence seemed to be to go on the offensive, so I asked him why his men had looted this house. 'This house belonged to Mr Joe, a US diplomat. Why did your men do this? Baba Saddam said there is no looting in Kuwait!' I said, pointing indignantly to the mess inside. The Iraqi was a little taken aback. He said that his men had not done it, but we should not be here. They seemed to be

Illustration 2. POWER TO THE AMERICANS

Plans by Tony Hordern for 'water-boring' a tunnel from the US Embassy, Kuwait to a nearby power source to provide them with electricity

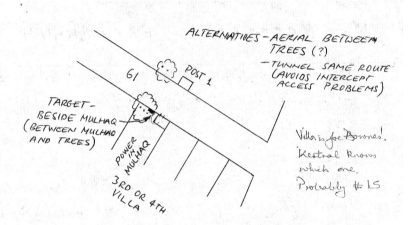

1. CALCULATE LENGTH AND DRIVE PIPE TO CLEAR TARGET WALL BY ABOUT 300 MM (1 FOOT)

2. ADVISE DEPTH FOR INTERCEPT PIT – ADVISE APPROX. LOCATION IN PLAN (OFF PERPENDICULAR WALLS)

3. THREAD PIPE WITH STIFF WIRE (FENCING WIRE) FOR CABLE PULLING

4. 1½ TO 2 INCH (40 TO 50 MILLIMETRE) DIAMETER IRON WATER PIPE IS PROBABLY SUFFICIENTLY STIFF TO AVOID DEFORMATION.

5. ESTIMATED TOTAL DRIVING LENGTH 12 – 14 METRES. TEST STIFFNESS OF THIS LENGTH OF PIPE IN AIR TO ASSESS SUITABILITY – THINNER PIPE MAY SUFFICE.

6. WHEN PROVIDING CABLE ALLOW SUFFICIENT LENGTH FOR UNDERGROUND RUNNING TO AND INSIDE MULHAQ

7. STARTING DEPTH DEPENDS ON STARTING WALL FOOTINGS BUT IF VERY DEEP (OVER 1 METRE – 3 FEET) CONSIDER DRILLING A HOLE THROUGH WALL AT THAT DEPTH TO AVOID EXCESSIVE TRENCHING AT EITHER END. BELOW THAT DEPTH MAY FOUL STREET UTILITIES. STREET AND SUPPLY POWER CABLES PROBABLY ABOVE THAT DEPTH.

Illustration 2. POWER TO THE AMERICANS (cont.)

Plans by Tony Hordern for 'water-boring' a tunnel from the US Embassy, Kuwait to a nearby power source to provide them with electricity

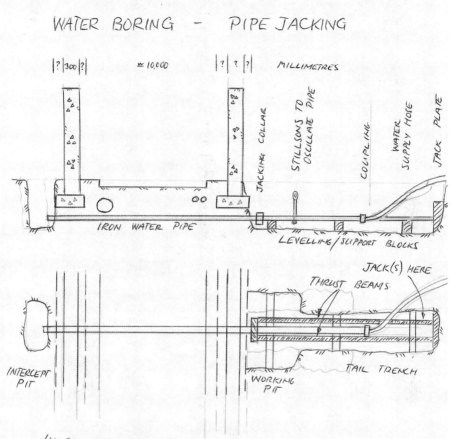

IN SANDY SOIL IT MAY BE POSSIBLE TO JACK PIPE FORWARD USING WATER PRESSURE ALONE. FLOW, NOT PRESSURE, REMOVES DEBRIS. PROVIDE A SUMP DRAIN FOR CONVENIENCE OF WORKERS. JACK FROM CLOSE TO HOLE COLLAR TO AVOID DEVIATION. USE HYDRAULIC OR MECHANICAL JACKS AT END OF TAIL TRENCH, PUSHING IN LINE WITH PIPE. USE STILLSONS TO OSCILLATE PIPE IF NECESSARY TO CLEAR STONES AND PEBBLES. IT WOULD HELP TO FILE DOWN THE NOSE OF THE PIPE ABOUT 60° – NOT TOO SHARP TO AVOID DEFORMATION. PIPE MAY BE JOINED WITH COUPLERS TO ACHIEVE LENGTH – PREFERABLY LAST 1/3 TO HELP AVOID DEVIATION. SINGLE LENGTH WOULD BE BEST.

in two minds as to whether to arrest us. However, they had been at fault in even allowing us to get this far, and wanted rid of us as soon as possible. They told us to go, and not to come back.

That evening, Tony drew up plans for the waterboring, and British warden Sandy Macmillan faxed them to Barbara, who apparently passed them on to the engineers in the compound. I suggested that we defer commencement of the project for a week as Tony was going to Baghdad, and we did want to return to the house for a while in case the Iraqis were on the lookout for us. We waited a few days until the Americans had a chance to study the plans. When I asked Barbara's opinion, I was surprised at the tone of her voice. She was usually very perky and friendly, but this time seemed annoyed. 'That's not possible,' she said sharply. 'We haven't got explosives in here, and even if we did, we wouldn't use them.' I was shocked. We had said nothing about explosives.

It took some time to clear up the misunderstanding. From what we could gather, her engineers had said they would need explosives to get through the perimeter wall, which had foundations going down four metres. We had not expected it to be that deep, but water-boring under the wall would have been very difficult as it was below the level of the water table. She said she would keep the plans, and let us know if they could use them. We took this to be a diplomatic 'No way!' However, her main concern was that we were getting too blasé about our safety, especially after our encounter in Joe's back yard.

As it turned out, all the Westerners were released before the American generators ran out of fuel, and the power was not needed. Nevertheless, it was close. They had very little left at the end, perhaps three weeks maximum at greatly reduced transmission time. The British were even worse off. Their Ambassador fired up his generator when he returned in February 1991; it ran out of fuel in minutes. Nevertheless, we felt better that we had at least given the problem serious attention, and got so close to the blockaded Americans.

It is one of the great mysteries of the crisis that a country as paranoid about security as Iraq would allow dozens of highly-motivated potential amateur spies to operate with such freedom of movement. We never learned why the Iraqis allowed us to move around in this manner. They must have known that we had American and British friends whom we would not leave. They must have known that we could see their forces, and that most of us were itching for a chance to get back at them for the invasion by reporting whatever we could see to the Allied military. Perhaps they were simply too busy to consider a hundred Westerners from lesser Coalition nations. Whatever the reason, we were grateful for the freedom, as were those who benefited from it.

14. THE EMBASSIES, KUWAIT

After most of the Western women and children had left Kuwait, the diplomats who had been confined to their embassy compounds by the Iraqis settled in for the long wait.

The diplomatic hold-outs were in a curious state of limbo. The Iraqis claimed not to recognize the immunity of diplomats accredited to Kuwait, but stopped short of treating them in the same way as their civilian nationals. They knew exactly where they were but, with the exception of the September raids, left them pretty much alone. The diplomats were, after all, providing a Human Shield in Kuwait, at little or no trouble to the Iraqis.

The embassy sieges were essentially a waiting game, with the Iraqis not allowing anything into the compounds, and expecting the diplomats to come out after finishing their food, water, or fuel to run their communications. When they did, the Iraqis escorted them to Baghdad, or allowed them to travel there to join their colleagues in the embassies accredited to Iraq.

Within days of the closure order of 24 August, the Iraqis cut power, water and most phone services to the Western embassies, and several ambassadors' residences outside the compounds. The electricity was particularly important for running air-conditioning in the heat of summer, and for refrigerating perishable food. The diplomats therefore found themselves in a great deal of discomfort, with much of their food rotting.

The Iraqis never actually disconnected all embassy telephone lines, although they did cut some. It was unclear whether they had not found them all, or deliberately kept the few lines working in order to talk to the diplomats if they had to. In the case of the British and West German embassies, the Iraqis cut only the numbers on the embassies' letterheads, but left all others. They had actually turned some of them back on after cutting them earlier in August so that the ambassadors could pass on the order to assemble in hotels to their communities. After that, the Iraqis either forgot to cut the lines again, or left them open so they could tap them. We simply had to assume that the lines were bugged. Most of the diplomats did too.

The Americans were particularly conscious of the security risk . They never, ever discussed over the phone the number of people in their compound, their roles, the names of their nationals in hiding, or their reserves of food or fuel. Later in the occupation, when the free nationals servicing men in hiding needed a list of Americans in Kuwait to ensure they were all covered if the diplomats were forced to leave, the US diplomats would not fax it out to us. Instead, it was encrypted, transmitted by satellite to their embassy in Baghdad, and brought back to Kuwait by Eoin MacDougald. The British, however, were more open. This made things easier for those who needed help and for those helping them, but caused constant concern that security had been breached. It was a never-ending trade-off between pragmatism and security.

Curiously, beyond the fiasco of the September raids and cutting utilities, the Iraqis took little definite action to force the diplomats out of the compounds. Some troops periodically fired shots over the buildings, but this was more of a nuisance than a real danger. The Iraqis could have played high-volume Arabic music through loudspeakers outside the embassies to increase the mental stress on the diplomats. The Americans even set up their own high-decibel sound system which they planned to use to counter this, or to create a diversion during any military rescue attempt, using, somewhat appropriately, Wagner's *Dance of the Valkyries*.

The Iraqis were in sporadic contact with some of the diplomats, especially the Americans, despite officially refusing to recognize their status. This was necessary for the practical matters of organizing evacuations, and liaising with the Iraqis when a US citizen was shot and wounded. The diplomats and Foreign Ministries kept quiet about this vital piece of Iraqi inconsistency as Iraqi withdrawal of this limited communication would have compromised their consular function. The political gain was not worth the consular price.

The British diplomats did not have quite the same relationship with the Iraqis, although several of their civilians in Kuwait died or were killed during the siege. The only Iraqis the British spoke to after being sealed off were a few troops guarding the compound. In the main, the Western embassies used their Indian or Arab staffers to deal with the Iraqis. This was extremely brave of these individuals. The Iraqis had threatened to hang anybody helping Westerners in hiding, and these men were not accredited diplomats.

Every Western country except Australia, Cyprus, Iceland, Ireland, Luxembourg, Malta, New Zealand and Portugal had an embassy in Kuwait, as did most Arab, Asian and East European countries. Even Cuba had one. Only southern and central Africa, Latin America and Oceania were poorly represented, but they had few nationals in Kuwait.

Most of the embassies initially refused to close, but because few African, Asian, Latin American and East European embassies had the resources to hold out, they shut their doors within days of the closure order. This left mainly the US, Canadian, EC and GCC embassies, and other diehards such as Indonesia, Iran, Japan, Senegal and the Philippines. By 26 August only 26 of the 60 diplomatic missions in Kuwait were still manned, but several left each week from then on. By late September, fewer than 20 foreign missions in Kuwait remained, some with as few as two diplomats. The Belgians, Danes, Dutch, Greeks, Italians and Spanish were still in town, but left in early October. The West Germans went on 11 October, and the Canadians on the 18th, against the wishes of a number of their resident diplomats.

The Indians had been among the first to comply with the closure order, but had moved their consular operations to a school in Salmiya, beefed up their Basra consulate to service their thousands of people in Kuwait, and removed any political presence in a compromise which satisfied the Iraqis. The Philippines Embassy, still with power and water, was struggling along. A few diplomats were trying to organize evacuations, and cope with 3,000 desperate civilians camped in nearby abandoned houses or building sites.

By mid-October, Indonesia was the only Far Eastern country still operating, but Iraq was loath to alienate the world's most populous Muslim nation. Nevertheless, they too left. By the month's end, only the American, British, Iranian, and a handful of Asian and Arab embassies were left. The French had gone in the last week of October, when their nationals were released.

The Iranians were in a particularly enviable position. The Iraqis did not dare antagonize them for fear of upsetting the uneasy peace Saddam had just established with his long-time foe, and reopening another front on his eastern flank. This proved particularly useful to the Kuwaitis as the Iranians were prepared to issue papers to Kuwaitis of Persian origin, especially military officers being sought by the Iraqis. Many of these people escaped through the Iraq-Iran border post of Shalamcha, and rejoined the Kuwaiti forces regrouping in Saudi Arabia. The Bahrainis also issued their passports to wanted Kuwaitis, especially members of the Al-Sabah, thus allowing them to escape through Iraq into Jordan or Iran. So too did the Yemenis. Of all the diplomats, the only one who stayed in Kuwait throughout the entire occupation was the gutsy Ambassador of tiny Bahrain.

The major diplomatic mission in Kuwait at the time was undoubtedly the US Embassy, on the Gulf Road, a kilometre south of the Dasman Palace. It was on a 5-acre seaside compound leased from the Amir of Bahrain, surrounded by a three-metre high tank-proof concrete wall, topped with razor wire and dubbed by the besieged Americans 'Camp Kuwait'.

After the non-essential personnel had left in the 23 August 'Convoy to Hell' there were 28 individuals in the compound: eight diplomats, 19 American civilian men who were granted safe-haven, and the Ambassador's Pakistani houseboy. Only the houseboy and three men of Arab extraction left before the release of all hostages in December; two of these joined the Human Shield.

The ranking US diplomat in Kuwait was Ambassador W. Nathaniel Howell III, a distinguished diplomat who had served in Kuwait since August 1987. Howell was no stranger to crisis, having been in Cairo during the 1967 Six-Day War, in the UAE during the 1973 war, and in Lebanon from 1974 to 1976, when his Ambassador and several colleagues had been killed. He was determined to keep the embassy staffed as long as possible, 'until,' as he told his son early in the occupation, 'I could accept the Iraqi surrender'.

The compound was run on a day-to-day basis by Deputy Chief of Mission (DCM) Barbara Bodine, a very capable and feisty thirty-something lady with one year's service in Kuwait. Although Howell was popular and capable, his usual job was to deal with the government on matters of policy. In occupied Kuwait, the legitimate government was in exile, so the key roles in the embassy became those of the DCM, as his Chief of Staff, and the Consul.

The Consul was also a young lady, Gale Rogers, who had first arrived in Kuwait days before the invasion. Gale had hardly seen anything beyond her office before the Iraqis arrived. Her husband had not even arrived to join her. It was a credit to her that she coped in the circumstances.

The other five US diplomats were Chief Administrative Officer Wayne Logsdon, his wife Mimi, Administrative Officer Mark Hertzberg, and Communicators Jeff Jugar and Connie Parrish. The communicators were probably the most critical people in the compound. Without them, the embassy could not talk with Washington. It would have had to close.

Although Howell was undoubtedly the formal authority in the compound, most people who talked to the embassy from outside were under the impression that Bodine was running the show. Very few Americans or other nationals – including other diplomats – spoke to the Ambassador during the crisis. Some of us were not even sure if he was in the embassy. Most of the civilian men in the compound actually found him quite aloof until late September, when most of the US women and children had been evacuated. After that, he seemed to drop the facade, and became almost one of the boys, although to some he was always 'Sir', or 'Mr Ambassador'.

Although the Americans had to destroy or bury all the perishable food when the Iraqis cut their power, the compound was well stocked with bulk rice, canned tuna, breakfast cereals, and MREs (Meals-Ready-To-Eat), thanks mainly to the foresight of the departed USLOK personnel in the first three weeks of the occupation. The embassy started out with 6,000 cans of tuna, various other canned goods, 400 kilograms of rice, 200 frozen turkeys, plenty of pasta and tomato and hot sauce. They still had 4,000 cans of the tuna and most of the MREs, and 100 days of drinking water, when they left in December - enough to survive beyond Easter 1991, not that anyone wanted the ordeal to go on for that long.

The US communications equipment allowed the embassy to speak with and exchange faxes and telexes with Washington, and any other US embassy in the world, by satellite. The transmissions were encrypted so the Iraqis could not read them. All other secure communications systems had been destroyed or disabled, along with their encryption codes. In the event of a sudden Iraqi move on the embassy, the one remaining system could be destroyed quickly. Both communicators slept in the communications room, known as 'The Snakepit', so they could react instantly in the event of a night-time attack.

This satellite communications equipment, and the local phones, provided the main practical service of the embassy to their community in hiding by allowing them to pass brief messages to loved ones at home, and co-ordinate the evacuation efforts. Curiously, it would have been incredibly easy for the Iraqis to disable the Americans' communications with a single sniper shot into their satellite dish, which was visible from the Kuwait International Hotel.

The US communications were a blessing to many other countries, particularly when the equipment of those such as Canada and France failed, and for countries without embassies in Kuwait, or who had left, leaving civilians behind. The US eventually provided communications for 17 different nationalities in Kuwait. Those people provided a fine source of intelligence for the Americans, but caused a great deal of work for Barbara Bodine and her communicators. We have always been very grateful for that service.

All the US diplomats who stayed behind in Kuwait were volunteers. Ambassador Howell and DCM Bodine had selected the various specialities and skills they required for a siege prior to the evacuation of non-essential personnel. This came to about 16 individuals, which was initially approved by Washington.

Howell reduced this in an attempt to get as many people out as possible. Washington then cut the number to eight. To their delight, Howell and Bodine had more volunteers than they could accept.

The work of liaising with people outside the compound was split between Gale Rogers and Barbara Bodine. Rogers dealt almost exclusively with the Americans, and ran the 'Air Rogers' evacuations. Bodine dealt with the free-nationals, other embassies and, infrequently, the Iraqis. There was a reason for her being the contact with the Iraqis. If they demanded an instant answer on some issue, she could buy time by saying she had to consult the Ambassador.

One of Gale's main problems in running the air evacuation was actually convincing women still in Kuwait that the current flight was their absolutely final opportunity to leave. Many of the people qualified to leave on these flights were Arabs with US passports who wanted to stay as long as possible. The Americans took them all out, but tried to get them to leave quickly. Gale did not want a panicked rush if the crisis suddenly took a turn for the worse.

Some of the dealings with Arab nationals taken out on the evacuation flights were extremely frustrating. US immigration law at the time apparently allowed all immediate family members of a US passport holder, comprising parents, children and siblings, to be evacuated. In some cases, the only US passport holder in a family was a child who had been 'conveniently' born in the US. One family of 11 went out on the strength of a two-year-old's passport, but the case that took the prize for cheek was that of a woman who had delivered her baby in the US shortly before or after the invasion, obtained a US passport for the child, then returned to Kuwait via Jordan and Iraq, and took out about 20 family members on an evacuation flight to the US. They could have gone overland to their real home country, but used the system to go directly to the US where, to no one's surprise, they applied to stay.

The 19 US civilian men taking refuge in their embassy were a mixed but very capable bunch, and the diplomats were exceedingly fortunate that these men brought a wide range of handyman skills with them. In fact, it was largely due to them that the embassy survived, especially when trouble arose with the generators for the communications systems.

The embassy's main problems during the crisis were the shortage of diesel fuel for the generators, and mechanical problems. The compound actually had three generators: a diesel-powered main set which could run everything in the compound; a second, smaller diesel unit exclusively for the satellite communications; and a small Honda gasoline unit to power lights and appliances such as the fax machine, power tools, TV and video.

In the early stages of the occupation, they had been using the main generator, but stopped doing so after 23 August because of its heavy fuel consumption. If the main set had been kept running after the compound was sealed off, it would have consumed all the fuel within a few days. To use the second, smaller, communications generator, two engineers among the men, Jack Rinehart and Ron Webster, had to rewire the compound's electrical distribution boards – without the manuals. This was a major feat in itself, one which no one would have believed possible under the circumstances.

During the early weeks of the siege, the diplomats ran their communications for eight hours a day. They then cut it down to four to conserve fuel, then three and two. By late November, they were talking to Washington only every second day. Their fuel at the end of the siege was enough for only a few more days. Unknown to Saddam, if he had delayed releasing the Westerners by a week, he may well have forced the embassy out of business.

The skills and energy of these men were useful in other ways. The embassy had plenty of long-life milk and drinking water. The big problem was water for washing, which was a real issue without air conditioning in the summer heat, and later with the autumn humidity. The swimming pool was full of water, but without mains power they could not run the pump. Contrary to news reports at the time, which were disinformation put out by a departee, the Americans never drank the pool water, although it made a great siege story.

One of the civilians, Paul Brown, a landscape architect, decided that the compound was so close to the coast that the water table must not be very deep. The men had dug a hole to fill sandbags - using State Department mailbags - for a bunker in the embassy basement. Paul kept on digging after all the sandbags were full. The others initially laughed at him, but the laughter subsided when he struck water four metres down in mid-October after two weeks of digging. The water was not potable, but was fine for bathing, laundry, and irrigation. In fact, there was so much of it that it gushed 50 feet into the air when connected to a pump. Some of the diplomats took to washing their cars parked inside the compound, much to the disgust of the Iraqis watching them from atop the Kuwait International Hotel across the road.

This not only provided delightful propaganda for the State Department, but Paul and another man, Charles Carradine, then built a primitive hot water system by pumping the water through pipes laid out on the hot iron roofs of the buildings, and through tanks painted black to absorb the sun's heat. The residents of the compound were thus able to have warm showers every afternoon until winter began to set in during November.

More importantly, the water irrigated a 200-foot long vegetable garden, fertilised with the destroyed perishable food, and started with seeds provided by the Ambassador. It was lovingly tended by a Moroccan-American, El-Miloudi Hamid, from Tennessee. The Americans were able to enjoy home-grown onions, radishes, lettuce, peas, beans, watermelon and turnips with their scant Thanksgiving dinner in late November.

Bennie Mitchell, one of the HAWK missile men, proved invaluable in maintaining the local phone service so that the Americans could talk to people outside the compound. The Iraqis progressively cut off most of the embassy's lines as they found them, but Mitchell always found new local lines which had lain dormant for years. This was particularly difficult as there were no wiring diagrams of incoming lines available. He had no previous training in phone systems, and had to teach himself as he went along.

The other men generally pitched in where they could, especially with the cooking, cleaning, laundry, watch-keeping and answering the phone to the Americans in hiding, and other Westerners dealing with the embassy. There were a few exceptions, but most people pulled their weight. With 24 men on the premises for most of the siege, none of the four women had to lift a finger to do the cooking or most other chores.

With limited water and primitive plumbing, there was one toilet and one shower stall for the men. The women had separate facilities. Health and hygiene were taken very seriously. One man whose duty it was to keep the men's facilities clean literally stood guard outside them every morning to ensure no one entered them until they had dried. Getting rid of the sewage was also critical, but this too had to be kept quiet from the Iraqis. The embassy is connected to the city's main sewer system, but the effluent is pumped out electrically from a cistern. Each week, under cover of darkness, from a position behind the wall, the Americans had to manually pump their own wastes out of the compound into the city system. If the Iraqis had discovered this, they could have blocked the pipes and made life even more uncomfortable for them.

Jack Rinehart, one of the men who kept the generators going, had another useful skill. He was an amateur gunsmith, and the embassy was woefully short of arms. The US Marine guards had disabled all the embassy's original weapons early in August following a misunderstanding over orders from Washington, and the only weapon available was the Beretta pistol brought in by USLOK commander Colonel Mooneyham on 14 August. Rinehart set to work with Communicator Jeff Jugar and between them they managed to get four shotguns in working order, cannibalizing parts from other weapons. If there was an attack, and they needed to buy enough time to get a message out and then smash the communications equipment, at least now they had the means. The guns were secured in the communications area, and allocated to Jeff, his colleague Connie Parrish, Jack, and Ron Webster, under the direction of the DCM. They were to be used only as a last resort.

In any event, the use of deadly force was the sole prerogative of the Ambassador, and Howell was not about to have anyone make a heroic last stand and go home dead. There was never any intention to defend the compound against an Iraqi attack. The basement bunker was to be used if the Iraqis came over the wall shooting, to give them time to calm down and realize that no one was firing back at them, or in case of war or a Special Forces rescue attempt. The bunker interior was barricaded with sturdy tables, and reinforced with steel safes welded together. A steel basketball goal post was used to brace the roof. It was equipped with food, water, medical supplies, toilet facilities and gas masks – one for everyone on the compound. Even the high-decibel diversionary sound system could be controlled from it.

The Americans were not above using a little deception on the Iraqis to reduce the risk of a forced takeover. They constantly tried to convey the impression that they were running out of food, so the Iraqis would expect that they would give themselves up soon, and avoid the trouble of moving in. In mid-September, just after the raids on other missions, the State Department said that the earliest the lack of food, water and other necessities would cause the embassy to close would be about September 17 or 19. At the end of October, Washington was saying quite openly that the embassy was down to a three-to-four week supply of canned tuna fish and rice, and was running low on generator fuel. The latter part was true, but they had far more food than that.

The compound was in fact under almost constant satellite surveillance, day and night. The Americans prepared for almost every eventuality they could, and even had a series of prearranged visual signals with Washington which could be seen by the satellite. This included an infra-red reflector which could be seen at night from space, but looked totally innocuous to the Iraqis. In the event of a takeover where communications had to be rapidly destroyed or had failed, the Americans simply had to tip over the reflector. Washington would then know that the Iraqis were in control.

With the internal power and intercoms out, and two dozen people spread across a sprawling compound, each individual or group was issued with a walkie-talkie, and a codename. The Americans knew the Iraqis would be listening, so took delight in confounding them. For example, one of Ron Webster's jobs was to read the fuel level in the generators, and radio this to the communicators. He would transmit the quantity in units of 'goat bladders'.

Ron was a large southerner who looked like an Alabama sheriff. When in the Plaza Hotel before moving to the embassy, he had been nicknamed 'Deputy Dawg'. In the embassy, he was 'Longhorn'. The Ambassador was '99', Barbara Bodine, 'Kestrel', and Gale Rogers, 'Gazelle'. Two other men were 'Ramblin' Wreck' and 'Chicken'. I became 'Skippy', as their main Australian contact. The Irish warden was Leprechaun I, and his deputy Leprechaun II.

To keep the radio batteries charged without using up precious diesel, Ron rigged up a charging system using an alternator from one of the cars in the compound. Cars were cannibalized for other purposes. Radiator fans were used as cooling fans, powered by car batteries, and dome lights rigged up in living quarters, also run off the batteries, allowed the Americans to read at night.

Not all the plans to improve the lot of the Americans in the compound were successful. The diplomats asked Washington for advice on making 'turkey jerky' by drying the meat over a children's jungle gym, and curing it in a smokehouse. The results had to be buried as unchewable. Another man, Sergio Ado, caught a few pigeons for the Thanksgiving dinner, but when they told Washington, the State Department said that they couldn't eat city pigeons. It wasn't clear whether they meant Washington DC pigeons or Kuwait City pigeons, which were probably far less affected by pollution. Paul Brown offered to try one, but was voted down. The birds were reprieved.

Once the basic requirements of food, water and hygiene had been catered for, and the diplomats and men with them had done everything they could for the Americans in hiding, they had to keep their own morale up. Tennis tournaments, backgammon, and pool competitions were held. They even organised the First Annual Hostage Halloween Ball in October. The DCM turned up as Mickey Mouse, and one of the men as 'Superhostage', complete with red cape and boots. The Ambassador, who had a set of US Army desert camouflage fatigues, came as 'The Liberating Allied Forces'.

Although the Americans had the the largest mission in Kuwait, the nearby British Embassy was responsible for the majority of Westerners in the country.

When the Iraqis ordered the embassies to close, Ambassador Michael Weston reportedly started to pack up, but Whitehall told him that he was staying. Her Majesty's Government was not about to accede to an illegal Iraqi order. At the time, the diplomats fully expected that the Iraqis would enter their compound within two or three days of the closure order.

A few days after the compounds were sealed off, just as it was clear that the Iraqis were unlikely to move in, the morale of the four British diplomats was buoyed by messages from the Queen and Mrs Thatcher telling them what splendid chaps they were. The FCO then posed a serious question: 'How long can you last?' At the time, they estimated they could go to the end of September, barely five weeks. In fact, Ambassador Weston and Larry Banks stayed until mid-December, and could have gone longer, with difficulty.

The core of the besieged British team comprised Ambassador Weston, who had been in Kuwait since March 1990, and his Consul, Larry Banks. A further two men, Commercial Attaché Don Macauley, and Security Officer Brian McKeith remained in the embassy until they left for Baghdad on 6 October. All other British diplomats and their dependents had been evacuated to Baghdad in August. The diplomats also had Malcolm, the Sri Lankan Club Steward, together with his two daughters, but he proved to be a rotten cook and was asked to leave the premises in early September. The Ambassador himself then took over the cooking, and by all accounts did a good job of it.

The men actually lived on the verandah of Ambassador's Residence, which is over the embassy's offices. With the heat, and in the absence of fans or air-conditioning, they made up beds on the verandah, using the swimming pool lounging beds, in the hope of gaining some relief from the heat through the breeze. Their one phone was moved there thanks to a long length of wire they found, and the verandah became their office, bedrooms, dining room and salon.

There were no civilian Britons in Her Majesty's compound. In fact, several people who sought refuge were turned away. The reasons for this were that the diplomats did not have the supplies to feed them and, more importantly, they fully expected that the Iraqis would take over the embassy. The Ambassador was vindicated in this assessment when the three French civilians arrested during the September raid on the French Ambassador's Residence were taken away, but the sole French diplomat was released.

After Macauley and McKeith left, Messrs Weston and Banks had only each other for company. The compound had a high concrete security wall, so they felt relatively safe. They were a little more fortunate than the Americans in that the nearest tall buildings were far enough away from the perimeter to allow them some privacy from prying Iraqis.

When asked by London in October how they were coping, the two British diplomats sarcastically reported that they were spending their evenings sipping champagne by candlelight on the balcony of the Ambassador's Residence. It was classic British stiff upper lip. London passed the comment on to the BBC, who broadcast it and caused a storm of criticism to descend on the heads of the two men from their community in hiding. No one wanted people at home to think that their ordeal even remotely resembled a holiday. The two berated diplomats began to wonder just who their enemies were: the Iraqis outside, or a loose-lipped colleague back home who liked to talk to the press. They had enjoyed champagne by candlelight on the first night they were sealed off. After that, they had insufficient electricity from their generators to waste on refrigeration, so drank warm beer by streetlight.

With fewer people, supplies were less critical for the British, but they did have shortages, especially of fresh produce. They had plenty of water in roof tanks, ground tanks, and 1,000 gallons in the fire system for a new office building. They also had a swimming pool and garden pond which could be used for washing and irrigation. The British also dug a well. They actually had a six-foot head start on the Americans, and struck water after only a metre of digging, two days after Paul Brown. Their well was started in an open grave which had been prepared for Dame Violet Dickson, the widow of Kuwait's most distinguished British Political Agent. At the time of the invasion, Dame Violet had been hospitalized for several months, and was expected to pass away at any time. The ground in which the grave rested had already been consecrated, so the British well was known as 'Holy Water'.

They too planted a vegetable garden, and Mr Banks became known affectionately throughout the British community in hiding as 'Larry the Gardener'. The British diet was a little more varied than that of the Americans, with canned chicken frankfurters, curries, rice, and home-grown vegetables once Larry Banks' garden began to bear fruit.

When they left in December, Messrs Weston and Banks had enough rice and pasta for six months, but only half a tin of protein each day between two of them until the end of January 1991. Despite the vegetable garden, their main problem was lack of vitamin C. Prophetically, after several weeks in the embassy, they had told London they they could go until 28 February, 1991, which was two days after Allied forces actually reached Kuwait City.

Like the Americans, the British also had three generators, and limited, if secure, communications comprising a secure radio telex, rather than a sophisticated satellite telephone/telex/fax unit, and a voice radio which could be run off car batteries, with a range as far as Abu Dhabi. However, they only had 170 gallons of diesel on the compound at the start of the siege, which was merely enough to cope with an ordinary power cut.

The main British generator used a gallon of diesel an hour, and was the only one that could power the secure communications. A second set provided emergency power for the new office building. It was never used. The final unit was a small Tooley-Hatz model which only consumed a gallon every four hours, and was run for two hours each day to pump water, make ice, charge batteries, and power a hotplate after the diplomats used up their cooking gas.

Mike Weston apparently decided that there was no real need for secure communications, so the main generator was dispensed with early on, especially with their dire fuel situation. Instead, they relied exclusively on the Tooley-Hatz and the battery-powered voice radio, speaking to Abu Dhabi up to four times a day. This caused some concern to the men in hiding as they knew the Iraqis could listen in with ease. A few people saw their own embassy as a security risk. Nevertheless, there was nothing they could do. Of more importance was the fact that with the higher number of people involved, the security risk of identifying to the Iraqis just who was in Kuwait, and the sheer workload, the British diplomats could not pass personal messages for the men in hiding as the Americans were doing. An individual's status was reported home only if there were a serious problem, such as death or capture. The British had secure communications available for an emergency as they could have turned on the main generator, but they never used it.

They could also use the car batteries, salvaged from 15 vehicles in the compound, to power a 4" black-and-white TV. This supplemented the battery-powered shortwave radio which was used to listen to the BBC World Service. Unfortunately, they could only pick up Iraqi TV, but at least they knew what both the BBC and the Iraqis were saying.

The British community were more in need of embassy staff than the Americans purely because there were so many more of them. After the evacuation of the women and children, about 600 British men were in hiding, compared to fewer than 200 Americans. British groups in hiding averaged about four individuals; some men were on their own; others in groups of up to twelve. It was impossible for only two British diplomats to keep in touch with about 150 groups.

Messrs Weston and Banks were therefore fortunate to have a far more effective warden system than the Americans, and a locally employed Indian Vice-Consul, Mr Raj Gopolan, who had been in the embassy's service for a generation, and his Palestinian colleague, Mr Musallim. In fact, it was widely considered that the British wardens ran their community during the crisis, with the embassy functioning as an adjunct of the warden system.

Whatever the shortfalls of the British Embassy during the occupation, it was widely credited with redeeming itself immediately after liberation in February 1991. The 30 or so British who stayed throughout the occupation were granted easy access to Ambassador Weston, who even arranged for them to meet Prime Minister John Major when he flew in. Weston supplied these diehards with all manner of requirements such as gas cylinders, portable generators, lamps, food and water before basic services were restored. The British were way ahead of the other embassies in this regard.

All Western embassies other than the Americans, the British, and the French left Kuwait before their civilians were allowed to leave Kuwait and Iraq, although the Italian diplomats left Kuwait for Baghdad with all their civilians. The story behind this is a sorry tale of ambassadors and Foreign Ministries deceiving the public, and abandoning their nationals against the wishes of more junior staffers on the ground.

There seemed to be a conspiracy between most of the Continental European ambassadors and their Foreign Ministries at home to present a more desperate picture of the suffering of their diplomats in Kuwait than was the case. News reports were heard on the shortwave services about European diplomats facing starvation. When we called our diplomat friends, they knew nothing of this. They were not comfortable, but their situation was by no means desperate, and most of the younger diplomats were determined to stay in Kuwait until their civilian nationals were allowed to leave. The Foreign Ministries were actually using these broadcasts to lay the groundwork for the withdrawal of their diplomats from Kuwait.

In fact, the Belgian DCM, Bart Ouvry, and his Dutch colleague reportedly threatened to quit on the spot rather than leave their nationals behind, but they were forced to go. Swiss DCM Bernhard Bischoff was also unhappy about going. In fact, Bischoff was actually running the Swiss Embassy as his Ambassador seemed to have all but disappeared.

There was a similar split in the German and Italian ranks. During September, a young West German diplomat, Oliver Rentschler, manned the embassy alone. All other remaining German male diplomats were in the Ambassador's Residence nearby, and the females had been evacuated to Baghdad. The West Germans had been using the residence as living quarters, and staffing the embassy, where the communications equipment was installed, 24 hours a day, on a roster. The Iraqis suddenly sealed off the embassy with Oliver alone inside, and cut those telephone lines they were aware of.

This did not bother Oliver, who reconnected the phone to a little-known fax line to maintain contact with his community and his colleagues in the residence. He had supplies of canned food and drinking water. His main problem was that the weather was still hot in September, and there was no water for washing, or power for air-conditioning. Every hour during the night, the Iraqi soldiers outside fired a round or two over the building to keep him awake. Nevertheless, Oliver, whose nationals were candidates for the Human Shield if caught, was able to maintain contact with Bonn.

Oliver was probably the only member of the West German Embassy staff in Kuwait at the time that his community would not have cheerfully lynched. However, he had to follow orders. Both the German Foreign Ministry and his Ambassador wanted the diplomats to move to Baghdad without losing face, so greatly exaggerated their hardships. Oliver and some of his other European and Canadian colleagues left with great reluctance.

The disagreements within embassies was given a strange twist as German Reunification had been agreed before the invasion, but not yet formalized. At the time, both the East and West German embassies were functioning in Kuwait. In the early days of the occupation, East Germany was virtually an ally of Iraq. Some Iraqi security services had been modelled on or trained by the *Stasi*. Men on East German passports could therefore leave Iraq, but West Germans became Human Shields. In fact, the East German Ambassador had issued passports to several Britons who came to him, and they left Iraq successfully on these. He himself gained a great deal of sympathy within the Diplomatic Corps. Not only did he lose his embassy, but also his job and his country when he returned home, because of Reunification.

In the midst of this unseemly rush to evacuate Kuwait, even if it meant leaving nationals behind who had a well-founded fear of relocating to Baghdad, the French were particular heroes, especially their *chargé d'affaires*, Jean-Pierre Galtier, and Military Attaché Colonel Edouard Crespin. Not only did they stay until all their nationals were allowed out in late October, but earlier in the crisis, when the US and British embassies were advising people against cross-desert escape attempts to Saudi Arabia, Crespin was handing out maps to all-comers.

The recipients did not necessarily get out successfully, but at least they had the option, and a map. Later, when the French were released, they smuggled out three Americans disguised as Frenchmen, and Martin Sullivan, the British husband of a Frenchwoman.

The problems of the major Western embassies and their nationals were insignificant compared with those of embassies from Bangladesh, the Philippines, Sri Lanka and Thailand. Although the Iraqis were less intent on closing them down and did not cut their power, water and telephones, the Third World diplomats faced incredible problems with thousands of their desperate and impoverished nationals, and limited resources.

In particular, many of the Filipinos in Kuwait were single females working as domestic helpers. Thousands of these women were left alone to fend for themselves when their Kuwaiti and other employers left, or were caught outside Kuwait at the time of the invasion. Others were turned back at the Saudi border. Some were able to live off the food left behind in their employers' houses, or sell electrical goods to survive, but many had nowhere to turn except to their diplomats.

The embassy, with only four diplomats, tried to accommodate the crowds on their premises, and in vacant houses nearby. Finding food for them was a desperate battle. The US Embassy helped by arranging a US$35,000 line of credit with the Kuwait Danish Dairy, and providing rice and milk. Many Kuwaitis also helped with cash and rice, but it was impossible to feed everyone. The only solution was to get them out of Kuwait.

To aggravate matters, the Popular Army, which had replaced most of the disciplined Iraqi troops in the suburbs, was now guarding the embassy. Some of the Popular Army and PLO men, and Arab Liberation Front militia imported from Baghdad, would take the women almost at will to rape them.

The problems of these people were publicized by the Norwegian Ambassador to Kuwait, Hans Longva, whose wife is Vietnamese, when he left Kuwait in early September. He described them as dwarfing the trials of the tens of thousands of refugees in the camps on the Iraq-Jordan border, and told how hundreds of thousands of poor Asian workers were trapped in Kuwait without food or shelter when their residential camps were taken over to house Iraqi troops. The world at that time was mobilizing to address the problems of the refugees in Jordan, but could do little for the people in Kuwait. They were out of sight of the TV cameras, so were all but forgotten.

Despite being ostensibly firm allies in the Saudi desert, the American and British embassies in Kuwait were seldom on the best of terms. In fact for several weeks they were not even talking to each other.

The main reason for this appeared to be the American perception that the British diplomats were staying purely to keep the flag flying, and were doing very little for their people. The Americans felt they were staying to help their people in hiding, whereas the British seemed to believe that staying was its own goal. This seemed to be confirmed later when the last US diplomats left almost as soon as Saddam released all their nationals in December. The British made a point of gallantly staying an extra day so as to be the last Western diplomats out of Kuwait. The American attitude at that time was that 400,000 Americans and a division of crack British troops in Saudi Arabia could make the point to Saddam far more effectively than a few diplomats sticking their necks out unnecessarily.

The trouble between the Americans and the British seemed to start when the BBC virtually advised British nationals to comply with the Iraqi order of 15 August to report to specified hotels in Kuwait. This advice had been given to the BBC by the FCO acting in turn on the advice of its embassy in Kuwait. The Americans also relayed the same order, but gave less of an impression that the US Government endorsed it. The British Ambassador was supposedly furious at the Americans, and baffled. He and the Americans had consulted on the advice to be given to their people, and it seemed as if the Americans were acting differently from the agreed course of action.

The Americans were again horrified in early September at the hastily organized British road evacuation of the women and children to Baghdad, without an accompanying Baghdad-based diplomat, especially after the harrowing experiences of the British Embassy convoy of 16 August and the American Embassy convoy of 23 August. The Americans felt that the British had not learned anything from the previous convoys.

Several of the US diplomats, unaware that the British had expected to be overrun within days of the closure order and had not stocked up for the siege, were also annoyed at the British refusal to give refuge on their embassy compound to British civilians, or Commonwealth nationals without embassies in Kuwait. They were also upset that the British initially declined to help the Canadians and the French when their communications failed, although the British diplomats had more than enough on their hands with their own large community. The Americans did not mind helping out the other countries, but a few of them felt that the British should be doing more to help fellow Commonwealth and EC countries. For much of the time, the Americans felt that the British were out of touch, and simply 'on another planet'.

Despite the shortcomings of the embassies in Kuwait, we were certainly glad to have them around. They offered a vital if tenuous link to legitimate authority in an otherwise lawless environment, and particularly a vicarious link to our loved ones at home. Those of us who did not have our own diplomatic missions in Kuwait seldom took them for granted.

The diplomats had to be admired for staying. It took courage to remain at their posts in the besieged embassies. This applied particularly to the Americans, British and French who stayed until all their people could leave. They could have left at any time for the relative safety of their accredited embassies in Baghdad. The diplomats did more than keep the flag flying, or even service their nationals. They showed the Iraqis in a very practical way that the world was prepared to stand up to them, even at a price.

15. THE WARDEN SYSTEMS

The greatest asset of most foreign communities in occupied Kuwait was their national warden system. In normal circumstances, over 11,000 Westerners and Japanese lived in Kuwait. Given these numbers, it was impossible for the embassy consular staffs to maintain direct contact with everyone. Furthermore, those countries without embassies in Kuwait needed someone on the ground. Prior to the invasion, many embassies had therefore appointed volunteers as wardens. These people generally attended regular briefings at the embassies, or whenever the level of tension rose. Their primary function was to allow the embassies to disseminate information to their communities quickly and efficiently. A warden was responsible for passing messages from his embassy to anywhere from thirty to several hundred people or family groups. The better organized embassies maintained databases of people registered with them, and distributed lists to the wardens. This original function grew to encompass far more critical tasks during the occupation.

There were three main structures for warden systems: *national, cascade* and *geographic.* The national system applied to smaller communities without embassies in Kuwait where one or two wardens could keep in touch with everyone in their community, and act as a single point of contact for their own embassy or the embassy responsible for their interests in Kuwait. The cascade and geographic systems were used by major embassies such as the American and British. In each, the wardens' main point of contact was the Consul.

In the geographic system, which was used by the British, wardens were appointed for specific suburbs, and were responsible for some or all of their nationals in that suburb. They had about 40 wardens in normal times, each responsible for about 50 to 100 families. The system was supplemented by specific wardens for organizations with a large number of British employees.

The cascade system, adopted by the Americans, used people who were generally in contact with a large number of their compatriots, such as senior business executives, hotel general managers, and others such as the pastor of the Evangelical Church, and representatives of the American Women's League (AWL). In fact, the AWL wardens were among the most effective, as many of them were married to Kuwaitis. The idea was for each warden to pass information on to other people, who would pass it on again, 'cascading' it down the system like a fountain until, in theory, everyone had received it.

Each system had its pros and cons. In normal circumstances, the cascade system allowed easier passage of information. Some cascade wardens could use their organizations' own internal systems for this. However, the information could get lost or changed between the multiple levels, and it did not necessarily cover all nationals in the country. It depended on links that worked fine in peacetime but were completely disrupted after the invasion.

The flow of information in the geographic system was not quite as smooth.

The wardens did not always know the people in their area personally. However, it could potentially cover everyone in the country, and was less dependent on a particular individual warden. It had built-in redundancy. If the warden for a particular area was missing, then it was far easier for someone from that same area to replace him, regardless of who he worked for. It had some notable gaps, but most people were covered.

The differing features of these systems were to prove crucial to the ability of the Western communities in Kuwait, and their embassies, to care for themselves and avoid capture under occupation conditions.

The operation of the warden system in practice was a mix of good fortune, individual dedication, and failure. There were only about 5,000 Westerners and Japanese in Kuwait at the time of the invasion. Many people were on leave, particularly families taking advantage of the summer school holidays, and hundreds of teachers employed by the University and foreign schools were out of the country, leaving only a handful taking summer schools. The embassies and warden systems therefore had far fewer people to cope with than they would have had if Saddam had invaded a month later. This was to be one of their great salvations.

Working against this was the absence of many wardens themselves on leave. Two weeks before the invasion, when the tension was rising, the Americans found that many of their key wardens were away, and so had to look for replacements. They were still doing so when the Iraqis arrived.

The British had placed an advertisement in both of Kuwait's English-language newspapers during late July, reminding people to register with the embassy. There was no particular sense of urgency about the notice. The British then asked the Americans over to compare notes on what arrangements they had made for the summer. At the time, most of the wardens' lists were hopelessly out of date or non-existent. Many people had not bothered to register with their embassy, or to advise it when they left the country. In fact, since the August 1988 ceasefire in the Iran–Iraq War, the warden systems had become almost dormant in the absence of any identifiable threat.

Despite the generally better pre-invasion preparation on the part of the Americans, their warden system fell apart in the first week as wardens escaped from Kuwait across the desert, moved into safer houses or, with a few notable exceptions, simply failed to perform. Most Americans did not know who their wardens were, and even where wardens knew who they should be contacting, many people had moved in with others, and were not contactable at their usual home numbers. The Americans were thus at a particular disadvantage with their cascade system. It was based on the contacts people had in normal circumstances, but the invasion turned everything on its head. Many Americans began to contact their embassy directly, thus circumventing the warden system and defeating its purpose.

A week after the round-up order, two major incidents shattered the confidence in the embassy of the American civilians, and some of their wardens. The final wardens' meeting was called in the embassy for the evening of 22 August. The round-up order had been in effect for a week, but some of the Iraqi troops on the checkpoints were still unaware of it. The wardens who attended had to risk getting picked up on their way to or from the embassy. They felt that the embassy was seriously out of touch with the situation, and had put them in danger unnecessarily.

The American wardens then heard that the non-essential diplomats, and all the diplomats' dependents and pets, would be leaving for Baghdad on 23 August. Up to that point, the embassy had been telling the civilians that everyone would go out together in an evacuation. The civilians and wardens, however unfairly, felt that they had been strung along.

The remains of the American system suffered another body-blow when the American women and children left in September. With them went most of the AWL ladies, who were some of their most pro-active wardens.

There was never a real attempt to reconstruct the American warden system after that. The American diplomats, assisted by civilians taking refuge with them, had to contact most of their nationals directly. With a summer population of probably fewer than 800 Americans without dual Arab or Asian nationalities, in about 200 family or other groups, this was just manageable. Later, in November, when wardens of various countries started holding co-ordinating meetings, the US Embassy appointed Mrs Beth-Ann Mutairi, the American wife of a Kuwaiti, as their representative to this group, but a broad-based warden system never grew from this. However, at that stage, there was less need for American wardens as there were only slightly over 100 American men in hiding. The US diplomats were able to handle this number by telephoning them directly, where the phone system allowed this.

The British got off to a slower start. There were no calls to the wardens from the embassy in the early hours of 2 August to warn people to stay inside, mainly because the British Consul himself had been captured on his way to the embassy. Several Britons were therefore captured on their way to work, and were either released after a few hours, or became the first members of the Human Shield. There were also no orders from the BLT's Colonel Duncan for his men and their families to evacuate the IBI Camp – an obvious target – and move in with colleagues in the suburbs. Contingency plans to evacuate the camp in an emergency were simply never implemented beyond the first stage.

However, the British wardens out in the suburbs, acting largely on their own initiative, started to compile and correct their lists by contacting people in their areas. Areas without wardens were identified, and wardens found for most of them. This is how I became one. Within ten days of the invasion, most British nationals in Kuwait had a local warden.

In time, the British warden system became the most effective and certainly the most important system of any major country in occupied Kuwait. Many people saw it as virtually taking over the management of the British community from its embassy. The embassy was still vital for communicating with the outside world, but most other critical tasks were carried out by the wardens. Whereas the US Embassy arranged for medicine and food for those in dire need, or refuge for those with nowhere to go, it was the British wardens or free-nationals helping them who did this for their people.

The two pillars of the British system were a 44-year-old Scottish engineer, Sandy Macmillan, and the organization that became known amongst parts of the community as 'Command Central', run by Englishmen Brian Ashwell, Mike Devey, Geoff French and Mel Gage. As luck would have it, these men lived in or near the suburbs in which about 65% of their nationals lived. Another warden, Richard Hattersley, covered the suburb of Jabriya where a further 15% of the British were in hiding. The wardens began to describe their people as their 'parishioners', as though the wardens were pastors or shepherds with flocks. It was not an inaccurate metaphor.

All of these wardens were initially geographically based, which made it much easier for them to keep in touch with the people in their areas and to build up a comprehensive picture of what was going on around them. This proved invaluable on many occasions. If an explosion or house-to-house search occurred nearby, they were able to ring around and place it fairly accurately and quickly, thus scotching the inevitable wild rumours. Similarly, if people had to be visited personally to be talked out of depression or given supplies, the wardens could usually do so at night within the boundaries of the suburb without attracting Iraqi attention. The geographic system also allowed captured wardens to be replaced easily, and new wardens to join the system.

The only two British wardens not initially geographically based were Colonel Bruce Duncan, codenamed 'Big Nose', and a middle-aged banker, Ralph Williams. Duncan covered his remaining uncaptured men until he himself left for Baghdad in tragic circumstances in late October. Ralph Williams covered all Western employees of the National Bank of Kuwait, and scores of British women married to Kuwaitis in his area. Most of these ladies had been out of touch with the British community for years.

The distribution of wardens by area blurred as time went on. This seldom mattered as most contact between the communities and wardens was by phone, and free-nationals could do any necessary visiting. Some individuals felt more comfortable dealing with certain wardens. It was a matter of personality. I initially reported to Command Central before I became the warden for my own area, although I was well outside their area. If someone did not have a warden, or was in an unrepresented area, Sandy Macmillan or Command Central took them onto their books. Similarly, if people moved into safer accommodation in an area with a different warden, they usually maintained contact with their original man to build on the rapport and avoid double-counting, but the local warden was advised of the new man in his area. Command Central itself had to move to another suburb at one stage when its security was thought to have been compromised. In fact, this was accomplished by the Director General of Kuwait Airways, Ahmad Al-Zabin and several of his men, moving 22 people through Iraqi-occupied streets, the Western men dressed in *dishdashas* like Kuwaitis, and the women in *abayas*.

There were about eleven other active British wardens. Ideally, they should have been long-term residents, maybe even Arabists. In practice, the embassy was happy to get anyone who was prepared to get involved. Many chose to do the job out of a sense of duty. About the only thing most of them had in common was at least five years in Kuwait. Most of them who were still in Kuwait from September onwards had the contacts and experience to have escaped successfully across the desert to Saudi Arabia in the first week of the invasion, but had made a conscious decision to stay and help.

Most British wardens were typical middle-aged expatriates. Mike Devey was a young grandfather in his mid-forties. He had been a career REME NCO, but had no other training for the crisis. Mel Gage was the Managing Director of a printing press. The others were accountants, engineers, or salesman. I was the youngest, at 30. The eldest was in his 50s. The wardens with the fewest people on their lists covered perhaps a dozen individuals, whereas Sandy Macmillan and Command Central each had over a hundred. Only three of the British wardens, Dr Garry Burns, a university professor with Canadian nationality, Mike McMurtree, who was later able to obtain an Irish passport, and I, as an Australian, were ever able to move around Kuwait. All the other British wardens had to carry out their duties from their hiding places.

The British system worked so well that when it later became apparent that the Americans needed their own community-based warden system in case their embassy had to close, we suggested to the US diplomats that we simply allocate their civilians to the nearest British warden, instead of trying to build a new American system from scratch. They were against this, partially because they were reluctant to have Americans reporting to them through non-Americans, and partly due to the strained relations between the US and British embassies. Nevertheless, we quietly told any Americans we knew who the local British warden was, and left it up to them to contact him. Most did.

One area with a unique warden system, and a uniquely difficult situation, was the cluster of coastal suburbs south of Sixth Ring, which was cut off from phone contact with the rest of the country. These were Fintas, Abu Halifa, Mahboula and Mangaf. The area had a large number of Westerners living in several dozen large, prominent multi-storey apartment buildings. They had very little contact with their embassies and it was readily apparent to the Iraqis and to Palestinian collaborators that there was a high percentage of Westerners in the area. They were very exposed.

The American warden for the area was originally Odessa Higgins, the lady who was seriously injured on the US Embassy convoy to Baghdad on 23 August. She was a locally-employed embassy staffer, not a diplomat, but had a walkie-talkie which could reach the embassy. The British warden was a civilian man who was happy to carry out his duties in the local area but was not prepared to run the risk of going into town through the checkpoints to the embassy for the wardens' meetings.

Into the British breach had stepped a Mrs Dorothy Goodwin, whose husband was later caught on the second British evacuation convoy, disguised as a woman. Mrs Goodwin was also a locally-engaged embassy employee but had no walkie-talkie. She set about organizing a warden system in this area, under very difficult circumstances, using several people from each residential building. Within days, she had a pyramid of nearly twenty individuals of various nationalities, reporting to her. She established links with Mrs Higgins, and was able to pass messages to the British Embassy via the US Embassy through the American walkie-talkie.

The Americans in the area had their own problems. Mrs Higgins sought refuge in her embassy after the first few days, taking her walkie-talkie with her. The Americans and the British now had no means of contacting the embassy short of going to an area from where they could phone, or visiting the embassy itself. Both were risky propositions. At the time, the American diplomats, still in a state of near chaos, simply did not think to appoint another warden for this particularly needy area.

One of the HAWK men, Tal Ledford, the local manager for Raytheon Corporation, was already incensed at having been told by the embassy to lie low and stay in Kuwait when he and his staff could have escaped in the first days. He drove into town, running the gauntlet of checkpoints, and forced the embassy to give him a radio. He and a colleague, Guy Seago, then started going around all the apartment buildings in their area, especially those they suspected Americans of living in, knocking on doors to find where people were.

In the meantime, Mrs Goodwin and her group had not been idle. As the area faced the Arabian Gulf instead of Kuwait Bay, it was in the front-line for the expected amphibious assault. They established shelters in the basement carparks of several apartment blocks. Thanks to the structure which Mrs Goodwin's group established, the Westerners in the area were able to organise the first major escape attempt, down the Salmi Road to Saudi Arabia, with about 100 vehicles, on 7 August. It failed after the Iraqis turned them back, but at least people felt they had made a serious attempt. The endeavour gave some people the courage to make their own attempts later on, and taught them that they stood a better chance if they went out in small groups.

The Americans in the area suffered another blow when the diplomats ordered Ledford and his Raytheon colleagues into the embassy compound on 10 August. This time, however, Mr Ledford handed his walkie-talkie over to another American, who picked up the task.

Without phone communication to other areas, the people in these areas suffered a greater sense of abandonment and desperation than their compatriots elsewhere, and during the second week of the invasion, the warden system in the area fell apart as people began to look out for themselves, and some even tried to make their own escapes, including the redoubtable Mrs Goodwin and her husband. When one British man called up Mrs Goodwin as his warden, she said she was no longer doing the job, and gave him the phone number of another man. When called, the man said that he had not even agreed to do the job, and asked the caller not to phone him again.

Fate eventually caught up with most of these Americans and British. They were captured in early September, although a few dozen remained in hiding, concealed either by free-national friends or Palestinians, or in cleverly constructed hideaways. One particularly brave Pakistani woman, Mrs Rukhsana Khan, kept in contact with many of them, and travelled up to the city each day to call the embassies from her office, and pass messages back and forth, but the warden system in the area never re-established itself.

Virtually every other Western country with an embassy in Kuwait also had its own warden system. The Canadians had the basic structure of a system before the invasion, and were particularly fortunate to have two very active and effective individuals as key wardens, Fred Skovberg and Eoin MacDougald, reporting to *chargé d'affaires* Bill Bowden and Consul Ron Waugh inside the besieged Canadian Embassy. A third very active warden was Britt Mockridge, a Calgary lawyer who had just arrived in Kuwait.

The Canadian system went to work for the Americans when the US system collapsed, helping particularly with the evacuation of women and children. Barbara Bodine and Gale Rogers depended heavily on Eoin whenever they needed errands run, or food or medicine delivered to Americans in hiding.

The French had a different approach. There were seven French diplomats in Kuwait under *chargé d'affaires* Jean-Paul Galtier. Four of these remained in the French Embassy or Residence. The other three apparently went out and lived in the community, and acted as wardens. Once the French women and children had left, there were perhaps 80 Frenchmen in Kuwait. The diplomats could easily handle this themselves. More importantly, the diplomats outside the embassy ensured that the community could still function even if the Iraqis took over the embassy. The French were particularly fortunate to have excellent connections with the French-speaking Maronite Lebanese community, who were able to move around freely and support them.

The Germans also had their own warden system. The main German warden apparently escaped in November by being smuggled out of Kuwait, through Iraq, and into Jordan, in a truckload of furniture. One of the other key German wardens was a huge bearded photographer, Uwe Wruck, with a great sense of humour. Barbara Bodine would call him whenever she wanted just to talk and escape from the tense atmosphere in her own compound. The Germans certainly needed their sense of humour when their own diplomats left for Baghdad before their nationals were free to go. They were essentially left on their own, before being taken under the wing of the US Embassy.

One of their great advantages was that there was a relatively large number of German women in Kuwait who were married to Kuwaitis and were able to support the German men in hiding. Perhaps the most active was Monika Al-Khashti-Horstmann, who was later decorated by the German Government for her courage. She and her husband and sons cared for some 30 Germans, 4 Americans, 4 British and 2 Frenchmen, in hiding. At one stage, she sold her jewellery to buy food for her family and the men in hiding, and on another occasion she was arrested by the Iraqis after foolishly insulting them at a checkpoint. They held her in the local police station for several days, only allowing her home at night in deference to her age and sex – and provided her son took her place overnight. Mother and son were finally released after a hefty bribe had been paid.

People without their own embassies in Kuwait faced particular challenges. None of them had warden systems in place at the time of the invasion. They had to build them as they went along, and also establish some means of communicating with their embassies in Baghdad.

The Irish had several different wardens during the crisis. The first was Cathal O'Connell, an Aer Lingus computer specialist. As a visitor with very little knowledge of Kuwait, Cathal was a most unlikely warden. His two main qualifications were that he rose to the occasion as a natural leader, and that his team of five other Aer Lingus computer specialists and a visiting independent businessman they teamed up with comprised the single largest group of adult Irish in the country. He was always calm, friendly and reassuring, even when under great stress. His sense of humour, and that of his colleagues, carried him through. Cathal single-handedly established relations with the Italian Embassy, and had about half of the Irish women and children evacuated to Baghdad on an Italian bus in early September.

The second Irish warden was Paul Kennedy, a 44-year-old management consultant with the National Bank of Kuwait. He took over when Cathal's group was persuaded to relocate to Baghdad in mid-September. Paul was particularly active in trying to obtain Irish documentation for American and British nationals. He was an intense and meticulous individual, the antithesis of the laid-back Cathal, and did a tremendous job for his people.

Many of the British with qualifications for obtaining Irish documentation had reason to be grateful to Paul. He went to Baghdad on their behalf several times to argue their cases vociferously with Ambassador Antoin MacUnfraidh, who was reluctant to issue such documents. Whenever Paul was away, Brian Durnin, from ICL, stepped in and did a fine job.

The Australian and New Zealand warden systems started from a similar zero base. Neither country had wardens when the invasion occurred, and their embassies with responsibility for Kuwait were in Riyadh, on the other side of the front line, so the Baghdad embassies took over. I was appointed warden for the 80 Australians in town, assisted by another Australian, Stephen Tubb. Stephen later relocated to Baghdad, but by then the Australians had only 13 men and one woman in Kuwait. One man could handle this. The New Zealanders, for their part, with wardens Alistair Lane and Ron Houston, became most active in supporting Americans and British in hiding.

Although most of us had been appointed wardens by our own embassies, and asked to do our best to maintain contact with our diplomats, we were not given a written outline of our duties, nor anything that gave us an independent communication capacity. No arrangements were made with the other embassies in town by our own diplomats. The Australians were supposed to go through the Canadians, but their communications failed. The British were overworked with only two diplomats and a radio voice link. I therefore had to initially use the Swiss, where a personal friend, Bernhard Bischoff, was maintaining the embassy, and the West Germans. The New Zealanders first used the Danish Embassy, and the Irish initially went through the Italians.

When the Danish and Italian diplomats left, the Danes and New Zealanders transferred to the Belgians. The Irish sent a few messages out with the British, before giving up on them out of frustration – and the perceived security risk of the British using an open line – and transferring to the Belgians. They were joined a week or so later by the Australians after the Swiss were pulled out. At one stage, Bart Ouvry, the young diplomat manning the Belgian Embassy, was providing communications for at least four other countries. When he was ordered to Baghdad, we all moved over to Barbara Bodine in the US Embassy, who was already handling communications for the Bahrainis, Canadians and French. Later on, she took over the Germans after their diplomats were ordered out by Bonn. It was truly an exercise in international co-operation, rivalling the military in the Saudi desert.

The only qualifications required of a warden were the willingness to be involved, and diligence. The wardens were unpaid volunteers sticking their necks out, and their embassies in Baghdad were able to offer them little support other than passing messages on to their families, or offering advice on certain developments in the crisis which might directly affect them. However, the final decision on courses of action such as relocating to Baghdad or staying in Kuwait, or even going back into hiding, always had to be up to us first as individuals, and secondly as a community.

The Baghdad embassies were also limited as to how much financial assistance they could provide. The Irish Embassy was particularly generous with its people, giving everyone several hundred dollars each. Phil Coggan, the Australian diplomat who visited Kuwait in August and again in September, gave me US$100, KD100, and a couple of hundred Iraqi dinars as emergency funds for the entire community, but that was all. Even this caused a few problems. I consulted Stephen Tubb on how we should distribute it. He very wisely said to keep quiet about it, and any real need would soon become apparent. The last thing we needed was money squabbles. Stephen's foresight was vindicated when two of the best provisioned men came up with all sorts of messages to the embassy in Baghdad requesting funds which they did not really need. We were tempted to tell them to sell one of the several televisions in their house. When the last few members of the community left in December, we still had most of the money, so distributed it evenly among them to help pay for their trip to Baghdad.

The primary role of the wardens was to serve as a channel of communication between their communities and the embassies, and within the communities.

Perhaps their most important secondary role was as a source of information and advice. Wardens were never in a position to give orders. They could only give their opinion. The people in Kuwait were predominantly well-educated professionals with minds of their own. The advice of the wardens was usually followed, if only because it often confirmed individuals' own assessments, or their experience gave them a useful degree of insight and common sense.

Practically, the wardens were often able to direct people to sources of food, supplies or other services. A British gynaecologist in Kuwait, Dr Brian Bethell, and several Kuwaiti physicians, could provide medical advice. Bethell could not visit people, as this would have compromised his own security, but the knowledge that emergency medical advice or even care could be summoned through the warden system provided a great deal of comfort. Two Danish dentists, Claus and Esther Schmith, continued to run their clinic throughout the crisis, even making housecalls when necessary. The greatest problem was circulating this information. It was not until late October that the system was running smoothly enough to take advantage of most of the services on offer. It never worked perfectly, but it was a difficult situation.

Many wardens spent a great deal of time and energy sorting out difficulties in interpersonal relationships. This ranged from chivying people out of depression, to breaking up fights within groups. One warden described himself as an 'Agony Aunt'. On at least one occasion, a warden had to talk a despondent man in hiding alone out of suicide. They were not always successful in plucking men out of their despair. Another British man did not try to take his life, but turned himself in to the Iraqis on 1 November through depression.

Other incidents were less serious, but made the experience of hiding for weeks on end even more unpleasant. They arose mainly from the stress of unrelated people living together in confined spaces for long periods, under conditions of great stress. They got on each other's nerves; the smallest peeves could set off blazing rows. Some wardens had to put up with the different sides in a dispute asking them to tell the other party something, like feuding parents communicating with each other through their children.

Some concerns were more pressing, particularly with pick-ups. The wardens, and sometimes the diplomats, usually phoned recent captives in the Regency Palace Hotel and debriefed them. We needed to determine if there was a pattern to the pick-up, such as an informer, or an organized door-to-door search, or whether it was just pure chance. If the pick-up was from a door-to-door search, we could warn people to go into deeper hiding, or even move, if circumstances allowed. If it was an informer, then we had to identify whether any other men were at risk, and if they should move. If so, the wardens might be able to find a safe house, or arrange transport. Some wardens had the Kuwaiti contacts to arrange the execution of the informer, but never went that far. However, a story later emerged that one Resistance group had actually executed one Kuwaiti for attempting to betray Westerners.

The telephone debriefing of captives had another side benefit: it allowed people to know what to expect if they were caught. One of the greatest fears was that of the unknown. Knowing that the Iraqis were being relatively civil, especially to women, and were not subjecting people to harsh interrogation, put many minds at ease.

One incident which caused a great deal of concern to several British wardens was when a Scotsman, Norrie Atack, died on 30 September of a perforated ulcer. He had been living alone in the flat of the local Mercedes-Benz General Manager, Uwe Danzer, and consuming large quantities of home-made wine to ease himself through the crisis. He had actually called another Scotsman the night before his death to say that he was coughing up blood. Tragically, the US embassy, with whom he was also in contact, were making arrangements with a girl from the Kuwait Resistance to move him in with some other people who were prepared to care for him.

Atack was found dead in an armchair by a horrified maid who had been bringing him food. She told some Germans who were hiding in the same building, who told Oliver Rentschler in their own embassy, who in turn advised the British diplomats. The matter had to be handled very carefully as the British needed to have the body removed, but could not implicate the maid, who could have been hanged for aiding Westerners, or the German neighbours, who could have joined the Human Shield if they had been found.

Rumours arose apparently from two separate reports from either the ambulance driver who retrieved the body or the mortuary that Atack's body was bruised, as if he had been beaten up. Command Central therefore became concerned that the situation had deteriorated to a stage where looters were prepared to assault their victims. It was unclear whether the ulcer had burst spontaneously, or because of a beating. They wanted to determine whether they should try to move men into larger groups for safety. In Command Central's opinion, the British diplomats did not take their concerns seriously.

Atack's body had been checked by the embassy's Indian Vice-Consul Raj Gopolan, but Raj may not have been able to tell whether he had been assaulted without a closer examination. Command Central was being understandably jumpy, maybe even paranoid, but they and the embassy had not talked the issue through. Apart from the tragedy of Atack's death, it was a classic failure of communication which demonstrated the power-plays between the embassy and some wardens.

Another major concern was rumour-control. Scared people believe the strangest things, craving some hope to cling to. One of the most sudden and widespread rumours occurred late on the evening of 28 October, with reports that the hospitals had gone on alert, a chemical attack alert had gone out, and Iraqi vehicles were moving in force on Sixth and Seventh Ring. As the wardens and embassies tried to ascertain exactly what was going on, and calm people, the rumour gathered momentum. Each link in the chain added its own embellishment. Within half an hour of the rumour starting, the American in our building was talking as if liberation would occur before breakfast, and breaching all his own telephone security rules. It took several hours to control the rumour, but it was indicative of how people were grasping at straws.

Another example of near panic in some quarters arose from a rumour on 15 November, when Iraqi soldiers occupied the apartment of Henk Looy, a Dutchman who had travelled to Baghdad to call his wife. Several reports reached various wardens that 11 Britons in the same building had been arrested. This caused a great deal of concern as one of the men in the building was a warden who had a list of other people in the area. In fact, there were only four British in the building and none of them had been taken. The wardens had to quash such rumours before they got out of hand.

Not all the wardens' tasks were as burdensome as dealing with deceased or depressed parishioners. After physical and security requirements, the next most important task was to maintain morale. Many people took care of this themselves with exercise, a routine, and humour, but one of the critical aspects of the job was simply calling men up for a chat, and letting them know they had not been forgotten.

Humour was critical to sustaining morale. The main source was jokes passed from man to man by phone. They could be some of the weakest, silliest jokes ever told, usually with black humour, but they generated great mirth. They invariably sprang from some aspect of the situation, ranging from the lack of female company to the quality of Iraqi troops, and particularly Saddam's foibles.

One man with a healthy contempt for the Iraqi Army's courage told how the Russians had sold Iraq a special model T-72 tank, with four reverse gears and one forward. The reverse gears were readily understood: the joke was that the forward gear was in case they were attacked from behind.

One round of jokes covered how to identify the various ranks in the Iraqi Army. The major was the one who 'hung around cranes', in reference to the man identified as an Iraqi Army major who had been hanged publicly from a road crane to discourage looters. The colonel was 'the one in the big, black Mercedes with no wheels' in reference to the propensity of Iraqi officers to loot cars, and the tendency for any car left unattended for more than a day to be stripped; the private was 'the one with the wheels'.

The warden joke machine seemed to revolve around Britons Sandy Macmillan and Chris Bell, and a French-Canadian, Jean-Louis Pellerin. Both Sandy and Chris produced 'jokes-of-the-day' which were injected into the system. Sandy even started sweepstakes on the date of liberation, as did the two young British men in my Al-Muthanna group.

A number of the wardens' activities overlapped with their roles as individuals. For example, several men in Command Central had excellent Resistance contacts, and were actively assisting their Kuwaiti friends. On one occasion they hid weapons, ammunition and explosives for a Resistance cell. The guns were private hunting and target rifles, not military weapons, but if the Kuwaitis had been caught with them, they could have been executed. The wardens might have faced harsh questioning from the Iraqis, or maybe even a jail sentence, but were confident they would not be killed.

In other cases, wardens with military experience answered Kuwaiti Resistance queries on how to operate certain weapons, or passed on advice from other men – including one held on a site in Kuwait – on how to build car bombs. These Resistance contacts paid off. When the wardens needed people moved in a hurry, or certain errands run, the Resistance were happy to oblige.

However, some of these activities did not endear Command Central to the British Embassy, who saw them as a bit of a 'Boys' Own' outfit. The last thing the embassy needed was British civilians implicated in Resistance activities, or even hurt or killed. The embassy was painfully aware that any incident in which British individuals were linked to the Resistance would make life much more difficult for the broader community. The US Embassy went so far as to instruct its community to desist from taking action against Iraqi forces.

Some of the wardens' extra-curricular activities were more altruistic. Sandy Macmillan became the Kuwait end of one of the first reliable two-way mail systems into and out of Kuwait. An Englishwoman who had stayed with him before she was evacuated, Nicola Benwell, had a Palestinian visitor to her London office who said he was going back into Kuwait. Nicola was aware of the immense value of mail to the men in hiding, so collected a few messages from women she knew, and sent them into Kuwait for Sandy to distribute.

The next problem was to increase the number of letters, without compromising the security of the couriers. Sandy therefore took letters from people in Kuwait, usually transmitted to him by fax or modem, and put them onto a diskette. Each diskette held about 25 letters, and attracted no attention from the Iraqi customs or security at the airport or border. Nicola at the other end printed off the letters and sent them to the families, and then compiled another batch for the next outward trip to Kuwait. There were about four diskette mail runs, and a further two using hardcopy alone.

Sandy later told of calling Gale Rogers in the US Embassy and asking her if she wanted a copy of the current edition of *Newsweek*. Gale and her compatriots, dependent on Iraqi TV, CNN, VOA and State Department news summaries for their news, said they would like this very much. 'Alright!', said Sandy. 'Turn on your fax.' He then apparently faxed in the entire current edition of *Newsweek* which he had just received through his mail system.

One of Sandy's more ambitious schemes never came to fruition, but had great potential. As a consultant to the Kuwait Ministry of Communications, he knew the telephone wiring system within Kuwait, and its connections to other countries. An underground landline to Saudi Arabia runs alongside one of the north-south motorways. The Iraqis had cut the international switch at the exchange in the city, but the line itself was still intact. Sandy had identified an access manhole to the landline, and was trying to figure out how to get someone into it without attracting Iraqi attention, and tap into the line below the disabled switch. According to him, it was technically possible. The hard part was getting a qualified engineer into the hole. If he had been able to do so, he maintained that he could have patched every phone in Kuwait through to Saudi Arabia. With the co-operation of the Saudis, every person in Kuwait with access to a phone could have spoken directly to their families.

Despite the handful of generally early and isolated problems – and with the notable exception of the Americans – the warden systems worked well once they were up and running.

The dedication of the wardens was perhaps best demonstrated in December, when the civilians were released. Eoin MacDougald was at Kuwait Airport together with Sandy Macmillan on the day the British men left, poring over a list of names to ensure that everyone had been accounted for. They only left when they were certain that they had everyone who wanted to go.

That same day, the Command Central men ran a shuttle service to the airport, and one of them got arrested for their trouble. The Irish warden at the time, Paul Kennedy, stayed behind in Kuwait for a week after most other Westerners had left to gather further information on human rights abuses and looting, despite having been allowed to leave Iraq nine days before the general release. At least three British wardens, Mike Graham and his wife Margaret, Bruce Parry and his wife Edna, and Brock Matthews, declined to leave Kuwait when the opportunity presented itself. They had seen the Iraqis come in, Kuwait was their home, and they wanted to be there to see the Iraqis kicked out.

16. THE ASIANS' STORY

During late August and into September 1990, a human tragedy far greater than that of the repressed Kuwaitis or Iraq's Human Shields threatened to explode. This was the plight of hundreds of thousands of Asian and Arab refugees from Kuwait and Iraq, their ordeal in squalid refugee camps in Jordan and Turkey, and the plight of those still trapped in Kuwait. These displaced people had less political significance than the ten thousand trapped Westerners and Japanese, but the potential human suffering was far greater.

The scale of the problem was massive. Both Kuwait and Iraq relied heavily on Third World expatriate manpower. In Kuwait, jobs stopped with the invasion. Even in Iraq, the sanctions put many expatriates out of work. These people could not possibly survive for long without their pay.

However, the brunt of the suffering fell squarely onto those from Kuwait because of the different ethnic structure of the workforce and the security situation. About 40% of Kuwait's expatriates hailed from Asia. They had further to go home than the mainly Egyptian and Sudanese workers in Iraq, and less wherewithal to pay for the trip. There wasn't even much to go home to. Food, perhaps, and family, but no jobs. Furthermore, while most expatriates in Iraq continued working for some time after the invasion, and enjoyed interrupted law and order, those in Kuwait lost their jobs, had little access to their savings, and lived in constant fear of looting, assault and, for the women, rape.

The Asians in Kuwait were particularly hard hit. Whereas most Arab expatriates in Kuwait were Palestinians with a family structure and enough reserves to manage for several months, and a common language with the Iraqis, many of the Asians were labourers living in pre-fabricated contractors' camps or hostels, and fed by catering companies. Most caterers stopped working as the money dried up, or their staff fled. Others kept working as long as they could, but there was a limit to what they could do. Without money and food, the labourers faced starvation. There were substantial food supplies in Kuwait, but it took some time for the Indian and other Asian communities to gain access to them. Fears grew of mobs armed with sticks and knives roaming the city, hunting for food wherever they could find it.

Tens of thousands of domestic staff, particularly single female Indians, Filipinas and Sri Lankans faced similar problems. When Kuwaiti or Palestinian employers fled, many of the maids, drivers and cooks were deposited at their overworked embassies. The Westerners and some Kuwaitis fleeing into Saudi Arabia took their domestic staff with them, but the numbers were small. By the second week of the crisis, several Asian embassies in Kuwait looked like refugee camps for thousands of desperate females.

During the first week of the occupation, Asian and Arab expatriates faced as much uncertainty as the Westerners and Japanese. At the time, Iraq had closed its borders. Only diplomats accredited to Baghdad could leave.

This changed on 11 August. Saddam allowed all non-Kuwaiti and non-Iraqi Arab nationals and Asians out, but many of the Asians and thousands of poorer Arabs could not afford to leave. Only Jordanians, Palestinians with Jordanian nationality, and some wealthier Egyptians could get home relatively easily.

The major overland route out of Kuwait and Iraq was through Jordan. The only remaining regular air link between Baghdad and the outside world was the daily Iraqi Airways flight to Amman, and this could not handle the flood. The Iraqis – and Saudis – had blocked the shortest logical departure route through Saudi Arabia. In any event, the Saudis did not want to deal with a refugee problem as well as the influx of thousands of Allied troops.

The Iraqis allowed only Iranians to cross their borders into Iran. Indians and Pakistanis trying to go home overland, especially in their own cars, usually had to go all the way to the far north of Iraq, into Turkey, and then into Iran, a route that added several thousand kilometres to what was already an arduous journey. The Syrian border was supposedly open, but decades of Iraqi-Syrian antagonism, and the deployment of Syrian troops to Saudi Arabia, all but closed it off to anyone except Syrians.

Estimated numbers of Third World nationals in Kuwait and Iraq, August 1990.

	Kuwait	Iraq	Combined
ARABS and IRANIANS			
Egypt and Sudan	120,000	1,200,000	1,320,000
Palestinians/Jordanians	450,000	170,000	620,000
	570,000	1,370,000	1,940,000
Iran	40,000	—	40,000
Lebanon	10,000	—	10,000
Morocco	6,000	30,000	36,000
Syria	30,000	10,000	40,000
Tunisia	2,000	2,000	4,000
	658,000	1,412,000	2,070,000
ASIANS			
Bangladesh	60,000	15,000	75,000
China	3,000	5,000	8,000
India	172,000	10,000	182,000
Indonesia	1,000	—	1,000
Korea	100	900	1,000
Pakistan	30,000	15,000	45,000
Philippines	45,000	5,000	50,000
Sri Lanka	85,000	—	85,000
Thailand	6,000	6,000	12,000
Vietnam	—	5,000	5,000
	402,100	61,900	464,000
TOTAL	1,060,100	1,473,900	2,534,000

The Iraqis further complicated matters by insisting that any evacuation ships entering Iraqi or Kuwaiti ports must bring in food and medicines. Such deliveries were permissible as humanitarian supplies, but only in the presence of a clear need, which was not yet apparent. They also refused to deal with the International Committee of the Red Cross (ICRC), whose function under the 1949 Geneva Conventions was the protection of war victims, on the pretext that Kuwait was not occupied, but was part of Iraq. This was particularly galling to the ICRC at the time as they were providing substantial assistance to Iraq with the repatriation of its own POWs from Iran.

Following the opening of the Jordanian border, 20,000 refugees poured across daily, mainly poorer Egyptians and Indians, Bangladeshis and Sri Lankans. Within ten days, 185,000 had entered, but only 67,000, mostly Egyptians, had been repatriated. Many of the Asians could not afford the air fare home. Without evacuation flights to their home countries, they languished in makeshift desert camps under the scorching summer sun, kept out of Jordanian cities, with little food and water, and growing fears of disease.

The Jordanian Government was immediately swamped. They received little help from outside and felt that they were being made to pay the price for their support of Saddam. Most of the assistance initially came from the overworked Indian and other Asian embassies in Amman, and private Jordanian citizens and charities. It was not until 22 August, eleven days after Iraq opened the border, that Jordan first asked for UN help, and closed their own border to allow about 118,000 refugees to be relocated to hastily constructed refugee camps. It took until 24 August before a joint Jordanian Red Crescent/ICRC reception and First Aid centre was operating at the Jordan–Iraq border at Ruwaishid. They then opened a transit camp at Sha'alan, further into Jordan. It was intended to hold 3,000, but soon contained 10,000. Within days, it had swelled to 20,000, then 60,000.

By the end of August, an estimated 330,000 of the 2.5 million Arab and Asian expatriates in Kuwait and Iraq had entered Jordan. A further 100,000 people, mainly Iranians and Pakistanis from Kuwait were fleeing through Iran. To the north, 26,000 people had entered Turkey, 16,000 of whom had moved on. Tens of thousands were camped on the Iraqi side of the border in Kurdistan, with minimal food, water and shelter.

However, the numbers in the Jordanian camps remained constant as the more numerous Egyptians were moved on. Cairo organized ferries from Jordan's port of Aqaba, through the UN naval blockade. In one unfortunate incident, an evacuation ship was turned back by the blockading warships. The desert trip to Aqaba initially took up to four days, but it was better than a desperate existence of weeks in a camp. Jordan and Egypt even came to a preliminary understanding with Israel to allow Egyptians home through Eliat, by crossing the Allenby Bridge and transitting through the Israeli-occupied West Bank, but this was abandoned. Neither Jordan nor Egypt wanted to be seen to be too closely associated with Israel when Saddam was accusing the Coalition's Arab states of collaborating with that country. Nevertheless, by the end of August, 85,000 Egyptians were home. A further 5,000 followed each day.

Over 200,000 individuals had been moved through Jordan in 20 days, or were Palestinians who resettled in Jordan. However, only about 30,000 of those repatriated were Asians, mainly people who could afford to pay their own way home. A further 65,000 to 70,000 Asians were suffering terrible deprivation in the overcrowded camps. About 350,000 remained in Kuwait. When they saw the distressing TV pictures of the crowded camps, and heard the radio reports, many of them felt they were better off staying where they were as long as their food lasted. Not everyone had this choice. The poorer workers in particular, with little food, simply had to get out.

The only people paying much attention to the situation in early September were the Jordanian Red Crescent (JRC) and the ICRC, and even when foreign help arrived, the operation was dogged with indecision and mistakes. Jordan was so dissatisfied with the performance of the responsible UN official that Crown Prince Hassan publicly demanded his removal on 4 September. It was 12 September before a full-time competent UN official, Prince Sadruddin Aga Khan, was appointed to help with the crisis. A horrified King Hussein's wife, Queen Noor, visited the camps, followed by TV crews. The pictures of the refugees beamed across the world galvanized the West into action.

During September, the Jordanians got on top of the problem as other governments, including Kuwait, helped with the evacuations, and the initial rush subsided. The UK contributed an initial £500,000 to the ICRC's efforts. The EC provided £21 million. Other countries sent relief supplies, tents, water purification equipment, personnel and money.

In the first week of the month, a further 90,000 people entered Jordan, but the numbers in the camps fell slightly from 114,000 to 105,000. The second week was even better. The ICRC and JRC opened a 30,000-capacity camp at Azraq, near Amman, on 12 September to take the pressure off the more remote Sha'alan, which by then had 35,000 inhabitants. Another 50,000 refugees arrived, but the numbers in the camps fell to 45,000. As importantly, the camp conditions improved greatly and the danger of starvation and disease all but disappeared. During the second half of September, only another 40,000 refugees arrived, and by month's end the camps held a manageable 33,000.

Over half a million individuals had crossed into Jordan from Iraq in seven weeks. People continued to arrive at a rate of up to 20,000 per week into October and November. The camp numbers sometimes rose to as high as 43,000, but the crisis was under control.

This was not achieved without a great deal of work. The Indian Government chartered Air India aircraft, and sent Air Force transports to build an air bridge from Amman to Dubai, and on to Bombay. From 7 September through to 12 October, 21,508 Indians were repatriated through Dubai on 125 flights. Thailand had repatriated 4,500 of its 6,000 nationals from Kuwait by the first week of September. Seventy-two aircraft had been chartered to airlift 19,000 Bangladeshis and Sri Lankans home.

The situation was also critical in Turkey. Although Bangladeshi President Hussein Ershad visited the Turkish camps in mid-September (which by then held 40,000 Bangladeshis and Pakistanis), his Government and several others could not afford to charter aircraft. The International Organization for Migration (IOM) stepped in, financed in part by another £2 million from the UK. Aircraft came from everywhere. British Airways, with one of its 747s trapped in Kuwait, provided a Tristar. Air Canada was involved. Giant Soviet Antonov freighters took out 500 workers on each trip, crowded into the holds on mattresses. By mid-September, the IOM had repatriated more than 31,500 people on 107 flights. Even the US Air Force flew Sri Lankans home from Jordan after delivering troops and equipment to Saudi Arabia.

The camps themselves gradually became quite habitable. The initial Sha'alan site, in a desolate no man's land, was replaced by a transit camp, known cryptically as T1/28, near the border. By the time Azraq was handed over to the League of Red Cross and Red Crescent Societies on 15 November, it had sheltered nearly 70,000 Indians, whose average stay was four days.

Not surprisingly in a crisis of that magnitude, there were problems of co-ordination between the aid agencies and the Jordanian Government. On one occasion, the Jordanians asked that the camp at Azraq be pulled down after giving permission for it to be built when they belatedly realized that it might pollute Amman's water supply. Nevertheless, the hospitality of the Jordanians, with a per capita GDP on a par with Fiji or Paraguay was a tribute to them when they were in an invidious political and economic cleft between their Western friends and Iraq.

The problems of the refugees from Iraq were generally not as acute as those from Kuwait, but there were significant cases of hardship. Perhaps the greatest was that of thousands of Vietnamese labourers at a dam site in northern Iraq. When the construction contract was terminated with the sanctions, these workers were abandoned by their own government, and the Iraqis. They had little food, no money, no transport, and could speak neither Arabic nor English. At the same time, on 18 August, the Iraqi Ministry of Labour and Social Affairs was saying that 'in keeping with their humanitarian principles, equal attention was being given to the physical needs of foreign families and Iraqis'. They were being less than straightforward. This applied only to those in the view of the TV cameras, especially Westerners from the Coalition countries. The starving Vietnamese were outside Baghdad, and of little interest to war-hungry Western TV editors. It was left to the US and British diplomats in Baghdad to force the Iraqis to evacuate the Vietnamese by threatening to expose this scandal.

Only a relatively few affluent Asians could drive through Iran to Pakistan or India, but first they had to go into Turkey and on into Iran and then to the sub-continent. Most Asian refugees from Kuwait had to make the arduous journey to Jordan via Baghdad. Even when the Iraqis opened the Saudi border in September to encourage Kuwaitis to leave, the Asians could not go that way.

Those with money tried to fly from Baghdad to Amman. They had to travel overland to Baghdad as there were only one or two Iraqi Airways daily flights from Kuwait to Baghdad, and few people knew about them. Those with families could not afford to stay in Baghdad for long, so intrepid young Indian men drove to Baghdad from Kuwait to buy airline tickets and confirm reservations, financing these trips by bringing cartons of liquor back into Kuwait. If they could get tickets, the families could then go to Baghdad, and board the aircraft almost immediately. Once in Amman, they could join scheduled flights home, or the evacuation flights. Nevertheless, only two aircraft flew from Baghdad to Amman each day, so seats were at a premium.

Of the Arab refugees, some of the most annoyed were the Palestinians. Most of them were firmly against what had happened in Kuwait, and incensed at the PLO's stand, but they knew their privileged positions were gone forever, whatever happened. If the Iraqis stayed, they would take the good jobs for themselves. If the Kuwaitis returned, they would not forgive the PLO's treachery. Yasser Arafat had broken the compact. The Palestinians had fought for the PLO to be recognized as their sole, legitimate representative. They now had to live with that choice. After giving up to 450,000 Palestinians shelter, education and jobs for two generations, and substantial direct aid to the PLO, Kuwait had asked only for political support when she needed it. Arafat had failed to pay the bill when it was presented.

Most of the Palestinians had Jordanian passports and relatives in Jordan. They entered the country with ease, and went straight home. As Arabs, they could handle the Iraqi system, and were able to export most of their possessions. Chrysler and Mercedes sedans, loaded with complete Palestinian families and their possessions, and followed by truckloads of furniture, headed west from Baghdad towards Amman, past hordes of destitute Asians and Egyptians on the roadside. They were dubbed the 'Mercedes Refugees'.

However, one group of about 20,000 Palestinians had no choice but to stay in Kuwait or Iraq. They were the holders of Egyptian *laissez-passe* documents from the occupied Gaza Strip, or Lebanese documents. The only countries that would accept these people were Kuwait and Iraq. Most of them elected to remain in their homes in Kuwait, and are still there today.

In contrast to the Palestinians and their trucks, most Asians and Egyptians salvaged only what they could carry in a suitcase or on their backs. Nevertheless, the Iraqi soldiers at the Abdaly-Safwan border post and the Jordanian border regularly looted them of even these meagre possessions.

During the first weeks of the crisis, some of the poorer embassies in Kuwait had thousands of people camped in their grounds, and outside their walls. The Sri Lankan and some other embassies took over nearby schools and abandoned houses, or building sites, to accommodate their people.

The Indian Embassy, under Ambassador Arun Budhiraja, was besieged by crowds of low-income construction workers demanding assistance. Many of these people were hungry, angry and scared, and did not have their passports, which were held by employers who were nowhere to be found. The embassy deftly defused the crisis by typing onto a piece of paper the standard request from the Indian Foreign Ministry at the front of a passport to let the bearer proceed without let or hindrance, signing it, and handing out thousands of copies to the crowds. The piece of official paper in their hands kept them happy for a while, and allowed the diplomats to catch their breath.

The 172,000 strong Indian community itself was riven with schisms. Most of the embassy officials were north Indians, from Delhi and nearby, whereas most Indians working in Kuwait were from the south. Suspicions arose that certain people were getting preferential treatment from the embassy. Feelings were running so high that the Ambassador was manhandled on one occasion.

During the first week of the occupation, Ambassador Budhiraja asked several leading members of his community to establish a committee to help feed the endangered contract workers. This became known as the Indian Citizens' Committee (ICC). Its two leading lights were Mr Harbhajan Singh Vedi, an eminent architect, and Mr Sunny Mathews, who had established the Toyota dealership in Kuwait. Another half-dozen community patriarchs, known locally as the 'Old Boys', completed the ICC, with a cadre of volunteers working beneath them. Many of these men put in huge amounts of their own time and money to feed those in need. They liaised with local Indian and Kuwaiti food merchants, and supplied the workers' camps with enough rice and essentials to keep the men going until they could be evacuated.

To maintain communications with New Delhi, the embassy enlisted the aid of Shaji Varghese, a young electronics engineer and ham radio enthusiast. He brought one of his two sets into the embassy in the Ambassador's car, and trained the diplomats how to use it. However, after some time, the diplomats said that they alone would have to use it because of the 'confidential' nature of the traffic. Shaji was out, and apparently never got his radio back.

When the Indian Embassy became the first major mission to comply with the Iraqi closure order, the ICC established itself in the Indian School in the suburb of Salmiya. The diplomats relocated to the Indian Consulate in Basra, a hundred kilometres away. Ambassador Budhiraja left for India in early October, but his Deputy, Mr Makhija, stayed in Basra and visited Kuwait regularly to liaise with the Committee.

Scores of volunteers worked in the school, registering people, and distributing rice and other supplies. Five distribution centres were established around Kuwait in suburbs with high concentrations of Asian nationals. Retired Indian military officers delivered lectures on protection against missile attack, bombardment and gas attack. People were shown how to tape up their windows to prevent them being shattered by blast. It wasn't much, but it produced a sense that someone was in control and doing something.

Later, in January 1991, Shaji Varghese brought his second ham radio into the Indian School, and re-established communications with India. This time, he operated the set himself. He spoke in the Malayalam language, in case the Iraqis were listening, but was still at grave risk. If caught operating the radio outside the embassy, he could have been shot.

The other Asian countries faced similar challenges, albeit with lesser numbers. The Iraqis did not generally prevent Asians from moving around freely, although they were not averse to looting them. One brief exception was the Pakistanis. At one stage in September, when Pakistan sent troops to Saudi Arabia, the Iraqis started rounding up Pakistani professionals, mainly doctors and engineers, apparently in case they needed them in case of war. However, the Iraqis seemed to relent after a while. The Pakistanis did not need telling twice. Their exodus went into immediate overdrive.

In the meantime, the Indian Government had been negotiating with the Iraqis to help get Indians out of Kuwait and Iraq, but this deal partially collapsed on 9

September. India had agreed to close its Kuwait Embassy in return for Iraqi help with the refugees, but Baghdad reneged on this after the closure.

Part of the deal involved the Indian Foreign Minister, Mr I.K. Gujral, visiting Baghdad, one of the first and few senior foreign Government Ministers to do so. Actually, his visit originally had little to do with his beleaguered people in Kuwait. Unlike Kuwait, most Indian business in Iraq was carried out by major Indian Government firms, and Gujral's mission was apparently to salvage as much of this as he could. He was filmed embracing Saddam, a sight which inflamed many Indians and Kuwaitis, although many Indians assumed that this was just for show, to help get his people out.

However, once in Baghdad, the Indian community and diplomats prevailed upon him to visit Kuwait, where there were far more Indians. Gujral flew to Kuwait on 20 August, with Saddam's permission, in an Indian Air Force *Iluyshin* 76 transport. He was accompanied by the Indian Ambassador to Baghdad, Mr K.N. Bakshi, and five other officials. On the evening of his arrival, Gujral addressed a crowd of thousands of Indians and Kuwaitis at the Indian School in Salmiya. The Indians were less certain that the Minister's cuddles with Saddam had been for show when he started praising him, and lambasting the Kuwaitis, without even the excuse of having to play to TV cameras. Most of the crowd could have cheerfully lynched him.

That evening, and into the following morning, the ICC was swamped with angry calls from Kuwaitis who had been helping them. The Minister had given the distinct impression that India was more pro-Saddam than the Palestinians. When a chastened Gujral met the ICC for breakfast on 21 August, he was left in no doubt where the Indian community stood. His next speech to a crowd at the Indian Embassy was more restrained, but he had not quite learned his lesson. This time, he suggested that the crisis had little to do with India, so his people should go back to work. Besides being totally impractical in the circumstances, he was advocating breaking the Kuwaiti Resistance boycott of working under Iraqi rule for anything other than essential services. He left the meeting under a storm of abuse.

 Gujral eventually left Kuwait with a planeload of 200 people on the night of 21 August. They were supposed to be heavily pregnant women, elderly people and medical cases, but influence came to play a part. Many of the passengers were well-connected, single, female and pretty, or wealthy. Only six were ill. One young lady talked her way onto the aircraft by virtue of her job as an air hostess with Kuwait Airways, arguing with that they needed trained people to care for the medical cases on the flight. Even the Iraqis at the airport were shocked to see members of the Indian élite turn up with mountains of baggage, dressed up to the nines, some in their jewellery. Wheelchairs and stretchers were conspicuous by their absence. The plane overnighted in Baghdad, and then flew direct to India. There was only one obvious pregnancy case on the aircraft, and she had been forced on, against the wishes of Gujral's staff, by her relatives and a neighbour.

The only real service Mr Gujral provided to the broader Indian community was to take out sacks of mail for them. The visit left a bitter taste in the mouths of many Indians in Kuwait, most of whom were delighted when the Minister lost his job soon afterwards. Relations between the local Indians and the Kuwaitis cooled for some time, but recovered when the Kuwaitis realised that Gujral did not represent the vast majority of his people.

As August drew to a close with no end to the crisis in sight, the ICC turned its attention to evacuations. At the time, there was no programme of evacuation flights from Amman, and the Jordanian camps were still in chaos. With Mr Gujral safely back in India, it was now up to the ordinary members of the Indian community to cope with the real problems.

The priority cases were was the sick and heavily pregnant, women whose husbands were out of Kuwait on leave or business at the time of the invasion, and single girls who were more at risk. There were 800 pregnant women, 4,000 heart patients, 65 cancer patients and 15 kidney dialysis patients. All of these could have been adequately cared for under the regular Kuwaiti health system, but were at increasing risk with the Iraqi takeover of the hospitals.

The Committee established a medical corps under a Dr Prakash to assess priorities for evacuation. People were rated on a scale of 'A' to 'D'. The first attempt on 29 August to evacuate those most at risk was a disaster. The Committee, in co-ordination with the Iraqi and Indian Governments, tried to charter an Iraqi jet to take 332 of the most serious medical cases direct from Kuwait to Bombay. However, with the Minister gone and little chance for another worthwhile photo opportunity, the Iraqis only agreed to fly them out of Baghdad, so the patients had to be bussed north. When they arrived there, they found that the Iraqis had inexplicably cancelled the flight. Without money to remain in Baghdad, they had no option but to return to Kuwait, where at least they had people who could care for them.

To complicate matters, the bus company initially refused to take them back without advance payment. After extended argument, the convoy backtracked, only to arrive in Kuwait after curfew. Iraqi troops at a checkpoint would not let the buses proceed, and the patients were forced to sleep on the roadside until the curfew was lifted at dawn.

In the meantime, the Indian Government and its Ambassador in Baghdad had been working hard behind the scenes with the Iraqis. At the end of August, the *Al-Safir*, a Panamanian-flagged Indian cargo ship which had been caught in Kuwait's Shuwaikh Port, was allowed to leave for Dubai. This ship had been carrying rice, most of which was looted by the Iraqis. The ICC loaded the empty vessel with women, teenage girls, and a few families, 1,500 individuals in all, but as it was a cargo ship, it was considered too risky to send the sick, and those advanced in pregnancy. Nevertheless, the two-day voyage was surprisingly pleasant, with people housed in the ship's holds and camping on deck. They were safe, and had food and water. The Gulf was calm, with a cooling breeze, and flights from Dubai would take them home.

A more regular air and sea evacuation programme started at the end of August. A total of 10 Indian Air Force transport flights direct from Basra to Bombay took out about 250 people each from 28 August to 2 October, and two Indian passenger vessels, the *Tippusultan*, with a capacity of 700, and the *Akbar*, with room for 1,800 were chartered. *Tippusultan* made four voyages from Umm

Qasr to Dubai, and *Akbar* three, with a round trip of five days. The passengers had to be bussed to Umm Qasr, but this was far preferable to Jordan. Evacuees from all but the last trips for each vessel were flown from Dubai to Bombay, with the ships going to Bombay on their final trips. The priority passengers on the aircraft and vessels were the sick, pregnant, and elderly, defined by Dr Prakash's medical corps as 'A' and 'B' class evacuees.

The Indian Embassy staff, however, took good care of their own property. Another ship, the *Viswasidhi*, was allowed to berth at Umm Qasr in December to take out their belongings.

In parallel with the air and sea evacuations, two other Committee members, Shiva Basin and K. K. Nair, ran a larger bus evacuation to Amman. This linked up with Air India and other flights home. From 16 September to 12 October, an average of 70 buses left daily for the Jordanian border, each carrying 35 passengers, or 2,450 people per convoy. The main organized bus evacuations concluded on 18 November, after 1,500 busloads, leaving behind only about 18,000 Indians in Kuwait, and 6,000 in Iraq. Convoys continued on an irregular basis after that, with the last leaving during the last week of December.

Mr Mathews and several key organisers of the evacuations left on one of the last major convoys on 18 October when everyone who wanted to go at that stage had left. Mr Vedi and several other men remained behind to continue the relief work, and organise further convoys. In all, about 143,000 Indians from Kuwait went out on ICC-organised evacuations.

Iraq and the UN sanctions committee eventually allowed an Indian Red Cross relief ship, the *Shiva*, into Umm Qasr, with 6,000 tonnes of rice, dry goods and medicine for the Indians in Kuwait. The vessel arrived on 23 September, but the Iraqis initially prevented it from being unloaded. When they relented, they looted a sizeable share of the cargo. In any event, by the time the supplies got to Kuwait in October, most of the Indians had left.

The distribution of the relief supplies was supervised by the Indian Red Cross Society people, including its Secretary-General, Mr Ajit Bhowmick, who came into Kuwait, in conjunction with a team of volunteers organised by a Maersk Shipping Line executive, Mathew Kuruvilla, and banker Abraham Mathew, who was one of the most active members of the Committee.

While the refugee problem was massive, it was neither as big as it could have been, nor did it extend for as long as feared, thanks to the combined efforts of the Western, Jordanian and Asian governments, aid agencies, and dedicated private individuals. With the camps and evacuation flights well-organized in late September, and the initial surge past, new arrivals in Jordan could be promptly repatriated. Despite earlier fears of widespread death and sickness, actual deaths were few, and disease did not take hold.

A number of Arabs and Asians chose to stay in Kuwait and Iraq, despite the prospect of war. They were better off remaining in Kuwait as long as their food supplies lasted, and hoping that they could survive the war and pick up their jobs again once Kuwait was liberated.

The Palestinians with Egyptian and Lebanese documents had no choice but to stay as even the countries who issued their documents would not accept them, but many with Jordanian passports also stayed. In all, about 100,000 of the estimated 450,000 Palestinians in Kuwait on 2 August were still there at liberation. Almost all the poorest Asians left, but about 15,000 Indians and 4,000 Filipinos remained behind. Many of them worked in hospitals as nurses, doctors or technicians, as domestic staff, and in essential services. A few would be killed at their posts during the air war. In Iraq itself, hundreds of thousands of Egyptians whose jobs were unaffected by sanctions opted to stay.

In all, over a million Arab and Asian refugees passed through Jordan, Turkey and Iran from August to December 1990, with about 350,000 Palestinians resettling in Jordan. At the time, it was one of the greatest dislocations of people since Pol Pot's Cambodia.

After most of the Asians had left Kuwait, those remaining behind turned their attention to surviving the occupation. Their reasons for staying varied, but usually had to do with protecting businesses or property. A few people simply had nowhere to go back to, and feared that if they left, it would be almost impossible to get back in to resume their jobs after liberation.

Of the original ICC members, only Mr Vedi stayed. The Committee was reconstituted with some of the men who had been already active, particularly Mathew Kuruvilla, who became Vedi's right hand man. Vedi's deputy was Mr Raman Sharma, a prominent businessman. From then on, the ICC's major task was organizing the distribution of food, and protecting the property of the Indian schools and convents.

In the confusion following liberation, the Indian community found itself at odds with a number of Kuwaitis for its government's less than enthusiastic support for the Coalition. Food had been brought in from Saudi Arabia, and was being distributed through the local co-op supermarkets, but many Indians were not getting their share, and were even being beaten. The ICC then went to the US forces, was given truckloads of food, and used their structure and network to distribute it equitably. They also worked closely with the Kuwait Red Crescent Society which came into Kuwait on the heels of the troops.

One objective of Saddam's release of the Third World nationals was to split the world community in a divide-and-conquer strategy. He hoped to remove Third World support for the Western-led Coalition by letting their people home. It backfired badly. While most of the Asians were mightily annoyed at being caught up in what they saw as a Western–Iraqi conflict, they laid the blame for their misfortune squarely at the feet of Saddam. The displaced Asians became vocal advocates of the Kuwaiti cause. The quicker Iraq was out of Kuwait, the quicker they could get back to their jobs, and see justice done.

17. THE KUWAITI RESISTANCE

The role of the Kuwaiti Resistance is perhaps the greatest untold story of the crisis. It is impossible to do justice to it, or to the brave men and women, young and old, who risked and even gave their lives as part of it. The Resistance's casualty rate far exceeded that suffered by the Coalition military and the Western hostages. Their deeds are all the more remarkable for being carried out mostly by ordinary people under threat of execution if caught. The full stories of many of their activities died with those who paid the highest price, or are locked in minds too modest or too traumatized to relate them.

During the crisis, the Western media perpetuated the easy cliché of the Kuwaitis as a nation of five-star refugees paying the US to liberate them. The Resistance, if mentioned at all, was portrayed as tiny bands of hit-and-run snipers. The Resistance did have its 'wild boys', as the Kuwaitis dubbed them, but the overall effort was far more comprehensive and sophisticated. It did have some outside help, mostly from its own Government, but most activities were initiated, planned and executed from inside Kuwait. In fact, the Resistance gave such great service to the Allies that General Colin Powell sought out its surviving leaders after liberation to thank them personally.

Although many were military and police personnel, most Resistance members were ordinary Kuwaiti working men and women who chose to stay behind and fight for their country. Some other Arabs, especially Egyptians, Palestinians, Saudis and *bidoons* – stateless Arabs – also joined up. Even a few Westerners helped with minor operations, or provided technical advice.

The low-level military attacks were certainly important in keeping the Iraqi military off balance, but they proved prohibitively expensive in terms of Kuwaiti lives. The greatest victories were won by Kuwaiti wits, not firepower. The Resistance was thus able to maintain the honour of its country, provide significant leverage to the Allies in Saudi Arabia, and reduce the environmental damage which Saddam later wreaked on the region.

The main organizational feature of the Resistance was its lack of formal structure, particularly in its early days. It was very much a grass-roots movement. There was never any sole chief, nor were all activities, military or otherwise, ever co-ordinated through one single central command. Several key figures who liaised with the exiled Kuwaiti Government did emerge, a higher co-ordinating committee developed, and the Resistance became more integrated with time, but it was always a movement of the people.

The shape of the Resistance, such as it existed, was a reflection of Kuwaiti society. Kuwaitis are remarkably pluralistic – politically, religiously and ethnically. They are predominantly Arab Shi'ite and Sunni Muslims, with a few Christians, but regardless of origin, society is based on close-knit extended families which tend to intermarry and deal within their own sub-groups.

The two major bonds uniting these disparate camps are a common Kuwaiti identity, and wide recognition of the legitimacy of the ruling Al-Sabah as an institution of government. A strong system of consultative hereditary rule is seen as the most effective means of balancing the country's competing interests.

The Resistance grew out of these family and religious groups. The armed forces and police had been shattered. There was no military structure to build on. People therefore formed small groups of seldom more than a dozen family members and friends or colleagues. In a situation where betrayal could mean death, they were loath to answer to anyone they could not trust completely.

Another feature of Kuwaiti society kept these groups small and provided the Resistance with one of its greatest strengths: its cell structure. In Kuwait, every Kuwaiti wants to be their own boss. Economically, it is a nation of small managers and bureaucrats. Only 5% of employed Kuwaitis work in the private sector. The remainder are civil servants, in the military or police, or in oil or banking, usually in managerial jobs. The building blocks of the Resistance were therefore several hundred small cells, each with its own ideas on how to best take the fight to the Iraqis. It was not the most efficient structure, but if one cell were compromised, the Iraqis could seldom go further than other members of that cell. Staying alive was as important as getting things done.

The leaders of various cell groups did not always see eye to eye. Some felt driven to attack the Iraqis, whereas others argued that the cost in Kuwaiti lives did not justify this, and that they should help with the real liberation by providing the Allies with intelligence on the Iraqis. Some of the problems came from differences of opinion between fundamentalist Sunni Islamist groups, primarily the Muslim Brotherhood, and other more secular people. The Brotherhood also did not want to work with the Shi'ites. An inordinate amount of effort was spent trying to get some groups to pull together. The Islamists generally believed in a more passive Resistance, and - sensibly - that any armed resistance should be carried out by military professionals, and not civilians. In fact, with Western forces gathering in Saudi Arabia, some of the more religious elements had to struggle with theological questions about whether it was permissible to ask for military help from non-Muslims against a Muslim invader. The secularists saw this debate as irrelevant.

There were other petty jealousies, but never to the extent that groups fought each other. They were all Kuwaitis with a national crusade. In the end, every group went away and carried on the Resistance as they saw fit, but the differences prevented it from ever becoming a completely integrated effort.

In conjunction with these cells, suburb-based area committees established themselves to maintain essential services. These used the existing structures of Co-operative Societies, whose peacetime task was running the local shopping complex, Islamic organizations, the local *diwaniahs* where neighbourhood men would gather in the evenings, and the mosques. These suburban organisations, usually based on one of the two main Islamist parties, became known as the *Al-Takaful* or 'Solidarity Committees'. Together the Resistance cells and the local committees formed a comprehensive web of indigenous opposition to the Iraqis with one message: they wanted the Iraqis out, and were prepared to take whatever steps necessary to achieve this as soon as possible, without losing an unnecessary number of Kuwaiti and Allied lives.

In the early days of the occupation, several senior military and police officers were sent in by the Government to act as leaders, notably Major-General Abdul Wahab Al-Muzain, and police Brigadier Yousef Al-Mishari. They had flown from London to Saudi Arabia the day after the invasion. Four days later, they had been infiltrated into Kuwait, with authority to co-ordinate the civil and military Resistance wherever they could.

Al-Muzain and Al-Mishari met up with Major-General Mohammed Al-Bader, who worked for the Cabinet, KAF Colonel Fahd Al-Ameer, and several other senior officers. Al-Muzain's main role was acting as co-ordinator between the Government-in-exile, and those in Kuwait. Al-Mishari's was to organize the gathering of intelligence in Kuwait, and to get it out to Saudi Arabia. Al-Bader's task was to co-ordinate the civil and military groups.

Tragically, both Al-Muzain and Al-Mishari were captured on 14 October along with seven others, most of whom are still unaccounted for. Major-General Al-Bader himself barely escaped.

After the capture of Al-Muzain and Al-Mishari, the Resistance formed a co-ordinating committee with representatives from every major interest group in Kuwait. The military, represented by men such as Major-General Al-Bader, Colonels Fahd Al-Ameer, Mohammed Al-Harmi, and Talal Musallem joined with Sheikh Ali Salem Al-Ali and Sheikh Sabah Nasir as representatives of the ruling family, Faisal Marzouk for the leading merchants, Jawad Bu Khamseen and Abdulwahab Al-Wazzan for the well-organized Shi'ite community, and Jassim Al-Oun, who was active in the suburban committees.

The committee's main function was to distribute Government instructions, policy and guidance to the Popular Committees. Sheikh Ali Salem Al-Ali was initially the only man authorized to write government cheques in Kuwait, so the authority came from the source of funds.

The Resistance eventually settled into four main areas of activity: military, which involved armed attacks on Iraqi troops, and gathering intelligence for the Allies; essential services, which covered maintaining power, water, telephones, medical care and the oil industry; civil disobedience, which initially included public demonstrations, but was mainly the Kuwaiti boycott of all jobs except essential services; and solidarity and support, which involved keeping food, money and medicines flowing to Kuwaitis and hunted Westerners, especially when the Iraqis refused to issue ration cards to Kuwaitis who would not adopt Iraqi nationality.

Within a week of the invasion, the Kuwaiti Government had re-established itself in exile in Taif, Saudi Arabia, and elements of the Resistance in Kuwait began to communicate with it, and with the Kuwaiti Embassy in Washington.

The most important means of communication was initially a clandestine satellite telephone retrieved from the home of Sheikh Salem Hmoud Salem in the suburb of Nuzha on a tip from a Kuwaiti Ministry of Communications technician, Mustafa Qattan. He got it to Sheikh Ali Salem Al-Ali, who had re-entered Kuwait from Saudi Arabia on 4 August, and quickly established a link with the exiled Government. Mustafa was later arrested by the Iraqis, and is still missing. During early September four more US$50,000 satellite phones, arranged by the Kuwait Oil Tanker Company from its offices in Dubai, were smuggled across the Saudi border, concealed in the bodywork and fuel tanks of cars or pick-ups. Later, the Kuwait security services, or *Amn Dawla*, smuggled in another two via Jordan and Iraq.

Each set was more than just a phone with a satellite dish. They could also send faxes and telexes, so were used for written reports, maps, even photographs. All used the INMARSAT Atlantic and Indian Ocean satellites. These links to the legitimate Government conferred a *de facto* authority on the holders of the sets, particularly Sheikh Ali Salem Al-Ali himself, Sheikh Sabah Nasir, and Colonel Al-Ameer. Major-Generals Mohammed Al-Bader and Khalid Boodai also obtained systems later in the occupation.

These systems were perhaps the greatest tool of the Resistance, enabling it to maintain direct contact with the outside world, to co-ordinate actions, arrange for support such as funds, and identify the intelligence needs of the Coalition military. Sheikh Sabah Nasir and Major-General Boodai spoke almost daily with the Crown Prince and Prime Minister Sheikh Sa'ad Al-Abdullah, Foreign Minister Sheikh Sabah Al-Ahmad, and their Embassy in Washington. The sets were also used to communicate with Western TV networks to keep the plight of those in Kuwait in the public eye.

A number of the systems either broke down or were captured, including Brigadier Al-Mishari's. His last call was reportedly to his wife in October, several weeks after his capture, with the Iraqis standing over him. It was the last she ever heard of him. By the end of the occupation, only Major-General Boodai's set was operational.

Later, during Operation *Desert Storm*, the sets were used to direct Allied air strikes. To escape aerial bombing, the Iraqis hid some armoured vehicles under road bridges. However, the Kuwaitis on the ground could see them, and identify the location and nature of the target to the US Air Force in Riyadh. The Americans would tell the Resistance to ensure that all civilians were out of the area and within hours an aircraft would roar up the highway at low level, and destroy the vehicles with cluster bombs or rockets, without seriously damaging the bridge. On one occasion, when the Allies planned to bomb a huge Iraqi ammunition dump near Ahmadi, they were able to call the Kuwaitis first and tell them to clear any civilians out of nearby houses.

The first widespread civilian resistance began on the fourth day of the occupation when the Iraqis ordered everyone back to work. The Kuwaitis stayed away in droves. Only those required for essential services, or to prevent damage to machinery or take computer back-ups went to work.

Within days, the Kuwaitis were printing leaflets and newsletters on their home PCs, photocopying them, and passing them around by hand or fax. However, the newsletter campaign fizzled out in mid-September after several young Kuwaitis had been shot or tortured for distributing them.

The first public acts against the occupation were demonstrations, mostly by women and children carrying banners and photos of the Amir and Crown Prince. The earliest of these - videoed by the Kuwaitis to show people outside what they were doing - occurred on 3 August. The Iraqi troops initially fired over the crowd to disperse them, but during two marches on 8 August, they first fired over the rally, and then into it. The video cameraman dived for cover, but the mike continued recording the screams and gunfire. A young university chemistry major, Miss Sana'a Al-Foderi, was fatally wounded. Another student, Abdulrahman Hassan, was killed in a separate demonstration.

Anti-Iraqi graffiti, including derisory comments about the so-called Provisional Free Kuwait Government, appeared all over Kuwait from the first day, and on the night of 11 August, most Kuwaitis went onto the roofs of their houses, and called 'Allah Akhbar' (God is Great), for a full half hour. This was repeated on 1 September, on instructions from the exiled government.

It was spine-chilling inspiration to hear the thousands of voices rising out of the darkness like the keening of damned souls. The Iraqis were so unnerved that they fired machine guns and Kalashnikovs over the rooftops to try to stop it. The green and red tracers arcing low over the city, and the crackle of the weapons alongside the chanting was surreal. Voices against bullets. The danger very real. The Iraqis did not always aim high; a bullet fired into the air must come down somewhere. A young Kuwaiti friend of mine, Susi Al-Mutawa, was almost killed by a round which cracked past her ear. She was not the only one.

The military resistance maintained a steady low-level campaign against the Iraqis throughout the occupation, especially in the first six weeks before it was slowed down by savage Iraqi retribution, the capture of several key leaders, and the Iraqis 'encouraging' Kuwaitis to leave from mid-September.

Iraqi casualties from such attacks probably never exceeded a thousand, more likely hundreds, but the invaders got the message that they were unwelcome. More importantly, the Resistance probably tied down an estimated 30,000 Iraqi troops – more than 10% of those in Kuwait. The Iraqis had to garrison each of the 60 or so suburbs in Kuwait with between a company and a battalion, often using Special Forces, some of Saddam's best.

Initial military operations were amateurish affairs by untrained young men and women, using hunting rifles, shotguns, pistols, anything they could lay their hands on. In some cases, they were more danger to themselves and civilians than to the Iraqis. On one occasion, a Palestinian colleague with his two small children was at an Iraqi vehicle checkpoint when the Resistance fired on it. The Iraqi soldiers returned fire from behind the car. No one was hurt, but the children were long-traumatized from it.

Most Resistance weapons initially came from Kuwait Ministry of Defence stores, or police stations. In the first hours of the invasion, the Kuwaiti police had cleared out their suburban station armouries, handing out guns and ammunition to the citizens, or hiding them. Over the next two days, several Kuwaiti officers took great risks to retrieve weapons, ammunition, explosives and even a few shoulder-launched SAM-7 'Strella' anti-aircraft missiles from Army stores. Other weapons, especially RPGs which could be used against armour, trucks and buildings from 300 metres, were bought from Iraqi troops.

Once armed, some cell leaders tried to co-ordinate activities to concentrate on high-value targets. One of the most active was led by Colonel Mahmoud Al-Dossari, the Kuwait Airport Security Chief, and merchant Mohammed Al-Fajji.

They later worked with Sheikh Athbi Fahd Al-Ahmad, whose natural authority as part of the Al-Sabah and the son of the fallen Sheikh Fahd could be particularly useful in gaining other cells' co-operation.

Targets engaged by the military groups included police stations, schools housing Iraqi troops, isolated vehicles and troops, and senior officers. On many occasions, Iraqi vehicles that had broken down were torched as targets of opportunity. Other attacks were more planned. A favourite technique using a two-man team was to drop grenades or Molotov cocktails onto trucks or APCs passing under flyovers. The first man's task was to drop the explosive, while the second manned a getaway car. These attacks caused the Iraqis to close many of the flyover bridges, and divert traffic around them. It caused more inconvenience to the Kuwaitis than the Iraqis, but the point was made.

Not all attacks were on the roads. In early October, the Al-Dossari/Al-Fajji group used a SAM-7 missile to attack an Iraqi transport aircraft leaving Kuwait Airport. The team was led by Kuwait Army Captain Salah Jassim Al-Harban. They apparently hit an engine, but reports differ as to whether the aircraft was brought down, or landed safely in Basra. Either way, the Iraqis were forced to move their flight operations to the more secure and less convenient Ali Al-Salem KAF base outside the city.

This group also took the fight into Iraq itself by planting several car bombs in Basra and Zubair. Both Al-Dossari and Al-Fajji were captured in Baghdad in November, and brutally tortured. They received a death sentence on 15 February 1991, but the ceasefire came before it was carried out.

The most widely known Resistance attack was the 6 October car-bombing of the Kuwait International Hotel, where a delegation of senior Iraqi officials were staying. It was carried out by a cell later known as the '25th February Group', after Kuwait's national day. The hotel was across the road from the US Embassy, so eyewitness accounts soon reached Washington. The operatives were three young Kuwaitis, Miss Suad Al-Hassan, Thamer Dokar, and Miss Wafa Al-Amer; a Palestinian, Ashraf Abdullah, and an Iraqi from Kuwait, Abdulrahman Ali. The bomb missed the delegation, but killed two soldiers and brought the Resistance to the doorstep of the seniormost Iraqis in Kuwait.

One of the biggest Resistance operations was the truck-bombing of an Iraqi encampment in the Sulaibiya area, well-removed from residential suburbs. The Resistance used a water tanker truck, with the tank divided into three sections. The mid-section, with the filler opening, contained water so that it could pass inspection as an ordinary tanker. The other two sections contained twelve 81mm and four 120mm mortar shells, 200 kilograms of TNT, and home-made diesel-ammonium nitrate explosive. The truck was driven into the camp like a normal delivery, with a 15-minute fuse. It worked beautifully. The Kuwaitis could not ascertain the Iraqis' casualties, but the greater value was in showing them that they were at risk even in their own camps.

The military resistance also took on the difficult task of dealing with the Iraqis to get people out of custody. This often involved befriending the Iraqis, and running the risk of being labelled a collaborator, or of being arrested, because if the Iraqis became suspicious, they could easily lay a trap. In any event, the Iraqis seldom cared whether a man was innocent or not. Their attitude was that it was better to shoot an innocent man than to run any risk of missing a guilty one. This at least had the effect of keeping people terrorized.

The Kuwaitis never gave up on captured people. They always tried to bribe them out of custody or to convince the Iraqis that they had the wrong man – or woman. One very important person was an imam, or mosque prayer leader, Sheikh Jassim Mohalhal Al-Yaseen, who talked a number of Kuwaitis out of custody, using his authority as an eminent Muslim scholar to good effect.

Retribution for military Resistance attacks increased in severity from late August when Ali Hassan Majeed had established himself as the Governor of Kuwait, and the *Mukhabarat* had settled in. They countered with brutal force, not necessarily concerning themselves with finding the culprits. If an attack occurred in a certain area, they might burn a house which sniper fire may have come from, and the houses on either side. The occupants had five minutes to get out. The younger men were usually taken away.

When this did not stop the attacks, the Iraqis took to rounding up teenage boys and young men from the area at random, and holding them for a few days while they were beaten up, and then ransomed. In a number of cases, they took these youths back to their homes, let them out of the car to stumble towards their distraught families, and then shot them in the back of the head.

A number of murders of Resistance people were particularly brutal. One of Colonel Al-Dossari's men, 32-year-old Captain Ahmad Qabazard, of the police VIP Protection Squad, was captured on 7 September after walking back into Kuwait from Saudi Arabia disguised as an Afghan gardener. He was arrested at his home in Jabriya, after an informer's tip-off. On 16 September his neighbours saw him delivered back to the house, beaten and bloody, by the Iraqis. He had to be carried from the car, and supported as he stood. The neighbours could see him being questioned, and an exchange of sharp words. An officer then shot him three times in the neck and head with a pistol. Qabazard fell dead, and the Iraqis torched the house.

The Iraqis left Qabazard's body outside the burning house and his father was called by the neighbours. According to him, his son's palms had been drilled through with a power drill. All his nails had been extracted, and the inside of both his knees had been sliced, and the legs bound together so that the wounds had coagulated against each other. He had also been tortured with electricity. Incredibly, he had not compromised his colleagues. No members of his cell were arrested in the immediate aftermath of his death.

It was not only military operatives who were targeted. Treating wounded Resistance members was also punishable by death. Physician Dr Hisham Al-Obaidan, who was thought to have provided poison to inject into food for the troops, was arrested leaving the Sabah Hospital – renamed the Saddam Hospital by the Iraqis – and found with medical equipment in his car. This was enough. He was shot dead on 3 October, and his body left in the street.

The Iraqis could use the slightest pretext for execution. In one instance, on 13 September, the supermarket manager in the suburb of Ardiya, Mubarak Al-Nout, apparently refused to display Iraqi-supplied pictures of Saddam. He was shot dead outside his shop.

The Iraqis did not give up on chasing Resistance people who had caused them particular trouble or embarrassment. This could often lead to the deaths of a whole group of people. On 9 January 1991, Miss Suad Al-Hassan, the 19-year-old student who had taken part in the bombing of the Kuwait International Hotel was arrested, more than three months after the attack. The following day, her friend Wafa Al-Amer was picked up from her home. The Iraqis then came for Ashraf Abdullah, the hotel's Palestinian cashier, who had been involved. He was taken from his room at the hotel on 13 January, along with his Kuwaiti colleague, Thamer Doker. A total of 14 individuals associated with the group were rounded up. Several members of their families were also taken into custody, but later released.

Thamer's family initially traced him to the Naif Palace, in the Kuwait Governorate building. The Iraqis denied he was there, but phoned the family on 26 January to say he was in the Juvenile Prison, and that they could bring him food, blankets and cigarettes. Both Thamer's and Ashraf's families brought the supplies to the gate, but were not allowed to see the men.

Over the next week, the third of the air war, the Iraqis called the families asking for gold, clothes, and a generator in return for the release of the men. Thamer's mother was even allowed to visit her son on 4 February, and was told that he would be released in the next two days. The following morning at 6.30 a.m., he was brought to his home and shot dead in front of it. His colleague, Ashraf, was found dead outside his home on the same day, with one bullet in the chest, and one in the head. However, his head been chopped with an axe. Half of it, and both of his eyes, were missing, apparently gouged out. His legs and hands had been tied, and his mouth taped shut. His family could only pray that the mutilation had occurred after he was shot.

Wafa Al-Amer's fate is more uncertain. She too was found dead on 5 February, with signs of torture on her neck. Her friend, Suad Al-Hassan, was found in the suburb of Kheitan on 13 February, less than two weeks before liberation, dead from strangulation, with evidence of other torture. In all, nine members of the group died. Several are still unaccounted for. Few of the surviving members can bring themselves to talk about their activities.

There were a number of other cases where it is thought that the capture of one cell member led to the capture and eventual death of others. Surprisingly, within Kuwait, there is little bitterness on the part of the families of murdered Resistance members that their colleagues may have given them away under torture. In the belief of many bereaved families, no one could be expected to stand up to the treatment meted out by the *Mukhabarat*.

Apart from torturing captured Resistance members, the Iraqis also systematically repressed the general public. They had no intention of maintaining hospitals for their conquered people. In Iraq, mentally ill people are usually left to die, and so it was in Kuwait under Iraqi rule.

Similarly, although emergency care continued to be available, thanks to the volunteer efforts of Kuwaiti, Egyptian, Indian and Palestinian doctors and nurses, specialist patients such as those with cancer, or requiring kidney dialysis, or diabetics, were denied treatment, forcing them to leave for Saudi

Arabia. Some died before the borders were opened to Kuwaitis in mid-September. The hospitals were reserved for Iraqis and emergency cases.

In a more public programme of repression, Kuwaitis would be picked up, almost randomly, and held in the local police station or school, where they were beaten and humiliated. The idea was often to obtain ransoms from their relatives in the form of money, electronic equipment or cars.

Again, the women bore the brunt of the repression. The number of Kuwaiti women raped during the occupation will never be known, but it is certainly in the thousands. The victims also included Palestinians and Asians, and the British wife of a Kuwaiti was gang-raped by three soldiers in Ahmadi. Unlike attacks on Western women, there was little official retribution on Iraqi soldiers for attacks on Kuwaitis and Asians. Being predominantly Muslims, the Iraqis were aware that rape would be a particularly difficult trauma for conservative Kuwaiti society to deal with effectively.

Against this background of repression, maintaining food supplies was one of the Resistance's most important functions. Initially, this was not a problem as local storehouses held enough supplies to sustain the country for over a year, and with the higher food prices, supplies flowed in from Jordan and Iraq. The main problem was not obtaining supplies, but paying for them, safeguarding and rationing them, and distributing them to retail outlets without having them looted. Obtaining fresh produce and dairy products was also difficult.

The usual source of groceries in Kuwait is the local Co-operative Society, known as the 'Co-op', of which there are about forty. There were also several privately-owned major supermarkets, notably The Sultan Center (TSC) in Salmiya, and Americana Safeway, the latter which was burned out in the first week. In their efforts to get the country back to 'business-as-usual', the Iraqis were happy to allow the co-ops and TSC to continue working. They even posted guards to maintain order. However, after a few weeks the *Mukhabarat* became aware of the assistance they were providing to the Resistance. They began harassing the store managers, even imprisoning them for days or weeks.

The co-ops were supplied from warehouses in the industrial area of Subhan, near the airport. These huge stores held about KD140 million worth of supplies. To protect them, men such as Tareq Barak, Chairman of the Central Stores Company, which runs the government's basic ration stores, Abdullah Al-Baijan, the Chairman of the Kuwaiti Union of Foodstuff Importers and Manufacturers, and Abdulatief Al-Kharaza, the Chairman of the Co-operative Societies, met early in the occupation with representatives of the Iraqi Ministry of Commerce and bought time by agreeing to 'guarantee a return to pre-invasion normalcy'. They obtained an order to all Iraqi checkpoints and patrols not to interfere with representatives of co-ops, even if they were carrying large sums of money. Incredibly, none of the co-ops took advantage of the situation to raise their prices, or to divert their stock to the black market.

As time went on, the Kuwaitis moved much of the inventory into basements of large houses in the suburbs, and then resupplied the retail outlets by van. The Kuwaiti warehouse managers were treading a very fine and dangerous line, trying to keep the Iraqis from moving into the stores, while co-operating with the Resistance and spiriting the supplies out to less obvious locations.

Another major source of food was the Kuwait Danish Dairy (KDD), also in Subhan. The Iraqis allowed it to continue production as part of the charade that Kuwait was operating normally under their benign rule. KDD's main product line was reconstituted milk. With enough raw materials to keep them going for months in normal times, they were able to supply the much reduced population until the plant was bombed by the US Air Force during the air war. Perhaps as important as dairy products were their reconstituted fruit juices.

The Kuwait Livestock Transport and Trading Company, which usually imports thousands of live sheep from Australia monthly, continued to operate its slaughterhouses, using stock on hand. Fortunately, all its vessels were outside Kuwait at the time of the invasion. Nevertheless, they had to close down in December when the Iraqi Army took the last of their sheep, an experimental flock and gene pool built up over 20 years.

To supplement these major sources, street markets sprang up on traffic roundabouts and anywhere people gathered. These often sold goods at inflated prices, but they were accessible. They also had items that the co-ops had run out of, especially eggs, chickens and fruit.

Later, when there were fewer people in Kuwait, the co-ops organized home deliveries of staples such as rice, flour and sugar directly from the underground suburban stores to minimize losses to the Iraqis. Neighbourhood bakeries continued working, using volunteer Kuwaiti and Palestinian workers to replace departed Asians. Kuwaiti women baked at home, and planted vegetable gardens. Some families moved sheep, cattle and chickens into their gardens. Elegant residential areas began to sound like farmyards.

This close community co-operation seemed to instill a sense of bonding among many of the Kuwaitis in a way not experienced since before the easy wealth of oil. 'We were like this before!' was the comment of one old Kuwaiti lady I spoke to. 'I hope it continues when they are gone.'

The parallel issue to food was money. The major food outlets took in money more as a means of rationing supplies and financing replacement staple goods from Iraq than of making profits. However, the greatest need for money was not to buy food, but to buy captured Kuwaitis out of custody. This could be very expensive, with ransoms ranging from ID1,000 to ID100,000, or US$35,000.

The Kuwaitis could bring money in from Saudi Arabia with relative ease during the first fortnight before the Iraqis sealed the border. Substantial sums of government cash continued to come in this way, with increasing difficulty, until October. Some Palestinian friends brought in cash via Jordan and Iraq.

During the first month of the occupation, the Kuwaitis tapped whatever sources they could inside the country, particularly the safes and cash boxes from the KNPC petrol stations and the cash floats of the Ministry of Social Affairs and Labour social services centres. In some cases, the Kuwaiti managers had to cut the safes open with oxy-acetylene torches. Not being experienced safe-crackers, they sometimes set the money inside afire, and had to douse it. This money, soaking wet at times, was passed to Sheikh Sabah Nasir, who then distributed it to where it was needed. However, this money ran out by the end of August, and the Resistance had to turn to merchants inside Kuwait for funds. About KD2 million was moved from KNPC, and a further KD100,000 from the Ministry of Social Affairs.

The Government-in-exile authorized two Resistance leaders in Kuwait, Sheikh Ali Salem Al-Ali and, much later, Major-General Boodai, to sign chits on behalf of the Government to take money from Kuwaiti merchants and currency traders, and to guarantee payments to major food suppliers, with the equivalent amount payable outside through the Kuwait Investment Office in London. They also bought Iraqi dinars from individual Iraqis by transferring an equivalent amount of hard currency into their Swiss bank accounts.

A copy of every chit signed by Sheikh Ali was sent to his London home, and another to an office of the Central Bank of Kuwait in London, who then passed it on to the Finance Minister in Taif. In effect, the Kuwaiti banking community went to war. After liberation, it was estimated that the government paid out about KD30 million in payments guaranteed during the occupation.

A further critical activity of the Resistance was locating and then supplying the Kuwaiti military prisoners-of-war who had been captured and taken to prison camps in Iraq in the first couple of days.

For the first two months of the occupation, the relatives of the interned servicemen frantically searched for any news of them, unsure if they were alive or dead. Although the Iraqi military were treating the men largely in accordance with the Geneva Conventions, they ignored one critical part of the accords – advising the families of the condition of the men.

One breakthrough was made by the mother of Captain Ahmad Qabazard, who was so brutally murdered in September. Her second son, Salman, was a Naval officer who had been captured at Ras Al-Jalayh. Through a senior Iraqi Shi'ite cleric, Ayatollah Ali Akbar Al-Khoui, who was later murdered by Saddam, she found that the Kuwaiti armed forces and some police officers were being held in a camp near Mosul, where they had been from 26 August.

The family was eventually able to bribe a senior Iraqi into allowing them to see the men. The price was six cars and ID80,000. They got to see Salman on 25 September and got a list of all the other 637 officers, with the addresses and phone numbers of their families in Kuwait. Other families had been making their own enquiries, which bore fruit at the same time. They promptly returned home, and contacted all the other families with the first firm news of their men. The Resistance then organised a supply network for the families of the POWs. The manager of The Sultan Center, Riad Sultan Al-Essa, told the families to take food, money, and anything else they needed for free.

The POWs were held in four castles, like old English castles. One was for officers, and the others for enlisted men. Each had 12 barracks, with room for seventy men. With the high castle walls, the men were unable to see outside. The conditions were better than the earlier Rasheed Army Camp, but they had no mattresses, and only received blankets in October, after three months.

On 6 November, the Iraqis moved the Kuwaiti officers by train to Ba'qouba Army Camp, an hour's drive north of Baghdad, and opened an office in Baghdad so that families could register each Wednesday morning to visit them that day. Each week, the families would make up food parcels, with warm

clothes, cigarettes, and changes of underwear, and travel from Kuwait to
Baghdad by car or bus. They were allowed to see the men from 10.00 a.m. to 4.00
p.m. until shortly before the air war started in January 1991. For all the
repression in Kuwait, the Iraqis acted with decency in allowing the visits.

There were four other POW camps, mainly for enlisted men, at Rasheed, near
Baghdad, west of the capital at Ramadi, and at Mosul and Takrit.

Mention the name Asrar in Kuwait today, and every Kuwaiti will know who
you mean: Asrar Al-Qabandi. Asrar is generally hailed as Kuwait's Joan of Arc.
The comparison is not an overstatement. At 30 years old, she was a woman a
generation ahead of her time. Although from a typical, conservative middle-
class family, she had studied in the US, preferred jeans and T-shirts to traditional
dress, and had an American accent and habits. She was a stoutly built five-foot
powerhouse of energy, with a feisty sense of humour, a fiery temper, and an
utter contempt for the Iraqis. This latter quality was to lead to her capture in
early November, and a terrible death.

Wearing her dark hair pulled back in a bun or pony-tail, and sporting large
spectacles, Asrar exuded drive and confidence. Life was too short for all she had
to do. She rushed everywhere. Naturally headstrong, she was absolutely
convinced that her way of doing things was right. Whether it was democracy,
women's rights, or care of the handicapped, she spread her message vocally. Her
favourite hours before the invasion were spent holding endless discussions,
sipping beverages, with friends in the family's beach chalet.

Her first mission in early August, with her friend, Hind Al-Bahar, had been
to find a secure haven for Sheikh Ali Salem Al-Ali, Sheikh Sabah Nasir and his
wife, and the satellite phone system that Mustafa Qattan had retrieved and
passed to Sheikh Ali. Asrar's next task was to get 15 Al-Sabah children out of the
country. Some of their parents had been outside the country at the time of the
invasion, leaving the children in the care of relatives or governesses. Other Al-
Sabah parents would stay in the Kuwait underground, but needed to get their
kids out. Asrar arranged for the youngsters, their nannies and an Al-Sabah
woman to go out across the desert to Saudi Arabia on 12 August with a guide,
together with an American friend, Katherine Baker, German dentist Claus
Spitzer, an Arab friend, and Ms Baker's two dogs.

Asrar soon teamed up with Dr Hashem Behbehani, a distinguished lecturer
at Kuwait University. He moved out to his cousin's house, and Asrar took over
his Mishref residence as a more permanent base for her group's operations.

Asrar worked mainly with Sheikh Sabah Nasir and his wife, Sheikh Ali
Salem Al-Ali, Salah Al-Rayes, the brother of the Kuwaiti Ambassador to the UK,
her friend, Hind Al-Bahar, Dr Behbehani, and young Sheikh Mishal Yousef.
Nazeeh Khajah, the nephew of Ahmad Khajah, joined the group after his
American wife was evacuated in September.

The young woman seemed to be everywhere, with an unshakable belief that
Kuwait would be liberated. Like most other people in the country at the time,
she could hardly understand why the Allies in Saudi Arabia did not simply
drive into Kuwait. Everyone expected the Iraqis to flee at the first sight of a US
Marine. Her motto, and that of the Resistance as a whole, became *'Allah, Al-*

Watan, Al-Amir!' (God, The Nation, The Amir!). Her colleagues have a video of her spray-painting this on a wall.

Asrar's activities included forging driving licences for Kuwaitis, Americans and British in hiding to identify them as safe nationalities, forging car registration books, supporting Kuwaitis and Westerners in her immediate area, setting up safe houses, and assisting the Bahraini Ambassador to issue his passports to Kuwaitis who were particularly vulnerable. Her main link to the Westerners in Kuwait at the time was a Lebanese Armenian lady, Lucia Topalian, and one of the British wardens, Dr Stuart Dick. Together, they arranged the distribution of tens of thousands of Iraqi dinars of smuggled Kuwaiti Government money to Westerners in hiding.

Once, using her dark skin to advantage and disguised as an Indian, she smuggled vital computer disks out of a ministry. When orders came from Taif to cease military attacks in urban Kuwait because of Iraqi reprisals, she and Nazeeh Khajah scouted targets in Basra for car bomb attacks in Iraq itself.

Asrar's Achilles' heel was that she felt the Iraqis were too stupid to catch her. She was so contemptuous of them that she seemed oblivious to the risks. Her one concession to security was to assume the false identity of Sarah Mubarak, named after her paternal grandfather, and to arrange a cover story with her father that she had left home two years previously.

Asrar spoke almost daily to her boss, Foreign Minister Sheikh Sabah Al-Ahmad, in Taif on the satellite phone. She also telephoned and faxed her elder brother Adnan, who was working with the exiled government, providing comprehensive information on conditions in Kuwait, and passing messages between separated families. She also organized interviews with US, British and French TV networks to keep Kuwait in the public eye.

When the Committee of the Kuwait Red Crescent Society was arrested by the Iraqis, it was Asrar who got the news out to the West within hours, via her brother Adnan, allowing the ICRC in Geneva to pressure Baghdad for their release even before the Iraqi Government was aware of the arrests.

In late October, Asrar left for Saudi Arabia through the Nuwaisib border post, which the Iraqis had opened to Kuwaiti women, children and older men. She stayed overnight at Khafji with her brother Bassam. The plan was for her to go to Taif, and then to the US to testify before Congress. With her US education and accent, go-getter attitude, and the credibility of undercover satellite phone interviews on network TV, she would be Kuwait's star witness.

However, from Khafji, Asrar could see the lights of Kuwait's Al-Zoor twinkling across the border. She decided to return. At the time, she suspected that the Iraqis knew her false identity, but her contempt for them was undiminished. Bassam pleaded with her not to go; she had done more than enough already. She would not hear of it. It was the last time he saw her. Asrar found a lift back into Kuwait on a pick-up smuggling money concealed in the vehicle's bodywork. Within hours, her brother Adnan in Taif got a call from her on the satellite phone. 'Guess where I am?', she said. He thought she was in Riyadh. Asrar laughed. 'No, back in Kuwait!'

Asrar was only one of many Kuwaiti woman active in the Resistance. In fact, many people in Kuwait consider the women to have been the Resistance's backbone. They carried weapons and forged papers, and provided many of the organizational and technical skills required to run a complex campaign.

Despite a spate of rapes in the first week, the Iraqi troops seem to have been given orders to behave respectfully toward females in the early days. The Kuwaiti women played this for all it was worth by carrying concealed weapons and ammunition through checkpoints where men would have been searched. It was an incredibly dangerous task requiring great courage. They were very much on their own if their cargo was discovered.

A number of young women stood out in this task, including 23-year-old radiographer Wafa Al-Amer, who took part in the Kuwait International Hotel bombing, journalist Kholoud Al-Khamis, and Amy Bahman, the pretty teenage daughter of a Kuwait Airways pilot and an Englishwoman. Amy's widowed mother was outside Kuwait at the time of the invasion, and unable to return. Amy turned her house in a quiet street of the exclusive suburb of Mishref into a Resistance meeting place. She took full advantage of her diminutive size and striking looks to bluff her way through Iraqi checkpoints with weapons. She still shivers when recalling the danger: the almost paralysing fear she dealt with approaching the checkpoints is still evident.

Wafa, for her part, took part in at least two other bombings, including restaurants catering to Iraqi soldiers, in the Kheitan and Hasawi areas, and was one of the key sources of false identification cards. She was not as fortunate as Amy or Kholoud, and was eventually captured and killed.

The Resistance also looked after many Westerners in hiding. Numerous Americans, British, French and Germans were sheltered by Kuwaitis in their own homes and in safe houses, at great risk to the Kuwaitis' lives and those of their families. Fortunately, there are no known confirmed cases of Kuwaitis being killed for hiding Westerners, but several had very close escapes.

The Resistance supported scores of other Westerners who were hiding in their own homes by supplying them with food and cigarettes. Once the Kuwaitis got their food pipeline working properly, most Westerners being provisioned by the Resistance were stocked up for many months ahead.

The relationship between the Resistance and the Westerners was not all one-way. In fact, many Westerners in Kuwait felt a deep bond of shared suffering with the Kuwaitis. The country was their home, and they felt as much rage as many Kuwaitis. A group of Germans taught the Resistance how to build timers for explosives, and others helped them build a better car bomb.

In fact, the Command Central British warden group, with several ex-military men in it, became the proposed contact point for British Special Forces which were to be infiltrated into Kuwait to serve as the local co-ordinators for an exfiltration operation for those in hiding, and the diplomats in the embassies. The Allies could not communicate through the British Embassy as its voice link to Abu Dhabi was insecure. The diplomats were apparently considered a security risk. The idea was for the commandos to enter Kuwait, link up with the Resistance who would then take them to Command Central where they could be then put in contact with the free-Westerners in Kuwait who could brief them in detail on the local conditions.

To do this, the Allies had to prove to Command Central that the initial message was not a hoax, and to test the speed and security of the Resistance communication channels. An officer in the UK visited Mike Devey's wife, and asked her to how they could prove to Mike that the message was valid. She came up with the expression *'Thora Third has gone greenroading,'* explaining that *'Thora Third'* was Mike's old Land Rover in England, and 'greenroading' was the family expression for taking it driving in the backwoods.

Sure enough, the message found its way through to Mike via Major-General Boodai's satellite phone. The Kuwaiti officer who delivered it, Lieutenant-Colonel Ahmad Al-Rahmani, code-named 'Abu Fahd', was just as puzzled as British Intelligence, but it made perfect sense to Mike.

Unfortunately, the message took too long to reach Mike to be of much use. The message path was too slow. Fortunately, the need for rescue by the commandos abated with the release of the Westerners and Japanese in early December. Nevertheless, the initial planning had been done.

The satellite phones were the most secure means of communication the Resistance had with the outside world, but they could not cope with the demand for messages, and were kept secret because of the security risk to their operators. Kuwait's ham radio fraternity stepped into the breach, and maintained a message service throughout the occupation.

The most active of these hams was Abdul Jabbar Marafie, a retired Ministry of Communications engineer and father of eight, who ran his station from his basement in the suburb of Salwa. He used the AMTOR (Amateur Transmission Over Radio) system, whereby contact is established from computer to computer rather than by voice, using radio signals as the link. He used a Bahraini call sign instead of his own 9K2DZ, which would have identified him as a Kuwaiti station. At least one other ham in Kuwait, Muhsen Al-Ajeel, also used AMTOR, but most used the regular ham radio voice system.

Abdul Jabbar's role was later immortalized in a TV documentary, *'The Last Voice From Kuwait'*, and has been credited with helping to shape US public opinion in support of military action. His messages started out as a simple health and welfare service, but at the suggestion of one of his contacts, Frank Moore of WANE-TV in Indiana, he started sending out descriptions of day-to-day life under the occupation. Abdul Jabbar was the individual who broke the news of the premature babies being taken from their incubators at Kuwaiti hospitals – later embellished in the US – and gave vivid accounts of the Iraqi atrocities in Kuwait. Moore passed these accounts to the State Department, and other media sources, after ensuring that Abdul Jabbar's security was not compromised and the intelligence could not be traced back to him. Other contacts relayed messages to the Kuwaiti Government-in-exile in Taif.

The health and welfare messages always formed the basis of Abdul Jaber's service. He felt that they had a more direct effect on easing the suffering of people in Kuwait at the time. Nevertheless, later on, he sent out military intelligence as part of the life reports. At one stage, the Iraqis were building dummy tanks using steel plate and six-inch pipes, and placing them in the desert under camouflage to fool US satellites as to the number of armoured vehicles in Kuwait. The decoys not only looked like tanks from above, but gave off infra-red signatures similar to the real tanks. Oil men in Ahmadi had independently identified these, including the location of the workshop. The Allies were therefore alerted from two separate sources to be aware of decoys, and were able to structure their plans accordingly.

In August, Abdul Jabbar relayed news that two BA149 crew had been seen at a dental clinic in the company of the Iraqis. Several companies in Germany with people in Kuwait made contact through the German part of his network, especially Siemens, Mercedes Benz and Lufthansa, and were able to pass messages. The link was so effective that when one large group of Germans was captured in mid-September, the German Government was able to lodge a protest with the Iraqis, complete with names, ages and occupations, before the Iraqi Government itself knew that the men had been taken.

Abdul Jabbar's overseas network was massive. The outgoing messages were initially passed through a fellow ham in Holland, and then from the beginning of September through Scott Ward, the chief radio operator on the aircraft carrier USS *John F. Kennedy* in the Red Sea. This simplified matters as the vessel was closer to Kuwait and could obtain better reception. Ward continued to communicate with Abdul Jabbar until his ship was required to maintain radio silence from mid-January 1991 with the onset of the air war. He could then receive, but not transmit. Other contacts were the Kuwait Embassy in London, and hams in Guatemala, Egypt, Germany, Lebanon, Pakistan, Sweden and Switzerland. Two exiled Kuwaitis in Egypt collected messages to be transmitted to Abdul Jaber in bulk. One Guatemala contact relayed about 4,000 messages for Kuwaiti hams from September onwards.

The internal network within Kuwait was just as important for gathering outgoing messages and relaying incoming messages. Abdul Jabbar was simply too busy operating the radio to field the calls. The key part of his team was Mrs Nargis Qabazard, a woman with boundless energy. She handled an average of 50 incoming messages each day - on some days, there were up to 150 - found the answers they requested, or passed them on, and then prepared the replies. Abdul Jabbar was almost relieved when the phone lines were cut during the air war as it allowed him to rest for the first time in months.

Curiously, throughout the occupation, the Iraqis did not tell him to take his aerial down, although it was in plain view. It may have been mistaken for a large TV aerial. They did find his name from the records of the Kuwait Amateur Radio Society and visited him once. However, by an incredible stroke of luck, they first went to the wrong house. Abdul Jabbar heard of this, and visited the police station to see who was after him. He left a message, and returned home to find the Iraqis there. They asked him if he had a radio. He said he only had two old sets which had been in storage since the invasion. They were apparently convinced of his innocence because of his age and voluntary visit to the police station, and took the two old radios. However, the portable set which he actually used was safely hidden.

The Kuwaiti oil fields and the companies operating them are the country's greatest physical assets. Although the oil industry is controlled by Kuwait

Petroleum Corporation, the two principal operating companies are Kuwait Oil Company (KOC), which runs the fields and produces crude oil and gas, and Kuwait National Petroleum Company (KNPC), which refines the crude oil for export and local sale. These operations had given Kuwait her huge investment portfolio which financed much of the Allied deployment in Saudi Arabia, and would be critical in rebuilding the country after liberation.

The objectives of the Resistance in this area were to preserve those assets as much as possible, and to enable others to fight the Iraqis more effectively. The members of what became known as the 'Oil Sector Resistance' had therefore to work alongside the Iraqis to influence them, instead of confronting them directly. To their credit, they lost not a single Kuwaiti life, although a KOC accountant and several KNPC employees were executed elsewhere.

The first priority immediately after the invasion was for KOC to almost shut down the 2 million-barrels-per-day crude oil production from the fields. The Iraqis had ordered the KNPC refineries shut down on the second day of the occupation, as with the trade embargo in force the refinery storage tanks would eventually overflow. However, the oilfields had to be kept going at a reduced level. The Kuwaiti power generation and water desalination systems used local oil and the associated gas as feedstock. In the heat of summer, no one in Kuwait could have survived long without power or fresh water. The hospitals and bakeries also needed gas for their ovens and other machinery. The hospitals had emergency generators, but would have soon run out of fuel, and the cooking gas could not be replenished. Apart from these basic needs, most other fuel requirements were drawn from refinery stocks.

The Iraqis initially tried to take over the oil industry using people who had previously worked with the Kuwaitis, particularly on a pipeline from southern Iraq to Kuwait, and others who had trained in Kuwaiti refineries. In the early days, the Iraqis installed these men to supervise the industry. They called in all oil sector employees, but were faced with a boycott of everyone except a few Palestinians, emergency workers and others who had to stay on the job to prevent damage to the installations. The Iraqis then brought down executives and engineers from the South Basra Oil company and the Iraqi National Oil Company to take over KOC and the three KNPC refineries.

In the meantime, the Kuwaitis formed their own underground management team, comprising mainly mid-level executives such as Shuaiba Refinery Manager Riyadh Al-Saleh; Mina Al-Ahmadi Refinery Manager Bader Hajji Yousef; Shuaiba Refinery Operations Manager Toufic Al-Mughni; KOC Manager for Operations, Projects and Planning Ahmad Al-Arbeed; KOC Maintenance Manager Mohammed Al-Jazzaf, and Musab Al-Yaseen, the KOC General Superintendent of Reservoirs. Al-Yaseen was the group's main contact with the Government-in-exile through Brigadier Al-Mishari, Sheikhs Ali Salem Al-Ali and Sabah Nasir, and later Major-General Boodai.

Other key individuals included Ali Al-Qabandi, a KOC chief accountant; Bader Al-Khashti, who took care of KOC's safety and firefighting; Ahmad Al-Rayyis, a Maintenance Superintendent; Ahmad Murad, the Systems Development Manager; Abdullah Al-Bannai from the Personnel Department; Services Manager Mohammed Jassim Abdul Salam, and a dozen others. Murad and Al-Bannai had actually infiltrated back into Kuwait from Saudi Arabia in mid-August on their ninth attempt. The senior KOC and KNPC managers and board members had either gone into hiding or escaped to Saudi Arabia.

The first task of this team was to obtain permission from their Government to work alongside the Iraqis in the greater interests of preserving the oil sector. They did not want to be labelled as collaborators after liberation. Once clearance was obtained, they then went to work, on the Iraqis.

The relationship between the Iraqi and Kuwaiti oilmen was tense, but the Iraqis knew they did not have the capability to run the sector properly, so initially let the Kuwaitis have a reasonably free rein. Besides, with the minimal levels of production up to September, it hardly mattered. They had control of the refinery stocks, which met all their fuel requirements.

Then, in late September, the Iraqis told the KOC men that they wanted to boost production to 1 million barrels per day – half the usual level. The KNPC managers were also told to get the refineries operating again. The Kuwaitis presumed that this was so the Iraqis could produce fuel for their army, although there was plenty of fuel available in Iraq with its exports embargoed. Unknown to the Kuwaitis at the time, the Iraqis had other plans.

The Kuwaiti managers resisted, but the Iraqis brought in an unsavoury character called Ali Zubair, who would not take no for an answer. He threatened to charge them with treason – for which the penalty in Iraq was execution – if they did not co-operate. Some of the Kuwaitis decided that this was enough, and went into hiding. Others decided that the Iraqis would get the refineries working with or without their help. The real question was whether they would damage them in the process, and whether Kuwaiti involvement could help prevent this. There was a further consideration. If the Iraqis wanted to produce crude oil, they would have to allow the Kuwaitis into the oilfields to check the facilities there, and that would allow them to observe the Iraqi troop deployments. Furthermore, without oil, there would be no power generation, and no water desalination for the several hundred thousand civilians in the country. Eventually, the Kuwaitis agreed to start one of the units at the Mina Al-Ahmadi refinery, and by mid-October were refining 200,000 barrels per day, or 25% of the country's refining capacity.

The Iraqis then tried to establish more direct control, and tried unsuccessfully to re-start the other two refineries. They brought down about 500 more of their own men at the end of October – drew up a new organization chart, and tried to slot the Kuwaitis into positions they dictated.

The Kuwaitis started to lose what little *de facto* control they had, but this was difficult to prevent in the circumstances. The underground management team feared that if the Iraqis identified their real roles, they would be simply removed. They had to find a way to protect themselves, yet still influence the operation. They therefore nominated certain members of the official management to act as a buffer between themselves as the real Kuwaiti management, and the Iraqis. The official management would ostensibly take instructions from the Iraqis, and then pass them on to the real management, who would consider how they served their own interests at the time. The official management would then go back to the Iraqis with various reasons why things could or could not be done. It was impossible to control everything, but the Iraqis were a generation behind the Kuwaitis in oilfield technology and not sufficiently familiar with their captive oil industry, so were inclined to believe the bluff. In reality, the Kuwaitis were running parts of the operation, but letting the Iraqis think that they were doing it.

Miraculously, when the Iraqis burned the KOC Head Office in February 1991, they did not touch the computer centre, which was in a separate building. The Iraqis were still largely unaware of the full use of computers in a modern oil company, and did not appreciate the trouble they could have caused by destroying them. Within months of liberation, the Kuwaitis had restored their pre-invasion data, and were even able to produce financial statements.

One of the Iraqis' reasons for boosting crude oil production only became apparent late in the occupation. They had two projects in mind, one named 'Great Saddam', the other 'Tareq'. Both were nothing less than incredible acts of environmental terrorism, with little or no military value. The Kuwaitis could only assume that Saddam himself had dreamed them up, and that no one in Baghdad had dared to tell him they were a monumental waste of time.

'Great Saddam' involved digging a line of trenches throughout southern Kuwait, between the Iraqi troops and the Allied forces in Saudi Arabia, and filling them with oil, fed by pipelines. 'Tareq' was the marine version. It involved pumping oil into the Subiya waterway between the Kuwaiti mainland and Bubiyan Island from twin 16-inch pipelines, and letting it flow down into the Gulf, as well as pumping oil directly into Kuwait Bay from Doha. In both instances, the Iraqi intention was to set fire to this oil – an impossibility for the oil dumped in the Gulf as it would sink to just below the surface and was too heavy to burn fiercely. 'Great Saddam' was to have created a wall of fire around south-western Kuwait, fed by oil from Ahmadi.

It took the Kuwaitis some time to figure out what the Iraqis were up to, and even then, it wasn't until the air war that they fully realized what Tareq was for. They had seen the Iraqis stealing 110 kilometres of 16-inch pipe stored from a deferred project. They knew the Iraqis had connected this pipe to the main 30-inch transit line between north and south Kuwait, and had even noticed the two twin 16-inch pipelines under construction. Still, the Kuwaitis suspected that the Iraqis were planning to pump Kuwaiti oil across Bubiyan Island to Iraq or Iran, although some of the Kuwaitis had a suspicion of what was to come when the Iraqis started loading five of their oil tankers which had been allowed through the UN blockade with crude, and installed pipes on the ships to enable them to discharge the cargo into the sea.

Throughout the occupation, the Kuwait underground management reported on the local state of affairs in the oil sector to the Government-in-exile by faxing reports produced on a home PC to Taif, using Sheikh Sabah Nasir's or Major-General Boodai's satellite phones. It was too dangerous to have a set in Ahmadi. They had noticed an Iraqi radio tracking unit nearby and were not sure whether it could also pinpoint the satellite phone transmissions.

During August, the oilmen advised the government that the well-heads had been mined. The Government – desperate at the time for anything to use against the Iraqis – promptly broadcast this as part of their propaganda. This caused great concern on the part of the underground management and the Iraqis helping them. It would be obvious where the reports had come from as only a limited number of Kuwaitis were allowed into the fields, and only a few Iraqis had the authority to let them go there.

Fortunately, Iraqi intelligence did not pick up on this. In any event, it suited them to have the Coalition aware of their preparedness to blow the fields, as they eventually did. However, this early information allowed the Government to plan to bring in firefighting teams after liberation, and for the military to plan for the effects on their operations of oilfield smoke.

In fact, the Kuwaiti oilmen had apparently smuggled Kuwaiti National Guard ordnance specialists into the oilfields and refineries, disguised as engineers, complete with KOC identification papers. They even put them on the payroll in case the Iraqis checked. The Guardsmen were able to identify the type of explosive, and the detonation wiring systems.

The Kuwaitis then apparently started bribing the Iraqis to remove the detonators from the well-heads, and rewire the detonation circuits so that they would show up as complete if tested. They concentrated on high-pressure wells which would cause the greatest trouble if blown. The Kuwaitis could not do this themselves as they were not explosives specialists, and their access to the fields was limited. This activity had an additional benefit for the Kuwaiti military resistance in the city. Their oil sector resistance colleagues passed on some of the removed detonators for use in car bombs.

About ten days before the land war, in February 1991, another gaffe outside Kuwait may have undone much of this good work. The Resistance had told their government that they had sabotaged the Iraqi oilfield sabotage, and that most of the wells apart from the low-pressure Wafra field and a few others were safe. A senior official foolishly broadcast this. The Iraqis may have heard, or may have simply decided to test the circuits for real. They tried to blow up a number of wells at Raudhatain, in northern Kuwait, and discovered the sabotage. For the next few days, Iraqi Army engineers frantically reset the charges, and then blew the wells. About 720 were destroyed, but the Iraqis did not have time to reset and blow the other 300.

Other pieces of oil sector Resistance intelligence, which the Kuwaiti Government passed to the Americans, but did not broadcast, had more direct military relevance. The Kuwaitis in the oilfields identified the Iraqi units deployed there, and their condition, and faxed details out, including even the names and ranks of several senior Iraqi officers they met. They even knew the name of the Iraqi in charge of mining the wells, a Major-General Sa'ad.

This was the priceless 'human intelligence' which the Coalition forces could get nowhere else. Thanks in part to this and their own electronic sources, when the US Marines attacked southern Kuwait in January 1991, they knew almost exactly which Iraqi units they were up against.

Although the Kuwaitis did not tumble completely to the Tareq Project until during the air war, they were aware that the Iraqis intended to pour crude oil into the Gulf from the export terminals near Ahmadi to foil an Allied amphibious attack. They could not prevent this entirely, so concentrated on minimizing the flow of oil pumped directly into the Gulf from land storage.

The refineries and crude oil tanker loading points in Kuwait are fed from two huge tank farms on a ridge eight kilometres inland, one on the north side of Ahmadi, and one on the south. The northern farm has 24 tanks with a total capacity of 8 million barrels. The southern one has 35 tanks with 6 million barrels capacity. Prior to the dumping, an estimated 10.7 million barrels were in the tanks, and almost unlimited reserves in the nearby Burgan oilfield.

From the tank farms, the crude oil can go to one of four main destinations: the three coastal refineries for refining and then export; two export loading piers, known respectively as North and South Pier; another spur manifold which pumps oil to the power stations and water desalination plants; and finally to a Very Large Crude Carrier oil loading point, known as 'Sea Island Terminal', twelve kilometres offshore. Two main loading manifolds (valve systems) control the flow of crude from the tank farms to these destinations.

The ridge on which both tank farms sit is 120 metres above sea level, so the flow of oil is assisted by gravity. Sea Island is connected to the last onshore manifold by a 48" undersea crude oil pipeline, and a 20" bunker pipe. The 48" line, twelve kilometres long, contains about 100,000 barrels of oil. The Iraqi plan was to dump oil into the Gulf from Sea Island, North and South Piers, and three 200,000-tonne tankers, each with a capacity of 1.4 million barrels, which would load at South Pier, sail offshore, and dump the oil overboard.

To stop the flow of oil from the land, the Kuwaitis had to close the valves in the pipeline system from the two tank farms. They could not get into the tank farms, or the two major loading manifolds outside the tank farms, so first concentrated on the 48" pipe to Sea Island. Several ingenious engineers changed the indicator plate on the coastal manifold feeding this pipe to read 'Open' when it was in fact closed, and rewired the feedback loop to the control room so that it would read similarly. Unfortunately, the plate was changed back in error, and up to 5 million barrels of oil flowed into the Gulf.

The Iraqis had placed anti-aircraft guns on Sea Island, and docked two missile boats there. The guns had been firing at Allied warplanes, so they and the missile boats were bombed. Conveniently for the Allies, the attacks took place around the time the Iraqis opened the taps for the 48" pipeline, and also set alight one of the three tankers which were dumping oil overboard. The bombs and resultant fires ignited the oil, some of which burned off.

This still left the problem of the two piers from which the tankers loaded. The Allies had seen the oil spill from Sea Island early on 25 January, and feared that the massive reserves of oil in the tank farms and the Burgan field would soon find their way into the Gulf. The slick already covered 1,000 square kilometres of sea. The potential for further pollution was incredible.

The Allies needed intelligence on how to stop the flow, without causing unnecessary damage, so requested advice from the Resistance inside Kuwait. The oilmen identified the two key loading manifolds outside the tank farms, and faxed out the information and co-ordinates on a satellite phone.

The Americans were given alternative targets, depending on their accuracy. 'If you are as good as we've seen on CNN, where you hit the Defence Ministry in Baghdad, then hit the two loading manifolds for the most effective results. You will need to be accurate because civilian houses are near one of them,' advised the Kuwaitis. 'If you can't be that precise, hit the secondary target, which is another manifold. It is further away from Ahmadi so there is less chance of casualties. It will be less effective as the Iraqis can still pour oil from the North Farm into North Pier, but it will substantially cut the flow.'

The Americans decided to go for the two main loading manifolds, and on the night of 26 January, shortly before the 11.00 p.m. curfew, they successfully bombed them with a single GBU-15 glider bomb each. The two bombs were launched four minutes apart, from separate USAF FB-111s flying almost five kilometres high. The first aircraft released its weapon five kilometres out to sea, half-way between the coast and Sea Island, before turning away. The bomb would take 120 seconds to glide 13 kilometres to impact. Two other FB-111s, flying parallel to the coast 100 kilometres offshore, prepared to guide the bomb in using TV images transmitted from a camera in its nose.

As the first bomb fell, the data link to the guiding FB-111 was lost, jeopardizing the mission. Fortunately, Captain Brad Seipal, the weapons systems officer in the second offshore FB-111, picked up the link, and guided the bomb onto the target. He then did the same with the bomb from the second attack aircraft for the most stressful and successful six minutes of his career.

The bombs blew the manifolds to pieces, spewing burning oil onto the ground, but leaving the tanks intact. The blazing crude from the South Tank Farm flowed down a road on the southern edge of Ahmadi, past the Iraqis' decoy-tank workshop, and towards the coast. The Iraqis downhill panicked, abandoned their checkpoints, and fled, as did many Kuwaitis. Three hundred people took refuge in the KOC Hospital. No one cared for curfew.

This was exactly the type of confusion the Kuwaitis needed. The KOC fire brigade was sent on a wild goose chase to a minor fire at Al-Shuaiba refinery, further down the coast. A number of KOC men ran to the South Tank Farm, one of them, Bader Al-Khashti, shouting at the shocked guards in an Iraqi accent that they had to get in and turn off the valves otherwise everyone in Ahmadi, Iraqis included, would burn. This was a bluff. The Kuwaitis knew that the folds in the land would channel the flaming oil away from the houses, but the Iraqis were panicked. They opened the gates, and the Kuwaitis went in, closed the tanks manually, and set the valves to manual so that they could not be opened automatically from the control room. The only oil which trickled into the Gulf after that from the southern fields was what was left in the pipelines, the surviving tankers, and a few other minor sources.

At the time, to protect the Kuwaitis who had done the work, credit was given to KOC oil engineers who were supposedly in Saudi Arabia, and to the US pilots. The real experts, and the men in the firing line, were in Kuwait.

The Kuwaitis were also able to pass intelligence to the Allies on the Tareq Project. During the air war, they suddenly noticed pressure in the pipes. At the time, they were sending heavy fuel oil from the refineries to the Doha power station, but Doha suddenly started receiving crude oil from the northern fields, to which it was also connected. The Iraqis had restarted these fields, but not shut the Doha line. The Kuwaitis realised then that the Iraqis intended to pour crude into the Gulf from the new lines. They told the Allies, who bombed the two lines on land, and prevented further marine spillage.

The oil sector Resistance also offered to help with the expected US Marines' amphibious assault. The Americans had chosen Shuaiba Port south of Ahmadi as the most promising landing site, but a nearby LPG plant was causing them concern. If it was hit during the fighting, it could conceivably blow up and cause casualties among the Marines. The Resistance offered to drain the tanks in advance of the assault. In the end, this proved unnecessary.

The Resistance intelligence operation went far beyond the efforts of the oil sector. For most of the occupation, the Coalition's military options included a direct attack into the suburbs of Kuwait City, and amphibious landings.

The Resistance was able to plot individual units, sometimes down to specific tanks and types of artillery dug in along the coast, and four Iraqi gunboats anchored at Fahaheel. They could map out concentrations of Iraqi troops within suburbs and identify the types of units. The details were transcribed onto estate agents' maps and sent to Saudi Arabia. The information was seldom complete, but was nevertheless extremely useful.

A key part of the intelligence-collecting operation was the Kuwait Fire Brigade, which the Iraqis allowed to operate relatively unhindered. The firemen were allowed to travel into areas where other people could not go, and fed whatever information they gleaned back to the Resistance.

The Kuwaitis have verified that about 300 of their people died as a direct result of the invasion and occupation. Nine were women. The males included young boys. About 62 people were executed; 13 are thought to have died during torture. Several were killed during civilian resistance such as anti-Iraqi demonstrations, and 13 during armed resistance. The remaining 190-odd died in battle on 2 August, 1990, as a result of the war in early 1991, mines, traffic accidents with Iraqi military vehicles, or lack of specialist medical care.

A figure of 110 individuals killed as a result of Resistance attacks or retribution hardly seems large in the overall context of the crisis. However, the numbers belie some chilling facts. First, many of those deaths were often barbaric, and followed days, or weeks, of brutal torture. The Kuwaitis have documented most methods of torture practised on them by the Iraqis. This has been further independently verified by the US Army Judge Advocate-General. In the Iraqi rush to leave Kuwait in February 1991, several of their torture chambers were left intact, complete with the implements. Secondly, the effect of hundreds, perhaps thousands of rapes and other assaults are not reflected in the numbers of dead. Finally, about 560 Kuwaitis are still unaccounted for. With the passage of years since liberation, hope for them is fading. A total of about 860 Kuwaitis out of population of 650,000 are either dead or missing as a direct result of the invasion and occupation.

The role of the Kuwaiti Resistance in the eventual liberation of Kuwait, and in sustaining those who remained there during the occupation, cannot be overstated. The military and political value of their efforts went far beyond

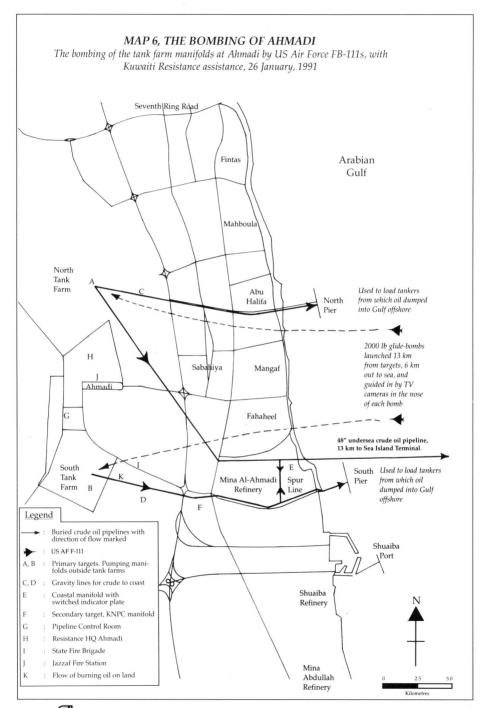

MAP 6, THE BOMBING OF AHMADI

The bombing of the tank farm manifolds at Ahmadi by US Air Force FB-111s, with Kuwaiti Resistance assistance, 26 January, 1991

Seventh Ring Road

Fintas

Arabian Gulf

Mahboula

North Tank Farm

A

C

Abu Halifa

North Pier

Used to load tankers from which oil dumped into Gulf offshore

2000 lb glide-bombs launched 13 km from targets, 6 km out to sea, and guided in by TV cameras in the nose of each bomb

H

Sabahiya

Mangaf

J

Ahmadi

G

Fahaheel

48" undersea crude oil pipeline, 13 km to Sea Island Terminal.

South Tank Farm

B

I

K

D

F

E

Spur Line

Mina Al-Ahmadi Refinery

South Pier

Used to load tankers from which oil dumped into Gulf offshore

Legend

→ : Buried crude oil pipelines with direction of flow marked

◄ : US AF F-111

A, B : Primary targets. Pumping manifolds outside tank farms

C, D : Gravity lines for crude to coast

E : Coastal manifold with switched indicator plate

F : Secondary target, KNPC manifold

G : Pipeline Control Room

H : Resistance HQ Ahmadi

I : State Fire Brigade

J : Jazzaf Fire Station

K : Flow of burning oil on land

Shuaiba Port

Shuaiba Refinery

N

Mina Abdullah Refinery

0   2.5   5.0
Kilometres

BASE MAPS © SALEM AL-MARZOUK AND SABAH ABI-HANNA WLL

Explanatory notes to Map 6, The Allied bombing of oil facilities at Ahmadi, with Kuwait Resistance help, to cut the flow of oil into the Gulf

- **Prior to bombing**

1. Fires started at Mina Abdullah and Mina Shuaiba refineries, on coast south of Ahmadi around 21 January 1991.
2. 24 January: Oil taps on Sea Island, North Pier, and South Pier opened. Tankers filled at South Pier dump oil into Gulf.
3. 25 January, early morning. US reconnaissance detects oil slick from Sea Island Terminal, and tankers, now empty, riding high in the water.
4. Allied forces in Saudi Arabia ask for and receive Kuwait Resistance intelligence on best targets to bomb to stop flow. Oil men in Kuwait identify the two key manifolds at Tank Farm North and Tank Farm South, and send advice and co-ordinates out by satellite telephone. Alternate targets of manifolds between Maghreb-Assafar and Fahaheel Expressways, through which oil is pumped to power stations and water desalination plants, also identified.
5. 25 January, evening: Coalition forces attack Iraqi anti-aircraft positions on Sea Island Terminal, and missile boats, suspected of laying mines, docked there. Oil flowing from Sea Island Terminal ignited, burning much of it off. However, within 24 hours, spillage covers 1,000 square kilometres of the Arabian Gulf.

- **Bombing**

6. 26 January, 10.30 p.m.: Four US Air Force FB-111 bombers in two pairs from Saudi Arabia bomb manifolds. One aircraft from each pair launches GBU-15 TV-guided glide-bombs from 15,000 feet, thirteen kilometres from the manifolds, half-way between coast and Sea Island Terminal. Aircraft standing 100 kilometres off the coast guides bombs onto target. Weapons take two minutes from launch to impact.
7. Ruptured pipes spew burning oil from destroyed manifolds. Oil flows down hill alongside Ahmadi, past decoy tank workshop, panicking Iraqis.
8. Kuwaiti Resistance enter tank farms in confusion, and turn off valves manually. Prior to this, local fire brigade despatched to Mina Shuaiba to prevent any attempts to put out manifold fires.

inflicting several hundred casualties on the Iraqi Army, and has been widely acknowledged by senior Coalition military officers.

Militarily, the Resistance provided leverage to the Allied forces by helping them to assess the Iraqis' combat-effectiveness, and pinpoint targets. The destruction of the Ahmadi oil manifolds is the most public example of a joint Resistance–Coalition operation, but by no means the only one.

The contribution of the Resistance to the political will to go to war was at least as important. The accounts of life under occupation, the atrocities, and the courage of the ordinary Kuwaitis transmitted out by people like Asrar Al-Qabandi, Abdul Jabbar Marafie and Muhsen Al-Ajeel were critical in helping to keep the Western public focused on the crusade.

The actions of the Resistance helped to retain the moral high ground for Kuwait in a way that diplomats and PR consultants could not. That ground was paid for in blood. A number of Westerners who were in hiding in Kuwait are convinced that they owe their lives to the Resistance. During rallies in London during early 1991 in support of military action, some of these people carried signs saying 'I AM ALIVE BECAUSE OF A KUWAITI.'

There have been many words of thanks offered to the Resistance on a personal level. The Kuwait Government has not seen fit officially to recognize the efforts of many of its members ostensibly because of the continuing tragedy of hundreds of missing Kuwaitis, and perhaps because it is so very difficult to verify deeds carried out in secrecy. Indeed, the stories of some of these people cannot yet be told as they are thought to be still in Iraqi custody.

The greatest tragedy of the Resistance is the loss of the young lives of many of its members who would have been at the forefront of the next generation of Kuwait's leadership. The next greatest tragedy is the plethora of self-made 'retrospective heroes' in the wake of liberation. This unpleasant phenomenon dishonours the memory of the real heroes. While the deaths of the likes of Wafa Al-Amer, Suad Al-Hassan, Ashraf Abdullah, Dr Hisham Al-Obaidan, Asrar Al-Qabandi and Ahmad Qabazard speak volumes of silent testimony to their courage, their living colleagues are remarkably reticent to speak of their deeds. They know the true extent of the risks they took, the fear they dealt with, and the reasons why they did it. It was not for praise or medals, but for the sake of their country, and because someone had to do it.

No one hears much in Kuwait these days from people such as Sheikh Ali Salem Al-Ali, Major-Generals Mohammed Al-Bader and Khalid Boodai, Abdul Jabbar Marafie or Sheikh Sabah Nasir. Colonel Fahd Al-Ameer is now a Major-General and Deputy Chief of Staff of the Kuwaiti Armed Forces, but is remarkably low profile. People like Hind Al-Bahar and Nazeeh Khajah, and the oilmen of Ahmadi, have simply gone back to their work or studies, happy to be alive. Some of the survivors will struggle for the rest of their lives with the trauma of having taken human lives. Most just want to put the nightmare behind them.

But there are some people other than those in Kuwait at the time who do not forget the Resistance, and recognize the value of their contribution. At least one senior American officer took time out in the hectic days after the ceasefire to pay tribute to the brave men and women of the Resistance. The following letter was received by a number of individuals, including Major-General Boodai, Colonel Fahd Al-Ameer and Sheikh Sabah Nasir:

Department of the Air Force
United States Central Command Air Forces (USCENTAF)
Shaw Air Force Base S. C. 29152-6001

Office of the Commander   8 March 1991

Subject: Letter of Appreciation

I would like to take this opportunity to express the Allied Air Forces' gratitude to members of your staff who often risked their lives to provide critical information during the battle to liberate Kuwait.

Throughout the long months before the outbreak of actual hostilities, the resistance succeeded in developing a number of ingenious and innovative methods for communicating vital intelligence about enemy dispositions and intentions in the Kuwaiti theater of operations.

Their success in passing information to us during Operation Desert Shield facilitated the efforts of coalition targeters to develop the highly effective targeting strategies which eventually resulted in the destruction and defeat of Iraqi forces during the Desert Storm campaign.

We are specifically grateful to your people for pinpointing locations of deployed enemy forces, ammunition depots, and chemical/biological ordnance storage areas. It is not at all inconceivable that the struggle to liberate Kuwait might have proven much more costly to both the coalition forces and the people of Kuwait had we not received precise and timely information about these facilities from the brave soldiers of the Kuwaiti resistance.

You, your staff and the people of Kuwait can be justly proud of the key role played by the resistance in the success of the air war against Iraq and the ultimate liberation of Kuwait.

CHARLES A. HORNER
Lieutenant General, USAF
Commander

18. THE PAPERCHASE

'The Paperchase' described the struggle to obtain documents to conceal the real identities of Kuwaitis wanted by the Iraqis, such as military and police officers, members of the Al-Sabah, senior bureaucrats and members of the Resistance, and to provide false identification for potential Human Shields.

This involved everything from completely changing a man's nationality quite legally to preparing false papers to help him lie his way through an interrogation. It included forging drivers' licences, ID cards, vehicle registrations, and passports. The Kuwaitis at risk engaged in the paperchase from the earliest days of the occupation, but it was not until a week or so after the August round-up order that the Westerners started considering it seriously.

The Kuwaiti Government requires every resident, Kuwaiti and expatriate alike, to obtain and carry a civil identification card, known as the 'civil ID' issued by the Public Authority for Civil Information (PACI). Only diplomats are exempted. Almost everyone dealing with government bodies, from vehicle registration to medical services and marriage, requires this card.

In 1990, the civil ID card represented the very latest technology in national identification systems, short of magnetic coding. It was printed on highest quality watermarked paper stock, blue for expatriates, pink for Kuwaitis, in a heat-sealed plastic sleeve. The sleeve had its own embedded pattern and national crest separate from the watermark in the underlying paper. It was very well thought out – almost a security document – so much so that the Iraqis themselves immediately accepted it at face value as proof of identity.

The front of the card carried the individual's photograph overstamped by PACI, full name, nationality, civil ID number, birth date, and date of expiry, all computer-printed in Arabic. The reverse had the sponsor's name for expatriates, the civil number again, the individual's address, and blood group. Home phone numbers were included for men, but not for women.

A second form of identification, held by most of the Western and Kuwaiti adults was a Kuwaiti driving licence. This was a simple affair compared to the civil ID. It was also encased in a heat-sealed sleeve, with a photograph of the individual overstamped by the Traffic Department, and the usual details, including nationality. However, the paper was standard stock, with a Government crest and spaces for details printed in black. The plastic sleeve had no impregnated pattern, and could have been used for any commercial identification card. The details were written by hand. In addition to this, the registration books of cars, or *dufftars* in Arabic, contained the owner's nationality, again hand-written in Arabic.

Furthermore, every expatriate living in or visiting Kuwait, babies included, has to have a passport. Into this is stamped the residence or visitor's visa, in Arabic, clearly identifying the sponsor.

In the early days, the Kuwaitis' priority was to protect the greatest number of people, and their population records, by retrieving the latest copies of the PACI database. Fortuitously, PACI was having great problems with the disk drives in its main computer centre. It would have been impossible for the Iraqis to fix these without expert help, so they could not have accessed the main database. For good measure, PACI staff further sabotaged the drives.

The backup copies of the database were on 16 Betamax-type computer tape cartridges, at PACI's Farwaniya complex, separate from the main computer centre. The tapes were identified by numbers, so only those familiar with the system level would know what to look for.

During the first week of the occupation, the PACI managers plotted how to get the tapes out of Farwaniya. Incredibly, the Iraqis had not yet moved into the PACI facilities in force, or tried to access the database, but this was only a matter of time. During recent years, PACI had hosted their Iraqi opposite numbers, and demonstrated the system to them. Sooner or later, some bright *Mukhabarat* officer would realize the potential of the system. In principle, if it were working, it would be a simple affair for the Iraqis to put a gun to an operator's head, and obtain lists, showing nationality, employer, address and phone number, of almost everyone in Kuwait, especially the military and police, and key Government people. The implications were far-reaching. It would greatly help the Iraqis to track down almost anyone they wanted.

It was too risky for the Kuwaitis to go to Farwaniya personally and get the tapes, as the Iraqis would be suspicious of them, so they contacted Ehab Younis, an Egyptian in PACI's Database Administration Group. He in turn teamed up with an Indian colleague, Soumitra Marvin.

Ehab and Marvin, as they were known, went to Farwaniya as if returning to work as ordered by the Iraqis, and retrieved the box of tapes with ease. They then encountered one of those bizarre wartime moments when the remnants of the peacetime system threatened to blow the entire operation. The regular PACI Kuwaiti securityman, who had also returned to work, refused to let them out with the tapes unless they signed for them. They tried to reason with him, but he stood firm. Neither man wanted to sign as they knew that the Iraqis could then trace them, and might hang them for espionage. They rang one of the senior Kuwaiti managers at home who told the dutiful securityman to let them go. He refused. Standing orders were standing orders.

Eventually, fearing they would be caught red-handed, Ehab signed the log, and made a hurried departure. They got the tapes to the Kuwaitis, who smuggled them out to Taif. Ehab, for obvious reasons, promptly left Kuwait. As for the diligent securityman, the Kuwaitis did not know whether to try him for treason, or reward him for unswerving devotion to duty.

A number of 'Desert Storm' servicemen, particularly pilots, may owe their lives to Ehab's and Marvin's courage. If the tapes had fallen into the wrong hands, the Iraqis could conceivably have found people to help them get captured Kuwaiti HAWK missiles working, and shot down more Allied warplanes. Many more Western men who remained successfully in hiding in their homes in Kuwait until they were released in December are also indebted to these few men, as are thousands of Kuwaiti servicemen and police.

Meanwhile, as the Iraqis started rounding up certain Westerners, the paperchase problem was how to back up a claim by a captured American, Briton, Frenchman or German that he was actually an Australian, Canadian, Cypriot, Dane, Dutchman, Irishman, or New Zealander.

Only the few Arabic-speaking Westerners of Arabic appearance could pass themselves off as Arabs. Nor could most Westerners pass for Asians. One African–American, however, did successfully masquerade as a Somali.

Besides identity documents, we had to consider the risk of being identified by accent. Enough Iraqis had been educated in the West for this danger to be real, if remote. To be on the safe side, we generally tried to turn Americans into Canadians or Irishmen, with closer accents, and Britons into Australians, New Zealanders or Irishmen.

The simplest method of identifying oneself as a 'safe national' was to throw away all ID papers, claim that they were lost, and state blandly that you were anything but American, British, French or German. The Iraqis seldom fell for this, but a particular quirk of Kuwaiti employers added a little credibility to this tale, and made the use of photocopies more believable, at least for passports. Most employers retained employees' passports. They had no legal right to do so, but it was standard practice. The Iraqis learned of this during the first week when they had to let hundreds of frantic Arab and Asian workers into their workplaces to retrieve their passports. Thus, the Scotsman or American trying to convince an Iraqi officer that he really was from Perth, Australia, and not Perth, Scotland or Perth Amboy, New Jersey, could quite credibly say that his Australian passport was in his office. However, to prevent the Iraqi digging a little deeper and perhaps going along to the office to discover the truth, he had to offer a little more. Westerners were not generally careless enough to lose their driving licence and civil ID as well.

The civil ID itself was almost impossible to replicate without the proper supplies of blanks, sleeves and machinery, but the simpler driving licence was easier. Fortunately, several Kuwaiti policemen with great foresight had taken out blanks for the licences, empty plastic sleeves, and the necessary rubber stamps from the Traffic Department in the first days of the occupation.

Additionally, the Iraqis themselves were running the Traffic Department to change all Kuwaiti vehicle registrations to Iraqi, so with a little bribery, some Kuwaitis obtained supplies to make driving licences. Failing this, they used plastic sleeves from commercial identity cards, and made their own blanks using photocopies of licences and corrector fluid. One Resistance group made their stamps out of rubber erasers. Later, they had the stamps made professionally in Jordan and Syria, and smuggled them into Kuwait.

In principle, it was then a relatively simple matter of transcribing the individual's details with a false name or nationality, pasting in a passport photo, stamping it, forging the traffic colonel's signature, and sealing the plastic sleeve with a household iron. The result was almost indistinguishable from the real thing, so much so that after liberation the Kuwaiti authorities had to change the format and colour of all driving licences issued.

In practice, for the Westerners, it was never quite so simple. The first step was to contact someone from the Kuwaiti Resistance who could get this done. It was very much a matter of who you knew. These people were preoccupied with fighting for their country, so seldom appreciated Westerners' urgent requests for false ID. It was not until late October that we could arrange forged driving licences almost on demand.

Further practical difficulties abounded, particularly with photos. Many men had no spare passport-type photos at home. We simply had to work with what we had. It was impossible to remove the heat-sealed photograph from the existing licence without wrecking it. In the absence of Polaroid film and cameras, the solution was usually to cut out the man's face from a family photo. This was seldom satisfactory, as most family snaps are dissimilar to posed ID photos. In some cases where men could not produce any photos at all, we used photos of other similar-aged men, clean-shaven, back-dated the issue date of the licence ten years, and the recipient grew a beard.

Once the driving licence was done, we then had to change the man's nationality on his car registration booklet, or *dufftar*. These had numbered pages, pre-printed in Arabic, held together by two ordinary spine staples. Each *dufftar* contained the vehicle's details, and records of previous owners, including nationality, all hand-written. If a man's car was still outside his home, then the Iraqis knew they could check his nationality from the *dufftar*,

Additionally, some free-Westerners had to borrow cars, especially if theirs had been stolen, so needed to change the entire registration into their names. Troops at checkpoints would regularly ask for the *dufftar,* as well as personal ID, and would take the car if it was not registered to the driver.

Unfortunately, the Kuwaitis were not as successful in getting blank *dufftars* from the Traffic Department as they had been with driving licence blanks, and since the preprinted *dufftar* pages were on distinctive paper, photocopy forgeries were easy to spot. The demand for whatever blank *dufftars* had been obtained was therefore particularly high, as the Kuwaitis themselves were converting the registrations for cars belonging to friends and family members to keep them out of Iraqi hands. They were also busy changing the identities of people who worked in the Ministries of Defence and Interior. The high level of car ownership in Kuwait also added to demand. I met one Kuwaiti who, although he had not been obliged to change his own identity, now had in his name ten vehicles belonging to relatives, or friends in the police and military.

One option when changing the nationality for a wanted Westerner was to carefully scrape out his true nationality with a razor blade and write in the false nationality, in Arabic, matching it to his false licence. This was a very delicate job. Few people could do this and make it appear natural. The trick was therefore to get the right blank numbered pages, and replace them, but this needed the Traffic Department stamp. Several men had *dufftars* returned to them with all pages except those containing their vehicle's details replaced. The pages from their books had gone to reconstruct some other book.

Several Westerners were told by Kuwaitis that false driving licences and *dufftars* would cost substantial sums of money. The most widely quoted figure was KD200. Most men could not pay as very few had any cash. To the credit of the Resistance, these profiteers were soon put in their place. I am not aware of a single Westerner who paid for forged documents obtained from a Kuwaiti.

A forged driving licence and *dufftar* were only one set of documents, and not always easy to obtain, especially in the early days. Men in danger of spending the rest of what might be very short lives at one of Saddam's installations understandably wanted as much protection as they could get.

Attention turned to the civil IDs and passports. Unknown to the Westerners then, the Kuwaitis initially had limited supplies with which they could make civil IDs, but the priority demand for these came from Kuwaitis in real danger, such as the Al-Sabah and key Resistance figures. In any event, the blank paper the Kuwaitis had was for their own pink cards, not the blue ones for expatriates. The latter were on their own when it came to forging civil IDs.

The expatriates could not make real forgeries, but we could make photocopy forgeries. It is standard practice in Kuwait to keep photocopies of key documents at home, separate from the originals, just as people maintain a list of travellers' cheque numbers separately. We could therefore claim that the real documents were lost, but the photocopies would be *prima facie* evidence of nationality. The technique was perfected by Tony Hordern, an Australian BA149 transit passenger. He became its leading exponent.

The prerequisite was a photocopier. This in itself was difficult. Most offices were closed or looted, or in heavily guarded downtown Kuwait City. It was impossible to explain a visit to an office when the whole country was at a standstill. Tony and I attracted undue Iraqi attention the one time we tried it. Only luck and some fast talking prevented our arrest with the incriminating evidence of photocopier toner in our possession. We had to rely on home photocopiers. Later on, we took material to Baghdad to produce documents on embassy copiers when the local supply of toner ran out.

To make a photocopy forgery of a civil ID, Tony first photocopied the real card of a safe national, cut out the Arabic word for the nationality, and then pasted this onto the real card of the targeted national. He then photocopied that card front and back, with all the details, so that the only item changed was the nationality. In the case of people with sensitive employers, we also changed the sponsor's name. The rest of the card was very convincing, as the Iraqis could match up the photograph to the man's face, and the address and telephone number to wherever they were, if they were still at home.

Forging passport photocopies was much more involved. Several Kuwaiti Resistance leaders had blank real Kuwaiti passports which they could use to change the identity of their own people, but only into other Kuwaitis. Again, the Westerners had to make do with photocopy forgeries.

To create such a document, you first needed a safe national's passport as a template. The most popular at first were the Australian and New Zealand passports as they did not have watermark strips running across the photograph. We later used a few others. The forger would type out the beneficiary's details, cut out the strips of paper, and paste them over the details on the genuine safe passport. Tony even cracked the alphanumeric codes which some countries place on the bottom of the passport details page.

The beneficiary's photograph was then placed over the real photograph, and the details page photocopied several times until any marks that might distinguish it as a forgery were sufficiently blurred. The result was a passable photocopy of what looked like a genuine passport.

A further refinement was to photocopy the beneficiary's residence visa from his own passport, carefully cut out any background marks that identified it as having come from a US or British passport, and then photocopy it using a blank page of a safe passport as the background. The photocopied residence visa would then match up to the details on the photocopied civil ID.

Add the photocopy of the passport to the forged driver's licence, *dufftar,* and civil ID, and the potential Human Shield had a fighting chance. The one condition attached to these false documents was that they were to be used only as a last resort, if the Iraqis raided the holder's hiding place. They were not to be used for moving around. We were only too aware how little attention would be needed to expose what was a very amateurish scheme.

The passport-forging exercise has several amusing stories. The best concerns Bob Jaggard, an Englishman initially known as 'One-Day Bob'. He had arrived in Kuwait from Dubai on the afternoon of 1 August for a one-day visit, and was trapped in Kuwait until December.

Bob had one of the first New Zealand passports forgeries. He had been staying in the Kuwait International Hotel, where a New Zealander, Robin Van Kempen, worked. Bob had moved out into hiding, but maintained contact with the hotel. He asked one of the staff, who was actually Iraqi, if a copy of Robin's passport was on file, and if he get a copy of it. She extracted it, copied it, erased Robin's details with corrector fluid, and typed in Bob's.

The only photo Bob had with him was on the permit issued to him by the Dubai Government to allow him to buy alcohol for his personal consumption. To complicate matters, part of the photo was covered with the stamp, in Arabic, of the issuing authority. It was apparent the stamp was intended to be both on the photograph, and the underlying document.

The precious photo was carefully removed from the permit, and pasted onto the amended passport blank. The remainder of the stamp was very carefully drawn in with the name of the New Zealand Department of External Affairs, and the existing part of the stamp on the photograph suitably altered. The paper was then run through a fax machine photocopier to produce a facsimile of sufficiently poor quality to hide any imperfections. It almost fooled the New Zealand Ambassador to Baghdad when it was shown to him later.

Shortly after receiving this tenuous lifeline, Bob moved to another hiding place which already had four men. It was raided by the *Mukhabarat* soon afterwards. They had information that four Britons were there. One of these was fortunately in a back room, and fled quietly out the back door when he heard the Iraqis. The Iraqis were satisfied that they had caught the four men they had been told about, and took them to the Regency Palace.

Bob boldly produced his poorly-forged New Zealand passport to the officer in charge and was told that as a New Zealander, he was free to go. Delighted, but never one to pass up a lead, Bob asked if he could have a letter saying that as a New Zealander he was free to move around Kuwait, so as to avoid further inconvenience. The officer declined, but turned over the paper, wrote in Arabic that Bob had been to the hotel, was a New Zealander, and was not required again. He then signed and dated it. Bob, who then became known as 'Bob the Kiwi', therefore became the only man in Kuwait to have a forged New Zealand passport authenticated by the Iraqi Secret Police.

The use of New Zealand passports photocopy forgeries became so widespread that when the real New Zealanders were released several weeks before most other men, there was a scramble to reconvert the false New Zealanders to another safe nationality which was still around in sufficient numbers. Only one genuine New Zealander had stayed behind. At the time, there were innumerable Britons with false New Zealand papers, far more than there had ever been New Zealanders in all of Iraq and Kuwait combined.

The practice of using the documents of 'safe' nationals to protect those who were wanted by the Iraqis did not meet with universal approval.

Opposition came not so much from the governments of the safe nationals, represented by their Baghdad diplomats, but from safe nationals in Kuwait. To their credit, most diplomats who were aware of the practice turned a blind eye to the whole affair, but at least one Australian and several Canadian civilians became quite upset that their relative freedom might be compromised if it were discovered that Americans and Britons were passing themselves off as safe nationals with the assistance of genuine safe nationals.

The general view was that this was a rather selfish attitude. We were all in this together as Westerners, and there but for the Grace of God, could go we. Most of the safe nationals felt an obligation to help out the Americans and British, even if it involved some risk. Besides, argued the forgers, genuine safe nationals had genuine documents which could prove their identities conclusively. Any fallout from the discovery of a forgery would most likely rest on the person carrying the forged documents.

By the time this issue came to a head, the Iraqis seemed to be trying to back out of the hostage problem. Nevertheless, it was a real concern to several people.

In one particularly shameful incident, another Australian, Peter Byrnes, and I were in the Canadian Ambassador's Official Residence, making forged photocopies of civil IDs for the 14 men he was looking after in Ahmadi, which was close enough to two oil tank farms for there to be great concern for the residents' safety when the war started. Our intention was to turn all the men there into false Australians, with passport and civil ID photocopies, and forged drivers' licences, and then to smuggle them up to a safe area.

The Canadian civilian placed in charge of the Residence after the departure of the Canadian diplomats saw what we were doing and became very upset, saying that we were compromising the safety of all the Canadians, and that if the Iraqis raided the Residence then, everyone there would be in trouble. We were particularly piqued as he was in fact a BA 149 passenger, and not part of the regular Canadian community. Furthermore, we were being careful to ensure that any evidence could be quickly swept away if there was a raid. To top it all, the Residence had already been raided in mid-September. It was most unlikely that the Iraqis would return.

Several other Canadians remonstrated with him, and he agreed that we should finish what we were doing and then leave, but not carry out such activities in the Residence again. This was a particularly heavy blow to us as the Canadian Residence photocopier was one of the few functional photocopiers we still had access to.

Curiously, the American and British men were quite understanding of this attitude. They appreciated us sticking our necks out, but did not seem to resent someone who felt he had to protect himself, and to hell with everyone else.

Not all identity changes were false. In a number of cases, people were able to obtain genuine documents, which they may or may not have been entitled to. Perhaps the first of these were several East German passports handed out in early August to Britons on a first-come, first-served basis by the East German Ambassador. The Iraqis at that stage still distinguished between East and West Germany. The former was seen as a friend of sorts; the latter as a member of the West and the EC, and a major player in the Coalition.

Some Westerners, especially those of Arab extraction, had maintained documents for their original nationalities, so simply hid the Western ones. Being fluent in Arabic, they were generally able to move freely. In any event, from mid-August, the Iraqis allowed such people to leave if they wished – even some who were Human Shields – regardless of documented nationality.

Others were able to revert to previous safe nationalities such as Indian, Pakistani or Filipino, held before taking citizenship of Western countries. Generally, countries issuing these documents to people who had given up their previous citizenship, or who were not legally entitled to hold dual citizenship, were flexible in applying their rules. On the other hand, very few people received papers from major countries to which they were not entitled. This was vital in maintaining the integrity of the documents which were issued, and the position of the real nationals of the major countries. This explains why no Americans I am aware of were issued with Canadian documents, as had been done to get Americans out of Iran during the 1979 Revolution. The Iraqis would have been alert to any repeat performance.

The issue of genuine documents was not limited to Westerners. Several members of the Al-Sabah family escaped on Bahraini passports, through Iraq. The Bahrainis are to be admired for sticking their necks out for their Kuwaiti cousins. Certain Al-Sabah women went out as Yemenis.

Perhaps the most widespread example of using legitimate documents to change nationality was that of 'converting' Americans and Britons to Irish. Under the Republic of Ireland's Constitution, anyone with a parent or grandparent born on the island of Ireland, including Northern Ireland, is entitled to Irish citizenship. Most Northern Irish in Kuwait held UK passports, in preference to Irish. In fact, a UK passport was favoured as it allowed one to travel into Bahrain and the UAE without a prearranged visa.

When the Baghdad-based Irish Consul, Dr Niall Holohan, first visited

Kuwait in mid-September, he was swamped by Americans and Britons who
had, usually quite genuinely, discovered Irish ancestors. He issued temporary
travel documents (TTDs) to those he could. When the Iraqis prevented him from
visiting Kuwait again, the new Irish warden, Paul Kennedy, did a sterling job in
carrying applications for Irish citizenship to Baghdad, and Irish TTDs back to
Kuwait. During the occupation, 25 of these documents were issued.

The spectacle of Unionist Britons scrambling for Republican Irish passports
caused a great deal of amusement among what became known as the 'full Irish'.
By mid-September, US and British wives at home were bombarding Irish
embassies, the Foreign Ministry and various Catholic bishops and cardinals of
Irish extraction with requests for their husbands to be issued with the
documents to which their heritage entitled them.

The TTDs issued by the Irish Embassy were really 'one-way' passports of the
kind issued to travellers who lose their passports in more normal circumstances.
They allow the bearer to travel one-way to Ireland, where he then has to make
arrangements to replace the regular passport.

By November 1990, so many Americans and Britons had discovered their
Irish roots that the Irish Ambassador, Anton MacUnfraidh, expressed concern
that there would soon be more holders of these TTDs in Kuwait than there were
holders of full Irish passports. 'If by any chance the Irish are released tomorrow
ahead of everyone else, the Iraqis are going to be wondering why so many
Irishmen carelessly lose their passports,' he once said to me.

It was a genuine concern. If the Iraqis started questioning people about their
birthplaces, he would be hard put to convince the authorities that Ireland was
not breaking or bending the rules to frustrate Iraq. Foreign countries with
embassies in Iraq not only had to act correctly, but had to be seen to be acting
correctly so as not to undermine their own legitimacy.

On top of that, Oliver North had used false Irish passports during his
shenanigans in Iran several years before, so it was known to the Iraqis that
Ireland had been used in this way before.

By November, the Westerners' paperchase objective was to provide everyone
who wanted it with 'safe ID'. We never achieved this, but were well on the way
to it before the need was removed by the release of all the hostages.

One idea put to the embassies was to get the US and UK Governments
together with the exiled Kuwaitis and the foreign firms which supplied the
PACI system. We suggested that they match the list of Americans and British
still hiding in Kuwait, including each individual's new false nationality, as
provided by their forged driver's licence and forged passport photocopy, to the
PACI computer records smuggled out of the country, and produce new, original
civil IDs for each individual, with the nationality suitably altered.

This would have required the men's families to provide passport-type
photos for the new cards which, about 600 in all, would be flown into Baghdad
in diplomatic pouches, and then smuggled down to Kuwait by the free-
nationals. The plan was feasible in principle, but was thought to be impractical
because of the co-ordination required.

Unknown to us, the Western intelligence services were working along these same lines, and had set up a facility with the Kuwaitis in Bahrain to do this, at least for the Kuwaiti Resistance. For the Westerners, the Americans had even gone back to original passport applications to get the photos of men to issue diplomatic passports for the 19 civilians taking refuge on the US Embassy compound, and now 'employed' by the State Department. We never discovered whether the CIA or MI-6 got as far as planning to issue new, nationality-amended civil IDs for all the US and British civilians hiding in Kuwait, but the idea had been put to their people in Kuwait. It was possible.

Strangely enough, some men declined offers of false identification, and even efforts on their behalf to obtain genuine documents based on inherited entitlement. One Christian friend, Gerald Selous, felt that it was against his beliefs to engage in such skullduggery, and that God would protect him. He was vindicated. Although he had a Lebanese wife who could cover for him, Gerald had some escapes which could only be described as miraculous.

Other men of principle but less religious conviction considered that if they were going to go, they would not pretend to be someone they were not. A few were concerned that being caught with forged documents would have made the situation worse for them, and resulted in them being tried in Iraqi criminal courts. It was their option. We had to respect it, and to admire their example.

19. OCTOBER 1990: MITTERRAND'S MONTH

As October opened, Saddam seemed to be winning the diplomatic battles. He had held Kuwait for two full months in the face of world condemnation. Western leaders were seen as merely reacting to his moves. Presidents Bush and Mitterrand had just made what sounded to us like conciliatory UN General Assembly speeches. In particular, Bush's suggestion that Iraq's pullout from Kuwait might be linked to a future Arab-Israeli deal sounded very much like acceptance of Saddam's so-called 'August 12th initiative'.

Conflicting signals abounded. After meeting with the Kuwaiti Amir in September, Bush had said 'the UN would be asked to look at a military option if sanctions did not work', but he set no deadline. The Security Council had also said that sanctions must have time to work. Allied forces continued pouring into Saudi Arabia, but there was little talk of liberating Kuwait.

Those of us in Kuwait, impatient for solid results, doubted the Coalition's will to resolve the problem expediently. To us, this could only be done by force, but it looked as if the Allies would simply sit in Saudi Arabia for years while the sanctions slowly achieved what the troops could do in days. There was no empty jingoism in Kuwait. No one wanted war for its own sake. It was simply a matter of solving the problem, and military action was seen as the only way to deal with Saddam. It might even give some meaning to our ordeal.

Throughout Iraq and Kuwait, about 661 Human Shields were at strategic sites, complemented by the hundreds of foreigners and diplomats still in Iraq with relative freedom, and 800 others in hiding or moving around in Kuwait. Thousands of Kuwaiti military POWs were held in Iraq, where they would remain until March 1991. However, they had been located by the Kuwaitis and could at least see their families, even if the Human Shields could not.

October 1st was a holiday throughout Iraq and Kuwait to celebrate the Prophet Mohammed's Birthday, but nine Frenchmen were celebrating their release after what Iraq described as a 'humanitarian gesture'. It was the first substantial release of men since Kurt Waldheim's Austrians in August.

We had another small but sweet victory that day. The clocks in Iraq went back onto winter time, which was the same as Kuwaiti time. Kuwait does not practice summer daylight-saving, so Iraq had tried to eliminate the one-hour time difference by decreeing that the time would be the same in both places. The sun had caught up with Saddam. To us, Iraq was going onto Kuwait time.

One item on Iraqi TV two days later was Saddam's first known visit to Occupied Kuwait. This explained a clean-up operation we had noticed in Kuwait City in late September. The Iraqi Army had been acting like schoolboys preparing for the form master's inspection. We were incensed at Saddam's arrogance in strutting around Kuwait, but his message was unmistakable. Kuwait was his, and he was going to keep it.

International opinion swung sharply against Iraq on 4 October with the release of an Amnesty International report on the Iraqi atrocities in Kuwait. Saddam then proceeded to shoot himself in the foot again by warning the US of 'thousands of coffins' if it went to war. The effect of this was to stiffen the resolve not only of the troops, but also of the wavering politicians.

Within days, however, things seemed to go Saddam's way again. On 6 October, President Gorbachev's envoy Yevgeny Primakov, a noted Arabist and member of the Soviet Presidential Council, came away from a meeting with Saddam in Baghdad with news that did not square with the facts as we saw them. 'Sanctions were working', he said. 'Saddam cannot survive very long under them.' We felt that Primakov's judgement must be flawed. Despite his long experience, he seemed to have no idea of Iraqi self-sufficiency, or of the ability of Saddam's security apparatus to keep the population in check.

People in Kuwait were almost universally hawkish, regardless of the risk of being on the receiving end of a war. The remaining embassies in Kuwait received more calls from men in hiding urging their leaders to attack now before the fragile Coalition fell apart. For many of those in hiding, it was a race against time between the liberation, and an Iraqi knock on the front door.

Primakov's mission did, however, have some tangible results for his own people. Shortly after he left Baghdad, Iraq said that 1,500 of the 5,174 Soviets still in Iraq could leave within a month, and that the remaining 140 Soviet military advisors could leave when their contracts expired. The Iraqis had said earlier that the Soviets could leave, and about 2,600 had already gone, but they refused to issue exit visas to most of those still under contract to their oil industry and the military. With the situation in the USSR at the time, many of the Russians actually preferred to stay.

Tareq Aziz then repeated his offer to release all the hostages in return for a US undertaking not to attack Iraq. It was a tempting opportunity for the Allies to get their men back without bloodshed, and one which many hostages desperately wanted Bush to accept. Others felt that it would leave far greater issues unresolved. The debate was academic. The offer was dismissed.

Saddam then surprisingly found himself with a most unlikely ally: Israel. On 8 October, Israeli border police killed 21 unarmed Palestinians and wounded 140 others during a riot on Jerusalem's Temple Mount. TV clips clearly showed the policemen aiming squarely at the backs of fleeing youths. The ricochets hit the Coalition right where it hurt, in the contradiction of Arab states being aligned with Israel's greatest supporter against another Arab and predominantly Muslim state.

The Saudis were in a particularly embarrassing position. We did not expect King Fahd to expel the US forces, but the incident could have seriously weakened the Coalition to the extent of making an attack to liberate Kuwait impractical. It was now clear that Saddam was not going to attack Saudi Arabia, but the Allied military mission was still explicitly to defend that country, not liberate Kuwait. There was less need of the US if Saudi Arabia was not directly threatened, but active Saudi co-operation was vital to the liberation of Kuwait.

But the US spoke first, leading the charge to condemn Israel, publicly rebuking Tel Aviv with uncharacteristic harshness. The combination of this US action and the interests of Arab Coalition partners kept Coalition unity solid, if not unshaken. The Egyptians were sufficiently annoyed at Saddam for his Nasserite pretensions, sending home hundreds of dead Egyptian workers from Iraq, and destroying the jobs of scores of thousands of others to be too principled about Israeli atrocities against Palestinians. The Syrians - basking in their new-found international acceptance - had bigger fish to fry in Lebanon. They made only the requisite diplomatic protests. However, the question of enforcing action against Israel distracted UN attention from the Kuwait crisis into November, and seriously impeded the diplomatic offensive.

On 10 October, British Foreign Secretary Douglas Hurd put the crisis back into focus by saying that the Coalition must decide 'within weeks' whether to go to war. At the time, the economic impetus for war to restore stability in the oil market and avoid a world recession seemed compelling. The oil price had more than doubled from US$14 barely three months earlier.

In Kuwait, such was the importance placed on every nuance coming from senior ministers that some of us calculated a precise date for commencement of military action, based on Hurd's words. He had said 'weeks' in the plural, but not 'month' or 'months', so the minimum time was seen as two weeks, and the maximum four. Popular opinion in Kuwait settled on the tidy date of 31 October as the day for war, three weeks from the date of Hurd's comments.

In fact, the oil issue was not as relevant as it seemed. Supplies were assured from other OPEC producers taking up the slack of Kuwaiti and Iraqi production. Since the 1973 oil shock, conservation measures had been implemented, and strategic reserves built up. The temporary price problem arose from the fear of disruption to Saudi supplies in case of war, but the oil price alone would not provide enough impetus for war.

On 14 October the Soviets dropped another bombshell from the Primakov meeting, reporting that Saddam might be willing to leave Kuwait if he were allowed to keep the northern Rumaillah/Ratga oilfield, and Warba and Bubiyan Islands which controlled his access to the Gulf. Saddam vehemently denied this, claiming that all of Kuwait would for evermore be Iraqi.

However, this was the first time that what had become known as 'the nightmare scenario' was mentioned officially as a distinct possibility. This involved Saddam withdrawing from Kuwait City, but keeping some or all of the northern half of the country. We had visions of the Kuwaitis returning to their shattered city from Saudi Arabia, and having to live under the barrels of Iraqi artillery overlooking them from Mutla'a Ridge. Such a solution was no solution at all; it was capitulation. The crisis had gone too far for that.

The Kuwaitis agreed. Their country was tiny enough as it was without giving more of it away. They quite understandably wanted to keep all of it. So, it seems, did Saddam. We were perversely delighted at this because it meant that he would eventually have to leave all of Kuwait, and pay the price for taking it in the first place. If he withdrew only from the south, he would still have the north with its not inconsiderable oilfields, and could soon dictate Kuwaiti and Saudi oil policy at the point of a nuclear gun.

Contradictory signals continued to emanate from Western leaders. On 15 October, five days after Douglas Hurd said that the Coalition must decide 'within weeks' on war, US Defense Secretary Dick Cheney and his British counterpart Tom King warned against quick military action because – incredibly – they believed that sanctions were working. It was not what we wanted to hear. In Kuwait, some saw these comments as a ploy to deceive Saddam on a 31 October attack, but most felt that war would slip until after the November US half-term elections, or, at the latest, Thanksgiving on 22 November. Few were prepared to revise the deadline by more than a month.

The US then countered the 14 October Primakov report by rejecting any deal which let Saddam keep any part of Kuwait. Primakov persisted in his search for a diplomatic solution, jetting between Rome, Paris, Washington and London, but toning down his earlier suggestion of a partial withdrawal, saying now that full withdrawal was both possible and necessary.

In the meantime, President Bush, deeply affected by the Amnesty International report released two weeks earlier, was echoing Margaret Thatcher's comments of early September that Saddam should be held responsible for atrocities in Kuwait, and recalled the Nuremberg trials. The US started working on a UN Security Council Resolution on this.

Life in Kuwait itself during the first two weeks of October was far quieter than in September. To our surprise, the midnight rooftop chanting of 1 September was not repeated on 1 October. The Kuwaiti Resistance had reassessed its role after the casualties suffered during the Iraqi crackdown in September. Massive car bomb explosions were still occasionally heard in certain parts of Kuwait, but most activities were kept well away from populated areas. Futile gestures were not worth one more Kuwaiti life.

The Resistance generally redirected their efforts towards collecting intelligence on Iraqi troop dispositions, weapons, food supplies, morale and all the little things the Allies in Saudi Arabia needed to know. Their aims shifted from killing individual Iraqis to providing leverage to the Coalition forces, and keeping as many Kuwaitis as possible alive until the Allies arrived. Women and children were advised to take advantage of the opportunity to leave through the Saudi border, which the Iraqis had opened to them in mid-September. Thousands left, but to their credit, many Kuwaiti women chose to stay with their men and their homes.

The Resistance was also acutely aware of the value of Western public opinion. They arranged more live satellite phone interviews on US network TV with men in hiding, to convey the urgency of military action, capitalizing on America's abhorrence of hostage-taking and its memories of the Teheran US Embassy episode, and smuggled out photos and videos of atrocity victims.

The pressure of up to two months in hiding began to tell on many of the Western men in Kuwait. News from home was scant, with only a brief message once or twice a week on the international shortwave services.

Those of us who could move around, or were busy with warden's duties, hardly felt the pressure. In fact, several of us quite perversely enjoyed the adventure, despite the risk. However, one problem we had not foreseen was the Iraqi cancellation of the Kuwaiti currency. Iraq now declared that the Kuwaiti dinar was no longer legal tender. Soldiers at checkpoints started searching people for it, and confiscating it. Most of us had been trying to use any Iraqi dinars we had, and conserve the far more valuable Kuwaiti ones. The Iraqis had decreed in August that the Kuwait and Iraqi dinar were at parity, but a healthy black market had developed where one KD bought four or five ID. Now we would have difficulty doing even that.

The Iraqis also continued taking a census in Kuwait, as if there were no crisis at all. Two-man teams went around suburbs with clipboards and rang doorbells, but left if there was no reply. It was a terrifying time for many men in hiding who thought they were *Mukhabarat*, or that their flats had been marked down as empty, so the Iraqis could return to loot them. Some men in houses found green or red spray-painted marks on their gateposts. We never discovered precisely what they meant, but it was incredible. The Iraqis were facing the greatest military force gathered in one place since Korea, and their bureaucrats were going around town counting heads and painting gateposts.

Most men, and the few remaining women, were now living in groups. The largest was Command Central, with up to 20 men in one house. The average was four or five men per group. Perhaps 50 men lived on their own, some by choice to escape the pressures of living with the same individuals 24 hours a day. Thankfully, the pick-ups declined during the first half of October. The Iraqis had already taken the easy targets. Those remaining were generally very security conscious. Nevertheless, there were constant reminders against complacency. On 22 October, 29 men were picked up. We never found out how or why, but suspected that the Iraqis had known where at least some of them were for a while, and took them to replace people to be released the following day with British ex-Prime Minister Edward Heath, then in Baghdad.

A number of men suffered so much from the cabin fever induced by being forced to stay inside that they suffered nervous breakdowns. Their thoughts turned solely inwards, to the exclusion of others. Our own group in the Al-Muthanna Complex was a classic case, even though it was particularly fortunate in having two people who could move around. In the weeks since gaining freedom of movement, we had, with the assistance of our Syrian guardian angel, Imad Ghawji and several others, acquired enough food for eight months at a pinch. Once our own group had been taken care of, Paul Kennedy and I turned our attention to those in the broader community who did not have free-nationals living with them.

However, we met with fierce protests from our American. As far as he was concerned, his security took absolute priority. He feared that our moving in and out of the building would attract attention, and have him captured. This was all the more unreasonable as we had obtained genuine Irish papers for him, and a forged driver's licence identifying him as Irish. No similar protests were put forward by the Britons who were in far more danger, nor had the American objected when we first went out to get supplies. Nevertheless, we had earlier sworn to look after each other faithfully. He had done his best for us then. We could not now ignore his wishes.

Suddenly, the American's case was given a boost in the worst possible way. Ken and Magda Hoyle, the elderly couple living two floors above us returned one afternoon to their flat from walking their poodle, Samson, on the roof. They encountered a Jordanian trucker who was moving the household effects of their Syrian neighbours. He asked Ken if he was English. Ken said he was Czech, as Magda was Czech-born. The man seemed unconvinced.

The Hoyles were concerned that their security and that of the others in the building may have been compromised. They moved to an empty flat several floors below, and Paul and I agreed to not go out for the time being to minimize any risk of discovery. After several days with no sign of trouble, the Hoyles concluded that the Jordanian could not have reported them. They moved back to their own flat, but the ban on movement in and out of the building remained.

That afternoon, the Hoyles were playing bridge in the American's flat when their Kuwaiti neighbour, Mr Al-Awadi, called to say that the Iraqis had broken into their home. The Jordanian must have reported them, but the Iraqi machine had taken time to work. Unknown to us then, the Iraqis had threatened Mr Al-Awadi's sons with death if he did not help them find the couple. He could have directed the Iraqis straight to the American's flat, and those of the other British, but instead he played for time with great courage.

It was a difficult situation. The Hoyles' papers, clothes and Samson were all in their flat. It was obvious that the Iraqis would know they were somewhere in the building, and come looking for them door-to-door if they did not return. Paul and I suggested that one of us should go up to their flat, confront the Iraqis, and claim the flat as our own, but we would be unable to explain the different papers or Magda's clothing , and we had to assume that the Jordanian trucker had given Ken and Magda's description to the Iraqis.

While the rest of the group discussed what to do, Ken and Magda simply stood up, said that they had to give themselves up to protect those in hiding, and walked out of the flat. We could not stop them. It was the strangest feeling to watch these two such dignified people walk out of the door to an uncertain fate. Every one of us felt an overwhelming sense of impotence and tragedy, as if we might never see them alive again. In fact, by giving themselves up they probably saved Mr Al-Awadi's sons from a severe beating, at the very least, and the other British from capture.

We later learned that the Hoyles had walked in on two surprised *Mukhabarat*, and four Special Forces men. The officer asked them where they had been, and seemed satisfied when they explained they had just been for a walk on the roof. The interrogation was civilized and unpressured. In response to questions about their large food stocks, they explained that Magda had plenty before the invasion, and that departing Indian and Arab friends had given them more. The final question was whether there were any other Westerners in the building. They said no. The Iraqi seemed satisfied. They were given time to pack, and then taken to the Regency Palace Hotel.

The capture caused concern - almost panic - among the rest of the group. We went into 'deep hiding'. We knew that the Iraqis might leave a man behind in the Hoyles' flat in case any visitors called by, and would probably watch the building more closely. There was now no question of Paul and me going out.

On 13 October, the Amir of Kuwait convened in Jeddah a broad-based conference of 1,200 leading Kuwaiti politicians from all persuasions, former

Parliamentarians, and businessmen. It was an impressive achievement in the circumstances, given that the total population of Kuwaitis is only about 650,000, and about 200,000 of these were still in Kuwait.

The conferees demonstrated remarkable solidarity. Crown Prince and Prime Minister Sheikh Sa'ad Al-Abdullah promised that the 1962 Constitution, suspended for security reasons during the Iran-Iraq War, would be restored in liberated Kuwait, and many of the demands of the democracy movement would be met. There were even allusions to extending the vote to women.

The conference contributed greatly towards changing the views of critics who saw Kuwait as a feudal anachronism. It was clear that the Al-Sabah as the ruling institution of Kuwait enjoyed broad popular support. More importantly, it provided confirmation of Kuwait's progress, largely unique in the region, towards genuine participative democracy. The crusade to liberate Kuwait was elevated to the defence of democracy against dictatorship.

In a surprisingly magnanimous gesture, the conference distinguished between Kuwait's feelings for the Iraqis and Palestinians, and their respective leaders. It said that Kuwait did not bear any grudges or hatred against the ordinary people, and that the Iraqi people themselves were as much in need of salvation from Saddam as were the Kuwaitis.

Some inside Kuwait were unimpressed, seeing the conference as more of a PR exercise to educate foreign critics than saying anything new. We wanted more action and less talk. One leading Resistance figure, Asrar Al-Qabandi summed up the feelings of many of her colleagues by saying, 'We haven't even got a country...! Why are they wasting time talking about democracy!'

Nevertheless, the Kuwaitis outside took every opportunity to fly the flag, even if they were a country without land. On the eve of the Jeddah conference, Kuwait Airways announced resumption of its operations, using Cairo as its base, and eight of its 23 aircraft which were outside Kuwait at the time of the invasion. KAC 747s would soon be ferrying US reinforcements to Saudi Arabia.

Meanwhile, back in the Al-Muthanna, the question of Paul and me going out arose again, but with the recent scare, we could not guarantee to the others that our movements would not compromise their security. However, the need of those in hiding in the suburbs was growing more acute. Few of them were as well stocked up as us, and those supporting them were becoming overworked.

The only way out of the conflict was to leave the building entirely and not return, but the American vetoed this on the grounds that we might be seen leaving. He had become paranoid to the point of paralysis since the Hoyles' capture. The issue eventually came to a head when Paul Kennedy proposed going to Baghdad to see a delegation of three Irish Parliamentarians who were travelling there to plead with Saddam for the release of the Irish. The American with his Irish papers saw this as a chance to get out. He changed his tune so rapidly that he insisted Paul went to ensure that he was on their list, but he still did not accept that other people in Kuwait needed our help.

This hypocrisy and the demands from outside were too great to ignore. I insisted that if I could only leave the building by doing so surreptitiously and not returning, then so be it. I found a place to stay in the suburbs with Norma

Armstrong, a British woman who had taken in several other men who had been looted or felt unsafe in their own homes, and enlisted the help of Fred Skovberg, a Canadian with an apartment in our complex. Fred had moved out in August, but came in to check his apartment every week or so. Furthermore, if he was coming in without attracting Iraqi attention, then things must be safe. I arranged for Fred to take me out of the underground carpark in his vehicle. Imad would then drive my car out, park it around a corner, and I would transfer into it. I would not return to the complex at all unless it was safe for Americans and Britons to move around. In fact, I did not return to the building, or my own flat, until after the release of all the hostages, two months later.

14 October saw the Kuwaiti Resistance suffer one of its most grievous blows, with the capture of several of its key military leaders.

That day, Major-Generals Mohammed Al-Bader and Abdulwahab Al-Muzain, together with Brigadier Yousef Al-Mishari and a group of their officers were meeting in a suburban house when the Iraqis raided it. Accounts of how this happened vary. One says that the officers were using the vacated house of a family who had left to Saudi Arabia, and a neighbour saw them, assumed that they were looters and reported them to the Iraqi police. Another says that the Iraqis had noticed an unusual number of people going into the house, and became suspicious.

Either way, Al-Muzain, Al-Mishari and seven other officers were in the house at the time, with a satellite phone. They were apparently smoking heavily. Al-Bader, a non-smoker, had gone out to get some air. Suddenly, he saw the Iraqis moving in, but could do nothing to warn his friends. He had no choice but to flee over the neighbourhood fences, and alert other Resistance people.

The nine captured officers were taken to the local police station for questioning, with Al-Bader frantically trying to find a way to spring them from Iraqi custody. He could not go to the station himself as he would eventually be recognized. Finally, he approached Issam Al-Sager, a young Managing Director at the National Bank of Kuwait. Al-Sager was from an eminent merchant family, and had no military connections. Al-Bader pleaded with him to try to arrange the release his colleagues. He agreed, went to the police station, and was promptly arrested himself.

The officers and Al-Sager were eventually taken to Iraq, and held in various jails. The young banker and four others, Colonel Abdullah Sept, State Security Colonel Abdullah Jiran, Captain Abdulsalam Sumait, and Lieutenant Abdullah Al-Anzi were released during the March 1991 Shi'ite revolt, and got back to Kuwait. Al-Muzain, Al-Mishari, and three other officers, Police Colonel Yacoub Al-Sijari, Adel Abdulrazzak from the Air Force, and Safa Anbar from State Security are still missing, possibly in Iraqi custody.

Following the Kuwaiti Jeddah Conference, news from Iraq suggested that the sanctions were biting, but this would prove to be a false hope. On 18 October Baghdad offered bargain-price oil to countries who would come and get it, with payment to be made into an escrow account which was not to be touched until after the crisis. This was an attempt to win over poorer Third World countries such as India and Pakistan who were suffering particularly from the higher oil prices and reduction of remittances from expatriate workers in the Gulf. The offer was ignored, but recognized as a sign of Iraqi desperation.

The next day, Iraq announced that petrol rationing would start the following week. Private cars would be allowed 30 litres per week, taxis 60 litres. This was inconceivable in a country with over 10% of the world's oil reserves, but was initially seen as an indication that the sanctions were working by denying Iraq the chemical catalysts required to refine oil. However, a number of petroleum engineers in our midst knew the approximate stock of catalysts held by both Kuwait and Iraq. There should have been enough to supply the Iraqi refineries for several years. In retrospect, it may have been an attempt to con the world into believing that sanctions were working, and so feed the anti-war lobby. Although initially implemented in Kuwait for two days, petrol rationing was never pursued seriously, and was soon called off, with the dismissal of Iraq's Oil Minister.

The Iraqis had gone to great lengths to overcome the sanctions. Hoarding of food had become a capital offence, and rationing had been introduced. Uncultivated privately-owned agricultural land was expropriated, and farmers were exempted from military service, and allowed to use certain State-owned land. Prices paid by the Iraqi Government for their produce were raised, and the price of seeds and fertilizer lowered. Urban Iraqis were encouraged to take up fishing, grow their own vegetables, and raise chickens.

 Early American estimates suggested that Iraq had four to five months' supply of wheat and rice. Another authoritative estimate had said eight months for wheat, two for rice, and one for sugar, even with the harvest. They had not counted on the untapped agricultural potential of Iraq, a bumper wheat harvest of 400,000 tonnes, up from 100,000 in 1989, or Saddam's tight control over his centrally-planned economy. Prices went up, shortages occurred, luxury goods - except those looted from Kuwait - disappeared and ordinary Iraqis did suffer, but sanctions posed no real threat to Saddam or his regime. Food was also coming in from Jordan in considerable quantities.

Unknown to us at the time, the Human Shields were also being hurt by the sanctions. The black market was working to provide the Iraqi and Kuwaiti populace with their needs, but the money allowed to the camp managers to feed the hostages was generally fixed, so the quantity and quality of the food continued to deteriorate. Even where camp managers had a generous budget and were not skimming for their own pockets, their purchases of food for the hostages were limited by the rationing system. A few of the guards had become nasty as the crisis mounted. In fact, for about a week after the shooting of the Palestinians on Temple Mount, most medical care had been withdrawn from the Human Shields.

In Kuwait, of more concern to us was the Iraqi order that foreigners in Kuwait had two weeks to register with the authorities, or face sanctions. Although this was most likely a result of the Iraqi bureaucracy going through the motions of incorporating Kuwait into Iraq, it was seen as a cynical attempt to flush out the remaining Westerners in hiding.

The embassies in Kuwait told people that there was no assurance that Americans, British, French and Germans would not be incarcerated if they went to register, there was no point in doing so. However, one Englishman was in such a state of mind that he did in fact go to register and promptly became a Human Shield. No other wanted nationals followed suit.

The order was of more practical concern to those moving around. We were worried that our freedom would be curtailed if we did not register, or we might even be put back into the same category as those on the sites. Our Baghdad embassies could only suggest that the decision whether or not to register was up to us, although we should not give our correct addresses.

Arab friends were unable to discover the punishment for not registering, but we knew from pre-invasion times that breaching Iraqi immigration laws could mean up to seven years in jail. Free nationals who had moved to Baghdad were required to register with the authorities there; most had done so.

A great debate ensued among the free nationals in Kuwait. A few principled individuals saw registration as collaboration. Most of us were more pragmatic. The Iraqis were running Kuwait, and the greater requirement of being able to continue moving around outweighed our distaste for playing their little game. Some Americans and British with Irish TTDs, and several Australians with new passports - without Kuwaiti visa stamps - were concerned that the Iraqis would question their documents and incarcerate them as wanted nationals masquerading as free-nationals.

Again, it was the Canadians and New Zealanders who moved first. The registration office was in a villa near the huge Kazma Sports Stadium which, unknown to us at the time, was being used as a prison and torture centre for captured Resistance people.

The procedure was actually quite simple. You completed a form with the usual details, and were supposed to hand in your passport with two passport photos with a letter from your employer, a medical report and an AIDS-free certificate. The first Canadian to visit the office, Fred Skovberg, had a pleasant surprise. The Iraqi officials were very friendly. A particularly co-operative individual, Mr Raad, told him 'No, you cannot have residence visa. We must give you exit visa. You can leave Iraq. Give me your passport and come back tomorrow.' He did not even require the AIDS-free certificate, accepting that it was impractical under the circumstances.

This caused a great deal of excitement. We waited expectantly for the result. Perhaps the Iraqis had decided to release all the Canadians. Nevertheless, there was a strange sense of reluctance. When faced with the prospect of the option to leave, or even the requirement to do so, many of those who had elected not relocate to Baghdad felt an obligation to stay in Kuwait and maintain those in hiding. Secondly, we expected war in barely a month, and wanted to see the Iraqis chased out. Set against this was the compelling desire to return home to loved ones. Some of us faced a cruel dilemma.

In any event, the Canadians' hopes were dashed the next day. Mr Raad had erred. He could give them a two-month residence visa, but no exit visa.

Once these first residence visas for the so-called Iraqi province of Kuwait had been issued to the Canadians and New Zealanders, most other free-nationals decided to comply. The debate over whether or not to register had consumed most of the two-week grace period. There was a rush to the Kazma Stadium. When we arrived, the scene was pandemonium. We had not seen so many people in one place in Kuwait since before the invasion. Thousands of Arabs and Asians were standing in the huge carpark in national groups, with Iraqi officials calling out names from boxes of passports, and tossing the precious documents like Frisbees into the crowd whenever a voice answered.

There seemed to be a separate procedure for Westerners. Our task was to get into the villa to see Mr Raad. We had to press through the crowd, pleading 'Mr Raad, Mr Raad!', holding up our passports. A number of Palestinians or Iraqis scowled at us, but most were friendly, just concerned with getting their families' documents processed. When we finally got past the gate, we were seated in the reception area and asked to fill in the forms.

We went through the same rigmarole as the Canadians. Like them, we had to part with our passport photos and even more precious passports. We asked for a receipt, but were assured 'No problem. Come back tomorrow!' We had heard that promise so many times from officials in pre-invasion Kuwait that we feared it was the last we would see of the passports for at least a week, despite the Canadians' successes. This would leave us in a very difficult position if our nationalities were suddenly released. Nevertheless, we had to bite the bullet. If we did not register, maybe they would not let us out at all.

We completed the forms. I put down a false local address, and hoped they would not check it. One question asked for details of how and when we had entered Iraq. I had returned to Kuwait through the airport on 25 July, but did not consider Kuwait to be part of Iraq even now. We had that much principle left, even if we were playing the Iraqi registration game. In a stupidly dangerous piece of defiance at the time, I put down 'Invasion, Occupation, Annexation, August 2nd 1990' for the date and means of entry. Either Mr Raad and his staff did not read the form, or ignored my futile little protest. No comment was passed, and the form accepted.

True to Mr Raad's promise, when we returned at the appointed time and forced our way through the crowd, the passports were waiting for us, with an impressive-looking 'Republic of Iraq, Directorate of Residence' visa sticker, with one month's residence, and room for two extensions. The date of arrival in Iraq was shown as the date the visa was issued. It had proved easier to obtain residency in Iraq than it ever had in pre-invasion Kuwait.

Curiously, a fellow free-national who registered later queried why he had been issued a one-month visa, when the Canadians had two months. Mr Raad or one of his staff looked at him with long-suffering weariness and told him that it would not matter in a month. This promptly started a rumour that the Iraqis would be withdrawing by the end of November.

Much to our chagrin, after having gone to the trouble of getting the visa, the Iraqis at checkpoints seldom looked at it. They still asked for the Kuwaiti civil ID. The whole exercise seemed to have been a waste of time, but it amused us that the troops relied more on the Kuwaiti ID than Iraqi visas. I would later learn how valuable the Iraqi visa was in maintaining our freedom. At least one Indian, a part-owner of a private hospital, was jailed for not registering. The Iraqis could be serious if they chose to be.

A further blow in Kuwait was Canada's announcement on 20 October that she was withdrawing her diplomats. The last Dutch, Italian and Polish diplomats had left two weeks earlier, and the Belgians and Germans the previous week. The reason given was that it was unsafe for them to remain, and they were serving no useful purpose. This was despite the fact that a dozen Canadian civilians remained in Kuwait, and considered themselves safer in Kuwait than in Baghdad in the event of hostilities.

In fact, there was little the Canadian Embassy could do other than fly the flag. It was blockaded, its independent communications had failed, and the Canadian civilians were looking after themselves and many others quite capably. *Chargé d'affaires* Bill Bowden believed he could hold out, and argued with Ottawa in favour of doing so. He was given a direct order to go.

We were disappointed to see the Canadian diplomats leave, but on balance it was for the best. With their departure, only the US, Bahraini, British, French, Iranian and Omani embassies were holding on.

Perhaps the most important development in late October was the visit to Saudi Arabia by the Chairman of the US Joint Chiefs of Staff, General Colin Powell. He arrived on 21 October for consultations with General Schwarzkopf and the Saudis. These meetings marked the shift in military preparations from a primarily defensive mission to an offensive one to liberate Kuwait. The deployment of the tank-heavy US VII Corps from Germany, plus the 1st Mechanized Infantry Division and an additional US Marine division, was agreed on. Air and naval forces were to be greatly increased.

The day after Powell's arrival, King Fahd declared that Saudi Arabia's stance towards 'Iraq's criminal aggression against Kuwait' was 'firm, irrevocable, clear and unambiguous ... not subject to any change or negotiations in any of its details'. We were delighted. The King had never spoken so firmly before. There had been concern that the Saudis were prepared to live with at least a partial Iraqi occupation of Kuwait. The King's comments were irrefutable confirmation that the liberation of Kuwait was a foregone conclusion. The only question was when.

After Powell's return to Washington, President Bush authorized a doubling of US forces to more than 400,000 troops. Bush maintained later that he still hoped for a peaceful solution, but he was prepared to use force if that failed. The deployments would take several months, but it was endgame for Saddam.

However, Liberation would be too late for one British Human Shield, Ron Duffy, who died in a camp of a heart attack on 20 October, and Alex Duncan, a British youth accidently killed in Iraqi custody on his way to being released.

The first releases of a few of the French hostages on 1 October was ostensibly a result of groveller Gilles Munier's efforts, but there was more than met the eye. That minor release actually arose from President Mitterrand's UN speech of 24 September where he seemed to breathe new life into Saddam's faltering 12 August proposal for linking the Kuwaiti and Palestinian issues. The Iraqis had been privately trying to get France to send a senior Minister for direct talks. If Saddam could engage a key Coalition member in dialogue, especially a permanent member of the Security Council, it would be more difficult for anyone to attack him. The Soviets did not offer sufficient leverage as they had not sent troops. China was sitting out the crisis, and the US and UK were far too hardline. Of the five permanent members, that just left France.

In a craftily-drafted speech, Mitterrand appeared to recognize the legitimacy of some of Iraq's claims and suggested that the resolution of the crisis could be followed by a comprehensive Middle East peace conference. Everything was possible if Iraq withdrew and released the hostages.

The speech was compared by some to Neville Chamberlain's appeasement of Hitler. French diplomats were soon busy explaining that Mitterrand had been over-interpreted. However, the Iraqis were delighted. To Saddam, it must have seemed as if the wall of Western solidarity against him was cracking. His reward to the French was the minor release of 1 October. Nine men were not many, but it was a start, a token that the Iraqis wanted to talk.

The Iraqis immediately went to work again on the French. A message was passed to Paris suggesting a meeting with Yasser Arafat to receive an important message from Saddam. French Foreign Minister Roland Dumas went to Tunis to meet secretly with Arafat on 14 October, but the message was merely a plea for a face-saving formula to allow Saddam to extricate himself from the crisis, and a request for Dumas or another senior Minister to visit Baghdad. Dumas indicated that he would go if he received a meaningful signal from Baghdad, but that France could go no further than Mitterrand's UN speech. The signal was presumably the release of all French hostages.

On 16 October, former French Foreign Minister and Presidential Envoy Claude Cheysson visited Tunis as part of an EC delegation. This time Tareq Aziz was there, and reportedly admitted that the invasion had been a mistake. Iraq was looking for a way out. Cheysson reiterated the official line. Cheysson then met separately with Arafat, who reportedly promised to 'take care of the hostages'.

Within days, a third French envoy, Edgar Pisani, met with Arafat in Tunis. He too reiterated that the Human Shield was damaging Iraq's cause. Arafat seemed convinced that the French were serious about a diplomatic effort, but that their main priority was the hostages, and conveyed this to Saddam in Baghdad on 20 October. This apparently led to the general release of the French two days later. The French then fell back into line with everyone else, and closed the doors on Saddam. When the Iraqis protested, the French replied that they had meant all the hostages, and Americans, British, Germans and Japanese were still being held as Human Shields.

Soviet envoy Yevgeny Primakov returned to Baghdad on 28 October after a hectic four-nation tour to brief Western leaders on his earlier meeting.

Primakov met with Saddam and his senior generals in the morning, and Tareq Aziz in the afternoon. He apparently found Saddam more sombre than earlier in the month. This time, instead of simply stating that Kuwait was part of Iraq, he wanted to know how and when the withdrawal of US troops from Saudi Arabia would be accomplished if he agreed to leave Kuwait; whether the sanctions would be lifted; how Iraq's concerns for a better outlet to the sea would be addressed, and whether there would be linkage between an Iraqi withdrawal and a solution to the Palestinian question. Without answers to these questions, he said he could do nothing. For the first time, he seemed to be seriously considering withdrawal, but he needed a *quid pro quo*.

Primakov and Saddam both claimed that their talks had been useful, but they gave the Coalition precious little to work with. At a summit in Paris on the 29th, Mitterrand and Gorbachev, both of whom were sensitive to accusations of having done special deals to get their people out, jointly called for the release of all hostages and - aware that time was running out for a peaceful solution - reassured Saddam that he would not be attacked if he withdrew.

As the month drew to a close, the French prepared to leave. There had been an unusual delay of several days between Saddam's recommendation to his Parliament, on 22 October, that they should be allowed to leave, and the actual departure. We did not know that he was trying to gain maximum political advantage from the release, and time the arrival in Paris of the returning French with the Mitterrand-Gorbachev summit there on 29 October.

Shortly before the French were to depart, I got a call from Barbara Bodine of the US Embassy, asking if the American in my apartment complex would like to take the chance of leaving with them. In his mental state, he had boycotted the embassy, so this was the only way for her to talk to him. The French had offered to issue documents to a limited number of American men who preferably spoke French, or were ill. Barbara made it quite clear that anyone who went risked being discovered and sent to a site. The offer was couched in terms suggesting that it was available only to Americans. Unknown to us at the time, the British Embassy had apparently turned the French down, much to the later annoyance of many French-speaking British.

I recommended the scheme to our American, who dismissed it as hare-brained. Three other Americans elsewhere in Kuwait decided it was worth it. Barbara then asked if the Australians could help get the documents. Our task was to go to the three Americans' separate hiding places, get their passport photos, and take them to the French Consul, who would issue the papers. We would then take the papers back to the three pseudo Frenchmen, and take them to the departure rendezvous. All this had to be done in a matter of hours.

On the morning of the departure, the Iraqis came to the front gate of the French Residence to escort the French to Baghdad. When they found no one waiting they banged on the bars of the gate. They were in a hurry, but the Consul, Jean-Pierre Galtier, was not going to be rushed. He came to the gate after a suitable delay, dressed only in his swimming trunks, to see what they wanted. The Iraqis were obviously impatient. Jean-Pierre explained to the officer with exquisite politeness that he had yet to finish his breakfast, and would be with them when he had completed both that and his packing.

At the time, I was in contact with Jean-Pierre by phone to co-ordinate the documents for the three American Frenchmen, and happened to call him shortly after this. He was in his element. 'If these bastards can lock me in here for months and kidnap my people,' he said, 'they can damn well wait until I finish my coffee and croissants!' The Iraqis had to wait. If Jean-Pierre had been aware of the Iraqi plan to time the arrival of the French in Paris to coincide with the Mitterrand–Gorbachev summit – as perhaps he was – he may have delayed them for another day to foil their plan completely.

Elsewhere in Kuwait, the Iraqis collected three young French BA149 passengers who were Human Shields at IBI Camp, and two of the three women remaining there, Jo Best and Wendy Majors, and took them first to the airport, and then to Ali Al-Salem KAF base by bus.

Wendy had stayed there with her father, Don, and a BA steward with whom she had struck up a romance. A number of the men in the camp had become concerned at the attention paid to Wendy by the troops. Wendy did not help matters by dressing fine for Club Med, but not quite appropriately for Iraqi soldiers. The camp boss, Ken Best, asked his wife, Jo, to leave so that Wendy would go. It would be the last time Wendy saw her father alive.

The French from Kuwait were joined by Martin Sullivan, the English husband of a French woman, who was issued with the appropriate papers. Everyone destined to leave, including the three plucky Americans, rendezvoused at Ali Al-Salem. They flew to Baghdad, where they joined their compatriots from the Iraqi camps, and the French from Baghdad, and then on to Paris, arriving on the night of 29 October to a rapturous welcome.

The following day, a coded message came over RFI: 'Your three parcels have arrived safely.' It was the three Americans, the first to escape from Kuwait since August. All three were sworn to secrecy until the crisis passed, in case the ploy could be reused. Those Americans in Kuwait who had rejected the chance were dejected, but could blame no one but themselves.

The French were the heroes of the hour. Speculation persisted that Mitterrand had done a deal with Iraq, but the wags in Kuwait insisted that it had more to do with getting them home in time for the *Nouveau Beaujolais.*

The release of the French was a mixed blessing for the men left behind in the camps and in Kuwait. The French took out mail for some of them, and would eventually make their conditions known to the press, thus generating even more outrage. However, when the French left, the Iraqis moved the Human Shields in Iraq closer to their strategic sites. In August and September, they had been held in reasonably comfortable accommodation near the sites. Now they were placed directly in the hearts of the installations, on the factory floors of uranium enrichment facilities, ammunition plants, or in dam turbine rooms. Conditions deteriorated. For some men, the noise of machinery working around the clock next to their beds made sleep impossible.

At the Al-Qaim uranium plant, the hostages were moved from their comfortable chalets into small rooms next to the machinery, pipes and silos. The uranium processing section where the men were was surrounded by a seven-metre concrete wall on three sides, and sandbags on the fourth. Outside this area was a regular fertilizer plant. The uranium plant was actually hidden inside the fertilizer factory, and the men had been placed right next to it.

At some camps, the changes in location and of the seasons exposed the hostages to more mosquitoes and flies. The Iraqi idea of sanitation was primitive. They simply threw waste into compost heaps, and sewerage systems often broke down. With the arrival of winter rains, hostages in some locations found it impossible to venture outside for more than a few minutes before the insects and smell drove them back inside. This, the meagre diet, and the lack of physical exercise, placed great strains on their health.

Of even greater concern to several particularly fearful men were reports on shortwave radio services that the Iraqis had said that hostages 'would be abused in the event of an attack on Iraq'. This coincided with further news of atrocities coming out of Kuwait. In their heightened state of fear, they believed that they might face such torture in the event of war, and prayed more fervently for rescue or, failing that, a quick war. Better a quick death from a US bomb than a slow death at the hands of vengeful Iraqis.

The arrival home of the French coincided with the passing of UN Security Council Resolution 674 demanding an immediate end to hostage-taking, and calling on Iraq to rescind the closure order against the embassies in Kuwait, and ensure immediate access to food, water and basic services for the protection of Kuwaitis and third-country nationals in Iraq and Kuwait, including diplomats. This was a direct request to the Iraqis to stop blockading the only two remaining Western embassies in Kuwait, the US and British, and to allow the diplomats access to their hundreds of nationals in hiding.

The Resolution also hit Iraq in the pocket by asking member states to collect evidence of Iraqi human rights abuses in Kuwait, and of financial losses caused by the invasion. The French, with all their hostages home, backed this up. The Iraqi Ambassador to Paris, the senior Iraqi diplomat in Europe, Mr Abdul Razzaq Al-Hashimi, was called to the Quai d'Orsay to hear protests about the privations suffered by the French Embassy in Kuwait. He received not a word of thanks for their release. As far as the French were concerned, the hostages should never have been taken in the first place.

More importantly, Saddam never got his much-coveted visit from a senior French official. He may have assumed that his supposedly generous gesture of releasing the French would obtain this. Saddam actually went to even further lengths to woo the French. When three French soldiers somehow wandered across the Saudi border into Iraqi hands on 29 October, they were taken to Baghdad and released to their embassy, arriving back in France shortly afterwards. The only person Mitterrand was prepared to send to Baghdad was a senior administrative figure to arrange the departure of the hostages, not to negotiate or enter into a dialogue. The French once again reminded the Iraqis that they had been talking about the release of all hostages, not just theirs.

Mitterrand had to endure accusations of doing a secret deal with Saddam, but the French had outfoxed the Iraqis, and got their people home. More importantly, Mitterrand reaffirmed France's continued support for enforcing UN Security Council Resolutions.

The EC also hardened. On 28 October, at a summit in Rome, aware of how Saddam was using the 'grovel' system and trying to lure a senior Coalition Minister to Baghdad without first agreeing to the UN demands, they agreed not to send any Government representatives to talk with him. They left the door open by allowing the appointment of a special UN representative to go to Baghdad for the purposes of gaining the release of the hostages, but drew a distinction between 'negotiating', and 'pressing for the release of the hostages'.

The international community, which had seemed almost conciliatory a month earlier was now presenting a more unified front.

After releasing the French for nothing in return, the Iraqis were loath to let go any more hostages go. Saddam was in a dilemma. The Human Shield was bad public relations, but was one of his few remaining cards. The military force now facing Iraq was formidable. Saddam had no immediate way out of the crisis without losing face. He needed to play for time.

His solution reached new heights in cynicism. On 31 October, the Iraqis announced that the families of 'those staying as our guests' could visit them for Christmas and New Year. Iraq even offered to accommodate the families, but there was no indication that the men could leave with them, although it was widely assumed that the women could. This would give Iraq at least another two months, and reinforce the Human Shield with hundreds of additional women and children. The Coalition could perhaps attack with the men in the sites. It was an entirely different matter with women and children.

The reaction from the men hiding in Kuwait was swift and almost universal. Embassies were swamped with messages from men ordering their families not to come anywhere near Iraq. Many free-Westerners in Kuwait travelled to Baghdad just to call their wives and tell them not to come. A number of men did want their wives to visit, but these were relatively few.

The women at home were divided. Some were determined to go, especially as the prospect of war was not as stark as when they had left, and their children were now safe. Many struggled with the guilt of having left their men to an uncertain fate. Others saw Saddam's Christmas offer as playing into his hands, and elongating their husband's ordeal. Nevertheless, women worldwide started consulting each other about going.

It was clear as October closed that Saddam was now on the defensive, searching desperately for a way to delay any attack. The hostages were central to these efforts, but were a two-edged sword. He could gain diplomatic points only by releasing them, but he would then reduce their perceived military value as Human Shields. In any event, their military value had declined with the consistent Coalition message that their presence would not deter an attack. The Allies had regained the initiative. In Kuwait, we felt they should press home their advantage. They would do so in November.

20. THE BAGHDAD SAFARI PARK

The first free Western nationals to arrive in Baghdad in September 1990 found a city of paradox. The Iraqi capital was an eerie contrast to a tense and ravaged Kuwait. Basking in the glorious sunshine of a Mesopotamian summer, it appeared surprisingly relaxed for a city supposedly on the verge of war.

Many Iraqi men in Baghdad – and even some women – were in uniform, but more smartly presented than their colleagues in Kuwait. Soldiers were usually armed only if on duty. Anti-aircraft guns were evident on many of the higher buildings, but the crews were relaxed.

Baghdad was flooded with Kuwaiti loot. There was a bonanza of everything from electronics to food or fashion, often with Kuwaiti labels still attached. Baghdad's city bus fleet had been augmented with the Kuwait Public Transport Company's distinctive blue-and-white Mercedes vehicles, and yellow-and-cream TATAs, with new Iraqi licence plates and their logos hastily painted over. Looted Kuwaiti automobiles were everywhere.

The first stop for free Westerners arriving from Kuwait was usually their embassies. The diplomats left them in no doubt as to the reason for the apparent peace and security in Baghdad: in Saddam's capital, it was 'Police State Rules', referred to as 'Moscow Rules'. Despite the genuine warmth of many ordinary Iraqis, the relaxed atmosphere was entirely superficial. The populace was intimidated by a ruthlessly efficient security apparatus.

The basic rule in the embassies was to say nothing that might be construed as anti-regime or that might compromise one's own or someone else's security. Assume that every phone was tapped, that every Iraqi, including those working in the embassies and the taxi drivers, was a spy; that every embassy, diplomatic residence, hotel room, lobby, elevator and restaurant was bugged. If you wanted to speak your mind, do so outside, well away from any buildings. We were told that the *Mukhabarat* were trained by the East German *Stasi*, and knew what they were doing. It was a most sinister feeling. One diplomat drove the point home by explaining that even if we as Westerners did not suffer personally for an indiscretion, an Iraqi whom we unwittingly compromised could quite possibly die, and we would know nothing of it.

The Iraqi preoccupation with security was so Orwellian that it was impossible to buy street maps of Baghdad. They were unavailable. I was lucky to have a third-generation photocopy of a simple map published many years previously, but most people had to get by with hand-drawn sketches and memory. Western residents of Baghdad were therefore uncommonly skillful amateur cartographers.

Some Westerners in Baghdad had developed a curious code of communication based on diplomats' techniques used in the Eastern bloc to minimize the risks of surveillance. Saddam was seldom referred to by name, unless respectfully, and then usually simply as 'The President', or *Al-Rais*. Otherwise, he was 'Boris', and then 'Eric' when someone suggested that with all the talk about 'Boris' among non-Russians, the eavesdroppers had surely tumbled to the ploy. Long-term expatriates also called him 'Stan The Man', or simply 'Stan'.

The game was actually more in the minds of the Westerners. The Iraqis could never bug every single conversation, let alone process such a mass of words into useful intelligence. However, the spy's great strength is that you are never sure when you are being spied upon. The use of Boris or whatever name was chosen for the day was a subtle way of having a joke at the expense of the Iraqis, and of thumbing your nose at Saddam right under his.

The humour could be even more subtle. Japanese Ambassador Kunio Katakura dubbed Baghdad 'The Safari Park'. He saw those hostages who could 'roam' Baghdad's streets but not leave Iraq as the 'safari park' hostages, and those on strategic sites as 'behind bars', or the 'zoo' hostages.

But the pun went even further. The Arabic for 'Embassy' is *Safara*, and life for most foreigners in Baghdad revolved around their embassies. They were a place of shelter, a source of funds, a means of communication with home. Foreign journalists and TV crews visited the embassies regularly where the Ambassadors and *chargés d'affaires* were often good for a briefing or interview. The image of hordes of wide-eyed journalistic tourists doing the rounds of the embassies fitted quite neatly into the 'Safari Park' metaphor.

Yet, if the surveillance could not be everywhere, Saddam himself did his best to be omnipresent. He gazed down from the wall of every hotel room, office, restaurant and lobby in one of his many roles as soldier, statesman, bedouin or pilgrim. Even Iraqis with no love for him had a portrait in their living rooms lest it seemed they did not have the beloved *Al-Rais* as the head of their household. Taxi drivers had him on their dashes. The street portraits I recalled from pre-invasion trips to Iraq seemed more numerous, and bigger, as if to underline the man's new international status.

In another interpretation of Mr Katakura's 'Safari Park', the exotic animals were a metaphor for the visitors, and Saddam-cum-Boris or Eric was very much the King of the Jungle, the Boss Gorilla who everyone wanted to see.

From mid-August 1990, Baghdad was host to an incredible range of human creatures from all corners of the globe. Some were regulars on a perennial migration, such as Yasser Arafat and Javier Perez de Cuellar, usually seeking a solution to whatever international crisis Saddam had created for that year.

The far more numerous lesser species were generally on their first trips to the park. Foremost among them were the hostages. They were sighted briefly, if at all, on their way through Baghdad to hidden lairs in the hinterland to become Human Shields. Most were Caucasian or Japanese adult males, with a few Negroes. They appeared on Iraqi TV now and then looking hunted and harried to mumble platitudes dictated by the Boss Gorilla, and send messages of love to far-away mates and offspring. Except for a few elderly or sick specimens held in the Mansour Melia, they were rarely seen in the flesh.

The hostages formed the basic krill of an incredibly complex intercontinental food chain. The two higher orders of this unique dietary system were the international media, and those who became known as the 'Grovellers'. This latter species visited the park voluntarily to plead for the release of various hostages. Their objectives ranged from a genuine desire to help these people, to a far more cynical appetite for personal glory. Sadly, the latter type seemed prevalent, but the entire species was characterized by a naive misconception that their efforts could make any difference at all.

The international media were the ultimate predators and scavengers – the sharks in the food chain. Their diet was information, for which they had an insatiable appetite. Many were extremely professional, but others cared little where they got their sustenance from, or who got hurt in the process. Once snared in Baghdad, the prey was often spiced up with a dash of sensationalism, and transmitted to the distant family home where a parent figure known as an 'editor' might add further spice before broadcasting it from the final part of the digestive tract to a news-hungry public.

Like the grovellers, the media comprised several sub-species. The most visible were TV news crews. They hunted in packs, usually led by a cunning creature known as a 'producer'. The extreme demands of their editor-parents made them voracious, so they were not always selective in their reporting.

A more scholarly sub-species were newspaper and magazine reporters. They usually prowled alone, or with a mate known as a 'photographer'. They were usually better informed and under less pressure to produce a visual story for tonight's news, so their feeding was less frenzied than their electronic cousins.

These groups formed a symbios. The hostages provided the rationale for the grovellers, and great groveller glory if the Boss Gorilla condescended to release a few. Boss Gorilla himself thrived on the international publicity generated by his meetings with the more distinguished grovellers. In turn, the hostages placed great hope on the grovellers getting them out of the park. The media were delighted at the local interest provided by the grovellers, many of whom were eminent opposition politicians, ex-statesmen, or has-been sportsmen. In turn, those grovellers in pursuit of glory depended on the media to provide their stage. They could not have existed without each other.

The major species of creatures in Baghdad which most often went unnoticed were the Kuwaiti visitors to the military POW camps. However, these people generally preferred to avoid all media attention lest they or their imprisoned menfolk attracted the ire of the *Mukhabarat* once the cameras were turned off. The Kuwaiti POWs themselves never found their way onto TV screens, so by definition, did not exist in the media world.

The free-Westerners, or 'Safari Park hostages', came in several distinct classes. Most were Australians, Canadians, New Zealanders, and Europeans other than British, French and Germans who had been persuaded to move to Baghdad from Kuwait. The rest had been working in or visiting Iraq on business or pilgrimages at the time of the invasion. They included British, predominantly Irish, and a few Canadian medical personnel at the PARC Ibn Al-Bitar hospital; US, British and Canadian Bechtel engineers; British construction workers, and advisors from the Australian Wheat Board. None of these people qualified as Human Shields, although several Americans and British who had been working in Iraq had been sent to camps by mistake.

There were great benefits to being in Baghdad, notably access to consular personnel still recognized by the Iraqis, medical care, assured food supplies, relative safety and, most importantly, communication with home. After the departures of the women and children, there was the hope that being in Baghdad placed one in a better position to get out when the time came.

The down-side, however, was particularly grim. Few people believed that the city would escape an Allied attack. They feared they could not win either way, either being blown to smithereens by Allied bombs, or torn to pieces by irate Iraqis. The greatest ghost in Baghdad was the 1958 Iraqi revolution, when a number of foreigners had been lynched by mobs. Despite fervent wishes in foreign capitals for the prompt demise of Saddam, some diplomats with an eye to history dreaded that this would precipitate a complete breakdown of law and order as the repressions of millions of Iraqis exploded.

The two streams of free Westerners in Baghdad, those from Iraq and those from Kuwait, did not always see eye-to-eye. On one occasion, an Irishman from Kuwait was drinking in a hotel with a compatriot from the PARC hospital, who was bemoaning his predicament, and the fact that he could not leave. The Kuwait Irishman turned on him in disgust, lecturing him on how he didn't know how good he had it: 'You're up here, in phone contact with your wife and kids. You still have your job, you can send your worldly goods out in an orderly manner, and there's law and order everywhere. Do you realize that there's a war in Kuwait, and that any one of us could get topped by some nasty *Mukhabarat* goon just to prove himself? And what about the guys at the sites? If the war starts, you'll be in that nice safe hospital with a Red Cross on the roof, well protected by local troops who want you to treat them if they get hurt. The guys on the sites will be dead, as well as some of us in Kuwait.'

The Iraqis encountered in Baghdad were vastly different from the military we had known in Kuwait. They were generally well educated, respectful, often fluent in English, even the taxi drivers and shopkeepers. Few seemed to bear any great resentment towards the West. Almost exclusively, they would not discuss the crisis for fear that their conversation might be reported. Many who spent time in Baghdad came to appreciate the spirit and finer qualities of the Iraqis as individuals, and the fear and apprehension haunting them.

The first large group of free Western men to relocate to Baghdad without being taken there in Iraqi custody were Scandinavian and Dutch men who had gone north in national convoys in late August and early September, followed by a group of Irish in mid-September. The next arrivals were free Westerners who were ill, and felt they could be better cared for in Baghdad, and those who had only recently arrived in Kuwait, or were visitors.

Many of those who lived in Kuwait were reluctant to relocate to Baghdad. For some, this smacked of collaboration. Kuwait was their home and Baghdad was, after all, the enemy capital. To move there was an admission of defeat and a desertion of Kuwaiti friends. Others, with a role in the support function for people in hiding, or acting as wardens, felt they would be letting down those who desperately needed them if they moved north.

Some had more practical reasons for staying where they were. We anticipated, correctly as it turned out, that the Allies would bomb Baghdad - General Michael Dugan, the US Air Force Chief, had said so himself - but not capture it. The Allied armies would concentrate on freeing Kuwait and those in Baghdad would be 600km behind the front line, trapped amidst two million irate Iraqis, whereas those in Kuwait could lie low until the Allies arrived.

When the crisis settled down to a waiting game, more free Westerners from Kuwait did move north, but some only temporarily. They were grateful for the chance to phone their families, but found the atmosphere too sinister, and the carefully balanced views of some of their diplomats and the journalists too forgiving of the Iraqis. In their opinion, many people in Baghdad, even some who were paid to be objective, seemed affected by Iraqi propaganda, and divorced from reality. The horrors of Kuwait were totally alien to their experience. Once these free Westerners had phoned home, they stocked up on funds and supplies, and hurried back to Kuwait. They preferred to take their chances with the occupation troops and live in hope of liberation, rather than look over their shoulder during every conversation.

The Westerners from Kuwait were probably too harsh in their assessment of those from Baghdad as sympathisers of Iraq, and those from Baghdad had difficulty understanding the conviction among many of those from Kuwait that war was not only necessary, but morally imperative and well-overdue.

However, the decision to return to Kuwait was not always for the best. An elderly Australian lawyer did so, only to find that if he had stayed in Baghdad, he could have left much sooner with the first Australian groveller.

Others from Kuwait chose to stay, encouraged by their families, the medical care, and the prospect of grovellers' visits which might result in their release. A few felt that they could escape from Iraq into Turkey, Jordan or Syria, and hatched plans to do so.

For Westerners visiting or working in Iraq itself at the time of the invasion, the question of their relocating to Baghdad never arose.

The Americans, British, French, Germans and Japanese among them were particularly nervous of being interned along with their compatriots from Kuwait. Many of them therefore stayed on diplomatic premises, not venturing onto the streets. About 25 Americans, mainly Bechtel men, took refuge in their Ambassador's Residence, and 55 Britons in their embassy. Five of the eight Canadians in their Ambassador's Residence, and one American with a Canadian family, were Bechtel men. Some other Westerners were also worried about being interned, but in the main they went about unhindered.

Few of the Westerners in Baghdad, whether from Iraq or Kuwait, were idle. The city had plenty of tourist sites and interesting *souqs*, but these active men needed something more meaningful to occupy their time. Some took over the jobs of diplomats who had been evacuated by acting as unpaid ambassadors' secretaries, or consular assistants. Some did volunteer work at the UN High Commission for Refugees or British Council. Others took responsibility for co-ordinating incoming mail for the people in Kuwait. Some intrepid individuals even used their enforced stay in Iraq to see the country.

This relative freedom of movement was a curious concession in a country so paranoid about security. Every free Westerner was a potential spy, and many did become amateur spies. However, the information gathered was usually low-level intelligence on the state of the Iraqi economy and the effect of sanctions. Free Westerners travelling around Iraq could see troops, but their military intelligence was of minimal significance. In any event, their own embassies and countrymen discouraged them from spying on military matters as it could lead to serious retribution if they were to be caught.

In fact, almost paradoxically, the sanctions boosted parts of the Iraqi economy. The higher prices made some previously uneconomical areas viable. Farmers were quick to cash in by growing market-garden crops. Iraq had purchased strategic supplies of wheat before the Invasion, so although the quality of the bread was poor, and everything very expensive, Iraq would not starve. Add to this looted food from Kuwait, the porous Turkish, Iranian and Syrian borders, plus trade from Jordan, and the futility of the sanctions as a timely means of making Saddam mend his ways was apparent.

Now and then, a particular shortage of drugs or some other vital commodity would become public. On further investigation, it was usually discovered that similar shortages had existed prior to Iraq's invasion of Kuwait. They were endemic in Iraq's war-ravaged Stalinist economy.

Some of the intelligence provided by Westerners in Iraq was, however, of direct use to the Allied military. Many of Iraq's vital dams, power plants and bridges had been built by Western contractors, and some of the very engineers who had built these facilities were being held in Iraq. They knew exactly how to destroy them. Some of them were sufficiently incensed at the situation to share their information with the embassies by showing them how to put the installation out of operation, without killing the workers.

At a more immediate level for those in Baghdad, the USLOK men from Kuwait, now in their Embassy in Baghdad, plotted the location of every Iraqi checkpoint on the main roads from Kuwait to Baghdad, and to Jordan and Turkey, using information culled from a host of sources. This was particularly significant as these men, led by Colonel John Mooneyham, an ex-Special Forces man, were busy preparing escape, evasion, exfiltration and evacuation plans. From the Embassy, Mooneyham had intermittent secure-telephone contact with Central Command elements at MacDill Air Force Base in Florida.

Despite this surreal and sinister atmosphere, life could be surprisingly normal. When Iraqi TV was not broadcasting news of Saddam's latest speech or accomplishment, the day's 'spontaneously organized' demonstration against the US, or the Human Shields sending messages to their families, the viewing hours were filled with old US and Australian series such as 'The Love Boat' and 'The Flying Doctors', and even old Audie Murphy Westerns.

For those who ventured out for a night on the town, there were excellent fish restaurants on the banks of the Tigris. The five-star hotels had nightclubs that would not have been out of place in a Western capital, even if the drinks selection was limited. The crisis generated a boom in concerts and art exhibitions, as the Iraqi intelligentsia grasped their first real opportunity in many years to prove that there was a more cultured side to their country.

The diplomats in Baghdad were often seen as a breed apart from the civilians in that they had diplomatic immunity, and were perceived to be trained for such a difficult situation. In truth, they were just ordinary men and women with the same concerns for their families at home as the civilians. Most of them were under no illusions as to what their fate might be if things turned nasty. Diplomatic immunity had done nothing for the US diplomats in Teheran in 1980, and Saddam was already flouting the Geneva Conventions.

As with the civilians, there were two streams of diplomats: those accredited to Baghdad, and those who had relocated from Kuwait. Most of the Baghdad-based diplomats had evacuated their spouses, dependants and all non-essential personnel. There was no point in maintaining commercial sections in Baghdad with sanctions in force, and even less to gain by putting families at risk. The embassies were run by skeleton staffs.

There was no change in the status of the accredited diplomats, although some were expelled as part of the crisis's gamesmanship. The Iraqis meticulously allowed those who had finished their tour to be replaced by fresh diplomats who were in turn accredited, and for the ambassadors' own superiors and security specialists to visit Iraq for consultations. In fact, the Canadian Ambassador, Chris Poole, even received *agrément* from the Iraqis after the invasion, arriving in September. His predecessor had completed his term shortly before 2 August, and left. Ottawa was keen to get Poole in to deal with the problem of Canadians who could not leave. Yet, in the midst of all this business-as-usual, the Iraqis consistently refused to allow diplomats from Kuwait to be officially reassigned to the Baghdad embassies, or to leave Iraq.

The diplomats who had relocated from Kuwait, including those from the countries whose nationals were Human Shields, found themselves in a limbo similar to the free Westerners. Unlike their civilian compatriots, they were not sent to camps, but they could not leave Iraq. The women among them had been allowed out in September, but the men had to stay until their Kuwait embassies closed, with the Iraqis refusing to recognize their diplomatic status.

These relocated diplomats, particularly the Americans, actually had less freedom than the free Westerners. The Iraqis generally refused all diplomats – whether Baghdad-accredited or relocated from Kuwait – permission to travel more than 25km from the city centre. This was in line with a similar restriction on Iraqi diplomats in Allied capitals. It had been in effect before the invasion, but receiving permission to go further had been a mere formality. Now, the Iraqis maintained it more strictly. At one stage, the diplomats were unsure whether they could go to Saddam International Airport, just outside the limit, to help with evacuation flights, but the Iraqis didn't stop them.

Although the accredited diplomats could leave Iraq when they wished, most of their trips were harried shopping and courier missions to Amman to get spare parts and tyres for embassy vehicles, generator parts, and food in case they had to endure the war in the Iraqi capital and feed their nationals. They also delivered and collected mail for hostages and others stuck in Iraq. The tyres were especially important, as there was an acute shortage of them in Iraq, and most embassy evacuation plans involved drives of up to several hundred kilometres, some of it cross-country, in four-wheel drive vehicles.

It was not only the male diplomats who made sometimes superhuman efforts. The Australian Ambassador's wife, Mrs Libby Lloyd, an irrepressibly optimistic woman who was afflicted with arthritic hands, was seen on one occasion carrying heavy tyres across the Amman airport tarmac to load into the hold of the jet. She stayed in Baghdad to help run the UN High Commissioner for Refugees' office in a bid to get as many of the Iranian and other refugees as possible out of the country before war. Other female diplomats and wives also stayed behind, and served with great distinction.

Curiously, a small minority of the Baghdad-based ambassadors had difficulty in bringing themselves to believe that the crisis would come to war. Their pre-invasion job had been to maintain good relations with the Iraqis. Their social circles revolved around sophisticated members of the Iraqi elite, often the liberals who had managed to avoid falling foul of the Ba'ath Party. They knew the Iraqis as individuals and as a people, and may even have absorbed some of their general antipathy towards the Gulf States. Their earnest desire that war did not come to the city they knew was as heartfelt as any Baghdadi's. They certainly did not sympathize with Iraq's invasion, but they did not seem to feel the same outrage as their colleagues, superiors, and compatriots from Kuwait. In the opinion of some, they had 'gone native'.

Perhaps the most surprising thing about the Baghdad embassies was their number. The whole world seemed to be represented in Iraq. Even minor countries such as Ireland, New Zealand, Portugal, Sri Lanka and Vietnam had missions, sometimes staffed with as few as two diplomats.

The reason for this plethora of embassies was trade. The world did not send its diplomats to Baghdad in admiration of Saddam, or to service large numbers of pilgrims or tourists. Egypt, the USSR and Vietnam had thousands of workers in Iraq, but most relations with Iraq were about commerce. Ireland sold beef and medical personnel; New Zealand sheep; Sri Lanka tea; the USSR military equipment and advice; Vietnam labour, and Australia wheat.

The permanent members of the UN Security Council had a political interest in Iraq as a key Arab League member and a major military power, but until Saddam's belligerence blossomed anew in early 1990, Baghdad had been a low priority. After all, the Iran–Iraq War was over. Australia, Canada, Ireland, New Zealand and the Scandinavians joined the US and UK in making Iraq aware of their concern for its human rights abuses, but the diplomats' main job was to sell anything, bar weaponry, to a large import-dependent economy.

The result of the diplomatic emphasis on commerce was that the Baghdad embassies were singularly unprepared for the monumental consular task that befell them in the wake of the invasion.

The two messages the embassies had for Iraq were to leave Kuwait, and let the hostages go. The invasion, occupation and hostage-taking were all illegal under international law, so both demands were non-negotiable. As such, the diplomats could not be seen to be offering concessions in return for the release of any hostages. This would have amounted to entering into negotiations.

However, the embassies had a particularly unenviable conflict of duties. Their capitals' political hard stands clashed with their consular role of assisting their distressed nationals. The diplomats were in a heart-wrenching dilemma. They often witnessed at first hand the misery of the Human Shield programme, but could not help their people by granting concessions to the Iraqis because of the broader political considerations.

The result was a crafty piece of diplomatese which did not acknowledge that negotiations were being undertaken, but made the point that certain categories of people, such as the sick and elderly, required special consideration. In effect, the embassies prioritized people in an effort to get at least some of them out. Lists were compiled by age and medical condition on the assumption that the sick and oldest would be the first beneficiaries of any Iraqi compassion. Those over 55 were thought to stand a better chance, and in fact the first few French and Australian men released were in this category. Other special lists included full-time students over 18, BA149 transit passengers, and those employed in or visiting Iraq at the time of the invasion.

The US Embassy in Baghdad was a remarkably sparse affair. In contrast to the large Kuwait compound, it was little more than a large, old, three-storey house bristling with communications antennae, surrounded by a high-security wall topped with razor wire.

The Embassy was in the middle-class suburb of Masbah, near the Australian, German, Japanese and Polish missions, but it was clearly the poorer cousin of the Poles' well-appointed property. This was a legacy of America's mixed history of diplomatic relations with Baghdad, which had only been renewed in 1984 after being broken by the 1967 Six-Day Arab–Israeli War. The Americans were late-comers to the Baghdad diplomatic scene.

During the crisis, the Embassy was under the command of Mr Joseph Wilson IV, the mission's *chargé d'affaires* and number two man. Wilson, a brash, cigar-smoking 40-year-old, Connecticut-born Californian was not at all the distinguished diplomatic type, and proud of it. His Ambassador, April Glaspie, an accomplished Arabist and highly respected professional diplomat, had not returned to Baghdad after departing on leave less than 48 hours before the invasion. Publicly, the State Department was saying that her return might send the wrong message to the Iraqis. In actual fact, she was in need of medical treatment, which had been deferred as the crisis developed. She would later be criticized unfairly by some who should have known better for giving Saddam the green light to move into Kuwait, but was completely vindicated before a US Congressional Committee in March 1991.

Glaspie's misfortune was, nevertheless, Wilson's windfall. It was his chance to excel, and he promptly did so. He was neither an Arabist, nor even a Middle East specialist. In Baghdad for about 18 months, his diplomatic career until then had been unspectacular, mainly as an Administrative Officer in Africa. Overnight, he became the world's most listened-to US diplomat, after the Secretary of State and UN Ambassador. As the representative of the sole remaining superpower, he became Baghdad's senior foreign diplomat, outranking men a decade older, without being an Ambassador.

Wilson proceeded, successfully, to juggle the demands of representing the US position to a hostile Iraqi regime, evacuating his nationals where possible, trying to service his people held at strategic sites, and supporting the Americans in Kuwait. Despite these burdens, he never displayed anything less than an unshakeable sense of purpose in his dealings with the Iraqis, and maintained scrupulous objectivity in his reports to Washington.

Wilson's greatest asset was his staff, but their numbers were pitifully low. With thousands of US troops flooding into Saudi Arabia, the State Department initially had only eight diplomats in Baghdad. Unlike the military, their numbers actually went down. Wilson had only Ambassador's Secretary Ardith Miller, Economic/ Political Officer Charlie Sidel, Defense Attaché Colonel Jim Ritchie, Communicator Wally Eustis, Administrative Officer Jim Van Laningham, PR man Steve Theibault, and Consul Melvin Ang.

The staff situation was exacerbated when Ang came to the end of his tour and was pulled out, and Baghdad expelled several of the accredited US diplomats on 20 September, including Colonel Ritchie, in retaliation for Washington's expulsions of Iraqi diplomats. Ang was replaced first by Bill Colwell, the retiring Consul from Kuwait, and then by Jeanette Pina, an accredited officer who had been outside Iraq at the time of the invasion. This left the official strength of the Embassy at only six. By December, their number had been further reduced to only four.

As if he did not have enough problems, Wilson also had to find accommodation for and cope with the requirements of about 50 US male diplomats and military personnel from Kuwait who had arrived with the 23 August convoy and were now stranded in Baghdad. They were eventually accommodated in four residential buildings, which had previously been occupied by evacuated Baghdad-based diplomats, and in the Embassy itself.

The strandees, who became known as 'the men who came to dinner' were - despite their diplomatic or official passports - considered by the Iraqis as ordinary American civilians from Kuwait, and thus equally qualified to be sent to strategic sites. Several direct and veiled threats were made to do so, but never followed through. They were free to move around Baghdad, but could not travel beyond the checkpoints at the edge of the city, nor were they allowed too far into the airport. They lived in constant fear that the Iraqis would tire of their game, and one day turn them into regular Human Shields, especially as they had relatively few Americans at the strategic sites.

The real reason for the Iraqis refusing to recognize the Kuwait-based diplomats' immunity had more to do with pressuring Washington to close its Kuwait embassy than the niceties of diplomatic accreditation. Joe Wilson was told that this group could leave Iraq only when the US Embassy in Kuwait closed. The Americans were not prepared to do this as it would have meant abandoning their nationals in hiding in Kuwait, and surrendering the 19 civilians in the Kuwait Embassy. Constant pressure on the Iraqis to allow the 50 men to go, including attempts to reassign them officially to the Baghdad Embassy, failed. The stranded men became hostages of principle.

Wilson then turned these men into an asset by replacing his own evacuated or exhausted staff. All of them were resentful at being detained in Baghdad: the military in particular. They wanted to be out in the thick of things, but had to follow orders to restrain themselves. In fact, the Iraqis would have served their own cause better by letting them go. They were an angry body of trained men, looking for every chance to get back at Saddam. By releasing them, he could have severely disrupted the Embassy's ability to function both politically and in support of the hostages, as well in the gathering of military intelligence which was later put to good use in January 1991.

As these men gained confidence in their new roles, and the Iraqi threat to send them to sites receded, they took on more duties within the embassy. This included liaison with other embassies, debriefing free nationals who visited Baghdad from Kuwait, running evacuations, dealing with low-level officials, and trying to meet US hostages during their brief passage through Baghdad.

The senior diplomat among them, 36-year-old Economic Counselor Emil Skodon, from Chicago, became the Embassy's Acting DCM , directing its day-to-day activities and personnel, thus freeing Mr Wilson to concentrate on the crisis. Skodon established himself in the DCM's office on the Embassy's top floor, with black drapes covering all the windows and walls to foil any Iraqi eavesdropping. The room was in darkness, except for a sole desk lamp. A phone maintained an open line to Washington through a scrambler and the regular Iraqi phone system. The line was promptly re-established as soon as it went down. The scene was classic Le Carré. Less seriously, there was a half-joking suggestion that Iraq's Ministry of Communications would be a priority target in the bombing of Baghdad because the bill for the five-month open line had not been received. The Ministry was indeed hit on the first night of the war, and the invoice has apparently never been received.

The USLOK men were also particularly active. Colonel Mooneyham's men took over tracking and supporting the 100 or so US Human Shields at strategic sites. They also collated whatever intelligence they could obtain on Iraqi forces in Kuwait from free Westerners and others travelling there. The Embassy had a full set of *Jane's* military reference books, and USLOK men would brief interested Australians and Irishmen from Kuwait on how to distinguish a T-72 tank from a T-62 or T-55. They were particularly interested in ballistic missiles and anti-aircraft defences in Kuwait, and taught us how to identify SCUD and SCALEBACK missiles and their launchers.

Other men had their own tasks. Commercial Counselor Paul Scogna, USLOK Major Fred Hart, and CWO4 Dave Forties went on combined shopping trips and spy missions to assess the impact of the sanctions. The US Marine guards from Kuwait under Staff Sergeant Jimmy Smith took over embassy security after their accredited colleagues had left Baghdad. A young first-tour diplomat from Kuwait, Kevin Briscoe, had the unenviable job of receiving the regular 'spontaneously organized' Iraqi demonstrations which found their way to the embassy. The image of young Mr Briscoe, a clean-cut, church-going Christian, alone outside the Embassy gate, receiving with aplomb a mob of Iraqi women waving empty milk formula tins and trying to sound fierce for the cameras is one of the enduring images of the madness that was Baghdad. The diplomats were somewhat bemused by this, as the sanctions specifically excluded humanitarian supplies, including baby formula, but once Saddam had decreed that there was a shortage, and that Iraqi children were dying as a result, then the Iraqis doggedly insisted that this was so.

Relationships within the US Embassy were not always harmonious, particularly between some of the diplomats and some of the younger military officers. As in Kuwait, there were differences of opinion on courses of action and policy recommendations, and even the leadership of the Embassy, but the chain of command ran through the State Department, not the Pentagon. The diplomats called the shots, to the chagrin of a number of the military, but Colonel Mooneyham's leadership, and their own discipline, generally prevented their personal reservations from standing in the way of their jobs.

Mooneyham, a lanky, relaxed Southerner, earned the respect of both the diplomats and his own men with his leadership and initiative. He could always see an angle to problems which others had missed, and knew how to motivate people. After one briefing session, one of the diplomats was heard to say 'Goddamn! I'd follow that Colonel over any hill in the world!'

Critical roles carried out by the US diplomats and military from Kuwait included running the Baghdad end of the 'Air Rogers' evacuation flights from Kuwait, steering the media towards stories of Iraqi atrocities, looting and sanctions-busting, and verifying the latest street rumours about withdrawals from Kuwait, Army morale, various imagined or failed assassination attempts against Saddam, and the effect on local industry of shortages of spare parts.

A number of the military had the task of contingency planning for a rescue operation or hurried evacuation if an Allied attack became imminent, or Iraq moved into Saudi Arabia. For security, only those men who were co-ordinating with the Allied Special Forces and intelligence services were aware of the arrangements. Even the senior diplomats were told only in general terms. It was the one area where the military did not defer to the diplomats.

For the civilian diplomats, responsibilities were seldom cut and dried. When Administrative Officer Jeanette Pina returned to Iraq and was assigned consular duties, she initially objected that this was outside her area of training. When told that the US State Department could live with the problem of the Embassy's books not balancing, but could not accept any avoidable harm to US citizens, Miss Pina took to her new tasks with relish.

The hands-on approach extended to the top. As the senior diplomat, Joe Wilson had plenty to do without getting involved in the evacuation of the women and children, but when the Iraqis stopped some of the 'Air Rogers' evacuees from leaving Baghdad, ostensibly because of irregularities in their documentation, he went to the airport for the stopover of every flight. The main problem was American children of Kuwaitis, especially those with American mothers. Several evacuees got out of Iraq simply because Wilson bellowed and intimidated Iraqi officials into letting them board the plane.

During these evacuations, the relocated diplomats ran their own airline check-in facility in the street between two embassy buildings. They had a passport control desk, baggage check-in, waiting room, and bus to Saddam International. Bill Colwell's performance stood out particularly. He had stayed on in Kuwait for a few extra days before the invasion to help break in his replacement, Gale Rogers. He should not even have been there on 2 August. Day after day in Baghdad, until he was allowed to leave on 15 November because of his age, he counselled his younger colleagues, and spent long hours cheerfully helping evacuees obtain the paperwork needed to leave.

Some of the duties were far more basic. Food was a concern as the Iraqis refused to issue ration cards to the men from Kuwait. This was overcome by assigning several of the more resourceful fellows to work the Baghdad black market. Among other things, they traded disposable diapers from vacated embassy apartments for food. CWO4 Dave Forties in particular became so proficient that he was nick-named 'Scrounger' after the character in *King Rat*. This operation also allowed the Americans to assess how the average Baghdadi was coping with sanctions, and monitor the black market.

The responsibilities of the US Embassy in Baghdad extended beyond its own nationals. Because the Embassy in Kuwait had the best secure telecommunications system in the occupied city, and was eventually handling communications for about 17 different countries, the Americans in Baghdad were constantly passing messages from other embassies to their people in the US Embassy in Kuwait, and vice versa. This was critical in helping those other countries, especially Australia, Canada, France, Ireland and New Zealand, maintain contact with their nationals in Kuwait.

The British Ambassador to Baghdad, 57-year-old Harold Walker, an accomplished Arabist, was, like April Glaspie, out of Iraq at the time of the invasion, but returned within days. He initially had a full staff of about 25 diplomats, some of whom, with their dependents, were evacuated.

The UK Defence Attaché, Colonel John Cochrane, and two NCOs were expelled along with the Americans' Colonel Jim Ritchie on 20 September in the tit-for-tat expulsions following the Iraqi raids on diplomatic premises in Kuwait, leaving ten British diplomats and nine support staff. Later expulsions further reduced this, but Walker was able to bring in additional lower-level staff, notably the very capable Miss Caroline Cross.

Walker needed all the staff he had. Three times as many British men as Americans were at the sites or in Kuwait, and within Iraq itself there were about 700 British residents compared to about 100 Americans. Some of these were married to Iraqis, or Anglo-Iraqi children, with no intention of leaving Iraq. Nevertheless, several hundred British residents turned to their Embassy for refuge or for assistance of some sort. However, the British had to handle only eight relocated male diplomats from Kuwait, the last two of which did not arrive until October. Whereas the US military advisors in Kuwait were on diplomatic passports, their British counterparts enjoyed no such privilege and were therefore either Human Shields, or in hiding in Kuwait.

Her Majesty's Embassy compound was on the opposite side of town to most other missions, set in huge grounds with rolling lawns, almost within sight of the infamous Mansour Melia. Unlike the high-security US mission, the British perimeter wall was a glorified high garden fence of brick, stone and wrought-iron railings. There was less need for fortifications. Any car bomber would first have had to get through the concrete obstacles separating the Embassy's road entrance from the main thoroughfare, past the Iraqi troops guarding the gate, and then up a long and winding driveway to the buildings.

The large British compound was a product of the UK's long relationship with Iraq. As the League of Nations mandate power in the wake of World War I until independence in 1932, and having maintained forces there for another 30 years, the UK had played a central role in Iraqi history. However, despite the sumptuous grounds, the buildings, constructed many years ago in impressive colonial style, were somewhat run-down and neglected.

Mr Walker's deputy was initially Mr Robin Keeley, who was replaced on 7 September at the end of his term by 39-year-old Mr Christopher Segar. Both Walker and Segar were archetypical British diplomats, each in his own way. The Ambassador, affectionately known by all as 'Hookey', was tall, calm and polished, with a relaxed patrician air. His time in Baghdad had been short, but eventful. He had first arrived in early 1990, only to be recalled over the March judicial murder of Farzad Bazoft. Segar, on the other hand, was bespectacled, short, and intense. He radiated energy and unflappability and could intimidate Iraqi officials a full head taller than himself with ease.

As key members of the Coalition, the British were as concerned as the Americans with monitoring sanctions and gathering intelligence. One of their number, James Tansley, convened a local sanctions-monitoring committee comprising diplomats from all OECD countries. He also had the job of receiving protesters at the embassy gate, and was later expelled by the Iraqis, ostensibly for using inappropriate language to one of the delegations.

The British also had to cope with a greater number of grovellers and media. Tragically, they also had to handle the repatriation of the bodies of four of their nationals who died in camps or in hiding, or were killed accidentally in Iraqi custody, as well as support several of their nationals languishing in Iraqi jails on trumped-up charges of corruption and spying. The Americans had to repatriate one dead Human Shield, and had no one in jail.

Despite the efforts of the British diplomats in Baghdad, they did not always find favour with their colleagues in Kuwait. Ambassador Michael Weston and Consul Larry Banks in the besieged Kuwait compound often saw their Baghdad Embassy as having little appreciation of the situation in Kuwait. The FCO Emergency Unit in London was supposed to be tasking Baghdad with compensating where possible for functions that the besieged Kuwait embassy could no longer perform. This was not happening. Baghdad seemed to treat the Kuwait embassy as if it were still a fully functioning facility, instead of two men holding out in difficult conditions. On several occasions, Baghdad sent to Kuwait the names of people who had escaped into Saudi Arabia, and asked Weston and Banks to look for them, instead of checking first with Saudi Arabia. Several people gained the impression that Baghdad saw Kuwait as a bit of a nuisance.

The other embassies had their own problems, particularly the French, Germans and Japanese, with their own men at sites, and their own relocated diplomats from Kuwait. They handled the crisis similarly. The French were perhaps the most fortunate in that their hostages were released in October. The Germans, for their part, had to cope with the merging of the West German and East German Embassies into one during the crisis.

The Australians, Canadians, Dutch and Irish each had a couple of their dual-nationals who had been captured with their UK passports at sites, but there was little the diplomats could do other than insist to the Iraqis that these men really were citizens of the lesser countries. The Iraqis generally contended that it was impossible for people to hold the nationalities of two or more countries at the same time. When they did concede the point, they argued that the men had UK passports, so were British. However, in several instances, the diplomats, particularly Australian Ambassador Peter Lloyd, were able to prevail on the Iraqis to allow these men to stay in the Mansour Melia for at least some time, rather than being sent to sites.

Embassies of countries without people at sites, but whose nationals were prevented from leaving Iraq, had their own peculiar problems. Several of them, particularly the Irish, had many people working in Baghdad. Most of them strongly encouraged their people in Kuwait to relocate to Baghdad, where they could supposedly be placed under the nominal protection of the embassies, and maintain contact with their families at home. However, the embassies were unable to guarantee their nationals from Kuwait that they could fully protect them if war came, or if the Iraqi populace turned against them. To their credit, these embassies often paid for the food and hotel accommodation of their people when they came to Baghdad, or accommodated them in the quarters of evacuated diplomats.

The embassies liaised regularly with one another, with the ambassadors meeting every three or four days to compare notes. There were three distinct groups: the EC; the East Europeans; and what became known as the 'Non-Group', comprising Australia, Canada, Japan, New Zealand, Switzerland, Sweden, the US and various other countries not in a particular grouping. There was also regular liaison between those countries and the men at sites.

The embassies with perhaps the greatest consular task were the Asians, especially Bangladesh, India, the Philippines, Sri Lanka, Thailand and Vietnam. Their people were not prevented from leaving Iraq, but the sheer weight of numbers was crushing, and made all the more difficult to handle by their limited resources. Most of the evacuation efforts from Kuwait through to Jordan were organised by committees of private individuals in Kuwait, but many Asian nationals arrived in Baghdad destitute, or with no papers.

Embassy support for the men held at sites was generally provided by diplomats who had relocated from Kuwait. In the case of the Americans and Japanese, most of the diplomats in their Embassies had come from Kuwait, and so felt a closer affiliation with the hostages.

The UK diplomats from Kuwait, on the other hand, were in the minority to their Baghdad-based colleagues, so there was a perception that the hostages did not enjoy the same level of priority from the embassy as a whole, but this may have been due to the sheer weight of numbers. Several of these diplomats were spoken of highly by the hostages, but there was a consistent belief on the part of many British hostages that their embassy could have tried harder.

The main tasks of the diplomats trying to support the Human Shields were to track the hostages, contact them if at all possible, and get supplies and mail to them. The only chance they had of speaking to them was when they passed through the Mansour Melia. The diplomats used these brief visits to pass cash, clothes, toiletries, cigarettes and even alcohol to the men.

The source of many of these supplies was not necessarily the Western governments, but often members of the Baghdad's British community, particularly two local businessmen, Tug Wilson, the Chairman of the British Club, and ICL's Barry Cooper, and individual diplomats. When the governments provided funds to support the Human Shields, they would come in as dollars, be handed over to trusted members of the British community to change on the black market into Iraqi dinars, and then used to purchase supplies for comfort parcels. The diplomats themselves could not risk their broader function by being caught changing currency illegally.

Each of the five major embassies with people at sites maintained lists of their hostages, and the sites at which they thought they were being held. Perhaps the most effective of the Americans was USLOK Lieutenant-Colonel Tom Funk, who had the job of tracking the Human Shields, and improving their lot where he could. He maintained a map of all known strategic sites, which was constantly updated with scraps of information from all sources. Weekly meetings were held to compare notes between the UK, French, German and Japanese embassies. Funk also prepared a newsletter and provided whatever information was available to friends and relatives. The Japanese also had a good idea of where their men were, and were especially helpful.

Other information came from East European workers who were allowed to leave; from Kurdish opposition groups; from expatriate US and European site managers who were allowed to travel to Baghdad, and from the French who were released in October. The various embassies pooled this information, and were constantly in touch with each other to try to track their men.

The main problem with tracking Human Shields was that information was usually at least several days out of date by the time it reached the diplomats, because of the Iraqi 'shell-game'. The Baghdad diplomats knew from their colleagues in Kuwait whenever someone was captured, and would expect them to arrive in the Mansour Melia within a week, when limited access was sometimes allowed, but they lost track of them when they were taken away.

The embassies also tried to send food and clothing to the sites, especially when they learned of the poor diet, and colder weather arrived. At the time of the Human Shields' release in December, they were assembling Christmas boxes for each one, including candy, soap, toothpaste, toothbrushes, shaving gear, writing paper, ballpoint pens, Christmas cards and blankets.

The diplomats were never allowed to visit the sites, so had to rely on the Iraqi Red Crescent as the means of delivery. Despite these efforts, the Iraqis even used the food parcels to sow dissent among the hostages. They allowed packages through to Germans and Japanese, but stopped those for the Americans and British. The same applied to much of the incoming mail.

A further important function of the embassies was acting as a punching bag for the hostages. These people were understandably angry and frustrated at their plight, which some saw as a result of their governments' firm line against Iraq, or the lack of advice to get out of Kuwait when they could. The Iraqis simply ignored the hostages' complaints: the hostages' own government representatives were an easier target.

In retrospect, the embassies might sometimes have been able to do more, but were largely constrained by a lack of resources, and by their own capitals. In such a crisis, little things such as toiletries and a little spending money made a great difference. It was the first time that many of the Human Shields had anything to do with their diplomats, and they expected a more comprehensive handling of their plight. There was little appreciation of how thinly the diplomats were stretched, their limitations, and their difficulties with the Iraqis. In fact, the embassies did spend a great deal of money on the hostages. They chartered buses and aircraft to evacuate them when this became possible, and passed messages out of Iraq for them through their own communications. The Iraqis even billed them for hostages' hotel bills in some cases, a cost which the embassies were obliged to pay to get their people out.

A sub-group of people supported by the diplomats were nationals who had sought refuge at the embassies. Most of these had been working in Iraq, but a few had courageously made their way up from Kuwait with false papers.

While the Americans, Australians and Canadians in this category were accommodated at their ambassadors' residences or diplomats' quarters, the British, comprising 55 Bechtel men and one woman, camped out in the grounds of their Embassy. There was no accommodation available in the buildings. At least two of their US colleagues and another Briton visiting Iraq had been taken to sites, so they were understandably fearful of the same fate. Whereas the Americans and others were generally unseen in the suburbs, these British were plainly visible to anyone at the Embassy gates, and were particularly nervous of being filmed. To their credit, the media respected this.

The British diplomats gave the Bechtel refugees whatever assistance they could, including taking them shopping in diplomatic vehicles. However, a number of them seemed to expect the Embassy to cater more fully for them, and did not quite appreciate its limitations. It seemed to some that these men were on an extended holiday. A few of them even went drinking at the British Club, when they were supposed to be too scared to leave the Embassy grounds.

Several members of the British community in Baghdad saw the Bechtel men as their own worst enemies, who had been panicked into running into the Embassy by their US colleagues. This fear was probably initially justified, but passed. More seriously, at least one of them wrote to a leading British newspaper, and gave a BBC interview accusing the Embassy of being unhelpful. It was unnecessarily divisive. The whingers were in the minority, but poisoned the situation. Most of the men were positive, and even helped with some improvements to the Embassy buildings.

The refugees did cause some trouble for the diplomats with the Iraqis. On 27 September, the Iraqi Ministry of Foreign Affairs (MFA) circulated the following note to the embassies effectively saying that ambassadors who did not register people they were sheltering would be hanged:

Revolutionary Command Council Resolution No. 341 dated 26/8/90 stipulates that housing a foreigner for the purpose of hiding him or her from the authorities is a crime of espionage. The punishment of death shall be imposed on the individual who commits such a crime.

The Ministry will appreciate it if the esteemed Mission would kindly inform the Ministry of whether any of its citizens or any other nation's citizens are residing in the Mission's embassies and/or diplomatic residences whether or not these citizens have contracts with the Government or are working with foreign companies operating in Iraq.

The note arose from the Iraqi threat to hang anyone sheltering foreigners in Kuwait. In retrospect, it was merely badly drafted, but it was not the type of treatment to which ambassadors take kindly. It was taken very seriously indeed, and even released to the Press by US Secretary of State James Baker.

Joe Wilson phoned the Iraqi Undersecretary of the MFA, Nizar Hamdoun, to seek clarification. Hamdoun was not in, so Wilson left a message, in his most pleasant voice, saying, 'Does Revolutionary Command Council Resolution 341 mean that he intends to hang me?' He then visited the Ministry with a noose, fashioned by one of the Marine guards, around his neck.

The diplomats categorically rejected the Iraqi request for the names of the non-diplomats living on diplomatic premises, and protested strongly to the MFA. The note was soon withdrawn, with the Iraqi Government's apologies, but there was no backdown on the Human Shield policy, or the threat to apply the death penalty to non-diplomats sheltering targeted nationals.

The Baghdad embassies are seldom given the credit they deserve. It is often forgotten that the diplomats were working under great pressure, and were simply trying to do their best in impossible circumstances. All the accredited diplomats could have left at any time, but most stayed. Those who did leave were ordered out, had become exhausted, or had finished their tour. Many of these were assigned to the hostage support function in their home capitals.

The Baghdad diplomats were seldom able to support their people as much as they would have liked, but without them, the ordeal for many hostages could have been far worse. Some diplomats took great risks; several were threatened or humiliated at gunpoint, and those who were unaccredited always ran the risk of joining those they were trying to help.

A comment often made by some hostages was that it was the diplomats' job to do what they had to do. The truth is quite different. As with the diplomats in Kuwait, their role is primarily to represent their Government to the host country. Few of them were fully prepared or trained for the situation they found themselves in, and for the most part they performed with distinction.

The Resistance car bomb attack on the Kuwait International Hotel, where senior Iraqis were staying, early October 1990. The aftermath of the attack was photographed from inside the nearby US Embassy compound. Several Iraqi soldiers were killed, but many members of the '25th February Group' involved in the attack were later captured and executed.

Members of a key civilian Resistance group. Left to right, back row : Sheikh Sabah Nasir, his wife, Sheikha Sheikha, Lieutenant-Colonel Abdulaziz Al-Farhan, Nazeeh Khajah. Front row: Ghanema Al-Fahd, Asrar Al-Qabandi, the dynamic young woman who met a horrible death at the hands of the Iraqis.

Seen in happier days at celebrations to celebrate the extinguishing of the last oil fire, a few of the KOC oilmen involved in the Resistance. Left to right : Ahmad Al-Arbeed, Abdulhussein Shehab, Aisa Bou Yabes, Musab Al-Yaseen, Ahmad Al-Rayyis, Bader Al-Khashti, Ahmad Murad, Abbas Al-Qallaf, Abdullah Baroun.

KOC's Mohammed Abdul Salam, who used the cover of the Ahmadi Hospital 'Red Crescent' to help fight a losing battle to retain law and order against Iraqi looting in Ahmadi.

Asrar Al-Qabandi, Captured 4 November, 1990. Executed 14 January, 1991.

Mohammed Abulhassan, Kuwaiti Ambassador to the United Nations, where Security Council and General Assembly Resolutions ranging from the trade embargo to use-of-force were crafted.

Ghazi Al-Rayyis, Kuwaiti Ambassador to the UK and Ireland.

Sheikh Saud Nasir Al-Sabah, Ambassador to the US, Canada and Venezuela and Kuwait's man in Washington, who spearheaded the nation's diplomatic and public relations campaign.

Dr. Hassan Al-Ebraheem, the driving force behind Washington-based Citizens for a Free Kuwait (CFK), which, with its colleague organisation in London, the Association for a Free Kuwait run by Dr Jaffer Behbehani and the Free Kuwait Campaign, waged a valuable lobbying and public relations campaign.

A postcard used as part of the Free Kuwait Campaign. Hard-hitting PR.

British Consul-General Christopher Segar, who took up his post as Ambassador Harold Walker's deputy in Baghdad's British Embassy after the invasion.

US diplomats Emil Skodon and Joe Wilson IV. Wilson took over as Chargé d'Affaires from Ambassador April Glaspie who departed Baghdad on the eve of the invasion, and earned the praise of President Bush for his exemplary performance. Skodon, who led the 23 August 'Convoy to Hell' road evacuation of US diplomats, military personnel, and their dependents from Kuwait to Baghdad, stepped in as Number 2 in Wilson's understaffed Mission.

Members of the Indian Citizens' Committee who remained in Kuwait after the mass evacuations. Left to right: Mathew Kuruvilla, H.S. Vedi (Chairman), Mrs. Indira Sharma and Prakash Shaw.

Half way to Amman ... Asian refugees walking across the Jordanian border from Iraq with their last few remaining possessions...

And with hundred of thousands of troops flooding into Saudi Arabia, someone had to pay the bill for Desert Shield.

SAUDI ARABIAN MONETARY AGENCY   1740/10586
RIYADH, SAUDI ARABIA RIYADH US$ ***760,000,000,00
                          COPY NOT   30th October   19 90   1-23/210
PAY
TO THE
ORDER OF THE GOVERNMENT OF UNITED STATES OF AMERICA...............US$ 760,000,000.00
THE SUM OF SEVENHUNDRED SIXTYMILLION.....................................US DOLLARS
                                                                        ONLY.....
     JPMorgan Morgan Guaranty
                Trust Company of   Negotiable
                New York

FOR

⑆000 10586⑆ ⑈021000238⑈ 662 92 517⑈

Minefields, some of which were exposed by the wind, barred the way of Allied troops.

Colonel Ahmad Al-Mulla, Acting Commander of the Kuwaiti Navy during the war.

Colonel Jesse Johnson, the commander of General Schwarzkopf's Special Forces, including the US Navy SEALs on board KNS 'Happy Duck', and Lieutenant-Colonel Nasser Husseinan, the Kuwaiti Flotilla Commander for Task Element Kilo.

Iraqi troops trying to walk home to Iraq from Abraq Kheitan in suburban Kuwait, prior to the arrival of Allied forces.

US Marine officers from Lieutenant-General Walter Boomer's command group raise the Kuwaiti and US flags as they cross into Kuwait. Boomer's Kuwaiti liaison officer, Lieutenant-Colonel Mahmoud Boushahri is on the right.

Kuwaiti and US Special Forces search Iraqi POWs handed over to them by members of the Kuwaiti Resistance (in background, in dishdashas, with rifles).

Amir Sheikh Jaber Al-Ahmad Al-Jaber arrived to an emotional reception on 14 March, 225 days after narrowly escaping capture or death.

The end of the line for ill-fated BA149. Only the engines were partially recoverable.

Oil fires, some of about 700 set by the Iraqis. All were extinguished in just under nine months. A greater long-term problem has been the 20 million barrels of oil in oil lakes.

The Kuwaitis had some of their own damage to inflict on the many portraits of Saddam which the Iraqis had installed around Kuwait. One here is seen in front of the Ministries Complex.

A young girl, maimed by one of the hundreds of thousands of mines and other items of ordnance left behind by the Iraqis, or dropped from the air by the Allies during the war.

Nightime at noon. It was June 1991 before the residents of Kuwait could be assured of clear skies for more than a day or two at a time.

A montage of a cross-section of the 604 Kuwaiti and other nationals still unaccounted for, and thought by the Kuwaitis - and others - to be still held in Iraq. This was prepared by the mother of Samira Marafie, the young woman in the ninth row, fifth from the right, with permission of the families of all individuals shown.

21. MEDIA MADNESS

In any contemporary crisis, the international media are major players. We expect instant news on TV, radio and in our newspapers. The anchors and journalists who provide it are household names, and are now almost as important an institution in our democracies as the government. However, they are no longer dispassionate observers, but active participants, with the power to affect opinions, influence decisions, and even get people killed.

The overall performance of the international media during the Kuwait crisis did them no great credit. Their actions during Operation Desert Storm, and the way they were used then by both the Iraqis and Allies, has been well documented. Less well appreciated is their role during the occupation itself. In fact, many hostages considered elements of the media a great danger to their safety, and in some cases, collaborators with the Iraqis.

Although there were many examples of brilliant and responsible journalism, the media's own tragedy is that they failed to police the irresponsible elements who cared for nothing other than a good story, even if they caused suffering or endangered lives. These were a minority, but the enduring legacy of the media in the minds of most people involved in the crisis is something the Fourth Estate cannot be proud of.

A major criticism of the media was that they broke the UN sanctions with impunity, and collaborated with Saddam by pouring millions of dollars into blockaded Iraq. The sums were simple. Each media visitor paid Iraqi Airways several hundred dollars for an Amman–Baghdad return fare. Then add excess baggage for heavy TV gear, hotels, food, drinks, international phone calls, taxis, everything required to keep a team functioning, all in hard currency. TV crews also paid about US$400 for each satellite feed. With at least 200 media personnel in Baghdad from September 1990 to mid-January 1991, Iraq's economy benefited by at least US$250,000 per week.

In the first weeks after the invasion, world attention turned to the Iraqi capital, but there was not one Western or Japanese camera crew in Baghdad.

The first Western journalist to arrive was Ted Koppel of America's ABC network at 10.00 p.m. on 14 August, after a week cooling his heels in Amman. He was on the air in the US four hours later, using his embassy's phone. His sudden arrival on a special Iraqi aircraft was made possible by Jordan's King Hussein and Queen Noor. He was followed shortly by Dan Rather of CBS.

The Iraqis were not quite as ready for Koppel as they thought. On 15 August he and a cameraman got into the Al-Rasheed Hotel where 38 US hostages were held, and managed to interview several of them before being thrown out. It was one of the few times that the media gained access to hostages destined for the sites. The journalists would leave after a few days, apparently much relieved not to have joined their compatriots on the strategic sites.

The first British journalists into Baghdad were BBC TV's John Simpson and three colleagues, on 23 August, accompanied by CNN. ITN's Trevor McDonald and Brent Sadler and their crews, and the *Daily Telegraph's* Patrick Bishop followed on the 26th. They were a week behind ABC and CBS, but were fortunate in their timing as they could cover the evacuation of the British women and children from Kuwait. As soon as the bulk of the women and children had left, the journalists followed. They had enough footage for now.

However, there was an even greater scoop in the early hours of 30 August, which went to CBS after intense competition from all the networks. This was an interview with Saddam himself. Dan Rather was two days into his second trip to Baghdad when he found himself summoned to the Ministry of Foreign Affairs (MFA) on the night of 29 August. Two military policemen picked him and whisked him not to the MFA, but to Saddam's residence. Much to his chagrin, he was left without his own producer or crew. The Iraqis insisted on using theirs, but an interview with Saddam was an interview.

To his credit, Rather was typically hard-hitting, even quoting George Bush's comparison of Saddam to Hitler. Nevertheless, the interview was an anti-climax. Saddam said nothing that had not already been covered in official communiques beyond admitting that the hostages were 'guests against their will', and did nothing to dispel the growing conviction around the world that he was indeed a dangerous fellow.

When editors abroad realized that their own crews were unlikely to end up as hostages, what seemed like every Western TV and radio network and newspaper descended on Iraqi embassies for visas. They knew that media manipulation would be a major part of Saddam's strategy, and there was little mileage for the Iraqis in alienating the media by holding them hostage. The market wanted news. There was money to be made.

By early September, the US hostages in the Al-Rasheed had been cleared out to the Mansour Melia or the sites, and it was teeming with 200 media people from 50 organizations. There was good reason for corralling the media in the Al-Rasheed. It had been purpose-built to accommodate and spy on delegates to a Non-Aligned Movement summit which Saddam had tried to stage during the Iran–Iraq War. It was widely suspected that Saddam's personal bunker was directly under the hotel or the Conference Centre directly across the road.

The Al-Rasheed was bugged throughout. The surveillance systems were actually designed into the building. Not only were there microphones in the phones and light sockets, but even the signs near the elevators contained hidden cameras. One Irishman, Martin Phillips, found a bug in a bedboard, presumably designed to monitor pillow talk. It was suspected that some of the TVs in the rooms had inbuilt videocameras to spy on the occupants. The elevators were certainly bugged, and some bathroom mirrors were one-way glass. The lobby always had a crowd of shifty-eyed young men in leather jackets sitting around with studied casualness reading well-thumbed newspapers. Putting all the journalists into this nest of the *Mukhabarat* was the best way for the Iraqis to keep an eye on them. They were directly wired into the surveillance system.

The men heading the Iraqi information campaign were Minister of

Information and Culture, Latif Nsayyif Jassim, and his Director-General, Naji Al-Hadithi. The Minister's limited grasp of English hardly qualified him to carry the media battle to the world. He was little more than a Ba'athi thug with connections, and relied greatly on his far more fluent subordinate. Al-Hadithi, for his part, was a confirmed Anglophile with a refined sense of humour. Nevertheless, both men could be so charming that it was easy to forget that they spoke for a regime with the blood of thousands on its hands.

Actually, Iraq's media blitz in early August had little to do with the West. It was to convince the other Gulf States that Saddam had no designs on them, and that Kuwait was a one-off special case. Saddam knew that the GCC could not evict him from Kuwait without help, and gambled that they would accept the loss of Kuwait as a *fait accompli* if they themselves did not feel threatened. The idea was to deny the GCC a reason to call in the Americans.

As such, the Iraqi information campaign first concentrated on slandering the Amir of Kuwait, referring to him as the 'Qaroon', or the Arabic equivalent of Croesus. This failed due to the new-found unity of the GCC, and the awakening of the Saudis to the fact that they really were in danger.

When it was clear that the GCC would not accept the annexation of Kuwait, Saddam tried to bring the less wealthy Arabs onto his side. He attacked the legitimacy of the GCC leaders by calling them 'bedouins', and Saudi Arabia 'the lands of the *Nejd* and the *Hijaz'*, two of the constituent elements from which the Kingdom had been formed in the 1920s. There was even suggestions that the crisis would give the Jordanian Hashemites the opportunity to regain the Saudis' *Hijaz* region with Jeddah, and the Holy Cities of Mecca and Medina, which they had lost to the Saudis after World War I. He also began to portray himself as the pre-eminent leader who was going to redistribute the oil wealth of the Gulf to the poorer Arab masses.

When Western forces arrived in Saudi Arabia, Saddam tried to sell himself as the defender of Islam, notwithstanding his regime's secular nature. Many North African Arabs and Asian Muslims were fooled that the US troops were invaders, *infidels* intent on defiling Mecca and Medina. In fact, the only foreign troops defending the Holy Cities were Muslim Pakistanis.

Then Saddam tried to link the Palestinian question to Kuwait, much to the initial delight of many Palestinians and Jordanians. He rekindled a feeling of pride in the hearts of many ordinary Arabs, reminiscent of the days of Nasser, as they saw one of their leaders stand up to the West. The Arabs had lost four wars to Israel since 1948, mainly because of Western support for the Jewish State. Now someone was turning the tables. Kuwait hardly mattered.

Saddam's opening of Baghdad to the Western media kicked off Round Two. If he could not stop Allied forces landing in Saudi Arabia, he would try to use the hostages and Western public opinion, shaped for him by the media, to stop them attacking him.

The Iraqi media objectives with the West were surprisingly simple and inextricably bound up with the fate of the hostages: it was to drive home to the Western public that they could have their people back if their governments improved their attitude towards Iraq, thereby weakening and eventually wrecking the Coalition. There would then be little effective opposition to Iraq retaining control of Kuwait.

The Iraqis pushed the line that their quarrel was not with the American and British people, but with their leaders who were leading them to a faraway war. The hypocrisy of Iraq's professed affection for ordinary people when they were holding hundreds of them as Human Shields was conveniently ignored.

They seemed to figure that if they could stall the Coalition long enough, it would eventually fall apart under its own internal political and financial pressures. After all, Iraq was the hero-nation which had fought the feared Iranians to a standstill. Iran was the US's nemesis, so was not Iraq really a Western ally? The Iraqis wanted desperately to present themselves as regular guys, the people next door, whom no one in their right mind would bomb.

This strategy required a delivery mechanism, and this is precisely where the Western media could be of great service. But this meant little to the Western journalists in Baghdad. They knew that they would be controlled by the Iraqis, but this was an occupational hazard, and they had a job to do.

Iraqi control of the media started even before the journalists got to Baghdad. They simply chose who they wanted, by the judicious granting of visas.

Tabloids were definitely out, perhaps, as one diplomat joked, 'because they would be more likely to dig up the dirt on Saddam's love-life than serve his cause'. There was some logic in this. With Saddam trying to present himself as a family man, the father of the Iraqi nation, it would not have helped his image to break the story that he had actually dumped his wife for an air hostess several years earlier. Mrs Saddam Hussein was a wife in name only.

The Iraqis carefully selected those organizations that could be expected to report reasonably objectively, or at least not be inherently hostile, and those from countries with particular leverage in the Coalition. 'Objective' meant that the organization knew to temper its reporting if it wanted to be allowed in again. The availability of visas was directly proportional to the utility of the network or publication to the Iraqis. As such, the US, British and French electronic media, with their potential for conveying pictures of smiling, ordinary Iraqis into Western living rooms, were well represented. German and Japanese TV crews, from countries with less influence on the Coalition, were less numerous, as were print journalists of all nationalities. The Iraqis were well aware that the electronic media play to emotions whereas the print media informs. Without a good cause, they had to work on gut reactions.

Each media team, especially TV crews, was usually assigned an Iraqi 'minder', whose job was to accompany them and ensure that they did not report on matters that might cast Iraq in a poor light, or film Saddam's residence or military installations. If anything slipped through the minders, the censors at Iraqi TV would intercept it on the satellite feed. The media were seldom allowed outside the capital. With few exceptions, all of which were carefully orchestrated to convey the Iraqi message - including several trips to Kuwait - Baghdad or nearby Babylon was as far as they could go.

Nevertheless, the Iraqis could be their own worst enemies. An ill-placed statement by a senior official could undo hours of careful media management.

The Information Minister himself once told a US network that the Iraqi people would 'eat any captured American paratroopers'. When it was suggested that he may have gone a little too far, he toned this down by saying the captured Americans would be fed to the dogs. First Deputy Prime Minister Taha Yassin Ramadan made his own contribution. When asked why foreign journalists were prevented from visiting Kuwait, he said that it was a military zone, and he would 'break the legs of any journalist who went there'.

The Human Shields, the people in hiding in Kuwait, and many free Westerners had a love-hate relationship with the media. On the one hand, we depended greatly on them for news. On the other, we felt that they had little business being in Baghdad. Most meaningful reporting on the crisis was being done outside Iraq, and the media presence there was seen as giving Saddam a direct line to the world, and thus potentially prolonging the crisis.

The main objection of men in hiding to the media, particularly the electronic type, were that they had very little grasp of how their reports may have put us in more danger. This was more than just the knee-jerk reaction of frightened men. The media could only report what the Iraqis allowed them to, and not the true situation in Kuwait. With such an untenable position, we felt they should have boycotted Iraq if they could not tell both sides of the news. Half a story is worse then no story at all: it is distorted.

However, the media are not a monolithic whole, and commercial considerations were powerful forces. The news programmes were some of the highest rating broadcasts at the time. Everyone had to have their slice of the action. The electronic media did, however, belatedly make it clear when they were broadcasting under Iraqi control, particularly after incurring newspaper criticism for simply relaying Iraqi footage.

One example of the media not covering the Kuwait side even when they were aware of it was when several British women were interviewed by ITN's Brent Sadler in Baghdad during their evacuation. Their accounts of the fear and horrors of Kuwait, and their concern for the men still in hiding brought tears to Sadler's eyes, but he said that he just could not transmit such stories from Iraq. What then, asked the ladies, was the point of him being there?

Later in the crisis, the media were perhaps unfairly credited with generating pressure on President Bush to finish the war prematurely, thereby allowing the Iraqi Republican Guard to escape from the Basra area with their heavy weapons. The tragic consequences of this to the Kurds and southern Iraqi Shi'ites are now well known. The media supposedly did this by over-reporting Iraqi casualties at Mutla'a during the Iraqi retreat from Kuwait, but not balancing this in a timely manner with the horrendous Iraqi atrocities in Kuwait. Many who had been in Kuwait felt that the will to continue the war for the extra day to put the Republican Guard out of business would have been stronger if the media had told the full story. Again, to their credit, the media did later cover the atrocities, but the momentum had been lost.

Our opinion of the media was shared by such distinguished figures as the Commander of Allied Forces in Saudi Arabia, General Schwarzkopf, and the Commander of the British forces, Lieutenant-General Sir Peter de la Billière.

Schwarzkopf was convinced that the Western electronic media were the Iraqis' best source of military intelligence on his forces. Not only did some US networks publicize the vulnerability and problems of his forces in the early days, but later, CNN broadcast information that allowed the Iraqis to identify some units facing them in particular locations, and their mission. Even the print media were not innocent. *Newsweek*, which should have known better, used its extensive sources to speculate on the Coalition's plan of attack, and published a version uncomfortably close to the actual plan.

Peter de la Billière found it difficult to accept that the Western media had any legitimate role in Baghdad. The principle of free speech, as he understood it, was that the media report everything. He felt that reporters in the heart of enemy territory were, in effect, mouthpieces for the enemy, whose aim was to kill Allied servicemen. In de la Billière's opinion, the reports of the media in Baghdad should not have been broadcast, as they worked against the Coalition and offered no real extension of the information available to the public. It was often difficult for the military to determine whose side the media were on. In principle they were neutral, but in practice some seemed to do their best to damage the Coalition and its commanders.

The first major instance of this occurred with the US Air Force Chief of Staff, General Michael Dugan, who told journalists in September that the Allies would bomb Baghdad, and specifically target Saddam. He effectively gave them a status report on the deployment and mission of Allied air forces. This was incautious on the General's part, to say the least, but many of his comments had been offered as background briefing. The journalists knew that publishing them would probably force his superiors to fire him, destroy his career, and damage US Air Force morale. This is precisely what happened.

Other reports seemed to do their best to sabotage the delicate relationship the US military had with the Saudis. In recognition of local sensibilities there was a ban on overt non-Muslim religious services, and what the Saudis considered risqué entertainment, such as dancing girls. In one case, a group of ARAMCO female staff put on a show for US troops in their walled compound, an area generally off-limits for Saudis where Westerners are largely free to practise their own culture. However, ARAMCO is still on Saudi soil, and publicizing activities that are unacceptable elsewhere in Saudi Arabia did not enhance US–Saudi relations. This mattered not to CNN, who delighted in showing the troops having a good time, with views of the ladies' shapely legs. Complaints from conservative Saudis went all the way up to King Fahd.

Other eminent critics of the media included Jordan's Crown Prince Hassan. During August his country was inundated with impoverished Asian and Egyptian refugees, yet most of the journalists going to Baghdad boarded air-conditioned Iraqi airliners in Amman, or chartered executive jets, and flew blithely over the wretches in the border camps below, sometimes sipping champagne and lunching on smoked salmon. This was too much for the Prince. He complained that 'the plight of these persons has evoked only the faintest of responses from a world press more interested in war scenarios than in humanitarian relief'. He had a point. Within days, chastened editors sent crews to the camps, and the Third World refugee crisis was belatedly covered.

For most of September there was little to report on in Baghdad. It was a time of phoney war, when the battles were fought with words at the UN headquarters, accompanied by an inexorable military build-up on either side. Once the media had filmed a few Western families resident in Iraq, exhausted stories on the fish restaurants by the Tigris, visited Babylon, and the British Council library, there was not much else to do. The Baghdad diplomats soon became a reliable fallback for comments on the latest developments in the crisis, and background briefings.

The US Embassy in Baghdad established a routine whereby *chargé d'affaires* Joe Wilson held a daily press conference at 9.00 a.m., and his Acting Deputy Emil Skodon provided supplemental one-on-one briefings thereafter. They soon learned which journalists they could trust. The real professionals accepted the situation gracefully when the diplomats said there was good reason why they could not disclose further information, or were prevented from discussing a particular subject. The responsible journalists therefore got more co-operation from the diplomats when they could help, but their lesser colleagues took their frustrations out on the diplomats. Joe Wilson himself was a particularly easy target. As a young, relatively inexperienced diplomat, suddenly in the limelight, he did not handle the press as adeptly as some of his older peers, and came across as somewhat brash. He was just the type of man George Bush appreciated in the situation, but did not fit the journalist's preferred stereotype of a distinguished senior diplomat.

On the other hand, British Ambassador Harold Walker was far more popular with the media. He had a talent for being unstuffy, and knew how to craft the easily digestible sound bites relished by the electronic media. As an Arabist, he could always offer a deeper insight into the issue of the day.

Other diplomats were sought out not only by their own national networks, but also by the major US and UK organizations. Some of these gentlemen, such as Australian Ambassador Peter Lloyd, had served in Iraq for several years, and had developed deep personal friendships with the Iraqi intelligentsia, as distinct from the regime. Lloyd had a good grasp of how ordinary Iraqis ticked, and with opinions not as hard-line as many of his colleagues, he was regularly courted by reporters for his insights into the Iraqi character.

The difficulty of getting hard facts out of Kuwait led many media organizations to revert to the age-old journalist fallback: if there's no news, then speculate, or make it up, especially if it can't be verified. This led to the much-vaunted CNN being labelled 'Conjecture Network News' by some.

According to one diplomat in the besieged US Embassy in Kuwait, CNN reported several times on the basis of unconfirmed rumours that the Iraqis had overrun the compound. They were more interested in breaking a story first rather than breaking it right. This was particularly irresponsible given CNN's trusted place in the minds of most Americans. It apparently took several hours for the State Department to reassure the families and friends of those in the embassy compound that CNN had got it wrong, again.

This was not the only incident of speculation affecting the Western embassies. In late October there was talk of resupplying the besieged missions, and a UN Security Council resolution was passed demanding that Iraq allow this. The US had said that it hoped for Iraqi agreement to a resupply operation. Force could not be used as any resupply ship would have to cross a wide swathe of Iraqi-held territory to get anywhere near the compounds. It was not worth risking the lives of troops on an opposed mission, or those of the diplomats for a piece of meaningless political symbolism.

This was not good enough for CNN. They jumped on the story, and interviewed so-called military experts on how this might be done by force. It was pure speculation, complete with footage of a US Navy destroyer in a sweeping turn at high speed. Given the authority commanded by CNN, some Iraqis apparently believed that such a mission was in the offing, and fears grew that they might actually pre-empt it by entering the US Embassy.

In fact, another resupply scheme was partially torpedoed by the media. US Special Forces in Saudi Arabia had considered dropping supplies into the Embassy from remotely controlled parachutes, which could be dropped from a high altitude and steered into the compound. Each parachute could carry 100 kilograms. Enquiries went to the manufacturers in the US, and some bright media man got word of it. Through a combination of media attention and the manufacturer's indiscretion, the mission was blown. The Iraqis watched American TV, so would be on the lookout for the parachutes.

The loved ones of those trapped in Iraq and Kuwait were also caused suffering by this kind of speculation. The media regularly reported conditions in Kuwait as being much worse than they were, with Westerners near starvation, and roaming bands of looters terrorizing the city. Conditions were very difficult at times, but not as bad as portrayed. The general image given by the media was drawn from isolated reports, and ignored more balanced accounts. As a result of these reports, my own family had visions of my friends and me sleeping on concrete floors in a concentration camp.

As small consolation, the speculation was a two-edged sword which, at times, helped the Allies. When the West turned up the military pressure in October, the outrage provided by these reports helped provide public support.

Nevertheless, some of the speculation was so amateurish as to be laughable. In one discussion of possible war scenarios, CNN showed a map with arrows indicating US forces striking at Iraq from Saudi Arabia, Turkey, Syria and, of all places, Jordan, Saddam's ally, where there were no US forces at all. In Kuwait, we wondered sarcastically whether CNN had stumbled on secret US plans for the invasion of Jordan. The only saving grace of this nonsense was that it did not show an arrow for US troops moving in from Iran.

A slightly less serious sin than the media making up stories was their failure to at least try to verify horror stories reaching them from evacuees, free Westerners, and hostages. Unfortunately, a number of these people felt that they had to embellish. However, verification was possible in some cases. An American who had been at IBI Camp with his wife and a group of Britons, related on his departure how the 48 men, women and children had dug trenches and bunkers while the guards watched and laughed. In fact, most of the women and all the children had left in August, and no one had dug any trenches. The journalist did not check with any of the other 46 hostages.

More serious was the failure to verify stories published some time after the event. Some men had become unbalanced by their experiences, and expanded on the truth. Others just thrived on the mischief of telling tall stories to journalists who swallowed them. Such tales included Iraqi soldiers chopping off a Kuwaiti's leg with a shovel after a minor traffic accident, and people driving over dead bodies left on the road. Most Kuwaitis who were killed died either in the torture chambers, or were shot in front of their own homes. These things could not have happened, and could have been checked.

The main objection to embellishment felt by people in Kuwait and Iraq was that the ordeal was bad enough as it was. There was no call to cheapen it by adding to it. The second objection was that the lies, when uncovered, cast doubt on the validity of all the horrific true stories. Finally, the Iraqis were portrayed by these tales to be monsters. There were indeed some vicious individuals, but the stories did a grave injustice to the ordinary Iraqis with no wish to be in Kuwait, and some of those who were even helping the Kuwaitis.

The lack of concern for the possible effect of broadcasts on people's fears was not confined to the tabloid newspapers, or their electronic equivalent, CNN. It extended in some cases to such well-respected institutions as the BBC.

For example, the two British women who were on the Dutch evacuation bus from Kuwait in August recall that most networks gracefully accepted when they declined their requests for on-camera interviews. The women did not want the Iraqis putting a name to a face who spoke her mind, and then taking their frustrations out on her husband if he was captured. However, the women were prepared to speak anonymously on radio, and be filmed for TV with innocuous comment. This was not enough for the BBC's John Simpson. When one of the women explained that she and her family and friends in Kuwait were very grateful for the BBC's reporting, but that she could not speak on camera, he replied sharply: 'Well, some of us are prepared to stick our necks out!'

The lack of sensitivity for people who were experiencing trauma was particularly apparent in some journalists back home in their hunt for grief and controversy. In the UK, the country with the greatest number of trapped people, several volunteer helplines were established to assist relatives and friends of the hostages and those in hiding. Some reporters were very co-operative, and thoughtful, but others regularly called the helplines looking for sorrow stories. A few particularly loathsome individuals even posed as friends or relatives to get confidential information. Many relatives had to have unlisted phone numbers installed after being discovered by the media.

Another casualty of the rush for news was objectivity. Many media organizations did allow their people to report what they found in Baghdad, as long as they could get it past the Iraqi censors, but others had a preconceived notion of what they wanted. Their editors virtually wrote the story, and then told their people to go and find footage or interviews to fill it.

One incident concerned the Dutch women on their evacuation. As chance would have it, most of these ladies were of Arab or Indian extraction. There were no typically fair, blue-eyed, Dutchwomen. This caused the Dutch reporter looking for tearful blonds great annoyance. He asked one Dutch–Indian wife where the families from The Netherlands were, as he would like to interview a Dutchwoman. 'We're here, all around you,' she said, indicating the dark women in her group, and holding out her passport, 'and I'm Dutch.' This wasn't good enough. The man wanted a blond.

Creating false impressions by writing the story before the facts were discovered extended to the subject of the Iraqi forces, particularly the Republican Guard. The journalists could see the no-nonsense élite troops which Saddam kept in Baghdad, and extrapolated this impression to the rest of the supposed 1 million-man Iraqi Army. Few TV journalists seemed to question the demographic impossibility of having a million men under arms and functioning effectively as an army in a country of only eight million males of all ages. If they had consulted any good reference book on Iraq's order of battle, or even some of the better newspaper articles, they would have discovered that perhaps only 500,000 of these men were regular troops - and then of mixed quality - and that only 1,000 of Iraq's 5,500 tanks were T-72s. The other half million men were poorly trained reservists, and the other tanks were T-54s, T-55s and T-62s. The numbers refer roughly to the year of design, so these machines were obsolete before most of their crews could shave.

The media therefore built up the Iraqi Army into a creature far more fearsome than it actually was. To be sure, it had chemical weapons, excellent artillery, and its sheer mass was daunting, but its air support, intelligence, communications, command and control, and artillery fire-control were woeful. Allied commanders, however, were delighted. The more the Iraqis were made to look like a real threat, the easier it was to obtain the forces to counter it.

A major concern of those in Kuwait was that the media were simply unqualified to assess when their actions might put us in more danger with the Iraqis. This criticism also extended to editors at home, and journalists in other Gulf States. One man expressed a widely held view: 'It's not their ass on the line, so they don't care if we get ours shot off, as long as they get their story?'

Some errors of judgement had serious consequences. During early August, when Westerners were dashing across the Kuwaiti desert into Saudi Arabia, they arrived high on adrenalin. Some of these people were full of stories of their adventure, and told anyone who would listen. The media broadcast details, including descriptions of the escape routes. But the Iraqi Army also had radios and TVs, and people whose job it was to monitor them. Within hours of the reports going on air, the routes were closed, and scores of people who might have escaped were trapped. Some became Human Shields or spent months in hiding because of this, and one man died using a route he might not have been on if earlier ones had not been shut off.

Another escape story which caused trouble was when a British couple passed themselves off as Indians, and boarded an Indian evacuation ship carrying Indians from Kuwait to Dubai. They also foolishly told their story, much to the annoyance of the Indians covering for them.

There were several other incidents. Shortly after the Iraqis rounded up 36 British BLT servicemen in Kuwait on 3 August, the soldiers appeared on Iraqi TV walking into the Mansour Melia. One resourceful journalist discovered that the team comprised 77 men, 66 of whom had been in Kuwait at the time of the invasion. These numbers were broadcast on BBC-TV. Not surprisingly, it alerted the Iraqis that there were another 30 BLT men to find. This caused a great deal of anguish among those still in hiding because they knew that the Iraqis would be looking for them all the more diligently. In fact, 21 of the remaining 30 BLT men were eventually captured.

Even the much-loved *Gulf Link*, the BBC hostage message service, fell into the trap. Their most serious gaffe lay in not properly checking the content of messages sent by relatives of hostages. Many of the wives had heard of the possibility of suitably qualified people obtaining Irish passports. They were working on obtaining such documents, but broadcast this to the men, and to the Iraqis, who also had shortwave radios. Most of the messages, and the men's identities, were suitably cryptic such as: 'We're seeing if the Dublin cousins can help,' or 'Your granny will be sending you a green letter from her home town,' but others were far more obvious. I recall Irish warden, Paul Kennedy, the man responsible for obtaining these documents, in apoplexy when he heard one wife say over the air: 'The Irish PP is on its way,' and another tell her husband about her visit to the Irish Embassy in London on his behalf.

The main concern of the Irish was that the Iraqis would dismiss as invalid the legally-issued one-way Irish passports, and punish the broader Irish community for helping Americans and British evade the Human Shield. It was difficult to blame *Gulf Link* for this security breach, especially as the relatives had been counselled not to identify their men by surname. Nevertheless, it was felt that a distinguished organization such as the BBC, being aware of the risk, should have screened the messages more carefully.

Some segments of the media never did learn. Insensitivity to the predominant religion of the region the Allies were defending was widespread.

In late October, the Royal Australian Navy filmed sailors on the destroyer HMAS *Darwin* engaging in an irreverent parody of Muslims at prayer as the vessel crossed the equator on its way to the Gulf. It was simple fun to the servicemen, and would have gone unnoticed if the RAN had not passed the video over to an Australian network. The editors broadcast it, forgetting that there were still several dozen Australian men trapped in Kuwait and Iraq.

The error did not remain harmlessly in the Antipodes. It was a time when the public was satiated with shots of F-15s taking off, and US Marines in the desert. This was fresh material, and other networks in turn broadcast it worldwide. Even British Airways, with several crews and dozens of passengers trapped in Iraq and Kuwait, displayed an extraordinary absence of judgement by featuring it on their Middle East in-flight news programmes.

The Iraqis, needless to say, were delighted. One of the main strings to their propaganda bow in their campaign for the hearts and minds of the Arab masses was the invasion of the Holy Lands of Saudi Arabia by *infidels* with no respect for Islam. This was all the proof they needed.

For their part, the Australians in Iraq and Kuwait, who at that stage had enjoyed freedom of movement for about a month, were appalled. Their first groveller was due in Baghdad within days, and hopes were high that at least some of the older or sick men would get out with her. The incident dashed some of these hopes, and made the task of the diplomats and the groveller all the more difficult. The Australian men in Baghdad wrote a scathing letter of complaint to the *Sydney Morning Herald*, which quickly found its way back to Baghdad, and also apologised to the Iraqis. The men in Kuwait went underground for a few days in case there was a local backlash. Fortunately for the Australians in Iraq and Kuwait, and unfortunately for the British, the Iraqis identified *Darwin* as a British warship. They could get far more mileage out of this, so the British paid the price of the Australian folly. Meanwhile, back in Australia, the Chief of Naval Operations was obliged to make a humiliating public apology to the country's Muslim community.

Some organizations did learn as they went along, but never fully. In October 1990, the video interviews which my American neighbour and I had made in September were aired worldwide. We had identified ourselves at the beginning of the tape so that it could be authenticated, and our families could be informed, but had specifically requested that our identities not be broadcast. Our faces were unrecognizable to anyone who did not know us as we had placed lights behind our heads. The networks complied largely with our wishes, but identified our nationalities.

However, in the month it had taken to smuggle the tape out, the Australians had gained freedom of movement. The networks knew this from their correspondents in Baghdad. I was one of only a dozen Australians moving around Kuwait at the time, and we were in the process of registering with the Iraqi authorities so that we could continue to do so. The Iraqis would not have had great difficulty identifying me if they had really tried. Far worse, they could also have found the American, and perhaps also the British in hiding with him. The networks should simply have identified us as 'Westerners'.

CNN again became a villain of this piece. The tape was dramatic enough as it was, but CNN had to dramatize it even more by saying that it had been smuggled out by the Kuwaiti Resistance, when in fact it had gone out in the toilet bag of Shirin Monteiro, our Indian neighbour. To viewers overseas, the means by which the tape left Iraq meant nothing, but such hype by CNN put us and our Kuwaiti friends in great danger. It implied that we were in contact with the Resistance, which by this time was being brutally suppressed. If the Iraqis had followed up the tape and caught either of us, it could have meant torture or death for any Kuwaitis whose names they extracted from us.

Fortunately, the Iraqis failed to pursue this, but it caused great concern for my family and Foreign Ministry at home, my embassy in Baghdad, and the US Embassy in Kuwait. Most wanted me to relocate immediately to Baghdad before the Iraqis came looking for me. They felt they could offer me some protection against a backlash if I was in Baghdad. However, with war expected within weeks, the last thing I wanted was to be in the enemy capital. Besides, there was a great deal to do in Kuwait for those in hiding. The hostage support effort would not fail for the loss of one man, but our numbers were down to only several dozen active free-nationals to service hundreds of men in hiding. We could not afford more losses. I replied to Baghdad thanking them for their concern, and suggesting that they might like to relocate to Kuwait for their safety as we would be able to hide them from the Iraqis in the event of war, whereas this was not possible in Baghdad.

Later, on a trip to Baghdad, I happened to be in the Al-Rasheed Hotel, where CNN had their offices. I visited them and took to task John Holliman, one of their reporters, for putting people in danger. Holliman protested that he was a professional reporter who was doing his job, and that it was CNN's mission and responsibility to report the news. Beyond that, he was not prepared to listen to me, or to hear of the fears which their methods were causing.

I got nowhere with Holliman, who became increasingly agitated, so I walked out. However, his producer, Ingrid Formanek, caught up with me. To her credit, she took note of my points and apologised for any concern they may have caused. We did not notice any improvement in CNN's reporting, and there were several other security breaches, but at least it did not deteriorate.

'Conjecture Network News' was not the harshest label applied to CNN. This was 'Collaboration Network News', with good reason. CNN seemed particularly close to the Iraqis, and would do almost anything on Saddam's terms to get a story. Several individuals called it the 'TV whore' as it seemed prepared to prostitute itself to the Iraqi cause for the sake of any story.

These men felt that their opinions were vindicated when CNN became the only major Western media organization allowed to remain in Baghdad and transmit out in late January 1991. However, there was ample evidence of real CNN collaboration earlier in the crisis. As early as August, CNN reporter Doug James was quoted as saying: 'I think Saddam Hussein is very TV-wise .... He certainly knows the power of TV ...' This was just after CNN had given Saddam over an hour's air time in his second major appearance with foreign hostages, appropriately dubbed *'The Saddam Hussein Show'* by US newspapers. CNN was certainly not ignorant of their service to Saddam.

In October 1990, news of Iraqi atrocities found its way out to the West, particularly overblown tales of premature babies being taken out of incubators and killed. To counter this, the Iraqis took CNN to Kuwait to film the Al-Adan Hospital which had been especially spruced up for the trip, with babies in incubators. They were not allowed to see any other hospitals, visit the besieged US Embassy, or film anything else. The Iraqis could have done the filming themselves. That was the essence of CNN's collaboration. They sold their credibility to the Iraqi propaganda machine and its charades.

Another CNN favourite was to cover a minority of what they said were Kuwaiti civilians relaxing in hotels in the Gulf States, or partying in Cairo or European nightclubs. These people should have been more careful about their behaviour, but were more likely to be other Gulf nationals. Any misbehaving Kuwaitis among them were soon brought to task by their countrymen.

This practice of only reporting selected angles gave the impression that the Kuwaitis were not worth fighting for. In the opinion of those in hiding, this was doing the Iraqis' job for them, all the more effectively because of the high regard in which CNN was held. To their credit, however, CNN reported the secondment of Kuwaiti students in the US to Allied forces as liaison officers, and showed them going through basic training , but this was too little too late.

Another disturbing aspect of the media, not limited to CNN, was the use of so-called experts. These people were usually retired generals or think-tankers on contracts of up to US$1,000 per day. Very few of them were independent academics. Even fewer were suitably qualified to comment on the situation. The networks seemed to think that an expert on Egypt could comment knowledgeably on the Gulf and Iraq. This was like asking a Greek to comment on Iceland on the basis that they are both European countries.

More seriously, most of the networks' Arab 'experts' were Levantines, often Palestinians or Lebanese with a grudge against the Gulf Arabs. The producers could not assess this. To them, they were Arabs so must have special insights. In effect, the networks gave a stage to anti-Kuwaiti and anti-Saudi elements.

The manner in which the experts were used was also disturbing. Instead of providing background, context or analysis, they were frequently asked for predictions, which usually turned out to be wrong. This explains why the Western public found so much difficulty in understanding the nuances of the crisis. Many of the experts served only to confuse the issue.

CNN were not the only journalists to visit Kuwait during the occupation. A team from the US's syndicated *Inside Edition* accompanied Jesse Jackson on his two brief Iraqi-controlled trips there on 30 August and 1 September.

Apart from locally-based newspaper reporters and correspondents, all of whom wisely kept a very low profile, or left as soon as they could, there were four credible Western journalists in Kuwait at the time of the invasion: Vic Mallet of the London *Financial Times*, who had landed on BA149, Giancarlo Gumuccio, a stringer for *The Times* of London, Hetti Lubberding of Dutch Radio, and Caryle Murphy, the Cairo correspondent of the *Washington Post*. There were also several Asian journalists, particularly a Filipino who covered the plight of his own community with distinction.

Vic Mallet stayed for a little over a week after the invasion, and then escaped across the desert on his second attempt. He was the first Western journalist to get out of Kuwait with eye-witness details of the invasion. Mallet had more reason than most to leave. The *Financial Times* had done an exposé on Iraqi arms purchases under his name. We lost track of the *Times'* Gumuccio; he presumably left with the Italians, or got out across the desert.

Caryle Murphy, however, stayed for 26 days. During this time, she sent out some excellent articles for which she later shared a Pulitzer Prize. These accurately described the invasion, the fear, the activities of the nascent Resistance, and the Kuwaiti boycott of non-essential services under Iraqi rule.

However, like many of her colleagues in Baghdad, Murphy seemed to have little concept of her power to put people at risk. Among other things, she tried to ascertain the number of people in the US Embassy, and their status as diplomats or otherwise. The US did not want the Iraqis to know this in case they had to pass off the civilians and military in the compound as diplomats.

In fact, Murphy was sheltered by the Kuwaiti Resistance. At one stage, she had been trying to contact the editor of *Al-Qabas* newspaper, one of Kuwait's leading dailies. He was out, so instead she spoke to his brother, Issam Al-Sager, a young Managing Director at the National Bank of Kuwait. Al-Sager told

Major-General Mohammed Al-Bader about Murphy. Al-Bader, aware of the need to get word out of what was happening in Kuwait, wanted to see her urgently. She met with him and Brigadier Yousef Al-Mishari, who gave her access to a satellite telephone to get her copy out. Al-Bader sheltered her in his own house, and then moved her to Al-Sager's home.

When the round-up order came, Murphy refused to destroy her notes, hiding them in a refrigerator. If she had been caught with these, the people sheltering her and those identified in the notes might have been in great danger. The Kuwaitis decided to get her out of the country for her own safety, and their own. She was in Saudi Arabia by the end of August.

Despite the widespread criticism of the media by most other Western participants in the crisis, they did have their uses. To balance the humanitarian image the Iraqis tried to convey of themselves, diplomats in Baghdad grew adept at judiciously steering the media towards stories of Iraqi looting or human rights abuses. Then some of the US diplomats from Kuwait who had moved to Baghdad found that their own State Department was not quite diligent in supporting them with funds and providing for their evacuated families. They had to cash personal cheques with the journalists. This did nothing for their independence, but they had no other choice.

The Allies enlisted the media on several occasions to convey footage of US Marines practising amphibious assaults, particularly the meaningfully-named 'Exercise Imminent Thunder'. Besides boosting the morale of the men in hiding, it helped to con the Iraqis to divert forces uselessly to beach defences.

On several occasions, US and British networks were linked to men in hiding by the Kuwaiti Resistance satellite phones, and even spoke on air several times with active Resistance figures. These interviews helped to keep the plight of the men in hiding and the hostages in the public eye, and reassure Western leaders that the men in hiding fully supported the use of force.

Perhaps the most useful role of the media for the Western men in hiding was their coverage of the arrival of the evacuated women and children in Baghdad. It was a great relief for the men to see their families on TV within 36 hours of saying goodbye to them. Most of them had heard over the BBC or VOA, and through their embassies in Kuwait that the families had arrived safely in Baghdad, but the evidence of their own eyes was great reassurance.

As for the women themselves, the presence of the media in Baghdad provided a measure of protection against unwanted Iraqi attentions. For the most part, the Iraqis in Baghdad acted properly, but there were exceptions. The women knew how much store the Iraqis set by their public image, so felt more comfortable when the cameras were around. This was particularly useful at the airport when the families were flying out of Baghdad.

The media provided a similar service to the men when they were leaving. Some of them, including the Irish warden, Paul Kennedy, had amassed evidence of Iraqi human rights abuses and looting in Kuwait, as well the names of firms whose goods had found their way into Kuwait during the occupation in breach of the UN sanctions. They were concerned that the Iraqis might find and confiscate this evidence, and perhaps punish them. They therefore enlisted the help of the BBC's John Simpson to escort them into the airport departure hall. The officials checking them out of Iraq were on their best behaviour in front of the cameras. The evidence got out safely.

Several other men in hiding besides my neighbour and me also made videotapes of scenes in Kuwait, and did interviews with themselves to describe their plight. Some of these videos had an unexpected benefit, thanks to the media. With the dearth of news and footage from Kuwait, the media were prepared to pay for almost anything. At the time, the free Westerners in Kuwait needed funds to help support those in hiding, and were having little success in obtaining them from the Baghdad embassies. During a trip to Baghdad in November, I told an Australian TV journalist about one of these videos. He put me onto the American ABC TV News, who gave us US$500 for the tape, sight unseen. In retrospect, this was a giveaway price. The TV crews paid that for a single satellite feed, but we were not to know the real value.

On the same trip to Baghdad, I met two Canadian newspapermen who wanted stories out of Kuwait. We had a cloak-and-dagger breakfast meeting in the Al-Rasheed. The only diners were ex-World Champion boxer Mohammed Ali with his aides. One free Westerner in Kuwait was *Arab Times* reporter Jadranka Porter. I thought that she might like to help. The journalists and I set up a channel with secret addresses whereby the next visitor to Baghdad could pass the stories out, and they gave me a US$100 advance on the first article. As it happened, Jadranka was already committed elsewhere, and the hostages were released before we could find an alternate source, but the money was useful. A total of US$600 was ID3,000 – which bought a lot of fresh fruit and vegetables and cigarettes for the men in hiding.

Despite the antipathy for the media among many of those directly involved in the crisis, there were some very respected journalists. For example, Chris Dickey of *Newsweek* worked for a responsible organization which did not seem to require him to produce a story for its own sake, even though his editors later let him down by publishing General Schwarzkopf's battle plan.

Most of these men and women had visited Iraq and the region many times, and were wise to the real nature of the Iraqi regime. They were prepared to receive information as 'deep background', and not use it until the danger to individuals was past. Their deeper knowledge of the situation showed in the quality and depth of their reporting. As a result, they were not inveigled by the Iraqis. Unfortunately, their voices were often drowned in the din of the instant TV wisdom. Their industry depends on developing more like them.

22. THE GROVELLERS

'Grovellers' was the term used to describe individuals who visited Baghdad to plead for the release of their nationals. They were a mixed bunch, arousing perhaps more mixed feelings than the media. Some were also referred to somewhat grandly as 'peace envoys'.

The prevailing opinion in Kuwait was that the grovellers simply lent credibility to Saddam, and lengthened the hostage ordeal. This view was shared to a lesser extent by the Human Shields. Those in Baghdad were more in favour of the grovellers as they saw them as a more immediate means by which they might leave Iraq, and had more contact with them. Those in Kuwait, being out of sight, were usually at the bottom of the grovellers' lists. The grovellers had little use for them, and they little use for the grovellers.

A number of people suspected that some individuals who left Iraq early had used undue influence to get on the grovellers' lists. Indeed, while some grovellers asked for the release of all hostages, or at least all their own nationals, most of them pushed small sub-groups such as employees of particular companies, or friends, relatives, or employees of those paying their expenses. Most Human Shields and those in hiding felt that except for the female, young, elderly and ill, everyone should be freed together, and that grovelling for sub-sets prolonged the ordeal of those left behind.

Most governments of people held hostage were universally opposed to grovellers, although they could not and did not stop them travelling to Baghdad, and generally respected their convictions. White House Press Secretary Marlin Fitzwater summed up the feelings of most governments, saying of the grovellers: '... they walk a very fine line between trying to help their countrymen and being used by Saddam Hussein ...'

From the Iraqi standpoint, the grovellers were one of three groups of puppets, together with the hostages and the media, that could be used in a self-sustaining spiral to maintain Saddam's campaign to defer military action, and to present himself as a reasonable man. If the grovellers wanted any success, they had to be nice to Saddam. Despite his faults, he can be so charming as to seduce the most hardened political operators into seeing him as a man of good faith. This led to such respected figures as Sir Edward Heath, Yasuhiro Nakasone, Willy Brandt and Tony Benn making gratuitously favourable comments about him. With the Iraqis refusing to call the hostages anything but 'guests' or 'ambassadors of peace', the grovellers were obliged to play Saddam's game and use his terminology. Their credibility and the media's was inveigled brilliantly into Iraq's cause.

About 70 'grovel teams' visited Baghdad, ranging in size from one person, to 16 for the American–Iraqi Friendship Foundation. Some such as America's Jesse Jackson even came with their own TV crews.

The first and most successful was Austrian President Dr Kurt Waldheim. He took out all those of his nationals who wanted to leave. It was a brilliant, perfectly-timed move. Austria was neutral, not even in the EC, and Waldheim enjoyed great credibility in Baghdad from his peace-making efforts early in the Iran–Iraq War as UN Secretary-General. He also knew that Saddam had to demonstrate that he would let people go to persuade other grovellers to visit. After Waldheim, there would be diminishing returns, but he got all his Austrians home.

Jesse Jackson was the only other groveller to visit Baghdad in August. During September, there were six: two Japanese parliamentary delegations, one from Italy, and three from France. The first French team was led sensibly by Algerian ex-President Ahmad Ben Bella, and the second by Gilles Munier, a neo-Gaullist ex-Minister, of the Franco–Iraqi Friendship Group. The third was a delegation of French volunteers. The French got a dozen between them, in early October. The Italians and Japanese got nobody.

The pace quickened in October with about 20 grovel teams. The Japanese returned with three more parliamentary groups, and a Friendship Society. The Spanish sent a group of intellectuals and artists to play on historic Arab links to Spain, and a parliamentary delegation. Two parliamentary groups arrived from Germany and got four people, ostensibly as an Iraqi gesture of joy at German reunification. The Spanish got 15, and the Japanese nobody, again.

October saw the advent of the Western Islamic delegations. With Saddam presenting himself as a great Muslim leader standing up to an *infidel* West, and questioning the House of Saud's custodianship of the Holy Cities of Mecca and Medina, he could hardly ignore other Muslims.

The first of these Islamic delegations was the converted British pop singer, Yusuf Islam, previously Cat Stevens, who left with four men. However, all of these were British Shi'ite Muslim pilgrims visiting Iraq at the time of the invasion. It was hardly a major victory. None of them had been Human Shields. Then came Dr Salim Mansour of the American–Iraqi Friendship Foundation who got 14, and a Swedish–Palestinian–Islamic Friendship Group who won four. Two further Swedish non-Islamic delegations who took out six men between them. Few, if any, of those released were from sites or Kuwait.

Meanwhile, two delegations arrived from Finland, and one each from Italy and Greece. The Finns had five people released. The Italians and Greeks had less success. Finland was one of the ten non-permanent members of the UN Security Council at the time. Releasing the Finns could potentially take some of the heat off Iraq at the UN. However, nine out of the 14 Finns in Kuwait and Iraq were held back to ensure that Helsinki got the message. The reasons for releasing the Spanish were less clear, but may have been to pre-empt criticism from Latin America. Saddam did nothing out of the goodness of his heart. There was always a *quid pro quo*.

Late in the month, one of the more unusual grovellers arrived, the first from Australia - Mrs Anne Fairbairn, a flamboyant, 60ish, eccentric poetess. Largely unknown, even in the Antipodes, she had far more experience with Iraq than most other grovellers, having visited the country several times to compile an anthology of poems. She was devastated to get only two older hostages, but this was relatively better than most of her co-grovellers considering that she had no political power at home.

The big winners in October were the Bulgarians, when their Vice-President was granted the release of all his 700 nationals; the French, who had all their 327 men released on the 22nd; and 80 Swedes and 35 Portuguese who were also allowed out. Saddam need not have bothered with the Bulgarians; many of them apparently preferred to stay in Iraq.

Former British Prime Minister Sir Edward Heath had less luck. He departed on 24 October with 33 men, some of them elderly or ill, and promises that certain British workers in Iraq would be allowed to leave when their contracts expired, and that British youths aged between 18 and 21 could go. However, Heath's visit was tragically blighted by the accidental death of one of these youths in Iraqi custody on the way to the airport in Kuwait.

Heath's visit and the French release marked a watershed. The French were the first nationality with men serving as Human Shields to enjoy a general release, and Heath was the first major groveller from a leading Coalition country. His haul represented only three per cent of all British men then in Iraq and Kuwait, but it was the most British men released so far.

Eight days after Heath left, the Speaker of the Iraqi National Assembly, Sa'di Mehdi Saleh, announced that all hostages would be released in return for a guarantee of non-aggression. From then on, the Iraqis seemed to be looking for ways to get rid of the hostages while squeezing as much mileage out of them as possible. Nevertheless, at the end of October, there were still about 2,000 Western men prevented from leaving, plus several thousand Soviets whose contracts had not expired. In the first three months of the crisis, the grovellers had got out fewer than five per cent of their beleaguered nationals.

The pace of groveller visits became almost frenetic from then until all hostages were released in December, with an average of one mission per day arriving in Baghdad. The US, UK and others stepped up diplomatic pressure for a general release by citing the inhuman experiences of the people released in October, and turning Saddam's argument on its head. They told the Iraqis 'not only is holding hostages *not* preventing military action, but it is making it more likely because of growing resentment in the West.'

Against this hardening background, the seven major missions in November were led by Japanese former Prime Minister Yasuhiro Nakasone, West German former Chancellor Willy Brandt, Danish former Prime Minister Anker Jorgensen, New Zealand former Prime Minister David Lange, British leftist politician Tony Benn, French right-winger Jean-Marie Le Pen leading an EC delegation, and former Greek Catholic Patriarch of Jerusalem, Archbishop Hilarion Capucci. Grovelling created some of the most unlikely bedfellows.

This was the level of groveller which Saddam wanted. It paid him some respect. Brandt met Saddam twice, and got 170 individuals out, of which 120 were German, leaving about 180 behind, 44 of them on strategic sites. The others were 25 Italians, 10 Dutch, and 15 Americans and British thrown in just to keep the big powers in the game. The small number of Americans and British compared to the other nationals was particularly pointed.

Jorgensen received 16 out of about 75 Danes, one of whom was the Danish Ambassador to Kuwait. Le Pen took out 82 people, of whom 35 were British, 4 Irish, 15 German, 15 Italian, and the rest a sprinkling of other Europeans; Archbishop Capucci got 68 Italians out of about 170. Only Tony Benn was short-changed, with 15 out of over 1,000 British. Saddam was not quite ready to let too many Americans or British go, and Mr Benn was not even an ex-Prime Minister. To show who was still in charge, he gave nobody to the Netherlands or Australian Red Cross, the Italian Green Movement, a Belgian Friendship Association, a Swedish 'Peace Messenger', or parliamentary delegations from Ireland, Japan, Spain and the UK. However, Italian parliamentarians got 20, the Swiss 36, and the Canadians five out of 60. This was particularly galling for the three visiting Irish Deputies, as Ireland had sent no forces, was owed a fortune for beef sold to Iraq, and staffed Baghdad's Ibn Al-Bitar hospital.

Perhaps the most controversial November grovel mission, and the one with most potential, was that of Willy Brandt, given his unquestioned stature. Following a demonstration by the families and friends of German Human Shields, Brandt had said as early as 19 October that he would involve himself in the hostage issue, and made preparations to go to Baghdad.

However, on 28 October an EC summit in Rome had decided that the hostage issue was getting out of hand with Saddam trying to play off each country against the other. In order to present a united front, they agreed not to send government representatives to Iraq in any capacity to negotiate the release of hostages, to discourage others from doing so, and to ask the UN Security Council to continue its efforts for the immediate departure of all hostages.

As with the French, Iraq had secretly offered to release all the 352 Germans if Foreign Minister Hans-Dietrich Genscher went to Baghdad to collect them. Genscher refused to play the game. Brandt, for his part, wanted to go, but had indicated to the German hostages' relatives that he could not go against the wishes of the German Government.

However, popular concern over the fate of the hostages and its potential effect in upcoming elections prompted Chancellor Helmut Kohl and Genscher to about face, and support Brandt. This contradicted the Rome Agreement, much to the displeasure of the UK and others. In order to reconcile this, the Germans tried to elevate the status of the mission by including former European External Affairs Commissioner Willy de Clerq, inviting Italy to send former Prime Minister Emilio Colombo with Brandt, and asking UN Secretary-General Javier Perez de Cuellar to designate Brandt as the special representative authorized by the Rome Agreement, arguing that the trip was in line with Security Council Resolution 674, which called for a Secretary-General's special commission to press for the release of the hostages.

However, the Iraqis would not talk to the UN about the hostages, so Perez de Cuellar's approval was not forthcoming. Besides, the Aga Khan had been appointed to this role on the 29th. With this, Colombo and de Clerq backed out. Brandt decided to go unilaterally, arriving in Baghdad on 5 November with the German Government's ambiguous blessing and a very unambiguous Lufthansa Airbus full of medical supplies and children's food.

During the second half of November, the number of releases per groveller seemed to be determined mathematically in advance by the Iraqis as a function of the nationality and eminence of the visitor, the remaining numbers of the respective nationals, and previous releases.

Significantly, the price had been set for the British and Americans. At the time there were about 350 Americans and 1,150 British in Kuwait and Iraq. Edward Heath had taken out one in 15 of the British, and Mansour 1 in 25 Americans, whereas Brandt got about half his people, Nakasone a fifth, and all the French were released without any grovellers. A US or a British hostage was worth about seven Frenchmen, two Germans, or four Japanese.

Saddam seemed to have realized by mid-November that the hostages were damaging him, as they were galvanizing Western public opinion against him. A flurry of major releases followed. On the 24th, Saddam ordered the release of most of the remaining 300 Italians, and 30 Irish nurses at the PARC hospital. The few dozen remaining Greeks and the 56 Swedes were allowed out, followed on the 28th by all the Belgians. A further 40 Czechs and 36 Japanese left in December just before the general release.

However, of the hundreds who left in November, only 19 were Americans and 62 British. The grovellers had concentrated the Iraqi hostage policy on these two nationalities. By late November, it looked as if everyone except these people would get out within weeks, before the war started.

The rush of grovellers in November actually became so great that they began tripping over each other, and even fighting amongst themselves. There was insufficient glory to go around. After various politicians and other individuals at home had seen the media attention accorded to the first wave, they rushed to the nearest Iraqi Embassy for visas. However, the grovellers already in Baghdad were incensed as the Iraqis would now have to save some hostages for the next wave, thus reducing their potential score.

Some countries ended up with four different delegations in Baghdad concurrently, all pretending to be on the best of terms with each other and working for the common good of their nationals, yet at each other's throats privately. With the rush of grovellers and media to Baghdad, the hotels could hardly cope, so many grovellers and so-called peace activists were housed on a resort complex on an island in the Tigris, sarcastically termed 'The Peace and Friendship Camp', 'Honeymoon Island' or 'The Island of Brotherly Love' by free-Westerners in Baghdad. It was anything but that.

The flood of grovellers pouring into Baghdad actually posed a problem for the Iraqis. Not everyone could get to see Saddam. He was a busy fellow coping with a world crisis. Besides, if every groveller got to see him, it would diminish the value of meeting the great man. Personal appearances were therefore limited to the significant grovellers. The Americans usually got to see him as they were such a rarity. Most of the British also got an audience.

To cope with the rush, the Iraqis set up the 'Friendship, Peace and Solidarity Organisation' to orchestrate the activities of the lesser grovellers and set their itineraries. The grovellers had to be given something to do as they worked their way up the ladder. The first stop was always their own contacts if they had any.

Artists usually went to the Minister of Information and Culture. Female grovellers were often sent to the Iraqi Women's Federation, where they were well looked after, and told how many Iraqi babies were dying because of sanctions. A trip to Babylon was always a good fill in. After several encounters with successively higher levels of the Iraqi hierarchy, they usually found themselves with the Speaker of the Iraqi Parliament, or the First Deputy Prime Minister. This was generally the last stop unless they were sufficiently eminent to see Saddam. Sometimes they had to go back for a second meeting, or say something nice about Iraq and Iraqis to the press. A day or so after this, they got their ration of hostages.

As with the media, there were good grovellers and bad grovellers. Sensible delegations such as Western nationals of Arab extraction or Western Muslims who called Saddam's Arab–Muslim bluff were viewed more favourably than has-been politicians attempting to rekindle fading glory. Grovellers from countries not actively participating in the Coalition, such as Ireland and New Zealand, were seen as simply stating their case that their country was not really involved, so their people should be let go.

Those in hiding and the Human Shields were divided in their attitudes. The majority were firmly against the visits as they saw them as playing into Saddam's hands, and failing to address the real problem of getting everyone out immediately. They saw the grovellers as divisive by pandering to Saddam's view that the world was not really united against him, and that he could split or wait out the Coalition. A number of hostages were so thoroughly disgusted by the spectacle of respected people fawning on Saddam that they vowed they would refuse to leave if released ostensibly through the grovellers' efforts, or even demand that a more needy individual go in their place.

Others were grateful for any efforts to get them out. To them, every man out was a gain. In fact, several groups, including some of the Australians, Canadians and Danes in Kuwait, actually wrote to their own Governments and potential grovellers requesting that they go to Baghdad on their behalf. Some men strongly objected to these letters, and insisted that they be worded to make it clear that they did not represent a unanimous view. Furthermore, the grovellers were doing a disservice to families at home by getting their hopes up, only to have them cruelly dashed. Some grovellers did give hope to families desperate for any straw to cling to, but the depression after the failure of most of these missions was a heavy price to pay.

Opinion on the usefulness of the grovellers was as divided at home as it was in Kuwait and Iraq. For many family members, the grovellers were respected people who provided a ray of hope for the release of their men. However, in late October, many wives noticed a pattern to the releases and pick-ups. It seemed that captures of people hiding in Kuwait increased immediately after a groveller-inspired release. The Iraqis seemed to be letting people out at one end, but filling up the pipeline at the other. A case in point was Sir Edward Heath's visit. Within 24 hours of 33 men leaving with him, another 40 were captured or sent to sites. The same happened in November when Saddam moved the

Human Shields in Kuwait to Baghdad, and sent them out to sites in Iraq itself at the same time as he released 15 men to Tony Benn. Days later, he released 11 men to their relatives and 15 more men became Human Shields.

Although the pattern may have been co-incidence, even some diplomats in Baghdad were convinced that the Iraqis were running a 'topping-up' operation, described by one as 'industrial'. In Kuwait, we were fairly sure that men in hiding were picked up as soon as the Iraqis knew where they were. However, on occasions, the Iraqis seemed so well-informed that it appeared they had known about the men for some time, but had left them alone until a release was made. This pattern was observed quite independently by people in Kuwait, by wives back home, and by diplomats. As such, many wives of men still in hiding turned against the groveller system as it seemed to put their husbands in more danger. Wives of Human Shields at the sites remained in favour of it. These two camps, understandably, could never see eye-to-eye.

The American grovellers were Jesse Jackson, Salim Mansour, Ramsay Clark, Mohammed Ali, the American Fellowship of Reconciliation led by Roman Catholic Bishop Michael Kenny, and Oscar Wyatt of Coastal Corporation - a major importer of Iraqi oil - with former Texas Governor John B. Connally in his capacity as a member of the Coastal Board of Directors. The only two of these groups who left a favourable impression were Mohammed Ali and Bishop Kenny. Ali in particular was seen as having great courage and dignity, and the conviction of his faith, by going to Baghdad while suffering from Parkinson's disease, and dealing with Saddam as an American and a Muslim in equal parts.

No one ever quite knew what Ramsay Clark's agenda was, but he arrived in Baghdad almost unnoticed in November and left just as quietly, with four men. There was always a suspicion that such ex-politician grovellers might be carrying some secret message from George Bush to Saddam. This gave too much credit to conspiracy theories: it is illegal for anyone other than the State Department to negotiate on behalf of the US. The US Embassy in Baghdad was quite capable of passing the American President's messages to Saddam.

The most widely criticized grovel trip was that of Jesse Jackson. His objective seemed to be personal glory, regardless of the fate of people he could have helped with ease, particularly women and children. There seemed to be a great lack of sincerity about him. For a start, he could not decide whether he was a journalist or a groveller. He initially entered Baghdad as a reporter for the *Inside Edition* TV programme. This was the means he used to provide funding for his trip. In a way, he was using Saddam just as Saddam was using him. TV footage with the great man in August was at a premium, and a joint appearance would assure Jackson of TV time at home.

What annoyed people most was that Jackson continued to claim credit when events had already overtaken him. When he first visited Kuwait from Baghdad on 30 August in an Iraqi plane, the Iraqis had already said on the 28th that all women and children were free to go. This news had even been in US newspapers, but the embassies in Baghdad had not had time to organize evacuations. After speaking briefly to the diplomats in the US Embassy compound in Kuwait, Jackson returned to Baghdad to interview Saddam on 31 August *without taking any US women and children from Kuwait with him*. It was inconceivable that he or his aides were unaware that Saddam had already released them, and that the problem now was getting them out.

Back in Baghdad, during his TV interview with Saddam, Jackson asked for the release of the sick people on the Embassy compound, including four men. Saddam went along with the game, not budging an inch during the interview. Jackson never pointed out that the women and children were already free to go, so he just had to collect them. At the end of the interview, Saddam suddenly made one of his staged 'spontaneous magnanimous gestures', and told Jackson that he could take the four ill men, and the sick women and their children from the Embassy compound. Apparently, Jackson still did not mention the hundreds of other women and children in Kuwait and Iraq.

The charade continued the next day when Jackson returned to Kuwait, accompanied by Saddam's personal interpreter, Dr Saadoun Joubaydi. At the time, the US Embassy was relying on advice from the State Department that the women and children could go. The Washington bureaucrats were apparently not doing their job, so the Embassy seemed ignorant of the release order. The US Embassy man from Baghdad accompanying Jackson to Kuwait, Consul Melvin Ang, seemed, incredibly, similarly uninformed.

Jackson and the Iraqis then proceeded to take advantage of this to make him look good. This show started in the nearby Kuwait International Hotel. A US woman of Arab extraction, Furiel Allen, had been hiding in one of the rooms, similarly unaware that she was free to leave. Mrs Allen apparently pretended to have cervical cancer, and appealed to Jackson, who came to the rescue and haggled with the Iraqis for her release. This took several hours, as the *Inside Edition* crew filmed the negotiations. Jackson reportedly heroically told the Iraqis that they would have to keep him if they kept Mrs Allen. In the meantime, hundreds of other women and children released from the sites were waiting at Baghdad Airport, ignorant of the problem, for Jackson to arrive so that they could leave Iraq on the same Iraqi Airways 747.

As soon as the Iraqis in Kuwait had relented to what they had agreed to almost four days earlier, Jackson went to the Embassy to collect the people there. This time, DCM Barbara Bodine and Consul Gale Rogers haggled for the remaining five women and children with them but not on Jackson's list. Jackson had enough glory for the day. He cut Barbara off short, and agreed with Dr Joubaydi that their names would be submitted to the US and Iraqi authorities in Baghdad. They had to stay for now. Neither Jackson, his aides, the Iraqis, Ang, nor the *Inside Edition* team pointed out that these five people and every other woman and child in Kuwait were already free to go.

In the meantime, Gale Rogers had been pressuring the Iraqis over the phone about getting other sick and injured individuals out on Jackson's Iraqi aircraft. She eventually shamed them into accepting another half-dozen particularly needy cases by asking them if they wanted to take responsibility for their deterioration or death. Hundreds of other US women and children were left behind. Jackson's plane could not have taken them all, even with both trips, but scores of them were needlessly obliged to spend another week in Kuwait.

When Jackson boarded the Iraqi 747 in Baghdad with the women and children released from the sites for the trip out of Iraq already aboard, he presented himself as the 'Great Liberator' to people who had been waiting for him for hours. He was told in no uncertain terms to sit down and shut up and retreated to the first-class lounge, while some of the released BA149 stewardesses and several British youths got his camera crew inebriated elsewhere on the plane. In a delightful piece of poetic justice, they were apparently too drunk to film Jackson's speech at the first stop at Orly.

Some members of the media also had a poor opinion of the Jackson, and an insight into his motives. When the BBC's team in Baghdad asked Jackson's business manager if they could have seats on his aircraft to Kuwait, the reply was apparently, 'We aren't into chequebook journalism, but that will be US$100,000.' It sounded very much like chequebook journalism to the BBC.

The Iraqis were similarly unimpressed. Three months later, Dr Joubaydi confided to another groveller, 'Jesse Jackson is a complete fake. He came with a TV crew; Saddam Hussein wanted to talk about the crisis, and Jackson said, "I'm just here doing TV programmes."' However, to Jackson's credit, the US diplomats in Kuwait said later that he was the only groveller who did them any good, but that there was not one word of follow-up after he left.

Perhaps the most disturbing aspect of Jackson's trip was that he had little or no grasp of the real issues. In an interview after arriving back in the US, Jackson summarized the problems between Iraq and Kuwait as an oil price–territorial dispute. There was no mention of nuclear, chemical, or biological weapons, or Saddam's expansionism. It was a good thing he didn't want to talk with Saddam about the crisis. He knew nothing about it.

The second US grovel mission also turned the groveller system into a farce which cast aspersions on the motives of the more sincere visitors. In October, Salim Mansour, an Iraqi-American heading the so-called American-Iraqi Friendship Foundation was granted 14 people, without specific names. He tossed the selection of who could go back to the US diplomats, insisting that those released travel with him to New York for a press conference. If they refused, he would select another 14. It was outright blackmail.

This decision of who should go was particularly painful at the time. Mansour was the first groveller to be granted American men being held as Human Shields, as distinct from medical or special humanitarian cases, and there was no way of knowing whether there would be any other releases. Those left behind may have been essentially condemned to death by war.

The US Embassy people, particularly the USLOK personnel, referred to Mansour as 'Slime Mansour', instead of Salim. They found him despicable. The prevailing joke was that the American-Iraqi Friendship Foundation's 16 individuals comprised the sum total of Iraq's friends in the US.

The final US grovel team, Coastal Corporation's Oscar Wyatt and John B. Connally, also came in for criticism. They had circulated various US corporations with people in Iraq, saying that they could use their long-standing connections with Baghdad to get 100 people out, and reportedly arrived with such a list. At that time, there were perhaps 250 US men in Kuwait and Iraq. It soon became apparent that the Iraqis might give them about 12. They then went to the embassy asking for more names, but said publicly that the Embassy had pleaded with them to take more.

Not surprisingly, this caused some unpleasantness with the diplomats. Wyatt and Connally met with Saddam on 5 December, the night before the general release was announced, and claimed credit for 23 of the hostages released, although Saddam had at that time decided to release everyone. Their aircraft left two days later, with two-thirds of its 175 seats empty.

Wyatt's and Connally's people accused the Embassy of not pushing hard enough to get more Americans on the flight. They did not mention that the Iraqis prevented this so that the remaining Americans would have had to leave on chartered Iraqi flights. Neither man had even phoned the Embassy about the matter. More importantly, those on their list were invariably executives of major US corporations. The groveller system actually discriminated blatantly not only against those in Kuwait, but also against those ordinary hostages who lacked a big corporate sponsor.

Perhaps the most admired of the six US groveller teams was that of Catholic Bishop Michael Kenny. His American Fellowship of Reconciliation came in late October. When the rest of his team left empty-handed after a week, Kenny refused to go without taking people back. He finally hectored the Iraqis so much that they gave him four. It wasn't much, but it was something.

While waiting, the Bishop gave spiritual counsel to the US hostages, diplomats and military in Baghdad, and even celebrated Mass in Baghdad's Catholic Churches. Kenny was not the only visitor whose heart seemed to be in the right place. A number of greater and lesser politicians who made the pilgrimage to Baghdad, including Australia's Janine Haines, paid their own way and shied away from publicity. Others, including New Zealand's David Lange and Britain's Tony Benn made a point of leaving before people could be organized to go with them to deny Saddam the additional publicity.

The only British grovellers of any consequence out of the five from the UK were parliamentarians Sir Edward Heath and Tony Benn. Although these two senior statesmen hailed from opposite sides of the political divide, they were united in a heartfelt aversion to a military solution, even if it meant compromises from Kuwait and the Allies, and their personal and political opposition to Prime Minister Margaret Thatcher.

Heath was undeniably the senior of the two. Even the Iraqis recognized this. They accommodated him in a Government guest-house. Benn had to make do with a suite in the Al-Rasheed. Heath initially had the implicit support of the FCO, but this was withdrawn when Mrs Thatcher learned of it. Both he and Benn left London under a great deal of official criticism, but carrying with them the hopes of many of the Human Shields' relatives.

The factors driving these two men to Baghdad seemed to be a strange mix of genuine concern for the hostages, and an opportunity to snipe at the UK Government. The best interests of the hostages was by no means the only item on their agendas. As with some US grovellers, there were suspicions that they had come to deliver messages, especially as Heath had met in Washington with several members of the US Cabinet before his trip, but both made it quite clear in their meetings with Saddam that they had no power to negotiate.

Heath arrived in Baghdad on Saturday 20 October with a priority list of about 70 people whose families, friends and contacts had lobbied him in the UK. This included the sick, the British passengers on BA149, and the young men between 18 and 21 who were considered borderline adult males. The omens were good as Cat Stevens/Yusuf Islam had just left with four British men.

However, many of the men in Kuwait suspected later that the 'old-boy' network had played a part in the compilation of the list, especially as one of the boys on it was attending Balliol College at Oxford, Heath's *alma mater*. In any event, the list was supplemented by the British Embassy in Baghdad giving Heath the names of the old and sick Britons in Baghdad. His list eventually totalled about 200. There was a distinct feeling among people in Baghdad that the Iraqis had kept these people as bait for Heath.

On the day of his arrival, Heath and his two offsiders visited the sick and elderly British in the hotels and Ambassador's residence, and the British medical staff at the PARC Ibn Al-Bitar Hospital, before dining that evening with Iraqi Foreign Minister Tareq Aziz and British Ambassador Harold Walker. This act in itself caused outrage among some men in Kuwait, with Aziz seen as at best the chief apologist for the invasion.

The following afternoon, Heath met Saddam for three hours without having to navigate the usual obstacle course, but he did not bring up specific names, nor did he receive any specific promises of releases. Various categories of hostages were discussed, but the selection of who could go was to be left up to Saddam's minions. Saddam kept the discussion general and refused to say how many could go. Heath apparently did not criticize Iraq for its invasion of Kuwait, or for the atrocities that were occurring there, and left the meeting impressed with Saddam's desire for a peaceful solution.

The working part of the trip came that night. The team worked until 4.00 a.m. the following morning presenting their lists to the ubiquitous Dr Saddoun Joubaydi, to determine who could go. It was an unpleasant and degrading process, with Joubaydi denying that the sick men were as ill as they claimed, and accepting or rejecting them with little or no discussion. As dawn broke, they thought they had a list of 38 whom the Iraqis agreed to let go, but they could not be sure. Over the next two days, the Iraqis brought in up to 30 men from the sites to the Mansour Melia. Heath's team eventually left Baghdad on Wednesday with 33 hostages, and promises of about 37 more to follow.

None of the people who left Baghdad with Sir Edward Heath were from Kuwait, but two should have been. In fact, Heath should have taken out 38, not 33. The five were young men between 18 and 21.

This episode was the most tragic affair of the crisis as far as most Westerners in Kuwait were concerned. The two from Kuwait were the sons of BLT Commander Colonel Bruce Duncan. The boys, Alex, 19, and Rory, 18, had been visiting their parents on holiday when the invasion happened. Both were strapping lads who could not have passed for less than their years and had opted not to leave on the evacuations with their mother and sisters.

Both boys were students. Alex was the one attending Balliol College. The Iraqis had agreed to let them go, apparently ignorant of their father's identity, and the two had bid him farewell and come out of hiding to rendezvous with the Iraqis, who were driving them to Kuwait Airport for the flight to Baghdad. The car, with an Iraqi driver, an Iraqi MFA representative, and the two boys was hit by an Iraqi Army truck coming the other way on the wrong side of the road. The driver had no chance. The MFA man and Alex Duncan were both killed outright. The driver and Rory Duncan were seriously injured, Rory with a badly hurt back.

The casualties were taken to Kuwait's Al-Sabah Hospital - now renamed Saddam Hospital - where Rory, who was not given painkillers, was finally able to call British Ambassador Michael Weston, who in turn had the unenviable task of contacting Colonel Duncan. With one son dead, Duncan had no choice. He came out of hiding and went direct to the hospital.

There was little Weston or his Consul could do for Colonel Duncan and his surviving son, blockaded as they were in their compound. Weston's counterpart in Baghdad made representations to allow a visit by Weston to Rory in hospital on compassionate grounds, and to permit his father and him to leave Kuwait and Iraq without being detained. The Iraqis did not reply. However, the Duncans are devout Catholics, so Weston contacted the Catholic Bishop and Vicar Apostolic for Kuwait, Francis Micallef, a Maltese. The next morning, he and one of his Lebanese priests went to visit Rory, who was in acute pain. Colonel Duncan was there, beside himself with grief at the double tragedy. The Bishop tried to console the distraught father as best he could.

The men were then taken to where Alex's body was lying in the mortuary, wrapped in a sheet. His jewellery and a number of other possessions had looted. Colonel Duncan had to identify his son's body. The three men were so overcome that they found it almost impossible to pray over the body. The Colonel was weeping openly, as were the priests, both of whom knew the family well. When they regained their composure, the Bishop commended Alex to God, praying for the bereaved family's consolation.

Colonel Duncan and Rory were allowed to leave after Rory's condition had been stabilized in Baghdad, and were then flown to the UK with Alex's body.

The death of young Alex Duncan, and Rory's injuries, came as a great shock to those of us in Kuwait. It seemed to sum up the waste of all the human potential of those who had died for no reason other than Saddam's misguided ambition. The Iraqis had been doing their very best to get the boys to Baghdad for Heath's flight, but that did not make it easier for us to accept.

Opinion among many in Kuwait turned on Heath in particular and the grovellers in general. In retrospect, this was grossly unfair to Heath. He could not be blamed for Alex Duncan's death any more than he could be blamed for the invasion, but the sentiment was heartfelt. To Heath's great credit, he attended Alex Duncan's funeral and Requiem Mass in the UK.

The incident also shook up the Iraqis, and caused further trouble for some of the other Human Shields. The other three boy-men held at sites had been brought back to Baghdad, one of them with his mother, Mrs Pauline Barlow. They expected to leave with Heath. However, when Alex Duncan was killed, they were taken back to the sites. This was particularly traumatic as they had no idea what was going on. Mrs Barlow even feared that it was a ploy to separate her son, Julian, from her and her husband. They were eventually released several weeks later with Jean-Marie Le Pen's EC delegation.

The origins of Tony Benn's trip were less altruistic than Sir Edward Heath's. He came at the invitation of the Iraqis, not at the request of the families of hostages. With the dearth of credible British grovellers in the pipeline after Heath's return, Benn was approached by the Iraqi Ambassador to London, Dr Shafiq Al-Salihi, on 6 November, and told that in view of his anti-war stance he would be welcome in Baghdad. He arrived in Baghdad on 26 November with an Irish Arabist, Paul Lalor, as his translator.

Whereas Heath had gone to ask for hostages, Benn felt that he might be able to convince Saddam to withdraw from Kuwait. It was a naive hope, but he was quite explicit that the purpose of his trip was political, not humanitarian. His conditions were that he meet Saddam, and King Hussein, and have some hostages released. However, his main aim seemed to be to pour maximum criticism on the UK Government and its Baghdad Embassy, and establish his place in history by persuading Saddam of the error of his ways.

I observed Benn's attitude first-hand when I visited him at the Al-Rasheed in Baghdad on 27 November. I thought at the time that he would appeal to Saddam especially for the sick and elderly, as Heath had. At the time, I was particularly concerned for two British men in Kuwait, Lawrence Miall, who required a delicate brain operation and Mike Meade, a cancer patient. The UK Embassy in Kuwait had also given me a list of 15 other ill men. I assumed that they would all be on Benn's list, but wanted to make sure.

After finding Benn's suite, I first had to speak with Lalor and explain the function of the free Westerners supporting the men in hiding in Kuwait, being suitably vague to frustrate any bugging. Lalor understood, and checked the list of people to be presented to Saddam, but neither name was on it. In fact, no men in Kuwait, sick or otherwise, were listed. Lalor wrote in the first two names I had. He then called in Benn, and told him about the missing names.

'Oh, they're in Kuwait, aren't they?' said Benn. 'We aren't going to submit the names of any men in Kuwait because that might help the Iraqis find them. We will only discuss those sick men in Iraq.'

I was both impressed and appalled. For one thing, Benn had considered the security of those in hiding. On the other hand, he was all but ignoring those in Kuwait. The men in Baghdad and at sites seemed to have far more priority. I explained to him that the Iraqis could not find men in Kuwait just from their names. It was far more important to give them access to medical treatment.

Benn was unmoved. He explained to me that his approach to the problem of the men in hiding in Kuwait was to ask Saddam to grant them the same freedom of movement as British residents of Baghdad enjoyed. This, he would stress, would help ease the pressure coming from these men and their families for war, as they were taking a much harder line than the British in Baghdad. The man struck me as having a very sharp mind. He had demonstrated an excellent grasp of the differing streams of opinion between those in Kuwait, and those in Baghdad, but I could not believe that such an intelligent man could be so naive as to expect Saddam to go along with his suggestion.

As far as he was concerned, the discussion was closed. Lawrence's and Mike's names were removed from the list, despite my protests. I was even more incensed later when I learned Benn had accepted a list of compassionate cases of those in Iraq from the local UK Ambassador. It was blatant discrimination between the British who were ill in Baghdad, and those still in Kuwait.

I then tried to explain to Benn that there was no chance of Saddam giving freedom of movement to the men hiding in Kuwait, but he asked me about the co-operation I had received from the British and Australian embassies in supporting the men in hiding. I was not about to criticise anybody with or without reason in case the comments back-fired on me. This did not please him. My audience was terminated. It struck me as I left that he was more interested in dirt on the diplomats than the fate of the men in Kuwait.

This impression was confirmed a quarter of an hour later as Benn was leaving the Al-Rasheed. The media were waiting for him on the front steps. The moment the cameras went on, he thrust his chest and chin out, drew himself up to his full height, assumed a look of studied statesmanship, and injected a tone of high moral purpose into his voice. I have never seen such a comprehensive transformation in a human being. He was aware that millions of Britons would be watching him on TV that night. Most of the questions were about the hostages, and his expectations for the meeting with Saddam the following day, but he managed to skillfully dominate the interviews with stinging criticism of the local British Embassy, and the British Government.

Benn's visit with Saddam the following day lasted three hours. Although he asked for all the hostages, and delivered some letters from relatives of hostages to Saddam, he got so caught up in discussing the higher aspects of the crisis that he forgot to ask how many hostages he could have, and when they would be allowed out. In the end, he received 15 British men, half the number released with Sir Edward Heath upon his departure.

Interestingly, Saddam told him 'Within a week, every 'foreign resident' of Iraq could have freedom of movement restored.' To Saddam, Iraq no doubt included Kuwait. This was only eight days before Saddam announced the general release. It seems that he had already decided to let the hostages go. There was no point sending more than he needed to with Benn.

Nevertheless, there were some fascinating revelations on Saddam's reasons for keeping Kuwait. They had little to do with the publicly touted line of Kuwait originally being part of Iraq. Saddam seemed to admit that he had not really wanted to go all the way into Kuwait, but now that he was there, he had to keep it to prevent America using it as a base from which to attack him. In effect, Saddam was aware that the main Western objective was to cripple his weapons of mass destruction in Iraq proper. He seemed to think that while the Allies would fight him out of Kuwait, they would not go as far as Iraq itself. Kuwait would be the first line of defence against the Coalition armies before they could go into Iraq. He did not seem to appreciate that the Coalition had the power and intention to do both.

Relations between the grovellers and the diplomats in Baghdad were mixed, but mostly cordial. People such as the Wyatt/Connally team, Salim Mansour and Tony Benn aside, most grovellers got on quite well with their embassies, and worked closely with them in the common interest of their nationals.

Despite the official government opposition to most grovellers, many diplomats saw them as a second string to their own efforts. If the embassies' message was not getting through to the Iraqis because the Iraqis did not like the messenger, then the ambassadors were delighted for someone more acceptable to the Iraqis to reinforce it. Some of the governments were secretly happy that the grovellers presented a chance for at least some people to get out. Every man out was one less to worry about rescuing if it came to war.

Despite their limitations, the embassies could often render substantial assistance to the grovellers with briefings on Iraqis they would meet, international phone calls, and extra lists of people to plead for. The embassies were also able to discern patterns in the releases, although this was more of an art than a science. They were more in tune with what categories the Iraqis might be prepared to release, such as older men, or full-time students, and could therefore counsel the grovellers on how best to structure their own lists.

However, the embassies and some of the lesser grovellers preferred to distance themselves from each other to avoid compromising the grovellers' supposedly independent negotiating positions. This subterfuge sometimes involved the grovellers avoiding their respective embassies altogether. They met their diplomats, or nationals who were free to move around Baghdad, in hotels, at the Ambassador's Residence, or at the homes of other diplomats.

A final class of visitor to Baghdad consisted of the wives, fiancees, mothers and children of men held at sites. These women were a particularly vulnerable target of the Iraqi propaganda machine. Their sole concern was for the men they loved. They were incredibly frustrated at the lack of solid results by their own governments and the grovellers. Nevertheless, they were used by the Iraqis in an even more cynical manner than the public figures.

The best evidence of this exists in a letter purporting to be from the wives of British hostages in Iraq, but actually written by the Iraqis. These women had gone to Iraq on 11 November in response to Saddam's offer to allow women to visit their husbands, and with the encouragement of the Iraqi Embassy. The Iraqis had accommodated them free-of-charge in the Mansour Melia.

The letter reads as follows, exactly as written, with spelling and grammar:
'From: Wives of British guests in Iraq to Women of the World.

Dear peace, justice and freedom loving women of the world,

We are a group of British women hosted by Iraq at this serious time of his history and history of the world. We visited our husbands in Iraq, to get acquainted with their conditions seizing the kind invitation made by Iraq to allow families visit their men in Iraq. We made this visit in spite of the warnings we received from many western governments and circles, however, we arrived in Iraq. Since the first instance we realized the wide-scale distortion practised by western media against Iraq and its people. When we met our husbands we found out that they have been provided with utmost care and attention which some people lack even at their homes. We are now aware of the human motive which forced Iraq and its people to host the foreign guests. We realise that Iraq is doing all that to protect its people and property with all human means possible. Iraq wants to attract the attention of the world to the danger of the American and foreign military presence on world peace.

By doing that, Iraq does not want to hold the freedom of anyone but rather to drive off the spectre of war from the whole world; this war which the U.S. wants to trigger off to repeat the Vietnam tragedy.

Dear freedom-fighting women of the world,

We denounce the presence of American and allied forces in the Arab Gulf region. We believe that peaceful dialogue is the best way to solve all the problems of the region because it makes humanity avoid catastrophies of war. Some countries want war, dominate the world and exploit the wealthes of the peoples.

From Baghdad with its nice, hospitable people who cherish peace and justice we appeal to you through your women organisations to raise your voices for the withdrawal of foreign troops from the Arab Gulf region and abandon the war option for the benefit of peace and dialogue. By adopting such an honest position you will contribute to exercising pressure on the U.S. and its allies to avoid war and its catastrophies you will also strengthen the spirit of peace based on justice. President Saddam Hussein's initiative on November 18, 1990 to allow Iraq's guests to leave on batches as from December 25, 1990 over a period of three months, affirms Iraq's peace desire.

We are looking forward to all the women organisations in the world to call for peace and to renounce war and destruction.'

The letter arose when the group met the Iraqi Women's Federation, an organization with considerable behind-the-scenes clout, as they worked their way up to Saddam. The British played up the suffering of Iraqi widows and orphans from the Iran–Iraq War, emphasizing that Iraqi families stood to lose even more men without a peaceful resolution, and that releasing the hostages could help achieve this. The Iraqi women seemed sympathetic and suggested that the letter would be useful, and helpfully drafted it.

There was some discussion among the British as to whether they should correct the atrocious English, or to even sign the letter at all. They eventually signed it unchanged so it would be obvious that it came from the Iraqis. By the evening of 26 November, the Iraqi Press Office in London had faxed the letter to all the major UK papers who, to their credit, did not publish it.

In effect, the women were obliged to sign a collaborationist document. It was outright blackmail, but it was impossible to blame them for agreeing to this.

These people were neither the first nor the only families to appeal directly to Saddam. In September, an American woman had won her 25-year-old asthmatic son's freedom. A British woman, Gilly Battersby, flew into Baghdad with Edward Heath in October, entirely independently of his mission. Her husband was not released then, but they had ten precious days together in the Mansour Melia. She returned in November, and was allowed to take him with her then. Several US women had previously visited Baghdad unsuccessfully, but during November, another American, Jean Hromatka, whose British husband, Nigel Nightingale, had once been detained with me in Kuwait, went to Baghdad. She and the women from the large British group eventually met with Saddam, got all their men, and left on 29 November.

By 5 December, another 25 British women had left with their men, and a further 50 had just arrived in Baghdad, together with a US group of 15 women, one boy whose mother was unable to travel, and one man for his father, led by Bishop Gumbleton of Detroit.

The real measure of the success of the grovellers lies in how many people left Kuwait and Iraq significantly before they would otherwise have done so.

For the Americans, about 50 of their 300 men left Iraq prior to the 6 December general release as a result of grovellers. Of these, 20 left less than a week before everyone else. The remaining 30 went in three lots in early September, mid-October, and early November. In effect, the US grovellers only achieved the early release of 30 out of 300 American men.

The British fared even worse. About 1,150 British left Baghdad in December. Approximately 400 of these had been at camps, another 350 had remained in hiding in Kuwait, and another 400 had been resident in Baghdad. About 110 had left prior to this, 68 in the two weeks prior to the general release. Thus, the real British success rate was a lowly 42 out of 1,260.

Of the countries with men on sites, the French were the most fortunate, but their early release had more to do with deft maneuvering by their politicians than grovellers. The Germans were all released in late November, two weeks before most other nationalities, but this was also unrelated to the grovellers. Of their 300 or so men, about 122 left in early November. The grovellers gained only an extra two weeks of freedom for barely 40% of the Germans. The final nationality with people on sites were the Japanese. About 230 of these left in December. Only 77 left previously with Yasuhiro Nakasone in November.

Overall, the grovellers were a waste of time. A few score individuals left Iraq substantially before they might otherwise have done, but the 2,000-odd left behind - and a number of the diplomats in Baghdad - generally feel that the grovellers extended our ordeal by at least three weeks.

As a final indictment of the grovellers, as of today there are over 600 Kuwaitis and others unaccounted for by Iraq. The only crisis-era groveller to have returned to Baghdad to plead their case is Mohammed Ali. Sir Edward Heath went back to collect several Britons who wandered across Iraq's borders, but did not ask for any Kuwaiti or other POWs. The grovellers who were so conspicuously concerned for others in 1990 are remarkably silent now.

Illustration 3. GROVELWATCH
Estimates of releases ostensibly as a result of 'grovellers'

Name/Group	Affiliation/ Status	Approximate date of visit	MAJOR FIVE NATIONALITIES (PROSPECTIVE HUMAN SHIELDS)					Other Nationalities
			American	British	French	German	Japanese	
AUGUST, 1990								
1 President Kurt Waldheim, Ex-UN Sec. Gen.	Austria	25 Aug						95 Austrians
2 Jesse Jackson	USA	31 Aug	4 +					
SEPTEMBER, 1990								
1 Mario Campana, Parliamentary Delegation	Italy	11 Sept						
2 Ahmad Ben Bella, Algerian ex-President	France	15 Sept			Few			
3 Parliamentary Delegation	Japan	19 Sept						
4 'Friendship Society'	France	21 Sept			9			
5 Parliamentary Delegation, Social Democratic Party	Japan	30 Sept						
6 'Volunteers'	France	28 Sept						
OCTOBER, 1990								
1 Senior Politicians	Japan	1 Oct						
2 Intellectuals/ Artists	Spain	4 Oct						
3 Parliamentary Delegation	Germany	5 Oct						
GENERAL RELEASE, without groveller	Brazil	7 Oct						78 Brazilians
4 Parliamentary Delegation	Japan	8 Oct						
5 Parliamentary Delegation	Spain	15 Oct						15 Spanish
6 Yusuf Islam (Cat Stevens)	Britain	13 Oct		4				
7 Social Democratic Party	Germany	15 Oct						
8 'Peace Delegation'	Finland	16 Oct						
9 Dr Salim Mansour	USA	17 Oct	14					
10 Ex-PM Edward Heath	UK	23 Oct	1	33				
11 Social Democratic Party	Finland	21 Oct						
GENERAL RELEASE	France	23 Oct			327			
12 Vice-President	Bulgaria	23 Oct						All Bulgarians (approx. 700)
13 'Peace Delegation'	Italian	23 Oct						
14, 15 Two Delegations	Sweden	25 Oct						6 Swedes
16 Panhellenic Social Democratic Movement	Greece	25 Oct						
MAJORITY RELEASE, without groveller	Portugal	26 Oct						35 Portuguese
PARTIAL RELEASE, without groveller	Sweden	26 Oct						80 Swedes
17 Anne Fairbairn, poetess	Australia	27 Oct						2 Australian
18 'Friendship Society'	Japan	28 Oct						
19 Swedish-Palestinian Friendship Society	Sweden	31 Oct						5 Swedes
20 'Peace Delegation'	Japan	31 Oct						
NOVEMBER, 1990								
1 Fellowship of Reconciliation, Bishop Kenny	USA	1 Nov	4					
2 Ex-PM Yasuhiro Nakasone	Japan	4 Nov					77	
3 Parliamentary Delegation	Italy	4 Nov						20 Italians
4 Friendship Association	Belgium	4 Nov						
5 Ex-Chancellor Willy Brandt	Germany	6 Nov				120		50 various Europeans
6 Netherlands Red Cross	Netherlands	6 Nov						
7 International Trade Union Federation	?	7 Nov				2		2 Portuguese
8 Green Movement	Italy	7 Nov						
9 Peace Messenger	Sweden	7 Nov						
10 Parliamentary Delegation	Japan	7 Nov						

Illustration 3. GROVELWATCH (cont.)
Estimates of releases ostensibly as a result of 'grovellers'

Name/Group	Affiliation/ Status	Approximate date of visit	MAJOR FIVE NATIONALITIES (PROSPECTIVE HUMAN SHIELDS)					Other Nationalities
			American	British	French	German	Japanese	
NOVEMBER, 1990 (cont.)								
11 Australian Red Cross	Australia	10 Nov						None
12 Ex-PM Anker Jorgensen	Denmark	11 Nov						16 Danes
13 Ex-PM David Lange	New Zealand	11 Nov						All New Zealanders (17)
14 Parliamentary Delegation	Ireland	11 Nov						None
15 Parliamentary Delegation	UK	12 Nov						None
16 Jean Marie Le Pen	EC	14 Nov		35		15		33 various Europeans
17 Parliamentary Delegation	Switzerland	14 Nov		2				16 Swiss, 20 other Europeans
18 Clinton Condon (Australian Wheat Board)	Australia	17 Nov						4 Australians
19 Arab Australians	Australia	17 Nov						2 Australians
20 & 21 Ex-politicians	Australia	19 Nov						1 Australian
GENERAL RELEASE	Germany	20 Nov				180		
22 Parliamentary Delegation	Spain	20 Nov						
23 Ron Brown MP	UK	24 Nov	5					
MAJORITY RELEASE, without groveller	Italy	24 Nov						300 Italians
PARTIAL RELEASE, without groveller	Ireland	24 Nov						30 Irish nurses, PARC Hospital
24 Mohammed Ali	USA	26 Nov	15					
25 Pacifist Group	Greece	26 Nov						10 Greeks
26 Peace Delegation	Switzerland	26 Nov						
27 Tony Benn MP	UK	26 Nov		15				
28 Parliamentary Delegation	Canada	26 Nov						6 Canadians
GENERAL RELEASE	Sweden	26 Nov						All remaining Swedes (approx. 56)
29 Archbishop of Jerusalem, Hilarion Cappucci	Italy	26 Nov						68 Italians
30 Parliamentary Delegation	Belgium	28 Nov						All Belgians (approx. 36)
31 Parliamentary Delegation	Japan	26 Nov						
TOTAL RELEASES PRIOR TO GENERAL RELEASE			38	94	9+	137	77	Total foreign nationals released, 6 December 1990:
APPROXIMATE NUMBERS RELEASED AT GENERAL RELEASE			200	1,000	327	180	305	approx. 3,400 individuals.
Date of General Release, 1990			6/12	6/12	23/10	20/11	6/12	

NOTES:

(1) Groveller visits for December 1990 of Miroslav Vacek (ex-Defence Minister, Czechoslovakia), an Italian and an EC Parliamentary Delegation, John B. Connally and Oscar Wyatt of Coastal Corporation (USA), Ramsay Clark (USA), and Parliamentarian Antonio Anoki (Japan) are excluded as it is reasonably certain that Saddam had decided on the general release of all Western annd Japanese hostages by the end of November 1990; therefore their efforts did not contribute to any early releases.

(2) With the exception of Austrians, the number of persons released refers to adult males, as women and children were allowed to leave from the end of August 1990. Austrian women and children were the only non-adult males allowed to leave before any other women and children.

(3) Where no numbers are indicated for a groveller, no releases were obtained by that groveller or his/her team.

(4) Details compiled from various sources. Not necessarily precise, but reasonably correct. Excludes releases as a result of visits by families of hostages.

23. THE HOSTAGE SUPPORT GROUP

As the crisis moved into November 1990, about 500 Westerners - Americans, British and Germans - remained in hiding, in about 175 different locations. A further 80 or so Westerners had freedom of movement. The Germans were well served by German wives of Kuwaitis and the one Japanese family had passed themselves off as Chinese, so the main concern was for the Americans and British. Saddam was obviously concentrating on them.

In the weeks since the free Westerners first started moving around, most men in hiding had been resupplied by these people, the Kuwaitis, or Arab and Asian friends. Anyone supporting those in hiding had become known as a 'minder', after the character Terry in the British TV series of that name.

During late October and early November, a number of people in Kuwait started trying to improve the effectiveness of the minder system. There were several pressing reasons for this. First, the people being served best were those with the best contacts, whereas the poorly connected actually needed more help. Secondly, the grovellers and a realization that war was unlikely before Christmas led many free nationals to relocate to Baghdad in the hope of getting out. There were simply fewer people available in Kuwait to carry the load. Finally, the threat of having cars with Kuwaiti plates confiscated or denied petrol was a worry. The efforts who were active as minders were not being co-ordinated effectively. They were covering an inordinate amount of ground, running too many risks with checkpoints, becoming frayed, and were unable to take full advantage of the available supplies and skills.

One of the first attempts to co-ordinate efforts was a meeting in early November of a leading British warden, Sandy Macmillan, the main Canadian warden, Fred Skovberg, and me, at Sandy's home. Our major concerns at that time were integrating the various national warden networks, improving the mail system between Kuwait and home, obtaining money for Westerners in hiding and those helping them, and ensuring that everyone who wanted safe identification got it. It was designated an International Wardens' Meeting.

We worked on the mail and the money aspects by formulating proposals which were put to the embassies in Kuwait. These involved establishing a regular courier service between Baghdad and Kuwait, using the free-nationals. The US and UK Embassies in Baghdad, at the insistence of their Kuwait colleagues, agreed to finance these trips. Baghdad's Irish Embassy had already agreed to finance any courier engaged by the Irish warden.

This group did not get much further as the New Zealanders were released shortly afterwards. With their departure, we lost some of our most active operatives. However, this was a blessing in disguise as it galvanised several other free-nationals into action. The magnitude of the task, with an ever-decreasing number of free-nationals in Kuwait, was driven home.

Conveniently, the apartment block called 'Kiwi House', where several of the

New Zealanders had lived, had become an informal meeting place for free-nationals. It had always been a main drop-off point for mail to Baghdad, and a prime venue for parties, so was well known. It was so busy with free national visitors that the Iraqis hardly gave it a second glance. Most of these visitors were full of ideas about how things could be better run, but no one was bringing it all together. Few of us had known each other before the invasion. The situation called for a military structure or a recognized central authority but this was impossible given the temperaments involved. Lise Hertz, a Dane who had moved to Kiwi House, and I therefore decided to hold an informal meeting of all interested people soon after the New Zealanders left.

This first meeting of this wardens' and minders' group, which later became known as the Hostage Support Group, started slowly. The discussion initially went around in circles with people chatting in small groups. As one of those who had called the meeting, I eventually took on the role of Chairman to try to bring it back on track. The effect of the imposition of some sort of authority was startling. People were brimming with ideas and enthusiasm, but just needed a structure to pour these into. In the atmosphere of a controlled meeting, they could give their opinions, have them assessed, and gain broad approval for specific courses of action. The spirit of co-operation was quite remarkable. By the end of this first meeting, there was a real sense of achievement that we were working together. People no longer felt so isolated in their efforts to help.

The first major consideration was improving the minder system itself. The main problem was that minders usually serviced people widely dispersed across Kuwait. I was covering several groups and individuals spread over four suburbs. Eoin MacDougald and Lise Hertz were serving even more. This had come about as people were minding their own friends and acquaintances, without reference to where they lived, and those who had become minders early such as Eoin and Lise had built up a huge portfolio of men in their care.

The solution was to allocate minders geographically, like the British warden system, with at least one per suburb. That minder would concentrate on those in his own patch. This meant that he seldom needed to move far from his home, except when coming to Kiwi House. It meant less trouble with checkpoints, and less time spent travelling around. The whole objective of this was to help the minders to operate more effectively, and ensure that everyone in hiding had someone who could take over if his own minder went north.

We did not seek to supplant minder relationships which were already working well, or where minders were happy to continue serving people outside their own area. As importantly, many men in hiding had built up trust and friendships with their minders. It was vital for their psychological well-being that we should not interfere with this.

There was another important objective in having free Westerners as minders. The Kuwaiti Resistance were directly helping perhaps a hundred of the men in hiding, and risked being hanged if caught. We passed the word that the free nationals were prepared to take over from Kuwaitis in the interests of their safety. We had no takers. The Kuwaitis counted it as a point of honour to continue minding the Westerners, even under threat of death.

Another major consideration was supplies. We often spent an inordinate amount of time shopping for small amounts of varied items for certain people, when the same time could be devoted to buying bulk supplies, if only we could spread them around effectively. It was also a waste of our limited funds. The solution was for certain people to source bulk supplies, and to split these into smaller 'handypacks' which could be used effectively by groups.

In deference to the particularly active Canadians, we suggested holding the next meeting at the Canadian Ambassador's Official Residence, known as the 'OR' with Eoin MacDougald or Fred Skovberg chairing it. Kiwi House was crowded. The OR had a huge formal dining table which looked as if it came from IBM's boardroom. However, the first meeting eventually went so well, and the risks of getting the British members of the group to the OR were so great, that everyone preferred to keep it at Kiwi House. We held only one meeting at the Canadian OR, the day after Saddam freed all Westerners.

Despite this organization, we had no wish for the men in hiding to know how the minder system really worked, and who was behind it. This was to protect our security, and ultimately theirs. They needed to know only who their minder was, and what he or she could do for them. Information on how we were co-ordinating ourselves would leak out soon enough. We could be compromised by the capture of one scared man who hoped to get better treatment for himself by telling the Iraqis everything he knew. We did not expect anyone to betray us deliberately, but we knew that frightened men do strange things.

The core of the Hostage Support Group comprised six individuals: Lise Hertz; three British men in hiding, Keith Chandler, Bob Jaggard and David Neal; one of the leading Canadian wardens, Eoin MacDougald, and me, as the Australian warden and one of the two British Embassy wardens with freedom of movement. Only Eoin and I did not live at Kiwi House.

There was no real leadership structure to this core. This was one of its main strengths as it avoided power plays and dented egos. However, the driving force of the group was definitely Lise Hertz. She was a natural organizer, had been actively involved in the support function from September, and was recognized as one of the most active and bravest of the minders.

The roles of the three Britons were less visible as they were in hiding. They were none the less indispensable. Keith Chandler was a computer buff, so he maintained our database. David Neal became our postmaster. He also had another critical role. He was a very quiet fellow who listened to our various discussions, and then often provided an entirely new and sensible perspective. As a candidate for the Human Shield, he kept us free nationals focused on security risks which a few of us were becoming blasé about. I had started to answer the phone with a flippant 'Hostage Headquarters. Can we help you?' Dave pointed out that the lines might be tapped, and that even if the Iraqis could not match the number to an address, it was unwise to attract attention to ourselves. Dave also became the housekeeper. He was always 'minding the shop', so to speak, so was dubbed 'Granville' after the TV character who played opposite Ronnie Barker in *Open All Hours*. The third Briton, Bob Jaggard, became our Registrar and Secretary, and maintained our list of safe houses, and the minutes of the group's more formal meetings.

The Canadian member of the core group, Eoin MacDougald, was perhaps the most active minder, having never actually gone into hiding since he was first captured and released on 19 August. He was our main link to the Canadians, and our principal liaison with the US Embassy. I was the group's main liaison with the British Embassy, and the Australian community. I also acted as Chairman for the more formal co-ordinating meetings of the group, as a secondary liaison with the US Embassy, and as a minder in my own right.

The people outside the core group were equally vital as many of them had exclusive access to certain skills or resources. Almost anyone who wanted to help was welcome. The only prohibitions were on those who might be a security risk, or disruptive. For security, we were obliged to consider only Palestinians such as Nasser Bakir, and his Pakistani wife, Rukhsana, who had a track record as minders. We were even leery of the Christian Iraqi wife of a Canadian Scot, although she did help greatly by obtaining documents to 'prove' that we were trying to change our Kuwait licence plates to Iraqi ones.

One of the most important people outside the core was Lucia Topalian, an Armenian–Lebanese executive who lived with Asrar Al-Qabandi of the Kuwaiti Resistance. Asrar was our main source of the money that the Kuwaiti Government had sent into the country to support the Kuwaitis remaining there. During October, Asrar had approached Sheikh Ali Salem Al-Ali, one of the main sources of government funds in Kuwait, and told him that the Westerners were in just as much need of cash as the Kuwaitis. Asrar asked Lucia to get the numbers of Westerners. These were only available through our group. The Kuwaitis were shocked, and then pleasantly surprised, to learn that so many of us were still hiding successfully in Kuwait. The money gradually started coming through via Lucia, even after Asrar was captured.

Another vital individual was Shakir Abul, a Kuwaiti with access to Traffic Department rubber stamps that could be used to forge driving licences and car registration booklets. As a Kuwaiti, Shakir was incredibly brave to be even seen at Kiwi House. If our operation had been broken by the Iraqis, he would have been liable for execution, as would Lucia. Shakir's stamps had actually been brought in from Syria. The main problem with them was they were so sharp that they had to be smudged to make them look more realistic.

Shakir started a quick-turnaround document service. Once he had a man's photograph, he could usually produce a perfectly forged and laminated driver's licence in 24 hours. Given more time, he could forge car registration books for free nationals who needed to use the cars of men in hiding.

Several other individuals, notably women, were especially important. An Irishwoman, Astrid Kenny, married to a Kuwaiti physician, Dr Sabah Al-Hadeedi, was a source of bulk flour, sugar, live sheep, and chickens. Her husband never visited Kiwi House, but he was always available for house calls to men in hiding. Again, he could have been executed if caught helping Westerners in this way. The Iraqis had already shot his colleague, Dr Hisham Al-Obaidan. An Englishwoman, Rose Lambert, worked for KDD, and became our major source of dairy products and fruit juices after the New Zealanders left. She had excellent contacts with the Resistance through her friend, Colonel Fawzi Al-Ali, but we never asked about his role. To us, he was just Fawzi. We did not discover his rank until after liberation.

Of the 80-odd free nationals, only about 30 individuals were active minders. Some of the Irish had only temporary travel documents, and were loath to move around on them. Many free nationals' cars had been looted and there was a continuous flow of these people to Baghdad as their grovellers arrived. More seriously, some people simply did not want to get involved.

One of the most important assets of the support group was its database of almost every Westerner in Kuwait, including those in hiding and the free nationals. Its main purpose was to help us ensure that everyone was covered in the most effective manner possible, and to keep track of which wardens and minders were looking after whom. This was later expanded to incorporate control of the disbursement of the Kuwait Government funds, planning for exfiltration, and identifying people who needed safe identification.

The database was maintained on Keith Chandler's Macintosh computer, using EXCEL. There were columns for each individual's name, phone number, warden, minder, suburb, location within suburb, and nationality. Everything except the names and phone numbers was coded. There were no headings to the columns, nor legends for the codes, in case it fell into the wrong hands.

We were acutely aware of the dangers involved. It was no coincidence that we used a Mac. If the Iraqis got hold of the disk, and tried to read it, there was less chance of their having access to a Macintosh than to an IBM machine. The database was kept on a disk innocuously labelled 'Games', and buried several directories deep, with its own false name. The only people who knew how to get to it and to read the codes were Keith Chandler and me. The EXCEL application software needed to run the database was kept on a separate disk, so that anyone who happened to capture it would need both disks before they could run it.

No other item in the group's function was as sensitive, or caused as much concern for security. This database eventually included about 85% of the Westerners in Kuwait at the time. The *Mukhabarat* would have killed to get it. The information would not have allowed them to catch those on it directly unless they extracted the codes from us, but Keith and I were under no illusion that they could have done so if they wanted to. Even with only a printout, they could have focused on certain areas, and made their job much easier.

Whenever the database disk was not in use, it was kept in a box of random disks as if it were just ordinary personal correspondence. We later hid it in a ceiling cavity for additional security. We only made one back-up copy, and that was hidden in another house, in a different suburb, in a box of IBM disks.

We took a full printout of the database on only two occasions. The first was to show other members of the group what we were doing. There was so much concern about this printout that it was destroyed immediately. All further work on the database was carried out on the screen. The second occasion was after Saddam said that all Westerners were free to go. We just wanted to see what the database looked like on paper, and used it to check off people to ensure that they all had transport to the airport for the evacuation flights.

EXCEL's sorting function was particularly useful. Each individual, regardless of nationality, had a record of the suburb they were in, and the number of their group within that suburb. Thus, we could sort the database by various keys, and identify whether a group had a free national living with them or nearby. If so, then their allocated minder was usually that person. We then allocated minders to people without one. The only exceptions were those in the US Embassy. They were on the list in case we had mail for them, so we could fax it to them. Their suburb was coded as 'H/O' for 'Head Office'.

The database could also be used to search for people with incoming mail, so that we could get it to that person's minder. It could be sorted by nationality to determine how many nationals of each country were still in Kuwait.

There were difficulties in compiling the database. The first 60% of the people were easy, as the core group itself knew who and where they were. The next stage was getting information out of the British wardens, and the US and British Embassies. Some of the wardens were not convinced that we really needed this data, so were reluctant to part with it. A few were jealously guarding their territories. The US Embassy was even more security-conscious, and rightly so. They suspected that their lines were tapped, so could not give us the information over the telephone or fax. They had to encrypt it, and send it to their embassy in Baghdad by satellite. Eoin MacDougald then had to go there, pick it up, and physically bring it back to Kuwait with him.

Perhaps the two potentially most important functions of the database, which we thankfully did not have to use, were in planning to support people if the US or British embassies ceased to function, or were taken over by the Iraqis, and planning for exfiltration. If the embassies were knocked out, then the group was one of the few reliable means of communication with the outside world, and the most comprehensive. The British wardens could take up some of the slack if their embassy was lost, but the Americans were more at risk as their warden system rested on their Consul instead of men in hiding.

In fact, we had discovered that despite the cut-off of international phone lines, you could still send telegrams from the suburban Kuwaiti telecoms centres now under Iraqi management. We deliberately avoided using these so as not to draw attention to ourselves, but if we lost the embassies, Iraqi telegrams were one option. Secondly, a few of us were aware that the Resistance had at least one satellite phone, although we did not know how to find it. We learned later that Lucia knew more, but for the security of its operators could say nothing. There were also a few ham radios in Kuwait, one of which was with a Palestinian minder, Nasser Bakir. He had given the frequencies to the Australian Embassy in Baghdad in case we had to use it.

Exfiltration and rescue was something we almost did not want to think about, as someone was sure to get killed during it. However, the database identified which suburbs people were in, and thus would allow military planners to focus on those areas. If a rescue operation were proposed, then given time, people in outlying areas could be smuggled into the four suburbs where most people were in hiding, greatly limiting the area and number of landing zones the troops would have to secure, and saving lives. The intelligence passed to the Baghdad embassies on this never exceeded estimated totals of men in particular areas, but they were astounded that we could even provide this and, with sufficient notice, consolidate people.

Incoming mail was one of the greatest morale boosters for everyone, especially for the men in hiding. With the exodus from Kuwait, it was not difficult to get mail out within a week if one could catch a departee. The greater problem was getting incoming mail from home into Kuwait. There were only two ways in which external mail could get into Kuwait: through the embassies in Baghdad, and via Arab friends coming into Kuwait via Iraq from abroad.

The incoming mail systems were actually quite complicated, even in the home countries. For mail brought in through the embassies, the senders had to write to their addressee, care of a Foreign Ministry address in their country. The mail was then consolidated and dispatched by courier to Jordan, where it waited in the Amman embassies until a diplomat was travelling to Baghdad. Fortunately, we had the Kuwait General Manager of DHL Worldwide Express, Steve Bushby, in our midst. Using the outgoing mail system, he arranged for mail to be couriered, free, from the respective capitals to Amman, but even DHL could not get it into Iraq. With the Baghdad embassies severely short-staffed, the Amman embassies tried to co-ordinate this so that a diplomat from any Coalition country would take the mail in for all others. Even some grovellers and journalists were enlisted as couriers.

Once the mail was in Baghdad, it was sorted into letters for men in Kuwait, those in camps, and those with freedom of movement in Iraq. The mail for Kuwait then had to be sent there. Again, the Baghdad embassies had to co-ordinate among themselves. We tried to use the Australian Embassy as the central collection point so that couriers with limited time in Baghdad did not have to do the rounds of all the embassies. Invariably, there were hitches.

The couriers themselves had to be secure, both for the sake of the men in hiding, and for their own safety. The embassies could not simply release mail to any Palestinian who called in saying he had Western friends in Kuwait. Secondly, the couriers could not carry too much mail in case this drew Iraqi attention to them. We also had to limit the exposure of men in hiding if the Iraqis found the mail and searched it for clues to their locations. We therefore established a roster for a regular weekly Kuwait-Baghdad shuttle, with the express purpose of bringing mail back in not too large quantities.

Once in Kuwait, the mail was generally delivered to Kiwi House, sorted by postmaster Dave Neal into bundles for the respective minders. This was seldom easy as the envelopes usually showed only the men's names. Dave had to use his own knowledge of where they were, and then Keith's database, and then finally call the embassies if he still could not find the man.

The outgoing mail system worked in reverse. The minder picked up the mail, took it to Kiwi House, where Dave got it to the next traveller to Baghdad. The courier then gave it to the embassies who sent it out of Iraq with the next diplomatic courier, co-operative groveller or trusted journalist, to their respective Foreign Ministry, from where it was posted. In some cases, it went to DHL in Amman, and then from there to the respective home country. The minders in each area were the suburban post offices, Kiwi House the central GPO, and the Baghdad embassies the international department.

Even the courier leg between Baghdad and Amman was not simple, though accredited diplomats generally carried the mail. Apparently, diplomatic convention prohibits personal mail being carried in diplomatic pouches, so it had to be carried separately. This seemed petty to us in the circumstances, but the embassies had to remain above reproach. They managed this by sending the mail out with the person carrying the official bag, and did not enlighten the Iraqis that the mailbag was not *bona fide* diplomatic baggage.

The group's embassy-based mail system was not the only means of getting mail in and out, but it was the most reliable, once Foreign Ministries in the home countries organized their central addresses, and it certainly handled the most incoming mail. During November, literally hundreds if not thousands of letters came into occupied Kuwait, right under the Iraqis' noses.

Never the less, the mail systems were not without their problems. Strangely, these were usually at the home end, rather than in Kuwait or Iraq. The US State Department was never able to organize a US address for families at home to send their mail to. The Pentagon could provide hundreds of thousands of troops in the Saudi desert with an excellent mail service, but Washington could not arrange mail for a couple of hundred hostages. We therefore gave the Americans in hiding the addresses which the Australian, UK, Canadian, Danish and German Foreign Ministries had set up. Some of the Americans sent these out, and got mail in that way. However, to their great credit, the State Department was extremely diligent in transmitting brief messages between men in hiding and home, via the US Embassy in Kuwait.

One of the more contentious aspects of the support group's operation was handling money, with all the problems of deciding how it was to be spent, and accounting for it. This required a fine balance between openness and discretion, and a great deal of trust.

We needed money for several reasons. Cars needed fuel and repairs. We had to pay air fares for the courier runs to Baghdad before the embassies agreed to finance these, and to pay for the bulk purchases of food. For most of October, the free nationals were very short on funds. On some of my earlier food deliveries, I was obliged to ask men in hiding to pay for the supplies. This was distasteful, but I needed the cash to buy my own petrol, and fresh produce for them. One of the other Australians with access to the pre-invasion takings of a fast-food chain had given me a couple of thousand Iraqi dinars, but this did not go far when buying supplies for scores of men.

One of our major sources of funds was the Kuwaiti Resistance, through Asrar Al-Qabandi. Most members of the group never met Asrar – she was captured before the group really got moving – but the flow of funds that she put in place served us well even after this. The first instalment per man was ID200. It was not a great sum, but at least allowed them to pay for cigarettes and alcohol and gave them some self-respect. More was promised later.

One strong lobby suggested that the money should not be distributed to the men, but used to buy food for them, which we could then deliver. The argument was that the only things men in hiding could spend money on if they were stocked up with food were cigarettes and alcohol. In the circumstances, some saw using money to buy these as wasteful. However, the core group felt that although we had the power to withhold the cash, we had no moral authority to do so. Besides, if men were captured, they might need it in captivity.

The arguments that clinched the decision to distribute all the money to the men was the fact that a smoke and a drink were important psychological crutches for men in hiding. We were vindicated in this later on when Lucia told us that Asrar had intended the money to go directly to the men to use as they saw fit, and to let them know that Kuwait had not forgotten them.

However, Lucia was so horrified at what she saw as the security risk posed by our method of administering the funds that she backed right out of the group, and communicated with us through one of the Canadians, Britt Mockridge. We had made up short handwritten lists of recipients from the database and other sources, and asked them to sign for the cash. This reduced the risk of double-deliveries, when other men had received none. With the limited funds available, we had to do this. For the first few deliveries, we even had to break the individual instalment of ID200 into ID50, delivered first, followed by ID150 a few days later once more money came in, so that more men would at least get something. Some men refused to sign for the funds in case the lists fell into Iraqi hands, so we had to do so on their behalf.

The departure of the New Zealanders also provided a financial windfall. One of them, Tony Strange, sold his car for ID15,000, and distributed the money among members of the group. Several of the New Zealanders who had been working at KDD left their salaries with Lise Hertz. It was extremely generous. They were returning home to unemployment and could have used the money, but they were aware of the predicament of the men in hiding, and the prospect that they could be there for several more months.

A number of commercial organizations with Irish staff in Baghdad, particularly ICL and PARC, were particularly generous. We later obtained some cash from media organizations for videos and advances for newspaper items. The Irish Embassy in Baghdad was the most forthcoming of all embassies with financial support equivalent to about ID16,000. It was not until late November that the US and UK embassies chipped in, and then in much smaller amounts. The British in particular were hamstrung with bureaucracy.

The support group never actually had its own central fund, but we knew where we could call upon funds. The Resistance money went straight in and out. All other funds such as money left behind by departing New Zealanders and Germans were held by the individuals to whom they had been entrusted, but the wider group could call on those people to help if necessary.

The food distribution system followed the minder system which was, after all, the original function of the minders. The main improvements were on the supply side, and the equity of distribution.

The larger group allowed us to take advantage of bulk flour and sugar acquired by Astrid Kenny. A few men then set up home bakeries where they used the flour to bake bread for others. The bread was delivered fresh. It gave the men in hiding a great sense of achievement to know they were running bakeries under the very noses of the Iraqis. Astrid was even able to source live sheep and chickens, although we had enough frozen meat and poultry.

On the equity side, the organization of the group allowed us to reduce hoarding of supplies by better-connected people to the detriment of others. Every minder could know what was available, and how to get it. One of these resources was the KDD dairy and fruit juice products which had been supplied primarily to men the New Zealanders were serving. The group was able to ensure that those who had not previously received them now did so.

Fortunately, much of the food was supplied by Kuwaiti merchants direct from warehouses. We did not have to pay for it. In late October, the US Embassy in Kuwait had set up a system with a Lebanese minder, Christian Geargeoura. The Americans in hiding ordered their requirements through the Embassy, who then passed the orders on to Christian. He and a Maltese friend, Ray Alamango, made up food packages, and the minder responsible for the particular Americans in hiding would pick up the order and deliver it.

As time went on, we set up 'food banks' within suburbs where a large number of Westerners were hiding in case we were later prevented from using our cars. The plan was to then resupply people in hiding from these food banks, on foot if necessary. For example, Norma Armstrong, an Englishwoman living in Jabriya, had plenty of freezer space, so kept large strategic stocks to service that area. She kept most of her freezers sealed, and as cold as possible, so that the food would last as long as possible in the event of power failure.

Thankfully, we had very few medical problems with were life-threatening in the short-term. A number of men had cancer, or were in need of operations, but held out. Besides Astrid Kenny's husband, Dr Sabah Al-Hadeedi, other Kuwaiti, Arab and Turkish doctors were prepared to make house calls, and the Resistance could obtain drugs for high blood pressure and some other medical conditions. We were even able to get specialized medication in from the US or PARC via the US Embassy in Baghdad for several Americans in hiding. It was hardly a fully-fledged hospital service, but it was something.

There were also two Western physicians in town. One was paediatrician Dr James Carroll, who was holed up in the US Embassy. His services were limited to phone counselling, but it was better that he stay in the Embassy as we could get any man in hiding to emergency treatment, but without a resident physician the Americans would have had to come out. The other, Dr Brian Bethell, was an obstetrician and gynaecologist. There was little demand for his specialist services among the hundreds of men in hiding, but he knew medicine.

We also had several Danish dentists, particularly Drs Claus and Esther Schmith. No one could remain in hiding with a severe toothache, so the Schmiths were particularly useful.

The other source of medical skills was a number of Filipina and Indian nurses who had remained behind, and Kuwaiti, Egyptian, Indian and East European doctors who remained at their posts at the hospitals. We preferred not to call on them for their own safety, but it was reassuring to know they were there if we needed them.

Another service of the group was maintaining a register of safe houses which

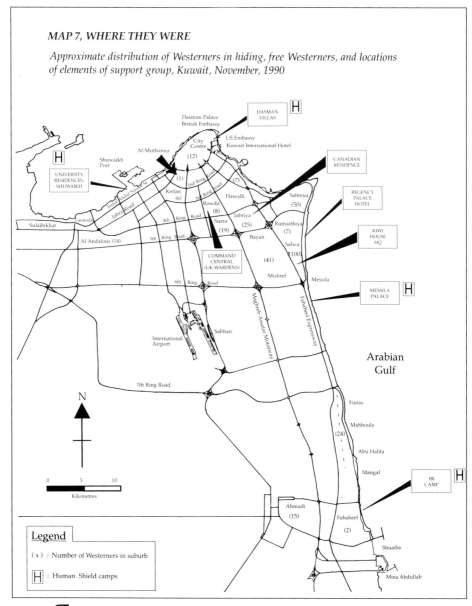

MAP 7, WHERE THEY WERE

Approximate distribution of Westerners in hiding, free Westerners, and locations of elements of support group, Kuwait, November, 1990

DASMAN VILLAS H

Dasman Palace
British Embassy

City Centre

US Embassy
Kuwait International Hotel

Al-Muthanna

(12)

Shuwaikh Port

UNIVERSITY RESIDENCES, SHUWAIKH H

CANADIAN RESIDENCE

REGENCY PALACE HOTEL

(1)

2nd Ring Road

3rd Ring Road

(7)

Keifan
(6)

Hawalli

Salmiya
(50)

Rawda
(8)

Jamal Abdul Nasser St.
Jahra Road

Grenada

Sulaibikhat

4th Ring Road

Surra
(19)

Jabriya
(25)

Rumaithiya
(7)

KIWI HOUSE HQ

Al Andalous (14)

5th Ring Road

Bayan

Salwa
(100)

COMMAND CENTRAL
(UK WARDENS)

(41)

Mishref

Messila

MESSILA PALACE H

6th Ring Road

Maghreb-Assabar Motorway

Fahaheel Expressway

International Airport

Sabhan

Arabian Gulf

7th Ring Road

N

Fintas

Mahboula
(24)

Abu Halifa

Mangaf

IBI CAMP H

0   5   10
Kilometres

Ahmadi
(15)

Fahaheel
(2)

Shuaiba

Mina Abdullah

Legend

(x) : Number of Westerners in suburb

H : Human Shield camps

BASE MAPS © SALEM AL-MARZOUK AND SABAH ABI-HANNA WLL

people could be moved to if the Iraqis got too close to their hiding place, or if groups had to be broken up. These were empty houses and apartments in relatively safe suburbs, and occupied homes where existing occupants were prepared to take in others. This function duplicated much of what the British wardens were doing, but our advantage was that we could move people without putting Kuwait Resistance people at risk. The notice board in Kiwi House was filled with bunches of keys on hooks, with coded labels on them.

Perhaps one of the most important functions of the group was simply to visit people. This was brought home to Lise Hertz when she visited a man hiding on his own after dropping in on Command Central. The larger group was well catered for in almost everything except female company, but this man was on the verge of despondency from lack of human contact. The psychological strain was much greater on small groups or men on their own, especially those with small children, or whose wives had recently had babies. A number of men had been working in Kuwait for several months before the invasion on single status, and had been unable to contact their wives before the international lines went out, and so had not seen their families for at least six months.

The wardens could phone most men for a chat, and pass jokes around, but a personal visit made a great difference. We used to just sit and let them talk, and give us their opinions on how the crisis was moving, or simply tell us about themselves or their families. In fact, some of them were so delighted at visits that they cooked special meals and invited us to lunch or dinner. We looked after the men on their own and in the small groups, and they looked after us in their own way. We even went so far as to make a formal decision to leave the larger groups for the time being, and to concentrate on visiting lone men. The moral support was not one-way. The appreciation on their faces when we called around helped keep us going.

By the time the Westerners were released, the support group had developed into the nearest thing possible to a publicly accountable underground administration for the men in hiding. Its major advantage over the embassies and UK wardens was that its members could move around, and shuttle between Kuwait and Baghdad. It had responsibility for the most comprehensive mail system in Kuwait, access to significant funds and food supplies, and responsibility for getting these to the men in hiding equitably. We also had the most comprehensive database of all Westerners in Kuwait at the time.

The peak period of the group's operations was during the last of the four months in which Westerners were trapped in Kuwait. We were prepared to go through until Christmas and beyond. In fact, when the Westerners were released, we had become so involved, and the system was functioning so well, that we were almost sorry that our entire *raison d'etre* had disappeared.

24. NOVEMBER 1990: A DEADLINE IS SET

Despite Saddam's isolation, November opened with contradictory indications on the likelihood of an early war. General Schwarzkopf said he could obliterate Iraq, but also, with all due political correctness, that he still hoped for a peaceful settlement. President Bush, armed with UN Security Council Resolution 674 condemning the mistreatment of Kuwaitis, the hostages and diplomats, fired off a broadside at Saddam, saying, 'I have had it with Iraq's efforts to starve out the US Embassy in Kuwait, and its treatment of American citizens.' He also said he was still giving sanctions time to work, which suggested that he wasn't quite as fed up as he claimed.

We welcomed what we saw as Bush's belated attention to the hostage issue, but were disappointed at his preference for sanctions. He continued to work on a Security Council resolution giving the Coalition explicit permission to use force against Iraq, and this became the central diplomatic theme of the month. The need for this was more political than legal. The Allies were already authorized under international law to strike Iraq, but Bush needed both to undercut his anti-war opponents in Congress, and to give the military an unassailable mandate. The Americans were also working against the clock. The Presidency of the Security Council would pass on 1 December from them to Yemen, one of Iraq's few sympathisers. If the 'use-of-force' resolution were not passed by the month's end, the Yemenis might stall it until the New Year.

On 3 November, US Secretary of State James Baker started a gruelling three-week twelve-country tour to line up support for the resolution. However, when he asked the Kuwaitis for financial assistance into 1991, we feared that war was many months away. The Kuwaitis obliged, but were not the only ones impatient for action. When Baker spoke to troops in Saudi Arabia, he was told: 'This is a waste. Let's go do something, or go!'

In Iraq, Saddam was sincere about his 31 October offer to allow Christmas family visits for the hostages. From early November, most Human Shields in Iraq were allowed to call home, some on the condition that they invited their wives for Christmas. When they spoke to them, several men found that the local Iraqi Embassy had already contacted them about the Christmas visits.

Those in the four camps in Kuwait were not given calls home, perhaps because all international circuits from Kuwait were cut. Suddenly, being in camps in Iraq rather than in hiding or in a camp in Kuwait was an advantage of sorts as those in Iraq could talk directly to their families, instead of merely receiving brief radio messages every few days on the BBC or VOA.

The phone calls were generally a great relief. The hostages and their families had not spoken since the women's evacuations two months earlier, some even before that. Most men made it clear surreptitiously that they had no wish whatsoever for their wives to accept Saddam's Yuletide hospitality. The phone calls were also a mixed blessing. Through them, the families learned just how difficult life was for the men, particularly psychologically. Many of the men felt that not enough was being done at home to secure their release, and pleaded with their wives to keep their plight in the public eye.

The Iraqis also told the hostages they would be able to send mail. Letters which had been held back by them until then poured into the camps. Some men received dozens in one day.

At the same time, Saddam tried to play his German and Japanese cards. With Willy Brandt on his way and Yasuhiro Nakasone in Baghdad, he announced on 4 November that all hostages would be freed if either Germany or Japan and one of three named permanent members of the UN Security Council, France, China or the USSR, stated that they were opposed to military action. Saddam was trying to split the US and Britain from the rest of the world, and looking for a veto, or at least a pre-empting of the agenda, on the use-of-force resolution. The message was clear. Brandt and Nakasone could have everyone if such guarantees were forthcoming. No one took the bait.

The Kuwait Resistance suffered three of its most grievous losses in early November. Asrar Al-Qabandi, the young woman who was one of its most active members, was arrested around lunchtime on 4 November at a checkpoint in Mishref. She had just returned through the desert to Kuwait from her final trip to Saudi Arabia. She suspected that her false identity had been compromised, and had visited her uncle Abdullah to borrow the ID papers of his daughter, who was about her age. It was the last time he saw her alive.

That night, as curfew fell at 11.00 p.m., 20 *Mukhabarat* men raided her family home, arresting her elderly father Mohammed, her uncle Abdullah, and brother Ghassan. They searched the house, taking great interest in a photo of Asrar's eldest sister, Anwar. 'Where is this girl?' they asked the next sister, Iqbal. Fortunately for Anwar, she was out of Kuwait. The Iraqis took the men and left the women and kids, telling Iqbal to stay. Iqbal had no intention of doing so, and moved them all out to different houses at first light.

Asrar's father was questioned in front of his daughter, but he stuck to the cover story of not having seen her for two years. The Iraqis then played back a tape of a phone conversation between them. He knew then that his daughter was likely to die. At one stage, the Iraqis beat Asrar in front of him, throwing the diminutive girl between two large men. She rode the blows to avoid further punishment. When they threatened to rape her, she jumped up, spitting at them, yelling they were not men enough to do so. Fortunately, she had kept most of her activities secret from her father. He knew very little, and the Iraqis eventually tired of their game. Her uncle Abdullah and brother Ghassan were questioned separately, but also knew nothing.

It took two weeks for Asrar's colleagues to locate her, but all attempts to buy her out of custody failed, although her father, uncle and brother were bribed out on 29 December. The Iraqis had apparently found her by torturing the information out a captured colleague. They knew the extent of her activities, and that she had access to a satellite phone. Asrar, however, never betrayed her friends, or any of those she had been working with.

Two other important Resistance losses were Colonel Mahmoud Al-Dossari, and Mohammed Al-Fajji, a young businessman, the leaders of one of the most active military groups. Al-Fajji had extensive interests in Iraq, and knew Saddam personally. The two men were in Baghdad, en route to Turkey. They were going to meet with representatives of the Government-in-exile to co-ordinate activities in Kuwait, and had arranged a car to Kurdistan through Al-Fajji's Baghdad agent. The *Mukhabarat* had got to him first. They were stopped between Baghdad and Sammara on the morning of 7 November.

Al-Dossari and Al-Fajji were both questioned separately at length by Sabawi Ibrahim Al-Hassan, Saddam's half-brother and the Chief of General Intelligence. He was particularly interested in their activities in Iraq, and seemed more concerned that they were helping elements in Iraq plotting against the regime. He hardly seemed to care about their deeds in Kuwait.

Both men were imprisoned in Iraq for two weeks, then transferred to the *Mishatel*, an agricultural complex in Kuwait which the *Mukhabarat* were using as their main prison. There, they saw Asrar. After almost two months, during which they were brutally tortured, they were shifted back to Baghdad just before the air war. They were later sentenced to death, but were spared, perhaps through Al-Fajji's connections. Asrar would not be so fortunate.

The focus of the crisis shifted to the military on 5 November with news of the departures to the Gulf from German bases of the first of a further 200,000 US troops and 1,000 tanks – primarily the US VII Corps, virtually doubling the US commitment. That same day, more Syrian troops arrived in Saudi Arabia.

Egypt's Hosni Mubarak also sent more armour, saying 'sanctions should be given a further two to three months to work, but force should be used if they have not worked by then'. President Bush himself echoed this on 9 November, saying he hoped sanctions would work 'within a two-month period'. For us, this set a war date for January. The Amir of Kuwait spoke for most of us when he called for an immediate attack.

There was some satisfaction that the eventual use of these new forces was implicit in their deployment, tempered by disappointment that the war was at least two months away. The Allies could already whip Iraq. We did not see why Bush was delaying things.

Iraq was also suffering diplomatically. The General Committee of the UN General Assembly refused its request that an item labelling the US presence in the Gulf a threat to Arab and international peace and security be placed on the Assembly agenda. It instead labelled Iraq as the threat, and accused it of distortion, immoral acts, bad faith, and perversion of UN procedures.

In the US, the anti-war lobby was becoming more effective, but Congress - particularly the House of Representatives - was quietly behind Bush. In early November, major reserve units were called up for service after Congress quietly doubled their call-up limit to 360 days. The numbers - amounting to 12,000 by 11 November - were not large, but calling reservists from their civilian lives underlined the greatly increased likelihood of action. A further indication of American seriousness came when plans to rotate troops were cancelled. Everyone deployed would stay until the job was done.

Saddam, however, was not one to buckle under pressure. On 8 November he replaced his Army Chief of Staff, Lieutenant-General Nazir Al-Khazraji, who had reportedly opposed the invasion, with the more hardline Lieutenant-General Hussein Rashid, a Republican Guard officer. Ten days later, Iraq announced it would send another 250,000 troops to Kuwait and southern Iraq, bringing its total army strength in the theatre to 680,000. However, in a country of 18 million, most of these were reservists, who would be more trouble than use to their officers when the shooting started.

Throughout this military build-up, Saddam continued to try to split the Coalition. He had failed with the French, and had little leverage with China, so he turned up the charm on the Soviets. They, however, were rapidly losing patience with him. Foreign Minister Eduard Shevardnadze, during a break in consultations with James Baker, said that use of force could not be ruled out if diplomacy failed. His main disagreement with Baker was not if force should be used, but when, and under what limitations.

A week later, Soviet envoy Yevgeny Primakov, one of the leading proponents of a diplomatic solution, called for delaying the use-of-force resolution to allow for a final negotiating effort, but said if this failed, the UN should adopt the resolution, and military action should follow.

Chinese Foreign Minister Qain Qichen visited Saddam on 11 November after meeting Baker at Cairo Airport on the 6th, and the Kuwaiti Amir in Taif on the 8th. Significantly, this was the only visit to Baghdad by a major power's Minister during the crisis. Qain had not given his explicit support to the use-of-force resolution, but had indicated that China would not veto it if diplomacy failed. This was enough for Baker. China had too much to gain in its international rehabilitation after the 1989 Tianamen Square massacre to throw it all away for Saddam. In Baghdad, Qain related China's position to Saddam, leaving him in little doubt that he could not depend on old Cold War rivalries to save him from the resolution.

November 11th saw a last futile attempt by the Arab League to resolve the crisis peacefully. King Hassan of Morocco and King Hussein of Jordan tried to convene a summit in Casablanca but despite the support of most Arab leaders, Saddam's preconditions rendered it an impossibility. He said that no summit should be held with foreign troops in Saudi Arabia, disputed the venue, demanded linkage of the Palestinian question to Kuwait, and required that the League's earlier resolution to send troops to Saudi Arabia be rescinded. Saddam condemned the summit as a front for the US. In fact, he seemed more concerned that he would be facing a majority of the Arab world against him.

Curiously, in early November, conditions in some strategic sites improved. Apparently, the Iraqis realized if they were going to let the hostages call home, they had better provide them with something positive to say.

Those men who had been moved in October from more comfortable accommodation to the heart of sites were not returned to their earlier quarters, but their food improved, and they were allowed outside for exercise. In some sites where groups of hostages had been segregated, they were now allowed to mix. Coupled with the phone calls and getting mail out, these little changes were immensely welcome. Incredibly, in several camps, the men were even measured up for and supplied with smart grey double-breasted suits.

The changes seemed to come from the top. Several camp managers told the hostages that they had orders from Baghdad to ask them to prepare lists of whatever medicines they required. Some men were even asked to list the contents of their flats in Kuwait, and any other assets such as bank accounts and cars they may have lost. Incredibly, Saddam seemed to be considering compensating them. A consensus developed in the camps that the hostages were now an embarrassment, and that Saddam was looking for ways to release them with maximum political payback. It was a great boost to morale.

In Kuwait, the men in hiding continued to try to occupy themselves and keep their minds off their predicament. The stress and depression after three months was so great that one Briton turned himself in to the Iraqis. The smallest things could trigger heated arguments, even among close friends.

Once food supplies had been assured, the main requirement was to maintain morale. The British in particular were adept at the black humour born of adversity. One lasting example of this came from Britons Ray Washer and Ian Smith, two of the men held in the Kuwait University residential complex. They used a salvaged IBM PC to produce a double-sided foolscap newsletter entitled *The Hostage Herald*, or *Q8. The Long Wait*. When Danish minder Lise Hertz and New Zealander Robin Van Kempen made their first delivery of food to them on 30 October, Ray gave them the first few of an eventual nine issues before his group were taken to Baghdad in late November.

The *Herald* poked cynical, sarcastic fun at the situation, the ineptitude of the Iraqi guards, the poor quality of the food, the grovellers, almost everything. The Classified Ads carried an item for a used British Airways 747, only parked once, with increasingly low mileage for its age, in reference to BA149. The 'Top Ten' in edition four was headed by *Born Free*.

Around the same time as the *Herald* appeared on home faxes and in food deliveries to men in hiding, another group, led by a Gulf Bank computer specialist Dave Dorrington, produced *The Kuwait Invasion Times*. This only went to three weekly editions: the fourth was under preparation when the group was captured. Their specialities were anniversary announcements, Letters to the Editor, and Peanuts, Wizard of Id and B.C. cartoons modified to suit the situation. The Baghdad B.C. Dictionary gave the definition of a guest as 'A person who accepts your hospitality for as long as YOU want.'

The *Times* was even quick to pick up on topical news from home. When a British Conservative MP, Sir John Stokes, admonished hostages' relatives for 'mewling and puking' about their menfolk's plight instead of keeping a stiff upper lip, it started a kidnap fund to have Sir John snatched and brought to Kuwait to share the experience for himself. The *Times* faithfully reported that Stoke's castigation of the hostages' families had given rise to suggestions that the wives carry out a similar-sounding surgical operation on him.

A circulation war of sorts developed between the two newsletters. This was particularly difficult as copies had to be passed from group to group due to the shortage of copier toner and paper. The *Times* printed only 20 copies to go around over 600 men, and had to tell their readers to pass it on.

Two young men hiding in the Al-Muthanna Complex, David Hough and Neil Beevor, produced an inspired 32-page document entitled *The Official Expat's Guide to the 19th Province*. It was a play on the name of a series of well-known guides to Gulf countries. They did not have the luxury of desktop publishing software, a fax, or a photocopier, so it was done entirely by hand. The *Expat's Guide* excelled in sarcasm against the incompetence of the Iraqi troops and the British Embassy, and caricatures of the foibles of respective group members. Nothing was sacred. It included a 'Hotel Guide' with the Regency Palace listed as 'suitable for short-term stopovers. Advance booking unnecessary.' Lists included 'Things NOT to say at Iraqi checkpoints' ('Saddam WHO?'), how to identify Iraqi Army ranks (The colonel is the one in the looted Mercedes with no wheels; the private is the one with the wheels), and two poems entitled *The Saddamic Verses* and *More Saddamic Verses*. A section on *Famous Quotes From The Invasion* included a Kuwaiti border guard to his mate while observing the Iraqi Army build-up on 1 August: 'Go on, give them the finger...they can't do anything'; a Kuwaiti in bed early on the morning of 2 August saying to his wife as gunfire woke her, 'Go back to sleep, dear. Its probably just the kids,' and an American later on the same day promising, 'Don't worry, guys. George will get us out of here in a day or two.'

The humour was not confined to paper. Two men in hiding together, Briton Nick Cate and German Ottmar Lange made a series of home-video skits entitled ITV (Invasion Television) and INN (Invasion Network News). They dressed up as CNN anchormen, with the requisite affectations, and presented their news on *The Station of the Invaded Nation*. Special features included *Hostages on Holiday* with activities to keep one's mind and body occupied, and a tongue-in-cheek cookery lesson on how to catch locusts and turn them into tasty sandwiches. They even had a weather report with isobars showing a depression moving in from the north and settling on the southern Kuwaiti border (the Iraqi Army), and a high pressure system moving up from the south (the Allies), causing dust and unstable conditions (war) when they met.

Although the humour brought some relief to the tedium, there were far less pleasant moments. The pick-ups continued, in smaller numbers, but danger often came from looters, mainly local Palestinians. Several groups of men had to watch helplessly as their cars were taken from in front of their houses. They could not go out and stop the thieves for fear of being incarcerated.

Strangely, whenever people reported looters, the local Iraqi police were unusually diligent in pursuing them, and even posted guards on certain buildings. A number of men in hiding credited the Iraqi police with unwittingly protecting them when they posted guards around their residential buildings to deter looters, but did not search the buildings.

On one occasion, three Iraqi soldiers were caught looting by the Iraqi police at the Pearl Marzouk residential building in Salmiya. Several days later, they were taken to a seaside location nearby, and joined by three other Iraqi prisoners. The Iraqi authorities forced everyone from the surrounding streets to gather around and watch. All six men were shot by firing squad, and then given the *coup de grace* by an officer. The event was witnessed and photographed by a number of horrified Danes in the building. This spectacle was repeated in an identical pattern in several locations around Kuwait.

However, other Iraqis seemed to loot with impunity. In fact, the looting of the most valuable items was official. The Kuwait National Museum's collection was trucked to the Baghdad Museum, minus a few very valuable gems which were probably pocketed by soldiers. Kuwait Airways Corporation's aircraft caught on the ground had been flown out to Basra. All educational, scientific and medical institutions in Kuwait were placed under the administration of the respective Iraqi Ministries, who simply relocated property to their less well-equipped facilities in Iraq. Even blackboards and chalk were taken. Casual looters without Ba'ath Party sanction were dealt with severely, while those with power lined their pockets.

Tragically, the Iraqi Army were not the only people who killed looters. During November, a Palestinian with a pistol entered a villa in Mishref where four Americans and a Briton were hiding. Two of the Americans were a father and his adult son, the householder. The son, a Vietnam veteran, feared for his father's life, and ambushed the looter with a machete, killing him. The Resistance helped him to dispose of the body, but it was a very unpleasant affair. This, fortunately, was the only known incident of its type.

Lise Hertz's food deliveries to the Kuwait University hostages were the most significant contacts between the Hostage Support Group and people in the Kuwait camps, but not the only one. During early November, a few letters from the UK came through the mail system for men who were not on our database. Ambassador Michael Weston told us they were Human Shields in IBI.

Garry Burns, a British warden with a Canadian passport, and I decided to try to deliver the letters, so drove down to the camp, parking a little distance away at a nearby fish market for a few minutes to reconnoiter. We could see no military presence around the camp, so drove slowly down the access road to its outer gate. We did not try to hide. If anyone saw us, we did not want them to think we were up to no good. A small group of soldiers were brewing tea just off the road, but they paid us scant attention. We stopped at the unguarded and locked gate, and waited until we were noticed. It was better act openly rather than risk getting shot. Within minutes, the tea-drinkers caught up with us by foot, having realised that a couple of Westerners should not be there. They were more embarrassed than aggressive. It would have been incredibly easy for Allied Special Forces to have got into the camp and got the hostages out.

While we were showing these troops our identification, a soldier came to the gate from inside the camp. His poor English matched our poor Arabic, so he asked us to come inside, but to leave the car outside. We were escorted to a hut near the inner camp gate, but still outside the camp itself. Inside, an Iraqi in an officer's uniform, but without any badges of rank, introduced himself in fluent English as the doctor in charge of the camp. He seemed at a loss as to how to handle us, so, as Arab hospitality demands, sat us down and made tea.

We told him we had mail for the men in the camp. He asked how we had got it, and how we knew the men were there. We lied that we had got the letters from the British Embassy in Baghdad, and they had told us where to find the men. He seemed satisfied, and took our details. By now, we were worried. We were inside a hostage camp, and no one else knew we were there. We realised that we should have told someone what we were up to.

After some small talk, the doctor said he would get what he called the 'Chief Guest Representative'. A lone, sunburnt Briton, clad only in shorts, soon arrived. He his eyes widened when he saw us. 'British!' he exclaimed.

Garry and I were horrified. If the Iraqis thought we were British, then we would join the hostages. 'He's Australian; I'm Canadian!' said Garry. 'He's Canadian; I'm Australian!' I said, as we pointed meaningfully at each other.

The man was George Parris, a BA149 cabin crew member. The doctor asked him to sit down, but would not let us give the mail to George directly, or allow him to tell us who else was in the camp. He was in fine shape, but we nevertheless asked him if there was anything he needed. The doctor seemed to take offence at this as if we were suggesting he was not doing his job. We were unwelcome, so took our leave, and were walked back to the car. As we were leaving, the doctor suggested it would not be a good idea to come back.

We left, relieved not to be detained, and that everything had been so easy. It was a little victory, and we were delighted to have got the mail in to the men. British Ambassador Michael Weston was similarly impressed.

A week or so later, more mail came in for the men at IBI, so I went there again with another Australian, Tony Hordern. This time, the Iraqis were ready. We did not get beyond the fish market. The doctor came out to us, with some of the soldiers. They were not overtly threatening, but we had to stay there until 'some officer' came. We had to wait for three hours in the open while someone went to get this man. The doctor and his men were as polite as they could be, even offering us tea, but the temperature dropped as night fell, and a cold breeze came in from the Gulf. The men were obviously foregoing their evening meal to be there. It looked serious. There was a little talk. The doctor was circumspect about where he came from, but told us of his service during the Iran-Iraq War, stressing that as an Iraqi Army doctor, he had also treated wounded Iranians. All our suggestions that we had to get home for dinner, or before curfew, were politely but firmly turned down. We were prisoners at least until the man with the authority arrived.

Eventually, a pick-up drove up with a short, broad man who commanded attention by his mere presence. Everything about him was as tough as nails. I will never forget his eyes. They were as hard and as cold as a shark's. His handshake was like iron. He questioned us through the doctor, who addressed him respectfully as *Mumtaza*, or 'Excellency'. We later learned that this was his rank, the most senior rank of a non-commissioned or warrant officer.

The *Mumtaza* asked us the same questions the doctor had earlier, and copied down all our personal and vehicle details into a school exercise book. It was obvious that the doctor had been told to summon him if we came again, and we should not have been allowed to get so close to the camp earlier. We were eventually dismissed, much to our relief, but the doctor would not even take the letters. This time the warning was more explicit. We should not come again. It was not just a matter of the hostages, but he would get into serious trouble himself. He seemed terrified of the *Mumtaza*; I shared his fear. The *Mumtaza* looked as if he would enjoy killing someone, and had done so.

Strange rumours of an Iraqi civilian withdrawal began to circulate around mid-November. Iraqi and Jordanian businessmen who had been crowding the Kuwaiti hotels were told to leave by the 20th. Apparently, so many Iraqis had taken their savings out from under their beds to share in the bonanza from the looting of Kuwait that it was causing inflation in Iraq. From then on, anyone entering Kuwait from Iraq's 'other provinces' had to prove that they lived there, or that they were on official Iraqi Government business.

A particularly memorable day for many of those in hiding was 16 November when Colonel Bruce Duncan, whose teenage son Alex had been killed in October on his way to freedom with Sir Edward Heath, sent a very moving message on *Gulf Link*. This brought down to earth many men who were bemoaning their predicament. When they compared their situation to the suffering of Duncan and his bereaved family, and the quiet dignity and courage with which he spoke, the complaints receded.

In the meantime, Saddam was searching frantically for ways to undercut the Coalition. Leading UK and US newspapers had rediscovered the probable extent of his nuclear weapons programme, and were recalling Israel's 1981 bombing of Iraq's Osirak nuclear reactor. He seemed to fear that the Allies might go to war just to wreck his nuclear programme, even without his chemical and far more secret biological weapons programmes. This issue above all was in the West's interests: far more important than liberating Kuwait.

The Iraqis therefore invited the International Atomic Energy Agency (IAEA) to Iraq to verify that their small stock of highly enriched uranium reactor fuel had not been made into nuclear weapons. The inspection results would be announced on the eve of the UN vote on the use-of-force resolution; Iraq had not diverted the fuel to weapons. It took some of the urgency out of the crisis, but matters had gone too far already, and there were no guarantees that Iraq did not have another, secret programme.

During the IAEA inspections, American, British and Israeli intelligence leaked their conclusions that Iraq's nuclear weapons capacity could enable it to begin manufacturing and using nuclear missiles and bombs within less than ten years. These assessments increased the Coalition's resolve to take this opportunity to trounce Saddam. If they did not take out his nuclear weapons programme now, they might be facing a nuclear war with him before the turn of the Century. Indeed, after the defeat of Iraq in 1991, these assessments were proved partially right. UN inspectors discovered a secret Manhattan Project level nuclear programme, far more advanced than the spies had concluded, but with technical bottlenecks that could have been overcome by the late 1990s. The IAEA was found to have been the victim of a massive deception.

Saddam's increasing isolation gave rise to an announcement on 16 November that all hostages could leave if Bush promised he would not attack. When no such assurance was forthcoming, Iraq said on the 18th that all 'guests' would be released in batches over three months, starting from Christmas, 'unless', as Saddam put it, 'some other event occurred to disturb the climate of peace.'

This cunning ploy was the work of Tareq Aziz. It meant that the hostages would be retained over the best time of year for the Allies to attack. By April, the weather would be warm and the Allies would run into the Muslim holy month of Ramadan. The offer was also timed to coincide with the meeting in Paris of Bush, Gorbachev and European Heads of Government at a Conference on Security and Co-operation in Europe (CSCE) summit.

The ploy was transparent, and was dismissed. Saddam was playing for time. He needed to impose such a heavy cost on the Coalition in maintaining the huge force in Saudi Arabia that it would eventually have to be reduced. His strategy had potential. On several occasions, Operation Desert Shield would have been bankrupt had the Japanese not come to the rescue.

There was mixed joy in Kuwait and Iraq at this announcement. It placed a time limit on the ordeal, and was the first comprehensive announcement to contemplate the release of all hostages. But 25 March, 1991 was 18 weeks away. It had been difficult enough surviving so far.

Saddam was now confident that there would be no attack until at least January 1991. Not only would the Allied reinforcements need time to deploy, but the women now crowding Jordanian and Iraqi missions in Europe, the US and Japan applying for visas for the Christmas visits would deter any attack until they had left Iraq. Saddam also boosted the case of the West's anti-war lobby that there was no point going to war while the hostages were being released, as it meant that some would die for the sake of a mere 90-day delay. The peaceniks seemed not to realize that the delay would mean a far heavier toll among the Kuwaitis from Iraqi atrocities, and among Allied troops.

More ominously, Saddam needed time to complete his nuclear weapons, to make the consequences of any attack too fearful to contemplate. He could not have done so in the months he was trying to buy, but no one could guarantee this. The bluff of possibly having the Bomb was almost as useful having it.

Despite the previous general US-Soviet agreement, major differences showed up at the CSCE summit. Gorbachev, under domestic pressure, preferred to delay war. Even after two hours of discussions, Bush failed to get his agreement on the use-of-force resolution. The best he got was Gorbachev's undertaking to ensure that Security Council deliberations continued.

The Europeans themselves were divided, but not critically. At a pre-summit meeting with Bush, German Chancellor Helmut Kohl had referred repeatedly to the idea of conducting negotiations with Saddam. Thatcher, for her part, said quite bluntly that 'military force would have to be used' if Saddam did not withdraw. Britain then committed a further 14,000 troops, bringing her ground forces up to a full armoured division, with more aircraft.

However, James Baker's shuttle was bearing fruit. By the time Bush was in Paris, Ethiopia, Ivory Coast and Zaire, all non-permanent members of the

Security Council, had told Baker that they would support the use-of-force resolution. Together with the UK, France and Canada, Baker now had seven of the nine votes needed to carry the day, barring a Soviet or Chinese veto.

Despite his offer to release all hostages over three months from Christmas, Saddam seemed to have realized that they had already outlived their usefulness. With the Allied reinforcements in Saudi Arabia, his only option was to go on the peace offensive on the one hand, and dig in on the other.

On 20 November, the day Saddam committed another 250,000 troops to Kuwait, Iraq announced the release of all the 180 remaining Germans, 44 of whom were at strategic sites, and seven of whom were still hiding in Kuwait. Ostensibly, this was in appreciation of an anti-war remark which Kohl was heard to have made at the CSCE summit. Two days after the German release, 83 Europeans, including 35 British, were allowed to leave with Jean-Marie Le Pen. A Swiss delegation also took out 36, mainly Swiss, but including two British. The 234 Western employees at the Ibn Al-Bitr hospital were told that they could leave. The releases were gathering such pace that they overlapped. The Germans released with Le Pen went both as part of his quota, and as part of the general German release. However, except for the Germans and four of the 37 Britons, none of these people were from the camps.

In Kuwait, this sharper focus on the Americans and British caused further consternation among many of those still in hiding. They foresaw a time when the free-Westerners were allowed to leave, and could not be blamed for going. Hundreds of men were afraid that when their food ran out in the New Year, with no one around to resupply them, they would have to give themselves up to the Iraqis on the eve of a war. It was a difficult situation for the free nationals. Few of us wanted to be faced with the choice of having to go or stay. It had been an easy decision for the New Zealanders earlier in November. Then, there were still enough other free-nationals and Kuwaitis in Kuwait to service those in hiding. The decision would be more stark next time around.

Thursday, 22 November was the US holiday of Thanksgiving. In preparation for this, the minders in Kuwait tried to stock up groups in hiding, especially Americans, with turkeys, pumpkins, corn, beer and whisky.

The turkeys were relatively easy. The sanctions were pitifully ineffectual. The Kuwaitis made a point of bringing in scores of birds. The Americans in hiding were deeply touched that the Kuwaitis would do so much to help them maintain their traditions. As a result, most Americans ended up with at least a duck or chicken. Some even had a second one in the freezer for Christmas.

Even the Iraqis in charge of the Human Shields entered into the spirit, pooling several groups of hostages in a model camp and putting on a good turkey dinner with a great deal of hard liquor and beer, and a band. Iraqi TV was on hand to film the proceedings. The Iraqis failed to appreciate the irony that most of those who were being filmed were British, to whom the occasion was little more than the opportunity for a good meal and plenty of alcohol.

This was repeated at several sites in Iraq, but not in the camps in Kuwait. In some cases, the Iraqis made a genuine effort, without the propaganda payback.

A number of men gained the impression that the camp managers had arranged the party on their own initiative, and paid for it themselves. One group was even invited after dinner to a local Kurdish wedding.

Several hundred kilometres to the south, George Bush and his wife joined US troops in the Saudi desert for their festivities, after meeting King Fahd and the Kuwaiti Amir the previous day. Meantime, hard-working James Baker was in Yemen, trying to garner its support, or at least its acquiescence, as one of the non-permanent Security Council members, for the use-of-force resolution.

As far as many of the Americans in Kuwait and Iraq were concerned, the biggest turkey on TV that day was their own President, tagged by many Americans in hiding as 'Mush Bush'. They were galled to see him visiting the greatest US military force assembled in recent times, and not ejecting the rag-tag Iraqi Army from Kuwait. To them, he was giving Saddam time to build defences which would ultimately cause more Allied casualties. The men in Kuwait could see the Iraqis digging in for street fighting. Positions that had merely been trenches and sandbags in October were now concrete bunkers with anti-tank weapons and mortar pits. Buildings in strategic locations were fortified by replacing windows with concrete breeze blocks, with firing ports. One Iraqi unit which only weeks previously had been bivouaced in an open field north of the airport was now dug in so deep that the men lived almost totally underground. They were well and truly preparing for a long stay.

Despite their morale problems, it was obvious that the Iraqis had got their supply system working. When the weather turned cool, they appeared in field jackets, balaclavas, and gloves. They looked healthy and well-fed, if not motivated. No one doubted the outcome of the battle, but the longer Bush waited, the greater the price of liberation would be in Allied lives.

The media with Bush in Saudi Arabia had a field day, interviewing US soldiers in the desert and sending their Thanksgiving messages home. One story, probably apocryphal, went around Kuwait saying that a Marine had told the cameras he thought he had been sent to Saudi to 'kick ass and take names', but was just 'sitting on his ass, and giving his name to CNN'.

The Iraqis themselves had cause for thanksgiving on that day when British Prime Minister Margaret Thatcher resigned.

Although Britain was a secondary power, Mrs Thatcher was widely seen by many as the driving force behind the Coalition. She had an effect far beyond the potential of the British military. As leader of the country that had created Iraq, she was indeed more of a nemesis to Saddam than George Bush.

The Iraqis were so jubilant at Thatcher's fall that they even claimed credit for it. Although many of the British hostages were disappointed at her demise, there was a quiet pride that their system of government - unlike Iraq's - allowed continuity of her stance without her as an individual being in power. There was some concern that John Major's less forceful style would result in a softening of British policy, but this was soon dispelled.

The hostage humour machine in Kuwait was particularly active that day. The most memorable rumour doing the rounds was that Thatcher's resignation was a conspiracy agreed with Washington. She would step down with her Cabinet and the country so firmly behind the cause that her absence would make no difference. She would then take over the US Presidency from George Bush, because 'if he didn't have the balls for the job, then she certainly did'.

That night, I had one of my more enlightening meetings with an Iraqi officer. I was on my way home, close to curfew, after trying to deliver a turkey and some alcohol to my previous group in the Al-Muthanna, when I was stopped at a checkpoint by a young Iraqi lieutenant. This was unusual as officers seldom manned checkpoints. The search of the car was unusually thorough.

The lieutenant's main problem was a school notebook I was using for coded shopping lists of those in hiding. It had a picture of the Kuwaiti Amir on the back cover. Annoyed at the inconvenience, I told him if he did not like it, then that was his problem, not mine. He could tear off the cover if he wanted.

I immediately regretted the outburst, and tensed for the response, but his attitude suddenly changed. He invited me to join him for tea at a little fire in the lee of an adjacent flyover. He was an intelligent man, with excellent English. I was terrified sitting there drinking tea with Iraqi troops as the Resistance often hit checkpoints at night, but I was in no position to refuse.

The lieutenant knew about Mrs Thatcher's fall earlier that afternoon. He was delighted. I was impressed. I tried to explain to him that it would make no difference. He seemed to appreciate the chance to discuss an opposing view with someone who would not report back to the *Mukhabarat,* but stuck firmly to the Iraqi line. We touched on the sanctions, and how Iraq could not sell its oil or import its needs. He gave the standard line that Iraq was a powerful country that could grow all its own food. Iraq's Army, he said, could survive on dates from Basra, and water from its two rivers. They didn't need foreign food. Nevertheless, he was obviously unhappy with his country's isolation.

The political discussions were getting nowhere, so I asked him about his family. He asked me how old I was. 'Thirty,' I said. He said he was the same age, also unmarried. I asked him why, as Arab men generally marry young.

'John,' he said, taking a sip of tea, and looking me straight in the eye, 'I was taken from University at 20 to fight Iran. I have been in the Army since then. I am an engineer by education, but have never had a chance to work at it. I have no career but the Army, and that does not pay enough to allow marriage.' He sighed, before going on. . . 'Yesterday the Iranians may have killed me; tomorrow it might be America. If we leave here, our President may send me to be killed by Israel. I do not want to leave a widow and orphans, or to bring children into a world such as this. Your people have been 'our guests' for a few weeks. In Iraq, we have been hostages for a generation.'

He tossed the dregs of his tea away with a scowl, looked briefly around him, and suddenly the mask of the professional Iraqi officer was back on his face. 'Curfew is soon. You better get home. The officer at the next checkpoint may not be as nice as I am,' he said, smiling. I rose to shake his hand.

'I hope you come out of this alive,' I said, meaning it.

'*Inshallah!* (God willing), he said, tightening his grip momentarily.

Upon leaving Saudi Arabia after Thanksgiving, President Bush met Hosni Mubarak in Cairo, and then Hafez Al-Assad in Geneva. It was a measure of the depth of the crisis that Bush was prepared to meet Al-Assad, with Syria still on the State Department list of countries that sponsored terrorism.

More importantly, it seemed that President Gorbachev was losing patience with Saddam, saying that the UN Security Council should meet urgently to discuss implementing its resolutions, and to see what other steps could be taken to get Iraq out of Kuwait, and the hostages released. Gorbachev met with Tareq Aziz yet again in Moscow, warning him of a tough UN resolution if Iraq did not comply. In uncharacteristically angry remarks, he charged for the first time that some 3,000 Soviets were being prevented from leaving, and demanded their release. With days to go before the UN use-of-force vote, the US saw these remarks as suggesting that Gorbachev would go along with it.

Two days after Thanksgiving, a large group of mainly British women who had arrived in Baghdad on 9 November met Saddam. Their men had been brought in from the camps or from the Baghdad hotels to join them.

The group was led by Carol Cox and Dorothy Goodwin, the British lady whose husband had tried to sneak out in a women and children's evacuation convoy in September, disguised as a woman. Originally, the group comprised just the two of them. Mrs Cox had gone on TV in late October saying she would go back to Baghdad, and Mrs Goodwin had teamed up with her. When they went to the Iraqi Embassy in London to get visas, the Ambassador hinted they would stand more chance of success if they went as a larger group.

The British women were not without their own internal problems. One of them, Mrs Herbert, brought her cute little daughter, Abigail, with her. Several of the others objected to this, aware of the August incident where Saddam had let out BLT WO2 Jerry Blears because of his daughter Rachel's birthday, but had kept the other men. They felt that Abigail might get her father Patrick released at the expense of their men.

Mrs Cox was the group leader, but Goodwin was a formidable personality who virtually forced the Iraqis to deal with her alone. However, she had not counted on Saddam being used to having his orders obeyed to the letter. When they were leaving the hotel to meet him, Goodwin refused to go if little Abigail accompanied them. The Iraqi escorts tried to dissuade her but she prevailed, much to Mrs Herbert's distress. However, when they arrived, Saddam asked for Abigail, and sent for her before he would receive them.

Ken and Magda Hoyle, the elderly couple who had been captured from my apartment complex in October, were also there. Their daughter, Gina, was with the group, so they joined the dozen hostages who also met Saddam.

After shaking hands with Saddam, and listening to a long diatribe on the integrity of Iraq's position, the injustice of the sanctions, and the plight of the Palestinians, Saddam announced that they could all leave Iraq. The Hoyles' wedding anniversary was the following day. It was the best present they could have hoped for. On 28 November they left for Amman.

On the same day this group met Saddam, 215 foreign workers on contract with Dutch dredging companies working for the Iraqis in the Shatt Al-Arab waterway were allowed out. Most of the 300 Italians were freed, thirty Irish nurses, ten Greeks and all of the 56 Swedes were allowed to go. On 28 November, Saddam asked his parliament to release the 32 Belgians. Perhaps more importantly, in an effort to obtain Moscow's veto for the UN war resolution then being debated, Iraq finally allowed out 1,000 Soviets who had been told almost three weeks earlier that they could go.

Of these hundreds of releases, only the eleven British and one American whose relatives had come out were from the strategic sites. Saddam was reaping good press throughout the world, but giving relatively little away.

On 25 November, the Iraqis moved the 64 hostages held in the four camps in Kuwait to Baghdad.

The change in attitude of some of the Iraqis at this stage was enlightening. Just before the move, I had been driving near IBI with another Australian, Peter Byrnes, after visiting two British men living in a shack atop a nearby office building. We passed a roundabout where we saw the Iraqi Army doctor from IBI talking to a few Military Policemen. He recognized me, and indicated that he wanted to talk, out of sight of the MPs. We met him later, near the fish market. He was, he told us, totally fed up with his task, and sympathized with the hostages. They were innocent people held unnecessarily. If we had mail to pass to them, he would be happy to do oblige.

We did not know whether to believe the doctor, or whether the *Mukhabarat* or the cold-eyed *Mumtaza* had set him up to draw us in. We decided that it was best to play safe, and not trust him, but his outrage seemed genuine. We said that we could give him some money or food for the people, but he said he had enough. It was his duty to take care of them properly.

We never saw the doctor again, but I am now convinced that he was genuine. We later learned that the men in the camp had the same impression. The doctor put his own safety on the line for a principle, for people to whom he owed no obligation, and for a rare chance to maintain what was left of his professional dignity and integrity.

On the morning of the 25th, two coaches with the people from the four sites left Kuwait for the Mansour Melia. A truck accompanied them with their remaining personal effects, including beer supplies rescued from their flats and from the IBI brewing room. After calling at the first two sites, the buses stopped at the Regency Palace where the seven released Germans and 11 other Britons, including the *Kuwait Invasion Times* publishers, were being transferred a flight to Baghdad, but the two groups were denied any contact.

Around this time, the Hostage Support Group in Kuwait found it needed to go to Baghdad to liaise directly with the embassies about support for those in hiding. There were several reasons for this.

First, the diplomats in Baghdad did not yet know us face-to-face. In mid-November, Americans hiding in Kuwait were told by their embassy that they might only be able to send messages for another two or three weeks. The Embassy was having problems with its generators. The British had only a radio voice link via Abu Dhabi, which could be monitored. We needed to set up our own links with Baghdad before the existing ones failed entirely.

Secondly, we were concerned that there would be insufficient resources to maintain those in hiding until liberation. It was still uncertain whether a war deadline would be imposed. We might still have to wait out sanctions. At this stage, the earliest date we had to plan for release was 25 March, 1991, four months away. Everyone expected the people in hiding, especially the Americans and British, to be the last out if Saddam kept his word to release people over the three months from Christmas. Although we did have some funds from various sources in Kuwait, including from the Resistance, these would not last long. The Baghdad embassies were supporting people in the camps and in Baghdad where possible with food and money. We felt our men deserved at least the same, especially as they were still out of Iraqi custody.

Thirdly, the traffic of free-nationals between Baghdad and Kuwait was now largely one way as a result of the arrival of more grovellers, and various releases. This was affecting our mail system. It was increasingly difficult to find people to carry mail back to Kuwait. There were also problems with collecting the mail in the countries of origin. We wanted to sort this out.

A number of other pressing matters needed personal attention. The embassies in Baghdad were not in a position to search out alternative nationalities for their people without compromising their own positions. As civilians, we could do so without fear of the consequences. We had asked some of the men in hiding to consider what alternate passports they might legally be entitled to. We would determine the paperwork requirements from the respective embassies, and take whatever we could north on the next trip.

Finally, we needed to brief the Baghdad embassies on precisely what we could and could not do if it came to exfiltrating people. I was scheduled by the group to make the first trip, followed a week later by Dr Garry Burns.

The first trip was a mixed success, especially with the British. The Americans could not have been more helpful. Our main US contact was Emil Skodon. He was astounded at what we could do, and how we could help a rescue mission, and took careful note of our capabilities and limitations. We later learned that plans had been laid for a rescue, but for security Skodon did not know details. Nevertheless, he could pass our information along.

When it came to financial support, Skodon gave us all the ready cash he had at the time, only ID500, but promised ten thousand the following week. He offered embassy transport to take us to other embassies where we were to pursue alternative identities for Americans, but we declined as this might draw unwelcome attention from the *Mukhabarat*. He gave us open access to the Embassy's international phones so that we could call relatives of those in hiding in Kuwait, wherever they might be, free of charge.

The British, with several exceptions, were not so accommodating. Three of the eight diplomats who had relocated from Kuwait, led by First Secretary Tony Milson, had responsibility for keeping track of and assisting both the men in camps and those in Kuwait. They worked from the office of the now expelled Defence Attaché. They were understandably preoccupied with the 350 men at the sites and the hundreds of other British in Baghdad. Until we visited, they seemed to think that there was very little that they could do for the men in hiding in Kuwait.

For the most part, the Embassy seemed to us to consider the Kuwait crisis as an interruption to its normal functions. This criticism was patently unfair, but the atmosphere was so tense that we lashed out at anything. A senior UK diplomat later explained to me that the embassy had insufficient staff to handle both major issues of the men hiding in Kuwait, and in the camps. The work involved in getting Red Crescent parcels to the Human Shields and lists for the grovellers was enormous, and the Iraqis were being obstructive.

Our first problem was funds. British civilians with freedom of movement in Baghdad, but without employers to support them, could claim £250 per month as reasonable living expenses, or about ID2,000 on the black market. This was ten times what was required to support a man in Kuwait for a month.

I was told that there were three main sources of financial support for the 400 British men hiding in Kuwait, all of which would have to come from the UK. First, employers could deposit funds with the FCO in London, to be transferred to the Embassy in Baghdad, who could then pass them on to authorized people for carriage to Kuwait. Relatives or friends could do the same thing. Finally, British Airways could be approached to help those of its passengers and crew still in Kuwait in the same manner as it was helping those free-national passengers who had gone to Baghdad. However, it was now three months into the crisis, and no one had thought to activate these sources. Apparently, although the Embassy knew that we were coming, no one had even called BA in Baghdad to have their representative meet us.

I could hardly believe this. The FCO knew that those in Kuwait worked mainly for Kuwaiti firms whose funds outside Kuwait were largely frozen. As for relatives, the men in Kuwait were for the most part their families' breadwinners. Both avenues were completely impractical for all but a few men. They simply did not seem to appreciate the situation. There was a low-level war in Kuwait, hundreds of their nationals were in hiding, and no one of any authority seemed to have given serious consideration to how they could be helped. It was as if they did not exist. We did not require a great deal of money per man, perhaps about US$50 a month. This was half the cost of a Baghdad hotel room for a single day.

I almost got into an argument with the British diplomats. They were as sympathetic as possible, but severely constrained by their bureaucracy. All three were personally embarrassed that they could not do more.

Tony Milson suggested that the British in hiding apply for assistance under the 'Distressed British Subjects', or DBS, scheme. This was an emergency fund which British consulates abroad can draw on to lend small amounts to Britons who find themselves short of funds in extreme emergencies as a result of being robbed, or losing their passports. It was designed to allow vacationers to tide themselves over until they could have funds sent from home. The usual advance was US$50. The diplomats told me, with perfectly straight faces, that the situation in Kuwait would qualify as an extreme emergency.

I jumped at this. US$50 was ID225, a lot of money in Kuwait, and even more if pooled and used efficiently. But there was a snag. Each person who needed the funds had to write a letter of application, which meant me going back to Kuwait and collecting the letters in time for the following week's trip. It was not possible to advance the funds to me. As I would return to Kuwait only a few days before the next trip, it was going to be difficult to generate much money from this source until perhaps the third trip. Nevertheless, it was a start.

When I later reported the meeting to the British Consul in Kuwait, Larry Banks, he held out little hope of getting significant DBS funds out of a worldwide budget of only £100,000. It was unbelievable. We were in a war situation, hundreds of Britons had been in hiding for months, and we were still talking about consular budgets as if we were careless tourists.

Telephone calls were another problem. Many of those in hiding had asked us to call their wives in the UK. The Embassy allowed us to use their lines, but we had to pay for the calls from our meagre funds. Incredibly, the Iraqis were now paying for daily phone calls by Human Shields, but unlike the Americans, the British could not finance 20 calls for a few men in hiding.

At this point, British Ambassador Harold 'Hookey' Walker, walked in. It was not an opportune moment for His Excellency to arrive, given my increasing frustration with the perceived lack of support for his nationals in Kuwait. I was introduced as 'JL'. All the messages from the Embassy in Kuwait which referred to our group used only initials for brevity, if not security. He welcomed me to Baghdad, but assumed that I was staying, or awaiting release with a groveller. He did not understand why I was returning to Kuwait.

'Why?' he asked. 'It's so much more comfortable here in Baghdad.'

'Because, Sir,' I said, 'there are 400 of your people still down there in Kuwait in hiding, plus the Americans. There are barely two dozen of us available to move around and support them, and bugger-all official support for them from Baghdad. In effect, if we all move up here to what you see as safety and comfort, we will be abandoning your people in Kuwait, and we'll be 600 km behind enemy lines when the war stops on the Kuwait-Iraq border.'

The Ambassador retained his composure admirably. He was obviously used to angry Westerners. To his great credit, he took our concerns to heart. Proposals were put to London and funding requested. We still had to pay for the phone calls that week but the following week the diplomats placed the calls officially, so they were free as far as we were concerned. More importantly, by the time Garry Burns arrived the following week, they had the DBS money ready for any application letters he had, and paid him US$500 which covered his airfare, taxis, two nights in the Sheraton, and left US$200, or ID900, for the pool of funds in Kuwait.

Not all our dealings with the British were difficult. After my session with Walker and the three ex-Kuwait diplomats, I was taken to see a bright young diplomat, also from the Embassy in Kuwait. He was in charge of the military and intelligence aspects, and I was to brief him on the situation in Kuwait. We walked outside to talk, in the best spy movie tradition of avoiding bugs.

The quality and deployment of the Iraqi troops were generally well-known by now, but the young man seemed as surprised as the Americans to hear what we could do in terms of moving people around. I gained the impression that the

British had given far more consideration to exfiltrating people militarily than the Americans had, and that he was actively looking for help on the ground in doing so. He was unable to give me any details of what might or might not happen, but was very happy to have another string to his bow.

The second individual of note was a young lady by the name of Caroline Cross. She was only a temporary staffer, but she made every effort within her powers to help whoever she could. One of the British I was minding was being supported by an Iraqi doctor who had lived in Kuwait for many years, and could not return safely to Iraq after Kuwait was liberated. He was concerned for his family's safety after liberation as some Kuwaitis would not take kindly to Iraqis in their midst, even those who had helped. His assistance to the British was adequately documented, and his British friend had asked for an embassy letter of safe conduct for him. Miss Cross went out of her way to provide this, in Arabic and English. The doctor later credited it with saving his life on several occasions in the aftermath of liberation.

While the Hostage Support Group was visiting Baghdad, the Human Shields transferred to Baghdad from the Kuwait camps were in the Mansour Melia.

On the 27th, one of the men discovered that British MP Tony Benn, in town on his grovel mission, was due to see Saddam the next day. The hostage asked an Iraqi minder to contact Benn, to ensure that they were on his list. The Iraqi gave him the number of the Al-Rasheed where Benn was staying. A list of the people at the Mansour Melia was compiled, and Benn's assistant contacted.

That evening, Benn visited the Mansour Melia, and addressed the group in one of the restaurants. He impressed a number of the men as being very forthright, with a quick mind. With the various releases occurring that week, there was great hope that they might be going home. However, as soon as Benn left, they were told to pack. Fifteen minutes later, the first of them were taken off in a great thunderstorm to various sites to replace those released. Ominously, it was the same night that Kuwait saw its first winter rains.

I was in the British Embassy when a call came in from the Mansour Melia to say what was happening. We threw supplies of tracksuits, alcohol and sports shoes into a pick-up, and sped through the pouring rain to the hotel. The US Embassy had also been alerted, and one of their officers, Jeanette Pina, was there. Australian Ambassador Peter Lloyd and his wife Libby arrived soon afterwards because one of the men from Kuwait, Greig Pollock, was an Australian on a UK passport. Within minutes, a Western TV crew turned up.

Most of the men were still upstairs, awaiting the call to come down. They were furious. After coming to Baghdad where there seemed at least some prospect of getting out of Iraq and being able to phone home, they were now going to disappear again to unknown destinations. Some of the men were in tears at the unexpected turn of events; others were aggressive.

At the time, I still had a bundle of letters for the men who had been at IBI, so in the confusion I took an unguarded elevator to the floor the men were on. The Iraqis there were busy trying to calm them, so I simply stood outside the elevator calling out names from the envelopes, and asking one of the men to get a list of who was there, unaware that a list had already been given to Benn.

There were a number of leftover letters, presumably for the men already taken away, so I continued to call out names of people who were not there, and false names, while the list was obtained. However, the Iraqis forced me back into the elevator and back down to the lobby before I could get it.

By now, a number of the men had been taken downstairs, and were awaiting their coaches, within sight of, but separated from, their diplomats. The TV crew was prohibited from filming them, but the cameraman was an old hand. He walked around nonchalantly with his camera on his shoulder, turned on, but with his eye removed from the eyepiece as if he was merely carrying it. His game was given away when one of the hostages in a steel army helmet he had picked up in his travels noticed this, and stood up to make the 'V for Victory' sign. A battle for the tape ensued between the crew and the Iraqis. The TV crew were quick. They switched the real tape for a blank, and then put up a commendable fight for the false one. The real tape eventually got out.

There was little the diplomats could do other than press tracksuits, shoes, bottles of whisky, cigarettes, food, and Iraqi money onto the men as they passed by. The British DHM, Christopher Segar, a dapper little man in a dark suit, remonstrated vociferously with the Iraqis. He held a rolled-up umbrella he had used as protection against the rain outside, and was suppressing the urge to clout the Iraqis with it. The only piece of costume missing was a London gent's bowler hat. He was telling a visibly embarrassed Iraqi that Her Majesty's Government objected most strongly to the treatment accorded Her subjects by Iraq. The Iraqi was suggesting to Segar that he could take it up with the MFA the following day, but Segar insisted unsuccessfully that his citizens be released into his custody, or at least left where they were. Any lingering doubts I might have had about the courage and commitment of the British diplomats in Baghdad were rapidly dispelled.

The Australian Ambassador adopted a softer, more successful approach, but he had only one man to care for. He was allowed to sit quietly and talk with Greig for quite some time before he too was taken away. A number of Australians who had relocated from Kuwait were with him, and knew several of the British. One of the women, Gail Barro, was in tears at how much weight one of her friends had lost, and how he had aged. It was pitiful to see these men come so close to freedom, and then be dragged off again.

When one of the British men from IBI, Don Majors, left the Mansour Melia for a strategic site at Shuaiba Iraqi Air Force Base, near Basra, it was the last time most of his fellows saw him alive. Don was 57, with a history of heart trouble. The day after arriving at the new camp, Don and fellow-hostage Eric Watson, were boarding a bus after a jog around the camp perimeter. Suddenly Don clutched his chest in pain, and collapsed dying into Eric's arms.

Don Majors was the last of the five Western hostages to die. His death was of natural causes, but was arguably brought about by the stress. Tragically, it was only a week before he would have been released and sent home.

Inexplicably, in late November, Saddam replaced his cousin, Ali Hassan Majeed - the architect of the infamous chemical gas attack on Kurdish Halabja - as Governor of Kuwait with one Aziz Saleh Nouman.

It seemed to some that Saddam wanted to distance his inner circle from the fiasco of Kuwait. Nouman was hardly a high flyer in the Ba'athi hierarchy. He was accessible, but seemed to have little authority. When the Catholic Bishop of Kuwait went to see him on 27 November about an exit visa which had already been arranged with Saddam for the American Pastor in the US Embassy, the new Governor was not much help. He was, however, able to direct the Bishop and his priests to the appropriate officials so that they could change their Kuwaiti car licence plates and continue to move around.

Yet with every Iraqi favour, there was always a *quid pro quo*. When Nouman realised that Christian clergy were still functioning in Kuwait, they were all invited to a Christian Congress for Peace to be held in Baghdad on 3 December. Saddam had failed to mobilise the Muslim world, so was now sponsoring a Christian conference as part of his grasping at straws. To a man, the clergy refused. The priests were not going to betray Kuwait for a charade.

In Kuwait, on 27 November, the Iraqis pulled a devious trick to capture two men from inside the US Embassy compound.

One of the few categories of Western men allowed out of Iraq early were those who had been born in an Arab country, spoke Arabic, and had an Arabic name. An American of Moroccan extraction, El Maloudi Hamid, qualified on all points. He had taken refuge in the Embassy in August, and later negotiated his way out with the Iraqis. El Maloudi had gone to Baghdad, where he had agreed to remain and act as a liaison between the Iraqis and the US hostages.

He had innocently given the Iraqis the names of two other men of Arab extraction in the compound, Sergio Ado and B. George Saloom, but both men were US-born and spoke no Arabic. To the surprise of the Americans in Kuwait, an Iraqi major asked for both men by name, saying they would be released. After great discussion, the men decided that the Iraqis were sincere.

The Iraqis were supposed to collect Ado and Saloom for the flight to Baghdad at 9.00 a.m. on the 28th. Instead, they came at 11.00 a.m. on the 29th, and took them to the Regency Palace. There, they questioned them about who was in the compound, their roles and identities, who were the diplomats, how many were women, how much food, water and fuel was available, and their mental state. They also wanted to know who the various codenames used on the walkie-talkie radios referred to. The questioning was without undue pressure. It certainly did not get physical. The men gave out little. Finally, the Iraqis asked what the Americans wanted in terms of resupply. One recalls the question being put as 'What can we do to get Barbara to like us?' Barbara Bodine, the DCM, was the Embassy's main point of contact with the Iraqis.

The main requirement was fresh fruit and vegetables. Apart from what they had grown themselves, it had been three months since they had enjoyed such luxuries, especially citrus fruits. The result was a delivery on 30 November of several plastic shopping bags containing 45 tangerines, 80 oranges, 85 bruised apples, 155 golf-ball-sized cucumbers, and 45 cartons of Iraqi Sumer cigarettes. The Iraqis also had Pepsis, but would not hand them over until the Americans gave them back the equivalent number of empty bottles. The Iraqis returned the following day when the Americans had the empties ready, and handed over 10 cases of Pepsi. The only other Western embassy still manned in Kuwait, the British, received nothing.

Bodine and her colleagues had mixed feelings about accepting the Iraqi gifts. Although a smoker, she wanted the world to know that there were many things they needed more than cigarettes, and to understand that this did not constitute a resupply. If Saddam wanted to make a gesture, then all he had to do was turn on the power and water.

The incident sent journalists in Baghdad into a frenzy of analysis. Some reported that the resupply may have been ordered directly by Saddam in compliance with October's UN Security Council Resolution 674 requiring Iraq to allow resupply for the embassies in Kuwait, or even with a recent General Assembly resolution condemning violence against consular missions in Kuwait. In reality, the local Iraqis were probably simply trying to gain Bodine's favour. Saloom got the distinct impression that the chief Iraqi had an unrequited crush on Barbara.

As for Ado and Saloom, they were flown north late on the 29th with eight captive Britons. They still hoped to be freed, but the fact that they were not allowed to take their luggage with them was disconcerting. They had been told that US Embassy representatives would meet them at Baghdad Airport. Only a local employee was there, not a diplomat, and they were prevented from going with him. They knew then that they were in trouble. The Iraqis took them to the Mansour Melia, where they met El Maloudi. His face dropped when he saw them. Apparently the Baghdad Embassy had sent a message to Kuwait saying that the release offer was a trick, but the Kuwait Embassy never received it. Ado and Saloom soon joined the Human Shield at the camps.

The last ten days of November 1990 were dominated by a build-up in the UN for the Security Council use-of-force resolution. James Baker's shuttle diplomacy marathon was paying off, aided by Saddam's intransigence and Bush's wooing of Gorbachev. The Soviets had given up on Iraq, and were now prepared to vote for the resolution. China might not support it but would not veto it. In the circumstances, an abstention was as good as a vote. Since Thanksgiving, the US Administration had stopped sending mixed signals and seemed to adopt a firm line. Bush's popularity in Kuwait had soared.

By the 26th, the resolution looked like a foregone conclusion, with a few details to be worked out. The US was prepared to accept a deadline of 30 January. Kuwait was pressing for 1 January, as contained in the most recent draft. An earlier draft had mentioned mid-January. The 15th became the date. This would not give the newly-arrived Allied ground forces time to deploy properly, but the air war had been ready to go for several months. The ground troops could get into place while the airmen did their work.

Domestically in the US, Senator Edward Kennedy called the resolution 'a constructive step and an impressive achievement', but wanted to change the deadline to 2 August, 1991, to give sanctions more time. It was a nice tidy date, but would have meant hundreds more, if not thousands, Kuwaiti and Allied deaths. Incredibly, similar idiotic advice came from two retired Chairmen of the Joint Chiefs of Staff, Admiral William Crowe and General David Jones.

Thankfully, no one listened to them.

The British were more unified. Opposition Leader Neil Kinnock announced that his party supported the Resolution. Polls showed overwhelming public support for war, even from some of those with most to lose from it. Days earlier, the families of 89 of the 350 British Human Shields had presented a letter to the Prime Minister demanding the use of force to free the hostages.

On 27 November, the Security Council heard extensive testimony on Iraqi atrocities in Kuwait. The horrifying details dispelled any lingering doubts as to the righteousness of the anti-Saddam crusade. In Moscow, President Gorbachev told Tareq Aziz that Iraq needed to get out of Kuwait and release the hostages, especially the Soviets as already agreed. 'Otherwise,' he was warned, 'the world would take firm measures.'

On 28 November, the UN General Assembly, in an overwhelming 148 to 1 vote, with Iraq as the lone dissenter, condemned acts of violence against consular missions and representatives in Occupied Kuwait. The Security Council then adopted Resolution 677 condemning Iraq's attempt to alter the demographic composition of Kuwait and destroy the civil records of the legitimate government. It authorized the Secretary General to take custody of the copy of the population register up to 1 August, 1990, that is, the PACI computer tapes which had been smuggled out of Kuwait.

Then, on 29 November, came the king-hit. The Security Council, meeting at Foreign Minister level, voted 12 to 2 with Yemen and Cuba against and China abstaining, to pass Resolution 678 approving 'the use of all necessary means' if Iraq did not withdraw from Kuwait by 15 January, 1991. In comments after the vote, the Security Council members said they would observe a 'pause of goodwill', but the US warned that the 47-day respite would end if Saddam harmed any of the foreign hostages, or made any other provocative moves.

Bush then called an emergency session of Congress to give him a domestic mandate in line with the UN resolution. He had outflanked his domestic opponents through the UN. The peace lobby would now be pre-empted by the will of the American people. At last, the war deadline was firmly in place.

In Kuwait, we were jubilant. The action would not be immediate, but it now had a reasonable timeframe. Our ordeal would be given some meaning. After four months of occupation; another two against a firm deadline would be manageable. The end was in sight, despite the danger of war. The hostage humour machine cranked into action; invitations for *Kuwait Liberation Day Parties, January 15th 1991*, RSVP James Baker III, flew across the fax lines.

However, it was clear that Saddam had lost the propaganda war, and would now have to fight the military one. We thought that our utility had changed back overnight from potential rewards for various grovels to Human Shields to deter an Allied attack. We now had more value being kept in Iraq and expected all releases to stop. Furthermore, the Iraqi Christmas invitation for families still stood, so Saddam could conceivably double his hostage population within weeks. We saw no mileage for him in releasing anyone at this stage. Even if he honoured his 18 November pledge to release people over three months from Christmas, we fully expected that this would be cancelled as soon as the first bombs fell on 15 January.

To no one's surprise, Iraq rejected the UN ultimatum as 'illegal and invalid'. However, what did surprise us was George Bush's invitation of 30 November for Tareq Aziz to visit Washington within two weeks, and his suggestion to Saddam that he receive James Baker in Baghdad at a mutually convenient time between 15 December, and 15 January, 1991. This was what became known as Bush's 'extra mile for peace'.

It seemed to us that Bush was now giving Saddam an opportunity to talk his way out of the crisis, and what he had been asking for all along: direct talks. The salient difference now was that this was against a clear mandate for use of force, with that force in place. Yet, in our frame of mind, the Bush olive branch was seen as weakness rather than the high statesmanship it was. A US visit by Tareq Aziz was tentatively agreed for 10 December. However, Iraq made the talks almost impossible by insisting that all Middle East problems be included. 'No-way!' said the US.

Saddam also had an even bigger surprise for us. Defying all expectations, his position did not harden in the days after the UN vote. On the contrary, he announced on 1 December that he would release all the hostages if the UN decided on a peaceful solution. It seemed so out of character for him not to react more aggressively. Instead, people who had been released before the vote, and who had not yet left, were allowed out. However, his men in Kuwait were still after Americans and British. This reinforced our fear that eventually only they and those who elected to stay and support them would remain.

Unknown to us, Saddam was sitting on a time bomb of his own making. His Christmas invitation to the Human Shields' families, combined with the earlier success of the women who had gone to Baghdad to get their men back, was backfiring. Hundreds of women and more grovellers were on their way. Many were already in Baghdad, including relatives of a fifth of the 90 remaining US Human Shields. The Iraqi bureaucracy was overwhelmed.

The men in hiding in Kuwait were in quite a different situation. Although unable to phone their wives about the Christmas visits, most had sent messages through their embassies urging them not to come. Many Human Shields felt similarly, but the wives were coming regardless. The result was that by 5 December, relatives of scores of Human Shields were in Baghdad or on their way, but few womenfolk of men in hiding had arrived. It now seemed that those in the camps would be rescued not by the SAS or Delta Force, but by their own wives and mothers. Those left behind would be the men in Kuwait.

In early December, our main concern in Kuwait was to secure our position for war. We feared that the searches for Americans and British would intensify. The Hostage Support Group did not defer plans to bring in Christmas presents from home - via the Baghdad embassies - for those in hiding as Christmas would be the most difficult time for them, but we concentrated on ensuring that everybody had enough food for two months, safe identification, and a secure hiding place. We were going to be in a battlefield, and wanted to be ready.

25. THE HOME FRONT

With Allied forces in Saudi Arabia preparing for action against Iraq, another war was being fought thousands of miles from the Gulf. This was a campaign of many battles: the fight by the Kuwaitis for the hearts and minds of a Western public unsure of the cause for which their troops might be asked to fight; the struggle by governments and volunteer groups to support the families of the hostages; and the Kuwaitis' own battle to support their people outside Kuwait, and assist the Resistance. This was the Home Front.

The Kuwaitis were acutely aware that a public relations defeat, particularly in the US, could delay Liberation, or even prevent any Liberation at all. The bastions of the Kuwaiti home front were therefore Washington, New York, London and, to a lesser extent, Cairo. Similarly, the families of the Human Shields and the men in hiding knew that they could not hold out forever, physically or mentally. Most saw an early war as imperative.

Kuwait's Field Marshal in the American campaign was Sheikh Saud Nasir, the Ambassador to the US, Canada and Venezuela. A former Ambassador to the UK – appointed at age 31 – and envoy to Washington since 1981, he was one of the most successful Arab ambassadors. Although not as flamboyant as his Saudi colleague, Prince Bandar Sultan, Saud was no stranger to crisis, having steered Kuwaiti-US relations throughout the Iran–Iraq War.

During the first hours of the invasion, the Ambassador was the senior functioning member of Kuwait's Government. No one knew whether the Amir and Crown Prince and the Cabinet were alive, dead, or captured. Even before their fate was known, Sheikh Saud and his colleague Ambassador to the UN, Mohammed Abulhassan, were in action, mustering support, and arrange to secure the unfreezing of Kuwaiti assets for the fight ahead.

Throughout the crisis, Sheikh Saud had the heavy responsibility of mobilizing the US Government and public opinion to liberate Kuwait as soon as possible. If he put one foot wrong and antagonized the wrong individuals, then his entire people stood to lose their country. Every day's delay meant more Kuwaiti dead, more torture, more destruction. The dignified and firm demeanour of Saud and Abulhassan alike impressed politicians, diplomats and journalists alike whose initial reaction was that the crisis was about oil, a sliver of disputed desert, and two worthless islands. At first, there was little mention of Saddam's weapons of mass destruction, the rule of law, or the atrocities. A substantial element of the Democrat-controlled Congress were all for letting him keep Kuwait provided he left Saudi Arabia alone.

Sheikh Saud also had to bear his own personal agony. His wife, Awatif, had returned to Kuwait just before the invasion with their son and daughter. Other eminent expatriate Kuwaitis protected their families inside Kuwait by keeping a low profile, but Sheikh Saud's job was to be seen and heard. Until his family escaped in late September, he lived in constant fear of a message from the Iraqis saying that they had them, and to behave accordingly.

The early days of the crisis were the most difficult. Although the UN condemned the invasion within hours, the Kuwaitis were acutely aware that Security Council resolutions only work if major countries get behind them. Without enforcement, the resolutions were all but worthless. In this case, only the US had the clout to ensure Iraqi compliance. As importantly, until Saudi Arabia agreed to accept foreign troops on her soil, even the US would find it impossible to eject Saddam from Kuwait, short of waging nuclear war on him.

It was not until five days into the occupation that formal Saudi approval was forthcoming. Two days later, Sheikh Saud met with President Bush for the first time since the invasion. 'Don't worry. Kuwait will return,' said Bush. Only then could he breathe easily after a week of intense anxiety.

Although Bush had declared from the beginning that 'this aggression will not stand', there was no specific talk of how it might be undone. It was obvious that the sanctions were no more than a stopgap measure, but on 2 August, only 37% of the US public supported military action. Bush could not possibly go to war on that basis. At Sheikh Saud's first news conference on the day of the invasion, at which he asked for US military intervention, many of the correspondents present made fun of his request. It was almost inconceivable at the time that the US would fight on behalf of Kuwait. Defending Saudi Arabia was one matter, but going to war to reverse what was seemingly a *fait accompli* was an entirely different proposition.

The key to American public opinion was the media, in all its forms. Sheikh Saud's battles were thus fought in newspaper columns and on prime-time TV. Every network wanted him as Kuwait's number one man. Almost every one of the 6,000 US radio stations wanted to interview him personally. He spoke well, could carry an argument, had the facts at his fingertips, handled hardball questions deftly, and came across well on both TV and radio.

The initial challenge was very basic: to educate the US public about Kuwait. Most Americans had no idea where it was. Many had swallowed the initial Iraqi tale of an internal revolution, and Saddam's story about Kuwait historically being part of the Ottoman Basra. Sheikh Saud had to point out that Kuwait had been an independent State since 1961, with a 200-year history before that as a sovereign entity separate and distinct from modern-day Iraq and its predecessors. He pointed out Kuwait's membership of every major international organization from the Arab League to the UN, and that Kuwait had maintained diplomatic relations with Iraq since the early 1960s. How then could Kuwait be part of Iraq if Iraq had itself recognized Kuwait?

Once the basics were established, the case had to be made for military action. Sheikh Saud had to tread a very fine line between appearing to promote a war in which Americans would inevitably die for Kuwait, and America's own interests. The question of oil arose repeatedly. Although immensely relevant, it was a two-edged sword. It lent ammunition to those who argued that American boys should not die for the price of gas, but some astute commentators turned this around, saying that it was more about old ladies on welfare freezing to death in winter than petrol. Cheap oil meant not only a high standard of living for most Americans, but survival for many.

Ironically, Sheikh Saud had an unlikely ally: Saddam Hussein himself, and his regime. The atrocity stories coming out of Kuwait were too numerous to be dismissed as propaganda. Previous news items on the vicious nature of Saddam's rule were resurrected. Despite Saddam's clumsy attempts to present himself as a reasonable man, the use of civilians as Human Shields, and later the sieges of the embassy compounds in Kuwait, proved that this was not so.

Sheikh Saud also had an important secret weapon inside Kuwait: his own brother, Sabah, and his satellite phone. The two men spoke almost daily. The Washington Embassy knew exactly what was going on in Kuwait. They filtered out the stories of horror, repression, rape, torture, murder, and looting, ensuring that the sources were protected. When these accounts were first passed to the media, they were hardly believed, but once foreign women and children started arriving home in September, the Kuwaitis were able to back these up independently. This had a massive impact on public opinion.

Sheikh Saud's enemies came not only from the Iraqis and their Jordanian and Palestinian allies, but also from a large body of influential US isolationists. To them, despite the bitter lessons of history, America could not be the world's policeman. They argued that all international problems should be solved by the United Nations, forgetting that the UN itself is impotent without the leadership of the big powers.

Most of these individuals - described in the US as liberals - were intelligent people of great integrity. They could not be dismissed easily, especially as they were particularly influential. The challenge was thus to turn their views around so that they would support war. The Kuwaitis never had complete success with this, but with the news of the atrocities and Saddam's weapons programmes, a significant proportion of these individuals came to see war against Iraq as the lesser of two evils.

More obvious opposition came from Iraq's own diplomats in the US, but Sheikh Saud put paid to these fairly quickly. In one televized half-hour debate on *Crossfire* with the Iraqi Ambassador, Mohammed Al-Mashat, the Kuwaiti Ambassador so outclassed Al-Mashat that he declined a rematch.

Nevertheless, even some members of President Bush's own party had themselves to be educated. In one TV debate with Sheikh Saud, Pat Buchanan asked, 'Why should the US be asked to defend an undemocratic country?' Sheikh Saud simply picked up a copy of the Kuwaiti Constitution, handed it to Buchanan, and said, 'This is our Constitution, and this says we are a democracy.' It apparently came as a complete surprise to Buchanan that Kuwait had a Constitution that provided for an elected parliament.

One of Sheikh Saud's most important tasks in the first weeks of the crisis was organizing the visit of the Kuwaiti Amir, Sheikh Jaber Al-Ahmad, to the US, where he addressed the UN General Assembly on 27 September, and met with President Bush and his Cabinet in Washington the next day.

This visit had a profound effect on both the UN and the Americans. It drove home that the Amir was Kuwait's legitimate Head of State, and that Kuwait was using every means at its disposal to ensure its liberation. The Jeddah Conference was still two weeks away, but it was already apparent that the Kuwaiti people were firmly behind the Amir. Not one opposition Kuwaiti politician had taken political advantage of the crisis.

With the Amir's return to Saudi Arabia, Sheikh Saud threw himself back into the routine of media appearances, and building support in the US Government and UN. He was constantly on the move, attending ceremonies for Kuwaiti students graduating from military training, attending debates, organizing support for stranded expatriate Kuwaitis, and giving interviews.

October and November were filled with even more atrocity stories than the first two months, but the main theme of Sheikh Saud's and Mohammed Abulhassan's work during this period was the UN use-of-force resolution. However, the joy of the resolution passing was dampened by the pain of knowing that Saddam had been given a month and a half to continue his dismantling of Kuwait.

Even after the UN vote of 29 November, the battle was far from won. There was still the US Congress. President Bush may have had a UN mandate for war against Iraq, and his forces may have been in place, but it would have been political suicide for him to attack without the approval of Congress.

Like most Presidents before him, Bush saw no constitutional need to seek Congressional approval. Most Congressmen, including many who supported Bush, felt otherwise, citing the 1975 War Powers legislation which had arisen out of the Vietnam War. Bush's main problem – and that of Kuwait – was that Congress was controlled by the Democrats, many of whom were making partisan political mileage out of the crisis. However, American public opinion had completely turned around since 2 August. Now 63% supported war. Through a combination of the Kuwaiti information campaign, outrage at the Iraqi atrocities and hostage-taking, and ordinary Americans supporting the massive troop deployment, public opinion was firmly behind President Bush.

To complement normal diplomatic channels, the Kuwaitis established a grass-roots movement in Washington known as 'Citizens For A Free Kuwait' (CFK). The members were Kuwaiti academics, executives, students and public servants, some with American spouses. CFK's function was to harness the efforts of ordinary Kuwaitis in the US, present the human face of Kuwait, and maintain public pressure for early military action.

In addition to CFK, the National Union of Kuwait Students–USA, working from Boulder, Colorado, established 'Friends of Free Kuwait'. Several other expatriate Kuwaitis formed their own small groups, but the main organization was always CFK. Finance came from the members' own pockets, and wealthy exiled Kuwaitis in the US, Europe and Saudi Arabia.

CFK was headed by Dr Hassan Al-Ebraheem, the Chairman of the Kuwait Society for the Advancement of Arab Children and former Minister for Education and Rector of Kuwait University, and Mr Fawzi Sultan, a Kuwaiti expatriate economist working with the World Bank. Al-Ebraheem, who was in Washington on business at the time of the invasion, immediately established a loose network of displaced Kuwaitis, Americans, and other people with links to Kuwait. This grew into CFK within days. The 'Citizens' part of its name distinguished it from the official Kuwait Government effort.

CFK was run by a core of 13 Kuwaiti exiles, with several chapters and hundreds of volunteers throughout North America. Al-Ebraheem himself was primarily responsible for dealings with the US Government, his own Government, and public relations. Sultan concentrated on the finance, economics and legal area, together with Dr Abdullah Al-Obaidan. Other key individuals were Dr Mohammed Al-Abduljaleel, whose main responsibility was the media; Ahmad Khajah and Dr Athmar Al-Salem who ran what became known as 'grass roots' support; Dr Mohammed Al-Awadi, who covered research and information, and Khalid Bishara and Dr Fatma Nazar.

Al-Ebraheem, Sultan, and their team had to build CFK from a zero-base. Kuwait's Washington Embassy did not have a single fact sheet on Kuwait, other than a few pictures of Government figures. Apart from the overworked Ambassador, who could not be everywhere, there were few people in the Embassy who came over well on the electronic media, or could speak to groups of Americans. CFK had to commission, produce and distribute publicity material, and find people to carry their message.

CFK concentrated on educating the American public on the nature of the Kuwaiti people, Kuwait's history, and the background of the crisis. They delivered literally thousands of speeches and interviews to everyone from high school groups and Rotary Clubs to Congressional Committees and the UN Security Council. By late November, on the eve of the use-of-force resolution, they were organising at least 20 speeches and other activities each day. Promotional material went as far afield as the UK, Egypt and Bahrain, and perhaps more importantly, copies of the Kuwaiti Constitution, which they explained to many surprised Americans was modelled in part on theirs.

Together with the embassy, CFK built up a comprehensive picture of the horrors inside Kuwait, and fed this to the media. In the area of human rights, most Americans erroneously associated Kuwait with other conservative regional states, particularly in freedom of political expression. The Kuwaitis had to counter this, broaden the debate into the human dimension, and convince the American public that the crusade was worth embracing.

One of the first misimpressions CFK had to counter was that Kuwaitis were fleeing to Europe and the US, and leaving foreign troops to die on their behalf. In September they organized media briefings with an escaped Resistance figure, known as 'Major Sam', who described – without compromising security inside Kuwait – how the Resistance was organized by Kuwaiti officers. A Kuwaiti spokesman said at the briefing 'When the war starts, you can be sure that Kuwaiti blood will be the first to be shed.' He should have spoken in the past tense. The war was already under way inside Kuwait.

The Kuwaitis pulled out all stops in the public relations battle, and hired a renowned public relations firm, Hill and Knowlton, and six other firms to help them. Hill and Knowlton put together an extremely professional campaign, and the Kuwaitis slotted their own people into various roles in it. Hill and Knowlton's bill for their 40 days of involvement with CFK came to millions of dollars, but the Kuwaitis got excellent value, even though they had to endure criticism of the cost, mostly by journalists who had never had their own country invaded. The Kuwaitis were not in a position to take risks. They had to sell hard, or risk losing their country.

One of the most significant events in the Kuwaiti battle for American public opinion was testimony delivered to the International Committee of Red Cross and Red Crescent Societies in Geneva and later to the UN Security Council in New York by people who had escaped Kuwait, particularly Dr Ebraheem Behbehani of the Kuwaiti Red Crescent. Behbehani and several of his colleagues had been arrested by the Iraqis in September, and held for 26 days. News of the arrests had been transmitted out of Kuwait by satellite phone. His appearance was like a man appearing from beyond the grave.

Behbehani was backed up in New York by six other escapees from Kuwait, including an Indian surgeon, Dr Satish Shander Sharma, a Kuwaiti journalist, Fatma Hussein, and a dialysis patient. Further individuals testified before Congress, particularly about the lack of care in Kuwaiti hospitals under Iraqi rule, and premature babies being removed from incubators. This latter story became blown out of proportion, with allegations of Iraqi troops killing these babies. The truth was more prosaic, but no less tragic. The Iraqis who took over the hospitals simply removed the babies from the incubators, and placed them in their mothers' arms, where, predictably, some of them died.

In October, CFK organized ten witnesses to testify before the Congressional Human Rights Caucus. The legislators were deeply moved by the accounts. Later, after the release of the Western hostages, CFK arranged the visit to Washington of a group of 30 Americans who had been Human Shields or in hiding in Kuwait. This group spoke to Representatives and Senators. Three of them testified to the House Committee on Foreign Affairs on 8 January, 1991 together with Dr Al-Ebraheem, Dr Fawziah Al-Qattan, a Kuwaiti gynaecologist who had treated victims of Iraqi rape in Kuwait, John Healy of Amnesty International USA, and Andrew Whitley of Middle East Watch.

Many Kuwaitis outside Washington worked tirelessly and selflessly for the cause. Perhaps the most active was Dr Adnan Shehab El-Din, a Visiting Professor at Berkeley in California. He almost single-handedly carried the Kuwaiti campaign in the San Francisco Bay area. El-Din – and many others – spent thousands of dollars of their own money, seldom seeking reimbursement.

Many young Kuwaitis in the US went beyond the public relations battle. About 550 of them were studying at American universities. Most of the medically fit males withdrew from their studies and went through basic military training before joining US units as liaisons to Arab forces in Saudi Arabia, intelligence officers, and translators. They were particularly useful given their bilingual abilities and local knowledge of Kuwait.

However, according to some people, the Kuwaitis could be their own worst enemies in the public relations war. Senior State Department people described them as 'babes in the media woods'. They had to handle the cultural differences between a media campaign in the US, and at home. The most obvious example of this was the use of graphic pictures of atrocity victims in an attempt to generate sympathy in the Western public. The images were very real, but the US public recoiled from them, and hence from the issue.

Most importantly, when critics pointed out deficiencies in the Kuwaiti political system, the natural Kuwaiti reaction was to deny that a problem existed, instead of simply acknowledging that their country was as imperfect as any other, and was working through it. This tendency undermined their public credibility on the more salient issues to the extent that they never quite held the moral high ground as firmly as they should have.

On a more subtle level, some people in the Kuwaiti Embassy in Washington tried to control what Kuwaitis throughout America were saying, to ensure that a unified front was presented. This stifled the natural spontaneity which was far more important in establishing the credibility of the message. The Embassy need not have worried. The Kuwaitis may have had differences between themselves, but they buried these for the crisis.

On a practical level, planning for post-liberation rehabilitation of Kuwait started in late September, following the Amir's visit. Even then, the Kuwaitis already knew that the Iraqis would wreck the infrastructure even if they left peacefully. CFK put together a reconstruction plan through World Bank consultants organized by Dr Al-Ebraheem and Mr Sultan, with a prominent Kuwaiti merchant, Fawzi Musaad Salah, and a previous Minister of Commerce and Industry, Mr Abdulatief Al-Hamad. It was predicated on three scenarios: total devastation, medium destruction, and minimal damage.

As a result of this, representatives of every Kuwaiti Ministry established themselves in Washington in October as part of the Kuwait Emergency Recovery Office (KERO), a joint US–Kuwaiti task force. Their mission was to plan to manage Kuwait from the day of liberation with power, water, sanitation, food distribution, medical services, police, virtually everything. KERO was tied into the US military's Civil Affairs group and its representatives would follow closely the troops into Kuwait. Its main function was to deal with contractors who would be involved in the reconstruction, and to arrange procurement and services based on the CFK–World Bank plan.

Sheikh Saud Nasir's colleague as Ambassador to the UK was Ghazi Al-Rayes, a capable diplomat. Al-Rayes enjoyed so much British Government and public support for his cause that he was overwhelmed with offers of help.

London, however, assumed an importance far greater than might have first appeared. Most of Kuwait's substantial foreign investments were run from London's Kuwait Investment Office. The British had saved Kuwait from Ottoman Turkey, from tribal raiders in the 1920s, and from Iraq in 1961. Many Kuwaitis had close British friends, and thousands of them had been educated in the UK. London was their European spiritual home.

Margaret Thatcher was far more popular than George Bush among the Kuwaitis. While he had spoken earlier of lines in the sand, she had stated unequivocally that Kuwait would be liberated. British complicity in giving two-thirds of Kuwait to Saudi Arabia in 1922 was forgotten by the Kuwaitis.

On a practical level, two of Kuwait's largest corporations, Kuwait Petroleum Corporation under its International Vice-President Nader Sultan, and the National Bank of Kuwait, had offices in the City, with the funds to support their people. As importantly, the Kuwaitis were wise to the seminal influence of the

British media, from which commentators in other English-speaking countries, including the US, often took their lead.

The UK version of CFK was the 'Association for a Free Kuwait' (AFK) headed by Dr Jafaar Behbehani. It carried out much the same functions as Hassan Al-Ebraheem's organization, with very effective political lobbying and media work.

In addition to AFK, a separate organization known as the 'Free Kuwait Campaign', or 'Free Kuwait', was formed. It was originally established in early August and first known as the 'Kuwait Committee' of the National Union of Kuwaiti Students in Britain and Ireland. Much of the credit for forming Free Kuwait goes to Mike Lorrigan, a history teacher who had previously worked in Kuwait. Although a forceful individual who made a number of enemies, he was very savvy in the ways of the media and politics, and suggested forming Free Kuwait from the Student Union's Kuwait Committee. From then on, Free Kuwait took on a life of its own.

Free Kuwait was run jointly by Kuwaitis and their British volunteer friends, many of whom were ordinary expatriates on summer leave from their jobs in Kuwait, such a schoolteacher Caroline Tshering, Lorrigan himself, and others. After the hostages were released, a number of them joined up.

The key Kuwaitis were young men and women living, studying, or caught in London, such as Ali Al-Mulaifi, Dina Mustapha, and Sundus Hamza Abbas. Other Kuwaitis working in the UK would finish their day jobs, and then spend evenings and weekends at Free Kuwait designing publicity material, or writing letters to newspapers, other parts of the media, and politicians. Muna Al-Mousa, a young woman working at Kuwait Petroleum International, designed a very effective postcard showing a picture of Saddam and Stuart Lockwood, dated 1990, alongside a similarly posed photo of Hitler and a German boy, dated 1940. It was hard-hitting, no-holds-barred publicity.

Free Kuwait was always more amateur than the high-powered CFK in the US and its more official AFK partner in London, but nevertheless effective given its resources. Several of its members – including Lorrigan – went to the US during the crisis to swop ideas and experiences, and co-ordinate with others involved in generating grass-roots support.

Campaign finance came from the National Bank of Kuwait's London Office, the Kuwaiti Embassy through the Kuwait Investment Office, and wealthy individuals, usually anonymously. On one occasion, when the campaign desperately need a large printing job done quickly, Sheikha Souad Al-Sabah, a prominent Kuwaiti writer, put the entire cost on her account. At other times when the Kuwaitis were handing out badges and leaflets in the London Underground, people wanted to give them money. They had to decline as they would not take money from the public, but they were touched by the offers.

Free Kuwait divided its activities into three main areas. The first was building general public support by distributing items such as Amnesty International reports on Iraqi atrocities in Kuwait, and posters, badges, stickers, leaflets, baseball caps, T-shirts and sweatshirts. The 'Free Kuwait' logo which went worldwide was designed in the campaign's basement, and the production of thousands of items bearing it was financed by the Kuwait Investment Office.

From London, the material was shipped to Washington for distribution by CFK, and to Riyadh, Cairo or wherever else it was needed.

The second major area was disseminating information through the media, arranging press conferences, providing credible expert opinion, and organizing rallies and marches. The final area involved lobbying the UK Government and Parliament, preparing briefing papers, and speaking to anyone who would listen. The Campaign made a point of replying to newspaper letters and articles by noon, to ensure they could be considered for the next day's issue.

On occasions, the BBC and other news organisations would contact the Campaign to verify the accuracy of information which had come to them from other sources, including, on one occasion, satellite photographs. The Campaign also maintained quiet links with the UK Ministry of Defence to channel information which could be militarily useful. There was a great deal of information - some of it very good - coming out of Kuwait through a variety of sources, and much of it ended up at the Campaign offices.

Besides countering preconceived notions of Kuwait, one of the Campaign's main challenges was dealing with a naive but powerful peace movement, some of whose members sincerely believed that the West should not go to war in the Middle East, while others, as in the US, were using the crisis for their own agenda. Although the UK Government and public were firmly behind the Kuwaitis, a hard core of well-organized and vocal peace campaigners was a constant thorn in their side.

The Kuwaiti strategy to counter this was simple: they turned the focus of the Campaign onto the violation of basic human rights in occupied Kuwait. Oil was never mentioned. Campaign advertisements ran with the slogan: 'Face Up To The Real Issue', which was presented as the fate of a whole nation, and the murder, torture, rape and fear. A supporting theme was the distinct nature of the Kuwaiti people, and their contribution to world prosperity through the transfer of wealth to the poorer countries. The punchline was: 'The World Can't Afford To Wait'.

The Kuwaitis in Britain held a series of rallies, marches, and vigils. Before the Campaign itself got off the ground, Kuwaiti students organized a march of 700 Kuwaitis from their Embassy to the Prime Minister's Residence on 8 August to urge stronger British action against Iraq. They were not disappointed. Mrs Thatcher was one of their firmest supporters.

The Campaign's own first major event was a 'Free Kuwait' rally with 2,000 marchers on 9 September, with a second, larger march on 7 October. A vigil was held outside Parliament on 24 October for those Kuwaitis who had died in the invasion and in the Resistance. The three-month anniversary of the invasion, 2 November, was designated 'Free Kuwait Day', with a church service in St Martin's in the Fields, and the symbolic release of yellow balloons over London in remembrance of those trapped. Over 120 universities and colleges participated, with distribution of leaflets and promotional material in more than 200 cities and towns throughout the UK and Ireland.

All the marches were held in silence to make the point in a dignified manner. As news of the atrocities in Kuwait grew, photographs smuggled out of Kuwait found their way onto Campaign posters and banners, and as in America, they became one of the focal points of the Campaign. Prompted by these, a 'Stop the

Atrocities Day' was held on 24 November. A 'Stop the Atrocities March' through London on 2 December drew over 6,000 marchers.

The Kuwaitis in the UK also went into the provinces, especially to Scotland, whose people were particularly well-represented in Kuwait and in the British forces in Saudi Arabia, and where many Kuwaiti students and pilot-trainees were based. As in the US, the Campaign felt the need to build support among the families of the troops. These people were almost as directly involved in the crisis as the Kuwaitis. It was important that they understood the human element and justice of the cause for which their people might die. The British forces had their own regional family support groups, and these were visited by Campaign volunteers who talked about the Kuwait they had lived in, gave whatever moral support they could, explored areas where practical help could be extended, and corrected many misconceptions.

The Campaign's activities did not stop after the hostages were released in December. This was a double cause for celebration for many members of the Campaign. Their friends were now home and safe, and the decision to go to war was easier with them out of the way. Later, after the hostages had a chance to settle in back home, a 'Save the People March' was held on 13 January, drawing over 8,000. At its close, 3,000 black balloons were released, representing the 300,000 civilians of all nationalities still in Kuwait.

The January march came just before the commencement of Operation Desert Storm, and in the wake of virulent last-gasp anti-war protests. The peace protesters' arguments were effectively countered by the Chairman of the House of Commons Select Committee on Foreign Affairs, David Howell, who said '...those who supported peace at any price would only encourage Iraq to commit future atrocities. The war began on 2 August and that war can be ended by Saddam Hussein if he wishes. But if he refuses to end it, we will have to use force to prevent even worse horrors.'

Although the largest concentrations of Kuwaitis outside the Middle East were in the US and UK, there was substantial support elsewhere. Some of the most active supporters were in India, particularly Goa which was home to many displaced Indians. An organisation known as 'Friends of Kuwait' was formed there. Many Kuwaitis had been educated in India, with family connections dating back to the days when Kuwaiti dhows rode the trade winds.

Marches, vigils, and sit-ins were held in parts of India, the Philippines, and Sri Lanka. However, people in these countries often had to contend with the perception of poorly-educated Muslim elements, propagated by the Iraqis, that Western troops were defiling the Holy Lands of Islam. A number of local political leaders capitalised on residual resentment of the First World to whip up support for their own causes. On several occasions, Asian supporters of Kuwait were attacked and even stoned by their own countrymen.

The wives and families of the Western and Japanese men trapped in Iraq and Kuwait faced their own problems. They were totally preoccupied with the fate of their men, but had to get on with life, especially where children were involved. These families often had to compete for public attention with the families of the troops. Some people sympathized more with the soldiers' families as their men had been sent to fight overseas, while the hostages were seen as people who had taken the risk of working abroad themselves. This was unfair. Many were diplomats or people visiting on business or holiday, or airline passengers and crew caught in transit. As for those who worked in the region, their governments had encouraged them to do so.

The Western military had their own support networks, designed for exactly this type of crisis, but there were no existing support systems for the hostages' families. Major corporations such as Bechtel, British Airways and ICL, most of which still had offices functioning in Baghdad, established counselling helplines for the families, and continued to pay the men's salaries. Some large Kuwaiti firms such as Kuwait Petroleum Corporation did likewise, but others – including some KPC subsidiaries – were not particularly helpful.

However, most people caught up in the crisis did not work for such companies. Many of the women and children returnees still had breadwinners trapped in Kuwait and Iraq, and needed special support. Furthermore, most of them had never previously had to turn to welfare agencies. With husbands held hostage, income cut off and assets frozen, some women found themselves almost destitute, and in desperate need of specialized financial and psychological support. As a result, the Foreign Ministries' functions – which usually cease the moment their nationals re-enter their home country – expanded to include a limited amount of welfare counselling.

Even some US and UK Government organizations with men trapped failed to appreciate the families' plight. After an initial warm welcome home, wives of service personnel held hostage were often left to their own devices. Some could not get their husbands' pay because the men were held at sites, and could not personally authorize this. Others were denied medical treatment for their children as their husbands had no official designated assignment. The problem was particularly acute in the US, where returning families were seen as just another family of one of thousands of men going to the Gulf. The distinction between a hostage and a man on regular duty was lost.

Despite the overwhelming support for the Kuwait cause in the West, businesses were not always sympathetic to the plight of hostages and their families. The Foreign Ministries could intervene in certain areas, but usually only when the situation had become desperate. In one instance, the Australian Foreign Minister's staff had to go to the top level of a major bank to prevent foreclosure on a hostage's mortgage. Other businesses were more sympathetic.

Help for some US and British families came from an unexpected source: the Kuwaiti embassies. This applied mainly to people whose spouses worked in senior positions for the Government, but was all the more meaningful as many of the Kuwaiti diplomats had their own families trapped in Kuwait.

In America, an interagency Task Force was established in the State Department's offices, bringing together representatives from every interested arm of the US Government, including State, Defense, the CIA, Treasury, refugee aid agencies, and the military themselves. Its function was to serve as a co-ordinating unit for all US Government actions.

Political input from all sources, as distinct from military intelligence, was fed into the Task Force, which then had the unenviable job of checking, verifying and disseminating it. The nature of the crisis was such that they received almost as much rumour as useful information. The Task Force was the first point of contact for the Kuwaiti Embassy in Washington, CFK, families of the hostages and those caught in Kuwait, journalists, and even ordinary Kuwaitis who just wanted to help. At its height, it numbered 200 people, including retired foreign service officers recalled for their crisis expertise. The State Department's policy was to call families at least every 48 hours, even if there was no new information, just to keep in touch. Relatives of known captives and other special cases were called daily.

Two of the most vital Task Force contacts were the besieged US Embassy in Kuwait, and the Baghdad Embassy, through their satellite phones and, for Baghdad, scrambled regular lines. This dialogue was particularly poignant for the staff in Washington. They were talking to colleagues whom they might never see alive again if the crisis took a turn for the worse.

The first Task Force Director was the Ambassador-designate to Kuwait, Edward Gnehm, with State's Country Director for Kuwait, David Ransom, as his deputy. Gnehm left to accompany Defense Secretary Cheney on his second visit to Saudi Arabia in late August. He was replaced by Ryan Crocker, who left six weeks later to become Ambassador to Lebanon. Crocker's replacement was Mary Ryan, a competent official, but with little expertise in the Gulf.

This last change was particularly inconvenient to the US diplomats holding out in their Embassy in Kuwait. At the time, they had to minimize their communications to conserve diesel fuel for the generators. By November 1990, they were down to about 15 minutes of communication time daily. US Ambassador Nat Howell and his staff not only had to cope with their own dire situation, but also had to get to know Ryan over the phone.

An invaluable member of the Task Force was Howell's wife, Margie. In the US at the time of the invasion, she was on the Task Force within a week. As a public figure in Kuwait for the previous three years, Margie Howell had excellent contacts among displaced Americans and Kuwaitis. She became a lightning rod for officials, businesspeople, and displaced Americans alike. Most importantly for people with men trapped in Kuwait and Iraq, she could identify with them as her own husband was in the same situation.

The Task Force was also caught between a legal rock and a hard place. The *Freedom of Information Act* required it to make information available to the public where possible, but other legislation prevents personal information from going even to a man's wife unless he specifically authorizes its release. It was impossible for Human Shields and even some of the men in hiding to give their permission, so Task Force staff simply had to use their own judgement.

On occasions, families were given information about people other than their relatives, or incorrect information. Complaints ranged from constantly busy phone lines to rude officials. On the day of the invasion itself, they had 600 calls per hour. In the first six weeks of the crisis, before the women and children arrived home, the Task Force logged 50,000 calls. Problems were inevitable. Some personnel working the phones became so stressed that they had to be relieved. They were dealing with thousands of frustrated and angry people, many of whom were prepared to lash out at any symbol of authority.

Other people had nothing but praise for the Task Force. They felt that it was doing everything it could in the circumstances. In fact, some of the Task Force's problems arose from the families themselves. The number of people enquiring about a single hostage might number dozens, each expecting to be dealt with individually. Many families did not organize themselves so that they had a structure for sharing the information among themselves.

The UK, with more people trapped, had a much larger job than the Americans. On 3 August the FCO established an Emergency Unit, manned 24 hours a day, comprising a consular arm, led by the Crisis Manager, Christopher Denne, who was the Head of the Consular Services Department, and a political arm headed by Rob Young, the Head of the Middle East Department. The Unit initially had only ten people to answer thousands of telephone calls. This was later expanded to 25.

The Unit co-ordinated the evacuation flights with the UK Embassy in Baghdad, liaised with the BBC and financed their *Gulf Link* programme, tried to arrange for post and parcels for the trapped men, and issued briefings.

The British and Americans shared the problem of callers desperate for information suspecting that the Unit was holding out on them. Some relatives did not appreciate the government's limitations. There was even a sense among some of the more distraught that the crisis was more the fault of their Government than of Saddam Hussein. One of the greatest problems of the Unit was that it seldom had new information, and had to tell callers the same thing repeatedly. This was often seen as a lack of concern. More seriously, the news was sometimes that a man had been captured. In several cases, it was of a man's death. In others, they had to pass news to Kuwait of parents who had died while their children were held hostage, or of wives who miscarried.

The Unit adapted as the crisis developed. In September, when the financial plight of some of the evacuated families became apparent, the FCO established a Gulf Families Support Centre. This was a steering group of the various Government departments involved, particularly Social Services. It also helped to try to unfreeze bank accounts affected by the UN sanctions. Nevertheless, it took up to three months for some people to gain access to their funds.

The problems with the Department of Social Services were often more of communication than a lack of concern. A crisis line was provided, but the number was not publicized. Social Services people met evacuation flights with emergency funds, but few needy returnees were made aware of the facility. Offices throughout the UK were often ignorant of special arrangements for returning families.

Few other countries involved in the crisis had as many people trapped in Kuwait and Iraq for as long as the Americans and British. There were far more Asians, but they were allowed to leave within a matter of weeks, and most of those who wanted to leave were out in a couple of months.

All of the countries with hostages in Kuwait and Iraq had their own support functions for relatives at home, with much the same problems as the US and UK, but the pressure eased on those whose people were not Human Shields as it became apparent that their nationals could move around freely. Nevertheless, the lack of direct communication with Kuwait, and the decision of many free-nationals to stay there instead of moving to Baghdad, greatly complicated the Ministries' task of keeping relatives informed.

For some of the smaller countries, the numbers involved were far less than they had handled in other crises. The Australians and Belgians had coped with more in Bougainville and the Congo respectively. However, the uncertainty, the dearth of information, duration of the crisis, and inability of the Governments to get their people out added a new dimension to the problem. The consular aspect overshadowed the political function as most of these countries had sent only token military forces – or none at all in the case of Ireland – and they were not permanent members of the UN Security Council.

The Australian support operation was generally typical of the smaller countries. It was run as a Task Force, headed by a First Assistant Secretary, Ric Smith. The other key members were David Rutter, the Assistant Secretary for Consular Affairs, Leo Cruise, the Director of Consular Operations, and Sue Boyd, who handled the media. The Task Force served as an umbrella organization for all officials directly involved with the crisis. As for the larger countries, the problems extended beyond Kuwait and Iraq. Relatives and employers were concerned about their people in other Gulf countries, and Jordan, despite uninterrupted communications. Nevertheless, the families of those trapped in Kuwait and Iraq received absolute priority.

Task Force members toured the country to meet personally with families. In smaller countries such as New Zealand, relatives were brought to the capital for briefings. A few surprises came to light at these meetings. The Ministries generally assumed that employers with substantial numbers of people in the area were providing adequate support to the families. This was not always so. Similarly, relatives were less in contact with each other than anticipated. Some found it useful to maintain contact with those in similar straits; others did not want to add the burden of other families' suffering to their own.

The grovellers also greatly complicated the Ministries' task by raising false hopes, and took their time with briefings. Most grovellers were well-respected individuals, so desperate relatives understandably believed that they might be able to help. However, once they got to Baghdad, they simply became more pawns for Saddam. Nevertheless, they often gave the erroneous impression they were doing something that the Governments were refusing to.

Several senior members of the Task Forces actually went quietly to Baghdad to assess matters for themselves, and to report back to the relatives more accurately. These diplomats achieved far more for the hostages by working quietly behind the scenes than the high profile grovellers ever did.

The official organizations in countries with large numbers of people affected by the crisis were supplemented by volunteer groups made up primarily of the friends and wives of men still trapped in Kuwait and Iraq. Some of these groups filled an important need which the Ministries could not.

The major function of these groups was simply to listen to people and network families into self-help groups. The therapeutic effect of being able to talk and share with other women in similar circumstances was critical. The emotional ordeal of many people at home, whether they had been there at the time of the invasion or were evacuated, was actually greater than that of some hostages. They had been forced to flee from their homes, leaving behind husbands, sons and friends, and the possessions and attachments of a lifetime. Homecoming was not a happy event for them. They had to cope with constant talk of war, in which their people would be on the receiving end.

The men in hiding or held as Human Shields had the comfort of knowing their own condition on a daily basis, and that their families were safe. However, most families had no way of knowing how the men were. The sparse information filtering out of Kuwait and Iraq was usually weeks old, and often inaccurate, or distorted. Furthermore, the families were often without a breadwinner. The bills did not stop just because the husband was a hostage. The stress of ignorance, media harassment, fear that they might never see their men again, and financial hardship all conspired to make the families at home hostages in their own right. To make matters worse, many returned wives suffered a sense of guilt at abandoning their men, even though their departure was the best course of action, especially for their children. The children also suffered greatly. They understood far more than most adults gave them credit for, including the prospect of losing their fathers.

The two major support groups in the US were 'Coming Home, Ltd', and the appropriately named 'Ku-WAITing for News'. Their main challenge was the wide geographical spread and relatively low number of US hostages. There was hostage for every million Americans, but one for every 80,000 Britons. However, the hostage issue struck a particularly painful chord in the American psyche with memories of Lebanon and Teheran. The Americans seemed to have many more women married to Kuwaitis still in Kuwait, so the organizations served the American wives of both American and Kuwaiti men.

Coming Home, Ltd was started by Michael Saba, of Champaign, Illinois, an Arab–American who had been allowed out of Iraq. With his experience of the situation there, he felt keenly for the men left behind. The main function of his organization was to provide information and referral services to the families, and to press for a quick release of the hostages. He produced an excellent sample letter for people to use in asking their Congressmen to demand that the State Department invoke the Fourth Geneva Convention for the protection of civilians in wartime. Chapters of Coming Home were established throughout the US, particularly in Nevada and California.

Each organization issued newsletters as the most effective way of reaching people across the country. Ku-WAITing went to four eight-page issues, and had contact numbers on both coasts. Coming Home provided an '800' number. The groups could be very useful in networking people to help each other. They were even recognized by Mrs Bush, and calls from the White House.

Whereas the US support groups were led by people who knew Kuwait or Iraq, the British volunteer groups were an unlikely collection of people with little or no connection with Kuwait.

There were three main groups, based in London, Bristol and Coventry. The leader of the London group, Joanna (Jo) Copley, her brother Jon, and husband Tony, were spurred into action when Jo and Jon's sister was caught in Kuwait as a BA149 transit passenger. By the time she was home after five weeks, the group was so active that it kept going until all the hostages were home.

The founders of the other two major groups, Stephen and Josie Brookes in Coventry, and Parliamentarian Robert Hayward in Bristol, each had an adult male friend from BA149 held hostage at sites until December. The Bristol and London groups soon merged, and then organized themselves together with the Brookes' Coventry group as the Gulf Support Group (GSG), under the auspices of the Gulf Support Group Trust. The Brookes operated as the Midlands GSG, fielding up to 40 calls a day. The Copley/Hayward organization became the London GSG, with even more calls.

London was a large operation, complete with offices, a full-time press officer, Andy Charles, a part-time fundraiser, Steve King, and a computer system which never quite worked. There were four full-time staff and three dozen volunteers organized into shifts of telephone operators, each supervized by a trained counseller from the National Association of Bereavement Societies, or the Samaritans. The FCO paid their rent and electricity; British Telecom eventually paid part of the phone bill, and Reuters provided a news machine free of charge. It was the closest any volunteer group got to a professional operation. The Midlands GSG operated from the Brookes' spare bedroom and dining room table, initially with two shoeboxes of index cards.

As a recognized organization, the GSG could claim to represent a sizable group of people, and collate their individual problems into a coherent whole, thus bringing pressure to bear on financial institutions seeking to foreclose on housing mortgages, and enlisting FCO support on such matters. It also provided a focal point for a media ravenous for information and fresh angles.

The group was able to respond swiftly and effectively to criticisms of the families. When a Conservative MP, Sir John Stokes, insensitively criticised the wives of the hostages, a GSG spokesman replied in the same news cycle, putting Stokes firmly in his place. In other cases, when a few people expressed resentment that so much attention was being paid to people who had been making big money abroad, the GSG was able to point out that most of them made little more than they would at home, and worked longer for it, and that many hostages were in fact people who did not even live in the Middle East.

Members of the GSG met every evacuation flight with a stall and information leaflets on how they could help. They explored other avenues for maintaining pressure on behalf of the hostages. On several occasions, the Brookes visited the Iraqi Ambassador in London to plead the hostages case, without success. British grovellers who were considering the pilgrimage to Baghdad used the GSG as a source of names of particularly needy hostages.

From October 1990, the group had to fight hard against the hostage story dying. Their main problem was that the public's primary source of information was TV, and without pictures there was no story. Most hostage footage was of men in hotels. There were no cameras at the sites, or in Kuwait, so nothing was happening there as far as the networks were concerned.

On 2 December, the same day as the Free Kuwait Campaign's 'Stop the Atrocities March', the GSG held a 'Yellow Ribbon Day' to focus attention on the hostages, who had been overshadowed by the UN use-of-force resolution. This campaign went to the US, France, Germany, Ireland, Japan, Australia, Cyprus and even Iraq, and involved tying yellow ribbons on hostages' homes and in public places. In London, yellow ribbons were tied in Piccadilly Circus, and then 1,400 yellow balloons released, one for every trapped Briton.

More established organizations also became involved, particularly with the evacuations. Forty-five Red Cross volunteers met the second wave of flights. Travelcare, a charity to help people arriving at airports, was also on hand, with the airport chaplains. The Salvation Army helped with clothes and housing for people who had left everything behind.

The small support groups of wives who knew each other from Kuwait and Iraq were not as noticeable as the larger GSG, but were probably more important for mutual support. While none of the GSG leaders had been to the region or been held hostage, these women could relate to each other. A number of them, based around four wives of Kuwait Oil Company engineers, became particularly active. They called themselves the Gulf Support Campaign, and organized a march in London on 28 October, attended by 300 people. Several members of Free Kuwait joined them. They presented a letter to Mrs Thatcher, then organized a letter-writing campaign to Saddam and presented 150 letters to the Iraqi Embassy, with a petition for the release of their men.

On 2 November, two of the four women, Anne Mansell, whose husband Steve was a Human Shield, and Jackie Hurley, organized a picket of 60 women outside the Iraqi Embassy to mark three months since the invasion, but the police tried to keep them away from the Embassy. The media attention attracted in the ensuing tussle had an added benefit for the men back in the Gulf: they heard the news on the BBC that their wives were virtually fighting physically to get them out, and felt less abandoned.

The Home Front was a reflection of the world-wide scale of the crisis. People from virtually every country were involved. Some had relatives and friends who got out of Iraq and Kuwait within days of the invasion, or who could leave whenever they wished. Others, particularly wives of Kuwaitis, had to wait for many months to be reunited with their loved ones. Some never were.

The war at home was seldom in as sharp a focus as the events in Kuwait and Iraq. It was nevertheless a hard-fought battle, with casualties. It was a holding action, a war of attrition. There was as much daily heroism and sacrifice as on the battlefield. It was difficult to define victory, but the overwhelming Western public support for the eventual war against Iraq, and the survival of the vast majority of displaced families from all countries are its greatest honours.

26. ESCAPE AND EXFILTRATION

During October and November 1990, with the prospects for peace receding daily, Westerners and Japanese still in Iraq and Kuwait feared they would be caught in the middle of a shooting war. The pressure eased with the various releases, but this still left over 2,000 individuals in the firing line. About 600 of these were at sites throughout Iraq and, until late November, in Kuwait. Most were British men. The rest were Americans, Japanese, a few unfortunate individuals of mistaken identity, and several women who had stayed with their men. A further 500 were in hiding in Kuwait, with about another 100 free Westerners, and those in the besieged embassies in Kuwait City.

Baghdad hosted an entire community of over a hundred diplomats, some of whom were accredited to Iraq. There were also hundreds of Westerners with relative freedom of movement, mostly from the regular communities in Iraq, but also from Kuwait. Transients such as the media and a few misguided peace fanatics rounded out the numbers, but they were free to leave at any time. Of the non-transients, only the accredited diplomats could leave. Others were leaving with grovellers, but few of these were from the sites or from Kuwait. The only bright spot was that East Europeans were being allowed out in sufficiently large numbers that most of them would be home by Christmas.

The problem was obvious. Conventional wisdom at the time held that both Baghdad and Kuwait could be flattened in the war. The US Air Force had made no secret of this in Baghdad's case. It looked as if most Westerners and Japanese would survive only if they managed to escape from Iraq on their own initiative or through a military rescue. The Baghdad diplomats could give refuge to their non-accredited colleagues and some of their people, but there was no guarantee that the Iraqi populace would not turn on them.

Those in Kuwait could gamble on lying low until the Allies had crushed Iraq, but this was a huge risk. The Human Shields were even more unfortunate. At the time, the military option seemed their only hope. Yet, the scale of any mass rescue was daunting, It amounted to the equivalent of exfiltrating six jumbo-jet passenger loads from an acutely hostile area larger than the State of California, against a large, well-armed army and some of the world's heaviest air defences.

A few individuals did manage to escape from Iraq and Kuwait after the borders were sealed in August. These daring escapades required a great deal of personal courage, nerve and good fortune. The numbers involved had little impact on the overall problem and were almost exclusively through Iraq into either Jordan or Turkey, rather than from Kuwait into Saudi Arabia.

One of the earliest escapes from Kuwait to Jordan was by a young Texan. In early September, he disguised himself in a *dishdasha* and sandals, obtained false papers identifying him as an Arab, and pretended to be deaf, dumb and mentally retarded. He drove with a Jordanian friend to Basra, where they sold the car, and then took a taxi through Baghdad to the Jordanian border.

The Jordanian crossed the border unhindered, but the Texan's false papers and deaf-and-dumb act were only good enough to fool internal Iraqi checkpoints, not a proper border check. He waited until nightfall, changed into dark trousers and a navy blue sweatshirt, and struck out into the desert away from the road, hoping to avoid patrols, before turning west towards Jordan. He had only the sandals for footwear, so his feet were soon scorched and cut by the burning desert sand, still hot from the daytime sun.

His first obstacle was a series of barbed wire fences, but he could not tell whether they marked the actual border, or were on the Iraqi side. After crossing them, he saw the lights of what proved to be a military vehicle heading towards him. It was impossible to identify it as Jordanian or Iraqi, so he lay flat on the open desert. The vehicle stopped nearby, but the soldiers, whoever they were, did not see him in the dark, and finally drove away.

The next scare was potentially more dangerous. He heard the barking of a pack of wild dogs, so went to ground again. The pack passed by upwind, howling and yapping, and did not detect him. He finally reached Amman in time to join the first evacuation flight of US women from Kuwait.

Nevertheless, at least three Britons with freedom of movement in Iraq did escape into Saudi Arabia in October. Two of them worked for Baghdad's PARC hospital. They spent two days driving across the Iraqi desert, and crossed over at the Saudi town of Ar Ar, far to the west of Kuwait. When news of the escape reached Baghdad, PARC management immediately condemned it as it put the far more numerous remaining staff at risk of further restriction.

A more sophisticated version of the young Texan's route was used in October and November by some US engineers and an Australian colleague from Bechtel Corporation. It became known as the 'Bechtel Sausage Machine'.

The Americans, most of whom were taking refuge at their Baghdad Ambassador's Residence, were particularly concerned that the Iraqis would incarcerate them. Their American country manager, Jim Roach, one other Bechtel American, and several other Americans living in or visiting Iraq at the time of the invasion were already languishing on sites. Saddam had plenty of Britons, but was short of Americans.

The Americans contacted colleagues in Jordan, who then liaised with the US Embassy in Amman, and arranged with the Jordanian military to pick them up at a rendezvous on the Jordanian side of the border. The men in Baghdad then debriefed diplomats who had driven the road to Jordan to determine the lie of the land, and took lessons in basic nighttime celestial navigation from the Kuwait-based USLOK people still in Baghdad. They were unable to ascertain whether the border was patrolled by the Iraqis, or mined, but they figured that the Iraqi Army must be so stretched by this time that they would hardly protect their only friendly border in depth.

Each man prepared himself with dark clothing and a little rucksack with the bare essentials. On the appointed dates, usually moonless nights, groups of four to six men left Baghdad and were driven to a point just short of the border, arriving at dusk. As they were generally allowed the freedom of Iraq and travelled by day, they had little trouble at checkpoints. Each of these self-contained groups was known as a 'sausage', as the escape process was akin to forcing sausages through a sausage-making machine into the safety of Jordan.

The driver of each sausage stopped just out of view of the last petrol station before the border, and the men struck out at right angles to the road on foot, while the driver returned to Baghdad. After several kilometres they turned west, and walked about 30km in the dark across the desert, into Jordan. Each sausage was designed to be small enough to avoid attracting attention, but large enough to provide help to any member who was disabled, and protection against the wild dogs. Several dozen men made it out in this way, with the last sausage going out shortly before the general hostage release in December.

Not all escapes from Iraq were over land. Perhaps one of the most daring, particularly from an almost landlocked country, was by three British engineers, Ivan Manning, Mike Teasdale and Keith Barkworth, and two French colleagues, Amadee du Pate and Gamel du Burean. Their firm had just completed a gas loading terminal 60km upstream from the Gulf, near Basra.

The men were staying on-site at the terminal when the invasion occurred. They thought they would be unaffected, but when the shipments were cancelled with the UN sanctions, they prepared to leave. The Iraqis had other ideas, and confined them to the site. However, they still had a contract, and there was work to be done, so they pretended to be gainfully employed to maintain good relations with the Iraqis. This enabled them to avoid becoming part of the Iraqi shell game, and to get off the site for short periods.

They had considered several avenues of escape, including into Iran, but they stood a good chance of encountering the millions of mines on the border. A waterborne escape seemed to offer the best potential, so they made a regular practice of going out on the waterway to fish, so that the Iraqis would get used to seeing them on the water. They then stole a marine radio from one of the ships at the terminal, and established a radio link with St Lise Radio in France, through which they could speak to their wives and superiors. They also acquired an Iraqi flag which would be essential if they were to pass themselves off as an Iraqi boat, and set aside rations for the attempt.

By late September, the site's labour force of 200 Asians and Egyptians had left, making the charade of continuing to work more difficult to maintain. Finally, on Monday, 1 October, a public holiday in Iraq for the birthday of the Prophet Mohammed, when the Iraqis would be more likely to be off duty, the five men made their move. They used the radio to request a tugboat from Dubai to pick them up outside Iraqi waters, and went fishing again at midday in a five-metre fibreglass lifeboat. They puttered slowly down the waterway, their Iraqi flag flying in the breeze, waving to the infrequent Iraqi Navy patrols as they went past, and hit the Gulf estuary at dusk.

In the estuary, they encountered unseasonable three-metre seas with whitecaps. They pressed on into the Gulf, past Kuwait's Bubiyan Island, trying to navigate by an old 1956 chart, using oil terminals as reference points. However, a generation of offshore development and the ravages of the Iran–Iraq War had made it useless. It took them some time to regain their bearings.

The tugboat from Dubai was nowhere to be seen. Nor, for that matter, were any other vessels. They had the impression from Iraqi TV and BBC Radio that the Gulf was crowded with Allied warships, but there were none to be seen anywhere. However, Dubai had alerted the Iranians. They could hear Iranian helicopters searching for them, but they were too close in to the coast to be seen, and in any case had no idea whose helicopters they were.

Their greatest danger was the high seas. They had to work the bilge pump constantly, but the engine kept them going steadily south, with the lights of Kuwait to starboard. They were picked up the next day by a Japanese work barge off the Saudi port of Khafji. Five other men on the site who had wanted nothing to do with the scheme spent another two-and-a-half months in Iraq.

These men were not the only ones to escape by sea. In the first days of the crisis, about 50 US engineers and construction workers from Brown and Root Inc., living on a work barge off Iraq's Fao Peninsula, sailed the barge 450km down the Gulf, past the occupied Kuwaiti coast, to Bahrain.

The Baghdad embassies had to be extremely circumspect about helping escapees. The diplomats were obliged to follow Iraqi law, no matter how ridiculous this might be, and aiding and abetting an unauthorized departure from Iraq was a criminal offence, and illegal. Any assistance traced back to the embassies would greatly compromise their ability to support the far more numerous people who had little or no opportunity to get out.

Notwithstanding this, a number of people did escape with official help. They included three Americans and one Briton in hiding in Kuwait who were taken out with the French in October. A lesser-known group comprised, among others, J. Hunter Downes, the Kuwait CIA Station Chief, USLOK's Major Fred Hart, and Major John Feeley, a Central Command briefer. All three had moved to Baghdad on the US road convoy of 23 August. The wisdom of exfiltrating the CIA man was obvious. Despite his diplomatic cover, Downes was a spy, and the Americans did not need the Iraqis parading a CIA man across their TV screens and turning him into yet another bargaining chip. Details on how these men and several others escaped are still classified.

Some men had more than the Iraqi military and *Mukhabarat* to deal with, and found themselves in front of the courts. However, the Iraqi judges seemed to have a sense of humour, and most of these cases ended happily.

The best known is that of Peter Goodwin, who was arrested from an evacuation convoy of British women and children, disguised as a woman. Goodwin had been sent to a site near Basra. After five weeks there, he was woken early one morning and flown to Baghdad. Instead of the Mansour Melia, he found himself in a nondescript building, being photographed. He was then put into the back of a truck with a group of Arabs, all handcuffed in pairs. When he asked where he was going, he was told: 'Calaboos', or 'Jail'.

Sure enough, Goodwin found himself in a low security prison courtyard with 40 other prisoners, most of whom seemed to be there for passport or immigration offences. One of the more interesting individuals was a Syrian who had killed three people at home and then fled to Iraq. The Iraqis were more concerned about him breaching their immigration regulations upon entering Iraq than his domestic homicidal activities.

A fortnight later, Goodwin and three Danes who had also fallen foul of the law were taken to court. The Danes were acquitted, but the court dissolved into fits of laughter as a prosecutor explained how Goodwin had dressed up in a wig and a woman's blouse, with little elephants on it. The judge regained his composure sufficiently to declare: 'Not guilty, Mrs Goodwin!' explaining his verdict by saying firstly that the defendant could not have been trying to leave Iraq illegally when arrested at the old border as Kuwait and Iraq were now one country, so he had been still inside Iraq; secondly that while it was not usual for Iraqis to dress up as women, it was certainly not illegal to do so.

The prosecutor did not share the judge's humour, and appealed the verdict. In the meantime, Goodwin went back to the jail, and then to the Mansour Melia, a free man but still a hostage. Presumably the appeal failed.

Another individual who found himself on the wrong side of the law was Andrew Whitcombe, a British man from Kuwait, in his 20s. He had put his passport through a washing machine, and tried to travel to Baghdad as a very mature-looking 17-year-old, with a plucky, middle-aged Australian girlfriend who claimed to be his aunt. The judge threw the case out, saying he did not have jurisdiction as it should properly be tried by a minors' court.

The handful of successful escapes still left over 2,000 stranded Westerners and Japanese in three distinct categories: those with relative freedom of movement in Baghdad; those in Kuwait; and the Human Shields. Each category presented a uniquely different challenge to potential rescuers.

For those in Baghdad, there were three main approaches to handling the outbreak of war. The first was for the diplomats and civilians in Baghdad to button up in their missions, and hope they would not be stormed by the Iraqis when the first bombs fell. This was not a viable option for the Americans and the British in particular, as they were providing most of the bombs. Nevertheless, it was a distinct possibility for most other nationalities. The Westerners could also take refuge in East European embassies, which were less obvious mob targets. The Irish could take cover in the PARC Ibn Al-Bitar hospital, as the Iraqis would need them to tend their wounded.

The second option was to drive towards Jordan, Syria or Turkey either by road or across the desert in national groups during the confusion of the early attacks, and hope that the convoys would not be stopped. This avenue was viable only for national groups of fewer than 50 people, such as the Australians, Canadians, and some of the Europeans. Any large convoy would attract too much attention, and be impossible to keep together. It was nevertheless a dangerous proposition as the journeys are up to 600km, and there was no way of telling how the Iraqis would react to groups of Westerners driving around the countryside when their cities were being bombed.

The third option was exfiltration by the military, or in diplomatic parlance a 'services-assisted evacuation'. The only countries capable of carrying this out, and with the Special Forces in the area to do so, were the US and UK. As leading members of the Coalition, their nationals were the ones most at risk, and hence most in need of rescue.

The Americans and the British faced a moral dilemma with this option. Their first duty was to exfiltrate their own men, but they could not necessarily also take their Australian, Canadian and European friends with them. If these people were still in Iraq when the war started, some would just have to stay behind and take their chances. This was particularly galling to the US and UK diplomats who had received substantial assistance from them.

The obvious means of extracting people militarily was by helicopter, but Baghdad's dense air defences made it suicidal to try to land them in the city. There was a small civilian airport in central Baghdad known as Al-Muthanna. One option was to capture that in an airborne assault, get all the civilians there, and take them out by large helicopters or Hercules C-130s. However, the chances of getting hundreds of civilians safely through Baghdad to Al-Muthanna, and then out of Iraq without being shot down were nil. Even holding Al-Muthanna against the several divisions of Iraqi troops on call in Baghdad would have required a huge force. This option would effectively have required the capture of central Baghdad.

A barely more viable plan was for the diplomats and civilians to drive to the outskirts of Baghdad, and rendezvous with low-flying helicopters as far away as possible from the city's air defences, while the first air attacks struck home and held the Iraqis' attentions. This depended on the cars being able to get through the city's checkpoints, especially with an Allied attack imminent. This in itself was extremely unlikely. The diplomats were actually prevented from venturing more than 25km from the city centre. Special Forces men may have had to infiltrate into Iraq to ensure that the convoys made the rendezvous, and to guide the helicopters in. There was simply too much that could go wrong, and this still left the problem of the Human Shields.

Advance preparation on the ground in Baghdad for any military exfiltration operation was crucial. The first priority was to minimize the number of people to be rescued, and thus the number of rescue aircraft required. Not only do more aircraft complicate co-ordination: but they also require more back-up for potential mechanical failure, refuelling, covering fire and radar suppression. Rescue helicopters would have to go into small landing zones, perhaps under fire, in the dark, so the risk of aircraft collision greatly increased with every extra machine used. The spectre of the debacle of the 1979 attempt to rescue the Teheran US Embassy hostages haunted everyone.

With this in mind, the Baghdad diplomats had to get as many people as possible out in advance by other means. They maximized departures with grovellers, continually pressed the cases of elderly or sick men, tried to obtain legal alternative nationalities for Americans and Britons, and allowed all but the most crucial accredited diplomats to leave through normal channels.

The Americans and British in Baghdad were able to provide significant intelligence for the rescue planners. The USLOK commander, Colonel John Mooneyham, was a Vietnam veteran in the US Special Forces, and was familiar with the planning and intelligence requirements for a rescue operation. By November, his men had plotted most of the Iraqi checkpoints between Baghdad and Kuwait, west to Jordan, and north to Turkey. They had contact with Central Command at MacDill Air Force Base, Florida through a secure phone at the embassy. Presumably, once out of the Baghdad's environs, they could have driven in one of several directions to a rendezvous, or even to Jordan or Turkey, with Allied aircraft bombing the checkpoints ahead of them.

However, despite the best efforts of the world's élite forces, some men would be left behind in Baghdad. The Iraqis always had people in the Mansour Melia, or on the move between sites or between Kuwait and Baghdad.

Rescuing the 600 Americans, British and Japanese on strategic sites presented even greater problems. By late November, with war imminent, the Allies had – or should have had – relatively comprehensive information on the sites where men were being held. There were enough pieces of the jig-saw available to build up a reasonable picture of who was where. In fact, the Iraqis wanted the Allies to know roughly where the men were so that these sites, most of which were in fact bombed during the war, would be spared.

However, the hostages were spread over about 80 sites, many of them well defended, over 400,000 square kilometres of Iraq. Some of the sites were in central Baghdad, or in huge army complexes. They were not guarded by crack troops, but the volume of air defences around them, and the difficulty of finding the precise location of a few men on the sprawling bases, made any rescue mission virtually impossible. They were needles in a massive haystack.

With clear skies over Kuwait and Iraq in autumn, information was coming down from satellites and surveillance aircraft in such detail that, according to the British Commander in the Gulf, Lieutenant-General Sir Peter de la Billière, every time Saddam's men dug a new slit trench, the Coalition knew about it. However, the satellites were not so successful in tracking hostages. They could not provide human intelligence. De la Billière was extremely frustrated at the desperate lack of good intelligence about the Human Shield.

It is surprising that the military's human intelligence was so limited. If de la Billière's complaints are valid, then it was not because the intelligence was unavailable. It was either not co-ordinated, not obtained, or not passed on to the military, although many released hostages were extensively debriefed. Many of the sites had been built by non-Iraqi companies, so detailed information on their layout was available from the contractors and satellite imagery. The men in Baghdad responsible for tracking hostages on the basis of the limited information available to them – Lieutenant-Colonel Tom Funk at the US Embassy and Don Macauley at the British Embassy – certainly passed on their information but, according to de la Billière, it does not seem to have reached those who needed it to plan exfiltration operations.

To be fair, the General was restricted in just how much he could disclose, but it was extremely difficult to confirm suspected sites and numbers of hostages with satellites. Many were operational facilities where hostages were kept indoors. Even with clear skies, the best cameras in the world cannot see through buildings. Nevertheless, there is a great difference between knowing where people are, and exfiltrating them. In October, with most of the hostages being British, the Special Air Service examined ways of rescuing them, and started working with the FCO to build as complete a picture as possible of where they were. They were aware from the beginning that they would never know where all of the men were at a given time, so any rescue operation could never be a complete success. Furthermore, any rescue attempt required all sites to be hit almost simultaneously to prevent the Iraqis from moving or even killing the men as soon as they heard about attacks elsewhere.

To have any chance of success, the rescue mission would have required about 60 helicopters just to lift the men out, plus aircraft to get the rescue teams to and from the sites, suppress Iraqi air defences, and provide covering fire. The scale of such an operation, particularly when combined with the need to exfiltrate the hundreds of Westerners in Baghdad, and those in Kuwait, would have stretched the Western world's Special Forces beyond their limits.

The gravity of the situation was later confirmed by de la Billière who at no stage felt that he could have recovered more than half of the Human Shields. At least 300 out of the 600 men on sites would have been left behind, or killed in any rescue operation. Nevertheless, as early as 1 November, an FCO spokesman, interviewed on the BBC, said that there were contingency plans for getting the hostages out in case of war. People were working on it.

Although the people in Kuwait were much closer to Allied bases in Saudi Arabia, their rescue also presented serious problems. First, Kuwait was almost as heavily defended as Baghdad, so getting helicopters safely into the city, and out again, was nigh on impossible. Secondly, the 600 Westerners in Kuwait in November were spread across about 200 separate locations. The 500 Americans and Britons among them were unable to move around freely, so it was much more difficult to concentrate them in a few places, and impossible for them to rendezvous on the city outskirts. A problem unique to Kuwait was the 27 people in the US Embassy, the two men in the British Embassy, and, until late November, the Human Shields at four sites in Kuwait.

With Saudi Arabia so close, there was a temptation, especially among the free-nationals, simply to try to drive there. From September, the Iraqis had allowed Kuwaiti women, children and men over 45 to leave. It seemed worth a try. However, when two Australians attempted it in November, they were stopped just south of Ahmadi, and politely told to go back home.

With November's cooler weather, other men contemplated getting out to Saudi Arabia by walking the 80km parallel to the road by night, and hiding out somewhere by day. In theory, they could cover the distance in two nights, but it would have been almost impossible to find somewhere to hide in the desert. To the best of my knowledge, no one tried this. If they had, they would have eventually found their way blocked by Iraqi troops and minefields.

The general official attitude towards a military rescue of the men in Kuwait was that it was a 'mission impossible'. It was safer for them to stay in hiding until the Iraqis had withdrawn or been expelled. Another two months, especially over Christmas, would place great strain on them, but was preferable to dying in an impossible rescue attempt. This attitude changed in November, especially for the British, when the Baghdad diplomats were briefed on what the Hostage Support Group could do. The major problem with a Kuwait rescue operation prior to this was that the rescuers would have to get hundreds of frightened men out of their widely-dispersed hiding places to the landing zones, against Iraqi opposition. They would have no idea where the men were hiding.

The time the rescuers would have had to spend on the ground would give the Iraqis plenty of time to regroup. In effect, the Allies would have to capture all of Kuwait City before this operation was viable, in which case there would no longer be a problem for those in Kuwait.

Now, the embassies realized that with sufficient support, the Hostage Support Group could concentrate the men near landing zones. They could then board the helicopters as soon as they landed. This shorter time on the ground, and the fewer troops required, may have made the operation just possible.

The general idea was to move up to 20 men for a single helicopter load into an apartment or villa near a landing zone several days before the operation. Up to 50 men may have had to share accommodation for some time, in a dozen different places, thus increasing the risk of capture. The operation would have had to be very carefully managed on the ground, but it was a calculated risk. We knew that we would not be able to reach some men, and were never sure that every man would go along with it as it meant placing their lives in the hands of others. Nevertheless, it gave them a fighting chance.

The landing zones and nearby Iraqi deployments could be reconnoitered by satellite, and this information confirmed by the Hostage Support Group on the ground. Our main advantage was that most men in hiding were in the coastal suburbs. Iraqi defences in those areas were oriented seaward. If helicopters landed behind them, then the Iraqis could counter them with little more than personal weapons, which was still a risk. Furthermore, at night, the Iraqis fortified themselves in the local schools they were using as billets, with only a few checkpoints outside which we could plot. In effect, we knew with a high degree of certainty where most troops within a kilometre of the landing zones would be, as long as the operation was conducted at night. Finally, perhaps only a hundred men had to be moved between suburbs to consolidate them, so we did not need peak concentrations until a few nights before the mission. Several landing zones were suggested to the diplomats. Perhaps up to six would be needed, as it would require about 30 large helicopters to get everyone out, all at once.

A final target would have been the Kuwait Regency Palace Hotel where captured Human Shields were held before being transferred to Baghdad. Fortunately, this was also on the coast, near the suburbs with the highest concentrations of men in hiding. Security around it was relatively light, but as the rescuers would actually have to go into the building to get those held inside, it would have to be captured quietly, perhaps by Special Forces infiltrated into Kuwait before the mass rescue.

It is by no means certain that every man in hiding or in the Regency Palace would have got out alive and unhurt, but for many of them, the risk of rescue was preferable to more months in hiding. It was imperative that any operation exfiltrated as many men as possible simultaneously as there would undoubtedly be Iraqi casualties from covering fire. Any men left behind would bear the brunt of Iraqi anger at this. A shuttle service would not work.

We never discovered whether the information passed to the Baghdad diplomats on what could be done on the ground reached the military in time for them to work it into their plans, but every Westerner in Kuwait then is grateful that they were released before a rescue attempt had to be made.

Unknown to us at the time, the US Special Forces had asked the Kuwaiti Resistance in Ahmadi to mark a landing site on the maps they could fax out on the satellite phones, together with all safe houses within 500 metres of the site. They wanted to infiltrate men and equipment. Ahmadi was the most isolated suburb, and the closest to Saudi Arabia. It also had a Resistance group with proven reliability. The Resistance were shocked, saying that the ground was covered with Iraqis who would be sure to hear the helicopters. The Americans told the Kuwaitis not to worry about the noise. They just needed the site and maps. Apparently, the Americans had silent helicopters.

Nevertheless, the Americans were most welcome. The Resistance could hide and help them, and even make them false IDs, as long as they could pass for Arabs or Africans. For one week, the Resistance were on tenterhooks before the Americans, inexplicably, cancelled the operation.

The diplomats in the US and British Embassies in Kuwait had two options. The first was to close shop and relocate to Baghdad. The Iraqis were preventing their male colleagues who had earlier relocated there from leaving Iraq in order to pressure them to shut their Kuwait missions. The implication was that if the Americans and British complied, then all the Kuwait-based diplomats would be allowed to leave Iraq.

However, the situation was more complicated than this. First, no one knew whether they could trust the Iraqis to let them out of Iraq if the Kuwait diplomats moved north. Secondly, 19 of the men on the US compound were not bona-fide diplomats, although they had been put onto the State Department payroll, and had diplomatic passports waiting for them in Baghdad. It was uncertain whether the Iraqis would recognise them as diplomats. It later transpired that they would not. If the Americans had closed their Kuwait Embassy, they may have had to give up these men to join the Human Shield.

As a compromise, the four women on the US compound could have moved to Baghdad, and would have been allowed out of Iraq. However, three of these ladies were crucial to the Embassy's operations. Free Westerners could have brought the diplomatic passports from Baghdad for the 19 civilians so that they could have walked out with them in their hands, and at least put the Iraqi on the back foot in arguing that they were not diplomats. Getting the passports to Kuwait was not the problem. Getting them into the Embassy was.

More seriously for the men in hiding, the US Embassy's satellite phone provided the only means of prompt and secure communications out of Kuwait. With the Americans gone, the communications required to co-ordinate a rescue operation would be unavailable, unless the Resistance satellite phones could be used, or Special Forces with their own independent communications were infiltrated into Kuwait. We had ham radios, but these were insecure.

The second option for rescuing the people in the embassy compounds was a military operation. This would have to be done either just before the rescue operation for the men in hiding, or simultaneously. If those in hiding were exfiltrated first, then the Iraqis guarding the diplomatic compounds would be alerted to move in and capture those inside.

Both compounds were on Kuwait Bay, but 20km inside the bay. Any rescue helicopters would have had to come in low over the water. Fortunately, they could vector on the distinctive Kuwait Towers, with the team for the British going to the right and the larger team for the Americans to the left.

The American compound was a far more difficult rescue than the British, not just because of the numbers involved. The landing space inside the compound was more limited, and it was overlooked by the Kuwait International Hotel, and several other high buildings. The Iraqis had placed a heavy machine gun pointing out to sea on the hotel roof. Strangely, they had not placed any troops on top of the taller buildings behind the hotel, a fact which we verified by climbing up them and checking them physically. Mortars had been set up on the beach across the road from the Embassy. The aiming stakes were clearly visible from the roofs of some Embassy buildings. Additionally, there were still many civilian workers in the hotel. The Iraqis had also established a barracks opposite the compound, and the Americans had noticed them holding prisoners, probably Kuwaitis, in there.

During November, the Americans set up a landing zone in the compound by clearing all debris which could be sucked into helicopters' air intakes, and cutting down an inconveniently placed basketball goal. All this had to be done carefully at night to avoid arousing the suspicions of the watching Iraqis.

It was later reported that the US Joint Special Operations Command had devised a plan codenamed 'Pacific Wind' to rescue the people in the two compounds. It involved 18 F-15 fighter-bombers, four F-117 Stealth bombers, four F-14 Tomcat fighters, rescue helicopters, several electronic jamming aircraft, and a C-130 command plane from which the operation would be run. Two of the Stealths would each bomb a Kuwaiti power station to knock out the lights around the Embassies, and most of Kuwait City into the bargain. The other two Stealths would flatten the International Hotel to kill the Iraqis inside, and neutralize the roof-top machine-gun. The F-15s would then attack the Iraqis along the beach and on the roads around the compounds, presumably seeding the roads with cluster bomblets to hinder reinforcements. Simultaneously, Delta Force commandos would land in the compounds.

The people in the US compound were to take shelter in the fortified basement of the chancery during the attack. Once the compound was secure, they were to emerge and run along a marked path to the rescue helicopter. They would be pulled inside and counted, and the helicopter would take off as soon as everyone was on board. The troops securing the compound would then withdraw. Up until 25 November, when they were moved to Baghdad, the Human Shields in the nearby Dasman Villas were included in the plan.

Apparently, on at least two occasions, the Americans were within an hour of launching the rescue mission when satellite reconnaissance around the Embassy suggested that the Iraqis were about to move in. Fortunately they were false alarms, and nothing happened.

The British Embassy was a little more simple, if such an operation were needed at all. A safer option for Mike Weston and Larry Banks was simply to relocate to Baghdad in the hope that they and their colleagues who had moved there earlier would then be allowed out of Iraq. However, if they had to go out the hard way, all nearby high buildings were far enough away from the compound not to pose a threat, and the Ambassador's garden provided a ready-made landing zone. It would have been sufficient for a single helicopter to make a quick touchdown behind the Embassy walls, and for the two diplomats to dash for it while other gunships provided cover.

The plan as reported had several major drawbacks, especially for the American compound. First, the International Hotel housed not only Iraqi troops and administrators, but also African, Asian and Kuwaiti civilian employees. There were also several groups of Americans and Britons in hiding within 300 metres of the Embassy. The rescue force would have had to capture the entire area to get them out, a far more complicated job than taking over two compounds and the nearby hostage site. If they had gone in with the simple plan to isolate the compounds by destroying a large part of the neighbourhood, many Kuwaitis and other civilians, including perhaps these men in hiding and the civilians in the hotel would have died. Furthermore, rescuing this handful of diplomats without simultaneously exfiltrating the Human Shields and men in hiding would have meant that those left behind would pay the real price of the rescue at the hands of the Iraqis.

Perhaps most importantly, General Schwarzkopf is reported to have told the officers planning the operation: 'If I direct you to conduct this, then I may need to go ahead and execute the rest of the war plan.' In other words, the plan could only be implemented as part of the main attack.

The question of exfiltrating people from Iraq and Kuwait was deadly serious. Despite Western leaders' statements that the hostages made no difference as to whether they went to war against Iraq, and the preference by the majority of the hostages for war, the danger to 2,000 innocent Western and Japanese men would have greatly complicated the decision to strike on 16 January, 1991.

As confirmed to me by General Schwarzkopf, who said, 'If Saddam had not released the hostages, we would have had to conduct the war differently to try to avoid hitting our own people on targets we wanted to bomb,' the presence of Human Shields would have fundamentally changed the nature of the air war. Concern for these people would have increased pressure for an early, even premature, ground war. In retrospect, this might have saved hundreds of Kuwaiti lives by denying the Iraqis the opportunity for a final orgy of blood-letting and hostage-taking as they withdrew, but the price might have been more Allied military casualties.

The difficulties in exfiltrating such a large number of people in such circumstances were paramount. Certainly, some people would have been left behind. Others, including some members of the rescue teams, would have died. Whatever else people who were in Kuwait and Iraq may think of Saddam, and whatever his reasons, they are grateful to him for their release before they had to go through the risk of a rescue operation, or war.

27. RELEASE

Thursday, 6 December, at 3.00 p.m., was a sleepy time in Kuwait and Iraq. The men in hiding and in the camps often took a post-lunch nap, or did their daily exercises. Very few were listening to the radio. After four months, most only tuned in to the news a couple of times a day. The minders in Kuwait were doing their rounds. It was not prime listening time. As such, most people missed the first BBC announcement that Saddam was releasing all the hostages. It came as a short, simple, single sentence before the main news bulletin:

'Before we read the news, it has just been announced that all travel restrictions on foreigners in Iraq have been lifted.'

During the next 55 minutes, the phones in Kuwait went wild. Men checked around with all their other contacts to see if anyone knew more. Others stayed glued to the radio, expecting further details, but there was nothing. By 4.00 p.m., the phones were silent. Everyone with access to a shortwave radio was tuned in. The announcement was confirmed on the hourly bulletin. It was the lead item, but details were sparse. It seemed too good to be true.

In retrospect, the general release was probably a foregone conclusion. We were largely unaware of the Arab negotiations behind the scenes. For all practical purposes, the hostages had outlived their usefulness. Although they provided Saddam with a continuous stream of grovellers and TV cameras to Baghdad, they had not prevented a military build-up, nor enticed the Coalition into negotiations. In fact, their detention had created far greater public outrage than had the invasion of Kuwait.

Meanwhile, the releases of the hostages was turning into a circus. The Iraqis were overwhelmed. So many wives of men still held at the sites were applying for visas that the Iraqi Embassy in London had to stop issuing them.

Most of the senior grovellers who visited Baghdad claimed at least some credit for convincing Saddam to release the hostages, but the catalyst that precipitated the general release appears to have been a 4 December meeting between Saddam, King Hussein of Jordan, Yasser Arafat, and Yemeni Vice-President Ali Salem Al-Bid. Arafat and the King argued strongly for the release, apparently confirming Saddam's own impression that this would greatly improve the prospects for a peaceful settlement; releasing the hostages immediately and unconditionally could capitalize on the growing public demands in the West for peace in preference to war.

This meeting was held against a background of an apparently significant softening of the European and US positions in the wake of the 29 November UN use-of-force resolution, and Bush's offer of talks. Bush was coming under fire from leading Democrats who demanded that the sanctions be given more time, even though they had been shown to be ineffectual. A domestic debate raged on whether he had the constitutional powers to go to war without clear authorization from Congress. To Saddam, a properly-handled general release might allow him to retain at least some of Kuwait, regain some credibility, and emerge from the crisis with some dignity. He was wrong. If it had come a few weeks earlier, and been accompanied by at least a partial withdrawal, UN approval for war may have been less certain. He had missed his chance.

Nevertheless, such considerations of higher policy were of little concern to most foreigners in Iraq and Kuwait. All that mattered was going home.

The initial reaction to the announcement in Kuwait was one of shock, and then scepticism. Men there were resigned to the idea of spending Christmas in hiding, and being freed only by the Allies retaking Kuwait in January. Many of the Human Shields in Iraq felt similarly, although some were hopeful that their wives could get them out. Several dozen had in fact been moved back to the Mansour Melia to be with their wives who had arrived in Baghdad.

A number of men in hiding feared it was an Iraqi trick to get them to give themselves up, only to be incarcerated. The announcement had mentioned only those in Iraq, but some men in Kuwait felt that because Iraq considered Kuwait part of Iraq, they must be included. Few men were prepared to venture outside until we knew more. Saddam was putting the release question to his Parliament, which would meet in special session the following day. However, one member of the Hostage Support Group, Keith Chandler, was convinced that the release was genuine. He sent a fax to the Iraqi authorities at the Regency Palace Hotel, in travel agency format, dated 4.03 p.m., 6 December, just after the BBC bulletin finished. It read, in effect:

Please confirm booking for 350 double rooms for ex-guests from 7 December until departure. Meals, accommodation, laundry and sports facilities to the account of the Revolutionary Command Council Baghdad. Wine, women and song to personal account. Please confirm as soon as possible.

It was signed: 'Ex-potential detainees, South Salwa and surrounding areas.'

This message would have been unremarkable, except that the Iraqis, or someone else, took it seriously. Perhaps they too had a sense of humour. A faxed reply asked for more information to allow them to confirm the booking.

That evening, a few other men in Kuwait who were equally certain of the announcement ventured out to visit friends they had not seen in four months. Most remained in hiding. Even if the announcement were true, few expected that the troops on the street would know of it. The embassies and wardens advised people not to lower their guard. The following day, 7 December, the BBC confirmed that it did in fact include those in Kuwait, but advised the men in hiding to wait until it was ratified by the Iraqi Parliament.

That same Friday, the minders of the Hostage Support Group were due to hold our weekly co-ordination meeting. We went ahead with it, wondering what was left for us to do. Strangely, there was a terrible feeling of anti-climax.

We were ecstatic for the men who were going home without having to face war, but somehow the final act of the play had been stolen from us. The organization was operating smoothly now. We were getting the co-operation we needed from the Baghdad embassies. Although some communities such as the Canadians still had their own internal problems, the system in general was working beautifully. We were short of minders in some suburbs, but the mail was coming in and going out reliably and regularly. Our bulk-buying of food and document-forging in conjunction with the Kuwaiti Resistance was going well. Suddenly, the release announcement had rendered us redundant.

The only tasks left for us now were to ensure that everybody had transport to the airport, and that foodstocks and money left behind were distributed to the Kuwaitis and Filipinos who had been helping us, and to the Westerners who had decided to stay.

Remaining in hiding was too much for some of the men. A few more of them ventured outside tentatively the day after the announcement, blinking in the direct winter sunlight. Some had last been outside in the scorching heat of a Kuwaiti summer, and were pallid. Others looked tanned and fit from sunning themselves on the roofs of their apartment complexes, or in their gardens. The ecstasy of being able to stride across a street or a patch of open ground, or see the outside of one's building instead of the inside, to breathe in a lungful of fresh air, or to simply scream and shout at the top of one's voice, was indescribable.

The sight greeting those venturing out was not pleasant. The sight of the stripped cars and looted shops, burned houses, and ubiquitous portraits of Saddam, some three meters high, came as a shock. Every single electronics store, clothes outlet, toy shop, takeaway, video shop and jewellers had been looted. The only businesses open were barbers, a few supermarkets, the petrol stations and cigarette and vegetable stalls, and a couple of Palestinian-operated car repair shops. Kuwait was a ghost town. Perhaps only 200,000 Kuwaitis were still in the country, and a similar number of Palestinians. The Kuwaitis were keeping a low profile to avoid the enforced change to Iraqi citizenship. The once-bustling city was dead. The most noticeable features were the crude Iraqi checkpoints. Men emerging from hiding expressed surprise that the free-nationals could have coped with moving around such a depressing landscape for so long.

Other people had even more unpleasant surprises. Some who had moved into hiding with others went back to their own homes to find them completely looted. Others found that the Iraqi Army had taken over their buildings, sometimes for billets, other times as a strongpoint. Usually, nothing was left, not even photographs. Some found their Palestinian neighbours, people they had lived next to for years, living in their homes. There was nothing they could do but turn around burning with anger, and return to their hiding places.

By Saturday 8 December, incredibly, parties were organized. The British led the way; the Americans for the most part stayed inside. They did not want to take any last-minute risks, with freedom was so close now, and they were still the main force in the Coalition. The parties were unforgettable. There was now no need to ration food, and alcohol was freely available. After being confined to

Illustration 4. PLEASE MAKE A RESERVATION

Correspondence with Regency Palace Hotel, Kuwait, 6 and 7 December, 1990, concerning release of hostages.

Original Keith Chandler fax of 6 December, 1990, to Iraqi authorities, Regency Palace Hotel, with transmission confirmation slip.

4:03 PM Thu, Dec 6, 1990

TO :IRAQI AUTH REG PLC HTL KWT.

FM:EX HSTGS KWT

URGENT URGENT URGENT URGENT URGENT URGENT URGENT

PLS CNF BKG 350 DBLE RMS FR EX GSTS 7 /12 TILL DEP.
MEALS ACCOM,LNDRY + SPRT FACS TO ACC OF REV CON BAG.
WINE WOMAN SONG TO P/ACC.
PLS CNF ASAP.

RGDS
      EX -PTNTIAL DTAIN⁻
S SALWA & SURROUNDING AREAS..

[ACTIVITY REPORT]				14	
		265		HOUSE	
MODE	CONNECTION TEL	CONNEC		AGE T.	PAGES
TX	5723109	KREGPLH	12/06 16:14	20'39	01(00)

Illustration 4. PLEASE MAKE A RESERVATION (cont.)

Correspondence with Regency Palace Hotel, Kuwait, 6 and 7 December, 1990, concerning release of hostages.

7 December, 1990, reply of Regency Palace Hotel to Keith Chandler's fax of 6 December.

'90 12/07 10:30   ☎ 5723109   KREGPLH KT   01

Kuwait Regency Palace

TO: EX-PINTIAL OTAIN   06.12.1990.

FROM: KUWAIT REGENCY PALACE.

SIR,

    IN ORDER TO CONFIRM YOUR RESERVATION, WOULD YOU BE KIND ENOUGH TO SEND THE
FOLLOWING INFORMATIONS.

1. THE EXACT NO OF ROOMS YOU REQUIRE & NO.OF PERSONS WHO ARE GOING TO
   OCCUPIED THESE ROOMS.

2. THE NATIONALITY OF EACH GUESTS.

3. PLEASE INFORM US IF THERE ARE ANY WOMAN OR CHILDREN AMONG THEM.

4. ANY COUPLES AMONG THEM?

LOOKING FORWARD FOR YOUR REPLY.
                                        BEST REGARDS
                                    (KUWAIT REGENCY PALACE)

The Leading Hotels of the World

P.O. Box 1139, Kuwait 22012 Salmiyah Kuwait Telephones: 5728000 Telex: 46082 KT KREGPLH FAX: 5723100 their homes for so long, the men simply had to get out and see those they had been speaking to on the phone for months, but had yet to meet.

A few of the women who had remained in Kuwait came to one of the British parties, including Lorraine Dyer, a stunning former air hostess, Fiona Underwood, an effervescent blond Anglo-Irishwoman, and another vivacious British woman, Norma Armstrong. The effect on the men was astounding. Many had not seen a woman in months. They just wanted to sit down and talk with a female, to be reminded what a woman looked like, and to smell a perfume other than the sweat of men they were hiding with. The men would be home with their own families soon, but these few brave women were a tangible reminder that a normal life remained beyond the current experience.

At one of these parties, I phoned Barbara Bodine, still inside her Embassy compound, held the phone out for her to hear the music, singing, and conversation, and said: 'Listen, Barbara! The sounds of freedom!' She laughed. Her people would be going out soon. There was now no need for her to stay. 'There's 400,000 US troops down there in Saudi who can make the point far better than a few diplomats sitting it out without power or water in the Embassy,' she said, a note of anticipation in her voice.

The release announcement itself was not simple. Saddam went through the charade of democracy by making a recommendation to his rubber-stamp Parliament that the 'guests' be released. A number of delegates dutifully voted against it, but the result was never in doubt. They even worked overtime, on Friday 7 December, the Arab week-end, to authorize the release.

With the release, Saddam offered Iraq's apologies for all harm caused, and asked forgiveness from God, saying that the hostages were no longer needed, and could be home for Christmas, as if he were a benevolent Scrooge giving his workers a Yuletide break. He went on to say that their presence 'had given Iraqi forces the time needed to prepare their defences, and great service to the cause of peace'. He reconciled the general release to his earlier offer of a phased release from 25 December by saying that he was bringing forward the release as Iraq no longer needed the Human Shield.

The apology and request for forgiveness as if the ordeal of the invasion and occupation were little more than the inconvenience of a delayed train incensed the hostages, but they held their counsel until they were safely out of Iraq.

From late on 7 December and over the next two days, the Iraqis bussed and flew the Human Shields in from the camps to the Mansour Melia. Even then, they needed more PR in the US, so the Americans were often the first to leave.

The departures from camps where the men had half-expected to die from Allied bombs were filled with a mix of elation and poignancy. Many of them had formed deep friendships, and wept as they left, promising to keep in touch. Even some of the guards shared their joy. At several camps, they allowed curious locals up to the fences. The men were touched at their abject poverty, and handed out fruit, other food, and medicines through the wire. Crowds gathered, and soon anything the Human Shields would not be taking with them was being handed over.

Upon arriving at the Mansour Melia, they found the atmosphere charged with emotion. Men were reunited with wives who had come to try to get them out. Others met friends from whom they had been separated in the Iraqi shell-game of moving hostages between sites. The hotel was full of embracing, weeping couples and groups. The media were there in force, and soon pictures of the happy men were being beamed back home to their delighted families.

Initially, there was little ill-feeling against the Iraqis: there was too much to be happy about. A number of men, and some of the women, were aggressive, but the Iraqis generally smiled it off. They were genuinely worried about the prospect of war, but they also seemed happy for the hostages that they were going home. Exit visas were obtained for most of the Americans by the afternoon of 9 December in anticipation of a flight out that night. Only a fraction of the hundreds of British had their visas, but their diplomats were working through the night to complete the processing.

In the meantime, other diplomats in Baghdad were working feverishly on chartering planes to take their people out of Kuwait and Iraq. The Americans in Kuwait were told early on the 8th that their Baghdad Embassy was trying to arrange a blanket visa for all Americans. They could expect to leave on the 10th or 11th. Things then moved faster than expected: they were told that evening they should get to Kuwait Airport by 9.00 a.m. the following morning.

The Americans expected only 150 people to go. Barbara Bodine told us that they could take out the sick British with them. From what we could gather, she had virtually given up talking with the British Embassy, and was dealing with their community through the minders and wardens. I called around those men we knew were ill. Several jumped at the chance.

The British were also trying to charter a flight and arrange a blanket visa, but their departure was expected to be on the 11th. Strangely, most of the British were not worried about the extra two days. A number were touring the city. For the few BA passengers and crew still in town, it was their first chance to see the city that had been their unintended home for four months.

Curiously, the main problem in those days was finding dog and cat boxes. Talk of claiming compensation from Iraq increased. Priorities had changed completely. On one occasion, Barbara Bodine asked me to drive to the Fintas area which was out of phone contact with the rest of Kuwait, and obtain the permission of the few Americans hiding there to have their names given to the Iraqis for the exit visas, and to ask if they had any questions. One couple wanted to drive their car out through Saudi Arabia so they could salvage it and some of their household goods. It all seemed so petty in the light of what people had gone through. Yet, there was a comforting ordinariness about people being worried about trivia rather than the Iraqi knock on the door.

At this time, about 100 of the 400 Britons still in Kuwait were considering staying, as were about 20 of the Americans and the sole remaining Japanese family, the Moriwakis. Like some of the free-nationals in the Hostage Support Group, they wanted to see the crisis through.

Kuwaiti friends were touched that so many wanted to stay, but tried to talk us out of it. 'You can do far more for us outside by telling people back home the truth about what is going on in Kuwait, and that the Kuwaiti people are really worth fighting for,' said one. Another Kuwaiti had a particularly stubborn British friend, so told him, with remarkable prescience, that by staying he would put Kuwaitis in danger as they would try to protect him when the Iraqis changed their mind and came looking for him.

The overriding factor that changed people's minds about staying was not the risk of war, but the fact that some of the families at home had suffered far more psychologically than the hostages or those in hiding. The wives and children had not and would not know from day to day whether their loved ones were alive or dead. With the embassies also leaving, there would be no means of communication other than the scarce Resistance satellite phones to which few men had access, or the ham radios. It was 40 days to the war deadline of 15 January. Everyone expected that it would be about a week beyond that before Kuwait was free. With Christmas looming, more and more men decided that they could not put their families through any more suffering, no matter how much they felt at one with Kuwait.

As more people changed their minds, the resolve of others fell. No one could blame them. In the end, about 37 Westerners and the Moriwakis stayed. Some were women married to Kuwaitis, or long-term residents with nowhere else to go, or with deep links to the Kuwaiti community. One was a Yugoslav-British reporter at the local *Arab Times*, Jadranka Porter, who wanted to write about the experience. Her American editor, Taddeusz Karwecki, also initially decided to stay, but soon changed his mind. There would be no way of getting copy out, and he drew a distinction between journalism and spying.

On Sunday, 9 December, the US men who had remained successfully hidden in Kuwait flew to Baghdad on an Iraqi 727, together with a handful of Britons.

The British Embassy in Baghdad spent the two days following the release announcement negotiating unsuccessfully with the Iraqis to bring a BA 767 and a Virgin Atlantic 747 into Baghdad. The Americans had chartered an Iraqi plane. It may have contributed to Iraq's economy, but this was not a time to stand too firmly on principle. The Americans wanted their people out fast.

Two of the eight US diplomats from the Kuwait embassy, Gale Rogers and Mark Hertzberg, joined the men from Kuwait, together with the 17 civilians still in the US Embassy. The remaining six diplomats would stay behind until Thursday, 13 December, to close the embassy, and ensure as best they could that all Americans who wanted to go had been given an opportunity to leave.

Most of the Americans in hiding had little trouble making their way to the airport at 9.00 a.m. for the scheduled departure time of noon. British friends who were due to leave on the 11th, their Kuwaiti minders, and the Hostage Support Group took them. The Iraqis would not let them drive any closer than the checkpoint on an overpass one kilometre from the airport, a security precaution against Resistance attacks. The men were forced to pay ten Iraqi dinars for the short taxi ride to the terminal. Some had driven their own cars, and had to leave them behind at the checkpoint. As they did so, looters moved in and took them, under the noses of the *Mukhabarat* and soldiers.

In the meantime, I was trying to get the American diplomats out of their compound. The exit of this first batch of US diplomats and civilians from their embassy turned into yet another farcical episode of Iraqi incompetence.

Barbara Bodine and I had organised a minibus from the Regency Palace Hotel. Several Americans living in an apartment complex near the Embassy had organised their own minibus, and met at the embassy. A further two private cars, driven by Arab employees of the hotel, made up our convoy, which met outside the Embassy early in the morning.

The hotel's Palestinian manager, Ghassan Rwanjhi, had arranged frozen chicken, fresh fruits and vegetables, and beer for the diplomats, who had been living on rice, pasta and canned tuna for months. As soon as his driver arrived, we transferred the supplies into my car for his safety. The Iraqis might shoot an Arab for trying to smuggle food into the Embassy, but not a Westerner. As it was, the man was taking a tremendous risk even being there.

We had expected the diplomats to be waiting outside for us, but there was only an old soldier opposite the Embassy gate. We stood by the barrier blocking the access road to the gate, 30 metres away, for what seemed like an eternity, trying in vain to attract the diplomats' attention. The drivers of the other vehicles grew increasingly nervous, as did the old soldier. One driver wanted to leave. I told him curtly that the Americans had spent four months inside the Embassy, and had sent 400,000 troops to liberate his country, so he could wait another ten minutes. Unknown to me, he was Yemeni, not Kuwaiti. Eventually, I had to go into the nearby International Hotel to phone the Embassy and tell them we were there.

As I arrived back, much relieved that the drivers were still there, Barbara and Gale came out of the Embassy just as a middle-aged Kurdish-looking Iraqi lieutenant turned up. It was the first time I had set eyes on these two ladies throughout the crisis, after speaking with them almost daily for four months. It was a very special moment to meet these two brave women face-to-face.

The old soldier seemed to be trying to tell the ladies that he would have to shoot them if they came out any further, but they dismissed him with a contemptuous wave. The poor old fellow did not know what to do. The only authority which the lieutenant seemed to have was to take the numbers of our cars, much to the consternation of the Arab drivers.

Eventually, a fat Iraqi major turned up. The two women had walked half-way up the access road, and the major and I walked half-way down to meet them. The old sentry saluted the major, and then stood there looking useless.

The major seemed to be unaware of the release. He was also unused to dealing with women on an equal basis, and the Americans were not about to make any concessions to Iraqi sensitivities. At first, he turned to talk to me as the only foreign man there, but I had to tell him that the ladies were in charge; I was only a driver. The Americans could not have delivered a more subtle insult if they had tried. Barbara and Gale are both youngish-looking, attractive women. The message to the major was 'You are not worth us sending our men to talk to. We will not even send you our women; talk to our girls!'

Eventually the major was made to understand that Saddam had said that the Americans could go. But first, the Ambassador himself had to come out, go over to the International Hotel, and phone an Iraqi MFA official.

This little visit by Ambassador Howell to the hotel caused a minor panic in Washington and the Embassy. It was the first time he had been off the compound since August. He came out onto the road, spoke to the major, and then strode over to the hotel. Suddenly, the implications of the situation hit the diplomats. The Ambassador was off the compound, alone, and in Iraqi custody. The satellite phone generator was fired up, and a message flashed to Washington. There was nothing the diplomats or the State Department could do other than pray that the Iraqis were acting in good faith.

Meanwhile, Howell was sitting in the hotel lobby, waiting for the call, when he too suddenly realized the situation. Here he was, the ranking US representative in Kuwait, with the Iraqis supposedly not recognizing his diplomatic status. After successfully withstanding the four month siege, he was now sitting in the lions' den, completely cut off from his colleagues. Fortunately, the Iraqis had no ulterior motives, and Howell soon returned to his much relieved subordinates, carrying a small camel whip which the MFA man, who had turned up full of apologies, had given him as a gift.

Once permission had been given for the departure, there was a rush to get the baggage. I suggested to Ambassador Howell that it might be easier to ask the Iraqis if we could drive the cars to the gate instead of having to carry the bags to the road. He said it was no trouble to carry the bags. I winked at him, saying: 'It's not what we want to get out, Sir, it's what we want to get in.' One of the ladies caught his eye, and he understood in a flash. 'Fine!' he said.

All of a sudden it became a great problem to carry the bags to the road. Howell put on a consummate performance. The soldiers were displeased at having to open the barriers, but obliged. We drove the car around, the diplomats distracted the Iraqis, and we slipped the food and beer into the compound under cover of the outcoming cases. It was one small, final delicious victory. The six remaining diplomats would eat and drink well that night.

In the meantime, the US civilians at the airport were becoming agitated at the delay. They were sitting at a trashed terminal, completely vulnerable, with Iraqi security all around. The Iraqis were not harassing them, but they stopped them wandering around the carpark. After hiding successfully for four months, they were suddenly at the Iraqis' mercy, and things were moving slowly. They were unaware of anyone actually having left Iraq yet. Several men still feared that it was a ploy to get them to Baghdad, and into custody.

When the people from the embassy finally arrived, everyone was loaded onto buses for the hour-long trip to Ali Al-Salem KAF base. The Iraqis lost track of the baggage on the way, so security had to be repeated before they boarded a 727 for the flight to Baghdad, finally leaving at 3.00 p.m.

Late that afternoon in Baghdad, the 90 remaining American Human Shields, more Americans from Baghdad, 93 Britons who had exit visas, and a number of others, were bussed to Saddam International to rendezvous with the Americans from Kuwait. Those with visas had been told to be ready by 8.00 a.m. They were seething with impatience when they finally arrived at the airport in the afternoon. There was a further delay with obtaining overflight clearance for the Iraqi 747 which would take them to Frankfurt.

When the details were finally resolved, the Americans and a handful of British who had arrived from Kuwait at 4.10 p.m. boarded the aircraft, together with the Americans from the camps and Baghdad, while the British from Baghdad were held back. A number of them began to swear at the Americans, unaware that the aircraft had been chartered by Uncle Sam.

The first aircraft actually to leave that evening was another Iraqi 747 with the Italians who had been allowed to go just days before the general release. It carried 176 of them, 14 Dutch, 11 British, 11 Australians and 9 Irish. It had been due to depart at 1.30 p.m., but there were similar delays with overflight permission, and a fresh crew had to be found as the original crew had exceeded their duty time. They eventually left at 7.28 p.m. There was a cheer as it cleared Iraqi airspace, and champagne was passed around.

The US-chartered Iraqi 747 to Frankfurt finally left at 9.20 p.m., fully loaded, to loud applause from the passengers as it cleared the ground. Most people on board had spent time in camps, or had been in hiding, so were understandably more nervous and distrustful of the Iraqis than the Italians had been. *Mukhabarat* were on board. The tension remained throughout the flight, especially until they were out of Iraqi airspace.

The passengers had one last scare as the pilot approached the runway just before 2.00 a.m. The aircraft was almost on the ground when the Iraqi pilot applied full power, and roared back into the German night sky. A number of passengers reported hearing the stall warning siren; others say the wheels had actually touched the tarmac before the pilot executed his go-around. It seems the pilot feared overshooting, but many of the terrified passengers thought he was going to crash, or that they would be flown back to Baghdad.

Several of the Americans from Kuwait were apparently armed with pistols from the Resistance which had gone undetected by Iraqi security in Kuwait, and during the transfer at Baghdad. They had decided that no matter what, they were not going back to Baghdad. Each man picked a *Mukhabarat* man. They were determined to control the aircraft, if necessary. They had at least two pilots on board as passengers, and could get the aircraft on the ground. As the aircraft banked around for a second approach, the passengers were silent, strapped in their seats, praying silently, some of the women weeping quietly. The Iraqi pilot put the 747 safely on the runway on his second attempt.

As the aircraft taxied towards the terminal, many of the American men stood up, chanting 'U-S-A! U-S-A! U-S-A!', punching their fists into the air in unison. The Iraqi cabin crew and *Mukhabarat* began to fall back towards the cockpit. An immense feeling of pride swept the cabin, especially among those who had remained successfully in hiding. They had beaten Saddam. The overriding emotion was of relief. They were safe, almost out of Iraqi control.

The Japanese also took their people out, together with several Australians and others destined for the Far East. Within fours days of the release announcement, over 500 Westerners and Japanese and others had flown out of Iraq. It would take another two days before all but a handful remained.

As the Americans and a sprinkling of others who had left with them landed safely in Frankfurt on the morning of 10 December, most Britons in Baghdad and Iraq were waking up to their last dawn under Saddam's control.

They expected to leave Iraq that day, but one particularly unfortunate group of about 30 were some of the BLT men and others, who had been among the first Human Shields. They had no passports, and their Baghdad Embassy had not yet issued them with replacements. Without these, the Iraqis could not issue exit visas, so these men feared spending another day in Iraq. They were furious. Frantic efforts were made to complete the formalities, but they left for the airport without the documents. To complicate matters, the Iraqi official who was to issue the visas was nowhere to be found.

At the airport, Ambassador Harold Walker tried to explain the situation to the men, who were becoming increasingly agitated at seeing others passing through the check-in. Fortunately, the flight was delayed with more overflight clearance problems, and the passports and visas arrived with minutes to spare. At 11.30 p.m., the Iraqi 747 with 277 ex-Human Shields and 120 contract workers and others landed at Gatwick to a tumultuous welcome.

The British from Kuwait flew to Baghdad on 11 December, two days after the Americans, and a day after the British Human Shields had left. They were joined by a few other free-nationals who had stayed behind, including Canadians, Irishmen, the last Frenchman and Dutchman in Kuwait, plus dogs, cats, and birds in cages. All other Australians had gone to Baghdad earlier.

The belated departure of this last major group served to confirm the belief of many of them that they were the FCO's bottom priority. This was unfair, as the diplomats in Baghdad chartered whatever planes were available, and got those closest at hand out first, but cynicism was running strong.

A great effort was made by the wardens, minders, Kuwaitis and other Arabs to ensure that everyone had transport to the airport, and no one was left behind. The previous day, one man who no one had been aware of had come out of hiding from near the US and British embassies. Our main concern was that there might be others like him. They might be out of phone contact, and not have a shortwave radio, and simply be waiting for the US Marines to arrive. A number of men encountered minor problems at the checkpoints with troops asking for their watches and money, but the soldiers did not press the point.

Command Central's Mike Devey and Geoff French ran a shuttle service to the airport, alternating runs so that Geoff, who was staying, could drop Mike on the last run. Even then, some of the troops were unaware that they could go. They were stopped and ordered from their car on the last trip; it was only by luck that a passing *Mukhabarat* officer told the soldiers to let them go.

One of the main British wardens, Sandy Macmillan, and Canadian Eoin MacDougald worked until the very end, checking people in, ensuring that no one was missed, and allocating people to the aircraft. Two British diplomats from Baghdad, Martyn Roper and Julian Lyons, flew down with the plane to assist, but Sandy and Eoin had everything under control.

Whereas the Americans had left in a subdued mood, the British went in style. They were greeted at the airport by a piper in kilt and sporran, skirling out traditional Scottish tunes. The scene was high paradox, but a tremendous morale booster. This man was piping his heart out in a trashed airport terminal, with Kuwaiti women in *abayas* and veils from the arriving flight scuttling past him incredulously. A few of the British and Irish women who had stayed behind dressed up for the occasion. One man came in his tuxedo. The Iraqi security were just as bemused, and even more so by the hundreds of Britons arriving at the airport. We could imagine them wondering how so many people had evaded capture for four months.

Most of the British had arrived early for the planned departure time of 9.00 a.m., but did not leave for Ali Al-Salem until the afternoon. There was no food or water available, but many of these experienced survivors had brought their own. Once at Ali Al-Salem, they had to wait a further two hours in a hangar while the aircraft were readied. The Iraqis seemed to make a point of making things difficult. Hand luggage was searched thoroughly and the British forced to remove batteries from their radios as a security precaution. Fortunately, none of the men had tried to smuggle weapons, as the Americans had. They had to load their own limited baggage into the hold of the aged Iraqi Airways 707 and 727, and finally arrived in Baghdad after dark.

In Baghdad, they were greeted by their Ambassador, some of the staff from the Embassy in Kuwait, and Western and Japanese media clamouring for interviews. A buffet was provided, paid for by the journalists. Some of the home mail which had not yet found its way down to Kuwait was available. Most welcome of all were clean toilets after twelve hours without any. The piper who had greeted them at the airport in Kuwait started playing. The men relaxed and there was the sound of laughter. Some groups even began to sing. They were ecstatic to be going home, and so close to departure.

There was minor Iraqi harassment. Most arose from standard bureaucratic exit visa requirements and restrictions on exporting Iraqi currency, but was interpreted by the men as deliberate. The Iraqis asked for their UK addresses for the visas. They were reluctant to provide these, so gave false ones, including 10 Downing Street, or Buckingham Palace. Then one man said his home was in Kuwait. The Iraqis pressed him for a UK address, insisting that he did not live in Kuwait any more. He would not budge. After that, in a final little act of defiance, almost every other man gave his address as Kuwait.

They boarded an Iraqi 747 after a couple of hours' for a relatively uneventful trip. A few *Mukhabarat* were aboard, but there was no trouble. The crew went through the motions of serving a meal, but several men handed it back. They wanted nothing more to do with Iraq, and were more interested in drink than food. Duty free was available in-flight, but the stewards seemed to have trouble finding the miniatures until some of the BLT men who had remained in hiding threatened to kill the purser. The drinks were found.

They landed at Gatwick just before 11.45 p.m., 19 hours after those from Kuwait had left their hideouts. A great cheer went up as the wheels touched British soil. They were home. As they taxied in, a voice came over the tannoy, quite professionally: 'Thank you for flying Iraqi Airways, and we hope to see you again very soon.' No one was listening.

With the departure from Kuwait of the last of the British and Americans who wanted to leave on the 11th, there were perhaps four dozen Westerners in

Kuwait, a few of whom were from the Hostage Support Group, including Lise Hertz and me. There was little left for us to do but distribute remaining foodstocks to the Kuwaitis, Filipinos and Westerners who were staying.

Lise and a few others were adamant. They would not go. They all had their reasons. One common thread was a desire to see the Iraqis leave. They knew that war would come within weeks, and were strangely calm about it.

With the men gone, it was dawning on me that my only reason to remain was a selfish desire to see justice done. I was torn between a burning desire to see Kuwait free again and the Iraqis running, and an equally keen realization that this would be at the price of great suffering for my family at home. I had to stay for a little while anyway. One of the other Australians had gone to Baghdad to phone home just before the release, with the intention of returning to Kuwait and staying. In Baghdad, he had been persuaded to leave, but his luggage was in Kuwait. He had asked me to take his suitcase to Baghdad. I had to collect it, and pack my own bags. The last charter flight would leave in two days on Thursday 13th with the six remaining US diplomats.

After seeing the British off, I visited the flat where we had run the Hostage Support Group from. Lise was there. We sat down for a coffee, but there was nothing to say. A black cloud of depression and anti-climax settled over us. The people we had become so intensely close to over the four months of adversity were now gone. Our entire function in life had been taken from us. It was as though we were parents, and a family of hundreds of children had left home all at once. In a way, our involvement in the group had given us a sense that we were fighting the Iraqis, and beating them. In our own little way, we felt almost a part of the huge Allied force in Saudi Arabia. It was like being relieved of command just before the end of the battle, and having the fruits of victory stolen from us at the last minute. We should have been happy, but we had never felt so down. Both of us needed to be alone. I left, driving home through the deserted streets without even noticing the Iraqis at the checkpoints. They seemed to sense the mood, and never once asked for my ID.

Over the following day, I pulled myself together. There was still work to be done. Food had to be redistributed. Cars left behind had to be hidden or immobilized to reduce the risk of their being looted. Final good-byes had to be said. But there was still a great magnet drawing me to remain.

The departure of the remaining six US diplomats was almost as difficult as when the first batch had left. I would go to Baghdad with them, with my compatriot's suitcase, and planned to return to Kuwait to salvage some of my property. I could not drive them to the airport as I would have to leave my car at the airport, and it would be gone by the time I returned. Besides, Barbara Bodine was concerned that my profile was becoming far too high with the Iraqis. In any event, the Iraqis had offered to take them to the airport.

The flight from Kuwait was due to take off at about 8.30 a.m. Imad Ghawji, the Syrian engineer who had given so much selfless help to my original group in the Al-Muthanna, myself, and a sprinkling of other Americans and Britons who had not gone out earlier were to be the only civilians on it. It was now a full week after the release announcement. Most hostages were out of Iraq, but

Coalition governments were making it clear that the releases would make no difference to maintaining the war option for 15 January. These comments seemed to be irritating the Iraqis. We were concerned that they might suddenly close the door, and trap those still in Iraq and Kuwait, including the diplomats. A small Human Shield could be almost as effective as a large one.

We went to the airport to await the US diplomats, but there was no sign of them for an hour. The scheduled departure time for the aircraft passed. We feared that something had gone badly wrong, and that the Iraqis had decided to keep them as hostages at the last minute. Finally, we spied a minibus, with the unmistakable bulk and white mane of Ambassador Howell inside, but the Iraqis drove them directly onto the tarmac to meet the bus to Ali Al-Salem.

All other people on the flight would be carrying on directly to Frankfurt. I would be getting off in Baghdad with my compatriot's case. The Iraqis eventually agreed to put it in Hold 1A, so it would not end up in Frankfurt. We boarded the bus to Ali Al-Salem, with the diplomats still confined to their minibus. We learned later that the Iraqi security had kept them separate from the public ostensibly for their own safety. From Imad's and my knowledge of the ordinary Iraqis, it was more likely that they would have shaken the diplomats' hands for their having survived the siege.

There were further delays at Ali Al-Salem, and security checks. The diplomats were still kept separate. We could speak with them only after the plane had boarded. It was the first real opportunity to sit down face to face with Barbara, who had been of immense assistance to countless people.

At Baghdad, the US diplomats and the others were ushered into a lounge to have their exit visas issued. It would be the last I saw of them. I was more concerned with getting the suitcase off before it went to Frankfurt. I should have gone with the others for the exit visa. Not unexpectedly, the Iraqis in Kuwait had failed to alert their Baghdad colleagues that a bag had to come off. By the time I had retrieved it, the airport was deserted, and the American diplomats, and others, were on their way to freedom.

Australian diplomats had come to the airport to collect me, and get the exit visa, but we had missed each other. I therefore took a taxi to the embassy, but it was closed for the week-end. I tried the Ambassador's Residence instead, and found the diplomats celebrating the departure of the last of the other hostages. The party was well under way, so they suggested that we obtain the visa when the Iraqi Ministry re-opened on Sunday. That is, of course, if I did not mind spending the week-end in Baghdad. I had no objection to this, as long as I could call home, so spent a delightful final week-end in Baghdad, between writing up a final report for the local US Embassy on bits of intelligence on the Iraqi forces in Kuwait.

The trouble started on Sunday when the Ambassador's driver went for the exit visa. He returned to say that the special arrangements whereby visas could be issued in Baghdad for those registered in 'other provinces' had expired the previous day. Anyone registered elsewhere, including Kuwait Province, had to obtain their visa from the residence office in that province.

The Ambassador was horrified. He had his last national safely in Baghdad; this was a final, unforeseen hitch in a long line of difficulties. He approached

Tareq Aziz's office, and the Chief of Protocol at the MFA, but to no avail. The rules were the rules. The Iraqis insisted that everyone had been given a week, sufficient time to take advantage of the special arrangement.

I told the Ambassador that it was no real problem to go back to Kuwait, but he was most reluctant that I do so. To further complicate matters, the last two British diplomats in Kuwait, and with them all forms of communication with the outside world except for the inaccessible Kuwaiti Resistance satellite phones and ham radios, had left Kuwait that day. After the week-end in Baghdad, and speaking with my family, I was convinced that I should leave.

British Ambassador to Kuwait, Michael Weston, and his Consul, Larry Banks, arrived in Baghdad that afternoon. Like some of us, they would have preferred to stay and see the crisis through, but they had to leave.

Weston had phoned each of the British and the locally employed staff who were staying behind in Kuwait to make a last minute appeal for them to go. They then did all the things that diplomats abandoning embassies do, locked the doors and gates from the inside, and climbed out of the Embassy using a ladder lowered from an upstairs window. They met the same reception as Barbara Bodine and Gale Rogers had when they emerged from their compound the previous Sunday. A ragged group of soldiers tried to order them back into the Embassy which the Iraqis had been insisting for four months that they vacate. Weston looked disdainfully at a man pointing a Kalashnikov at his chest, and said, with inimitable aplomb 'You'll have to shoot me, I'm afraid.'

Officers were summoned, and then the MFA man, and finally the last two Western diplomats in Kuwait went to Baghdad. The only foreign diplomat left behind was the Bahraini Ambassador, Mr Issa Al-Jamea. This brave man would stay all the way through, incommunicado, until liberation. Messrs Weston and Banks also took out about ten other individuals.

That evening, a Sunday, with Christmas only nine days away, a Carols Service was held at St George's Anglican Church in Baghdad. Most of the congregation were diplomats and journalists. Like almost everything in Baghdad, the incongruity was inescapable. The church was a classical, old building, arched, with stained-glass windows and carved pews. This leftover from Baghdad's past, dedicated to the service of mankind, could not have been more different from the monolithic Mansour Melia nearby.

I attended the service with the Australian Ambassador, Peter Lloyd. There was even greater irony. We were singing of Peace On Earth, and Goodwill To All Men, of the coming of The Saviour, and every one of us was acutely aware that the war deadline was less than a month away. There was a storm outside. The lightning and thunder seemed almost a harbinger of the man-made storm looming in the New Year. I have never sensed the Hope of Peace which comes with Christmas felt so keenly as among that congregation.

As we were leaving the service, we learned of the arrival of Mike Weston and Larry Banks, and that a reception was being held for them at a British diplomatic residence. I promptly asked myself along. After all that time, and almost daily phone conversations with these men since September, it was the first chance to meet them face to face. The US *chargé d'affaires* in Baghdad, Joe Wilson, was there, along with several other diplomats. The British Ambassador was out of town. His deputy, Christopher Segar, was host, with the highly-regarded junior officer, Caroline Cross. After the non-British diplomats had left the reception, Mike, Larry, Christopher, Caroline and I settled down to dinner. It was a fascinating evening, swopping stories of the past four months, and putting together the pieces that different individuals among us were unaware of, as if it were a great adventure.

For all the criticism he had incurred in Kuwait, Michael Weston was refreshingly self-effacing. He was cast in the classic colonial diplomatic mould, public-school background, articulate, with a polished upper crust accent, and pince-nez. When interviewed by the BBC the following day and asked inanely if he and Larry considered themselves heroes, Michael was quick to give credit where it was due: 'Not in the least,' he said. 'The real heroes are firstly the British community who stayed on; secondly the people who helped us and them: the Australians and New Zealanders, the Irish, the Canadians; and thirdly, our wardens and the local staff.'

Ambassador Weston had not mentioned the Kuwaitis and the Danes, but was probably unaware of their involvement as it had been kept very quiet. Nevertheless, he left Kuwait and Baghdad well respected for having sat out the crisis in the true British tradition. His delayed departure from Kuwait may have been one last dig at the Americans, and a stubbornness to be the last to go. The extra few days he and Larry Banks spent there contributed nothing to the resolution of the crisis, but the gesture was not lost on the Kuwaitis.

The following afternoon, the Australian Ambassador and I decided that the quickest way to get the exit visa was for me to go back to Kuwait. His efforts had come to naught. It was then back onto the Iraqi Airways flight to Kuwait. Curiously, the Iraqis at the airport did not query why a Westerner should be going to Kuwait when everyone else had left, but my papers were in order, so they followed their own rules to the letter and let me proceed. This time, I was armed with a letter from the Embassy requesting every assistance from the residence office in issuing an exit visa.

Arriving in Kuwait, and meeting some of those who were staying behind, I was again sorely tempted to stay. I was still torn between my family and the all-consuming intensity of the occupation experience. The following day I went back to the villa where our residence visas had been issued. This time, there were no crowds, and no problems getting in. The Iraqi bureaucrats themselves were nervous, and seemed to be packing up.

Sitting waiting in the Iraqis' office, there was no doubting the scope of their organisation. In a rack by one wall were a stack of manila files, with preprinted covers, one for each Westerner who had registered in Kuwait. I could not get a close look at them, but the names were neatly written in the appropriate space, in English. Some of the files were a centimetre thick. It was obvious that the Iraqis were keeping tabs on us, registering information every time we came in contact with their organisations.

The Iraqis would not talk freely when there was more than one of them in the room, or identify themselves by their name. They even avoided saying where in

Iraq they came from. When Iraq's 'current problem with America' was broached gently with a group of them, I would get the standard line of the numerical superiority and experience of the Iraqi Army, but without any great sense of conviction. Once, when I was alone with one of them, he asked me what I thought would happen. I told him, as gently as I could: 'The Americans are going to bomb you out of here in four weeks' time.' He looked at me, without a hint of hostility, and sighed wearily. 'I think they will,' he said, looking away sadly. 'We should not have come here.'

Finally, the exit visa was ready. I had two weeks to leave, and was supposedly allowed to reenter within three months. The next day, I flew to Baghdad, and out of Iraq on 21 December, arriving home on the 24th after a foreign affairs debriefing.

Another half dozen Westerners left Kuwait within those few days, leaving the hard core who would sit out the war with the Kuwaitis, the Palestinians and 20,000 Asians who had remained behind, the several hundred thousand pitiful troops which Saddam was prepared to sacrifice, the *Mukhabarat* torturers who would leave behind a legacy of horror, and the lone, brave, Bahraini Ambassador.

On that last Iraqi Airways flight to Baghdad, I was seated beside a tall, handsome, Iraqi Army major. He spoke good English, and told me he was an accountant in Baghdad, but was now in charge of a tank company in Kuwait's Burgan oilfield. He was going home for a week to visit his family. I gave him a US Army MRE (Meal-Ready-To-Eat) pouch which the American diplomats had given me. He smiled, amused that he was probably the only Iraqi officer in Baghdad or Kuwait with a US Army ration. He was conversational on the plane where he knew he was not under surveillance, but as soon as we were in the airport concourse, he would not even acknowledge my presence. It was another lesson in the nature of the giant hostage camp that was Iraq.

Just over two months later, when images of columns of Iraqi POWs filled Western TV screens, I noticed a tall, handsome, educated-looking man in the front ranks, with the officers, a head above the other men around him. His rank was not visible, but I hoped it was the major. If so, he was alive, and could hopefully go back to accounting, not soldiering.

The elation of homecoming was indescribable. The first British, Irish, Dutch and Australians to land in Rome on 10 December were flown home the following day. Most of the Americans who arrived in Frankfurt hours later were flown on to their final destinations, usually free-of-charge by various airlines. There were scores of reporters but only two State Department people to meet the hundreds of Americans in Germany. With the delays, a number of men simply found their own hotels, and arranged their own flights home.

Gulf Air flew the Australians home First Class on their new Sydney service. A number of other airlines went out of their way to get the men home quickly, treating them like royalty. Governments worldwide assigned Foreign Ministry officers to meet the returnees and ease their passage. Immigration officers processed them ahead of aircrew. Customs officers waved them through with whatever meagre possessions they had salvaged. The whole world, except Iraq, was delighted that their hostages were home.

The larger groups of men were a mixed bunch as they deplaned. Some were gaunt and mentally and physically shattered. A few had lost up to a fifth of their body weight, and aged years in four months. Others were fit and tanned from relaxation at the camps, exercise which they had been unable to fit into their regular lives, and sunning themselves. A few were drunk, yet there was a pride among virtually all of them at having survived, and beaten Saddam.

The first British arrivals on the morning of 10 December were greeted with cheers, hugs, kisses, screams and applause by their relatives and friends - and TV cameras. The media intrusion hardly mattered. No one could steal this most intense, precious moment from families as they were reunited. They were safe, alive, and together again. Families just stood in the arrival halls, holding each other, weeping with joy, oblivious to anyone else.

I recall this moment of being reunited with my family as the most special of the crisis, not wanting to let go again, just wanting to look at them and the joy in their faces, hardly believing that I was finally home. There was not a Kalashnikov, or a checkpoint, or an Iraqi soldier in sight. It was beautiful. Some of the men had no jobs, no homes, no money to return to, having lost everything, but that was inconsequential in those sweet moments of reunion.

Yet in Kuwait, the nightmare was continuing. War was barely a month away. The Kuwaitis themselves were still hostages in their own land. Many would die, some horribly. The Westerners who chose to leave were home, but many had left their hearts in Kuwait.

Kuwait, despite its ordeal, found time to share in the joy. Every ex-hostage its Embassies were able to locate received a gift basket, usually of plants, and the following letter:

Please accept our warmest congratulations on your safe return home, just in time to spend Christmas with your loved ones.

Some of you have lived in a safe and peaceful Kuwait for many years and have greatly contributed to its development. We are indeed grateful for the benefits we have gained from your skills and expertise, and very much regret that you have been subjected to such an ordeal.

We very much hope and pray that we will be able to thank you properly very soon in a liberated Kuwait.

Please join us in prayers for the liberation of the largest hostage population, namely the citizens and residents of Kuwait.

May we finally pay tribute to the courage and dignity shown by your families throughout their ordeal.

The Government and People of Kuwait.

28. THE EVE OF THE STORM

By Christmas week, 1990 there were still about 200,000 Palestinians, 100,000 *bidoons*, or stateless Arabs, several thousand Egyptians and Syrians and 20,000 Asians in Kuwait, besides the Kuwaitis and Iraqis. Kuwaitis continued to trickle out through the Saudi border until the Iraqis sealed it just before the expiry of the UN deadline of 15 January.

About 100 Westerners not of Arabic origin stayed in Kuwait. Thirty of these were British. One of the Britons was gynaecologist and obstetrician Dr Brian Bethell. He went back to work. The babies would not wait until liberation. The other Westerners were six Danes, a handful of Americans including wives of Kuwaitis and several single men, a sole New Zealander, two Dutchmen, a few Cypriots, Poles and Yugoslavs, the Maltese Roman Catholic Bishop of Kuwait Francis Micallef, and a number of German wives of Kuwaitis.

The Bishop and his Indian, Filipino and Arabic priests had their pastoral duties. The Danes included Lise Hertz and dentists Claus and Esther Schmith. Others were medicos who felt an obligation to be on hand when the inevitable war casualties occurred, and to continue providing care for the civilians in Kuwait. The New Zealander, Graham Gaston, was engaged to an Indian midwife, Priscilla Punita, who was staying. He was working as the Kuwait Danish Dairy Plant Maintenance Manager in what had become an essential service. Others wanted to protect their property. A few felt that they had been in Kuwait during the good times, so should stay with the Kuwaitis during the bad. Others simply wanted to be there to see the Iraqis kicked out.

There was little doubt in the minds of anyone in Kuwait that the Allies would go to war. This had been patently clear since the UN use-of-force resolution of 29 November. The last-minute diplomatic shuttles and appeals for peace were seen as little more than theatrics playing to domestic audiences. Saddam was intransigent. His troops were digging in. It was a final countdown. The Coalition could not defer action much beyond 15 January and retain its credibility unless Saddam withdrew, and that was not happening.

In Kuwait, a peaceful withdrawal was seen as worse than a forced withdrawal as Saddam's forces would still be intact for further mischief. This view was not held as universally outside Kuwait. The world seemed to want to believe there would be peace. As late as 31 December, President Bush was expressing a 'gut feeling' that Saddam would withdraw peacefully. Soviet envoy Yevgeny Primakov described Saddam's attitude eloquently as a 'Massada Complex', whereby he would choose death, in battle or by suicide, over capture. This was a brave but inaccurate attempt to characterize the man. He would not be the one doing the dying or being captured. His ego would not allow him to withdraw from Kuwait without war, even if he had to sacrifice innocent Iraqi lives. Experts who predicted war were in a minority, and accused of being overly hawkish. In the midst of this, the plight of the Kuwaitis still under Iraqi occupation was largely forgotten.

Those in Kuwait were not the only ones unconvinced of Saddam's good faith. On 5 December, Iraq had formally accepted President Bush's proposal for a top-level exchange of visits, which was widely hailed as the 'extra mile for peace'. Tareq Aziz would meet Bush in Washington, and James Baker would meet Saddam in Baghdad. This had raised great hopes for a peaceful settlement, which had quickly dissipated as Iraq failed to follow through.

The Iraqis originally wanted to base the talks on Saddam's initiative of 12 August, linking Kuwait to the Palestinian problem. The Americans had no intention of mixing one can of worms with another. Aziz sought to spend five days in Washington, and meet the Congressional leaders. It was a smart attempt to outflank Bush by playing to the isolationist Democrats in Congress, but the US would allow only two days and one night. 17 December was set as the tentative date for Aziz's visit, but this could not be confirmed until the date for Baker's trip to Baghdad was settled. The Iraqis said that Saddam could not meet Baker before 12 January, more than three weeks after Aziz's trip to Washington. The Americans were happy with anytime between 20 December and 3 January, but would not accept a date just before the deadline.

Saddam was actually offering nothing at all by trying to base the talks on his so-called 12 August initiative. In effect, he required that the Palestinian problem be settled, not merely discussed, before anything else could even be addressed. Even then he would give only a vague commitment to discuss - but not necessarily settle - Kuwait. With the best will in the world, the settlement of the Palestinian problem would take many years – as it indeed has – and Saddam would still be in Kuwait. The Iraqis were stalling.

On 14 December, with most US hostages home and only a skeleton crew manning his Baghdad embassy, Bush's patience ran out. He put the meetings on hold unless Baghdad agreed to receive Baker no later than 3 January. On the same day, Algerian President Chadli Benjedid ended his own mission to Baghdad with no result. Aziz then announced that he would not go to Washington, and that Iraq alone would set the date for Baker to visit Baghdad. It was stalemate.

There was no let up of the pressure on Iraq. There would be no further UN Security Council Resolutions until after the cessation of hostilities in March 1991 - although there were several attempts by the French and Secretary General Perez de Cuellar to push through a final resolution - but on 18 December, the General Assembly overwhelmingly condemned Iraq's serious human rights violations against the Kuwaiti people and third-state nationals in a vote of 144 to 1. Iraq's was the only dissenting voice.

The following day, Amnesty International issued a comprehensive report citing Iraq for numerous human rights violations in Kuwait. The report documented extensive eye-witness accounts of murder and various forms of torture inflicted on Kuwaitis, as recounted by Kuwait Red Crescent doctors, foreign nationals, and other people from Kuwait. It made chilling reading.

Saddam continued his belligerence. On 21 December, he staged an elaborate evacuation drill of about 10,000 people from one of Baghdad's working class areas, claiming that a million people had been involved. It seemed more like a clumsy attempt to persuade Western journalists that Iraq was really ready for war, than a genuine attempt to prepare his people.

In Saudi Arabia, US Defense Secretary Dick Cheney, and Joint Chiefs of Staff Chairman General Colin Powell visited warships, air bases and desert camps, and declared their 300,000 troops in the Gulf ready to fight. This time it seemed to be for real. Iraqi forces in and near Kuwait were now estimated – over-estimated in retrospect – at 500,000, and showed no sign of withdrawing.

In Kuwait, people tried to maintain a sense of normality. Roman Catholic Bishop Francis Micallef, and his staff held a Christmas Tree Party for children in the Cathedral. Some of the Westerners and Kuwaitis organized their own Christmas parties in a personal act of defiance. They were not going to let Saddam get in the way of their traditions.

The Christmas services in Kuwait were surprisingly well attended. People seemed to come out of the woodwork. There were no midnight Masses because of the risk of travelling around at night, but those churches that were still operating held morning services, some of which were attended by Christian Iraqi troops, who stood singing the hymns with their Kalashnikovs over their shoulders. The atmosphere was particularly poignant. The congregations were singing about peace and a time for reconciliation between all men, with a million men and women-at-arms preparing to do battle nearby.

With slightly over three weeks until the deadline, people were either settling in for war, or preparing to leave. On Christmas Eve, the Indian Embassy in Baghdad sent word to Kuwait that the last convoy of buses to Baghdad from Kuwait would leave on 27 or 28 December, with further evacuation direct to Bombay by air.

Saddam's Christmas present to the world was a threat to destroy Tel Aviv if war broke out. He continued to peddle his discredited thesis that Kuwait was historically part of Iraq. The ordinary people in Baghdad were not so confident as their leader. After all, they did not have well-protected bunkers. An air of great nervousness and tension pervaded the city, and people spoke openly of going to spend time with relatives in the country in January.

The week between Christmas and New Year was remarkably quiet both in Kuwait, and on the diplomatic front. It seemed to be a lull to presage a final flurry of diplomatic activity in early January. Both sides took a brief respite.

Behind the scenes in Baghdad, US *chargé d'affaires* Joe Wilson was working on a compromise date for a high-level American-Iraqi meeting. If reciprocal visits to capitals were impossible, then a meeting on neutral ground between the latest date acceptable to the US of 3 January, and the earliest date acceptable to the Iraqis of the 12th, might still be possible. Bush needed to make one last effort to cast Saddam firmly as the intransigent party.

The EC were also active in seeking a diplomatic solution without departing from the agreed Allied message. The French led in this, with hints that Foreign Minister Roland Dumas might go to Baghdad if nothing came of the US-Iraqi dialogue. However, German Foreign Minister Hans-Deitrich Genscher identified Yugoslav Foreign Minister Budimir Loncar as a potential intermediary between the EC and Iraq. Loncar had several distinct advantages, foremost of which were good Yugoslav commercial and military links with Iraq prior to the imposition of sanctions, and shared membership with Iraq of the Non-Aligned Movement. Loncar arrived in Baghdad on 28 December, but he too got nowhere.

The next EC move was an expression of readiness to travel to Baghdad by the then President of the Council of Ministers, Luxembourg Foreign Minister Jacques Poos. The Europeans had decided that direct talks were needed. The Americans were getting worried that the plethora of peace missions would damage the Coalition's overall position, so stepped up their own attempts to arrange a final high-level US-Iraqi meeting, and preempt the Europeans.

In Kuwait, the generally quiet atmosphere between Christmas and New Year masked a breakdown in the Iraqi civil administration.

The Iraqi campaign to force Kuwaitis to change their nationalities had been so spectacularly unsuccessful that the deadline was extended to mid-January, as if the Iraqi civil servants were unaware that the war would start then. However, rationing was still in force. It was harder for the Kuwaitis to get into the supermarkets without bribing their way past the Iraqi troops, so they came to rely more and more on the Resistance food network.

Cars and petrol were a greater problem than food. Any car travelling around with Kuwaiti plates was subject to confiscation, so many families changed the plates on at least one of their cars, usually the oldest one. The Iraqi Traffic Department seemed to have dropped their requirement that Kuwaiti owners change their nationality before changing the licence plates.

With the prospect that they would face war, some of the Iraqi security forces became even nastier. People were arrested and detained on the flimsiest of pretexts. One Kuwaiti family, including the children, was arrested because the husband had not changed his car licence plates. This particular family was taken to Baghdad, and then back to Basra before the air war, and finally released by Shi'ite rebels in March 1991 after three months in custody.

The Managing Director of the Kuwait Danish Dairy, Mr Ezzat Mohammed Jaafar, who was in his late 70s, was arrested with his son, Mohammed, and accused of being in contact with the Amir – who he had tutored in the Amir's youth – and of subsidizing the Resistance. They too were jailed in Basra and Baghdad. Both were badly tortured, but survived, and were finally released on 28 March, after being told the previous night that they would be executed that day.

Elsewhere in Kuwait, people were largely ignorant of these horrors. There were even more New Year's Eve parties among the Westerners than there had been Christmas celebrations: 1991 was going to be the year of liberation, and a new start for Kuwait. The Kuwaitis themselves did not forget the Westerners who had stayed behind. They presented each of them with a cake and ID1,000. Also, British Ambassador Michael Weston had left behind a bottle of Scotch and a greetings card for each of the British to aid their festivities.

The New Year opened with a sudden increase in diplomatic efforts to achieve a peaceful withdrawal, but in Kuwait, there was an air of great apprehension and impatience, and the Iraqi troops looked ever more nervous. The Kuwaitis and

Westerners felt almost smug. The Iraqis' hour of reckoning would be their hour of salvation. However, for many, the worst was yet to come.

More Coalition forces poured into Saudi Arabia and NATO deployed aircraft from Europe to Turkey to help deter any action by Iraq. Saddam, for his part, made a conspicuous visit to his troops in northern Kuwait, and was said to have awarded his officers a pay rise of ID50 per month.

The Kuwaiti Resistance continued to make their presence felt with a few random car bombs, but with little military effect. Their leaders were concentrating on sending out last-minute intelligence to the Coalition.

On 3 January, President Bush said he would be willing to send James Baker to Geneva to meet with Tareq Aziz. Joe Wilson's efforts during the Christmas–New Year week in Baghdad were paying off. After a little haggling, the date was set at January 9th. This meeting carried neither the symbolism of visits to national capitals, nor the level of contact of Foreign Minister to Head-of-State, but was senior enough for each side's purposes. Bush told the Congressional leaders that this was his last set of proposals. They in turn agreed to hold off any Congressional vote until after the Baker–Aziz meeting.

At the same time, UN Secretary-General Javier Perez de Cuellar expressed concern about what he saw as 'war-fever', and a wish to convene the Security Council for another resolution. However, there was little time left before the withdrawal deadline expired. He was prepared to do whatever he could for peace, but the earlier Resolutions stood. At the same time, the EC Foreign Ministers met with a view to playing a mediating role. By the evening of 4 January, the Iraqis had agreed that Aziz would meet Baker on the 9th in Geneva, and a delegation of EC Foreign Ministers in Luxembourg on the 10th.

Meanwhile, the people who had served as Saddam's Human Shields, or remained successfully in hiding from his forces, had not forgotten Kuwait.

In the US, 30 of them blitzed Capitol Hill with CFK (Citizens For A Free Kuwait). On 8 January, three of them, Ernie Alexander, Paul Pawlowski and Jerry Willis, testified before the House Committee on Foreign Affairs' hearings on Iraqi human rights abuses in Kuwait and Iraq. They were joined by the Executive Director of Amnesty International USA, John Healy; the Executive Director of Middle East Watch, Andrew Whitley; the President of CFK, Dr Hassan Al-Ebraheem; and Kuwaiti gynaecologist and obstetrician Dr Fawziah Al-Qattan, who had fled Kuwait in November, after treating rape and torture victims. The testimony was riveting, and was later credited with contributing to Congressional support for US forces going to war against Iraq.

CFK, and the Association for a Free Kuwait and the Free Kuwait Campaign in London, pulled out all the stops with last-minute media interviews in the lead-up to Parliamentary votes around the world. Dr Al-Ebraheem and his colleague, Mr Fawzi Sultan, were liberally quoted in a *Time* magazine cover story on *'Is Kuwait Worth Liberating?'* which made a deep impact on many members of the US public who were still unsure of the cause.

The lead-up to the Baker-Aziz talks in Geneva was almost as important as the meeting itself.

There was concern in US political circles that the meeting would be futile if it were only a rehashing of positions. To keep his options open, Bush announced that he would meet with Perez de Cuellar to review the situation. The implication seemed to be that if Baker was not going to Baghdad to see Saddam, then the UN chief would.

On 5 January, a French envoy, Michel Vauzelle, Chairman of the French National Assembly's Foreign Affairs Committee, met with Saddam and Yasser Arafat. Although Vauzelle was acting as an unofficial envoy of President Mitterrand, French Foreign Minister Roland Dumas made it clear that Vauzelle had no mandate for negotiation. Nevertheless, Vauzelle was not visiting Baghdad for his own health only ten days before the deadline.

The only substantive result of Vauzelle's five hours with Saddam was a hint that he would be prepared to withdraw if the deadline were extended. The Americans and British – greatly irritated that the French seemed to be trying to do a separate deal – dismissed this. Saddam had already enjoyed more than seven weeks' grace. However, Vauzelle's talks lasted far longer than discussions with any other Western envoy. Saddam was obviously getting worried and still held out hopes of using the French to save his skin.

Upon returning to Paris, Vauzelle encouraged Mitterrand to send an official envoy, such as Dumas, to Baghdad, but Mitterrand - unconvinced of Saddam's sincerity - would not send anyone until Saddam first made a concrete gesture. This was not forthcoming, so the French started working on an initiative involving Algeria and Morocco to be launched after the expected failure of the Baker-Aziz talks. In the end, this too came to nothing.

Saddam, in the meantime, continued to dig himself a bigger hole, but the tragedy was that his ordinary troops, and many Kuwaitis, would be buried in it. In an address on Army Day in Baghdad on 6 January, he, looking tired and drawn, warned his armed forces to prepare for a long battle and heavy sacrifices, and reiterated that Kuwait would remain Iraq's 19th Province. He warned that 'the Mother Of All Battles' would soon begin, and would grow into a greater war for the Holy Places, and the rights of the Palestinians.

The Iraqis then announced that Aziz would not meet the EC Foreign Ministers in Luxembourg on the 10th - only two days after they had agreed that he would - but anyone was welcome to come to Baghdad. None of the Europeans took up the invitation. British Prime Minister John Major, for his part, was more interested in visiting his troop in Saudi Arabia in anticipation of their going into action, rather than allowing Saddam to play for time.

At the time, Saddam seemed to hold to a belief that the Allies would have time to launch no more than a few air-strikes on Baghdad before the Western public called upon their leaders to desist. This was why there were still over 300 Western journalists in Baghdad. They were Saddam's self-financing secret weapon, his channel to the Western public. He seemed to have no idea that the pinpoint bombing of Baghdad would - at least initially - fail to produce the footage of massacred Iraqi civilians he was after.

On 8 January, James Baker and his delegation arrived in Geneva after stopping off to meet Allies in France, Germany and Italy. Tareq Aziz arrived the same day. Bush kept the pressure on by calling Baker's mission 'perhaps the final chance' to resolve the conflict without war. He then called on the US Congress to adopt a resolution stating its support of UN Security Council Resolution 678, and the Resolutions leading up to that. Bush argued that such a resolution would send the clearest possible message to Saddam that he must withdraw unconditionally from Kuwait without delay.

As widely expected, the Baker–Aziz meeting was a failure. This was no reflection on the professional abilities of Aziz; Saddam had given him absolutely no room for movement. Baker did not move beyond the UN Resolutions, and Aziz did not budge from Saddam's 12 August initiative. The talks lasted six-and-a-half hours, with Aziz refusing to accept a letter from Bush to Saddam, maintaining that it was not politely written.

Perhaps the most interesting aspect of the meeting was the US threat to exact revenge on Iraq if Saddam used chemical or biological weapons. Baker made it quite clear that the US had the means to do this, and that if matters reached such a point, their objectives would include toppling the Iraqi regime.

The threat against Saddam, as the Commander-in-Chief of his forces, was barely masked. It was less clear what means the Americans would use, but there was speculation that Baker was referring to tactical nuclear weapons, or even a drive all the way to Baghdad. In fact, Defense Secretary Dick Cheney had said in late December, 'If Saddam were foolish enough to use weapons of mass destruction, the US response would be absolutely overwhelming and ... devastating'. He had also said that the use of chemical or nuclear weapons by the Coalition had 'never been on the table'. President Bush had already ruled out nuclear weapons, but had not been quite as explicit as he might have been, presumably to keep Saddam guessing. It was more likely that the Americans were telling Saddam that his regime would be allowed to survive if he did not use chemical or biological weapons. This is precisely what happened.

At the post-meeting news conference, Baker expressed regret that he had heard nothing which suggested any Iraqi flexibility on complying with the UN Resolutions. In Washington, Bush called Aziz's refusal to accept his letter to Saddam Hussein 'one more example that the Iraqi Government is not interested in direct communications', but he had not given up on a peaceful solution. The choice for peace or war, he said, was Saddam's to make.

The Iraqis seemed resigned to the prospect of war. Aziz, in his usual restrained style, said he would not be surprised if the Allies decided to attack Iraq. His boss was less diplomatic. 'The American troops,' Saddam said, 'were falling into a trap, and would swim in their own blood.'

Saddam's decision to send Aziz to Geneva in the first place seems to have been little more than a ploy in the same league as the Jeddah meeting with the Kuwaitis on the eve of the invasion, after the decision to invade had been made, only this time it was for the dubious benefit of the Iraqi people, to convince them that the war they would face was one imposed from outside.

With the failure of the Geneva talks, the Americans reverted to Plan B. After priming Javier Perez de Cuellar in the days before the meeting, Bush indicated that he would back a diplomatic visit by him to Baghdad. That evening, Perez de Cuellar announced that he would travel to Baghdad to meet with Saddam. Baker, meanwhile, flew to Saudi Arabia to brief King Fahd.

The EC initiative effectively died with the failure of the Geneva talks. Aziz said he would only be interested in talking to the EC Ministers if they had something more to offer than the US, and came to Baghdad. This was unacceptable to the EC, so any final European diplomatic efforts fell to individual Governments. The day after Geneva, French envoy Edgar Pisani met with Saddam's half-brother, Barzan Al-Takriti, who had been part of Aziz's delegation. Again, nothing happened.

People in Kuwait had mixed feelings about the failure of the talks. Some wondered why the Americans had even bothered. Others were devastated at the failure of what was seen as the last chance for peace. Both camps agreed that war was now one step closer.

Out in the desert between Kuwait City and Saudi Arabia, the Iraqis had built five defensive lines of trenches, minefields, barricades and oil-filled fire trenches. A line of trenches extended along the entire Kuwaiti coast, behind beaches strewn with barbed wire, mines and tank-traps. Kuwaiti holiday chalets and homes all the way down the coast had been taken over as sleeping quarters and stores. The coastal trench systems came complete with concrete bunkers for sleeping and ammunition storage every 20 metres or so. Behind that first line of trenches was another, fall-back system of lesser trenches. The Iraqis were not great soldiers, but they knew how to dig.

Some of the trench patterns were actually quite artistic, in zig-zags and curves to allow the troops to fire in a number of directions at oncoming ground forces. It did not seem to occur to them that unlike the Iranian human waves they were used to fighting, the Allies would simply fly over them.

Most striking of all was the orientation of the artillery and tanks. Each major position on the coastal defences had at least one T-55 tank or a medium artillery piece. There were thousands more such weapons out in the desert. Their main problem was not so much lack of firepower, but the fact that they were pointed east out to sea, and south towards Saudi Arabia. It would not be a simple matter to turn them around to deal with an attack from behind.

In the city, those freeway flyovers that had not previously been sealed were now blocked off, and anti-aircraft guns mounted on them. Other guns were placed on tall buildings, even in residential areas, and on boats in Kuwait Bay and in the ports. The Iraqis even tried to mount guns on the roof of the Roman Catholic Cathedral, but were persuaded against doing so by the Bishop. Some of the hospitals and nurses' residential quarters were not so fortunate.

Other city troops dug mortar pits, and sighted the weapons on key routes and intersections. More houses were taken over and fortified with sandbags and bricks in the windows. Even more barbed wire and tank obstacles were placed along the beaches. Signals units seemed particularly active. There had been very little evidence of field phones or radios among Iraqi troops up to that point, but suddenly they were laying cable everywhere.

In fact, on several occasions, some people in Kuwait thought that the war had started when the Iraqis test-fired their heavy weapons out to sea, or ranged them. There had been a few test-firings earlier, but nothing like this.

In the urban area, most of the Iraqi civilian administration, including the police, cleared out of Kuwait in the first week of January. People with ration cards were told to use them by the 10th. Iraqi settlers who had moved into abandoned homes were told by the authorities to go back to Iraq. The local Iraqi propaganda sheet, *Al-Nida'a*, ceased publication. The printing press for Kuwait's *Al-Qabas* newspaper, where it had been produced, was dismantled and joined the procession of loot northwards. Curfews were more strictly enforced, but few people were going out anyway.

The soldiers were not the only ones getting ready. Gulf radio stations broadcast do-it-yourself instructions on preparing for war. Those civilians who had not already prepared basement shelters now did so. Some areas had only a few houses with basements; these were designated local community shelters and stocked up with mattresses, canned and dried food, water, first-aid kits, cooking gas, radios, torches, rugs and blankets. Windows that had not already been taped up now sported 'X's in masking tape to prevent them from shattering, and sealed rooms were set up in case of gas attack.

Nevertheless, people did not allow the prospect of war to get in the way of style. Some neighbours competed with each other for the best decorated and supplied basement shelter. If there were a chance they were going to die, then they would do so as elegantly as possible. Opinion was divided as to whether or not there would be street-fighting, but most people thought that the Iraqis would run as soon as the going got tough. They were less certain that Saddam would not fire a few parting chemical or biological shells into the urban areas.

On 11 January, UN Secretary-General Perez de Cuellar met with the EC Foreign Ministers in preparation for his 13 January meeting with Saddam, and obtained their support for his last-minute mission. He then met twice with King Hussein in Amman before flying to Baghdad. He was not optimistic. The fateful meeting would be held barely 60 hours before the deadline.

That same day, the White House released the text of President Bush's letter to Saddam, which Aziz had declined to accept. It said, among other things, 'This is a war that can be ended only by Iraq's full and unconditional compliance with UN Security Council Resolution 678. We prefer a peaceful outcome.... However, anything less than full compliance with UN Security Council Resolution 678 and its predecessors is unacceptable.'

With little more than 80 hours until the deadline, the US Congress sent Saddam the message Bush had asked for. Both Houses passed a joint resolution giving Bush the authorization to use US armed forces pursuant to UN Security Council Resolution 678, once he had determined that the US had exhausted all appropriate diplomatic and other peaceful means. The Senate vote was uncomfortably close, at 52 to 47. The House of Representatives was more in tune with reality. They cleared it 250 to 183. The major battle on the 'Home Front' was won. The Allied troops could now go to work in earnest.

On 11 January in Kuwait there was a sudden flurry of military traffic. There were rumours that the Iraqis were withdrawing, but in fact they were only redeploying. A crackdown on foreigners without Iraqi residence permits intensified. During the previous few days, hundreds of Asians had been detained for not having the correct papers. A final rush of Kuwaitis made the crossing into Saudi Arabia before the Iraqis sealed the border completely.

With the increasing fear and tension, the Iraqis in Kuwait seemed to become more vindictive to just about anybody who crossed their paths. Even children were not immune. Indian Mohammed Ali, and his 12-year-old daughter Alia, were arrested while out shopping for not having the correct papers. They were shuffled from one police station to another, without being fed, and had to sleep in bare cells in the cold of winter. Their relatives tracked them down, and managed to get a blanket to them. Alia gave it to her sick father, while she managed with an oversized towel. From Kuwait, they were moved first to Basra, then to Baghdad, where they were held separately in a jail. During the air war, they were terrified by the bombing and din of the anti-aircraft fire, trapped as they were in their stone cages.

Finally, Alia was released with two Indian women. Incredibly, they made it back to Kuwait. Alia's father was not repatriated until March 1991.

The looting increased noticeably with the departure of Iraqi civilians, some troops, and the last of the Palestinians to leave. The lack of Iraqi civilian police made the looters more brazen. Civilian air traffic to and from Baghdad was halted. From 13 January, a 6.00 p.m. to 6.00 a.m. curfew was imposed. Strangely, the street lights were still functioning normally on their automatic timers. There was no blackout. The weather was dark, wet and cold. The clouds over the city seemed a portent of the coming storm.

On Thursday 10 January, the last Western diplomats started evacuating Baghdad. There could have been no clearer message to Saddam that his capital was in the Coalition's sights. The Soviets maintained their Embassy, as did the Poles, Swedes and Yugoslavs, but were very much on their own.

Curiously, the last major Western country to abandon its Kuwait embassy was one of the first to leave Baghdad, but a single brave man stayed on until the last minute. The British diplomats drove out to Jordan at dawn on 10 January, leaving behind only Consul-General Christopher Segar. He was staying to attend the trial of one of his citizens, Patrick Trygg, who had been arrested in September 1990 for helping other British subjects to escape from Iraq.

The Germans followed later that day. The Australians, New Zealanders and Irish had already gone, but the Americans, Canadians, Japanese and several other EC people were still in town. With war looming, they had been all but forgotten by their capitals. In fact, some capitals had asked their envoys whether there was any alternative to going out with the Americans, for appearances. This seemed largely irrelevant to then in the circumstances.

The diplomats had arranged a code between them to say when to move. Joe Wilson was to ring them up with a cryptic 'Follow my suitcases.' Everyone was packed and ready to go, but most of them wanted to stay as late as possible, and leave together in a last demonstration of solidarity.

It was the morning of Saturday, 12 January, the day after UN Secretary-General Perez de Cuellar arrived in Baghdad, before Joe Wilson's suitcases went into action. He and his last five colleagues took an Iraqi charter flight to Frankfurt shortly before noon, accompanied by seven private US citizens, six Canadians, five Dutch, three Norwegians, three Swiss, a couple of Belgians, an

Algerian, a Finn, and a Turk – all of whom were diplomats – and nine other individuals. The French *chargé d'affaires*, Andre Janier, and his British colleague, Christopher Segar – who was to attend Trygg's trial that morning – were the only major Western diplomats left in Baghdad. Fortunately for both Segar and Trygg, one of the three judges did not turn up, and the case was dismissed. They drove out at lunchtime, leaving the intrepid Mr Janier to hold the fort. He would fly out less than 48 hours before the deadline expired.

On 13 January, after two days in Baghdad, Perez de Cuellar met Yasser Arafat in the morning, and then Saddam for three-and-a-half hours. Again, the talks were fruitless. Saddam also acted exceedingly rudely by keeping the world's senior diplomat waiting for hours, while he met with a largely irrelevant envoy, Mrs Takako Doi, Secretary of the Japanese Socialist Party.

Perez de Cuellar made absolutely no progress in persuading Saddam to pull out of Kuwait by the deadline, now less than three days away, saying later that he had 'not been offered anything from the Iraqi authorities which I can consider a step towards peace. As far as I am concerned, I have done what I have to do – I don't know whether others will do something, but it appears to me that it is perhaps a little late for embarking on any other peace efforts. Only God can tell whether there will be peace or war, if you believe.'

It was a sad and poignant moment. If this senior man of peace, with his vast experience in dealing with Saddam during the Iran–Iraq War, was washing his hands of the whole affair, then the prospects for peace were all but dead.

That Friday, 11 January, the last Muslim week-end before war, the mosques in Baghdad had been packed. Despite Saddam's rhetoric, the populace were nervous, although they put on a defiant show for the journalists.

As Perez de Cuellar was leaving Baghdad after his failed mission, Kuwait was suffering its own tragedy. On that day, 13 January, Asrar Al-Qabandi was brutally executed by the *Mukhabarat*.

Details of her fate in the 71 days of captivity since 4 November are uncertain, but she was apparently chained to a desk for at least the first 17 days. No amount of money could bribe her out of custody. The Iraqis were aware of her activities, and seemed to have orders from the most senior level. They were convinced she had access to a satellite phone, and had been contacting CNN and ABC in the US. When she denied this, they showed her faxes which had been sent to her through another captured system.

In the third week of her captivity, Asrar was moved into a room with three other girls, where she was held until at least 28 December. The number of girls increased to nine, and then back down to three as some were released. The beatings were reduced when the Iraqis asked the women to cook for them, and wash their clothes. During this time, they could hear the horrifying screams of Kuwaiti men being tortured in adjoining rooms every night after midnight.

That winter was the coldest and wettest in many years. Many of the prisoners had been captured in their summer clothes. After some time, the Iraqis grew to respect the fiery young woman. Asrar used this to talk them into letting her get warm clothing for some of the prisoners by providing the Iraqis with electronics from one of her abandoned safe-houses.

Asrar's ordeal during the last two weeks of her 31 years of life is uncertain. One story says she was taken to Baghdad, sentenced to death, and then taken back to Kuwait. That is unlikely, because she would probably have been killed in Baghdad. What is certain is that she was murdered on 13 January with four bullets to the chest, and one in the head. Her hands had been tied in front of her with plastic tubing, and her head sliced in two with an axe, from the right hand side. The Iraqis then dumped her body on the rain-soaked street outside her family's empty home, still dressed in the jeans and shirt she had been captured in. Her face was unrecognizable.

Her father Mohammed, and uncle Najeeb, in hiding in the home of one of Asrar's sisters, were told by neighbours that 'something had been dumped outside the house'. They knew instinctively that it was Asrar. They recovered the body, took it to a relative's house, photographed it for evidence, and had three Kuwaiti doctors perform an autopsy. She had been violated and severely beaten before being killed. A physician who examined her body, Dr Abdullah Behbehani, described it as 'completely mutilated'. To this day, he cannot speak of it without visible emotion.

As a final insult, the Iraqis required that a death certificate be obtained before she could be buried. The cause of death was listed as 'gunshots in the chest and head', and the place of death as a 'hospital' instead of a torture centre. Asrar was buried by her grieving father on a dark and gloomy day, the day before the expiry of the UN deadline. Eerily, as she was laid to rest and the remains of her face uncovered and turned towards Mecca in the Islamic tradition, the Iraqis were test-firing some of their artillery nearby. It was as if they were paying their own final salute to this brave young woman.

Several of her Resistance colleagues from other groups would die similarly horrible deaths as the Iraqis cleared out their cells over the next few weeks.

On the day of Asrar's death, King Fahd of Saudi Arabia, and President Hosni Mubarak of Egypt indicated that they were prepared to join in action against Iraq if necessary. Up to that point, the Arab members of the Coalition, Kuwait excluded, had been lukewarm on actually hitting Iraq, although they were prepared to provide support and bases to the Western Allies.

This was followed by last-minute calls for peace from such eminent people as the Secretary-Generals of the Organization of the Islamic Conference, and the Organization for African Unity, and Pope John Paul II.

There was one last attempt at mediation by President Mitterrand of France. Yasser Arafat, acting again as Saddam's messenger boy, tried to convince the French that there was still hope. Late on 14 January, after seeing Perez de Cuellar that morning, Mitterrand met with the Iraqi Ambassador to Paris, Abdul Razzak Al-Hashimi, and President Mobutu of Zaire, whose country then held the rotating Presidency of the UN Security Council. The idea was for French Foreign Minister Roland Dumas to visit Baghdad and discuss an arrangement involving an Iraqi withdrawal from Kuwait, deployment of a UN peacekeeping force, and an eventual Middle East peace conference.

The Security Council discussed the proposal, with barely disguised US and British irritation at France's last-minute meddling, but Dumas never went to

Baghdad. Mitterrand had no intention of exposing him to the humiliation endured by Perez de Cuellar. Following the fruitless Security Council discussions, Perez de Cuellar urged Saddam, for the last time, to 'commence without delay, the total withdrawal of Iraqi forces from Kuwait'.

The silence from Baghdad to these last anguished appeals was deafening.

The withdrawal deadline was 8.00 a.m., 16 January, in Kuwait. On the afternoon of 15 January, Saddam is thought to have made his last visit to his troops in Kuwait. He was filmed talking to a group of soldiers manning the beach defences. The footage shown on Iraqi TV may have been from his earlier visit in late December. No one knew for sure.

He chatted amicably with the men as a security cordon kept everyone else at a safe distance. Saddam had asked them what they were having for lunch. 'Chicken, Sir,' they replied, 'and eggplant'. Saddam then asked where they had got the eggplant. They had grown it themselves, they said, pointing to a nearby barren stretch of ground. This caused great mirth among the Kuwaitis. Not only could that desert plot not have grown anything, but eggplant was out of season. There was speculation that the chicken was stolen, and Saddam's staff had created the best-fed squad of Iraqi troops in Kuwait for the cameras.

For the Kuwaitis, the spectacle of Saddam's PR people unwittingly making a fool of him was heartening, but with the deadline barely 24 hours away, there was more to look forward to. Few people expected the war to start as soon as the deadline passed. The consensus was that the attack would come at night, at least ten hours later, when the Iraqis were virtually blind. The Kuwaitis were happy to see the Iraqis sweat throughout the day of 16 January. The anti-aircraft gun crews in the city were visibly nervous. The only traffic was of Iraqi military vehicles and a few cars and trucks, mostly heading north. Kuwait City had the atmosphere of 'High Noon'. Saddam's 'Mother Of All Battles' was about to become reality, but as he expected.

As dusk fell on 16 January, a cold and drizzly day in occupied Kuwait, soldiers and civilians alike battened down. Those with access to satellite TV were glued to CNN. Anyone with a shortwave radio had it tuned to the BBC or the other services. At that moment, hundreds of Allied pilots on airbases throughout the Gulf, and on aircraft carriers at sea, were reviewing their plans. Some were strapping themselves into their ejector seats. The armourers conducted their final checks. Targetters ran their last tests on hundreds of cruise missiles. B-52s from US bases were already in the air over the Atlantic. By dawn, the Desert Storm campaign which would later be known in Kuwait as the Liberation War would have begun. The waiting was over. A finger was tightening on the trigger, only this time it was General Schwarzkopf's, not Saddam Hussein's, and his objective was liberation, not occupation.

29. LIBERATION

The Liberation of Kuwait started as the invasion had: in the early hours of a Thursday morning. The similarity ended there. It was now a wintry 17 January, not the summer of 2 August, and while the invasion had been largely a surprise, almost everybody in Kuwait expected the war to start that night. The deadline was nearly 20 hours old.

Most of those in Kuwait heard the opening shots of the war in precisely the same way as people around the world – on TV and radio. People with access to CNN watched the fireworks show of anti-aircraft fire over Baghdad at 2.40 a.m. on 17 January with fascination. Others heard the news on the BBC Radio. Gulf TV stations were off the air at that time of night, so only those with satellite TV could see the images. At no time during the occupation had they ever seen anything like the tracer fire over Baghdad that morning. Yet, there was a curious sense of detachment. Baghdad was 700km away, and there was no sound of firing or bombing in Kuwait. It was almost as if they were watching a movie. Incredibly, the phones in Kuwait were still working, and were alive with people excitedly passing the news around. The five-and-a-half months of waiting were over. A great sense of relief swept over everyone.

Then, just before 4.00 a.m., the first attacks struck Kuwait City. They seemed to be pinpoint air strikes on the buildings housing Iraqi troops. Fierce blasts shook windows, and shattered some. Those who were not already in their shelters raced for them. The noise of the repeated blasts was deafening. It was impossible to determine whether the noise was of bombs exploding or outgoing anti-aircraft fire, but it seemed as if the entire military might of the Western world was being concentrated on the city and its suburbs.

This first attack on Kuwait was over within minutes. Amazingly, the street lights were still on, but the Iraqis soon put them out, and imposed a complete curfew. The next raid came just before 9.00 a.m. By then, people had realized that the bombing was directed with incredible accuracy at military targets, so did not necessarily take shelter. The pilots knew precisely where the Iraqis were as a result of their own reconnaissance and Resistance intelligence. On that first day, US, British, Kuwaiti and Saudi planes took part in 400 raids on 60 targets. Early indications spoke of spectacular results, with few losses.

Within hours, President Bush announced his decision to launch the attack. Saddam's response was typical. 'The 'Mother Of All Battles' had started, and 'the Devil Bush' and his 'evil allies' had begun the showdown,' he said. 'God was on Iraq's side, and with His help, victory would be Iraq's.'

The early hours of the second day, Friday 18 January, brought another scare. At 3.03 a.m., Saddam fired the first of eight *Al-Hussein* missiles into Israel. There were fears that they might be chemically armed. Suddenly the prospect of gas warfare in Kuwait was very real. The Iraqis had been issued with gas masks and atropine. This may have been to protect them from an Allied attack, but it was equally likely to shield them from their own gas.

There was little those in Kuwait could do other than prepare home-made gas masks with crushed charcoal, and improvised protection suits of plastic garbage bags. They kept poultry close by as an early-warning system. If the chickens started dying, then it was time to start using their scant protection. There was great relief when the Israelis reported no chemicals, but the fear persisted - with great justification, as was later discovered.

The main success of the Iraqi missiles was to divert a significant part of the Allied air forces to so-called 'SCUD hunting' for the rest of the war, and to remove some of the air support for which ground commanders were crying out. Saddam had indeed acted on his threat to burn half of Israel, only it was the half with the Arabs who would suffer most. During the war, he would fire a total of 93 SCUDs, 43 at Israel, 47 Saudi Arabia, and three at Bahrain.

On the early afternoon of 18 January, the first black rains came to Kuwait, accompanied by a heavy smell of kerosene in the air. The Iraqis had not yet blown the Kuwaiti oil wells or refineries, but had shelled a Saudi refinery at Khafji, just south of the border. It was 100km south of Kuwait City, but a southerly wind carried the oil smoke and carbon into the rain clouds.

That night, the emphasis of the air attacks in Kuwait seemed to shift towards the Republican Guard divisions in northern Kuwait and southern Iraq, and was reportedly supported by ship-launched cruise missiles, or B-52s.

With the world focused on the air war, Kuwaiti and US forces were in action at sea. Apart from the air and missile attacks launched from US carriers, cruisers and submarines, the sharp end of the Allied Naval operations was a tiny force of the Kuwaiti Navy's two surviving Lurssen fast patrol boats, *Istiqlal* and *Sanbouk,* the renamed and greatly-modified Coastguard barge, *Happy Duck,* and the frigate USS *Nicholas,* whose function was to provide air defence for the Kuwaiti boats, and link them with the US Naval Command through the USS *Oldendorf,* and the flagship, USS *Wisconsin.*

These four vessels were designated Task Element K, or *Kilo,* the radio phonetic for the letter 'K', for Kuwait. The Kuwaiti squadron commander was Lieutenant-Colonel Nasser Husseinan. *Nicholas* was under Commander Dennis Moral. The two Kuwaiti Lurssens were skippered by the same men who had led them in battle on 2 August, 1990, Major Jassim Al-Ansari and Captain Yacoub Al-Muhanna. *Happy Duck* was under Captain Khalid Al-Kandari.

Kilo's mission was five-fold. Of all the Allied forces, the Kuwaitis knew the Gulf's northern waters best. They were to provide search-and-rescue for pilots who might be downed, reconnaissance of Iraqi naval activity in the area, skirmishing with Iraqi vessels as the opportunity arose, mine detection, and support for special operations against the Kuwaiti coast. To carry out the latter two functions, a unit of US Navy SEAL commandos under Lieutenant-Commander David Olsen was on *Happy Duck,* together with several two-man submarines equipped with sonar, and a number of heavily armed speedboats.

The Kuwaitis had trained extensively with Olsen's men, and the *Nicholas.* From September, they had realized that the only way they would be able to get into the front line would be by involving themselves with the Special Forces. The Kuwait Navy Acting Commander, Colonel Ahmad Al-Mulla, had successfully integrated his boats with the Americans, and found a place for them in the massive Allied war scheme. The Acting Kuwaiti Chief of Staff, Major-General Jaber Al-Khalid had spoken to his old classmate, Colonel Jesse Johnson, who headed Schwarzkopf's Special Forces, and ensured that his men would be involved. Now, finally, they would strike back.

The mine detection mission was perhaps the most critical to the overall Allied naval effort. Belatedly, Allied commanders had realized that they had not kept an eye on where the Iraqis were laying mines during the previous five months. It would be up to the Kuwaitis and Olsen's men to find them.

The Kuwaitis also had their own agenda. On board *Happy Duck* were several platoons of Kuwaiti volunteer Marines who had been trained by Kuwaiti Army officers, Major Faisal Al-Adwani and Captain Abdulnasser Al-Sayegh in the UAE with the help of the local armed forces. Al-Mulla and Husseinan were keen to get these men onto the Kuwaiti offshore islands of Qaro and Umm Al-Maradem before anyone else, particularly the Saudis, got there. These two tiny islets lay off the northern sector of what had been the Neutral Zone established between Kuwait and Saudi Arabia by the British in 1922. Since then, the Saudis had always claimed at least co-sovereignty over them, but the Kuwaitis claimed them fully as their own – including their offshore mineral rights. If the Kuwaitis could liberate the islands, then it would seal this claim. If the Saudis got there first, they might never leave.

Kilo's first job was to neutralize eleven offshore oil platforms in Kuwait's Dorra and Hout oilfield, 35km north of the Kuwait-Saudi border, and 60km off the coast. Allied pilots had reported anti-aircraft fire from the area, and it was thought that the platforms were part of an Iraqi early-warning system. During 18 January, *Nicholas* sent a Seahawk helicopter to reconnoitre. It returned with a video showing Iraqi emplacements, and 12.7mm or 23mm anti-aircraft guns installed atop the platforms, nine of which seemed occupied.

Istiqlal crept towards the platforms from the east just before dusk for a closer look, with Sanbouk remaining farther offshore to guard *Happy Duck*, and *Nicholas* situated between them. The intention was to neutralize the platforms by capturing the occupants, not to kill them. If the Iraqis surrendered, then so much the better. However, no one was taking any chances.

After consultations, *Istiqlal* – with two SEALs on board as observers — and *Nicholas* divided the nine targets between the two vessels, and *Nicholas'* Seahawk and two small Army helicopters which were operating off *Nicholas*. At 8.50 p.m., with their long-range infra-red cameras trained on the targets, *Istiqlal* and *Nicholas* opened fire with their forward 76mm guns from a range of about three kilometres, aiming high on the platforms to knock out the anti-aircraft guns. The helicopters launched Hellfire missiles at the two platforms closest inshore, and farthest away from the vessels. There was no reaction from the Iraqis – some of the platforms were unmanned, including all four being attacked by *Nicholas* – so *Istiqlal* moved in closer and opened fire from 2000 metres with her rear 40mm guns, with their higher rate of fire.

There was still no reaction, so *Istiqlal* closed in with her .50 calibre machine guns at the ready, to within 25 metres of the first platform, and was able to shout to the Iraqis. This time, they surrendered.

Over the next 12 hours, the Iraqis were taken off the platforms by joint parties of Kuwaitis and the SEALs. Twenty-three survivors, three of whom were wounded, and five dead, including a lieutenant, were recovered. Most were conscripts, but they were commanded by a Republican Guard lieutenant.

The following day, *Istiqlal* and the SEALs returned to the platforms, boarded them, and threw all the guns and ammunition overboard so that other Iraqis could not retrieve them. Much to the later discomfort of the helicopter pilots, they also found a stock of shoulder-fired surface-to-air missiles.

Back on the Kuwaiti mainland, there was a respite from air attacks on the urban area on the nights of 19 and 20 January, but they were renewed with a vengeance on the 21st. After the initial shock, speculation arose that the war might go on for weeks, if not months.

These fears were laid to rest prematurely on the afternoon of 21 January with news of Allied forces in Saudi Arabia moving towards the Kuwaiti border, increased bombing of the coastal defences, and news of the oil platforms operation. It seemed at the time that the Iraqis would be facing a two-pronged attack from the sea and from directly across the Saudi border within days. From the very beginning, the Allies encouraged the Iraqi belief that an amphibious attack was coming. Actually, General Schwarzkopf was against such an operation, but did not rule it out until 2 February. He wanted to retain the option of launching one, if only to take pressure off the land troops.

The Allied deception worked. The Iraqis seemed convinced that the attack would come from the south, so they torched the oil facilities at Wafra, on the border. They then began quietly moving an armoured strike force to the southern borders. A few men stuck on platforms in the Gulf might be prepared to surrender, but the Iraqi Army was not about to give up just yet.

The air raids on Kuwait soon assumed a pattern. They were mostly on the two KAF bases outside the city, Bubiyan and Failaka Islands, the coastal defences, and the troops in the desert between the city and the Saudi border. Nevertheless, there were quite a few strikes on targets in the urban area.

For several nights in a row, there would be few attacks on the city, and then a wave of bombing would start late in the evening, and continue all night. The first indication was usually a rumble of what could have been approaching aircraft, travelling at high subsonic speed. The anti-aircraft guns then opened up with a tremendous sustained roar. They had little chance of hitting the planes. Most of the guns were manually sighted, and traversed by soldiers frantically winding handles. Those with radar guidance were quickly put out of action by radiation-homing missiles. The Iraqis' only hope was to put up a wall of metal and hope that the planes would fly into it. The pilots were at more risk from heat-seeking missiles, but used decoy flares liberally.

The Kuwaiti pilots were perhaps the most highly motivated of the Allied flyers. At last, it was their chance to hit back. With 39 fixed-wing combat aircraft, and various helicopters and support aircraft, the Kuwaitis accumulated over 800 missions during the war, second only to the Saudis among Arab forces in missions per aircraft, and marginally better than the French.

However, one Kuwaiti A-4 Skyhawk was shot down in the Burgan oilfield, south of Ahmadi. The pilot, Lieutenant-Colonel Mohammed Mubarak, apparently tried again to hit a target he missed on his first run, using the same direction of attack, thus giving the Iraqi gunners a chance to hit him. He ejected safely, was captured, and was later paraded on Iraqi TV with downed US, British and Italian airmen. The Americans also lost an observer plane over Kuwait on 18 January, with two Marine crewmen captured.

It was seldom safe to be out during raids, although the danger was less from the attackers than from the defenders. Some of the Iraqis were so nervous that they fired on anyone they saw. Furthermore, they were putting so much fire into the air that anyone on the ground was at grave risk from falling spent shrapnel, which could kill after falling thousands of metres under gravity.

There were a number of spectacular hits in the urban area. On the morning of 18 January, French planes bombed a huge Iraqi ammunition dump on the southern edge of Sixth Ring. Windows several kilometres away were smashed with the explosions. A week later, there was an unusual prelude to some particularly heavy raids. Suddenly all shortwave radios in Kuwait went dead, as if the power had failed. Within minutes, bombers struck, and the radios came back on. The Allies had just jammed every frequency in Kuwait, and hit Iraqi radar-guided anti-aircraft missile sites.

On the night of 12 February, the Allies knocked out a single room in the city telecommunications centre with one missile. The accuracy was incredible. The destruction was total. The room held equipment which the Iraqis were using to talk to Baghdad. The bomb went in through the roof, and sliced through several floors before exploding almost precisely where it should have.

Not all the targets were on land. On 1 February, an Iraqi Osa missile craft was struck in Shuwaikh Port by US Navy A-6 bombers. There must have been a massive amount of ammunition on board, as pieces of the vessel rained down on the suburb of Kaifan, a kilometre inland.

Civilian casualties were light, but did occur. The first deaths came on the night of 20 January, when a family were killed in their Ahmadi home. A week later, an errant missile struck a block of flats near the airport, and a man lost a leg. Other injuries were caused, and houses damaged, in Ahmadi on 6 February when a nearby ammunition dump of the Iraqi III Corps was hit.

Four people were killed in the nurses' quarters of the Al-Adan Hospital, ten kilometres north of Ahmadi, in the afternoon of 9 February. They were two Indian men, the wife of an Egyptian doctor, and a five-year-old Filipino. Three other Filipinos were seriously injured by flying glass and blast. One of these lost both eyes. The others each lost an eye. The Iraqis had placed anti-aircraft guns on the hostel roof, so the Allies bombed the open space between two of the buildings to try to knock them out, without directly hitting the hostel. Unfortunately, after three weeks of bombing, people had become blasé and had not taken shelter during the raids. Some were at the windows when the bombs struck, blowing in the glass and window frames onto them. The Egyptian woman was walking from her car to the hostel.

In the first days, many Kuwaitis who had hidden their weapons after the retribution against the Resistance retrieved them, and sat waiting for the Allies to arrive. However, the bombing just went on, and on. The Iraqis were obviously petrified, but showed no sign of withdrawal, and the Allies seemed happy to pound them from the air indefinitely. The guns were reburied.

The greatest fears were of an Iraqi massacre or round-ups of Kuwaitis, such as the Iraqi Army had practised when withdrawing from captured Iranian territory. These fears were not unfounded. The Iraqis had stepped up arrests of Kuwaitis, and killings of anyone suspected of having Resistance links. Being impotent against the Allied onslaught, and irate at the the bombing of Baghdad and Iraq, they took their frustrations out on the Kuwaitis.

After the first couple of days of winter sunshine, the weather for most of the air war was atrocious. There were a few clear days, but mostly there was rain, sometimes torrential. In a way, this was a blessing as it kept the Iraqis indoors. The men in the desert trenches and bunkers must have been miserable.

By 23 January, petrol sales to civilians ceased, with all fuel reserved for the Army. Even people who had acquired Iraqi licence plates were turned away. In any event, anyone who went out in a car risked having it confiscated, or even being arrested. The checkpoints became even worse, with the troops being particularly vindictive. They were joined by whatever Iraqi police were left in town, the *Mukhabarat,* and Arab Liberation Front Palestinian militia, most of whom had come from Iraq. Soldiers even came to houses, asking for cars on the pretext that they were needed as ambulances, or taking them anyway. The only way to keep cars was to bribe the local Iraqi commander, completely immobilize them, lock them behind high walls, or even bury them. One man used a crane to hide his Jaguar sedan in his empty swimming pool. He then filled it in with soil, and planted a vegetable garden on top.

When the initial shock of the first raids wore off, life returned to a sort of normality. Street traders reappeared on roadsides. The noise of the bombs and anti-aircraft fire became almost like background noise. People only took shelter if an attack was particularly close. Late in the first week, the curfew was either lifted, or the Iraqis did not bother to enforce it.

Incredibly, truckloads of Jordanian produce continued to run the gauntlet of air raids through Iraq and into Kuwait until February. The prices in Kuwait apparently made it worthwhile, and there was always the chance of a backload of personal effects. The drivers must have been brave, stupid, or desperate. Allied pilots could not differentiate between Army and civilian vehicles, and several of the trucks were hit.

In some respects, people in Kuwait were probably better off than those in Baghdad. The Iraqi capital lost electricity in the first days of the air war, but Kuwait did not experience its first major power interruptions until mid-February. Despite being in the middle of the war, most of those in Kuwait heard it rather than saw it, and followed it with the rest of the world, on TV and radio, as long as their electricity or batteries lasted. The glowing reports of early Allied successes greatly boosted morale, but even after two weeks of bombing, the Iraqis did not seem on the verge of withdrawal, although a scattered few gave themselves up to Kuwaiti civilians, asking for refuge.

With world attentions focused on the air war, Allied ground troops were having their own piece of the action. The main plan of attack was already in place, whereby US, UK and French troops would outflank the Iraqis in a broad sweep into the desert west of Kuwait, with a supporting attack directly into Kuwait by the US Marines and Arab Coalition troops.

There had been many small sporadic exchanges of artillery and short-range missiles between Saudi and Iraqi troops across the border near Khafji. These were not part of any overall plan. However, Marine Commander Lieutenant-General Walter Boomer wanted to deceive the Iraqis about where his main ground assault would fall, and to disrupt their forces. To do this, he arranged with the local Saudi commander, Major-General Sultan Al-Mutairi, for Marine artillery to conduct a series of raids. The first was on the night of 21 January, on an Iraqi artillery unit near Khafji. The second struck the following night, much farther to the west in the Marines' own sector, on the Iraqi-occupied Al-Minagish Kuwaiti Police post, near the 'elbow' of the border.

Another ten Marine artillery raids were conducted over the next month, with several Saudi Multiple Launch Rocket System barrages on Iraqis north of Khafji, inside Kuwait. Both forces were supported by co-ordinated air strikes. One of the earlier Marine raids was on an Iraqi build-up near the Umm Al-Hjul police post at the heel of the Kuwaiti border. The Americans did not know it at the time, but the concentrations were probably a prelude to an Iraqi strike across the border into Saudi Arabia a few days later.

At sea, Task Element *Kilo* was back in action. Since the platforms operation, the Kuwaiti boats had been trying to find the Iraqi minefields. *Istiqlal* and *Sanbouk* would escort *Happy Duck* closer to the Kuwait shore from their holding positions, and the US Navy SEAL mini-submarines - which could not operate far from their mother ship - would be hoisted over the side. They did not find a single mine at that stage, and would only discover why later.

The main operation on the Kuwaitis' minds was the liberation of Qaro, the tiny one-kilometre-square coral island 50km due east of Ras Al-Jalayh. Now that it was apparent that at least those Iraqis stationed in the Gulf waters wanted to surrender, the plan had been for a US helicopter to fly over the island, and to demand surrender in Arabic through a loudspeaker. The Allies were fairly confident that the Iraqis wanted to give up. However, there was still a danger. *Nicholas*, *Istiqlal* and *Sanbouk* would station themselves four nautical miles east of the island, and fire bursts of five 76mm shells onto it if the Iraqis did not give up immediately. Once the Iraqis had surrendered to the helicopters, *Istiqlal* would sail to the island and take them off.

On the morning of 23 January, at about 9.30 a.m., *Istiqlal* and *Sanbouk* were ten to fifteen nautical miles south of Qaro, out in front of the larger US ships, when they detected an Iraqi vessel about 12 nautical miles west of the island, heading for it at 12 knots. The Kuwaitis could have blown the Iraqi boat out of the water with their Exocets, but held their fire. They advised the USS *Curts*, which had replaced *Nicholas* as their air defence, and urged the captain to execute the plan to capture Qaro immediately. *Curts* agreed.

The Kuwaiti troops who were supposed to land on Qaro were not yet in place so the *Curts'* Kuwaiti liaison officer, Major Faisal Habib and two other officers boarded the *Curts'* Seahawk with the Americans, and flew over the island. They appealed in Arabic over loudspeakers for the Iraqis to surrender, which they did. The helicopter landed and Habib became the first Kuwaiti to set foot on the first piece of liberated territory. Further US and Kuwaiti forces moved in on the Rigid Inflatable Boats (RIBs) to take care of the Iraqis.

By this time, the Iraqi boat was nearing the island. It too surrendered. Eventually, a total of 53 Iraqis from both the island and the boat were taken prisoner, without, mercifully, any casualties on either side.

The Americans and Kuwaitis searched the island, finding it honeycombed with bunkers full of Jordanian ammunition. However, a shock awaited them. They discovered charts of some of the nearby minefields, and finally realized why *Happy Duck* and the SEALs had not been able to find them. They had unknowingly sailed right through them on their way inshore to launch the mini-subs, and were looking for the mines *inside* the mine-barrier. The mines had been laid farther offshore than anyone realized.

The following day, more Kuwaitis landed, with representatives from all three vessels. The flag was first raised on a piece of freed Kuwait by Major Faisal Al-Adwani, who commanded the men who would occupy Qaro and Umm Al-Maradem. Twenty men were left on Qaro, and the boats withdrew.

The Kuwait Navy Acting Commander, Colonel Ahmad Al-Mulla, arranged for the flag-raising to be filmed, by helicopter, so that there could be no mistake about the location, and to show the world Kuwaitis liberating their own land. He passed this tape to the media; it went worldwide within hours, providing clear evidence that Qaro was indisputably and indivisibly Kuwaiti.

Four days later, on 29 January, Umm Al-Maradem, further south, was retaken. It was abandoned, although the Iraqis had been there. More Kuwaiti *Happy Duck* volunteers were posted there to occupy it, and the flag raised the following day. Curiously, several of the Kuwaitis who knew Qaro and Umm Al-Maradem from pre-invasion days noticed something amiss. Both islands had previously had plenty of rabbits on them. Now there were none. Apparently, the hungry Iraqis had eaten every single rabbit on both islands.

On 24 January, the Iraqis started pouring oil into the Gulf from the Mina Al-Ahmadi Sea Island terminal, and from tankers modified to pump oil overboard from their tanks. It seems that the objective of this vandalism was to forestall an amphibious attack, which they believed to be imminent.

The tankers were relatively easy for the Allies to put out of action with missiles from Royal Navy Lynx helicopters. The flow of oil from the terminal - which was fed by the oil in two huge tank farms - was more difficult to stem. The US Air Force had to ask the Kuwaiti Resistance in Ahmadi to identify the key onshore loading manifolds which they needed to strike to cut the supply of oil at its source. On 26 January, they struck the two manifolds, setting them ablaze. In the confusion, members of the Resistance slipped into the tank farms and closed the valves on the tanks themselves.

However, there was little the Allies or the Resistance could do to prevent the Iraqis from blowing the oil wells. As early as the night of 26 January, people in

Kuwait City could see huge fires shooting up into the air beyond Kuwait International Airport. Entire sections of the skyline turned red, with an evil, pulsating glow. The roar of the flames was clearly audible in southern residential areas, as clouds of dirty black smoke joined the rain clouds, and then descended on the city in carbon and oil-filled raindrops. Black rain had already been falling for a week, fed by the smoke from a burning Saudi refinery at Khafji. This was far worse. By morning, the normally pristine white seagulls picking at the soaked rubbish piles were all a dirty grey.

However, there were a few bright points on the horizon. People figured that the Iraqis could not be intent on staying if they were destroying the oil industry; the country would be free again within days, if only they could survive. Secondly, late on the 26th, only nine days into the air war, Iraqi Air Force planes started fleeing to Iran. Eighty left over four days, and then another 55 in February. This seemed unfathomable. Some feared an unholy conspiracy between Iraq and Iran to unite against the Allies. To others, it was the best confirmation yet that Saddam was hurting. Strangely, some of the aircraft flown out were Kuwait Airways airliners he had stolen from Kuwait.

At the end of January, the Iraqi Army took the initiative after two weeks of solid pounding. These engagements, although dismissed as militarily irrelevant by an embarrassed General Schwarzkopf, would kill 25 US servicemen, one-sixth of all Americans killed in action during the crisis, 18 Saudis – almost half of all Saudis killed – and scores of Iraqis.

Across the border from Kuwait in Saudi Arabia, 1,200 US Marines, designated Task Force *Shepherd*, formed a screen to protect their parent unit, the 1st Marine Division, 48km to the south. Some of *Shepherd's* men, and reconnaissance troops from the 2nd Marine Division, had occupied a series of observation posts, or 'OPs', in Saudi border police stations facing Kuwait. Several companies from *Shepherd*, in wheeled light armoured vehicles, were stationed a few kilometres behind the westernmost posts as mobile reserves.

The easternmost of these OPs, Number 8, was just inland from the coast, 11km north of Khafji. It was manned by Marines, US Special Forces and Saudis. Another important post, OP-4, was 70km inland, at the heel of the border, straddling the three-metre high sand berm built by the Saudis to deter smugglers. OP-4 was opposite Kuwait's Umm Al-Hjul area, which had been hit days earlier by Marine artillery. It was manned by 30 Marines under Lieutenant Steven Ross, and a number of Saudis. A third critical post, OP-6, was 40km north of OP-4, and 10km south of the elbow.

During 29 January, spotters had seen unusual movement in the trees around Wafra, and had called in airstrikes. Three Iraqis had surrendered to OP-8, perhaps as a ruse, saying that their officers had fled north. Underestimating the Iraqis, the Americans did not expect an immediate attack.

However, at 6.30 p.m., the Iraqis started trying to jam the Marines' radios, with some success. Then, *Shepherd's* 'C' Company, looking east into Kuwait from Saudi high ground near OP-6, saw Iraqi armour heading south. Ninety minutes later, 'D' Company, four kilometres north-west of OP-4, spotted presumably the same vehicles, numbering about 50. A US F/A-18 was called in and attacked just as the Iraqis neared OP-4 at around 9.30 p.m., but failed to stop them. Ross' men in OP-4 opened fire, and hit one tank, stalling the attack. Outnumbered and outgunned, Ross called for help.

In response, 'D' Company moved towards OP-4. Thinking that they were within range of the Iraqis, three of the Marine vehicles opened fire with an anti-tank missile each. Two fell short, but the third tragically struck another 'D' Company vehicle, blowing it to pieces and killing all four Marines inside.

With the Iraqis distracted by the sudden firing and the massive explosion of the destroyed Marine vehicle on their flank, the OP-4 men sprinted to their vehicles, and sped away, past the burning wreckage and carnage of 'D' Company's vehicle. The Iraqis then moved forward, capturing the post.

At the same time, other Iraqi units moved towards OP-6, and the nearby OP-5. The reconnaissance Marines quickly abandoned them.

As 'D' Company was assessing its casualties, US troops further to the east opposite Wafra detected about 100 Iraqi armoured vehicles emerging from a grove of trees, and heading east towards the coast, parallel to the border. An officer tried to call in air-strikes, but all available aircraft had been sent to the crisis at OP-4. It was a classic diversion. The Iraqis had drawn the Americans' attention to a relatively unimportant area, and launched their real attack elsewhere. The Americans soon abandoned two other OPs along the border. Both US Marine divisions were now under attack by what was later learned to be elements of the Iraqi 20th Mechanized and 26th Armoured brigades. The Iraqis had launched a well-coordinated attack across a 70-kilometre front, and were getting the better of the Americans.

OP-8 north of Khafji was also having problems. At 9.00 p.m., they had heard Iraqi tanks on the Kuwaiti side of the border, and radioed a warning to their colleagues in the Khafji desalination plant, two kilometres south. Suddenly, the Iraqis were upon them. The Americans and Saudis ran for their lives, pulling back into Khafji in confusion, with the Iraqis hot on their heels.

The Saudi area commander, Major-General Sultan Al-Mutairi, called for airstrikes from Marine aircraft, which were supposed to provide him with air cover. He had a company of Saudi Marines in Khafji, but their weapons were no match for Iraqi armour. Despite US promises, no aircraft arrived.

Meanwhile, elements from the 5th Battalion of the Saudi National Guard 2nd Brigade were trying unsuccessfully to engage the Iraqis from the desert west of Khafji. After further repeated Saudi calls for airstrikes, the Marines said that the National Guard was too close to the Iraqis, and would have to be pulled back, otherwise they might be inadvertently hit by the Marine helicopters. Al-Mutairi ordered the National Guard to withdraw.

By then, a full battalion of Iraqi armour was closing in on the desalination plant. The men from OP-8 and the plant, and the Saudi Marines in Khafji, fled further south, inadvertently leaving behind two newly-arrived six-man US Marine reconnaissance teams. The border and Khafji had been abandoned, and a dozen Marines trapped. An armoured battalion from the 15th Brigade of Iraq's 5th Mechanized Division now held Khafji, and was soon reinforced by a mechanized battalion and an armoured company, with another brigade approaching. Other Iraqis held a thin strip of Saudi territory along the line of the east-west OPs. A number of Saudis left behind in Khafji were captured.

At around the same time, the Kuwaiti vessels in Task Element *Kilo*, patrolling near the coast after retaking Umm Al-Maradem earlier in the day detected many small boats moving south towards Khafji, close inshore. The Iraqis had come out of the harbours at Al-Zoor and the Khiran Resort, and were trying to support the Khafji operation. The command ship, USS *Oldendorf*, asked the Kuwaitis to deal with them, and alerted helicopters to back them up. Whatever else may be said about the Iraqis, they were making a concerted and co-ordinated effort to hold Khafji, even without air support.

The Coalition was now very firmly on the defensive. The greatest fear was that the Iraqis were headed for the Saudis' and US Marines' supply base at Al-Mishab Port on the Saudi coast, 40km south of Khafji, or the Marines' forward inland base at Kibrit, 50km south of Wafra. Successful attacks on these locations, especially the huge ammunition dump at lightly-defended Kibrit, would be a disaster. Allied engineers hurriedly mined the Khafji-Mishab road. Kibrit called for US armour from further south.

In the west, at OP-4, the bloodied 'D' Company was still in action. Its commander had moved his surviving vehicles two kilometres southwest of the post, and called in US Air Force A-10 tankbuster aircraft onto the Iraqi armour. More tragedy awaited him. At around 10.30 p.m., an A-10's missile hit another of his vehicles, killing seven of the eight crew. 'D' Company pulled back further, and were relieved by 'A' Company just before midnight.

At sea, *Istiqlal* and *Sanbouk* moved in to within 6km of the coast to get a fix on the Iraqi boats moving towards Khafji. Most of the Iraqi vessels were too small to present a good radar picture, so the Kuwaitis requested eight armed speedboats to assist. Four Saudi and four US Navy SEAL boats arrived. The Kuwaiti warships then opened fire with their forward 76mm guns, and *Sanbouk* fired an Exocet at a larger Iraqi boat still near Khiran. Several vessels were hit and sunk, and all but one of the Iraqi boats withdrew back into Khiran. One brave Iraqi kept going south, dodging between buoys and surface structures to try to confuse the Kuwaitis' targeting radar. He was sunk with 76mm fire. A RIB was sent to rescue any survivors, but none were found.

Back on land, in the early hours of 30 January, the Iraqis moved into the now abandoned OP-6. This time, it was their turn to fire on each other. 'C' Company could see two Iraqi units in a firefight for ten minutes near the post before they sorted themselves out. They then called in airstrikes on the Iraqi armour, and counter-attacked later, destroying eleven vehicles without loss.

Back at OP-4, more US aircraft struck the Iraqis, together with 'A' Company, which was also trying to find the casualties from the two destroyed 'D' Company vehicles. The Iraqis counter-attacked, but daylight allowed the Americans to use their airpower with effect. By mid-morning, OPs-4, 5 and 6 were back in Allied hands, the sole US Marine survivor from the destroyed vehicles had been found and evacuated, and nine Iraqis captured.

Meanwhile, at Khafji, Saudi Major-General Sultan Al-Mutairi had moved towards the western perimeter of the town with two armoured companies and two anti-tank platoons, one each from the 8th Saudi (King Fahd) Mechanized

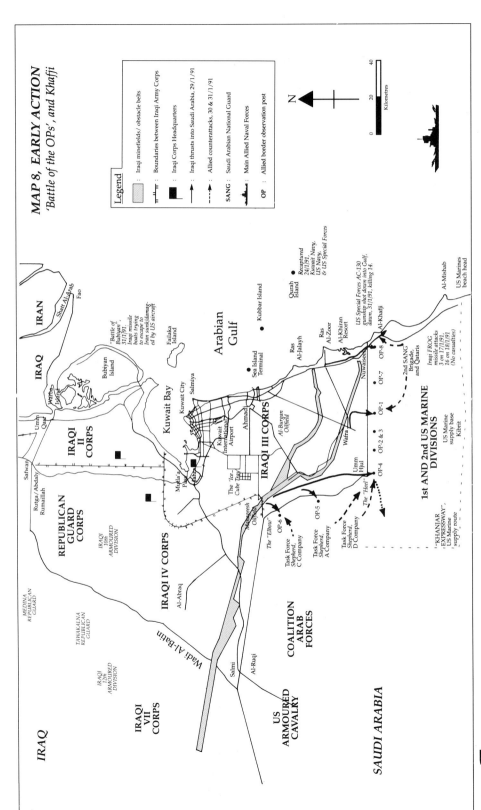

MAP 8, EARLY ACTION
'Battle of the OPs', and Khafji

Legend

▨	:	Iraqi minefields/ obstacle belts
⊥⊤	:	Boundaries between Iraqi Army Corps
■	:	Iraqi Corps Headquarters
→	:	Iraqi thrusts into Saudi Arabia, 29/1/91
⇠	:	Allied counterattacks, 30 & 31/1/91
SANG	:	Saudi Arabian National Guard
⬗	:	Main Allied Naval Forces
OP	:	Allied border observation post

N

0   20   40
Kilometres

IRAQ

IRAN

Shatt Al-Arab
Fao

"Battle of Bubiyan", 31/1/91. Iraqi missile boats trying to escape to Iran sunk/damaged by US aircraft

IRAQ

Bubiyan Island

Warba Island

Umm Qasr

Failaka Island

Arabian Gulf

IRAQI II CORPS

Kuwait Bay

Salmiya

Kuwait City

Sea Island Terminal

Kubbar Island

Qurah Island

Recaptured 24/1/91, Kuwaiti Navy, US Navy, & US Special Forces

Safwan

Ratqa / Abdaly
Rumaillah

REPUBLICAN GUARD CORPS

IRAQI 10th ARMOURED DIVISION

Mutla'a Pass

Jahra

The 'Ice-Cube'

Kuwait International Airport

Ahmadi

Al-Burqan Oilfield

Ras Al-Jaleyh

Ras Al-Zoor

Al-Khiran Resort

Nuwaiseeb

OP-8

OP-7

2nd SANG Brigade, and Qataris

Al-Khafji

US Special Forces AC-130 gunship shot down into Gulf, dawn, 31/1/91, killing 14.

MEDINA REPUBLICAN GUARD

TAWAKALNA REPUBLICAN GUARD

IRAQI 12th ARMOURED DIVISION

IRAQI VII CORPS

IRAQI IV CORPS

Al-Abraq

Wadi Al-Batin

Manageesh Oilfield

The 'Elbow'

OP-6

Task Force Shepherd, C Company

OP-5

Task Force Shepherd, A Company

Task Force Shepherd, D Company

Umm Hjul

OP-4

The 'Heel'

OP-2 & 3

Wafra

OP-1

COALITION ARAB FORCES

Salmi

Al-Ruqi

US ARMOURED CAVALRY

SAUDI ARABIA

1st AND 2nd US MARINE DIVISIONS

US Marine supply base Kibrit

"KHANJAR EXPRESSWAY", US Marine supply route

Iraqi FROG missile attacks 3 on 17/1/91, 16 on 18/1/91 (No casualties)

Al-Mishab

US Marines beach head

IRAQI III CORPS

BASE MAPS ©

SALEM AL-MARZOUK AND SABAH ABI-HANNA WLL.

Explanatory notes to Map 8, Early Action (late January, 1991)

1. During the day of **29 January,** Allied spotters notice Iraqi activity around Wafra, and call in air strikes. No further major action expected.

2. 6.30 p.m.: Iraqis start jamming US Marine radios. Task Force *Shepherd's* 'C' Company notice Iraqi armour moving south inside Kuwait.

3. 9.00 p.m., *Shepherd's* 'D' Company notice presumably same armour closing in on OP-4. F/A-18 called in, but fails to stop Iraqis. Lightly armed force in OP-4 opens fire as Iraqis close in, and signal desperately for help.

4. With American attention drawn to OP-4, Iraqis move in on OP-8 on the coast. American forces flee.

5. At OP-4, 'D' Company closes in. Fires on Iraqis. Misses, but destroys one of their own vehicles, killing four. With the Iraqis distracted, the men in OP-4 make their escape.

6. With action under way at OP-4 and OP-8, Iraqis move towards the now abandoned OP-5 and OP-6 further north.

7. As 'D' Company reforms, large Iraqi force noticed moving near Wafra. Air strikes called for, but all available aircraft heading for OP-4 and OP-8. Iraqis move into OP-1 and OP-7 virtually unopposed.

8. At Khafji, US and Saudi forces retreat south of the town, inadvertently leaving behind two US Marine reconnaissance teams. Armoured battalion of Iraqi 5th Mechanized Infantry Division occupies Khafji.

9. Small Iraqi boats move out of Al-Zoor and Khiran harbours in occupied Kuwait, and move south, close inshore, to support Iraqis in Khafji. USS *Oldendorf* requests Kuwait Navy patrol boats *Istiqlal* and *Sanbouk* to deal with them.

10 Near OP-4, US Air Force A-10 aircraft supporting 'D' Company strikes a second Marine vehicle, killing seven. 'D' Company pulls back, relieved by 'A' Company.

11. US forces, fearing that the Iraqis may be heading for their port at Al-Mishab, or their major inland logistics base at Kibrit, mine the Khafji–Mishab road, and form a hasty defence around Kibrit. Armoured units from 1st Marine Division put on alert, and start moving north.

12. Kuwait Navy vessels engage Iraqi small boats trying to support Khafji, destroying several and chasing the remainder back into Khiran.

13. OPs 4, 5, and 6 recaptured in daylight, **30 January**, with help of air strikes. No need for US armour.

14. Saudi and Qatari forces probe into Khafji 9.00 p.m., and rescue trapped US Marines. Iraqis try to reinforce town, but are beaten back by air strikes.

15. Dawn, **31 January:** Iraqis shoot down US Special Forces AC-130 gunship, killing all fourteen men on board.

16. During **31 January,** Saudi and Qatari forces retake Khafji.

17. Kuwaiti Resistance reports high-level meeting of Iraqi commanders at base of Kuwait's 15 Brigade, near Ras Al-Jalayh. Air strikes called in, reportedly killing senior Iraqi officers.

18. US Navy battleships off the coast are unable to come sufficiently close inshore to support Khafji actions because of threat of mines. During the week following these engagements, mines are cleared, and US battleships shell Iraqi positions in Khiran Resort, and Ras Al-Jalayh.

Brigade, and his Qatari battalion. They spotted Iraqi armour on the town's edge, and the Qataris engaged them. After a brief exchange, about 20 Iraqis surrendered. After learning from them that there were another 1,500 Iraqis in Khafji, Al-Mutairi pulled back, but sent the Saudi company to hold the road north of the town, between it and the border, to block Iraqi reinforcements.

That evening, a company of the 2nd Saudi National Guard Brigade and armour from the Saudi 8th Mechanized Brigade probed into Khafji, rescued the trapped US Marines, and withdrew. The Iraqis then tried to reinforce Khafji overland, drawing intense air attack. US aircraft continued to strike them throughout the night, beating back two brigades trying to reach Khafji. A further two Iraqi divisions assembling inside Kuwait for what seemed to be a follow-up attack were also hit. The Allied air forces, now recovered from the surprise, and finding the Iraqis in the open, attacked them ferociously.

However, three of the aircraft used were Hercules AC-130 Special Forces gunships. With their slow speed they were supposed to operate only at night to minimize the risk from ground fire. Two of the aircraft had returned to base as the sky lightened. The third was flying over OP-8, when it was ordered to break-off. The pilot acknowledged, but seconds later, the gathering daylight allowed an Iraqi gunner to hit the aircraft with a missile, breaking off the left wing. The aircraft spiralled into the Gulf, killing all 14 men on board.

Later that morning, the Saudis cut off Khafji from the north by reinforcing the their armoured company holding the road from Kuwait into the town, and placing a battalion of Saudi Marines south of the town to prevent the Iraqis from coming any further. Two battalions of the 2nd Saudi National Guard Brigade under Colonel Turki Al-Firmi, assisted by a company of Qatari armour, a company of Qatari mechanized infantry, and US Marine artillery and aircraft, then moved into Khafji. As they were engaging the Iraqis, another brigade of Iraqi armour from inside Kuwait sped towards the town, and was stopped by the Saudis on the road from the border. The Iraqis retreated back into Kuwait, and were further bombed by Coalition aircraft.

After street-by-street fighting, during which the attackers had to cope with Iraqi artillery from north of the border, the Saudis and Qataris retook Khafji by dark. Several hundred Iraqis escaped, but the Saudis and Qataris killed 32 and captured about 500 at the cost of 18 Saudis killed and 49 wounded.

Diplomatic efforts to secure a withdrawal continued throughout the air war. Iraqi Foreign Minister Tareq Aziz visited Teheran in the first days of February, presumably by road, and met with Iranian President Hashem Rafsanjani. However, Rafsanjani admitted afterwards that he saw no sign of flexibility from Saddam, even after two weeks of bombing. Iranian mediation efforts involving France, Syria, Turkey, and the USSR continued into early February, but to no avail. On 11 February, Gorbachev's envoy, Yevgeny Primakov, travelled to Baghdad yet again, but with similar results.

Saddam's initial hopes that the Allied bombing of Baghdad would produce heavy civilian casualties with resultant Western public outrage were dashed by the precision bombing. His only remaining strategy after the failure of the armoured thrusts into Saudi Arabia seemed to be to absorb the punishment, and then to fight what he thought would be a pitched ground battle of attrition, using his superior numbers and the natural advantage of a defender.

As the US Marines recovered from their first real encounter with the Iraqis, the war was continuing on a more one-sided basis at sea, but not without problems. In an engagement on 30 January, later known as the 'Battle of Bubiyan', naval aircraft damaged or sank a number of Iraqi missile craft and other vessels trying to flee to Iran. One of these boats was *Istiqlal's* captured sister ship, *Sabhan,* which was disabled by a British Lynx helicopter with a Sea Skua missile. The crew were taken off by the British, and *Sabhan* - too far north to be salvaged safely - was finished off by an American A-6 bomber.

However, despite the best efforts of the Kuwaiti Navy and the US Navy SEALS in trying to find the remainder of the Iraqi minefields, their success was limited. The British had some very effective minehunters, but could not bring them in close enough to shore to operate effectively without exposing them to Iraqi coastal batteries. The Iraqis had the world's greatest naval powers on the defensive with the simple naval mine, and shore-based missiles. This threat had prevented the US battleships *Missouri* and *Wisconsin* coming close enough inshore to support ground troops during the Khafji and related incidents, even with the 32-km range of their 16-inch guns. The Allies' fear of mines was not misplaced. Two weeks after this, the USS *Tripoli* and USS *Princeton*, two major vessels, were seriously damaged by mines. Both ships had to be withdrawn from service for repairs.

With the commencement of the ground war scheduled then for 21 February, less than three weeks away, the Allied commanders formally decided on 2 February to dispense with a real amphibious attack unless it was absolutely needed to take pressure off the forces attacking from Saudi Arabia. Nevertheless, the US Navy was tasked to deceive the Iraqis that it was a distinct possibility, and thus tie up three Iraqi divisions in coastal defence.

Following the Khafji incident, Task Element *Kilo* continued its mine-detection mission, and expanded it to include laying decoy marker buoys along approach routes to possible Marine landing sites. On 15 February, they landed on Kubbar Island, north of Qaro, but found that it had not been occupied by the Iraqis. The island was in range of Iraqi coastal Silkworm missiles and was of little military value, so the Kuwaitis stayed one night, then withdrew.

Meanwhile, in Kuwait, living conditions continued to deteriorate. The local phones failed completely on 6 February. The only means of communication now between areas was by word of mouth, or VHF radios in the local fire stations.

The phones were a major loss. They had been essential for keeping people in touch with each other for the three weeks of bombing, and maintaining morale. Now the news was limited to what people could glean from the radio and TV and immediate neighbours. The sense of isolation became more acute.

Shortly afterwards, the water supply was disrupted. By 10 February, it failed almost entirely. This had been expected, and people had stockpiled water in virtually every container. Mercifully, the weather was cold and wet. Electrical power continued for the time being, with intermittent interruptions.

One of the hardest aspects to endure was not having a time limit on the ordeal.

It was worse than before the imposition of the 15 January UN deadline. Now there was no countdown, only endless bombing. A ground war was inevitable, but had been expected within a week of the first air raids. It was as if the Allies wanted to win the war from the air alone.

Throughout this time, the Allies continued to bomb strategic targets in Baghdad. On Ash Wednesday, 13 February, Saddam got his wish for TV footage of massive civilian casualties. Two Stealth fighters bombed a bunker which was thought to be a command centre in the Baghdad suburb of Amariya. Tragically, it contained hundreds of mainly women and children. About 204 died. Later that day, an errant British bomb killed about 130 in the southern riverside town of Fulaijah. Both incidents were undoubtedly errors, but too little too late to cause the uprising of Western public opinion Saddam hoped for.

In Kuwait, the reaction was even more cynical. After all they had been through, few people trusted any Iraqi story. They readily believed the Allies' explanation that the lower levels of the Amariya bunker was a military target, and that the civilians had been placed there by Saddam in the knowledge that it would be hit, to provide the requisite horrifying images for the Western TV crews in Baghdad. They had become so inured to Iraqi duplicity that they even suspected that the genuine grief of those around the smoking bunker was staged. The undeniable tragedy was lost on them.

On the day following Amariya and Fulaijah, President Gorbachev advised President Bush that his envoy Yevgeny Primakov had sensed a change in attitude in Saddam, in that he could now contemplate an unconditional withdrawal. With Tareq Aziz on his way to Moscow yet again, and the ground war imminent, the Soviet message was to hold off.

Saddam was indeed prepared to withdraw, but hardly unconditionally. On 15 February, his Revolutionary Command Council did say that Iraq was prepared to leave Kuwait, but the offer was no more than an opening position at best. The conditions were a complete ceasefire; an annulment of all UN Resolutions on the crisis; a complete withdrawal of all Coalition forces from the region within a month of the ceasefire; an Israeli withdrawal from the occupied West Bank, the Golan Heights, and Lebanon, or the passage of UN Resolutions against Israel as a result of these occupations, identical to those passed against Iraq; and finally, that 'political arrangements for Kuwait be agreed based on the people's will and in accordance with democratic practice.' The latter condition presumably referred to a plebiscite to be held in Kuwait, with the existing population, the majority of whom were Palestinians and Iraqis, after Saddam had terrorized most of the Kuwaitis into leaving.

Furthermore, Saddam had the cheek to claim war reparations, the cancellation of Iraq's debts to Coalition countries and cancellation of debts from other regional non-Coalition countries, such as Jordan and Yemen. Bush was in no mood to haggle. By evening, Kuwait time, he had dismissed the proposal as a 'cruel hoax', and called on the Iraqis to topple Saddam.

The Iraqi troops in Kuwait were however, ecstatic, on hearing the news. They thought they were going home, and would be spared the ground assault. They fired so much ammunition into the air that some people thought that the ground war had started. The following morning brought a massive hangover when they realised that the Allies would not be conned. They would not be withdrawing. After glimpsing a light at the end of the tunnel, the troops knew that they were facing almost certain defeat at best, or death.

Unknown to the troops, they had actually gained a brief respite from their fate as a Valentine's Day present. The ground war, slated for the 21st, was then rescheduled for 24 February. Those three days would greatly assist the Allies, but would lead indirectly to the deaths of hundreds more Kuwaitis.

At midnight on 15 February, most of Kuwait lost electrical power entirely. This eliminated TV news except for those with generators. Worse, radio batteries were running low. Candles and kero-lamps had to be used for light.

The sense of isolation and fear, after nearly a month of the air war, was equalled only by the impatience for the ground war to start. Power was restored to most areas on the evening of 17 February, and continued intermittently for a further week until the Iraqis blew the power stations.

Strangely, that evening, when Allied aircraft overflew the Kuwaiti urban area, hardly a shot was fired at them. The Iraqis had either used up their supply of ammunition in their celebrations the previous afternoon, or simply did not care any more. Whatever fight may have been in them had gone.

After the Allies' rejection of the Iraqi offer, Saddam apparently concluded that withdrawal would eventually be necessary. On the evening of 17 February, the Iraqis in Kuwait started destroying local monuments. The first to go was the old city gate from the wall that surrounded Old Kuwait City as recently as the 1920s. They used a bulldozer to flatten an artifact which was to the Kuwaitis what the Statue of Liberty is to Americans, and Big Ben is to the British.

However, the imminent withdrawal was not immediately apparent to those in Kuwait City. Indeed, there was a tremendous amount of military traffic, away from the coastal areas into the suburbs. The Iraqis were probably consolidating in preparation for the big move north, but it seemed to some that they were going to fight house-to-house in a war of attrition. The Allies would surely win, but people in Kuwait began to fear that they might die in the crossfire, or that the Iraqis might massacre them as they fell back.

In the meantime, Tareq Aziz was in Moscow conferring with President Gorbachev on plans to prevent a full-scale ground war. He returned home on 19 February, and went back to Moscow late on the 21st. Saddam was as defiant and as inflexible as ever. The bombing of Kuwait and Iraq continued unabated.

Then, suddenly, the early morning news on 22 February indicated that Baghdad had given a positive response to Moscow's latest peace plan, and began to spell it out. Initial reactions were mixed. Most people in Kuwait saw it for what it was: another attempt by Saddam to buy time. President Bush evidently agreed with the Kuwaitis. He had had enough. On the afternoon of 22 February, Bush issued his ultimatum to Saddam: start a substantive withdrawal within 24 hours, or face a ground offensive.

The terms of the ultimatum were firm. Iraq was to begin a withdrawal by 8.00 p.m. local time on 23 February, and complete it within seven days. All Iraqi forces were to be out of Kuwait City and the legitimate Government allowed to return within the first 48 hours; Iraqi forces were to withdraw from all defences along the Saudi–Kuwait and Saudi–Iraq borders, and from the Kuwaiti portion of the Rumaillah/Ratga oilfield. All POWs and detainees were to be released within 48 hours, and all explosive and booby-trap devices were to be removed from Kuwait. Finally, Iraq was to cease all combat air fire and aircraft flights except for planes carrying troops out of Kuwait. In return, Bush promised that retreating troops would not be attacked.

Much to the annoyance of Western leaders, Moscow continued to try for a settlement with a second, tougher plan. Despite his earlier critical role in the Coalition, Gorbachev was looking increasingly irrelevant. Events were overtaking the Soviets faster than they could draft new peace plans.

Although the Iraqi decision to leave may have been made as early as 17 February, it was not until the 23rd that Saddam apparently gave the order to do so. The Iraqi communications lag prevented the order being carried out quickly enough to make it apparent. Saddam had played his brinkmanship just a little too long. The withdrawal order actually came before the expiry of Bush's deadline, but was not broadcast by Baghdad until nearly 60 hours later, early on 26 February. The Allies could hardly be blamed for missing it.

The Iraqis took advantage of the respite from the ground war offered by the Primakov-Aziz shuttle to prepare for withdrawal in their own style. In a last spiteful orgy of destruction, they tried to destroy or steal anything of value left in Kuwait, and capture as many Kuwaiti men as possible.

They had started blowing up Kuwait's oil wells, gathering centres and refineries in earnest on 18 February. By the time Bush issued his ultimatum on the 22nd, hundreds of wells were ablaze. By noon on the 23rd, smoke was so thick over Kuwait City that the sun was invisible. That evening there were reports of Iraqi executions of Kuwaiti civilians, and horrendous atrocities.

On February 22nd and 23rd, the Iraqis torched and shelled most of the major hotels, and the main shopping centres. Only the Kuwait International Hotel, the Plaza, and the Holiday Inn remained relatively unscathed. The senior Iraqis were staying at the International. They left it until last, so did a rush job and tried to set it on fire from the eighth floor. The General Manager would later say that only an Iraqi would try to burn down a hotel from the top.

However incompetent the Iraqis were with some acts of destruction, they were primitively effective in others. They shelled my own building with tanks. The few remaining tenants had less than five minutes to evacuate. A number of other buildings were set on fire, especially the symbolic National Assembly Parliament building, and Kuwait Oil Company's offices in Ahmadi.

More seriously, the last throes of violence extended to people, often the most defenceless. The Iraqi troops in the city went after Filipinas still working or sheltering in the hotels for a last final fling. Many of these women had to flee with just the clothes on their backs. Some did not escape.

During these last violent days of the occupation, the Iraqis undertook a far more serious campaign of destruction: they virtually tried to wipe out the remaining Kuwaiti adult males by relocating them to Iraq.

Late on 18 February, they started rounding up all Kuwaiti men between 18 and 40. The age-bracket was so precise that the order could only have come from on high. It was not immediately apparent what was happening as the phones were out, and the first pick-ups were isolated. At the time, there were perhaps 130,000 Kuwaitis in Kuwait. The arrests continued at a low level over the next three days, but the Iraqis struck with a vengeance on Friday, 22 February - the day after the ground war had originally been scheduled to start - when hundreds of men attended the mosques as part of the weekly ritual. The Iraqis were waiting for them.

In all, about 8,000 out of an estimated 23,000 Kuwaiti men in Kuwait were taken away to Iraq over five days - often under air attack. Some were taken as far north as Mosul, or to Baghdad, but most were held in atrocious conditions in Basra until they were released after the ceasefire, either by the Iraqis, or the Shi'ite rebellion. In the Basra jails, 300 men were held in cells designed for 20. They slept in shifts so that at least some of them could lie down. They had to defaecate on the floor, and pass the dead over their heads to the door.

The round-up was a repeat of a tactic used by the Iraqis in the Iran–Iraq War. During that conflict, they had taken Iranian civilians – even women and children – as hostages whenever they retreated. Many of these Iranians are still missing years after the cessation of hostilities. Of the Kuwaitis taken during the occupation, about 544 are still unaccounted for at the time of writing, as are 15 Gulf nationals and 46 others. Mercifully, for the 90% of captured Kuwaitis who were released, the Iraqis did not have sufficient time to carry out the extermination orders as they were overtaken by the Allied victory. Nevertheless, despite gratitude for liberation, there is still a feeling in Kuwait that if the Iraqis had been chased out sooner, they would have been too busy making good their own retreat to capture many of those now missing.

Within eight hours of Bush's deadline, the Allies struck into Kuwait, at 4.00 a.m. on Sunday, 24 February, 1991. The long-awaited land attack had come.

At 4.30 a.m., all electricity failed. The Iraqis had blown the power stations. News was sketchy because of the media blackout. The noise of bombing increased, and was now joined by the rumble of heavy artillery. The day dawned cold and drizzly, with a heavy pall of black smoke over the city. An orange, pulsating glow from hundreds of burning oil wells lit the southern horizon. People living in suburbs near Ahmadi could feel the intense heat from the raging fires. They even had trouble making themselves heard above the roar of the flames. The air stank of oil, cordite and fear. It was a scene from hell. Deliverance was at hand but, for some, the worst was yet to come.

On the eve of the ground war, the Iraqis held Kuwait and the contiguous areas in Iraq with five army corps. The heaviest of these in Kuwait itself was Lieutenant-General Salah Abud Mahmoud's III Corps, with nine infantry divisions, and one each of armour and mechanized infantry. It occupied all of southern Kuwait from Kuwait Bay to the Saudi border. Eight infantry divisions covered the border, and the coast. The ninth infantry division, the 15th Division, was in reserve in Jahra, west of Kuwait City, where General Mahmoud had made his HQ in the barracks of Kuwait's 80 Brigade. The Corps' armour, the 3rd Armoured Division, was at Kuwait Airport and at an agricultural complex 20km west of the airport, known as the 'Ice-Cube Tray' because of its appearance from the air. The final division, the remains of the bloodied 5th Mechanized, which had carried out the OPs and Khafji operations, was in the Burgan oilfield, southwest of Ahmadi.

North Kuwait was held lightly by II Corps, with only two infantry and one light armoured divisions. Western Kuwait from Jahra across to the Iraqi border at Wadi Al-Batin was held by IV Corps with seven divisions, five of which were infantry, the 6th Armoured Division in the north of their sector, and the 1st Mechanized near Ali Al-Salem KAF base. The Corps HQ was in a massive underground bunker between Ali Al-Salem and the Abdaly Road.

The vast area west of the Wadi Al-Batin, in Iraq itself, was held by the Iraqi VII Corps, with seven infantry divisions, and the 12th Armoured Division. Perhaps poetically, the Iraqi VII Corps would face the armoured might of the US VII Corps, together with the UK 1st Armoured Division.

North-west Kuwait was held mainly by Iraq's 10th Armoured Division, as part of the Republican Guard Forces Corps. However, on their own side of the border, the Iraqis had five of their best units, the *Tawakalna* Mechanized, 52nd Armoured, 17th Armoured, *Medina* Armoured, and *Nebuchadnezzar* Infantry. These forces were positioned either to defend Basra from an attack from the west, as eventually happened, or to move into Kuwait. Around Basra, were four other Guard Divisions: the *Hammurabi* Armoured, *Al-Fao, Adnan* and *Baghdad* Infantry, plus Special Forces. Whatever else may be said about the Iraqis, they were not entirely unaware that the Allies might try a wide sweep through the desert to their west. They would not otherwise have deployed their best forces in this way. In fact, Allied officers later expressed admiration for the way the Republican Guard Commander's strategy.

Facing the 11 divisions of Iraq's III Corps in southern Kuwait were two reinforced divisions of US Marines, the 1st and 2nd, operating as I Marine Expeditionary Force (I MEF), under Lieutenant-General Walter Boomer, and a division-sized force of Saudi, Kuwaiti and GCC forces on their right, or east, designated Joint Forces Coalition-East (JFC-E). Far to I MEF's west was Joint Forces Coalition-North (JFC-N), a four division-sized Saudi, Egyptian, Syrian and Kuwaiti force, facing Iraq's IV Corps. Kuwaiti liaison and intelligence officers were attached to the I MEF units. A second Marine force, the 4th and 5th Marine Expeditionary Brigades, was on ships in the Gulf.

The Marines' and Arab forces' mission was to hold the Iraqis in Kuwait in place while two huge US-British-French Army Corps swept into Iraq far to the west, to the rear of the Iraqis, destroyed the Republican Guard to the north of Kuwait, and recaptured northern Kuwait. It was feared that the Iraqis in Kuwait could turn north or west to help their embattled colleagues once they realized what was going on. The Marines' major task was to prevent this by engaging them. They were to be a magnet to fix the Iraqis in place in Kuwait, not a piston to push them out. They were not to liberate Kuwait City. That job, potentially the most bloody part of the campaign with street-fighting, was assigned to Kuwaiti forces, with Arab support.

The Marines' battle plans had developed through four different versions as further US, British – and Iraqi – reinforcements were added during the crisis. They had finally settled on a breach point near the heel of the border, near OP-4. It was just about the farthest they could get from Kuwait City, but was less well defended, harder for Iraqi III Corps to support or reinforce, and would be less affected by smoke from burning oilfields. In any event, a longer drive to the city served well the Marines' purpose of holding the Iraqis in place. This plan, which survived until early February, envisaged the two divisions going through the same breach, essentially in single file, followed by JFC-E.

The larger of the two Arab forces, JFC-N, with two arms under Egyptian Major-General Salah Halaby and Saudi Major-General Suleiman Al-Wahaib respectively, would attack Iraq's IV Corps, west of the Marines. Halaby's men, which would take the left – or western – part of the sector comprised Egypt's 3rd Mechanized and 4th Armoured Divisions, and a Ranger regiment. Al-Wahaib had the Saudi 20th Mechanized Brigade Group, the Saudi 4th Armoured Brigade, Major-General Ali Habib's Syrian 9th Armoured Division, a Syrian Ranger regiment, and two small Kuwaiti brigades, the reconstituted 35 (*Shaheed*, or Martyrs') Armoured under Colonel Salem Al-Sarour, and the 15th (*Tahrir*, or Liberation) Mechanized under Colonel Khalid Al-Rhodani. The commander of Kuwaiti JFC-N forces was Colonel Rashid Mubarak.

However, following Khafji, JFC-E's Saudi commanders, infused with their victory, elected to attack on line with the Marines, conduct their own breaches, and take on the Iraqis themselves. Significantly, at the time, the Marine generals were increasingly concerned that their two divisions and JFC-E going through a single breach would cause a massive traffic jam, and expose them to Iraqi artillery at their most vulnerable time. Then, Kuwaiti oil men working with the 2nd Marine Division advised its commander, Major-General Bill Keys, that they could traverse the Umm Gudayr oilfield, further north. Keys, already uncomfortable with the single breach, took the idea to Boomer.

On 5 February, it was decided that each Marine division would conduct its own breach. This would get them through the minefields and into Kuwait quicker, before the Iraqis could counter-attack. The 1st Division would still breach at the heel, but the 2nd Division would move 25km northwest. The 1st Division's 19,500 men were first to take Ahmad Al-Jaber KAF base, 45km beyond their breach, for use as a resupply point. They would then attack north past Burgan to Kuwait Airport, 35km from Al-Jaber. At the time, the Marine generals expected that it would take five days for them to reach the airport.

The 2nd Marine Division's 16,000 troops, along with the 4,700-man 1st Armored Brigade of the US Army's 2nd Armored Division, the *Tiger* Brigade, would race 60km north for the interchanges west of Jahra, and seal the exits from Kuwait City, to prevent Iraqi III Corps from reinforcing IV Corps, or the Republican Guard further north. *Tiger* Brigade had replaced the British 7th

Armoured Brigade which had been previously assigned to the Marines, but which had now joined up with the British 4th Armoured Brigade to comprise the UK 1st Armoured Division, under the US VII Corps. It was expected that the 2nd Marine Division and *Tiger* would take four days to reach Jahra.

The Marines, *Tiger,* and the Arab forces faced two main obstacle and minefield belts. The first was 10 to 15 kilometres into Kuwait, almost paralleling the frontier. The second was between two and 20 kilometres behind the first, depending on the location. The Iraqis were expected to let the Marines through the first belt, and then attack them at the second, more formidable belt, when they were all but trapped between the two barriers.

At the same time as the Marines attacked, Lieutenant-General Gary Luck's US XVIII Corps - with the 82nd Airborne, 101st Air Assault, and 24th Mechanized Divisions, and the French 6th Light Armoured Division - west of VII Corps and the British, would thrust deep into Iraq to provide a screen for VII Corps' armour. VII Corps itself, and JFC-N on the coast, would move out 24 hours later, VII Corps into Iraq and JFC-N directly into Kuwait. Whilst VII Corps' job was to smash the Republican Guard, JFC-N was to hold Iraq's IV Corps in place inside Kuwait by moving across the border between Salmi and Al-Minagish, then across the Salmi Road to Al-Abraq barracks, before turning east and taking Ali Al-Salem. They would then pass through the Marines' lines to clear Kuwait City, with Kuwaiti troops in the lead.

Between JFC-N and US VII Corps was the US 1st Cavalry Division, near Salmi. It was to feint up the Wadi Al-Batin to draw Iraqi IV Corps away from JFC-N and the Marines to the east, and then to act as a tactical reserve.

The two US Marine divisions were organized slightly differently. The 1st, which had been in Saudi Arabia since August under Major-General Mike Myatt, comprised eight 'task forces', each equipped for its respective job. The two most heavily armoured, *Papa Bear* and *Ripper,* would be the main force and reserve respectively. Each had a reinforced battalion of tanks, and the equivalent of three battalions of infantry. Two other task forces, *Taro* and *Grizzly*, comprised primarily two battalions of infantry each, with reconnaissance companies. They would infiltrate undetected into Kuwait on foot, up to the first obstacle belt, so that they could cross over quickly when the attack commenced and provide flank protection for *Papa Bear* and *Ripper.* The 1st Marine Division also had task force *Shepherd,* which had seen action at OPs 4, 5 and 6, and *X-Ray,* which was an infantry battalion. The division's artillery was task force *King.* The final task force, appropriately named *Troy,* had the mission of making enough noise in the wrong place to convince the Iraqis that the attack was still coming from the Wafra area.

Major-General Key's recently-arrived 2nd Marine Division was organized more simply. Its main units were the 6th Regiment, which would lead the way, and the 8th Regiment. *Tiger* Brigade would fight alongside them.

The Marines' and JFC-E's target areas of operation comprised that part of Kuwait held by Iraq's III Corps. JFC-E's sector encompassed roughly a 20-kilometre-wide swath of coastal territory north from the Saudi border to the city, and all of Kuwait City. This force was centred on the 2nd Saudi National Guard

Brigade, the Saudi 8th and 10th Mechanized Brigades, with Kuwaiti forces, a Bahraini infantry company, a small Qatari mixed armoured and infantry brigade, a UAE infantry battalion, and an Omani infantry battalion.

JFC-E's Kuwaiti forces comprised four small battalion-sized brigades, under the overall command of Colonel Mohammed Al-Harmi, who had led Kuwait's 15 Brigade in the defence of Jiwan Camp in Kuwait on the morning of the invasion. The strongest of these units with the greatest proportion of regulars was the *Al-Fatah* (Conquest, or Victory) with Egyptian *Fahd* wheeled APCs, and BMP-2s which had escaped from Kuwait. It was commanded by Colonel Fouad Al-Haddad, and comprised the 43rd Mechanized Battalion under Lieutenant-Colonel Sa'ad Saleh, the 90th Mechanized Battalion under Lieutenant-Colonel Nasser Al-Za'abi, and the 95th Mechanized Battalion under Lieutenant-Colonel Abdulaziz Alghanim.

The other three brigades were a tactical reserve of mainly infantry whose job was to move forward once the advance reached the urban area, and to clear it street-by-street if necessary. These units were the *Kholoud* (Immortality), *Al-Haq* (Justice, or Right), and *Bader* (named after the historic Battle of Bader in Islamic history), commanded respectively by Colonel Abdulwahab Al-Anzi, Colonel Ibrahim Wasmi, and National Guard Colonel Abdulhadi Al-Rajahi. Many of the men in these smaller units were volunteers.

The general direction of the Marine and JFC-E attack would be northwards. On Allied maps, Kuwait was marked with roughly east-west 'phase lines', to provide points of reference during the advance. The border was Phase Line 'Black'. The limit of the Marines' advance, at Sixth Ring, was 'Green'. In between were other phase lines, the most important of which was 'Red', running through the centre of Iraq's III Corps to Ahmadi and the Gulf Coast.

The first Allied troops to enter Kuwait in force was a strong Saudi JFC-E reconnaissance unit, on 20 February, to probe the Iraqi defences. They encountered the first barriers 13km inside Kuwait, and came under artillery fire, without casualties. Significantly, an engineering platoon managed to clear a 30-metre wide gap all the way through the first minefield. More Saudi engineers went in the next day and opened up three more lanes. The Saudis also captured the now-abandoned Kuwaiti border post of Nuwaisib, and brought up Kuwaiti troops and a band to raise the Kuwaiti flag.

On the day as the first Saudi mission, Colonel Randolph House's 2nd Brigade of the US Army's 1st Armored Cavalry Division conducted a strong reconnaissance ten kilometres up the Wadi Al-Batin, the gully marking Kuwait's western border with Iraq. This was over 100km west of where the main Marine attack would fall, and was intended to convince the Iraqis that the Allied strategy was a four-pronged assault into Kuwait up the Wadi Al-Batin, at the border elbow, up the coast road, and amphibiously from the Gulf.

House's men made early contact with the Iraqis, inflicting casualties with the help of US Air Force A-10s, and capturing some prisoners. However, the Iraqis drew them into a clever ambush. Three Americans were killed and nine wounded before they withdrew into Saudi Arabia that evening.

The next major foray into Kuwait was by a Marine reconnaissance unit, the

2nd Division's 2nd Light Armored Infantry (LAI) Battalion. It was more successful than the Cavalry's costly mission. They crossed the border near the elbow on 21 February with 159 vehicles to probe the Iraqis, and deceive them as to where the division's main breach point would be, further south. The next day, they ignited some of the oil-trenches, which took up to 12 hours to burn out. They drew fire, suffered some wounded, but no deaths, and captured some 200 Iraqis. In fact, they, the Cavalry and the Saudis made such an impact that Baghdad Radio announced that the ground war had started.

A quieter series of incursions occurred on 22 and 23 February. The 1st Marine Division's *Grizzly* and *Taro*, with four battalions, infiltrated on foot 25km into Kuwait - between the Iraqi 29th and 42nd Divisions - and prepared to cross the first minefield so that they could move across promptly and protect *Ripper* and *Papa Bear* as they breached the second, more formidable obstacle belt. Their mission was not simple. Starting on 19 February, *Grizzly* engineers had tried to find paths through the first minefield, but were persistently chased out by the US Air Force, rather than the Iraqis. They finally got through late on the 23rd, with barely twelve hours to go until the main attack, after being shown a safe lane by surrendering Iraqis. *Grizzly's* and *Taro's* job was in stark contrast to the high-tech TV war seen worldwide. Their work was done mostly by lone infantrymen, on foot, or hands and knees, tentatively probing ahead of themselves with fibreglass sticks and bayonets.

To the east, JFC-E's Saudi engineers had cut six lanes in their sector of the obstacle belt. Baghdad Radio was right. By 23 February, the ground war was under way, but the Allies had not committed their ground forces fully. If the Soviet initiative pulled off an unconditional withdrawal, then the ground forces were in a position to hold off. However, many Iraqi troops on the front lines had little faith in eleventh-hour diplomacy. Scores of them surrendered during the night of 23 February, but others were prepared to fight.

Off the coast, the USS *Missouri* shelled Failaka Island, as if in preparation for an amphibious landing. US Navy SEALs laid strings of buoys and set explosive charges along the coast, with timers primed at predetermined intervals, to keep the Iraqis focused on that area.

The main attack of I MEF and JFC-E was made by the 1st Marine Division, led by *Grizzly* and *Taro*, which were already inside Kuwait, at 4.00 a.m. on 24 February, preceded by a B-52 strike on the Iraqis in front of them. The 2nd Division, located further north, attacked at 5.30 a.m. The times were staggered so that the two divisions would eventually swing in side-by-side.

It was cold, dark, and drizzly, with clouds of stinking, black smoke billowing into the wintry sky from the distant torched oilfields. Visibility on the ground in places was barely 100 metres at times, with low clouds and the smoke hampering close air support. The 1st Division wore chemical-protection suits in anticipation of an Iraqi gas attack which never came. Fortuitously, the prevailing wind shifted to the southeast, blowing the oilfield smoke across the Coalition troops' line of advance, obscuring them from the Iraqis.

There were a few surprises. The first obstacles were the stripped carcasses of hundreds of cars abandoned by civilians fleeing into Saudi Arabia almost seven months earlier. Behind the minefields were well-built fighting positions and decoy tanks. Fortunately for the Americans, most of the Iraqis had fled. Yet, for all the claims of the air war, some Iraqis still had fight in them. They lobbed over 300 artillery rounds onto the Marines, but caused no casualties. The Marines had more problems with their rocket-fired minefield-clearing charges not working, or getting hung up on power lines, and the mines damaging their mine-ploughs. Nevertheless, by 7.00 a.m., with *Ripper* through the first obstacle belt, I MEF was eight hours ahead of schedule.

Despite some stiff resistance at the second obstacle belt, *Ripper* breached it by noon with remarkably light casualties of four wounded. They then turned left towards a road intersection north of Al-Jaber base to prepare to attack into it from the rear, and sent forces into the Al-Subayhiya Oasis in front of their breach point. *Shepherd* followed through the breach to screen *Ripper's* move towards Al-Jaber, as *Grizzly* and *Taro* held positions between the minefields. The main impediment was Iraqis surrendering rather than fighting.

In the meantime, *Papa Bear* made their own separate breach of the first belt in mid-morning, slightly to the east of *Ripper's,* but it was late afternoon before they managed to get through the second belt. They then advanced into the southern edges of the Burgan oilfield, and attempted to establish a landing zone for Task Force *X-Ray.* They too were swamped with prisoners.

To the north, the 2nd Division cut six lanes through the minefields across a four-kilometre front, into the Iraqi 14th Division. The first major contact was made by the division's right flank at 9.30 a.m., with a small Iraqi armoured unit. They were beaten off, and the division lead elements reached Phase Line Red, ten kilometres beyond the second obstacle belt, by afternoon.

That afternoon, *Tiger* Brigade crossed over, and took the 2nd Division's left flank, slicing between the Iraqi 7th and 14th Divisions. The 8th Regiment started through the breach during the night, and took the right flank, alongside the 1st Marine Division, between the Iraqi 14th and 29th Divisions. The Marines made a point of attacking along the boundaries of Iraqi units to complicate the Iraqi commanders' task by forcing them to co-ordinate movement and artillery fire across divisional boundaries.

It took until the early morning of the second day to get both divisions through the obstacle belts. This was far quicker than expected. As early as 9.30 a.m. on the first day, Lieutenant-General Boomer and General Schwarzkopf became concerned that I MEF's left flank would be exposed to the Iraqi IV Corps, particularly the 6th Armoured Division near Ali Al-Salem, as they moved north of Phase Line Red. JFC-N, the US VII Corps and the British were not scheduled to move until the following morning. Iraqi forces in West Kuwait had therefore not been engaged by anything heavier than cross-border artillery, and feints. The Marines were held back and the timetable for the other forces advanced by 12 hours. Instead of moving off at 4.00 a.m. on 25 February, they would go at 4.00 p.m. on the 24th. VII Corps and the British set off on time; JFC-N a little later. Included in JFC-N was Kuwait's 35 Brigade, under Colonel Salem Al-Sarour, operating with the Saudi 20th Brigade, with the mission of recapturing their own base, and Ali Al-Salem KAF Base, and then linking up with the 2nd Marine Division before entering Kuwait City.

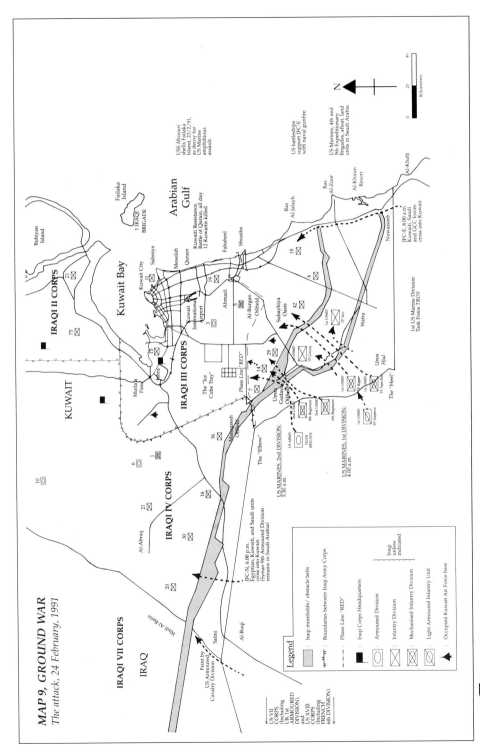

MAP 9, GROUND WAR
The attack, 24 February, 1991

IRAQI VII CORPS

IRAQ

US VII CORPS (including UK 1st ARMOURED DIVISION), and US XVIII CORPS (including FRENCH 6th DIVISION).

Feint by US Armoured Cavalry Division

Salmi

Al-Ruqi

Wadi Al-Batin

IRAQI IV CORPS

Al-Abraq

21

30

20

16

6

1

36

JFC-N, 6.00 p.m. Egyptian, Kuwaiti, and Saudi units cross into Kuwait. (Syrian 9th Armoured Division remains in Saudi Arabia)

KUWAIT

IRAQI III CORPS

Mutlaa Pass

Jahra

75

Kuwait City

Kuwait International Airport

Salmiya

Messilah

Qurain

Fahaheel

Shuaiba

Kuwait Bay

Bubiyan Island

Failaka Island

1 IRAQI BRIGADE

IRAQI II CORPS

21

Arabian Gulf

Kuwaiti Resistance, Battle of Qurain, Battle of Qurain, all day 12 Kuwaitis killed

USS Missouri shells Failaka Island, 23.2/.91, as decoy for US Marine amphibious assault.

US battleships support JFC-E with naval gunfire.

US Marines, 4th and 5th Expeditionary Brigades, afloat, land units in Saudi Arabia.

The "Ice Cube Tray"

Phase Line "RED"

Magwa Oilfield

The "Elbow"

Umm Gudayr Oilfield

US MARINES, 2nd DIVISION: 5.30 a.m.

US MARINES, 1st DIVISION: 4.00 a.m.

US ARMY TIGER BRIGADE

8th Regiment

6th Regiment

1st USMD

2nd USMD

1st USMD

TF Shepherd

TF Pope Bob

TF Ripper

TF Grizzly

TF Taro

Umm Hjul

The "Heel"

1st USMD

1st USMD

Al-Burgan Oilfield

Subayhiya Oasis

Ahmadi

Wafra

Ras Al-Jalayh

Ras Al-Zoor

Al-Khiran Resort

Al-Khafji

Nuwaseeb

1st US Marine Division Task Force TROY

JFC-E, 8.00 a.m. Kuwait, Saudi and GCC forces cross into Kuwait

7

14

29

42

5

3

19

11

18

8

N

0   20   40
Kilometres

Legend

:	Iraqi minefields/ obstacle belts
:	Boundaries between Iraqi Army Corps
:	Phase Line "RED"
:	Iraqi Corps Headquarters
:	Armoured Division
:	Infantry Division
:	Mechanised Infantry Division
:	Light Armoured Infantry Unit
:	Occupied Kuwait Air Force base

Iraqi unless indicated

Explanatory notes to Map 9, Ground War

1. **13 February** onwards: US Marine reconnaissance teams slip across the border to survey Iraqi defences, and confirm intelligence on Iraqi forces.
2. **19 February:** *Grizzly* and *Taro* combat engineers of 1st Marine Division infiltrate mainly on foot to find a path through Iraqi minefields. They are chased out of the area by US Air Force.
3. **20 February:** JFC-E engineers and heavy reconnaissance troops venture into Kuwait, and clear a lane through minefield, before withdrawing, without casualties. 2nd Brigade, 1st US Armored Cavalry Division pushes ten kilometres up the Wadi Al-Batin. Engage Iraqis, capture several prisoners. Falls into ambush. Withdraws with three dead.
4. **21-22 February:** 2nd LAI Battalion of 2nd US Marine Division probes into Kuwait. Ignites oil-filled trenches. Draws Iraqi fire, incurring wounded, but no deaths. Withdraws into Saudi Arabia, 23 February. Baghdad Radio announces that the ground war has started.
5. **22 and 23 February**: *Grizzly* and *Taro* infiltrate four infantry battalions 25km into Kuwait, ready to move across first obstacle belt/minefield when the main ground attack is launched, and provide flank protection for *Ripper* and *Papa Bear* armour as they make their own breaches.
6. USS *Missouri* shells Failaka Island as if in preparation for amphibious US Marine assault. Frogmen lay route-marking buoys off the Kuwaiti coast, and set off timed explosive charges, as decoys.
7. **24 February,** 4.00 a.m.: *Grizzly* and *Taro* infantry move into the area between the two obstacle belts, as *Ripper* and *Papa Bear* armour start from Phase Line 'Black' in Saudi Arabia.
8. 5.30 a.m.: 2nd US Marine Division's 8th Marine Regiment starts breaching obstacle belt.
9. 7.00 a.m.: *Ripper* through first obstacle belt. Continues on to second belt.
10. 8.00 a.m.: JFC-E moves across the obstacle belts in its sector. Engages the Iraqi 18th Division.
11. Eighteen-member Kuwaiti Resistance group in Al-Qurain engaged by Iraqi troops rounding up civilian Kuwaiti men. Day-long firefight develops.
12. Mid-morning: *Papa Bear* makes its own breach of the first obstacle belt, to the east of *Ripper's*. Marines' rapid progress causes timetable for JFC-N and US VII Corps attack to be advanced 12 hours. 2nd US Marine Division's 8th Regiment completes its breaches, into 14th Iraqi Division.
13. Noon: *Ripper* completes breach of second obstacle belt. Most of *Ripper* turns towards an intersection north of Al-Jaber KAF base. Rest proceeds into Al-Subayhiya Oasis, or 'Emir's Farm'. *Papa Bear* completes its passage through the first obstacle belt. *Shepherd* moves through *Ripper's* breach, to screen its move on Al-Jaber. *Grizzly* and *Taro* retain positions between the belts.
14. Early afternoon: 2nd US Marine Division's lead elements reach Phase Line 'Red'.
15. Mid-afternoon: US Army *Tiger* Brigade, operating alongside 2nd US Marine Division, completes its breach, and moves out onto the extreme left flank, between the Iraqi 7th and 14th Divisions.
16. Late afternoon: *Papa Bear* completes its breach of the second obstacle belt.
17. 5.30 p.m.: Iraqis overpower Kuwaiti Resistance group in Al-Qurain. 12 Kuwaitis killed or captured; 7 escape. Those captured are later killed. In this engagement, the Resistance loses more men than the entire Allied forces in the first day.
18. 6.00 p.m.: JFC-N, including Kuwait's 35 Brigade, moves across border west of the US Marines.
19. After dark: 2nd US Marine Division's 6th Regiment makes its breach, and takes right flank, linking up with left flank of the 1st US Marine Division. Attacks between Iraqi 14th and 29th Divisions. Allied forces in Kuwait laager for the night.

To the east, JFC-E had crossed the border at 8.00 a.m., 30km inland, near the settlement of Ragwa, about ten kilometres east of Wafra. Reaching the Wafra-Gulf road safely, they turned east along it towards the coast. Their first objective was the Al-Zoor coastal power station and desalination plant, 20km inside Kuwait. However, first they had to clear the Khiran Resort, 10km north of the border, in case any Iraqis were trapped behind them. The Arab units were accompanied by Marine ANGLICo (Air and Naval Gunnery Liaison Company) teams to co-ordinate fire support from the US battleships off the coast. They soon ran into the Iraqi 18th Infantry Division, as it fell back towards the city. JFC-E spent most of the day duelling with them.

By nightfall on 24 February, the 1st Division's Task Force *Ripper* was consolidated around the north and eastern edges of Al-Jaber base, but darkness prevented them from retaking it safely until the morning. An attempt was made to fly in *X-Ray* to a point north of the second obstacle belt, but this had to be deferred until the following day. The two Marine divisions in Kuwait laagered overnight just south of Phase Line Red. Ahmadi and the Arabian Gulf coast were only 35km to the east, beyond the fog, mist, and smoke from the raging fires of the Burgan oilfield. JFC-E camped at Al-Zoor.

At sea, the Kuwaiti Navy vessels in Task Element *Kilo* reoccupied Kubbar Island. By then, there were no Iraqi movements at sea, with the main remaining danger being from mines. However, as would become apparent only a few hours later, the Iraqi coastal defences were not quite yet out of the fight.

With news of the start of the ground war, elements of the Kuwaiti Resistance started attacking Iraqi forces in the expectation that liberation was imminent. Most of these actions were hit and run sniping attacks, but one incident in particular grew into a major firefight, with tragic consequences.

On the morning of 24 February, Iraqi troops were still rounding up Kuwaiti males to take to Iraq. In the suburb of Al-Qurain, on the coast between Sixth Ring and Ahmadi, a group of 18 armed Resistance fighters led by Saeed Al-Alawi had gathered in a house, and planned to harass the Iraqis in the nearby areas. However, as the first men left the premises, just before 8.00 a.m., they were surprised by troops, and retreated into the house. The Iraqis soon brought up reinforcements, and surrounded the house with about 60 infantry.

The soldiers were initially unable to dislodge the Kuwaitis, so brought in two tanks. Two of the Kuwaitis tried to draw the Iraqi fire while their colleagues attempted to escape, but both men, Jassim Ghloum and Mubarak Mansour, were critically wounded as soon as they broke cover. Another, Lieutenant Amer Al-Anzi, was hit by an RPG, and killed instantly. The Iraqis, however, did not press the attack with the tanks as they seemed to want to take some of the Kuwaitis alive. The fight lasted throughout the day until most of the Kuwaitis, including Al-Alawi, were dead or badly wounded.

However, several of the Kuwaitis had managed to sneak into an adjacent house. Three of them broke through the Iraqi lines and disappeared into the surrounding area. Another two men, Mohammed Yousef and Hazem Al-Saleh hid in a cavity above the bathroom, as did two other men in the first house, Jamal Al-Bannai, and Sami Al-Alawi, the son of the now dead group leader.

The Iraqis finally entered the houses at 5.30 p.m., but did not find the hidden men. Most of the remaining eleven were dead. They took away the wounded, and the unfortunate owner of the house into which the Resistance men had retreated. Their bodies were found dumped in the street later.

During this engagement, the Resistance lost more men than the entire Allied forces had in the first day. The tragedy was all the more poignant as they died less than 36 hours before the Iraqis abandoned the area.

Throughout the city, the sun was almost blotted out by the black smoke from the burning oil wells. When it was visible through the haze, it looked more like the moon. For the first time, residents of Kuwait City experienced eerie near night-time conditions during the day. The only sunlight was that reflected in horizontally under the low, dark cloud stretching to the horizon.

A few brave souls who peered outside noticed that many of the Iraqi anti-aircraft positions had been abandoned. Troops were still around, but most of them seemed to be preparing to leave. News was pouring in of mass surrenders. The few people in Kuwait with access to emergency power and TV were astounded at the images of Iraqi troops emerging gratefully from their bunkers to give themselves up, but no one in the city had seen a single Allied soldier.

Out in the desert, the night of 24 February saw a reassessment of the Marines' plans. It became clear that Al-Jaber base was largely abandoned. *Ripper's* armour could be better employed in the drive north towards the International Airport. The mission of clearing Al-Jaber was reassigned to *Grizzly's* infantry.

During the night, captured documents reviewed by a Kuwaiti officer with *Ripper*, and reports from prisoners, indicated that an Iraqi counter-attack would come 'out of the flames'. There were blazing oil wells along much of the 1st Division's front, but the most likely prospect was the huge conflagration of Burgan. At first, the Marine commanders thought that no one could survive in the smoke, with what was presumed to be high concentrations of hydrogen sulphide gas. However, it became apparent that the gases were being burned off, and that the oilfield itself was a potential hiding place for the Iraqis.

Overnight, a 1st Division intelligence captain reported to his superiors that two Iraqi brigades were probably hiding in Burgan. Initially, they did not believe him, but the Kuwaiti officer's reports backed up his concerns. At the time, the division's command post was situated roughly half-way between *Ripper* and *Papa Bear*, near Al-Subayhiya Oasis, on the southwest edge of Burgan. *Papa Bear* was told to send an infantry battalion into Burgan at first light to reconnoitre it, and a massive artillery barrage was arranged to strike the presumed locations of the hidden Iraqi brigades after 8.00 a.m. Fortuitously, the 1st Division's officers reinforced the security around their own command post at dawn with a company from *Shepherd*.

The first action on the second day of the ground war was actually at sea. At 4.00 a.m., the 4th Marine Expeditionary Brigade, afloat off the coast, staged a feint towards Shuaiba, with naval gunfire support from the USS *Missouri*. The Iraqis fired two Silkworm missiles at the ships. One fell short. The other was shot down by HMS *Gloucester*, after it had already gone past the ship!

At the same time, on land, 1st Marine Division radio eavesdroppers reported that Iraqi forces were on the move in Burgan in front of *Papa Bear*. The Kuwaiti officer's and the Marine captain's intelligence had been right. Then, at about 5.15 a.m., in the west of the division's sector, well away from Burgan, *Shepherd* noticed Iraqi vehicles moving south towards Al-Jaber. *Shepherd* chased after them, knocking out five tanks and a truck from the rear of the column. An hour later, *Ripper's* tanks, still near Al-Jaber, engaged the column's front. The bloodied Iraqis withdrew north.

Shortly afterwards, 10km northwest, in the 2nd Division's sector, an Iraqi armoured battalion stumbled out of the early-morning fog past a reserve Marine tank company, operating with the 8th Regiment. The Americans were laagered south of Phase Line Red, on their division's right flank, off the main road from Kuwait City to Al-Jaber. An Iraqi counter-attack was expected, but on the left flank, against *Tiger* Brigade's sector. This Iraqi unit had actually slipped past the 2nd Division's main force three kilometres to the north, unnoticed in the dark and haze. The Marine tank crews spotted the Iraqis through their thermal sights before the Iraqis saw them, and opened fire. Not realizing what has happening, following Iraqi vehicles continued to roll out of the mist into the US fire. In a ten-minute fight which became known as the 'Reveille Engagement', 13 Marine M1A1 tanks destroyed 30 Iraqi T-72s, 4 other tanks, 7 APCs, and captured about 200 prisoners, for no losses.

Back in the 1st Marine Division's sector, one of *Papa Bear's* infantry battalions moved into the southern Burgan oilfield as arranged, at 7.30 a.m. Conditions were atrocious, with visibility less than 200 metres.

At around the same time, a battalion of the Iraqi 5th Mechanized Division's 22nd Brigade made its move towards *Papa Bear's* command post, slipping past the screen of scouts around the command post. The first thing *Papa Bear's* commanders knew of the Iraqi attack was when they looked up into the muzzle of an Iraqi tank, 50 metres away. Fortunately, these Iraqis – a major and 20 of his men – wanted to surrender, but they could have destroyed the lightly-defended command post by surprise if they had been attacking.

Minutes later, the rest of the Iraqis arrived, with 50 vehicles, looking for a fight. The Marines just managed to beat them off. *Papa Bear's* officers warned their tank battalion, which was facing north, ready for the drive to the airport. Within minutes, they too were attacked, but managed to stall the Iraqis. The Marine tanks then thrust 2,000 metres north into Burgan, encountering the Iraqi 8th Infantry Division's 501st Brigade, which had pulled back from the border, and the rest of the 5th Division's 22nd Brigade.

Back at *Papa Bear's* HQ, a Kuwaiti liaison officer went through the captured major's vehicle. Besides a useful map of III Corps' positions, he found radios set on the Iraqis' nets, with officers on the other end shouting orders. The major refused to divulge the call-signs, so the Kuwaiti tried to bluff his way through on the radios. They suddenly went silent as the Iraqi officers recognized his accent. They could now no longer use their frequencies.

Shortly afterwards, the prearranged Marine artillery barrage fired nearly 700 rounds onto the areas in Burgan where the two Iraqi brigades were thought to be hiding. There was no reaction. The Iraqis had already moved. However, an hour later, the infantry battalion from *Papa Bear* which had earlier set off into the oilfield ran into part of the 3rd Armoured Division's 15th Brigade. It had escaped the artillery, and was attacking from the east, out for revenge. After destroying several vehicles and capturing 29 men, the Marines continued on their way north, eventually capturing 400 Iraqis by 11.00 a.m.

This action set off an unexpected chain of events. *Papa Bear's* infantry battalion's initial contact had struck only the southern flank of the westward-moving Iraqis, who then pivoted south as the Marines went north. The two units passed by each other in the dark like ships in the night. At 9.30 a.m., the Iraqis, now heading south, ran into the 1st Marine Division command post itself. It was almost a repeat of the surprise attack on *Papa Bear's* command post, except that none of these Iraqis wanted to surrender.

It took a half hour for the division security troops to beat off an initial attack of about 40 armoured vehicles. The Iraqis regrouped, and reattacked, but the Marines had called in helicopter gunships. The Iraqis were beaten back a second time, but regrouped yet again behind the burning oil wells, safe from the gunships, and attacked for a third time at 11.00 a.m. This time, the Marines turned the attack, and beat them decisively.

By 4.00 p.m, *Papa Bear's* infantry battalion and tank battalion attacking north through Burgan reached the limit of their advance, roughly half-way through the oilfield, and linked up with *Shepherd* on their left. During the day, fighting under the filthy black smoke of the burning oilfields in almost night–time conditions, the two battalions had taken more than 800 prisoners, and destroyed or disabled several hundred vehicles, for the cost of 3 wounded.

Around midday, *Grizzly's* infantry, now on trucks, started to relieve one of *Ripper's* battalions, which was holding the northern flank of Al-Jaber.

Trouble came from III Corps' artillery further north, which fired on *Grizzly*, killing one man. It was after 4.00 p.m. by the time they started tentatively into the undefended base, but no one was taking any chances. Over the next four hours, in very poor visibility, they crept as far as they could to the edge of Al-Jaber's main buildings, and then stopped for the night.

Earlier that morning, the 2nd Division had planned to seize the 'Ice-Cube Tray,' half-way between Al-Jaber and Jahra. However, following the 1st Division's Burgan engagements, the attack was deferred. In fact, the Marines were moving so fast at the time, relative to VII and XVIII Corps, and JFC-N to their west, that General Schwarzkopf asked them to hold at Phase Line Red for a while. Nevertheless, by evening, the 2nd Division held a line north of the Ice-Cube Tray. By then, it was too dark to continue. Both divisions stopped for the night, planning for the 1st Division to move out in the morning to Kuwait International Airport, and for the 2nd Division with *Tiger* Brigade to take the key Sixth Ring Road highway interchanges west of Jahra.

To the Marines' west, in the Iraqi IV Corps' sector, JFC-N continued their steady advance. By 5.00 p.m., Kuwait's 35 Brigade under Colonel Salem Al-Sarour had reoccupied its own base south of the Salmi road, against minimal

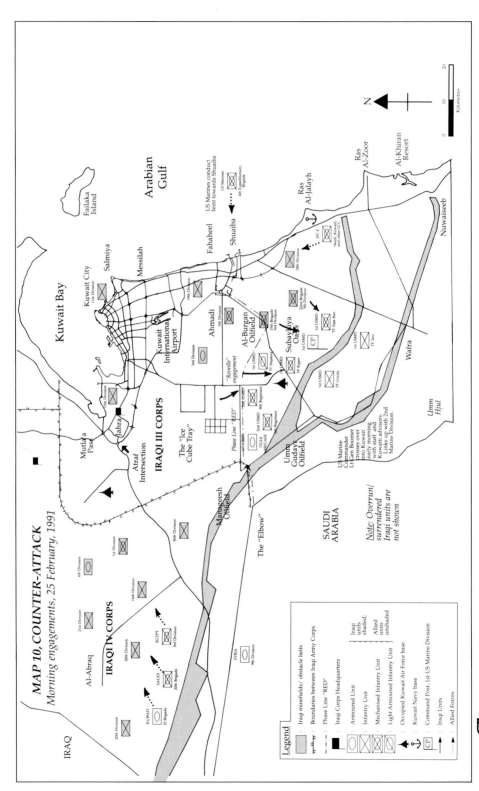

MAP 10, COUNTER-ATTACK
Morning engagements, 25 February, 1991

IRAQ

Al-Abraq

IRAQI IV CORPS

Kuwait Bay

Mutla'a
Pass

Jahra

Atraf
Intersection

IRAQI III CORPS

Kuwait City

Salmiya

Messilah

Kuwait
International
Airport

The "Ice
Cube Tray"

Phase Line "RED"

Ahmadi

Al-Burgan
Oilfield

"Reveille"
engagement

Mamageesh
Oilfield

The "Elbow"

Umm
Gudayr
Oilfield

Subayhiya
Oasis

**SAUDI
ARABIA**

Fahaheel

Shuaiba

Arabian
Gulf

Failaka
Island

US Marines conduct
feint towards Shuaiba

Ras
Al-Jalayh

Ras
Al-Zoor

Al-Khiran
Resort

Nuwaiseeb

Wafra

Umm
Hjul

US Marine
Commander
Lt-Gen Boomer
crosses over
into Kuwait
early morning
with staff and
Kuwaiti
advisors.
Links up with 2nd
Marine Division.

*Note: Overrun/
surrendered
Iraqi units are
not shown*

N

Kilometres
0   10   20

Legend

	Iraqi minefields / obstacle belts
	Boundaries between Iraqi Army Corps
	Phase Line "RED"
	Iraqi Corps Headquarters
	Armoured Unit
	Infantry Unit
	Mechanised Infantry Unit
	Light Armoured Infantry Unit
	Occupied Kuwait Air Force base
	Kuwait Navy base
CP	Command Post, 1st US Marine Division
	Iraqi Units
	Allied Forces

Iraqi
units
shaded.

Allied
units
unshaded.

Explanatory notes to Map 10, Engagements with Iraqi forces, particularly morning Iraqi counter-attacks, 25 February, 1991.

1. During the night of **24/25 February,** plans made to take largely abandoned Al-Jaber KAF base with *Grizzly's* infantry, and to free *Ripper* for the drive north. Intelligence then picked up that Iraqis might counter-attack out of the smoke and flames of the Burgan oilfield. *Papa Bear* ordered to send an infantry battalion into Burgan at first light.

2. 4.00 a.m.: 4th US Marine Expeditionary Brigade, on ships in the Gulf, stages amphibious landing feint towards Shuaiba, with naval gunfire support from USS *Missouri*. Iraqis fire two Silkworm missiles at US Navy ships. One falls short. The second is shot down by HMS *Gloucester.*

3. 5.15 a.m.: 1st Marine Division's Task Force *Shepherd* detects Iraqi vehicles moving south towards Al-Jaber. Destroys several vehicles from the rear of the column. The front of the column is engaged by *Ripper* about an hour later.

4. 5.50 a.m.: Reveille Engagement. Iraqi armoured battalion heading southwest stumbles into a US tank company. 41 Iraqi tanks and APCs destroyed and 200 prisoners taken for no Marine losses.

5. 7.30 a.m.: *Papa Bear* infantry battalion from moves into Burgan oilfield, towards KOC Gathering Centre 4.

6. 8.00 a.m.: A battalion from the Iraqi 5th Mechanized Division's 22nd Brigade bypasses *Papa Bear's* infantry battalion in Burgan and scouts screening *Papa Bear's* command post. Surprises *Papa Bear's* commanders. The first Iraqis to arrive want to surrender, but others, in 50 armoured vehicles, fight. They are narrowly beaten back.

7. 8.17 to 8.25 a.m.: US Marine artillery barrage strikes presumed locations in Burgan oilfield of the Iraqi 5th Mechanized Division's 22nd Brigade, and Iraqi 3rd Armoured Division's 15th Brigade.

8. About 8.30 a.m.: *Papa Bear's* tank battalion comes under attack. They counter-attack, advancing 2,000 metres into the Burgan oilfield, and engage Iraqi 8th Infantry Division's 501st Brigade, and the rest of the Iraqi 5th Mechanized Division's 22nd Brigade.

9. About 9.15 a.m.: *Papa Bear's* infantry battalion advancing through the Burgan oilfield comes into contact with southern flank of the Iraqi 3rd Armoured Division's 15th Brigade, which was headingwestwards. Following this skirmish, the Iraqis turn south, as *Papa Bear's* infantry battalion proceeds north in the opposite direction.

10. 9.30 a.m.: Iraqi 3rd Armoured Division's 15th Brigade, now heading south, runs into command post of 1st US Marine Division, and is finally beaten off over several hours.

11. Up to 11.00 a.m.: *Papa Bear's* infantry battalion continue their way north through the Burgan oilfield, capturing about 400 Iraqis.

12. About midday: Task Force *X-Ray* flown up to occupy *Papa Bear's* previous positions, and *Grizzly* starts an overland move to relieve *Ripper* at Al-Jaber.

13. 2.00 p.m.: 2nd US Marine Division advances from Phase Line Red to beyond 'Ice-Cube Tray.'

14. 4.00 p.m.: *Papa Bear's* infantry battalion and tank battalion reach the limit of their advance, half-way through Burgan, and link up with *Shepherd. Grizzly* starts infiltrating into Al-Jaber. One Marine from *Grizzly* killed by Iraqi artillery from the north prior to this.

15. JFC-E on the Marines' right flank continue a steady advance up the coast road, nearing Ahmadi by evening. Saudi, Egyptian and Kuwait forces from JFC-N on the Marines' left flank continue advancing in their sector, and turn east towards Kuwait City. By 5.00 p.m., Kuwait's 35 Brigade retakes its own camp, without opposition.

Iraqi opposition. Meanwhile, the Syrian 9th Armoured Division was still in Saudi Arabia, and did not cross into Kuwait until the following day, after the fighting in Kuwait was done. In the east, JFC-E were making steady progress up the coast, hampered mainly by the chore of taking and caring for prisoners.

In the meantime, in the city, with the Allies consolidating barely 30km away, the Iraqis continued their last minute round-up of Kuwaiti men.

At 00.32 a.m. on 26 February, Baghdad radio announced that Iraq would comply with the UN Resolutions. Whatever Saddam may have hoped to achieve with this, it was too late to save his army. Most of his men in Kuwait were on the run, or surrendering. That afternoon, a longer statement declared a complete troop withdrawal, but ground combat had already been joined for three days; it could not be stopped until the Iraqis surrendered completely.

People in Kuwait City were subjected to a continuous, deafening barrage throughout the night. It was so loud that it almost drowned out the now familiar roar of the burning oil wells. No one knew exactly what it was, but many presumed that it was the leading edge of artillery duels between the Marines, who were thought to be on the very outskirts of the city, and the Iraqis. It may have been the the *Missouri's* huge guns shelling the International Airport in preparation for the morning attack.

The Iraqi retreat from Kuwait City actually started on the evening of 25 February, Kuwait's 30th National Day, but it was not immediately apparent that a full scale withdrawal was under way. The withdrawal was so sudden that many were left behind. Soldiers simply abandoned their weapons and ran to catch whatever transport they could: tanks, APCs, cars, buses, anything that would move, heading west towards the exit of Kuwait City at Mutla'a Pass. By dawn on the 26th, the city was almost devoid of Iraqi troops.

Tragically, on this last but one day of the occupation, the Iraqis scored their most effective hit on the Coalition. A single SCUD missile, one of the last fired, fell on a US billet in Dhahran, killing 28 reservists and wounding over 100, most of whom had arrived in Saudi Arabia barely a week earlier.

In JFC-E, late on 25 February, a Kuwaiti Gazelle helicopter arrived with instructions for the commander of JFC-E's Kuwaiti troops, Colonel Mohammed Al-Harmi, and *Al-Fatah's* Colonel Fouad Al-Haddad, saying that the Iraqis were running, and to get to Kuwait City as soon as possible. The Kuwaitis were keen to be the first into their own capital, despite the risks.

Al-Harmi and Al-Haddad could not move in force without authorization from the Saudi JFC-E commander, and certainly couldn't put the entire brigade on the road in the dark. However, a strong reconnaissance element was possible. Lieutenant-Colonel Sami Al-Faraj, a reservist working with *Al-Fatah's* ANGLICo unit, together with Lieutenant Baker Dashti, and ANGLICo and US Army Special Forces men with the brigade were keen to go. *Al-Fatah* put together 60 men, comprising Al-Faraj and Dashti, a reinforced platoon of 48 under Major Adnan Behbehani, and ten ANGLICo/ Special Forces men under Captain Daniel Smith, and a Captain Jones. They set off in the early hours of 26 February in a motley convoy of *Fahd* APCs and jeeps.

In the pre-dawn winter darkness and rain, with the smoke from the inferno of Burgan ahead of them, the little convoy slowly, steadily, crept up the pitch-black coastal highway, half expecting an ambush. The pulsating glow of the burning oil wells lit the western horizon, with the occasional flash out to sea as US battleships hurled more 16-inch shells into Kuwait. Nearing the urban area, they broke out the Kuwaiti and US flags so that they would not be mistaken for Iraqis by any Allied troops or Resistance they might meet.

At about 1.00 a.m. on the 26th, US surveillance aircraft detected huge Iraqi convoys heading out of Kuwait. They were taking two main routes; the first through Mutla'a and then directly up the Abdaly Road; the second along the north coast of Kuwait Bay, and then parallel to Bubiyan Island. Movement was also picked up at Ali Al-Salem as early as 8.00 p.m. on the 25th as Iraq's IV Corps, particularly the 6th Armoured and 1st Mechanized Divisions, grouped and started north in a long line, parallel to the Abdaly Road.

Apart from getting the Iraqis out of Kuwait City, this was exactly what the Allies wanted to avoid at the time. Once in Iraq, Iraqi III and IV Corps troops from Kuwait would be able to reinforce the Republican Guard who had yet to feel the full fury of the US VII Corps still racing into southern Iraq in its huge loop. The Marines' advance had been so swift in the 45 hours since they entered Kuwait that VII Corps was not yet in place to block the Iraqi retreat from Kuwait. Instead of acting like a magnet to keep the Iraqis in Kuwait in place, the Marines had become a piston to push them out. The Iraqis were ruining the timing of General Schwarzkopf's plan by running away too soon.

Allied aircraft were scrambled to stop the convoys, but were initially unable to locate them in the rain and smoke. They finally found and struck the main convoy at its most dense at the Mutla'a chokepoint at 2.00 a.m. on 26 February, and then the rear, five kilometres away, on the outskirts of Jahra.

Contrary to later news reports, the first attacks were not on the front of the convoy, nor on the only route out of Kuwait. Thousands of vehicles escaped ahead of the bombers. Others fled along the other two main exit routes, but the 1,000-vehicle segment of the convoy at Mutla'a was trapped. Most of the Iraqis fled their vehicles and started walking home as US planes pounded the three routes throughout the pre-dawn hours. In fact, by the time the second wave went in, most of the Iraqis who could escape from the vehicles had done so. Reliable estimates of Iraqis actually killed at Mutla'a are about 400 men.

By 4.00 a.m., the party of 60 Kuwaitis and Americans from *Al-Fatah* were making their way tentatively up the empty Maghreb-Assafar Motorway into Kuwait City. Suddenly, as they neared the intersection with Fourth Ring, they came under rifle fire, which stopped as quickly as it had started. No one was hurt, but they later learned that it was the Resistance who – having difficulty differentiating between the Kuwaiti and Iraqi flags in the dark – had initially mistaken them for retreating Iraqis. Luckily, one of their number had noticed the US flag flying from a following vehicle.

Several kilometres further on, they heard the sound of women ululating in joy in the dark. It was a great morale booster. Now, the question was where to go to link up with the Resistance. They headed for the Sheraton, near the city centre, and met there with one of the leaders, Major-General Mohammed Al-Bader and Colonel Abdulrahman Al-Hajeri in the pre-dawn darkness. Central Kuwait City was liberated, barely 48 hours into the ground war.

Elsewhere in Kuwait, other intrepid troops were linking up with the Resistance, barely two hours after the Iraqis had fled the city. In Ahmadi, at 5.00 a.m., a group of the local Resistance coordinators were in their HQ in the house of one of their members, Abu Abdullah. They were canvassing the suburban fire stations around Kuwait on a VHF radio to track what was happening, when two JFC-E Marine ANGLICo officers, Dave Landersman and Andrew Hewitt, walked in. Using a Resistance satellite phone, Abu Abdullah's colleagues had earlier faxed out a map of their location to the Allies so that they could link up. Landersman and Hewitt had it with them.

Abu Abdullah could hardly believe his eyes. This was Liberation, the moment they had waited and prayed for, after nearly seven months. The Americans and Kuwaitis hugged each other, laughing and jumping up and down like little boys. It was a sweet, sweet moment.

26 February is marked as Liberation Day in Kuwait. Perhaps no more than a few hundred Allied soldiers had actually entered the city itself, but most of the Iraqis had left. By lunchtime, the Resistance was in control of most of the city, although a strong Iraqi force remained on the outskirts at the airport, and was desperately trying to extract itself. That evening, the Kuwaiti Amir in Saudi Arabia issued a decree appointing Crown Prince and Prime Minister Sheikh Sa'ad Al-Abdullah, Military Governor, and imposing martial law.

The early morning news confirmed Iraq's order for its troops to retreat to positions they held on 1 August, 1990. However, the Allies continued the war as Iraq had not yet indicated compliance with the UN Resolutions. After months of duplicity, no one was prepared to take Saddam seriously until he personally, or his Government, made a formal and public statement ordering a complete withdrawal, and accepting all the UN Resolutions.

There was a limbo period in the city between the exit of the Iraqis and the entry of the main Allied forces, as the Marines fought their way through the remnants of the Iraqis on the city outskirts. Small arms fire could be heard, and planes overhead, invisible above the smoke clouds. There was great anticipation that the liberators would march triumphantly in at any moment.

By mid-morning, a few small intrepid groups ventured out to see for themselves, constantly checking over their shoulders for any sign of Iraqis. Little crowds gathered in the suburbs, and at the Sheraton Roundabout in the city centre, next to the burnt-out hotel, congratulating each other, crying with relief. More congregated at the Kuwait Towers, and the nearby US and British embassies, where Allied troops were expected to rendezvous.

The sound of Arab women ululating in joy cut the air above the crackle of sporadic small arms fire. Men tore down or set fire to the portraits of Saddam installed all over the city, or riddled them with bullets from abandoned Kalashnikovs. Iraqi flags above public buildings were ripped down and replaced with Kuwaiti ones. People tentatively picked their way through abandoned equipment, everything from rifles and ammunition to chemical warfare kits, jeeps and tanks. The Iraqis had just dropped everything and run.

The entire city had been vandalized. Litter, graffiti and faeces were everywhere. Not a single shop had been left unlooted. All the major hotels and shopping centres had been torched. The National Museum had been shelled and burned, as had the National Assembly building. A huge wooden dhow in the museum courtyard, a link with Kuwait's seafaring past, was nothing but ashes and blackened iron nails. In the dhow harbour itself across the road from the museum, all the boats had been either sunk or burned to the waterline. The Amir's Residence at Dasman had been completely trashed; and his workplace at the Seif Palace had been shelled and partially burned.

Most distressing was the human cost. As the residents of Kuwait City poked their way through the abandoned Iraqi bunkers on the coast, perhaps their most disturbing find was an underground room full of discarded women's clothing where the Iraqi troops had apparently held women of various Arab and Asian nationalities. The fate of these unfortunate women is unknown.

To the residents of Kuwait City, savouring their first moments of freedom in nearly seven months, the physical damage hardly mattered. It was heartbreaking, but nothing beside the joyous realization that the Iraqis really were gone. Despite all the destruction, newly liberated Kuwait had never looked more beautiful. Not even the glowering, smelly, black clouds over the city could spoil the mood. In mid-afternoon, the sky opened up, and the rain poured down as if the entire country was weeping with relief.

Although Kuwait City was largely devoid of Iraqi troops at dawn on 26 February, the outlying desert was still a very dangerous place for the liberators. Apart from mines, some Iraqis were still prepared to resist, perhaps through a fear that this was their only chance of surviving.

To the south, the 1st Marine Division kicked off its advance from Burgan at 7.00 a.m., to bring it on line with the 2nd Division. Both divisions then struck north at noon, abreast, while *Grizzly* stayed behind to complete clearing Al-Jaber. *Ripper's* first objective was the intersection of Sixth and Seventh Ring Roads, ten kilometres west of the airport. *Papa Bear* and *Shepherd* turned towards the airport itself. Meanwhile, *Tiger* Brigade raced out on the 2nd Division's left for the intersections outside Jahra. To the west, JFC-N had taken Al-Abraq, and was moving steadily eastwards towards Ali Al-Salem.

Although the previous morning's fog had disappeared, the south-easterly wind which had offered so much protection from the Iraqis in the early hours of the ground war was now blowing the oil smoke over both Marine divisions, blotting out the sun and reducing visibility in places to less than 100 metres. A tremendous sandstorm blew up during the day, making progress extremely difficult. They had to advance carefully in stop-start style to deal with scattered Iraqi resistance and navigate around oil installations and quarries. One of the greatest dangers was unexploded air-dropped Allied ordnance on the ground. Most Iraqi vehicles they engaged had already been abandoned. Those which were manned were seldom in formed units, but there were a few firefights. It was clear that not all Iraqis were prepared to give up, or were perhaps unaware

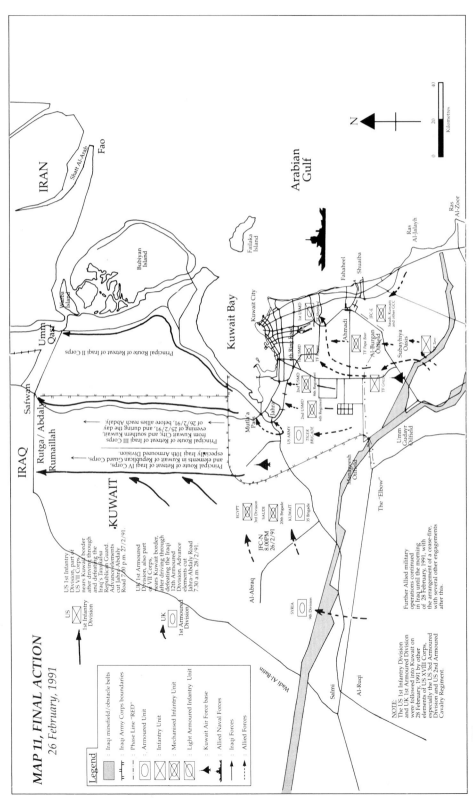

MAP 11, FINAL ACTION
26 February, 1991

Legend
: Iraqi minefield/obstacle belts
: Iraqi Army Corps boundaries
: Phase Line "RED"
: Armoured Unit
: Infantry Unit
: Mechanised Infantry Unit
: Light Armoured Infantry Unit
: Kuwait Air Force base
: Allied Naval Forces
: Iraqi Forces
: Allied Forces

NOTE:
The US 1st Infantry Division
and UK 1st Armoured Division
were followed into Kuwait on
28 February 1991 by other
elements of US XVIII Corps,
especially the US 3rd Armoured
Division and US 2nd Armoured
Cavalry Regiment.

US 1st Infantry
Division, part of
US VII Corps,
nears Kuwait border
after driving through
and defeating the
Iraqi's Tawalkana
Republican Guard.
Advance elements
cut Jahra-Abdaly
Road 7.00 p.m. 27/2/91.

UK 1st Armoured
Division, also part
of VII Corps,
nears Kuwait border,
after driving through
and defeating the Iraqi
12th Armoured
Division. Advance
elements cut
Jahra-Abdaly Road
7.30 a.m. 28/2/91.

Further Allied military
operations continued
in Iraq until the morning
of 28 February, 1991, with
the arrangement of a cease-fire,
with several other engagements
after this.

Principal Route of Retreat of Iraqi IV Corps,
and elements in Kuwait of Republican Guard Corps,
especially Iraqi 10th Armoured Division.

Principal Route of Retreat of Iraqi III Corps
from Kuwait City, and southern Kuwait,
evening of 25/2/91, and during the day
of 26/2/91, before allies reach Abdaly.

Principal Route of Retreat of Iraqi II Corps

IRAQ
Rutga / Abdaly
Rumaillah
Safwan

IRAN
Fao
Shatt Al-Arab

Umm Qasr
Warba Island
Bubiyan Island
Failaka Island

Kuwait Bay
Kuwait City
Mutla'a Pass
Jahra

Arabian
Gulf

Fahaheel
Shuaiba
Ras Al-Jalayh
Ras Al-Zoor

KUWAIT

Al-Abraq
Al-Ruqi
Salmi
Wadi Al-Batin

Ahmadi
Al-Burgan Oilfield
Subayhiya Oasis
Umm Gudayr Oilfield
The "Elbow"
Maqwaah Oilfield

EGYPT
3rd Division
SAUDI
20th Brigade
KUWAIT
35 Brigade

JFC-N
8.00PM
26/2/91

SYRIA
9th Division

US
1st Infantry
Division

UK
1st Armoured
Division

N
Kilometres
0   20   40

BASE MAPS ©   SALEM AL-MARZOUK AND SABAH ABI-HANNA WLL

Explanatory notes to Map 11, Final movements of Allied forces in Kuwait, 26 February, 1991

1. **25 February,** 8.00 p.m.: Iraqis start retreating from Kuwait, using three routes north.
2. Overnight: USS *Missouri* shells Kuwait International Airport.
3. **26 February,** 00.32.a.m.: Baghdad Radio announces that Iraq will comply with UN Security Council Resolutions.
4. 1.00 a.m.: US reconnaissance detects Iraqi retreat. Confirmed by Kuwaiti Resistance.
5. 2.00 a.m.: First air attacks on retreating Iraqis at Mutla'a Ridge.
6. 5.00 a.m.: First link-up between Kuwaiti Resistance and Kuwaiti/American troops in Kuwait City, and in Ahmadi, with US Marine ANGLICo unit from JFC-E.
7. 7.00 a.m.: US 1st Marine Division departs overnight positions in Burgan oilfield, to come on line with the 2nd Marine Division. Task Force *Grizzly* stays behind to clear Al-Jaber base.
8. Noon: US 1st Marine Division's Task Force *Ripper* advances in poor visibility and sandstorm towards intersection of Sixth and Seventh Ring Roads. *Papa Bear* and *Shepherd* advance towards Kuwait International Airport. 2nd Marine Division's 6th and 8th Marine Regiments advance towards the sector of Sixth Ring Road west of the intersection with Seventh Ring. *Tiger* Brigade races ahead, to the left, towards the strategic interchanges west of Jahra.
9. Late afternoon: A battalion of US Army's *Tiger* Brigade, operating alongside 2nd US Marine Division, takes the Atraf interchange, blocking any exit out of Kuwait along Sixth Ring. Destroys 55 retreating Iraqi vehicles. Two other *Tiger* battalions cut the Jahra-Abdaly Road at dusk.
10. 1st US Marine Division's Task Force *Ripper* takes Sixth Ring Road from the Seventh Ring Road Intersection, across to the western perimeter of Kuwait International Airport, a front of ten kilometres.
11. Dusk: The remainder of *Tiger* Brigade – two battalions – takes the high ground overlooking Mutla'a Pass. Destroys 33 Iraqi armoured vehicles, and takes 720 prisoners.
12. 7.00 p.m.: US Marine reconnaissance unit links up with Kuwaiti Resistance, and retakes the US Embassy compound in Kuwait City, unopposed.
13. 8.00 p.m.: JFC-N halts its advance for the day four kilometres west of Ali Al-Salem KAF base. Syrian 9th Armoured division operating as part of JFC-N crosses border into Kuwait from Saudi Arabia.
14. Late evening: 1st US Marine Division's Task Force *Papa Bear* arrives on southern perimeter of Kuwait International Airport. *Shepherd* moves along western edge of Maghreb-Assafar Motorway, and stops at racetrack south of Sixth Ring.
15. **27 February,** 4.30 a.m.: Task Force *Shepherd* starts moving into Kuwait International Airport precinct. Controls the airport by 7.00 a.m.
16. 9.00 a.m.: JFC-N troops, with Kuwaitis in lead, pass through US Marine lines west of Jahra, and start into Kuwait City, as main force of JFC-E troops come up the Maghreb-Assafar Motorway.
17. Afternoon: US Marine Commander, Lieutenant-General Boomer, enters Kuwait City.
18. 7.00 p.m.: US VII Corps' 1st US Infantry Division cuts the Jahra-Abdaly Road just south of the Iraqi border, after most of Iraqi III Corps and IV Corps have left Kuwait.
19. **28 February,** 7.30 a.m.: British 1st Armoured Division cuts Jahra-Abdaly Road north of Mutla'a. Suspension of hostilities.
20. 8.00 a.m.: Suspension of hostilities. During the day, US, British and French embassies secured by respective Special Forces. Further elements of US VII Corps enter Kuwait.

of the retreat from the city of their fellows. If the announcement from Baghdad to withdraw had come a day earlier, many more Iraqis would have lived.

That afternoon, a *Tiger* battalion took control of the Sixth Ring-Atraf interchange. Anything trying to leave Kuwait along Sixth Ring would now encounter US armour. This was where Kuwait's 35 Brigade had engaged the invading Iraqis on 2 August; now the Iraqis were heading home in retreat.

Tiger's two other battalions swung around into the desert between Ali Al-Salem and Jahra, and climbed the high ground which would bring them to the crest of a rise overlooking Mutla'a Pass. In the process of doing so, they destroyed a further 33 Iraqi armoured vehicles, and took 720 prisoners.

As dusk fell, *Tiger's* soldiers gazed down on the destruction wrought by the American pilots that morning, awed by the carnage of bombed and burned vehicles stretching for five kilometres from Jahra along the road running up the ridge. There were tanks, APCs, trucks, buses, cars, water tankers, ambulances, almost every type of vehicle. Above the crackle of the flames and the howling of the winter wind, the Americans could hear the intermittent explosions of ammunition left in the burning vehicles cooking off.

By late afternoon, the 1st Marine Division's *Ripper* held a ten-kilometre front from the Sixth and Seventh Ring Roads intersection to the western edge of the airport. *Papa Bear* arrived on the airport's southern outskirts five hours later.

In the meantime, *Shepherd* moved east of the airport to form a screen on the western edge of the Maghreb-Assafar Motorway. They passed through a now-abandoned Kuwaiti Amiri Guard barracks near the Military Hospital and the Hunting and Equestrian Club, onto Sixth Ring Road around dusk.

The airport was now isolated with *Ripper* on the west, *Papa Bear* to the south, and *Shepherd* on the east, with Kuwait's suburbs on the other side of Sixth Ring, invisible in the smoke, sandstorm, and dark. It was too dangerous to move into the airport at night, so the Marines held their positions.

In the desert to the west, JFC-N had halted at 8.00 p.m. after a skirmish west of Ali Al-Salem. On the coast, the main JFC-E force drove up the motorway towards the city, with residents waving and shouting to them under the gloomy sky. One of the leading Marine ANGLICo teams, under Lieutenant Brian Knowles, linked up with the Kuwaiti Resistance, and was brought to the US Embassy, as Saudi forces headed for their own nearby compound. Although Army Special Forces were supposed to re-take the embassy, the Marines could not resist the temptation. They moved in at 7.00 p.m. Within hours, they were being interviewed by intrepid TV crews already in the city.

The fighting in Kuwait was all but over by dawn on 27 February. *Shepherd* had started moving into the airport at 4.30 a.m. and controlled it by 7.00 a.m., destroying about 100 Iraqi tanks in the process.

Iraqi tanks were not the only vehicles destroyed during the battle. The 747 of flight BA149 went up in flames. Only the tail and the four engines survived relatively unscathed. A nearby KAF DC-9 met a similar fate. The Iraqis took the blame, but later reports suggested that the planes were too tempting a target for an over-eager Marine pilot or gunner. One doesn't get a chance to blow up an airliner every day.

Prosaically, one of the first visitors to the site of the remains of BA149 was Victor Mallet, the London *Financial Times* journalist who had flown into Kuwait on it seven months previously. He had come full circle.

Meanwhile, to the west, near Jahra, the 2nd Marine Division linked up with the JFC-N Arab forces who had finally caught up. Fighting would continue for several days in Iraq, but all resistance in Kuwait had collapsed. By 9.00 a.m., JFC-N, with Kuwaitis in the lead, started through the Marines' lines, along Jahra Road, into Kuwait City, as JFC-E came in from the south.

On Kuwait's western border with Iraq, in US VII Corps' sector, the UK 1st Armoured Division had overrun the Iraqi 12th Armoured Division, and elements of at least three other divisions, while the Americans had taken on several Republican Guard divisions. The US 1st Infantry Division would reach Abdaly that evening. The British arrived north of Mutla'a, at 7.30 a.m. on 28 February, 38 hours behind *Tiger* Brigade, now on their right flank.

Far to the south, the US 1st Cavalry Division had been released from its job of protecting VII Corps' HQ in Saudi Arabia. It was now racing in a huge arc to encircle the main Iraqi forces north of Kuwait. The plan had been for VII Corps and the British to drive into the Iraqis from the south, with XVIII Corps hitting them from the west, while the Marines supported the Arab troops in any fighting that might need to be done in Kuwait City. These plans were brought to a halt by what was later widely considered a premature suspension of hostilities at 8.00 a.m. on the morning of the 28th, but at that point in time, the destruction of the Republican Guard seemed almost assured.

Apart from the few dozen Americans and Europeans who had stayed in Kuwait, the only Westerners in town on the morning of 27 February were bands of daring journalists and a few Marine reconnaissance and Special Forces units. The main column of Arab soldiers and US Marine Commander Lieutenant-General Boomer would not arrive until the afternoon. At the Catholic Cathedral, the priests fixed the previously unused bell, and pealed it in victory. The imams went up their mosque minarets and broadcast the call to prayer, without loudspeakers as the power was out, until they were hoarse.

For many people in Kuwait, the hangover soon set in as they searched frantically for missing friends and relatives. It would be several weeks before most of the prisoners were returned by Iraq. Others never would return. In the meantime, people went around the morgues and hospitals looking for their loved ones, almost hoping against hope not to find them there.

The journalists went chasing after blood, and found plenty. The Kuwaiti bodies were in the worst condition. Most had been shot, but many also had broken limbs, heads split open, missing eyes. Several had been very severely burned, even to the bone, from being thrown on rubbish fires, or immersed in acid. The shocked and silent observers in the cold, tiled morgues could only pray that the mutilations had occurred after death, but it was apparent to some of the more seasoned journalists that this had not always been the case.

Outside, the sky was dark with oil smoke and clouds, and the air stank of kerosene, but nothing could suppress the joy of the occasion. Crowds were out on the streets, cheering, clapping, sounding car horns, waving flags, carrying large posters of the Amir and Crown Prince which they had hidden under pain of death. Home-made banners thanking George Bush and Margaret Thatcher abounded. Although Thatcher had been deposed four months earlier, she was seen as responsible for putting backbone into the Coalition from Day 1. Conservative Kuwaiti women in *abayas* and veils danced in the streets like teenagers, ululating. Kuwaiti men and even some of the Coalition Arab troops fired off abandoned Iraqi Kalashnikovs in celebration. The public was at great risk from falling bullets. Several people were in fact wounded.

When the Marines arrived, they were completely overwhelmed at the heartfelt gratitude. Even the most cynical of the journalists were visibly moved. At Kuwait Airport, Lieutenant-General Boomer, flushed with victory, said he now had some idea of what the Liberation of Paris in World War II must have felt like. The nightmare, for most people, was almost over.

Once the military had gained control of the city, the diplomats wasted no time in returning. The British, who had been the last to leave in December, were the first back, on 28 February, within 48 hours of liberation.

But first, the embassies had to be secured. Despite the Marines upstaging the US Army by taking the US compound the previous evening, General Schwarzkopf wanted all three major embassies, the US, British and French, retaken concurrently, without any one-upmanship. His Special Forces commander, Colonel Jesse Johnson, was in charge of this for all three missions. Johnson's men would secure the US compound, the UK Special Boat Service (SBS) Her Majesty's, and the French Dragoons theirs. The Marines in the US Embassy were cleared out so that the Special Forces could do it again.

The French chose the eminently practical approach of simply climbing over the wall and opening the gate, but the Americans and SBS had to have their fun. At the UK Embassy, in a marvelously impressive operation in full view of gathered journalists, several helicopters surrounded the area from the air as commandos abseiled down ropes from a hovering Chinook onto the Chancery roof, and blew their way in. Ostensibly, they were checking for booby traps, but the Iraqis had left the compound undisturbed. In fact, the Union Flag which Ambassador Michael Weston had left flying upon his departure still fluttered defiantly above the compound, streaked black from the oily rain.

The troops could simply have asked the Embassy's Indian Vice-Consul, Raj Gopolan, who was standing nearby, for the key to the front gate, but this would have spoiled their fun. After shooting up the bullet-proof glass panels at the reception counter, generally turning the place upside down, and destroying an historic door, the grinning commandos reappeared, looking like a bunch of heavily armed schoolboys who had just had a lot of fun.

The Chinook left, but soon returned. Michael Weston emerged out of it to a rapturous reception from the gathered Kuwaitis, his faithful Indian local staff, and a few of the British who had stayed behind. Several people commented that the Iraqis had treated the Embassy with more respect than the SBS had, yet there was a reason behind the vandalism. Apparently, the SBS had spoken to BLT men who had been taken hostage in August. Much of the blame for leaving their families unprotected at IBI had been laid, rightly or wrongly, with the diplomats. The military were getting their own back.

The US Embassy did not fare any better. Its flag and compound had been as undisturbed as that of the British, although the Iraqis had been over the wall. Barbara Bodine, the DCM who had run the embassy during the occupation, was irate that the US Special Forces blew the door of her office off its hinges, setting her curtains ablaze. They made more of a mess of it than the Iraqis ever had. The new US Ambassador, Mr Edward Gnehm, flew in the day after Mr Weston, and was escorted off his helicopter by Colonel Johnson.

On the day the British diplomats returned, the Kuwaiti Navy came home, not to their destroyed base, but to Ras Al-Ardh in Salmiya, on Kuwait Bay.

After spending most of the ground war with little to do other than watch the bombardment of their homeland, *Kilo* received permission to land, at their own risk, on 28 February. At the time, there was still a great danger from mines, but they would not let that stand in their way. Several of the men had families in Kuwait, whom they had not seen in seven long months.

Approaching the coast was a sombre experience. They couldn't even see it with the oil smoke, and had to use all their local experience to find the harbour. As they neared shore, they were shocked at the utter devastation of the once pristine waterfront which was now a warren of trenches, bunkers and emplacements. The Kuwait they were returning to was far different to the one they had left. Finally, at 4.35 p.m., they set foot on land. *Kilo* was home.

On 2 March, 1991, two days after the Allied suspension of offensive operations, the UN Security Council adopted Resolution 686 setting out the conditions to be met by Iraq for a formal end to hostilities. It was the first Resolution on the crisis since November's use-of-force vote. Iraq was to rescind its purported annexation of Kuwait; immediately return all POWs and all detained third-country nationals and Kuwaitis, and return the remains of any who had died in action or in detention; return all Kuwaiti property and accept in principle liability for any loss, damage or injury as a result of the invasion and occupation; assist the Coalition in identifying mines, booby traps, and chemical and biological attacks on Israel and Saudi Arabia; and designate military commanders to meet with their counterparts from the allies to arrange for the military aspects of an earliest possible cessation of hostilities.

The following morning, Allied commanders General Schwarzkopf and Lieutenant-General Prince Khalid Bin Sultan met with Iraqi Deputy Chief of Staff Lieutenant-General Sultan Hashim Ahmad, and the Commander of Iraq's decimated III Corps, Lieutenant-General Salah Abud Mahmoud at Safwan Airfield, just north of the Kuwaiti border. Schwarzkopf's main concern seemed to be to prevent further fighting, such as had just occurred between his 24th Mechanized Division and the *Hammurabi* Republican Guard. His next priority was to get back Allied service personnel who had been taken prisoner, and the remains of airmen killed over Iraq.

The talks were long and complex, but one critical aspect which was not addressed sufficiently was the accounting of Kuwaitis taken by the Iraqis during the occupation, especially in the final days. Prince Khalid tried to ensure that the subject was given the attention it warranted, but the Iraqis gave a vaguely positive response, and discussions moved on to other matters.

Schwarzkopf later told me that, up to that point, the Iraqis had complied with all his demands, and it was perhaps out of largess and practicality that he allowed them concessions such as using helicopters in areas where the Shi'ite uprising later occurred. Either way, he was aware of the large numbers of Kuwaiti detainees, and failed to use his leverage over the Iraqis to ensure that they were all returned. Some people, generals and diplomats included, have suggested that Saddam himself, as Iraq's Commander-in-Chief, or at the very least a member of his Revolutionary Command Council, not two largely irrelevant generals, should have been brought to the negotiating table.

The day before the Safwan meeting, Shi'ite rebels in Basra had stormed the jails, killing some of the guards, and releasing many of the prisoners. One of these was Englishman Brock Matthews, who had stayed in Kuwait after most other Westerners had left in December, and had been arrested and held in Basra since late January. He fled into the Basra back streets amid the gunfire, with a Lebanese and a Sri Lankan, and scores of Kuwaitis. Hundreds of other prisoners never made it out as the guards regrouped and re-established control.

For two days, the fugitives were sheltered and fed by Iraqi Shi'ites, who had little enough themselves. After regaining their strength, they tried to walk back to Kuwait, past the remnants of the retreating Iraqi Army. Much of it was in disarray, but there were still enough formed units to put down the rebellion, and man the front line against the Americans. Brock's party were joined by hundreds of Kuwaitis and others trying to get home. Mostly, the Iraqis left them alone, but southern Iraq was still a dangerous place. Brock's Lebanese companion was hit by a bullet which went through his arm.

Four days after the prison break, they finally made it back to Kuwaiti territory. They were lucky to be able to cross over. For all the claims of utter defeat of the Iraqis, they were very much in control at the border. Once in Kuwait, on the Abdaly Road, they met with Caryle Murphy of the *Washington Post*, who had returned after her own escape into Saudi Arabia in August, and Bob Drogin of the *LA Times*, who gave them a lift to Kuwait City. The BBC had been looking for them, at the request of Ambassador Weston, who had learned of Brock's arrest; the word had gone around the journalists. Like many Kuwaitis, Brock almost literally came back from the dead.

Elsewhere in southern Iraq, particularly Nassiriyah, Iraqi Shi'ites rescued other Kuwaitis from the jails, and drove them on trucks across the desert as close as they could to the border. From there, they had to walk, keeping the pall of smoke from the burning oilfields ahead of them like a lodestar. The Iraqi Shi'ites turned back into their shattered country, with the unending gratitude of the Kuwaitis, to face the wrath of Saddam's Republican Guard which it had been the task of the Western members of the Coalition to smash.

Over the next few weeks, thousands of people would return to Kuwait from Iraq on foot or by air, on Red Cross flights, or on buses run by Kuwait's Indian Citizens' Committee, but hundreds still remain unaccounted for to this day.

One member of the last batch to return was Ghassan Al-Qabandi, whose sister Asrar was so brutally murdered on the eve of the air war. He hoped to see a number of his compatriots he had last seen earlier in an Iraqi jail, but they were never heard of again. In the rush to agree to the ceasefire terms and retrieve Allied military POWs, the main victims of the crisis were all but forgotten, and the Iraqi Shi'ites were left to Saddam's tender mercies.

On the day of the Safwan meeting, the last piece of Kuwait still occupied by the Iraqis was liberated. Not that the Iraqis concerned were in a position to do much, particularly after the pounding they had received from US Navy battleships and Air Force B-52s. They were trapped on Failaka Island, a mixture of Iraqi Navy and Marines, with 35 officers and 1405 men. Many of the other officers had managed to escape to Umm Qasr by small boat.

Over the previous two days, leaflets had been dropped on the island telling the Iraqis to surrender, and to gather at the TV transmitter site. On 3 March, a Chinook from USS *Okinawa* picked up several Kuwaiti and US officers from Ras Al-Ardh, including *Kilo's* Squadron Commander, Lieutenant-Colonel Nasser Husseinan, *Istiqlal's* and *Sanbouk's* skippers, and Captain Abdullah Shuaib, who had been born on Failaka, and whose father had been the mayor.

At 9.15 a.m., the first Chinook landed on Failaka. Graciously, the Marines insisted that Husseinan, as the senior Kuwaiti officer present, have the honour of being the first to set foot on the island. He deferred to Captain Shuaib, saying that it was his island more than anyone's. Shuaib went first.

The strangest of sights greeted the liberators. Scores of Kuwaiti flags were hoisted on the island, all upside down. Then they discovered one grizzled old fisherman, Ahmad Mallalah, who had somehow managed to be the only Kuwaiti to stay on the island after the Iraqis had ejected everyone else. Apparently, before the helicopters had arrived, Mallalah had found a stock of flags in the island school, and had asked the Iraqi commander if he could hoist them. The officer had asked him to at least wait until they were captured, but Mallalah put the flags up anyway. However, he couldn't remember which colour went at the top, and picked the wrong way.

The old man had a wealth of stories, and a few complaints. Apparently, the Iraqis had been stealing fish from his traps. He was glad the Marines had arrived as they would put a stop to that. Then, on one occasion, the Iraqis had said they were going to execute him when they found 'Death to Saddam' written on a road. 'Don't be stupid,' Mallalah had said. 'I can't even read, let alone write. It must have been one of your guys!' He was let go. Mallalah also recounted the human reaction to the B-52s. 'Your heart doesn't stop jumping for half an hour after they finish,' he said, awed at the bombardment.

At 4.00 p.m., the Kuwaiti officers hoisted the Kuwaiti flag - right way up - at Captain Shuaib's house, and the Iraqi POWs left by helicopter.

Kuwait's Crown Prince and Prime Minister, Sheikh Sa'ad Al-Abdullah, returned to Kuwait on 4 March, to a rapturous reception, and a reunion with his daughter, Hussa, who had remained in Kuwait. His home had been all but destroyed, so he and his wife stayed with friends.

Sheikh Sa'ad had been appointed Military Governor, but much of his time was taken up with senior Coalition Ministers visiting him to congratulate him on the Liberation, and remind him how much they had done to help free his country. They all wanted a piece of the reconstruction cake, even before the blood was dry, amid highly inflated estimates of the business available.

Some of these visitors were more sincere. British Prime Minister John Major flew in a couple of days after Sheikh Sa'ad to meet his troops, the Ambassador, and the 30 Britons who had stayed throughout the occupation.

Despite the freedom, the first weeks of Liberation were as difficult as some of the occupation's darkest days. There was little food, no power and water, and some elements took the law into their own hands before the Army could impose order. Civilians carried guns with impunity. Several people were killed and others wounded by stray bullets from random celebratory gunfire.

On the day Failaka was liberated, a Kuwaiti Special Forces soldier, Sergeant Faiz Al-Thiab, was killed ferreting out a group of Palestinian collaborators. Another brave officer, Lieutenant-Colonel Ahmad Shamsaldeen set about clearing many local areas of mines almost single-handedly, arguing that Allied troops should not be put at risk doing the job. He and First Sergeant Shaberem Al-Fuzli were killed by a mine three months after Liberation. At least a dozen other Kuwaitis and several others were killed by these insidious devices. Scores more were maimed.

On 11 March, 1991, Iraq formally renounced its purported annexation of Kuwait in a letter to the UN Secretary-General, although neither its Parliament nor Saddam put their names to this. At the time, the world's attention had shifted to the tragedy of the Kurds in northern Iraq and the brutal repression of the Shi'ite uprising in southern Iraq.

Kuwait's Amir, Sheikh Jaber Al-Ahmad, returned to his country on 14 March once security was re-established, 225 days after narrowly escaping capture by the invading Iraqis. As if an omen of a brighter future, the wind changed as the Amir's plane landed, and the black, oily skies above the city cleared to a springtime blue. It would be one of the few times over the next six months that people in Kuwait City would see the sky as it is meant to be.

Overcome, the Amir dropped to his knees, and kissed the ground. Kuwait was free again, its legitimate Government restored. The long, hard, task of extinguishing the oil fires and reconstructing the shattered country lay ahead.

30. EPILOGUE

No conflict ever has a tidy ending. Kuwait's liberation was no exception.

The burning question in the aftermath of the war - and even now - was why did the Allies not go all the way to Baghdad and get Saddam. The answer is simple. They had no UN mandate to do so. More practically, the job was beyond even the combined capabilities of the US, British and French forces. The Americans had enough trouble getting Manuel Noriega in Panama. They never found Mohammed Aideed in Mogadishu, and indicted war criminals are still publicly at large in Bosnia. It would have been virtually impossible to get Saddam, even if they had occupied Baghdad. As importantly, the cost in Allied lives would have been prohibitive. Public support would have evaporated overnight. Iraq is a well-armed country. The Iraqis did not fight to keep Kuwait, but they would have fought for Baghdad.

Even if Baghdad had been taken and Saddam deposed, what then? The US would have been left holding a huge country, with the occupier's responsibility to re-establish an indigenous government. This would have taken years, and more money and lives than the Allies were prepared to pay. During this time, US troops would have faced Iran, Syria and Jordan on Iraq's borders, with unlimited potential for further crises, and criticism of a new imperialism. Arab support for a large US presence in the Middle East would at best have disappeared, but more likely turned into vehement opposition.

Paradoxically, Saddam serves Western interests far better by staying in power. His principal service, even with his reduced strength, is to provide a regional counterbalance to Iran, and prevent Iraq from breaking up into a northern Kurdish sub-state, a southern Arab Shi'ite one, and an Arab Sunni fiefdom in the middle, with Turkey, Syria and Iran nibbling at the edges. Less obviously, Saddam concentrates the minds of GCC leaders on their impotence against him. They are now far more amenable to Western access to their military facilities. The Americans are now welcome guests at the party.

This change is significant. For years, despite generally warm relations with the West, the major GCC states firmly resisted an overt Western military presence. The Saudis allowed US AWACS aircraft to operate from their soil, but not ground forces. Even warships escorting Kuwaiti oil tankers during the Iran–Iraq War did not call at Kuwaiti ports. US advisors wore civilian clothes; the BLT wore Kuwaiti uniforms. Today, in Kuwait, US and British servicemen wear their own uniforms openly. Allied warships visit Kuwait regularly, and hold well-publicized exercises with Kuwaiti forces.

There are two qualifiers to the view that the Allies were right not to go to Baghdad. First, they could have done away with Saddam's nuclear, biological, chemical, missile and supergun weapons programmes once and for all. These have taken a body blow from the Allied bombing and UN inspectors, but Iraq continued to frustrate the UN for more than three years before finally agreeing to comprehensive weapons monitoring. It still retains the knowledge to resume this work. Secondly, over 600 Kuwaitis and others remain unaccounted for. A captive Iraq would have had either to account for these individuals' remains, or release them if they were still alive.

The enormity of the longer-term threat posed by Saddam's weapons programmes only became clear after the war. In fact, the full extent may still be unknown. After four years of deceiving UN inspectors, Baghdad was finally forced by the defection of Saddam's son-in-law, Lieutenant-General Hussein Kamil Al-Majeed, to hand over documents which, it said, 'Al-Majeed had been hiding.' These proved that the programmes were far more extensive than even the inspections had found. Earlier, defecting Iraqi scientists had claimed that Saddam was trying to build an A-bomb by late 1991. Although over-ambitious, this was still too close for comfort. The implications of a nuclear-armed Iraq facing nuclear-armed Israel, and holding a nuclear dagger to the throats of Saudi Arabia, Iran and Kuwait, are too chilling to contemplate.

Iraq's nuclear bomb programme was at the level of the 1940s US Manhattan Project, with improvements. It had produced fissile material in three distinct, parallel processes: gas centrifuge, electromagnetic separation, and thermal diffusion, and a little plutonium, had acquired deuterium oxide and lithium 6, both vital Bomb ingredients. While a more powerful H-bomb was still some years beyond the classic Hiroshima/Nagasaki A-bombs devices, Iraq had many H-bomb elements which could significantly enhance the yield of simple atomic bombs. The improved-SCUDs which could have been used to deliver the nuclear weapons were barely more advanced than Hitler's V-2 rockets, but these were potentially effective systems for this purpose.

Only three of Iraq's seven nuclear sites were hit in the war. During January 1991, General Schwarzkopf reported that all known nuclear facilities had been destroyed. He was wrong. They had only been damaged. The unknown ones had not even been touched. The removal of this threat with the war and post-war UN inspections completely vindicated the West for hitting Iraq far harder than was necessary merely to liberate Kuwait. It explains the ceasefire terms that all of Iraq's weapons of mass destruction be destroyed. This was the real agenda.

As such, the Kuwaitis paid the price of the invasion and occupation of their country to give the international community a basis for pre-empting a far more serious global threat. Although Kuwait's liberation in itself was a worthy goal, there was far more at stake. The world fought Iraq to defend itself from a greater future - even a nuclear - war, with much of the human and financial bill paid by Kuwait and Saudi Arabia.

Yet, the idea that America came to Kuwait's rescue in her own interests is not a popular notion, even in Kuwait. When Mr Abdulaziz Al-Masaeed, a newspaper editor and the popularly-elected Speaker of the now-defunct Kuwaiti National Council, which served the function of Kuwait's suspended Parliament between early 1986 and the invasion, suggested in 1992 that the US had acted in its own interests, he was greeted with howls of protest in his own country. Kuwait's Crown Prince and Prime Minister went so far as to place ads in US newspapers explaining that these were one man's comments in a democracy, and in no way reflected any widespread ingratitude to America.

Al-Masaeed was, however, only expressing what many Kuwaitis were saying privately. He meant no ingratitude, but as an eminent individual in his eighties who had seen more history than most, he felt entitled to call it as he saw it. In retrospect, he could have said more clearly that Kuwaitis appreciated that America's and Kuwait's interests ran in parallel. However, few Kuwaitis doubt that America would not have stepped in so quickly had it not been in her own best interests to do so. Such is the nature of the world, a lesson driven home more recently with far greater bloodshed in Bosnia.

To Kuwaitis, the realization that the US went after Iraq in her own interests is not purely of academic interest. They know from history that Middle East alliances can shift as quickly as the desert sands. Pre-World War I, Britain helped Kuwait against the Ottomans only when her own interests were threatened. Similarly, Kuwait sheltered Ibn Saud, enabling him to recapture Riyadh and eventually build his Saudi Kingdom, only to have much of her land coveted by him in the 1920s, and handed over by the British. More recently, America was Iran's strongest supporter until the fall of the Shah, but in the 1980s, she virtually entered the Iran–Iraq War on Iraq's side. Even Egypt, the major Arab Coalition power after Saudi Arabia, once supported a Yemeni war with Saudi Arabia, and bombed Saudi towns.

Kuwait was lucky this time, and again in October 1994, that her interests coincided with those of Washington. She may not be so fortunate next time.

If the case for not capturing Baghdad is relatively clear-cut, the argument for stopping the war early is less so. Another day's fighting would certainly have caused much greater damage to the Iraqi Army, and robbed it of much of the equipment which it later used to suppress the internal uprisings, and even to threaten Kuwait again in October 1994, but that day would surely have seen more Allied deaths. The Shi'ites and Kurds paid the price of the tragic reality that a US or British soldier's life is worth more than many of theirs.

However, this has to be put into perspective. Much comment has been passed on George Bush's words at the time which were interpreted as saying that he would support the Iraqi rebellions. In such cases, people hear what they want to. The US had no arrangements with any rebels to come to their aid. Whatever the feelings of individual Allied soldiers, US intervention in Iraq beyond that required to free Kuwait, repatriate military POWs, and wreck Saddam's weapons programmes was simply not on the agenda.

The military campaign against Iraq was a triumph and a victory, even if it was incomplete and qualified. In fact, Saddam was an unsolved problem well before he invaded Kuwait, but had not been dealt with because it was impossible to marshal the necessary collective action needed to move against him. Kuwait was liberated, and the Western powers got what they wanted: the emasculation of Iraq's military potential, relative regional stability, easier access to military facilities in the Gulf, and the rule of international law. To the Allies, breaking the back of Saddam's military power was an objective at least as important as the liberation of Kuwait.

Every crisis has its postmortem. This one will be analysed for decades. However, a number of questions demand immediate attention.

The first is why Saddam invaded Kuwait when he did, on 2 August. If he had waited another two days, the Kuwaiti Crown Prince and Prime Minister and several of his Ministers, including the Amir's own brother, Sheikh Sabah Al-Ahmad, would have been in Baghdad for the continuation of the aborted Jeddah talks, and could have been held hostage, or even killed, with ease.

There are indications that the invasion itself – although planned for some time – was hastily executed, even botched, especially the Iraqi Special Forces operation to capture the Amir. Given their experience, and the infiltration of Iraqi commandos into Kuwait in July 1990, this should have been an easy operation. Iraqi forces were not quite ready for the operation when they were ordered to execute it. The limited use of the Iraqi Air Force in failing to bomb the camps of Kuwait's 35 Brigade and 15 Brigade, the hasty although masterful operation against the Ras Al-Jalayh naval base, and the failure to capture Kuwaiti oil tankers in port before they could set sail, bear this out.

One explanation is that after the Jeddah talks on 1 August, Saddam expected Kuwait to call in the Americans, as the UAE had two weeks earlier, thus rendering any incursion impossible as it would have brought him into direct conflict with US forces. He had to get in before the Americans arrived.

A second question is why Saddam did not simply stop at Mutla'a, or even withdraw to there any time after the invasion. The US would have found it more difficult to go to war if only half of Kuwait were occupied. As early as 2 August, the US Joint Chiefs of Staff Chairman, General Colin Powell, said he thought the US would go to war over Saudi Arabia, but doubted whether it would do so over Kuwait. Sanctions may have been applied, but not force, and Saddam may have got the cash he coveted, and maybe even the territory.

The 'best guess' answer is that by leaving half of Kuwait, and the Government alive, Saddam would have given the Kuwaitis the opportunity to mobilize international support, and turn what was left of the country into a US military camp. It was by no means certain at the time that other regional countries would oppose him with as much vigour on behalf of Kuwait.

The broader question is why Saddam even invaded at all. In the six-month build-up to the invasion, his main demand was for money. Kuwait and Saudi Arabia had eventually agreed to provide at least some of the funds he wanted, and to support a higher oil price. He must have known that the invasion would result in sanctions which would not only prevent him getting at Kuwaiti oil and financial assets, but also prevent him from selling his own oil, even if the Allies were not prepared to liberate Kuwait. By invading, he lost far more than he could ever have gained through extortion.

The answer to this question is probably that Saddam simply did not expect such strong international reaction. He may have gambled that the West would not embargo the 20% of the world's oil reserves he would control with Iraqi and Kuwaiti resources combined. If so, he miscalculated OPEC's ability to take up the slack, and the extent of strategic stocks held by importers. It is also possible that he was making even more money out of affecting the oil price on the oil futures and options markets. By putting pressure on the markets and then easing it, he has the ultimate insider trader's track, and can put profits directly into his own pocket without moving one drop of oil.

The popular answer to the question of why Saddam invaded at all, and when he did, is that it was an irrational, spur-of-the-moment decision by an egotistical dictator. That is an over-simplification. Iraqi preparations for taking Kuwait had been under way for at least several years. Documents captured by Kuwaiti forces in August 1990 suggest that ACC military exercises in Jordan earlier in 1990 were used as a rehearsal for the invasion. The extent of Iraqi infiltration into Kuwait in the months before the invasion is now well documented. Most of the official looting was extremely well planned.

Saddam certainly did not believe his own rhetoric, inherited from King Ghazi in the 1930s, and Abdul Karim Qassim in the 1960s, that Kuwait was part of Iraq. He would not otherwise have gone through the charade of an internal coup in the first week. He knew that an outright land grab would be internationally unacceptable. Another possible answer is that Saddam's judgement is simply atrocious. This is supported by his invasion of Iran, which he expected to be little more than a limited incursion. Instead, it cost Iraq eight years of war, and hundreds of thousands of casualties. Perhaps Saddam is just a slow learner with a big ego and a dangerous grasp on power.

Even if Kuwait had given in to Saddam's demands, it is by no means certain that he would not have invaded. Kuwait was well within her rights not to succumb to extortion. To have done so would have only invited more.

The burning question in the minds of many of the Human Shields and hostages is why Saddam let them go just 40 days before the UN war deadline. It is now known that Saddam regretted this. In fact, during the air war, his troops in Kuwait went looking for Westerners who had stayed behind.

The answer seems to be that Saddam thought that such a bold move at the time would remove Western public support for military action. It was not to be so. Saddam misunderstands the Western mentality. This was perhaps best demonstrated by his TV appearances with the hostages, especially little Stuart Lockwood. Saddam thought he was playing the kindly uncle; to viewers in the West, he came across as the incarnation of evil, even a pervert.

Only Saddam Hussein himself can answer these questions fully. Perhaps one day he will. What is certain is that the taking of Westerners as hostages worked against him from the beginning by confirming in the eyes of the Western public that he really was an evil man. It made the issue personal.

The greatest cost of war is the loss of human life. Much press coverage was given in the aftermath of the war to an estimate of Iraqi casualties of 100,000. Later, more reliable estimates suggested as few as 1,500 to 6,000 dead.

This is not inconceivable. Front-line Iraqi troops were so well dug-in that casualties from artillery and air attack were relatively light. Few were treated by Kuwaiti hospitals, most of which were operating throughout the war. Most Iraqi armour destroyed by the Allies had been abandoned. US forces, which captured the areas of heaviest fighting, buried only 577 bodies. Most vehicles on the much-photographed 'Highway of Death' at Mutla'a were in fact empty after the occupants fled the first attacks on foot. The highest estimate of dead from that was 400, all of which are included in the earlier US figure of 577. The Saudis killed 32 Iraqis at Khafji, although others died at sea, and in the incursions west of Khafji. Allied forces did kill Iraqi troops in ground combat, but the numbers were not huge.

Perhaps the next highest single casualty toll after Mutla'a was about 204 from the tragic attack on the Amariya bunker in Baghdad, and a reported 130 from Fulaijah. These innocent people and their families paid the price of Saddam's folly. Victory did not come cheaply for the Allies. They lost about 240 killed in action, and a further 776 wounded, a very high proportion by their own fire, and to single incidents such as the Iraqi SCUD missile attack on Dhahran, and the downing of a US Special Forces AC-130 gunship. Another 138 were killed and 2,978 injured in non-combat incidents before or during the fighting, and another several dozen Allied troops and civilians were killed by unexploded Allied or Iraqi ordnance after the cessation of hostilities. Six Western civilians – five British and one American – died either trying to escape from Kuwait, or in hiding or in Iraqi custody. A number of others are thought to have subsequently committed suicide as a result of the experience.

However, it was the Kuwaitis who paid the highest human price, relative to their population. An estimated 300 Kuwaitis died as a direct result of the invasion and occupation. This excludes premature infants born during the crisis who died from lack of care, or as a result of being removed from incubators. Another 604 individuals, mainly Kuwaitis, are unaccounted for, or thought by Kuwaiti authorities to be still held by Iraq. It took Iraq until September 1994 to admit that it had in fact held 45 of these people, for whom the Kuwaitis held captured documents proving that they had been in Iraqi custody, and until December 1994 to admit that they had held a further 11. In late 1995, Iraq admitted to having had 126 of them in custody, but claims to have lost track of such people, explaining that they fled from jails in Southern Iraq during the Shi'ite revolt, and have not been seen since. This is ridiculous. Several were senior officers of the rank of Colonel to Major-General, captured as part of the Resistance. Another was the head of the Ba'ath movement in Kuwait, and a personal friend of Saddam who refused to help him form a puppet government. A police state like Iraq does not simply lose such people.

With the passage of years, hope is fading for these people. Under Islamic law, missing people can be declared dead after four years, upon application to the court. This process can start at any time now, especially with women with missing husbands, and who want to remarry. Other people, especially parents of the young, will never write them off. Without bodies, there is still hope.

In total, Kuwait may have lost almost 1,000 citizens, proportionately equivalent to about 400,000 Americans, or 100,000 British.

Yet, the Kuwaiti deaths are only part of the story. The full extent of the atrocities inflicted on those in Kuwait became apparent only after liberation. The way in which many of those people died, and how the survivors suffered, is so horrible that even the Kuwaitis have not reported some of the worst cases. A number of people outside Kuwait during the occupation had exaggerated reports coming out of Kuwait. The media had eventually seen through this, and some of the reports had been turned against Kuwait, suggesting that they were universally unreliable. However, no amount of exaggeration could have prepared the world for the truth. All of these incidents are harrowing. Most have been independently verified.

The unofficial Kuwaiti explanation for not publicizing details of these horrors this is that people have suffered enough. There is little to gain at the cost of further suffering by surviving family members.

A more visible consequence of the occupation was the 650 raging oil fires the Iraqis left behind and oil pollution in the Gulf. For months, every day, up to four million barrels of crude, twice Kuwait's pre-invasion daily output, went up in flames, or gushed into oil lakes on the desert floor. Millions more gallons dumped into the Gulf by Iraq threatened the marine environment.

Initial fears of a mini nuclear winter proved unfounded. Kuwait pulled out all the stops to control the inferno. Kuwait Oil Company organised perhaps the largest and fastest airlifting of civilian equipment ever. The Kuwaiti Amir ceremoniously extinguished the last fire on 8 November, 1991, only 36 weeks after liberation. Experts, including the venerable Red Adair, who had predicted it would take four years to control the fires, were stunned.

Another challenge was the rivers of oil flooding into huge oil lakes from blown wells that had not caught fire. It took five years to clean up most of these. The process of decontaminating the sand will go on for many years.

Saudi Arabia actually bore more of the marine pollution than Kuwait. The prevailing tides and currents pushed the oil dumped into the Gulf away from Kuwait, and back onto Saudi beaches further south.

The fires were not the only pressing problem the Kuwaitis had to deal with. The Government returned to find a populace heavily armed with abandoned Iraqi weaponry, and angry at having endured the occupation. They were in no mood to be told what to do by anyone, especially those who had left. Elements of the Resistance felt more qualified to handle the country's security than returning soldiers who had seen little or no fighting. People wanted essential services restored immediately, and democracy reintroduced just as quickly.

This anger took time to pass. In fact, a noticeable schism between those who had stayed and those who had left persisted for at least a year. The stayers were far more outspoken, and their basic values had changed. Money and possessions meant less. Their priorities were family, friends, life's simple pleasures, and freedom of political expression.

A more serious problem was people who felt they had something to prove, particularly a few hotheads who tried to settle scores with local Palestinians and others for real or imagined sins of collaboration. Most Palestinians had acted honourably - some had even fought with the Resistance - but a few turncoats gave most of them a bad name. About 20 were killed. Even more were detained. Some were tortured. The spirit of hatred had not left with the Iraqis. Sixty more Palestinians are still missing, whether in Iraq or Kuwait, or buried with the anonymous dead of Mutla'a Ridge.

Most of the misbehaving seemed to come from people who had spent the occupation outside the country, and felt that they had something to prove.

Those who had stayed throughout were less inclined towards vengeance. They knew what the score was, and were tired of fear and torture and killing.

None of this was condoned by the Government, and occurred while it was still trying to re-establish law and order. However, those Kuwaitis who had stayed were aware of who had collaborated, and who had not. Many Palestinian families were protected by Kuwaiti neighbours until the rage subsided. Tragically, most of the Palestinians killed were innocent. Most of those who had worked with the Iraqis had long since left town for Jordan.

Large numbers of Palestinians left or were deported from Kuwait over the next two years, mainly because there were no jobs for them. The Government had decided to reduce reliance on expatriates in every sector, and without jobs, they had no place in Kuwait. A few were seen as security risks. Those who had left were not allowed to return, even if they had jobs waiting for them.

The Palestinians had come to Kuwait as a business arrangement and had broken the contract. A number protested that they had built modern Kuwait, so deserved special consideration. The Kuwaiti reply was simple: if they had been interested only in building civilizations, they should have gone to Mali or Somalia. They had come to work, and, like any expatriates, had been rewarded for their efforts. There have indeed been injustices but, tragically, the Kuwait Palestinians had to pay for the PLO's lack of support for Kuwait.

There were even suggestions from foreign journalists that Kuwait should have given citizenship to Palestinian long-term residents. This imposes foreign notions of naturalization on Kuwait. As a huge importer of labour, if Kuwait conferred citizenship on all long-stayers, even just Arabs, it would soon dilute its national identity out of existence. Furthermore, the PLO and the Arab League are themselves against this; Palestinians who are given citizenship of other countries will soon forget about Palestine.

There are still about 40,000 Palestinians in Kuwait today, with their breadwinners working in the private sector or embassies. The numbers are down from about 450,000 pre-invasion, and 100,000 at liberation, but this is still a relatively high proportion of their world population. A similar ratio of Egyptians would be 520,000. Despite Egypt's key Coalition role, barely half that number of Egyptians are working in Kuwait. In effect, Kuwait is still giving preferential treatment to Palestinians despite the PLO's treachery.

Later on, Kuwait received criticism for heavy sentences, including the death penalty, handed down by State Security Courts, on collaborators. No death sentences were carried out, nor will they be. Unfortunately for Kuwait, the trials were conducted in Arabic, and some reporters got their translation wires crossed. All the trials were public, and well-attended by recognized international observers. The justice may have been harsh, but collaboration is a serious matter, and implicated the guilty in the deaths of innocent people.

At one time, some 260 individuals were actually serving time in Kuwait for collaboration. About 20 of these were once on death row, but their sentences have been effectively commuted to a custodial term. The only people executed judicially in Kuwait since Liberation – about half a dozen in all – met their fate for murder and rape crimes unconnected with the occupation.

One man who is in little danger from his death sentence is Ala'a Hussein Ali, the head of the short-lived 'Provisional Free Kuwait Government'. He was tried and sentenced in absentia as he is still living in Iraq. The other seven members of his puppet government, all Kuwaitis, returned and were cleared after investigations proved that they had been forced into the charade.

If you land at Kuwait Airport today and drive into the city, you may notice an occasional rumbling as your tyres pass over the impressions made in the road by Iraqi tanks. You may even see a few burned-out houses. The greatest damage visible in the city today is the burned-out Salam Palace Hotel, a beached converted cruise liner. If you happen to visit the International Hotel, now renamed the Safir International, you may see the bullet holes where the sleeping car park attendant was wounded in the early hours of 2 August , 1990.

It doesn't look much considering the scale of the conflict, and reports of wholesale devastation immediately after liberation. The Kuwaitis made a massive effort to repair most of the damage. Relatively few buildings were completely destroyed, despite the Iraqis' best efforts. Most of the damage was looting, and trashing of the interiors of buildings. The Iraqis had a curious habit of defaecating everywhere they could. The clean-up took months.

The most serious damage was out of the public eye, in power stations, desalination plants, oil refineries, and KAF bases. Kuwait's own hardened aircraft shelters were destroyed by the Allies in case the Iraqis were using them to hide missiles, or chemical or biological weapons. Nevertheless, much of the power, water production and refining capacity has been restored. Intermittent power and water were back within six weeks of liberation.

The Iraqis could have done much more damage if they had known how to. They were essentially a 1930s army trying to wreck a 1990s infrastructure. For example, they did not realize the trouble they could have caused simply by destroying computers and databases. They did so to a certain extent, stealing computers and years of research data from the Kuwait Institute for Scientific Research, but they left the computers of the banks, and KOC, virtually intact.

This is not to understate the magnitude of Kuwait's losses. Compensation which Kuwait can claim from Iraq through the UN is preliminarily estimated at US$117 billion for the public and private sector, and individuals, and US$53 billion for the oil sector. This excludes the losses of foreign firms, and expatriates. As part of the ceasefire terms, Iraq is obliged to pay 30% of its oil revenues into a compensation fund, but it will be many years before anyone is paid in full, if at all. In addition to this, Kuwait will be pursuing as yet undetermined losses for foregone oil production, and damage to her reservoirs, through the World Court in The Hague.

Less visible than the physical damage, but infinitely harder to repair, is the human damage. Although perhaps only 100,000 out of 650,000 Kuwaitis remained in Kuwait at the time of the liberation, many of those had suffered trauma. Thousands more had been held in Iraqi POW camps, or by the *Mukhabarat*. Most were not tortured, but many were. For the lesser torture victims, extracted fingernails have grown back, burns have healed with ambiguous scars, and broken bones have been reset. Visitors to Kuwait have asked where the serious torture victims are. The answer is simple. The Iraqis killed their serious torture victims.

Perhaps the greatest burden of the occupation fell on the Kuwaiti women. Conservative estimates put the number of rapes at several thousand. Other estimates range higher. About 400 Kuwaiti women reported their cases to psychiatric centres set up by the Government after liberation, but a far greater number of women are thought to have hidden the event out of shame.

The inevitable consequences of some of these rapes were unwanted pregnancies. This was very difficult for a conservative Muslim society such as Kuwait to accept, but it has done its best. Abortion is generally illegal under Islam, but the problem was so serious that local religious leaders issued a *Fatwa* (Muslim religious ruling) allowing women to travel abroad to obtain abortions provided the foetus was no more than sixteen weeks old. Many women took advantage of this, but those who were raped and conceived in the first four months of the occupation had to carry their babies to full term.

A number of families have cared for the babies as their own. Others have been unable to cope with bringing up a child fathered by an enemy in violence, and given them up to the Kuwait Orphanage. About 37 children who are thought to be the offspring of Iraqi rape are cared for there. They are treated with all the privileges of citizenship. No mention is allowed of their origins.

For the traumatized, the mental scars run deep, but their society does not encourage them to deal openly with mental pain. The Amiri Diwan has therefore established a Social Development Office to try to change this ingrained cultural attitude. In December 1991, the Kuwait Health Ministry established a centre manned by Danish clinical psychologists experienced in the trauma of torture, as well as by Kuwaiti doctors. This aspect of the crisis will run for many years as Saddam's lasting wound on Kuwait.

America asked Kuwait for two things in return for liberation: that the country pay its share of the bill, and that it would re-establish democracy. The first request was met in full. The second has been largely honoured.

Critics of Kuwait during the crisis charged that it was a feudal state, without any meaningful public participation in the political process. Few of these people had been to Kuwait, could even define feudalism, or knew what they were talking about. Kuwait does have democracy, but of a version which owes more to its own history and Islamic culture than to the traditions of Westminster or Washington. In fact, it is the only Gulf State with a political system that even resembles a participative democracy.

This was amply demonstrated in October 1992 and again in October 1996 when elections were held for a 50-member National Assembly. Both campaigns was as feisty as any, with an 80% - plus voter turnout. The elections were hailed internationally as free and fair. Parliaments considered strongly independent of the Government were elected. The Cabinet is still largely made up of unelected appointees, as in the US, but a number of Ministers are drawn from the Parliament. The final say still rests with the Al-Sabah, but they have to listen to the people's representatives, as they always have.

However, the greatest criticism of the process was that the electorate - especially for the 1992 elections - was limited to males over 21, with first-class citizenship: that is, those able to trace their family heritage in Kuwait back to 1920. Out of a population of 650,000, of which about 400,000 are of voting age, only 81,400 could vote. The balance comprises those holding other classes of citizenship, armed forces personnel, the police, and women. According to many Kuwaitis, their democracy is standing on one leg.

More citizens were enfranchized for the 1996 elections, and even more will be for the year 2000, but the question of women getting the vote is the major issue. It has the support in principle of the Crown Prince and Prime Minister, and equality of men and women before the law is guaranteed by the Constitution. Against this is arrayed centuries of tradition, patriarchy, and an election law which allows only men to vote. Some men would be quite happy to see women voting and holding office. Others want women to have the vote, but not to be eligible to run for Parliament. Still others see the issue of women being denied the vote as non-negotiable.

The issue is more complicated than it ever was for the suffragettes in the West. The greatest inhibitor is the social mores which prevent unrelated men and women from socializing with each other outside work. Most political discussions are held in traditional *diwaniahs*, generally an all-male environment. It would be impossible for conservative women to attend such meetings, and difficult even for more liberated women. Furthermore, there is a fear - perhaps unfounded - that extending the vote to women would in fact result in a more conservative Parliament. This might ultimately reduce the extensive rights of independence such as working, driving and education which Kuwaiti women enjoy, and which are denied to most of their Gulf sisters. The reason: many of the more conservative voters have several wives, who will vote as their husbands tell them, for traditionalist candidates.

It will take time for these barriers to fall. In the meantime, the women are leading the assault. They picketed electoral offices in the runup to both the 1992 and 1996 ballots. They continue to be vocal. One of their main arguments is women's performance during the Occupation as effective members of the Resistance. Some of them died just as bravely and brutally as the men. Many women hold senior posts in public service, academia and commerce. The current Kuwait University rector, Dr Faiza Khorafi, is a conservative woman. Women serve as Faculty Deans, and Ministerial Undersecretaries. Others run major businesses, or hold senior executive positions, including Miss Seham Razouki, a Managing Director of Kuwait Petroleum Corporation.

However, for many women, electoral rights takes second place to social rights. Single women are more concerned with being able to live away from the family home if they choose to do so, or marry their chosen husband. If they marry a non-Kuwaiti, then their children bear his nationality, but cannot be Kuwaitis. These basic rights are more keenly missed than the vote.

Kuwait will have to deal with these problems itself. Nevertheless, there is one aspect of political life on which almost all parties agree. This is the role of the Al-Sabah. One body of opinion favours reducing their influence, but the strongest suggestion so far has been that the posts of Prime Minister and Crown

Prince be held by separate individuals. Even this has not received popular support. The Al-Sabah have played a central role in governing Kuwait for over 240 years. Most see no need to change a system that works.

The crisis has brought about a sea change in Kuwaiti attitudes. Prior to the invasion, they were strong supporters of broader Arab interests. The local press was full of the standard Arab rhetoric.

This has changed markedly. In March 1991, the six GCC States joined together with Egypt and Syria under the 'Damascus Declaration' whereby Egypt and Syria would provide troops to defend the GCC in return for economic aid. That alliance never got off the ground. Kuwait soon sent the Egyptian and Syrian troops home because of trouble with them looting and allowing Iraqi infiltrators to bribe their way into Kuwait through their lines. The alliance has held perhaps half a dozen Foreign Minister level meetings. Its communiques generally discuss anything but the substance of the declaration.

The Kuwaitis know that their real friends are the Western permanent members of the UN Security Council, even if they have to pay for that friendship through major contracts. Joint military exercises are held regularly with Western forces, while GCC Ministers still talk about a joint local force, as they did for years prior to the invasion. The wisdom of moving closer to the West was starkly illustrated in October 1994, when Iraqi forces moved to the Kuwaiti border. Only the Americans and British were able to leave no doubt in Saddam's mind that he was in for a second drubbing if he went too far.

The change in Kuwaiti thinking was best demonstrated to me by a conversation with a Kuwaiti friend in July 1991, when Coalition soldiers of a dozen nationalities could still be seen walking around Kuwait City.

'Bader,' I said, 'it's fantastic that all these fellows from all over the world came to help you!' I then added a little joke which I immediately regretted for its lack of taste, saying:'The only ones who aren't here besides the Iraqis are the Israelis!' Bader smiled and said: 'John, the Israelis, they are more than welcome. We will even build a camp for them next to the Americans.'

Kuwait has not forgotten the dead of the other nations who came to its rescue. The Kuwait-based British Memorial Fund, made up of Kuwaitis and British expatriates, brought to Kuwait the families of the 47 British servicemen who died, and some of those who were seriously injured in 1992 and again in 1993. In 1994 and 1995, they hosted summer holidays for them in the UK. The US relatives visited in early 1993, under the aptly-named 'Project Hope'. These family members have been overwhelmed by the gratitude and generosity of the Kuwaitis. Nothing but God and time can truly heal their sense of loss, but being able to visit the country which their loved ones died for, and see it free, has reassured many of them that the sacrifice was not in vain. The public at home may have forgotten, but Kuwait has not.

Many of the expatriates caught up in the invasion have returned to their jobs in Kuwait. For the vast majority of returnees, the sight of Kuwait free again was the best therapy they could have had. They needed that closure to lay to rest an experience that no one who was not there can fully understand.

Colonel Salem Al-Sarour of Kuwait's 35 Brigade, which took on the invading Iraqis in a tank battle, is now a major-general, and heads Kuwait's Land Forces. His KAF colleague, Colonel Saber Al-Suwaiden, who stayed behind with his men at Ali Al-Salem base and became a POW instead of escaping, is also now a major-general, and leads the reconstituted KAF. Colonel Fahd Al-Ameer, who became one of the Resistance leaders, also now a major-general, is the Deputy Chief of Staff of the Kuwaiti Armed Forces.

Most of the other surviving Resistance figures such as Sheikh Sabah Nasir, Major-Generals Mohammed Al-Bader and Khalid Boodai, Colonel Mahmoud Al-Dossari, and the Ahmadi oilmen have simply faded back into what they were before, been promoted, or retired. Sheikh Ali Salem Al-Ali is now chief of the Kuwait Ports Authority. All of them are the most reluctant of heroes.

The Home Front did not collapse after Liberation. In the US, Citizens for Free Kuwait eventually gave birth to the Kuwait-America Foundation.

In the UK, the Association for a Free Kuwait and the Free Kuwait Campaign wound up. The London Gulf Support Group folded shortly after the hostages returned, but the couple running the Coventry branch continued and turned it into a living for a while. Of more immediate value was an organisation called Hostages Of the Middle East, or HOME, which arranged for UK wardens Chris Bell, Mike Devey and Sandy Macmillan, and Dave Dorrington, and Paul Cienciala, the son of a Human Shield, to return to Kuwait shortly after Liberation. They flew in by RAF Hercules to conduct property surveys of the homes of members, and to secure or repatriate whatever they could. The task was heartbreaking. Almost every residence had been thoroughly looted, even of things such as family photos which were of no value to the looters. Many homes had been wantonly trashed, to the extent of excrement being deposited liberally on floors. Now, even HOME has folded.

Iraq did, however, comply with some of the terms of the ceasefire resolution by returning looted bullion, and almost all the collection of the Kuwait National Museum. In fact, early in the Occupation, the Iraqis had sent archaeologists from their Antiquities Department in Baghdad to pack up the collection and transfer it to Baghdad. Most of the collection which was stored in the museum itself was undamaged, but items held in Kuwait outside the museum at the home of the owners were looted and have not been recovered.

However, according to the Security Council, Iraq still holds about 9,000 pieces of Kuwaiti military equipment - including such items as APCs and missile launchers - and 6,000 dual-use items. It has returned many other items, including aircraft and tanks, but has been most reluctant to give everything back, even refusing to admit in the face of satellite photo evidence that it still has them. Apparently, according to the Americans, Saddam even had the cheek to use some of it when he threatened Kuwait in October 1994.

The great Arab losers besides Iraq were Jordan, the Palestinians, and Yemen. Jordan had been in a particularly unfortunate position before the invasion.

Jordan had apparently aligned herself with Iraq, notably at the May 1990 Arab Summit, to secure her regular supply of cheap Iraqi oil. This required King Hussein to be uncharacteristically critical of the West and those Arab countries, notably Kuwait and the other GCC states, that did not support Iraq.

Because of her close relations with Iraq, Jordan was widely and unfairly considered guilty by association. She was in a no-win situation. Although not the target of the UN embargo against Iraq, she became one of its greatest victims. Her losses in exports, transit trade, private remittances, and official aid were in the billions of dollars. She also had to absorb hundreds of thousands of refugee Palestinians and Jordanians from the Gulf.

However, Jordan was not a complete loser. The arrival of the Palestinians and Jordanians from Kuwait initially strained her economy, but they brought Kuwaiti funds and skills with them. Jordan received an even greater cash injection during 1991 and 1992 when the Kuwaiti Government, and some companies, paid the end-of-service benefits due to these people. Jordan is now consequently far healthier economically, with improved prospects.

Yet, there remains a lurking suspicion in some corners that all may not be what it seems as far as King Hussein is concerned. Those with an eye to history recall that he has never forgiven the Iraqis for the brutal 1958 murder of his cousin and closest boyhood friend, Faisal II of Iraq, in the revolution that overthrew the Iraqi Hashemite monarchy. There is still a dormant Hashemite claim to the Iraqi throne which the king subtly resurrected in August 1995, following the defection of Saddam's sons-in-law to Jordan.

The King, an astute man, may even have been concerned in 1990 that Saddam had designs on his kingdom. There is a theory that Jordan's great encouragement of Iraq during the Iran–Iraq war was more to keep Saddam off the king's back, which it did very effectively. With the Iran–Iraq war over, Saddam was again in a position to cast his expansionist eye elsewhere. Jordan, a country with barely the financial means to survive as an independent state, was a prime candidate. Saddam's Arab Cooperation Council may have been seen as a first step in him forming an Iraqi–Jordanian political entity, which he would eventually come to dominate. King Hussein's recruiting of Egypt and Yemen into the ACC may have been an attempt to offset Iraqi influence in it.

The wily king may then have concluded that trouble elsewhere was the best way to ensure that Saddam was too preoccupied to pursue any ambitions over Jordan. Little Kuwait, and to a lesser extent, the UAE, were perfect bait.

Those who watch Saddam closely know that, at the time, he placed great store by King Hussein's counsel. If the king had suggested that the Western response to Iraq taking Kuwait would be limited to sanctions, a breaking off of diplomatic relations, and a few meaningless UN Resolutions, that the Saudis would never allow sufficient Western forces into their lands to eject Iraq from Kuwait, and that he might just get away with it, this may have been enough to convince Saddam to move. The king, for his part, knew that if Kuwait were taken, then Saudi Arabia was threatened, and therefore in the long run the US would have to pull Saddam's teeth more effectively than the Iranians were ever able to. This is precisely what happened. With Saddam's military smashed, his economy in ruins, and his influence limited to his own back yard, King Hussein was free to pursue the closer ties he craved with Israel, and to receive the massive US aid he needs to stay afloat. On top of that, he still gets cheap oil from Iraq, and acts as its major port. He may even eventually put a Hashemite back on the Iraqi throne at some time in the future. The king was neither for Saddam nor against Kuwait. His priority was the survival of his Hashemite kingdom, and Kuwait was sacrificed to that end.

The PLO was also in a difficult position before the invasion. It had become dangerously isolated in the Arab world after making significant compromises over Israel. However, the US had cut its links with the PLO after a dissident faction had attacked an Israeli beach just two months before the invasion, thus stalling the Middle East peace process. On top of its problems with the Arabs, the PLO had found itself losing its new-found acceptance in the West.

Yasser Arafat's solution was to try to force the US back to the negotiating table by taking a harder line on other regional issues. Saddam's confrontation with the West in early 1990 provided the perfect opportunity for this. Unfortunately for Arafat, this dispute grew into the invasion of Kuwait, one of his greatest benefactors. He was unable to get off the speeding bandwagon when he needed to. This undid years of his own careful diplomacy, and alienated many of his Western supporters, and the Arabs' friends among Israeli liberals. He can count himself fortunate that the West and the Israelis are prepared to deal with him. Most of the Gulf States know him too well to do so.

As far as most of the world is concerned, the Gulf War is over. This is not quite so. Saddam continues to flaunt UN Resolutions where he can, and cause untold suffering to his own people. Allied warplanes still patrol recently-expanded no-fly zones in the south and north of Iraq. It took until October 1994, another stand-off with Allied forces, and another UN Resolution, before Iraq accepted the UN demarcation of the border, and recognized Kuwaiti sovereignty in terms acceptable to the UN. Saddam was even implicated in an assassination attempt on George Bush when the latter visited Kuwait to receive the gratitude of the Kuwaiti people in May 1993.

Kuwait has recovered and is again prosperous and peaceful. The Allied troops are home, as are the Human Shields. However, the world has all but forgotten the 604 Kuwaiti and other individuals who are unaccounted for by Iraq. For all their platitudes, none of the 'grovellers' have seen fit to travel to Baghdad and plead for these people. The Western media are similarly uninterested. There simply is not enough glory in it. This task is now left up to Kuwait, the ICRC, and the professional diplomats at the UN.

It is not only these 604 people, and the families awaiting news of them, who are prisoners. The entire Iraqi nation, all 17 million of them, excluding Saddam and his inner circle, are themselves hostages of sorts. They have been brutalized for a generation, and deserve better. The wealth of Iraq has been squandered futilely. There will be no stability in the region until Saddam and his clique are gone, and the Iraqis themselves learn to be productive members of the world community. Kuwait is free, and grateful for it. Iraq is not.

MARTYRS AND MISSINGS

This Appendix is divided into four parts. The first (pages 635-643) includes the lists of all known Kuwaitis who died as a direct result of the invasion and occupation, the foreign spouses of such people, and non-Kuwaiti individuals who served in the Kuwaiti Armed Forces, or Resistance. In Kuwait, these people are referred to as 'Martyrs'.

The second part (page 643) lists the names, where available, or otherwise, the summary numbers by nationality of all known civilian foreigners who died as a direct result of the invasion and occupation, including Human Shields. The third part (pages 644 and 645) is the list of all known Western Allied service personnel who are generally accepted have lost their lives as a result of the crisis. It excludes non-Kuwaiti Arab, African and Asian service personnel and Iraqis as information on their names is either unavailable, or was excessively difficult to obtain reliably. However, where possible, numbers of these individuals by nationality are included.

The fourth and final part (pages 646-649) is a list of those who are still unaccounted for as a result of the crisis, known as 'The Missings' in Kuwait.

These lists are not exhaustive, but are the most comprehensive I have been able to compile from a variety of sources, including the Kuwaiti Ministries of Defence and Interior, Amiri Diwan, the UN Compensation Claims Commission, various foreign embassies in Kuwait, the US Department of Defense, and several religious organisations in Kuwait who have taken an interest in the Missing Persons. Although believed to be substantially complete and correct, with the exception of the lists of US, British and French service personnel, they are not officially approved, nor are they verified by the respective Governments, UN, or International Committee of the Red Cross.

In Part 1, the list of Kuwaiti Martyrs is in order of presumed date of death, showing brief details of how the individual met their death. The actual date of death, particularly for deaths during the occupation, may differ from that recorded because of difficulties in determining when death occurred. In such cases, the recorded date is generally that of when the body was identified or recovered. Such details were not generally available for the people listed in Part 2, so they have been listed generally by name. For service personnel in Part 3, in order to put matters in perspective, I have provided summary figures of those killed in action, as most service personnel died in accidents.

Part 4, the list of Missings, is in alphabetical order, by family name, and shows the estimated age of each individual at the time of their disappearance. It is based on a translation of the only publicly available list of those who are unaccounted for as a result of the crisis, or who are thought by the Kuwaiti authorities to be still in Iraqi custody, as provided by the Islamic World Committee of the Social Reform Society. It includes only names and nationalities, and ages where this is known. Dates of disappearance, and circumstances of going missing are only available for certain individuals so, for brevity and consistency, are excluded for everyone.

The Kuwait National Committee for Missing and Prisoners of War Affairs, an official organisation established on 5 May, 1991, separate from the Social Reform

Society, and the body officially charged with pursuing the issue of the Missing Persons, maintains that 604 non-Iraqi individuals are still missing or unaccounted for as a result of the crisis. 537 of these are Kuwaiti males, and 6 are Kuwaiti females. The remainder, comprising 2 women and 59 men, are Saudis, Iranians, Egyptians, Syrians, Indians, Lebanese, Stateless individuals with an association to Kuwait and one individual each from Bahrain, Oman, and the Philippines. There are also an undetermined number of missing Jordanians, Palestinians and Yemenis which are not included on this list.

Of the 543 Kuwaitis which the Kuwaiti National Committee for Missing and Prisoners of War Affairs claims are being held by Iraq, Iraq has apparently admitted to having held a total of 126 of these individuals during the occupation, but claims to have lost track of them, as they were supposedly held in prisons in southern Iraq, and escaped during the Shi'ite uprisings in March 1991. According to Iraq, they are 'Missing in Action'. According to the Kuwaitis, they are 'Prisoners of War'. It is unlikely that the two sides will come to a common understanding anytime soon.

The issue of the Missing Persons is extremely complex. These individuals went missing in a variety of ways. Some were arrested as part of the Kuwaiti Resistance and are thought to have been executed, but their remains have never been found, perhaps because were held and killed in Iraq, and are buried there. They may even have been in the *Mishatel* Agricultural Complex in Kuwait itself, which the *Mukhabarat* were using as a prison, when it was bombed by the Allies. Others left Kuwait in the early days of the occupation either as members of the armed forces, to bring salvaged Kuwaiti military vehicles and aircraft to Saudi Arabia, or as civilians to bring their families to safety, and then tried to infiltrate back into Kuwait. They were seen leaving Saudi Arabia, but never reached their destinations in Kuwait. Presumably, they were intercepted by Iraqi troops on the border.

By far the greatest number of Missing Persons were arrested in the last weeks of the occupation, particularly young men. These round-ups also included other Arabs, Indians and Iranians, often because they had not changed the number plates of their cars to Iraqi ones, or had not registered with the occupying authorities. Most were held in prisons in southern Iraq, and may have been killed in the Shi'ite uprising, when there were massive prison break-outs, and Iraqi Government forces ruthlessly restored order. The Iraqi Government have admitted that they held Kuwaitis in southern Iraq at the time, and have lost track of them as a result of the turmoil then.

The possibility that such people may have lost their lives in the circumstances described above has been confirmed by other Kuwaitis, Arabs, Asians, and a sole Westerner who escaped from the jails, and successfully made their way back to Kuwait. If such people were killed, it is unlikely that, as escaped prisoners, they would have had identification documents on them. They would have been buried as persons unknown.

However, people who were held in prisons other than where the uprising took place may be alive, but imprisoned under false names, perhaps as Iraqi citizens. Many Kuwaitis, when arrested, routinely gave false names to protect their families, and had forged documentation to back up their new identity.

Actually, in the month following the ceasefire, Iraq repatriated about 4,000 Kuwaiti military POWs - including, without exception, all members of the

Kuwaiti military and police captured in early August 1990 - and 3,000 civilian internees. They later returned 21 members of the Al-Sabah family. The initial releases concentrated on people who had been held together in relatively large groups. At the time, the Iraqis seemed to be sticking to their word to release everyone, but the co-operation stopped when Allied forces withdrew from Iraqi territory. Those left behind had generally been arrested individually or in small groups, and had never been held with their compatriots. A few such people were seen in Iraqi jails by earlier returnees, and had been expected to follow on later repatriations, were never seen again.

The Kuwaiti cause has not been helped by the fact that early lists of Missing Persons were manifestly inaccurate. The first two lists, prepared in March and April 1991 before the establishment of the Kuwait National Committee, contained over 11,000 names, many of which were duplications. Other people were listed several times under different variations of their names, which is a common problem with the construction of Arabic names. By June 1991, the National Committee had settled on a list of about 3,800 names, which was further reduced to 2,443 by September 1991 as more information came to light, although very few, if any, Kuwaitis had been repatriated since May 1991. This third list also omitted Stateless Arabs who had not worked for the Kuwaiti Government, Jordanians and Palestinians, who were then considered not to be the responsibility of the Kuwaiti Government.

A fourth National Committee list was compiled in October 1991, but still contained inaccuracies. By March 1992, three lists later, this had been reduced to about 850. Later that year, the list settled at 625 individuals, and had been properly and professionally verified, with advice from the ICRC. Many of the changes between the lists were Kuwaiti women who were married to Iraqis, and are living in Iraq of their own free will.

During 1995, the list was further reduced to the present 604 as the remains of several individuals who had been listed as missing were identified. A number of other individuals had been on the list of 625 under two names, although it was known by the Kuwaitis that this was the case. The reason behind this was to ensure that Iraq accounted for these people under whatever name was available for them. During ICRC-sponsored discussions with the Iraqis, it was agreed to treat these people under one name. As such, the list of 604 is unlikely to reduce any further. However, the inaccuracies in the earlier lists have bolstered Iraq's contention that the issue of the Missing Persons is a political ploy to ensure that UN sanctions remain indefinitely on Iraq.

Further information on the Missing Persons may be available from the Kuwait National Committee for Missing and Prisoners of War Affairs on Kuwait (965) 552-3164, 552-3162 or 3, or fax 552-4749, or from the Social Reform Society on Kuwait, (965) 257-2208 or 9, fax 257-2206.

2 AUGUST, 1990
6 BRIGADE, MUTLA'A
1. Al-SHAMMERI, Obeid S. 33
   Sergeant
   Killed in early engagement at Mutla'a from several gunshots after Iraqis ignored his orders to stop.
2. Al-ANZI, Mufreh K.   33
   Sergeant
   Called to report for duty in the early hours of the Invasion. Shot by the Iraqis on his way. Died of wounds 4 August, 1990.

80 BRIGADE, JAHRA
3. Al-KANDARI, Abdelkarim T.   24
   Captain
4. Al-MUTAIRI, Rafie A.   45
   Warrant Officer
5. Al-THUFEIRI, Falah S. 45
   Warrant Officer
   (Saudi national serving in Kuwaiti forces)
6. Al-ANZI, Khalaf A.   32
   First Sergeant
7. Al-SHAMMERI, Idris B. 34
   Sergeant
8. Al-ANZI, Ahmad N.   34
   Private

KUWAIT NAVY, JALAYH
9. Al-SALEM, Jamal S.   33
   First Lieutenant
   Wounded at entrance to Ras Al-Jalayh Naval Base when trying to enter the base around dawn to assist in its defence. According to several reports, the Iraqis attacking the base prevented him from receiving medical treatment, and beat him as he lay wounded. Died of haemorrhage.

KUWAIT COASTGUARD
10. IBRAHIM, Abduljaleel I.   21
    Died of wounds when struck early morning by Iraqi gunfire in Shuwaikh when attempting to report for duty.

35 BRIGADE, ATRAF
11. Al-MUTAIRI, Mutlaq M.40
    First Sergeant
12. Al-SHAMMERI, Freih B. 30
    Lance Corporal
13. Al-ANZI, Mo'hd Q.   35
    Sergeant
14. Al-SHAMMERI, Hamoud M.   37
    Lance Corporal

15. Al-THUFEIRI, Safnan M.   33
    Lance Corporal
16. Al-SHAMMERI, Hassan R.   32
    Sergeant

JIWAN/ MUBARAK CAMPS
15 BRIGADE
17. Al-SHAMMERI, Ghazwan H.   32
    First Sergeant
18. Al-THUFEIRI, Rashid K.36
    Sergeant
19. Al-ANZI, Ahmad K.   32
    Sergeant
20. Al-SHAMMERI, Daham H.   32
    Private
21. Al-SABEAI, Sahami M. 45
    Lance Corporal

SIGNALS CORPS
22. MARWAN, Abbas A.   32
    Warrant Officer
23. Al-ANZI, Abbas S.   46
    Warrant Officer,
24. Al-ANZI, Mohsen A.   37
    First Sergeant
25. Al-THUFEIRI, Ibrahim J.   31
    Sergeant
26. Al-SUBAYEE, Ibrahim A.21
    Lance Corporal
27. AMIN, Mohammed O.   24
    Conscript

OTHER ARMY UNITS/ CORPS
28. Al-MUTAIRI, Jashayn A.32
    Captain, HQ Company
    Unable to reach his own base on the morning of 2 August, so reported to Jiwan Camp. Killed by rocket-propelled grenade.
29. Al-ANZI, Salem M.   32
    Warrant Officer,
    Military College
30. Al-FADLI, Jassim N.   38
    First Sergeant
31. HATHAB, Abdulrahman N.   39
    Sergeant
    (Jordanian national serving in Kuwaiti forces)
32. Al-SHAMMERI, Moh'd J.27
    Lance Corporal
    Personnel and Manpower
    Administration Unit
    Died of wounds, August 10th.
33. Al-ANZI, Ahmad S.   26
    Private, Kuwait Army
    Training Corps

34. Al-FARHAN, Kulaib S. 40
    Warrant Officer
    Public Affairs and Moral
    Guidance Directorate
35. Al-ANZI, Marai N.   36
    First Sergeant
    Public Affairs and Moral
    Guidance Directorate
36. TURKI, Abdullah A.   35
    First Sergeant, Public
    Affairs and Moral
    Guidance Directorate

NATIONAL GUARD
37. Al-MAJIDI, Muttar G. 37
    Warrant Officer,
    National Guard
38. Al-ABANI, Mohammed J.   31
    Corporal, 3rd Infantry
    Battalion, National Guard
39. Al-LANGWI, Jamal S. 28
    Lance Corporal, Economic
    Services, National Guard
40. Al-KHRENAIGH, Ali S. 24
    Lance Corporal, Financial
    Department
41. Al-AZMI, Salman N.   32
    Lance Corporal,
    Mechanised Infantry
    Battalion
42. Al-KHOUSALI, Majid R.21
    Lance Corporal, Public
    Services
43. Al-FADHLI, Tarek M.   18
    Economic Services
44. Al-KHASEELI, Mansour K.   20
    Guardsman, 1st Ifantry
    Battalion
45. Al-SHAMMERI, Hamad K.   19
    Guardsman, National
    Guard Special Forces

AMIRI DIWAN
46. Al-AZMI, Rajan W.   25
    Lance Corporal, 3rd
    Infantry Battalion,
    National Guard
    Killed by gunshot to chest, early morning.

DASMAN PALACE
47. Al-SABAH, Fahd A.   44
    Chairman, Olympic
    Committee
48. Al-SHAMMERI, Musheb M.   28
    Lance Corporal,
    Amiri Guard
49. Al-ADWANI, Mishal N. 21
    Conscript, Amiri Guard/
    Operator, KNPC

50. Al-ANZI, Eid K.   61
    Civil Servant, Amiri Diwan
51. Al-RUWAILI, Farhan S.45
    Retainer in Amiri Diwan
    (Saudi national resident in Kuwait.)

KUWAIT AIR FORCE
52. Al-RASHEEDI, Faiz A. 31
    Lieutenant Colonel
53. Al-SAYAGH, Thia A.   36
    First Lieutenant
54. JABER, Kamil R.   28
    First Sergeant
55. Al-FADAGH, Hassan T. 18
    Lance Corporal
    All four were killed when their Puma helicopter was shot down by 'friendly fire' in error near Ahmadi.
56. SAEEDI, Fahaid R.   27
    Corporal
57. Al-THUFEIRI, Warid M. 31
    Warrant Officer
    Killed in Commander's office and operations building at Ali Al-Salem KAF base, 5:45p.m. during Iraqi bombing attack.

KUWAIT FIRE BRIGADE
58. Al-SULTAN, Hamad Y. 23
    Called to attend fire at Dasman Palace ealy in the morning. Caught in cross-fire and hit in the chest.

KUWAIT POLICE
59. Al-SHAMMERI, Mitab S.41
    Senior Constable
60. Al-ABDULAZIZ, Suleiman A.   22
    Policeman

CIVILIANS
61. Al-QALAF, Hadi M.   29
    Civil Servant,
    Ministry of Defence
    Struck early evening by a stray bullet which passed through his chest while standing outside with several colleagues.
62. BU HAMAD, Zacharia A.18
    Student
    Died of gunshot to the head.
63. Al-DHAEDI, Mohammed H.   43
    Civil Servant,
    Ministry of Justice
    Died of gunshot wound.

---

*: Females; KNPC: Kuwait National Petroleum Company; PAAET: Public Authority for Applied Education and Training.

3 AUGUST, 1990
KUWAIT AIR FORCE
64.Al-REFAI, Anwar A.   29
  Captain
65.Al-ANZI, Hamdan M.   24
  Lieutenant
66.Al-BAIJAN, Khalid A.   22
  Lieutenant
67.Al-OBEID,
  Mohammed M.   22
  Lieutenant
Killed when their Gazelle helicopter crashed in undetermined circumstances near Saudi border during evacuation.
68.SABRI, Ra'ad M.   22
  Airman
(Jordanian national serving in Kuwait Armed Forces.) Shot at Air Defence Base, near Kuwait Airport.

5 AUGUST, 1990
69.Al-SALAILI,
  Abdulaziz S.   17
  Student
Hit by four bullets during Resistance action against Iraqi troops at overpass at Al-Jahra.

6 AUGUST, 1990
70.Al-ANZI, Mohammed S.35
  Corporal, Kuwait Army
Struck by bullet inthe chest during exchange of fire between Iraqis and Kuwaiti Resistance in Keifan area.
71.Al-HIAIH, Adel A.   25
  Corporal, Army Signal Corps
Killed in exchange of fire with Iraqis in front of Al-Qadsiya Co-operative supermarket.

7 AUGUST, 1990
72.HASSAN,
  Abdulrahman M.   20
  Engineering student
Shot and fatally wounded in chest during peaceful demonstration against the Invasion in the Rumaithiya area.
73.MAHMOUD,
  Mahmoud M.   34
  Carpenter
Shot in juvenile prison.
74.SHANATER, Miseer F.   32
  First Sergeant
  Kuwait Air Force
Hit with a bullet in the back and lung near Al-Jahra Club.

8 AUGUST, 1990
75.Al-ASKARI, Mousad A. 32
  Lance Corporal
  National Guard
Shot in the neck. Body initially not identified, and buried in mass grave 21 August, 1990. Later identified from hospital records.
76.Al-FODERI, Sana A. * 20
  Student, PAAET
Died of a bullet wound to the abdomen suffered when Iraqi troops fired on peaceful street demonstration staged in the Rumaithiya area by Kuwaiti women to protest the invasion.
77.SAFRI, Waheed M.   19
  Student
(Iranian national resident in Kuwait.) Killed with gunshot in the chest.

9 AUGUST, 1990
78.Al-HARSHABI, Moh'd S.58
  Retired
Shot in the Al-Ardiya area.
79.Al-SUBEH, Ali A.   45
  Taxi driver
Shot dead after falling into an argument with an Iraqi soldier at Dasman Co-oper-ative bakery.

10 AUGUST, 1990
80.Al-KANDARI, Ibrahim I.26
  Civil Servant, PAAET
Killed with multiple gunshots.
81.Al-RAIHAN, Ali I.   17
  Student
Arrested for distributing anti-Iraqi leaflets, and raising the Kuwaiti flag in the Kaifan area. Executed in front of his house with five gunshots.

11 AUGUST, 1990
82.Al-BU GHBAISH,
  Abdulhussein A.   24
(Iranian national resident in Kuwait.) Supervisor, Jabriya Co-op Society. Arrested in Jabriya area. Executed.

12 AUGUST, 1990
83.Al-HASHAN, Nawaf M. 19
  Civil Servant, Ministry of Interior
Died after being shot running a checkpoint near the intersection of Fifth Ring Road and Maghreb-Assafar Motorway, following a Kuwait Resistance operation. One colleague escaped. Others captured.

15 AUGUST, 1990
84.Al-SHAMMERI,
  Najma A.   39
85.Al-NAJDI, Khalid A.   6
Mother and son. Car accident on Sixth Ring Road with Iraqi military vehicle. Mother died immediately. Son died later of a fractured skull.

18 AUGUST, 1990
86.ABDULKARIM,
  Bassam M.   19
  Student
  Kuwait Resistance
Wounded in chest, right hand, and abdomen in engagement with Iraqis in Sabah Al-Salem area. Dead on arrival at hospital.
87.Al-ADWANI,
  Abdullah M.   35
  Border Guard
(Egyptian national serving in Kuwaiti Forces.) Shot and wounded in the back at Jiwan. Died of his wounds.

19 AUGUST, 1990
88.Al-SHAWAF,
  Mohammed J.   43
  Occupation unknown
Died of inadequate medical care as a result of the Invasion.

23 AUGUST, 1990
89.Al-MUTAIRI,
  Nuwaier S. *   14
  Student
Killed near the Saudi border of a gunshot, trying to escape to Saudi Arabia with her family.

25 AUGUST, 1990
90.Al-JARALLAH,
  Munira A. *   43
  Housewife
Car accident with Iraqi vehicle.

26 AUGUST, 1990
91.Al-BAHAR, Faisal B.   40
  Civil Servant,
  Civil Aviation Direcorate
Arrested about 6 August because of Kuwait Resistance attack on Iraqi troops. Executed behind dispensary in Nugra area.
92.Al-HAMDAN,
  Abdulatief A.   39
  Immigration Officer
Was working as manager of Fintas Co-op. On 25 August, 1990, his neighbourhood was

surrounded by Iraqis, and his home searched by Mukhabarat. Firearms found. He and his in-laws arrested. Died of torture during captivity.
93.HAMOUD, Munzer H.   20
  Lance Corporal,
  National Guard
Killed by gunshot, near Abdullah Salem High School.

27 AUGUST, 1990
94.GHLOUM,
  Abdulrasool H.   36
  Technician, Ministry of Communications
  Kuwait Resistance
Caught at checkpoint carrying a weapon in his car. Car fired upon and burned, presumably after being struck by an RPG round.

28 AUGUST, 1990
95.BU HAMDI, Ahmad A.   3
  Child
Killed by stray bullet. Source of fire unknown.

29 AUGUST, 1990
96.RABIEH, Sayer K.   50
  Border Guard,
  Ministry of Interior
Heart, respiratory and renal failure. Cause not given.
97.Al-SHAMMERI, Moh'd 0.56
  Retired policeman
Car accident.

30 AUGUST,1990
98.IBRAHIM, Ali G.   37
  Policeman
Shot in the right shoulder after passing through a checkpoint without stopping, 14 August, 1990. Taken to hospital, but inadequate treatment available. Family then left to Iran with him. Operated on for the bullet wound, but died from infection one week after the operation.

31 AUGUST, 1990
99.Al-SHEIKH, Habib M.   51
  Telephone Operator,
  Ministry of Justice
Brought to hospital dead. Cause of death unclear.

---

*: Females; KNPC: Kuwait National Petroleum Company; PAAET: Public Authority for Applied Education and Training.

2 SEPTEMBER, 1990

100.Al-ADWANI, Nasser G.23
Guardsman
National Guard
Shot in the head.

101.Al-JASSIM,
Mahmoud K.   29
Technician, Ministry of
Electricity and Water
*Arrested late August for
distributing anti-Iraqi leaflets.
Held in Bayan Police Station.
Found in Hawally, dead of a
gunshot to the head.*

102.JOUDA, Malakia R. * 30
Educational Administrator
*Shot in the heart in front of
her house.*

4 SEPTEMBER, 1990

103.Al-SAMHAN, Khalid A.25
Fireman,
Kuwait Fire Brigade
*Arrested during the first two
weeks of the Occupation on his
way to work. Accused of having
anti-Iraqi leaflets in his car.
Held in Keifan Police Station.
Executed with a gunshot.*

8 SEPTEMBER, 1990

104.Al-ANZI, Sabar A.   32
Sergeant
Kuwait Air Force
*Captured, August 1990.
Executed in front of his house.*

105.Al-KANDARI, Salem A.29
Senior Police Constable
Executed in front of his house.

106.Al-MOUSAWI, Baker A.21
Civil Servant,
Ministry of Social Affairs
and Labour
*Captured 3 September, 1990.
Tortured during captivity. On
8 September, brought to his
home in Bayan with Ahmad
Al-ANZI (See also 16
September, 1990). Executed
with a gunshot to the head.*

107.Al-OTAIBI, Ghazi F.   54
Ministry of Awkaf and
Religious Affairs
*Son was found with a
firearm. Acting on this,
Ghazi's home was searched,
and he was arrested after
weapons were found hidden
in a ceiling cavity. Kept in
Bayan Police Station for ten
days, then brought back to
the street in front of his
house and executed with a
gunshot to the head.*

108.HUSSEIN, Salah H.   23
Engineering Student
*Captured 1 September, 1990.
Held for one week, then
executed in front of his house
with a gunshot to the head.*

9 SEPTEMBER, 1990

109.Al-TAQI, Jaffar A.   30
Teacher,
Ministry of Education
Killed by stray bullet.

11 SEPTEMBER, 1990

110.AHMAD, Bader R.   35
Accountant,
Kuwait Oil Company
*Had been administering food
distribution through a Co-
operative Society. Fell into an
argument with Iraqi troops or
Mukhabarat. They returned
later, and arrested him. Body
discovered with signs of
torture. Apparently killed by
gunshot to the head.*

12 SEPTEMBER, 1990

111.Al-ANZI, Madhkhar G.54
Retired National Guard
*Shot and killed as he was
trying to leave for Saudi
Arabia across the desert with
his family.*

112.Al-KHARJI,
Miriam I. *   68
Housewife/ Widow
*Shot and killed as she was
trying to leave for Saudi
Arabia across the desert with
her family.*

13 SEPTEMBER, 1990

113.Al-NOUT, Mubarak F. 43
Supermarket Manager
Manager of Al-Ardiya
Co-operative Society
Supermarket
*Shot in the head because he
refused to hang Saddam's
picture in the supermarket.*

15 SEPTEMBER, 1990

114.Al-SHAMMERI,
Hamad S.   20
University student

115.Al-SHAMMERI, Saad S.25
Occupation unknown
*Brothers. Executed together
in front of their house with
gunshots to their heads.*

116.Al-THUWASH,
Mohammed H.   30
Manager, Civil Aviation
Administration
*Executed in front of his house
in Kheitan.*

16 SEPTEMBER, 1990

117.ABDULATIEF,
Ibrahim A.   24
Unemployed
Kuwaiti Resistance
*Captured at the Mishref home
of his friend, Ahmad A. Dashti.
Tortured. Died of gunshot
wounds to head and chest.*

118.Al-ANZI, Ahmad A.   24
Policeman
Kuwait Resistance
*Captured 2 September, 1990.
Accused of having weapons
and forging identity cards for
military officers in the
Resistance. Executed in front
of his friend's home. See also
Baker A. Al-MOUSAWI, 8
September, 1990.*

119.Al-KHAMIS, Issa A.   78
Retired businessman
*Was with his son in his car
when struck by an Iraqi
military vehicle which went
through a red light between
Qadsiya and Mansouriya
areas. Died of his injuries.
Son survived.*

120.Al-RUMADHEEN,
Mohammed J.   40
Lieutenant-Colonel,
Kuwait Navy
Kuwait Resistance
*Arrested at Khalid Al-Dashti's
house. Tortured in captivity,
and then executed with
gunshot to the head and
chest.*

121.QABAZARD, Ahmad M.32
Captain, Police VIP
Protection Unit
Kuwait Resistance
*Out of Kuwait in Lebanon at
the time of the invasion.
Took his family to Bahrain
then infiltrated back into the
country 10 August, 1990.
Captured from his home in
Jabriya 4 September, 1990.
Tortured severely during
captivity. Brought back to his
now abandoned home, early
mornning, 16 September.
Killed with gunshots to the
neck and head. His home was
then set alight.*

17 SEPTEMBER, 1990

122.ALI, Yacoub Y.   24
Assistant Electrical
Engineer, Ministry of
Electricity and Water
*Ordered by the Iraqis to go to
Ahmad Al-Jaber KAF base,
then occupied by the Iraqis, to
repair a high voltage
generator. During the
operation, the generator
exploded, causing severe burns
to 45% of his body, and
severely injuring two of his
colleagues. Died of his injuries.*

18 SEPTEMBER, 1990

123.ROUIAH, Amal A. *   37
Secretary,
Ministry of Education
*Died from haemorrage after
Caesarean-section childbirth,
due to inadequate natal care
under the occupation.*

19 SEPTEMBER, 1990

124.Al-KANDARI, Bader A.22
University Student/
Postal Officer
*Left his home, 14 September,
1990. Body found 19
September, 1990 by his
brother with evidence of
torture. Died of gunshot.*

23 SEPTEMBER, 1990

125.ABBAS, Adel G.   23
Administrator,
Al-Adan Hospital
*Arrested 5 a.m. 11
September, 1990. Accused of
possessing weapons and
participating in the
Resistance. Beaten in custody
before being brought to say
goodbye to his family five
hours later. Thirteen days
later, at 5 a.m. brought to
the street in front of his
father's house in Al-Riggae
with several other members of
the Resistance, and executed
with a gunshot to the head.*

126.Al-BALHAN,
Abdulhameed A.   45
Deputy Director, Hussain
Makki Al-Juma Cancer
Centre
*Arrested from his workplace.
Later executed with gunshot
to the head.*

127.Al-BALOUSHI,
Ibrahim A.   31
Civil servant, Ministry of
Defence
128.Al-BALOUSHI,
Najam A.   30
Corporal, Kuwait Navy
Kuwait Resistance
*Brothers. Captured 10
September, 1990. Brought
back to the family house at
7:00 a.m. and executed with
gunshot to the head,
following severe torture.*
129.Al-MUNIR,
Abdulatief A.   27
Civil servant, Ministry of
Social Affairs and Labour
130.BU ARKI, Faiz H.   24
First-Lieutenant,
Kuwait Army
*Arrested in Bayan 23 August
after Iraqis found a map and
plans for getting into an
armoury in the Faiha area.
After one month in captivity,
brought to the street in front
of Faiz's house and executed
together.*
131.ALI, Issa M.   23
Student
*Arrested 11 September. Held
in captivity, then executed in
front of his house.*
132.DASHTI,
Mohammed Q.   23
Civil Servant, Ministry of
Public Health
*Executed with gunshot to the
head*
133.MAHDI, Majeed A.   43
Civil Servant, Ministry
of Health
134.MAHDI, Ali M.   20
135.MAHDI, Hamoud M.   18
*Father and two sons. Anti-
Iraqi leaflets and weapons
found in house during
search. Arrested, tortured,
then executed together with
gunshots to the head.*
136.SANASIRRI,
Ahmad H.   20
Caterer, Al-Adan Hospital
*Arrested 13 September, 1990
from Al-Adan Hospital.
Accused of membership in/
aiding Kuwait Resistance.
Tortured during captivity.
Brought to his family home,
6:00 a.m. and executed in
front of his family.*

137.Al-MUTAIRI,
Aeeyedh S.   46
Security Guard,
Kuwait Municipality
*Shot in the back. Died in
Farwaniah Hospital.*

29 SEPTEMBER, 1990
138.Al-AZMI,
Mohammed A.   22
Lance Corporal,
National Guard
*Shot in the head in a park in
Rumaithiya area, near his
home.*
139.Al-QALAF,
Mohammed Y.   24
Lance Corporal,
National Guard
*Executed in front of his
house by gunshot to the
head.*
140.Al-JOUWAISRI,
Hamad A.   20
Foreman, Ministry of
Public Works
Member of *25th February
Group, Kuwait
Resistance*
*Captured in Rumaithiya mid-
September 1990. Brought
back to his home, 29
September, and shot in front
of his mother and siblings.*
141.Al-MANSOUR, Walid   32
Occupation unknown
Gunshot to the head.
142.ZAMAL, Saud A.   27
Telephone operator,
Kuwait Municipality
Gunshot to the head.

30 SEPTEMBER, 1990
143.KHREBAT,
Abdulhamid I.   37
Engineer
Arrested. Died from torture.

3 OCTOBER, 1990
144.Al-DHAMER, Khalid A.18
Engineering Student
*Captured 9 September, 1990.
Brought to his family home,
and shot in the head
outside.*
145.Al-DHAMER, Adnan A.19
Trainee,
Kuwait Oil Company
Kuwait Resistance
*Captured with firearms.
Tortured in captivity, then
executed with a gunshot to
the head in front of his
house.*

146.Al-ABEDLI, Issa H.   17
Student
Gunshot to the head.
147.Al-OBAIDAN,
Dr. Hisham M.   31
Physician, Ministry of
Public Health/ Reservist
First-Lieutenant, Kuwait
Army Medical Corps
*Arrested with medical
equipment used to treat
wounded Kuwait Resistance
fighters in his car. Thought
to have been involved in
supplying poison to inject
into food/drink offered to
Iraqi soldiers. Executed,
gunshot to the head.*
148.Al-FALAH, Yousef I.   37
Major, Kuwait Army,
15 Brigade.
Kuwait Resistance, part
of Colonel Al-Dossari's/
Mohammed Al-Fajji's
group
*Captured 22 September,
1990, then executed in front
of his house with a gunshot
to the head.*
149.Al-RAFIE, Salah M.   22
Imam (Prayer leader at
neighbourhood mosque)
*Arrested from his house in
Kheitan September 1990
after he refused to honour
Saddam in his Friday sermon.
Anti-Iraqi leaflets and
weapons found in his house.
Killed in front of his own
mosque with a gunshot to
the back of the head.*

7 OCTOBER, 1990
150.MARZOUK, Ismael M. 19
151.MARZOUK, Sultan M. 21
152.FALAKAWI, Sadiq A.   20
Brothers and friend
*Captured 7 September, 1990
from the Marzouk home
together. Held for one
month, then brought back to
the Marzouk family home
and shot dead in front of it.*
153.Al-DARMI,
Abdullah A.   35
Occupation unknown
*Arrested at a checkpoint
after being found with anti-
Iraqi leaflets and firearms in
his car. Held for one and a
half months. Executed with a
gunshot in the head.*

154.Al-AJMI, Ali M.   46
Technician,
Mina Abdullah Refinery,
KNPC
*Arrested in front of his
house. Held for one month
and six days, after which he
was brought to the street in
front of his house, and
executed by gunshot to the
head.*
155.Al-DOSSARI, Moh'd F. 40
Social worker,
Ministry of Education
*Arrested 6 October, 1990.
Tortured, taken back to his
house the following day, and
shot outside.*
156.AHMAD, Mahmoud A. 26
KNPC employee
157.Al-AJMI, Mathi S.   21
KNPC employee
*Arrested for smuggling
weapons into Kuwait from
Saudi Arabia. Executed
together by gunshots to the
head and back.*
158.Al-MAJOUB, Saad T.   45
Civil Servant,
Ministry of Health
Died of gunshot.
159.Al-MUTAWA,
Jassim M.   31
Teacher,
Ministry of Education
Died of gunshot to the head.
160.Al-SURRI, Yousef K.   32
Teacher,
Ministry of Education
*Arrested 9 September, 1990
from in front of a Co-
operative Society
Supermarket where he was
working as a volunteer at the
time. Shot in front of his
house.*
161.MALALLAH, Younis M.24
Accountant,
Ministry of
Communications
Kuwait Resistance,
25th February Group
*Captured with his brother
when the Iraqis surrounded
their house. Held in Umm
Salim School in Salwa, then
transferred to Rumaithiya
Police Station. Held in
custody for a total of 35
days, then brought back to
the street in front of his
house, and executed. Brother
eventually released.*

*: Females; KNPC: Kuwait National Petroleum Company; PAAET: Public Authority for Applied Education and Training.

10 OCTOBER, 1990
162.Al-KHALDI, Mousad H.20
  Policeman
Wounded by gunshot.
Operated on in Mubarak Al-
Kabeer Hospital, died after 9
days following operation.
163.ASHKANANI,
  Mahmoud G.   62
  Gulf Food Supply Co.
Car accident with Iraqi
military vehicle.

15 OCTOBER, 1990
164.Al-LAHEEB,
  Suleiman M.   18
  High School Student
Arrested in Faiha area with a
firearm. Later shot in neck,
head and hip in front of his
house.
165.Al-MAYAS, Saad R.   22
  Civil Servant, Civil
  Aviation Directorate
Arrested in a trap set for the
Iraqis by his Palestinian
colleagues. Taken to Fahaheel
Police Station, and then to
another prison. Kept in
custody for 25 days until
brought with another group
of captive Kuwaitis to the
street in front of his house in
Fahaheel, where he was shot.
166.HUSSEIN,
  Maitham H.   20
  Student, PAAET
Captured with anti-Iraqi
leaflets. Held for 45 days, then
killed in front of his house
with a gunshot to the face.
167.MIRZA, Fadel A.   20
  Policeman
Arrested in September from a
checkpoint in Bayan area.
Had been working in
Rumaithiya Co-op. Held in
captivity. Underwent severe
torture, including burning of
the body with a clothes iron
and cigarettes, burning of his
beard, and electrical torture.
Brought back to his house
where he was shot in front of
the door.
168.AL-SAEED, Ali H.   21
  Realtor
(Iraqi national resident in
Kuwait.) Admitted to
Farwaniah Hospital with
gunshot wound.
Died after 25 days.

17 OCTOBER, 1990
169.Al-OSAIMI,
  Mohammed S.   60
Died of complications arising
from diabetes. Adequate
medical care unavailable.

21 OCTOBER, 1990
170.Al-HUSSEINI, Badi M.47
  Warrant Officer, Kuwait
  Army Military College
Died of illness in captivity.

24 OCTOBER, 1990
171.Al-SHEHAB, Abbas H.50
  Retired Civil Servant,
  Ministry of Finance
Went out shopping with his
son. Stopped at checkpoint
and asked for ID. After
passing through the
checkpoint, one of the Iraqi
soldiers hit him in the
shoulder with his gun,
causing his car to swerve into
a concrete road divider. Died
in hospital of injuries
sustained.

6 NOVEMBER, 1990
172.Al-RASHEEDI,
  Al-Homaidi D.   22
  University student
Went missing 3 November.
Found by younger brother
hanging from ceiling fan in
an empty house.

7 NOVEMBER, 1990
173.ABBAS, Yacoub Y.   19
  Student
Gunshot in the back, Firdous
area.

10 NOVEMBER, 1990
174.DASHTI, Khalid A.   29
  Industrial Engineer,
  Ministry of
  Communications
  Kuwait Resistance
Captured, tortured, and
brought to his family home,
where he was executed with a
gunshot to the head.

11 NOVEMBER, 1990
175.BOOR, Ibrahim M.   50
  Driver, Ministry of
  Electricity and Water
(Iranian national resisent in
Kuwait.) Killed in vehicle
collision with Iraqi military
vehicle during the course of
his duties.

27 NOVEMBER, 1990
176.Al-HUSSEIN, Habib G.27
  Detective,
  Ministry of Interior
  Kuwait Resistance
Arrested, held, tortured and
executed. Body found in
Shuwaikh.

19 NOVEMBER, 1990
177.Al-ANZI, Salem F.   30
  Civil Servant, Ministry of
  Commerce and Industry
Arrested September 1990,
held in custody, then executed
in front of his house.

1 DECEMBER, 1990
178.Al-KANDARI,
  Mohammed A.   42
  Driver, Prime Minister's
  and Cabinet Office
Died as a result of burns to
60% of his body sustained in
accident when working as a
volunteer in Ardiya bakery.

4 DECEMBER, 1990
179.Al-OTAIBI, Mutlaq M. 27
  Sergeant, Kuwait Army
Killed in traffic accident
whilst serving with Kuwaiti
forces in Saudi Arabia.

11 DECEMBER, 1990
180.Al-ASFOOR, Fatma A.*34
  Teacher,
  Ministry of Education
Died of unavailability of
adequate medical care.

12 DECEMBER, 1990
181.Al-AJMI,
  Mohammed N.   28
  High School Counsellor
Traffic accident.

17 DECEMBER, 1990
182.Al-AZMI, Bader M.   27
  Fireman
Died as a result of injuries
received attempting to rescue
a fire victim.

18 DECEMBER, 1990
183.Al-ZANKI, Jamal A.   34
  Supervisor, PAAET
Died as a result of injuries
sustained in car accident.

22 DECEMBER, 1990
184.AL-SHAMMERI,
  Bader S.   23
  Merchant
Captured and tortured.

Released, but later died of
renal failure in Al-Adan
Hospital as a result of the
torture.

31 DECEMBER, 1990
185.HUSSEIN, Jassim M. 18
  Student
Found dead near his father's
home in the Ardiya area
following capture and torture.
186.SADDOUN,
  Khaldiya A. *   33
  Housewife/ Widow
Fell into an argument with
Iraqi soldiers at a checkpoint.
When she tried to drive away,
they fired into the air,
panicking nearby drivers. Her
vehicle struck by Iraqi trailer.
Died of injuries sustained in
the collision.

4 JANUARY, 1991
187.Al-KHALIDI,
  Ghalia H. *   23
  English teacher,
  Ministry of Education
Died of medical complications
as a result of inadequate
health care.

5 JANUARY, 1991
188.Al-SHATTI, Fouad M. 28
  Corporal,
  Kuwait Army Intelligence
Shot and killed when Iraqi
troops stormed his father's
house.

6 JANUARY, 1991
189.Al-YACOUB, Ahmad K.30
  Security Guard,
  Ministry of Education
Killed in vehicle collision with
Iraqi military vehicle.
190.MANSOUR, Ali S.   28
  Public Relations,
  Ministry of Health
Gunshot to the head.

14 JANUARY, 1991
191.Al-QABANDI,
  Asrar M. *   31
  Founder, administrator,
  and teacher, Khalifa
  School for Autistic and
  Downs Syndrome
  Children. Computer
  Specialist, Ministry of
  Foreign Affairs.
  Kuwait Resistance
Involved in communications
with Government-in-exile and
Western media via satellite

---

*: Females; KNPC: Kuwait National Petroleum Company; PAAET: Public Authority for Applied Education and Training.

telephones, distribution of funds to Kuwaitis and Westerners in hiding, and numerous other activities. Captured at a checkpoint in Mishref, early afternoon, 4 November, 1990. Father, brother and uncle were arrested from the family home later that evening. Tortured in captivity. Executed with gunshots to the head and chest. Head sliced in two with an axe. Brain and eyes removed by Iraqis. Body dumped outside family home.

15 JANUARY, 1991
192.MAJID, Abdulhameed M.　42
Technical Inspector, Ministry of Communications
Arrested, tortured, and executed with gunshot to the head.

18 JANUARY, 1991
193.Al-MUTAIRI, Jazza S. 39
Unemployed
Died of heart failure.

19 JANUARY, 1991
194.KARIMI, Hamza M.　55
Retiree, Ministry of Communications
Captured 18 January, 1991 with his two sons and son-in-law, Ali Bin Nakhi (see below). Held in Rumaithiya Police Station where he was tortured. Executed with a gunshot to the head. Sons released.
195.BIN NAKHI, Ali A.　18
Supervisor, Central Telephone Exchange, Ministry of Communications
Captured with father in-law, Hamza M. Karimi. Killed with gunshot to the head after torture in captivity.
196.BIN JEBEL, Mishari Y.　43
Retiree, KNPC
According to his wife, was a member of a Kuwaiti Resistance group, and executed in Rumaithiya Police Station for not changing his car licence plates from Kuwaiti to Iraqi. Gunshot to the head, and one of his eyes removed.

20 JANUARY, 1991
197.DASHTI, Amir A.　21
198.DASHTI, Hamza A.　22
Security Guards.
Amir for Kuwait Municipality; Hamza for PAAET
Brothers. Captured together. Bodies found in hospital refrigeration unit after Liberation. Marks of torture were evident, including being burned on the back with a domestic clothes iron. Gunshots to the forehead, and heads split with an axe blow.
199.Al-SALEH, Walid S.　23
Chief Refueller, Kuwait Aviation Refuelling Company.
Kuwait Resistance
Arrested leaving a mosque in Rumaithiya. Tortured in captivity, and then executed near the home of a friend, Yayha Ahmad.
200.MOHAMMED, Mohammed B.　25
Private, Kuwait Army Air Defence Unit
Arrested, tortured, and executed with gunshot to the head.

22 JANUARY, 1991
201.Al-ABDULWAHAB, Majeed I.　61
In hospital intensive care unit when Iraqis removed the medical equipment for transfer to Iraq, and transferred him to a general ward. Died as a result of this.

25 JANUARY, 1991
202.Al-AJMI, Abdullah F. 17
Student. Volunteer with Kuwait Forces in Saudi Arabia
Fire accident in tent housing volunteers. Severe burns to 90% of his body.

26 JANUARY, 1991
203.Al-AJMI, Mohammed S.　42
Driver, Ministry of Communications
Arrested and held for 15 days after weapons found in his car. Body found near his house, dead of a brain haemorrhage.

28 JANUARY, 1991
204.Al-ANZI, Mohammed M.　21
Policeman
Took his family out to Saudi Arabia on 10th day of Occupation, then returned to Kuwait across the desert to engage in Resistance activities. Shot and wounded during an operation. Taken to Al-Adan Hospital. Arrested from there by the Iraqis. Taken to his house, and executed with gunshot to the head.

31 JANUARY, 1991
205.Al-SHAMMERI, Eman M.*　17
Student
Killed when her home was struck during the air war.
206.Al-MUTAIRI, Falah S. 13
Child
Playing in the street with a friend during a lull in the air war. Killed by an explosion, either from a bomb, or unexploded ordnance. Friend wounded in the feet.

1 FEBRUARY, 1991
207.Al-SHATTI, Ismael A. 59
Retired security guard
Shot at random on his way to mosque. His daughter, who was accompanying him, was wounded, but survived.
208.RAHMA, Rahma A.　17
Student
Died from explosion.

2 FEBRUARY, 1991
209.Al-KHUDEER, Ibrahim A.　23
Policeman
In Cairo at the time of the Invasion. Infiltrated back into Kuwait September 1990 with several other officers. Last seen leaving his home, 30 January, 1991. Brought to Mubarak Al-Kabeer Hospital, dead of gunshot to the head. Fate prior to death unknown.

3 FEBRUARY, 1991
210.Al-AJMI, Salem A.　6
Child
Killed by landmine.

5 FEBRUARY, 1991
211.Al-BADER, Ali F.　20
Kuwait Police Special Forces
*Arrested with his father and brother 13 January, 1991 from his father's house. Charged with leading a Resistance cell. Three men taken to Basra and imprisoned. Ali's body found 5 February in Kuwait, near his home, with evidence of torture by electricity and cigarettes. Killed Gunshot to the head.
Father released from prison in March 1991 with Shia uprising. Returned home to the news of his son's death, and died himself of grief four days later.*
212.Al-WAHIB, Abdulaziz R.　21
Fireman
Shot twice in the head, once in chin, once in the neck and once in left knee. Body dumped in a park in the Faiha area. Buried as unidentified, but later identified from fingerprints taken before burial.
213.Al-MUBARAK, Mansour M.　27
214.Al-MUBARAK, Moused M.　23
215.Al-MUBARAK, Shakir M.　30
Three brothers. Captured together early in the air war. Each was shot in the head in front of their family home.

5/6 FEBRUARY, 1991
'25th FEBRUARY'
RESISTANCE GROUP
216.Al-AMER, Wafa A. *　23
Radiography Technician
217.HASSAN, Souad A. *　19
Law Student
218.Al-AHMAD, Ahmad A.20
Coastguard
219.Al-AHMAD, Khalid A. 27
Airport Policeman
220.ALI, Abdulrahman Q. 30
Policeman
(Iraqi national resident in Kuwait.)
221.Al-SHARHAN, Abdulaziz S.　31
Businessman

---

*: Females; KNPC: Kuwait National Petroleum Company; PAAET: Public Authority for Applied Education and Training.

222.ABDULLAH, Ashraf M.21
  Insurance clerk,
  Y.A. Alghanim and Sons
(Jordanian resident of Kuwait.)
223.ALI, Abdulrahman Q. 30
(Iraqi national serving in Kuwait Police.)
224.ABDULFATTAH,
  Samer M.   21
  University Student.
(Jordanian national resident in Kuwait.)
225.RAJAB,
  Osama A.   22
  Civil Defence Officer,
  Ministry of Interior
  Members of '*25th February*' Kuwait Resistance group, which carried out October 1990 car bomb attack on Iraqi delegation at the Kuwait International Hotel.

• *Miss Al-AMER captured 11 January, 1991 with the cousins she was staying with at the time. Cousins later released. Tortured, and strangled with a chain. Body dumped in the Adaliya area near her house. Found 6 February, 1991.*
• *Miss HASSAN arrested 11 January, 1991 with her mother and sisters, who were later released. Held in custody, and then strangled with a chain. Body dumped in the street near her home. Found 6 February, 1991.*
• *Al-AHMAD brothers, Ahmad and Khalid arrested from their home in Salmiya 13 January, 1991, with brother-in-law, Abdulrahman Q. ALI. All 3 found dead, 5 February, 1991, with gunshots to the head, and evidence of torture by electric drill to their faces.*
• *Al-SHARHAN captured from his home 13 January, 1991, found dead in Khaifan area 5 February, 1991 with 4 shots to the chest, head, shoulder and neck, and a broken jaw. Buried unidentified, but later identified by family after Liberation from hospital photographs.*
• *ABDULLAH captured 13 January, 1991. Executed with gunshots to the head and chest, 5 February. Head*

sliced with an axe. Body dumped outside his home.
• *ALI arrested 13 January, 1991. Executed in front of his house.*
• *ABDULFATTAH arrested 13 January, 1991 from the hotel where he had been working throughout the crisis. Executed in front of his house.*
• *RAJAB captured 15 January, 1991. Tortured in captivity. Found dead near his home, early morning, 5 February, dead of gunshot wounds.*

9 FEBRUARY, 1991
226.Al-MAZATI,
  An'am S. *   39
  Nurse, Al-Adan Hospital
(Egyptian resident of Kuwait.)
227. JAYANN, Manchala B. 42
228.GODAWAN , Rajinder 35
  Radiography technicians
  Al-Adan Hospital
(Indian nationals resident in Kuwait.)
Killed during Allied air attack on Iraqi anti-aircraft positions situated on or near the staff residences in the grounds of Al-Adan Hospital.

10 FEBRUARY, 1991
229.SHEER, Adnan A.   30
  Senior Constable. Military Court Reporter
Arrested 9 February, 1991 on suspicion of possession of weapons, and membership of Resistance. Found dead of gunshots to head, chest and back near his uncle's home.

11 FEBRUARY, 1991
230.Al-SAAD, Aish A.   28
  Businessman
(Saudi national resident in Kuwait.)
231.Al-NATEFI,
  Abdulrahman M.   30
  Policeman
232.JARAR,
  Mohammed A.   29
  Al-Homaidi Co.
(Jordanian Palestinian resident in Kuwait.)
233.Al-OSTAD, Jassim R. 41
  Trainer, PAAET
234.SULTAN, Emad Y.   31
  Businessman
  Kuwaiti Resistance
Captured about 2 February, 1991. Tortured. Brought to

car park of Sawaber Residential Complex in Kuwait City, and executed with gunshots to the head and body.
235.ABDULLAH,
  Ibrahim A.N.   30
  Occupation unknown
(Iraqi national resisent in Kuwait.)
Captured from his home, 6:00 a.m. 3 February, 1991. Accused of having arms and military equipment. Held and tortured in Salwa Police Station. Electric drill applied to his face. Burned. Died of gunshot.
236.A'SI, Jaber J.   30
  Policeman
Found dead in his car, dead of gunshots, with multiple bullet holes in the car.
237.Al-ROUMI, Jaber H.   10
  Child
238.Al-ROUMI, Fahd H.   8
  Child
Brothers. Landmine explosion near a mosque near their house. Shrapnel wounds to chest and abdomen caused extensive internal bleeding.

13 FEBRUARY, 1991
239.Al-MUHANNA,
  Ibrahim H.   30
  Policeman
  Kuwaiti Resistance
Had been obtaining weapons from outside Kuwait for the Resistance. Captured 25 January, 1991 from his home. Beaten in front of his children. Tortured extensively during his three weeks in captivity. Executed, and his body dumped in the street in Rumaithiya area.

14 FEBRUARY, 1991
240.FOUZAIH,
  Abdullah H.   16
  Student
Various gunshots to the head and body.
241.Al-MANSOUR, Fahd S.45
  Civil Servant, Ministry of Education
Bodies of Iraqi soldiers killed by the Kuwaiti Resistance found in a school adjacent to the family's house. Local residents accused of complicity in the killings. Al-

MANSOUR's wife, who was an Iraqi national, was taken into custody for three days as part of the investigation. Stress of the incident seriously affected his health, and he was hospitalised. Died in hospital.

15 FEBRUARY, 1991
242.Al-FUZIEH, Nasser A. 27
  Computer Operator, KNPC
243.Al-FUZIEH,
  Abdulhameed A.   33
  Management Executive, Kuwait Airways
Brothers. Killed by gunshots, Awkaf Complex. Bodies found in shallow grave, 1993.
244.BOURSLI, Tarek B.   19
  Officer Cadet, Kuwait Army
Several gunshots to the head.

19 FEBRUARY, 1991
245.Al-MUTAIRI, Walid K. 25
  Fireman
246.Al-SALEH, Yousef J. 47
  Businessman
Arrested during an Iraqi door-to-door search of Rumaithiya are, block 4 in late January 1991 when he opened his front door to see what was going on. Body found one month later, dead of a gunshot wound, and showing signs of torture.

20 FEBRUARY, 1991
247.BANDER, Walid I.   23
  Student
Left his home, 19 January, 1991, and did not return. Body later identified after Liberation in Al-Sabah Hospital by his father with signs of torture, and gunshots to head and shoulder.

24/25 FEBRUARY, 1991
Al-QURAIN BATTLE 'MESSILAH' RESISTANCE GROUP
248. ABBAS, Khalid A.   25
  Refinery Operater, Mina Abdullah Refinery, KNPC
249.Al-ALAWI, Saeed H.   41
  Civil Servant, Kuwait Municipality

---

*: Females; KNPC: Kuwait National Petroleum Company; PAAET: Public Authority for Applied Education and Training.

250.ALI, Yousef K.   35
Captain, Kuwait Army
251. Al-ANZI, Amer F.   26
First-Lieutenant,
Kuwait Army, 15 Brigade
252.AL-BELOUSHI,
Khalil K.   26
Civil Servant,
Public Ports Authority
253. GHLOUM, Jassim M. 30
Unemployed
254. MANSOUR,
Ibrahim A.   35
Security Guard, Ministry
of Social Affairs and
Labour
255.MANSOUR,
Mubarak A.   27
Security Supervisor,
Bayan Hall
256.MENDENI,
Abdullah A.   41
Senior Constable
257. RIDA, Hussein A.   20
Policeman
258. Al-SHAYA,
Mohammed O.   30
Civil Servant, Ministry of
Communications
Part of a 19-member
Kuwaiti Resistance group

Discovered accidentally and then surrounded, morning of 24 February, 1991 - four hours after the start of the ground war, and 36 hours before the commencement of the Iraqi retreat - in two houses in the suburb of Al-Qurain by Iraqi forces as they were conducting a round-up of Kuwaiti males prior to their retreat. Ensuing firefight lasted throughout most of the day, until the Iraqis overran the house. Five of the 19 hid in cavities in the houses and avoided capture. Another three had escaped during the day. Other surviving members of the group, all wounded, were captured and executed that evening or the following day.

25 FEBRUARY, 1991
259.AL-THUFEIRI, Munir S.25
Sergeant, Kuwait Army
2nd Infantry Battalion,
15 Brigade. Attached to
35 Brigade as part of
JFC-E during Allied
attack into Kuwait
Pin of grenade on his webbing caught and pulled

on a protuberance in his armoured vehicle, exploding the grenade behind him.

26 FEBRUARY, 1991
260.AL-AEDAN, Bader N. 29
Prison Officer
Owner of house next to where Messilah Kuwait Resistance Group gathered before being surprised by Iraqi troops, 24 February. During initial engagement with Iraqi forces, this group retreated into Al-AEDAN's house. He was wounded in the subsequent firefight, and later captured. Tortured prior to being executed.
261.AL-AJMI, Naif M.   35
Chemical engineer
Gunshot to the head.
262.AL-ANZI, Ahmad S.   21
Student
Killed by explosion while manning a police station in aftermath of Liberation, presumably from unexploded ammunition.
263.AL-ADWANI, Dala A. *41
Housewife
Died of gunshot to the head.
264.AL-RANDI,
Dalal A. *   67
Housewife
Died at her home.
265.AL-FOUZAN, Qattan A.57
266.AL-FOUZAN, Zainab Q.41
(Zainab: Indian wife of Qattan, a Kuwaiti businessman.)
Both killed in their house in Ahmadi as a result of the airwar. Date of death likely to have been earlier. Son injured, but survived.
267.AL-ANZI, Ramadan D. 30
Refinery Operator, KNPC
Died of gunshots to the face, head, and chest.
268.AL-THUFEIRI,
Beasan M.   26
Lance Corporal, Kuwait
Army Special Forces
269.ISMAEL,
Abdulrazzak S.   19
Police bandsman
Manning a checkpoint on the day of liberation at overpass in Al-Riqqa, when a car with Iraqi soldiers trying to escape Kuwait approached the checkpoint. The Iraqis opened fire, killing him.

270.Al-TARKEET,
Ghalia A.*   25
Psychiatrist, Mental
Hospital
Went out on the day of liberation with her sons and uncle to greet Allied troops. Hit and killed by a stray bullet. Uncle also injured, but survived.
271.BEHBEHANI,
Leila A. *   35
Secretary, Ministry of
Health
Gunshot in the stomach.

27 FEBRUARY, 1991
272.Al-GHANIM,
Ahmad M.   14
Student
Killed by landmine in central city precinct, immediately after liberation.
273.AL-AZMI, Mubarak A. 25
Customs officer, serving
in *Fatah* Brigade, Kuwait
Army
Died of gunshot wound to the head, after entering Kuwait following liberation. Presumably accidental.
274.AL-KHALDI,
Madhkhar D.   52
Retired, Ministry of
Interior
Wounded by Allied airstrike on Sixth Ring Road during Iraqi retreat of 26 February, 1991. Died of his wounds the following day.
275.AL-MILHEM,
Abdulatief A.   58
Retiree from Public Ports
Authority
Died as a result in inadequate medical care.
276.AL-ROUMI, Yousef M. 6
Child
Hit in the chest with stray bullet.
277.BU HAMAD,
Shathi, N.   11
Child
Hit by stray bullet.

1 MARCH, 1991
278.Al-AZMI,
Mohammed M.   25
279.MOHAMMED,
Habib H.   18
Volunteers, *Fatah*
Brigade, Kuwaiti Army
Died of gunshot wounds sustained after liberation.

280.MUSALLAM,
Hassan K.   32
Captain, Kuwait Army,
Public Relations and
Moral Guidance
Directorate
Killed by landmine in front of his home.
281.SUROOR, Khalifa M. 19
Student
Killed by landmine near his home in Ardiya.

2 MARCH, 1991
282.Al-GHAYEB, Ahmad A.38
Bank Manager, National
Bank of Kuwait
Kuwait Resistance
Captured in Wafra area. Found in Mubarak Al-Kabeer Hospital, dead of gunshots to the neck and heart.
283.AL-SHAMMERI,
Hadi M.   25
Switchboard operator,
Jahra Police Station
Immediately after liberation, he was gathering Iraqi POWs and handing them over to the police, when a mine planted near the police station exploded, critically wounding him.

3 MARCH, 1991
284.Al-THIAB, Faiz G.   30
Sergeant, Kuwait Army
Intelligence
Was serving with Special Forces. Encountered a group of Palestinian collaborators in a house in the Abdullah Al-Salem area. Shot and killed during operation to capture them.
285.Al-SHAMMERI   25
Ministry of Interior
Killed by landmine.

8 MARCH, 1991
286.Al-RASHID,
Abdullah A.   24
Public servant, Ministry
of Education
Arrested, and initially transferred to Basra. Body later found in Al-Sabah Hospital. Fate unknown.

---

*: Females; KNPC: Kuwait National Petroleum Company; PAAET: Public Authority for Applied Education and Training.

11 MARCH, 1991 287.Al-MUJADI, Abdulaziz A. 40 Lieutenant-Colonel, Kuwait Army *Killed in accident at* *checkpoint, after liberation.* **19 MARCH, 1991** 288.Al-DUJEENE, Ahmad M. 22 Guardsman, National Guard *Killed by landmine near SAS* *Hotel.* **28 MARCH, 1991** 289.Al-ANZI, Khalaf G. 24 Lance Corporal, Kuwait Army. 7th Armoured Battalion, 35 Brigade *Killed by landmine near* *Abdaly.* 290.Al-SHAMMERI, Abdullah N. 6 Child *Killed by landmine.*	**1 APRIL, 1991** 291.Al-SULILI, Nasser E. 20 Corporal, Kuwait Army. 2nd Infantry Battalion, 15 Brigade (attached to 35 Brigade) *Killed by landmine near* *Jahra.* **6 APRIL, 1991** 292.Al-MUTHERAT, Nahar M. 31 Corporal, Kuwait Army *Killed by landmine.* **9 APRIL, 1991** 293.Al-BADER, Fouad N. 45 Head of Information Department, Ministry of Education **11 APRIL, 1991** 294.AJMI, Khalid G. 31 Student, and volunteer helper for Ministry of Defence *Killed by landmine.*	**26 MAY, 1991** 295.SHAMSALDEEN, Ahmad S. 41 Lieutenant-Colonel 296.AL-FUZLI, Shaberem K. 34 First Sergeant Both members of Kuwait Army Ordnance Corps *Both killed by landmine.* **16 JULY, 1991** 297.Al-HARBI, Khalid R. 25 First-Lieutenant, Kuwait Army, 35 Brigade *Killed by landmine.* **29 JULY, 1991** 298.Al-RASHID, Mohammed K. 32 Captain, Kuwait Navy *Captured mid-February 1991* *on suspicion of being military.* *Transferred to Iraq. Released* *mid-March after ceasefire.* *Went to London for medical* *care as result of treatment in* *captivity. Died in London.*	**11 MARCH, 1992** 299.Al-RASHEEDI, Abdi A.18 Lance Corporal, Kuwait Army *Killed by landmine.* 300.Al-THUFEIRI, Fadoui M. 25 Lance Corporal, Kuwait Army *Killed by landmine.* 301.Al-ANZI, Madad K. 31 Lance Corporal, Kuwait Army *Killed by landmine.* **25 SEPTEMBER, 1992** 302.TAWEEM, Fahd S. 12 Student *Killed by landmine.*

PART 2, CIVILIANS

The number of non-Kuwaiti and non-Iraqi civilians who died as a direct result of the crisis is uncertain, but is thought to be approximately as follows, based on various sources including the United Nations Compensation Commission: <u>European Countries and USA/Canada:</u> Britain 5 United States 2 Poland 2 Canada, Australia, New Zealand, and others: No known deaths	<u>Asian and Arab Countries:</u> China 3 India 13 Iran 1 Jordan 218 Pakistan 4 Sri Lanka 16 Thailand 3 Other countries such as Egypt, Lebanon and The Philippines did have civilian deaths, but the numbers and names unless already noted in Part 1, are unavailable.	Individuals known to have died and whose names are available are as follows: **BRITAIN** 1. ATACK,William(Norrie) 2. CROSKERY, Douglas 3. DUFFY, Ron 4. DUNCAN, Alexander 5. MAJORS, Don **UNITED STATES** 1. WORTHINGTON, James	**INDIA** 1. ALI, S.M. 2. CHERRYAN, S. 3. DIYAR, Abdul B. 4. GATANJI, K. 5. GODAWAN, R. 6. HUSSAN, A. 7. JAYANN, M.B.P. 8. KHUNBA, M. J. 9. LA SHARH, L.B.R. 10. MEMMENCHERIAN, M.M. 11. MEMMENCHERIAN, P.M. 12. MEMMENCHERIAN, S. 13. OSHETTI, N.

Most countries who publicise the numbers and names of those who died make no distinction between those who were killed in action, and those who died in accidents or training related to the crisis.

The names of individuals are only available for Kuwaiti (see earlier) and for Western military members of the Coalition, as below.

The number of non-Kuwaiti Arab Coalition service personnel killed in action, according to the Commander of Joint Coalition Forces, Saudi Lieutenant-General Khaled bin Sultan, is approximately as follows:

Saudi Arabia	38
Egypt	11
Syria	3
UAE	5

BRITAIN

ROYAL FLEET AUXILIARY:
1. FOY, MM1 M.J.
2. HARRIS, MM1 P.J.

ARMY:
16th/5th The QUEEN'S ROYAL LANCERS:
3. WHITEHEAD, Lt E.A.
ROYAL ARTILLERY:
4. KEEGAN, Gnr P.P.
ROYAL ENGINEERS:
5. WRIGHT, LtCol A.J.
6. KINGHAN, Maj J.S.
7. DENBURY MM QGM, Cpl D.E. 8. LANE MM, Cpl S.J. ¶
9. ROYLE, Spr R.A.
ROYAL SIGNALS:
10. HAGGERTY, Pte T.
COLDSTREAM GUARDS:
11. NAPIER, Gdsm C.A.
ROYAL REGIMENT of FUSILIERS:
12. ATKINSON, Fus P.P.
13. BUNNEY, Fus A.
14. COLE, Fus C.P.
15. GILLESPIE, Fus R.A.
16. LEECH, Fus K.
17. SATCHELL, Fus S.T.
18. THOMPSON, Fus L.J.
STAFFORDSHIRE REGIMENT:
19. MOULT, Pte C.
20. TAYLOR, Pte S.P.
QUEEN'S OWN HIGHLANDERS:
21. DONALD, Pte N.W.D.
22. FERGUSON, Pte M.
23. LANG, Pte J.W.
ARGYLL and SUTHERLAND HIGHLANDERS:
24. MacKINNON, CSgt D.A.
PARACHUTE REGIMENT:
25. CONSIGLIO MM, Cpl R.G. ¶
ROYAL CORPS of TRANSPORT:
26. BOLAM, Cpl C.A.E.
27. CROFTS, LCpl S.R.

28. HILL, LCpl T.T.W.
29. ROBBINS, LCpl R.
30. WELLINGTON, LCpl L.
31. McFADDEN, Dvr J.P.
ROYAL ARMY ORDNANCE CORPS:
32. PHILLIPS, SSgt V.D. ¶
33. FOGERTY, Pte A.J.
ROYAL ELECTRICAL and MECHANICAL ENGINEERS:
34. BURCH, Maj A.J.
35. DOWLING MM, Sgt M.J.
36. EVANS, LCpl F.C.
ROYAL MILITARY POLICE:
37. TITE, SSgt D.C.
ROYAL ARMY MEDICAL CORPS:
38. GOING, Cpl R.H.
ROYAL ARMY PIONEER CORPS:
39. KINNEAR, Sgt D.B.
ROYAL AIR FORCE:
40. ELSDON, WgCdr T.N.C.
41. LENNOX, SqnLdr G.K.S.
42. WEEKS, SqnLdr K.P.
43. COLLIER, FltLt R.M.
44. COLLISTER, FltLt K.
45. DENT, FltLt N.T.
46. DUFFY, FltLt K.J.
47. HICKS, FltLt S.M.

MM : Military Medal;
QGM : Queen's Gallantry Medal

FRANCE
FRENCH AIR FORCE:
1. AMISSE, Lt
FRENCH ARMY:
2. BURGART, SSgt
3. CORDIER, Cpl
4. GUICHARD, SSgt
5. SCHMIDTT, Sgt
6. SUDRE, WO1
FRENCH FOREIGN LEGION:
7. VAN SUONG, Lgnr

SPAIN
ROYAL SPANISH NAVY:
1. ROMERO, Cpl I.R.
2. del PINO DIEZ, PFC J.A.

UNITED STATES
1. ADAMS, LCpl T.R.
2. ALANIZ, SP A.
3. ALLEN, LCpl F.C.
4. ALLEN, SSgt M.R.
5. AMES, SSgt D.R.
6. ANDERSON, CWO M.F.
7. APPLEGATE, Sgt T.R.
8. ARTEAGA, 1stLt J.I.
9. ATHERTON, SP S.E.
10. AUGER, Cpl A.M.
11. AVEY, PFC H.C.
12. AWALT, R.
13. BARTUSIAK, Cpl S.W.
14. BATES, D.
15. BATES, 1stLT T.
16. BAXTER, J.
17. BEAUDOIN, SP C.M. *
18. BELAS, Sgt L.A.
19. BELLIVEAU, AEM3 M.L.

20. BENNINGFIELD, A.
21. BENTZLIN, Cpl S.E.
22. BENZ, Cpl K.A.
23. BETZ, Cpl D.W.
24. BIANCO, Cpl S.F.
25. BLAND,T.
26. BLESSINGER, J.
27. BLOWE, Mr J.
28. BLUE, Sgt T.A.
29. BNOSKY, Capt J.J.
30. BOLIVER, SP J.A.
31. BONGIORNI, J.P. III
32. BOWERS, PFC T.
33. BOWMAN, C.
34. BOXLER, Sgt J.T.
35. BRACE, SP W.C.
36. BRADT, Capt D.L.
37. BRIDGES, PFC C.D.J. *
38. BRILINSKI, Sgt R.P. Jnr
39. BRIOSKY, J.
40. BROGDON, T*
41. BROOKS, BTFR T.M.
42. BROWN, ANA C.B.
43. BROWN, ANA D.K.
44. BROWN, J.
45. BUDZIAN, ANA S.A.
46. BUEGE, P.
47. BUNCH, SSgt R.L.
48. BURT, Sgt P.L.
49. BUTCH, ASM2 M.R.
50. BUTLER, SP T.D.
51. BUTTS, SSgt W.T.
52. CADY, PO2 A.T.
53. CALDWELL, Capt T.R.
54. CALLOWAY, PFC K.L.
55. CAMPISI, SSgt J.
56. CARR, Sgt J.C.
57. CARRANZA, H. Jnr.
58. CARRINGTON, SM M.C.
59. CASH, SP C.A.
60. CHAPMAN, Sgt C.J.
61. CHASE, Maj R.W.
62. CHINBURG, Capt M.L.
63. CLARK, B.
64. CLARK, SP B.S. *
65. CLARK AN L.M.
66. CLARK, MSgt O.F.
67. CLARK, SP S.D.
68. CLEMENTE, Mr S.J.
69. CLEYMAN, SSgt M.H.
70. CODISPODO, E.
71. COHEN, PFC G.A.
72. COLLINS, PFC M.R.
73. CONNELLY, Maj M.A.
74. CONNER, M.R. Snr
75. CONNOR, P.
76. COOKE, B.
77. COOKE, Cpl M.D.
78. COOPER, PFC A.B.
79. COOPER, Capt C.W.
80. COOPER, Sgt D.
81. CORMIER, Capt D.T.
82. COSTEN, Lt W.T.
83. COTTO, Cpl I.
84. CRASK, SP G.W.
85. CRAVER, Sgt A.B.

86. CROCKFORD, PO J.F.
87. CRONIN, Capt W.D. Jnr
88. CRONQUIST, SP M.R.
89. CROSS, S.*
90. CRUMBY, Sgt D.R. Jnr.
91. CRUZ, Mr G.
92. CUNNINGHAM, LCpl J.B.
93. CURTIN, CWO3 J.J.
94. DAILEY, PFC M.C. Jnr.
95. DAMIAN, SP R.T. Jnr.
96. DANIEL, C. *
97. DANIELS, SP M.D.
98. DANIELSON, Sgt D.
99. DAUGHERTY, PFC R.L. Jnr
100. DAVILA, SP M.A.
101. DAVIS, PFC M.R.
102. DEES, SSgt T. *
103. DELAGNEAU, Cpl R.A.
104. DELGADO SN3 D.
105. DELGADO, SP L.
106. DIERKING, Sgt R.A.
107. DIFFENBAUGH, WO1 T.M.
108. DILLON, Capt G.S.
109. DILLON, Sgt Y.
110. DOLVIN Capt K.R.
111. DONALDSON, CWO P.A.
112. DOUGHERTY, LCpl J.D.
113. DOUTHIT, LtCol D.A.
114. DOUTHIT, Sgt D.Q.
115. DURREL, R.
116. DWYER, Lt R.J.
117. EDWARDS, Capt J.R.
118. EICHENLAUB, Capt P.R. II
119. FAILS, Pte D. *
120. FAJARDO, Capt M.
121. FARNEN, SP S.P.
122. FELIX, LCpl E.
123. FIELDER, SP D.L.
124. FINNERAL, AMM3 G.S.
125. FITZ, Pte M.L.
126. FLEMING, AO3 A.J.
127. FLEMING, Pte J.J.
128. FONTAINE, AS G.A.
129. FOREMAN, Sgt I.L.
130. FOWLER, SP J.C.
131. GALVAN, A.
132. GARDNER, MSgt S.M. Jnr
133. GARRET, SSgt M.A.
134. GARVEY, CWO P.M.
135. GARZA, LCpl A.O.
136. GARZA, SP J.
137. GAY, PFC P. *
138. GENTRY, Sgt K.B.
139. GILLESPIE, Maj J.H.
140. GILLILAND, BT3 D.A.
141. GODFREY, CWO R.G.
142. GOLOGRAM, Sgt M.J.
143. GORDON, Maj J.M.
144. GRAYBEAL, 1stLt D.E.
145. GREGORY, LCpl T.L.
146. GRIMM, Capt W.D.
147. GUERRERO, AN J.L.
148. HADDAD, Cpl A.G. Jnr.
149. HAGGERTY, 1stLt T.J.
150. HAILEY, SSgt G.V.
151. HAMPTON, Sgt T.

*: Females
¶: Died on service with the Special Air Services Regiment.
French Army ranks are translated into their English equivalent.

UNITED STATES (cont)

152. HANCOCK, LtCol J.H. Jnr.
153. HANSEN, SSgt S.
154. HARRIS, SSgt M.A.
155. HARRISON, SSgt T.R.
156. HART, SP A.J.
157. HATCHER, SSgt R.E. Jnr
158. HAWS, Sgt J.D.
159. HAWTHORNE, Sgt J.D.
160. HECTOR, SP W.E.
161. HEDEEN, 1stLt E.D.
162. HEIN, WO K.P.
163. HEIN, Sgt L.E. Jnr
164. HENDERSON, Maj B.K.
165. HENRY-GARAY, L.
166. HERR, Capt D.R. Jnr
167. HERRERA, MSgt R.
168. HEYDEN, SP J.
169. HEYMAN, SP D.L.
170. HILL, SP T.
171. HILLS, AEA K. J.
172. HOAGE, PFC A.T.
173. HOCK, Maj P.S.
174. HODGES, R.
175. HOGAN, L.
176. HOLLAND, B.
177. HOLLEN, SP D.W. Jnr
178. HOLLENBECK, Sp D.C.
179. HOLT, AET3 W.A.
180. HOLYFIELD, R.
181. HOOK, Maj P.S.
182. HOPSON, Mr T. Jr
183. HORWATH, Cpl R.L.
184. HOWARD, PFC A.W
185. HUGHES, CWO R.
186. HULEE, SSgt R.J.
187. HULL, Lt D.V.
188. HURLEY, SgtMaj P.R.
189. HURLEY, Capt W.J.
190. HUTCHINSON, BT2 M.E.
191. HUTTO, PFC J.W.
192. HUYGHUE, FN W.L.
193. JACKSON, Sgt A.
194. JACKSON, PFC K.J.
195. JACKSON, M.
196. JACKSON, FCT3 T.J.
197. JAMES, SP J.W.
198. JARRELL, SP T.R.
199. JENKINS, LCpl T.A.
200. JOCK, MMFA D.W
201. JOEL, Cpl D.D.
202. JONES, AA A.
203. JONES, EM3 D.M.
204. JONES, SP G.D.
205. JONES, Cpl P.J.
206. JOSIAH, PO2 T.
207. KAMM, SSgt J.H.
208. KANUHA, D.
209. KELLER, Sgt K.T.
210. KELLY, 2ndLt S. *
211. KEMP, MSSA N.H.
212. KEOUGH, SP F.S.
213. KIDD, SP A.W.
214. KILKUS, Sgt J.R.
215. KILKUS, Mr A.
216. KIME, Capt J.G. III

217. KING, PFC J.L.
218. KIRK, PFC R.G. III
219. KNUTSON, TSgt L.A.
220. KONTZ, T.
221. KRAMER, PFC D.W.
222. KUTZ, Sgt E.B.
223. LAKE, Cpl V.T. Jnr
224. LaMOUREAUX, PFC D.C.
225. LANE, LCpl B.L.
226. LANG, LCpl J.M.
227. LARSON, Lt T.S.
228. LAWTON, 2ndLt L.K.
229. LEE, CWO R.R.
230. LEWIS, SSgt R.E.
231. LINDERMAN, LCpl M.E. Jnr
232. LINDSEY, SP S.J.
233. LONG, J.
234. LOVE, Lt J.H.
235. LUMPKINS, LCpl J.H.
236. LUPATSKY, EM2 R.H.
237. McCARTHY, Maj E.
238. McCOY, Cpl J.R.
239. McCREIGHT, AN B.A.
240. McDOUGLE, Sgt. M.
241. McKINNEY, CW2 C. *
242. McKINSEY, BTFA D.C.
243. McKNIGHT, SP B.L.
244. MADISON, SP A.
245. MAHAN, SP G.
246. MAKS, 1stLt J.D.
247. MALAK, G.
248. MANNS, FM M.N.
249. MARTIN, C.
250. MASON, SP S.G.
251. MATHEWS, K.
252. MAY, J.II.
253. MAYES, SP C.L. *
254. MIDDLETON, SP J.T.
255. MILLER, SP J.R.
256. MILLER, PFC M.A.
257. MILLS, SP M.W.
258. MILLS, R.
259. MITCHELL, Pte A.L. *
260. MITCHEM, E.
261. MOBLEY, SP P.D.
262. MOLLOR, Sgt N.A.
263. MONGRELLA, Sgt G.A.
264. MONROE, 1stLt M.N.
265. MONSEN, SSgt L.M.
266. MONTALVO, Sgt C.
267. MORAN, SSgt. T.J.
268. MORGAN, SSgt D.
269. MORGAN, WO J.K.
270. MULLIN, J.
271. MURPHY, 1stSgt J.
272. MURPHY, SFC D.T.
273. MURRAY, PFC J.C. Jnr
274. MYERS, SP D.R.
275. NEBERMAN, J.F.
276. NEEL, ANA R.L.
277. NELSON, AFC R.J.
278. NOBLE, S.*?
279. NOLINE, PFC M.A.
280. NOONAN, SP R.
281. O'BRIEN, Sgt C.L. *
282. OELSCHLAGER, J.

283. OLIVER, LCpl A.D.
284. OLSON, Capt J.J.
285. OLSON, 1stLt P.B.
286. ORTIZ, Spt P.E.
287. PACK, Cpl A.A.
288. PADDOCK, CW04 J.M.
289. PALMER, SP W.E.
290. PARKER, BT2 F.R. Jnr
291. PATTERSON, Pte A.T.
292. PAULSON, SP D.L.
293. PEREZ, TSgt D.G.
294. PERRY, SP K.J.
295. PHILLIPS, SP K.D.
296. PHILLIS, Capt S.R.
297. PLASCH, WO D.G.
298. PLUMMER, ABF2 M.J.
299. PLUNK, 1stLt J.
300. POOLE, SAN R.L.
301. POREMBA, LCpl K.A.
302. PORTER, LCpl C.J.
303. POULET, Capt J.B.
304. POWELL, Sgt D.R.
305. PRICE, Maj R.M.
306. RAINWATER, N.
307. RANDAZZO, Sgt R.M.
308. REEL, PFC J.D.
309. REICHLE, CWO H.H.
310. REID, Capt F. A.
311. RENNISON, SP R.D.
312. RITCH, PFC T.C.
313. RIVERA, Capt M. Jnr
314. RIVERS, Sgt E.
315. ROBINETTE, S.
316. ROBSON, SSgt M.R.
317. RODRIGUEZ, MSgt E.A. Jnr
318. ROLLINS, Sgt J.A.
319. ROMEI, Cpl T.W.
320. ROSE, 1stLt P.
321. ROSSI, Maj M.T. *
322. RUSH, PFC S.A.
323. RUSS, Sgt L.A.
324. SAN JUAN, LCpl A.P.
325. SANDERS, 1stSgt H.J. Jnr
326. SAPIAN, SP M.B. Jnr
327. SATCHELL, Sgt B.
328. SCHIEDLER, DS3 M.J.
329. SCHOLAND, T.
330. SCHRAMM, Maj S.G.
331. SCHROEDER, PFC S.A.
332. SCHULDT, Capt B.R.
333. SCHUMAUSS, M.
334. SCOTT, Sgt B.P
335. SEAY, DK3 T.B.
336. SETTIMI, MSSA J.A.
337. SHAW, SSgt D.A.
338. SHAW, PFC T.A.
339. SHEFFIELD, SSgt E.E.
340. SHERRY, 2ndLt K.M. *
341. SHUKERS, FCC J.W.
342. SIKO, SP S.J.
343. SIMPSON, Cpl B.K.
344. SMITH, MM3 J.A.
345. SMITH, SSgt J.M. Jr
346. SMITH, Sgt M.S.
347. SMITH, SFC R.G. Jnr
348. SNYDER, LCpl D.T.

349. SNYDER, Lt J.M.
350. SPACKMAN, SP B.K.
351. SPEICHER, PFC J.W.
352. SPEICHER, LtCdr M.S.
353. SPELLACY, Capt D.M.
354. SQUIRES, SP O.B. Jr
355. STEPHENS, SSgt C.H.
356. STEPHENS, J.
357. STEPHENSON, PFC D.J.
358. STEWART, LCpl A.D.
359. STEWART, RM R.T.
360. STOKES, Sgt A.
361. STONE, SP T.G.
362. STREETER, SFC G.E.
363. STREHLOW, Sgt W.A.
364. STRIBLING, Maj E.K.
365. SUMMERALL, R.
366. SYLVIA, Cpl J.H.
367. SWANO, SP P.L. Jnr
368. SWARTZENDRUBER, WO G.R.
369. TALLEY, Pte R.D.
370. TAPLEY, SFC D.L.
371. TATUM, SP J.D.
372. THOMAS, AMS3 P.J.
373. THORP, Capt J.K.
374. TILLAR, 1stLt D.P III
375. TORMANEN, LCpl T.R.
376. TRAUTMAN, SP S.R.
377. TURNER, C.
378. UNDERWOOD, Capt R.C.
379. VALENTINE, Lt(jg) C.E.
380. VALENTINE, Pte R.E.
381. VEGA, M.
382. VELAZQUEZ, Sgt M.V.
383. VIGRASS, Pte. S.N.
384. VILLAREAL, SMSgt C. Jnr
385. VIQUEZ, C.
386. VOLDEN, BT1 R.L.
387. WADE, PFC R.C.
388. WALDRON, LCpl J.E.
389. WALKER, PFC C.S.
390. WALKER, LCpl D.B.
391. WALLS, SP F.J.
392. WALRATH, Sp T.E.
393. WALTERS, Capt D.L. Jr
394. WANKE, PFC P.A.
395. WARE, SP B.M.
396. WEAVER, AE2 B.P.
397. WEAVER, P.
398. WEDGEWOOD, SP T.M.
399. WELCH, Sgt L.N.
400. WEST, ASMA J.D.
401. WHITTENBURG, Sgt S.L.
402. WIECZOREK, PFC D.M.
403. WILBOURN, Capt J. N.
404. WILCHER, Sgt J.
405. WILKINSON, MSS2 P.L.
406. WILLIAMSON, Cpl J.M.
407. WINKLE, PFC C.L.
408. WINKLEY, CWO B.S.
409. WITZKE, SSgt H.P. III
410. WOLVERTON, SP. R.V.
411. WORTHY, SP J.E.
412. WRIGHT, SP K.E.
413. ZABEL, Sp C.W.
414. ZOUGNER, Maj T.C.

*: Females

KUWAITI FEMALES	AGE
1. AL-AJMI, A.T.	(45)
2. AL-AIDAN, A. T.	(28)
3. AL-MUTAWA, J.M	(20)
4. AL-ABER, N.K.	(26)
5. AL-DOSSARI, N.M.	(20)
6. MARAFIE, Samira A.	(26)

KUWAITI MALES

1. ABBAS, Mohammed A. (21)
• ABDULLAH,
2. Khalid Y. (21)
3. Khalid A. (27)
4. Safa A. (40)
5. ADNAN, Matham R. (18)
• AHMAD,
6. Ahmad I. (39)
7. Ahmad A. (24)
8. Nasser M. (21)
9. Osama A. (15)
• Al-ABDALY,
10. Hamad A. (27)
11. Musaad S. (25)
12. Al-ABDELKARIM, Fahd A. (21)
13. Al-ABDULHUSSEIN, Bashar A. (27)
14. Al-ABDULJALIL, Fawzi I. (37)
15. Al-ABDULRAZZAK, Adel S. (39)
16. Al-ABRASH, Mohammed A. (46)
• Al-ADWANI,
17. Barges S. (20)
18. Khaleef M. (20)
19. Mutlaq A. (22)
20. Al-AESI, Abdelkarim (25)
21. Al-AFASI, Abdulla N. (24)
• Al-AHMAD,
22. Mohammed S. (32)
23. Salem K. (26)
24. Samah K. (31)
• Al-AJEEL,
25. Abdulla A. (31)
26. Faisal Z. (27)
27. AJMETMU, Mansour F. (21)
• Al-AJMI,
28. Abdulla S. (19)
29. Abdulla M. (25)
30. Aqab A. (24)
31. Fahd A. (37)
32. Hamad M. (21)
33. Hamad M. (41)
34. Hamad A. (24)
35. Hamdan A. (23)
36. Khalid M. (26)
37. Khalid N. (25)
38. Mohsen M. (20)
39. Mohammed S. (36)
40. Mohammed A. (27)
41. Mohammed N. (46)
42. Mansour A. (15)
43. Nasser A. (19)
44. Nasser F. (25)
45. Nawaf H. (16)
46. Shujam M. (49)
47. Saad M. (17)
48. Tareq M. (21)
49. Al-AKEEL, Mohammed H. (19)
50. Al-ALATI, Saad S. (20)
• Al-ALI,
51. Abdulla M. (37)
52. Abdelwaheb A. (35)
53. Hassan A. (26)
54. Salem A. (31)
55. Al-AMEERI, Nasser S. (24)
56. Al-AMIR, Abdulla S. (35)
• Al-ANZI,
57. Ahmad M. (26)
58. Ahmad S. (28)
59. Attallah A. (18)
60. Fahd A. (39)
61. Fahd S. (23)
62. Faisal A. (19)
63. Feras M. (28)
64. Jamaan S. (23)
65. Khalaf S. (25)
66. Khalifa A. (17)
67. Majid J. (31)
68. Matar A. (24)
69. Matar S. (19)
70. Mishal J. (29)
71. Misharif A. (28)
72. Mohammed A. (16)
73. Mohammed F. (24)
74. Mohammed J. (22)
75. Mohammed N. (29)
76. Mousa S. (20)
77. Mousa S. (23)
78. Nasser A. (21)
79. Nasser H. (50)
80. Saad M. (29)
81. Sakhnan (28)
82. Salah H. (26)
83. Salah M. (20)
84. Al-AREFAN, Abdulatief (32)
85. Al-ASAWASI, Azzam F. (23)
• Al-ASFOOR,
86. Abdulla A. (26)
87. Ali A. (16)
88. Ahmad H. (19)
89. Al-ASOUSI, Suleiman F. (25)
90. Al-ASSAF, Walid S. (21)
91. Al-ATEYA, Khalid H. (19)
92. Al-ATTAR, Jamal A. (27)
93. Al-ATWAN, Othman J. (29)
94. Al-AWAD, Ali Y. (29)
• Al-AWADI,
95. Mohammed N. (36)
96. Mohammed S. (21)
97. Al-AYAZ, Faeq M. (42)
• Al-AZMI,
98. Ahmad M. (20)
99. Ali A. (18)
100. Ali F. (39)
101. Hadi D. (26)
102. Hadi F. (23)
103. Ibrahim M. (25)
104. Lafer S. (15)
105. Al-AZRAN, Yousef B. (21)
106. Al-BAHAR, Ahmad A. (20)
• Al-BANNAI,
107. Emad M. (31)
108. Nabil K. (22)
• Al-BARAISI,
109. Makhled H. (35)
110. Saad M. (32)
111. Walid M. (18)
112. Al-BASEERI, Mohammed A. (38)
113. Al-BELOUSHI, Bader A. (27)
• Al-BERAISI,
114. Bader M. (22)
115. Hamad T. (?)
116. Al-DAKHEEL, Mohammed (36)
• Al-DARBAS,
117. Khalid J. (37)
118. Salah K. (30)
119. Al-DAREES, Khalid A. (42)
120. Al-DARIEH, Hussein J. (30)
• Al-DEEHANI,
121. Ayed F. (17)
122. Fahd A. (22)
123. Makhled J. (22)
124. Musaad A. (18)
125. Nawaf M. (21)
126. Saud N. (19)
127. Tareq M. (16)
128. Al-DEERI, Nawaf M. (18)
129. Al-DOKHI, Salah A. (21)
• Al-DOSSARI,
130. Ahmad M. (21)
131. Ali M. (20)
132. Ibrahim A. (26)
133. Musaad M. (22)
134. Salem F. (17)
135. Salem R. (45)
136. Saud A. (25)
137. Al-DOUWAILA, Rashid Z. (25)
138. Al-DOUWAISAN, Ali A. (38)
139. Al-EID, Khalid A. (28)
• Al-FADHLI,
140. Bader F. (18)
141. Hamoud M. (20)
142. Nasser H. (17)
143. Sami A. (68)
144. Sayer A. (22)
145. Al-FAHAID, Ahmad M. (19)
• Al-FAHD,
146. Bader F. (30)
147. Khalid H. (20)
148. Nawaf S. (22)
149. Walid H. (25)
150. Al-FAIZ, Kamal A. (24)
151. Al-FALAH, Zafar J, (23)
152. Al-FAZIEH, Adel F. (28)
153. Al-FODERI, Ahmad S. (24)
• Al-FOUZAN,
154. Abdulrazzak A. (37)
155. Jassim M. (38)
156. Yousef M. (31)
• Al-FULAIJ,
157. Amman A. (24)
158. Safi M (21)
• Al-GHARIB,
159. Abdullah R. (33)
160. Falah R. (33)
161. Saud M. (19)
162. Al-HABISHI, Fouaz S. (22)
163. Al-HABLAH, Nasser A. (29)
164. Al-HADDAD, Abdullah S. (28)
165. Al-HAIFI, Nasser S. (24)
166. Al-HAJANI, Salah A. (34)
• Al-HAJERI,
167. Falah H. (16)
168. Hamad M. (22)
169. Khalifa R. (18)
• Al-HAMAD,
170. Adel F. (23)
171. Ahmad A. (20)
172. Bader A. (32)
• Al-HARSHANI,
173. Bader N. (20)
174. Hamoud (39)
• Al-HASHASH,
175. Khalifa A. (22)
176. Yasser A. (20)
177. Al-HATLANI, Mohammed H. (24)
178. Al-HAWLA, Mohammed H. (26)
179. Al-HAYYAN, Abdulmohsen F. (17)
180. Al-HOULI, Jamal A. (31)
181. Al-HUBAISHI, Saud A. (35)
182. Al-HUSSEINI, Mohammed J. (29)
183. Al-IBRAHIM, Mansour S. (15)

KUWAITI MALES (cont)

184. Al-JADAIE, Khalifa M. (36)
185. Al-JADI, Shakir A. (22)
186. Al-JAHAMA, Mohammed A. (32)
187. Al-JANAIE, Khalid N. (20)
188. Al-JASSAR, Nasser F. (32)
189. Al-JAZZAF, Jamal M. (23)
190. Al-JEDI, Nabil N. (22)
191. Al-JEERAN, Walid I. (25)
192. Al-JEHMAN, Noori A. (29)
193. Al-JOWAISRI, Nawaf I. (22)
194. Al-JUHMAH, Nabil A. (25)
195. Al-KADRI, Zachria A. (35)
196. Al-KAHAIDI, Abdulla J. (34)
• Al-KANDARI,
197. Ahmad A. (24)
198. Bader G. (28)
199. Al-KARAZ, Mohammed A. (63)
200. Al-KENEENI, Abdulaziz A. (55)
201. Al-KHADHER, Salah A. (17)
202. Al-KHALAF, Abdulmohsen M. (27)
203. Al-KHALAF, Fawzi A. (24)
• Al-KHALAIFI,
204. Mishal I. (25)
205. Mousa I. (25)
• Al-KHALDI,
206. Abdulrasool S. (17)
207. Anwar A. (23)
208. Barges A. (29)
209. Fahd K. (17)
210. Jassim M. (20)
211. Khalid D. (19)
212. Mutlaq A. (20)
213. Nasser S. (31)
214. Sahan N. (27)
215. Al-KHANNA, Salah N. (22)
216. Al-KHARAZ, Abdulaziz A (36)
217. Al-KHIAT, Rida I. (34)
218. Al-KHOUWARI, Ahmad M. (22)
219. Al-KREENEGH, Ali M. (57)
• Al-KOUAH,
220. Khalid A. (26)

221. Saud A. (26)
222. Al-LOMEAH, Jassim H. (17)
223. Al-MAHEENI, Mohammed S. (25)
224. Al-MAJID, Salah A. (23)
225. Al-MAKHEIL, Khalid A. (20)
226. Al-MALLA, Fawzi A. (22)
• Al-MANAH,
227. Adnan F. (67)
228. Hani F. (21)
229. Walid F. (28)
• Al-MANAIE,
230. Bader A. (25)
231. Khalid A. (23)
232. Al-MARAISHID, Rashid I. (33)
233. Al-MAREEKHI, Fahd K. (21)
234. Al-MARHASH, Nasser S. (19)
235. Al-MARRI, Ali H. (23)
236. Al-MARZOUQ, Mohammed A. (32)
237. Al-MASAHLAK, Nasser A. (41)
238. Al-MASOUD, Mohammed Q. (21)
239. Al-MATHKOUR, Jamal A. (32)
240. Al-MEKAYEL, Nasser H. (20)
241. Al-MERUSHAID, Adel I. (26)
242. Al-MESSILAH, Hani A. (18)
243. Al-MISFER, Abdulaziz A. (27)
244. Al-MISHARI, Yousef T. (50)
245. Al-MOOSA, Basil B. (24)
• Al-MOUEEL,
246. Abdulla J. (26)
247. Makki J. (21)
248. Al-MOUNS, Mouns M. (27)
249. Al-MOWAIZRI, Najem F. (17)
250. Al-MUHANNA, Saeed F. (22)
251. Al-MULAITI, Abdulaziz T. (20)
252. Al-MUNAS, Jamal M. (21)
253. Al-MUSALAM, Mishal A. (18)
254. Al-MUTAIR, Al-Mohaidi M. (23)
• Al-MUTAIRI,
255. Abdullah F. (16)

256. Abdullah S. (25)
257. Ali S. (48)
258. Bader M. (19)
259. Bader S. (22)
260. Fahd M. (20)
261. Fahd S. (23)
262. Falah J. (21)
263. Feahan M. (55)
264. Feras A. (18)
265. Fouaz B. (18)
266. Hamdan M. (15)
267. Hilal S. (59)
268. Jathli M. (33)
269. Khalid M. (21)
270. Lafi F. (23)
271. Mansour T. (27)
272. Mazi H. (23)
273. Misfer S. (50)
274. Mohammed A. (18)
275. Mohammed F. (28)
276. Muslet M. (36)
277. Mutlaq A. (36)
278. Mutlaq S. (21)
279. Naif M. (23)
280. Nasser M. (21)
281. Nawaf A. (18)
282. Obeid F. (20)
283. Rajah D. (19)
284. Rashid M. (26)
285. Saeed M. (24)
286. Safah B. (50)
287. Salem O. (21)
288. Sami M. (18)
289. Saad A. (22)
290. Salah M. (17)
291. Al-MUTAWA, Hisham A. (42)
292. Al-MUZAIN, Abdelwahib A. (50)
293. Al-NASHI, Khalid R. (28)
294. Al-OBEID, Mohammed A. (29)
295. Al-OMAR, Abdulla Y. (39)
• Al-OSAIMI,
296. Bader A. (19)
297. Hussam M. (17)
298. Al-OSTAD, Yacoub Y. (27)
• Al-OTAIBI,
299. Abdulrahman A. (17)
300. Hamdi H. (25)
301. Hamdan H. (24)
302. Khalid R. (20)
303. Khunaiser M. (24)
304. Matab M. (17)
305. Misfer S. (26)
306. Mishal O. (19)
307. Mohammed M. (23)
308. Mohammed N. (18)
309. Nasser A. (19)
310. Obeid M. (24)
311. Salem M. (29)
312. Talal M. (18)

313. Al-OWAIHAN, Abdulla A. (38)
314. Al-QADEEFI, Abdulla I. (22)
• Al-QALAF,
315. Ahmad A. (20)
316. Hussein A. (22)
• Al-QATTAN,
318. Faisal A. (28)
319. Khalil S. (25)
320. Mustapha N. (23)
• Al-QHATANI,
321. Feras A. (19)
322. Majid F. (27)
323. Mutlaq F. (24)
324. Tareq M. (31)
325. Al-QOUBAH, Bader M. (25)
326. Al-RABEEDI, Abdulrahman S. (17)
327. Al-RAHELI, Jassim M. (20)
328. Al-RAJAB, Nabil M. (22)
329. Al-RAQM, Adel A. (38)
• Al-RASHEEDI,
330. Abdulla F. (21)
331. Ajmi A. (27)
332. Emad F. (22)
333. Fahd B. (27)
334. Hajab S. (23)
335. Marshad A. (24)
336. Marshad J. (23)
337. Nahi A. (25)
338. Saad B. (20)
339. Saeed A. (21)
340. Salah A. (18)
341. Salah E. (25)
342. Saleem A. (19)
343. Saqar T. (25)
344. Shafi M. (27)
345. Suroor F. (24)
346. Zafar A. (23)
• Al-RASHID,
347. Emad Y. (20)
348. Khalid A. (23)
349. Mohammed A. (26)
350. Sami K. (25)
351. Al-REHAN, Abdullah I. (20)
• Al-RIFAI,
352. Adnan M. (34)
353. Ahmad A. (19)
354. Fawzi A. (38)
355. Al-ROQAI, Abdulla A. (25)
• Al-ROUMI,
356. Azzam A. (28)
357. Emad A. (33)
358. Fahd K. (26)
359. Al-RUSHOOD, Nabil A. (31)
360. Al-SADANI, Mubarak (25)

KUWAITI MALES (cont)

- Al-SAEEDI,
361. Hamad S. (39)
362. Hamoud M. (18)
363. Al-SAFAR,
Samir J. (20)
- Al-SAHALI,
364. Hamoud I. (32)
365. Raja H. (33)
366. Al-SAHOUD,
Jassim S. (20)
367. Al-SAIF,
Munzer N. (18)
368. Al-SAMAK,
Jassim H. (20)
369. Al-SAMEEM,
Mohammed M. (19)
- Al-SANE,
370. Abdulaziz S. (20)
371. Faisal A. (53)
372. Khalid A. (33)
373. Nasser A. (47)
374. Al-SARHEED,
Meshid M. (35)
375. Al-SEEKAN,
Suleiman, R. (46)
376. Al-SERAFAI,
Abdelwahab A. (28)
377. Al-SEYAFI,
Hussam A. (26)
378. Al-SHAHAB,
Jassim M. (52)
- Al-SHAHEEN,
379. Fahd A. (23)
380. Shaheen A. (23)
381. Al-SHAMLAN,
Adel A. (20)
- Al-SHAMMERI,
382. Abdullah F. (20)
383. Abdulrahman A. (24)
384. Abdulrahman N. (35)
385. Ahmad A. (20)
386. Ali S. (30)
387. Arak S. (19)
388. Hamoud M. (22)
389. Hussein A. (28)
390. Hussein A. (23)
391. Hussein S. (21)
392. Jarallah K. (34)
393. Khalid M. (33)
394. Khalid M. (33)
395. Khalifa T. (26)
396. Mamdouah H. (37)
397. Mohammed N. (37)
398. Muter A. (33)
399. Salem A. (20)
400. Salah M. (27)
401. Tareq F. (21)
402. Al-SHARAF, Issa A. (28)
403. Al-SHARAN,
Walid A. (25)
404. Al-SHAREEDA,
Khalid A. (25)
405. Al-SHARHAN,
Khalid A. (22)

406. Al-SHARQAWI,
Bader A. (29)
- Al-SHATTI,
407. Faisal M. (28)
408. Mustapha A. (25)
409. Al-SHAWI,
Anwar A. (19)
- Al-SHAYEJI,
410. Bader A. (21)
411. Lowai A. (19)
412. Al-SHEIDI,
Salah M. (17)
413. Al-SHIRAZI,
Azzam F. (22)
414. Al-SHOUMANI,
Abdulrahman H. (24)
415. Al-SHUREEFI,
Mohammed A. (16)
416. Al-SIJARI,
Yacoub Y. (47)
417. Al-SOUAGH,
Mohammed S. (17)
418. Al-SOUAIDI,
Obeid A. (21)
- Al-SUBAYEE,
419. Khalid N. (17)
420. Shafi M. (22)
421. Al-SULTAN,
Assad A. (20)
- Al-SULTANI,
422. Saud R. (20)
423. Saud S. (21)
424. Al-SULUBEY,
Mohammed M. (61)
425. Al-TAMIMI,
Mansour G. (44)
426. Al-TARARWA,
Ahmad I. (23)
427. Al-TAWASH,
Mohammed H. (30)
428. Al-TAYYAR,
Mohammed B. (20)
429. Al-THANAYAN,
Mohammed J. (24)
430. Al-THAQAB,
Mansour F. (18)
- Al-THUFEIRI,
431. Bader D. (34)
432. Fahd A. (15)
433. Faisal G. (20)
434. Noori K. (15)
435. Saud A. (18)
436. Zaben M. (32)
- Al-TOWAIJRI,
437. Khalid S. (30)
438. Riad I. (32)
439. Al-TOWALA,
Abdulrazzak D. (22)
440. Al-WUHAIB,
Abdulatief N. (18)
- Al-YACOUB,
441. Abdullah R. (40)
442. Yousef Y. (37)
443. Al-YACOUT,
Tareq M. (26)

444. Al-YAMANI,
Abdulaziz Y. (29)
445. Al-ZAMEL,
Yousef Z. (27)
- Al-ZAQAH,
446. Habib H (42)
447. Mohammed A. (40)
- ALI,
448. Faiz H. (23)
449. Hussein M. (27)
450. Mishal Y. (20)
451. Yacoub H. (24)
452. ANBAR, Safa (40)
453. ALIABDUL,
Amer Z. (19)
454. ARAB,
Yasser A. (59)
455. ASHKANANI,
Amair A. (28)
456. AYEDH,
Khalid A. (23)
457. AZRAN,
Ahmad N. (28)
458. BAHMAN,
Hussein S. (35)
459. BEHBEHANI,
Adnan M. (20)
- BOUSHAHRI,
460. Nabil A. (40)
461. Abdulrazzak A. (26)
462. BUARKI,
Abdullah M. (29)
463. BURISLI, Talal B. (24)
464. BUHADEDA,
Mohammed F. (20)
465. BURAHMAN,
Mohammed A. (23)
466. BURESLI,
Nasser B. (27)
467. DOWALIAH,
Mohammed R. (19)
- FAHD,
468. Ahmad K. (24)
469. Omar A. (20)
- FAIZ,
470. Ahmad I. (27)
471. Khalid A. (23)
472. Suleiman I. (22)
473. FARAJ, Khalid B. (23)
- GHLOUM,
474. Jamal A. (31)
475. Mousa M. (27)
476. Samir A. (21)
477. HAJJIA,
Mohammed A. (34)
478. HAMZA,
Mohammed S. (50)
- HASSAN,
479. Fadel I. (19)
480. Hassan G. (38)
481. Mohammed J. (37)
482. HAZRAN,
Mubarak S. (34)
- HUSSEIN,
483. Ahmad A. (33)

484. Bashar M. (16)
485. Hussein M. (19)
486. Mohammed A. (38)
- IBRAHIM,
487. Khalid M. (17)
488. Walid M. (22)
- ISMAEL,
489. Walid A. (18)
490. Walid S. (28)
491. ISSA,
Khalid A. (17)
492. JAFFAR,
Naji F. (24)
- JASSIM,
493. Mustapha A. (26)
494. Taleb A. (24)
495. KHALID,
Khalid A. (22)
496. KHALIL,
Raed A. (20)
- MARAFI,
497. Abdelmahdi A. (26)
498. Adnan S. (23)
- MALLALAH,
499. Faisal H. (30)
500. Hamad A. (26)
501. MANSOUR,
Salah H. (20)
502. MENDENI,
Salah J. (21)
- MOHAMMED,
503. Ahmad A. (35)
504. Faisal A. (26)
505. Mohammed A. (36)
506. Nasser H. (26)
507. Rida K. (29)
508. Saud M. (36)
509. Salah F. (26)
510. Ziad M. (17)
511. MUKBEL,
Abdullah M. (18)
512. MURDA,
Bader H. (20)
513. MUSTAPHA,
Ahmad A. (35)
- NASSER,
514. Abdulrazzak A. (64)
515. Ahmad B. (20)
516. Khalid B. (19)
517. QABANDI,
Hussein A. (22)
518. QAMBAR,
Hassan A. (35)
519. QATAH,
Suleiman K. (18)
- RASHID,
520. Adnan A. (32)
521. Shaalan H. (22)
522. ROUWAIH,
Jalal A. (19)
- SAAD,
523. Hani A. (25)
524. Marzouq A. (35)
525. Riad A. (25)
526. SALEM, Abdullah S. (17)

KUWAITI MALES (cont)
527. SALMAN, Salem A. (20)
528. SAMIRA,
     Abdullah A. (56)
529. SAUD, Saud F. (25)
530. SAYED, Sayed M. (32)
531. SHAKIR, Shehab A. (31)
532. SHOWAISH,
     Jamal A. (32)
533. SUKER, Salem A. (31)
534. TEOW,
     Mohammed (40)
535. TURKI, Mansour (39)
•   YOUSEF,
536. Azzam Y. (22)
537. Yousef M. (31)
538. ZAMAN, Essam (28)

BAHRAINI NATIONAL
1. BURKUBA,
    Hussein I. (26)

EGYPTIAN NATIONALS
1. ABDARBA,
    Mahmoud A. (?)
2. ABDULFATTAH, A.A. (?)
3. AL-HATAB,
    Ahmad M. (28)
4. AL-MISRI, Adel A. (39)

INDIAN NATIONALS
1. SINGH, Surinder (32)
2. KANT, Nano A. (29)
3. MOHAMMED, Boor (?)

IRANIAN NATIONALS
1. Al-MAAS, Issa F. (36)
2. Al-QATTAN, Amir H. (27)
3. Al-QATTAN,
    Mustapha H. (23)
4. ALI, Hussein A. (24)
5. BORASHARNI,
    Ali A. (20)

LEBANESE NATIONALS
1. Al-HARIRI, Raad O. (33)
2. ALI, Mohammed M. (18)
3. NASOHI, Subhi K. (28)

OMANI NATIONAL
1. AL-BELOUSHI,
    Mohammed Y. (24)

PHILIPINNES NATIONAL
1. LEEBID, Francisca H. (?)

SAUDI NATIONALS
1. Al-ASFOOR,
    Anwar M. (29)
2. Al-BADAWI,
    Abdulaziz I. (23)
3. Al-DOSSARI,
    Barges M. (23)
4. Al-DOSSARI,
    Khalid A. (19)
5. Al-DOSSARI,
    Misfer S. (23)
6. Al-DOSSARI,
    Salem A. (25)

7. Al-SALAM,
    Khalid J. (22)
8. AL-TAYYAR,
    Mohammed A. (51)
9. Al-THUFEIRI,
    Ali Z. (18)
10. Al-THUFEIRI,
    Fahd A. (19)
11. Al-THUFEIRI,
    Mohammed A. (19)
12. Al-ZAWAIHER,
    Arif I. (19)
13. ZAID,
    Zaid S. (21)

SYRIAN NATIONALS
1. Al-ABDULHUSSEIN,
    Bashar A. (?)
2. Al-AJAM,
    Mohammed Y. (19)
3. AWAZ,
    Ahmad M. (38)
4. Al-HAFADH,
    Abdulrazzak A. (?)

STATELESS PERSONS
1. AFAT, Abdulla A. (?)
2. AHMAD, Ahmad A. (?)
3. AL-ADWAN, Obeid R (42)
4. AL-ANZI, Hamad B. (32)
5. AL-ANZI, Kazi A. (45)
6. AL-ANZI, Nasser M. (24)
7. Al-HARBI, Maouf J. (41)
8. Al-MALKI, Ali Y. (27)

9. Al-MASEERI,
    Bassee T. (?)
10. AL-MUFFAZI, Ali E. (38)
11. AL-MUTAIRI, Rafie A. (?)
12. Al-ONAIDI,
    Abdulla A. (22)
13. Al-RASHEEDI,
    Rouak M. (?)
14. Al-SATTI,
    Abdulla J. (28)
15. Al-SHAMMERI,
    Fahd W. (25)
16. Al-SHARIF,
    Matar M. (?)
17. Al-SHATTI,
    Khalid M. (24)
18. Al-THUFEIRI,
    Abdulla T. (33)
19. AL-THUFEIRI,
    Farhan H. (30)
20. ALI, Ali M. (25)
21. FARHAN,
    Abdelkarim M (27)
22. MUSTAPHA,
    Kader A. (21)
23. REZA,
    Mohammed S. (38)
24. SABAH, Salal H. (16)
25. SHADID, Jaber H. (45)
26. ZAHER, Hilal S. (31)

UN SECURITY COUNCIL RESOLUTIONS ON THE CRISIS

660 *Condemning Invasion,* 2 August, 1990

661 *Imposing Trade Sanctions,* 6 August, 1990

662 *Declaring Iraq's Annexation of Kuwait Null and Void,* 9 August, 1990

664 *Demanding Freedom for Foreign Hostages, Diplomats,* 18 August, 1990

665 *Authorising Enforcement of Trade Embargo,* 25 August, 1990

666 *Allowing Humanitarian Supplies into Iraq,* 13 September, 1990

667 *Condemning Iraqi Raids on Diplomatic Premises in Kuwait,* 16 September, 1990

669 *Humanitarian Relief,* 24 September, 1990

670 *Imposing Air Embargo on Iraq,* 25 September, 1990

674 *Condemning Iraqi Hostage-Taking, Human Rights Abuses,* 29 October, 1990

677 *Entrusting Kuwait's Population Records to the UN,* 28 November, 1990

678 *Authorising Use of Force, if Iraq does not leave Kuwait,* 29 November, 1990

686 *Temporary Cease-Fire Resolution,* 2 March, 1991

687 *Permanent Cease-Fire Resolution,* 2 April, 1991

688 *Demanding Iraq Cease Repression of Kurds,* 5 April, 1991

689 *Establishing UNIKOM,* 9 April, 1991

692 *Establishing UN Compensation Fund,* 20 May, 1991

699 *Authorising Inspection of Iraq's Weapons of Mass Destruction,* 17 June, 1991

700 *On Arms Embargo,* 17 June, 1991

705 *Setting Percentage of Iraqi Oil Sales to go to Compensation Fund,* 15 August, 1991

706 *Allowing Iraq to Sell Oil to Finance Humanitarian and UN Work,* 15 August, 1991

707 *Condemning Iraqi Non-Cooperatioan with Weapons Inspections,* 15 August, 1991

712 *Concerning the Humanitarian Needs of the Iraqi Population and the Financing of their Requirements,* 19 September, 1991

715 *Concerning the Inspection and Verification of Iraq's Weapons of Mass Destruction, particularly Nuclear,* 11 October, 1991

773 *On Demarcation of the Land Border between Iraq and Kuwait,* 26 August, 1991

778 *Requiring the Transfer of Iraqi Funds held outside Iraq to a UN Escrow Account to Finance the Requirements of Various Preceding UN Security Council Resolutions, and the Sale of Iraqi Petroleum and Petroleum Products held outside Iraq for the Same Purposes,* 2 October, 1992

806 *On Border Incidents,* 5 February, 1993

878 *On Compensation for Displaced Iraqis,* 3 March, 1994

949 *Condemning Moves by Iraqi Troops to Kuwaiti Border,* 15 October, 1994

BIBLIOGRAPHY

Abu-Hakima, A. *History of Eastern Arabia: The Rise and Development of Bahrain, Kuwait and Wahhabi Saudi Arabia*, London: Probsthain, 1967

Abu-Hakima, A. *The Modern History of Kuwait 1750-1965*, London: Luzac, 1983

Al-Damkhi, Dr A. *Invasion: Saddam Hussein's Reign of Terror in Kuwait*, London: Kuwait Research and Advertising, 1992

Al-Faras, N. *Diary of a Prisoner of War*, Kuwait: National Committee for Missing and POW's, 1993

Al-Gosaibi, G. *The Gulf Crisis: An Attempt to Understand*, London: Kegan Paul, 1993

Al-Hammadi, Dr A. & Al-Abdalrazaq, A. *Atlas of Iraqi War Crimes in the State of Kuwait*, Kuwait, Al-Qabas Press, 1994

Al-Khalil, S. *Republic of Fear: The Inside Story of Saddam's Iraq*, London: Hutchinson Radius, 1989

Al-Sadani, N. *Asrar Al-Qabandi* (Arabic), London: Noureya Al-Sadani, 1992

Al-Saud, HRH General Prince K. bin S., & Seale P. *Desert Warrior: A Personal View of the Gulf War by the Joint Forces Commander*, New York: HarperCollins, 1995

Allen, T., Berry, F. & Polmar N. *War in the Gulf*, London: Maxwell-Macmillan, 1991

Al-Qabas, *Various* (Arabic)

Al-Watan, *Various* (Arabic)

Amnesty International, *Iraq's Occupation of Kuwait*, December 19th, 1990

Arab Times, The, *Various*

Atkinson, R. *Crusade. The Untold Story of the Gulf War*, London: HarperCollins, 1993

Belohorska, I. *My Second Homeland, Kuwait*, Kuwait, 1991

Babcock, F. *Caught in Kuwait. A Story of God's Miraculous Care in Modern Times*, Boise ID: Pacific Press, 1992

Bishop, P. *Famous Victory*, London: Sinclair-Stevenson, 1991

Braybrook, R. Air Power: *The Coalition and Iraqi Air Forces. Desert Storm Special 2*, London: Osprey, 1991

Canby, T. *After the Storm*, National Geographic, August 1991

Casey, P. *Forgotten Victims: Kuwait's Prisoners in Iraq*, London: Planet Publishing, 1994

Chicago Tribune, The, *Various*

Cienciala, G. *A Guest of Saddam Hussein*, Contact, December 1991, English Language Congregation, National Evangelical Church In Kuwait

Cohen, R. & Gatti, C. *In the Eye of the Storm*: The Life of General H. Norman Schwarzkopf, London: Bloomsbury, 1991

Cureton, Lieutenant-Colonel C. *U.S. Marines in the Persian Gulf, 1990-1991: With the 1st Marine Division In Desert Shield and Desert Storm*, Washington: History and Museums Division, Headquarters, U.S. Marine Corps, 1993

Darwish, A. & Alexander, G. *Unholy Babylon*, London: Gollancz, 1991

David, P. et al. *Triumph in the Desert*, New York: Random House, 1991

De La Billière, General Sir P. *Storm Command*, Dubai: Motivate Publishing, 1992

Dolman, J. *My Testimony*, Contact, December 1991, English Language Congregation, National Evangelical Church In Kuwait

Duncan, Colonel B.A.C. *Cruelty and Compassion: an Englishman in Kuwait*, Army Quarterly and Defence Journal, Vol. 121, No. 2, Gulf War Issue, 1991

Easton, Dr J. & Turner, Dr S. *Detention of British Citizens as Hostages in the Gulf –*

Health, Psychological, and Family Consequences, British Medical Journal, Volume 303, November 16th, 1991

Edakitil, G. *Our God Reigns*, Contact, December 1991, English Language Congregation, National Evangelical Church In Kuwait

Freedman, L. & Karsh, E. *The Gulf Conflict 1990-1991*, London: Faber and Faber, 1993

Fremont, C. *Eyewitness to Invasion: Hiding Out in Occupied Kuwait*, Soldier of Fortune, May 1991

Fronabarger, J. *God Will Never Let Us Down*, Contact, December 1991, English Language Congregation, National Evangelical Church In Kuwait

Gilchrist, P. Sea Power: *The Coalition and Iraqi Navies. Desert Storm Special 3*, London: Osprey, 1991

Guardian Weekly, The, *Various*

Heikal, M. *Illusions of Triumph. An Arab View of the Gulf War*, London: HarperCollins, 1992

Hiro, D. *Desert Shield to Desert Storm: The Second Gulf War*, London: HarperCollins Paladin, 1992

Hiro, D. *The Longest War*, London: Grafton Books, 1989

Hogan, J., Hogan, R. & Meyer, L. *Trapped in Kuwait; Countdown to Armageddon*, Lynnwood WA: Chas Franklin, 1991

Horwitz, A. *Baghdad Without a Map, and other Misadventures in Arabia*, New York: Plume 1991

International Herald Tribune, The, *Various*

International Institute For Strategic Studies. *The Military Balance 1990-1991*, London: Brassey's, 1990

International Institute For Strategic Studies. *The Military Balance 1987-1988*, London: IISS, 1987

Jowers, K., *Kuwait Assignment*, Married to the Military, Issue Unknown

Keenan, B. *An Evil Cradling*, London: Random House Vintage, 1992

Kelly, M. *Martyrs' Day. Chronicle of a Small War*, London: Macmillan, 1993

Kirkland, F. (Ed.) *Operation Damask. The Gulf War, Iraq-Kuwait 1990-1991*; Macarthur Press, Sydney, 1992

Kuwait Times, The, *Various*

Lacey, R. *The Kingdom*, London: Hutchinson, 1981

Lambert, L. & Lambert, E. *The Other Kuwait*, Worthington OH: Lambert, 1993

Latham, D. *Occupation Diary, Kuwait*: Noureya Al-Sadani, Kuwait, 1992

Lauterpacht, E. et al (Editors). *The Kuwait Crisis: The Basic Documents*, Cambridge International Documents Series Volume 1, Cambridge U.K.: Grotius, 1991

Lewis, T. & Brookes, J. *The Human Shield*, Lichfield, U.K., Publication date unknown

Lockwood, G. *Diary of a Human Shield*, London: Bloomsbury, 1991

Melson, Major C., Englander, E. & Dawson, Captain D. (Compilers), *U.S. Marines in the Persian Gulf, 1990-1991: Anthology and Annotated Bibliography* Washington: History and Museums Division, Headquarters, U.S. Marine Corps, 1992

Moore, M. *A Woman at War: Storming Kuwait with the U.S. Marines*, New York: Macmillan, 1993

New Arabia, *Various*

New York Times, The, *Various*

Newsweek, *Various*

Nichols, Flight-Lieutenant J. & Peters, Flight-Lieutenant J. *Tornado Down*, London: Michael Joseph, 1991

Peake, A. *Guest of the President*, Dulwich, South Australia: Tudor, 1991

Porter, J. *Under Siege in Kuwait*, London: Gollancz, 1991

Powell, General C. & Persico, J. *My American Journey*, New York: Random House, 1995

Quilter, Colonel C., *U.S. Marines in the Persian Gulf, 1990-1991: With the I Marine Expeditionary Force in Desert Shield and Desert Storm*, Washington: History and Museums Division, Headquarters, U.S. Marine Corps, 1993

Rajab, J. *Invasion Kuwait, An English Woman's Tale*, London: Radcliffe, 1993

Ripley, T. *Land Power: The Coalition and Iraqi Armies. Desert Storm Special 1*, London: Osprey, 1991

Sasson, J. *The Rape of Kuwait*, New York: Knightsbridge, 1991

Schwarzkopf, General H. & Petre, P, *It Doesn't Take a Hero*, New York: Bantam

Schofield, R. (Editor) *Territorial Foundations of the Gulf States*, London: Geopolitics and International Boundaries Research Centre, School of Oriental and African Studies, University College London, 1994

Sifry, M. & Cerf, C. (Editors) *The Gulf War Reader. History, Documents, Opinions*, London: Times Books, 1991

Simpson, J. *From The House of War: John Simpson in the Gulf*, London, Arrow Books, 1991

State Organization For Tourism, General Establishment For Travel And Tourism Services, *Iraq: A Tourist Guide*, Baghdad, 1982

Stevens, P. (Editor) *The Iraqi Invasion of Kuwait: American Reflection*s, Washington D.C.: International Education and Communications Group

U.S. News And World Report. *Triumph Without Victory: The Unreported History of the Persian Gulf War*, New York: Random House, 1992

U.S. Army War Crimes Documentation Center, International Affairs Division, Office of the Judge-Advocate General, *Report on Iraqi War Crimes (Desert/ Shield/ Desert Storm) [Unclassified Version]*, Washington, 1992

U.S. Information Service, *Inferno: The Legacy of Destruction in Kuwait*, 1991

U.S. Information Service, *Seven Months to Freedom*, 1991

Vine, P. & Casey, P. Kuwait, *A Nation's Story*, London: Immel, 1992

Woodward, R. *The Commanders*, New York: Simon and Schuster, 1991

Yergin, D. *The Prize. The Epic Quest for Oil, Money & Powe*r, New York: Simon and Schuster, 1991

Zorpette, G. *How Iraq Reverse-Engineered the Bomb*, Spectrum, April 1992, The Institute of Electrical and Mechanical Engineers (UK)

INDEX

The letter to participants, other preliminary material, photographs and their captions, illustrations and appendices are not included in this index.

Apart from obvious contractions of titles and military ranks, abbreviations used include: Affrs: Affairs; Agncy: Agency; Agree't: Agreement; Amb./ Ambass.: Ambassador; Amer: American; Armrd: Armoured/ Armored; artlly: artillery; Assmbly: Assembly; Assoc.: Association/ Associates; athr. author; Att.: Attaché; Aust.: Australian; Batt: Battalion; Bghdd: Baghdad; Brig./ brig.: Brigade; Brit.: British; Broad.: Broadcasting; cdr: commander; Corp'n: Corporation; Ch/ Chf: Chief; Cncl.: Council; Comm.: Commercial; Cnsl: Consul; Conf.: Conference; Coy: Company (military); C'tee: Committee; concess.: concession(s); Cres.: Crescent; Ctr: Centre/Center; deleg(s): delegation(s); Dep: Deputy; Dpt/ Dept.: Department; dipl(s), dplmt(s): diplomat(s); desig.: designate; Dir: Director; Div'n: Division (military); Emb.: Embassy; evac.: evacuation; fed'n: federation; FM: Foreign Minister; For./ frgn: Foreign, foreign; Fr. French; Gd/ gd: Guard/ guard; Gen.: General (as in Secretary General); Germ.: German; GM: General Manager; Gov't: Government; Gvnrt: Governorate; Grp: Group; hstg: hostage; Inf: Infantry; Inst.: Institute; Inter'l/ Internat'l: International; Ire.: Ireland; Kt: Kuwait; Mech.: Mechanized (infantry); Lge: League; Lgn: Legion; Lib'n: Liberation; medic.: medical; Mil.: Military; Min.: Minister; mvmnt: movement; Nat'l: National; Orgnztn: Organization; Parl't: Parliament; prlmntry: parliamentary; Plce: Palace; PM: Prime Minister; Pres.: President; pres.: present; Prov.: Province; Rdg: Ridge; Resist.: Resistance; rte: route; Sec.: Secretary or Security; Shk: Sheikh; Socy: Society; Soc's/Soc'ies: Societies; Sprt: Support; St.: State (as in Secretary of State); Std'ts: Students; Stf: Staff; stn.: station; sub.: suburb; s'wave: shortwave; Trde: Trade; w': with; W.: West; W.G.: West German(y); Wash.: Washington (D.C.); wpns: weapons.

KNS stands for 'Kuwait Naval Ship', as HM(A)S stands for Her Majesty's (Australian) Ship, and USS stands for United States Ship. Unless otherwise stated or obvious from an individual's identity, all listed persons with military, police or maritime rank are members of the Kuwaiti armed forces or police.

Arab names commencing with the definite article 'Al-' are all listed alphabetically together under 'Al-'. Members of Arab nobility are generally listed by their first name (e.g., 'Jaber Al-Ahmad Al-Jaber; Saud Nasir Al-Saud). The title 'Sheikh/ Sheikha' generally denotes a member of the Al-Sabah family, with the exception of one religious figure.